# CCNP and CCIE Data Center Core [ Official Cert Guide

## Companion Website and Pearson T                    e

Access interactive study tools on this book's companion website, including ........., .....ware, review exercises, Key Term flash card application, a study planner, and more!

To access the companion website, simply follow these steps:

1.  Go to www.ciscopress.com/register.

2.  Enter the print book ISBN: **9780138228088**.

3.  Answer the security question to validate your purchase.

4.  Go to your account page.

5.  Click on the **Registered Products** tab.

6.  Under the book listing, click on the **Access Bonus Content** link.

When you register your book, your Pearson Test Prep practice test access code will automatically be populated with the book listing under the Registered Products tab. You will need this code to access the practice test that comes with this book. You can redeem the code at **PearsonTestPrep.com**. Simply choose Pearson IT Certification as your product group and log into the site with the same credentials you used to register your book. Click the **Activate New Product** button and enter the access code. More detailed instructions on how to redeem your access code for both the online and desktop versions can be found on the companion website.

If you have any issues accessing the companion website or obtaining your Pearson Test Prep practice test access code, you can contact our support team by going to **pearsonitp.echelp.org**.

# CCNP and CCIE Data Center Core DCCOR 350-601

**Official** Cert Guide

Second Edition

SOMIT MALOO, CCIE NO. 28603, CCDE NO. 20170002

ISKREN NIKOLOV, CCIE NO. 20164, CCSI NO. 32481

FIRAS AHMED, CCIE NO. 14967

Cisco Press

# CCNP and CCIE Data Center Core DCCOR 350-601 Official Cert Guide, Second Edition

Somit Maloo, Iskren Nikolov, Firas Ahmed

Copyright© 2024 Cisco Systems, Inc.

Published by:
Cisco Press

Hoboken, New Jersey

1 2023

Library of Congress Control Number: 2023946984

ISBN-13: 978-0-13-822808-8

ISBN-10: 0-13-822808-6

## Warning and Disclaimer

This book discusses the content and skills needed to pass the 350-601 CCNP Data Center Core certification exam, which is the prerequisite for CCNP as well as CCIE certification. Every effort has been made to make this book as complete and as accurate as possible, but no warranty or fitness is implied.

The information is provided on an "as is" basis. The authors, Cisco Press, and Cisco Systems, Inc. shall have neither liability nor responsibility to any person or entity with respect to any loss or damages arising from the information contained in this book or from the use of the discs or programs that may accompany it.

The opinions expressed in this book belong to the author and are not necessarily those of Cisco Systems, Inc.

## Trademark Acknowledgments

All terms mentioned in this book that are known to be trademarks or service marks have been appropriately capitalized. Cisco Press or Cisco Systems, Inc., cannot attest to the accuracy of this information. Use of a term in this book should not be regarded as affecting the validity of any trademark or service mark.

## Special Sales

For information about buying this title in bulk quantities, or for special sales opportunities (which may include electronic versions; custom cover designs; and content particular to your business, training goals, marketing focus, or branding interests), please contact our corporate sales department at corpsales@pearsoned.com or (800) 382-3419.

For government sales inquiries, please contact governmentsales@pearsoned.com.

For questions about sales outside the U.S., please contact intlcs@pearson.com.

# Feedback Information

At Cisco Press, our goal is to create in-depth technical books of the highest quality and value. Each book is crafted with care and precision, undergoing rigorous development that involves the unique expertise of members from the professional technical community.

Readers' feedback is a natural continuation of this process. If you have any comments regarding how we could improve the quality of this book, or otherwise alter it to better suit your needs, you can contact us through email at feedback@ciscopress.com. Please make sure to include the book title and ISBN in your message.

We greatly appreciate your assistance.

**Vice President, IT Professional:** Mark Taub

**Alliances Managers, Cisco Press:** Jaci Featherly; James Risler

**Director, ITP Product Management:** Brett Bartow

**Executive Editor:** James Manly

**Managing Editor:** Sandra Schroeder

**Development Editor:** Ellie Bru

**Senior Project Editor:** Tonya Simpson

**Copy Editor:** Chuck Hutchinson

**Technical Editor:** Donald S. Bacha

**Editorial Assistant:** Cindy Teeters

**Cover Designer:** Chuti Prasertsith

**Composition:** codeMantra

**Indexer:** Ken Johnson

**Proofreader:** Charlotte Kughen

# Pearson's Commitment to Diversity, Equity, and Inclusion

Pearson is dedicated to creating bias-free content that reflects the diversity of all learners. We embrace the many dimensions of diversity, including but not limited to race, ethnicity, gender, socioeconomic status, ability, age, sexual orientation, and religious or political beliefs.

Education is a powerful force for equity and change in our world. It has the potential to deliver opportunities that improve lives and enable economic mobility. As we work with authors to create content for every product and service, we acknowledge our responsibility to demonstrate inclusivity and incorporate diverse scholarship so that everyone can achieve their potential through learning. As the world's leading learning company, we have a duty to help drive change and live up to our purpose to help more people create a better life for themselves and to create a better world.

Our ambition is to purposefully contribute to a world where

- Everyone has an equitable and lifelong opportunity to succeed through learning

- Our educational products and services are inclusive and represent the rich diversity of learners

- Our educational content accurately reflects the histories and experiences of the learners we serve

- Our educational content prompts deeper discussions with learners and motivates them to expand their own learning (and worldview)

While we work hard to present unbiased content, we want to hear from you about any concerns or needs with this Pearson product so that we can investigate and address them.

Please contact us with concerns about any potential bias at https://www.pearson.com/report-bias.html.

# About the Authors

**Somit Maloo**, CCIE No. 28603, CCDE No. 20170002, is a content architect from the data center team in the Learning & Certifications' organization. He holds a master's degree in telecommunication networks and a bachelor's degree in electronics and telecommunication engineering. He is also a penta CCIE in routing and switching, service provider, wireless, security, and data center technologies. Somit holds various industry-leading certifications, including CCDE, PMP, RHCSA, and VMware VCIX6 in Data Center and Network Virtualization. Somit has extensive experience in designing and developing various data center courses for the official Cisco curriculum. He started his career as a Cisco TAC engineer. Somit has more than 13 years of experience in the networking industry, working mostly with data center networks. You can reach Somit on Twitter: @somitmaloo.

**Iskren Nikolov**, CCIE No. 20164, CCSI No. 32481, MCT Alumni, content architect, engineer, and developer with the Cisco Learning & Certifications' Data Center & Cloud team. He is responsible for designing, developing, and reviewing Data Center Official Learning Cisco courses, including lab infrastructures and exercises. He holds a master's degree in computer systems and management from the Technical University-Sofia, Bulgaria. Iskren has more than 26 years of experience in designing, implementing, and supporting solutions based on the data center, security, storage, wide area networks, software-defined networks, cloud, hybrid, and multi-cloud technologies, including 11 years of teaching, and developing Cisco Data Center & Cloud and Microsoft Azure courses. The huge experience across technologies from multiple vendors such as Cisco Systems, VMware, Microsoft, and Barracuda, combined with the different perspectives gained from the different roles in his work and experience with customers from different industries, allow Iskren to have a unique view of the current data center technologies and the future trends. You can reach Iskren on LinkedIn: https://www.linkedin.com/in/iskrennikolov.

**Firas Ahmed**, CCIE No. 14967, is a solution architect on the data center technologies team at Nile. He completed a master's degree in systems and control engineering following a bachelor's degree in computer engineering. Firas holds CCIE certificates in routing and switching, collaboration, wireless, security, and data center technologies in addition to industry-based certifications, including CISSP, PMP, VMware VCP6.5-DCV, ITIL, and GICSP. Firas has more than 18 years of experience in designing, developing, and supporting various data centers for enterprise and IoT customers. Firas has additional experience as a seasonal instructor in a number of community colleges in Toronto, where he taught various computer networking courses. You can reach Firas on Twitter: @dccor_firas.

## About the Technical Reviewer

**Donald Bacha** is an infrastructure manager with a health research organization in New York City. He's the technical lead responsible for designing and implementing network, compute, virtualization, storage, and disaster recovery solutions. During the past 18 years, Donald has supported Cloud Services Provider, Enterprise, and Data Center environments contributing to complex routing and switching, data center, storage, and virtualization projects in both greenfield and brownfield deployments. Donald's certifications include CCNP Data Center, CCNP Enterprise, and VCAP-DCV. Donald holds a master of science in network engineering from Southern Methodist University (SMU) Lyle School of Engineering and a master of business administration from the Commonwealth of Learning/University of Guyana. You can reach Donald on Twitter: @donald_bacha.

# Dedications

### Somit:

To my loving wife, Renuka, for her unending love and support.

To my wonderful parents, who supported me in every phase of my life.

To Navya and Namit, who agreed not to fight while Papa was working on the book.

To my aunt, Tara, for being the guiding angel in my life.

### Iskren:

To my loving family—my wife, Petya, and my kids, Diana and Valentin—for their continued support and unconditional love!

### Firas:

To my amazing wife, Nora, who has been extremely supportive throughout this process. Thanks for letting me spend long hours on my computer once again!

To Ibrahim and Maryam, you are growing so fast. Never give up on what you want. If at first you don't succeed, try and try again. I love you more than anything!

To my parents, you are still the guiding light that keeps me on the right path.

# Acknowledgments

**Somit Maloo:**

I would like to thank my coauthors, Iskren Nikolov and Firas Ahmed, for working as a team to complete this book. Without their support, this book would not have been possible. I am thankful to all our professional editors, especially James Manly and Ellie Bru, for their patience and guidance at every step of the book process. I would also like to thank our technical editor, Donald Bacha, for his keen attention to detail and for agreeing to review the book, taking time out of his busy schedule.

**Firas Ahmed:**

I would like to thank my co-author, Somit Maloo, for taking the initiative to form this partnership and for his dedication in putting together the outline of this book. Thank you for your valuable input and continuous support throughout the process.

Thanks to the Cisco Press team, especially James Manly, for believing in us, and Ellie Bru, for her guidance and extreme patience while editing and amending the chapters of the book.

A special credit to Hazim Dahir, distinguished engineer at Cisco Systems, for his help and support with the technical review of the book.

In addition, I want to thank my colleague Naveen Chapa for reviewing and providing constructive feedback that helped enhance the ACI chapter.

**Iskren Nikolov:**

I would like to thank my co-author, Somit Maloo—it's not that often one can work effortlessly as a team with someone. I am thankful to the whole production team, especially James Manly and Ellie Bru, for their professionalism and endless patience with me! Special thanks also to our technical editor, Donald Bacha, for providing this precious other perspective on how we can tell a better story about the technology!

# Contents at a Glance

Introduction   xxxv

**Part I**        **Networking**

Chapter 1     Implementing Routing in the Data Center   2

Chapter 2     Implementing Data Center Switching Protocols   90

Chapter 3     Implementing Data Center Overlay Protocols   150

Chapter 4     Describe Cisco Application Centric Infrastructure   172

Chapter 5     Cisco Cloud Services and Deployment Models   240

Chapter 6     Data Center Network Management and Monitoring   252

Chapter 7     Describe Cisco Nexus Dashboard   314

**Part II**       **Storage**

Chapter 8     Implement Fibre Channel   352

Chapter 9     Implement FCoE Unified Fabric   434

Chapter 10   Describe NFS and NAS Concepts   478

Chapter 11   Describe Software Management and Infrastructure Monitoring   488

**Part III**      **Compute**

Chapter 12   Cisco Unified Computing Systems Overview   530

Chapter 13   Cisco Unified Computing Infrastructure Monitoring   628

Chapter 14   Cisco Unified Compute Software and Configuration Management   658

Chapter 15   Cisco HyperFlex Overview   702

**Part IV**       **Automation**

Chapter 16   Automation and Scripting Tools   730

Chapter 17   Evaluate Automation and Orchestration Technologies   762

**Part V**        **Security**

Chapter 18   Network Security   798

Chapter 19   Compute Security   874

Chapter 20    Storage Security  896

Chapter 21    Final Preparation  932

Chapter 22    *CCNP and CCIE Data Center Core DCCOR 350-601 Official Cert Guide*
              *Exam Updates*  942

Appendix A    Answers to the "Do I Know This Already?" Quizzes  946

              Glossary  961

              Index  984

**Online Elements**

Appendix B    Memory Tables

Appendix C    Memory Tables Answer Key

Appendix D    Study Planner

              Glossary

# Contents

Introduction   xxxv

**Part I**   **Networking**

**Chapter 1**   **Implementing Routing in the Data Center   2**

"Do I Know This Already?" Quiz   2

Foundation Topics   5

Routing Protocols Support on Cisco Nexus Devices   5

OSPF   6

   OSPF Link-State Advertisements   7

   *OSPF Areas   10*

   *Designated Routers and Backup Designated Routers   12*

   OSPF Authentication   13

   OSPF Configurations and Verifications   13

Border Gateway Protocol   24

   BGP Peering   25

   BGP Path Selection   26

   *Step 1: Comparing Pairs of Paths   27*

   *Step 2: Determining the Order of Comparisons   28*

   *Step 3: Determining the Best-Path Change Suppression   29*

   Multiprotocol BGP   29

   BGP Configurations and Verifications   30

Bidirectional Forwarding Detection   37

   Rapid Detection of Failures   38

   BFD Configurations and Verifications   38

Multicast   42

   Internet Group Management Protocol   43

   Switch IGMP Snooping   46

   Multicast Listener Discovery   46

   Multicast Distribution Trees   47

   Protocol Independent Multicast   49

   *PIM Rendezvous Points   53*

   *PIM Designated Routers/Forwarders   54*

   Multicast Forwarding   55

   Multicast Configurations and Verifications   56

Hot Standby Router Protocol   69

Virtual Router Redundancy Protocol   73

VRRP Operation 73

VRRP Groups 75

VRRP Router Priority and Preemption 76

VRRP Authentication 77

VRRP Tracking 77

IPv6 First Hop Redundancy 77

HSRP/VRRP Configurations and Verifications 79

Exam Preparation Tasks 87

Review All Key Topics 87

Memory Tables 88

Define Key Terms 88

References 88

Chapter 2    Implementing Data Center Switching Protocols 90

"Do I Know This Already?" Quiz 90

Foundation Topics 93

Spanning Tree Protocols 93

STP Topology 93

STP Port Types 94

STP Extensions 94

STP Bridge Assurance 95

BPDU Guard 96

BPDU Filter 96

Loop Guard 96

Root Guard 97

Unidirectional Link Detection 97

Rapid PVST+ 98

Rapid PVST+ Ports 100

Spanning Tree Configurations and Verifications 102

Port Channels 117

Port Channel Load Balance 120

Virtual Port Channel 122

vPC Traffic Flows 125

vPC Dual-Control Plane 126

vPC Primary and Secondary Roles 127

vPC Configuration Consistency 128

vPC Duplicate Frames Prevention Mechanism 129

vPC HSRP Gateway Considerations 131

vPC ARP Synchronization   131

vPC Peer Gateway   131

Port Channel Configurations and Verifications   132

Exam Preparation Tasks   146

Review All Key Topics   146

Memory Tables   147

Define Key Terms   147

References   148

**Chapter 3     Implementing Data Center Overlay Protocols   150**

"Do I Know This Already?" Quiz   150

Foundation Topics   151

Virtual Extensible LAN (VXLAN) Overview   151

VXLAN Encapsulation and Packet Format   152

VXLAN Tunnel Endpoint   152

Virtual Network Identifier   153

VXLAN Control Plane   154

*VXLAN Flood and Learn Multicast-Based Control Plane*   154

*VXLAN MPBGP EVPN Control Plane*   156

VXLAN Gateways   157

VXLAN High Availability   157

VXLAN Tenant Routed Multicast   159

VXLAN Configurations and Verifications   159

Exam Preparation Tasks   169

Review All Key Topics   169

Define Key Terms   170

References   170

**Chapter 4     Describe Cisco Application Centric Infrastructure   172**

"Do I Know This Already?" Quiz   172

Foundation Topics   174

Cisco Application Centric Infrastructure (ACI) Overview   174

Cisco Application Policy Infrastructure Controller   176

Cisco Nexus 9000 Series Spine and Leaf Switches for Cisco ACI   179

Cisco ACI Initial Setup, Fabric Discovery, Fabric Upgrade, and Fabric Access
Policies   182

Cisco ACI Initial Setup   182

Cisco ACI Fabric Discovery   187

Startup with Cisco ACI Fabric Discovery and Configuration    188

Fabric Upgrade    189

Cisco ACI Fabric Access Policies    190

Cisco ACI Fabric Building Blocks, Policy Model, and VMM Domains    195

ACI Policy Model    197

Cisco ACI Tenants    198

*Virtual Routing and Forwarding    200*

*Bridge Domain and Subnets    200*

*Endpoint Group    202*

*Cisco ACI Virtual Machine Manager Domains    203*

*Cisco ACI Integration with Microsoft SCVMM    204*

*Cisco ACI Integration with VMware vCenter    205*

*Cisco ACI Virtual Edge    206*

*Integrating VMware Overlays with the Cisco ACI    206*

*Application Profiles    206*

*Microsegmentations    207*

*Attachable Entity Profile    207*

*ACI Contract    208*

Taboo Contracts    209

vzAny Rule    210

Filters and Subjects    213

Management Tenant    213

In-Band Management Access    214

*Out-of-Band Management Access    214*

ACI VXLAN    215

ACI Intersubnet Tenant Traffic    217

Policy Identification and Enforcement    218

ACI Fabric Traffic Storm Control    219

ACI Fabric Traffic Load Balance    219

ACI Fabric Loop Detection    220

ACI Design Best Practices    221

ACI LAB Configurations Example    221

Building ACI Fabric    224

Creating Tenant    227

Creating Contract and Filter    230

Deploying a Three-Tier Application    233

Integrating with vCenter    235

Exam Preparation Tasks   238

Review All Key Topics   238

Define Key Terms   239

References   239

**Chapter 5**   **Cisco Cloud Services and Deployment Models   240**

"Do I Know This Already?" Quiz   240

Foundation Topics   242

What Is Cloud Computing?   242

Cloud Service Models   245

Software as a Service   245

Platform as a Service   246

Infrastructure as a Service   246

Cloud Deployment Models   248

Private Cloud   248

Public Cloud   248

Hybrid Cloud   249

Community Cloud   250

Exam Preparation Tasks   250

Review All Key Topics   250

Define Key Terms   251

References   251

**Chapter 6**   **Data Center Network Management and Monitoring   252**

"Do I Know This Already?" Quiz   252

Foundation Topics   254

Cisco Nexus NX-OS Software Installation, Updates, and Their Impacts   254

PowerOn Auto Provisioning (POAP)   259

Data Center Infrastructure Software Lifecycle Management   263

Nexus Nondisruptive In-Service Software Upgrade   263

Nexus Disruptive and Nondisruptive Upgrade/Downgrade Procedure   265

Programmable Logical Devices Upgrade   269

Nexus Configuration Management   271

NX-OS Configuration Save and Backup   272

Nexus Config Rollback and Checkpoint   272

Network Time Management   274

Network Time Protocol   275

Precision Time Protocol   280

Network Infrastructure Monitoring   284

    NX-OS System Message Logging   284

    NX-OS Simple Network Management Protocol   286

    Nexus Smart Call Home   292

    Nexus NetFlow   293

    Switched Port Analyzer   298

Streaming Telemetry   306

Network Assurance Concept   310

Exam Preparation Tasks   312

Review All Key Topics   312

Memory Tables   313

Define Key Terms   313

References   313

**Chapter 7    Describe Cisco Nexus Dashboard   314**

"Do I Know This Already?" Quiz   314

Foundation Topics   316

Cisco Nexus Dashboard   316

    Cisco Nexus Dashboard Insights   318

    *Cisco Nexus Dashboard Insights Features and Benefits*   318

    *Cisco Nexus Dashboard Insights GUI Overview*   320

    Cisco Nexus Dashboard Orchestrator   323

    *Cisco Nexus Dashboard Orchestrator Features and Benefits*   324

    Cisco Nexus Dashboard Fabric Controller   325

    *Cisco Nexus Dashboard Fabric Controller Features and Benefits*   326

    *Cisco Nexus Dashboard Fabric Controller GUI Overview*   331

    Cisco Nexus Dashboard Data Broker   335

    *Cisco Nexus Dashboard Data Broker Features and Benefits*   337

Cisco Nexus Dashboard Platforms   337

Cisco Nexus Dashboard Cluster Nodes   339

Cisco Nexus Dashboard External Networks   341

Cisco Nexus Dashboard GUI Overview   342

    One View Page   343

    Admin Console Page   343

    *Overview Page*   344

    *Sites Page*   345

    *Services Page*   345

    *System Resources Pages*   346

*Operations Pages  347*

*Infrastructure Pages  348*

*Administrative Pages  348*

Exam Preparation Tasks  348

Review All Key Topics  348

Memory Tables  349

Define Key Terms  349

References  349

**Part II        Storage**

**Chapter 8        Implement Fibre Channel  352**

"Do I Know This Already?" Quiz  353

Foundation Topics  356

Cisco MDS 9000 Series Hardware  356

Cisco MDS 9700 Series Multilayer Directors  356

Cisco MDS 9300 Series Multilayer Fabric Switches  360

Cisco MDS 9200 Series Multiservice Switches  361

Cisco MDS 9100 Series Multilayer Fabric Switches  362

Fibre Channel Basics  365

Fibre Channel Topologies  365

Fibre Channel Port Types  368

*E Port  369*

*F Port  369*

*NP Ports  369*

*TE Port  369*

*TF Port  370*

*TNP Port  370*

*Fx Port  370*

*Auto Mode  370*

Fibre Channel Addressing  371

Flow Control  372

Switched Fabric Initialization  373

*Principal Switch Selection  374*

*Domain ID Distribution  375*

*FCID Allocation  377*

*Fabric Reconfiguration  377*

Device Registration: FLOGI, PLOGI, PRLI  378

FLOGI and FCNS Databases  378

CFS    380

    CFS Features    381

    CFS Fabric Lock    382

    CFSoIP and CFSoFC    382

    CFS Merge    384

    CFS Regions    384

VSAN    386

    VSAN Features    386

    VSAN Attributes    387

    VSAN Advantages    388

    Dynamic Port VSAN Membership (DPVM)    388

    VSAN Trunking    389

SAN Port Channels    396

    Types of SAN Port Channels    396

    Port Channel Load Balancing    398

    Port Channel Modes    399

Zoning    404

    Zoning Features    404

    Zone Enforcement    406

    Full and Active Zone Set    407

    Autozone    410

    Zone Merge    410

    Smart Zoning    411

    Enhanced Zoning    412

Device Alias    418

    Device Alias Features    419

    Device Alias Modes    419

    Device Alias Distribution    420

    Zone Aliases (FC Aliases) Versus Device Aliases    421

NPIV and NPV    424

Exam Preparation Tasks    431

Review All Key Topics    431

Memory Tables    432

Define Key Terms    432

References    433

**Chapter 9**    **Implement FCoE Unified Fabric    434**

"Do I Know This Already?" Quiz    434

Foundation Topics    436

FCoE Overview    436

  Ethernet Enhancements    438

  *Priority-Based Flow Control (PFC)    438*

  *Enhanced Transmission Selection (ETS)    439*

  *Data Center Bridging Exchange (DCBX)    440*

  FCoE Frame Format    442

  Virtual Fibre Channel (VFC)    444

  FCoE Elements and Port Types    445

  FCoE Addressing and Forwarding    447

  FCoE Initialization Protocol (FIP)    448

  Benefits of FCoE    451

FCoE Topology Options    451

  FCoE Single-Hop Topology    451

  *FCoE Direct-Attached Topology    452*

  *FCoE FEX Topology    453*

  *FCoE Remote-Attached Topology    454*

  FCoE Multi-Hop Topology    454

FCoE Implementations    455

  FCoE Configuration on Cisco Nexus 7000 Series Switches    456

  *Miscellaneous FCoE Configuration    457*

  FCoE Configuration on Cisco Nexus 5000 Series Switches    458

  FCoE Configuration on Cisco Nexus 9000 Series Switches    459

  FCoE over FEX    461

  FCoE NPV    463

  FCoE Verification    466

Exam Preparation Tasks    475

Review All Key Topics    475

Memory Tables    476

Define Key Terms    476

References    476

**Chapter 10**    **Describe NFS and NAS Concepts    478**

"Do I Know This Already?" Quiz    478

Foundation Topics    479

Describe NFS Concepts    479

Describe NAS Concepts   481

NAS Benefits   483

Cisco UCS S-Series Storage Servers   483

Exam Preparation Tasks   485

Review All Key Topics   485

Define Key Terms   485

References   486

**Chapter 11**   **Describe Software Management and Infrastructure Monitoring   488**

"Do I Know This Already?" Quiz   488

Foundation Topics   490

Cisco MDS NX-OS Setup Utility   490

Cisco MDS NX-OS Software Upgrade and Downgrade   498

Nondisruptive Upgrade on a Cisco MDS Fabric Switch   500

Disruptive Upgrade on a Cisco MDS Fabric Switch   505

Nondisruptive Downgrade on a Cisco MDS Fabric Switch   508

Disruptive Downgrade on a Cisco MDS Fabric Switch   513

EPLD Upgrade on Cisco MDS 9000 Series Switches   515

Infrastructure Monitoring   521

System Messages   521

Call Home   521

Embedded Event Manager   522

RMON   523

SPAN   523

*SPAN Configuration Example   526*

*Remote SPAN   526*

Exam Preparation Tasks   528

Review All Key Topics   528

Define Key Terms   529

References   529

**Part III**   **Compute**

**Chapter 12**   **Cisco Unified Computing Systems Overview   530**

"Do I Know This Already?" Quiz   530

Foundation Topics   532

Cisco UCS Architecture   532

Cisco UCS Components and Connectivity   534

Cisco UCS 5108 Blade Server Chassis   536

UCS Blade Servers   536

Cisco UCS Rack Servers   537

Cisco UCS Storage Servers   537

Cisco UCS Mini   539

Cisco UCS Fabric Infrastructure   539

Cisco UCS 6536 Fabric Interconnect   540

Cisco UCS 6454 Fabric Interconnect   541

Cisco UCS 6300 Series Fabric Interconnects   543

Fabric Interconnect and Fabric Extender Connectivity   544

Cisco UCS Virtualization Infrastructure   550

Cisco UCS-X System   555

Cisco UCS Initial Setup and Management   557

Fabric Interconnect Connectivity and Configurations   565

*Uplink Connectivity*   566

*Downlink Connectivity*   567

Fabric Interconnect Port Modes   567

Fabric Failover for Ethernet: High-Availability vNIC   569

Ethernet Switching Mode   570

UCS Device Discovery   577

Chassis/FEX Discovery   577

Rack Server Discovery Policy   577

Initial Server Setup for Standalone UCS C-Series   578

Cisco UCS Network Management   584

UCS Virtual LAN   584

*Named VLANs*   586

UCS Identity Pools   591

*Universally Unique Identifier Suffix Pools*   591

*MAC Pools*   593

*IP Pools*   593

*Server Pools*   596

Service Profiles   596

UCS Server Policies   599

UCS Service Profile Templates   602

Quality of Service   608

*QoS System Classes*   608

*QoS System Classes Configurations*   609

*Configuring Quality of Service Policies*   610

Cisco UCS Storage    611

UCS SAN Connectivity    611

UCS SAN Configuration    615

Virtual Storage-Area Networks    616

*Named VSANs Configurations*    616

*Zones and Zone Sets*    618

World Wide Name Pool    621

SAN Connectivity Policies    624

Exam Preparation Tasks    625

Review All Key Topics    625

Define Key Terms    626

References    626

**Chapter 13    Cisco Unified Computing Infrastructure Monitoring    628**

"Do I Know This Already?" Quiz    628

Foundation Topics    630

Cisco UCS System Monitoring    630

Data Management Engine    631

Application Gateway    631

Northbound Interfaces    631

Cisco UCS Monitoring Events and Logs    632

Cisco UCS Monitoring Policies    634

*Cisco UCS Simple Network Management Protocol*    636

*Cisco UCS Call Home and Smart Call Home*    636

*Cisco UCS Manager Database Health and Hardware Monitoring*    638

*Cisco UCS NetFlow Monitoring*    638

Traffic Monitoring    640

*Traffic Monitoring Across Ethernet*    641

*Traffic Monitoring Across Fibre Channel*    642

Cisco Intersight    647

Intersight Management as a Service    648

Intersight as a Telemetry Data Collection    650

Cisco Intersight Supported Software    650

Cisco Intersight Licensing    652

Exam Preparation Tasks    656

Review All Key Topics    656

Define Key Terms    657

References    657

**Chapter 14    Cisco Unified Compute Software and Configuration Management   658**

"Do I Know This Already?" Quiz   658

Foundation Topics   660

Cisco UCS Configuration Management   660

   Creating and Running a Backup Operation   661

   Backup Policies   666

   Backup Policy Configuration   666

   Import Backups   668

   Enable the Import Operation   669

   System Restore   670

   Restoring the Configuration for a Fabric Interconnect   671

UCS Firmware and Software Updates   672

   Firmware Version Terminology   679

   Firmware Upgrades Through Auto Install   680

   Direct Upgrade After Auto Install Procedure   684

   Install Infrastructure Firmware Procedure   688

   Upgrading the Server Firmware with Auto Install   691

   Standalone Cisco UCS C-Series Server Firmware Upgrade Using the Host Upgrade Utility (HUU)   693

   Downloading and Preparing the ISO for an Upgrade   694

Exam Preparation Tasks   700

Review All Key Topics   700

Define Key Terms   700

References   700

**Chapter 15    Cisco HyperFlex Overview   702**

"Do I Know This Already?" Quiz   702

Foundation Topics   704

Cisco HyperFlex Solution and Benefits   704

   HyperFlex Benefits   707

   *Intelligent End-to-End Automation   708*

   *Unified Management for All Workloads   709*

   *Independent Resource Scaling   710*

   *Superior Virtual Machine Density with Lower and Consistent Latency   711*

HyperFlex as an Edge, Hybrid, and All-Flash Nodes   712

   HyperFlex as an Edge Device   712

HyperFlex Hyperconverged Multicloud Platform (Hybrid or
All-Flash)   714

HyperFlex All NVMe   715

Cisco HyperFlex Data Platform   716

*HX Storage Cluster Physical Components   717*

*HX Data Platform High Availability   718*

*HX Data Platform Cluster Tolerated Failures   719*

*HX Data Platform Ready Clones   719*

*HX Data Platform Native Snapshots   719*

*HX Cluster Interfaces   720*

*HX Self-Encrypting Drives   720*

*Configuring a Local Encryption Key   721*

*Managing HX Disks in the Cluster   721*

*Managing HX Datastores   724*

*Expand Cisco HX System Clusters   725*

*Enabling HX Logical Availability Zones   726*

Exam Preparation Tasks   728

Review All Key Topics   728

Define Key Terms   728

References   728

Part IV        Automation

Chapter 16    Automation and Scripting Tools   730

"Do I Know This Already?" Quiz   730

Foundation Topics   733

EEM Overview   733

Policies   733

Event Statements   734

Action Statements   734

Configuring EEM   735

Verifying the EEM Configuration   736

Scheduler   736

Configuring Scheduler   737

Verifying Scheduler Configuration   739

Bash Shell for Cisco NX-OS   740

Managing Feature RPMs   742

Managing Patch RPMs   742

Guest Shell for Cisco NX-OS   743

Accessing the Guest Shell   743

Resources Used for the Guest Shell   744

Capabilities in the Guest Shell   744

Managing the Guest Shell   746

XML   748

Example   749

XML Syntax   750

JSON   751

Rest API   752

Authentication   753

Response   754

NX-API   755

NX-API Request and Response Elements   757

NX-API Developer Sandbox   759

Exam Preparation Tasks   760

Review All Key Topics   760

Memory Tables   761

Define Key Terms   761

References   761

**Chapter 17    Evaluate Automation and Orchestration Technologies   762**

"Do I Know This Already?" Quiz   762

Foundation Topics   764

Ansible   764

Ansible Components   765

Important Ansible Concepts   766

Ansible CLI Tools   767

Cisco NX-OS and Ansible Example   767

Python   768

Python Package for Cisco   769

Using the CLI Command APIs   771

Python in Interactive Mode   772

Python in Noninteractive Mode   773

UCS Manager Python SDK   775

Convert to UCS Python   777

PowerOn Auto Provisioning (POAP)   777

Limitations of POAP   778

Network Requirements for POAP   778

POAP Configuration Script   778

POAP Process   779

*Power-Up Phase*   *779*

*USB Discovery Phase*   *779*

*DHCP Discovery Phase*   *781*

*Script Execution Phase*   *782*

*Post-Installation Reload Phase*   *782*

Configuring a Switch Using POAP   782

HashiCorp Terraform   783

Terraform Concept   784

Terraform Components   784

Terraform Commands   786

PowerShell   789

Exam Preparation Tasks   795

Review All Key Topics   795

Memory Tables   796

Define Key Terms   796

References   797

**Part V         Security**

**Chapter 18   Network Security   798**

"Do I Know This Already?" Quiz   798

Foundation Topics   801

Authentication, Authorization, and Accounting   801

AAA Service Configuration Options   802

Authentication and Authorization User Login Process   803

AAA NX-OS Configurations   804

Role-Based Access Control   807

NX-OS User Roles and Rules   809

NX-OS RBAC Configurations   811

Nexus First-Hop Security   815

Nexus Dynamic ARP Inspection   816

NX-OS DAI Configurations   819

NX-OS DHCP Snooping   827

*DHCP Snooping Trusted and Untrusted Sources*   *827*

*DHCP Snooping Packet Validation*   *828*

*DHCP Snooping Option 82 Data Insertion*   *829*

*NX-OS DHCP Snooping Configuration* 829

Port Security 832

Nexus Port Secure MAC Address Maximum and Dynamic Address Aging 833

Port Security Violations and Actions 834

Nexus Port Types and Port Security 835

NX-OS Port Security Configuration 835

Nexus Control Plane Policing 837

Control Plane Packet 839

Classification for CoPP 840

*Rate-Controlling Mechanisms* 840

*Modular QoS Command-Line Interface* 842

NX-OS CoPP Configuration 844

Cisco ACI Contracts 851

Cisco ACI Contract Configuration Parameters 853

Create, Modify, or Remove Regular Contracts 854

Apply or Remove VRF Contracts 856

Inter-Tenant Contracts 857

Inter-Private Network Contracts Communication 858

Single Contract Bidirectional Reverse Filter 859

Single Contract Unidirectional with Multiple Filters 859

Multiple Contracts Unidirectional Single Filter 860

ACI Microsegmentation 860

Example: ACI Microsegmentation with VMs from a Single Application EPG 862

Example: ACI Microsegmentation with VMs in Different Application EPGs 863

ACI Microsegmentation Configurations 864

Keychain Authentication 868

NX-OS Keychain Configurations 868

Key Selection 871

Exam Preparation Tasks 872

Review All Key Topics 872

Define Key Terms 873

References 873

**Chapter 19 Compute Security 874**

"Do I Know This Already?" Quiz 874

Foundation Topics 875

Securing UCS Management Using Authentication, Authorization, and Accounting 875

    User RADIUS and TACACS+ Attributes 876

    Two-Factor Authentication 879

    UCS Web Session Refresh and Session Timeout Period 879

    UCS LDAP Providers and Groups 879

    *LDAP Group Mapping 885*

    RADIUS and TACACS+ Authentication Configurations 888

    UCS Remote Users Role Policy 892

    Multiple Authentication Services Configuration 894

Exam Preparation Tasks 895

Review All Key Topics 895

Define Key Terms 895

References 895

**Chapter 20 Storage Security 896**

"Do I Know This Already?" Quiz 896

Foundation Topics 898

Authentication, Authorization, and Accounting 898

    Authentication 899

    Authorization 899

    Accounting 900

    Server Groups 900

    AAA Service Configuration Options 900

    AAA Server Monitoring 900

    Remote AAA Services 901

    *RADIUS 902*

    *TACACS+ 904*

    *LDAP 907*

    Local AAA Services 911

    AAA Authentication and Authorization Process 912

    AAA Server Distribution 913

    Merging RADIUS and TACACS+ Configurations 914

User Accounts and RBAC 914

    User Roles 915

Rules   915

User Role Policies   917

RBAC Sample Configuration   918

Port Security   919

Port Security Configuration   921

*Method 1: Manual Database Configuration   921*

*Method 2: Auto-Learning Without CFS Distribution   922*

*Method 3: Auto-Learning with CFS Distribution   923*

Verification of Port Security   924

Fabric Binding   926

Fabric Binding Configuration   926

Port Security Versus Fabric Binding   928

Exam Preparation Tasks   929

Review All Key Topics   929

Memory Tables and Lists   930

Define Key Terms   930

References   930

**Chapter 21**   **Final Preparation   932**

Getting Ready   932

Tools for Final Preparation   933

Pearson Test Prep Practice Test Software and Questions on the Website   933

How to Access the Pearson Test Prep (PTP) App   933

Customizing Your Exams   934

Updating Your Exams   935

*Premium Edition   935*

Chapter-Ending Review Tools   935

Learn the Question Types Using the Cisco Certification Exam Tutorial   935

Suggested Plan for Final Review/Study   940

Summary   940

**Chapter 22**   **_CCNP and CCIE Data Center Core DCCOR 350-601 Official Cert Guide Exam Updates   942_**

The Purpose of This Chapter   942

About Possible Exam Updates   943

Impact on You and Your Study Plan   943

News About the Next Exam Release   944

Updated Technical Content   944

**Appendix A**   Answers to the "Do I Know This Already?" Quizzes   946

Glossary   961

Index   984


**Online Elements**

**Appendix B**   Memory Tables

**Appendix C**   Memory Tables Answer Key

**Appendix D**   Study Planner

Glossary

## Other Features

In addition to the features in each of the core chapters, this book has additional study resources on the companion website, including the following:

Practice exams: The companion website contains an exam engine that enables you to review practice exam questions. Use these questions to prepare with a sample exam and to pinpoint topics where you need more study.

An online interactive Flash Cards application to help you drill on Key Terms by chapter.

Glossary quizzes: The companion website contains interactive quizzes that enable you to test yourself on every glossary term in the book.

More than two hours of video training: The companion website contains multiple hours of unique test-prep videos.

To access this additional content, simply register your product. To start the registration process, go to www.ciscopress.com/register and log in or create an account*. Enter the product ISBN 9780138228088 and click **Submit**. After the process is complete, you will find any available bonus content under Registered Products.

*Be sure to check the box that you would like to hear from us to receive exclusive discounts on future editions of this product.

## Icons Used in This Book

Cisco Nexus 9500 Series

ATM Router

Cisco Nexus 7000

File Server

Laptop

Server

Switch

Cisco Nexus 5000

Cisco Nexus 2000

Terminal

Cloud

Cisco Nexus 9300 Series

API Controller

Generic/ Unknown

Database

Storage Array

Telephony Router

Net Ranger

Router with Firewall

IP Phone

## Command Syntax Conventions

The conventions used to present command syntax in this book are the same conventions used in the IOS Command Reference. The Command Reference describes these conventions as follows:

- **Boldface** indicates commands and keywords that are entered literally as shown. In actual configuration examples and output (not general command syntax), boldface indicates commands that are manually input by the user (such as a **show** command).

- *Italic* indicates arguments for which you supply actual values.

- Vertical bars (|) separate alternative, mutually exclusive elements.

- Square brackets ([ ]) indicate an optional element.

- Braces ({ }) indicate a required choice.

- Braces within brackets ([{ }]) indicate a required choice within an optional element.

# Introduction

Professional certifications have been an important part of the computing industry for many years and will continue to become more important. Many reasons exist for these certifications, but the most popularly cited reason is that of credibility. All other considerations held equal, the certified employee/consultant/job candidate is considered more valuable than one who is not.

## Goals and Methods

The most important and somewhat obvious goal of this book is to help you pass the 350-601 CCNP Data Center Core Exam. In fact, if the primary objective of this book were different, the book's title would be misleading; however, the methods used in this book to help you pass the 350-601 CCNP Data Center Core Exam are designed to also make you much more knowledgeable about how to do your job. Although this book and the companion website together have more than enough questions to help you prepare for the actual exam, the method in which they are used is not simply to make you memorize as many questions and answers as you possibly can.

One key methodology used in this book is to help you discover the exam topics that you need to review in more depth, to help you fully understand and remember those details, and to help you prove to yourself that you have retained your knowledge of those topics. So, this book does not try to help you pass by memorization, but helps you truly learn and understand the topics. The Data Center Core Exam is just one of the foundation topics in the CCNP and CCIE certification, and the knowledge contained within is vitally important to consider yourself a truly skilled data center engineer or specialist. This book would do you a disservice if it didn't attempt to help you learn the material. To that end, the book will help you pass the Data Center Core Exam by using the following methods:

- Helping you discover which test topics you have not mastered

- Providing explanations and information to fill in your knowledge gaps

- Supplying exercises and scenarios that enhance your ability to recall and deduce the answers to test questions

- Providing practice exercises on the topics and the testing process via test questions through the companion website

## Who Should Read This Book?

This book is not designed to be a general networking topics book, although it can be used for that purpose. This book is intended to tremendously increase your chances of passing the CCNP Data Center Core Exam. Although other objectives can be achieved from using this book, the book is written with one goal in mind: to help you pass the exam.

So why should you want to pass the CCNP Data Center Core Exam? Because it's one of the milestones toward getting the CCNP and CCIE certification—no small feat in itself.

What would getting the CCNP or CCIE mean to you? A raise, a promotion, recognition? How about to enhance your resume? To demonstrate that you are serious about continuing the learning process and that you're not content to rest on your laurels. To please your reseller-employer, who needs more certified employees for a higher discount from Cisco. Or one of many other reasons.

## Strategies for Exam Preparation

The strategy you use for the CCNP Data Center Core Exam might be slightly different from strategies used by other readers, mainly based on the skills, knowledge, and experience you already have obtained. For instance, if you have attended the DCFNDU course, you might take a different approach than someone who learned data center technologies via on-the-job training.

Regardless of the strategy you use or the background you have, the book is designed to help you get to the point where you can pass the exam with the least amount of time required. For instance, there is no need for you to practice or read about OSPF or BGP if you fully understand it already. However, many people like to make sure that they truly know a topic and thus read over material that they already know. Several book features will help you gain the confidence that you need to be convinced that you know some material already and to also help you know what topics you need to study more.

## The Companion Website for Online Content Review

All the electronic review elements, as well as other electronic components of the book, exist on this book's companion website.

### How to Access the Companion Website

To access the companion website, which gives you access to the electronic content with this book, start by establishing a login at ciscopress.com and register your book. To do so, simply go to ciscopress.com/register and enter the ISBN of the print book: 9780138228088. After you have registered your book, go to your account page and click the **Registered Products** tab. From there, click the **Access Bonus Content** link to get access to the book's companion website.

Note that if you buy the Premium Edition eBook and Practice Test version of this book from Cisco Press, your book will automatically be registered on your account page.

Simply go to your account page, click the **Registered Products** tab, and select **Access Bonus Content** to access the book's companion website.

### How to Access the Pearson Test Prep (PTP) App

You have two options for installing and using the Pearson Test Prep application: a web app and a desktop app. To use the Pearson Test Prep application, start by finding the registration code that comes with the book. You can find the code in these ways:

- **Print book or bookseller eBook versions:** You can get your access code by registering the print ISBN (9780138228088) on ciscopress.com/register. Make sure to use the print book ISBN regardless of whether you purchased an eBook or the print book. Once you register the book, your access code will be populated on your account page under the Registered Products tab. Instructions for how to redeem the code are available on the book's companion website by clicking the Access Bonus Content link.

■ **Premium Edition:** If you purchase the Premium Edition eBook and Practice Test directly from the Cisco Press website, the code will be populated on your account page after purchase. Just log in at www.ciscopress.com, click Account to see details of your account, and click the digital purchases tab.

**NOTE** Do not lose the activation code because it is the only means with which you can access the QA content with the book.

When you have the access code, to find instructions about both the PTP web app and the desktop app, follow these steps:

**Step 1.** Open this book's companion website, as shown earlier in this Introduction under the heading "How to Access the Companion Website."

**Step 2.** Click the **Practice Exams** button.

**Step 3.** Follow the instructions listed there both for installing the desktop app and for using the web app.

Note that if you want to use the web app only at this point, just navigate to www.pearsontestprep.com, establish a free login if you do not already have one, and register this book's practice tests using the registration code you just found. The process should take only a couple of minutes.

## How This Book Is Organized

Although this book could be read cover to cover, it is designed to be flexible and allow you to easily move between chapters and sections of chapters to cover just the material that you need more work with.

The core chapters, Chapters 1 through 20, cover the following topics:

■ **Chapter 1, "Implementing Routing in the Data Center":** This chapter discusses data center Layer 3 routing protocols, focusing on OSPF and BGP routing protocols. It also discusses multicast and First Hop Redundancy Protocols such as HSRP and VRRP.

■ **Chapter 2, "Implementing Data Center Switching Protocols":** This chapter discusses data center Layer 2 switching protocols, focusing on spanning tree and multiport aggregation. It also discusses virtual port channels (multichassis port channels).

■ **Chapter 3, "Implementing Data Center Overlay Protocols":** This chapter discusses data center overlay protocol Virtual Extensible LAN (VXLAN).

■ **Chapter 4, "Describe Cisco Application Centric Infrastructure":** This chapter discusses various aspects of Cisco ACI, including but not limited to fabric discovery, fabric access policies, fabric packet flow, tenants, and VMM domains.

■ **Chapter 5, "Cisco Cloud Services and Deployment Models":** This chapter discusses an overview of what cloud computing is along with cloud service models per the NIST 800-145 definition, such as Infrastructure as a Service (IaaS), Software as a Service (SaaS), and Platform as a Service (PaaS). It also discusses various cloud deployment models per the NIST 800-145 definition, such as public, private, community, and hybrid cloud.

■ **Chapter 6, "Data Center Network Management and Monitoring":** This chapter discusses data center network disruptive/nondisruptive upgrade procedures, network configurations, and infrastructure monitoring aspects in detail. It also discusses data center network assurance and data telemetry.

■ **Chapter 7, "Describe Cisco Nexus Dashboard":** This chapter discusses various services/applications for the Cisco Nexus Dashboard platform including Cisco Nexus Dashboard Insights (NDI), Cisco Nexus Dashboard Orchestrator (NDO), Cisco Nexus Dashboard Fabric Controller (NDFC), and Cisco Nexus Dashboard Data Broker (NDDB), along with their features and benefits. It also discusses various form factors, node types, and network types for Cisco Nexus Dashboard deployment along with a graphical user interface (GUI) overview of the Cisco Nexus Dashboard platform.

■ **Chapter 8, "Implement Fibre Channel":** This chapter discusses the MDS 9000 Series Hardware and Fibre Channel protocol in detail. It discusses Fibre Channel topologies, port types, switched fabric initialization, CFS distribution, VSAN, zoning, device alias, FLOGI, and FCNS databases. It also discusses NPV and NPIV features in detail.

■ **Chapter 9, "Implement FCoE Unified Fabric":** This chapter discusses the FCoE Unified Fabric Protocol in detail. It discusses various Ethernet enhancements that enable FCoE support on Ethernet interfaces. It also discusses FCoE topology options and various FCoE implementations—for example, FCoE over FEX and FCoE NPV.

■ **Chapter 10, "Describe NFS and NAS Concepts":** This chapter discusses NFS basics along with various NFS versions. It also discusses NAS basics with an overview of the Cisco UCS S-Series Storage Servers.

■ **Chapter 11, "Describe Software Management and Infrastructure Monitoring":** This chapter discusses how the Cisco MDS NX-OS Setup Utility helps to build an initial configuration file using the System Configuration dialog. It also discusses Cisco MDS NX-OS software upgrade and downgrade procedures, along with infrastructure monitoring features such as SPAN, RSPAN, RMON, and Call Home.

■ **Chapter 12, "Cisco Unified Computing Systems Overview":** This chapter discusses the Cisco Unified Computing System (UCS) architecture. It also discusses in detail UCS initial setup, along with network management aspects of Cisco UCS, such as identity pools, policies, QoS, and templates.

- **Chapter 13, "Cisco Unified Computing Infrastructure Monitoring":** This chapter discusses Cisco Unified Compute traffic monitoring and Intersight cloud management.

- **Chapter 14, "Cisco Unified Compute Software and Configuration Management":** This chapter discusses Cisco UCS configuration management such as backup and restore. It also discusses aspects of firmware and software updates on Cisco UCS.

- **Chapter 15, "Cisco HyperFlex Overview":** This chapter discusses the Cisco Hyperflex solution and benefits. It also discusses edge solutions that enable any application to be deployed, monitored, and managed anywhere.

- **Chapter 16, "Automation and Scripting Tools":** This chapter discusses various automation and scripting tools. It discusses the Embedded Event Manager (EEM), Scheduler, Bash Shell, and Guest Shell for Cisco NX-OS software, and various data formats such as XML and JSON. It also discusses how the REST API can be used to configure Cisco NX-OS devices.

- **Chapter 17, "Evaluate Automation and Orchestration Technologies":** This chapter discusses various automation and orchestration technologies. It discusses how Ansible, Python, and Terraform can be used to automate Cisco Data Center products. It also discusses the PowerOn Auto Provisioning (POAP) process, along with the UCS PowerShell modules, also referred to as UCS PowerTool Suite.

- **Chapter 18, "Network Security":** This chapter discusses network authentication, authorization, and accounting (AAA) and user role-based access control (RBAC). It also discusses various network security protocols in detail, including control plan policing, dynamic ARP inspection, DHCP snooping, and port security, along with the keychain authentication method.

- **Chapter 19, "Compute Security":** This chapter discusses Cisco UCS authentication and user role-based access control.

- **Chapter 20, "Storage Security":** This chapter discusses various storage security features in detail. It discusses authentication, authorization, and accounting (AAA), user accounts, and RBAC. It also discusses configuration and verification of port security and fabric binding features on the Cisco MDS 9000 Series switches.

- **Chapter 21, "Final Preparation":** This chapter suggests a plan for final preparation after you have finished the core parts of the book, in particular explaining the many study options available in the book.

## Certification Exam Topics and This Book

The questions for each certification exam are a closely guarded secret. However, we do know which topics you must know to *successfully* complete this exam. Cisco publishes them as an exam blueprint for the Implementing Cisco Data Center Core Technologies (DCCOR 350-601) Exam. Table I-1 lists each exam topic listed in the blueprint along with a reference to the book chapter that covers the topic. These are the same topics you should be proficient in when working with Cisco data center technologies in the real world.

**Table I-1** DCCOR Exam 350-601 Topics and Chapter References

| DCCOR 350-601 Exam Topic | Chapter(s) in Which Topic Is Covered |
|---|---|
| 1.0 Network | |
| 1.1 Apply routing protocols | 1 |
| 1.1.a OSPFv2, OSPFv3 | 1 |
| 1.1.b MP-BGP | 1 |
| 1.1.c PIM | 1 |
| 1.1.d FHRP | 1 |
| 1.2 Apply switching protocols such as RSTP+, LACP and vPC | 2 |
| 1.3 Apply overlay protocols such as VXLAN EVPN | 3 |
| 1.4 Apply ACI concepts | 4 |
| 1.4.a Fabric setup | 4 |
| 1.4.b Access policies | 4 |
| 1.4.c VMM | 4 |
| 1.5 Analyze packet flow (unicast, multicast, and broadcast) | 4 |
| 1.6 Describe Cloud service and deployment models (NIST 800-145) | 5 |
| 1.7 Describe software updates and their impacts | 6 |
| 1.7.a Disruptive/nondisruptive | 6 |
| 1.7.b EPLD | 6 |
| 1.7.c Patches | 6 |
| 1.8 Implement network configuration management | 6 |
| 1.9 Implement infrastructure monitoring such as NetFlow and SPAN | 6 |
| 1.10 Explain network assurance concepts such as streaming telemetry | 6 |
| 1.11 Describe the capabilities and features of Nexus Dashboard | 7 |
| 2.0 Compute | |
| 2.1 Implement Cisco Unified Compute System Rack Servers | 12 |
| 2.2 Implement Cisco Unified Compute System Blade Chassis | 12 |
| 2.2.a Initial setup | 12 |
| 2.2.b Infrastructure management | 12 |
| 2.2.c Network management (VLANs, pools and policies, templates, QoS) | 12 |
| 2.2.d Storage management (SAN connectivity, Fibre Channel zoning, VSANs, WWN pools, SAN policies, templates) | 12 |
| 2.2.e Server management (Server pools and boot policies) | 12 |

| DCCOR 350-601 Exam Topic | Chapter(s) in Which Topic Is Covered |
|---|---|
| 2.3 Explain HyperFlex Infrastructure concepts and benefits (Edge and Hybrid Architecture vs all-flash) | 15 |
| 2.4 Describe firmware and software updates and their impacts on B-Series and C-Series servers | 14 |
| 2.5 Implement compute configuration management (Backup and restore) | 14 |
| 2.6 Implement infrastructure monitoring such as SPAN and Cisco Intersight | 13 |
| 3.0 Storage Network | |
| 3.1 Implement Fibre Channel | 8 |
| 3.1.a Switch fabric initialization | 8 |
| 3.1.b Port channels | 8 |
| 3.1.c FCID | 8 |
| 3.1.d CFS | 8 |
| 3.1.e Zoning | 8 |
| 3.1.f FCNS | 8 |
| 3.1.g Device alias | 8 |
| 3.1.h NPV and NPIV | 8 |
| 3.1.i VSAN | 8 |
| 3.2 Implement FCoE Unified Fabric | 9 |
| 3.3 Describe NFS and NAS concepts | 10 |
| 3.4 Describe software updates and their impacts (Disruptive/nondisruptive and EPLD) | 11 |
| 3.5 Implement infrastructure monitoring | 11 |
| 4.0 Automation | |
| 4.1 Implement automation and scripting tools | 16 |
| 4.1.a EEM | 16 |
| 4.1.b Scheduler | 16 |
| 4.1.c Bash Shell and Guest Shell for NX-OS | 16 |
| 4.1.d REST API (NX-API, JSON, and XML encodings) | 16 |
| 4.1.e On-box Python | 17 |
| 4.2 Evaluate automation and orchestration technologies | 17 |
| 4.2.a Ansible | 17 |
| 4.2.b Python | 17 |
| 4.2.c POAP | 17 |
| 4.2.d Cisco Nexus Dashboard Fabric Controller | 7 |

| DCCOR 350-601 Exam Topic | Chapter(s) in Which Topic Is Covered |
|---|---|
| 4.2.e PowerShell | 17 |
| 4.2.f Terraform | 17 |
| **5.0 Security** | |
| **5.1 Apply network security** | 18 |
| 5.1.a AAA and RBAC | 18 |
| 5.1.b ACI contracts and microsegmentation | 18 |
| 5.1.c First-hop security features | 18 |
| 5.1.d Keychain authentication | 18 |
| **5.2 Apply compute security** | 19 |
| 5.2.a AAA and RBAC | 19 |
| **5.3 Apply storage security** | 20 |
| 5.3.a AAA and RBAC | 20 |
| 5.3.b Port security | 20 |
| 5.3.c Fabric binding | 20 |

Each version of the exam can have topics that emphasize different functions or features, and some topics can be rather broad and generalized. The goal of this book is to provide the most comprehensive coverage to ensure that you are well prepared for the exam. Although some chapters might not address specific exam topics, they provide a foundation that is necessary for a clear understanding of important topics. Your short-term goal might be to pass this exam, but your long-term goal should be to become a qualified data center professional.

It is also important to understand that this book is a "static" reference, whereas the exam topics are dynamic. Cisco can and does change the topics covered on certification exams often.

This exam guide should not be your only reference when preparing for the certification exam. You can find a wealth of information available at Cisco.com that covers each topic in great detail. If you think that you need more detailed information on a specific topic, read the Cisco documentation that focuses on that topic.

Note that as data center technologies continue to develop, Cisco reserves the right to change the exam topics without notice. Although you can refer to the list of exam topics in Table I-1, always check Cisco.com to verify the actual list of topics to ensure that you are prepared before taking the exam. You can view the current exam topics on any current Cisco certification exam by visiting the Cisco.com website, choosing **Menu**, and **Training & Events**, then selecting from the Certifications list. Note also that, if needed, Cisco Press might post additional preparatory content on the web page associated with this book at http://www.ciscopress.com/title/9780138228088. It's a good idea to check the website a couple of weeks before taking your exam to be sure that you have up-to-date content.

# Taking the CCNP Data Center Core Exam

As with any Cisco certification exam, you should strive to be thoroughly prepared before taking the exam. There is no way to determine exactly what questions are on the exam, so the best way to prepare is to have a good working knowledge of all subjects covered on the exam. Schedule yourself for the exam and be sure to be rested and ready to focus when taking the exam.

The best place to find out the latest available Cisco training and certifications is under the Training & Events section at Cisco.com.

# Tracking Your Status

You can track your certification progress by checking http://www.cisco.com/go/certifications/login. You must create an account the first time you log in to the site.

# How to Prepare for an Exam

The best way to prepare for any certification exam is to use a combination of the preparation resources, labs, and practice tests. This guide has integrated some practice questions and sample scenarios to help you better prepare. If possible, get some hands-on experience with ACI, Nexus, and UCS equipment. There is no substitute for real-world experience; it is much easier to understand the designs, configurations, and concepts when you can actually work with a live data center network.

Cisco.com provides a wealth of information about Application Centric Infrastructure (ACI), Nexus switches, and Unified Computing System—Blade and Rack servers, and data center LAN technologies and features.

# Assessing Exam Readiness

Exam candidates never really know whether they are adequately prepared for the exam until they have completed about 30 percent of the questions. At that point, if you are not prepared, it is too late. The best way to determine your readiness is to work through the "Do I Know This Already?" quizzes at the beginning of each chapter and review the foundation and key topics presented in each chapter. It is best to work your way through the entire book unless you can complete each subject without having to do any research or look up any answers.

# Cisco Data Center Certifications in the Real World

Cisco is one of the most recognized names on the Internet. Cisco Certified data center specialists can bring quite a bit of knowledge to the table because of their deep understanding of data center technologies, standards, and networking devices. This is why the Cisco certification carries such high respect in the marketplace. Cisco certifications demonstrate to potential employers and contract holders a certain professionalism, expertise, and dedication required to complete a difficult goal. If Cisco certifications were easy to obtain, everyone would have them.

## Exam Registration

The 350-601 CCNP Data Center Core Exam is a computer-based exam, with around 100 to 110 multiple-choice, fill-in-the-blank, list-in-order, and simulation-based questions. You can take the exam at any Pearson VUE (http://www.pearsonvue.com) testing center. According to Cisco, the exam should last about 120 minutes. Be aware that when you register for the exam, you might be told to allow a certain amount of time to take the exam that is longer than the testing time indicated by the testing software when you begin. The reason for this discrepancy is that the testing center will want you to allow for some time to get settled and take the tutorial about the test engine.

## Book Content Updates

Because Cisco occasionally updates exam topics without notice, Cisco Press might post additional preparatory content on the web page associated with this book at http://www.ciscopress.com/title/9780138228088. It is a good idea to check the website a couple of weeks before taking your exam to review any updated content that might be posted online. We also recommend that you periodically check back to this page on the Cisco Press website to view any errata or supporting book files that may be available.

## Figure Credits

Figures 17-5 through 17-8: HashiCorp

# CHAPTER 1

# Implementing Routing in the Data Center

Data centers are an essential element of the Internet and cloud infrastructure. It is the data networks that deliver data services around the world. This task would be impossible without routing. Even in the new generation of facilities like edge data centers, routers play an important role in connecting network services to end users.

**This chapter covers the following key topics:**

**OSPF:** This section discusses the NX-OS OSPFv2 and OSPFv3 routing protocols and includes OSPF area types, OSPF routing device functions, and NX-OS configuration commands plus an example.

**Border Gateway Protocol (BGP):** This section covers the NX-OS BGP external routing protocols, including Multiprotocol BGP (MBGP or MP-BGP), along with configuration commands and an example.

**Bidirectional Forwarding Detection (BFD):** This section covers NX-OS routing with BFD failure detection and configuration commands and an example.

**Multicast:** This section discusses the NX-OS Layer 2 and Layer 3 multicast protocols, which include IGMP, MLD, MDT, PIM, and multicast forwarding, along with configuration commands and examples.

**Hot Standby Router Protocol (HSRP):** This section discusses NX-OS HSRP as a First Hop Redundancy Protocol (FHRP) on the Ethernet network, including HSRP object tracking and load sharing along with configuration commands and an example.

**Virtual Router Redundancy Protocol (VRRP):** This section discusses the NX-OS VRRP operation, groups, and object tracking. In addition, this section covers IPv6 first hop redundancy and configuration commands and includes an example.

## "Do I Know This Already?" Quiz

The "Do I Know This Already?" quiz allows you to assess whether you should read this entire chapter thoroughly or jump to the "Exam Preparation Tasks" section. If you are in doubt about your answers to these questions or your own assessment of your knowledge of the topics, read the entire chapter. Table 1-1 lists the major headings in this chapter and their corresponding "Do I Know This Already?" quiz questions. You can find the answers in Appendix A, "Answers to the 'Do I Know This Already?' Quizzes."

**Table 1-1** "Do I Know This Already?" Section-to-Question Mapping

| Foundation Topics Section | Questions |
|---|---|
| OSPF | 1–5 |
| Border Gateway Protocol (BGP) | 6–7 |
| Bidirectional Forwarding Detection (BFD) | 9 |
| Multicast | 10–11 |
| Hot Standby Router Protocol (HSRP) | 12–14 |
| Virtual Router Redundancy Protocol (VRRP) | 15 |

**CAUTION**   The goal of self-assessment is to gauge your mastery of the topics in this chapter. If you do not know the answer to a question or are only partially sure of the answer, you should mark that question as wrong for purposes of the self-assessment. Giving yourself credit for an answer you correctly guess skews your self-assessment results and might provide you with a false sense of security.

1. When Open Shortest Path First (OSPF) starts neighbor negotiations, what setting must match between OSPF neighbors for them to be able to establish adjacencies?

    a. Router ID

    b. Hello intervals

    c. Link cost

    d. IP address

2. Which two parameters will assist in designated router (DR) elections? (Choose two answers.)

    a. IP address

    b. Router ID

    c. Priority

    d. Code version

3. Designated router elections occur on which type of network? (Choose two answers.)

    a. Point-to-Point

    b. Broadcast (Ethernet)

    c. NBMA mode

    d. Point-to-Multipoint

4. What are two enhancements that OSPFv3 supports over OSPFv2? (Choose two answers.)

    a. It requires the use of ARP.

    b. It can support multiple IPv6 subnets on a single link.

    c. It supports up to two instances of OSPFv3 over a common link.

    d. It routes over links rather than over networks.

**5.** Which statement about IPv6 and routing protocols are true?

    **a.** Link-local addresses are used to form routing adjacencies.

    **b.** OSPFv3 is the only routing protocol that supports IPv6.

    **c.** Loopback addresses are used to form routing adjacencies.

    **d.** MBGP does not support the IPv6 protocol.

**6.** When selecting the best path, the BGP protocol takes into account the following information in the stated order. (Choose one answer.)

    **a.** AS_Path, origin type, multi-exit discriminator, local preference

    **b.** AS_Path, origin type, local preference, multi-exit discriminator

    **c.** Local preference, AS_Path, origin type, multi-exit discriminator

    **d.** Local preference, AS_Path, multi-exit discriminator, origin type

**7.** Which command displays the iBGP and eBGP neighbors that are configured?

    **a.** show ip bgp

    **b.** show ip bgp paths

    **c.** show ip bgp peers

    **d.** show ip bgp summary

**8.** What kind of BGP session is established between two routers that are adjacent but in two different autonomous systems?

    **a.** eBGP

    **b.** iBGP

    **c.** dBGP

    **d.** mBGP

**9.** What is a BFD detect multiplier?

    **a.** The interval at which this device wants to send BFD hello messages

    **b.** The minimum interval at which this device can accept BFD hello messages from another BFD device

    **c.** The number of missing BFD hello messages from another BFD device before this local device detects a fault in the forwarding path

    **d.** The time between BFD hello packets

**10.** In Ethernet LANs, what is the functional equivalent to IGMPv3 in IPv6?

    **a.** IGMPv3 includes IPv6 multicast support; that's why it is v3.

    **b.** MLDv2.

    **c.** MLDv1.

    **d.** IPv6's native support for multicast routing deprecates this need.

**11.** What is the importance of the multicast RPF checking when running PIM sparse mode? (Choose two answers.)

    **a.** To prevent multicast source spoofing

    **b.** To prevent receiver spoofing

    **c.** To prevent multicast forwarding loops by validating that the receiving interface is the reverse path to the S address

    **d.** To prevent multicast forwarding loops by validating that the receiving interface is the reverse path of the G address

**12.** Which statements about HSRP operation are true? (Choose three answers.)

    **a.** The HSRP default timers are a 3-second hello interval and a 10-second dead interval.

    **b.** HSRP supports only cleartext authentication.

    **c.** The HSRP virtual IP address must be on a different subnet than the router's interface IP address.

    **d.** The HSRP virtual IP address must be on the same subnet as the router's interface address.

    **e.** HSRP V1 supports up to 256 groups.

**13.** Which HSRP feature was new in HSRPv2?

    **a.** Group numbers that are greater than 255

    **b.** Virtual MAC addresses

    **c.** Tracking

    **d.** Preemption

**14.** When a router with the highest HSRP priority recovers from failure, which option will ensure that the router immediately becomes the active router?

    **a.** standby preempt

    **b.** standby priority

    **c.** standby tracker

    **d.** standby delay

**15.** Which statement describes Virtual Router Redundancy Protocol (VRRP) object tracking?

    **a.** It monitors traffic flow and link utilization.

    **b.** It ensures the best VRRP router is the virtual router master for the group.

    **c.** It causes traffic to dynamically move to higher bandwidth links.

    **d.** It thwarts man-in-the-middle attacks.

## Foundation Topics

# Routing Protocols Support on Cisco Nexus Devices

The Cisco Nexus devices lineup at the time of writing this book consists of Cisco Nexus 9200, Cisco Nexus 9300, Cisco Nexus 9400, Cisco Nexus 9500, Cisco Nexus 9800, and the ultra-low latency Cisco Nexus 3550, as well as Nexus 3400 and 3600 switches.

**NOTE** The first edition of this book also covered the Cisco Nexus 7000/7700, Cisco Nexus 5000/5500/5600, and Cisco Nexus 3000 series of switches. In the current updated version of the book, the references to these model families have been removed as much as possible. Because the NX-OS has been and continues to be the operating system for all Cisco data center devices, the commands in the examples can be applied to the Cisco Nexus switches that are currently end-of-sale/end-of-life status, for multiple customers and lab facilities are still in operation.

Cisco Nexus devices run the Cisco NX-OS operating system. It is a modular operating system in which you can enable and disable the needed functionality. This capability leads to an optimized utilization of the device's hardware resources.

To enable a feature that is not enabled by default, you use the **feature** command, and to disable it, you use the **no feature** command. To use and configure a routing protocol on a Cisco Nexus switch, you must first enable the feature for that specific protocol and then continue with the configuration. If you do not enable the feature that you want to use, you will not be able to see the feature-specific command or perform any configuration. You also need to be careful when you disable a feature because all the feature-related configuration will be removed form the switch. That's why it is always a good approach to back up your configuration before disabling any features.

There are some differences in how the different types of dynamic routing protocols are configured in the Cisco NX-OS. For example, the Interior Gateway Protocols (IGPs) are configured using the following sequence:

1. Enable the routing protocol using the **feature** command.

2. In global configuration mode, create the routing process, usually with the command router.

3. Then, in the interface configuration, add the routing process.

This is a general sequence, and the specific commands for each of the routing protocols are covered in this book, but it shows a major difference with the configuration of a routing protocol in the Cisco IOS, where the routing process is created in global configuration mode and the networks are also added.

The Cisco NX-OS supports the following routing:

- **Connected routes:** Includes networks directly connected to the Cisco Nexus 9000 switch

- **Static routes:** Includes manually added static routes

- **Interior Gateway Protocols (IGPs):** Includes the following:

    - Routing Information Protocol (RIP)

    - OSPFv2 and OSPFv3

    - Enhanced Interior Gateway Routing Protocol (EIGRP)

    - Intermediate System-to-Intermediate System (IS-IS)

- **Exterior Gateway Protocol (EGP):** Supports the Border Gateway Protocol (BGP) and its advanced features, such as the Multiprotocol BGP (MP-BGP)

# OSPF

From the supported IGP protocols, we cover the Open Shortest Path First (OSPF). It is an IETF link-state routing protocol, which distributes information within a single autonomous system (AS).

OSPF has two versions: IPv4 OSPFv2 (version 2), which is described in RFC 2328, and IPv6 OSPFv3 (version 3), which is described in RFC 2740.

OSPF utilizes *hello packets* (multicast IPv4 224.0.0.5 or IPv6 FF02::5) for neighbor discovery. These hello packets are sent out on each OSPF-enabled interface to discover other OSPF neighbor routers. OSPF sends hello packets every 10 seconds (the OSPF default *hello_interval* is set to 10 seconds). In addition, OSPF uses hello packets for keepalive and bidirectional traffic. For keepalive, OSPF determines whether a neighbor is still communicating. If a router does not receive a hello packet within 40 seconds (the OSPF *dead-interval* is usually a multiple of the hello interval; the default is four times the hello interval), the neighbor is removed from the local neighbor table.

When a neighbor is discovered, the two routers compare information in the hello packet to determine whether the routers have compatible configurations. The neighbor routers attempt to establish *adjacency*, which means that the routers synchronize their link-state databases to ensure that they have identical OSPF routing information. Adjacent routers share link-state advertisements (LSAs) that include information about the operational state of each link, the cost of the link, and any other neighbor information. The routers then flood these received LSAs out every OSPF-enabled interface so that all OSPF routers eventually have identical link-state databases. When all OSPF routers have identical link-state databases, the network is *converged*. Each router then uses Dijkstra's Shortest Path First (SPF) algorithm to build its route table.

The key differences between the OSPFv3 and OSPFv2 protocols are as follows:

- OSPFv3 expands on OSPFv2 to provide support for IPv6 routing prefixes and the larger size IPv6 addresses, OSPF Hello address FF02::5.

- LSAs in OSPFv3 are expressed as prefix and prefix length instead of address and mask.

- The router ID and area ID are 32-bit numbers with no relationship to IPv6 addresses.

- OSPFv3 uses link-local IPv6 addresses for neighbor discovery and other features.

- OSPFv3 can use the IPv6 authentication trailer (RFC 6506) or IPSec (RFC 4552) for authentication. However, neither of these options is supported on Cisco NX-OS.

- OSPFv3 redefines LSA types.

## OSPF Link-State Advertisements

OSPF uses link-state advertisements (LSAs) to build its routing table. When an OSPF router receives an LSA, it forwards that LSA out every OSPF-enabled interface, flooding the OSPF area with this information. This LSA flooding guarantees that all routers in the network have identical routing information. LSA flooding depends on the OSPF area configuration. The LSAs are flooded based on the link-state refresh time (every 30 minutes by default). Each LSA has its own link-state refresh time.

OSPFv2 LSAs have seven different types (LSA type 1 to 7) and extensions (LSA 9 to 11) called Opaque, as shown in Table 1-2.

Opaque LSAs consist of a standard LSA header followed by application-specific information. This information might be used by OSPFv2 or by other applications. OSPFv2 uses Opaque

LSAs to support the OSPFv2 graceful restart capability. The three Opaque LSA types are defined as follows:

- **LSA type 9:** Flooded to the local network.

- **LSA type 10:** Flooded to the local area.

- **LSA type 11:** Flooded to the local autonomous system.

In OSPFv3, LSA changed by creating a separation between prefixes and the SPF tree. There is no prefix information in LSA types 1 and 2. You find only topology adjacencies in these LSAs; you don't find any IPv6 prefixes in them. Prefixes are now advertised in type 9 LSAs, and the link-local addresses that are used for next hops are advertised in type 8 LSAs. Type 8 LSAs are flooded only on the local link, whereas type 9 LSAs are flooded within the area. The designers of OSPFv3 could have included link-local addresses in type 9 LSAs, but because these are only required on the local link, it would be a waste of resources.

**Table 1-2**   OSPFv2 and OSPFv3 LSAs Supported by Cisco NX-OS

| Type | OSPFv2 Name | Description | OSPFv3 Name | Description |
|---|---|---|---|---|
| 1 | Router LSA | LSA sent by every router. This LSA includes the state and the cost of all links and a list of all OSPFv2 neighbors on the link. Router LSAs trigger an SPF recalculation. Router LSAs are flooded to the local OSPFv2 area. | Router LSA | LSA sent by every router. This LSA includes the state and cost of all links but does not include prefix information. Router LSAs trigger an SPF recalculation. Router LSAs are flooded to the local OSPFv3 area. |
| 2 | Network LSA | LSA sent by the DR. This LSA lists all routers in the multi-access network. Network LSAs trigger an SPF recalculation. | Network LSA | LSA sent by the DR. This LSA lists all routers in the multi-access network but does not include prefix information. Network LSAs trigger an SPF recalculation. |
| 3 | Network Summary LSA | LSA sent by the area border router to an external area for each destination in the local area. This LSA includes the link cost from the area border router to the local destination. | Inter-Area Prefix LSA | Same as OSPFv2; just the name changed. |
| 4 | ASBR Summary LSA | LSA sent by the area border router to an external area. This LSA advertises the link cost to the ASBR only. | Inter-Area Router LSA | Same as OSPFv2; just the name changed. |

| Type | OSPFv2 Name | Description | OSPFv3 Name | Description |
|------|-------------|-------------|-------------|-------------|
| 5 | AS External LSA | LSA generated by the ASBR. This LSA includes the link cost to an external autonomous system destination. AS External LSAs are flooded throughout the autonomous system. | AS External LSA | Same as OSPFv2. |
| 7 | NSSA External LSA | LSA generated by the ASBR within a not-so-stubby area (NSSA). This LSA includes the link cost to an external autonomous system destination. NSSA External LSAs are flooded only within the local NSSA. | NSSA External LSA | Same as OSPFv2. |
| 8 | N/A | | Link LSA (New OSPFv3 LSA) | LSA sent by every router, using a link-local flooding scope. This LSA includes the link-local address and IPv6 prefixes for this link. |
| 9 | Opaque LSAs | LSA used to extend OSPF. | Intra-Area Prefix LSA | LSA sent by every router. This LSA includes any prefix or link state changes. Intra-Area Prefix LSAs are flooded to the local OSPFv3 area. This LSA does not trigger an SPF recalculation. |
| 10 | Opaque LSAs | LSA used to extend OSPF. | N/A | |
| 11 | Opaque LSAs | LSA used to extend OSPF. | Grace L SAs | LSA sent by a restarting router, using a link-local flooding scope. This LSA is used for a graceful restart of OSPFv3. |

To control the flooding rate of LSA updates in your network, you can use the *LSA group pacing* feature. LSA group pacing can reduce high CPU or buffer usage. This feature groups LSAs with similar link-state refresh times to allow OSPF to pack multiple LSAs into an OSPF update message.

Each router maintains a link-state database for the OSPF network. This database contains all the collected LSAs and includes information on all the routes through the network. OSPF uses this information to calculate the best path to each destination and populates the routing table with these best paths.

LSAs are removed from the link-state database if no LSA update has been received within a set interval, called the MaxAge. Routers flood a repeat of the LSA every 30 minutes to prevent accurate link-state information from being aged out. The Cisco NX-OS operating system supports the LSA grouping feature to prevent all LSAs from refreshing at the same time.

### OSPF Areas

An *area* is a logical division of routers and links within an OSPF domain that creates separate subdomains. *LSA flooding is contained within an area*, and the link-state database is limited to links within the area, which reduces the CPU and memory requirements for an OSPF-enabled router. You can assign an area ID to the interfaces within the defined area.

The area ID is a 32-bit value that you can enter as a number or in dotted-decimal notation, such as 3.3.3.3 or 0.0.0.3. Cisco NX-OS always displays the area in dotted-decimal notation. If you define more than one area in an OSPF network, you must also define the *backbone area*, which has the reserved area ID of 0.0.0.0. If you have more than one area, one or more routers become *area border routers* (ABRs). An ABR connects to both the backbone area and at least one other defined area (see Figure 1-1).

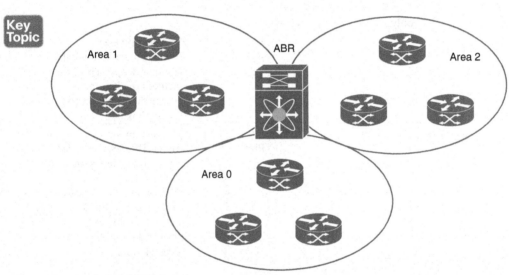

**Figure 1-1**   *OSPF Areas*

The ABR has a separate link-state database for each area to which it connects. The ABR sends *Network Summary (type 3) LSAs* from one connected area to the backbone area. The backbone area sends summarized information about one area to another area.

OSPF defines another router type as an *autonomous system boundary router* (ASBR). This router connects an OSPF area to another autonomous system. An autonomous system is a network controlled by a single technical administration entity. OSPF can redistribute its routing information into another autonomous system or receive redistributed routes from another autonomous system.

You can limit the amount of external routing information that floods an area by making it a *stub area*. A stub area is an area that does not allow AS External (type 5) LSAs. These LSAs are usually flooded throughout the local autonomous system to propagate external route information. Stub areas have the following requirements:

- All routers in the stub area are stub routers.

- No ASBR routers exist in the stub area.

- You cannot configure virtual links in the stub area.

Figure 1-2 shows an example of an OSPF autonomous system where all routers in area 0.0.0.5 have to go through the ABR to reach external autonomous systems. Area 0.0.0.5 can be configured as a stub area.

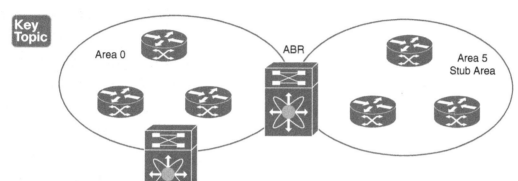

**Figure 1-2**  *OSPF Stub Area*

Stub areas use a default route for all traffic that needs to go through the backbone area to the external autonomous system.

There is an option to allow OSPF to import autonomous system external routes within a stub area; this is a *not-so-stubby area* (NSSA). An NSSA is similar to a stub area, except that an NSSA allows you to import autonomous system (AS) external routes within an NSSA using redistribution. The NSSA ASBR redistributes these routes and generates NSSA External (type 7) LSAs that it floods throughout the NSSA. You can optionally configure the ABR that connects the NSSA to other areas to translate this NSSA External LSA to AS External (type 5) LSAs. The ABR then floods these AS External LSAs throughout the OSPF autonomous system. Summarization and filtering are supported during the translation.

You can, for example, use NSSA to simplify administration if you are connecting a central site using OSPF to a remote site that is using a different routing protocol. Before NSSA, the connection between the corporate site border router and a remote router could not be run as an OSPF stub area because routes for the remote site could not be redistributed into a stub area. With NSSA, you can extend OSPF to cover the remote connection by defining the area between the corporate router and remote router as an NSSA.

**NOTE**  The backbone area 0 cannot be an NSSA.

All OSPF areas must physically connect to area 0 (backbone area). If one area cannot connect directly to area 0, you need a virtual link. Virtual links allow you to connect an OSPF area ABR to a backbone area ABR when a direct physical connection is not available. Figure 1-3 shows a virtual link that connects area 5 to the backbone area 0 through area 3.

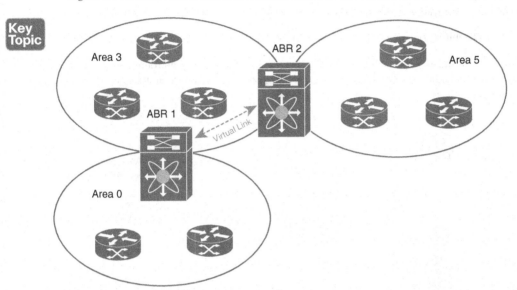

**Figure 1-3**  *OSPF Virtual Links*

You can also use virtual links to temporarily recover from a partitioned area, which occurs when a link within the area fails, isolating part of the area from reaching the designated ABR to the backbone area.

### Designated Routers and Backup Designated Routers

OSPF routers with the broadcast network type will flood the network with LSAs. The same link-state information needs to be sent from multiple sources. For this type, OSPF uses a single router, the *designated router* (DR), to control the LSA floods and represent the network to the rest of the OSPF area. OSPF selects a *backup designated router* (BDR). If the DR fails, the BDR will take the DR role of redistributing routing information.

Network types are as follows:

- **Point-to-point:** A network that exists only between two routers. All neighbors on a point-to-point network establish adjacency, and *there is no DR required.*

- **Broadcast:** A network with multiple routers that can communicate over a shared medium that allows broadcast traffic, such as Ethernet. OSPF routers establish a DR and BDR that control LSA flooding on the network. In OSPFv2, DR uses the well-known IPv4 multicast address 224.0.0.5 and the MAC address 0100.5e00.0005 to communicate with neighbors, and in OSPFv3, it uses the well-known IPv6 multicast address FF02::5 and the MAC address 3333.0000.0005 to communicate with neighbors. Likewise, in OSPFv2, each non-DR or non-BDR router uses the well-known IPv4 multicast address 224.0.0.6 and the MAC address 0100.5e00.0006 to send routing information to a DR or BDR, and in OSPFv3, it uses the well-known IPv6 multicast address FF02::6 and the MAC address 3333.0000.0006 to send routing information to a DR or BDR.

## OSPF Authentication

OSPFv2 supports authentication to prevent unauthorized or invalid routing updates in the network. Cisco NX-OS supports two authentication methods:

■ Simple password authentication

■ MD5 authentication digest

Simple password authentication uses a simple cleartext password that is sent as part of the OSPFv2 message. The receiving OSPFv2 router must be configured with the same cleartext password to accept the OSPFv2 message as a valid route update. Because the password is in clear text, anyone who can watch traffic on the network can learn the password.

Cisco recommends that you use MD5 authentication to authenticate OSPFv2 messages. You can configure a password that is shared at the local router and all remote OSPFv2 neighbors. For each OSPFv2 message, Cisco NX-OS creates an MD5 one-way message digest based on the message itself and the encrypted password. The interface sends this digest with the OSPFv2 message. The receiving OSPFv2 neighbor validates the digest using the same encrypted password. If the message has not changed, the digest calculation is identical, and the OSPFv2 message is considered valid.

MD5 authentication includes a sequence number with each OSPFv2 message to ensure that no message is replayed in the network.

OSPFv3 doesn't have an authentication field in its header like OSPFv2; instead, OSPFv3 relies on IPsec.

## OSPF Configurations and Verifications

Table 1-3 lists the OSPFv2/v3 default parameters. You can alter OSPF parameters as necessary. You are not required to alter any of these parameters, but the following parameters must be consistent across all routers in an attached network: ospf hello-interval and ospf dead-interval. If you configure any of these parameters, be sure that the configurations for all routers on your network have compatible values.

**Table 1-3**   Default OSPFv2/OSPFv3 Parameters

| Parameters | Default |
| --- | --- |
| Administrative distance | 110 |
| Hello interval | 10 seconds |
| Dead interval | 40 seconds |
| Graceful restart grace period | 60 seconds |
| OSPFv2/OSPFv3 feature | Disabled |
| Stub router advertisement announce time | 600 seconds |
| Reference bandwidth for link cost calculation | 40 Gbps |
| LSA minimal arrival time | 1000 milliseconds |
| LSA group pacing | 10 seconds |
| SPF calculation initial delay time | 200 milliseconds |

| Parameters | Default |
|---|---|
| SPF calculation maximum wait time | 5000 milliseconds |
| SPF minimum hold time | 1000 milliseconds |

Cisco NX-OS is a modular system and requires a specific license to enable specific features. Table 1-4 covers the NX-OS feature licenses required for OSPFv2/OSPFv3. For more information, visit the Cisco NX-OS Licensing Guide.

**Table 1-4** Feature-Based Licenses for Cisco NX-OS OSPFv2 and OSPFv3

| Platform | Feature License | Feature Name |
|---|---|---|
| Cisco Nexus 9000 Series | Enterprise Services Package | OSPF |
| | LAN_ENTERPRISE_SERVICES_PKG | OSPFv3 |

OSPFv2 and OSPFv3 have the following configuration limitations:

- Cisco NX-OS displays areas in dotted-decimal notation regardless of whether you enter the area in decimal or dotted-decimal notation.

- The OSPFv3 router ID and area ID are 32-bit numbers with no relationship to IPv6 addresses.

Tables 1-5 through 1-8 describe the most-used OSPFv2/v3 configuration commands. For a full list of the commands, refer to the Nexus Unicast Routing Configuration Guide links shown in the reference list at the end of this chapter.

**Table 1-5** OSPF Global-Level Commands

| Command | Purpose |
|---|---|
| feature ospf | Enables the OSPFv2 feature. |
| feature ospfv3 | Enables the OSPFv3 feature. |
| router ospf *ospf-instance-tag* | Creates a new OSPFv2 routing instance. |
| router ospfv3 *ospf-instance-tag* | Creates a new OSPFv3 routing instance. |

**Table 1-6** OSPF Routing-Level Commands

| Command | Purpose |
|---|---|
| router-id *ip-address* | (Optional) Configures a unique OSPFv2 or OSPFv3 router ID. *ip-address* must exist on a configured interface in the system. |
| area *area-id* authentication [message-digest ] | Configures the authentication mode for an area. |
| area *area-id* stub | Creates this area as a stub area. |
| area *area-id* nssa [no-redistribution] [default-information-originate]originate [route-map *map-name*]] [no-summary ] [translate type7 {always \| never } [suppress-fa ]] | Creates this area as an NSSA. |

| Command | Purpose |
|---------|---------|
| log-adjecency-changes [detail] | Generates a system message when a neighbor changes state. |
| address-family ipv6 unicast | Enters IPv6 unicast address family mode. |

**Table 1-7**   OSPF Interface-Level Commands

| Command | Purpose |
|---------|---------|
| ip ospf *cost number* | (Optional) Configures the OSPFv2 cost metric for this interface. The default is to calculate the cost metric, based on reference bandwidth and interface bandwidth. The range is from 1 to 65,535. |
| ip ospf dead-interval *seconds* | (Optional) Configures the OSPFv2 dead interval in seconds. The range is from 1 to 65,535. The default is four times the hello interval in seconds. |
| ip ospf hello-interval *seconds* | (Optional) Configures the OSPFv2 hello interval in seconds. The range is from 1 to 65,535. The default is 10 seconds. |
| ip ospf mtu-ignore | (Optional) Configures OSPFv2 to ignore any IP maximum transmission unit (MTU) mismatch with a neighbor. The default is not to establish adjacency if the neighbor MTU does not match the local interface MTU. |
| ospf network {broadcast \| point-point } | (Optional) Sets the OSPFv2 network type. |
| [default \| no] ip ospf passive-interface | (Optional) Suppresses routing updates on the interface. This command overrides the router or VRF command mode configuration. The default option removes this interface mode command and reverts to the router or VRF configuration if present. |
| ip ospf priority *number* | (Optional) Configures the OSPFv2 priority used to determine the DR for an area. The range is from 0 to 255. The default is 1. |
| ip ospf shutdown | (Optional) Shuts down the OSPFv2 instance on this interface. |
| ip ospf message- digest-key *key-id* md5 [0 \| 3 ] *key* | Configures message digest authentication for this interface. Use this command if the authentication is set to message-digest. The *key-id* range is from 1 to 255. The MD5 option 0 configures the password in clear text, and option 3 configures the pass key as 3DES encrypted. |
| ip router ospf *instance-tag* area *area-id* [secondaries none ] | Adds the interface to the OSPFv2 instance and area. |
| ipv6 router ospfv3 *instance-tag* area *area-id* [ secondaries none ] | Adds the interface to the OSPFv3 instance and area. |

**Table 1-8**   OSPF Global-Level Verification and Process Clear Commands

| Command | Purpose |
|---------|---------|
| show ip ospf [*instance-tag*] [ vrf *vrf-name* ] | Displays the OSPFv2 configuration. |
| show ip ospf interface [*instance-tag*] [ *interface-type interface-number* ] [brief] [ vrf *vrf-name* ] | Displays the OSPFv2 interface configuration. |

| Command | Purpose |
|---|---|
| **show ip ospf route** [ *ospf-route* ] [ **summary** ] [ **vrf** { *vrf-name* \| **all** \| **default** \| **management** }] | Displays the internal OSPFv2 routes. |
| **show ip ospf virtual-links** [ **brief** ] [ **vrf** { *vrf-name* \| **all** \| **default** \| **management** }] | Displays information about OSPFv2 virtual links. |
| **show running-configuration ospf** | Displays the current running OSPFv2 configuration. |
| **show ip ospf statistics** [ **vrf** { *vrf-name* \| **all** \| **default** \| **management** }] | Displays the OSPFv2 event counters. |
| **show ip ospf traffic** [ *interface - type number* ] [ **vrf** { *vrf-name* \| **all** \| **default** \| **management** }] | Displays the OSPFv2 packet counters. |
| **clear ip ospf** [instance-tag] **neighbor** {\* \| *neighbor-id* \| *interface-type number* \| *loopback number* \| *port-channel number*} [**vrf** *vrf-name*] | Clears neighbor statistics and resets adjacencies for Open Shortest Path First (OSPFv2). <br><br> **NOTE:** Clearing the OSPF **neighbor** command will reload the OSPF process, so take extra precaution before executing the command in a production environment. |
| **show** [*ipv6*] **ospfv3** [*instance-tag*] [ **vrf** *vrf-name* ] | Displays the OSPFv3 configuration. |
| **show** [*ipv6*] **ospfv3 interface** [*instance-tag*] [ *interface-type interface-number* ] [**brief**] [ **vrf** *vrf-name* ] | Displays the OSPFv3 interface configuration. |
| **clear ospfv3** [*instance-tag*] **neighbor** {\* \| *neighbor-id* \| **interface-type** *number* \| **loopback number** \| **port-channel** *number*} [**vrf** *vrf-name*] | Clears neighbor statistics and resets adjacencies for Open Shortest Path First (OSPFv3). <br><br> **NOTE:** Clearing the OSPF **neighbor** command will reload the OSPF process, so take extra precaution before executing the command in a production environment. |

Figure 1-4 shows the network topology for the configuration that follows, which demonstrates how to configure Nexus OSPF for IPv4 and IPv6.

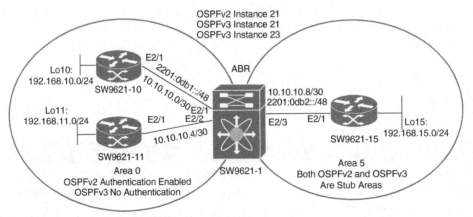

**Figure 1-4**   *OSPF Network Topology*

**NOTE**   To practice Nexus configuration, you can use the Cisco Virtual Internet Routing Lab (VIRL) from the Cisco Modeling Labs (https://developer.cisco.com/modeling-labs/). If you don't have VIRL in your lab, you can use Cisco dCloud (https://dcloud.cisco.com); in this case, search for "VIRL 1.6.65 Sandbox."

Example 1-1 shows SW9621-1 OSPFv2 feature enabling and router configurations.

**Example 1-1**   *OSPF Instance 21*

```
SW9621-1(config)# feature ospf
SW9621-1(config)# router ospf 21
SW9621-1(config-router)# router-id 1.1.1.1
SW9621-1(config-router)# area 0.0.0.0 authentication message-digest
SW9621-1(config-router)# area 0.0.0.5 stub
```

Example 1-2 shows SW9621-1 OSPFv3 feature enabling and router configurations.

**Example 1-2**   *OSPF Instance 21 and 23*

```
SW9621-1(config)# feature ospfv3
SW9621-1(config)# router ospfv3 21
SW9621-1(config-router)# router-id 1.1.1.1
SW9621-1(config)# router ospfv3 23
SW9621-1(config-router)# area 0.0.0.5 stub
```

**NOTE**   We didn't configure the router ID for OSPFv3 23; it is recommended that you configure the router ID.

Examples 1-3 and 1-4 show SW9621-1 OSFP interface and authentication configurations.

**Example 1-3**   *OSPF Interface Configurations*

```
SW9621-1(config)# interface loopback0
SW9621-1(config-if)# ip address 1.1.1.1/32
SW9621-1(config-if)# ip router ospf 21 area 0.0.0.0
SW9621-1(config)# interface Ethernet2/1
SW9621-1(config-if)# ip address 10.10.10.1/30
SW9621-1(config-if)# ip ospf authentication message-digest
SW9621-1(config-if)# ip ospf authentication key-chain mypass
SW9621-1(config-if)# ip router ospf 21 area 0.0.0.0
SW9621-1(config-if)# ipv6 address 2201:db1::1/48
SW9621-1(config-if)# ipv6 router ospf 21 area 0.0.0.0
SW9621-1(config-if)# no shutdown
SW9621-1(config)# interface Ethernet2/2
SW9621-1(config-if)# ip address 10.10.10.5/30
SW9621-1(config-if)# mtu 9216
SW9621-1(config-if)# ip ospf authentication message-digest
SW9621-1(config-if)# ip ospf authentication key-chain mypass
```

```
SW9621-1(config-if)# ip ospf network point-to-point
SW9621-1(config-if)# ip router ospf 21 area 0.0.0.0
SW9621-1(config-if)# no shutdown
SW9621-1(config)# interface Ethernet2/3
SW9621-1(config-if)# ip address 10.10.10.9/30
SW9621-1(config-if)# ip ospf hello-interval 25
SW9621-1(config-if)# ip router ospf 21 area 0.0.0.5
SW9621-1(config-if)# ipv6 address 2201:db2::1/48
SW9621-1(config-if)# ipv6 router ospf 23 area 0.0.0.5
SW9621-1(config-if)# no shutdown
SW9621-1(config-if)# exit
```

**NOTE**   Use the **ip ospf mtu-ignore** command for OSPFv2 or **ipv6 ospf mtu-ignore** command for OSPFv3 to disable MTU mismatch detection on an interface. By default, OSPF checks whether neighbors use the same MTU on a common interface. If the receiving MTU is higher than the IP MTU configured on the incoming interface, OSPF does not establish adjacencies. The **mtu-ignore** command will disable this check and allow adjacencies when the MTU value differs between OSPF neighbors. This command will help only if the OSPF LSA database packet size is less than the lowest interface MTU. If the OSPF LSA packet is greater than the interface MTU, the physical interface will drop the packet as defragment is disabled, and the OSPF neighbor will continuously change state between Down and Full.

**NOTE**   The dead interval default will be 4xhello-interval. In this example, it is set to 100 seconds. You can set the dead interval using the OSPF interface command **ospf dead-interval** *seconds.*

**Example 1-4**   *OSPF Authentication Shared Key Configuration*

```
SW9621-1(config)# key chain mypass
SW9621-1(config-keychain)# key 0
SW9621-1(config-keychain-key)# key-string cisco
SW9621-1(config-keychain-key)# exit
SW9621-1(config-keychain)# exit
```

Examples 1-5 and 1-6 show the SW9621-1 OSPF status.

**Example 1-5**   *OSFPv2 ABR Verification (SW9621-1)*

```
SW9621-1# show ip ospf neighbors

OSPF Process ID 21 VRF default
 Total number of neighbors: 3
 Neighbor ID    Pri State         Up Time Address      Interface
 1.1.1.10       10 FULL/BDR       00:20:19 10.10.10.2   Eth2/1
 1.1.1.11       1 FULL/ -         00:20:48 10.10.10.6   Eth2/2
 1.1.1.15       1 FULL/BDR        00:04:39 10.10.10.10  Eth2/3
```

```
SW9621-1# show ip ospf
 Routing Process 21 with ID 1.1.1.1 VRF default
 Routing Process Instance Number 1
 Stateful High Availability enabled
 Graceful-restart is configured
   Grace period: 60 state: Inactive
   Last graceful restart exit status: None
 Supports only single TOS(TOS0) routes
 Supports opaque LSA
 This router is an area border
 Administrative distance 110
 Reference Bandwidth is 40000 Mbps
 SPF throttling delay time of 200.000 msecs,
   SPF throttling hold time of 1000.000 msecs,
   SPF throttling maximum wait time of 5000.000 msecs
 LSA throttling start time of 0.000 msecs,
   LSA throttling hold interval of 5000.000 msecs,
   LSA throttling maximum wait time of 5000.000 msecs
 Minimum LSA arrival 1000.000 msec
 LSA group pacing timer 10 secs
 Maximum paths to destination 8
 Number of external LSAs 0, checksum sum 0
 Number of opaque AS LSAs 0, checksum sum 0
 Number of areas is 2, 1 normal, 1 stub, 0 nssa
 Number of active areas is 2, 1 normal, 1 stub, 0 nssa
 Install discard route for summarized external routes.
 Install discard route for summarized internal routes.
   Area BACKBONE(0.0.0.0)
         Area has existed for 00:37:14
         Interfaces in this area: 3 Active interfaces: 3
         Passive interfaces: 0 Loopback interfaces: 1
         Message-digest authentication
         SPF calculation has run 20 times
          Last SPF ran for 0.000420s
         Area ranges are
         Number of LSAs: 7, checksum sum 0x363a9
   Area (0.0.0.5)
         Area has existed for 00:37:14
         Interfaces in this area: 1 Active interfaces: 1
         Passive interfaces: 0 Loopback interfaces: 0
         This area is a STUB area
         Generates stub default route with cost 1
         No authentication available
         SPF calculation has run 20 times
          Last SPF ran for 0.000078s
```

```
        Area ranges are
        Number of LSAs: 11, checksum sum 0x5306a
SW9621-1# show ip ospf interface brief
OSPF Process ID 21 VRF default
Total number of interface: 4
Interface      ID    Area        Cost    State      Neighbors Status
Lo0            1     0.0.0.0     1       LOOPBACK 0          up
Eth2/1         4     0.0.0.0     40      DR         1         up
Eth2/2         3     0.0.0.0     40      P2P        1         up
Eth2/3         2     0.0.0.5     40      DR         1         up


SW9621-1# show ip ospf interface
loopback0 is up, line protocol is up
    IP address 1.1.1.1/32
    Process ID 21 VRF default, area 0.0.0.0
    Enabled by interface configuration
    State LOOPBACK, Network type LOOPBACK, cost 1
    Index 1
Ethernet2/1 is up, line protocol is up
    IP address 10.10.10.1/30
    Process ID 21 VRF default, area 0.0.0.0
    Enabled by interface configuration
    State DR, Network type BROADCAST, cost 40
    Index 4, Transmit delay 1 sec, Router Priority 1
    Designated Router ID: 1.1.1.1, address: 10.10.10.1
    Backup Designated Router ID: 1.1.1.10, address: 10.10.10.2
    1 Neighbors, flooding to 1, adjacent with 1
    Timer intervals: Hello 10, Dead 40, Wait 40, Retransmit 5
      Hello timer due in 00:00:05
    Message-digest authentication, using keychain mypass (ready)
    Number of opaque link LSAs: 0, checksum sum 0
Ethernet2/2 is up, line protocol is up
    IP address 10.10.10.5/30
    Process ID 21 VRF default, area 0.0.0.0
    Enabled by interface configuration
    State P2P, Network type P2P, cost 40
    Index 3, Transmit delay 1 sec
    1 Neighbors, flooding to 1, adjacent with 1
    Timer intervals: Hello 10, Dead 40, Wait 40, Retransmit 5
      Hello timer due in 00:00:02
    Message-digest authentication, using keychain mypass (ready)
    Number of opaque link LSAs: 0, checksum sum 0
```

```
Ethernet2/3 is up, line protocol is up
    IP address 10.10.10.9/30
    Process ID 21 VRF default, area 0.0.0.5
    Enabled by interface configuration
    State DR, Network type BROADCAST, cost 40
    Index 2, Transmit delay 1 sec, Router Priority 1
    Designated Router ID: 1.1.1.1, address: 10.10.10.9
    Backup Designated Router ID: 1.1.1.15, address: 10.10.10.10
    1 Neighbors, flooding to 1, adjacent with 1
    Timer intervals: Hello 25, Dead 100, Wait 100, Retransmit 5
      Hello timer due in 00:00:06
    No authentication
    Number of opaque link LSAs: 0, checksum sum 0
```

**Example 1-6**   *OSFPv3 ABR Verification (SW9621-1)*

```
SW9621-1# show ospfv3 neighbors

OSPFv3 Process ID 23 VRF default
Total number of neighbors: 1
Neighbor ID    Pri State          Up Time  Interface ID     Interface
1.1.1.15         1 FULL/DR          00:00:54 36               Eth2/3
   Neighbor address fe80::200:ff:feff:1ff
OSPFv3 Process ID 21 VRF default
Total number of neighbors: 1
Neighbor ID    Pri State          Up Time  Interface ID     Interface
1.1.1.10         1 FULL/DR          01:02:49 38               Eth2/1
   Neighbor address fe80::200:ff:fe00:2f

SW9621-1# show ipv6 ospfv3 interface

Ethernet2/3 is up, line protocol is up
    IPv6 address 2201:db2::1/48
    Process ID 23 VRF default, Instance ID 0, area 0.0.0.5
    Enabled by interface configuration
    State BDR, Network type BROADCAST, cost 40
    Index 1, Transmit delay 1 sec, Router Priority 1
    Designated Router ID: 1.1.1.15, address: fe80::200:ff:feff:1ff
    Backup Designated Router ID: 1.1.1.1, address: fe80::200:ff:feff:ddfe
    1 Neighbors, flooding to 1, adjacent with 1
    Timer intervals: Hello 10, Dead 40, Wait 40, Retransmit 5
      Hello timer due in 00:00:05
    Number of link LSAs: 2, checksum sum 0xe4da
```

```
Ethernet2/1 is up, line protocol is up
    IPv6 address 2201:db1::1/48
    Process ID 21 VRF default, Instance ID 0, area 0.0.0.0
    Enabled by interface configuration
    State BDR, Network type BROADCAST, cost 40
    Index 2, Transmit delay 1 sec, Router Priority 1
    Designated Router ID: 1.1.1.10, address: fe80::200:ff:fe00:2f
    Backup Designated Router ID: 1.1.1.1, address: fe80::200:ff:feff:ef22
    1 Neighbors, flooding to 1, adjacent with 1
    Timer intervals: Hello 10, Dead 40, Wait 40, Retransmit 5
      Hello timer due in 00:00:00
    Number of link LSAs: 2, checksum sum 0xbaac
```

Example 1-7 shows the SW9621-10 OSPFv2/v3 configurations and status.

**Example 1-7**  *Router 1 Configuration and Verification (SW9621-10)*

```
SW9621-10(config)# feature ospf
SW9621-10(config)# feature ospfv3
SW9621-10(config)# router ospf 21
SW9621-10(config-router)# router-id 1.1.1.10
SW9621-10(config-router)# area 0.0.0.0 authentication message-digest
SW9621-10(config)# router ospfv3 21
SW9621-10(config-router)# router-id 1.1.1.10
SW9621-10(config-router)# key chain mypass
SW9621-10(config-keychain)# key 0
SW9621-10(config-keychain-key)# key-string cisco

SW9621-10(config-keychain-key)# interface loopback0
SW9621-10(config-if)# ip address 1.1.1.10/32
SW9621-10(config-if)# ip router ospf 21 area 0.0.0.0

SW9621-10(config-if)# interface loopback10
SW9621-10(config-if)# ip address 192.168.10.1/24
SW9621-10(config-if)# ip router ospf 21 area 0.0.0.0

SW9621-10(config-if)# interface Ethernet2/1
SW9621-10(config-if)# no switchport
SW9621-10(config-if)# ip address 10.10.10.2/30
SW9621-10(config-if)# ip ospf authentication key-chain mypass
SW9621-10(config-if)# ip ospf priority 10 !# Note higher priorities win the DR
election
SW9621-10(config-if)# ipv6 address 2201:db1::2/48
SW9621-10(config-if)# ip router ospf 21 area 0.0.0.0
SW9621-10(config-if)# ipv6 router ospfv3 21 area 0.0.0.0
SW9621-10(config-if)# no shutdown
```

```
SW9621-10# show ip ospf neighbors
 OSPF Process ID 21 VRF default
 Total number of neighbors: 1
 Neighbor ID Pri State Up Time Address Interface
 1.1.1.1 1 FULL/DR 00:00:26 10.10.10.1 Eth2/1


SW9621-10# show ipv6 ospfv3 neighbors
 OSPFv3 Process ID 21 VRF default
 Total number of neighbors: 1
 Neighbor ID     Pri State       Up Time    Interface ID     Interface
 1.1.1.1          1 FULL/DR       00:01:54   37               Eth2/1
    Neighbor address fe80::200:ff:feff:ef22
```

Example 1-8 shows the SW9621-11 OSPFv2 configurations and status.

**Example 1-8**  *Router 2 Configuration and Verification (SW9621-11)*

```
SW9621-11(config)# feature ospf
SW9621-11(config)# router ospf 21
SW9621-11(config-router)# router-id 1.1.1.11
SW9621-11(config-router)# area 0.0.0.0 authentication message-digest
SW9621-11(config-router)# key chain mypass
SW9621-11(config-keychain)# key 0
SW9621-11(config-keychain-key)# key-string cisco
SW9621-11(config-keychain-key)# interface loopback0
SW9621-11(config-if)# ip address 1.1.1.11/32
SW9621-11(config-if)# ip router ospf 21 area 0.0.0.0
SW9621-11(config-if)# interface loopback11
SW9621-11(config-if)# ip address 192.168.11.1/24
SW9621-11(config-if)# ip router ospf 21 area 0.0.0.0
SW9621-11(config-if)# interface Ethernet2/1
SW9621-11(config-if)# mtu 9216
SW9621-11(config-if)# ip address 10.10.10.6/30
SW9621-11(config-if)# ip ospf authentication key-chain mypass
SW9621-11(config-if)# ip ospf network point-to-point
SW9621-11(config-if)# ip router ospf 21 area 0.0.0.0
SW9621-11(config-if)# no shutdown


SW9261-11# show ip ospf neighbors
 OSPF Process ID 21 VRF default
 Total number of neighbors: 1
 Neighbor ID     Pri State       Up Time  Address        Interface
 1.1.1.1          1 FULL/ -       01:23:31 10.10.10.5     Eth2/1

SW9261-11# show ipv6 osp?                    <-== Note: ospfv3 feature not enabled
                         ^
% Invalid command at '^' marker
```

Example 1-9 shows the SW9621-15 OSPF configuration and verification status.

**Example 1-9**   *Router 3 Configuration and Verification (SW9621-15)*

```
SW9621-15(config)# feature ospf
SW9621-15(config)# feature ospfv3

SW9621-15(config)# router ospf 21
SW9621-15(config-router)# router-id 1.1.1.15
SW9621-15(config-router)# area 0.0.0.5 stub
SW9621-15(config)# router ospfv3 23
SW9621-15(config-router)# area 0.0.0.5 stub
SW9621-15(config-keychain-key)# interface loopback0
SW9621-15(config-if)# ip address 1.1.1.15/32
SW9621-15(config-if)# ip router ospf 21 area 0.0.0.5
SW9621-15(config-if)# interface loopback15
SW9621-15(config-if)# ip address 192.168.15.1/24
SW9621-15(config-if)# ip router ospf 21 area 0.0.0.5
SW9621-15(config-if)# interface Ethernet2/1
SW9621-15(config-if)# no switchport
SW9621-15(config-if)# ip address 10.10.10.10/30
SW9621-15(config-if)# ip ospf hello-interval 25
SW9621-15(config-if)# ip router ospf 21 area 0.0.0.5
SW9621-15(config-if)# ipv6 address 2201:db2::2/48
SW9621-15(config-if)# ipv6 router ospfv3 23 area 0.0.0.5
SW9621-15(config-if)# no shutdown

SW9621-15# show ip ospf neighbors
 OSPF Process ID 21 VRF default
 Total number of neighbors: 1
 Neighbor ID     Pri State          Up Time  Address       Interface
 1.1.1.1           1 FULL/DR         01:08:08 10.10.10.9    Eth2/1

SW9621-15# show ipv6 ospfv3 neighbors
 OSPFv3 Process ID 23 VRF default
 Total number of neighbors: 1
 Neighbor ID     Pri State          Up Time  Interface ID  Interface
 1.1.1.1           1 FULL/BDR        00:07:55 39            Eth2/1
   Neighbor address fe80::200:ff:feff:ddfe
```

# Border Gateway Protocol

Border Gateway Protocol (BGP) provides loop-free routing between different autonomous systems, organizations, or domains. It uses a path-vector routing algorithm to exchange routing information between BGP speakers. Based on this information, each BGP speaker determines a path to reach a particular destination while detecting and avoiding paths with routing loops. The routing information includes the actual route prefix for a destination, the path of autonomous systems to the destination, and additional path attributes.

BGP selects a single path, by default, as the best path to a destination host or network. Each path carries *well-known mandatory*, *well-known discretionary*, and *optional transitive attributes* that are used in BGP best-path analysis. You can influence BGP path selection by altering some of these attributes by configuring BGP policies.

BGP also supports load balancing or equal-cost multipath (ECMP), where next-hop packet forwarding to a single destination can occur over multiple "best paths" that tie for top place in routing metric calculations. It potentially offers substantial increases in bandwidth by load-balancing traffic over multiple paths.

Cisco NX-OS supports BGP version 4, which includes multiprotocol extensions that allow BGP to carry routing information for IP multicast routes and multiple Layer 3 protocol address families. BGP uses TCP (Port 179) as a reliable transport protocol to create TCP sessions with other BGP-enabled devices.

The BGP autonomous system (AS) is a network controlled by a single administration entity. An autonomous system forms a routing domain with one or more Interior Gateway Protocols (IGPs) and a consistent set of routing policies. BGP supports 16-bit and 32-bit autonomous system numbers.

External BGP autonomous systems dynamically exchange routing information through external BGP (eBGP) peering sessions. BGP speakers within the same autonomous system can exchange routing information through internal BGP (iBGP) peering sessions.

BGP supports 2-byte or 4-byte AS numbers. Cisco NX-OS displays 4-byte AS numbers in plain-text notation (that is, as 32-bit integers). You can configure 4-byte AS numbers as either plain-text notation (for example, 1 to 42,94,967,295) or AS.dot notation (for example, 1.0).

## BGP Peering

A BGP speaker does not discover and peer with another BGP speaker automatically. You must configure the relationships between BGP speakers. A *BGP peer* is a BGP speaker that has an active TCP connection to another BGP speaker.

BGP uses TCP port 179 to create a TCP session with a peer. When a TCP connection is established between peers, each BGP peer initially exchanges all of its routes—the complete BGP routing table—with the other peer. After this initial exchange, the BGP peers send only *incremental* updates when a topology change occurs in the network or when a routing policy change occurs. In the periods of inactivity between these updates, peers exchange special messages called *keepalives*. The *hold time* is the maximum time limit that can elapse between receiving consecutive BGP update or keepalive messages. Cisco NX-OS supports the following peer configuration options:

- **Individual IPv4 or IPv4 address:** BGP establishes a session with the BGP speaker that matches the remote address and AS number.

- **IPv4 or IPv6 prefix peers for a single AS number:** BGP establishes sessions with BGP speakers that match the prefix and the AS number.

- **Dynamic AS number prefix peers:** BGP establishes sessions with BGP speakers that match the prefix and an AS number from a list of configured AS numbers.

Cisco NX-OS accepts a range or list of AS numbers to establish BGP sessions and does not associate prefix peers with dynamic AS numbers as either interior BGP (iBGP) or external BGP (eBGP) sessions until after the session is established.

For example, if you configure BGP to use IPv4 prefix 172.16.2.0/8 and AS numbers 10, 30, and 100, BGP establishes a session with 172.16.2.1 with AS number 30 but rejects a session from 172.16.2.2 with AS number 20.

> **NOTE**   The dynamic AS number prefix peer configuration overrides the individual AS number configuration that is inherited from a BGP template.

To establish BGP sessions between peers, BGP must have a router ID, which is sent to BGP peers in the OPEN message when a BGP session is established. The BGP router ID is a 32-bit value that is often represented by an IPv4 address. You can configure the router ID. By default, Cisco NX-OS sets the router ID to the IPv4 address of a loopback interface on the router. If no loopback interface is configured on the router, the software chooses the highest IPv4 address configured to a physical interface on the router to represent the BGP router ID. The BGP router ID must be unique to the BGP peers in a network.

Cisco NX-OS also supports some advanced functionality related to the configuration of BGP peers, which allows for better flexibility. These options include

- **BGP peer templates:** These constructs allow you to create a BGP configuration for the peers and reuse it across similar BGP peers. There are two subtypes of peer templates: (a) the peer-session template, which defines session attributes, timers, and AS, and (b) peer-policy templates, which define address-family-related dependent options, such as inbound and outbound policies, filter lists, prefix lists. Additionally, the peer-session and the peer-policy templates can be combined in one peer template that can be reused in the configuration.

- **BGP interface peering via IPv6 link-local for IPv4/6 address families:** Instead of specifying an IP address or a prefix for the neighbor, this feature allows you to define an interface to be used for automatic neighbor discovery. This capability is possible because of the ICMPv6 neighbor discovery (ND) route advertisement (RA) for automatic neighbor discovery and the ability to send IPv4 routes with IPv6 next hop, described in RFC5549.

> **NOTE**   If BGP does not have a router ID, it cannot establish any peering sessions with BGP peers.

## BGP Path Selection

The best-path algorithm runs each time a path is added or withdrawn for a given network. The best-path algorithm also runs if you change the BGP configuration. BGP selects the best path from the set of valid paths available for a given network.

Cisco NX-OS implements the BGP best-path algorithm in the following steps.

## Step 1: Comparing Pairs of Paths

This first step in the BGP best-path algorithm compares two paths to determine which path is better. The following sequence describes the basic steps that Cisco NX-OS uses to compare two paths to determine the better path:

1. Cisco NX-OS chooses a valid path for comparison. (For example, a path that has an unreachable next-hop is not valid.)

2. Cisco NX-OS chooses the path with the highest weight.

3. Cisco NX-OS chooses the path with the highest local preference.

4. If one of the paths is locally originated, Cisco NX-OS chooses that path.

5. Cisco NX-OS chooses the path with the shorter AS-path.

**NOTE**  When calculating the length of the AS-path, Cisco NX-OS ignores confederation segments and counts AS sets as 1.

6. Cisco NX-OS chooses the path with the lower origin. Interior Gateway Protocol (IGP) is considered lower than EGP.

7. Cisco NX-OS chooses the path with the lower multi-exit discriminator (MED).

   You can configure a number of options that affect whether this step is performed. In general, Cisco NX-OS compares the MED of both paths if the paths were received from peers in the same autonomous system; otherwise, Cisco NX-OS skips the MED comparison.

   You can configure Cisco NX-OS to always perform the best-path algorithm MED comparison, regardless of the peer autonomous system in the paths. Otherwise, Cisco NX-OS will perform a MED comparison that depends on the AS-path attributes of the two paths being compared:

   a. If a path has no AS-path or the AS-path starts with an AS_SET, the path is internal, and Cisco NX-OS compares the MED to other internal paths.

   b. If the AS-path starts with an AS_SEQUENCE, the peer autonomous system is the first AS number in the sequence, and Cisco NX-OS compares the MED to other paths that have the same peer autonomous system.

   c. If the AS-path contains only confederation segments or starts with confederation segments followed by an AS_SET, the path is internal and Cisco NX-OS compares the MED to other internal paths.

   d. If the AS-path starts with confederation segments followed by an AS_SEQUENCE, the peer autonomous system is the first AS number in the AS_SEQUENCE, and Cisco NX-OS compares the MED to other paths that have the same peer autonomous system.

**NOTE**  If Cisco NX-OS receives no MED attribute with the path, Cisco NX-OS considers the MED to be 0 unless you configure the best-path algorithm to set a missing MED to the highest possible value.

**e.** If the nondeterministic MED comparison feature is enabled, the best-path algorithm uses the Cisco IOS style of MED comparison.

**8.** If one path is from an internal peer and the other path is from an external peer, Cisco NX-OS chooses the path from the external peer.

**9.** If the paths have different IGP metrics to their next-hop addresses, Cisco NX-OS chooses the path with the lower IGP metric.

**10.** Cisco NX-OS uses the path that was selected by the best-path algorithm the last time that it was run.

   If all path parameters in step 1 through step 9 are the same, you can configure the best-path algorithm to compare the router IDs. If the path includes an originator attribute, Cisco NX-OS uses that attribute as the router ID to compare to; otherwise, Cisco NX-OS uses the router ID of the peer that sent the path. If the paths have different router IDs, Cisco NX-OS chooses the path with the lower router ID.

> **NOTE** When the attribute originator is used as the router ID, it is possible that two paths have the same router ID. It is also possible to have two BGP sessions with the same peer router, and therefore, you can receive two paths with the same router ID.

**11.** Cisco NX-OS selects the path with the shorter cluster length. If a path was not received with a cluster list attribute, the cluster length is 0.

**12.** Cisco NX-OS chooses the path received from the peer with the lower IP address. Locally generated paths (for example, redistributed paths) have a peer IP address of 0.

> **NOTE** Paths that are equal after step 9 can be used for multipath if you configure it.

### Step 2: Determining the Order of Comparisons

The second step of the BGP best-path algorithm implementation is to determine the order in which Cisco NX-OS compares the paths:

**1.** Cisco NX-OS partitions the paths into groups. Within each group, Cisco NX-OS compares the MED among all paths. Cisco NX-OS uses the same rules as in step 1 to determine whether MED can be compared between any two paths. Typically, this comparison results in one group being chosen for each neighbor autonomous system. If you configure the **bgp bestpath med always** command, Cisco NX-OS chooses just one group that contains all the paths.

**2.** Cisco NX-OS determines the best path in each group by iterating through all paths in the group and keeping track of the best one so far. Cisco NX-OS compares each path with the temporary best path found so far, and if the new path is better, it becomes the new temporary best path, and Cisco NX-OS compares it with the next path in the group.

**3.** Cisco NX-OS forms a set of paths that contain the best path selected from each group in step 2. Cisco NX-OS selects the overall best path from this set of paths by going through them as in step 2.

### Step 3: Determining the Best-Path Change Suppression

The next part of the implementation is to determine whether Cisco NX-OS will use the new best path or suppress it. The router can continue to use the existing best path if the new one is identical to the old path (if the router ID is the same). Cisco NX-OS continues to use the existing best path to avoid route changes in the network.

You can turn off the suppression feature by configuring the best-path algorithm to compare the router IDs. If you configure this feature, the new best path is always preferred to the existing one.

You cannot suppress the best-path change if any of the following conditions occur:

- The existing best path is no longer valid.

- Either the existing or new best paths were received from internal (or confederation) peers or were locally generated (for example, by redistribution).

- The paths were received from the same peer (the paths have the same router ID).

- The paths have different weights, local preferences, origins, or IGP metrics to their next-hop addresses.

- The paths have different MEDs.

> **NOTE**   The order of comparison determined in Step 2 is important. Consider the case where you have three paths—A, B, and C. When Cisco NX-OS compares A and B, it chooses A. When Cisco NX-OS compares B and C, it chooses B. But when Cisco NX-OS compares A and C, it might not choose A because some BGP metrics apply only among paths from the same neighboring autonomous system and not among all paths.

The path selection uses the BGP AS-path attribute. The AS-path attribute includes the list of autonomous system numbers (AS numbers) traversed in the advertised path. If you subdivide your BGP autonomous system into a collection or confederation of autonomous systems, the AS-path contains confederation segments that list these locally defined autonomous systems.

## Multiprotocol BGP

Cisco NX-OS supports multiple address families. Multiprotocol BGP (MBGP) can carry different sets of routes depending on the address family. For example, BGP can carry one set of routes for IPv4 unicast routing, one set of routes for IPv4 multicast routing, and one set of routes for IPv6 multicast routing. You can use MBGP for Reverse Path Forwarding (RPF) checks in IP multicast networks.

> **NOTE**   Because Multicast BGP does not propagate multicast state information, you need a multicast protocol, such as Protocol Independent Multicast (PIM).

You need to use the router address-family and neighbor address-family configuration modes to support Multiprotocol BGP configurations. MBGP maintains separate Routing Information Bases (RIBs) for each configured address family, such as a unicast RIB and a multicast RIB for BGP.

A Multiprotocol BGP network is backward compatible, but BGP peers that do not support multiprotocol extensions cannot forward routing information, such as address family identifier information, that the multiprotocol extensions carry.

## BGP Configurations and Verifications

Table 1-9 lists the BGP default parameters; you can alter BGP default parameters as necessary.

**Table 1-9**   Default BGP Parameters

| Parameters | Default |
|---|---|
| Administrative distance—External (routes learned from eBGP) | 20 |
| Administrative distance—Internal (routes learned form iBGP) | 200 |
| Administrative distance—Local (Applied to routes originated by the router) | 220 |
| BGP feature | Disabled |
| Keepalive interval | 60 seconds |
| Hold timer | 180 seconds |
| BGP PIC core | Enabled |
| Auto-summary | Always disabled |
| Synchronization | Always disabled |

Table 1-10 shows NX-OS feature license required for BGP. For more information, visit the Cisco NX-OS Licensing Guide.

**Table 1-10**   Feature-Based Licenses for Cisco NX-OS

| Platform | Feature License | Feature Name |
|---|---|---|
| Cisco Nexus 9000 Series | Enterprise Services Package LAN_ENTERPRISE_SERVICES_PKG | BGP |

BGP has the following configuration limitations:

- The dynamic AS number prefix peer configuration overrides the individual AS number configuration inherited from a BGP template.

- If you configure a dynamic AS number for prefix peers in an AS confederation, BGP establishes sessions with only the AS numbers in the local confederation.

- BGP sessions created through a dynamic AS number prefix peer ignore any configured eBGP multihop time-to-live (TTL) value or a disabled check for directly connected peers.

- Configure a router ID for BGP to avoid automatic router ID changes and session flaps.

- Use the maximum-prefix configuration option per peer to restrict the number of routes received and system resources used.

- Configure the update source to establish a session with BGP/eBGP multihop sessions.

- Specify a BGP policy if you configure redistribution.

- Define the BGP router ID within a VRF.

- If you decrease the keepalive and hold timer values, you might experience BGP session flaps.

- The BGP minimum route advertisement interval (MRAI) value for all iBGP and eBGP sessions is zero and is not configurable.

Tables 1-11 through 1-13 describe the most-used BGP configuration commands. For a full list of the commands, refer to the Nexus Unicast Routing Configuration Guide listed in the reference section at the end of the chapter.

**Table 1-11**   BGP Global-Level Configurations

| Command | Purpose |
|---|---|
| **feature bgp** | Enables the BGP feature. |
| **router bgp** *autonomous-system-number* | Enables BGP and assigns the AS number to the local BGP speaker. The AS number can be a 16-bit integer or a 32-bit integer in the form of a higher 16-bit decimal number and a lower 16-bit decimal number in *xx.xx* format. |

**Table 1-12**   BGP Routing-Level Configurations

| Command | Purpose |
|---|---|
| **router-id** *ip-address* | (Optional) Configures a unique BGP router ID. This IP address identifies this BGP speaker. |
| **description** *text* | (Optional) Adds a description for the neighbor. The description is an alphanumeric string up to 80 characters. |
| **neighbor** { *ip-address* \| *ipv6-address* } **remote-as** *as-number* | Configures the IPv4 or IPv6 address and AS number for a remote BGP peer. The *ip-address* format is *x.x.x.x*. The *ipv6-address* format is A:B::C:D. |
| **address-family** { **ipv4** \| **ipv6** \| **vpnv4** \| **vpnv6** }{ **unicast** \| **multicast** } | (Optional) Enters global address family configuration mode for the IP or VPN address family. |
| **network** *ip-prefix* [ **route-map** *map-name* ] | (Optional) Specifies a network as local to this autonomous system and adds it to the BGP routing table. For exterior protocols, the **network** command controls which networks are advertised. Interior protocols use the **network** command to determine where to send updates. |
| **timers** *keepalive-time hold-time* | (Optional) Adds the keepalive and hold time BGP timer values for the neighbor. The range is from 0 to 3600 seconds. The default is 60 seconds for the keepalive time and 180 seconds for the hold time. |
| **shutdown** | (Optional) Administratively shuts down this BGP neighbor. This command triggers an automatic notification and session reset for the BGP neighbor sessions. |

| Command | Purpose |
|---|---|
| neighbor *prefix* remote-as route-map *map-name* | Configures the IPv4 or IPv6 prefix and a route map for the list of accepted AS numbers for the remote BGP peers. The *prefix* format for IPv4 is x.x.x.x/length. The length range is from 1 to 32. The *prefix* format for IPv6 is A:B::C:D/length. The length range is from 1 to 128. |
| | The *map-name* can be any case-sensitive, alphanumeric string up to 63 characters. |

**Table 1-13**  BGP Verification and BGP Clear Commands

| Command | Purpose |
|---|---|
| show bgp all [summary] [vrf *vrf-name*] | Displays the BGP information for all address families. |
| show {ipv \| ipv6} bgp *options* | Displays the BGP status and configuration information. This command has multiple options. One important option is summary (**show ip bgp summary**). |
| show bgp convergence [vrf *vrf-name*] | Displays the BGP information for all address families. |
| show bgp {ip \| ipv6} {unicast \| multicast} [*ip-address* \| *ipv6-prefix*] community {regexp expression \| [community] [no-advertise] [no-export] [no-export-subconfed]} [vrf *vrf-name*] | Displays the BGP routes that match a BGP community. |
| show bgp *process* | Displays the BGP process information. |
| show running-configuration bgp | Displays the current running BGP configuration. |
| show bgp sessions [vrf *vrf-name*] | Displays the BGP sessions for all peers. You can use the **clear bgp sessions** command to clear these statistics. |
| show bgp statistics | Shows BGP statistics. |
| clear bgp all { neighbor \| * \| *as-number* \| peer-template *name* \| *prefix* } [ vrf *vrf-name* ] | Clears one or more neighbors from all address families. * clears all neighbors in all address families. The arguments are as follows: |
| | *neighbor:* IPv4 or IPv6 address of a neighbor. |
| | *as-number:* Autonomous system number. The AS number can be a 16-bit integer or a 32-bit integer in the form of higher 16-bit decimal number and a lower 16-bit decimal number in xx.xx format. |
| | *name:* Peer template name. The name can be any case-sensitive, alphanumeric string up to 64 characters. |
| | *prefix:* IPv4 or IPv6 prefix. All neighbors within that prefix are cleared. |
| | *vrf-name:* VRF name. All neighbors in that VRF are cleared. The name can be any case-sensitive, alphanumeric string up to 64 characters. |

| Command | Purpose |
|---|---|
| **clear bgp all dampening** [ **vrf** *vrf-name* ] | Clears route flap dampening networks in all address families. The *vrf-name* can be any case-sensitive, alphanumeric string up to 64 characters. |
| **clear bgp all flap-statistics** [ **vrf** *vrf-name* ] | Clears route flap statistics in all address families. The *vrf-name* can be any case-sensitive, alphanumeric string up to 64 characters. |

Figure 1-5 shows the network topology for the configuration that follows, which demonstrates how to configure Nexus BGP for IPv4 and IPv6.

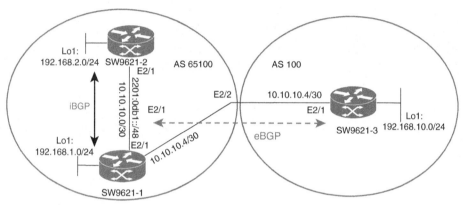

**Figure 1-5**  *BGP Network Topology*

Example 1-10 shows SW9621-1 BGP feature enabling and BGP router configurations.

**Example 1-10**  *BGP AS 65100 Creation Configuration*

```
SW9621-1(config)# feature bgp
SW9621-1(config)# router bgp 65100
SW9621-1(config-router)# router-id 1.1.1.1
SW9621-1(config-router)# address-family ipv4 unicast
SW9621-1(config-router-af)# network 192.168.1.0/24
SW9621-1(config-router)# neighbor 2201:db1::2 remote-as 65100
SW9621-1(config-router-neighbor)# address-family ipv6 unicast
SW9621-1(config-router)# neighbor 10.10.10.2 remote-as 65100
SW9621-1(config-router-neighbor)# address-family ipv4 unicast
SW9621-1(config-router-neighbor)# address-family ipv4 multicast
SW9621-1(config-router)# neighbor 10.10.10.6 remote-as 100
SW9621-1(config-router-neighbor)# address-family ipv4 unicast
```

Example 1-11 shows SW9621-1 interface configurations.

**Example 1-11**    *Interface Configurations*

```
SW9621-1(config)# interface loopback1
SW9621-1(config-if)# ip address 192.168.1.1/24
SW9621-1(config)# interface Ethernet2/1
SW9621-1(config-if)# ip address 10.10.10.1/30
SW9621-1(config-if)# no shutdown
SW9621-1(config)# interface Ethernet2/2
SW9621-1(config-if)# ip address 10.10.10.5/30
SW9621-1(config-if)# no shutdown
```

Example 1-12 shows the SW9621-1 BGP neighbors and summary.

**Example 1-12**    *BGP Verification*

```
SW9621-1(config)# show ip bgp summary


BGP summary information for VRF default, address family IPv4 Unicast
BGP router identifier 1.1.1.1, local AS number 65100
BGP table version is 14, IPv4 Unicast config peers 2, capable peers 2
3 network entries and 3 paths using 432 bytes of memory
BGP attribute entries [3/432], BGP AS path entries [1/6]
BGP community entries [0/0], BGP clusterlist entries [0/0]


Neighbor       V     AS    MsgRcvd MsgSent  TblVer  InQ OutQ   Up/Down  State/PfxRcd
10.10.10.2     4   65100   154     152          14   0    0    01:46:14 1
10.10.10.6     4     100   23      25           14   0    0    00:10:52 1
SW9621-1(config)# show ip bgp
BGP routing table information for VRF default, address family IPv4 Unicast
BGP table version is 14, local router ID is 1.1.1.1
Status: s-suppressed, x-deleted, S-stale, d-dampened, h-history, *-valid, >-best
Path type: i-internal, e-external, c-confed, l-local, a-aggregate, r-redist,
I-injected
Origin codes: i - IGP, e - EGP, ? - incomplete, | - multipath, & - backup


  Network          Next Hop        Metric    LocPrf   Weight   Path
*>l192.168.1.0/24  0.0.0.0                   100      32768    i
*>i192.168.2.0/24  10.10.10.2                100      0        i
*>e192.168.3.0/24  10.10.10.6                         0        100 i


SW9621-1(config)# show bgp all

BGP routing table information for VRF default, address family IPv4 Unicast
BGP table version is 14, local router ID is 1.1.1.1
Status: s-suppressed, x-deleted, S-stale, d-dampened, h-history, *-valid, >-best
Path type: i-internal, e-external, c-confed, l-local, a-aggregate, r-redist, I-injected
```

```
Origin codes: i - IGP, e - EGP, ? - incomplete, | - multipath, & - backup


   Network            Next Hop          Metric     LocPrf     Weight     Path
*>l192.168.1.0/24    0.0.0.0                      100        32768      i
*>i192.168.2.0/24    10.10.10.2                   100        0          i
*>e192.168.3.0/24    10.10.10.6                              0          100 i
SW9621-1(config)# show bgp sessions


Total peers 3, established peers 3
ASN 65100
VRF default, local ASN 65100
peers 3, established peers 3, local router-id 1.1.1.1
State: I-Idle, A-Active, O-Open, E-Established, C-Closing, S-Shutdown


Neighbor        ASN    Flaps    LastUpDn|LastRead|LastWrit St Port(L/R)    Notif(S/R)
10.10.10.2      65100  3        01:48:28|00:00:23|00:00:20 E  14994/179    0/3
10.10.10.6      100    1        00:13:05|00:00:20|00:00:04 E  16596/179    0/1
2201:db1::2     65100  0        00:27:27|00:00:25|00:00:25 E  179/46276    0/0


SW9621-1(config)# show ipv6 bgp sum


BGP summary information for VRF default, address family IPv6 Unicast
BGP router identifier 1.1.1.1, local AS number 65100
BGP table version is 3, IPv6 Unicast config peers 1, capable peers 1
0 network entries and 0 paths using 0 bytes of memory
BGP attribute entries [0/0], BGP AS path entries [0/0]
BGP community entries [0/0], BGP clusterlist entries [0/0]


Neighbor       V    AS     MsgRcvd MsgSent   Tbl  Ver  InQ OutQ    Up/Down  State/PfxRcd
2201:db1::2    4    65100    33      34       3    0    0           00:27:59    0
```

Example 1-13 shows SW9621-2 full configurations and BGP neighbors.

**Example 1-13**   *Router 2 Configuration and Verification (SW9621-2)*

```
SW9621-2(config-router-neighbor)# show run bgp


feature bgp
router bgp 65100
  router-id 2.2.2.2
  address-family ipv4 unicast
    network 192.168.2.0/24
  neighbor 2201:db1::1 remote-as 65100
    address-family ipv6 unicast
  neighbor 10.10.10.1 remote-as 65100
```

```
    address-family ipv4 unicast
    address-family ipv4 multicast
SW9621-2(config-router-neighbor-af)# show run int lo1
interface loopback1
  ip address 192.168.2.1/24


SW9621-2(config-router-neighbor)# show run int e2/1


interface Ethernet2/1
  no switchport
  mac-address 0000.0000.002f
  ip address 10.10.10.2/30
  ipv6 address 2201:db1::2/48
  no shutdown


SW9621-2(config-router-neighbor)# show bgp all
BGP routing table information for VRF default, address family IPv4 Unicast
BGP table version is 15, local router ID is 2.2.2.2
Status: s-suppressed, x-deleted, S-stale, d-dampened, h-history, *-valid, >-best
Path type: i-internal, e-external, c-confed, l-local, a-aggregate, r-redist,
I-injected
Origin codes: i - IGP, e - EGP, ? - incomplete, | - multipath, & - backup


   Network          Next Hop        Metric     LocPrf      Weight     Path
*>i192.168.1.0/24   10.10.10.1                 100         0          i
*>l192.168.2.0/24   0.0.0.0                    100         32768      i
 i192.168.3.0/24    10.10.10.6                 100         0          i
```

Example 1-14 shows SW9621-3 full configurations and BGP neighbors.

**Example 1-14**   *Router 3 Configuration (SW9621-3)*

```
SW9621-3(config-router-neighbor)# show run bgp
feature bgp
router bgp 100
  router-id 3.3.3.3
  address-family ipv4 unicast
    network 192.168.3.0/24
  neighbor 10.10.10.5 remote-as 65100
    address-family ipv4 unicast
      weight 100


SW9621-3(config-router-neighbor-af)# show run int lo
interface loopback10
  ip address 192.168.3.1/24
```

```
SW9621-3(config-router-neighbor-af)# show run int e2/1
interface Ethernet2/1
  no switchport
  mac-address 0000.0000.003f
  ip address 10.10.10.6/30
  no shutdown


SW9621-3# show bgp all
BGP routing table information for VRF default, address family IPv4 Unicast
BGP table version is 11, local router ID is 3.3.3.3
Status: s-suppressed, x-deleted, S-stale, d-dampened, h-history, *-valid, >-best
Path type: i-internal, e-external, c-confed, l-local, a-aggregate, r-redist,
I-injected
Origin codes: i - IGP, e - EGP, ? - incomplete, | - multipath, & - backup

  Network           Next Hop          Metric    LocPrf    Weight  Path
*>e192.168.1.0/24   10.10.10.5                            100     65100 i
*>e192.168.2.0/24   10.10.10.5                            100     65100 i
*>l192.168.3.0/24   0.0.0.0                               100     32768 i
```

## Bidirectional Forwarding Detection

Bidirectional Forwarding Detection (BFD) is a detection protocol designed to provide fast forwarding–path failure detection times for media types, encapsulations, topologies, and routing protocols. BFD provides subsecond failure detection between two adjacent devices and can be less CPU-intensive than protocol hello messages because some of the BFD load can be distributed onto the data plane on supported modules.

Cisco NX-OS supports the BFD asynchronous mode, which sends BFD control packets between two adjacent devices to activate and maintain BFD neighbor sessions between the devices. You configure BFD on both devices (or BFD neighbors). Once BFD has been enabled on the interfaces and on the appropriate protocols, Cisco NX-OS creates a BFD session, negotiates BFD session parameters, and begins to send BFD control packets to each BFD neighbor at the negotiated interval. The BFD session parameters include the following:

- **Desired minimum transmit interval:** The interval at which this device wants to send BFD hello messages.

- **Required minimum receive interval:** The minimum interval at which this device can accept BFD hello messages from another BFD device.

- **Detect multiplier:** The number of missing BFD hello messages from another BFD device before this local device detects a fault in the forwarding path.

Figure 1-6 shows how a BFD session is established. The figure shows a simple network with two routers running OSPF and BFD. When OSPF discovers a neighbor (1), it sends a request to the local BFD process to initiate a BFD neighbor session with the OSPF neighbor router (2). The BFD neighbor session with the OSPF neighbor router is now established (3).

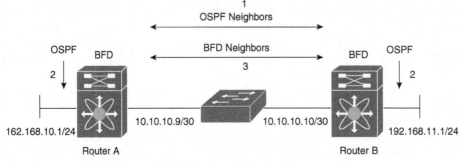

**Figure 1-6** *Establishing a BFD Neighbor Relationship*

## Rapid Detection of Failures

After a BFD session has been established and timer negotiations are complete, BFD neighbors send BFD control packets that act in the same manner as an IGP hello protocol to detect liveliness, except at a more accelerated rate. BFD detects a failure, but the protocol must take action to bypass a failed peer.

BFD sends a failure detection notice to the BFD-enabled protocols when it detects a failure in the forwarding path. The local device can then initiate the protocol recalculation process and reduce the overall network convergence time.

Figure 1-7 shows what happens when a failure occurs in the network (1). The BFD neighbor session with the OSPF neighbor router is torn down (2). BFD notifies the local OSPF process that the BFD neighbor is no longer reachable (3). The local OSPF process tears down the OSPF neighbor relationship (4). If an alternative path is available, the routers immediately start converging on it.

**NOTE** The BFD failure detection occurs in less than a second, which is much faster than OSPF hello messages could detect the same failure.

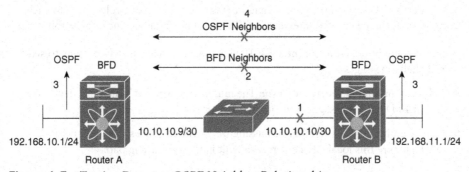

**Figure 1-7** *Tearing Down an OSPF Neighbor Relationship*

## BFD Configurations and Verifications

Table 1-14 lists BFD default parameters; you can alter BFD parameters as necessary.

**Table 1-14** Default Settings for BFD Parameters

| Parameters | Default |
|---|---|
| BFD feature | Disabled |
| Required minimum receive interval | 50 milliseconds |
| Desired minimum transmit interval | 50 milliseconds |
| Detect multiplier | 3 |
| Echo function | Enabled |
| Mode | Asynchronous |
| Port channel | Logical mode (one session per source-destination pair address) |
| Slow timer | 2000 milliseconds |
| Subinterface optimization | Disabled |

**NOTE** No license is required for BFD features.

BFD has the following configuration limitations:

- NX-OS supports BFD version 1.

- BFD supports single-hop BFD; BFD for BGP supports single-hop EBGP and iBGP peers.

- BFD depends on Layer 3 adjacency information to discover topology changes, including Layer 2 topology changes. A BFD session on a VLAN interface (SVI) may not be up after the convergence of the Layer 2 topology if no Layer 3 adjacency information is available.

- For port channels used by BFD, you must enable the Link Aggregation Control Protocol (LACP) on the port channel.

- HSRP for IPv4 is supported with BFD. HSRP for IPv6 is not supported with BFD.

Tables 1-15 through 1-18 described the most-used BFD configuration commands. For a full list of the commands, refer to the Nexus Unicast Routing Configuration Guide in the reference section at the end of the chapter.

**Table 1-15** BFD Global-Level Configurations

| Command | Purpose |
|---|---|
| feature bfd | Enables the BFD feature. |
| bfd interval *mintx* min_rx *msec* multiplier *value* | Configures the BFD session parameters for all BFD sessions on the device. You can override these values by configuring the BFD session parameters on an interface. The *mintx* and *msec* range is from 50 to 999 milliseconds, and the default is 50. The multiplier range is from 1 to 50. The multiplier default is 3. |

| Command | Purpose |
|---|---|
| bfd slow-timer *msec* | Configures the slow timer used in the echo function. This value determines how fast BFD starts up a new session and at what speed the asynchronous sessions use for BFD control packets when the echo function is enabled. The slow-timer value is used as the new control packet interval, while the echo packets use the configured BFD intervals. The echo packets are used for link failure detection, while the control packets at the slower rate maintain the BFD session. The range is from 1000 to 30,000 milliseconds. The default is 2000. |

**Table 1-16** BFD Routing-Level Configurations

| Command | Purpose |
|---|---|
| router ospf *instance-tag*<br>bfd | (Optional) Enables BFD for all OSPFv2 interfaces. |
| router bgp *as-number*<br>neighbor { *ip-address* \| *ipv6-address* }<br>remote-as *as-number*<br>bfd | Enables BFD for this BGP peer. |

**Table 1-17** BFD Interface-Level Command

| Command | Purpose |
|---|---|
| bfd echo | Enables the echo function. The default is enabled. |
| bfd optimize subinterface | Optimizes subinterfaces on a BFD-enabled interface. The default is disabled. |
| ip ospf bfd | (Optional) Enables or disables BFD on an OSPFv2 interface. The default is disabled. |

**Table 1-18** BFD Verification Commands

| Command | Purpose |
|---|---|
| show bfd neighbors [ *application name* ] [ details ] | Displays information about BFD for a supported application, such as BGP or OSPFv2. |
| show bfd neighbors [ interface *int-if* ] [ details ] | Displays information about BGP sessions on an interface. |

Figure 1-8 shows the network topology for the configuration that follows, which demonstrates how to configure Nexus BFD for OSPFv2.

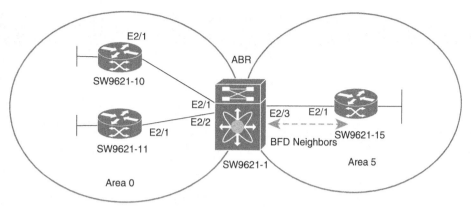

**Figure 1-8**   *BFD Network Topology*

Example 1-15 shows the SW9621-1 BFD feature enabling and its configuration.

**Example 1-15**   *SW9621-1 BFD Configuration*

```
SW9621-1(config)# feature bfd
SW9621-1(config)# interface Ethernet2/3
SW9621-1(config-if)# ip ospf bfd
SW9621-1(config-if)# no ip redirects
SW9621-1(config-if)# no ipv6 redirects
SW9621-1(config-if)# bfd interval 100 min_rx 100 multiplier 5
```

Example 1-16 shows SW9621-1 BFD neighbors.

**Example 1-16**   *SW9621-1 OSPFv2/BFD Verification*

```
SW9621-1# show bfd neighbors
OurAddr     NeighAddr    LD/RD             RH/RS  Holdown(mult)  State  Int     Vrf
10.10.10.9  10.10.10.10  1090519042/1090519042  Up    9193(5)        Up    Eth2/3  default


SW9621-1# show ip ospf interface
 Ethernet2/3 is up, line protocol is up
    IP address 10.10.10.9/30
    Process ID 21 VRF default, area 0.0.0.5
    Enabled by interface configuration
    State DR, Network type BROADCAST, cost 40
    BFD is enabled
    Index 2, Transmit delay 1 sec, Router Priority 1
    Designated Router ID: 1.1.1.1, address: 10.10.10.9
    Backup Designated Router ID: 1.1.1.15, address: 10.10.10.10
    1 Neighbors, flooding to 1, adjacent with 1
    Timer intervals: Hello 25, Dead 100; Wait 100, Retransmit 5
      Hello timer due in 00:00:04
    No authentication
    Number of opaque link LSAs: 0, checksum sum 0
```

Example 1-17 shows SW9621-15 BFD configurations and neighbors.

**Example 1-17** *Router 4 Config and Verification (SW9621-15)*

```
SW9621-15(config)# feature bfd
SW9621-15(config)# interface Ethernet2/1
SW9621-15(config-if)# ip ospf bfd
SW9621-15(config-if)# no ip redirects
SW9621-15(config-if)# no ipv6 redirects
SW9621-15(config-if)# bfd interval 100 min_rx 100 multiplier 5


SW9621-15# show bfd neighbors
OurAddr      NeighAddr   LD/RD                  RH/RS   Holdown(mult)   State   Int     Vrf
10.10.10.10  10.10.10.9  109051902/109051902    Up      9190(5)         Up      Eth2/1  default
```

# Multicast

The IP communication traditionally defines the unicast communication, when there is a host-to-host communication, or 1:1; and the broadcast type of communication, where one host sends to all other hosts. When you need to communicate with multiple but not all hosts, the broadcast communication is not effective because all hosts will receive it, and it also consumes more resources. This gap in functionality was closed through the introduction of multicast communication. With multicast communication, bandwidth and resources are saved because IP datagrams are sent to a group of receiving hosts in a single transmission.

In multicast communication, there are senders (this is the source of the IP datagrams) and receivers. The sender sends one copy of the data to multicast receivers, which are organized in a multicast group. The multicast group is assigned a group IP address, which is in the prefix 224.0.0.0/4 for the IPv4 multicast and ff00::/8 for the IPv6 multicast. These IP address ranges are officially defined by the Internet Assigned Numbers Authority (IANA). The group address is used by both the senders and the receivers. The senders use it as a destination address to send data to the multicast group of receivers without knowing who the specific receivers are. And the receivers use the group address to state their interest in receiving multicast traffic by registering to the group at the first-hop router by using either the Internet Group Management Protocol (IGMP) for IPv4 or Multicast Listener Discovery (MLD) for IPv6.

After a receiver has registered with a multicast group, the routers use the Protocol Independent Multicast (PIM) protocol to construct the multicast distribution tree for this group, which defines how the routers on the path will replicate and forward the datagrams of the communication.

Figure 1-9 shows one source transmitting multicast data that is delivered to two receivers. In the figure, because the center host is on a LAN segment where no receiver requested multicast data, no data is delivered to that receiver.

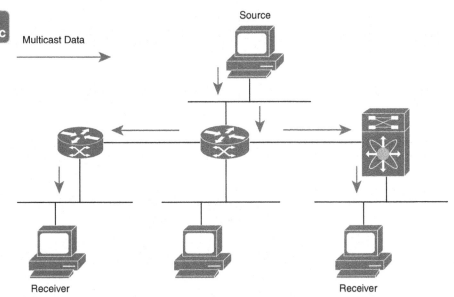

**Figure 1-9**  *Multicast Traffic from One Source to Two Receivers*

## Internet Group Management Protocol

The Internet Group Management Protocol (IGMP) is used by hosts that want to receive multicast data to request membership in multicast groups. Once the group membership is established, multicast data for the group is directed to the LAN segment of the requesting host.

IGMP is an IPv4 protocol that a host uses to request multicast data for a particular group. Using the information obtained through the IGMP, the software maintains a list of multicast group or channel memberships on a per-interface basis. The systems that receive these IGMP packets send multicast data that they receive for requested groups or channels out the network segment of the known receivers.

NX-OS supports IGMPv2 and IGMPv3. By default, NX-OS enables IGMPv2 when it starts the IGMP process. You can enable IGMPv3 on interfaces where you want its capabilities.

IGMPv3 includes the following key changes from IGMPv2:

- IGMPv3 supports source-specific multicast (SSM), which builds shortest path trees from each receiver to the source, through the following features:

  - Host messages that can specify both the group and the source.

  - The multicast state that is maintained for groups and sources, not just for groups as in IGMPv2.

- Hosts no longer perform report suppression, which means that hosts always send IGMP membership reports when an IGMP query message is received.

For detailed information about IGMPv2, see RFC 2236.

The basic IGMP process of a router that discovers multicast hosts is shown in Figure 1-10. Hosts 1, 2, and 3 send unsolicited IGMP membership report messages to initiate receiving multicast data for a group or channel.

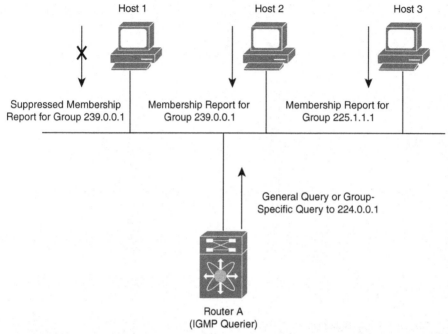

**Figure 1-10** *IGMPv1 and IGMPv2 Query-Response Process*

In Figure 1-10, router A, which is the IGMP designated querier on the subnet, sends periodic query messages to the all-hosts mulitcast group at 224.0.0.1 to discover whether any hosts want to receive multicast data. You can configure the group membership timeout value that the router uses to determine that no members of a group or source exist on the subnet.

The software elects a router as the IGMP querier on a subnet if it has the lowest IP address. As long as a router continues to receive query messages from a router with a lower IP address, it resets a timer that is based on its querier timeout value. If the querier timer of a router expires, it becomes the designated querier. If that router later receives a host query message from a router with a lower IP address, it drops its role as the designated querier and sets its querier timer again.

In Figure 1-10, host 1's membership report is suppressed, and host 2 sends its membership report for group 239.0.0.1 first. Host 1 receives the report from host 2. Because only one membership report per group needs to be sent to the router, other hosts suppress their reports to reduce network traffic. Each host waits for a random time interval to avoid sending reports at the same time. You can configure the query maximum response time parameter to control the interval in which hosts randomize their responses.

**NOTE** IGMPv2 membership report suppression occurs only on hosts that are connected to the same port.

In Figure 1-11, router A sends the IGMPv3 group-and-source-specific query to the LAN. Hosts 2 and 3 respond to the query with membership reports that indicate that they want to receive data from the advertised group and source. This IGMPv3 feature supports SSM.

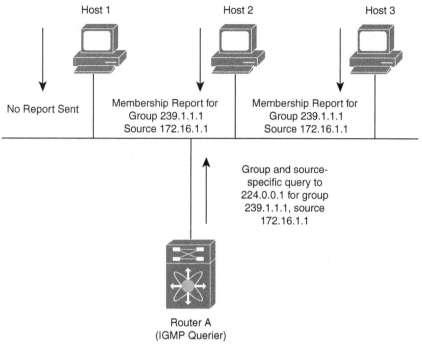

**Figure 1-11**   *IGMPv3 Group-and-Source-Specific Query*

> **NOTE**   IGMPv3 hosts do not perform IGMP membership report suppression.

IGMP messages sent by the designated querier have a time-to-live (TTL) value of 1, which means that the messages are not forwarded by the directly connected routers on the subnet. You can configure the frequency and number of query messages sent specifically for IGMP start-up, and you can configure a short query interval at start-up so that the group state is established as quickly as possible. Although usually unnecessary, you can tune the query interval used after start-up to a value that balances the responsiveness to host group membership messages and the traffic created on the network.

> **NOTE**   Changing the query interval can severely impact multicast forwarding.

When a multicast host leaves a group, a host that runs IGMPv2 or later sends an IGMP *leave message*. To check whether this host is the last host to leave the group, the software sends an IGMP query message and starts a timer that you can configure, called the *last member query response interval*. If no reports are received before the timer expires, the software removes the group state. The router continues to send multicast traffic for a group until its state is removed.

You can configure a robustness value to compensate for packet loss on a congested network. The robustness value is used by the IGMP software to determine the number of times to send messages.

Link-local addresses in the range 224.0.0.0/24 are reserved by the Internet Assigned Numbers Authority (IANA). Network protocols on a local network segment use these addresses; routers do not forward these addresses because they have a TTL of 1. By default, the IGMP process sends membership reports only for nonlink-local addresses, but you can configure the software to send reports for link-local addresses.

## Switch IGMP Snooping

IGMP snooping is a feature that limits multicast traffic on VLANs to the subset of ports that have known receivers. The IGMP snooping software examines IGMP protocol messages within a VLAN to discover which interfaces are connected to hosts or other devices interested in receiving this traffic. Using the interface information, IGMP snooping can reduce bandwidth consumption in a multi-access LAN environment to avoid flooding the entire VLAN. The IGMP snooping feature tracks which ports are attached to multicast-capable routers to help it manage the forwarding of IGMP membership reports. Multicast traffic is sent only to VLAN ports on which interested hosts reside. The IGMP snooping software responds to topology change notifications.

By default, IGMP snooping is enabled on the Cisco NX-OS system.

## Multicast Listener Discovery

Multicast Listener Discovery (MLD) is an IPv6 protocol that a host uses to request multicast data for a particular group. Using the information obtained through MLD, the software maintains a list of multicast group or channel memberships on a per-interface basis. The devices that receive MLD packets send the multicast data that they receive for requested groups or channels out the network segment of the known receivers.

MLDv1 is derived from IGMPv2, and MLDv2 is derived from IGMPv3. IGMP uses IP Protocol 2 message types, whereas MLD uses IP Protocol 58 message types, which is a subset of the ICMPv6 messages.

The MLD process is started automatically on the device. You cannot enable MLD manually on an interface. MLD is enabled automatically when you perform one of the following configuration tasks on an interface:

■ Enable PIM6.

■ Statically bind a local multicast group.

■ Enable link-local group reports.

Cisco NX-OS supports MLDv1 and MLDv2. MLDv2 supports MLDv1 listener reports.

By default, the software enables MLDv2 when it starts the MLD process. You can enable MLDv1 on interfaces where you want only its capabilities.

MLDv2 includes the following key changes from MLDv1:

■ MLDv2 supports source-specific multicast (SSM), which builds shortest path trees from each receiver to the source, through the following features:

  ■ Host messages that can specify both the group and the source.

  ■ The multicast state that is maintained for groups and sources, not just for groups as in MLDv1.

■ Hosts no longer perform report suppression, which means that hosts always send MLD listener reports when an MLD query message is received.

For detailed information about MLDv1, see RFC 2710. For detailed information about MLDv2, see RFC 3810.

The MLD process is similar to IGMP: MLD utilizes link-local addresses in the range FF02::0/16, as defined by the IANA. Network protocols on a local network segment use these addresses; routers do not forward these addresses because they have a TTL of 1. By default, the MLD process sends listener reports only for nonlink-local addresses, but you can configure the software to send reports for link-local addresses.

## Multicast Distribution Trees

A multicast distribution tree (MDT) represents the path that multicast data takes between the routers that connect sources and receivers. The multicast software builds different types of trees to support different multicast methods.

A *source* tree represents the shortest path that the multicast traffic takes through the network from the sources that transmit to a particular multicast group to receivers that requested traffic from that same group. Because of the shortest path characteristic of a source tree, this tree is often referred to as a *shortest path tree* (SPT). Figure 1-12 shows a source tree for group 239.1.1.1 that begins at host A and connects to hosts B and C.

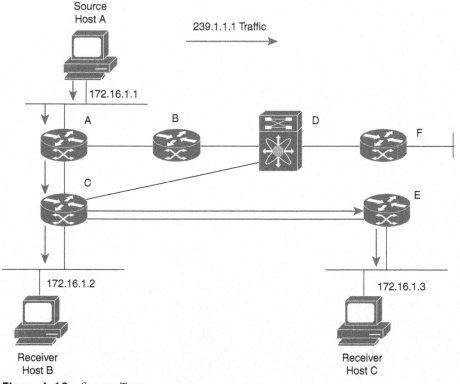

**Figure 1-12**   *Source Tree*

The notation (S, G) represents the multicast traffic from source S on group G. The SPT in Figure 1-12 is written (172.16.1.1, 239.1.1.1) and called "S comma G." Multiple sources can be transmitting on the same group.

A *shared tree* represents the shared distribution path that the multicast traffic takes through the network from a shared root or rendezvous point (RP) to each receiver. (The RP creates an SPT to each source.) A shared tree is also called an *RP tree* (RPT). Figure 1-13 shows a shared tree for group 239.1.1.1 with the RP at router D. Source hosts A and D send their data to router D, the RP, which then forwards the traffic to receiver hosts B and C.

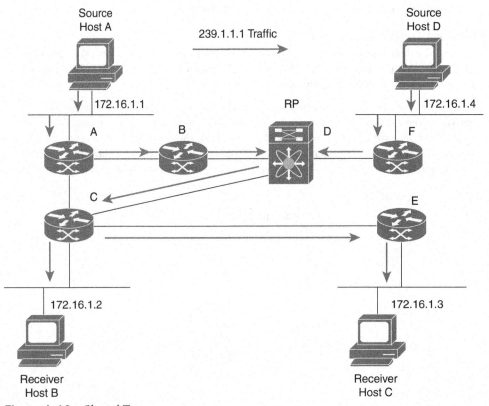

**Figure 1-13**   *Shared Tree*

The notation (*, G) ("star comma G") represents the multicast traffic from any source on group G. The shared tree in Figure 1-13 is written (*, 239.1.1.1).

A *bidirectional shared tree* represents the shared distribution path that the multicast traffic takes through the network from a shared root, or rendezvous point, to each receiver. Multicast data is forwarded to receivers encountered on the way to the RP. The advantage of the bidirectional shared tree is shown in Figure 1-14. Multicast traffic flows directly from host A to host B through routers B and C. In a shared tree, the data from source host A is first sent to the RP (router D) and then forwarded to router B for delivery to host B.

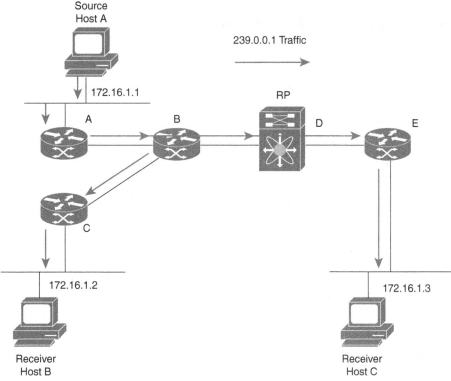

**Figure 1-14**  *Bidirectional Shared Tree*

The notation (*, G) represents the multicast traffic from any source on group G. The bidirectional tree in Figure 1-14 is written (*, 239.0.0.1).

## Protocol Independent Multicast

Cisco NX-OS supports multicasting with Protocol Independent Multicast (PIM) sparse mode. PIM (PIMv2) is an independent IPv4 routing protocol, and PIM6 is an independent IPv6 routing protocol. In PIM sparse mode, multicast traffic is sent only to locations of the network that specifically request it. PIM dense mode is not supported by Cisco NX-OS.

You need to enable the PIM or PIM6 feature before configuring multicast. Multicast is enabled only after you enable PIM or PIM6 on an interface of each router in a domain. You configure PIM for an IPv4 network and PIM6 for an IPv6 network. By default, IGMP and MLD are enabled on the NX-OS system.

PIM, which is used between multicast-capable routers, advertises group membership across a routing domain by constructing multicast distribution trees. PIM builds shared distribution trees on which packets from multiple sources are forwarded, as well as source distribution trees, on which packets from a single source are forwarded.

The distribution trees change automatically to reflect the topology changes due to link or router failures. PIM dynamically tracks both multicast-capable sources and receivers, although the source state is not created in Bidir mode.

The router uses the unicast routing table and RPF routes for multicast to create multicast routing information. In Bidir mode, additional routing information is created.

**NOTE** In this book, we use *PIMv2 for IPv4* and *PIM6 for IPv6* to refer to the Cisco NX-OS implementation of PIM sparse mode. A PIM domain can include both an IPv4 and an IPv6 network. Figure 1-15 shows two PIM domains in an IPv4 network.

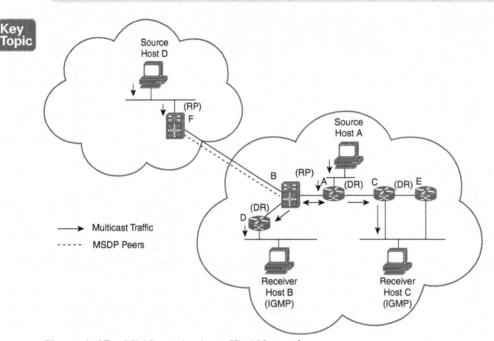

**Figure 1-15** *PIM Domains in an IPv4 Network*

Figure 1-15 shows the following PIM elements:

■ The lines with arrows show the path of the multicast data through the network. The multicast data originates from the sources at hosts A and D.

■ The dashed line connects routers B and F, which are Multicast Source Discovery Protocol (MSDP) peers. MSDP supports the discovery of multicast sources in other PIM domains.

■ Hosts B and C receive multicast data by using Internet Group Management Protocol (IGMP) to advertise requests to join a multicast group.

■ Routers A, C, and D are designated routers (DRs). When more than one router is connected to a LAN segment, such as C and E, the PIM software chooses one router to be the DR so that only one router is responsible for putting multicast data on the segment.

Router B is the rendezvous point for one PIM domain, and router F is the RP for the other PIM domain. The RP provides a common point for connecting sources and receivers within a PIM domain.

Figure 1-16 shows two PIM6 domains in an IPv6 network. In an IPv6 network, receivers that want to receive multicast data use the Multicast Listener Discovery (MLD) protocol to advertise requests to join a multicast group. MSDP, which allows for discovery of multicast sources in other PIM domains, is not supported for IPv6. You can configure IPv6 peers and use source-specific multicast (SSM) and Multiprotocol BGP (MBGP) to forward multicast data between PIM6 domains.

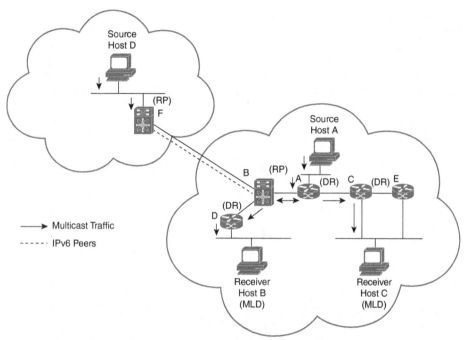

**Figure 1-16**   *PIM6 Domains in an IPv6 Network*

Cisco NX-OS supports a combination of three modes for different ranges of multicast groups. You can also define RPF routes for multicast.

*Any-source multicast* (ASM) is a PIM tree building mode that uses shared trees to discover new sources and receivers as well as source trees to form shortest paths from receivers to sources. The shared tree uses a network node as the root, called the rendezvous point. The source tree is rooted at first hop routers, directly attached to each source that is an active sender. The ASM mode requires an RP for a group range. An RP can be configured statically or learned dynamically by the Auto-RP or BSR group-to-RP discovery protocols. If an RP is learned and is not known to be a Bidir RP, the group operates in ASM mode.

The ASM mode is the default mode when you configure RPs.

*Bidirectional shared trees* (Bidir) is a PIM mode that, like the ASM mode, builds a shared tree between receivers and the RP but does not support switching over to a source tree when a new receiver is added to a group. In the Bidir mode, the router that is connected to a receiver is called the designated forwarder (DF) because multicast data can be forwarded directly from the designated router to the receiver without first going to the RP. The Bidir mode requires that you configure an RP.

The Bidir mode can reduce the amount of resources required on a router when there are many multicast sources and can continue to operate whether or not the RP is operational or connected.

*Source-specific multicast* (SSM) is a PIM mode that builds a source tree that originates at the designated router on the LAN segment that receives a request to join a multicast source. Source trees are built by sending PIM join messages in the direction of the source. The SSM mode does not require you to configure RPs.

The SSM mode allows receivers to connect to sources outside the PIM domain. PIM messages include the following:

■ **Hello:** The PIM process begins when the router establishes PIM neighbor adjacencies by sending PIM hello messages to the multicast address 224.0.0.13. Hello messages are sent periodically at an interval of 30 seconds. After all neighbors have replied, the PIM software chooses the router with the highest priority in each LAN segment as the designated router. The DR priority is based on a DR priority value in the PIM hello message. If the DR priority value is not supplied by all routers, or the priorities match, the highest IP address is used to elect the DR.

The hello message also contains a hold-time value, which is typically 3.5 times the hello interval. If this hold time expires without a subsequent hello message from its neighbor, the device detects a PIM failure on that link.

For security, you can configure an MD5 hash value that the PIM software uses to authenticate PIM hello messages with PIM neighbors.

■ **Join-Prune:** When the DR receives an IGMP membership report message from a receiver for a new group or source, the DR creates a tree to connect the receiver to the source by sending a PIM join message out the interface toward the rendezvous point (ASM or Bidir mode) or source (SSM mode). The rendezvous point is the root of a shared tree, which is used by all sources and hosts in the PIM domain in the ASM or the Bidir mode. SSM does not use an RP but builds a shortest path tree (SPT) that is the lowest cost path between the source and the receiver.

When the DR determines that the last host has left a group or source, it sends a PIM prune message to remove the path from the distribution tree.

The routers forward the join or prune action hop by hop up the multicast distribution tree to create (join) or tear down (prune) the path.

**NOTE** In this book, we use the terms *PIM join message* and *PIM prune message* to simplify the action taken when referring to the PIM join-prune message with only a join or prune action.

The software sends join-prune messages as quickly as possible. You can filter the join-prune messages by defining a routing policy. For information about configuring the join-prune message policy please refer to Table 1-24.

- **PIM register:** PIM register messages are unicast to the RP by designated routers that are directly connected to multicast sources. The PIM register message has the following functions:

  - To notify the RP that a source is actively sending to a multicast group.

  - To deliver multicast packets sent by the source to the RP for delivery down the shared tree.

  The DR continues to send PIM register messages to the RP until it receives a register-stop message from the RP. The RP sends a register-stop message in either of the following cases:

  - The RP has no receivers for the multicast group being transmitted.

  - The RP has joined the SPT to the source but has not started receiving traffic from the source.

  You can use the **ip pim register-source** command to configure the IP source address of register messages when the IP source address of a register message is not a uniquely routed address to which the RP can send packets. This situation might occur if the source address is filtered so that the packets sent to it are not forwarded or if the source address is not unique to the network. In these cases, the replies sent from the RP to the source address will fail to reach the DR, resulting in Protocol Independent Multicast sparse mode (PIM-SM) protocol failures.

PIM requires that multicast entries are refreshed within a 3.5-minute timeout interval. The state refresh ensures that traffic is delivered only to active listeners, and it keeps routers from using unnecessary resources.

To maintain the PIM state, the last-hop DR sends join-prune messages once per minute. State creation applies to both (*, G) and (S, G) states as follows:

- **(*, G) state creation example:** An IGMP (*, G) report triggers the DR to send a (*, G) PIM join message toward the RP.

- **(S, G) state creation example:** An IGMP (S, G) report triggers the DR to send an (S, G) PIM join message toward the source.

If the state is not refreshed, the PIM software tears down the distribution tree by removing the forwarding paths in the multicast outgoing interface list of the upstream routers.

### PIM Rendezvous Points

A rendezvous point (RP) is a router that you select in a multicast network domain that acts as a shared root for a multicast shared tree. You can configure as many RPs as you like, and you can configure them to cover different group ranges:

- **Static RP:** You can statically configure an RP for a multicast group range. You must configure the address of the RP on every router in the domain. You can define static RPs for the following reasons:

  - To configure routers with the Anycast RP address.

  - To manually configure an RP on a device.

■ **BSRs:** The bootstrap router ensures that all routers in the PIM domain have the same RP cache as the BSR. You can configure the BSR to help you select an RP set from BSR candidate RPs. The function of the BSR is to broadcast the RP set to all routers in the domain. You select one or more candidate BSRs to manage the RPs in the domain. Only one candidate BSR is elected as the BSR for the domain.

**CAUTION**    You should not configure both Auto-RP and BSR protocols in the same network.

■ **Auto-RP:** Auto-RP is a Cisco protocol that was used prior to the Internet standard bootstrap router mechanism. You configure Auto-RP by selecting candidate mapping agents and RPs. Candidate RPs send their supported group range in RP-Announce messages to the Cisco RP-Announce multicast group 224.0.1.39. An Auto-RP mapping agent listens for RP-Announce messages from candidate RPs and forms a Group-to-RP mapping table. The mapping agent multicasts the Group-to-RP mapping table in RP-Discovery messages to the Cisco RP-Discovery multicast group 224.0.1.40.

■ **Anycast RP:** An Anycast RP is used to define redundant and load-balanced RPs. An Anycast RP has two implementations:

   ■ Using Multicast Source Discovery Protocol (MSDP)

   ■ Using Protocol Independent Multicast (PIM)

An Anycast RP allows two or more RPs to share the load for source registration and to act as hot backup routers for each other. MSDP is the protocol that RPs use to share information about active sources. With an Anycast RP, the RPs are configured to establish MSDP peering sessions using a TCP connection. Group participants use the closest RP that is favored by the IP unicast route table.

You can use the PIM Anycast RP to assign a group of routers to a single RP address that is configured on multiple routers. The set of routers that you configure as Anycast RPs is called the Anycast RP set. This RP method is the only one that supports more than one RP per multicast group, which allows you to load balance across all RPs in the set. The Anycast RP supports all multicast groups.

PIM register messages are sent to the closest RP, and PIM join-prune messages are sent in the direction of the closest RP as determined by the unicast routing protocols. If one of the RPs goes down, unicast routing ensures that these messages will be sent in the direction of the next-closest RP.

You must configure PIM on the loopback interface that is used for the PIM Anycast RP.

### PIM Designated Routers/Forwarders

In PIM ASM and SSM modes, the software chooses a designated router from the routers on each network segment. The DR is responsible for forwarding multicast data for specified groups and sources on that segment. The DR for each LAN segment is determined as described in the hello messages.

In ASM mode, the DR is responsible for unicasting PIM register packets to the RP. When a DR receives an IGMP membership report from a directly connected receiver, the shortest path is formed to the RP, which may or may not go through the DR. The result is a shared tree that connects all sources transmitting on the same multicast group to all receivers of that group.

In SSM mode, the DR triggers (S, G) PIM join or prune messages toward the source. The path from the receiver to the source is determined hop by hop. The source must be known to the receiver or the DR.

In PIM Bidir mode, the software chooses a designated forwarder (DF) at RP discovery time from the routers on each network segment. The DF is responsible for forwarding multicast data for specified groups on that segment. The DF is elected based on the best metric from the network segment to the RP.

If the router receives a packet on the RPF interface toward the RP, the router forwards the packet out all interfaces in the OIF list. If a router receives a packet on an interface on which the router is the elected DF for that LAN segment, the packet is forwarded out all interfaces in the OIF list except the interface that it was received on and also out the RPF interface toward the RP.

> **NOTE**   Cisco NX-OS puts the RPF interface into the OIF list of the MRIB but not in the OIF list of the MFIB.

## Multicast Forwarding

Because multicast traffic is destined for an arbitrary group of hosts, the router uses *Reverse Path Forwarding* (RPF) to route data to active receivers for the group. When receivers join a group, a path is formed either toward the source (SSM mode) or the RP (ASM or Bidir mode). The path from a source to a receiver flows in the reverse direction from the path that was created when the receiver joined the group.

For each incoming multicast packet, the router performs an RPF check. If the packet arrives on the interface leading to the source, the packet is forwarded out each interface in the *outgoing interface* (OIF) list for the group. Otherwise, the router drops the packet.

> **NOTE**   In Bidir mode, if a packet arrives on a non-RPF interface, and the interface was elected as the designated forwarder, the packet is also forwarded in the upstream direction toward the RP.

Figure 1-17 shows an example of RPF checks on packets coming in from different interfaces. The packet that arrives on E2/1 fails the RPF check because the unicast route table lists the source of the network on interface E3/1. The packet that arrives on E3/1 passes the RPF check because the unicast route table lists the source of that network on interface E3/1.

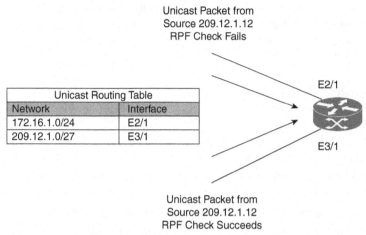

**Figure 1-17**  *RPF Check Example*

## Multicast Configurations and Verifications

Table 1-19 lists IGMP/MLD default parameters; you can alter these parameters as necessary.

**Table 1-19**   Default IGMP/MLD Parameters

| Parameters | Default |
|---|---|
| IGMP version | 2 |
| MLD version | 2 |
| Startup query interval | 30 seconds |
| Startup query count | 2 |
| Robustness value | 2 |
| Querier timeout | 255 seconds |
| Query timeout | 255 seconds |
| Query max response time | 10 seconds |
| Query interval | 125 seconds |
| Last member query response interval | 1 second |
| Last member query count | 2 |
| Group membership timeout | 260 seconds |
| Report link-local multicast groups | Disabled |
| Enforce router alert | Disabled |
| Immediate leave | Disabled |

Table 1-20 lists the default PIM/PIM6 parameters.

**Table 1-20**   Default PIM/PIM6 Parameters

| Parameters | Default |
|---|---|
| Use shared trees only | Disabled |
| Flush routes on restart | Disabled |

| Parameters | Default |
|---|---|
| Log Neighbor changes | Disabled |
| Auto-RP message action | Disabled |
| BSR message action | Disabled |
| SSM multicast group range or policy | IPv4: 232.0.0.0/8 |
| | IPv6: |
| | ff32::/32 |
| | ff33::/32 |
| | ff34::/32 |
| | ff35::/32 |
| | ff36::/32 |
| | ff37::/32 |
| | ff38::/32 |
| | ff39::/32 |
| | ff3a::/32 |
| | ff3b::/32 |
| | ff3c::/32 |
| | ff3d::/32 |
| | ff3e::/32 |
| PIM sparse mode | Disabled |
| Designated router priority | 1 |
| Hello authentication mode | Disabled |
| Domain border | Disabled |
| RP address policy | No message filtering |
| PIM register message policy | No message filtering |
| BSR candidate RP policy | No message filtering |
| BSR policy | No message filtering |
| Auto-RP mapping agent policy | No message filtering |
| Auto-RP RP candidate policy | No message filtering |
| Join-prune policy | No message filtering |
| Neighbor adjacency policy | Become adjacent with all PIM neighbors |
| BFD | Disabled |

**NOTE**  No license is required for IGMP/MLD.

Because PIMv2 required a license, Table 1-21 shows the required NX-OS feature licenses. For more information, visit the Cisco NX-OS Licensing Guide.

**Table 1-21** Feature-Based Licenses for Cisco NX-OS

| Platform | Feature License | Feature Name |
|---|---|---|
| Cisco Nexus 9000 Series | Enterprise Services Package<br><br>LAN_ENTERPRISE_SERVICES_PKG | PIMv2 (all modes)<br><br>MSDP |

PIM and PIM6 have the following configuration guidelines and limitations:

- Cisco NX-OS PIM and PIM6 do not interoperate with any version of PIM dense mode or PIM sparse mode version 1.

- Do not configure both Auto-RP and BSR protocols in the same network.

- Configure candidate RP intervals to a minimum of 15 seconds.

- If a device is configured with a BSR policy that should prevent it from being elected as the BSR, the device ignores the policy. This behavior results in the following undesirable conditions:

  - If a device receives a BSM that is permitted by the policy, the device, which incorrectly elected itself as the BSR, drops that BSM so that routers downstream fail to receive it. Downstream devices correctly filter the BSM from the incorrect BSR so that these devices do not receive RP information.

  - A BSM received by a BSR from a different device sends a new BSM but ensures that downstream devices do not receive the correct BSM.

You can configure separate ranges of addresses in the PIM or PIM6 domain using the multicast distribution modes described in Table 1-22.

**Table 1-22** PIM and PIM6 Multicast Distribution Modes

| Multicast Distribution Mode | Requires RP Configuration | Purpose |
|---|---|---|
| ASM | Yes | Any source multicast |
| Bidir | Yes | Bidirectional shared trees |
| SSM | No | Single-source multicast |
| RPF routes for multicast | No | RPF routes for multicast |

Tables 1-23 through 1-25 describe the most-used multicast configuration commands. For the full list of commands, refer to the Nexus Multicast Routing Configuration Guide in the reference section at the end of this chapter.

**Table 1-23** Multicast Global-Level Commands

| Command | Purpose |
|---|---|
| feature pim | Enables PIM. By default, PIM is disabled. |
| feature pim6 | Enables PIM6. By default, PIM6 is disabled. |

| Command | Purpose |
|---|---|
| [ip \| ipv6 ] [pim\|pim6] rp-address *rp-address* [group-list *ip-prefix* \| prefix-list *name* \| route-map *policy-name*] [bidir ] | Configures a PIM static RP address for a multicast group range. You can specify a route-map policy name that lists the group prefixes to use with the **match ip multicast** command. The default mode is ASM unless you specify the **bidir** keyword. The default group range for IPv4 is 224.0.0.0 through 239.255.255.255; for IPv6, it is ff00::/8.<br><br>Example 1 configures PIM ASM mode for the specified group range.<br><br>Example 2 configures PIM Bidir mode for the specified group range. |
| ip pim auto-rp {listen [forward ] \| forward [listen ]} | (Optional) Enables listening or forwarding of Auto-RP messages. The default is disabled, which means that the software does not listen to or forward Auto-RP messages. |
| ip pim bsr {listen [forward ] \| forward [listen ]} | (Optional) Enables listening or forwarding of BSR messages. The default is disabled, which means that the software does not listen or forward BSR messages. |
| [ip \| ipv6 ] [pim\|pim6] rp-address *anycast-rp-address* [group-list *ip-address*] | Configures a PIM Anycast RP peer address for the specified Anycast RP address. Each command with the same Anycast RP address forms an Anycast RP set. The IP addresses of RPs are used for communication with RPs in the set. |
| ip pim bidir-rp-limit *limit* | (Optional) Specifies the number of Bidir RPs that you can configure for IPv4. The maximum number of Bidir RPs supported per VRF for PIM and PIM6 combined cannot exceed 8. Values range from 0 to 8. The default is 6. |
| [ip \| ipv6 ] [pim\|pim6] register-rate-limit *rate* | (Optional) Configures the rate limit in packets per second. The range is from 1 to 65,535. The default is no limit. |
| ip pim spt-threshold infinity group-list *route-map-name* | (Optional) Configures the initial hold-down period in seconds. The range is from 90 to 210. Specify 0 to disable the hold-down period. The default is 210. |
| [ip \| ipv6 ] routing multicast holddown *holddown-period* | (Optional) Configures the initial hold-down period in seconds. The range is from 90 to 210. Specify 0 to disable the hold-down period. The default is 210. |
| ip igmp ssm-translate | Configures the translation of IGMPv1 or IGMPv2 membership reports by the IGMP process to create the (S,G) state as if the router had received an IGMPv3 membership report. |

**Table 1-24**   Multicast Interface-Level Commands

| Command | Purpose |
|---|---|
| [ip \| ipv6 ] [pim\|pim6] sparse-mode | Enables sparse mode on this interface. The default is disabled. |
| [ip \| ipv6 ] [pim\|pim6] dr-priority *priority* | (Optional) Sets the designated router priority that is advertised in PIM/PIM6 hello messages. Values range from 1 to 4,294,967,295. The default is 1. |

| Command | Purpose |
|---|---|
| [ip \| ipv6 ] [pim\|pim6] hello-authentication ah-md5 *auth-key* | (Optional) Enables an MD5 hash authentication key in PIM/PIM6 hello messages. You can enter an unencrypted (cleartext) key or one of these values followed by a space and the MD5 authentication key:<br><br>**0:** Specifies an unencrypted (cleartext) key.<br><br>**3:** Specifies a 3-DES encrypted key.<br><br>**7:** Specifies a Cisco Type 7 encrypted key.<br><br>The key can be up to 16 characters. The default is disabled. |
| [ip \| ipv6 ] [pim\|pim6] hello-interval *interval* | (Optional) Configures the interval at which hello messages are sent in milliseconds. The range is from 1000 to 18,724,286. The default is 30,000. |
| [ip \| ipv6 ] [pim\|pim6] neighbor-policy prefix-list *prefix-list* | (Optional) Configures which PIM/PIM6 neighbors to become adjacent to based on a route-map policy with the **match ipv6 address** command. The policy name can be up to 63 characters. The default is to become adjacent with all PIM6 neighbors.<br><br>**NOTE:** We recommend that you configure this feature only if you are an experienced network administrator. |
| [ip igmp \| ipv6 mld] version *value* | Sets the IGMP/MLD version to the value specified. The default is 2. |
| [ip igmp \| ipv6 mld] join-group { *group* [ **source** *source* ] \| **route-map** *policy-name* } | Statically binds a multicast group to the interface. If you specify only the group address, the (*, G) state is created. If you specify the source address, the (S, G) state is created. You can specify a route-map policy name that lists the group prefixes, group ranges, and source prefixes to use with the **match ip multicast** command.<br><br>**NOTE:** A source tree is built for the (S, G) state only if you enable IGMPv3.<br><br>**CAUTION:** The device CPU must be able to handle the traffic generated by using this command. Because of CPU load constraints, using this command, especially in any form of scale, is not recommended. Consider using the **ip igmp static-oif** command instead. |
| [ip igmp \| ipv6 mld] startup-query-interval *seconds* | Sets the query interval used when the software starts up. Values can range from 1 to 18,000 seconds. The default is 31 seconds. |
| [ip igmp \| ipv6 mld] query-timeout *seconds* | Sets the querier timeout that the software uses when deciding to take over as the querier. Values can range from 1 to 65,535 seconds. The default is 255 seconds. |
| [ip igmp \| ipv6 mld] query-interval *interval* | Sets the frequency at which the software sends IGMP host query messages. Values can range from 1 to 18,000 seconds. The default is 125 seconds. |
| [ip igmp \| ipv6 mld] access-group *policy* | Configures a route-map policy to control the multicast groups that hosts on the subnet serviced by an interface can join. |

| Command | Purpose |
|---|---|
| [ip igmp \| ipv6 mld] immediate-leave | Enables the device to remove the group entry from the multicast routing table immediately upon receiving a leave message for the group. Use this command to minimize the leave latency of IGMPv2/MLD group memberships on a given IGMP/MLD interface because the device does not send group-specific queries. The default is disabled. <br><br> **NOTE:** Use this command only when there is one receiver behind the interface for a given group. |
| [ip\|ipv6] pim ip-policy *policy-name* [in \| out] | (Optional) Enables join-prune messages to be filtered based on a route-map policy where you can specify group, group and source, or group and RP addresses with the **match ip multicast** command. The default is no filtering of join-prune messages. This command filters messages in both incoming and outgoing directions. |

**Table 1-25**   Multicast Global-Level BGP Verification Commands

| Command | Purpose |
|---|---|
| show [ip\|ipv6] pim rp | Displays rendezvous points known to the software, how they were learned, and their group ranges. For similar information, see also the **show ip pim group-range** command. |
| show [ip\|ipv6] mroute ip-address {*source group* \| *group*[ *source* ]} [ vrf *vrf-name* \| all ] | Displays the IP or IPv6 multicast routing table. |
| show [ip\|ipv6] pim group-range [*ip-prefix* \| vrf *vrf-name*] | Displays the learned or configured group ranges and modes. For similar information, see also the **show ip pim rp** command. |
| show running-configuration pim [ 6 ] | Displays the running-configuration information. |
| show [ip igmp \| ipv6 mld] interface [ interface ] [ vrf *vrf-name* \| all ] [brief] | Displays IGMP information about all interfaces or a selected interface, the default VRF, a selected VRF, or all VRFs. |
| show [ip igmp \| ipv6 mld] groups [ group \| interface ] [ vrf *vrf-name* \| all ] | Displays the IGMP attached group membership for a group or interface, the default VRF, a selected VRF, or all VRFs. |
| show [ip igmp \| ipv6 mld] route [ group \| interface ] [ vrf *vrf-name* \| all ] | Displays the IGMP attached group membership for a group or interface, the default VRF, a selected VRF, or all VRFs. |
| show [ip igmp \| ipv6 mld] local - groups | Displays the IGMP local group membership. |
| show running-configuration [igmp\|mld] | Displays the IGMP/MLD running-configuration information. |

Figure 1-18 shows the network topology for the configuration that follows, which demonstrates how to configure Nexus multicast routing.

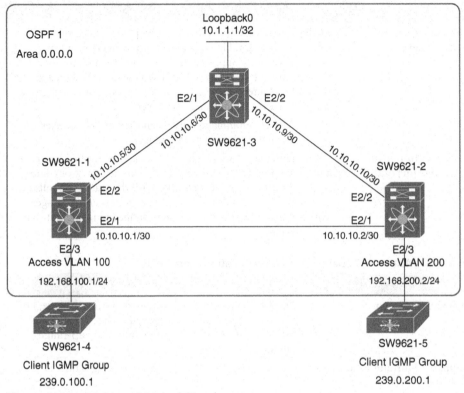

**Figure 1-18** *Multicast Network Topology*

Example 1-18 shows the SW9621-1 Multicast PIM feature enabling and IGMP configurations.

**Example 1-18** *Multicast IGMP SW9621-1 Configuration and Verifications*

```
SW9621-1(config)# feature interface-vlan
SW9621-1(config)# feature pim
SW9621-1(config)# vlan 100
SW9621-1(config)# interface vlan 100
SW9621-1(config-if)# ip pim sparse-mode
SW9621-1(config-if)# ip address 192.168.100.1/24
SW9621-1(config-if)# no shut
SW9621-1(config)# interface e2/3
SW9621-1(config-if)# switchport mode access
SW9621-1(config-if)# switchport access vlan 100

W9621-1# show ip igmp int vlan 100
IGMP Interfaces for VRF "default"
Vlan100, Interface status: protocol-up/link-up/admin-up
  IP address: 192.168.100.1, IP subnet: 192.168.100.0/24
```

```
   Active querier: 192.168.100.1, version: 2, next query sent in: 00:00:15
   Membership count: 0
   Old Membership count 0
   IGMP version: 2, host version: 2
   IGMP query interval: 125 secs, configured value: 125 secs
   IGMP max response time: 10 secs, configured value: 10 secs
   IGMP startup query interval: 31 secs, configured value: 31 secs
   IGMP last member mrt: 1 secs
   IGMP last member query count: 2
   IGMP group timeout: 260 secs, configured value: 260 secs
   IGMP querier timeout: 255 secs, configured value: 255 secs
   IGMP unsolicited report interval: 10 secs
   IGMP robustness variable: 2, configured value: 2
   IGMP reporting for link-local groups: disabled
   IGMP interface enable refcount: 1
   IGMP interface immediate leave: disabled
   IGMP VRF name default (id 1)
   IGMP Report Policy: None
   IGMP State Limit: None
   IGMP interface statistics: (only non-zero values displayed)
     General (sent/received):
       v2-queries: 33/33, v2-reports: 0/0, v2-leaves: 0/0
     Errors:
   Interface PIM DR: Yes
Interface vPC SVI: No
   Interface vPC CFS statistics:

SW9621-1# show ip igmp snooping vlan 100
Global IGMP Snooping Information:
   IGMP Snooping enabled
   Optimised Multicast Flood (OMF) enabled
   IGMPv1/v2 Report Suppression enabled
   IGMPv3 Report Suppression disabled
   Link Local Groups Suppression enabled

IGMP Snooping information for vlan 100
   IGMP snooping enabled
   Lookup mode: IP
   Optimised Multicast Flood (OMF) enabled
   IGMP querier present, address: 192.168.100.1, version: 2, i/f Vlan100
   Querier interval: 125 secs
   Querier last member query interval: 1 secs
   Querier robustness: 2
   Switch-querier disabled
```

```
IGMPv3 Explicit tracking enabled
IGMPv2 Fast leave disabled
IGMPv1/v2 Report suppression enabled
IGMPv3 Report suppression disabled
Link Local Groups suppression enabled
Router port detection using PIM Hellos, IGMP Queries
Number of router-ports: 1
Number of groups: 0
VLAN vPC function disabled
Active ports:
  Eth2/3
```

Example 1-19 shows SW9621-2 Multicast PIM configurations and IGMP status.

**Example 1-19**  *Multicast IGMP SW9621-2 Configuration and Verifications*

```
SW9621-2(config)# feature interface-vlan
SW9621-2(config)# feature pim
SW9621-2(config)# vlan 200
SW9621-2(config)# int vlan 200
SW9621-2(config-if)# ip address 192.168.200.1/24
SW9621-2(config-if)# ip igmp ver 3
SW9621-2(config-if)# ip pim sparse-mode
SW9621-2(config-if)# no shut
SW9621-2(config)# interface e2/3
SW9621-2(config-if)# switchport mode access
SW9621-2(config-if)# switchport access vlan 200
SW9621(config-if)# show ip igmp snooping vlan 200
Global IGMP Snooping Information:
  IGMP Snooping enabled
  Optimised Multicast Flood (OMF) enabled
  IGMPv1/v2 Report Suppression enabled
  IGMPv3 Report Suppression disabled
  Link Local Groups Suppression enabled

IGMP Snooping information for vlan 200
  IGMP snooping enabled
  Lookup mode: IP
  Optimised Multicast Flood (OMF) enabled
  IGMP querier present, address: 192.168.200.1, version: 3, i/f Vlan200
  Querier interval: 125 secs
  Querier last member query interval: 1 secs
  Querier robustness: 2
  Switch-querier disabled
  IGMPv3 Explicit tracking enabled
  IGMPv2 Fast leave disabled
  IGMPv1/v2 Report suppression enabled
```

```
IGMPv3 Report suppression disabled
Link Local Groups suppression enabled
Router port detection using PIM Hellos, IGMP Queries
Number of router-ports: 1
Number of groups: 0
VLAN vPC function disabled
Active ports:
  Eth2/3
```

Example 1-20 shows SW9621-1, SW9621-2, and SW9621-3 Multicast PIM configurations and IP PIM status.

**Example 1-20**   *Enabling PIM on Routers 1 to 3 (SW9621-1 to SW9621-3) and Verifications*

```
SW9621-1(config)# feature pim
SW9621-1(config)# interface e2/1
SW9621-1(config-if)# ip pim sparse-mode
SW9621-1(config)# interface e2/2
SW9621-1(config-if)# ip pim sparse-mode

SW9621-2(config)# feature pim
SW9621-2(config)# interface e2/1
SW9621-2(config-if)# ip pim sparse-mode
SW9621-2(config)# interface e2/2
SW9621-2(config-if)# ip pim sparse-mode

SW9621-3(config)# feature pim
SW9621-3(config)# interface e2/1
SW9621-3(config-if)# ip pim sparse-mode
SW9621-3(config)# interface e2/2
SW9621-1(config-if)# ip pim sparse-mode


SW9621-1# show ip pim neighbor
PIM Neighbor Status for VRF "default"
Neighbor        Interface .       Uptime    Expires   DR        Bidir- BFD
                                                      Priority Capable State
10.10.10.2      Ethernet2/1       01:23:13  00:01:38  1         yes    n/a
10.10.10.6      Ethernet2/2       01:22:01  00:01:36  1         yes    n/a


SW9621-2(config-if)# show ip pim neighbor
PIM Neighbor Status for VRF "default"
Neighbor        Interface         Uptime    Expires   DR        Bidir- BFD
                                                      Priority Capable State
10.10.10.1      Ethernet2/1       01:25:09  00:01:34  1         yes    n/a
10.10.10.9      Ethernet2/2       01:23:45  00:01:41  1         yes    n/a
```

```
SW9621-3# show ip pim neighbor
PIM Neighbor Status for VRF "default"
Neighbor        Interface      Uptime     Expires   DR       Bidir-  BFD
                                                    Priority Capable State
10.10.10.5      Ethernet2/1    01:24:15   00:01:37  1        yes     n/a
10.10.10.10     Ethernet2/2    01:24:04   00:01:18  1        yes     n/a
```

Example 1-21 shows SW9621-1 Multicast Static RP configurations and status.

**Example 1-21**  *Multicast Static RP Configurations and Verification*

```
SW9621-1(config)# ip pim rp 10.10.10.2


SW9621-1(config)# show ip pim rp
PIM RP Status Information for VRF "default"
BSR disabled
Auto-RP disabled
BSR RP Candidate policy: None
BSR RP policy: None
Auto-RP Announce policy: None
Auto-RP Discovery policy: None


RP: 10.10.10.2, (0),
 uptime: 00:00:14 priority: 0,
 RP-source: (local),
 group ranges:
 224.0.0.0/4


SW9621-1(config)# ip pim rp 10.10.10.6 group-list 239.0.200.0/24


SW9621-1(config)# show ip pim rp
PIM RP Status Information for VRF "default"
BSR disabled
Auto-RP disabled
BSR RP Candidate policy: None
BSR RP policy: None
Auto-RP Announce policy: None
Auto-RP Discovery policy: None


RP: 10.10.10.6, (0),
 uptime: 00:02:16 priority: 0,
 RP-source: (local),
 group ranges:
 239.0.200.0/24
```

Example 1-22 shows SW9621-1 multicast BSR RP configurations and status.

**Example 1-22**  *Multicast BSRs RP Configurations and Verification*

```
SW9621-1(config)# ip pim bsr bsr-candidate e2/1

SW9621-1(config)# show ip pim rp
PIM RP Status Information for VRF "default"
BSR: 10.10.10.1*, next Bootstrap message in: 00:00:53,
    priority: 64, hash-length: 30
Auto-RP disabled
BSR RP Candidate policy: None
BSR RP policy: None
Auto-RP Announce policy: None
Auto-RP Discovery policy: None


RP: 10.10.10.2, (0),
 uptime: 00:04:24 priority: 0,
 RP-source: (local),
 group ranges:
 224.0.0.0/4


SW9621-2(config)# ip pim bsr listen
SW9621-2(config)# show ip pim rp
PIM RP Status Information for VRF "default"
BSR listen-only mode
BSR: Not Operational
Auto-RP disabled
BSR RP Candidate policy: None
BSR RP policy: None
Auto-RP Announce policy: None
Auto-RP Discovery policy: None

RP: 10.10.10.6, (0),
 uptime: 00:03:39 priority: 0,
 RP-source: (local),
 group ranges:
 239.0.200.0/24
```

Example 1-23 shows SW9621-2 Multicast Auto RP configurations and status.

**Example 1-23**  *Multicast Auto RP Configurations and Verification*

```
SW9621-2(config)# ip pim auto-rp rp-candidate e2/1 group-list 239.0.0.0/24 bidir
SW9621-2(config)# ip pim auto-rp mapping-agent e2/1
SW9621-2(config)# ip pim auto-rp forward listen
```

```
SW9621-2(config)# show ip pim rp
PIM RP Status Information for VRF "default"
BSR listen-only mode
BSR: 10.10.10.1, uptime: 00:04:37, expires: 00:01:21,
     priority: 64, hash-length: 30
Auto-RP RPA: 10.10.10.2*, next Discovery message in: 00:00:05
BSR RP Candidate policy: None
BSR RP policy: None
Auto-RP Announce policy: None
Auto-RP Discovery policy: None

RP: 10.10.10.2*, (1),
 uptime: 00:00:16 priority: 0,
 RP-source: 10.10.10.2 (A),
 group ranges:
 239.0.0.0/24 (bidir) , expires: 00:02:43 (A)
RP: 10.10.10.6, (0),
 uptime: 00:08:54 priority: 0,
 RP-source: (local),
 group ranges:
 239.0.200.0/24
```

Example 1-24 shows SW9621-3 multicast anycast RP configurations and status.

**Example 1-24**   *Multicast Anycast RP Configurations and Verification*

```
SW9621-3(config)# int loopback 0
SW9621-3(config-if)# ip add 10.1.1.1/32
SW9621-3(config-if)# ip router ospf 1 area 0
SW9621-3(config-if)# no shut

SW9621-3(config)# ip pim anycast-rp 10.1.1.1 10.10.10.6
SW9621-3(config)# ip pim anycast-rp 10.1.1.1 10.10.10.9

SW9621-2(config)# ip pim auto-rp mapping-agent e2/1
SW9621-2(config)# ip pim auto-rp forward listen

SW9621-3(config)# show ip pim rp
PIM RP Status Information for VRF "default"
BSR disabled
Auto-RP disabled
BSR RP Candidate policy: None
BSR RP policy: None
Auto-RP Announce policy: None
Auto-RP Discovery policy: None

Anycast-RP 10.1.1.1 members:
 10.10.10.6 10.10.10.9*
```

Example 1-25 shows SW9621-1 multicast SSM range configurations and status.

**Example 1-25**  *Multicast SSM Configurations and Verification*

```
SW9621-1(config)# ip ssm range 239.0.100.0/24


SW9621-1(config)# show ip pim group-range
PIM Group-Range Configuration for VRF "default"
Group-range          Action Mode  RP-address      Shrd-tree-range   Origin


239.0.100.0/24          Accept SSM   -                   -              Local


224.0.0.0/4      -      ASM   10.10.10.2              -               Static
```

Example 1-26 shows the IP multicast routing table.

**Example 1-26**  *Multicast IP Route Example*

```
SW9621-1(config)# show ip mroute


IP Multicast Routing Table for VRF "default"
(*, 239.0.100.0/24), uptime: 00:03:07, pim ip
  Incoming interface: Null, RPF nbr: 0.0.0.0
  Outgoing interface list: (count: 0)


SW9621-2(config)# show ip mroute
IP Multicast Routing Table for VRF "default"

(*, 232.0.0.0/8), uptime: 00:30:21, pim ip
  Incoming interface: Null, RPF nbr: 0.0.0.0
  Outgoing interface list: (count: 0)


(*, 239.0.0.0/24), bidir, uptime: 00:10:46, pim ip
  Incoming interface: Ethernet2/1, RPF nbr: 10.10.10.2
  Outgoing interface list: (count: 0)


SW9621-3(config)# show ip mroute
IP Multicast Routing Table for VRF "default"


(*, 232.0.0.0/8), uptime: 00:29:36, pim ip
  Incoming interface: Null, RPF nbr: 0.0.0.0
  Outgoing interface list: (count: 0)
```

# Hot Standby Router Protocol

The First Hop Redundancy Protocols (FHRPs) are designed to keep the default gateway available for network participants. This goal is achieved by using two or more routers in a group to provide a backup for the router that carries the default gateway IP address. Such FHRP protocols are Hot Standby Router Protocol (HSRP) and Virtual Router Redundancy Protocol (VRRP).

HSRP allows a transparent failover of the first hop gateway router. It provides first hop routing redundancy for IP hosts on Ethernet networks configured with a gateway or default route. You can use HSRP in a group of routers for selecting an active router and a standby router. In a group of two routers, the active router is the router that routes packets; the standby router is the router that takes over when the active router fails or when preset conditions are met.

Many host implementations do not support any dynamic router discovery mechanisms but can be configured with a default router. Running a dynamic router discovery mechanism on every host is not feasible for a number of reasons, including administrative overhead, processing overhead, and security issues. HSRP provides failover services to these hosts.

When you use HSRP, you need an HSRP virtual IP address as the host's default router (instead of the IP address of the actual router). The virtual IP address is an IP address that is shared among a group of routers that run HSRP. Configuring HSRP on a network segment will provide a virtual MAC address and a virtual IP address for the HSRP group. You need to configure the same virtual address on each HSRP-enabled interface in the group. You also configure a unique IP address and MAC address on each interface that acts as the real address. HSRP selects one of these interfaces to be the active router. The active router receives and routes packets destined for the virtual MAC address of the group.

HSRP detects when the active router fails. At that point, a selected standby router assumes control of the virtual MAC and IP addresses of the HSRP group. HSRP also selects a new standby router at that time.

HSRP uses a priority mechanism to determine which HSRP-configured interface becomes the default active router. To configure an interface as the active router, you assign it with a priority that is higher than the priority of all the other HSRP-configured interfaces in the group. The default priority is 100, so if you configure just one interface with a higher priority, that interface becomes the default active router.

Interfaces that run HSRP send and receive multicast User Datagram Protocol (UDP)–based hello messages to detect a failure and to designate active and standby routers. When the active router fails to send a hello message within a configurable period of time, the standby router with the highest priority becomes the active router. The transition of packet forwarding functions between the active and standby router is completely transparent to all hosts on the network.

**NOTE**    You can configure multiple HSRP groups on an interface.

Figure 1-19 shows a network configured for HSRP. By sharing a virtual MAC address and a virtual IP address, two or more interfaces can act as a single virtual router.

The virtual router does not physically exist but represents the common default router for interfaces that are configured to provide backup to each other. You do not need to configure the hosts on the LAN with the IP address of the active router. Instead, you configure them with the IP address (virtual IP address) of the virtual router as their default router. If the active router fails to send a hello message within the configurable period of time, the standby router takes over, responds to the virtual addresses, and becomes the active router, assuming the active router duties. From the host perspective, the virtual router remains the same.

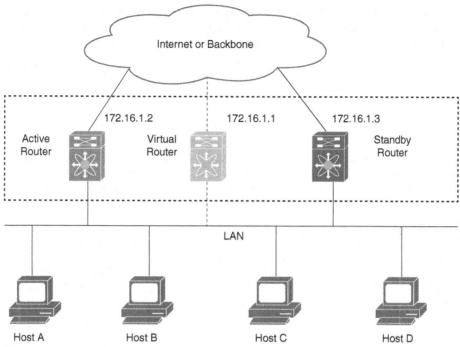

**Figure 1-19** *HSRP Topology with Two Enabled Routers*

Cisco NX-OS supports HSRP version 1 by default. You can, instead, configure an interface to use HSRP version 2.

HSRP version 2 has the following enhancements to HSRP version 1:

- Expands the group number range. HSRP version 1 supports group numbers from 0 to 255. HSRP version 2 supports group numbers from 0 to 4095.

- Uses the new IP multicast address 224.0.0.102 to send hello packets instead of the multicast address of 224.0.0.2, which is used by HSRP version 1.

- Uses the MAC address range from 0000.0C9F.F000 to 0000.0C9F.FFFF. HSRP version 1 uses the MAC address range 0000.0C07.AC00 to 0000.0C07.ACFF.

- Adds support for MD5 authentication.

When you change the HSRP version, Cisco NX-OS reinitializes the group because it now has a new virtual MAC address.

HSRP version 2 has a different packet format than HSRP version 1. The packet format uses a type-length-value (TLV) format. HSRP version 2 packets received by an HSRP version 1 router are ignored.

HSRP message digest 5 (MD5) algorithm authentication protects against HSRP-spoofing software and uses the industry-standard MD5 algorithm for improved reliability and security.

HSRP routers communicate with each other by exchanging HSRP hello packets. These packets are sent to the destination IP multicast address 224.0.0.2 (reserved multicast address used to communicate to all routers) on UDP port 1985. The active router sources hello packets from its configured IP address and the HSRP virtual MAC address while the standby router sources hellos from its configured IP address and the interface MAC address, which may or may not be the burned-in address (BIA). The BIA is the last 6 bytes of the MAC address that is assigned by the manufacturer of the network interface card (NIC).

Because hosts are configured with their default router as the HSRP virtual IP address, they must communicate with the MAC address associated with the HSRP virtual IP address. This MAC address is a virtual MAC address, 0000.0C07.ACxy, where xy is the HSRP group number in hexadecimal based on the respective interface. For example, HSRP group 1 will use the HSRP virtual MAC address 0000.0C07.AC01. Hosts on the adjoining LAN segment use the normal Address Resolution Protocol (ARP) process to resolve the associated MAC addresses.

HSRP version 2 uses the new IP multicast address 224.0.0.102 to send hello packets instead of the multicast address 224.0.0.2, which is used by version 1. HSRP version 2 permits an expanded group number range of 0 to 4095 and uses a new MAC address range of 0000.0C9F.F000 to 0000.0C9F.FFFF.

Routers that are configured with HSRP exchange the following three types of multicast messages:

- **Hello:** The hello message conveys the HSRP priority and state information of the router to other HSRP routers.

- **Coup:** When a standby router wants to assume the function of the active router, it sends a coup message.

- **Resign:** A router that is the active router sends this message when it is about to shut down or when a router that has a higher priority sends a hello or coup message.

HSRP enables you to configure multiple groups on an interface. You can configure two overlapping HSRP groups to load share traffic from the connected hosts while providing the default router redundancy expected from HSRP. Figure 1-20 shows an example of a load-sharing HSRP configuration.

Figure 1-20 shows two routers, A and B, and two HSRP groups. Router A is the active router for group 10 but the standby router for group 20. Similarly, router B is the active router for group 20 and the standby router for group 10. If both routers remain active, HSRP load balances the traffic from the hosts across both routers. If either router fails, the remaining router continues to process traffic for both hosts.

You can use object tracking to modify the priority of an HSRP interface based on the operational state of another interface. Object tracking allows you to route to a standby router if the interface to the main network fails.

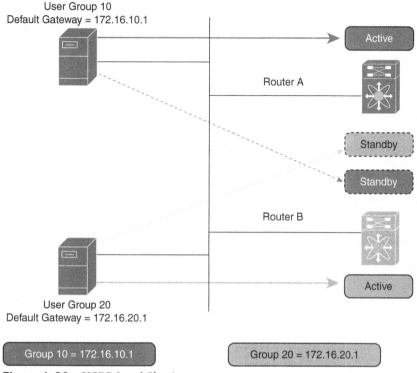

**Figure 1-20** *HSRP Load Sharing*

## Virtual Router Redundancy Protocol

The Virtual Router Redundancy Protocol (VRRP) allows for transparent failover at the first hop IP router, by configuring a group of routers to share a virtual IP address. VRRP selects a master router in that group to handle all packets for the virtual IP address. The remaining routers are in standby and take over in the event that the master router fails.

### VRRP Operation

A LAN client can determine which router should be the first hop to a particular remote destination by using a dynamic process or static configuration. Examples of dynamic router discovery are as follows:

- **Proxy ARP:** The client uses the Address Resolution Protocol (ARP) to get the destination it wants to reach, and a router will respond to the ARP request with its own MAC address.

- **Routing protocol:** The client listens to dynamic routing protocol updates (for example, from the Routing Information Protocol [RIP]) and forms its own routing table.

- **ICMP Router Discovery Protocol (IRDP) client:** The client runs an Internet Control Message Protocol (ICMP) router discovery client.

The disadvantage to dynamic discovery protocols is that they incur some configuration and processing overhead on the LAN client. Also, in the event of a router failure, the process of switching to another router can be slow.

An alternative to dynamic discovery protocols is to statically configure a default router on the client. Although this approach simplifies client configuration and processing, it creates a single point of failure. If the default gateway fails, the LAN client is limited to communicating only on the local IP network segment and is cut off from the rest of the network.

VRRP can solve the static configuration problem by enabling a group of routers (a VRRP group) to share a single virtual IP address. You can then configure the LAN clients with the virtual IP address as their default gateway.

Figure 1-21 shows a basic VLAN topology. In this example, routers A, B, and C form a VRRP group. The IP address of the group is the same address that was configured for the Ethernet interface of router A (10.0.0.1).

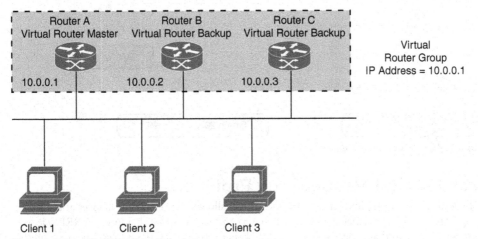

**Figure 1-21**   *Basic VRRP Topology*

Because the virtual IP address uses the IP address of the physical Ethernet interface of router A, router A is the master (also known as the *IP address owner*). As the master, router A owns the virtual IP address of the VRRP group and forwards packets sent to this IP address. Clients 1 through 3 are configured with the default gateway IP address of 10.0.0.1.

Routers B and C function as backups. If the master fails, the backup router with the highest priority becomes the master and takes over the virtual IP address to provide uninterrupted service for the LAN hosts. When router A recovers, it becomes the master again.

**NOTE**   Packets received on a routed port destined for the VRRP virtual IP address will terminate on the local router, regardless of whether that router is the master VRRP router or a backup VRRP router. This includes ping and telnet traffic. Packets received on a Layer 2 (VLAN) interface destined for the VRRP virtual IP address will terminate on the master router.

The benefits of VRRP are as follows:

- **Redundancy:** Enables you to configure multiple routers as the default gateway router, which reduces the possibility of a single point of failure in a network.

- **Load sharing:** Allows traffic to and from LAN clients to be shared by multiple routers. The traffic load is shared more equitably among available routers.

- **Multiple VRRP groups:** Supports up to 255 VRRP groups on a router physical interface if the platform supports multiple MAC addresses. Multiple VRRP groups enable you to implement redundancy and load sharing in your LAN topology.

- **Multiple IP addresses:** Allows you to manage multiple IP addresses, including secondary IP addresses. If you have multiple subnets configured on an Ethernet interface, you can configure VRRP on each subnet.

- **Preemption:** Enables you to preempt a backup router that has taken over for a failing master with a higher priority backup router that has become available.

- **Advertisement protocol:** Uses a dedicated Internet Assigned Numbers Authority (IANA) standard multicast address (224.0.0.18) for VRRP advertisements. This addressing scheme minimizes the number of routers that must service the multicasts and allows test equipment to accurately identify VRRP packets on a segment. IANA has assigned the IP protocol number 112 to VRRP.

- **VRRP tracking:** Ensures that the best VRRP router is the master for the group by altering VRRP priorities based on interface states.

## VRRP Groups

You can configure up to 255 VRRP groups on a physical interface. The actual number of VRRP groups that a router interface can support depends on the following factors:

- Router processing capability

- Router memory capability

In a topology where multiple VRRP groups are configured on a router interface, the interface can act as a master for one VRRP group and as a backup for one or more other VRRP groups.

Figure 1-22 shows a LAN topology in which VRRP is configured so that routers A and B share the traffic to and from clients 1 through 4. Routers A and B act as backups to each other if either router fails.

This topology contains two virtual IP addresses for two VRRP groups that overlap. For VRRP group 1, router A is the owner of IP address 10.0.0.1 and is the master. Router B is the backup to router A. Clients 1 and 2 are configured with the default gateway IP address of 10.0.0.1.

For VRRP group 2, router B is the owner of IP address 10.0.0.2 and is the master. Router A is the backup to router B. Clients 3 and 4 are configured with the default gateway IP address 10.0.0.2.

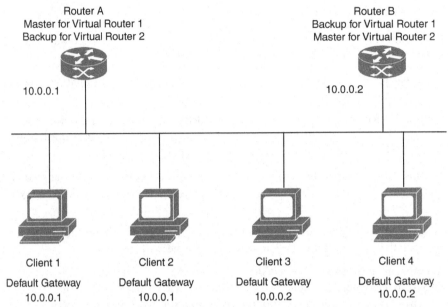

**Figure 1-22** *Load Sharing and Redundancy VRRP Topology*

## VRRP Router Priority and Preemption

An important aspect of the VRRP redundancy scheme is the VRRP router priority because the priority determines the role that each VRRP router plays and what happens if the master router fails.

If a VRRP router owns the virtual IP address and the IP address of the physical interface, this router functions as the master. The priority of the master is 255.

Priority also determines if a VRRP router functions as a backup router and the order of ascendancy to becoming a master if the master fails. For example, if router A, the master in a LAN topology, fails, VRRP must determine if backups B or C should take over. If you configure router B with the priority 101 and router C with the default priority of 100, VRRP selects router B to become the master because it has the higher priority. If you configure routers B and C with the default priority of 100, VRRP selects the backup with the higher IP address to become the master.

VRRP uses preemption to determine what happens after a VRRP backup router becomes the master. With preemption enabled by default, VRRP will switch to a backup if that backup comes online with a priority higher than the new master. For example, if router A is the master and fails, VRRP selects router B (next in order of priority). If router C comes online with a higher priority than router B, VRRP selects router C as the new master, even though router B has not failed.

If you disable preemption, VRRP will only switch if the original master recovers or the new master fails.

The VRRP master sends VRRP advertisements to other VRRP routers in the same group. The advertisements communicate the priority and state of the master. Cisco NX-OS encapsulates the VRRP advertisements in IP packets and sends them to the IP multicast address assigned to the VRRP group. Cisco NX-OS sends the advertisements once every second by default, but you can configure a different advertisement interval.

## VRRP Authentication

VRRP supports the following authentication mechanisms:

- No authentication
- Plain text authentication

VRRP rejects packets in any of the following cases:

- The authentication schemes differ on the router and in the incoming packet.
- Text authentication strings differ on the router and in the incoming packet.

## VRRP Tracking

VRRP supports the following two options for tracking:

- **Native interface tracking:** Tracks the state of an interface and uses that state to determine the priority of the VRRP router in a VRRP group. The tracked state is down if the interface is down or if the interface does not have a primary IP address.
- **Object tracking:** Tracks the state of a configured object and uses that state to determine the priority of the VRRP router in a VRRP group.

If the tracked state (interface or object) goes down, VRRP updates the priority based on what you configure the new priority to be for the tracked state. When the tracked state comes up, VRRP restores the original priority for the virtual router group.

For example, you might want to lower the priority of a VRRP group member if its uplink to the network goes down so another group member can take over as master for the VRRP group.

**NOTE**   VRRP does not support Layer 2 interface tracking.

VRRP supports stateful restarts and stateful switchover. A stateful restart occurs when the VRRP process fails and is restarted. Stateful switchover occurs when the active supervisor switches to the standby supervisor. Cisco NX-OS applies the runtime configuration after the switchover.

## IPv6 First Hop Redundancy

ICMPv6 Neighbor Discovery (ND) provides some sort of first hop redundancy. A router with the IPv6 interface enabled will send Router Advertisement (RA) ICMPv6 messages (Message value 134) every 200 seconds or when it receives Router Solicitation messages.

RA messages typically include the following information:

- One or more on-link IPv6 prefixes that nodes on the local link can use to automatically configure their IPv6 addresses

- Lifetime information for each prefix included in the advertisement

- Sets of flags that indicate the type of autoconfiguration (stateless or stateful) that can be completed

- Default router information (whether the router sending the advertisement should be used as a default router and, if so, the amount of time in seconds the router should be used as a default router)

- Additional information for hosts, such as the hop limit and MTU a host should use in packets that it originates

From RA messages, a router will send a suggestion to the client device on how to obtain address information dynamically and provide its own IPv6 link-local address as a default gateway.

IPv6 RA messages can be used to provide a first hop redundancy. Figure 1-23 shows the steps in IPv6 first hop redundancy.

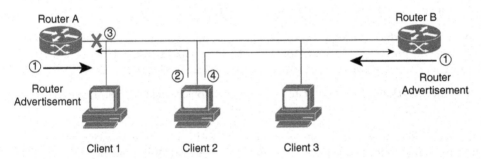

Router Advertisement Packet
ICMPv6 Type = 134
Src = Router Link-Local Address
Dst = All-Nodes Multicast Address
Data = Options, Prefix, Lifetime, Autoconfig Flag

**Figure 1-23**   *ICMPv6 Neighbor Discovery First Hop Redundancy*

1. Both router A and B send RA messages every 200 seconds to announce themselves as a default gateway for the network.
2. Client 2 receives these messages from both routers and installs both IPs in its default router list. Depending on preference or first received message, client 2 will select one router as the primary default gateway. As an example, client 2 will select router A as a default router and will start sending IPv6 traffic to router A.
3. If the link between router A and client 2 fails, client 2 will not receive any RA message from router A anymore. It will continue sending traffic to Router A and will keep router A as a default router until the lifetime expires (the lifetime sent to client 2 from router A via RA message data); the default lifetime is 30 minutes. ICMPv6 Neighbor Unreachability Detection (NUD) will determine if router A is not available anymore.
4. Client 2 will send an NS message to router B, the next default router in the list. When it receives an NA response, client 2 will update its default router and will use router B as the default router.

> **NOTE**  The default router update will depend on the client operating system.

In the preceding example, ICMPv6 Neighbor Discovery (NA) provides first hop redundancy, but it does have some drawbacks. For example, it will depend on the client operating system to determine if the primary router failed and start to use the second router as a default gateway.

For faster failover, Cisco NX-OS now supports IPv6 on both HSRP and VRRP protocols.

### HSRP/VRRP Configurations and Verifications

Table 1-26 lists HSRP default parameters; you can alter HSRP parameters as necessary.

**Table 1-26**  Default Settings for HSRP Parameters

| Parameters | Default |
|---|---|
| HSRP | Disabled |
| Authentication | Enabled as text for version 1, with *cisco* as the password |
| HSRP version | Version 1 |
| Preemption | Disabled |
| Priority | 100 |
| Virtual MAC address | Derived from HSRP group number |

Table 1-27 lists the default settings for VRRP parameters.

**Table 1-27**  Default Settings for VRRP Parameters

| Parameters | Default |
|---|---|
| VRRP feature | Disabled |
| Advertisement interval | 1 second |
| Authentication | No authentication |
| Preemption | Enabled |
| Priority | 100 |

Table 1-28 shows the NX-OS feature licenses required for HSRP and VRRP. For more information, visit the Cisco NX-OS Licensing Guide.

**Table 1-28**  Feature-Based Licenses for Cisco NX-OS

| Platform | Feature License | Feature Name |
|---|---|---|
| Cisco Nexus 9000 Series | No license required | |

HSRP has the following configuration limitations:

- You must configure an IP address for the interface where you configure HSRP and enable that interface before HSRP becomes active.

- The virtual IP address must be in the same subnet as the interface IP address.

■ We recommend that you do not configure more than one First Hop Redundancy Protocol on the same interface.

■ HSRP version 2 does not interoperate with HSRP version 1.

VRRP has the following configuration limitations:

■ You cannot configure VRRP on the management interface.

■ When VRRP is enabled, you should replicate the VRRP configuration across devices in your network.

■ We recommend that you do not configure more than one First Hop Redundancy Protocol on the same interface.

■ You must configure an IP address for the interface where you configure VRRP and enable that interface before VRRP becomes active.

■ When you configure VRRP to track a Layer 2 interface, you must shut down the Layer 2 interface and reenable the interface to update the VRRP priority to reflect the state of the Layer 2 interface.

Tables 1-29 to 1-31 show the most-used HSRP/VRRP configuration and verification commands.

**Table 1-29**   HSRP/VRRP Global-Level Commands

| Command | Purpose |
|---|---|
| feature hsrp | Enables the HSRP feature. |
| feature vrrp | Enables the VRRP feature. |
| hsrp version {1 | 2} | Configures the HSRP version. Version 1 is the default. |
| track *object-id* interface *interface-type number* {ip routing | line-protocol} | Configures the interface that this HSRP interface tracks. Changes in the state of the interface affect the priority of this HSRP interface as follows: |
| | You configure the interface and corresponding object number that you use with the **track** command in HSRP configuration mode. |
| | The **line-protocol** keyword tracks whether the interface is up. The **ip routing** keyword also checks that IP routing is enabled on the interface and an IP address is configured. |

**Table 1-30**   HSRP/VRRP Interface-Level Commands

| Command | Purpose |
|---|---|
| hsrp *group-number* [ipv4] | Creates an HSRP group and enters HSRP configuration mode. The range for HSRP version 1 is from 0 to 255. The range for HSRP version 2 is from 0 to 4095. The default value is 0. |

| Command | Purpose |
|---------|---------|
| **ip** [*ip-address* [**secondary**]] | Configures the virtual IP address for the HSRP group and enables the group. This address should be in the same subnet as the IPv4 address of the interface. |
| **name** *string* | Specifies the IP redundancy name for an HSRP group. The string is from 1 to 255 characters. The default string has the following format:<br><br>**hsrp**-*<interface-short-name>*-*<group-id>*. For example, **hsrp-Eth3/1-10.** |
| **preempt** [**delay** [**minimum** *seconds*][**reload** *seconds*] [**sync** *seconds*]] | Configures the router to take over as an active router for an HSRP group if it has a higher priority than the current active router. This command is disabled by default. The range is from 0 to 3600 seconds. |
| **timers** [**msec**] *hellotime* [**msec**] *holdtime* | Configures the hello and hold time for this HSRP member as follows:<br><br>*hellotime:* The interval between successive hello packets sent. The range is from 1 to 254 seconds.<br><br>*holdtime:* The interval before the information in the hello packet is considered invalid. The range is from 3 to 255.<br><br>The optional **msec** keyword specifies that the argument is expressed in milliseconds instead of the default seconds. The timer ranges for milliseconds are as follows:<br><br>*hellotime:* The interval between successive hello packets sent. The range is from 255 to 999 milliseconds.<br><br>*holdtime:* The interval before the information in the hello packet is considered invalid. The range is from 750 to 3000 milliseconds. |
| **priority** *level* [**forwarding-threshold lower** *lower-value* **upper** *upper-value*] | Sets the priority level used to select the active router in an HSRP group. The *level* range is from 0 to 255. The default is 100. |
| **track** *object-number* [**decrement** *value*] | Specifies an object to be tracked that affects the weighting of an HSRP interface.<br><br>The *value* argument specifies a reduction in the priority of an HSRP interface when a tracked object fails. The range is from 1 to 255. The default is 10. |
| **vrrp** *number* | Creates a virtual router group. The range is from 1 to 255. |
| **address** *ip-address* [**secondary**] | Configures the virtual IPv4 address for the specified VRRP group. This address should be in the same subnet as the IPv4 address of the interface.<br><br>Use the secondary option only if applications require that VRRP routers accept the packets sent to the virtual router's IP address and deliver to applications. |
| **priority** *level* [**forwarding-threshold lower** *lower-value* **upper** *upper-value*] | Sets the priority level used to select the active router in a VRRP group. The *level* range is from 1 to 254. The default is 100 for backups and 255 for a master that has an interface IP address equal to the virtual IP address. |

| Command | Purpose |
|---|---|
| **advertisement-interval** *seconds* | Sets the interval time in seconds between sending advertisement frames. The range is from 1 to 254. The default is 1 second. |
| **no preempt** | Disables the preempt option and allows the master to remain when a higher-priority backup appears. |
| **track interface type** *number* **priority** *value* | Enables interface priority tracking for a VRRP group. The priority range is from 1 to 254. |
| **no shutdown** | Enables the HSRP/VRRP group. Disabled by default. |

**Table 1-31** HSRP/VRRP Global-Level Verification Commands

| Command | Purpose |
|---|---|
| **show hsrp** [**group** *group-number*] | Displays the HSRP status for all groups or one group. |
| **show hsrp** [**interface** *interface-type slot/ port*] | Displays the HSRP status for an interface. |
| **show vrrp** | Displays the VRRP status for all groups. |
| **show vrrp vr** *group-number* | Displays the VRRP status for a VRRP group. |
| **show vrrp vr** *number* **interface** *interface-type port* **configuration** | Displays the virtual router configuration for an interface. |
| **show vrrp vr** *number* **interface** *interface-type port* **status** | Displays the virtual router status for an interface. |
| **show vrrp vr** *number* **interface** *interface-type port* **statistics** | Displays the virtual router information. |

Figure 1-24 shows the network topology for the configuration that follows, which demonstrates how to configure Nexus HSRP and VRRP.

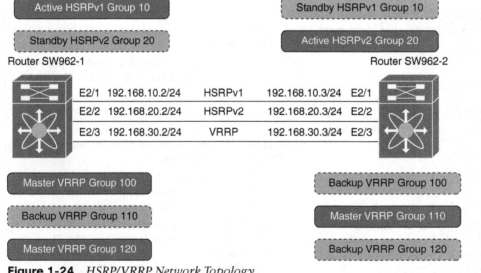

**Figure 1-24** *HSRP/VRRP Network Topology*

Example 1-27 shows SW9621-1 HSRP and VRRP feature enabling and interface configurations.

**Example 1-27**    *HSRP/VRRP SW9621-1 Full Configurations*

```
SW9621-1(config)# feature hsrp
SW9621-1(config)# feature vrrp

SW9621-1(config)# interface e2/1
SW9621-1(config-if)# ip add 192.168.10.2/24
SW9621-1(config-if)# no shut
SW9621-1(config-if)# hsrp 10
SW9621-1(config-if-hsrp)# ip 192.168.10.1
SW9621-1(config-if-hsrp)# preempt
SW9621-1(config-if-hsrp)# priority 255
SW9621-1(config-if-hsrp)# no shut

SW9621-1(config)# interface e2/2
SW9621-1(config-if)# ip add 192.168.20.2/24
SW9621-1(config-if)# hsrp ver 2
SW9621-1(config-if)# no shut
SW9621-1(config-if)# hsrp 20
SW9621-1(config-if-hsrp)# ip 192.168.20.1
SW9621-1(config-if-hsrp)# timers msec 300 msec 900
SW9621-1(config-if-hsrp)# no shut

SW9621-1(config)# interface e2/3
SW9621-1(config-if)# ip address 192.168.30.2/24
SW9621-1(config-if)# no shut
SW9621-1(config-if)# vrrp 100
SW9621-1(config-if-vrrp)# ip 192.168.30.100
SW9621-1(config-if-hsrp)# authentication text cisco
SW9621-1(config-if-hsrp)# advertisement-int 3
SW9621-1(config-if-hsrp)# no shut
SW9621-1(config-if)# vrrp 110
SW9621-1(config-if-vrrp)# ip 192.168.30.110
SW9621-1(config-if-hsrp)# advertisement-int 110
SW9621-1(config-if-hsrp)# no shut
SW9621-1(config-if)# vrrp 120
SW9621-1(config-if-vrrp)# ip 192.168.30.120
SW9621-1(config-if-hsrp)# no preempt
SW9621-1(config-if-hsrp)# no shut
```

Example 1-28 shows SW9621-2 HSRP and VRRP feature enabling and interface configurations.

**Example 1-28**    *HSRP/VRRP SW9621-2 Full Configurations*

```
SW9621-2(config)# feature hsrp
SW9621-2(config)# feature vrrp


SW9621-2(config)# interface e2/1
SW9621-2(config-if)# ip address 192.168.10.3/24
SW9621-2(config-if)# no shut
SW9621-2(config-if)# hsrp 10
SW9621-2(config-if-hsrp)# ip 192.168.10.1
SW9621-2(config-if-hsrp)# no shut


SW9621-2(config)# interface e2/2
SW9621-2(config-if)# ip address 192.168.20.3/24
SW9621-2(config-if)# hsrp ver 2
SW9621-2(config-if)# no shut
SW9621-2(config-if)# hsrp 20
SW9621-2(config-if-hsrp)# ip 192.168.20.1
SW9621-2(config-if-hsrp)# timers msec 300 msec 900
SW9621-2(config-if-hsrp)# priority 255
SW9621-2(config-if-hsrp)# preempt
SW9621-2(config-if-hsrp)# no shut


SW9621-2(config)# interface e2/3
SW9621-2(config-if)# ip address 192.168.30.3/24
SW9621-2(config-if)# no shut
SW9621-2(config-if)# vrrp 100
SW9621-2(config-if-vrrp)# ip 192.168.30.100
SW9621-2(config-if-hsrp)# authentication text cisco
SW9621-2(config-if-hsrp)# advertisement-int 3
SW9621-2(config-if-hsrp)# no shut
SW9621-2(config-if)# vrrp 110
SW9621-2(config-if-vrrp)# ip 192.168.30.110
SW9621-2(config-if-hsrp)# advertisement-int 110
SW9621-2(config-if-hsrp)# priority 254
SW9621-2(config-if-hsrp)# no shut
SW9621-2(config-if)# vrrp 120
SW9621-2(config-if-vrrp)# ip 192.168.30.120
SW9621-2(config-if-hsrp)# no preempt
SW9621-2(config-if-hsrp)# no shut
```

Example 1-29 shows the HSRP and VRRP status.

**Example 1-29**  *SW9621-1 and SW9621-2 Verifications*

```
SW9621-1# show hsrp brief
*:IPv6 group   #:group belongs to a bundle
                    P indicates configured to preempt.
                    |
 Interface   Grp  Prio P  State    Active addr      Standby addr     Group addr
 Eth2/1       10   255 P  Active   local            192.168.10.3     192.168.10.1   (conf)
 Eth2/2       20   100    Standby  192.168.20.3     local            192.168.20.1   (conf)
SW9621-1# show hsrp
Ethernet2/1 - Group 10 (HSRP-V1) (IPv4)
  Local state is Active, priority 255 (Cfged 255), may preempt
    Forwarding threshold(for vPC), lower: 1 upper: 255
  Hellotime 3 sec, holdtime 10 sec
  Next hello sent in 1.749000 sec(s)
  Virtual IP address is 192.168.10.1 (Cfged)
  Active router is local
  Standby router is 192.168.10.3 , priority 100 expires in 5.183000 sec(s)
  Authentication text "cisco"
  Virtual mac address is 0000.0c07.ac0a (Default MAC)
  1 state changes, last state change 00:55:33
  IP redundancy name is hsrp-Eth2/1-10 (default)


Ethernet2/2 - Group 20 (HSRP-V2) (IPv4)
  Local state is Standby, priority 100 (Cfged 100)
    Forwarding threshold(for vPC), lower: 1 upper: 100
  Hellotime 300 msec, holdtime 900 msec
  Next hello sent in 0.251000 sec(s)
  Virtual IP address is 192.168.20.1 (Cfged)
  Active router is 192.168.20.3, priority 255 expires in 0.058000 sec(s)
  Standby router is local
  Authentication text "cisco"
  Virtual mac address is 0000.0c9f.f014 (Default MAC)
  7 state changes, last state change 00:25:15
  IP redundancy name is hsrp-Eth2/2-20 (default)


SW9621-1# show vrrp
      Interface  VR IpVersion Pri   Time   Pre State   VR IP addr
-----------------------------------------------------------------
    Ethernet2/3 100    IPV4     100    3 s     Y  Master 192.168.30.100
    Ethernet2/3 110    IPV4     100  110 s     Y  Backup 192.168.30.110
    Ethernet2/3 120    IPV4     100    1 s     N  Master 192.168.30.120
```

```
SW9621-1# show vrrp detail

Ethernet2/3 - Group 100 (IPV4)
    State is Master
    Virtual IP address is 192.168.30.100
    Priority 100, Configured 100
    Forwarding threshold(for VPC), lower: 1 upper: 100
    Advertisement interval 3
    Preemption enabled
    Authentication text "cisco"
    Virtual MAC address is 0000.5e00.0164
    Master router is Local

Ethernet2/3 - Group 110 (IPV4)
    State is Backup
    Virtual IP address is 192.168.30.110
    Priority 100, Configured 100
    Forwarding threshold(for VPC), lower: 1 upper: 254
    Advertisement interval 110
    Preemption enabled
    Virtual MAC address is 0000.5e00.016e
    Master router is 192.168.30.3

Ethernet2/3 - Group 120 (IPV4)
    State is Master
    Virtual IP address is 192.168.30.120
    Priority 100, Configured 100
    Forwarding threshold(for VPC), lower: 1 upper: 100
    Advertisement interval 1
    Preemption disabled
    Virtual MAC address is 0000.5e00.0178
    Master router is Local

SW9621-2# show hsrp brief
*:IPv6 group   #:group belongs to a bundle
                   P indicates configured to preempt.
                   |
  Interface  Grp  Prio  P  State   Active addr     Standby addr    Group        addr
   Eth2/1     10   100     Standby  192.168.10.2    local           192.168.10.1  (conf)
   Eth2/2     20   255  P  Active   local           192.168.20.2    192.168.20.1  (conf)
SW9621-2# show vrrp
      Interface  VR IpVersion Pri   Time    Pre State    VR IP addr
-----------------------------------------------------------------
     Ethernet2/3 100   IPV4    100   3 s     Y  Backup 192.168.30.100
     Ethernet2/3 110   IPV4    254   110 s   Y  Master 192.168.30.110
     Ethernet2/3 120   IPV4    100   1 s     N  Backup 192.168.30.120
```

## Exam Preparation Tasks

As mentioned in the Introduction, you have a couple of choices for exam preparation: the exercises here, Chapter 21, "Final Preparation," and the exam simulation questions in the Pearson Test Prep software online.

## Review All Key Topics

Review the most important topics in the chapter, noted with the key topic icon in the outer margin of the page. Table 1-32 lists a reference to these key topics and the page numbers on which each is found.

**Table 1-32**   Key Topics for Chapter 1

| Key Topic Element | Description | Page |
|---|---|---|
| Section | OSPF Link-State Advertisements | 7 |
| Table 1-2 | OSPFv2 and OSPFv3 LSAs Supported by Cisco NX-OS | 8 |
| Paragraph | OSPF Areas | 10 |
| Figure 1-1 | OSPF Area | 10 |
| Figure 1-2 | OSPF Stub Area | 11 |
| Figure 1-3 | OSPF Virtual Links | 12 |
| Section | Designated Routers and Backup Designated Routers | 12 |
| Table 1-3 | Default OSPFv2/OSPFv3 Parameters | 13 |
| Section | Border Gateway Protocol | 24 |
| List | BGP Peering | 25 |
| Section | BGP Route Selection | 26 |
| Section | Multiprotocol BGP | 29 |
| Section | Bidirectional Forwarding Detection | 37 |
| Figure 1-6 | Establishing a BFD Neighbor Relationship | 38 |
| Section | Rapid Detection of Failures | 38 |
| Table 1-14 | Default Settings for BFD Parameters | 39 |
| Figure 1-9 | Multicast Traffic from One Source to Two Receivers | 43 |
| Section | Internet Group Management Protocol | 43 |
| Section | Multicast Distribution Trees | 47 |
| Section | Protocol Independent Multicast | 49 |
| Figure 1-15 | PIM Domains in an IPv4 Network | 50 |
| Section | PIM Rendezvous Points | 53 |
| Section | PIM Designated Routers/Forwarders | 54 |
| Section | Multicast Forwarding | 55 |
| Table 1-19 | Default IGMP/MLD Parameters | 56 |

| Key Topic Element | Description | Page |
|---|---|---|
| Section | Hot Standby Router Protocol | 69 |
| Figure 1-19 | HSRP Topology with Two Enabled Routers | 71 |
| Section | VRRP Operation | 73 |
| List | Benefits of VRRP | 75 |
| Table 1-26 | Default Settings for HSRP Parameters | 79 |

## Memory Tables

Print a copy of Appendix C, "Memory Tables" (found on the companion website), or at least the section for this chapter, and complete the tables and lists from memory. Appendix D, "Memory Tables Answer Key," also on the companion website, includes completed tables and lists to check your work.

## Define Key Terms

Define the following key terms from this chapter, and check your answers in the Glossary.

Address Resolution Protocol (ARP), any-source multicast (ASM), autonomous system (AS), Bidirectional Forwarding Detection (BFD), Cisco Nexus, Cisco NX-OS, equal-cost multipath (ECMP), First Hop Redundancy Protocol (FHRP), Gateway Load Balancing Protocol (GLBP), generic routing encapsulation (GRE), Hot Standby Router Protocol (HSRP), ICMP Router Discovery Protocol (IRDP), in-service software upgrade (ISSU), Interior Gateway Protocol (IGP), Internet Assigned Numbers Authority (IANA), Internet Control Message Protocol (ICMP), Internet Group Management Protocol (IGMP), Link Aggregation Control Protocol (LACP), link-state advertisements (LSAs), maximum transmission unit (MTU), Media Access Control (MAC) address, message digest 5 (MD5), Multicast Listener Discovery (MLD), Multicast Routing Information Base (MRIB), Multicast Source Discovery Protocol (MSDP), Multiprotocol BGP (MBGP), Neighbor Discovery (ND), Neighbor Unreachability Detection (NUD), Protocol-Independent Multicast (PIM), Reverse Path Forwarding (RPF), Router Advertisement (RA), Shortest Path First (SPF), shortest path tree (SPT), source-specific multicast (SSM), Switched Virtual Interface (SVI), time-to-live (TTL), type-length-value (TLV), User Datagram Protocol (UDP), Virtual Internet Routing Lab (VIRL), virtual port channel (vPC), Virtual Router Redundancy Protocol (VRRP), Virtual Routing and Forwarding (VRF)

## References

Cisco Nexus 9000 Series NX-OS Unicast Routing Configuration Guide, Release 10.3(x): https://www.cisco.com/c/en/us/td/docs/dcn/nx-os/nexus9000/103x/unicast-routing-configuration/cisco-nexus-9000-series-nx-os-unicast-routing-configuration-guide-release-103x.html

Cisco Nexus 9000 Series NX-OS Multicast Routing Configuration Guide, Release 10.3(x): https://www.cisco.com/c/en/us/td/docs/dcn/nx-os/nexus9000/103x/configuration/multicast/cisco-nexus-9000-series-nx-os-multicast-routing-configuration-guide-release-103x.html

Cisco Nexus 9000 Series NX-OS High Availability and Redundancy Guide, Release 10.3(x): https://www.cisco.com/c/en/us/td/docs/dcn/nx-os/nexus9000/103x/configuration/high-availability-and-redundancy/cisco-nexus-9000-series-nx-os-high-availability-and-redundancy-guide-release-103x/m-network-level-ha.html#ID50

Cisco NX-OS Licensing Options Guide: https://www.cisco.com/c/en/us/td/docs/switches/datacenter/licensing-options/cisco-nexus-licensing-options-guide.html

Relevant CiscoLive Presentations: https://ciscolive.com

Cisco Modeling Labs: https://developer.cisco.com/modeling-labs/

# CHAPTER 2

# Implementing Data Center Switching Protocols

Switching is an OSI Layer 2 (L2) process that uses a device's Media Access Control (MAC) address to perform forwarding decisions. For high availability, switches are normally interconnected using redundant links. Switching protocols prevent Layer 2 looping when deploying switches with redundant links.

**This chapter covers the following key topics:**

**Spanning Tree Protocols (STP):** This section provides an overview of the Layer 2 Spanning Tree Protocol, discusses the Rapid PVST+ protocol, and includes a configuration example.

**Port Channels:** This section discusses the Layer 2 port channel and command-line interface (CLI) commands and includes a configuration example.

**Virtual Port Channel:** This section covers the virtual port channel (vPC), vPC roles, vPC links, and types. It also includes a configuration example.

## "Do I Know This Already?" Quiz

The "Do I Know This Already?" quiz enables you to assess whether you should read this entire chapter thoroughly or jump to the "Exam Preparation Tasks" section. If you are in doubt about your answers to these questions or your own assessment of your knowledge of the topics, read the entire chapter. Table 2-1 lists the major headings in this chapter and their corresponding "Do I Know This Already?" quiz questions. You can find the answers in Appendix A, "Answers to the 'Do I Know This Already?' Quizzes."

**Table 2-1** "Do I Know This Already?" Section-to-Question Mapping

| Foundation Topics Section | Questions |
|---|---|
| Spanning Tree Protocols (STP) | 1–4 |
| Port Channels | 5–6 |
| Virtual Port Channel | 7–10 |

1. Which of the following bridge IDs would win an election as root, assuming that the switches with these bridge IDs were in the same network?

    a. 32769:0200.1231.1221

    b. 32769:0200.3322.1112

    c. 4097:0200.1122.1121

    d. 4097:0200.1122.2211

    e. 40961:0200.1111.1111

2. What STP feature causes an interface to be placed in a forwarding state as soon as the interface is physically active?

    a. STP

    b. RSTP

    c. Root Guard

    d. 802.1w

    e. PortFast

    f. Trunking

3. What are the IEEE standards that improve the original STP standard and lower convergence time? (Choose two answers.)

    a. STP

    b. RSTP

    c. Root Guard

    d. 802.1w

    e. PortFast

    f. Trunking

4. Which option describes how a switch in Rapid PVST+ mode responds to a topology change?

    a. It immediately deletes dynamic MAC addresses that were learned by all ports on the switch.

    b. It sets a timer to delete all MAC addresses that were learned dynamically by ports in the same STP instance.

    c. It sets a timer to delete dynamic MAC addresses that were learned by all ports on the switch.

    d. It immediately deletes all MAC addresses that were learned dynamically by ports in the same STP instance.

**5.** Which statements are true of the Link Aggregation Control Protocol (LACP)? (Choose three answers.)

   **a.** LACP also can be used to connect to non-Cisco devices.

   **b.** LACP packets are sent with the **channel-group 1 mode desirable** command.

   **c.** LACP packets are sent with the **channel-group 1 mode active** command.

   **d.** Standby interfaces should be configured with a higher priority.

   **e.** Standby interfaces should be configured with a lower priority.

**6.** Which statement is true regarding the Port Aggregation Protocol (PAgP)?

   **a.** Configuration changes made on the port channel interface apply to all physical ports assigned to the port channel interface.

   **b.** Configuration changes made on a physical port that is a member of a port channel interface apply to the port channel interface.

   **c.** Configuration changes are not permitted with Port Aggregation Protocol; instead, the standardized Link Aggregation Control Protocol should be used if configuration changes are required.

   **d.** The physical port must first be disassociated from the port channel interface before any configuration changes can be made.

**7.** Which Fabric Extender (FEX) topologies trade deterministic bandwidth for server-link stability during FEX uplink failure? (Choose two answers.)

   **a.** Port channel

   **b.** Static pinning

   **c.** Virtual port channel

   **d.** Dynamic pinning

   **e.** Equal-cost multipath

   **f.** RPVST

**8.** What protocol do vPC peers use to synchronize forwarding-plane information and implement necessary configuration checks?

   **a.** ARP

   **b.** Fabric Services

   **c.** IGMP

   **d.** Peer-Link

**9.** When does the vPC suspend the port channel?

   **a.** QoS config mismatch

   **b.** MTU config mismatch

   **c.** SVI config mismatch

   **d.** ACL config mismatch

**10.** Which of the following statements are correct regarding a vPC? (Choose two answers.)

    **a.** You can pair Cisco Nexus switches of different types. For example, you can deploy a vPC on Cisco Nexus Series 9300 and Cisco Nexus Series 9500 switches.

    **b.** You can configure only one vPC domain ID on a single switch or virtual device context (VDC). It is not possible for a switch or VDC to participate in more than one vPC domain.

    **c.** A vPC keepalive should run across a vPC peer link.

    **d.** You can use a vPC as a Layer 2 link to establish a routing adjacency between two external routers.

## Foundation Topics

# Spanning Tree Protocols

Spanning Tree Protocol (STP) operation prevents Layer 2 loops. It allows only one active path to exist between any Layer 2 devices. This operation is transparent to end devices (servers or hosts), and the end device cannot detect whether it is connected to a single Layer 2 switch or a group of multiple switches.

To create a Layer 2 network with redundancy, you must have a loop-free path between all nodes in a network. An STP algorithm calculates the best loop-free path throughout a switched network. When a local-area network (LAN) port becomes active, first it starts to send and receive STP frames, which are called bridge protocol data units (BPDUs) at regular intervals. Switches do not forward these frames but use the frames to construct a loop-free path.

Multiple active paths between switches cause loops in the network. If a loop exists in a Layer 2 network, end devices might receive duplicate messages, and switches might learn end-station MAC addresses on multiple ports. These conditions result in a *broadcast storm*, which creates an unstable network.

STP defines a tree with a root bridge and a loop-free path from the root to all switches in the network. It forces redundant data paths into a blocked state. If a network segment in the spanning tree fails and a redundant path exists, the STP algorithm recalculates the spanning tree topology and activates the blocked path.

When two ports on a switch are part of a loop, the STP port priority and path cost determine which port on the switch is put in a forwarding state and which port is put in a blocking state.

## STP Topology

All switches in an extended local-area network that participate in a spanning tree gather information about other switches in the network by exchanging BPDUs. This exchange of BPDUs results in the following actions:

- The system elects a unique root switch for the spanning tree network topology.

- The system elects a designated switch for each LAN segment.

- The system eliminates any loops in the switched network by placing redundant interfaces in a backup state; all paths that are not needed to reach the root switch from anywhere in the switched network are placed in an STP blocked state.

The topology on an active switched network is determined by the following:

■ The unique switch identifier Media Access Control (MAC) address of the switch that is associated with each switch

■ The path cost to the root that is associated with each interface

■ The port identifier that is associated with each interface

In a switched network, the root switch is the logical center of the spanning tree topology. STP uses BPDUs to elect the root switch and root port for the switched network, as well as the root port and designated port for each switched segment.

## STP Port Types

Cisco NX-OS has three main STP port types: an edge port, a network port, or a normal port. A port can be in only one of these states at a given time. The default spanning tree port type is normal. Depending on the type of device to which the interface is connected, you can configure a spanning tree port as one of these port types.

■ **Spanning tree edge ports:** Edge ports are normally connected to end hosts. An edge port can be either an access port or a trunk port. The edge port interface immediately transitions to the forwarding state without moving through the blocking or learning states. (This immediate transition was previously configured as the Cisco-proprietary feature PortFast.) Interfaces that are connected to hosts should not receive STP bridge protocol data units.

**NOTE**   If a port connected to another switch set as an edge port, that might create a bridging loop.

■ **Spanning tree network ports:** Network ports are normally connected only to switches or bridges. Bridge assurance is enabled only on network ports.

**NOTE**   If you mistakenly configure ports that are connected to hosts or other edge devices as spanning tree network ports, those ports automatically move into the blocking state.

■ **Spanning tree normal ports:** Normal ports can be connected to either hosts, switches, or bridges. These ports function as normal spanning tree ports. The default spanning tree interface is a normal port.

## STP Extensions

Different STP extensions are used to protect the switch against certain problems that can cause bridging loops in the network. Loops can be caused by several problems:

■ Unidirectional links

■ Device malfunctions

- Configuration errors

- External system forwarding (hub or non-STP switch, or end-host network bridging)

NX-OS has added many STP extensions that enhance loop prevention, protect against some possible user misconfigurations, and provide better control over the protocol parameters. Here's a quick summary of these extensions:

- **STP Bridge Assurance:** Spanning tree Bridge Assurance is one of those features that help prevent bridging loops in Layer 2 networks.

- **BPDU Guard:** This extension disables ports that receive a BPDU frame; it is useful for edge ports that should never be connected to another switch.

- **BPDU Filtering:** This extension prevents the switch from sending or even receiving BPDUs on a specified edge port.

- **Loop Guard:** This extension protects against network interfaces that malfunction. Loop Guard is useful only in switched networks where devices are connected by point-to-point links. On a point-to-point link, a designated bridge cannot disappear unless it sends an inferior BPDU or brings the link down.

- **Root Guard:** This extension prevents a port from becoming a root port or a blocked port.

### STP Bridge Assurance

When Bridge Assurance is enabled, BPDUs are sent on all switch interfaces, including blocked interfaces like the alternate or backup port. When an interface doesn't receive a BPDU for a certain time, the interface goes into the blocking state, as shown in Figure 2-1. When the second switch (SW2) fails and stops sending BPDUs, switches one (SW1) and three (SW3) disable the ports facing switch two to prevent any loop.

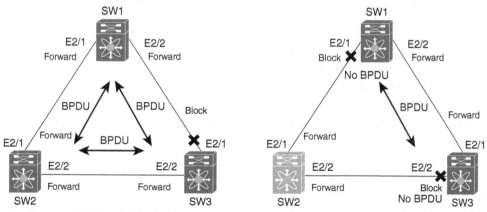

**Figure 2-1**  *STP Bridge Assurance*

When the interface receives BPDUs again, the interface is unblocked and goes through the normal spanning tree port states again. This helps prevent issues (that is, unidirectional link failures or switch failures where the switch does forward Ethernet frames, but STP is malfunctioning) where, for whatever reason, an interface doesn't receive BPDUs again and a blocked interface goes into the forwarding state, causing a bridging loop.

NX-OS has STP Bridge Assurance enabled by default, and it can only be disabled globally. Also, Bridge Assurance can be enabled only on spanning tree network ports that are point-to-point links. Finally, both ends of the link must have Bridge Assurance enabled. If the device on one side of the link has Bridge Assurance enabled and the device on the other side either does not support Bridge Assurance or does not have this feature enabled, the connecting port is blocked.

**NOTE** STP Bridge Assurance is supported only by Rapid PVST+ and MST. Legacy 802.1D spanning tree does not support Bridge Assurance.

### BPDU Guard

The BPDU Guard feature must be enabled on a port that should never receive a BPDU from its connected device—for example, a workstation, server, or printer. End devices are not supposed to generate BPDUs because, in a normal network environment, BPDU messages are exchanged only by network switches.

If BPDU Guard is configured globally, it affects only operational spanning tree edge ports. In a valid configuration, LAN edge interfaces do not receive BPDUs. A BPDU that is received by an edge LAN interface signals an invalid configuration, such as the connection of an unauthorized switch. BPDU Guard, when enabled globally, shuts down any spanning tree edge ports that receive a BPDU and generates an err-disable alert.

BPDU Guard provides a secure response to invalid configurations because an administrator must manually put the LAN interface back in service after an invalid configuration.

### BPDU Filter

BPDU Filter prevents the switch from sending or even receiving BPDUs on specified ports.

When configured globally, BPDU Filtering applies to all operational spanning tree edge ports. Ports should connect to hosts only, which typically drop BPDUs. If an operational spanning tree edge port receives a BPDU, it immediately returns to a normal spanning tree port type and moves through the regular transitions. In that case, BPDU Filtering is disabled on this port, and the spanning tree resumes sending BPDUs on this port.

**NOTE** Use care when configuring BPDU Filtering per interface. Explicitly configuring BPDU Filtering on a port that is not connected to a host can result in bridging loops because the port will ignore any BPDU that it receives and go to forwarding.

### Loop Guard

Loop Guard protects networks from loops that are caused by the following:

- Network interfaces that malfunction
- Busy CPUs
- Anything that prevents the normal forwarding of BPDUs

An STP loop occurs when a blocking port in a redundant topology erroneously transitions to the forwarding state. This transition usually happens because one of the ports in a physically redundant topology (not necessarily the blocking port) stops receiving BPDUs.

Loop Guard is useful only in switched networks where devices are connected by point-to-point links. On a point-to-point link, a designated bridge cannot disappear unless it sends an inferior BPDU or brings the link down.

You can use Loop Guard to determine if a root port or an alternate/backup root port receives BPDUs. If the port does not receive BPDUs, Loop Guard puts the port into an inconsistent state (blocking) until the port starts to receive BPDUs again. A port in an inconsistent state does not transmit BPDUs. If the port receives BPDUs again, the protocol removes its loop-inconsistent condition, and the STP determines the port state because such recovery is automatic. Loop Guard isolates the failure and allows STP to converge to a stable topology without the failed link or bridge. Disabling Loop Guard moves all loop-inconsistent ports to the listening state.

### Root Guard

Root Guard does not allow that port to become a root port. If a port-received BPDU triggers an STP convergence that makes that designated port become a root port, that port is put into a root-inconsistent (blocked) state. After the port stops sending superior BPDUs, the port is unblocked again. Through STP, the port moves to the forwarding state because recovery is automatic.

If Root Guard is enabled on a specific interface, it applies this functionality to all virtual local-area networks (VLANs) to which that interface belongs.

Root Guard is used to enforce the root bridge placement in the network. It ensures that the port on which Root Guard is enabled is the designated port. Normally, root bridge ports are all designated ports, unless two or more of the ports of the root bridge are connected. If the bridge receives superior BPDUs on a Root Guard–enabled port, the bridge moves this port to a root-inconsistent STP state. In this way, Root Guard enforces the position of the root bridge.

## Unidirectional Link Detection

Unidirectional Link Detection (UDLD) is a Cisco proprietary Layer 2 protocol that enables the devices to automatically detect the loss of bidirectional communication on a link. A unidirectional link occurs whenever traffic sent by a local device is received by its neighbor but traffic from the neighbor is not received by the local device.

All connected devices must support UDLD for the protocol to successfully identify and disable unidirectional links. When UDLD detects a unidirectional link, it disables the affected port and generates an alert. Unidirectional links can cause a variety of problems, including spanning tree topology loops.

UDLD supports two modes of operation: normal (the default) and aggressive. In normal mode, UDLD can detect unidirectional links due to misconnected ports on fiber-optic connections. In aggressive mode, UDLD can also detect unidirectional links due to one-way traffic on fiber-optic and twisted-pair links and to misconnected ports on fiber-optic links, as shown in Figure 2-2.

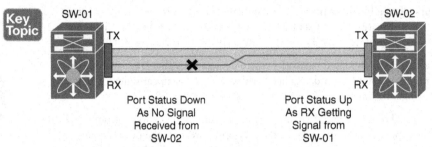

**Figure 2-2** *UDLD Detection of a Unidirectional Link*

## Rapid PVST+

Rapid PVST+ provides for rapid recovery of connectivity following the failure of a network device, a switch port, or a LAN. It provides rapid convergence for edge ports. Rapid PVST+ is the IEEE 802.1w (RSTP) standard implemented per VLAN. A single instance of STP runs on each configured VLAN (if you do not manually disable STP). Each Rapid PVST+ instance on a VLAN has a single root switch. You can enable and disable STP on a per-VLAN basis when you are running Rapid PVST+.

**NOTE** Rapid PVST+ is the default STP mode for Nexus switches.

Rapid PVST+ uses point-to-point wiring to provide rapid convergence of the spanning tree. The spanning tree reconfiguration can occur in less than one second with Rapid PVST+ (in contrast to 50 seconds with the default settings in the 802.1D STP).

**NOTE** Rapid PVST+ supports one STP instance for each VLAN.

Using Rapid PVST+, STP convergence occurs rapidly. Each designated or root port in the STP sends out a BPDU every two seconds by default. On a designated or root port in the topology, if hello messages are missed three consecutive times, or if the maximum age expires, the port immediately flushes all protocol information in the table. A port considers that it loses connectivity to its direct neighbor root or designated port if it misses three BPDUs or if the maximum age expires. This rapid aging of the protocol information allows quick failure detection. The switch automatically checks the PVID.

Rapid PVST+ ports are connected through point-to-point links as follows:

- **Edge ports:** When a port is configured as an edge port on an RSTP switch, the edge port immediately transitions to the forwarding state. You should configure only on ports that connect to a single end device as edge ports. Edge ports do not generate topology changes when the link changes.

- **Root ports:** If Rapid PVST+ selects a new root port, it blocks the old root port and immediately transitions the new root port to the forwarding state.

- **Point-to-point links:** If a port is connected to another port through a point-to-point link and the local port becomes a designated port, it negotiates a rapid transition with the other port by using the proposal-agreement handshake to ensure a loop-free topology.

Rapid PVST+ achieves rapid transition to the forwarding state only on edge ports and point-to-point links. Although the link type is configurable, the system automatically derives the link type information from the duplex setting of the port. Full-duplex ports are assumed to be point-to-point ports, and half-duplex ports are assumed to be shared ports.

Edge ports do not generate topology changes, but all other designated and root ports generate a topology change (TC) BPDU when they either fail to receive three consecutive BPDUs from the directly connected neighbor or the maximum age times out. At this point, the designated or root port sends out a BPDU with the TC flag set. The BPDUs continue to set the TC flag as long as the TC While timer runs on that port. The value of the TC While timer is the value set for the hello time plus one second. The initial detector of the topology change immediately floods this information throughout the entire topology.

When Rapid PVST+ detects a topology change, the protocol does the following:

- Starts the TC While timer with a value equal to twice the hello time for all the non-edge root and designated ports, if necessary

- Flushes the MAC addresses associated with all these ports

The topology change notification floods quickly across the entire topology. The system flushes dynamic entries immediately on a per-port basis when it receives a topology change.

Figure 2-3 shows Switch A (a root switch set the TC bits in its BPDU). This BPDU floods to the whole network. Normally, the TC bit is set by the root for a period of max_age + forward_delay seconds, which is 20+15=35 seconds by default.

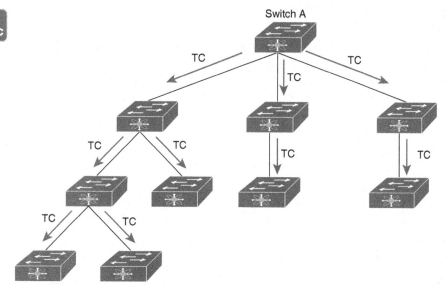

**Figure 2-3**  *Topology Change (TC) BPDU Flood*

**NOTE**  The TCA flag is used only when the switch interacts with switches running legacy 802.1D STP.

The proposal and agreement sequence then quickly propagate toward the edge of the network and quickly restore connectivity after a topology change.

### Rapid PVST+ Ports

Rapid PVST+ provides rapid convergence of the spanning tree by assigning port roles and learning the active topology. Rapid PVST+ builds on the 802.1D STP to select the switch with the highest priority (lowest numerical priority value) as the root bridge. Rapid PVST+ then assigns one of these port roles to individual ports, as in Figure 2-4:

- **Root port:** Provides the best path (lowest cost) when the switch forwards packets to the root bridge.

- **Designated port:** Connects to the designated switch, which incurs the lowest path cost when forwarding packets from that LAN to the root bridge. The port through which the designated switch is attached to the LAN is called the designated port.

- **Alternate port:** Offers an alternate path toward the root bridge to the path provided by the current root port. An alternate port provides a path to another switch in the topology.

- **Backup port:** Acts as a backup for the path provided by a designated port toward the leaves of the spanning tree. A backup port can exist only when two ports are connected in a loopback by a point-to-point link or when a switch has two or more connections to a shared LAN segment. A backup port provides another path in the topology to the switch.

- **Disabled port:** Has no role within the operation of the spanning tree.

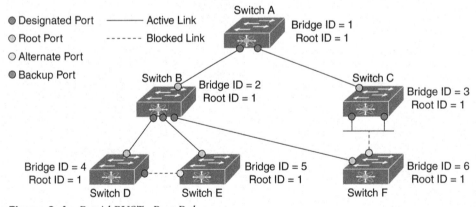

**Figure 2-4**   *Rapid PVST+ Port Roles*

In a stable topology with consistent port roles throughout the network, Rapid PVST+ ensures that every root port and designated port immediately transitions to the forwarding state while all alternate and backup ports are always in the blocking state. Designated ports start in the blocking state. The port state controls the operation of the forwarding and learning processes.

Due to propagation delays, topology changes can take place at different times and at different places in a Layer 2 network. When a switch LAN port transitions directly from nonparticipation in the spanning tree topology to the forwarding state, it can create temporary data loops. Ports must wait for new topology information to propagate through the switch LAN before starting to forward frames.

Each LAN port on software using Rapid PVST+ or MST exists in one of the following four states:

- **Blocking:** The switch LAN port does not participate in frame forwarding.

- **Learning:** The switch LAN port prepares to participate in frame forwarding.

- **Forwarding:** The switch LAN port forwards frames.

- **Disabled:** The switch LAN port does not participate in STP and does not forward frames.

Table 2-2 list the possible operational and Rapid PVST+ states for ports and the corresponding inclusion in the active topology.

**Table 2-2**   Port State Active Topology

| Operational Status | Port State | Is Port Included in the Active Topology? |
|---|---|---|
| Enabled | Blocking | No |
| Enabled | Learning | Yes |
| Enabled | Forwarding | Yes |
| Disabled | Disabled | No |

To control STP selection, you can set cost value to change the selection. Lower cost values to switch LAN interfaces are selected first, and higher cost values to switch LAN interfaces are selected last. If all switch LAN interfaces have the same cost value, STP puts the switch LAN interface with the lowest number in the forwarding state and blocks other interfaces.

On access ports, you assign port cost by the port. On trunk ports, port cost can be assigned by VLAN. The same port cost needs to be assigned to all the VLANs on a trunk port.

Cisco NX-OS supports two different path-cost methods: short and long methods. A short path-cost is a 16-bit value and ranges from 1 to 65,535. However, a long path-cost is a 32-bit value, which extends the value up to 200,000,000.

**NOTE**   Rapid PVST+ uses the short (16-bit) path-cost method to calculate the cost by default.

The STP port path-cost default value is determined from the media speed and path-cost calculation method of a LAN interface (see Table 2-3). If a loop occurs, STP considers the port cost when selecting a switch LAN interface to put into the forwarding state.

**Table 2-3**   Default Port Cost

| Bandwidth | Short Path-Cost Method of Port Cost | Long Path-Cost Method of Port Cost |
|---|---|---|
| 10 Mbps | 100 | 2,000,000 |
| 100 Mbps | 19 | 200,000 |
| 1 Gbps | 4 | 20,000 |
| 10 Gbps | 2 | 2,000 |
| 40 Gbps | 1 | 500 |
| 100 Gbps | 1 | 200 |
| 400 Gbps | 1 | 50 |

If a loop occurs and multiple ports have the same path-cost, Rapid PVST+ considers the port priority when selecting which switch LAN port to put into the forwarding state. Lower priority values are selected first, and higher priority values are selected last.

If all switch LAN ports have the same priority value, Rapid PVST+ puts the switch LAN port with the lowest LAN port number in the forwarding state and blocks other LAN ports. The possible priority range is from 0 through 224 (the default is 128), configurable in increments of 32. Software uses the port priority value when the LAN port is configured as an access port and uses VLAN port priority values when the switch LAN port is configured as a trunk port.

## Spanning Tree Configurations and Verifications

Table 2-4 lists STP default parameters, and Table 2-5 lists Rapid PVST+ and UDLD default parameters. You can alter these parameters as necessary to optimize protocol functionality.

**Table 2-4**   STP Extension Default Settings

| Parameters | Default |
|---|---|
| Port type | Normal |
| Bridge assurance | Enabled (on STP network ports only) |
| Global BPDU Guard | Disabled |
| BPDU Guard per interface | Disabled |
| Global BPDU Filtering | Disabled |
| BPDU Filtering per interface | Disabled |
| Global Loop Guard | Disabled |
| Loop Guard per interface | Disabled |
| Root Guard per interface | Disabled |

**Table 2-5**   Rapid PVST+ and UDLD Default Settings

| Parameters | Default |
|---|---|
| Spanning Tree | Enabled on all VLANs. |
| Spanning Tree mode | Rapid PVST+.<br><br>**NOTE:** Changing the spanning tree mode disrupts the traffic because all spanning tree instances are stopped for the previous mode and started for the new mode. |
| VLAN | All ports assigned to VLAN1. |

| Parameters | Default |
|---|---|
| Extended system ID | Always enabled. |
| MAC address reduction | Always enabled. |
| Bridge ID priority | 32769 (default bridge priority plus system ID extension of default VLAN1). |
| Port state | Blocking (changes immediately after convergence). |
| Port role | Designated (changes after convergence). |
| Port/VLAN priority | 128. |
| Path-cost calculation method | Short. |
| Port/VLAN cost | Auto. <br><br> The default port cost is determined by the media speed and path-cost method calculation, as follows: <br><br> **10 Mbps:** <br> short: 100 <br> long: 2,000,000 <br><br> **100 Mbps:** <br> short: 19 <br> long: 200,000 <br><br> **1 Gbps:** <br> short: 4 <br> long: 20,000 <br><br> **10 Gbps:** <br> short: 2 <br> long: 2,000 <br><br> **40 Gbps:** <br> short: 1 <br> long: 500 |
| Hello time | 2 seconds. |
| Forward delay time | 15 seconds. |
| Maximum aging time | 20 seconds. |
| Link type | Auto. <br><br> The default link type is determined by the duplex, as follows: <br><br> **Full duplex:** Point-to-point link <br><br> **Half duplex:** Shared link |
| UDLD global | Globally disabled. |
| UDLD per-port enable state for fiber-optic media | Enabled on all Ethernet fiber-optic LAN ports. |
| UDLD per-port enable state for copper media | Disabled on all Ethernet 10/100 and 1000BASE-TX LAN ports. |
| UDLD message interval | Disabled. |
| UDLD aggressive mode | Disabled. |

**NOTE**   No license is required for STP extensions. Any feature not included in a license package is bundled with the Cisco NX-OS system images. For a complete explanation of the Cisco NX-OS licensing scheme, see the Cisco NX-OS Licensing Guide.

STP, Rapid PVST+, and UDLD have the following recommended configurations and limitations:

- Port settings recommendations are as follows:

  - You should connect STP network ports only to switches.

  - You should configure host ports as STP edge ports and not as network ports.

  - If you enable STP network port types globally, ensure that you manually configure all ports connected to hosts as STP edge ports.

  - You should configure all access and trunk ports connected to Layer 2 hosts as edge ports.

  - You should enable BPDU Guard on all edge ports.

- Bridge Assurance runs only on point-to-point spanning tree network ports. You must configure each side of the link for this feature.

- Enabling Loop Guard globally works only on point-to-point links.

- Enabling Loop Guard per interface works on both shared and point-to-point links.

- Root Guard forces a port to always be a designated port; it does not allow a port to become a root port. Loop Guard is effective only if the port is a root port or an alternate port. You cannot enable Loop Guard and Root Guard on a port at the same time.

- Spanning tree always chooses the first operational port in the channel to send the BPDUs. If that link becomes unidirectional, Loop Guard blocks the channel, even if other links in the channel are functioning properly.

- If you group together a set of ports that are already blocked by Loop Guard to form a channel, the spanning tree loses all the state information for those ports, and the new channel port may obtain the forwarding state with a designated role.

- If a channel is blocked by Loop Guard and the channel members go back to an individual link status, the spanning tree loses all the state information. The individual physical ports may obtain the forwarding state with the designated role, even if one or more of the links that formed the channel are unidirectional.

**NOTE**   You can enable Unidirectional Link Detection (UDLD) aggressive mode to isolate the link failure. A loop may occur until UDLD detects the failure, but Loop Guard will not be able to detect it.

- It is recommended to enable Root Guard on ports that connect to network devices that are not under direct administrative control.

- The Rapid PVST+ maximum number of VLANs and ports is 16,000.

- The port channel bundle is considered a single port. The port cost is the aggregation of all the configured port costs assigned to that channel.

- For private VLANs, on a normal VLAN trunk port, the primary and secondary private VLANs are two different logical ports and must have the exact STP topology. On access ports, STP sees only the primary VLAN.

- Do not change timers because changing timers can adversely affect stability.

- Keep user traffic off the management VLAN; keep the management VLAN separate from the user data.

- Choose the distribution and core layers as the location of the primary and secondary root switches.

- When you connect two Cisco devices through 802.1Q trunks, the switches exchange spanning tree BPDUs on each VLAN allowed on the trunks. The BPDUs on the native VLAN of the trunk are sent untagged to the reserved 802.1D spanning tree multicast MAC address (01-80-C2-00-00-00). The BPDUs on all VLANs on the trunk are sent tagged to the reserved Cisco Shared Spanning Tree Protocol (SSTP) multicast MAC address (01-00-0c-cc-cc-cd).

Tables 2-6 through 2-8 show the most-used STP configuration commands. For a full list of commands, refer to the Nexus Interface Configuration Guide links provided in the "References" at the end of the chapter.

**Table 2-6**  STP Global-Level Commands

| Command | Purpose |
|---|---|
| feature udld | Enables UDLD for the device. |
| spanning-tree port type edge default | Configures all access ports connected to Layer 2 hosts as edge ports. Edge ports immediately transition to the forwarding state without passing through the blocking or learning state at linkup. By default, spanning tree ports are normal port types. |
| spanning-tree port type network default | Configures all interfaces connected to Layer 2 switches and bridges as spanning tree network ports. If you enable Bridge Assurance, it automatically runs on network ports. By default, spanning tree ports are normal port types. <br> **NOTE:** If you configure interfaces connected to Layer 2 hosts as network ports, those ports automatically move into the blocking state. |
| spanning-tree port type edge bpduguard default | Enables BPDU Guard by default on all spanning tree edge ports. By default, global BPDU Guard is disabled. |

| Command | Purpose |
|---------|---------|
| spanning-tree port type edge bpdufilter default | Enables BPDU Filtering by default on all operational spanning tree edge ports. Global BPDU Filtering is disabled by default. |
| spanning-tree loopguard default | Enables Loop Guard by default on all spanning tree normal and network ports. By default, global Loop Guard is disabled. |
| spanning-tree mode rapid-pvst | Enables Rapid PVST+ on the device. Rapid PVST+ is the default spanning tree mode. NOTE: Changing the spanning tree mode disrupts traffic because all spanning tree instances are stopped for the previous mode and started for the new mode. |
| spanning-tree vlan *vlan-range* | Enables Rapid PVST+ (default STP) on a per-VLAN basis. The *vlan-range* value can be 2 through 4094 except for reserved VLAN values. |
| spanning-tree vlan *vlan-range* root primary [diameter *dia* [hello-time *hello-time*]] | Configures a device as the primary root bridge. The *vlan-range* value can be 2 through 4094 (except for reserved VLAN values.) The *dia* default is 7. The *hello-time* value can be from 1 to 10 seconds, and the default value is 2 seconds. |
| spanning-tree vlan *vlan-range* root secondary [diameter *dia* [hello-time *hello-time*]] | Configures a device as the secondary root bridge. The *vlan-range* value can be 2 through 4094 (except for reserved VLAN values). The *dia* default is 7. The *hello-time* value can be from 1 to 10 seconds, and the default value is 2 seconds. |
| spanning-tree vlan *vlan-range* priority *value* | Configures the bridge priority of a VLAN. Valid values are 0, 4096, 8192, 12,288, 16,384, 20,480, 24,576, 28,672, 32,768, 36,864, 40,960, 45,056, 49,152, 53,248, 57,344, and 61,440. All other values are rejected. The default value is 32,768. |
| spanning-tree pathcost method {*long* | *short*} | Selects the method used for Rapid PVST+ path-cost calculations. The default method is the *short* method. |
| udld message-time *seconds* | (Optional) Specifies the interval between sending UDLD messages. The range is 7 to 90 seconds, and the default is 15 seconds. |
| udld aggressive | (Optional) Specifies UDLD mode to be aggressive. NOTE: For copper interfaces, you enter the interface command mode for those interfaces you want to configure for UDLD aggressive mode and issue this command in the interface command model. |

**Table 2-7**   STP Interface-Level Commands

| Command | Purpose |
|---------|---------|
| spanning-tree port type edge | Configures the specified access interfaces to be spanning edge ports. Edge ports immediately transition to the forwarding state without passing through the blocking or learning state at linkup. By default, spanning tree ports are normal port types. |
| spanning-tree port type network | Configures the specified interfaces to be spanning network ports. If you enable Bridge Assurance, it automatically runs on network ports. By default, spanning tree ports are normal port types. |

| Command | Purpose |
|---|---|
| **spanning-tree port type normal** | Explicitly configures the port as a normal spanning tree port and Bridge Assurance cannot run on this interface. |
| **spanning-tree bpduguard** {**enable** \| **disable**} | Enables or disables BPDU Guard for the specified spanning tree edge interface. By default, BPDU Guard is disabled on the interfaces. |
| **no spanning-tree bpduguard** | Falls back to the default BPDU Guard global setting that you set for the interfaces by entering the **spanning-tree port type edge bpduguard default** command. |
| **spanning-tree bpdufilter** {**enable** \| **disable**} | Enables or disables BPDU Filtering for the specified spanning tree edge interface. By default, BPDU Filtering is disabled. |
| **no spanning-tree bpdufilter** | Enables BPDU Filtering on the interface if the interface is an operational spanning tree edge port and if you enter the **spanning-tree port type edge bpdufilter default** command. |
| **spanning-tree guard loop** | Enables or disables Loop Guard for the specified interface. Loop Guard on specified ports is disabled by default.<br><br>**NOTE:** Loop Guard runs only on spanning tree normal and network interfaces. |
| **spanning-tree guard root** | Enables or disables Root Guard for the specified interface. Root Guard is disabled by default. |
| **spanning-tree** [**vlan** *vlan-list*] **port-priority** *priority* | Configures the port priority for the LAN interface. The *priority* value can be from 0 to 224. A lower value indicates a higher priority. The priority values are 0, 32, 64, 96, 128, 160, 192, and 224. All other values are rejected. The default value is 128. |
| **spanning-tree** [**vlan** *vlan-id*] **cost** [**value** \| **auto**] | Configures the port cost for the LAN interface. The cost value, depending on the path-cost calculation method, can be as follows:<br><br>**short:** 1 to 65,535<br><br>**long:** 1 to 200,000,000<br><br>**NOTE:** You configure this parameter per port on access ports and per VLAN on trunk ports.<br><br>The default is auto, which sets the port cost on both the path-cost calculation method and the media speed. |
| **udld** {**enable** \| **disable**} | (Optional) Enables UDLD on the specified copper port or disables UDLD on the specified fiber port.<br><br>To enable UDLD on copper ports, you use the **udld enable** command. To enable UDLD on fiber ports, you use the **no udld disable** command. |

2

**Table 2-8**   STP Global-Level Verification Commands

| Command | Purpose |
|---|---|
| **show spanning-tree** [**summary** \| **detail**] | Displays STP information. |
| **show spanning-tree mst instance-id interface** {*ethernet slot/port* \| *port-channel channel-number*} [*detail*] | Displays MST information for the specified interface and instance. |
| show running-config spanning-tree [**all**] | Displays STP configurations. |
| **show spanning-tree interface** {**ethernet** *slot/port* \| *port channel channel-number*} | Displays the STP configuration for the specified interface. |
| **show spanning-tree pathcost method** | Displays the STP path-cost method. |

Figure 2-5 shows the network topology for the configuration that follows, which demonstrates how to configure or modify a spanning tree.

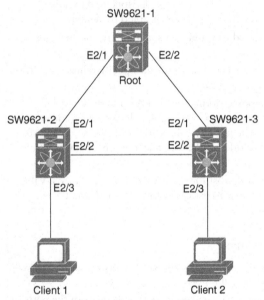

**Figure 2-5**   *STP Network Topology*

Example 2-1 shows the spanning tree configuration for the root switch (SW9621-1). The configuration changes the default spanning tree port to a network port and enables default bpduguard and bpdufilter for edge ports. It also lowers all VLAN priorities to make sure the switch will be elected as a root. Examples 2-2 and 2-3 show the interface configurations with a spanning tree summary and details.

**Example 2-1**   *SW9621-1 Global Configurations*

```
SW9621-1(config)# spanning-tree port type edge bpduguard default
SW9621-1(config)# spanning-tree port type edge bpdufilter default
SW9621-1(config)# spanning-tree port type network default
SW9621-1(config)# spanning-tree vlan 1-3967 priority 24576
```

**Example 2-2**  *SW9621-1 Interface Configurations*

```
SW9621-1(config)# interface Ethernet2/1
SW9621-1(config-if)# switchport
SW9621-1(config-if)# switchport mode trunk
SW9621-1(config-if)# spanning-tree guard root
SW9621-1(config)# interface Ethernet2/2
SW9621-1(config-if)# switchport
SW9621-1(config-if)# switchport mode trunk
SW9621-1(config-if)# spanning-tree guard root
```

**Example 2-3**  *SW9621-1 Verifications*

```
SW9621-1# show spanning-tree summary
Switch is in rapid-pvst mode
Root bridge for: VLAN0001, VLAN0100, VLAN0200
Port Type Default is network
Edge Port [PortFast] BPDU Guard Default  is enabled
Edge Port [PortFast] BPDU Filter Default is enabled
Bridge Assurance                         is enabled
Loopguard Default                        is disabled
Pathcost method used                     is short
STP-Lite                                 is enabled


Name                    Blocking Listening Learning Forwarding STP    Active
---------------------- -------- --------- -------- ---------- ----------
VLAN0001                     0         0        0          2      2
VLAN0100                     0         0        0          2      2
VLAN0200                     0         0        0          2      2
---------------------- -------- --------- -------- ---------- ----------
3 vlans                      0         0        0          6      6


SW9621-1# show spanning-tree
VLAN0001
  Spanning tree enabled protocol rstp
  Root ID    Priority    24577
             Address     fa16.3e93.f9cc
             This bridge is the root
             Hello Time  2  sec  Max Age 20 sec  Forward Delay 15 sec

  Bridge ID  Priority    24577  (priority 24576 sys-id-ext 1)
             Address     fa16.3e93.f9cc
             Hello Time  2  sec  Max Age 20 sec  Forward Delay 15 sec
```

```
Interface        Role Sts Cost      Prio.Nbr Type
---------------- ---- --- --------- -------- -------------------------------
Eth2/1           Desg FWD 4          128.257  Network P2p
Eth2/2           Desg FWD 4          128.258  Network P2p


VLAN0100
  Spanning tree enabled protocol rstp
  Root ID    Priority    24676
             Address     fa16.3e93.f9cc
             This bridge is the root
             Hello Time   2  sec  Max Age 20 sec  Forward Delay 15 sec


   Bridge ID  Priority    24676  (priority 24576 sys-id-ext 100)
              Address     fa16.3e93.f9cc
              Hello Time   2  sec  Max Age 20 sec  Forward Delay 15 sec


Interface        Role Sts Cost      Prio.Nbr Type
---------------- ---- --- --------- -------- -------------------------------
Eth2/1           Desg FWD 4          128.257  Network P2p
Eth2/2           Desg FWD 4          128.258  Network P2p


VLAN0200
  Spanning tree enabled protocol rstp
  Root ID    Priority    24776
             Address     fa16.3e93.f9cc
             This bridge is the root
             Hello Time   2  sec  Max Age 20 sec  Forward Delay 15 sec


   Bridge ID  Priority    24776  (priority 24576 sys-id-ext 200)
              Address     fa16.3e93.f9cc
              Hello Time   2  sec  Max Age 20 sec  Forward Delay 15 sec


Interface        Role Sts Cost      Prio.Nbr Type
---------------- ---- --- --------- -------- -------------------------------
Eth2/1           Desg FWD 4          128.257  Network P2p
Eth2/2           Desg FWD 4          128.258  Network P2p


SW9621-1# show spanning-tree detail
 VLAN0001 is executing the rstp compatible Spanning Tree protocol
   Bridge Identifier has priority 24576, sysid 1, address fa16.3e93.f9cc
   Configured hello time 2, max age 20, forward delay 15
   We are the root of the spanning tree
   Topology change flag not set, detected flag not set
   Number of topology changes 5 last change occurred 0:04:22 ago
         from Ethernet2/1
```

```
    Times:   hold 1, topology change 35, notification 2
             hello 2, max age 20, forward delay 15
    Timers: hello 0, topology change 0, notification 0


 Port 257 (Ethernet2/1) of VLAN0001 is designated forwarding
   Port path cost 4, Port priority 128, Port Identifier 128.257
   Designated root has priority 24577, address fa16.3e93.f9cc
   Designated bridge has priority 24577, address fa16.3e93.f9cc
   Designated port id is 128.257, designated path cost 0
   Timers: message age 0, forward delay 0, hold 0
   Number of transitions to forwarding state: 1
   The port type is network by default
   Link type is point-to-point by default
   Root guard is enabled
   BPDU: sent 4469, received 4466


 Port 258 (Ethernet2/2) of VLAN0001 is designated forwarding
   Port path cost 4, Port priority 128, Port Identifier 128.258
   Designated root has priority 24577, address fa16.3e93.f9cc
   Designated bridge has priority 24577, address fa16.3e93.f9cc
   Designated port id is 128.258, designated path cost 0
   Timers: message age 0, forward delay 0, hold 0
   Number of transitions to forwarding state: 1
   The port type is network by default
   Link type is point-to-point by default
   Root guard is enabled
   BPDU: sent 4470, received 4467


VLAN0100 is executing the rstp compatible Spanning Tree protocol
 Bridge Identifier has priority 24576, sysid 100, address fa16.3e93.f9cc
 Configured hello time 2, max age 20, forward delay 15
 We are the root of the spanning tree
 Topology change flag not set, detected flag not set
 Number of topology changes 5 last change occurred 0:04:22 ago
          from Ethernet2/1
  Times:   hold 1, topology change 35, notification 2
           hello 2, max age 20, forward delay 15
  Timers: hello 0, topology change 0, notification 0


 Port 257 (Ethernet2/1) of VLAN0100 is designated forwarding
   Port path cost 4, Port priority 128, Port Identifier 128.257
   Designated root has priority 24676, address fa16.3e93.f9cc
   Designated bridge has priority 24676, address fa16.3e93.f9cc
   Designated port id is 128.257, designated path cost 0
   Timers: message age 0, forward delay 0, hold 0
   Number of transitions to forwarding state: 1
```

```
    The port type is network by default
    Link type is point-to-point by default
    Root guard is enabled
    BPDU: sent 4468, received 4466


Port 258 (Ethernet2/2) of VLAN0100 is designated forwarding
   Port path cost 4, Port priority 128, Port Identifier 128.258
   Designated root has priority 24676, address fa16.3e93.f9cc
   Designated bridge has priority 24676, address fa16.3e93.f9cc
   Designated port id is 128.258, designated path cost 0
   Timers: message age 0, forward delay 0, hold 0
   Number of transitions to forwarding state: 1
   The port type is network by default
   Link type is point-to-point by default
   Root guard is enabled
   BPDU: sent 4469, received 4467


VLAN0200 is executing the rstp compatible Spanning Tree protocol
 Bridge Identifier has priority 24576, sysid 200, address fa16.3e93.f9cc
 Configured hello time 2, max age 20, forward delay 15
 We are the root of the spanning tree
 Topology change flag not set, detected flag not set
 Number of topology changes 5 last change occurred 0:04:22 ago
         from Ethernet2/2
 Times:  hold 1, topology change 35, notification 2
         hello 2, max age 20, forward delay 15
 Timers: hello 0, topology change 0, notification 0


Port 257 (Ethernet2/1) of VLAN0200 is designated forwarding
   Port path cost 4, Port priority 128, Port Identifier 128.257
   Designated root has priority 24776, address fa16.3e93.f9cc
   Designated bridge has priority 24776, address fa16.3e93.f9cc
   Designated port id is 128.257, designated path cost 0
   Timers: message age 0, forward delay 0, hold 0
   Number of transitions to forwarding state: 1
   The port type is network by default
   Link type is point-to-point by default
   Root guard is enabled
   BPDU: sent 4469, received 4468


Port 258 (Ethernet2/2) of VLAN0200 is designated forwarding
   Port path cost 4, Port priority 128, Port Identifier 128.258
   Designated root has priority 24776, address fa16.3e93.f9cc
   Designated bridge has priority 24776, address fa16.3e93.f9cc
   Designated port id is 128.258, designated path cost 0
```

```
Timers: message age 0, forward delay 0, hold 0
Number of transitions to forwarding state: 1
The port type is network by default
Link type is point-to-point by default
Root guard is enabled
BPDU: sent 4468, received 4467
```

Example 2-4 shows spanning tree configurations for the second switch (SW9621-2). The configuration changes the default spanning tree port to a network port and enables bpdugard and bpdufilter for edge ports. Examples 2-5 and 2-6 show the interface configurations for the root switch with a spanning tree summary.

**Example 2-4**  *SW9621-2 Global Configurations*

```
SW9621-2(config)# spanning-tree port type edge bpduguard default
SW9621-2(config)# spanning-tree port type edge bpdufilter default
SW9621-2(config)# spanning-tree port type network default
```

**Example 2-5**  *SW9621-2 Interface Configurations*

```
SW9621-2(config)# interface Ethernet2/1
SW9621-2(config-if)# switchport
SW9621-2(config-if)# switchport mode trunk
SW9621-2(config)# interface Ethernet2/2
SW9621-2(config-if)# switchport
SW9621-2(config-if)# switchport mode trunk
SW9621-2(config)# interface Ethernet2/3
SW9621-2(config-if)# switchport
SW9621-2(config-if)# switchport access vlan 100
SW9621-2(config-if)# spanning-tree port type edge
SW9621-2(config-if)# no shutdown
```

**Example 2-6**  *SW9621-2 Verifications*

```
SW9621-2# show spanning-tree summary
Switch is in rapid-pvst mode
Root bridge for: none
Port Type Default is network
Edge Port [PortFast] BPDU Guard Default  is enabled
Edge Port [PortFast] BPDU Filter Default is enabled
Bridge Assurance                         is enabled
Loopguard Default                        is disabled
Pathcost method used                     is short
STP-Lite                                 is enabled
```

| Name | Blocking | Listening | Learning | Forwarding | STP Active |
|------|----------|-----------|----------|------------|------------|
| VLAN0001 | 0 | 0 | 0 | 2 | 2 |
| VLAN0100 | 0 | 0 | 0 | 3 | 3 |
| VLAN0200 | 0 | 0 | 0 | 2 | 2 |
| 3 vlans | 0 | 0 | 0 | 7 | 7 |

```
SW9621-2# show spanning-tree


VLAN0001
  Spanning tree enabled protocol rstp
  Root ID    Priority    24577
             Address     fa16.3e93.f9cc
             Cost        4
             Port        257 (Ethernet2/1)
             Hello Time  2  sec  Max Age 20 sec  Forward Delay 15 sec


  Bridge ID  Priority    32769  (priority 32768 sys-id-ext 1)
             Address     fa16.3e4d.d715
             Hello Time  2  sec  Max Age 20 sec  Forward Delay 15 sec


Interface        Role Sts Cost      Prio.Nbr Type
---------------- ---- --- --------- -------- -------------------------------
Eth2/1           Root FWD 4         128.257  Network P2p
Eth2/2           Desg FWD 4         128.258  Network P2p



VLAN0100
  Spanning tree enabled protocol rstp
  Root ID    Priority    24676
             Address     fa16.3e93.f9cc
             Cost        4
             Port        257 (Ethernet2/1)
             Hello Time  2  sec  Max Age 20 sec  Forward Delay 15 sec


  Bridge ID  Priority    32868  (priority 32768 sys-id-ext 100)
             Address     fa16.3e4d.d715
             Hello Time  2  sec  Max Age 20 sec  Forward Delay 15 sec


Interface        Role Sts Cost      Prio.Nbr Type
---------------- ---- --- --------- -------- -------------------------------
Eth2/1           Root FWD 4         128.257  Network P2p
Eth2/2           Desg FWD 4         128.258  Network P2p
Eth2/3           Desg FWD 4         128.259  Edge P2p
```

```
VLAN0200
  Spanning tree enabled protocol rstp
  Root ID    Priority    24776
             Address     fa16.3e93.f9cc
             Cost        4
             Port        257 (Ethernet2/1)
             Hello Time  2  sec  Max Age 20 sec  Forward Delay 15 sec

  Bridge ID  Priority    32968  (priority 32768 sys-id-ext 200)
             Address     fa16.3e4d.d715
             Hello Time  2  sec  Max Age 20 sec  Forward Delay 15 sec


Interface          Role Sts Cost      Prio.Nbr Type
---------------- ---- --- --------- -------- --------------------------------
Eth2/1             Root FWD 4         128.257  Network P2p
Eth2/2             Desg FWD 4         128.258  Network P2p
```

Example 2-7 shows the spanning tree configuration for the third switch (SW9621-3). The configuration changes the default spanning tree port to a network port and enables bpduguard and bpdufilter for the edge ports. Examples 2-8 and 2-9 show the interface configurations for the root switch with a spanning tree summary.

**Example 2-7**  *SW9621-3 Global Configurations*

```
SW9621-3(config)# spanning-tree port type edge bpduguard default
SW9621-3(config)# spanning-tree port type edge bpdufilter default
SW9621-3(config)# spanning-tree port type network default
```

**Example 2-8**  *SW9621-3 Interface Configurations*

```
SW9621-3(config)# interface Ethernet2/1
SW9621-3(config-if)# switchport
SW9621-3(config-if)# switchport mode trunk
SW9621-3(config)# interface Ethernet2/2
SW9621-3(config-if)# switchport
SW9621-3(config-if)# switchport mode trunk
SW9621-3(config)# interface Ethernet2/3
SW9621-3(config-if)# switchport
SW9621-3(config-if)# switchport access vlan 200
SW9621-3(config-if)# spanning-tree port type edge
SW9621-3(config-if)# no shutdown
```

**Example 2-9**   *SW9621-3 Verifications*

```
SW9621-3# show spanning-tree summary
Switch is in rapid-pvst mode
Root bridge for: none
Port Type Default is network
Edge Port [PortFast] BPDU Guard Default  is enabled
Edge Port [PortFast] BPDU Filter Default is enabled
Bridge Assurance                         is enabled
Loopguard Default                        is disabled
Pathcost method used                     is short
STP-Lite                                 is enabled


Name                   Blocking Listening Learning Forwarding STP Active
---------------------- -------- --------- -------- ---------- ----------
VLAN0001                      2         0        0          1          3
VLAN0100                      1         0        0          1          2
VLAN0200                      2         0        0          1          3
---------------------- -------- --------- -------- ---------- ----------
3 vlans                       5         0        0          3          8


SW9621-3# show spanning-tree

VLAN0001
  Spanning tree enabled protocol rstp
  Root ID    Priority    24577
             Address     fa16.3e93.f9cc
             Cost        4
             Port        257 (Ethernet2/1)
             Hello Time  2  sec  Max Age 20 sec  Forward Delay 15 sec


  Bridge ID  Priority    32769  (priority 32768 sys-id-ext 1)
             Address     fa16.3ea2.53aa
             Hello Time  2  sec  Max Age 20 sec  Forward Delay 15 sec

Interface        Role Sts Cost      Prio.Nbr Type
---------------- ---- --- --------- -------- --------------------------------
Eth2/1           Root FWD  4          128.257  Network P2p
Eth2/2           Altn BLK  4          128.258  Network P2p


VLAN0100
  Spanning tree enabled protocol rstp
  Root ID    Priority    24676
             Address     fa16.3e93.f9cc
             Cost        4
```

```
Bridge ID  Priority    32868  (priority 32768 sys-id-ext 100)
           Port        257 (Ethernet2/1)
           Hello Time  2  sec  Max Age 20 sec  Forward Delay 15 sec


           Address     fa16.3ea2.53aa
           Hello Time  2  sec  Max Age 20 sec  Forward Delay 15 sec


Interface          Role Sts Cost       Prio.Nbr Type
---------------    ---- --- ---------  -------- -------------------------------
Eth2/1             Root FWD 4          128.257  Network P2p
Eth2/2             Altn BLK 4          128.258  Network P2p



VLAN0200
  Spanning tree enabled protocol rstp
  Root ID    Priority    24776
             Address     fa16.3e93.f9cc
             Cost        4
             Port        257 (Ethernet2/1)
             Hello Time  2  sec  Max Age 20 sec  Forward Delay 15 sec

  Bridge ID  Priority    32968  (priority 32768 sys-id-ext 200)
             Address     fa16.3ea2.53aa
             Hello Time  2  sec  Max Age 20 sec  Forward Delay 15 sec

Interface          Role Sts   Cost     Prio.Nbr Type
---------------    ---- ---   --------- -------- -------------------------------
Eth2/1             Root FWD   4         128.257  Network P2p
Eth2/2             Altn BLK   4         128.258  Network P2p
Eth2/3             Desg FWD   4         128.259  Edge P2p *BA_Inc
```

# Port Channels

In the Ethernet infrastructure, STP achieves a stable network. However, it does not utilize the available physical connectivity in the best way because some of the links between the same devices are put in a blocking state to avoid network loops. And as discussed previously, the goal of STP is to achieve a stable, loop-free environment for the networks to be operational. By design, the goal of better utilization for all the available physical links is not part of STP.

With the development of these technologies, the need for more and more bandwidth arose in the data center. The virtualization allowed for more virtual machines (VMs) to run on top of a single physical server, and because each VM provides an isolated environment to run an application, or an application framework, by mimicking a server, more applications were sharing the physical resources of a server. At the same time, the physical server's connectivity to the network infrastructure was the pipeline used for the communication of all the applications running on the multiple VMs on top of it. This bandwidth was shared at the level of the access layer switch to which it was connected with other servers, and all of them had to share the uplink bandwidth of the switch. So, the interconnectivity between the access, aggregation, and core layers in the data center infrastructures became the real bottleneck for the communication needs of the applications running in the data center.

To solve this challenge, the technologies needed to develop in several directions:

■ **Hardware improvements, or interfaces with higher bandwidths:** The technology went from 10/100 Mbps to 1 Gbps, then to 40 Gbps, and now interfaces operating at 100 and 400 Gbps are available.

■ **Optimized software-defined architectures:** More flexible designs were needed, such as spine-leaf architecture with the ability to redefine the connectivity using programmatic approach.

■ **Overcoming the limitations of the communications' protocols:** The STP blocks the communication over redundant links, which means that these capacities are not utilized. The port channel technology overcomes this limitation of STP.

A port channel is an aggregation of multiple physical interfaces to create one logical interface. Port channels provide three important benefits:

■ **Redundancy:** If a member port fails, traffic previously carried over the failed link switches to the remaining member ports within the port channel.

■ **Bandwidth:** Traffic is load-balanced across the links within the port channel members to increase the bandwidth.

■ **Spanning tree:** Port channels are seen as a single switchport by the Spanning Tree Protocol; all physical interfaces are in a forwarding state.

**NOTE** Port channels, EtherChannels, and port aggregation all refer to the same group of technologies that enable you to bond multiple physical links into a virtual one. Although *port channels* and *aggregation* of ports are general terms, *EtherChannel* is a Cisco brand name for its implementation of this technology.

Each physical port can be a member in only one port channel. Depending on the hardware or NX-OS software, port channels can bundle up to a maximum of 8 or 16 physical ports. All the physical ports in a port channel must be compatible; they must use the same speed and operate in full-duplex mode. Two channel modes are supported by NX-OS: Static or Link Aggregation Control Protocol (LACP). LACP is defined in IEEE 802.3ad and is more efficient than Static because the LACP link passes protocol packets. Table 2-9 shows the NX-OS channel modes.

**NOTE** Cisco NX-OS does not support Port Aggregation Protocol (PAgP) for port channels.

**Table 2-9**    Port Channel Individual Link Modes

| Channel Mode | Description |
|---|---|
| passive | This LACP mode places a port into a passive negotiating state, in which the port responds to LACP packets that it receives but does not initiate LACP negotiation. |
| active | This LACP mode places a port into an active negotiating state, in which the port initiates negotiations with other ports by sending LACP packets. |
| on | All static port channels—that is, those that are not running LACP—remain in this mode. If you attempt to change the channel mode to active or passive before enabling LACP, the device returns an error message.<br><br>LACP is enabled on each channel by configuring the interface in that channel for the channel mode as either active or passive. When LACP attempts to negotiate with an interface in the on state, it does not receive any LACP packets and becomes an individual link with that interface; it does not join the LACP channel group. |

Both passive and active modes allow LACP to negotiate between ports to determine whether they can form a port channel, based on criteria such as the port speed and the trunking state. The passive mode is useful when you do not know whether the remote system or partner supports LACP.

Ports can form an LACP port channel when they are in different LACP modes as long as the modes are compatible, as shown in the Table 2-10.

**Table 2-10**    Channel Mode Matrix

| PortA Channel Mode | PortB Channel Mode | Port Status |
|---|---|---|
| Active | Active | UP |
| Active | Passive | UP |
| Active | ON | Down |
| Passive | Active | UP |
| Passive | Passive | Down |
| Passive | ON | Down |
| ON | ON | UP (LACP disabled) |

Any configuration changes applied to the port channel are applied to each member interface of that port channel. For example, if Spanning Tree Protocol parameters on the port channel are changed, Cisco NX-OS applies those new parameters to each interface in the port channel.

**NOTE**    You cannot change the mode from ON to Active or from ON to Passive.

A port channel interface can be created directly or by associating an interface with a channel group. Cisco NX-OS creates a matching port channel automatically if the port channel does not already exist.

**NOTE**   The port channel is operationally up when at least one of the member ports is up and that port's status is channeling. The port channel is operationally down when all member ports are operationally down.

To add an interface to a channel group, NX-OS requires the physical interfaces to be compatible and checks certain interface attributes to ensure that the interface is compatible with the channel group—for example, adding a Layer 3 interface to a Layer 2 channel group. Cisco NX-OS also checks a number of operational attributes for an interface before allowing that interface to participate in the port channel aggregation. The compatibility check includes the following operational attributes:

- Network layer
- (Link) speed capability
- Speed configuration
- Duplex capability
- Duplex configuration
- Port mode
- Access VLAN
- Trunk native VLAN
- Tagged or untagged
- Allowed VLAN list

You can use the **show port channel compatibility-parameters** command to see the full list of compatibility checks that Cisco NX-OS uses. When the interface joins a port channel, some of its individual parameters are replaced with the values on the port channel, as follows:

- Bandwidth
- MAC address
- Spanning Tree Protocol

Many interface parameters remain unaffected when the interface joins a port channel, as follows:

- Description
- CDP
- LACP port priority
- Debounce

### Port Channel Load Balance

Cisco NX-OS load-balances traffic across all operational interfaces in a port channel by reducing part of the binary pattern formed from the addresses in the frame to a numerical value that selects one of the links in the channel.

Traffic load balance hashing will depend on the traffic header. A binary format will be generated from the packet header, and these binary values will be used to select a specific port channel member. It is hard to get even traffic distribution across all port channel members. To optimize traffic distribution, you can use the option that provides the balance criteria with the greatest variety in port channel configuration. For example, if Layer 2 (non-IP) traffic on a port channel goes only to a single MAC address and you use the destination MAC address as the basis of Layer 2 port channel load balancing, the port channel always chooses the same link in that port channel; using source MAC addresses might result in better load balancing, as shown in Figure 2-6.

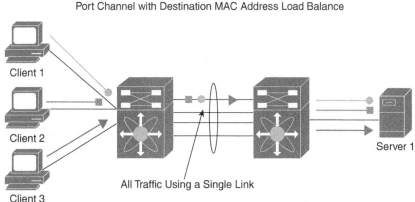

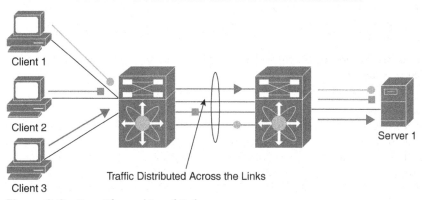

**Figure 2-6**  *Port Channel Load Balance*

The basic configuration uses the following criteria to select the link, as shown in Table 2-11:

- For a Layer 2 frame, it uses the source and destination MAC addresses.

- For a Layer 3 packet, it uses the source and destination MAC addresses and the source and destination IP addresses.

- For a Layer 4 segment, it uses the source and destination MAC addresses, the source and destination IP addresses, and the source and destination port number.

**Table 2-11**   Criteria Used for Each Configuration

| Configuration | Layer 2 Criteria | Layer 3 Criteria | Layer 4 Criteria |
| --- | --- | --- | --- |
| Destination MAC | Destination MAC | Destination MAC | Destination MAC |
| Source MAC | Source MAC | Source MAC | Source MAC |
| Source and destination MAC | Source and destination MAC | Source and destination MAC | Source and destination MAC |
| Destination IP | Destination MAC | Destination MAC, destination IP | Destination MAC, destination IP |
| Source IP | Source MAC | Source MAC, source IP | Source MAC, source IP |
| Source and destination IP | Source and destination MAC | Source and destination MAC, source and destination IP | Source and destination MAC, source and destination IP |
| Destination TCP/UDP port | Destination MAC | Destination MAC, destination IP | Destination MAC, destination IP, destination port |
| Source TCP/UDP port | Source MAC | Source MAC, source IP | Source MAC, source IP, source port |
| Source and destination TCP/UDP port | Source and destination MAC | Source and destination MAC, source and destination IP | Source and destination MAC, source and destination IP, source and destination port |

# Virtual Port Channel

A single end device can use a port channel across two upstream switches. Cisco Nexus switches with vPC appear to downstream devices as if they are a single device. The other device can be a switch, a server, or any other networking device that supports the IEEE 802.3ad port channel.

Cisco NX-OS software virtual port channel (vPC) and Cisco Catalyst Virtual Switching System (VSS) are similar technologies. Per Cisco EtherChannel technology, the term *multichassis EtherChannel* (MCEC) refers to either technology interchangeably.

The key difference between a vPC and a VSS is that the VSS creates a single logical switch. This results in a single control plane for both management and configuration purposes. With vPCs, each Cisco Nexus switch (vPC) is managed and configured independently. They remain two separate physical switches, and each of them is a logical switch. Only for the communication of the vPC, they present themselves in front of the third device connected to them using the vPC as one logical switch. In this way, the network devices communicating with the switches, which form the vPC pair, can see them as two separate network switches (if they do not use the vPC port-channel), or they will behave as a single logical device for the vPC port-channel communication. And this is a major difference with the VSS. A vPC allows the creation of Layer 2 port channels that span two switches.

vPCs eliminate STP block ports. Downstream devices can use all available uplink bandwidth and provide fast convergence upon link/device failure. vPCs consist of two vPC peer switches connected by a peer link. One is the primary, and the other is the secondary. The system formed by the switches is referred to as a vPC domain. Cisco Nexus switches form different topologies, as shown in Figure 2-7.

It is important to remember that with vPCs both switches are managed independently. Keep in mind that you need to create and permit VLANs on both Nexus switches.

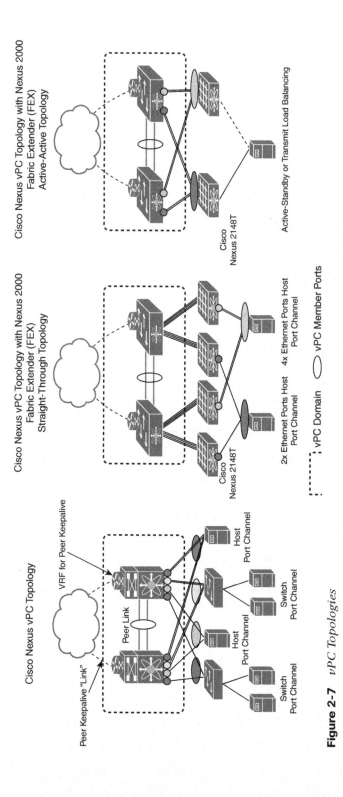

**Figure 2-7**  *vPC Topologies*

A vPC system consists of the following components:

- **vPC domain:** The domain includes the vPC peers, keepalive links, and port channels that use the vPC technology.

- **vPC peer switch:** This is the other switch within the vPC domain. Each switch is connected via the vPC peer link. It's also worth noting that one device is selected as primary and the other as secondary.

- **vPC peer-keepalive or fault-tolerant link:** A routed "link" (it is more accurate to say *path*) used to resolve dual-active scenarios in which the peer link connectivity is lost. This link is referred to as a *vPC peer-keepalive* or *fault-tolerant link*. The peer-keepalive traffic is often transported over the management network through the management port. The peer-keepalive traffic is typically routed over a dedicated virtual routing and forwarding (VRF) instance (which could be the management VRF, for example). The keepalive can be carried over a routed infrastructure; it does not need to be a direct point-to-point link, and, in fact, it is desirable to carry the peer-keepalive traffic on a different network instead of on a straight point-to-point link.

- **vPC peer link:** The most important connectivity element in the vPC system. This link is used to create the illusion of a single control plane by forwarding BPDUs or LACP packets to the primary vPC switch from the secondary vPC switch. The peer link is used to synchronize MAC addresses between aggregation groups 1 and 2 and to synchronize Internet Group Management Protocol (IGMP) entries for the purpose of IGMP snooping. It provides the necessary transport for multicast traffic and for the communication of orphaned ports. In the case of a vPC device that is also a Layer 3 switch, the peer link also carries Hot Standby Router Protocol (HSRP) frames. For a vPC to forward a VLAN, that VLAN must exist on the peer link and on both vPC peers, and it must appear in the allowed list of the switch port trunk for the vPC itself. If either of these conditions is not met, the VLAN is not displayed when you enter the **show vpc brief** command, nor is it a vPC VLAN. When a port channel is defined as a vPC peer link, Bridge Assurance is automatically configured on the peer link.

- **vPC member port:** A port that is assigned to a vPC channel group. The ports that form the virtual port channel are split between the vPC peers and are referred to as *vPC member ports*.

- **Non-vPC port:** The ports connecting devices in a non-vPC mode to a vPC topology are referred to as *orphaned ports*. The device connects to the Cisco Nexus switch with a regular spanning tree configuration: thus, one link is forwarding and one link is blocking. These links connect to the Cisco Nexus switch with orphaned ports.

Figure 2-8 illustrates the main vPC components.

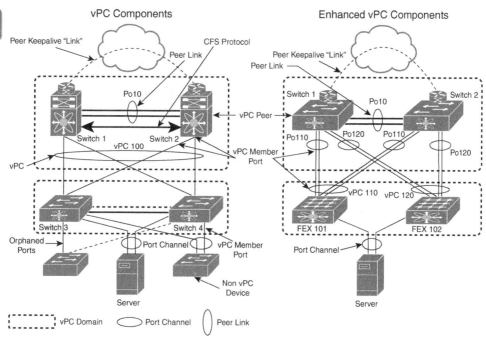

**Figure 2-8**  *vPC Components*

## vPC Traffic Flows

The vPC configurations are optimized to help ensure that traffic through a vPC-capable system is symmetric. In Figure 2-9, for example, the flow on the left (from Core1 to Acc1) reaching a Cisco Nexus switch (Agg1 in the figure) from the core is forwarded toward the access layer switch (Acc1 in the figure) without traversing the peer Cisco Nexus switch device (Agg2). Similarly, traffic from the server directed to the core reaches a Cisco Nexus switch (Agg1), and the receiving Cisco Nexus switch routes this traffic directly to the core without unnecessarily passing it to the peer Cisco Nexus device. This process occurs regardless of which Cisco Nexus device is the primary HSRP device for a given VLAN.

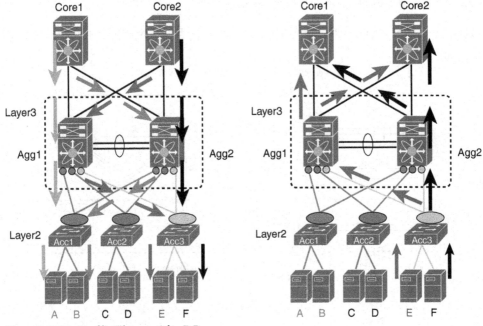

**Figure 2-9**  *Traffic Flows with vPC*

## vPC Dual-Control Plane

While still operating with two separate control planes, vPC helps ensure that the neighboring devices connected in vPC mode see the vPC peers as a single spanning tree and LACP entity. For this to happen, the system has to perform IEEE 802.3ad control-plane operations in a slightly modified way (which is not noticeable to the neighbor switch). IEEE 802.3ad specifies the standard implementation of port channels. Port channel specifications provide LACP as a standard protocol, which enables negotiation of port bundling. LACP makes misconfiguration less likely, because if ports are mismatched, they will not form a port channel. Switch MAC addresses are normally used by spanning tree and LACP, respectively—the bridge ID field in the spanning tree BPDU and as part of LACP LAGID. In a single chassis, they use the systemwide MAC address for this purpose.

For systems that use vPCs, a systemwide MAC address would not work because the vPC peers need to appear as a single entity. To meet this requirement, vPC offers both an automatic configuration and a manual configuration of the system ID for the vPC peers.

The automatic solution implemented by vPC consists of generating a system ID composed of a priority and a MAC address, with the MAC derived from a reserved pool of MAC addresses combined with the domain ID specified in the vPC configuration. The domain ID is encoded in the last octet and the trailing 2 bits of the previous octet of the MAC address.

By configuring domain IDs to be different on adjacent vPC complexes (and to be identical on each vPC peer complex), you help ensure the uniqueness of the system ID for LACP negotiation purposes. You also help ensure that the spanning tree BPDUs use a MAC address that is representative of the vPC complex.

## vPC Primary and Secondary Roles

In a vPC system, one vPC switch is defined as primary, and one is defined as secondary, based on defined priorities. The lower number has higher priority, so it wins. Also, these roles are nonpreemptive, so a device may be operationally primary but secondary from a configuration perspective.

When the two vPC systems are joined to form a vPC domain, the priority decides which device is the vPC primary and which is the vPC secondary. If the primary device reloads, when the system comes back online and connectivity to the vPC secondary device (now the operational primary) is restored, the operational role of the secondary device (operational primary) does not change, to avoid unnecessary disruptions. This behavior is achieved with a sticky-bit method, whereby the sticky information is not saved in the startup configuration, thus making the device that is up and running win over the reloaded device. Hence, the vPC primary becomes the vPC operational secondary.

If the peer link is disconnected, but the vPC peers are still connected through the vPC peer-keepalive link, the vPC operational roles stay unchanged.

If both the peer link and peer-keepalive link are disconnected, both vPC peers become operational primary, but upon reconnection of the peer-keepalive link and the peer link, the vPC secondary device (operational primary) keeps the primary role, and the vPC primary becomes the operational secondary device.

vPC modifies the way in which spanning tree works on the switch to help ensure that a vPC in a single domain appears as a single spanning tree entity on vPC ports. Also, the vPC helps ensure that devices can connect to a vPC domain in a non-vPC fashion with classic spanning tree topology. The vPC is designed to support hybrid topologies. Depending on the Cisco NX-OS release, this can be achieved in slightly different ways.

In all Cisco NX-OS releases, the peer link is always forwarding because of the need to maintain the MAC address tables and IGMP entries synchronized.

The vPC, by default, ensures that only the primary switch forwards BPDUs on vPCs. This modification is strictly limited to vPC member ports. As a result, the BPDUs that may be received by the secondary vPC peer on a vPC port are forwarded to the primary vPC peer through the peer link for processing.

**NOTE** Non-vPC ports operate like regular spanning tree ports. The special behavior of the primary vPC member applies uniquely to ports that are part of a vPC.

- The vPC primary and secondary are both root devices and both originate BPDUs.

- The BPDUs originated by both the vPC primary and the vPC secondary have the same designated bridge ID on vPC ports.

- The BPDUs originated by the vPC primary and secondary on non-vPC ports maintain the local bridge ID instead of the vPC bridge ID and advertise the bridge ID of the vPC system as the root.

The peer-switch option has the following advantages:

■ It reduces the traffic loss upon restoration of the peer link after a failure.

■ It reduces the disruption associated with a dual-active failure (whereby both vPC members become primary). Both devices keep sending BPDUs with the same bridge ID information on vPC member ports, which prevents errdisable from potentially disabling the port channel for an attached device.

■ It reduces the potential loss of BPDUs if the primary and secondary roles change.

The presence of a vPC domain does not hide the fact that two distinct Cisco Nexus switches are running. The Cisco CDP will show that there is a two-network device.

## vPC Configuration Consistency

Similar to regular port channels, virtual port channels are subject to consistency checks and compatibility checks. During a compatibility check, one vPC peer conveys configuration information to the other vPC peer to verify that vPC member ports can actually form a port channel. For example, if two ports that are going to join the channel carry a different set of VLANs, this is a misconfiguration.

Depending on the severity of the misconfiguration, a vPC may either warn the user (Type-2 misconfiguration) or suspend the port channel (Type-1 misconfiguration). In the specific case of a VLAN mismatch, only the VLAN that differs between the vPC member ports will be suspended on all the vPC port channels.

Inconsistencies can be global or interface specific:

■ **Global inconsistencies:** Type-1 global inconsistencies affect all vPC member ports (but do not affect non-vPC ports).

■ **Interface-specific inconsistencies:** Type-1 interface-specific inconsistencies affect only the interface itself.

Following are some examples of areas where Type-1 inconsistencies may occur:

■ Multiple Spanning Tree (MST) region definition (VLAN-to-instance mapping)

■ MTU value

■ Spanning tree global settings (Bridge Assurance, Loop Guard, and Root Guard)

■ Configuration changes to the following (these affect only individual vPCs for all VLANs on the vPC):

   ■ Port channel mode

   ■ Trunk mode

   ■ Spanning tree interface settings

**NOTE**   Mismatched quality of service (QoS) definitions were originally Type-1 inconsistencies but in newer releases are Type-2 inconsistencies.

The main inconsistencies that you need to be aware of are listed in Table 2-12. This table also shows which inconsistencies are global (that is, which bring down all vPCs) and indicates recommended operations to avoid disruptions.

**Table 2-12**   vPC Consistency Checks

| Type-1 Inconsistency | Impact | Recommendation |
|---|---|---|
| VLAN-to-MST Region mapping mismatch | Global | Preprovision and map all VLANs on the MST region. |
| System MTU | Global | Operate change during maintenance window. |
| Rapid-PVST+ Asymmetrically Disabled | Global | Disabling STP is NOT a best practice. |
| STP global settings (BA, Loop Guard, Root Guard) | Global | Use per-interface STP configurations. |
| STP mode mismatch | Global | None (Network misconfiguration). |
| Port channel mode (active/on) | vPC | Operate change during maintenance window. |
| Port MTU/Link Speed/Duplex mode/QoS | vPC | Operate change during maintenance window. |
| Trunk mode and Native VLAN | vPC | Operate change during maintenance window. |
| STP interface settings | vPC | Operate change during maintenance window. |
| Asymmetric VLANs on the trunk | VLAN on vPC | Acceptable impact. |

## vPC Duplicate Frames Prevention Mechanism

One of the most important forwarding rules for vPC is that a frame that enters the vPC peer switch from the peer link cannot exit the switch from a vPC member port.

Figure 2-10 shows switches 3 and 4 connected to switch 1 and switch 2 with vPCs Po51 and Po52. If one of the hosts connected to switch 4 sends either an unknown unicast or a broadcast, this traffic may get hashed to port eth2/2 on port channel 52. Switch 2 receives the broadcast and needs to forward it to the peer link for the potential orphan ports on switch 1 to receive it.

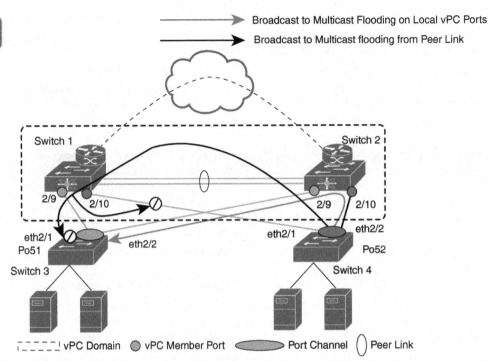

**Figure 2-10**  *vPC Blocking Duplicate Frames*

Upon receiving the broadcast, switch 1 detects that this frame is coming from the vPC peer link. Therefore, it does not forward it to port 2/9 or 2/10; if it did, a duplicate frame on switch 3 or 4, respectively, would be created.

If a host on switch 4 sends a broadcast, switch 2 will correctly forward it to Po51 on port 2/9 and place it on the peer link. Switch 1 will prevent this broadcast frame from exiting onto port 2/9 or 2/10 because this frame entered switch 1 from a vPC peer link. Should eth2/2 on switch 3 go down, port 2/9 on switch 1 would become an orphan port and as a result will receive traffic that traverses the peer link.

It is also important to realize that a topology based on port channels does not introduce loops, even if the peer link is lost and all the ports are forwarding. Figure 2-11 shows why.

Figure 2-11 shows the worst-case scenario of a vPC dual-active failure in which both peer-link and peer-keepalive-link connectivity are lost. In this particular case, one switch is running spanning tree (switch 4) with links that are not in port channel mode, and the other switches are configured in port channel mode.

With all links forwarding, a broadcast frame or an unknown unicast generated on switch 3, for example, is forwarded on both links directed to switches 1 and 2. When these two frames arrive on switch 4, they are not sent back to the port channel because that breaks the basic rule of Layer 2 forwarding: a frame cannot return to the port from which it originated.

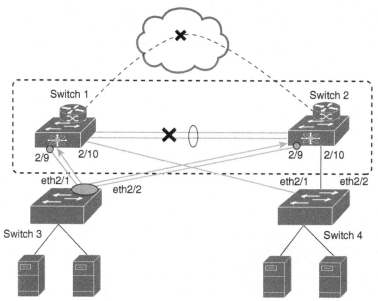

**Figure 2-11**  *Dual-Active Failure*

## vPC HSRP Gateway Considerations

In normal Hot Standby Router Protocol operation, the active HSRP interface answers ARP requests, but with a vPC, both HSRP interfaces (active and standby) can forward traffic.

The most significant difference between the HSRP implementation of a non-vPC configuration and a vPC configuration is that the HSRP MAC addresses of a vPC configuration are programmed with the G (gateway) flag on both systems, compared with a non-vPC configuration, in which only the active HSRP interface can program the MAC address with the G flag.

Given this fact, routable traffic can be forwarded by both the vPC primary device (with HSRP) and the vPC secondary device (with HSRP), with no need to send this traffic to the HSRP primary device.

Without this flag, traffic sent to the MAC address would not be routed.

## vPC ARP Synchronization

Layer 3 vPC peers synchronize their respective ARP tables. This feature is transparently enabled and helps ensure faster convergence time upon reload of a vPC switch. When two switches are reconnected after a failure, they use the Cisco Fabric Services protocol over Ethernet to perform bulk synchronization of the ARP table.

## vPC Peer Gateway

If a host or a switch forwards a frame to the Layer 3 gateway and this Layer 3 gateway is present on a vPC pair of switches, as long as the frame ID is destined to the HSRP MAC address, everything works as expected.

If the frame that is sent to the Layer 3 gateway uses the MAC burned-in address (BIA) instead of the HSRP MAC address, the port channel hashing of the frame may forward it to the wrong vPC peer, which would then just bridge the frame to the other vPC peer.

This scenario can be problematic because if the vPC peer that owns the MAC address routes the frame to a vPC member port, this frame will not be able to leave the switch because the vPC duplicate prevention rule would apply: no frame that comes from a peer link is allowed to exit the switch on a vPC member port.

Figure 2-12 shows the case in which device A sends traffic to remote MAC (RMAC) address A with a port channel hash that forwards the traffic to switch B. The result is that the frame cannot get to server B because of the duplicate prevention rule.

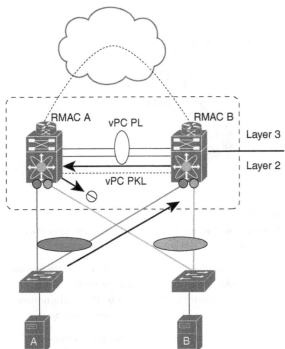

**Figure 2-12** *vPC Peer-Gateway*

To address this forwarding scenario, you should configure the **peer-gateway** command under the vPC domain. This command enables the vPC peers to exchange information about their respective BIA MAC addresses so they can forward the traffic locally without having to send it over the peer link.

## Port Channel Configurations and Verifications

Table 2-13 lists port channel default parameters. You can alter these parameters as necessary to optimize port channel functionality.

**Table 2-13** Port Channel Default Settings

| Parameters | Default |
|---|---|
| Port channel | Admin up |
| Load balancing method for Layer 3 interfaces | Source and destination IP address |
| Load balancing method for Layer 2 interfaces | Source and destination MAC address |
| Load balancing per module | Disabled |

| Parameters | Default |
|---|---|
| LACP | Disabled |
| Channel mode | On |
| LACP system priority | 32768 |
| LACP port priority | 32768 |
| Minimum links for LACP | 1 |
| Max bundle | 32 |
| Minimum links for FEX fabric port channel | 1 |

**NOTE**   No license is required for the port channel. Any feature not included in a license package is bundled with the Cisco NX-OS system images. For a complete explanation of the Cisco NX-OS licensing scheme, see the Cisco NX-OS Licensing Guide.

Port channeling has the following configuration recommendations and limitations:

- For Layer 2 port channels, ports with different STP port path costs can form a port channel if they are compatibly configured with each other.

- In STP, the port channel cost is based on the aggregated bandwidth of the port members.

- After you configure a port channel, the configuration that you apply to the port channel interface affects the port channel member ports. The configuration that you apply to the member ports affects only the member port where you apply the configuration.

- You must enable the LACP feature before you can use it.

- Do not put shared and dedicated ports into the same port channel.

- LACP does not support half-duplex mode. Half-duplex ports in LACP port channels are put in a suspended state.

- You must remove the port-security information from a port before you can add that port to a port channel. Similarly, you cannot apply the port-security configuration to a port that is a member of a channel group.

- Do not configure ports that belong to a port channel group as private VLAN ports. While a port is part of the private VLAN configuration, the port channel configuration becomes inactive.

- Channel member ports cannot be a source or destination SPAN port.

There are many considerations that you need to be aware of when you are implementing vPCs:

- You must configure the peer-keepalive link and form an adjacency between peers before the system can establish the vPC peer link.

- A vPC peer link must consist of Ethernet ports with an interface speed of 10 Gbps or higher. It is recommended that you use at least two 10-Gigabit Ethernet ports in dedicated mode on two different I/O modules.

- vPC peers must run the same Cisco NX-OS release. During a software upgrade, you must upgrade the primary vPC peer first.

- You must pair Cisco Nexus switches of the same type.

- When you are forming a vPC domain between two Cisco Nexus 9300 Series switches, both switches must be the exact same model to form a supported vPC domain. When you're forming a vPC domain between two Cisco Nexus 9500 Series switches, both switches must consist of the same models of line cards, fabric modules, supervisor modules, and system controllers inserted in the same slots of the chassis to form a supported vPC domain.

- A vPC keepalive should not run across a vPC peer link.

- A vPC domain, by definition, consists of a pair of switches that are identified by a shared vPC domain ID. It is not possible to add more than two switches to a vPC domain.

- A vPC is a Layer 2 port channel. A vPC does not support the configuration of Layer 3 port channels. Dynamic routing from the vPC peers to the routers that are connected on a vPC is not supported. It is recommended that you establish routing adjacencies on separate routed links.

- You can use a vPC as a Layer 2 link to establish a routing adjacency between two external routers. The routing restrictions for vPCs apply only to routing adjacencies between the vPC peer switches and routers that are connected on a vPC.

Tables 2-14 through 2-17 show the most-used port channel and vPC configuration commands. For a full list of commands, refer to the Nexus interface and virtual port channel configuration guide links in the "References" section at the end of this chapter.

**Table 2-14**   Port Channel and vPC Global-Level Commands

| Command | Purpose |
|---|---|
| **feature lacp** | Enables LACP on the device. |
| **feature vpc** | Enables vPCs on the device. |
| **vpc domain** *domain-id* | Creates a vPC domain on the device and enters the vpc-domain configuration mode for configuration purposes. There is no default; the range is 1 to 1000. |
| **port-channel load-balance** *method* {dst ip \| dst ip-port-vlan \| dst ip-vlan \| dst mac \| dst port \| src-dst ip [symmetric] \| src-dst ip-gre \| source-dst mac \| source-dst port \| src-ip port \| src-dst ip-l4port [symmetric] \| src-dst l4port \| src-dst mac \| src ip \| src mac \| src-port } [fex {*fex-range* \| all}] [rotate *rotate*] | Specifies the load-balancing algorithm for the device. The range depends on the device. The default for Layer 3 is **src-dst-ip** for both IPv4 and IPv6, and the default for non-IP is **src-dest-mac**. Use the **no port-channel load-balance src-dst mac asymmetric** command to revert back to the default system settings (symmetrical). NOTE: If a module-based configuration already exists, it takes precedence over the default system settings. |

| Command | Purpose |
|---|---|
| lacp system-priority *priority* | Configures the system priority for use with LACP. Valid values are from 1 through 65,535, and higher numbers have a lower priority. The default value is 32,768. |

**Table 2-15**   Port Channel and vPC Interface-Level Commands

| Command | Purpose |
|---|---|
| interface port-channel *channel-number* | Specifies the port channel interface to configure and enters the interface configuration mode. The range is from 1 to 4096. The Cisco NX-OS software automatically creates the channel group if it does not already exist. |
| switchport | Configures the interface as a Layer 2 access port. |
| switchport mode trunk | (Optional) Configures the interface as a Layer 2 trunk port. |
| switchport trunk {*allowed vlan vlan-id* \| *native vlan-id*} | (Optional) Configures necessary parameters for a Layer 2 trunk port. |
| channel-group *channel-number* [*force* ] [*mode* {*on* \| *active* \| *passive* }] | Configures the port in a channel group and sets the mode. The *channel-number* range is from 1 to 4096. This command creates the port channel associated with this channel group if the port channel does not already exist. All static port channel interfaces are set to mode on. You must set all LACP-enabled port channel interfaces to active or passive. The default mode is on. (Optional) Forces an interface with some incompatible configurations to join the channel. The forced interface must have the same speed, duplex, and flow control settings as the channel group. NOTE: The *force* option fails if the port has a QoS policy mismatch with the other members of the port channel. |
| speed {10 \| 100 \| 1000 \| auto } | Sets the speed for the port channel interface. The default is auto for autonegotiation. |
| duplex {auto \| full \| half } | Sets the duplex for the port channel interface. The default is auto for autonegotiation. |
| lacp min-links *number* | Specifies the port channel interface to configure the number of minimum links and enters the interface configuration mode. The range is from 1 to 16. |
| lacp max-bundle *number* | Specifies the port channel interface to configure max-bundle and enters the interface configuration mode. |
| lacp port-priority *priority* | Configures the port priority for use with LACP. Valid values are from 1 through 65,535, and higher numbers have a lower priority. The default value is 32,768. |
| load-interval [ counter { 1 \| 2 \| 3 } ] *seconds* | Sets three different sampling intervals to bit-rate and packet-rate statistics. |
| vpc peer-link | Configures the selected port channel as the vPC peer link and enters the vpc-domain configuration mode. |

**Table 2-16**  vPC Domain-Level Commands

| Command | Purpose |
|---|---|
| peer-keepalive destination *ipaddress* [ hold-timeout *secs* \| interval *msecs* { timeout *secs*} \| { precedence { *prec-value* \| network \| internet \| critical \| flash-override \| flash \| immediate priority \| routine}} \| tos { *tos-value* \| max-reliability \| max-throughput \| min-delay \| min-monetary-cost \| normal}} \|tos-byte *tos-byte-value*} \| source *ipaddress* \| vrf {*name* \| management vpc-keepalive }] | Configures the IPv4 address for the remote end of the vPC peer-keepalive link. NOTE: The system does not form the vPC peer link until you configure a vPC peer-keepalive link. The management ports and VRF are the defaults. NOTE: It is recommended that you configure a separate VRF and use a Layer 3 port from each vPC peer device in that VRF for the vPC peer-keepalive link. |
| peer-gateway | Enables Layer 3 forwarding for packets destined to the peer's gateway MAC address. |
| system-mac *mac-address* | Enters the MAC address that you want for the specified vPC domain in the following format: aaaa.bbbb.cccc. |
| system-priority *priority* | Enters the system priority that you want for the specified vPC domain. The range of values is from 1 to 65,535. The default value is 32,667. NOTE: It is recommended that you manually configure the vPC system priority when you are running LACP to ensure that the vPC peer devices are the primary devices on LACP. When you manually configure the system priority, ensure that you configure the same priority value on both vPC peer devices. If these values do not match, vPC will not come up. |
| role priority *priority* | Enters the role priority that you want for the vPC system priority. The range of values is from 1 to 65,636, and the default value is 32,667. NOTE: The lower role priority will be the primary vPC. |
| peer-switch | Enables the vPC switch pair to appear as a single STP root in the Layer 2 topology. Use the **no** form of the command to disable the peer switch vPC topology. |
| ip arp synchronize | Enables the ARP synchronization between the vPC peers. To disable the synchronization, use the **no ip arp synchronize** command. |
| ipv6 nd synchronize | Enables the ND synchronization between the vPC peers. To disable the synchronization, use the **no ipv6 nd synchronize** command. |

**Table 2-17**   Port Channel and vPC Global-Level Verification Commands

| Command | Purpose |
|---|---|
| show interface port-channel *channel-number* | Displays the status of a port channel interface. |
| show port-channel compatibility-parameters | Displays the parameters that must be the same among the member ports in order to join a port channel. |
| show port-channel load-balance | Displays the type of load balancing in use for port channels. |
| show port-channel summary | Displays a summary for the port channel interfaces. |
| show lacp { counters [interface port-channel *channel-number*] \| [interface *type/slot*] \| neighbor [interface port-channel *channel-number*] \| port-channel [interface port-channel *channel-number*] \| system-identifier ]]} | Displays information on LACP. |
| show running-config interface port-channel *channel-number* | Displays information on the running configuration of the port channel. |
| show running-config vpc | Displays running configuration information for vPCs. |
| show vpc brief | Displays brief information on the vPCs. |
| show vpc consistency-parameters | Displays the status of those parameters that must be consistent across all vPC interfaces. |
| show vpc peer-keepalive | Displays information on the peer-keepalive messages. |
| show vpc role | Displays the peer status, the role of the local device, the vPC system MAC address and system priority, and the MAC address and priority for the local vPC device. |
| show interface counters detailed [all] | Displays input packets, bytes, and multicast and output packets and bytes. |
| show interface counters errors | Displays information on the number of error packets. |
| show lacp counters | Displays statistics for LACP. |
| show vpc statistics | Displays statistics on the vPCs. |

Figure 2-13 shows the network topology for the configuration that follows, which demonstrates how to configure a virtual port channel.

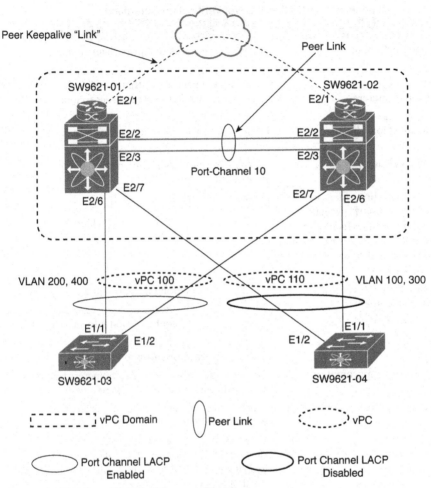

**Figure 2-13**   *Port Channel Network Topology*

Example 2-10 shows the first switch's (SW9621-01) vPC configuration, including the vPC keepalive and vPC peer-link interface.

**Example 2-10**   *SW9621-01 vPC Configurations*

```
SW9621-01(config)# feature vpc
SW9621-01(config)# feature lacp
SW9621-01(config)# vpc domain 10
SW9621-01 (config-vpc-domain)# peer-keepalive destination 10.10.10.2 source
10.10.10.1 vrf vPC_vrf
SW9621-01(config)# interface Ethernet2/1
SW9621-01(config-if)# vrf member vPC_vrf
SW9621-01(config-if)# ip address 10.10.10.1/30
SW9621-01(config-if)# no shutdown
```

```
SW9621-01(config)# interface port-channel10
SW9621-01(config-if)# switchport
SW9621-01(config-if)# switchport mode trunk
SW9621-01(config-if)# switchport trunk allowed vlan 10-1000
SW9621-01(config-if)# vpc peer-link
SW9621-01(config-if)# no shutdown


SW9621-01(config)# interface port-channel100
SW9621-01(config-if)# switchport
SW9621-01(config-if)# switchport mode trunk
SW9621-01(config-if)# switchport trunk allowed vlan 200,400
SW9621-01(config-if)# vpc 100
SW9621-01(config-if)# no shutdown

SW9621-01(config)# interface port-channel110
SW9621-01(config-if)# switchport
SW9621-01(config-if)# switchport mode trunk
SW9621-01(config-if)# switchport trunk allowed vlan 100,300
SW9621-01(config-if)# vpc 110
SW9621-01(config-if)# no shutdown

SW9621-01(config)# interface Ethernet2/2-3
SW9621-01(config-if)# channel-group 10 mode active
SW9621-01(config-if)# no shutdown

SW9621-01(config)# interface Ethernet2/6
SW9621-01(config-if)# channel-group 100 mode active
SW9621-01(config-if)# no shutdown

SW9621-01(config)# interface Ethernet2/7
SW9621-01(config-if)# channel-group 110 mode on
SW9621-01(config-if)# no shutdown
```

Example 2-11 shows the second switch's (SW9621-02) vPC configuration, including the vPC keepalive and vPC peer-link interface.

**Example 2-11**   *SW9621-02 vPC Configuration*

```
SW9621-02(config)# feature vpc
SW9621-02(config)# feature lacp
SW9621-02(config)# vpc domain 10
SW9621-02 (config-vpc-domain)# peer-keepalive destination 10.10.10.1 source
10.10.10.2 vrf vPC_vrf
SW9621-02(config)# interface Ethernet2/1
```

```
SW9621-02(config-if)# vrf member vPC_vrf
SW9621-02(config-if)# ip address 10.10.10.2/30
SW9621-02(config-if)# no shutdown


SW9621-02(config)# interface port-channel10
SW9621-02(config-if)# switchport
SW9621-02(config-if)# switchport mode trunk
SW9621-02(config-if)# switchport trunk allowed vlan 10-1000
SW9621-02(config-if)# vpc peer-link
SW9621-02(config-if)# no shutdown


SW9621-02(config)# interface port-channel100
SW9621-02(config-if)# switchport
SW9621-02(config-if)# switchport mode trunk
SW9621-02(config-if)# switchport trunk allowed vlan 200,400
SW9621-02(config-if)# vpc 100
SW9621-02(config-if)# no shutdown


SW9621-02(config)# interface port-channel110
SW9621-02(config-if)# switchport
SW9621-02(config-if)# switchport mode trunk
SW9621-02(config-if)# switchport trunk allowed vlan 100,300
SW9621-02(config-if)# vpc 110
SW9621-02(config-if)# no shutdown


SW9621-02(config)# interface Ethernet2/2-3
SW9621-02(config-if)# channel-group 10 mode active
SW9621-02(config-if)# no shutdown


SW9621-02(config)# interface Ethernet2/6
SW9621-02(config-if)# channel-group 110 mode on
SW9621-02(config-if)# no shutdown


SW9621-02(config)# interface Ethernet2/7
SW9621-02(config-if)# channel-group 100 mode active
SW9621-02(config-if)# no shutdown
```

Examples 2-12 and 2-13 show the end devices' (SW9621-03 and SW9621-04) port channel 100 and port channel 110 interfaces facing vPC switches with LACP configurations.

**Example 2-12**   *Port Channel 100/110 Configurations on SW9621-03*

```
SW9621-03(config)# feature lacp
SW9621-03(config)# interface port-channel100
SW9621-03(config-if)# switchport
SW9621-03(config-if)# switchport mode trunk
SW9621-03(config-if)# switchport trunk allowed vlan 200,400
SW9621-03(config-if)# no shutdown
SW9621-03(config)# interface E1/1-2
SW9621-03(config-if)# channel-group 100 mode active
SW9621-03(config-if)# no shutdown
```

**Example 2-13**   *Port Channel 100/110 Configurations on SW9621-04*

```
SW9621-04(config)# feature lacp
SW9621-04(config)# interface port-channel110
SW9621-04(config-if)# switchport
SW9621-04(config-if)# switchport mode trunk
SW9621-04(config-if)# switchport trunk allowed vlan 100,300
SW9621-04(config-if)# no shutdown

SW9621-04(config)# interface Ethernet1/1-2
SW9621-04(config-if)# channel-group 110 mode on
SW9621-04(config-if)# no shutdown
```

Example 2-14 shows the first switch's vPC and port channel LACP status, and Example 2-15 shows the second switch's vPC status.

**Example 2-14**   *SW9621-01 vPC and Port Channel Status*

```
SW9621-01# show vpc
Legend:
                (*) - local vPC is down, forwarding via vPC peer-link

vPC domain id                     : 10
Peer status                       : peer adjacency formed ok
vPC keep-alive status             : peer is alive
Configuration consistency status  : success
Per-vlan consistency status       : success
```

```
Type-2 consistency status            : success
vPC role                             : primary
Number of vPCs configured            : 2

Peer Gateway                         : Disabled
Dual-active excluded VLANs and BDs   : -
Graceful Consistency Check           : Enabled
Auto-recovery status                 : Enabled, timer is off.(timeout = 240s)
Delay-restore orphan ports status    : Timer is off.(timeout = 0s)
Operational Layer3 Peer-router       : Disabled
Self-isolation                       : Disabled

vPC Peer-link status
---------------------------------------------------------------------------------
id   Port   Status Active vlans                  Active BDs
--   ----   ------ -------------------------------------------------------------
1    Po10   up     100,200,300,400                   -

vPC status
Id              : 100
  Port          : Po100
  Status        : up
  Consistency   : success
  Reason        : success
  Active Vlans  : 200,400
Id              : 110
  Port          : Po110
  Status        : up
  Consistency   : success
  Reason        : success
  Active Vlans  : 100,300


SW9621-01# show vpc peer-keepalive

vPC keep-alive status          : peer is alive
--Peer is alive for            : (4159) seconds, (600) msec
--Send status                  : Success
--Last send at                 : 2019.07.24 00:39:59 917 ms
--Sent on interface            : Eth2/1
--Receive status               : Success
--Last receive at              : 2019.07.24 00:39:59 918 ms
--Received on interface        : Eth2/1
--Last update from peer        : (0) seconds, (17) msec
```

```
vPC Keep-alive parameters
--Destination                          : 10.10.10.2
--Keepalive interval                   : 1000 msec
--Keepalive timeout                    : 5 seconds
--Keepalive hold timeout               : 3 seconds
--Keepalive vrf                        : vPC_vrf
--Keepalive udp port                   : 3200
--Keepalive tos                        : 192   .


SW9621-01# show lacp interface E2/3
Interface Ethernet2/3 is up
  Channel group is 10 port channel is Po10
  PDUs sent: 287
  PDUs rcvd: 287
  Markers sent: 0
  Markers rcvd: 0
  Marker response sent: 0
  Marker response rcvd: 0
  Unknown packets rcvd: 0
  Illegal packets rcvd: 0
Lag Id: [ [(8000, e4-c7-22-15-2c-48, 9, 8000, 411), (8000, e4-c7-22-15-33-c8, 9,
  8000, 411)] ]
Operational as aggregated link since Tue Jul 23 23:36:30 2019

Local Port: Eth2/3   MAC Address= e4-c7-22-15-2c-48
  System Identifier=0x8000,  Port Identifier=0x8000,0x411
  Operational key=9
  LACP_Activity=active
  LACP_Timeout=Long Timeout (30s)
  Synchronization=IN_SYNC
  Collecting=true
  Distributing=true
  Partner information refresh timeout=Long Timeout (90s)
Actor Admin State=61
Actor Oper State=61
Neighbor: 0x411
  MAC Address= e4-c7-22-15-33-c8
  System Identifier=0x8000,  Port Identifier=0x8000,0x411
  Operational key=9
  LACP_Activity=active
  LACP_Timeout=Long Timeout (30s)
  Synchronization=IN_SYNC
  Collecting=true
  Distributing=true
```

```
Partner Admin State=61
Partner Oper State=61
Aggregate or Individual(True=1)= 1


SW9621-01# show port-channel summary
Flags:  D - Down        P - Up in port-channel (members)
        I - Individual  H - Hot-standby (LACP only)
        s - Suspended   r - Module-removed
        b - BFD Session Wait
        S - Switched    R - Routed
        U - Up (port-channel)
        M - Not in use. Min-links not met
--------------------------------------------------------------------------------

Group Port-        Type    Protocol  Member Ports
      Channel
--------------------------------------------------------------------------------

10    Po10(SU)     Eth     LACP      Eth2/2(P) Eth2/3(P)
100   Po100(SU)    Eth     LACP      Eth2/6(P)
110   Po110(SU)    Eth     NONE      Eth2/7(P)
```

**Example 2-15**   *SW9621-02 vPC Status*

```
SW9621-02# show vpc brief
Legend:
                (*) - local vPC is down, forwarding via vPC peer-link


vPC domain id                    : 10
Peer status                      : peer adjacency formed ok
vPC keep-alive status            : peer is alive
Configuration consistency status : success
Per-vlan consistency status      : success
Type-2 consistency status        : success
vPC role                         : secondary
Number of vPCs configured        : 2
Peer Gateway                     : Disabled
Dual-active excluded VLANs and BDs  : -
Graceful Consistency Check       : Enabled
Auto-recovery status             : Enabled, timer is off.(timeout = 240s)
Delay-restore status             : Timer is off.(timeout = 30s)
Delay-restore SVI status         : Timer is off.(timeout = 10s)
Delay-restore orphan ports status : Timer is off.(timeout = 0s)
Operational Layer3 Peer-router    : Disabled
Self-isolation                   : Disabled
```

```
vPC Peer-link status
-----------------------------------------------------------------------------
id    Port    Status Active vlans                      Active BDs
--    ----    ------ ------------------------------------------------------
1     Po10    up     100,200,300,400                   -


vPC status
-----------------------------------------------------
id     Port          Status Consistency Active VLANs
-----  ------------  ------ ----------- ----------------
100    Po100         up     success     200,400
110    Po110         up     success     100,300
```

Example 2-16 shows the end switches' port channel 100 and 110 status.

**Example 2-16**  *SW9621-03 and SW9621-04 Port Channel Status*

```
SW9621-03(config)# show port-channel summary
Flags:  D - Down        P - Up in port-channel (members)
        I - Individual  H - Hot-standby (LACP only)
        s - Suspended   r - Module-removed
        S - Switched    R - Routed
        U - Up (port-channel)
        M - Not in use. Min-links not met
-----------------------------------------------------------------------------
Group Port-       Type      Protocol  Member Ports
      Channel
-----------------------------------------------------------------------------
100   Po100(SU)   Eth       LACP      Eth1/1(P)    Eth1/2(P)


SW9621-03# show cdp neighbors
Capability Codes: R - Router, T - Trans-Bridge, B - Source-Route-Bridge
                  S - Switch, H - Host, I - IGMP, r - Repeater,
                  V - VoIP-Phone, D - Remotely-Managed-Device,
                  s - Supports-STP-Dispute



Device-ID               Local Intrfce Hldtme Capability  Platform     Port ID
SW9621-01
                        Eth1/1        132    R S I s     N7K-C7009    Eth2/6
```

```
SW9621-02

                        Eth1/2        165    R S I s   N7K-C7009         Eth2/7


SW9621-04# show port-channel summary
Flags:  D - Down        P - Up in port-channel (members)
        I - Individual  H - Hot-standby (LACP only)
        s - Suspended   r - Module-removed
        S - Switched    R - Routed
        U - Up (port-channel)
        M - Not in use. Min-links not met
--------------------------------------------------------------------------------

Group Port-       Type     Protocol  Member Ports
      Channel
--------------------------------------------------------------------------------

110   Po110(SU)   Eth      NONE      Eth1/1(P)    Eth1/2(P)


SW9621-04# show port-channel traffic
ChanId      Port Rx-Ucst Tx-Ucst Rx-Mcst Tx-Mcst Rx-Bcst Tx-Bcst
------ --------- ------- ------- ------- ------- ------- -------


   110    Eth1/1    0.0%    0.0%  30.72%  53.62%    0.0%    0.0%
   110    Eth1/2    0.0%    0.0%  69.27%  46.37%    0.0%    0.0%


SW9621-04# show port-channel load-balance


Port Channel Load-Balancing Configuration:
System: source-dest-ip


Port Channel Load-Balancing Addresses Used Per-Protocol:
Non-IP: source-dest-mac
IP: source-dest-ip source-dest-mac
```

# Exam Preparation Tasks

As mentioned in the Introduction, you have a couple of choices for exam preparation: the exercises here, Chapter 21, "Final Preparation," and the exam simulation questions in the Pearson Test Prep software online.

## Review All Key Topics

Review the most important topics in the chapter, noted with the key topic icon in the outer margin of the page. Table 2-18 lists a reference to these key topics and the page numbers on which each is found.

**Table 2-18** Key Topics for Chapter 2

| Key Topic Element | Description | Page |
|---|---|---|
| Section | STP Topology | 93 |
| Section | STP Port Types | 94 |
| Figure 2-2 | UDLD Detection of a Unidirectional Link | 98 |
| Paragraph | Rapid PVST+ | 98 |
| Figure 2-3 | Topology Change (TC) BPDU Flood | 99 |
| Section | Rapid PVST+ Ports | 100 |
| Table 2-2 | Port State Active Topology | 101 |
| Table 2-3 | Default Port Cost | 102 |
| Section | Port Channels | 117 |
| Table 2-9 | Port Channel Individual Link Modes | 119 |
| Table 2-10 | Channel Mode Matrix | 119 |
| Paragraph | Port Channel Load Balance | 120 |
| Figure 2-6 | Port Channel Load Balance | 121 |
| List | vPC system components | 124 |
| Figure 2-8 | vPC Components | 125 |
| Figure 2-9 | Traffic Flows with vPC | 126 |
| Figure 2-10 | vPC Blocking Duplicate Frames | 130 |
| Figure 2-12 | vPC peer-gateway | 132 |
| List | vPC implementation considerations | 133 |

## Memory Tables

Print a copy of Appendix C, "Memory Tables" (found on the companion website), or at least the section for this chapter, and complete the tables and lists from memory. Appendix D, "Memory Tables Answer Key," also on the companion website, includes completed tables and lists to check your work.

## Define Key Terms

Define the following key terms from this chapter, and check your answers in the Glossary.

Address Resolution Protocol (ARP), bridge protocol data units (BPDUs), Cisco Nexus, Cisco NX-OS, equal-cost multipath (ECMP), Hot Standby Router Protocol (HSRP), Internet Protocol (IP), Link Aggregation Control Protocol (LACP), local-area network (LAN), maximum transmission unit (MTU), Media Access Control (MAC) address, multi-chassis EtherChannel trunk (MCT), Port VLAN ID (PVID), Rapid per VLAN Spanning Tree (Rapid PVST+), Spanning Tree Protocol (STP), topology change (TC), Transmission Control Protocol (TCP), User Datagram Protocol (UDP), virtual device context (VDC), virtual LAN (VLAN), virtual port channels (vPCs), Virtual Routing and Forwarding (VRF)

## References

Cisco Nexus 9000 Series NX-OS Interfaces Configuration Guide, Release 10.3(x): https://www.cisco.com/c/en/us/td/docs/dcn/nx-os/nexus9000/103x/configuration/interfaces/cisco-nexus-9000-nx-os-interfaces-configuration-guide-103x.html

Cisco Nexus 9000 NX-OS Layer 2 Switching Configuration Guide, Release 10.3(x): https://www.cisco.com/c/en/us/td/docs/dcn/nx-os/nexus9000/103x/configuration/layer-2-switching/cisco-nexus-9000-nx-os-layer-2-switching-configuration-guide-103x.html

Relevant CiscoLive Presentations: https://ciscolive.com

# CHAPTER 3

# Implementing Data Center Overlay Protocols

The adoption of server virtualization has been increasing rapidly. Server virtualization provides flexibility and agility in provisioning and placement of computing workloads. However, network connectivity has not kept pace with such innovations in the computing environment, although it still offers a rigid approach to provisioning transport services.

As a solution, network overlays abstract the details of the physical network, making it much faster to connect virtual machines (VMs) and other devices. Rather than provision paths on physical devices, overlays encapsulate traffic using protocols such as Overlay Transport Virtualization (OTV) or Virtual Extensible LAN (VXLAN) across the physical network. These newer protocols allow operators to move beyond the limitations of VLANs, which support only 4096 virtual networks, so that they can better support multitenant services.

## This chapter covers the following key topics:

**Virtual Extensible LAN (VXLAN) Overview:** This section discusses the Layer 2 VLAN extension to provide multitenant flexibility, high segment scalability, and Layer 2 spanning tree improvement, along with a configuration example.

## "Do I Know This Already?" Quiz

The "Do I Know This Already?" quiz enables you to assess whether you should read this entire chapter thoroughly or jump to the "Exam Preparation Tasks" section. If you are in doubt about your answers to these questions or your own assessment of your knowledge of the topics, read the entire chapter. Table 3-1 lists the major headings in this chapter and their corresponding "Do I Know This Already?" quiz questions. You can find the answers in Appendix A, "Answers to the 'Do I Know This Already?' Quizzes."

**Table 3-1** "Do I Know This Already?" Section-to-Question Mapping

| Foundation Topics Section | Questions |
|---|---|
| Virtual Extensible LAN (VXLAN) Overview | 1–3 |

**CAUTION** The goal of self-assessment is to gauge your mastery of the topics in this chapter. If you do not know the answer to a question or are only partially sure of the answer, you should mark that question as wrong for purposes of the self-assessment. Giving yourself credit for an answer you correctly guess skews your self-assessment results and might provide you with a false sense of security.

1. In current data center networking architecture, which network layer is used to transmit VXLAN packets or other overlay packets?

   a. Overlay network

   b. SD-WAN

   c. Underlay network

   d. MPLS

2. How many available IDs can be assigned to a VXLAN at any given time?

   a. 4096

   b. 160,000

   c. 1 million

   d. 16 million

3. Which statement about VXLAN high availability is correct?

   a. For an anycast IP address, vPC VTEP switches can use the same VTEP IP address.

   b. For an anycast IP address, vPC VTEP switches must use the same secondary IP address on the loopback interface.

   c. Distributed anycast gateways must be connected with vPC.

   d. VTEP high availability will use unicast instead of multicast communications.

## Foundation Topics

# Virtual Extensible LAN (VXLAN) Overview

In partnership with other leading vendors, Cisco proposed the VXLAN standard to the Internet Engineering Task Force (IETF) as a solution to the data center network challenges posed by the traditional VLAN technology. The VXLAN standard provides for flexible workload placement and the higher scalability of Layer 2 segmentation that is required by modern application demands. VXLAN is an extension to the Layer 2 VLAN. It was designed to provide the same VLAN functionality with greater extensibility and flexibility. VXLAN offers the following benefits:

- **VLAN flexibility in multitenant segments:** It provides a solution to extend Layer 2 segments over the underlying network infrastructure so that tenant workload can be placed across physical pods in the data center.

- **Higher scalability:** VXLAN uses a 24-bit segment ID known as the VXLAN network identifier (VNID), which enables up to 16 million VXLAN segments to coexist in the same administrative domain.

- **Improved network utilization:** VXLAN solved Layer 2 STP limitations. VXLAN packets are transferred through the underlying network based on its Layer 3 header and can take complete advantage of Layer 3 routing, equal-cost multipath (ECMP) routing, and link aggregation protocols to use all available paths.

## VXLAN Encapsulation and Packet Format

VXLAN is a solution to support a flexible, large-scale multitenant environment over a shared common physical infrastructure. The transport protocol over the physical data center network is IP plus UDP.

VXLAN defines a MAC-in-UDP encapsulation scheme where the original Layer 2 frame has a VXLAN header added and is then placed in a UDP-IP packet. With this MAC-in-UDP encapsulation, VXLAN tunnels the Layer 2 network over the Layer 3 network. The VXLAN packet format is shown in Figure 3-1.

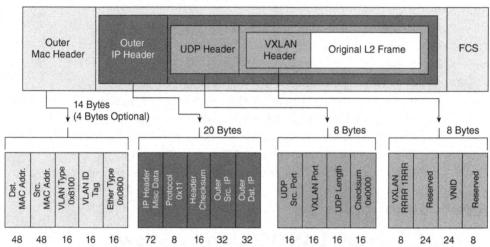

**Figure 3-1**  *VXLAN Packet Format*

As shown in Figure 3-1, VXLAN introduces an 8-byte VXLAN header that consists of a 24-bit VNID and a few reserved bits. The VXLAN header together with the original Ethernet frame goes in the UDP payload. The 24-bit VNID is used to identify Layer 2 segments and to maintain Layer 2 isolation between the segments. With all 24 bits in VNID, VXLAN can support 16 million LAN segments.

## VXLAN Tunnel Endpoint

VXLAN uses the VXLAN tunnel endpoint (VTEP) to map tenants' end devices to VXLAN segments and to perform VXLAN encapsulation and decapsulation. Each VTEP function has two interfaces: one is a switch interface on the local LAN segment to support local end-point communication, and the other is an IP interface to the transport IP network.

Infrastructure VLAN is a unique IP address that identifies the VTEP device on the transport IP network. The VTEP device uses this IP address to encapsulate Ethernet frames and transmits the encapsulated packets to the transport network through the IP interface.

A VTEP device also discovers the remote VTEPs for its VXLAN segments and learns remote MAC Address-to-VTEP mappings through its IP interface. The functional components of VTEPs and the logical topology that is created for Layer 2 connectivity across the transport IP network are shown in Figure 3-2.

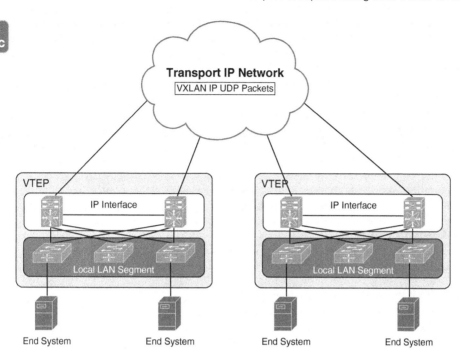

**Figure 3-2**  *VXLAN Tunnel Endpoint (VTEP)*

The VXLAN segments are independent of the underlying network topology; conversely, the underlying IP network between VTEPs is independent of the VXLAN overlay. It routes the encapsulated packets based on the outer IP address header, which has the initiating VTEP as the source IP address and the terminating VTEP as the destination IP address.

## Virtual Network Identifier

A virtual network identifier (VNI) is a value that identifies a specific virtual network in the data plane. It is typically a 24-bit value part of the VXLAN header, which can support up to 16 million individual network segments. (Valid VNI values are from 4096 to 16,777,215.) There are two main VNI scopes:

- **Network-wide scoped VNIs:** The same value is used to identify the specific Layer 3 virtual network across all network edge devices. This network scope is useful in environments such as within the data center where networks can be automatically provisioned by central orchestration systems.

    Having a uniform VNI per VPN is a simple approach, while also easing network operations (such as troubleshooting). It also means simplified requirements on network edge devices, both physical and virtual devices. A critical requirement for this type of approach is to have a very large number of network identifier values given the network-wide scope.

- **Locally assigned VNIs:** In an alternative approach supported as per RFC 4364, the identifier has local significance to the network edge device that advertises the route.

In this case, the virtual network scale impact is determined on a per-node basis versus a network basis.

When it is locally scoped and uses the same existing semantics as an MPLS VPN label, the same forwarding behaviors as specified in RFC 4364 can be employed. This scope thus allows a seamless stitching together of a VPN that spans both an IP-based network overlay and an MPLS VPN.

This situation can occur, for instance, at the data center edge where the overlay network feeds into an MPLS VPN. In this case, the identifier may be dynamically allocated by the advertising device.

It is important to support both cases and, in doing so, ensure that the scope of the identifier be clear and the values not conflict with each other.

## VXLAN Control Plane

Two widely adopted control planes are used with VXLAN: the VXLAN Flood and Learn Multicast-Based Control Plane and the VXLAN MPBGP EVPN Control Plane.

### VXLAN Flood and Learn Multicast-Based Control Plane

Cisco Nexus switches utilize existing Layer 2 flooding mechanisms and dynamic MAC address learning to

■ Transport broadcast, unknown unicast, and multicast (BUM) traffic

■ Discover remote VTEPs

■ Learn remote-host MAC addresses and MAC-to-VTEP mappings for each VXLAN segment

IP multicast is used to reduce the flooding scope of the set of hosts that are participating in the VXLAN segment. Each VXLAN segment, or VNID, is mapped to an IP multicast group in the transport IP network. Each VTEP device is independently configured and joins this multicast group as an IP host through the Internet Group Management Protocol (IGMP). The IGMP joins trigger Protocol Independent Multicast (PIM) joins and signaling through the transport network for the particular multicast group. The multicast distribution tree for this group is built through the transport network based on the locations of participating VTEPs. The multicast tunnel of a VXLAN segment through the underlying IP network is shown in Figure 3-3.

The multicast group shown in Figure 3-4 is used to transmit VXLAN broadcast, unknown unicast, and multicast traffic through the IP network, limiting Layer 2 flooding to those devices that have end systems participating in the same VXLAN segment. VTEPs communicate with one another through the flooded or multicast traffic in this multicast group.

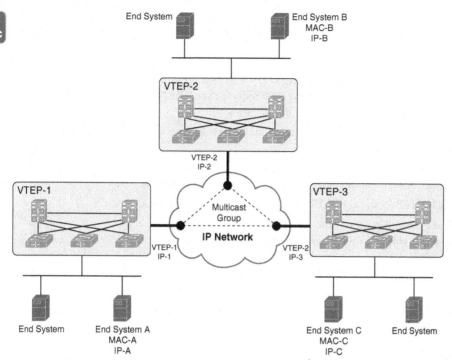

**Figure 3-3**  *VXLAN Multicast Group in Transport Network*

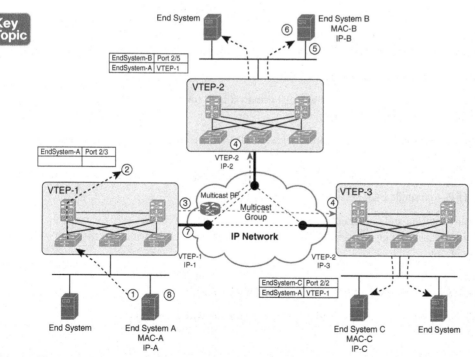

**Figure 3-4**  *VXLAN Multicast Control Plane*

As an example, if End System A wants to talk to End System B, it does the following:

1. End System A generates an ARP request trying to discover the End System B MAC address.

2. When the ARP request arrives at SW1, it will look up its local table, and if an entry is not found, it will encapsulate the ARP request over VXLAN and send it over the multicast group configured for the specific VNI.

3. The multicast RP receives the packet, and it forwards a copy to every VTEP that has joined the multicast group.

4. Each VTEP receives and deencapsulates the packet VXLAN packet and learns the System A MAC address pointing to the remote VTEP address.

5. Each VTEP forwards the ARP request to its local destinations.

6. End System B generates the ARP reply. When SW2 VTEP2 receives it, it looks up its local table and finds an entry with the information that traffic destined to End System A 180 must be sent to VTEP1 address. VTEP2 encapsulates the ARP reply with a VXLAN header and unicasts it to VTEP1.

7. VTEP1 receives and deencapsulates the packet and delivers it to End System A.

8. When the MAC address information is learned, additional packets are fed to the corresponding VTEP address.

## VXLAN MPBGP EVPN Control Plane

The EVPN overlay specifies adaptations to the BGP MPLS-based EVPN solution so that it is applied as a network virtualization overlay with VXLAN encapsulation where

- The PE node role described in BGP MPLS EVPN is equivalent to the VTEP/network virtualization edge (NVE) device.

- VTEP information is distributed via BGP.

- VTEPs use control plane learning/distribution via BGP for remote MAC addresses instead of data plane learning.

- Broadcast, unknown unicast, and multicast (BUM) data traffic is sent using a shared multicast tree.

- A BGP route reflector (RR) is used to reduce the full mesh of BGP sessions among VTEPs to a single BGP session between a VTEP and the RR.

- Route filtering and constrained route distribution are used to ensure that the control plane traffic for a given overlay is distributed only to the VTEPs that are in that overlay instance.

- The host (MAC) mobility mechanism ensures that all the VTEPs in the overlay instance know the specific VTEP associated with the MAC.

- Virtual network identifiers (VNIs) are globally unique within the overlay.

The EVPN overlay solution for VXLAN can also be adapted to enable it to be applied as a network virtualization overlay with VXLAN for Layer 3 traffic segmentation. The adaptations for Layer 3 VXLAN are similar to L2 VXLAN, except the following:

- VTEPs use control plane learning/distribution via BGP of IP addresses (instead of MAC addresses).

- The virtual routing and forwarding instances are mapped to the VNI.

- The inner destination MAC address in the VXLAN header does not belong to the host but to the receiving VTEP that does the routing of the VXLAN payload. This MAC address is distributed via the BGP attribute along with EVPN routes.

## VXLAN Gateways

VXLAN gateways are used to connect VXLAN and classic VLAN segments to create a common forwarding domain so that tenant devices can reside in both environments. The types of VXLAN gateways are

- **Layer 2 Gateway:** A Layer 2 VXLAN gateway is a device that encapsulates a classical Ethernet (CE) frame into a VXLAN frame and decapsulates a VXLAN frame into a CE frame. A gateway device transparently provides VXLAN benefits to a device that *does not support* VXLAN; that device could be a physical host or a virtual machine. The physical hosts or VMs are completely unaware of the VXLAN encapsulation.

- **VXLAN Layer 3 Gateway:** Similar to traditional routing between different VLANs, a VXLAN router is required for communication between devices that are in different VXLAN segments. The VXLAN router translates frames from one VNI to another. Depending on the source and destination, this process might require decapsulation and re-encapsulation of a frame. The Cisco Nexus device supports all combinations of decapsulation, route, and encapsulation. The routing can also be done across native Layer 3 interfaces and VXLAN segments.

  You can enable VXLAN routing at the aggregation layer or on Cisco Nexus device aggregation nodes. The spine forwards only IP-based traffic and ignores the encapsulated packets. To help scaling, a few leaf nodes (a pair of border leaves) perform routing between VNIs. A set of VNIs can be grouped into a virtual routing and forwarding (VRF) instance (tenant VRF) to enable routing among those VNIs. If routing must be enabled among a large number of VNIs, you might need to split the VNIs between several VXLAN routers. Each router is responsible for a set of VNIs and a respective subnet. Redundancy is achieved with FHRP.

## VXLAN High Availability

For high availability, a pair of virtual port channel (vPC) switches can be used as a logical VTEP device sharing an anycast VTEP address (shown in Figure 3-5).

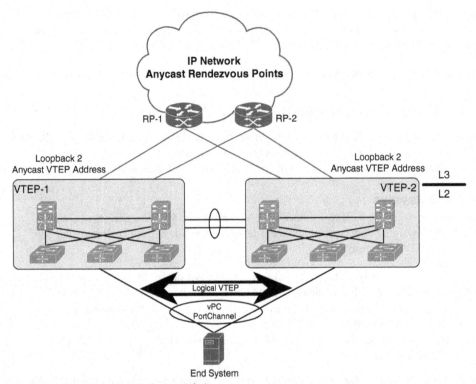

**Figure 3-5** *VXLAN High Availability*

The vPC switches provide vPCs for redundant host connectivity while individually running Layer 3 protocols with the upstream devices in the underlay network. Both will join the multicast group for the same VXLAN VNI and use the same anycast VTEP address as the source to send VXLAN-encapsulated packets to the devices in the underlay network, including the multicast rendezvous point and the remote VTEP devices. The two vPC VTEP switches appear to be one logical VTEP entity.

vPC peers must have the following identical configurations:

- Consistent mapping of the VLAN to the virtual network segment (VN-segment)

- Consistent NVE binding to the same loopback secondary IP address (anycast VTEP address)

- Consistent VNI-to-group mapping

For the anycast IP address, vPC VTEP switches must use a secondary IP address on the loopback interface bound to the VXLAN NVE tunnel. The two vPC switches need to have the exact same secondary loopback IP address.

Both devices will advertise this anycast VTEP address on the underlay network so that the upstream devices learn the /32 route from both vPC VTEPs and can load-share VXLAN unicast-encapsulated traffic between them.

In the event of vPC peer-link failure, the vPC operational secondary switch will shut down its loopback interface bound to VXLAN NVE. This shutdown will cause the secondary vPC switch to withdraw the anycast VTEP address from its IGP advertisement so that the upstream devices in the underlay network start to send all traffic just to the primary vPC switch. The purpose of this process is to avoid a vPC active-active situation when the peer link is down. With this mechanism, the orphan devices connected to the secondary vPC switch will not be able to receive VXLAN traffic when the vPC peer link is down.

## VXLAN Tenant Routed Multicast

Tenant Routed Multicast (TRM) brings the efficiency of multicast delivery to VXLAN overlays. It is based on standards-based next-gen control plane (ngMVPN) described in IETF RFCs 6513 and 6514. TRM enables the delivery of customer Layer 3 multicast traffic in a multitenant fabric, and this in an efficient and resilient manner.

While BGP EVPN provides a control plane for unicast routing, as shown in Figure 3-6, ngMVPN provides scalable multicast routing functionality. It follows an "always route" approach where every edge device (VTEP) with distributed IP Anycast Gateway for unicast becomes a designated router (DR) for multicast. Bridged multicast forwarding is present only on the edge devices (VTEP) where IGMP snooping optimizes the multicast forwarding to interested receivers. All other multicast traffic beyond local delivery is efficiently routed.

With TRM enabled, multicast forwarding in the underlay is leveraged to replicate VXLAN-encapsulated routed multicast traffic. A Default Multicast Distribution Tree (Default-MDT) is built per VRF. This is an addition to the existing multicast groups for Layer 2 VNI broadcast, unknown unicast, and Layer 2 multicast replication group. The individual multicast group addresses in the overlay are mapped to the respective underlay multicast address for replication and transport. The advantage of using a BGP-based approach is that TRM can operate as a fully distributed overlay rendezvous point (RP), with the RP presence on every edge device (VTEP).

A multicast-enabled data center fabric is typically part of an overall multicast network. Multicast sources, receivers, and even the multicast RP might reside inside the data center but might also be inside the campus or externally reachable via the WAN. TRM allows seamless integration with existing multicast networks. It can leverage multicast RPs external to the fabric. Furthermore, TRM allows for tenant-aware external connectivity using Layer 3 physical interfaces or subinterfaces.

## VXLAN Configurations and Verifications

VXLAN requires a license. Table 3-2 shows the NX-OS feature license required for VXLAN. For more information, visit the Cisco NX-OS Licensing Guide.

**Table 3-2**   VXLAN Feature-Based Licenses for Cisco NX-OS

| Platform | Feature License | Feature Name |
|---|---|---|
| Cisco Nexus 9000 Series switches | LAN_ENTERPRISE_SERVICES_PK | Cisco programmable fabric spine, leaf, or border leaf |

Tables 3-3 through 3-6 show the most-used VXLAN configuration commands along with their purpose. For full commands, refer to the Nexus VXLAN Configuration Guide.

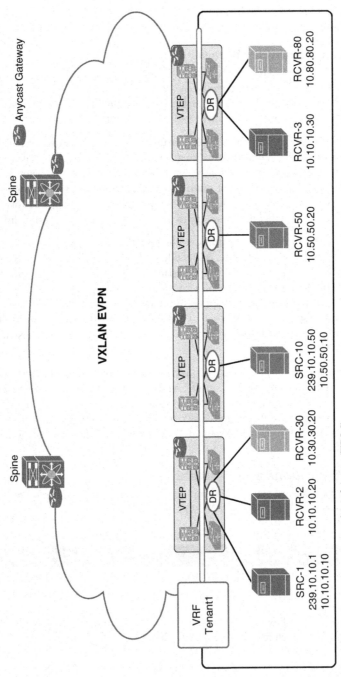

**Figure 3-6** *Tenant Routed Multicast (TRM)*

**Table 3-3**  VXLAN Global-Level Commands

| Command | Purpose |
|---|---|
| **feature nv overlay** | Enables the VXLAN feature. |
| **feature vn-segment-vlan-based** | Configures the global mode for all VXLAN bridge domains. |
| **vlan** *vlan-id* | Specifies VLAN. |
| **vn-segment** *vnid* | Specifies VXLAN virtual network identifier (VNID). |
| **bridge-domain** *domain* | Enters the bridge domain configuration mode. It will create a bridge domain if it does not yet exist. Use from the global configuration mode. |
| **dot1q** *vlan* **vni** *vni* | Creates mapping between VLAN and VNI. Use from the encapsulation profile configuration mode. |
| **encapsulation profile** *name_of_profile* **default** | Applies an encapsulation profile to a service profile. Use from the service instance configuration mode. |
| **encapsulation profile vni** *name_of_profile* | Creates an encapsulation profile. Use from the global configuration mode. |
| **service** *instance* **instance** *vni* | Creates a service instance. Use from the interface configuration mode. |
| **interface nve** *x* | Creates a VXLAN overlay interface that terminates VXLAN tunnels. |
| **mac address-table static** *mac-address* **vni** *vni-id* **interface nve** *x* **peer-ip** *ip-address* | Specifies the MAC address pointing to the remote VTEP. **NOTE:** Only 1 NVE interface is allowed on the switch. |
| **ip igmp snooping vxlan** | Enables IGMP snooping for VXLAN VLANs. You have to explicitly configure this command to enable snooping for VXLAN VLANs. |
| **ip igmp snooping disable-nve-static-router-port** | Configures IGMP snooping over VXLAN so that it does not include NVE as a static multicast router (mrouter) port using this global CLI command. The NVE interface for IGMP snooping over VXLAN is the mrouter port by default. |

**3**

**Table 3-4**  Interface-Level Commands

| Command | Purpose |
|---|---|
| **switchport vlan mapping enable** | Enables VLAN translation on the switch port. VLAN translation is disabled by default. **NOTE:** Use the **no** form of this command to disable VLAN translation. |
| **switchport vlan mapping** *vlan-id* *translated-vlan-id* | Translates a VLAN to another VLAN. The range for both the *vlan-id* and *translated-vlan-id* arguments is from 1 to 4094. ■ You can configure VLAN translation between the ingress (incoming) VLAN and a local (translated) VLAN on a port. For the traffic arriving on the interface where VLAN translation is enabled, the incoming VLAN is mapped to a translated VLAN that is VXLAN enabled. |

| Command | Purpose |
|---|---|
| | ■ On the underlay, this is mapped to a VNI; the inner dot1q is deleted and switched over to the VXLAN network. On the egress switch, the VNI is mapped to a translated VLAN. On the outgoing interface, where VLAN translation is configured, the traffic is converted to the original VLAN and egress out.<br><br>NOTE: Use the **no** form of this command to clear the mappings between a pair of VLANs. |
| **switchport vlan mapping all** | Removes all VLAN mappings configured on the interface. |

**Table 3-5**  Network Virtual Interface (NVE) Config Commands

| Command | Purpose |
|---|---|
| **source-interface** *src-if* | The source interface must be a loopback interface that is configured on the switch with a valid /32 IP address. The transient devices in the transport network and the remote VTEPs must know this /32 IP address. This is accomplished by advertising it through a dynamic routing protocol in the transport network. |
| **member vni** *vni* | Associates VXLAN virtual network identifiers (VNIs) with the NVE interface. |
| **mcast-group** *start-address* [*end-address*] | Assigns a multicast group to the VNIs.<br>NOTE: Used only for BUM traffic. |
| **ingress-replication protocol bgp** | Enables BGP EVPN with ingress replication for the VNI. |
| **ingress-replication protocol static** | Enables static ingress replication for the VNI. |
| **peer-ip** *n.n.n.n* | Enables peer IP for static ingress-replication protocol. |

**Table 3-6**  VXLAN Global-Level Verification Commands

| Command | Purpose |
|---|---|
| **show tech-support vxlan [platform ]** | Displays related VXLAN tech-support information. |
| **show bridge-domain** | Shows the bridge domain. |
| **show logging level nve** | Displays the logging level. |
| **show tech-support nve** | Displays related NVE tech-support information. |
| **show run interface nve x** | Displays NVE overlay interface configuration. |
| **show nve interface** | Displays NVE overlay interface status. |
| **show nve peers** | Displays NVE peer status. |
| **show nve peers** *peer_IP_address* **interface** *interface_ID counters* | Displays per-NVE peer statistics. |
| **clear nve peer-ip** *peer-ip-address* | Clears stale NVE peers. Stale NVE peers are those that do not have MAC addresses learned behind them. |
| **show nve vni** | Displays VXLAN VNI status. |
| **show nve vni ingress-replication** | Displays the mapping of VNI to an ingress-replication peer list and uptime for each peer. |
| **show nve vni** *vni_number* **counters** | Displays per-VNI statistics. |
| **show nve vxlan-params** | Displays VXLAN parameters, such as VXLAN destination or UDP port. |

Figure 3-7 shows the VXLAN network topology with configurations.

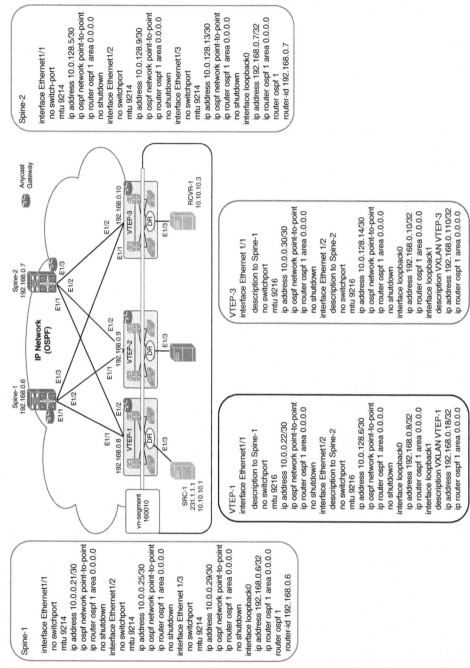

**Figure 3-7** *VXLAN Control Plane Topology*

Example 3-1 shows the spine router (Spine-1 and Spine-2) OSPF and multicast routing configuration, VTEP (VTEP-1 and VTEP-3) multicast routing configuration, and multicast routing verification.

**Example 3-1**  *PIM Multicast Configurations and Verifications*

```
Spine-1 Config
Spine-1(config)# feature pim
Spine-1(config)# interface loopback1
Spine-1(config-if)# ip address 192.168.0.100/32
Spine-1(config-if)# ip pim sparse-mode
Spine-1(config-if)# ip router ospf 1 area 0.0.0.0
Spine-1(config)# ip pim rp-address 192.168.0.100
Spine-1(config)# ip pim anycast-rp 192.168.0.100 192.168.0.6
Spine-1(config)# ip pim anycast-rp 192.168.0.100 192.168.0.7
Spine-1(config)# interface E1/1
Spine-1(config-if)# ip pim sparse-mode
Spine-1(config)# interface E1/2
Spine-1(config-if)# ip pim sparse-mode
Spine-1(config)# interface E1/3
Spine-1(config-if)# ip pim sparse-mode
Spine-1(config)# interface loopback0
Spine-1(config-if)# ip pim sparse-mode
Spine-2 Config (PIM Redundancy)
Spine-2(config)# feature pim
Spine-2(config)# interface loopback1
Spine-2(config-if)# ip address 192.168.0.100/32
Spine-2(config-if)# ip pim sparse-mode
Spine-2(config-if)# ip router ospf 1 area 0.0.0.0
Spine-2(config)# ip pim rp-address 192.168.0.100
Spine-2(config)# ip pim anycast-rp 192.168.0.100 192.168.0.6
Spine-2(config)# ip pim anycast-rp 192.168.0.100 192.168.0.7
Spine-2(config)# interface E1/1
Spine-2(config-if)# ip pim sparse-mode
Spine-2(config)# interface E1/2
Spine-2(config-if)# ip pim sparse-mode
Spine-2(config)# interface E1/3
Spine-2(config-if)# ip pim sparse-mode
Spine-2(config)# interface loopback0
Spine-2(config-if)# ip pim sparse-mode
VTEP-1 PIM Config
VTEP-1(config)# feature pim
VTEP-1(config)# ip pim rp-address 192.168.0.100
VTEP-1 (config)# interface E1/1
VTEP-1 (config-if)# ip pim sparse-mode
VTEP-1 (config)# interface E1/2
VTEP-1 (config-if)# ip pim sparse-mod
```

```
VTEP-1 (config)# interface loopback0
VTEP-1 (config-if)# ip pim sparse-mode
VTEP-1 (config)# interface loopback1
VTEP-1 (config-if)# ip pim sparse-mode
VTEP-3 PIM Config
VTEP-3(config)# feature pim
VTEP-3(config)# ip pim rp-address 192.168.0.100
VTEP-3(config)# interface E1/1
VTEP-3(config-if)# ip pim sparse-mode
VTEP-3(config)# interface E1/2
VTEP-3(config-if)# ip pim sparse-mode
VTEP-3(config)# interface loopback0
VTEP-3(config-if)# ip pim sparse-mode
VTEP-3(config)# interface loopback1
VTEP-3(config-if)# ip pim sparse-mode
Spine 1 Verifications
Spine-1# show ip pim neighbor
PIM Neighbor Status for VRF "default"
```

| Neighbor | Interface | Uptime | Expires | DR Priority | Bidir-Capable | BFD State |
|----------|-----------|--------|---------|-------------|---------------|-----------|
| 10.0.0.22 | Ethernet1/1 | 00:02:21 | 00:01:23 | 1 | yes | n/a |
| 10.0.0.26 | Ethernet1/2 | 00:01:50 | 00:01:20 | 1 | yes | n/a |
| 10.0.0.30 | Ethernet1/3 | 00:00:37 | 00:01:38 | 1 | yes | n/a |

```
Spine-1# show ip pim rp
PIM RP Status Information for VRF "default"
BSR disabled
Auto-RP disabled
BSR RP Candidate policy: None
BSR RP policy: None
Auto-RP Announce policy: None
Auto-RP Discovery policy: None
Anycast-RP 192.168.0.100 members:
  192.168.0.6* 192.168.0.7
RP: 192.168.0.100*, (0),
 uptime: 00:04:29 priority: 255,
 RP-source: (local),
 group ranges:
 224.0.0.0/4
Spine 2 Verifications
Spine-2# show ip pim neighbor
PIM Neighbor Status for VRF "default"
```

| Neighbor | Interface | Uptime | Expires | DR Priority | Bidir-Capable | BFD State |
|----------|-----------|--------|---------|-------------|---------------|-----------|
| 10.0.128.6 | Ethernet1/1 | 00:02:21 | 00:01:23 | 1 | yes | n/a |
| 10.0.128.10 | Ethernet1/2 | 00:01:50 | 00:01:20 | 1 | yes | n/a |
| 10.0.128.14 | Ethernet1/3 | 00:00:37 | 00:01:38 | 1 | yes | n/a |

```
Spine-2# show ip pim rp
PIM RP Status Information for VRF "default"
BSR disabled
Auto-RP disabled
BSR RP Candidate policy: None
BSR RP policy: None
Auto-RP Announce policy: None
Auto-RP Discovery policy: None
Anycast-RP 192.168.0.100 members:
  192.168.0.6 192.168.0.7*
RP: 192.168.0.100*, (0),
 uptime: 00:04:16 priority: 255,
 RP-source: (local),
 group ranges:
 224.0.0.0/4
```

**VTEP-1 Verifications**

```
VTEP-1# show ip pim neighbor
PIM Neighbor Status for VRF "default"
```

| Neighbor | Interface | Uptime | Expires | DR Priority | Bidir- Capable | BFD State |
|---|---|---|---|---|---|---|
| 10.0.0.21 | Ethernet1/1 | 00:03:47 | 00:01:32 | 1 | yes | n/a |
| 10.0.128.5 | Ethernet1/2 | 00:03:46 | 00:01:37 | 1 | yes | n/a |

```
VTEP-1# show ip pim rp
PIM RP Status Information for VRF "default"
BSR disabled
Auto-RP disabled
BSR RP Candidate policy: None
BSR RP policy: None
Auto-RP Announce policy: None
Auto-RP Discovery policy: None
RP: 192.168.0.100, (0),
 uptime: 00:03:53 priority: 255,
 RP-source: (local),
 group ranges:
 224.0.0.0/4
```

**VTEP-3 Verifications**

```
VTEP-3# show ip pim neighbor
PIM Neighbor Status for VRF "default"
```

| Neighbor | Interface | Uptime | Expires | DR Priority | Bidir- Capable | BFD State |
|---|---|---|---|---|---|---|
| 10.0.0.29 | Ethernet1/1 | 00:03:06 | 00:01:21 | 1 | yes | n/a |
| 10.0.128.13 | Ethernet1/2 | 00:02:48 | 00:01:35 | 1 | yes | n/a |

```
VTEP-3(config)# show ip pim rp
PIM RP Status Information for VRF "default"
BSR disabled
Auto-RP disabled
BSR RP Candidate policy: None
BSR RP policy: None
Auto-RP Announce policy: None
Auto-RP Discovery policy: None
RP: 192.168.0.100, (0),
 uptime: 00:03:11 priority: 255,
 RP-source: (local),
 group ranges:
 224.0.0.0/
```

Example 3-2 shows the VTEP (VETP-1 and VTEP-3) VXLAN and VXLAN Network Virtual Interface (NVE) configuration and status verification.

**Example 3-2**  *VXLAN Configurations and Verifications*

```
VTEP-1 Config
VTEP-1(config)# feature vn-segment-vlan-based
VTEP-1(config)# feature vn overlay
VTEP-1(config)# vlan 10
VTEP-1(config-vlan)# vn-segment 160010
VTEP-1(config)# vlan 20
VTEP-1(config-vlan)# vn-segment 160020
VTEP-1(config)# interface nve1
VTEP-1 (config-if)# source-interface loopback1
VTEP-1 (config-if)# member vni 160010 mcast-group 231.1.1.1
VTEP-1 (config-if)# member vni 160020 mcast-group 231.1.1.1
VTEP-1 (config-if)# no shutdown
VTEP-3 Config
VTEP-3(config)# feature vn-segment-vlan-based
VTEP-3(config)# feature vn overlay
VTEP-3(config)# vlan 10
VTEP-3(config-vlan)# vn-segment 160010
VTEP-3(config)# vlan 20
VTEP-3(config-vlan)# vn-segment 160020
VTEP-3(config)# interface nve1
VTEP-3(config-if)# source-interface loopback1
VTEP-3(config-if)# member vni 160010 mcast-group 231.1.1.1
VTEP-3(config-if)# member vni 160020 mcast-group 231.1.1.1
VTEP-3(config-if)# no shutdown
VTEP-1 Verifications
VTEP-1# show nve vni
```

```
Codes: CP - Control Plane      DP - Data Plane
       UC - Unconfigured       SA - Suppress ARP
       SU - Suppress Unknown Unicast

Interface VNI      Multicast-group   State Mode Type [BD/VRF]        Flags
--------- -------- ----------------- ----- ---- ----------------- -----
nve1      160010   231.1.1.1         Up    DP   L2   [10]
nve1      160020   231.1.1.1         Up    DP   L2   [20]


VTEP-1# show vxlan
Vlan           VN-Segment
====           ==========
10             160010
20             160020
VTEP-1# ping 10.10.10.3
PING 10.10.10.3 (10.10.10.3) : 56 data bytes
64 bytes from 10.10.10.3: icmp_seq=0 ttl=254 time=8.114 ms
64 bytes from 10.10.10.3: icmp_seq=1 ttl=254 time=5.641 ms
64 bytes from 10.10.10.3: icmp_seq=2 ttl=254 time=6.213 ms
64 bytes from 10.10.10.3: icmp_seq=3 ttl=254 time=6.119 ms
VTEP-1# show nve peers
Interface Peer-IP          State LearnType Uptime   Router-Mac
--------- ---------------  ----- --------- -------- -----------------
nve1      192.168.0.110    Up    DP        00:09:08 n/a
VTEP-1# show ip mroute
IP Multicast Routing Table for VRF "default"
(*, 231.1.1.1/32), uptime: 00:10:38, nve ip pim
  Incoming interface: Ethernet1/1, RPF nbr: 10.0.0.29
  Outgoing interface list: (count: 1)
    nve1, uptime: 00:10:38, nve
(192.168.0.18/32, 231.1.1.1/32), uptime: 00:02:34, ip mrib pim
  Incoming interface: Ethernet1/2, RPF nbr: 10.0.128.13
  Outgoing interface list: (count: 1)
    nve1, uptime: 00:02:34, mrib
(*, 232.0.0.0/8), uptime: 00:17:03, pim ip
  Incoming interface: Null, RPF nbr: 0.0.0.0
  Outgoing interface list: (count: 0)
```

**VTEP-3 Verifications**

```
VTEP-3# show nve vni
Codes: CP - Control Plane      DP - Data Plane
       UC - Unconfigured       SA - Suppress ARP
       SU - Suppress Unknown Unicast

Interface  VNI     Multicast-group   State Mode Type [BD/VRF]        Flag
---------  ------- ----------------- ----- ---- ----------------- -----
nve1       160010  231.1.1.1         Up    DP   L2   [10]
nve1       160020  231.1.1.1         Up    DP   L2   [20]
```

```
VTEP-3# show vxlan
Vlan            VN-Segment
====            ==========
10              160010
20              160020
VTEP-3# ping 10.10.10.1
PING 10.10.10.1 (10.10.10.1) : 56 data bytes
64 bytes from 10.10.10.1: icmp_seq=0 ttl=254 time=7.212 ms
64 bytes from 10.10.10.1: icmp_seq=1 ttl=254 time=6.243 ms
64 bytes from 10.10.10.1: icmp_seq=2 ttl=254 time=5.268 ms
64 bytes from 10.10.10.1: icmp_seq=3 ttl=254 time=6.397 ms
VTEP-1# show nve peers
Interface  Peer-IP         State LearnType Uptime    Router-Mac
---------  --------------- ----- --------- --------  -----------------
nve1       192.168.0.18    Up    DP        00:09:08  n/a
VTEP-3# show ip mroute
IP Multicast Routing Table for VRF "default"
(*, 231.1.1.1/32), uptime: 00:10:38, nve ip pim
 Incoming interface: Ethernet1/1, RPF nbr: 10.0.0.29
  Outgoing interface list: (count: 1)
    nve1, uptime: 00:10:38, nve
(192.168.0.18/32, 231.1.1.1/32), uptime: 00:02:34, ip mrib pim
  Incoming interface: Ethernet1/2, RPF nbr: 10.0.128.13
  Outgoing interface list: (count: 1)
    nve1, uptime: 00:02:34, mrib
(192.168.0.110/32, 231.1.1.1/32), uptime: 00:10:38, nve mrib ip pim
  Incoming interface: loopback1, RPF nbr: 192.168.0.110
  Outgoing interface list: (count: 1)
    Ethernet1/2, uptime: 00:09:39, pim
(*, 232.0.0.0/8), uptime: 00:17:03, pim ip
 Incoming interface: Null, RPF nbr: 0.0.0.0
 Outgoing interface list: (count: 0)
```

## Exam Preparation Tasks

As mentioned in the Introduction, you have a couple of choices for exam preparation: the exercises here, Chapter 21, "Final Preparation," and the exam simulation questions in the Pearson Test Prep software online.

## Review All Key Topics

Review the most important topics in the chapter, noted with the key topic icon in the outer margin of the page. Table 3-7 lists a reference to these key topics and the page numbers on which each is found.

**Table 3-7**   Key Topics for Chapter 3

| Key Topic Element | Description | Page |
|---|---|---|
| Section | VXLAN Encapsulation and Packet Format | 152 |
| Figure 3-1 | VXLAN Packet Format | 152 |
| Figure 3-2 | VXLAN Tunnel Endpoint (VTEP) | 153 |
| Section | Virtual Network Identifier (VNI) | 153 |
| Section | VXLAN Control Plane | 154 |
| Figure 3-3 | VXLAN Multicast Group in Transport Network | 155 |
| Figure 3-4 | VXLAN Multicast Control Plane | 155 |
| Section | VXLAN MPBGP EVPN Control Plane | 156 |

## Define Key Terms

Define the following key terms from this chapter, and check your answers in the Glossary.

Address Resolution Protocol (ARP); broadcast, unknown unicast, and multicast (BUM); Cisco Nexus; Cisco NX-OS; equal-cost multipath (ECMP); Ethernet VPN (EVPN); Internet Group Management Protocol (IGMP); local-area network (LAN); Media Access Control (MAC); Protocol Independent Multicast (PIM); User Datagram Protocol (UDP); virtual LAN (VLAN); virtual port channels (vPCs); virtual private network (VPN); virtual routing and forwarding (VRF); wide-area network (WAN)

## References

Cisco Nexus 9000 Series NX-OS VXLAN Configuration Guide, Release 10.3(x): https://www.cisco.com/c/en/us/td/docs/dcn/nx-os/nexus9000/103x/configuration/vxlan/cisco-nexus-9000-series-nx-os-vxlan-configuration-guide-release-103x.html

Relevant CiscoLive Presentations: https://ciscolive.com

A Summary of Cisco VXLAN Control Planes: Multicast, Unicast, MP-BGP EVPN: https://blogs.cisco.com/perspectives/a-summary-of-cisco-vxlan-control-planes-multicast-unicast-mp-bgp-evpn-2

# CHAPTER 4

# Describe Cisco Application Centric Infrastructure

The amount of data that businesses and individuals create is increasing rapidly year after year. As a result, data center networks continue to grow, and they are becoming more and more complicated to manage and monitor using traditional tools. Automation and programmability across data centers will be necessary to enhance network performance, redundancy, and visibility and also to reduce complexity. A software-defined networking (SDN) framework will reduce complexity and improve performance by decoupling control from underlying hardware and assigning it to a centralized software-based controller.

## This chapter covers the following key topics:

**Cisco Application Centric Infrastructure (ACI) Overview:** This section discusses the Cisco Application Policy Infrastructure Controller (APIC) and also discusses ACI automation and policy-driven application profiles, software flexibility, and hardware performance scalability.

**Cisco ACI Initial Setup, Fabric Discovery, Fabric Upgrade, and Fabric Access Policies:** This section discusses the ACI spine and leaf switch discovery and the ACI fabric upgrade process.

**Cisco ACI Fabric Building Blocks, Policy Model, and VMM Domains:** This section discusses the ACI fabric building blocks and traffic flow, focusing on east-west data center traffic. You learn how ACI tenants manage applications and networking and how servers include separation of duties by domain owner. This section also discusses how the Virtual Machine Manager (VMM) supports integration with multivendor hypervisors and provides configuration examples.

## "Do I Know This Already?" Quiz

The "Do I Know This Already?" quiz enables you to assess whether you should read this entire chapter thoroughly or jump to the "Exam Preparation Tasks" section. If you are in doubt about your answers to these questions or your own assessment of your knowledge of the topics, read the entire chapter. Table 4-1 lists the major headings in this chapter and their corresponding "Do I Know This Already?" quiz questions. You can find the answers in Appendix A, "Answers to the 'Do I Know This Already?' Quizzes."

**Table 4-1** "Do I Know This Already?" Section-to-Question Mapping

| Foundation Topics Section | Questions |
| --- | --- |
| Cisco Application Centric Infrastructure (ACI) Overview | 1–2 |
| Cisco ACI Initial Setup, Fabric Discovery, Fabric Upgrade, and Fabric Access Policies | 3–5 |
| Cisco ACI Fabric Building Blocks, Policy Model, and VMM Domains | 6–7 |

1. Which options outline the design requirements for spine nodes in a CLOS design? (Choose two answers.)

    a. Host connectivity

    b. High 40–100 Gbps ports

    c. Leaf-to-spine full-mesh interconnectivity

    d. APIC-to-leaf interconnectivity

2. The Cisco Application Policy Infrastructure Controller serves as the single point of automation and fabric element management in which environments? (Choose two answers.)

    a. Cloud-based environment

    b. Storage environment

    c. Physical server environment

    d. Virtual environment

3. In a Cisco ACI cluster, which protocol does the Cisco APIC use to discover new nodes?

    a. CDP

    b. DHCP

    c. LLDP

    d. IS-IS

4. Which network protocol is used for Cisco ACI fabric data plane forwarding?

    a. IS-IS

    b. FabricPath

    c. VLAN

    d. VXLAN

5. What is the minimum number of Cisco APIC controllers required to form a Cisco APIC cluster?

    a. Two controllers, N+1 redundancy

    b. Three controllers, N+2 redundancy

    c. One controller

    d. Three controllers, 3N redundancy

6. When you are creating endpoint groups in the Cisco ACI, what does this automatically create on an associated DVS?

   a. Port groups

   b. Access list

   c. VLAN

   d. VXLAN

7. Which options are supported by the Cisco ACI contract filters? (Choose two answers.)

   a. Ethertype

   b. COS marking

   c. TCP source port

   d. Logging type

## Foundation Topics

# Cisco Application Centric Infrastructure (ACI) Overview

The Cisco Application Centric Infrastructure, or ACI, is taking data centers to the next step in automation. The ACI is Cisco's data center software-defined networking (SDN) architecture. SDN enables the network to be centrally managed and automatically adjusts configuration to meet application needs. The Cisco ACI disassociates the control plane from the data (physical) plane. No more configurations are changed across an endless number of devices. As a result, the ACI architecture automates IT tasks, enhances business agility, and accelerates the data center.

Applications today behave differently than they did in the past. They are highly virtualized, run on multiple hypervisors, and are more distributed than ever. They also are developed differently. These newer applications require rapid and continuous delivery, shifting the communication needs within the data center. This new model is a transformation in data center design and scale, IT infrastructure management, provisioning, and consumption. Ease of provisioning and speed are now critical performance metrics for a data center network infrastructure that supports physical, virtual, and cloud environments without compromising scalability or security.

The Cisco ACI uses the concept of endpoints and policies. The endpoints are virtual machines (VMs) or physical servers. In network architecture designs, several endpoints have the same requirements, so they can be grouped together under endpoint groups. Then policies can be defined to determine with whom endpoint groups can communicate; for instance, a group of web servers may need to communicate with a group of application servers. The policy also defines other key parameters, such as which endpoint groups can access each other (or not), as well as quality of service (QoS) parameters and other services. Cisco ACI benefits include the following:

- **Centralized policy-defined automation management**

  - Holistic application-based solution that delivers flexibility and automation for agile IT

  - Automatic fabric deployment and configuration with a single point of management

  - Automation of repetitive tasks, reducing configuration errors

- **Real-time visibility and application health score**

  - Centralized real-time health monitoring of physical and virtual networks

  - Instant visibility into application performance combined with intelligent placement decisions

  - Faster troubleshooting for day-2 operation

- **Open and comprehensive end-to-end security**

  - Open APIs, open standards, and open-source elements that enable software flexibility for DevOps teams, and firewall and application delivery controller (ADC) ecosystem partner integration

  - Automatic capture of all configuration changes integrated with existing audit and compliance tracking solutions

  - Detailed role-based access control (RBAC) with fine-grained fabric segmentation

- **Application agility**

  - Management of application lifecycle from development to deployment to decommissioning in minutes

  - Automatic application deployment and faster provisioning based on predefined profiles

  - Continuous and rapid delivery of virtualized and distributed applications

The Cisco ACI architecture is a combination of high-performance hardware and software innovation and intelligence integrated with two important concepts from Cisco SDN solutions: overlays and centralized control.

The Cisco ACI solution consists of two main components following building blocks (see Figure 4-1):

- Cisco Application Policy Infrastructure Controller (APIC)

- Cisco Nexus 9000 Series spine and leaf switches for Cisco ACI

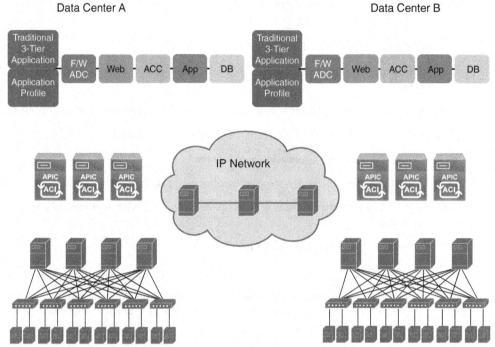

**Figure 4-1**  *Cisco ACI Architectural Building Blocks*

An ACI ecosystem handles the interaction with other solutions besides Nexus 9000 switches, which include Cisco Adaptive Security Virtual Appliances (ASAv) firewalls, Cisco Application Virtual Switch (AVS), VM managers such as VMware vCenter, Microsoft System Center Virtual Machine Manager (SCVMM), application delivery controllers from companies such as F5 and Citrix, and cloud orchestration systems such as OpenStack.

## Cisco Application Policy Infrastructure Controller

The Application Policy Infrastructure Controller is the main architectural component of the Cisco ACI solution. The APIC is the unified point of automation and management for the Cisco ACI fabric, policy enforcement, and health monitoring. The controller optimizes performance and manages and operates a scalable multitenant Cisco ACI fabric.

The APIC appliance or virtual machine is deployed as a cluster. A minimum of three infrastructure controllers are configured in a cluster to provide control of the scale-out Cisco ACI fabric (see Figure 4-2). The ultimate size of the controller cluster is directly proportionate to the size of the Cisco ACI deployment and is based on the transaction-rate requirements. Any controller in the cluster can service any user for any operation, and a controller can be transparently added to or removed from the cluster.

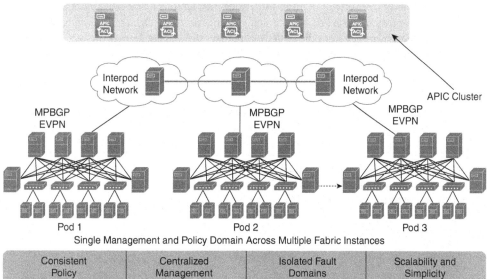

**Figure 4-2**  *Cisco ACI Fabric*

The APIC cluster is composed of multiple APIC controllers that provide operators a unified real-time monitoring, diagnostic, and configuration management capability for the ACI fabric. To assure optimal system performance, follow these general guidelines for making changes to or managing the APIC cluster:

■ Cisco recommends that you have at least three active APICs in a cluster, along with additional standby APICs. A cluster size of three, five, or seven APICs is recommended. A cluster size of four or six APICs is not recommended.

■ Disregard cluster information from APICs that are not currently in the cluster; they do not provide accurate cluster information.

■ Cluster slots contain an APIC ChassisID. After you configure a slot, it remains unavailable until you decommission the APIC with the assigned ChassisID.

■ If an APIC firmware upgrade is in progress, wait for it to complete and the cluster to be fully fit before proceeding with any other changes to the cluster.

■ When moving an APIC, first ensure that you have a healthy cluster. After verifying the health of the APIC cluster, choose the APIC you intend to shut down. After the APIC has shut down, move the APIC, reconnect it, and then turn it back on. From the GUI, verify that all the controllers in the cluster return to a fully fit state.

**NOTE**  Move only one APIC at a time.

■ When an APIC cluster is split into two or more groups, the ID of a node is changed, and the changes are not synchronized across all APICs. This can cause inconsistency in the node IDs between APICs, and also the affected leaf nodes may not appear in the inventory in the APIC GUI. When you split an APIC cluster, decommission the affected leaf nodes from the APIC and register them again so that the inconsistency is in the node IDs is resolved, and the health status of the APICs in a cluster is in a fully fit state.

■ Before configuring the APIC cluster, ensure that all the APICs are running the same firmware version. Initial clustering of APICs running differing versions is an unsupported operation and may cause problems within the cluster.

The ACI fabric renders policies from the APIC into a concrete model that runs in the physical infrastructure. The concrete model is analogous to compiled software; it is the form of the model that the switch operating system can execute. Figure 4-3 shows the flows of the logical model to the concrete model and the switch OS.

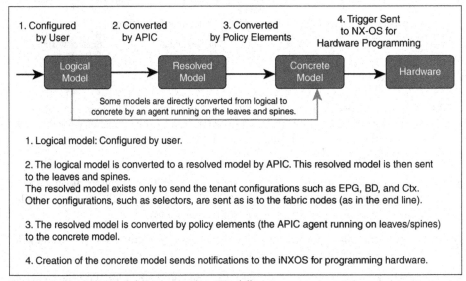

**Figure 4-3**  *ACI Model Conversation Workflow*

All the switch nodes contain a complete copy of the concrete model. When an administrator creates a policy in the APIC that represents a configuration, the APIC updates the logical model. The APIC then performs the intermediate step of creating a fully elaborated policy that it pushes into all the switch nodes where the concrete model is updated.

The APIC is responsible for fabric activation, switch firmware management, network policy configuration, and instantiation. Although the APIC acts as the centralized policy and network management engine for the fabric, it is completely removed from the data path, including the forwarding topology. Therefore, the fabric can still forward traffic even when communication with the APIC is lost.

**NOTE**   The Cisco Nexus 9000 Series switches can only execute the concrete model. Each switch has a copy of the concrete model. If the APIC goes offline, the fabric keeps functioning, but modifications to the fabric policies are not possible.

## Cisco Nexus 9000 Series Spine and Leaf Switches for Cisco ACI

Cisco Nexus 9000 Series switches offer modular and fixed 1-, 10-, 40-, and 100-Gigabit Ethernet switches. Nexus 9000 configurations can operate either in Cisco NX-OS standalone mode for compatibility and consistency with the current Cisco Nexus switches or run in ACI mode to take full advantage of the APIC's application policy-driven services and infrastructure automation features.

Cisco Nexus 9000 Series switches are designed for leaf-and-spine APIC deployment. Leaf-and-spine is a two-tier CLOS "fat-tree" architecture, as shown in Figure 4-4. Every lower-tier switch (leaf layer) is connected to each of the top-tier switches (spine layer) in a full-mesh topology. The leaf layer consists of access switches that connect to devices such as servers. The spine layer is the backbone of the network and is responsible for interconnecting all leaf switches. Every leaf switch connects to every spine switch in the fabric. The path is randomly chosen so that the traffic load is evenly distributed among the top-tier switches. If one of the top-tier switches were to fail, it would only slightly degrade performance throughout the data center.

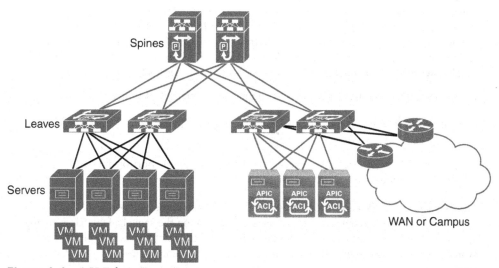

**Figure 4-4**   *ACI Fabric Overview*

Starting with the Cisco APIC Release 4.1(1), you can now create a multitier fabric topology that corresponds to the core-aggregation-access architecture. The new design for the Cisco ACI incorporates the addition of a tier-2 leaf layer for connectivity to hosts or servers on the downlink ports and connectivity to the leaf layer (aggregation) on the uplink ports, as shown in Figure 4-5.

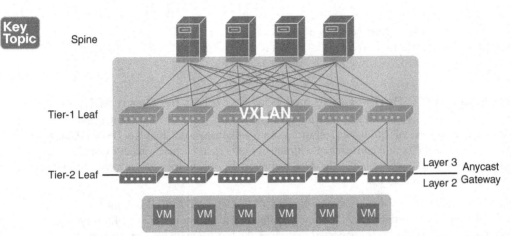

**Figure 4-5**  *Cisco ACI Multitier Architecture (Spine, Tier-1 Leaf, and Tier-2 Leaf) Topology*

In a multitier topology, all switch-to-switch links must be configured as fabric ports. You can also use ports that, by default, are downlink ports by configuring them to be fabric ports. Special care must be taken when choosing which port from tier-2 leaf switches is connected to tier-1 leaf switches. The reason is that the downlink to fabric link port conversion can be done only after the APIC discovers a leaf. If the APIC is connected to a tier-2 leaf, at least one tier-2 leaf default fabric port must be connected to a default fabric port on a tier-1 leaf. By ensuring this, the APIC can discover both the tier-2 leaf that is attached to the APIC and the tier-1 leaf that the tier-2 leaf is attached to. After this initial discovery, you can convert additional ports on the tier-1 and tier-2 leaf switches to be fabric ports. Also, each tier-1 leaf should have at least one default fabric port connected to a tier-2 leaf port.

In summary, these are the connectivity requirements for tier-2 leaf switches:

- If the APIC is connected to a tier-2 leaf, one default fabric port of the tier-2 leaf must be connected to a default fabric port of a tier-1 leaf.

- If no APIC is connected to a tier-2 leaf, one default fabric port of the tier-2 leaf must be connected to any port of a tier-1 leaf.

The ACI fabric provides consistent low-latency forwarding across high-bandwidth links (40 Gbps and 100 Gbps). Traffic with source and destination on the same leaf switch is handled locally, and all other traffic travels from the ingress leaf to the egress leaf through a spine switch. Although this architecture appears as two hops from a physical perspective, it is a single Layer 3 hop because the fabric operates as a single Layer 3 switch.

The Cisco Nexus 9000 product family consists of

- **Cisco Nexus 9800 Series Modular Chassis**

  - ACI or NX-OS mode

  - Cisco 9808 8-slot chassis

  - Cisco Nexus 9800 36-port QSFP-DD 400G line card with MACsec

  - Each 400G port also supports 2× 100G, 4× 100, 4× 25, and 4× 10G breakout options.

- **Cisco Nexus 9500 Series Modular Chassis**

  - ACI or NX-OS mode

  - Cisco 9504 (4-slot), 9508 (8-slot), and 9516 (16-slot) chassis

  - This chassis supports 10GE, 40GE, 100GE, and 400GE modules.

- **Cisco Nexus 9500 Series Modular Spine Switch Line Cards** (see Figure 4-6)

  - N9K-X9716D-GX: 16-port 400-Gigabit Ethernet Quad Small Form-Factor Pluggable Double Density (QSFP-DD) line card

  - N9K-X9736C-FX: 36-port 100-Gigabit Ethernet Quad Small Form-Factor Pluggable 28 (QSFP28) line card

  - N9K-X9732C-EX: 32-port 100-Gigabit Ethernet Quad Small Form-Factor Pluggable 28 (QSFP28) line card

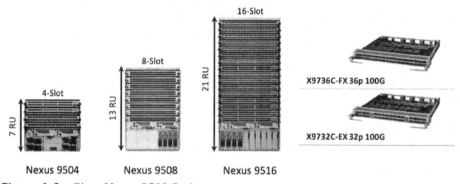

**Figure 4-6**  *Cisco Nexus 9500 Series*

- **Cisco Nexus 9300 Fixed Spine and Leaf Series** (see Figure 4-7)

  - Cisco Nexus 9316D: 16 × 400/100-Gbps QSFP-DD ports

  - Cisco Nexus 93600CD switch: 28 × 100/40-Gbps Quad Small Form-Factor Pluggable (QSFP28) and 8 × 400/100-Gbps QSFP-DD ports

  - Cisco Nexus 9364C Switch: 64 × 100/40-Gbps Quad Small Form-Factor Pluggable (QSFP28)

  - Cisco Nexus 9332C: 32-port 40/100G QSFP28 ports and 2-port 1/10G SFP+ ports

  - Cisco Nexus 9332D-GX2A: 32 × 400-Gbps QSFP-DD and 2 × 1/10-Gbps SFP+ ports

  - Cisco Nexus 9348D-GX2A: 48 × 400-Gbps QSFP-DD and 2 × 1/10-Gbps SFP+ ports

  - Cisco Nexus 9364D-GX2A: 64 × 400-Gbps QSFP-DD and 2 × 1/10-Gbps SFP+ ports

  - Cisco Nexus 93108TC-FX3P Switch: 48 × 100M/1/2.5/5/10G BASE-T ports and 6 × 40/100-Gbps Quad Small Form-Factor Pluggable 28 (QSFP28) ports

## Cisco Nexus 9300 CloudScale 40/100/400G Switches

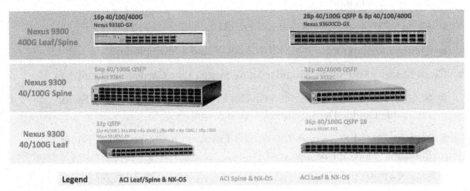

**Figure 4-7**   *Cisco Nexus 9300 Series*

# Cisco ACI Initial Setup, Fabric Discovery, Fabric Upgrade, and Fabric Access Policies

Cisco ACI technology enables you to integrate virtual and physical workloads in a programmable, multi-hypervisor fabric to build a multiservice or cloud data center. The Cisco ACI fabric consists of discrete components that operate as routers and switches, but it is provisioned and monitored as a single entity that allows application requirements via polces to define the network.

## Cisco ACI Initial Setup

Cisco ACI Fabric discovery prerequisites include

- Initial cabling of the Cisco ACI fabric

- Initial setup of the Cisco APIC cluster over the out-of-band network

- Running the same version of firmware on Cisco APIC nodes and switches

It is important to follow the mandatory prerequisites for the cabling of the Cisco ACI:

- Spines can be connected only to leaves. Spines cannot be interconnected.

- Leaves can be connected only to spines. There should be no cabling between the leaves.

- All endpoints, Layer 2, Layer 3, and Layer 4 through Layer 7 devices must connect to leaves.

- A Cisco APIC must be attached to a leaf and dual-homed, which means that it must be connected to two different leaves.

The Cisco ACI Fabric discovery is an automated process that uses the Link Layer Discovery Protocol (LLDP) and DHCP-based approach to discover the switch nodes, assign infrastructure VTEP addresses, and install the needed firmware. Before the start of the discovery process, you need to perform a minimal bootstrap configuration in the Cisco APIC console.

When you launch the Cisco APIC for the first time, the console presents a series of initial setup options. For many options, you can press Enter to choose the default setting that is displayed in brackets. At any point in the setup dialog, you can restart the dialog from the beginning by pressing Ctrl+C.

The following parameters are configured during the initial setup:

- **Fabric name, number of controllers, controller ID, and controller name:** First, you have to enter the fabric name, number of controllers (the default is 3), and controller ID. The controller ID is a unique ID number for the Cisco APIC instance (1, 2, or 3) and the controller name.

- **Address pool for TEP addresses:** Enter the address pool for tunnel endpoint (TEP) addresses. The default IP address pool for the TEP tunnel endpoint addresses is 10.0.0.0/16. This value is for the infrastructure virtual routing and forwarding (VRF) only. This subnet should not overlap with any other routed subnets in your network. If this subnet does overlap with another subnet, change this subnet to a different /16 subnet. The minimum supported subnet for a 3-APIC cluster is a /23.

- **VLAN ID for the infrastructure network:** Enter the VLAN ID for the infrastructure network. This infrastructure VLAN provides APIC-to-switch communication, including virtual switches. Reserve this VLAN for APIC use only. This VLAN ID must not be used elsewhere in your environment and must not overlap with any other reserved VLANs on other platforms. Cisco recommends VLAN 3967.

- **Out-of-band management IP address:** Enter the IP address for the out-of-band management, which is the IP address that you use to access the Cisco APIC through the GUI, CLI, or API.

- **Default gateway IP address:** Enter the IP address of the default gateway for communication to external networks using out-of-band management.

- **Admin password:** Set the password. The system administrator's password must be at least eight characters long with one special character.

If you are using a Cisco Integrated Management Controller (CIMC) for your setup, use only the port-side utility console port with the breakout cable. Set up the CIMC first, and then access the Cisco APIC through the CIMC KVM or continue to access the Cisco APIC locally through the port-side utility console port. Do not use the RJ-45 console port unless access to the port side is restricted. If you choose the CIMC KVM access, you will have remote access available later, which is required during operations.

It is recommended not to modify any parameters using CIMC. If there are any issues, ensure that the default setting for CIMC management node is dedicated mode and not shared. If dedicated mode is not used, it can prevent the discovery of fabric nodes.

Do not upgrade software or firmware using the CIMC user interface, XML, or SSH interfaces unless the modified property and software or firmware version are supported with your specific Cisco APIC version.

Set the NIC mode to dedicated, when setting up the CIMC, in the CIMC Configuration Utility.

During the initial setup, the system will prompt you to select IPv4, IPv6, or dual stack configuration. Choosing dual stack will enable you to access the Cisco APIC and Cisco ACI fabric out-of-band management interfaces with either IPv4 or IPv6 addresses.

The Cold Standby functionality for a Cisco APIC cluster enables you to operate the Cisco APICs in a cluster in active/standby mode. In a Cisco APIC cluster, the designated active Cisco APICs share the load, and the designated standby Cisco APICs can act as a replacement for any of the Cisco APICs in an active cluster.

An admin user can set up the Cold Standby functionality when the Cisco APIC is launched for the first time. We recommend that you have at least three active Cisco APICs in a cluster and one or more standby Cisco APICs. An admin user must initiate the switchover to replace an active Cisco APIC with a standby Cisco APIC.

Table 4-2 shows an active APIC setup, whereas Table 4-3 shows a standby APIC setup.

**Table 4-2**   Active APIC Setup Parameters

| Name | Description | Default Value |
|------|-------------|---------------|
| Fabric name | Fabric domain name. | ACI Fabric1 |
| Fabric ID | Fabric ID. | 1 |
| Number of active controllers | Cluster size. | 3<br>**NOTE:** When setting up the APIC in active/standby mode, you must have at least three active APICs in a cluster. |
| POD ID | POD ID. | 1 |
| Standby controller | Setup standby controller. | No |
| APIC-X | The Cisco APIC-X is a dedicated APIC cluster for running telemetry applications. | No |
| Controller ID | Unique ID number for the active APIC instance. | Valid range: 1–32 |
| Controller name | Active controller name. | apic1 |
| IP address pool for tunnel endpoint addresses | Tunnel endpoint address pool. | 10.0.0.0/16<br>This value is for the infrastructure Virtual Routing and Forwarding (VRF) only. This subnet should not overlap with any other routed subnets in your network. If this subnet does overlap with another subnet, change this subnet to a different /16 subnet. The minimum supported subnet for a three-APIC cluster is /23. |

| Name | Description | Default Value |
|---|---|---|
| VLAN ID for infrastructure network | Infrastructure VLAN for APIC-to-switch communication including virtual switches.<br><br>**NOTE:** Reserve this VLAN for APIC use only. The infrastructure VLAN ID must not be used elsewhere in your environment and must not overlap with any other reserved VLANs on other platforms. | — |
| IP address pool for bridge domain multicast address (GIPo) | IP addresses used for fabric multicast. For the Cisco APIC in a Cisco ACI multisite topology, this GIPo address can be the same across sites. | 225.0.0.0/15<br><br>Valid range: 225.0.0.0/15 to 231.254.0.0/15, prefixlen must be 15 (128k IPs) |
| IPv4/IPv6 addresses for the out-of-band management | IP address that you use to access the APIC through the GUI, CLI, or API. | — |
| IPv4/IPv6 addresses of the default gateway | Gateway address for communication to external networks using out-of-band management. | — |
| Management interface speed/duplex mode | Interface speed and duplex mode for the out-of-band management interface. | auto<br>Valid values are as follows:<br>auto<br>10baseT/Half<br>10baseT/Full<br>100baseT/Half<br>100baseT/Full<br>1000baseT/Full |
| Strong password check | Check for a strong password. | [Y] |
| Password | Password of the system administrator. This password must be at least eight characters with one special character. | — |

**Table 4-3** Standby APIC Setup Parameters

| Name | Description | Default Value |
|------|-------------|---------------|
| Fabric name | Fabric domain name. | ACI Fabric1 |
| Fabric ID | Fabric ID. | 1 |
| Number of active controllers | Cluster size. | 3<br><br>NOTE: When setting up the APIC in active/standby mode, you must have at least three active APICs in a cluster. |
| POD ID | POD ID. | 1 |
| Standby controller | Setup standby controller. | Yes |
| Standby Controller ID | Unique ID number for the standby APIC instance. | Recommended range: >20 |
| APIC-X | The Cisco APIC-X is a dedicated APIC cluster for running telemetry applications. | No |
| Controller ID | Unique ID number for the active APIC instance. | N/A |
| IP address pool for tunnel endpoint addresses | Tunnel endpoint address pool. | 10.0.0.0/16<br><br>This value is for the infrastructure Virtual Routing and Forwarding (VRF) only. This subnet should not overlap with any other routed subnets in your network. If this subnet does overlap with another subnet, change this subnet to a different /16 subnet. The minimum supported subnet for a three-APIC cluster is /23. |
| VLAN ID for infrastructure network | Infrastructure VLAN for APIC-to-switch communication including virtual switches.<br><br>NOTE: Reserve this VLAN for APIC use only. The infrastructure VLAN ID must not be used elsewhere in your environment and must not overlap with any other reserved VLANs on other platforms. | — |
| IPv4/IPv6 addresses for the out-of-band management | IP address that you use to access the APIC through the GUI, CLI, or API. | — |

| Name | Description | Default Value |
|---|---|---|
| IPv4/IPv6 addresses of the default gateway | Gateway address for communication to external networks using out-of-band management. | — |
| Management interface speed/duplex mode | Interface speed and duplex mode for the out-of-band management interface. | auto<br>Valid values are as follows:<br>auto<br>10baseT/Half<br>10baseT/Full<br>100baseT/Half<br>100baseT/Full<br>1000baseT/Full |
| Strong password check | Check for a strong password. | [Y] |
| Password | Password of the system administrator. This password must be at least eight characters with one special character. | — |

**NOTE**  To change the VLAN ID after the initial APIC setup, export your configurations, rebuild the fabric with a new infrastructure VLAN ID, and import the configurations so that the fabric does not revert to the old infrastructure VLAN ID.

## Cisco ACI Fabric Discovery

The Cisco APIC is a physically distributed but logically centralized controller that provides DHCP, bootstrap configuration, and image management to the fabric for automated start-up and upgrades, as shown in Figure 4-8. The Cisco Nexus ACI fabric software is bundled as an ISO image, which can be installed on the Cisco APIC appliance server through the serial console. The Cisco Nexus ACI Software ISO contains the Cisco APIC image, the firmware image for the leaf node, the firmware image for the spine node, default fabric infrastructure policies, and the protocols required for operation.

The APIC provides a simple and automated policy-based provisioning upgrade process and automated image management. Because ACI data centers can be very large, configuring switches or interfaces individually does not scale well, even using scripts. APIC pod, controller, switch, module, and interface selectors enable symmetric configurations across the fabric. To apply a symmetric configuration, an administrator defines switch profiles that associate interface configurations in a single policy group. The configuration is then rapidly deployed to all interfaces in that profile without the need to configure them individually.

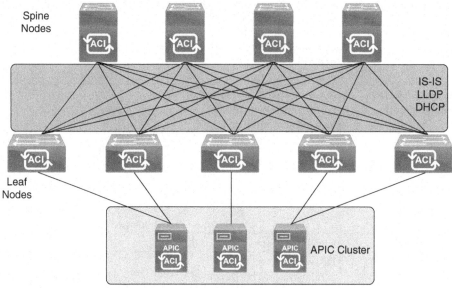

**Figure 4-8**    *Startup Discovery Configurations*

## Startup with Cisco ACI Fabric Discovery and Configuration

The Cisco ACI fabric bootstrap sequence begins when the Cisco ACI fabric is booted with factory-installed images on all the switches. Cisco Nexus 9000 switches running ACI firmware and Cisco APICs use a reserved overlay for the boot process. This infrastructure space is hard-coded on the switches. The Cisco APIC can connect to a leaf through the default overlay, or it can use a locally significant identifier. The Cisco ACI fabric is brought up in a cascading manner, starting with the leaf node directly attached to the Cisco APIC. Link Layer Discovery Protocol (LLDP) and control-plane IS-IS convergence occurs in parallel to this boot process.

All Cisco ACI fabric management communication within the fabric takes place in the infrastructure space using internal private IP addresses, the address assigned from an internal DHCP pool (TEP pool). Although Tunnel End Points (TEPs) are located inside the fabric, in some scenarios the TEP range may be extended beyond the fabric. Therefore, it is not advisable to use overlapping addresses between the internal TEP range and the external network in your data center. To avoid issues with address exhaustion in the future, Cisco strongly recommends that you allocate a /16 or /17 range for the TEP pool, if possible. This addressing scheme allows Cisco APICs to communicate with fabric nodes and other Cisco APICs in the cluster. The Cisco APICs discover the IP address and node information of other Cisco APICs in the cluster using the LLDP-based discovery process.

In this discovery process, a fabric node is considered active when the APIC and node can exchange heartbeats through the Intra-Fabric Messaging (IFM) process. The APIC also uses the IFM process to push policy to the fabric leaf nodes.

Fabric discovery happens in three stages, as shown in Figure 4-9. The leaf node directly connected to the APIC is discovered in the first stage. The second stage of discovery brings in the spines connected to that initial seed leaf. Then the third stage processes the discovery of the other leaf nodes and APICs in the cluster.

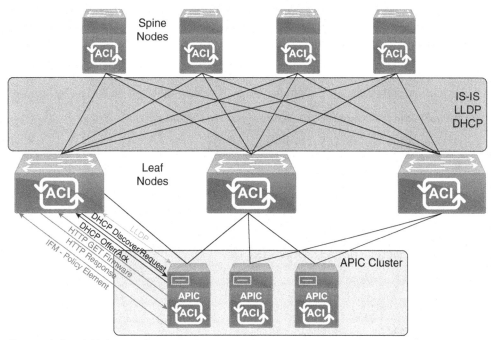

**Figure 4-9**  *ACI Auto Fabric Discovery*

Figure 4-9 illustrates the discovery process for switches that are directly connected to the APIC. The steps are as follows:

1. Link Layer Discovery Protocol (LLDP) Neighbor Discovery

2. Tunnel End Point (TEP) IP address assignment to the node from the TEP address pool (the default TEP pool is 10.0.0.0/16)

3. Node software upgraded if necessary, downloading the new software from APIC repository

4. Policy Element IFM setup

Prior to this automated process, a minimal bootstrap configuration must be performed on the Cisco APIC.

## Fabric Upgrade

Fabric upgrades are simple because the APIC allows you to manage upgrades for the entire fabric from a single dashboard (centrally). The Cisco APIC acts as the repository of the image and as the booting server. Leaf switches and spine switches have in-band connectivity to the Cisco APIC, and when upgrading, the switches download the firmware from the Cisco APIC. To complete an upgrade successfully, you must have connectivity from the leaf switches and spine switches that you are upgrading to the Cisco APIC. To maintain connectivity, you should define a minimum of two maintenance groups and upgrade one group at a time. Wait until the first group has successfully completed the upgrade before upgrading the second group.

At a high level, the steps to upgrade or downgrade the Cisco ACI fabric are as follows. (The procedure for upgrading and downgrading are the same unless stated otherwise in the release notes of a specific release.)

- Ensure that you have the required CIMC version required for the Cisco APIC upgrade.

- Download the Cisco ACI controller image (the Cisco APIC image) into the repository.

- Download the Cisco ACI switch image into the repository.

- Upgrade the cluster of the Cisco APICs.

- Verify whether the fabric is operational and the APIC cluster is "fully fit" before proceeding.

- Divide the switches into multiple groups, and upgrade the switches by group, verifying that the fabric is operational between switch group upgrades. For example, assume that you divided the switches into two groups—East and West. You could then go through the following upgrade process:

  - Upgrade the East group of switches.

  - Verify that the fabric is operational.

  - Upgrade the West group of switches.

  - Verify that the fabric is operational.

## Cisco ACI Fabric Access Policies

Fabric policies govern the operation of internal fabric interfaces and enable the configuration of various functions, protocols, and interfaces that connect spine and leaf switches. Users who have fabric administrator privileges can create new fabric policies according to their requirements. The APIC enables administrators to select the pods, switches, and interfaces to which they will apply fabric policies. Figure 4-10 provides an overview of the fabric policy model.

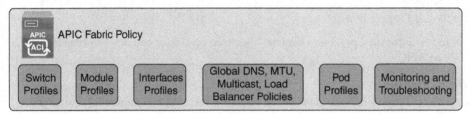

**Figure 4-10** *Fabric Policy Model*

Fabric policies are grouped into the following categories:

- Switch profiles specify which switches to configure and the switch configuration policy.

- Module profiles specify which spine switch modules to configure and the spine switch configuration policy.

- Interface profiles specify which fabric interfaces to configure and the interface configuration policy.

■ Global policies specify DNS, fabric MTU default, multicast tree, and load-balancer configurations to be used throughout the fabric.

■ Pod profiles specify date and time, SNMP, Council of Oracles Protocol (COOP), IS-IS, and Border Gateway Protocol (BGP) route reflector policies.

■ Monitoring and troubleshooting policies specify what to monitor, thresholds, how to handle faults and logs, and how to perform diagnostics.

The Cisco ACI has two main policies:

■ **Fabric policies:** Fabric policies configure internal interfaces that connect spine and leaf switches. Fabric policies can enable features such as monitoring (statistics collection and statistics export), troubleshooting (on-demand diagnostics and SPAN), IS-IS, Council of Oracles Protocol (COOP), SNMP, Multiprotocol Border Gateway Protocol (MP-BGP) route reflectors, DNS, or Network Time Protocol (NTP). Figure 4-11 shows the ACI Fabric Policies configuration page.

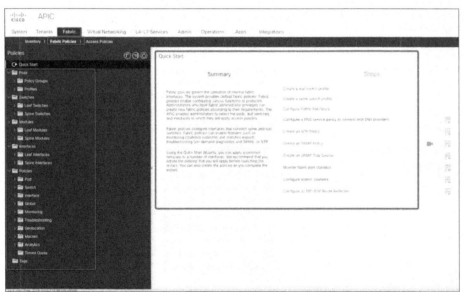

**Figure 4-11**  *ACI Fabric Policies Configuration Page*

To apply a configuration across the fabric, an administrator associates a defined group of policies to interfaces on switches in a single step. In this way, large numbers of interfaces across the fabric can be configured at once; configuring one port at a time is not scalable. Figure 4-12 shows how the process works for configuring the ACI fabric. This example has a monitoring policy with a health score. The Cisco ACI provides health scores that provide information on status, performance, and availability. Health scores are calculated using the number and importance of faults that apply to it. Faults, events, and statistics in the ACI fabric are represented as a collection of managed objects (MOs) within the overall ACI Object Model/Management Information Tree (MIT). All objects within ACI can be queried, including faults.

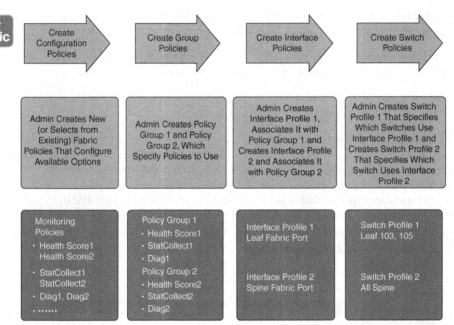

**Figure 4-12**   *Fabric Policy Configuration Process*

System health scores are a weighted average of the leaf health scores, divided by the total number of learned endpoints, multiplied by the spine coefficient, which is derived from the number of spines and their health scores.

Figure 4-13 shows the result of applying Switch Profile 1 and Switch Profile 2 to the ACI fabric.

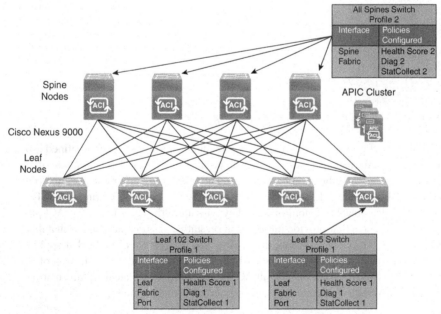

**Figure 4-13**   *Application of a Fabric Switch Policy*

This combination of infrastructure and scope enables administrators to manage fabric configuration in a scalable fashion. These configurations can be implemented using the REST API, CLI, or GUI.

- **Access policies:** Access policies configure external-facing interfaces that connect to devices such as virtual machine controllers and hypervisors, hosts, network-attached storage, routers, or Fabric Extender (FEX) interfaces. Access policies enable the configuration of port channels and virtual port channels, protocols such as Link Layer Discovery Protocol (LLDP), Cisco Discovery Protocol (CDP), or Link Aggregation Control Protocol (LACP), and features such as statistics gathering, monitoring, and diagnostics. Figure 4-14 shows the ACI Access Policies configuration page.

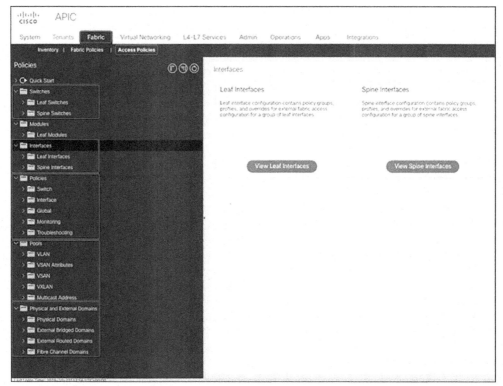

**Figure 4-14**  *ACI Policies Configuration Page*

To apply a configuration across a potentially large number of switches, an administrator defines switch profiles that associate interface configurations in a single policy group. In this way, large numbers of interfaces across the fabric can be configured at once. Switch profiles can contain symmetric configurations for multiple switches or unique special-purpose configurations. Figure 4-15 shows the process for configuring the interface profile.

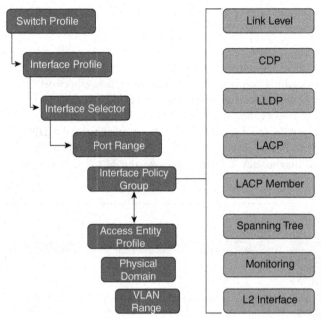

**Figure 4-15** *Interface Policy Configuration Process*

Figure 4-16 shows the result of applying Interface Profile 1 and Interface Profile 2 to the ACI fabric.

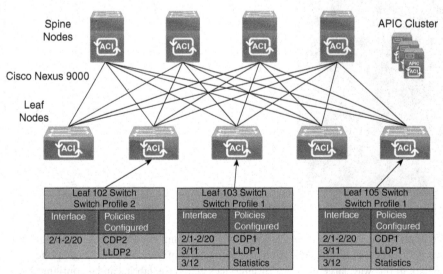

**Figure 4-16** *Applying an Access Interface Policy*

Fabric access policies are similar to folder organizers; most of the policies are folders and have subfolders. For example, under the Switch Policies folder, there are subfolders called Policies, Profiles, and Policy Groups. Figure 4-17 shows fabric access policies and the relationship between the folders.

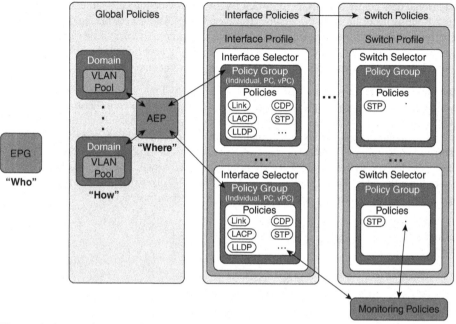

**Figure 4-17**  *Policy Configuration Relationship*

An AEP represents a group of external entities with similar infrastructure policy requirements. The infrastructure policies consist of physical interface policies that configure various protocol options.

## Cisco ACI Fabric Building Blocks, Policy Model, and VMM Domains

The main objective of the Application Centric Infrastructure is to decouple endpoints from the underlying physical network. It provides a distributed Layer 3 gateway that ensures optimal Layer 3 and Layer 2 forwarding. The ACI fabric supports standard bridging and routing without location restrictions (any IP address anywhere) and also removes flooding requirements for Address Resolution Protocol (ARP)/Gratuitous Address Resolution Protocol (GARP). All traffic within the fabric is encapsulated within VXLAN.

For application high availability and performance, the new application is designed to be distributed. Distributed applications drive east-west traffic from server to server through the data center access layer (Layer 2). Applications driving this shift include big data distribution, live virtual machine, or workload migration, as with VMware vMotion, server clustering, and multitier applications.

North-south traffic drives traditional data center design with core, aggregation, and access layers, or collapsed core and access layers. Client data comes in from the WAN or Internet, a server processes it, and then it exits the data center, which permits data center hardware oversubscription due to WAN or Internet bandwidth constraints. However, Spanning Tree Protocol (STP) is required to block loops. This limits bandwidth availability due to blocked links and potentially forces traffic to take a suboptimal path.

In traditional data center designs, IEEE 802.1Q VLANs provide logical segmentation of Layer 2 boundaries or broadcast domains. However, VLAN use of network links is inefficient, requirements for device placements in the data center network can be rigid, and the VLAN maximum of 4094 VLANs can be a limitation. As IT departments and cloud providers build large multitenant data centers, VLAN limitations become problematic.

A spine-leaf architecture addresses these limitations. The ACI fabric appears as a single switch to the outside world, capable of bridging and routing, as shown in Figure 4-18. Moving Layer 3 routing to the access layer would limit the Layer 2 reachability that modern applications require. Applications like virtual machine workload mobility and some clustering software require Layer 2 adjacency between source and destination servers. By routing at the access layer, only servers connected to the same access switch with the same VLANs trunked down would be Layer 2-adjacent. In ACI, VXLAN solves this problem by decoupling Layer 2 domains from the underlying Layer 3 network infrastructure.

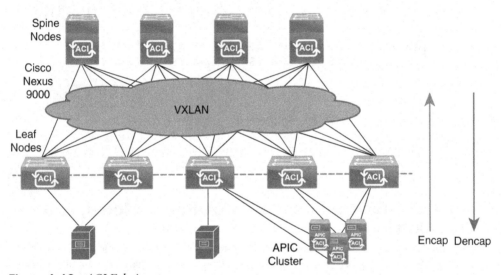

**Figure 4-18**  *ACI Fabric*

As traffic enters the fabric, the ACI encapsulates and applies policy to it, forwards it as needed across the fabric through a spine switch (maximum two-hops), and decapsulates it upon exiting the fabric.

Within the fabric, ACI uses IS-IS and Council of Oracles Protocol (COOP) for all forwarding of endpoint-to-endpoint communications. This enables all ACI links to be active, equal-cost multipath (ECMP) forwarding in the fabric, and fast-reconverging. ACI uses MP-BGP to propagate routing information between software-defined networks within the fabric and routers external to the fabric.

## ACI Policy Model

The ACI policy model enables the specification of application requirements policies. The APIC automatically renders policies in the fabric infrastructure. When a user or process initiates an administrative change to an object in the fabric, the APIC first applies that change to the policy model. This policy model change then triggers a change to the actual managed endpoint. This approach is called a *model-driven framework*.

Key characteristics of the policy model include the following:

■ As a model-driven architecture, the software maintains a complete representation of the administrative and operational state of the system (the model). The model applies uniformly to fabric, services, system behaviors, and virtual and physical devices attached to the network.

■ The logical and concrete domains are separated; the logical configurations are rendered into concrete configurations by applying the policies in relation to the available physical resources. No configuration is carried out against concrete entities. Concrete entities are configured implicitly as a side effect of the changes to the APIC policy model. Concrete entities can be, but do not have to be, physical (such as a virtual machine or a VLAN).

■ The system prohibits communications with newly connected devices until the policy model is updated to include the new device.

Network administrators do not configure logical and physical system resources directly but rather define logical (hardware independent) configurations and APIC policies that control different aspects of the system behavior.

Managed object (MO) manipulation in the model relieves engineers from the task of administering isolated, individual component configurations. These characteristics enable automation and flexible workload provisioning that can locate any workload anywhere in the infrastructure. Network-attached services can be easily deployed, and the APIC provides an automation framework to manage the lifecycle of those network-attached services.

The policy model manages the entire fabric, including the infrastructure, authentication, security, services, applications, and diagnostics. Logical constructs in the policy model define how the fabric meets the needs of any of the functions of the fabric. Figure 4-19 provides an overview of the ACI policy model logical constructs.

The fabric comprises the physical and logical components as recorded in the Management Information Model (MIM), which can be represented in a hierarchical Management Information Tree (MIT). The information model is stored and managed by processes that run on the APIC. Similar to the OSI Common Management Information Protocol (CMIP) and other X.500 variants, the APIC enables the control of managed resources by presenting their manageable characteristics as object properties that can be inherited according to the location of the object within the hierarchical structure of the MIT.

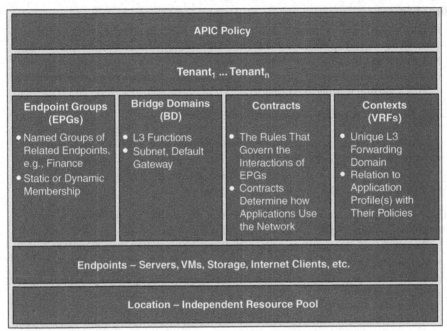

**Figure 4-19** *ACI Policy Model Logical Constructs Overview*

Each node in the tree represents a managed object or group of objects. MOs are abstractions of fabric resources. An MO can represent a concrete object, such as a switch, adapter, or a logical object, such as an application profile, endpoint group, or fault. Figure 4-20 provides an overview of the MIT.

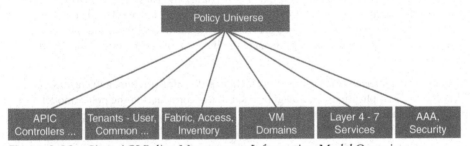

**Figure 4-20** *Cisco ACI Policy Management Information Model Overview*

As in Figure 4-20, the hierarchical structure starts with the policy universe at the top (Root) and contains parent and child nodes. Each node in the tree is an MO, and each object in the fabric has a unique distinguished name (DN) that describes the object and locates its place in the tree.

## Cisco ACI Tenants

Tenants (fvTenant) are top-level objects that identify and separate administrative control, network/failure domains, and application policies. A tenant's sublevel objects can be grouped into two basic categories: tenant networking and tenant policy.

The decision on how to leverage tenancy models is driven by a number of factors:

1.  Overall IT operations and support models in your organization to manage application, networking, servers, security, and so on

2.  Separation of environments from a software development lifecycle perspective: development, quality assurance, and production

3.  Separation of duties by domain owner, such as web, app, and database owners

4.  Fault domain size and scope to limit the impact of failures, such as different business units

*Tenant networking* is used to define networking policies and will be applied to the underlying hardware in a transparent way thanks to the layer of abstraction provided by ACI using VRFs, bridge domains, and subnets.

*Tenant policies* are where applications are defined. An application could consist of a combination of physical servers or virtual machines, which we will call *servers* from now on.

For example, a website could use a three-tier application model, composed of web servers, application servers, and database servers. When users browse the website, they might actually be communicating with a virtual IP address on a load balancer that, in turn, can distribute the web request to a number of different web servers. The web servers, in turn, communicate with core applications that can be divided among several application servers for load balancing or high-availability purposes. Finally, the application servers communicate with the database, which could also be a cluster of servers.

Each server is referred to as an *endpoint* in the ACI. Endpoints are classified in the ACI to apply policies. You need to create endpoint groups for endpoints that share the same types of policies, such as with whom they are going to communicate and what types of communication or restrictions are required. Therefore, an application can be formed by several endpoint groups, and they are grouped in an application profile.

Although the tenant networking and the tenant policies are defined separately, the networking policies used by an application are defined with a relationship between the endpoint groups and the bridge domain.

The following three tenants are preconfigured in the ACI system by default:

■  **Common:** This special tenant has unique abilities to easily share its resources with other tenants, with the purpose of providing "common" services to other tenants in the ACI fabric. Global reuse is a core principle in the common tenant. Some examples of common services are

  ■  Shared L3 out

  ■  Shared VRFs

  ■  Shared bridge domains

  ■  DNS

  ■  DHCP

  ■  Active directory

- **Infra:** This infrastructure tenant is used for all internal fabric communications, such as tunnels and policy deployment. This includes switch-to-switch (leaf, spine, Application Virtual Switch) and switch-to-Application Policy Infrastructure Controller communications. The infra tenant does not get exposed to the user space (tenants), and it has its own private network space (VRF) and bridge domains. Fabric discovery, image management, and DHCP for fabric functions are all handled within this tenant.

- **Mgmt:** The management tenant provides a convenient means to configure access policies for fabric nodes. While fabric nodes are accessible and configurable through the APIC, they can also be accessed directly using in-band and out-of-band connections. In-band and out-of-band policies are configured under the mgmt tenant:

  - In-band management access

  - Out-of-band management access

Figure 4-21 shows the components that can be configured within a tenant.

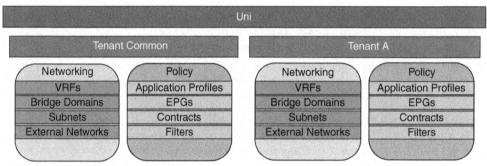

**Figure 4-21**   *Tenant Logical Model*

### Virtual Routing and Forwarding

Virtual Routing and Forwarding (VRF) is a unique Layer 3 forwarding and application policy domain. VRFs (fvCtx) are children of the tenant object. All of the endpoints within the VRF must have unique IP addresses because it is possible to forward packets directly between these devices if the policy allows it. One or more bridge domains are associated with a VRF.

The most common method to share VRFs between tenants is through the common tenant. VRFs created in the common tenant are shared globally within the fabric. However, a VRF that is intended to be used by multiple tenants and is not created in the common tenant requires explicit configuration to be shared.

### Bridge Domain and Subnets

A bridge domain (fvBD) is the logical representation of a Layer 2 forwarding domain within the fabric. A bridge domain is a child of the tenant object and must be linked to a VRF.

The bridge domain defines the unique Layer 2 MAC address space and a Layer 2 flood domain if flooding is enabled. While a VRF defines a unique IP address space, that address space can consist of multiple subnets. Those subnets will be spread across one or more bridge domains contained in the VRF.

Bridge domains will span all switches in which associated endpoint groups are configured. A bridge domain can have multiple subnets. However, a subnet is contained within a single bridge domain.

Figure 4-22 provides an example of a tenant that shows how bridge domains are contained inside of VRFs and how they are linked to endpoint groups and the other elements.

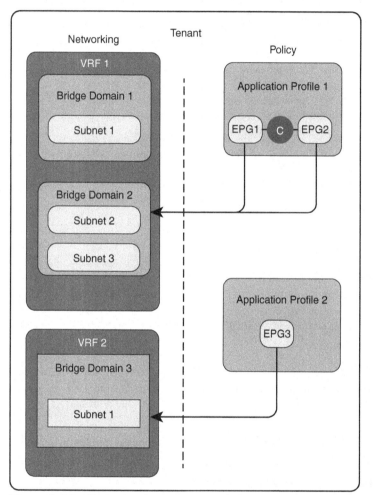

**Figure 4-22**  *Endpoint Group as Part of a Tenant Application Profile*

A bridge domain is not a VLAN, although it can act similar to one. Think of a bridge domain as a distributed switch, which, on a leaf, can be translated locally as a VLAN with local significance.

From a practical perspective, each bridge domain exists in a particular leaf if there is a connected endpoint that belongs to that endpoint group. Each bridge domain receives a VLAN ID in the leaf switches.

The VLAN ID used is also called the platform-independent VLAN or PI VLAN. This VLAN concept is different from traditional networking and is not used to forward traffic, but as an identifier. Each PI VLAN is then linked to a VXLAN ID that will be used for forwarding purposes inside the fabric.

Endpoint groups are also assigned with a PI VLAN ID that is locally significant in each leaf. This VLAN ID is different from the bridge domain. Therefore, in the Cisco ACI, several VLANs are used for endpoints inside one bridge domain.

When a subnet is defined in a bridge domain, the leaf switches are the default gateway for the endpoint groups using that subnet. If the endpoint groups have endpoints on multiple leaves, each leaf configures the default gateway. In that way, the default gateway for the endpoints is always the first switch of the fabric that is reached, also known as a *pervasive gateway*. This means that an SVI is configured under the VRF that represents the private network that the bridge domain is linked to. If a bridge domain has several subnets, there is only one SVI per bridge domain, but it uses secondary IP addresses.

Subnets are defined in one or more BDs that reference the corresponding VRF. The options for a subnet under a BD or under an EPG are as follows:

- **Advertised externally:** The subnet can be exported to a routed connection.

- **Private:** The subnet applies only within its tenant.

- **Shared between VRF:** The subnet can be shared with and exported to multiple VRFs in the same tenant or across tenants as part of a shared service. An example of a shared service is a routed connection to an EPG present in another VRF in a different tenant. This enables traffic to pass in both directions across VRFs. An EPG that provides a shared service must have its subnet configured under that EPG (not under a BD), and its scope must be set to advertised externally and shared between VRFs.

## Endpoint Group

Endpoint groups are used to create a logical group of hosts or servers that perform similar functions within the fabric and that share similar policies. Each EPG created can have a unique monitoring policy or QoS policy and is associated with a bridge domain.

An EPG is a child object of the application profile, and an application profile can contain multiple endpoint groups. Each endpoint within an EPG is susceptible to the same policy in the fabric.

All of the endpoints inside an EPG can communicate with each other. Communications between EPGs is governed by contracts and not traditional Layer 2/Layer 3 forwarding constructs. For example, Host A in EPG A can be on the same IP subnet with Host B in EPG B. In this case, they would not be allowed to communicate unless a contract that permitted connectivity existed between EPG A and EPG B.

Some types of endpoint groups within the fabric are not contained under application profiles, such as application endpoint groups, external bridge networks (aka Layer2 External), external routed networks (aka Layer3 External), and management endpoint groups. These EPGs might have special requirements; for example, in external bridge networks, MAC addresses of the endpoints are not learned by the leaf switches.

Endpoint groups are linked to bridge domains, but they will receive a VLAN ID different from the bridge domain, unless Bridge Domain legacy mode is used.

It is important to understand that a single subnet can be extended across several EPGs. Each EPG is identified by an encapsulation VLAN or VXLAN so that the same subnet uses different encapsulation IDs across the fabric. This concept is different from traditional networking.

## Cisco ACI Virtual Machine Manager Domains

The Cisco ACI enables the fabric administrator to integrate the APIC with various VMM solutions. For example, the administrator can use ACI as a single management portal (called a single pane of glass). This integration supports the VMware vCenter (with or without NSX), Microsoft System Center Virtual Machine Manager (SCVMM), Red Hat Virtualization (RHV), and OpenStack.

This integration brings the benefit of consolidated visibility and simpler operations because the fabric has a full view of physical and virtual endpoints and their location, as shown in Figure 4-23. The APIC can also automate provisioning of virtual networking within the VMM domain.

**Figure 4-23**    *ACI VM Network Page*

The essential components of an ACI VMM domain policy include the following:

- **Virtual Machine Manager domain profile:** Groups VM controllers with similar networking policy requirements. For example, VM controllers can share VLAN pools and application EPGs. The APIC communicates with the controller to publish network configurations such as port groups that are then applied to the virtual workloads. The VMM domain profile includes the following essential components:

  - **Credential:** Associates a valid VM controller user credential with an APIC VMM domain.

  - **Controller:** Specifies how to connect to a VM controller that is part of a policy enforcement domain. For example, the controller specifies the connection to a VMware vCenter that is part a VMM domain.

**NOTE**   A single VMM domain can contain multiple instances of VM controllers, but they must be from the same vendor (for example, from VMware or from Microsoft).

■ **EPG Association:** Regulates connectivity and visibility among the endpoints within the scope of the VMM domain policy. VMM domain EPGs behave as follows:

■ The APIC pushes these EPGs as port groups into the VM controller.

■ An EPG can span multiple VMM domains, and a VMM domain can contain multiple EPGs.

■ **Attachable Entity Profile Association:** Associates a VMM domain with the physical network infrastructure. An AEP is a network interface template that enables you to deploy VM controller policies on a large set of leaf switch ports. An AEP specifies which switches and ports are available and how they are configured.

■ **VLAN Pool Association:** Specifies the VLAN IDs or ranges used for VLAN encapsulation that the VMM domain consumes.

### Cisco ACI Integration with Microsoft SCVMM

For single network management, the Cisco Application Centric Infrastructure has an option to integrate with the Microsoft System Center Virtual Machine Manager. Any endpoint groups that were created in APIC will be created as VM networks in the SCVMM. Compute is provisioned in the SCVMM and can consume these networks.

Figure 4-24 shows a representative topology of a typical System Center Virtual Machine Manager deployment with Cisco ACI fabric.

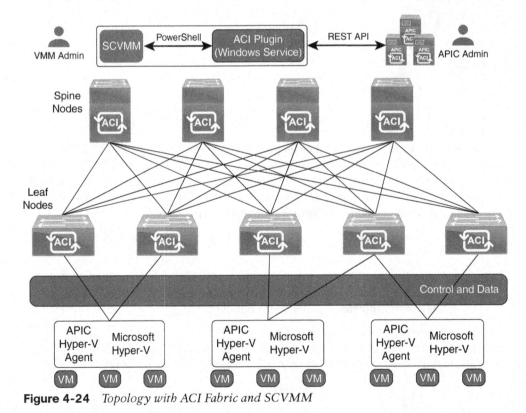

**Figure 4-24** *Topology with ACI Fabric and SCVMM*

A Microsoft SCVMM service can be deployed as a standalone service or as a highly available service on physical hosts or virtual machines but will logically be viewed as a single SCVMM instance that communicates to the APIC. Connectivity between an SCVMM service and the APIC is over the management network.

### Cisco ACI Integration with VMware vCenter

The APIC integrates with a VMware vCenter instance seamlessly to extend the ACI policy framework to vSphere workloads. The APIC uses Application Profiles to represent the ACI policy. The Application Profiles model is the logical representation of all components of the application and its interdependencies on the ACI fabric. This policy framework also includes an L4–L7 service insertion mechanism, providing full-service lifecycle management based on workload instantiation and decommission.

After these Application Profiles are defined in the APIC, the integration between vCenter and APIC ensures that these network policies can be applied to vSphere workloads. The network policies and logical topologies (VLANs, subnets, and so on) that have tradition-ally dictated application design are now applied based on the Application Profile through the APIC.

The Cisco APIC integrates with the VMware vCenter to simplify workload connectivity, as shown in Figure 4-25. For example, you do not have to use VLANs to define basic network-ing connectivity. To connect VMware workloads to the Cisco ACI fabric, the virtualization administrator simply needs to associate the virtual machines with the port groups that appear under the virtual distributed switch (VDS).

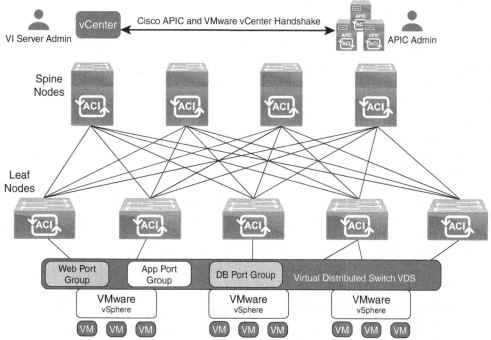

**Figure 4-25**   *Cisco ACI VMware Integration*

### Cisco ACI Virtual Edge

The Cisco Application Centric Infrastructure Virtual Edge is a hypervisor-independent distributed service virtual machine (VM) that is specifically designed for the Cisco ACI. It leverages the native distributed virtual switch that belongs to the hypervisor. The Cisco ACI Virtual Edge runs in the user space, operates as a virtual leaf, and is managed by the Cisco APIC. If you use the Cisco AVS, you can migrate to the Cisco ACI Virtual Edge; if you use the VMware VDS, you can run the Cisco ACI Virtual Edge on top of it.

The Cisco ACI Virtual Edge supports two modes of traffic forwarding: local switching and no local switching. The forwarding mode is selected during Cisco ACI Virtual Edge installation.

The Cisco ACI Virtual Edge is supported as a vLeaf for the Cisco APIC with the VMware ESXi hypervisor. It manages a data center defined by the VMware vCenter Server.

### Integrating VMware Overlays with the Cisco ACI

VMware virtualized overlay models use Virtual Extensible LAN (VXLAN) for tunneling. This tunneling allows virtual machine connectivity independent of the underlying network. In these environments, one or more virtual networks are built using the chosen overlay technology, and traffic is encapsulated as it traverses the physical network.

The Cisco ACI integration with VMware provides overlay independence and can bridge frames to and from VXLAN, Network Virtualization using Generic Routing Encapsulation (NVGRE), VLAN, and IEEE 802.1x encapsulation. This approach provides flexibility for heterogeneous environments, which may have services residing on disparate overlays.

The Cisco APIC integration with vCenter enables dynamic workload mobility, management automation, and programmatic policy. As workloads move within the virtual environment, the policies attached to the workloads are enforced seamlessly and consistently within the infrastructure.

This integration delivers a scalable and secure multitenant infrastructure with complete visibility into application performance across physical and VMware virtual environments.

### Application Profiles

An application profile (fvAp) defines the policies, services, and relationships between endpoint groups (EPGs). Application profiles contain one or more EPGs. Modern applications contain multiple components. For example, an e-commerce application could require a web server, a database server, data located in a storage-area network, and access to outside resources that enable financial transactions. The application profile contains as many (or as few) EPGs as necessary that are logically related to providing the capabilities of an application.

EPGs can be organized according to one of the following:

- The application they provide, such as a DNS server or SAP application (using API)

- The function they provide (such as infrastructure)

- Where they are located in the structure of the data center (such as a DMZ)

- Whatever organizing principle that a fabric or tenant administrator chooses to use

Application profiles provide a mechanism to understand groups of servers as a single application. This approach makes the Cisco ACI application aware and allows you to check the operational state for an application while monitoring all the servers that are part of an application as a whole. Furthermore, an administrator can become informed about relevant faults and health status for that particular application. Each application profile created can have a unique monitoring policy and QoS policy applied. An application profile is a child object of the tenant, and a single tenant can contain multiple application profiles

## Microsegmentations

Microsegments automatically classify endpoint groups from matching application profile "attributes." This type of endpoint group is also referred to as an attribute-based endpoint group. Some of the attributes that you can match against include VM properties (such as VM Name, VM ID, and Hypervisor), MAC addresses, and IP sets.

Some advantages of microsegmentation include the following:

- Stateless white list network access security with line rate enforcement.

- Per-microsegment granularity of security automation through dynamic Layer 4–Layer 7 service insertion and chaining.

- Hypervisor agnostic microsegmentation in a broad range of virtual switch environments.

- ACI policies that easily move problematic VMs into a quarantine security zone.

- When combined with intra-EPG isolation for bare-metal and VM endpoints, micro-segmentation can provide policy-driven automated complete endpoint isolation within application tiers.

After a uSeg endpoint group is created and eventually assigned to a VMM domain, it auto-matches on any endpoint within the VMM domain that exists within the tenant and moves any endpoints from their assigned application endpoint group to the uSeg endpoint group. When this occurs, any policies applied to the uSeg EPG (Contracts, QoS, monitoring policies, and so on) are now applied. Policies from their original application EPG are no longer applied to the endpoint.

## Attachable Entity Profile

The ACI fabric provides multiple attachment points that connect through leaf ports to various external entities such as bare-metal servers, virtual machine hypervisors, Layer 2 switches (for example, the Cisco UCS fabric interconnect), or Layer 3 routers (for example, Cisco Nexus 7000 Series switches). These attachment points can be physical ports, FEX ports, port channels, or a virtual port channel (vPC) on leaf switches.

An Attachable Entity Profile (AEP) represents a group of external entities with similar infrastructure policy requirements. The infrastructure policies consist of physical interface policies that configure various protocol options, such as Cisco Discovery Protocol (CDP), Link Layer Discovery Protocol (LLDP), or Link Aggregation Control Protocol (LACP).

An AEP is required to deploy VLAN pools on leaf switches. Encapsulation blocks (and asso-ciated VLANs) are reusable across leaf switches. An AEP implicitly provides the scope of the VLAN pool to the physical infrastructure.

The following AEP requirements and dependencies must be accounted for in various configuration scenarios, including network connectivity, VMM domains, and multi-pod configuration:

■ The AEP defines the range of allowed VLANs, but it does not provision them. No traffic flows unless an EPG is deployed on the port. Without defining a VLAN pool in an AEP, a VLAN is not enabled on the leaf port even if an EPG is provisioned.

■ A particular VLAN is provisioned on a leaf interface either through static port binding or based on VM events from external controllers such as VMware vCenter or Microsoft Azure Service Center Virtual Machine Manager.

■ Attached entity profiles can be associated directly with application EPGs, which deploy the associated application EPGs to all those ports associated with the attached entity profile. The AEP has a configurable generic function, which contains a relation to an EPG that is deployed on all interfaces that are part of the selectors that are associated with the attachable entity profile.

### ACI Contract

A *contract* is the policy that an ACI administrator uses to control traffic flow within the ACI fabric and between endpoint groups. These contracts are built using a provider/consumer model where one endpoint group provides the services it wants to offer (the provider) and another endpoint group consumes them (the consumer). Contracts are assigned a scope of global, tenant, VRF, or application profile, which limits the accessibility of the contract.

Contracts consist of one or more subjects. Each subject contains one or more filters. Each filter contains one or more entries. Each entry is equivalent to a line in an access control list (ACL) that is applied on the leaf switch to which the endpoint within the endpoint group is attached.

Specifically, contracts are composed of the following items:

■ **Subjects:** A group of filters for a specific application or service.

■ **Filters:** Feature used to classify traffic based on Layer 2 to Layer 4 attributes (such as Ethernet type, protocol type, TCP flags, and ports).

■ **Actions:** Predefined act to be taken on the filtered traffic. The following actions are supported:

  ■ Permit the traffic (regular contracts, only).

  ■ Mark the traffic (DSCP/CoS) (regular contracts, only).

  ■ Redirect the traffic (regular contracts, only, through a service graph).

  ■ Copy the traffic (regular contracts, only, through a service graph or SPAN).

  ■ Block the traffic (taboo contracts, only).

  ■ Log the traffic (taboo contracts, only).

■ **Labels (Optional):** Tags used to group objects such as subjects and endpoint groups for the purpose of increasing granularity in policy enforcement.

While different endpoint groups can only communicate with other endpoint groups based on the contract rules defined, there is no contract required for intra-endpoint group communication. Intra-endpoint group communication from endpoint to endpoint in the same endpoint group is allowed by default.

If a filter allows traffic from any consumer port to a provider port (for example, 8888), if reverse port filtering is enabled and the contract is applied in both directions (say for TCP traffic), either the consumer or the provider can initiate communication. The provider could open a TCP socket to the consumer using port 8888, whether the provider or consumer sent traffic first.

If you do not configure a contract, traffic is permitted only for the following types of packets as well as the types that are permitted by default for multicast traffic and class equal traffic. These packets must match specific IPv4 and IPv6 packets, identified by protocol type, protocol ID (prot), source port (sport) and destination port (dport):

- DHCP v4 (prot 0x11, sport 0x44, dport 0x43)

- DHCP v4 (prot 0x11, sport 0x43, dport 0x44)

- OSPF (prot 0x59)

- EIGRP (prot 0x58)

- PIM (prot 0x67)

- IGMP (prot 0x2)

- DHCP v6 (prot 0x11, sport 0x222, dport 0x223)

- ND-Sol ICMPv6 (prot 0x3a dport 0x0087)

- ND-Advt ICMPv6 (prot 0x3a dport 0x0088)

The following types of contracts can be applied in the ACI:

- Regular contracts

- Taboo contracts

- Out-of-band (OOB) contracts

## Taboo Contracts

Taboo contracts are used to deny and log traffic related to regular contracts and are configured into the hardware before the regular contract. For example, if the objective is to allow traffic with source ports 20 through 1200 with the exception of port 45, then the regular contract would allow all ports in the range of 20 through 1200 while the taboo contract would have a single entry denying port 45. The taboo contract denying port 45 would be programmed into the hardware before the regular contract allowing ports 20 through 1200. Out-of-band contracts apply only to out-of-band traffic from the management tenant.

Contracts govern the following types of EPG communications:

- Between application endpoint groups

- Between application endpoint groups and external networks

■ Between application endpoint groups and in-band management endpoint groups—for example, if in-band management is configured for the ACI fabric and certain endpoint groups are to be allowed to access it

## vzAny Rule

vzAny managed objects provide a convenient way of associating all endpoint groups in a Virtual Routing and Forwarding (VRF) instance to one or more contracts (vzBrCP) instead of creating a separate contract relation for each EPG. vzAny automates the process of configuring EPG contract relationships. Whenever a new EPG is added to a VRF, vzAny contract rules automatically apply. The vzAny one-to-all EPG relationship is the most efficient way of applying contract rules to all EPGs in a VRF.

To understand how the contract and vzAny work, assume you have an EPG called WebServer providing a contract called HTTPS being consumed by EPG users. The HTTPS contract is built on a filter-specifying destination port (DP)=443—without a specific source port.

The most straightforward way to apply this contract is with both the Apply Both Directions and Reverse Filter Ports options checked, as shown in Figure 4-26.

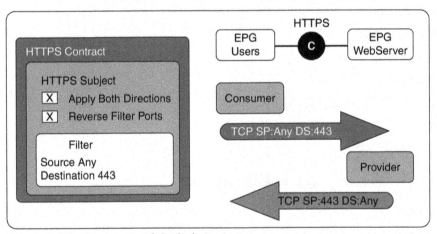

**Figure 4-26**  *Contract with Default Option*

The way the contract works is that the selected filter is applied to traffic coming from the consumer to the provider, so traffic with a DP=443 is permitted. When you enable Apply Both Directions, the filter is also used for traffic traveling from the provider to the consumer, but because the Reverse Filter Ports option is checked, the contract will reverse the source/destination port for reverse traffic and allow traffic with a source port (SP)=443.

In normal operation, this is the contract functionality. The contract permits forward traffic from the consumer to the provider and returns traffic in the opposite direction.

Now assume that you remove the Reverse Filter Ports option. The contract is still applied in both directions, but with DP=443 in each direction—essentially removing the whole idea of consumer and provider because only traffic with DP=443 would be allowed. No return traffic would get through, unless you added another contract to allow traffic with SP=443 to pass, as shown in Figure 4-27.

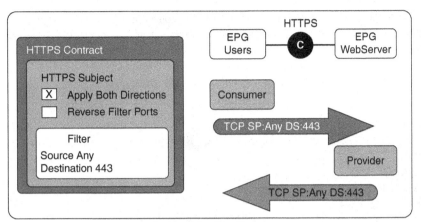

**Figure 4-27**   *Contract with One-Way Traffic*

If you disable both options, one direction of the traffic is permitted, but this option is optimal because it uses a single ternary content-addressable memory (TCAM) entry rather than two TCAM entries when both directions are enabled with the reverse path disabled, as shown in Figure 4-28.

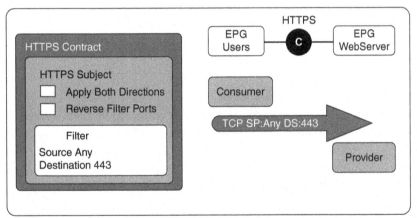

**Figure 4-28**   *Contract with Both Subject Options Disabled*

In the preceding example, you need a different contract and filter to allow the return traffic with SP=443, but there is a cleverer way of doing this using a special EPG called the *vzAny EPG*.

vzAny represents the collection of EPGs that belong to the same VRF. Instead of associating contracts to each individual EPG, you can configure a contract to the vzAny EPG, which is found under your VRF configuration's EPG collection for VRF.

The idea is that you can create a contract that allows all TCP traffic with the ACK flag set; you can use a predefined filter in the common tenant called est. You then make the vzAny EPG both a consumer and a provider of this contract, which then allows every EPG in that VRF to accept traffic with the ACK flag set but uses only a single TCAM entry for all EPGs.

In Figure 4-29, the HTTPS contracts allow traffic from the consuming EPGs to reach the providing EPGs, while the established contract allows universal traffic between EPGs as long as the TCP session is established. Essentially, the HTTPS contracts are only needed to allow the initial TCP SYN packet through to establish the session. All other traffic is handled by the vzAny EPG and its established contract, as in Figure 4-29.

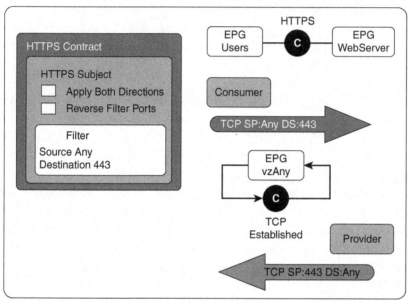

**Figure 4-29**  *vzAny Contract Example*

The ACI filter properties example in Figure 4-30 shows filter protocol, provider/consumer source port or range, and provider/consumer destination port or range.

**Figure 4-30**  *ACI Filter Configuration Page*

## Filters and Subjects

**Key Topic**

Labels, subjects, aliases, and filters enable mixing and matching among EPGs and contracts to satisfy various applications or service delivery requirements.

Contracts can contain multiple communication rules, and multiple EPGs can both consume and provide multiple contracts. Labels control which rules apply when communicating between a specific pair of EPGs. A policy designer can compactly represent complex communication policies and reuse these policies across multiple instances of an application.

Labels, subjects, aliases, and filters define EPG communications according to the following options:

- Labels are managed objects with only one property: a name. Labels enable classifying which objects can and cannot communicate with one another. Label matching is done first. If the labels do not match, no other contract or filter information is processed. The label match attribute can be one of these values: at least one (the default), all, none, or exactly one.

- Labels determine which EPG consumers and EPG providers can communicate with one another. Label matching determines which subjects of a contract are used with a given EPG provider or EPG consumer of that contract.

- The two types of labels are as follows:

  - Subject labels that are applied to EPGs. Subject label matching enables EPGs to choose a subset of the subjects in a contract.

  - Provider/consumer labels that are applied to EPGs. Provider/consumer label matching enables consumer EPGs to choose their provider EPGs and vice versa.

- Aliases are alternative names you can apply to objects, which can be changed, unlike the name.

- Filters are Layer 2 to Layer 4 fields, TCP/IP header fields such as Layer 3 protocol type, Layer 4 ports, and so forth. According to its related contract, an EPG provider dictates the protocols and ports in both the in and out directions. Contract subjects contain associations to the filters (and their directions) that are applied between EPGs that provide and consume the contract.

- Subjects are contained in contracts. One or more subjects within a contract use filters to specify the type of traffic that can be communicated and how it occurs. For example, for HTTPS messages, the subject specifies the direction and the filters that specify the IP address type (for example, IPv4), the TCP protocol, and the ports allowed. Subjects determine if filters are unidirectional or bidirectional. A unidirectional filter is used in one direction. Unidirectional filters define in or out communications, but not the same for both. Bidirectional filters are the same for both; they define both in and out communications.

## Management Tenant

The management (mgmt) tenant provides access to fabric management functions. While fabric management functions are accessible through the APIC, they can also be accessed directly through in-band and out-of-band network policies.

## In-Band Management Access

The APIC supports both static and dynamic in-band management access. For simple deployments where users manage the IP addresses of a few leaf and spine switches, configuring static in-band and out-of-band management connectivity is simpler.

Static in-band management is normally used for small deployments, but for complex deployments, where a large number of leaf and spine switches require managing many IP addresses, dynamic management access is recommended.

The management profile includes the in-band EPG MO that provides access to management functions via the in-band contract (vzBrCP). The vzBrCP enables fvAEPg (local connected devices), l2extInstP (L2 bridge connected devices), and l3extInstP (L3 connected devices) EPGs to consume the in-band EPG. This exposes the fabric management to locally connected devices, as well as devices connected over Layer 2 bridged external networks and Layer 3 routed external networks. If the consumer and provider EPGs are in different tenants, they can use a bridge domain and VRF from the common tenant.

Authentication, access, and audit logging apply to these connections; any user attempting to access management functions through the in-band EPG must have the appropriate access privileges.

Figure 4-31 shows an in-band management access scenario.

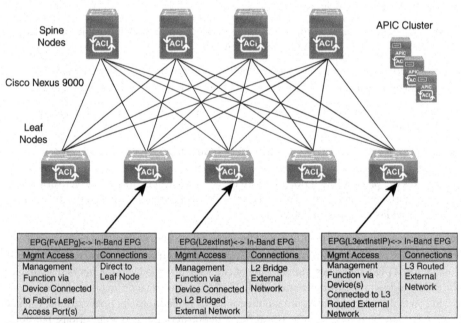

**Figure 4-31**  *In-Band Management Access Scenario*

## Out-of-Band Management Access

The management profile includes the out-of-band EPG MO that provides access to management functions via the out-of-band contract (vzOOBBrCP). The vzOOBBrCP enables the external management instance profile (mgmtExtInstP) EPG to consume the out-of-band

EPG. This exposes the fabric node supervisor ports to locally or remotely connected devices, according to the preference of the service provider. While the bandwidth of the supervisor ports will be lower than the in-band ports, the supervisor ports can provide direct access to the fabric nodes when access through the in-band ports is unavailable. Authentication, access, and audit logging apply to these connections; any user attempting to access management functions through the out-of-band EPG must have the appropriate access privileges. When an administrator configures an external management instance profile, it specifies a subnet range for devices that are allowed out-of-band access. Any device not in this range will not have out-of-band access.

Figure 4-32 shows how out-of-band management access can be consolidated through a dedicated switch.

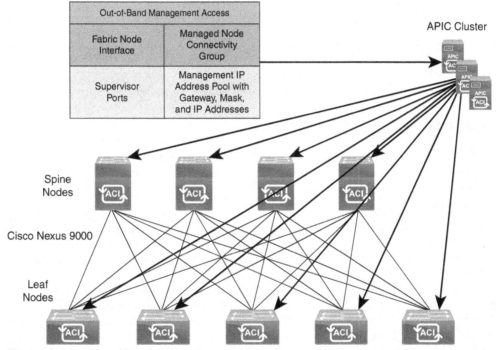

**Figure 4-32**  *Out-of-Band Access Scenario*

For security reasons, some service providers restrict out-of-band connectivity to local connections. Others can choose to enable routed or bridged connections from external networks. Also, a service provider can choose to configure a set of policies that include both in-band and out-of-band management access for local devices only, or both local and remote devices.

## ACI VXLAN

All traffic in the ACI fabric is normalized as VXLAN packets. At ingress, ACI encapsulates external VLAN, VXLAN, and Network Virtualization using Generic Routing Encapsulation (NVGRE) packets in a VXLAN packet. Figure 4-33 shows ACI encapsulation normalization.

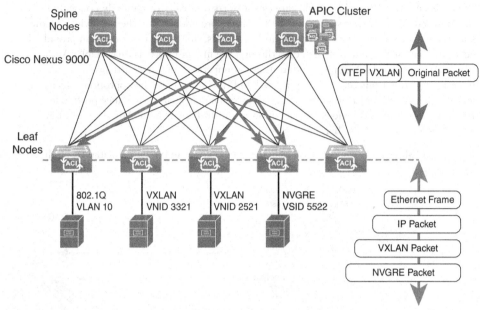

**Figure 4-33**   *ACI Encapsulation Normalization*

The ACI can consistently enforce policy in a fully distributed manner; every packet in the fabric carries ACI policy attributes. The ACI decouples application policy EPG identity from forwarding. Figure 4-34 shows how the ACI VXLAN header identifies application policy within the fabric.

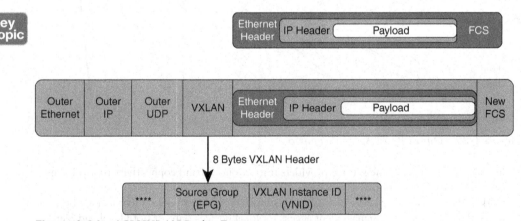

**Figure 4-34**   *ACI VXLAN Packet Format*

VXLAN enables the ACI to deploy Layer 2 virtual networks at scale across the fabric underlay Layer 3 infrastructure. Application endpoint hosts can be flexibly placed in the data center network without concern for the Layer 3 boundary of the underlay infrastructure, while maintaining Layer 2 adjacency in a VXLAN overlay network.

## ACI Intersubnet Tenant Traffic

As we mentioned earlier, ACI fabric provides tenants with default gateway functionality to route traffic between the ACI fabric VXLAN networks. The ACI does this at the ingress interface of the first leaf switch connected to the endpoint. All of the ingress interfaces across the fabric share the same router IP address and MAC address for a given tenant subnet.

The ACI fabric decouples the tenant endpoint address and its identifier from the location of the endpoint that is defined by its locator or VXLAN tunnel endpoint (VTEP) address. Forwarding within the fabric is between VTEPs. Figure 4-35 shows the decoupled identity and location in ACI.

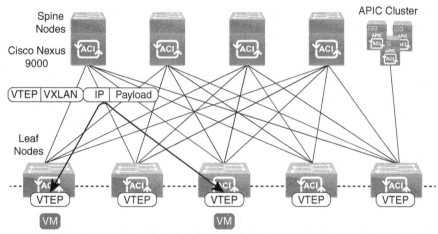

**Figure 4-35**   *ACI Decouples Identity and Location*

VXLAN uses VXLAN tunnel endpoint (VTEP) devices to map tenant end devices to VXLAN segments and to perform VXLAN encapsulation and decapsulation. Each VTEP function has two interfaces:

- A switch interface on the local LAN segment to support local endpoint communication through bridging

- An IP interface to the transport IP network

The IP interface has a unique IP address that identifies the VTEP device on the transport IP network known as the *infrastructure VLAN*. The VTEP device uses this IP address to encapsulate Ethernet frames and transmit the encapsulated packets to the transport network through the IP interface. A VTEP device also discovers the remote VTEPs for its VXLAN segments and learns remote MAC Address-to-VTEP mappings through its IP interface.

The VTEP in the ACI maps the internal tenant MAC or IP address to a location using a *distributed mapping database*. After the VTEP completes a lookup, the VTEP sends the original data packet encapsulated in VXLAN with the destination address of the VTEP on the destination leaf switch. The destination leaf switch decapsulates the packet and sends it to the receiving host. With this model, ACI uses a full-mesh, single-hop, loop-free topology without the need to use the Spanning Tree Protocol to prevent loops.

The VXLAN segments are independent of the underlying network topology. ACI routes the encapsulated packets based on the outer IP address header, which has the initiating VTEP as the source IP address and the terminating VTEP as the destination IP address. Figure 4-36 shows how routing within the tenant is done.

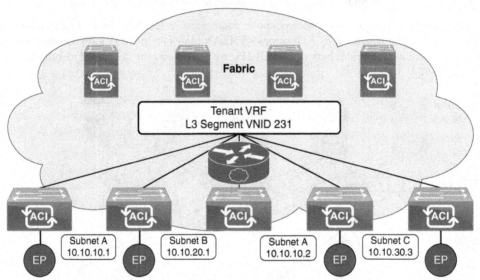

**Figure 4-36**  *Layer 3 VNIDs Transport ACI Intersubnet Tenant Traffic*

For each tenant VRF in the fabric, the ACI assigns a single Layer 3 VNID. The ACI transports traffic across the fabric according to the Layer 3 VNID. At the egress leaf switch, the ACI routes the packet from the Layer 3 VNID to the VNID of the egress subnet.

Traffic arriving at the fabric ingress that is sent to the ACI fabric default gateway is routed into the Layer 3 VNID. This provides very efficient forwarding in the fabric for traffic routed within the tenant. For example, with this model, traffic between two VMs belonging to the same tenant on the same physical host but on different subnets only needs to travel to the ingress switch interface before being routed (using the minimal path cost) to the correct destination.

## Policy Identification and Enforcement

An application policy is decoupled from forwarding by using a distinct tagging attribute that is carried in the VXLAN packet. Policy identification is carried in every packet in the ACI fabric, which enables consistent enforcement of the policy in a fully distributed manner. Figure 4-37 shows policy identification.

Fabric and access policies govern the operation of internal fabric and external access interfaces. The system automatically creates default fabric and access policies. Fabric administrators (who have access rights to the entire fabric) can modify the default policies or create new policies according to their requirements. Fabric and access policies can enable various functions or protocols. Selectors in the APIC enable fabric administrators to choose the nodes and interfaces to which they will apply policies.

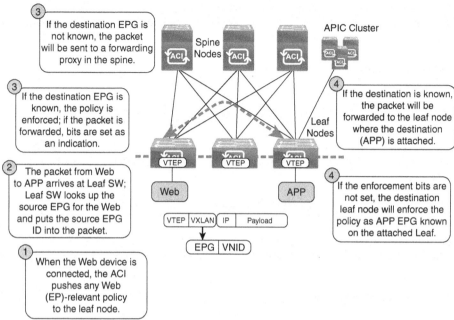

**Figure 4-37** *Policy Identification and Enforcement*

## ACI Fabric Traffic Storm Control

A *traffic storm* occurs when packets flood the LAN, creating excessive traffic and degrading network performance. You can use traffic storm control policies to prevent disruptions on Layer 2 ports by broadcast, unknown multicast, or unknown unicast traffic storms on physical interfaces.

By default, storm control is not enabled in the ACI fabric. ACI bridge domain Layer 2 unknown unicast flooding is disabled by default within the BD but can be enabled by an administrator. If disabled (default), the storm control policy applies only to broadcast and unknown multicast traffic. If Layer 2 unknown unicast flooding is enabled in a BD, then the storm control policy applies to Layer 2 unknown unicast flooding in addition to broadcast and unknown multicast traffic.

Traffic storm control (also called *traffic suppression*) enables you to monitor the levels of incoming broadcast, multicast, and unknown unicast traffic over a one-second interval. During this interval, the traffic level, which is expressed either as percentage of the total available bandwidth of the port or as the maximum packets per second allowed on the given port, is compared with the traffic storm control level that you configured. When the ingress traffic reaches the traffic storm control level that is configured on the port, traffic storm control drops the traffic until the interval ends. An administrator can configure a monitoring policy to raise a fault when a storm control threshold is exceeded.

## ACI Fabric Traffic Load Balance

The ACI fabric provides several load-balancing options for balancing the traffic among the available uplink. Static hash load balancing is the traditional load-balancing mechanism used in networks where each flow is allocated to an uplink based on a hash of its 5-tuple. This load balancing spreads the flows across the available links in a fairly even fashion. Usually, with a large number of flows, the even distribution of flows results in an even distribution of bandwidth as well. However, if a few flows are much larger than the rest, static load balancing might lead to suboptimal results.

ACI fabric dynamic load balancing (DLB) adjusts the traffic allocations according to congestion levels. It measures the congestion across the available paths and places the flows on the least congested paths, which results in an optimal or near optimal placement of the data.

DLB can be configured to place traffic on the available uplinks using the granularity of flows or flowlets. Flowlets are bursts of packets from a flow that are separated by suitably large gaps in time.

The ACI fabric adjusts traffic when the number of available links changes due to a link going offline or coming online. The fabric redistributes the traffic across the new set of links.

In all modes of load balancing, static or dynamic, the traffic is sent only on those uplinks or paths that meet the criteria for equal-cost multipath (ECMP); these paths are equal and the lowest cost from a routing perspective.

## ACI Fabric Loop Detection

The ACI fabric provides global default loop detection policies that can detect loops in Layer 2 network segments that are connected to ACI access ports. These global policies are disabled by default, but the port level policies are enabled by default. Enabling the global policies means they are enabled on all access ports, virtual ports, and virtual port channels unless they are disabled at the individual port level.

The ACI fabric does not participate in the Spanning Tree Protocol. Instead, it implements the Mis-Cabling Protocol (MCP) to detect loops. MCP works in a complementary manner with STP that is running on external Layer 2 networks and handles bridge protocol data unit (BPDU) packets that access ports receive.

A fabric administrator provides a key that MCP uses to identify which MCP packets are initiated by the ACI fabric. The administrator can choose how the MCP policies identify loops and how to act on the loops: use syslog only or disable the port.

Although endpoint moves such as VM moves are normal, they can be symptomatic of loops if the frequency is high and the interval between moves is brief. An administrator can choose how to act on move detection loops.

Also, an error disabled recovery policy can enable ports that loop detection and BPDU policies disabled after an interval that the administrator can configure.

The MCP runs in native VLAN mode where the MCP BPDUs sent are not VLAN tagged, by default. The MCP can detect loops due to mis-cabling if the packets sent in native VLAN are received by the fabric, but if there is a loop in non-native VLANs in EPG VLANs, it is not detected. The APIC now supports sending MCP BPDUs in all VLANs in the EPGs configured; therefore, any loops in those VLANs are detected. A new MCP configuration mode allows you to configure MCP to operate in a mode where MCP PDUs are sent in all EPG VLANs that a physical port belongs to by adding an 802.1Q header with each of the EPG VLAN IDs to the PDUs transmitted.

### ACI Design Best Practices

Following are the best practices for profile configuration. They might not work for all environments or applications, they but might help simplify day-to-day operation.

- Policies

  - Reuse policies whenever possible. For example, there should be policies for LACP active/passive/off, 1GE port speed, and 10GE port speed.

  - When naming policies, use names that clearly describe the setting. For example, a policy that enables LACP in active mode could be called "LACP-Active." There are many "default" policies out of the box. However, it can be hard to remember what all the defaults are, which is why policies should be clearly named to avoid making a mistake when adding new devices to the fabric.

  - Create a switch profile for each leaf switch individually, and additionally, create a switch profile for each vPC pair (if using vPC).

- Domains

  - Build one physical domain per tenant for bare-metal servers or servers without hypervisor integration requiring similar treatment.

  - Build one physical domain per tenant for external connectivity.

  - If a VMM domain needs to be leveraged across multiple tenants, you can create a single VMM domain and associate it with all leaf ports where VMware ESXi servers are connected.

- AEPs

  - Multiple domains can be associated with a single AEP for simplicity's sake. In some cases, you might need to configure multiple AEPs to enable the infrastructure VLAN, such as overlapping VLAN pools, or to limit the scope of the presence of VLANs across the fabric.

## ACI LAB Configurations Example

In this lab, we show you how to activate a new ACI cluster, auto fabric discovery (leaf and spine); then we show you how to create policies and tenants, apply the policies to EPG, and at the end integrate the ACI with vCenter. The main steps for this lab are as follows:

1. Build the ACI fabric.
2. Create a tenant.
3. Create contracts and filters.
4. Create a three-tier application.
5. Integrate the ACI with the VMware vCenter.

Figure 4-38 shows the APIC and Nexus 9000 lab topology.

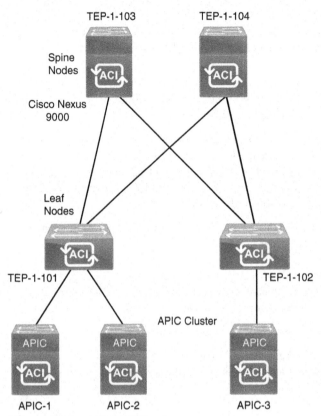

**Figure 4-38** *ACI LAB Topology*

In this lab, the APIC initial setup has already been completed, and all the switches and APIC are cabled and connected. Plus, you have access to the APIC GUI. Example 4-1 shows a sample of the initial setup dialog as displayed on the APIC console.

**Example 4-1** *APIC CLI Initial Setup*

```
Cluster configuration ...
  Enter the fabric name [ACI Fabric1]:
  Enter the fabric ID (1-128) [1]:
  Enter the number of active controllers in the fabric (1-9) [3]:
  Enter the POD ID (1-9) [1]:
  Is this a standby controller? [NO]:


  Is this an APIC-X? [NO]:
  Enter the controller ID (1-3) [1]:
  Enter the controller name [apic1]: sec-ifc5
  Note: The infra VLAN ID should not be used elsewhere in your environment and
should not overlap with any other reserved VLANs on other platforms.
```

```
   Enter the VLAN ID for infra network (2-4094): 3967
   Enter address pool for BD multicast addresses (GIPO) [225.0.0.0/15]:

Out-of-band management configuration ...
  Enable IPv6 for Out of Band Mgmt Interface? [N]:
  Enter the IPv4 address [192.168.10.1/24]: 172.16.10.30/24
  Enter the IPv4 address of the default gateway [None]: 172.16.10.1
  Enter the interface speed/duplex mode [auto]:

admin user configuration ...
  Enable strong passwords? [Y]:
  Enter the password for admin:

  Reenter the password for admin:

Cluster configuration ...
  Fabric name: ACI Fabric1
  Fabric ID: 1
  Number of controllers: 3
  Controller name: sec-ifc5
  POD ID: 1
  Controller ID: 1
  TEP address pool: 10.0.0.0/16
  Infra VLAN ID: 3967
  Multicast address pool: 225.0.0.0/15

Out-of-band management configuration ...
  Management IP address: 172.16.10.30/24
  Default gateway: 172.16.30.1
  Interface speed/duplex mode: auto

admin user configuration ...
  Strong Passwords: Y
  User name: admin
  Password: ********

The above configuration will be applied ...

Warning: TEP address pool, Infra VLAN ID and Multicast address pool
        cannot be changed later, these are permanent until the
        fabric is wiped.

Would you like to edit the configuration? (y/n) [n]:
```

## Building ACI Fabric

The following example accesses the ACI GUI. The APIC will discover leaf and spine switches. Also, you will verify network health and topology.

**Step 1.**   Log in to the APIC as the admin user, as shown in Figure 4-39.

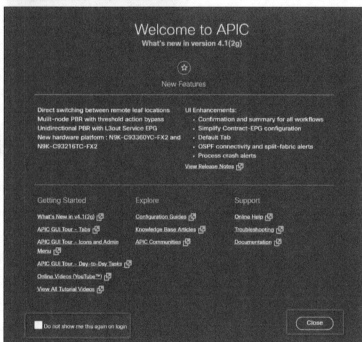

**Figure 4-39**   *APIC 4.1 Login and Welcome Screens*

**Step 2.**   Verify the fabric inventory by choosing **Fabric > Inventory > Fabric Membership**, as shown in Figure 4-40.

**Step 3.**   ACI starts fabric auto discovery. After two or three minutes, the first ACI leaf is detected and shows up under Nodes Pending Registrations. To register the node, assign the node ID and node name and verify the role, as shown in Figure 4-41.

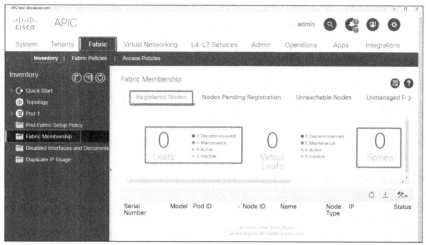

**Figure 4-40**   *APIC 4.1 APIC Fabric Membership Screen*

**Figure 4-41**   *Assign the Node ID and Confirm the Node Type to Register the Node*

**Step 4.**   After a couple of minutes, the first leaf is registered and gets an IP from the ACI. The IP address is populated, and other nodes are discovered. You need to register them. After four to five minutes, all nodes are registered and active, as shown in Figure 4-42.

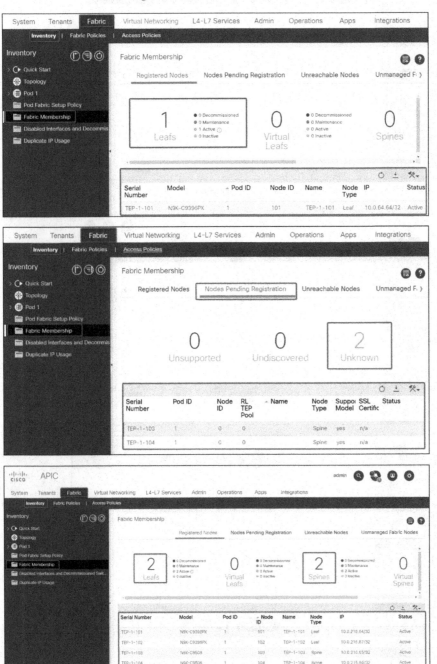

**Figure 4-42**  *APIC Fabric Member Registered Nodes Status*

**Step 5.**    You can verify the fabric topology that shows leaf-and-spine connectivity. The main system screen shows the health score for all nodes in the fabric (see Figure 4-43).

**Figure 4-43**   *Fabric Topology and Health Score*

## Creating Tenant

Creating a tenant requires you to create a VRF and bridge domain. In this example, you first create a tenant named ACILab and then can create a VRF named ACILab_DCCOR that has two bridges: ACILab_BD_DCCOR_1 and ACILab_BD_DCCOR_2.

**Step 1.**    Create a new tenant by choosing **Tenants > Add Tenant**, as shown in Figure 4-44. (Note that there are already three default tenants: common, infra, and mgmt.)

**Figure 4-44**   *Create a New Tenant Named ACILab*

**Step 2.**   After you click **Submit**, the tenant is created. Then you need to create a VRF and bridge domain. Figure 4-45 shows the many options under these new tenants. VRF and Bridge Domains are located under the Networking option.

**Figure 4-45**   *Tenant Options (Application Profiles, Networking, Contracts, Policies, and Services)*

**Step 3.**   Create a VRF named ACILab_DCCOR, and then create a bridge domain named ACILab_BD_DCCOR_1 (VRF Step 2) during VRF creation because VRF requires a minimum of one BD (see Figure 4-46).

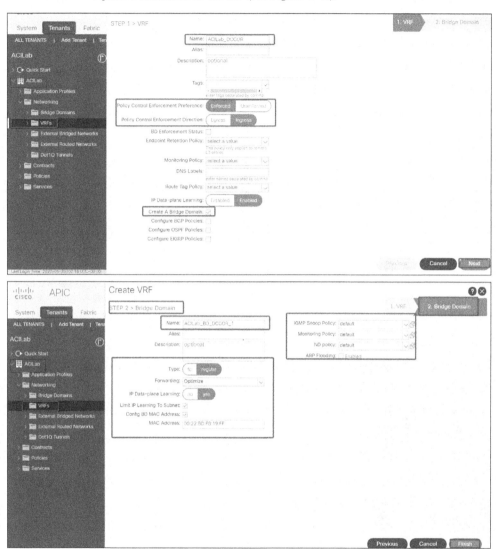

**Figure 4-46**   *Creating a VRF Named ACILab_DCCOR*

**Step 4.**   To create a second bridge domain and add it to the same VRF, right-click **Bridge Domains** and click **Create Bridge Domain**. The Create Bridge Domain page opens with four steps shown in Figure 4-47.

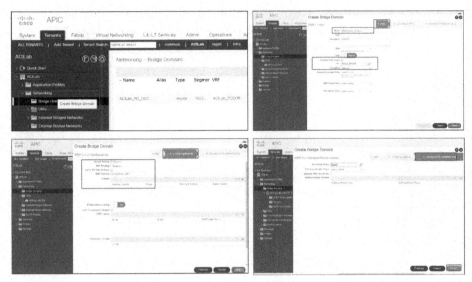

**Figure 4-47** *Creating a Bridge Domain and Assigning It to an Existing VRF*

**Step 5.** After creating the VRF and two BDs, verify the tenant network topology by selecting **Tenant > Specific Tenant (ACILab) > Networking**, as shown in Figure 4-48.

**Figure 4-48** *Tenant VRF Network Topology*

## Creating Contract and Filter

To create a contract and filter, follow these steps:

**Step 1.** Create a filter that passes only HTTPS traffic between the consumer and provider. To do so, choose **Tenants > Specific Tenant (ACILab) > Contracts**. Then right-click **Filter** and select **Create Filter** (see Figure 4-49).

**Figure 4-49**  *Creating a Contacts Filter*

**Step 2.**  Specify the filter name and click **+** (the plus sign) to add the filter. The filter has an Ether Type and IP Protocol type, source ports, and destination ports. For HTTPS, the Ether type is IP, the IP protocol is TCP, the source ports are any, and the destination ports are https/https, as shown in Figure 4-50.

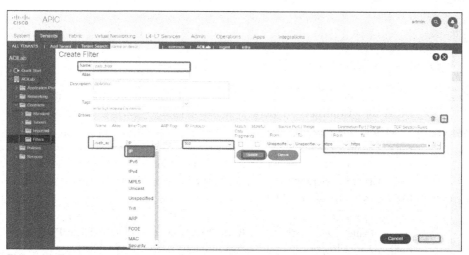

**Figure 4-50**  *Creating HTTPS Filter*

**Step 3.**   Repeat step 2 to create two additional filters for db and app, as shown in Figure 4-51.

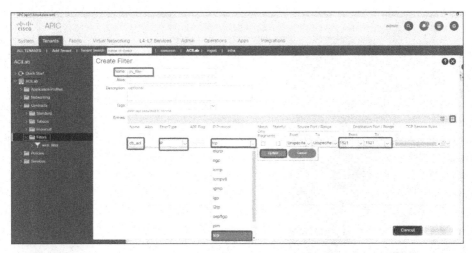

**Figure 4-51**   *Creating More Filters*

**Step 4.**   Verify that all filters are created by choosing **Tenants > Specific Tenant (ACILab) > Contracts > Filters**, as shown in Figure 4-52.

**Step 5.**   To allow communication between two end devices, you need to create a contract. A contract requires a subject with a filter chain to control the traffic. Choose **Tenants > Specific Tenant (ACILab) > Contracts**; then right-click, select **Create Contract**, and specify a contract name. It is important to select the correct scope option here.

To add a subject, click **+** (the plus sign). When the new window opens, fill in the subject name, select both **Apply Both Directions** and **Reverse Filter Path**, and then select a filter or filters, as shown in Figure 4-53.

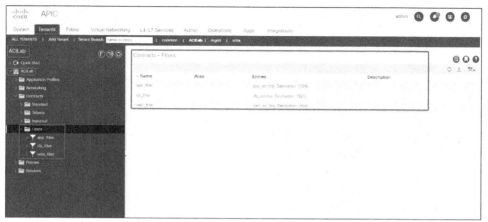

**Figure 4-52**  *ACI Contracts Filters List*

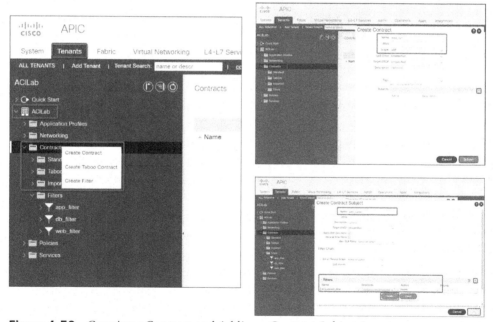

**Figure 4-53**  *Creating a Contract and Adding a Contract Subject*

## Deploying a Three-Tier Application

To create a multitier application, you need an application profile that contains endpoints. To create it, follow these steps:

**Step 1.**    To create a new application profile, choose **Tenants > Specific Tenant (ACILab) > Application Profiles.** Right-click, and then select **Create Application Profile,** as shown in Figure 4-54.

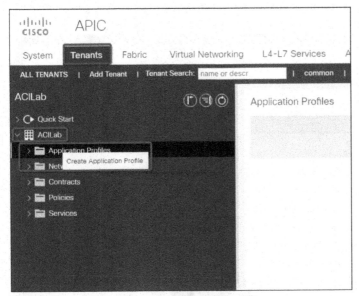

**Figure 4-54**    *Creating an Application Profile*

**Step 2.**    Fill in the name for the new application profile, and under EPGs, click **+** (the plus sign) to add an EPG, as shown in Figure 4-55.

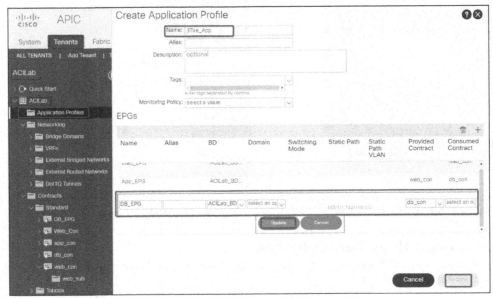

**Figure 4-55**    *Creating an Application Profile and Adding EPGs*

**Step 3.**    After adding the EPGs and assigning them to contracts and bridge domains, click **Submit** to create the profile.

**Step 4.**  Verify the profile you created and EPG topology by choosing **Tenants > Specific Tenant (ACILab) > Application Profiles > Specific Profile (3Tier_App) > Topology**, as shown in Figure 4-56.

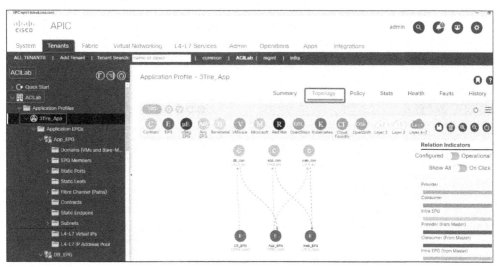

**Figure 4-56**  *Application Profile Topology*

## Integrating with vCenter

The ACI provides administrators with an option to integrate with hypervisors and manage VM switching. The ACI supports integration with Microsoft Hyper-V, OpenStack, and VMWare vCenter. In this example, you integrate ACI with VMWare vCenter as follows:

**Step 1.**  Choose **Virtual Networking > VMM Domains > VMware;** then click + (the plus sign) to add a new vCenter domain, as shown in Figure 4-57.

**Figure 4-57**  *Creating a New vCenter Domain*

**Step 2.**  To integrate, create a VLAN range that will be blocked for vCenter. Then use the range to create a VLAN pool, as shown in Figure 4-58, that creates a VLAN range 1000–1100, and add it to the VLAN pool.

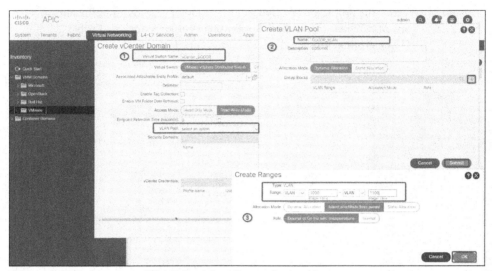

**Figure 4-58**    *Creating a VLAN Pool for vCenter Integration*

**Step 3.**    For integration, ACI requires vCenter admin account credentials to access vCenter. You can create the account and assign it to the domain, as shown in Figure 4-59.

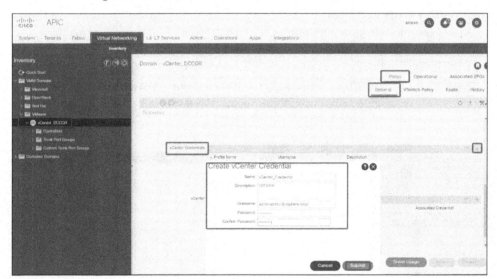

**Figure 4-59**    *Adding vCenter Administrator Credentials*

**Step 4.**    Enter a vCenter IP address or host name, distributed virtual switch type, and data center name so that the APIC can connect to the vCenter, as shown in Figure 4-60.

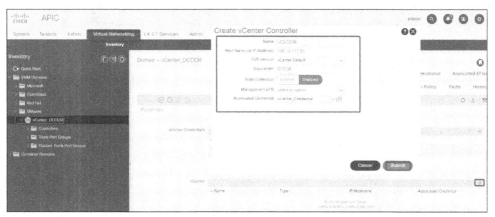

**Figure 4-60**   *Adding IP, Domain, and vCenter Switch Type*

**Step 5.**   Click **OK**. After three or four minutes, the ACI imports the VDS and all VM data, as shown in Figure 4-61.

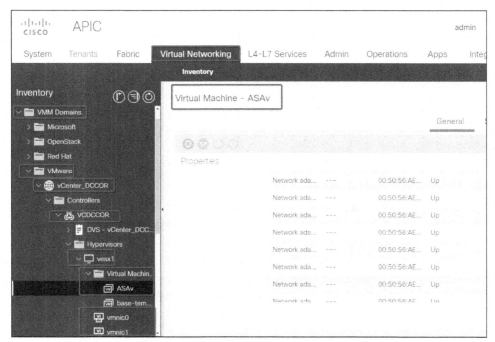

**Figure 4-61**   *APIC Manage vCenter VMs Showing vNICs and VDS*

**Step 6.**   Log in to vCenter and verify the VDS and virtual machines; compare them to the ACI VM networking, as shown in Figure 4-62.

**Figure 4-62**   *Comparing vCenter VMs to APIC VMWare Domain*

This lab shows that APIC is the unified automation and management portal for the ACI fabric and optimizes the application lifecycle for scale and performance by deploying three-tier application awareness. In addition, APIC supports flexible application provisioning across physical and virtual resources. Integrating with vCenter VMware provides a solution that enables next-generation cloud deployments driving business agility, lowers operational costs, and avoids vendor lock-in.

# Exam Preparation Tasks

As mentioned in the Introduction, you have a couple of choices for exam preparation: the exercises here, Chapter 21, "Final Preparation," and the exam simulation questions in the Pearson Test Prep software online.

## Review All Key Topics

Review the most important topics in the chapter, noted with the key topic icon in the outer margin of the page. Table 4-4 lists a reference to these key topics and the page numbers on which each is found.

**Table 4-4**   Key Topics for Chapter 4

| Key Topic Element | Description | Page |
|---|---|---|
| Figure 4-2 | Cisco ACI Fabric | 177 |
| Figure 4-5 | Cisco ACI Multitier Architecture (Spine, Tier-1 Leaf, and Tier-2 Leaf) Topology | 180 |
| Figure 4-6 | Cisco Nexus 9500 Series | 181 |
| Section | Cisco ACI Fabric Discovery | 187 |
| List | ACI Policies | 191 |
| Figure 4-11 | ACI Fabric Policies Configuration Page | 191 |
| Figure 4-12 | Fabric Policy Configuration Process | 192 |
| Figure 4-17 | Policy Configuration Relationship | 195 |

| Key Topic Element | Description | Page |
|---|---|---|
| Section | ACI Policy Model | 197 |
| Section | Cisco ACI Tenants | 198 |
| Section | Virtual Routing and Forwarding | 200 |
| Section | Bridge Domain and Subnets | 200 |
| Section | Cisco ACI Virtual Machine Manager Domains | 203 |
| Section | ACI Contract | 208 |
| Section | Filters and Subjects | 213 |
| Figure 4-34 | ACI VXLAN Packet Format | 216 |
| Section | ACI Intersubnet Tenant Traffic | 217 |
| Figure 4-37 | Policy Identification and Enforcement | 219 |

## Define Key Terms

Define the following key terms from this chapter, and check your answers in the Glossary.

Adaptive Security Virtual Appliances (ASAv), application programing interface (API), Application Virtual Switch (AVS), Cisco Discovery Protocol (CDP), Cisco Nexus, Cisco NX-OS, CLOS topology, Council of Oracles Protocol (COOP), Domain Name System (DNS), Dynamic Host Configuration Protocol (DHCP), dynamic load balancing (DLB), Intra-Fabric Messaging (IFM), Link Layer Discovery Protocol (LLDP), Microsegmentation (uSeg), Network Time Protocol (NTP), Network Virtualization using Generic Routing Encapsulation (NVGRE), Quality of Service (QoS), Simple Network Management Protocol (SNMP), software-defined networking (SDN), System Center Virtual Machine Manager (SCVMM), Virtual Extensible LAN (VXLAN), virtual machine (VM), Virtual Machine Manager (VMM), virtual private network (VPN), Virtual Routing and Forwarding (VRF)

## References

Cisco Application Policy Infrastructure Controller (APIC): https://www.cisco.com/c/en/us/support/cloud-systems-management/application-policy-infrastructure-controller-apic/tsd-products-support-series-home.html

Cisco Application Centric Infrastructure (ACI) Design Guide: https://www.cisco.com/c/en/us/td/docs/dcn/whitepapers/cisco-application-centric-infrastructure-design-guide.html

Cisco ACI Best Practices Quick Summary: https://www.cisco.com/c/en/us/td/docs/dcn/whitepapers/cisco-aci-best-practices-quick-summary.html

Frank Dagenhardt, Jose Moreno, and Bill Dufresne, *Deploying ACI: The Complete Guide to Planning, Configuring, and Managing Application Centric Infrastructure* (Cisco Press, 2018).

Cisco Nexus 9800 Series Switches Data Sheet: https://www.cisco.com/c/en/us/products/collateral/switches/nexus-9000-series-switches/nexus9800-series-switches-ds.html?ccid=cc002960&oid=dstdnc029386

Cisco Nexus 9500 Series Switches Data Sheet: https://www.cisco.com/c/en/us/products/collateral/switches/nexus-9000-series-switches/datasheet-c78-729404.html

Cisco Nexus 9500 Cloud-Scale Line Cards and Fabric Modules Data Sheet: https://www.cisco.com/c/en/us/products/collateral/switches/nexus-9000-series-switches/datasheet-c78-736677.html

# CHAPTER 5

# Cisco Cloud Services and Deployment Models

In today's world, cloud seems to be the answer to every question, from storing photographs to renting computing capability. But cloud computing history goes back to the 1950s when mainframes and time sharing were born. In this era, massive computers performed centralized computational operations, and an elite group of companies shared the computational power of these massive computers by paying a hefty price. In the 1960s, the first working prototype for ARPANET was launched, linking four geographically dispersed computers over what is now known as the Internet. In the 1980s and 1990s, more sophisticated machines capable of executing complex computational tasks at faster speeds were born and were cheaper than previous computers. In 1995, pictures of clouds start showing up in network diagrams, denoting anything too complicated for nontechnical people to understand. In the early 2000s, the era of the dot-com bubble, more cost-effective computing capabilities were sought, giving birth to the modern-era term *cloud computing*.

## This chapter covers the following key topics:

**What Is Cloud Computing:** This section provides an overview of what cloud computing is and what its characteristics are.

**Cloud Service Models:** This section covers different service models of cloud computing per the NIST 800-145 definition, such as Infrastructure as a Service (IaaS), Software as a Service (SaaS), and Platform as a Service (PaaS).

**Cloud Deployment Models:** This section covers different deployment models of cloud computing per the NIST 800-145 definition, such as public, private, community, and hybrid cloud.

## "Do I Know This Already?" Quiz

The "Do I Know This Already?" quiz enables you to assess whether you should read this entire chapter thoroughly or jump to the "Exam Preparation Tasks" section. If you are in doubt about your answers to these questions or your own assessment of your knowledge of the topics, read the entire chapter. Table 5-1 lists the major headings in this chapter and their corresponding "Do I Know This Already?" quiz questions. You can find the answers in Appendix A, "Answers to the 'Do I Know This Already?' Quizzes."

**Table 5-1** "Do I Know This Already?" Section-to-Question Mapping

| Foundation Topics Section | Questions |
|---|---|
| What Is Cloud Computing? | 1–2 |
| Cloud Service Models | 3–4 |
| Cloud Deployment Models | 5–6 |

1. What is cloud computing?

   a. A model for enabling ubiquitous, convenient, on-demand network access to a shared pool of configurable computing resources that can be rapidly provisioned and released with minimal management effort or service provider interaction

   b. A model for enabling ubiquitous, convenient, manual network access to a shared pool of configurable computing resources that can be manually provisioned and released with management effort or service provider interaction

   c. A model for automated provisioning of network connectivity solutions

   d. A model for enabling ubiquitous, convenient, on-demand network access to a shared pool of configurable computing resources that can be manually provisioned and released with management effort or service provider interaction

2. Which of the following is NOT a characteristic of cloud computing?

   a. Broad network access

   b. Rapid elasticity

   c. Measured service

   d. On-demand manual service

3. Which of the following are cloud computing service models? (Choose all the correct answers.)

   a. Platform as a Service (PaaS)

   b. Software as a Service (SaaS)

   c. Resource as a Service (RaaS)

   d. Infrastructure as a Service (IaaS)

4. In the Platform as a Service (PaaS) model, which layers are delivered as a service to cloud consumers?

   a. Networking, Storage, Servers, Virtualization, Operating System

   b. Networking, Storage, Servers, Virtualization, Operating System, Middleware, Runtime

   c. Networking, Storage, Servers, Virtualization

   d. Networking, Storage, Servers, Virtualization, Operating System, Middleware

5. Which of the following are cloud deployment models? (Choose all the correct answers.)

   a. Private cloud

   b. Community cloud

   c. Public cloud

   d. Software cloud

6. Which cloud deployment model provides better control over data security and regulatory compliance?

   a. Public cloud

   b. Hybrid cloud

   c. Community cloud

   d. Private cloud

## Foundation Topics

# What Is Cloud Computing?

For a long time, data centers have faced a critical challenge: the number of applications and amount of data in the data center continue their rapid growth, while IT struggles to provide the resources necessary to make services available to users and meet today's demands using existing infrastructure and organizational silos.

For too long, this siloed approach has hindered IT from adjusting dynamically to new business requests. In existing silos, application workloads are tightly coupled to physical assets, with software linked to operating systems to manage availability, enforce security, and help ensure performance. This tightly coupled model has resulted in the proliferation of server and storage devices, with attendant costs and maintenance overhead, to meet user demand.

Unfortunately, only a small portion of each dollar spent on IT today creates a direct business benefit. Customers are spending approximately 70 percent of their budgets on operations and only 30 percent on differentiating the business. Because data center IT assets become obsolete approximately every five years, the vast majority of IT investment is spent on upgrading various pieces of infrastructure and providing redundancy and recoverability: activities that consume approximately 60 to 80 percent of IT expenditures without necessarily providing optimal business value or innovation.

As a result, IT has been forced to focus on simply keeping the data center running rather than on delivering the kind of innovation that meets user needs for faster, better services while also meeting requirements and ensuring business agility.

What was needed is a solution with the scale, flexibility, and transparency to enable IT to provision new services quickly and cost effectively by using service-level agreements (SLAs) to address IT requirements and policies, meet the demands of high utilization, and dynamically respond to change, in addition to providing security and high performance.

Cloud computing provides a solution for meeting this challenge. Cloud computing is being proposed as one answer to the challenges of IT silos—inefficiencies, high costs, and ongoing support and maintenance concerns—and increasing user demand for services.

The term *cloud computing* has different connotations for IT professionals, depending on their point of view and often their own products and offerings. As with all emerging areas, real-world deployments and customer success stories will generate a better understanding of the term. Let's start with the National Institute of Standards and Technology (NIST) definition:

> The National Institute of Standards and Technology (NIST) defines cloud computing as a model for enabling ubiquitous, convenient, on-demand network access to a shared pool of configurable computing resources (e.g., networks, servers, storage, applications, and services) that can be rapidly provisioned and released with minimal management effort or service provider interaction.

In layperson's terms, cloud computing can be seen as a shared data center that emphasizes virtualization and automation, resulting in consolidation gains in both CAPEX (hardware) and OPEX (management).

Cloud computing provides the following benefits for users:

- **Cost reduction:** Cloud computing eliminates the CAPEX expenditure of buying new hardware and software and setting up and running on-site data centers. You can save money by avoiding the purchase of a large pools of servers, round-the-clock electricity and cooling, and IT experts for managing the infrastructure.

- **Faster deployment:** A large amount of computing power can be provisioned in minutes with some simple clicks, thus avoiding large delays of capacity planning.

- **Productivity:** Large data centers require a lot of IT experts for racking and stacking, cabling, setting up hardware, and patching software. Cloud computing eliminates many of these tasks, allowing IT experts to concentrate on more productive tasks.

- **Reliability:** Users can choose the service of data backup, disaster recovery, and business continuity from a cloud provider by mirroring data at multiple redundant sites.

- **Scalability:** Cloud providers support on-demand needs of customers to scale the services—for example, more or less storage, computing power, bandwidth—right when it's needed and from the right geographical location.

- **Performance:** Cloud providers regularly upgrade the servers to the latest generation of fast and efficient computing power. This offers performance benefits for users, including reduced network latency for applications and faster computing power.

NIST identifies cloud computing with the following five essential characteristics:

- **On-demand self-service:** A consumer can unilaterally provision computing capabilities, such as server time and network storage, as needed automatically without requiring human interaction with each service provider.

- **Broad network access:** Capabilities are available over the network and accessed through standard mechanisms that promote use by heterogeneous thin or thick client platforms (such as mobile phones, tablets, laptops, and workstations).

- **Resource pooling:** The provider's computing resources are pooled to serve multiple consumers using a multitenant model, with different physical and virtual resources dynamically assigned and reassigned according to consumer demand. There is a sense of location independence in that the customer generally has no control or knowledge over the exact location of the provided resources but may be able to specify location at a higher level of abstraction (such as country, state, or data center). Examples of resources include storage, processing, memory, and network bandwidth.

- **Rapid elasticity:** Capabilities can be elastically provisioned and released, in some cases automatically, to scale rapidly outward and inward commensurate with demand. To the consumer, the capabilities available for provisioning often appear to be unlimited and can be appropriated in any quantity at any time.

- **Measured service:** Cloud systems automatically control and optimize resource use by leveraging a metering capability at some level of abstraction appropriate to the type of service (such as storage, processing, bandwidth, and active user accounts). Resource usage can be monitored, controlled, and reported, providing transparency for both the provider and consumer of the utilized service.

Figure 5-1 describes cloud computing characteristics, service models, and deployment models per NIST.

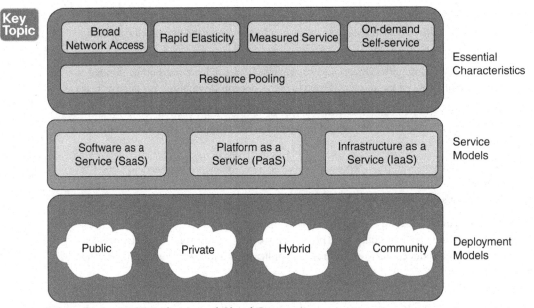

**Figure 5-1** *NIST Definition of Cloud Computing*

# Cloud Service Models

This section discusses some popular models of cloud computing that are offered today as services.

## Software as a Service

Consider the case of an enterprise with its set of software licenses for the various applications it uses. These applications could be in human resources, finance, or customer relationship management, to name a few. Instead of obtaining desktop and server licenses for software products it uses, an enterprise can obtain the same functions through a hosted service from a provider through a network connection. The interface to the software is usually through a web browser. This common cloud computing model is known as *Software as a Service* (SaaS) or a hosted software model; the provider is known as the *SaaS provider*.

SaaS saves the complexity of software installation, maintenance, upgrades, and patches (for example, for security fixes) for the IT team within the enterprise because the software is now managed centrally at the SaaS provider's facilities. Also, the SaaS provider can provide this service to multiple customers and enterprises, resulting in a multitenant model. The pricing of such a SaaS service is typically on a per-user basis for a fixed bandwidth and storage. Monitoring application-delivery performance is the responsibility of the SaaS provider. Salesforce.com is an example of a SaaS provider. The company was founded to provide hosted software services, unlike some of the software vendors that have hosted versions of their conventional offerings.

SaaS offers many benefits to the enterprise. The benefits include

- **Lower cost:** SaaS usually operates on a monthly subscription basis, and customers don't have to pay the license fees up front, resulting in lower initial costs. Also, SaaS providers maintain the infrastructure that removes the CAPEX expenditure for hardware and software.

- **Quick deployment:** In traditional networks, customers need to deploy the hardware and software solutions. SaaS solutions don't require any software to be installed or purchased to use SaaS services. Also, the hardware is managed by the SaaS provider. With SaaS solutions, only a web browser and Internet access are needed to get started.

- **Easier upgrades:** SaaS providers upgrade software solutions regularly and make them available to customers. Customers don't need to buy the upgrade package by paying an additional cost as in traditional software deployment.

- **Scalability:** SaaS providers provide flexible subscription options where customers can provide access to more users to the infrastructure as the business grows.

- **Time savings:** With SaaS solutions, software is already deployed in the cloud. Customers can directly start using the service, whereas in traditional networks customers need to deploy each software solution separately and integrate them, which may take weeks or even months to deploy.

## Platform as a Service

Unlike the fixed functions offered by SaaS, *Platform as a Service* (PaaS) provides a software platform on which users can build their own applications and host them on the PaaS provider's infrastructure. The software platform is used as a development framework to build, debug, and deploy applications. It often provides middleware-style services such as database and component services for use by applications. PaaS is a true cloud model in that applications do not need to address the scalability of the underlying platform (hardware and software). When enterprises write their applications to run over the PaaS provider's software platform, the elasticity and scalability are guaranteed transparently by the PaaS platform.

The platforms offered by PaaS vendors like Google (with its App-Engine) or Force.com (the PaaS offering from Salesforce.com) require the applications to follow their own *application programming interface* (API) and be written in a specific language. This situation is likely to change but is a cause for concern about lock-in. Also, it is not easy to migrate existing applications to a PaaS environment. Consequently, PaaS sees the most success with new applications being developed specifically for the cloud. Monitoring application-delivery performance is the responsibility of the PaaS provider. Pricing for PaaS can be on a per-application developer license and on a hosted-seats basis. Note that PaaS has a greater degree of user control than SaaS.

PaaS offers many benefits to the enterprise:

- Developers are focused on application development, not infrastructure management.

- The application is the unit of deployment and management, while the infrastructure is transparent.

- The development team's requirements for app tools and the operations team's requirements for app management are satisfied.

- The bottleneck in provisioning and deployment is eliminated.

- This service codifies the relationship between developers, IT, and globally distributed clouds.

## Infrastructure as a Service

Amazon is arguably the first major proponent of *Infrastructure as a Service* (IaaS) through its *Elastic Computing Cloud* (EC2) service. An IaaS provider offers "raw" computing, storage, and network infrastructure so that you can load your own software, including operating systems and applications, on to this infrastructure. This scenario is equivalent to a hosting provider provisioning physical servers and storage and letting you install your own operating system, web services, and database applications over the provisioned machines. Amazon lets you rent servers with a certain CPU speed, memory, and disk capacity along with the OS and applications that you need to have installed on them (Amazon provides some "canned" software for the OS and applications known as *Amazon Machine Images* [AMIs], so that is one starting point). However, you can also install your own OSs (or no OS) and applications over this server infrastructure.

IaaS offers you the greatest degree of control of the three models. You need to know the resource requirements for your specific application to exploit IaaS well. Scaling and elasticity are your—not the provider's—responsibility. In fact, it is a mini do-it-yourself data center that you have to configure to get the job done. Interestingly, Amazon uses virtualization as a critical underpinning of its EC2 service, so you actually get a virtual machine when you ask for a specific machine configuration, though VMs are not a prerequisite for IaaS. Pricing for the IaaS can be on a usage or subscription basis. CPU time, storage space, and network bandwidth (related to data movement) are some of the resources that can be billed on a usage basis.

IaaS offer many benefits to the enterprise. The benefits include

- **Greater financial flexibility:** The service offers a hosting IT system in a highly available, service-provider-class computing environment to reduce capital expenditures on servers, software, data center space, and network equipment.

- **Wider choice of services:** IaaS delivers services that are ubiquitously available and easily accessible and provide well-defined service options.

- **Cost-effective scalability:** IaaS offers a pay-as-you-go model, giving you the flexibility to scale up or down in line with business needs. Services are paid for by auditable-metered usage.

- **High availability:** Service providers offer high availability with SLAs based on fault-tolerant technologies, helping to assure that infrastructure is available 24 hours a day, 365 days a year.

- **Increased security:** High levels of service provider security provide a highly secure environment for applications and data.

Figure 5-2 describes cloud computing service models as per NIST.

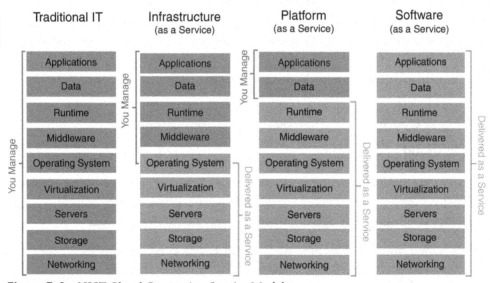

**Figure 5-2** *NIST Cloud Computing Service Models*

In summary, these are three of the more common models for cloud computing. They have variations and add-ons, including Data Storage as a Service (providing disk access on the cloud), Communications as a Service (for example, a universal phone number through the cloud), and so on.

# Cloud Deployment Models

In this section, we discuss various cloud deployment models.

## Private Cloud

In a private cloud, the infrastructure is provisioned solely for a single organization and may be managed internally or by a third party and hosted externally (as a virtual private cloud). Also in a private cloud, multiple business units can be separated by multitenants. The provider has full knowledge of resource locations because it owns the infrastructure.

The private cloud brings the benefits of cloud computing under the control of corporate IT. The benefits include

- **Superior performance:** In a private cloud, you can self-provision resources that match or exceed that of third-party providers.

- **Easy customization:** An enterprise can customize its cloud environment by deploying applications and services tailored to specific business needs.

- **Security and compliance:** A private cloud provides trusted security and regulatory compliance that is currently unavailable from public cloud providers because the infrastructure is not shared.

- **Scalability:** In a private cloud, the ability to scale resources with automatic provisioning permits high utilization and high agility.

- **Lower cost:** A private cloud decreases costs by consolidating workloads to optimize server utilization while maintaining performance and agility. In a traditional data center infrastructure deployment where resources are not shared, the CAPEX is very high.

- **Better control:** A private cloud offers better control over user data and information assets.

The major disadvantage of a private cloud is its cost intensiveness.

## Public Cloud

With a public cloud, the cloud infrastructure is provisioned by the cloud provider for open use by any type of customer. The infrastructure may be owned, managed, and operated by a business, academic, or government organization, or some combination of these entities.

A public cloud offers many benefits to the enterprise. These benefits include

- **Lower cost:** One of the main advantages of a public cloud is lower cost. A public cloud uses the "pay as you use" model, which results in lower costs.

- **No maintenance:** The enterprise doesn't need to purchase any hardware to set up the cloud infrastructure; therefore, no maintenance is involved here. The service provider that hosts the cloud provides the maintenance here.

- **Scalability:** The enterprise gets on-demand resources from the service provider, and the infrastructure can be scaled inward or outward to meet business needs.

- **Reliability:** The enterprise can choose data backup and disaster recovery services from the service provider for the data stored in the public cloud.

- **Available IT talent:** Because the data center is not managed by the enterprise here, the IT talent can be focused on more revenue-generating activities and new innovations that can improve the customers' experience and give an edge over the competition.

The major disadvantage of the public cloud is data security and privacy because the hardware is shared between multiple users.

## Hybrid Cloud

A hybrid cloud is composed of two or more clouds (private, community, or public) that remain unique entities but are bound together, offering the benefits of multiple deployment models. A hybrid cloud can also consist of multiple cloud systems that are connected in a way that allows programs and data to be moved easily from one deployment system to another.

A hybrid cloud model gives organizations the flexibility to put their workloads and data where they make most sense, deploying the right blend of public and private cloud services while addressing availability, performance, and security challenges. This model also often requires IT organizations to reduce complexity and manage strategic, financial, operational, and security risks that result from the need to manage multiple applications across multiple environments for multiple users.

A hybrid cloud offers many benefits to the enterprise. These benefits include

- **A platform for gradual cloud adoption:** Cloud adoption is a multistep journey. Designing workloads for the public cloud often requires organizations to redesign applications, understand new models and new terminology, and modify code to allow applications to control resources. A hybrid cloud allows customers to start by taking advantage of dedicated servers and virtualization using existing applications and resources, eventually evolving the infrastructure by moving the right workloads to a public cloud over time as needed. The flexibility to move specific applications between platforms enables IT organizations to transition to the cloud at their own pace and only with the workloads that make sense.

- **A platform for rapid innovation:** A hybrid cloud allows organizations to move at the speed of DevOps. With access to massive public cloud computing power fully integrated into existing infrastructure, new system enhancements and application updates proceed more quickly through the software life cycle, allowing businesses to get products to market faster. Developers can focus on developing products instead of waiting for IT to provision resources. IT can access resources as needed instead of tying up huge amounts of IT budget in seasonal projects.

- **Support for performance, security, and availability:** A successful hybrid cloud model addresses the performance, security, and availability limitations often experienced in public cloud services. An on-premises private cloud powered by all-flash storage eliminates performance and availability concerns while putting the IT department in control of data security and governance.

- **Reduced total cost of ownership (TCO):** Although the public cloud offers a lower-cost entry point, it is often not the most cost-effective approach at scale. A hybrid cloud model can weave cloud efficiencies into existing IT investments that aren't quite cloud ready while providing the flexibility to tap into public cloud resources as needed.

- **Prevention of vendor lock-in:** With so many vendors now offering public cloud services at various levels and prices, portability of workloads across the cloud is critical. The right hybrid cloud model has workload portability built in.

- **Scalability:** An enterprise can temporarily increase capacity in no time using a public cloud when business needs cannot be met by the private cloud. This is possible using cloud bursting, where an application running on a private cloud bursts to a public cloud when the demand for computing capacity increases.

The major disadvantage of the hybrid cloud is that the initial setup cost exceeds the cost incurred in a public cloud. Another disadvantage of a hybrid cloud is that if it is not picked correctly, there can be compatibility issues between the private and public cloud.

## Community Cloud

A community cloud shares infrastructure between several organizations from a specific community with common concerns (for example, security, compliance, or jurisdiction). A community cloud can be managed internally or by a third party and hosted internally (on-premises) or externally (off-premises).

A community cloud model helps offset common challenges across universities, government agencies, and enterprises, such as cost pressures, technology complexity, spending requirements, security concerns, and a lack of sector-specific services from service providers.

The advantages of a community cloud are cost reduction compared to a private cloud because the infrastructure is shared, ease of data sharing and collaboration across different enterprises that share common concerns, and improved security and privacy.

The major disadvantages of a community cloud are higher costs and low global scalability as compared to a public cloud and sharing of bandwidth and compute capacity.

## Exam Preparation Tasks

As mentioned in the Introduction, you have a couple of choices for exam preparation: the exercises here, Chapter 21, "Final Preparation," and the exam simulation questions in the Pearson Test Prep software online.

## Review All Key Topics

Review the most important topics in the chapter, noted with the key topic icon in the outer margin of the page. Table 5-2 lists a reference to these key topics and the page numbers on which each is found.

**Table 5-2**   Key Topics for Chapter 5

| Key Topic Element | Description | Page |
|---|---|---|
| Paragraph | Cloud Computing Definition as per NIST | 243 |
| List | Cloud Computing Characteristics as per NIST | 243 |
| Figure 5-1 | NIST Definition of Cloud Computing | 244 |
| Figure 5-2 | NIST Cloud Computing Service Models | 247 |
| Paragraph | Private Cloud | 248 |
| Paragraph | Public Cloud | 248 |
| Paragraph | Hybrid Cloud | 249 |
| Paragraph | Community Cloud | 250 |

## Define Key Terms

Define the following key terms from this chapter and check your answers in the Glossary.

community cloud, hybrid cloud, Infrastructure as a Service (IaaS), National Institute of Standards and Technology (NIST), Platform as a Service (PaaS), private cloud, public cloud, Software as a Service (SaaS)

## References

Private Cloud Computing for Enterprises: https://www.cisco.com/c/en/us/solutions/collateral/data-center-virtualization/cloud-computing/white_paper_c11-543729.html

NIST Cloud Computing Definition: https://nvlpubs.nist.gov/nistpubs/Legacy/SP/nistspecialpublication800-145.pdf

Relevant Cisco Live Presentation: https://www.ciscolive.com/

Cloud Computing—A Primer: https://www.cisco.com/c/en/us/about/press/internet-protocol-journal/back-issues/table-contents-45/123-cloud1.html

Private Cloud Solutions: https://www.cisco.com/c/dam/en/us/solutions/collateral/data-center-virtualization/private-cloud/private_cloud.pdf

Unified Computing Whitepaper: https://www.cisco.com/c/en/us/solutions/collateral/data-center-virtualization/unified-computing/whitepaper_c11-739168.pdf

Transitioning to Private Cloud White Paper: https://www.cisco.com/c/dam/en_us/training-events/le21/le34/downloads/689/rsa/Cisco_transitioning_to_the_private_cloud_with_confidence.pdf

Community Cloud Cisco Blogs: https://blogs.cisco.com/datacenter/emerging-cloud-models-community-cloud

Cisco IaaS Solutions: https://www.cisco.com/c/en/us/solutions/cisco-powered/iaas.html

# CHAPTER 6

# Data Center Network Management and Monitoring

Managing a data center infrastructure requires extraordinary uptime and reliability. Network monitoring, operation, and lifecycle management are required to sustain high uptimes and improve network performance.

The Cisco Nexus NX-OS provides best-in-class high availability, scalability, security, and management, allowing network engineers to deploy a high-performance data center infrastructure network. Cisco Nexus supports management and monitoring protocols such as syslog, SNMP, NetFlow, and Switched Port Analyzer (SPAN).

This chapter discusses the software management and infrastructure monitoring aspects of the Cisco Nexus family of switches relevant to the certification exam. It is assumed that you are familiar with the Cisco Nexus product family.

### This chapter discusses the following key topics:

**Cisco Nexus NX-OS Software Installation, Updates, and Their Impacts:** This section discusses the Cisco Nexus NX-OS software installation, software disruptive and non-disruptive upgrade and downgrade procedures, and the erasable programmable logical devices (EPLD) upgrade procedure.

**Network Configuration Management:** This section discusses the Nexus NX-OS configuration backup and restore operations and how to set a rollback point procedure. The configuration of NTP also is covered.

**Network Infrastructure Monitoring:** This section discusses various system management features used to monitor and manage a switch using the Cisco Nexus NX-OS software, including System Messages, SNMP, Call Home, SPAN, and NetFlow features.

**Streaming Telemetry:** This section discusses the Cisco Nexus streaming telemetry that exports system monitoring data in JavaScript Object Notation (JSON) or Google Protocol Buffers (GPB) format in an efficient way. It also includes a configuration example.

**Network Assurance Concepts:** This section discusses the Cisco Network Assurance Engine solution.

## "Do I Know This Already?" Quiz

The "Do I Know This Already?" quiz enables you to assess whether you should read this entire chapter thoroughly or jump to the "Exam Preparation Tasks" section. If you are in doubt about your answers to these questions or your own assessment of your knowledge of the topics, read the entire chapter. Table 6-1 lists the major headings in this chapter and their corresponding "Do I Know This Already?" quiz questions. You can find the answers in Appendix A, "Answers to the 'Do I Know This Already?' Quizzes."

**Table 6-1** "Do I Know This Already?" Section-to-Question Mapping

| Foundation Topics Section | Questions |
|---|---|
| Cisco Nexus NX-OS Software Installation, Updates, and Their Impacts | 1–2 |
| Network Configuration Management | 3–4 |
| Network Infrastructure Monitoring | 5 |
| Streaming Telemetry | 6 |
| Network Assurance Concepts | 7 |

**CAUTION** The goal of self-assessment is to gauge your mastery of the topics in this chapter. If you do not know the answer to a question or are only partially sure of the answer, you should mark that question as wrong for purposes of the self-assessment. Giving yourself credit for an answer you correctly guess skews your self-assessment results and might provide you with a false sense of security.

1. Which statements are true regarding the Cisco Nexus setup utility? (Choose two answers.)

   a. After bootup, the setup utility will start if there is a config file saved in NVRAM.

   b. After bootup, the setup utility will start if there is no config file saved in NVRAM.

   c. The setup utility is a dialog with steps that help you configure the final configuration on Nexus switch.

   d. The setup utility is a dialog with steps that help you with switch initial configuration only.

2. In which programming languages does Cisco offer configuration scripts for POAP? (Choose two answers.)

   a. JSON

   b. Python

   c. TCL

   d. Perl

3. The Cisco Nexus switch can act as an NTP stratum 1 server.

   a. True

   b. False

4. When is a Nexus switch system checkpoint generated? (Choose two answers.)

   a. When a license expires

   b. When the interface config changes

   c. When a specific feature is disabled

   d. When the Local admin password changes

**5.** Which protocol and port are used in SNMP polling by default?

   **a.** TCP 161

   **b.** UDP 161

   **c.** TCP 163

   **d.** UDP 163

**6.** Cisco NX-OS streaming telemetry allows you to push data off the device to a server endpoint as or using _____. (Choose two answers.)

   **a.** JavaScript Object Notation (JSON)

   **b.** Google Protocol Buffers (GPB)

   **c.** XML

   **d.** TCL

**7.** With the Cisco Network Assurance Engine, you can _____. (Choose two answers.)

   **a.** Predict the impact of changes

   **b.** Prevent network configuration changes

   **c.** Prevent a network security breach

   **d.** Verify networkwide behavior

## Foundation Topics

# Cisco Nexus NX-OS Software Installation, Updates, and Their Impacts

Cisco Nexus devices ship with the Cisco NX-OS operating system. NX-OS has the following images:

- BIOS and loader images combined in one file

- Kickstart image

- System image that includes a BIOS image that can be upgraded

A Nexus switch requires a basic setup to enable management. Cisco NX-OS offers a startup setup utility that guides you through a basic (also called a startup) configuration of the system. The setup utility allows you to configure only enough connectivity for system management.

Before creating a network management configuration and connecting the switch to the network, you must create a local management connection through a console terminal and configure the switch with basic management configurations.

You can also use the console to perform the following functions:

- Configure the switch using the command-line interface (CLI)

- Monitor network statistics and errors

- Configure Simple Network Management Protocol (SNMP) agent parameters

- Download software updates

A console local management connection is made between the asynchronous serial port on each Cisco Nexus switch and a console device capable of asynchronous transmission, such as a computer terminal or a laptop, as shown in Figure 6-1. Before you can connect the console port to a computer terminal, make sure that the computer terminal supports VT100 terminal emulation. The terminal emulation software makes communication between the switch and computer possible during setup and configuration. Figure 6-1 shows a laptop connection to a switch console port.

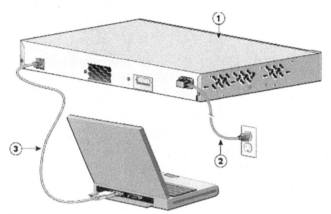

**Figure 6-1**   *Cisco Nexus Console Management Connection*

To connect the Cisco Nexus Series switch to a computer terminal, you need to match the following default port characteristics:

9600 baud

8 data bits

1 stop bit

No parity

When the switch boots, the golden BIOS validates the checksum of the upgradeable BIOS. If the checksum is valid, control is transferred to an upgradeable BIOS image. The upgradeable BIOS launches the kickstart image, which then launches the system image. If the checksum of the upgradeable BIOS is not valid, the golden BIOS launches the kickstart image, which then launches the system image.

You can force the switch to bypass the upgradeable BIOS and use the golden BIOS instead. If you press Ctrl+Shift+6 within two seconds after power is supplied to the switch, the golden BIOS is used to launch the kickstart image, even if the checksum of the upgradeable BIOS is valid.

Before the boot sequence starts, the BIOS performs internal tests on the switch. If the tests fail, the loader does not gain control. Instead, the BIOS image retains control and prints a message to the console at 9600 baud every 30 seconds to indicate a failure.

Figure 6-2 shows the normal and recovery boot sequence.

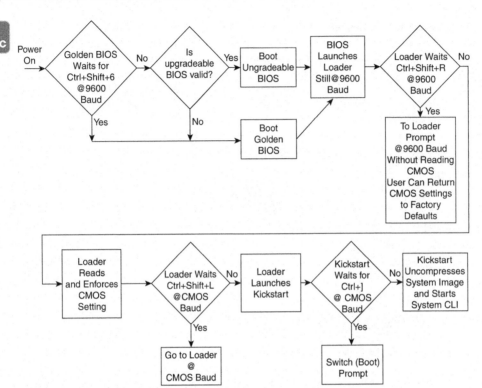

**Figure 6-2**   *Nexus NX-OS Boot Sequence*

When a boot is successful, you can use the setup utility to build an initial configuration file using the System Configuration dialog. The setup starts automatically when a device has no configuration file in NVRAM. The dialog guides you through the initial configuration. After the file is created, you can use the command-line interface to perform additional configuration.

You can press Ctrl+C at any prompt to skip the remaining configuration options and proceed with what has been configured up to that point, except for the Admin password. If you want to skip answers to any questions, press Enter. If a default answer is not available (for example, the device host name), the device uses what was previously configured and skips to the next question.

To configure basic management of the Cisco NX-OS device using the setup utility, follow these steps:

**Step 1.**   Power on the device.

**Step 2.**   Enable or disable password-strength checking.

```
---- System Admin Account Setup ----
Do you want to enforce secure password standard (yes/no) [y]: y
```

A strong password has the following characteristics:

■ Is at least eight characters long

■ Does not contain many consecutive characters (such as "abcd")

- Does not contain many repeating characters (such as "aaabbb")

- Does not contain dictionary words

- Does not contain proper names

- Contains both uppercase and lowercase characters

- Contains numbers

**Step 3.**   Enter the new password for the admin account.

```
Enter the password for "admin": <password>
Confirm the password for "admin": <password>
---- Basic System Configuration Dialog ----
```

This setup utility guides you through the basic configuration of the system. Setup configures only enough connectivity for management of the system.

Press Enter at any time to skip a dialog. Press Ctrl+C at any time to skip the remaining dialogs.

**Step 4.**   Enter the setup mode by entering **yes**.

```
Would you like to enter the basic configuration dialog (yes/no): yes
```

**Step 5.**   Create additional accounts by entering **yes** (no is the default).

```
Create another login account (yes/no) [n]: yes
Enter the User login Id : user_login
```

**NOTE**   Usernames must begin with an alphanumeric character and can contain only these special characters: (+ = . _ \ -). The # and ! symbols are not supported. If the username contains characters that are not allowed, the specified user is unable to log in.

```
Enter the password for "user1": user_password
Confirm the password for "user1": user_password
Enter the user role (network-operator|network-admin)
[network-operator]: default_user_role
```

**Step 6.**   Configure an SNMP community string by entering **yes**.

```
Configure read-only SNMP community string (yes/no) [n]: yes
SNMP community string: snmp_community_string
Enter the switch name: switch_name
```

**Step 7.**   Configure out-of-band management by entering **yes**. You can then enter the Mgmt0 IPv4 address and subnet mask.

```
Continue with Out-of-band (mgmt0) management
configuration? [yes/no]: yes
Mgmt0 IPv4 address: Mgmt0_ip_address
Mgmt0 IPv4 netmask: Mgmt0_subnet_mask
```

**Step 8.**   Configure the IPv4 default gateway (recommended) by entering **yes**. You can then enter its IP address.

```
Configure the default-gateway: (yes/no) [y]: yes
IPv4 address of the default-gateway: default_gateway
```

6

**Step 9.**   Configure advanced IP options such as the static routes, default network, DNS, and domain name by entering **yes**.

```
Configure Advanced IP options (yes/no)? [n]: yes
```

**Step 10.**   Configure a static route (recommended) by entering **yes**. You can then enter its destination prefix, destination prefix mask, and next hop IP address.

```
Configure static route: (yes/no) [y]: yes
Destination prefix: dest_prefix
Destination prefix mask: dest_mask
Next hop ip address: next_hop_address
```

**Step 11.**   Configure the default network (recommended) by entering **yes**. You can then enter its IPv4 address.

> **NOTE**   The default network IPv4 address is the same as the destination prefix in the static route configuration.

```
Configure the default network: (yes/no) [y]: yes
Default network IP address [dest_prefix]: dest_prefix
```

**Step 12.**   Configure the DNS IPv4 address by entering **yes**. You can then enter the address.

```
Configure the DNS IP address? (yes/no) [y]: yes
DNS IP address: ipv4_address
```

**Step 13.**   Configure the default domain name by entering **yes**. You can then enter the name.

```
Configure the default domain name? (yes/no) [n]: yes
Default domain name: domain-name
```

**Step 14.**   Enable the Telnet service by entering **yes**.

```
Enable the telnet service? (yes/no) [y]: yes
```

**Step 15.**   Enable the SSH service by entering **yes**. You can then enter the key type and number of key bits.

```
Enable the ssh service? (yes/no) [y]: yes
Type of ssh key you would like to generate (dsa/rsa) : key_type
Number of key bits <768-2048> : number_of_bits
```

**Step 16.**   Configure the NTP server by entering **yes**. You can then enter its IP address.

```
Configure NTP server? (yes/no) [n]: yes
NTP server IP address: ntp_server_IP_address
```

**Step 17.**   Specify a default interface layer (L2 for Layer 2 or L3 for Layer 3).

```
Configure default interface layer (L3/L2) [L3]: interface_layer
```

**Step 18.**   Enter the default switchport interface state (shutdown or no shutdown). A shutdown interface is in an administratively down state.

```
Configure default switchport interface state (shut/noshut) [shut]:
default_state
```

**Step 19.** Enter the best practices profile for Control Plane Policing (CoPP).

```
Configure best practices CoPP profile (strict/moderate/lenient/none)
[strict]: strict
```

The system now summarizes the complete configuration and asks if you want to edit it.

**Step 20.** Continue to the next step by entering **no.** If you enter yes, the setup utility returns to the beginning of the setup and repeats each step.

```
Would you like to edit the configuration? (yes/no) [y]: no
```

**Step 21.** Use and save this configuration by entering **yes.**

```
Use this configuration and save it? (yes/no) [y]: yes
```

**NOTE**   If you do not save the configuration at this point, none of your changes will be part of the configuration the next time that the device reboots. Enter **yes** to save the new configuration to ensure that the boot variables for the NX-OS image are also automatically configured.

## PowerOn Auto Provisioning (POAP)

PowerOn Auto Provisioning (POAP) automates the process of upgrading software images and installing configuration files on Cisco Nexus switches that are being deployed in the network for the first time.

When a Cisco Nexus Series switch with the POAP feature boots and does not find the startup configuration, the switch enters POAP mode, locates a DHCP server, and bootstraps itself with its interface IP address, gateway, and DNS server IP addresses. The switch also obtains the IP address of a TFTP server or the URL of an HTTP server and downloads a configuration script that enables the switch to download and install the appropriate software image and configuration file.

If a universal serial bus (USB) device that contains the required installation files is not available, POAP requires many services as shown in Figure 6-3. The network infrastructure requirements are as follows:

■ A DHCP server to bootstrap the interface IP address, gateway address, and Domain Name System (DNS) server

■ A TFTP server that contains the configuration script used to automate the software image installation and configuration process

■ One or more servers that contain the desired software images and configuration files

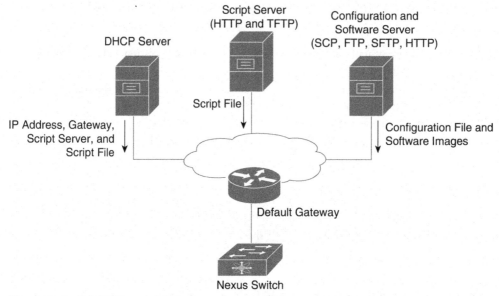

**Figure 6-3**   *POAP Network Infrastructure*

The reference script supplied by Cisco supports the following functionality:

■ Retrieves the switch-specific identifier—for example, the serial number.

■ Downloads the software image (system and kickstart images) if the files do not already exist on the switch. The software image is installed on the switch and is used at the next reboot.

■ Schedules the downloaded configuration to be applied at the next switch reboot.

■ Stores the configuration as the startup configuration.

Cisco offers sample configuration scripts that were developed using the Python programming language and Tool command language (Tcl). You can customize one of these scripts to meet the requirements of your network environment.

The POAP process has the following phases:

1. Power up
2. USB discovery
3. DHCP discovery
4. Script execution
5. Post-installation reload

Within these phases, other process and decision points occur. Figure 6-4 shows a flow diagram of the POAP process.

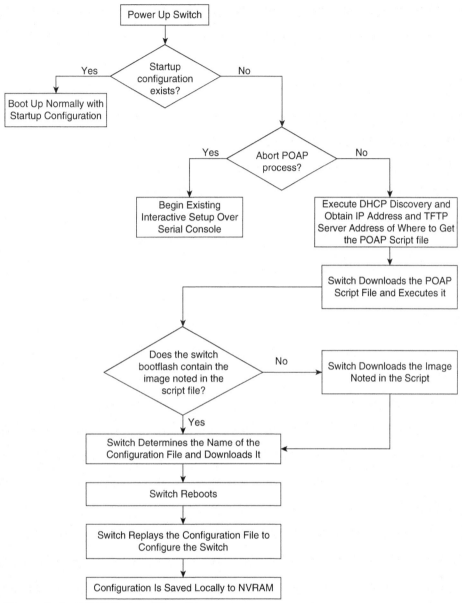

**Figure 6-4**   *POAP Process Flow Diagram*

To set up the network environment to use POAP, follow these steps:

**Step 1.**   Modify the basic configuration script provided by Cisco or create your own script.

The sample POAP script (poap.py) in Example 6-1 includes the personality feature.

**Example 6-1**   *Cisco poap.py Script Example*

```
#md5sum="b00a7fffb305d13a1e02cd0d342afca3"
# The above is the (embedded) md5sum of this file taken without this line, # can be
# created this way:
# f=poap.py ; cat $f | sed '/^#md5sum/d' > $f.md5 ; sed -i
"s/^#md5sum=.*/#md5sum=$(md5sum $f.md5 | sed 's/ .*//')/" $f # This way this
script's integrity can be checked in case you do not trust # tftp's ip checksum.
This integrity check is done by /isan/bin/poap.bin).

# The integrity of the files downloaded later (images, config) is checked # by
downloading the corresponding file with the .md5 extension and is # done by this
script itself.


from poap.personality import POAPPersonality import os


# Location to download system image files, checksums, etc.
download_path = "/var/lib/tftpboot"
# The path to the personality tarball used for restoration personality_tarball =
"/var/lib/tftpboot/foo.tar"
# The protocol to use to download images/config protocol = "scp"
# The username to download images, the personality tarball, and the # patches and
RPMs during restoration username = "root"
# The password for the above username
password = "C1$c04321"
# The hostname or IP address of the file server server = "1.1.1.1"


# The VRF to use for downloading and restoration vrf = "default"
if os.environ.has_key('POAP_VRF'):
    vrf = os.environ['POAP_VRF']


# Initialize housekeeping stuff (logs, temp dirs, etc.) p =
POAPPersonality(download_path, personality_tarball, protocol, username, password,
server, vrf)


p.get_personality()
p.apply_personality()


sys.exit(0)
```

**Step 2.**   (Optional) Put the POAP configuration script and any other desired software image and switch configuration files on a USB device that is accessible to the switch.

**Step 3.**   Deploy a DHCP server and configure it with the interface, gateway, and TFTP server IP addresses and a boot file with the path and name of the configuration script file. (This information is provided to the switch when it first boots.)

**NOTE**   You do not need to deploy a DHCP server if all software image and switch configuration files are on the USB device.

**Step 4.**    Deploy a TFTP server to host the configuration script.

**Step 5.**    Deploy one or more servers to host the software images and configuration files.

**Step 6.**    Power on the switch.

If no configuration file is found, the switch boots in POAP mode and displays a prompt that asks if you want to abort POAP and continue with a normal setup.

No entry is required to continue to boot in POAP mode.

**Step 7.**    (Optional) If you want to exit POAP mode and enter the normal interactive setup script, enter **y** (yes).

The switch boots, and the POAP process begins.

## Data Center Infrastructure Software Lifecycle Management

The Cisco NX-OS software-release methodology preserves the integrity, stability, and quality of mission-critical networks. The primary attributes of the release methodology include the following:

- Major releases introduce significant new features, functions, and platforms.

- Minor releases enhance the features and functions of an existing major release.

- Maintenance releases address product defects in a minor release.

If you want to improve data center security and reliability, installing regular NX-OS upgrades is a good exercise. Apart from having new features, defects, and vulnerabilities, fixes are more stable from a protocol perspective.

Cisco NX-OS supports normal upgrades/downgrades, nondisruptive upgrades (ISSU), Software Maintenance Updates (SMUs), and electronic programmable logic device upgrades (EPLDs) for Nexus modular switches (Nexus 7000/9500).

## Nexus Nondisruptive In-Service Software Upgrade

The Cisco NX-OS in-service software upgrade (ISSU) service allows you to upgrade Cisco Nexus device software while the switch continues to operate and forward traffic. The ISSU reduces or eliminates the downtime typically caused by software upgrades. The default upgrade process is disruptive, so the ISSU needs to be enabled using the CLI. Use of the nondisruptive option helps ensure a nondisruptive upgrade. The guest shell is disabled during the ISSU process and then reactivated after the upgrade.

When you perform an ISSU process, some Layer 2 and Layer 3 protocols will extend their values to accommodate the upgrade. For example, Unidirectional Link Detection (UDLD) and Bidirectional Forwarding Detection (BFD) will increase their hello timers so that adjacency is maintained during the ISSU process. Also, Border Gateway Protocol (BGP), Open Shortest Path First (OSPF), Intermediate System-to-Intermediate System (IS-IS), and Enhanced Interior Gateway Routing Protocol (EIGRP) perform a graceful restart. Because an allocated time is needed for the ISSU to successfully complete, aggressive timers are not supported for any Layer 2 and Layer 3 protocols. For example, a Link Aggregation Control Protocol (LACP) fast timer or an OSPF fast timer is not supported. For Layer 2 and Layer 3 protocols with sensitive timers, the timeout value should be increased. For applications for which you cannot increase the timeout value, the upgrade will be disruptive. Different

Nexus hardware platforms have different ISSU results. Here, we discuss the Nexus 9000 ISSU:

■ **Nexus 9000 ISSU:** The Cisco Nexus 9500 Platform switches are modular switches that are similar to Nexus 7000 switches; they require two supervisors. The minimum configuration required is two system controllers and two fabric modules.

Modular Cisco Nexus 9000 Series switches support parallel upgrades as the default method. The parallel method upgrades the modules in batches instead of one after the other for a faster upgrade. In the upgrade sequence, first the supervisors are upgraded (requiring a switchover), then the line cards, fabric modules, system controllers, and the Fabric Extender (FEX). After switchover is performed in a parallel upgrade, the secondary supervisor takes over, and the installer determines the current line cards and fabric modules. It then divides the components into buckets. It places the first half of the line cards in the first bucket, the first half of the fabric modules in the second bucket, the second half of line cards in the third bucket, the second half of the fabric modules in the fourth bucket, the first system controller in the fifth bucket, and the second system controller in the sixth bucket (see Figure 6-5). Each bucket is upgraded successfully before the upgrade process starts for the next bucket. The console shows which modules are assigned to which bucket and status of the upgrade. You have the option to choose a *serial upgrade* using the CLI.

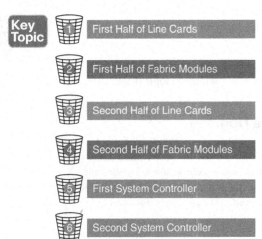

**Figure 6-5**  *Nexus 9500 Parallel Upgrade Process*

Cisco Nexus 9300 Series switches are standalone switches with single supervisors. The ISSU on the Cisco Nexus 9300 Series switches causes the supervisor CPU to reset and load the new software version. The control plane is inactive during this time, but the data plane keeps forwarding packets, leading to an upgrade with no service disruption. After the CPU loads the updated version of NX-OS, the system restores the control plane to a previous known configuration and runtime state and gets in sync with the data plane, thereby completing the ISSU process. Because the data plane keeps forwarding packets while the control plane is upgraded, any servers connected to the Cisco Nexus 9300 Series switch access layer should see no traffic disruption.

When an upgrade is performed, the control plane is reset. This reset causes spanning tree to time out to its neighboring devices, which results in a spanning tree topology change. In addition, if the switch undergoing the ISSU is the spanning tree root, it might not be able to send bridge protocol data units (BPDUs) during the ISSU process. If downstream switches are connected to devices undergoing the ISSU, as a best practice, you should use a vPC design for the ISSU. The vPC offers the advantage of running even if the two vPC peer devices operate with different NX-OS releases. During the transition phase, the vPC continues to work even if the peer devices use different NX-OS code. A configuration lock during the ISSU prevents synchronous upgrades on both vPC peer devices simultaneously (configuration is automatically locked on the other vPC peer device when the ISSU is initiated). This feature enables support for a nondisruptive upgrade for the vPC domain.

When the spanning tree primary switch undergoes the ISSU, it notifies the spanning tree secondary switch so that it can tune its spanning tree timers. If the switches are spanning tree root switches, the peer switch should be enabled. The peer switch allows both devices to share a common bridge ID when sending BPDUs. Because the peer switch is enabled, the spanning tree secondary switch continues to send BDPUs to its connected devices to avoid a spanning tree topology change while the spanning tree primary switch undergoes the ISSU.

## Nexus Disruptive and Nondisruptive Upgrade/Downgrade Procedure

The following steps show the upgrade/downgrade preparation process:

**Step 1.**    Log in to the device using a console port connection.

**Step 2.**    Download the required kickstart and system software files from Cisco.com to a server.

**Step 3.**    Ensure that the required space is available for the image file(s) to be copied. For a dual supervisor device, verify the standby supervisor also.

```
switch# dir bootflash:
49152 Dec 10 14:43:39 2015 lost+found/
80850712 Dec 10 15:57:44 2015 n9000-dk9.7.0.3.I1.1.bin
...


Usage for bootflash://sup-local
 4825743360 bytes used
16312102912 bytes free
21137846272 bytes total


For Standby Sup (Dual Sup device)

switch# dir bootflash://sup-standby/
49152    Dec 10 14:43:39 2015 lost+found/
80850712 Dec 10 15:57:44 2015 n9000-dk9.7.0.3.I1.1.bin
...
```

```
Usage for bootflash://sup-standby
 4825743360 bytes used
16312102912 bytes free
21137846272 bytes total
```

> **NOTE**   Cisco recommends that you have the kickstart and system image files for at least one previous release of the Cisco NX-OS software on the device to use if the new image files do not load successfully.

**Step 4.**   If you need more space on the active supervisor module, delete unnecessary files to make space available.

switch# **delete bootflash:n9000-dk9.7.0.3.I1.1.bin**

For a dual supervisor, delete the image from the standby supervisor also.

switch# **delete bootflash://sup-standby/n9000-dk9.7.0.3.I1.1.bin**

**Step 5.**   Copy the NX-OS kickstart and system images to the active supervisor module bootflash using a transfer protocol. You can use ftp:, tftp:, scp:, or sftp:. The examples in this procedure use scp:.

switch# **copy scp://user@scpserver.cisco.com//download/nxos.7.0.3.I2.1.bin bootflash:nxos.7.0.3.I2.1.bin**

**Step 6.**   Verify the SHA256 checksum for the file to verify the operating system integrity and ensure that the downloaded image is safe to install and use.

switch# **show file bootflash://sup-1/nxos.7.0.3.I2.1.bin sha256sum**

5214d563b7985ddad67d52658af573d6c64e5a9792b35c458f5296f954bc53be

**Step 7.**   Read the release notes for the related image file.

The following steps show how to use upgrade/downgrade prechecks:

**Step 1.**   Enter the **show incompatibility** command to verify that the target image is feature-wise compatible with the current image.

switch# **show incompatibility-all nxos bootflash:n9000-dk9.7.0.3.I1.1.bin**
Checking incompatible configuration(s)

No incompatible configurations

**Step 2.**   Enter the **show install all impact** command to identify the impact. This will show if you can upgrade using ISSU or it will be disruptive.

switch# **show install all impact nxos bootflash:n9000-dk9.7.0.3.I1.1.bin**
Installer will perform compatibility check first. Please wait.
uri is: /n9000-dk9.7.0.3.I1.1.bin
Installer is forced disruptive

Verifying image bootflash:/n9000-dk9.7.0.3.I1.1.bin for boot variable
"nxos".
[####################] 100% -- SUCCESS

```
Verifying image type.
[####################] 100% -- SUCCESS

Preparing "lcn9k" version info using image bootflash:/
n9000-dk9.7.0.3.I1.1.bin.
[####################] 100% -- SUCCESS

Preparing "bios" version info using image bootflash:/
n9000-dk9.7.0.3.I1.1.bin.
[####################] 100% -- SUCCESS

Preparing "lcn9k" version info using image bootflash:/
n9000-dk9.7.0.3.I1.1.bin.
[####################] 100% -- SUCCESS

Preparing "lcn9k" version info using image bootflash:/
n9000-dk9.7.0.3.I1.1.bin.
[####################] 100% -- SUCCESS

Preparing "lcn9k" version info using image bootflash:/
n9000-dk9.7.0.3.I1.1.bin.
[####################] 100% -- SUCCESS

Preparing "lcn9k" version info using image bootflash:/
n9000-dk9.7.0.3.I1.1.bin.
[####################] 100% -- SUCCESS

Preparing "lcn9k" version info using image bootflash:/
n9000-dk9.7.0.3.I1.1.bin.
[####################] 100% -- SUCCESS

Preparing "nxos" version info using image bootflash:/
n9000-dk9.7.0.3.I1.1.bin.
[####################] 100% -- SUCCESS

Preparing "lcn9k" version info using image bootflash:/
n9000-dk9.7.0.3.I1.1.bin.
[####################] 100% -- SUCCESS

Preparing "lcn9k" version info using image bootflash:/
n9000-dk9.7.0.3.I1.1.bin.
[####################] 100% -- SUCCESS

Performing module support checks.
[####################] 100% -- SUCCESS

Notifying services about system upgrade.
[####################] 100% -- SUCCESS
```

```
Compatibility check is done:
Module  bootable Impact          Install-type  Reason
------  -------- --------------  ------------  ------
1       yes      disruptive      reset         Reset due to
                                               single supervisor
21      yes      disruptive      reset         Reset due to
                                               single supervisor
22      yes      disruptive      reset         Reset due to
                                               single supervisor
23      yes      disruptive      reset         Reset due to
                                               single supervisor
24      yes      disruptive      reset         Reset due to
                                               single supervisor
25      yes      disruptive      reset         Reset due to
                                               single supervisor
26      yes      disruptive      reset         Reset due to
                                               single supervisor
27      yes      disruptive      reset         Reset due to
                                               single supervisor
29      yes      disruptive      reset         Reset due to
                                               single supervisor
30      yes      disruptive      reset         Reset due to
                                               single supervisor

Images will be upgraded according to following table:
Module Image Running-Version(pri:alt)  New-Version    Upg-Required
------ ----- ------------------------  -----------    -----------
1      lcn9k 7.0(3)I2(1)                   7.0(3)I1(1) yes
1      bios  v01.42(00               v01.42(00:v01.42(00 no
21     lcn9k 7.0(3)I2(1)                   7.0(3)I1(1) yes
21     bios  v01.42(00               v01.42(00:v01.42(00 no
22     lcn9k 7.0(3)I2(1)                   7.0(3)I1(1) yes
22     bios  v01.42(00               v01.42(00:v01.42(00 no
23     lcn9k 7.0(3)I2(1)                   7.0(3)I1(1) yes
23     bios  v01.42(00               v01.42(00:v01.42(00 no
24     lcn9k 7.0(3)I2(1)                   7.0(3)I1(1) yes
24     bios  v01.42(00               v01.42(00:v01.42(00 no
25     lcn9k 7.0(3)I2(1)                   7.0(3)I1(1) yes
25     bios  v01.42(00               v01.42(00:v01.42(00 no
26     nxos  7.0(3)I2(1)                   7.0(3)I1(1) no
26     bios  v01.42(00               v01.42(00:v01.42(00 no
27     nxos  7.0(3)I2(1)                   7.0(3)I1(1) no
27     bios  v01.42(00               v01.42(00:v01.42(00 no
29     lcn9k 7.0(3)I2(1)                   7.0(3)I1(1) yes
29     bios  v01.42(00               v01.42(00:v01.42(00 no
30     lcn9k 7.0(3)I2(1)                   7.0(3)I1(1) yes
30     bios  v01.42(00               v01.42(00:v01.42(00 no
```

After precheck, you can start the software upgrade/downgrade process. The following steps show the upgrade/downgrade process:

**Step 1.**   Enter the **install all** command to update to the latest Cisco NX-OS software.

```
switch# install all nxos bootflash:n9000-dk9.7.0.3.I1.1.bin
```

**Step 2.**   Peruse the installer impact analysis and accept to proceed.

After the upgrade/downgrade is complete, you can follow these steps to verify the upgrade/ downgrade status and software version:

**Step 1.**   Enter the **show install all status** command to verify the status of the installation.

```
switch# show install all status
```

**Step 2.**   Log in and verify that the device is running the required software version.

```
switch# show version
```

## Programmable Logical Devices Upgrade

Cisco Nexus modular switches contain several programmable logical devices (PLDs) that provide hardware functionalities in all modules. Cisco provides EPLD image upgrades to enhance hardware functionality or to resolve known issues for modular switches only. PLDs include EPLDs, field programmable gate arrays (FPGAs), and complex programmable logic devices (CPLDs), but they do not include application-specific integrated circuits (ASICs). In this chapter, the term *EPLD* is used for *FPGAs* and *CPLDs*.

The advantage of having EPLDs for some module functions is that when you need to upgrade those functions, you just upgrade their software images instead of replacing their hardware.

> **NOTE**   EPLD image upgrades for a line card disrupt the traffic going through the module because the module must power down briefly during the upgrade. The system performs EPLD upgrades on one module at a time, so at any one time the upgrade disrupts only the traffic going through one module.

EPLD image updates are not mandatory unless otherwise specified. The EPLD image upgrades are independent from the Cisco in-service software upgrade (ISSU) process, which upgrades the system image with no impact on the network environment.

When new EPLD images are available, the upgrades are always recommended if your network environment allows for a maintenance period in which some level of traffic disruption is acceptable. If such a disruption is not acceptable, then consider postponing the upgrade until a better time.

> **NOTE**   The EPLD upgrade operation is a disruptive operation. Execute this operation only at a programmed maintenance time. The system ISSU upgrade is a nondisruptive upgrade.

**NOTE** Do not perform an EPLD upgrade during an ISSU system upgrade.

To verify whether an EPLD is required, download and apply the EPLD as follows:

**Step 1.** Determine whether you need to upgrade an EPLD image with impact type or EPLD upgrade not required.

```
switch# show install all impact epld bootflash:n9000-s1-epld.5.1.1.img

Compatibility check:
Module  Type  Upgradable  Impact      Reason

------  ----  ----------  ----------  --------
1       LC    Yes         disruptive  Module Upgradable
2       LC    Yes         disruptive  Module Upgradable
4       LC    No          none        Module is not Online
5       SUP   Yes         disruptive  Module Upgradable
7       LC    Yes         disruptive  Module Upgradable
8       LC    Yes         disruptive  Module Upgradable
9       LC    Yes         disruptive  Module Upgradable
10      LC    Yes         disruptive  Module Upgradable
1       Xbar  Yes         disruptive  Module Upgradable
2       Xbar  Yes         disruptive  Module Upgradable
3       Xbar  Yes         disruptive  Module Upgradable
1       FAN   Yes         disruptive  Module Upgradable
2       FAN   Yes         disruptive  Module Upgradable
3       FAN   Yes         disruptive  Module Upgradable
4       FAN   Yes         disruptive  Module Upgradable

Retrieving EPLD versions... Please wait.
Images will be upgraded according to following table:

Module Type EPLD          Running-Version New-Version g-Required
------ ---- ----          --------------- ----------- -----------
1      LC Power Manager    4.008           4.008       No
1      LC IO               1.015           1.016       Yes
1      LC Forwarding Engine 1.006          1.006       No
1      LC FE Bridge(1)     186.005         186.006     Yes
1      LC FE Bridge(2)     186.005         186.006     Yes
1      LC Linksec Engine(1) 2.006          2.006       No
1      LC Linksec Engine(2) 2.006          2.006       No
1      LC Linksec Engine(3) 2.006          2.006       No
1      LC Linksec Engine(4) 2.006          2.006       No
1      LC Linksec Engine(5) 2.006          2.006       No
1      LC Linksec Engine(6) 2.006          2.006       No
1      LC Linksec Engine(7) 2.006          2.006       No
```

**Step 2.**    Download the EPDL image from Cisco.com.

**Step 3.**    Verify the EPLD upgrade version.

```
switch# show version module 7 epld


EPLD Device Version
------------------------------------------
Power Manager 4.008
IO 1.016
Forwarding Engine 1.006
FE Bridge(1) 186.008 << OK!
FE Bridge(2) 186.008 << OK!
Linksec Engine(1) 2.007
Linksec Engine(2) 2.007
Linksec Engine(3) 2.007
Linksec Engine(4) 2.007
```

**Step 4.**    Upgrade the EPLD for a specific module.

```
switch# install module 1 epld bootflash:n7000-s1-epld.5.1.1.img


Retrieving EPLD versions... Please wait.


Images will be upgraded according to following table:
Module Type EPLD          Running-Version New-Version Upg-Required
------ ---- ----          --------------- ----------- -------------
1      LC   Power Manager    4.008         4.008        No
1      LC   IO               1.015         1.016        Yes
1      LC   Forwarding Engine 1.006        1.006        No
1      LC   FE Bridge(1)     186.005       186.006      Yes
1      LC   FE Bridge(2)     186.005       186.006      Yes
1      LC   Linksec Engine(1) 2.006        2.006        No
1      LC   Linksec Engine(2) 2.006        2.006        No
1      LC   Linksec Engine(3) 2.006        2.006        No
1      LC   Linksec Engine(4) 2.006        2.006        No
1      LC   Linksec Engine(5) 2.006        2.006        No
1      LC   Linksec Engine(6) 2.006        2.006        No
1      LC   Linksec Engine(7) 2.006        2.006        No
1      LC   Linksec Engine(8) 2.006        2.006        No
Module 1 will be powered down.
Do you want to continue? (yes/no) [n]: y
```

# Nexus Configuration Management

Configuration Management (CM) enables you to control and track changes that are made to a device configuration. CM uses a change management feature to back up device configurations and also to set up a rollback checkpoint that helps clear all configuration changes.

## NX-OS Configuration Save and Backup

The Cisco NX-OS software has two types of configuration files: *running configuration* and *startup configuration*. The device uses the startup configuration (startup-config) during device startup to configure the software features. The running configuration (running-config) contains the current changes that you make to the startup configuration file. The two configuration files can be different. You might want to change the device configuration for a short time rather than permanently. In this case, you would change the running configuration by using commands in global configuration mode but not save the changes to the startup configuration.

Configuration files contain the Cisco NX-OS software commands used to configure the features on a Cisco Nexus device. Commands are parsed (translated and executed) by the Cisco NX-OS software when the system is booted (from the startup-config file) or when you enter commands at the CLI in a configuration mode.

To change the startup configuration file, you need to save the running-configuration file to the startup configuration using the following command:

```
copy running-config startup-config
```

The NX-OS **copy** command also can be used to back up the running configuration to the remote server using tftp: or ftp: or scp: or sftp: protocols:

```
copy running-config scheme://server/[url /]filename
```

You can configure Cisco NX-OS by using a file saved on the remote server. The command is similar, except that the source is the remote file and the destination is the running configuration:

```
copy scheme://server/[url /]filename running-config
```

Many automation tools provide config archive and config change tracking. Cisco Prime is one Cisco tool that offers regular configuration archives.

## Nexus Config Rollback and Checkpoint

The NX-OS rollback feature enables you to take a snapshot, or user checkpoint, of Cisco NX-OS configuration and then reapply that configuration to the device at any point without having to reload the device. A rollback allows any authorized user to apply this checkpoint configuration without requiring expert knowledge of the features configured in the checkpoint.

Cisco NX-OS automatically creates system checkpoints. You can use either a user or system checkpoint to perform a rollback. You can create a checkpoint copy of the current running configuration at any time by using this command:

```
checkpoint {[ cp-name ] [ description descr ] | file filename }
```

Cisco NX-OS saves this checkpoint as an ASCII file that you can use to roll back the running configuration to the checkpoint configuration at a future time. You can create multiple checkpoints to save different versions of your running configuration.

To roll back the running configuration, you use the following command:

```
rollback running-config { checkpoint cp-name | file cp-file } [ atomic | best-effort |
stop-at-first-failure ]
```

The rollback trigger types are

■ **atomic:** Implements a rollback only if no errors occur

■ **best-effort:** Implements a rollback and skips any errors

■ **stop-at-first-failure:** Implements a rollback that stops if an error occurs

The default rollback type is atomic.

When you are ready to roll back to a checkpoint configuration, you can view the changes that will be applied to the current running configuration before committing to the rollback operation using **show diff rollback-patch.**

```
show diff rollback-patch { checkpoint src-cp-name | running-config | startup-config |
file source-file } { checkpoint dest-cp-name | running-config | startup-config |
file dest-file }
```

If an error occurs during the rollback operation, you can choose to cancel the operation, or you can ignore the error and proceed with the rollback. If you cancel the operation, Cisco NX-OS provides a list of changes already applied before the error occurred. You need to clean up these changes manually.

After creating a checkpoint, you can verify the difference between the checkpoint and the running-config (if you made any changes to running-config) and rollback by skipping any errors.

**Step 1.** Create a checkpoint named **chk** with the description **first check point.**

```
switch# checkpoint chk description first check point
```

**Step 2.** Verify that the checkpoint was created.

```
switch# show checkpoint chk
--------------------------------------------------------
Name: chk
!Command: Checkpoint cmd vdc 1
!Time: Sun Sep 8 11:51:50 2019
version 7.3(0)D1(1)
power redundancy-mode redundant
vdc switch id 1
limit-resource module-type m1 m1xl m2xl f2e
allocate interface Ethernet2/1-48
allocate interface Ethernet3/1-48
allocate interface Ethernet4/1-48
```

**Step 3.** Apply any new configurations.

**Step 4.** Verify the difference between the checkpoint and current running configuration.

```
switch# show diff rollback-patch checkpoint chk running-config

Collecting Running-Config
#Generating Rollback Patch
!!
```

```
interface Ethernet2/1
no shutdown
exit
!
interface Ethernet2/2
ip address 10.10.20.1/24
no shutdown
```

**Step 5.** Roll back from chk, skipping any errors.

```
switch# rollback running-config checkpoint chk
Note: Applying config parallelly may fail Rollback verification
Collecting Running-Config
#Generating Rollback Patch
Executing Rollback Patch
Generating Running-config for verification
Generating Patch for verification
Verification is Successful.
Rollback completed successfully.
```

Cisco NX-OS can automatically generate system checkpoints to help you avoid a loss of configuration information. System checkpoints are generated by the following events:

■ When an enabled feature is disabled with the **no feature** command

■ When an instance of a Layer 3 protocol is removed, such as with the **no router bgp** command or the **no ip pim sparse-mode** command

■ When a feature's license expires

If one of these events causes system configuration changes, the feature software creates a system checkpoint that you can use to roll back to the previous system configuration.

The system-generated checkpoint filenames begin with "system-" and include the feature name. For example, the first time that you disable the BGP feature, the system creates the checkpoint named **system-fm-__inst_1__bgp**.

# Network Time Management

Time management, or time synchronization, is a critical component of any network. Every aspect of managing, securing, and debugging a network requires an accurate event time. Accurate timestamping is key to determine when a configuration changed or problems occurred and to find time correlations.

Cisco Nexus has an internal clock, and that clock needs to be configured to reflect the correct time. It is recommended that you sync the time with an accurate time source. If the time is set manually on all devices in a data center, these times will be ahead or behind a few seconds, or they will drift randomly, and after a while, all devices will be out of sync. If network devices are out of sync by a few milliseconds or, in extreme cases a few seconds, it can be very difficult for you to determine the sequence of events if a problem should occur.

Cisco NX-OS supports the Network Time Protocol (NTP) to synchronize time. NTP uses the User Datagram Protocol (UDP) as its transport protocol. All NTP communications use

Coordinated Universal Time (UTC). Cisco NX-OS also supports Precision Time Protocol (PTP); its hardware timestamp feature provides greater accuracy than NTP.

## Network Time Protocol

The Network Time Protocol (NTP) synchronizes the time among a set of distributed time servers and clients so that you can correlate events when you receive system logs and other time-specific events from multiple network devices.

An NTP server usually receives its time from a source such as a radio clock or an atomic clock attached to a time server and then distributes this time across the network. NTP is extremely efficient; no more than one packet per minute is necessary to synchronize two machines to within a millisecond of each other.

NTP uses a stratum to describe the distance between a network device and an authoritative time source, as shown in Figure 6-6:

- A stratum 1 time server is directly attached to an authoritative time source (such as an atomic clock).

- A stratum 2 NTP server receives its time through NTP from a stratum 1 NTP server.

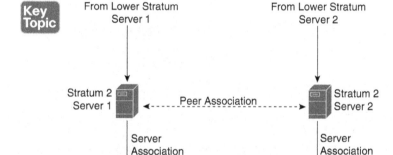

**Figure 6-6**  *NTP Stratum*

Before synchronizing, NTP compares the time reported by several network devices and does not synchronize with one that is significantly different, even if it is a stratum 1.

Because Cisco NX-OS cannot connect to a radio or atomic clock and act as a stratum 1 server, Cisco recommends that you use the public NTP servers available on the Internet.

If the network is isolated from the Internet, Cisco NX-OS allows you to configure the time as though it were synchronized through NTP, even though it was not.

The time kept on a device is a critical resource; it is strongly recommended that you use NTP security features to avoid any accidental or malicious setting of incorrect time. Two mechanisms are available: an access list-based restriction scheme and an encrypted authentication mechanism.

Table 6-2 lists the NTP default parameters. You can alter NTP parameters as necessary.

**Table 6-2**   NTP Default Settings

| Parameters | Default |
|---|---|
| NTP | Enabled |
| NTP authentication | Disabled |
| NTP port | UDP 123 |
| NTP access | Enabled |
| NTP logging | Disabled |
| NTP access group match all | Disabled |
| NTP broadcast server | Disabled |
| NTP multicast server | Disabled |
| NTP multicast client | Disabled |

Tables 6-3 and 6-4 describe the most-used NTP configuration commands. For a full list of the commands, refer to the Nexus System Management Configuration Guide links shown in the reference list at the end of this chapter.

**Table 6-3**   NTP Global Commands

| Command | Purpose |
|---|---|
| [no] feature ntp | Enables or disables NTP (on Nexus 7000, you can enable or disable in a particular VDC). NTP is enabled by default. |
| ntp master [*stratum*] | Configures the device as an authoritative NTP server. You can specify a different stratum level from which NTP clients get their time synchronized. The range is from 1 to 15. |
| ntp server {*ip-address* \| *ipv6-address* \|*dns-name*} [key *key-id*] [maxpoll *max-poll*] [minpoll *min-poll*] [prefer] [use-vrf *vrf-name*] | Forms an association with a server. Use the **key** keyword to configure a key to be used while communicating with the NTP server. The range for the *key-id* argument is from 1 to 65,535. Use the **maxpoll** and **minpoll** keywords to configure the maximum and minimum intervals in which to poll a peer. The range for the *max-poll* and *min-poll* arguments is from 4 to 16 seconds, and the default values are 6 and 4, respectively. Use the **prefer** keyword to make this the preferred NTP server for the device. Use the **use-vrf** keyword to configure the NTP server to communicate over the specified VRF. The *vrf-name* argument can be default, management, or any case-sensitive alphanumeric string up to 32 characters. **NOTE:** If you configure a key to be used while communicating with the NTP server, make sure that the key exists as a trusted key on the device. |

| Command | Purpose |
|---|---|
| **ntp peer** {*ip-address* \| *ipv6-address* \|*dns-name*} [**key** *key-id*] [**maxpoll** *max-poll*] [**minpoll** *min-poll*] [**prefer**] [**use-vrf** *vrf-name*] | Forms an association with a peer. You can specify multiple peer associations. |
| | Use the **key** keyword to configure a key to be used while communicating with the NTP peer. The range for the *key-id* argument is from 1 to 65,535. |
| | Use the **maxpoll** and **minpoll** keywords to configure the maximum and minimum intervals in which to poll a peer. The range for the *max-poll* and *min-poll* arguments is from 4 to 17 seconds, and the default values are 6 and 4, respectively. |
| | Use the **prefer** keyword to make this the preferred NTP peer for the device. |
| | Use the **use-vrf** keyword to configure the NTP peer to communicate over the specified VRF. The *vrf-name* argument can be default, management, or any case-sensitive alphanumeric string up to 32 characters. |
| **ntp** *authentication-key number* **md5** *md5-string*<br><br>**ntp** *trusted-key number* | Defines the authentication keys. The device does not synchronize to a time source unless the source has one of these authentication keys and the key number is specified by the **ntp** *trusted-key number* command. |
| | The range for authentication keys is from 1 to 65,535. Cisco NX-OS supports 16 or 32 alphanumeric characters for the MD5 string. |
| **ntp authenticate** | Enables or disables the NTP authentication feature. NTP authentication is disabled by default. |
| **ntp access-group** {**peer** \| **serve** \| **serve-only** \| **query-only** } *access-list-name* | Creates or removes an access group to control NTP access and applies a basic IP access list. |
| | ACL processing stops and does not continue to the next access group option if NTP matches a deny ACL rule in a configured peer. |
| | The **peer** keyword enables the device to receive time requests and NTP control queries and to synchronize itself to the servers specified in the access list. |
| | The **serve** keyword enables the device to receive time requests and NTP control queries from the servers specified in the access list but not to synchronize itself to the specified servers. |
| | The **serve-only** keyword enables the device to receive only time requests from servers specified in the access list. |
| | The **query-only** keyword enables the device to receive only NTP control queries from the servers specified in the access list. |
| **ntp source** *ip-address* | Configures the source IP address for all NTP packets. The *ip-address* can be in IPv4 or IPv6 format. |

6

| Command | Purpose |
|---|---|
| **ntp source-interface** *interface* | Configures the source interface for all NTP packets. Use the **?** keyword to display a list of supported interfaces. |
| **ntp broadcast** [*destination ip-address*] [**key** *key-id*] [*version number*] | Enables an NTP IPv4 broadcast server on the specified interface. *destination ip-address*: Configures the broadcast destination IP address. **key** *key-id*: Configures the broadcast authentication key number. The range is from 1 to 65,535. *version number*: Configures the NTP version. The range is from 2 to 4. |
| **ntp multicast** [*ipv4-address* \| *ipv6-address*] [**key** *key-id*] [*ttl value*] [*version number*] | Enables an NTP IPv6 broadcast server on the specified interface. *destination ip-address*: Configures the broadcast destination IP address. **key** *key-id*: Configures the broadcast authentication key number. The range is from 1 to 65,535. *ttl value*: The time-to-live value of the multicast packets. The range is from 1 to 255. *version number*: Configures the NTP version. **NOTE:** For an IPv4 multicast server, the range is from 2 to 4. |
| **ntp multicast client** [*ipv4-address* \| *ipv6-address*] | Enables an NTP IPv6 broadcast server on the specified interface. |
| **ntp logging** | Enables or disables system logs to be generated with significant NTP events. NTP logging is disabled by default. |

**Table 6-4** NTP Verification Commands

| Command | Purpose |
|---|---|
| **show ntp access-groups** | Displays the NTP access group configuration. |
| **show ntp authentication-keys** | Displays the configured NTP authentication keys. |
| **show ntp authentication-status** | Displays the status of NTP authentication. |
| **show ntp internal** | Displays internal NTP information. |
| **show ntp logging-status** | Displays the NTP logging status. |
| **show ntp peer-status** | Displays the status for all NTP servers and peers. |
| **show ntp peers** | Displays all the NTP peers. |
| **show ntp rts-update** | Displays the RTS update status. |
| **show ntp source** | Displays the configured NTP source IP address. |
| **show ntp source-interface** | Displays the configured NTP source interface. |
| **show ntp statistics** {**io** \| **local** \| **memory** \| **peer** {**ipaddr** {*ipv4-addr* \| *ipv6-addr*} \| **name** *peer-name*}} | Displays the NTP statistics. |
| **show ntp trusted-keys** | Displays the configured NTP trusted keys. |
| **show running-config ntp** | Displays NTP information. |

Example 6-2 shows the NTP configuration to sync with Internet NTP servers, sourcing NTP traffic from VLAN 10.

**Example 6-2**  *NX-OS NTP Configuration Example*

```
Nexus# configure terminal


!--- Form an association with a server. Use the prefer keyword to make this
!--- server as preferred NTP server.

Nexus(config)# ntp server 129.6.15.28 prefer
Nexus(config)# ntp server 129.6.15.29

!--- Configure the source interface for all NTP packets.

Nexus(config)# ntp source-interface vlan10

!--- Configure the device as an authoritative NTP server.

Nexus(config)# ntp master 1

Nexus(config)# interface vlan10
Nexus(config-if)# no shutdown
Nexu(config-if)# no ip redirects
Nexus(config-if)# ip address 172.20.100.34/24
```

Example 6-3 shows the NTP sync process. The NTP server is configured (including the local device) and the NTP is synced with preferred server 129.6.15.28.

**Example 6-3**  *NX-OS NTP Status*

```
Nexus# show ntp peers
-------------------------------------------------
 Peer IP Address            Serv/Peer
-------------------------------------------------
 127.127.1.0                Server (configured)
 129.6.15.28                Server (configured)
 129.6.15.29                Server (configured)


!--- Use the show ntp peer-status command in order to display the status for all NTP
servers and peers.
!--- For example:

Nexus# show ntp peer-status
Total peers : 3
* - selected for sync, + -  peer mode(active),
```

6

```
- - peer mode(passive), = - polled in client mode
    remote                  local                 st   poll   reach delay   vrf
--------------------------------------------------------------------------------
=127.127.1.0               172.20.100.34           1   64        0   0.00000
*129.6.15.28               172.20.100.34           1   64      377   0.03938 default
=129.6.15.29               172.20.100.34           1   64      377   0.01804 default
```

## Precision Time Protocol

The Precision Time Protocol (PTP) is a time synchronization protocol for nodes distributed across a network. Its hardware timestamp feature provides greater accuracy than the Network Time Protocol (NTP).

A PTP system can consist of a combination of PTP and non-PTP devices. These PTP devices include ordinary clocks, boundary clocks, and transparent clocks. Non-PTP devices include ordinary network switches, routers, and other infrastructure devices.

PTP is a distributed protocol that specifies how real-time PTP clocks in the system synchronize with each other. These clocks are organized into a master-member synchronization hierarchy with the grandmaster clock, the clock at the top of the hierarchy, determining the reference time for the entire system. Synchronization is achieved by exchanging PTP timing messages, with the members using the timing information to adjust their clocks to the time of their master in the hierarchy. PTP operates within a logical scope called a PTP domain. Figure 6-7 shows an example of a PTP domain.

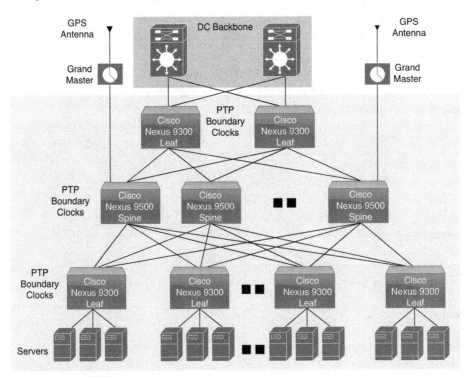

**Figure 6-7** *PTP Domain*

The following clocks are common PTP devices:

- **Ordinary clock:** Communicates with the network based on a single physical port, similar to an end host. An ordinary clock can function as a grandmaster clock.

- **Boundary clock:** Typically has several physical ports, with each port behaving like a port of an ordinary clock. However, each port shares the local clock, and the clock data sets are common to all ports. Each port decides its individual state, either master (synchronizing other ports connected to it) or member (synchronizing to a downstream port), based on the best clock available to it through all of the other ports on the boundary clock. Messages related to synchronization and establishing the master-member hierarchy terminate in the protocol engine of a boundary clock and are not forwarded.

- **Transparent clock:** Forwards all PTP messages like an ordinary switch or router but measures the residence time of a packet in the switch (the time that the packet takes to traverse the transparent clock) and in some cases the link delay of the ingress port for the packet. The ports have no state because the transparent clock does not need to synchronize to the grandmaster clock.

- **End-to-end transparent clock:** Measures the residence time of a PTP message and accumulates the times in the correction field of the PTP message or an associated follow-up message.

- **Peer-to-peer transparent clock:** Measures the residence time of a PTP message and computes the link delay between each port and a similarly equipped port on another node that shares the link. For a packet, this incoming link delay is added to the residence time in the correction field of the PTP message or an associated follow-up message.

The PTP process consists of two phases: establishing the master-member hierarchy and synchronizing the clocks.

Within a PTP domain, each port of an ordinary or boundary clock follows this process to determine its state:

- Examines the contents of all received announce messages (issued by ports in the master state).

- Compares the data sets of the foreign master (in the announce message) and the local clock for priority, clock class, accuracy, and so on.

- Based on this comparison, determines its own state as either master or member.

After the master-member hierarchy has been established, the clocks are synchronized as follows:

- The master sends a synchronization message to the member and notes the time it was sent.

- The member receives the synchronization message and notes the time it was received.

■ The member sends a delay-request message to the master and notes the time it was sent.

■ The master receives the delay-request message and notes the time it was received.

■ The master sends a delay-response message to the member.

■ The member uses these timestamps to adjust its clock to the time of its master.

Table 6-5 lists the PTP default parameters. You can alter PTP parameters as necessary.

**Table 6-5**   PTP Default Settings

| Parameters | Default |
|---|---|
| PTP | Disabled |
| PTP domain | 0 |
| PTP priority1 value when advertising the clock | 255 |
| PTP priority2 value when advertising the clock | 255 |
| PTP announce interval | 1 (one packet every 2 seconds) |
| PTP sync interval | 2 (one packet every 4 seconds) |
| PTP announce timeout | 3 |
| PTP minimum delay request interval | 2 (one packet every 4 seconds) |
| PTP VLAN | 1 |

Tables 6-6 through 6-8 describe the most-used PTP configuration commands. For a full list of the commands, refer to the Nexus System Management Configuration Guide links shown in the reference list at the end of this chapter.

**Table 6-6**   PTP Global Commands

| Command | Purpose |
|---|---|
| [no] feature ptp | Enables or disables PTP on the device. |
| ptp source *ip-address* [ vrf *vrf*] | Configures the source IP address for all PTP packets. The *ip-address* can be in IPv4 format. |
| ptp domain *number* | (Optional) Configures the domain number to use for this clock. PTP domains allow you to use multiple independent PTP clocking subdomains on a single network. The range is from 0 to 128. |
| ptp priority1 *value* | (Optional) Configures the **priority1** value to use when advertising this clock. This value overrides the default criteria (clock quality, clock class, and so on) for best master clock selection. Lower values take precedence. The range is from 0 to 255. |
| ptp priority2 *value* | (Optional) Configures the **priority2** value to use when advertising this clock. This value is used to decide between two devices that are otherwise equally matched in the default criteria. For example, you can use the **priority2** value to give a specific switch priority over other identical switches. The range is from 0 to 255. |

**Table 6-7**   PTP Interface-Level Commands

| Command | Purpose |
|---|---|
| [no] ptp | Enables or disables PTP on an interface. |
| ptp announce {*interval seconds* \| *timeout count* } | (Optional) Configures the interval between PTP announce messages on an interface or the number of PTP intervals before a timeout occurs on an interface.<br><br>The range for the PTP announcement interval is from 0 to 4 log seconds, and the range for the interval timeout is from 2 to 10. |
| ptp delay-request minimum interval *seconds* | (Optional) Configures the minimum interval allowed between PTP delay-request messages when the port is in the master state. The range is from −1 to 6 log seconds. |
| ptp vlan *vlan* | (Optional) Configures the PTP VLAN value on an interface. The range is from 1 to 4094. |

**Table 6-8**   PTP Verification Commands

| Command | Purpose |
|---|---|
| show ptp brief | Displays the PTP status. |
| show ptp clock | Displays the properties of the local clock. |
| show ptp clock foreign-masters record [interface *interface slot/ port*] | Displays the state of foreign masters known to the PTP process. For each foreign master, the output displays the clock identity, basic clock properties, and whether the clock is being used as a grandmaster. |
| show ptp corrections | Displays the last few PTP corrections. |
| show ptp parent | Displays the properties of the PTP parent. |
| show ptp port interface *interface slot/port* | Displays the status of the PTP port. |
| show ptp time-property | Displays the properties of the PTP clock. |

Example 6-4 shows how to configure PTP globally on the device, specify the source IP address for PTP communications, and configure a preference level for the clock:

**Example 6-4**   *NX-OS PTP Configuration Example*

```
switch# configure terminal
switch(config)# feature ptp
switch(config)# ptp source 10.10.10.1
switch(config)# ptp priority1 1
switch(config)# ptp priority2 1
```

Example 6-5 shows the PTP device boundary type. There is no port configured as a PTP port; all other parameters have default values.

**Example 6-5**   *NX-OS PTP Clock Status*

```
switch(config)# show ptp clock
PTP Device Type: Boundary clock
Clock Identity: 0:22:55:ff:ff:79:a4:c1
Clock Domain:0
Number of PTP ports: 0
Priority1: 1
Priority2: 1
ClockQuality:
Class: 248
Accuracy: 254
Offset(log variance): 65535
Offset From Master: 0
Mean Path Delay: 0
Steps removed: 0
Local clock time: Sun Jul 7 14:13:24 2019
```

# Network Infrastructure Monitoring

Network monitoring is important for data center visibility and management. Today's resource-intensive applications are causing network traffic to grow exponentially, putting high demands on the existing data center infrastructure. Companies are finding it challenging to differentiate critical applications from noncritical ones and to dynamically allocate network resources to higher-priority applications. To better manage network resources and be proactive, network administrators need visibility into the network traffic. Network monitoring will improve operational efficiency. The system management features of the Cisco Nexus switch allow you to monitor and manage your network for efficient device use, diagnostics, troubleshooting, and logging.

Cisco Nexus supports the following network monitoring tools:

- Notifications about network activity using system message logging

- Notifications about device status using logging or SNMP traps

- Cisco Call Home

- Export of network traffic flows using NetFlow

- Network traffic mirroring (SPAN)

## NX-OS System Message Logging

Logging can be used for fault notification, network forensics, and security auditing. Cisco Nexus log messages can be handled in five different ways:

- **Console logging:** By default, Cisco Nexus sends all log messages to its console port. Hence, only the users who are physically connected to the router console port can view these messages.

- **Terminal logging:** Similar to console logging, but it displays log messages to Cisco Nexus Telnet or SSH session instead. This is not enabled by default; Cisco recommends that you enable it on a second monitoring session.

- **Buffered logging:** This type of logging uses Cisco Nexus RAM for storing log messages. The buffer has a fixed size to ensure that the log will not deplete valuable system memory. The Cisco Nexus switch accomplishes this by deleting old messages from the buffer as new messages are added.

- **Syslog server logging:** Cisco Nexus can use syslog to forward log messages to external syslog servers for storage. This type of logging is not enabled by default.

- **SNMP trap logging:** The router can use SNMP traps to send log messages to an external SNMP server.

You can use system message logging to control the destination and to filter the severity level of messages that system processes generate. You can configure logging to terminal sessions, a log file, and syslog servers on remote systems.

Logging messages are categorized as having a severity level of 7. When you configure the severity level, the system outputs messages at that level and all lower levels. For example, if you configure the system to log severity level 4, the system will log severity levels 4, 3, 2, 1, and 0. Table 6-9 lists all the different severity levels.

**Table 6-9**   System Message Severity Levels

| Level | Description |
| --- | --- |
| 0 – Emergency | System unusable |
| 1 – Alert | Immediate action needed |
| 2 – Critical | Critical condition |
| 3 – Error | Error condition |
| 4 – Warning | Warning condition |
| 5 – Notification | Normal but significant condition |
| 6 – Informational | Informational message only |
| 7 – Debugging | Appears during debugging only |

The device logs the most recent 100 messages of severity level 0, 1, or 2 to the NVRAM log. You cannot configure logging to the NVRAM.

You can configure which system messages should be logged based on the facility that generated the message and its severity level.

Cisco Nexus can send logs to any syslog server. Syslog servers run on remote systems that log system messages based on the syslog protocol. NX-OS supports up to eight IPv4 or IPv6 syslog servers per device.

## NX-OS Simple Network Management Protocol

The Simple Network Management Protocol (SNMP) is an application layer protocol that provides a message format for communication between SNMP managers and agents. SNMP provides a standardized framework and a common language used for the monitoring and management of devices in a network.

The SNMP framework consists of three parts:

- **SNMP manager:** The system used to control and monitor the activities of network devices using SNMP.

- **SNMP agent:** The software component within the managed device that maintains the data for the device and reports this data, as needed, to manage systems. The Cisco Nexus device supports the agent and management information base (MIB). To enable the SNMP agent, you must define the relationship between the manager and the agent.

- **MIB:** The collection of managed objects on the SNMP agent.

SNMP is defined in RFCs 3411 to 3418. Cisco Nexus supports SNMPv1, SNMPv2c, and SNMPv3. Both SNMPv1 and SNMPv2c use a community-based form of security. Cisco NX-OS supports SNMP over IPv6.

A key feature of SNMP is the ability to generate notifications from an SNMP agent. These notifications do not require that requests be sent from the SNMP manager. Notifications can indicate improper user authentication, restarts, the closing of a connection, the loss of connection to a neighbor router, or other significant events.

Cisco NX-OS generates SNMP notifications as either *traps* or *informs*. A trap is an asynchronous, unacknowledged message sent from the agent to the SNMP managers listed in the host receiver table. Informs are asynchronous messages sent from the SNMP agent to the SNMP manager for which the manager must acknowledge receipt.

Traps are less reliable than informs because the SNMP manager does not send any acknowledgment when it receives a trap. The device cannot determine if the trap was received. An SNMP manager that receives an inform request acknowledges the message with an SNMP response protocol data unit (PDU). If the device never receives a response, it can send the inform request again.

You can configure Cisco NX-OS to send notifications to multiple host receivers.

Table 6-10 lists the SNMP traps that are enabled by default.

**Table 6-10**   SNMP Traps

| Trap Type | Description |
|---|---|
| generic | : coldStart |
| entity | : entity_fan_status_change |
| entity | : entity_mib_change |
| entity | : entity_module_status_change |
| entity | : entity_module_inserted |
| entity | : entity_module_removed |

| Trap Type | Description |
|-----------|-------------|
| entity | : entity_power_out_change |
| entity | : entity_power_status_change |
| entity | : entity_unrecognised_module |
| Link | : cErrDisableInterfaceEventRev1 |
| link | : cieLinkDown |
| link | : cieLinkUp |
| Link | : cmn-mac-move-notification |
| link | : delayed-link-state-change |
| link | : extended-linkDown |
| link | : extended-linkUp |
| link | : linkDown |
| link | : linkUp |
| rf | : redundancy_framework |
| license | : notify-license-expiry |
| license | : notify-no-license-for-feature |
| license | : notify-licensefile-missing |
| license | : notify-license-expiry-warning |
| upgrade | : UpgradeOpNotifyOnCompletion |
| upgrade | : UpgradeJobStatusNotify |
| entity | : entity_sensor |
| rmon | : fallingAlarm |
| rmon | : hcRisingAlarm |
| rmon | : hcFallingAlarm |

SNMPv3 provides secure access to devices through a combination of authenticating and encrypting frames over the network. The security features provided in SNMPv3 are the following:

- **Message integrity:** Ensures that a packet has not been tampered with in-transit.

- **Authentication:** Determines the message is from a valid source.

- **Encryption:** Scrambles the packet contents to prevent it from being seen by unauthorized sources.

SNMPv3 provides for both security models and security levels. A security model is an authentication strategy that is set up for a user and the role in which the user resides. A security level is the permitted level of security within a security model. A combination of a security model and a security level determines which security mechanism is employed when handling an SNMP packet.

The security level determines if an SNMP message needs to be protected from disclosure and if the message needs to be authenticated. The various security levels that exist within a security model are as follows:

- **noAuthNoPriv:** Security level that does not provide authentication or encryption. This level is not supported for SNMPv3.

- **authNoPriv:** Security level that provides authentication but does not provide encryption.

- **authPriv:** Security level that provides both authentication and encryption.

Three security models are available: SNMPv1, SNMPv2c, and SNMPv3. The security model combined with the security level determines the security mechanism applied when the SNMP message is processed. Table 6-11 identifies what the combinations of security models and levels mean.

**Table 6-11** SNMP Security Models and Levels

| Model | Level | Authentication | Encryption | What Happens |
|-------|-------|----------------|------------|--------------|
| v1 | noAuthNoPriv | Community string | No | Uses a community string match for authentication. |
| v2c | noAuthNoPriv | Community string | No | Uses a community string match for authentication. |
| v3 | authNoPriv | HMAC-MD5 or HMAC-SHA | No | Provides authentication based on the Hash-Based Message Authentication Code (HMAC) message digest 5 (MD5) algorithm or the HMAC Secure Hash Algorithm (SHA). |
| v3 | authPriv | HMAC-MD5 or HMAC-SHA | DES | Provides authentication based on the HMAC-MD5 or HMAC-SHA algorithms. Provides Data Encryption Standard (DES) 56-bit encryption in addition to authentication based on the Cipher Block Chaining (CBC) DES (DES-56) standard. |

Tables 6-12 through 6-15 describe the most-used SNMP configuration commands. For a full list of the commands, refer to the Nexus System Management Configuration Guide links shown in the reference list at the end of this chapter.

**Table 6-12** SNMP Global Commands

| Command | Purpose |
|---------|---------|
| **snmp-server** *user name* [ **auth** { **md5** \| **sha** } **passphrase** [auto ] [ **priv** [ **aes-128** ] **passphrase**] [engineID *id* ] [localizedkey ] ] | Configures an SNMP user with authentication and privacy parameters. The passphrase can be any case-sensitive alphanumeric string up to 64 characters. If you use the **localizedkey** keyword, the passphrase can be any case-sensitive alphanumeric string up to 130 characters. The **engineID** format is a 12-digit colon-separated decimal number. |

| Command | Purpose |
|---|---|
| **snmp-server** *user name* **enforcePriv** | Enforces SNMP message encryption for this user. |
| **snmp-server** *user name group* | Associates this SNMP user with the configured user role. |
| **snmp-server community** *name group* { **ro** \| **rw** } | Creates an SNMP community string. |
| **snmp-server community** *community-name* **use-acl** *acl-name* | Assigns an ACL to an SNMP community to filter SNMP requests. |
| **snmp-server host** *ip-address* { **traps** \| **informs** } **version 2c** *community* [ **udp_port** *number* ] | Configures a host receiver for SNMPv2c traps or informs. The *ip-address* can be an IPv4 or IPv6 address. The *community* can be any alphanumeric string up to 255 characters. The UDP port number range is from 0 to 65,535. |
| **snmp-server host** *ip-address* { **traps** \| **informs** } **version 3** { **auth** \| **noauth** \| **priv** } *username* [ **udp_port** *number* ] | Configures a host receiver for SNMPv3 traps or informs. The *ip-address* can be an IPv4 or IPv6 address. The username can be any alphanumeric string up to 255 characters. The UDP port number range is from 0 to 65,535. |
| **snmp-server host** *ip-address* **source-interface if-type if-number** [ **udp_port** *number* ] | Configures a host receiver for SNMPv2c traps or informs. The *ip-address* can be an IPv4 or IPv6 address. Use **?** to determine the supported interface types. The UDP port number range is from 0 to 65,535. This configuration overrides the global source interface configuration. |
| **snmp-server source-interface** { **traps** \| **informs** } **if-type if-number** | Configures a source interface for sending out SNMPv2c traps or informs. Use **?** to determine the supported interface types. |

**Table 6-13**   SNMP MIBs

| MIB | Purpose |
|---|---|
| All notifications | snmp-server enable traps |
| CISCO-AAA-SERVER-MIB | snmp-server enable traps aaa |
| | snmp-server enable traps aaa server-state-change |
| CISCO-BGP4-MIB | snmp-server enable traps bgp |
| CISCO-STP-BRIDGE-MIB | snmp-server enable traps bridge |
| | snmp-server enable traps bridge newroot |
| | snmp-server enable traps bridge topologychange |
| CISCO-CALLHOME-MIB | snmp-server enable traps callhome |
| | snmp-server enable traps callhome event-notify |
| | snmp-server enable traps callhome smtp-send-fail |
| CISCO-CFS-MIB | snmp-server enable traps cfs |
| | snmp-server enable traps cfs merge-failure |
| | snmp-server enable traps cfs state-change-notif |

6

| MIB | Purpose |
|-----|---------|
| CISCO-CONFIG-MAN-MIB | snmp-server enable traps config |
| | snmp-server enable traps config ccmCLIRunningConfigChanged |
| CISCO-EIGRP-MIB | snmp-server enable traps eigrp [ *tag* ] |
| ENTITY-MIB, CISCO-ENTITY- SENSOR-MIB | snmp-server enable traps entity |
| | snmp-server enable traps entity entity_fan_status_change |
| | snmp-server enable traps entity entity_mib_change |
| | snmp-server enable traps entity entity_module_inserted |
| | snmp-server enable traps entity entity_module_removed |
| | snmp-server enable traps entity entity_module_status_change |
| | snmp-server enable traps entity entity_power_out_change |
| | snmp-server enable traps entity entity_power_status_change |
| | snmp-server enable traps entity entity_unrecognised_module |
| CISCO-FEATURE- CONTROL-MIB | snmp-server enable traps feature-control |
| | snmp-server enable traps feature-control FeatureOpStatusChange |
| CISCO-HSRP-MIB | snmp-server enable traps hsrp |
| | snmp-server enable traps hsrp state-change |
| CISCO-LICENSE-MGR-MIB | snmp-server enable traps license |
| | snmp-server enable traps license notify-license-expiry |
| | snmp-server enable traps license notify-license-expiry-warning |
| | snmp-server enable traps license notify-licensefile-missing |
| | snmp-server enable traps license notify-no-license-for-feature |
| IF-MIB | snmp-server enable traps link |
| | snmp-server enable traps link IETF-extended-linkDown |
| | snmp-server enable traps link IETF-extended-linkUp |
| | snmp-server enable traps link cisco-extended-linkDown |
| | snmp-server enable traps link cisco-extended-linkUp |
| | snmp-server enable traps link linkDown |
| | snmp-server enable traps linkUp |
| OSPF-MIB, OSPF-TRAP-MIB | snmp-server enable traps ospf [ *tag* ] |
| | snmp-server enable traps ospf lsa |
| | snmp-server enable traps ospf rate-limit *rate* |

| MIB | Purpose |
|---|---|
| CISCO-PORT-SECURITY-MIB | snmp-server enable traps port-security |
| | snmp-server enable traps port-security access-secure-mac-violation |
| | snmp-server enable traps port-security trunk-secure-mac-violation |
| CISCO-RF-MIB | snmp-server enable traps rf |
| | snmp-server enable traps rf redundancy_framework |
| CISCO-RMON-MIB | snmp-server enable traps rmon |
| | snmp-server enable traps rmon fallingAlarm |
| | snmp-server enable traps rmon hcFallingAlarm |
| | snmp-server enable traps rmon hcRisingAlarm |
| | snmp-server enable traps rmon risingAlarm |
| SNMPv2-MIB | snmp-server enable traps snmp |
| | snmp-server enable traps snmp authentication |

**Table 6-14**  SNMP Specific Notification Commands

| Command | Purpose |
|---|---|
| snmp-server enable traps | Enables all SNMP notifications. |
| snmp-server enable traps aaa [ server-state-change ] | Enables AAA SNMP notifications. Optionally, enables the following specific notifications: |
| | **server-state-change:** Enables AAA server state-change notifications. |
| snmp-server enable traps bgp | Enables BGP SNMP notifications. |
| snmp-server enable traps callhome [ event-notify] | Enables Call Home notifications. Optionally, enables the following specific notifications: |
| | **event-notify:** Enables Call Home external event notifications. |
| | **smtp-send-fail:** Enables Simple Mail Transfer Protocol (SMTP) message send fail notifications. |
| snmp-server enable traps snmp [ authentication ] | Enables general SNMP notifications. Optionally, enables the following specific notification: |
| | **authentication:** Enables SNMP authentication notifications. |

**Table 6-15**  SNMP Verification Commands

| Command | Purpose |
|---|---|
| show interface snmp-ifindex | Displays the SNMP ifIndex value for all interfaces (from IF-MIB). |
| show snmp | Displays the SNMP status. |
| show snmp community | Displays the SNMP community strings. |
| show snmp context | Displays the SNMP context mapping. |
| show snmp engineID | Displays the SNMP engineID. |

6

| Command | Purpose |
|---------|---------|
| show snmp group | Displays SNMP roles. |
| show snmp host | Displays information about configured SNMP hosts. |
| show snmp session | Displays SNMP sessions. |
| show interface snmp-ifindex | Displays the SNMP ifIndex value for all interfaces (from IF-MIB). |
| show running-config snmp [ all ] | Displays the SNMP running configuration. |

Example 6-6 shows how to configure Cisco NX-OS to send the Cisco link Up or Down notifications to a notification host receiver using the Blue VRF and defines two SNMP users—Admin and NMS.

**Example 6-6**  *NX-OS SNMP Configuration Example*

```
switch# config t
switch(config)# snmp-server contact Admin@company.com
switch(config)# snmp-server user Admin auth sha abcd1234 priv abcdefgh
switch(config)# snmp-server user NMS auth sha abcd1234 priv abcdefgh engineID 00:00:
   00:63:00:01:00:22:32:15:10:03
switch(config)# snmp-server host 192.0.2.1 informs version 3 auth NMS
switch(config)# snmp-server host 192.0.2.1 use-vrf Blue
switch(config)# snmp-server enable traps link cisco
```

Example 6-7 shows how to configure SNMP to send traps using an in-band port configured at the host level.

**Example 6-7**  *NX-OS SNMP Destination Trap Server and Source Interface Configuration*

```
switch(config)# snmp-server host 171.71.48.164 version 2c public
switch(config)# snmp-server host 171.71.48.164 source-interface ethernet 1/2
```

Example 6-8 shows SNMP verification that shows the destination host with the SNMP version.

**Example 6-8**  *NX-OS SNMP Status*

```
switch(config)# show snmp host
-------------------------------------------------------------------
Host            Port  Version  Level   Type   SecName
-------------------------------------------------------------------
171.71.48.164   162   v2c      noauth  trap   public
  Source interface: Ethernet 1/2
-------------------------------------------------------------------
```

## Nexus Smart Call Home

Smart Call Home provides an email-based notification for critical system policies. A range of message formats is available for compatibility with pager services, standard email, or XML-based automated parsing applications. You can use this feature to page a network support engineer, email a network operations center, or use Cisco Smart Call Home services to automatically generate a case with the Cisco Technical Assistance Center.

Smart Call Home offers the following features:

- Automatic execution and attachment of relevant CLI command output.

- Multiple message format options such as the following:

    - **Short text:** Suitable for pagers or printed reports.

    - **Full text:** Fully formatted message information suitable for human reading.

    - **XML:** Machine-readable format that uses Extensible Markup Language (XML) and Adaptive Messaging Language (AML) XML Schema Definition (XSD). The AML XSD is published on the Cisco.com website. The XML format enables communication with the Cisco Technical Assistance Center.

- Multiple concurrent message destinations. You can configure up to 50 email destination addresses for each destination profile.

Example 6-9 shows how to configure Smart Call Home to send alerts via email when users configure a new routing protocol using the **show ip routing** command.

**Example 6-9**  *NX-OS Call Home Configuration Example*

```
switch(config)# snmp-server contact person@company.com
switch(config)# callhome
switch(config-callhome)# email-contact admin@Mycompany.com
switch(config-callhome)# phone-contact +1-800-123-4567
switch(config-callhome)# street-address 123 Anystreet st. Anytown,AnyWhere
switch(config-callhome)# destination-profile Noc101 full-text
switch(config-callhome)# destination-profile full-text-destination email-addr
    person@company.com
switch(config-callhome)# destination-profile full-text-destination message-level 5
switch(config-callhome)# destination-profile Noc101 alert-group Configuration
switch(config-callhome)# alert-group Configuration user-def-cmd "show ip routing"
switch(config-callhome)# transport email smtp-server 192.0.2.10 use-vrf Red
switch(config-callhome)# enable
switch(config-callhome)# commit
```

## Nexus NetFlow

Today data center administrators need detailed profiles of applications that traverse their networks. To efficiently operate, scale, and consolidate their networks, administrators need to know what applications are consuming bandwidth, who is using them, when they are being used, and what activities are prevalent in the data center. With this information, data center administrators have visibility into their networks, which is crucial in exerting control over the network, finding the precise reasons for performance problems and possible security concerns, and managing the overall end-user experience.

The capability to characterize IP traffic and understand who sent it, the traffic destination, the time of day, and the application information is critical for data center operations. It helps data center managers determine how to optimize resource utilization, plan network capacity, build traffic pattern models for consolidation, and determine where to apply quality of service (QoS), and it plays a vital role in network security for detection of DoS attacks and network-propagated worms (see Figure 6-8).

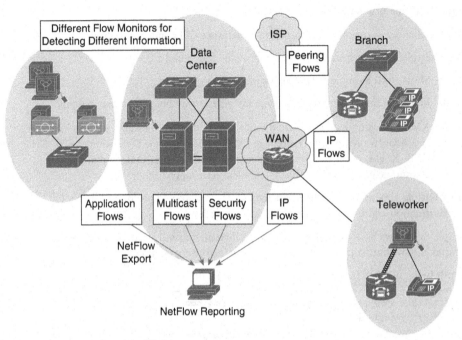

**Figure 6-8**   *NetFlow Traffic Export*

NetFlow identifies packet flows for ingress IP packets and provides statistics based on these packet flows. NetFlow does not require any change to either the packets themselves or any networking device.

NetFlow uses flows to provide statistics for accounting, network monitoring, and network planning. A flow is a unidirectional stream of packets that arrives on a source interface (or VLAN) and has the same values for the keys. A key is an identified value for a field within the packet. You can create a flow using a flow record to define the unique keys for your flow.

Cisco NX-OS supports the flexible NetFlow feature that enables enhanced network anomalies and security detection. Flexible NetFlow allows you to define an optimal flow record for a particular application by selecting the keys from a large collection of predefined fields.

All key values must match for the packet to count in a given flow. A flow might gather other fields of interest, depending on the export record version that you configure. Flows are stored in the NetFlow cache.

You can export the data that NetFlow gathers for your flow by using a flow exporter and export this data to remote NetFlow analytic tools, such as the Cisco Prime Network Analysis Module (NAM) or Cisco Stealthwatch.

Cisco NX-OS exports a flow as part of a NetFlow export UDP datagram under the following circumstances:

■ Flows are exported periodically as per the flow timeout value, which defaults to 10 seconds if not configured.

■ You have forced the flow to export.

The flow record determines the size of the data to be collected for a flow. The flow monitor combines the flow record and flow exporter with the NetFlow cache information.

Cisco NX-OS can gather NetFlow statistics and analyze all packets on the interface or subinterface.

Unlike other Cisco Nexus platforms, Cisco Nexus 9000 Series switches separate NetFlow processing into two layers:

- The first layer supports per-packet visibility for line-rate traffic. Packets do not need to be sampled and statistically analyzed. Instead, the packets can be processed and aggregated at line rate.

- The second layer enables the gathering of flows at scale. It can maintain hundreds of thousands of flows without losing any flows and periodically exports them to an external collector.

NetFlow configuration parameters are as follows:

- **Flow records:** A flow record defines the keys that NetFlow uses to identify packets and other fields of interest that NetFlow gathers for the flow. You can define a flow record with any combination of keys and fields of interest. Cisco NX-OS supports a rich set of keys. A flow record also defines the types of counters gathered per flow. You can configure 32- or 64-bit packet or byte counters.

  The key fields are specified with the **match** keyword. The fields of interest and counters are specified under the **collect** keyword.

  Cisco NX-OS enables the following match fields as the defaults when you create a flow record:

  - **match interface input**
  - **match flow direction**

- **Flow exporters:** A flow exporter contains network layer and transport layer details for the NetFlow export packet. You can configure the following information in a flow exporter:

  - Export destination IP address
  - Source interface
  - UDP port number (where the NetFlow Collector is listening for NetFlow packets): the default value is 9995

**NOTE** NetFlow export packets use the IP address that is assigned to the source interface. If the source interface does not have an IP address assigned to it, the flow exporter drops flows that were meant to be exported.

Cisco NX-OS exports data to the NetFlow Collector whenever a timeout occurs. You can configure a flush cache timeout (using the **flow timeout** command) to flush the cache and force a flow export.

- **Export format:** Cisco NX-OS supports the Version 9 export format. This format supports a more efficient network utilization than the older Version 5 export format and supports IPv6 and Layer 2 fields. In addition, the Version 9 export format supports the full 32-bit SNMP ifIndex values at the NetFlow Collector.

- **Layer 2 NetFlow keys:** You can define Layer 2 keys in flexible NetFlow records that you can use to capture flows in Layer 2 interfaces. The Layer 2 keys are as follows:

  - Source and destination MAC addresses

  - Source VLAN ID

  - EtherType from the Ethernet frame

  You can apply Layer 2 NetFlow to the following interfaces for the ingress direction:

  - Switch ports in access mode

  - Switch ports in trunk mode

  - Layer 2 port channels

**NOTE**   You cannot apply Layer 2 NetFlow to VLANs, egress interfaces, or Layer 3 interfaces such as VLAN interfaces.

Example 6-10 shows how to configure a NetFlow exporter configuration for IPv4.

**Example 6-10**   *NX-OS NetFlow Configuration Example*

```
switch(config)# feature netflow
switch(config)# flow exporter exporter1
switch(config-flow-exporter)# version 9
switch(config-flow-exporter-version-9)# flow record record1
switch(config-flow-record)# match ipv4 source address
switch(config-flow-record)# match ipv4 destination address
switch(config-flow-record)# collect counter bytes
switch(config-flow-record)# collect counter packets
switch(config-flow-record)# flow monitor flow1
switch(config-flow-monitor)# record record1
switch(config-flow-monitor)# exporter exporter1
switch(config-flow-monitor)# interface ethernet 2/2
switch(config-if)# ip flow monitor flow1 input
switch(config-if)# ip address 10.20.1.1/24
switch(config-if)# no shutdown
```

Example 6-11 shows a NetFlow exporter configuration for IPv4 from the Cisco Nexus switch to the NAM.

**Example 6-11** *NX-OS NetFlow to Cisco NAM Configuration Example*

```
switch(config)# flow exporter exp1
switch(config-flow-exporter)# destination 172.20.101.87 use-vrf management
switch(config-flow-exporter)# transport udp 3000
switch(config-flow-exporter)# source mgmt 0
switch(config-flow-exporter)# version 9
switch(config-flow-exporter-version-9)# flow record exp1
switch(config-flow-record)# match ipv4 source address
switch(config-flow-record)# match ipv4 destination address
switch(config-flow-record)# match ip protocol
switch(config-flow-record)# match ip tos
switch(config-flow-record)# match transport source-port
switch(config-flow-record)# match transport destination-port
switch(config-flow-record)# collect counter bytes long
switch(config-flow-record)# collect counter packets long
switch(config-flow-record)# collect timestamp sys-uptime first
switch(config-flow-record)# collect timestamp sys-uptime last
switch(config-flow-record)# collect ip version
switch(config-flow-record)# flow monitor exp1
switch(config-flow-monitor)# record exp1
switch(config-flow-monitor)# exporter exp1
switch(config-flow-monitor)# interface ethernet 2/3
switch(config-if)# ip flow monitor exp1 input
switch(config-if)# ip flow monitor exp1 output
```

Example 6-12 shows sample output for the **show hardware flow ip** command.

**Example 6-12** *NX-OS NetFlow Hardware Flow Status*

```
switch(config-if)# show hardware flow ip

D - Direction; L4 Info - Protocol:Source Port:Destination Port
IF - Interface: (Eth)ernet, (S)vi, (V)lan, (P)ortchannel, (T)unnel
TCP Flags: Ack, Flush, Push, Reset, Syn, Urgent


D  IF          SrcAddr         DstAddr         L4 Info       PktCnt      TCP Fl
--+----------- +------------+  ------------+   ------------+  -------+   ------
CP sup-eth1    010.020.001.002 010.020.001.001 001:00000:00000 0000000021 ......
```

Example 6-13 shows sample output for the **show running-configuration netflow** command.

**Example 6-13** *NX-OS NetFlow Status*

```
switch# show running-config netflow

!Command: show running-config netflow
!Time: Sun Jan  5 04:06:24 2020
```

```
version 7.3(0)D1(1)
feature netflow

flow exporter exporter1
  version 9
flow exporter exp1
  destination 172.20.101.87 use-vrf management
  transport udp 3000
  source mgmt0
  version 9
flow record record1
  match ipv4 source address
  match ipv4 destination address
  collect counter bytes
  collect counter packets
flow record exp1
  match ipv4 source address
  match ipv4 destination address
  match ip protocol
  match ip tos
  match transport source-port
  match transport destination-port
  collect counter bytes long
  collect counter packets long
  collect timestamp sys-uptime first
  collect timestamp sys-uptime last
  collect ip version
flow monitor flow1
  record record1
  exporter exporter1
flow monitor exp1
  record exp1
  exporter exp1

interface Ethernet2/2
  ip flow monitor flow1 input

interface Ethernet2/3
  ip flow monitor exp1 input
  ip flow monitor exp1 output
```

## Switched Port Analyzer

The Switched Port Analyzer (SPAN) feature, which is sometimes called *port mirroring* or *port monitoring*, is a method wherein a device sends a copy of all network packets seen on one port (or an entire VLAN) to another port. This feature allows the copied network to be analyzed for monitoring, troubleshooting, and other purposes. Figure 6-9 illustrates some of the key terms used in a SPAN implementation.

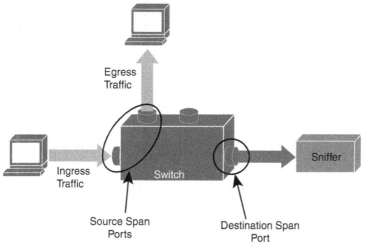

**Figure 6-9**  *SPAN Switch Port*

- **Ingress traffic:** Traffic that enters the switch.

- **Egress traffic:** Traffic that leaves the switch.

- **Source (SPAN) port:** A port that is monitored with use of the SPAN feature.

- **Source (SPAN) VLAN:** A VLAN whose traffic is monitored with use of the SPAN feature.

- **Destination (SPAN) port:** A port that monitors source ports, usually where a network analyzer is connected.

SPAN ports monitor all traffic for a source port, which sends a copy of the traffic to a destination port. The network analyzer, which is attached with a destination port, analyzes the traffic that passes through the source port.

The source port can be a single port or multiple ports or a VLAN, which is also called a *monitored port*. You can monitor all the packets for a source port that is received (ingress), transmitted (egress), or bidirectional (both). A replication of the packets is sent to the destination port for analysis.

For VLAN-based SPAN (VSPAN), all ports in the VLAN are source ports. So, the traffic in the VLAN is monitored. You can apply a VLAN-based filter on the trunk port of the switch to limit the SPAN traffic monitor.

The destination port is one that was connected to a device such as a SwitchProbe device or other Remote Network Monitoring (RMON) probe or security device that can receive and analyze the copied packets from a single or from multiple source ports.

A switch supports multiple SPAN sessions (up to 48 sessions), but only two sessions can be run simultaneously, and others are shut down. A port of the switch is configured as either the source port or the destination port.

Example 6-14 shows a SPAN destination port (interface E3/48) configuration.

**Example 6-14**  *NX-OS SPAN Port Configuration*

```
switch-1# configure terminal
switch-1(config)# interface ethernet 3/48


!--- Configures the switchport parameters for a port.


switch-1(config-if)# switchport


!--- Configures the switchport interface as a SPAN destination.


switch-1(config-if)# switchport monitor
switch-1(config-if)# no shut
switch-1(config-if)# exit
```

Example 6-15 shows a SPAN mirror port (interface E3/11) configuration and sends duplicate traffic to interface E3/48.

**Example 6-15**  *NX-OS SPAN Mirror Port (Source Port) Configuration*

```
switch-1(config)# monitor session 1

!---Configure the source port with traffic direction.

switch-1(config-monitor)# source interface ethernet 3/11 both

!--- Configure the destination port.

switch-1(config-monitor)# destination interface ethernet 3/48

!--- To enable the SPAN session, by default session in shutdown state.

switch-1(config-monitor)# no shut
switch-1(config-monitor)# exit
```

Example 6-16 shows active SPAN sessions with the source and destination of a single port/VLAN or group of ports/VLANs.

**Example 6-16**  *NX-OS SPAN Status*

```
!---The show monitor command gives the status of the SPAN sessions.
switch-1 #show monitor


Session  State       Reason                Description
-------  ----------  --------------------- ----------------------------
1        up          The session is up
!---The show monitor session all command gives a summary of the current SPAN
configuration.
```

```
switch-1# show monitor session all


  session 1
  ---------------
type             : local
state            : up
source intf      :
    rx           : Eth3/11
    tx           : Eth3/11
    both         : Eth3/11
source VLANs     :
    rx           :
    tx           :
    both         :
filter VLANs     : filter not specified
destination ports : Eth3/48
```

Cisco Nexus NX-OS also supports the Encapsulated Remote Switched Port Analyzer (ERS-PAN). ERSPAN transports mirrored traffic over an IP network. The traffic is encapsulated at the source router and is transferred across the network. The packet is decapsulated at the destination router and then sent to the destination interface. ERSPAN consists of an ERS-PAN source session, routable ERSPAN generic routing encapsulation (GRE)-encapsulated traffic, and an ERSPAN destination session, as shown in Figure 6-10. You separately configure ERSPAN source sessions and destination sessions on different switches.

- ERSPAN enables remote monitoring of multiple switches across your network.

- ERSPAN transports mirrored traffic from source ports of different switches to the destination port, where the network analyzer has connected.

- The traffic is encapsulated at the source switch and is transferred to the destination switch, where the packet is decapsulated and then sent to the destination port.

- ERSPAN consists of an ERSPAN source session, routable ERSPAN generic routing encapsulation (GRE)-encapsulated traffic, and an ERSPAN destination session.

- You can configure ERSPAN source sessions and destination sessions on different switches separately.

- ERSPAN does not monitor any packets that are generated by the supervisor, regardless of their source.

- ERSPAN source

  - The interfaces from which traffic can be monitored are called ERSPAN *sources*.

  - You can monitor all the packets for the source port that is received (ingress), transmitted (egress), or bidirectional (both).

- ERSPAN sources include source ports, source VLANs, or source VSANs. When a VLAN is specified as an ERSPAN source, all supported interfaces in the VLAN are ERSPAN sources.

■ ERSPAN destination

- Destination ports receive the copied traffic from ERSPAN sources.

- The destination port is a port that was connected to the device such as a SwitchProbe device or other Remote Monitoring (RMON) probe or security device that can receive and analyze the copied packets from a single source port or multiple source ports.

- Destination ports do not participate in any spanning tree instance or any Layer 3 protocols.

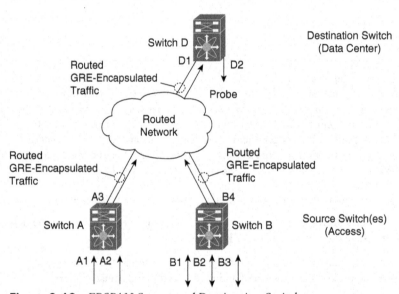

**Figure 6-10**   *ERSPAN Source and Destination Switches*

Example 6-17 shows an ERSPAN source switch configuration, SPAN source port (interface E2/10), and destination session (IP address 10.11.11.3).

**Example 6-17**   *NX-OS ERSPAN Source Switch Configuration*

```
switch_1# configure terminal

!--- Configures an ERSPAN source session.

switch_1(config)# monitor session 48 type erspan-source

!--- Configure the sources and traffic direction.
```

```
switch_1(config-erspan-src)# source interface Ethernet2/10 both

!--- Configure the destination IP address in the ERSPAN session.

switch_1(config-erspan-src)# destination ip 10.11.11.3

!--- Configure the ERSPAN ID.

switch_1(config-erspan-src)# erspan-id 902

!--- Configure the VRF.

switch_1(config-erspan-src)# vrf default

!--- Enable the ERSPAN source session (by default the session is !--- in shutdown
state).

switch_1(config-erspan-src)# no shut
switch_1(config-erspan-src)# exit
!--- Configure the ERSPAN global origin IP address.

switch_1(config)# monitor erspan origin ip-address 10.10.10.1 global

!--- Configure the IP address for loopback interface, which is used !--- as source
of the ERSPAN traffic.

switch_1(config)# interface loopback1
switch_1(config-if)# ip address 10.10.10.1/32
switch_1(config-if)# exit

switch_1(config)# interface Ethernet1/1
switch_1(config-if)# switchport
switch_1(config-if)# switchport mode trunk
switch_1(config-if)# no shutdown
switch_1(config-if)# exit
switch_1(config)# feature interface-vlan
switch_1(config)# interface Vlan 11
switch_1(config-if)# ip address 10.11.11.2/29
switch_1(config-if)# no ip redirects
switch_1(config-if)# no shutdown
switch_1(config-if)# exit
```

6

Example 6-18 shows an ERSPAN destination switch configuration, SPAN destination port (interface E2/34), and source session (IP address 10.11.11.3).

**Example 6-18**   *NX-OS ERSPAN Destination Switch Configuration*

```
switch_2# configure terminal

!--- Configures an ERSPAN destination session.

switch_2(config)# monitor session 47 type erspan-destination

!--- Configures the source IP address.

switch_2(config-erspan-src)# source ip 10.11.11.3

!--- Configures a destination for copied source packets.

switch_2(config-erspan-src)# destination interface Ethernet2/34

!--- Configure the ERSPAN ID.

switch_2(config-erspan-src)# erspan-id 902

!--- Configure the VRF
switch_2(config-erspan-src)# vrf default

!--- Enable the ERSPAN destination session (by default the session is !--- in
shutdown state).

switch_2(config-erspan-src)# no shut
switch_2(config-erspan-src)# exit

switch_2(config)# interface Ethernet2/34
switch_2(config-if)# switchport monitor
switch_2(config-if)# exit

switch_2(config)# feature interface-vlan
switch_2(config)# interface Vlan 11
switch_2(config-if)# ip address 10.11.11.3/29
switch_2(config-if)# no ip redirects
switch_2(config-if)# no shutdown
switch_2(config-if)# exit

switch_2(config)# interface Ethernet1/2
switch_2(config-if)# switchport
switch_2(config-if)# switchport mode trunk
switch_2(config-if)# no shutdown
switch_2(config-if)# exit
```

Example 6-19 shows the ERSPAN source switch session status.

**Example 6-19** *NXOS ERSPAN Status*

```
!---Use the show monitor command in order to display the status of the ERSPAN sessions:
switch_1# show monitor
Session  State        Reason                 Description
-------  -----------  ---------------------  --------------------------------
    48       up         The session is up
!---Use the show monitor session [session session_number] command in order to display
the ERSPAN session configuration:
switch_1# show monitor session 48
   session 48
---------------
type             : erspan-source
state            : up
erspan-id        : 902
vrf-name         : default
acl-name         : acl-name not specified
ip-ttl           : 255
ip-dscp          : 0
destination-ip   : 10.11.11.3
origin-ip        : 10.10.10.1 (global)
source intf      :
    rx           : Eth2/10
    tx           : Eth2/10
    both         : Eth2/10
source VLANs     :
    rx           :
    tx           :
    both         :
filter VLANs     : filter not specified
!---Use the show running-config monitor command in order to display the running
ERSPAN configuration:
switch_1# show running-config monitor

monitor session 48 type erspan-source
  erspan-id 902
  vrf default
  destination ip 10.11.11.3
  source interface Ethernet2/10 both
  no shut

monitor erspan origin ip-address 10.10.10.1 global
```

# Streaming Telemetry

The demand for data regarding network state, whether to detect hotspots in the network or to aid decision-making on workload placement, requires data at a pace that traditional methods just cannot deliver. SNMP, CLI, and syslog have limitations that restrict automation and scale.

SNMP polling can often be on the order of 5–10 minutes; CLIs are unstructured and prone to change, which can often break scripts, as shown in Figure 6-11.

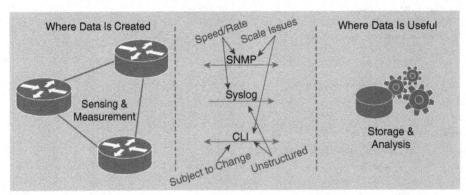

**Figure 6-11** *Traditional Management System Using SNMP, Syslog, and CLI*

The traditional use of the pull model, where the client requests data from the network, does not scale when what you want is near real-time data.

Cisco NX-OS streaming telemetry allows you to push data off the device to a defined endpoint as JavaScript Object Notation (JSON) or using Google Protocol Buffers (GPB) at a much higher frequency and more efficiently, as shown in Figure 6-12.

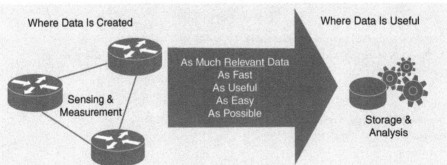

**Figure 6-12** *Management System with Streaming Telemetry*

Three simple steps are all that is required to configure telemetry:

**Step 1.** Set the format and destination to which the data is to be sent.

**Step 2.** Configure the data that is to be collected as part of the sensor group.

**Step 3.** Set the subscription between the sensor-group and the destination, along with the pace at which to send the data (in milliseconds).

This data collected can be sent to the collector of your choice, be it an in-house tool, a commercial application such as Splunk, or a Cisco-provided solution such as the Data Center Network Manager (DCNM).

To help aid in the adoption and understanding of the capabilities of telemetry, Cisco provided a sample collector, which is available on Docker Hub. This receiver can take GPB data streamed from the network, parse it into JSON, which can then be forwarded to the database of your choice.

With this telemetry data, you can see network state and changes in near real time, allowing easier and more timely visibility into your network, as shown in Figure 6-13.

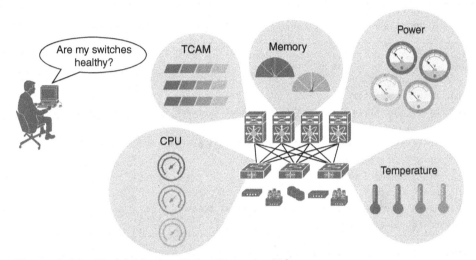

**Figure 6-13**  *Health Monitor Using Streaming Telemetry*

Using a combination of open-source tools and well-understood industry formats, you can begin your journey with telemetry data on Cisco NX-OS.

Example 6-20 shows a cadence-based collection of **show** command data every 750 seconds to monitor system health.

**Example 6-20**  *NX-OS Telemetry Configuration Example*

```
switch(config)# telemetry
switch(config-telemetry)# destination-group 1
switch(conf-tm-dest)# ip address 172.27.247.72 port 60001 protocol gRPC encoding GPB
switch(conf-tm-dest)# sensor-group 1
switch(conf-tm-sensor)# data-source NX-API
switch(conf-tm-sensor)# path "show system resources"
switch(conf-tm-sensor)# path "show version"
switch(conf-tm-sensor)# path "show environment power"
switch(conf-tm-sensor)# path "show environment fan"
switch(conf-tm-sensor)# path "show environment temperature"
switch(conf-tm-sensor)# path "show processes cpu"
```

```
switch(conf-tm-sensor)# path "show policy-map vlan"
switch(conf-tm-sensor)# path "show ip access-list test"
switch(conf-tm-sensor)# subscription 1
switch(conf-tm-sub)# dst-grp 1
switch(conf-tm-dest)# snsr-grp 1 sample-interval 750000
```

For security, SSL/TLS certificates can be used to encrypt all the data exchanged between the client and the server. Optional mechanisms are available for clients to provide certificates for mutual authentication.

A sample configuration, with encryption enabled, is shown in Example 6-21.

**Example 6-21** *NX-OS Telemetry with Encryption Configuration Example*

```
!---This example creates a subscription that streams data every 5 seconds to
destination IP 1.2.3.4 port 50003, and encrypts the stream using GPB encoding
verified using the test.pem.
switch(config)# telemetry
switch(config-telemetry)# certificate /bootflash/test.pem foo.test.google.fr
switch(conf-tm-telemetry)# destination-group 100
switch(conf-tm-dest)# ip address 1.2.3.4 port 50003 protocol gRPC encoding GPB
switch(config-dest)# sensor-group 100
switch(conf-tm-sensor)# path <show command>
switch(conf-tm-sensor)# subscription 100
switch(conf-tm-sub)# snsr-grp 100 sample-interval 5000
switch(conf-tm-sub)# dst-grp 100
```

Example 6-22 shows telemetry data collector details.

**Example 6-22** *NX-OS Telemetry Status*

```
switch# show telemetry data collector details
------------------------------------------------------------------------------
Succ Collections      Failed Collections       Sensor Path
------------------------------------------------------------------------------
150                   0                        <path>


! This command displays the statistic for the telemetry pipeline.
switch# show telemetry pipeline stats
Main Statistics:
    Timers:
        Errors:
            Start Fail      =     0

    Data Collector:
        Errors:
            Node Create Fail  =     0
```

```
      Event Collector:
          Errors:
              Node Create Fail  =    0    Node Add Fail    =    0
              Invalid Data      =    0
Queue Statistics:
      Request Queue:
          High Priority Queue:
              Info:
                  Actual Size    =   50    Current Size    =    0
                  Max Size       =    0    Full Count      =    0


              Errors:
                  Enqueue Error  =    0    Dequeue Error   =    0


          Low Priority Queue:
              Info:
                  Actual Size    =   50    Current Size    =    0
                  Max Size       =    0    Full Count      =    0


              Errors:
                  Enqueue Error  =    0    Dequeue Error   =    0


      Data Queue:
          High Priority Queue:
              Info:
                  Actual Size    =   50    Current Size    =    0
                  Max Size       =    0    Full Count      =    0


              Errors:
                  Enqueue Error  =    0    Dequeue Error   =    0


          Low Priority Queue:
              Info:
                  Actual Size    =   50    Current Size    =    0
                  Max Size       =    0    Full Count      =    0


              Errors:
                  Enqueue Error  =    0    Dequeue Error   =    0
```

! This command displays all configured transport sessions.

```
switch# show telemetry transport


Session Id    IP Address    Port      Encoding  Transport  Status
-------------------------------------------------------------------------------
0             192.168.20.123 50001    GPB       gRPC       Connected
```

## Network Assurance Concept

Digital transformation is rapidly accelerating because there are thousands of new applications, virtualized environments, and clouds. These applications can be hosted anywhere in the world. Building an enormous new data center with all network and security policies following those applications wherever they reside will be very challenging. The best approach is to build a new data center with network assurance and Cisco intent-based networking to address the new data center requirements.

Intent-based networking solutions enable conventional practices that require the alignment of manually derived individual network-element configurations to be replaced by controller-led and policy-based abstractions that easily enable you to express intent (desired outcome) and subsequently validate that the network is doing what you asked of it. Scale, agility, and security demands associated with digital transformation require that element-by-element network configuration be replaced by automated systemwide programming of network elements with consistent intent-based policies. Furthermore, the contextual analysis of data before, during, and after deployment enables continuous verification to help assure that the network is delivering the desired outcome and protection at any point in time. Continuous gathering of telemetry and other forms of data from a multitude of diverse sources provides a rich context of information to optimize a system and ensure it is secure.

The Cisco Network Assurance Engine solution provides continuous verification and analysis of the entire data center network, giving you confidence that your network is operating consistently with your intent. It combines mathematically accurate network models with codified Cisco domain knowledge to generate "smart events" that pinpoint deviations from intent and offer remediation recommendations.

Using comprehensive analysis spanning operator intent, controller policy, switch configurations, and data-plane state, the Network Assurance Engine helps you proactively detect network outages and security policy vulnerabilities before they impact business, reduces risk by predicting change impact, and rapidly determines the root cause of problems. With a unified network repository and compliance rules, the Network Assurance Engine simplifies audits and ensures compliance.

The Cisco Network Assurance Engine is the critical Intent Assurance pillar of Cisco's vision for intent-based data center networks. Built on Cisco's patented network verification technology, the Network Assurance Engine is a comprehensive intent-assurance solution that mathematically verifies the entire data center network for correctness. It gives you the confidence that your network is always operating consistently with your intent, even as it changes dynamically.

With the Cisco Network Assurance Engine, you can do the following:

- **Predict the impact of changes:** Proactively verify changes for correctness to drive increased change agility while significantly reducing risk of human error–induced network failures.

- **Verify networkwide behavior:** Continuously analyze and verify the dynamic state of the network against intent and policy to ensure connectivity and eliminate potential network outages and vulnerabilities before any business impact occurs.

- **Assure network security policy and compliance:** Assure network security policies and check for compliance against business rules to reduce security risk and achieve provable continuous compliance by policy and state.

The Cisco Network Assurance Engine achieves all of the above by reading the entire policy—every configuration, the networkwide state, and the operator's intent—and building from these comprehensive and mathematically accurate models of network behavior. It then combines these models with Cisco's operational domain knowledge of networking to generate smart events that instantly pinpoint any deviations from intended behavior and suggest expert-level remediation recommendations. By providing this continuous verification and validation of the entire data center network, the Cisco Network Assurance Engine fundamentally transforms the operations paradigm from reactive to proactive, as shown in Figure 6-14.

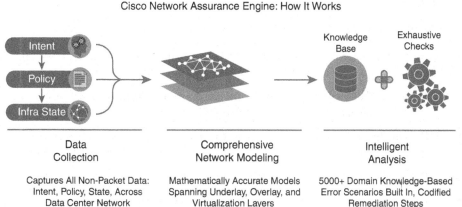

**Figure 6-14**  *Cisco Network Assurance Engine*

As the industry's most comprehensive intent-assurance suite, the Cisco Network Assurance Engine ushers in an operational paradigm that promises to bring to networking the advantages of verification-driven, agile, proactive change management for network operations. The Network Assurance Engine brings together unique capabilities, including

- **Most complete vision for intent-based networks:** Architected from the ground up for seamless integration with the Cisco Application Centric Infrastructure (Cisco ACI) solution, delivering on the vision of closed-loop intent-based networks for data centers.

- **Codified Cisco domain knowledge:** Includes 5000+ built-in failure scenarios in the initial version, powering smart events with remediation steps.

- **Deep policy controller integration:** Assures controller policy and configurations, correlating with dynamic network state.

- **Comprehensive analysis:** Captures, analyzes, and correlates entire network state–switch configurations plus hardware data-plane state.

The Network Assurance Engine enables you to provide these business benefits:

- **Increase change agility:** Exhaustive verification-driven methodology to drive faster change approvals and elimination of human error.

- **Avoid lost revenue and improve service-level agreements (SLAs):** Deep, continuous fabric analysis and visibility to reduce outages and dramatically reduce the mean time to repair issues.

- **Enhance operational maturity:** Detailed DevNet runbooks to empower tier 1 and tier 2 network operation center teams and reduce escalations.

- **Ensure network security:** Complete network security policy analysis and visualization, detailed Ternary Content Addressable Memory (TCAM) optimization, and ability to check for compliance against business intent.

- **Accelerate migrations:** Day-zero configuration analysis and accelerated learning curve of the software-driven networking paradigm to reduce uncertainty in migration timelines.

Operational benefits to using the Network Assurance Engine include the following:

- **Operator playbook:** Smart events that precisely convey the diagnosis, cause, impact, and remediation of complex network issues in a context-specific human-readable manner.

- **Codification of knowledge:** Multiple years' worth of Cisco Technical Assistance Center and autonomous system cross-customer domain knowledge codified for use.

- **DVR audit trail:** Complete record of historical configuration, along with state and assurance analysis data that is easily retrievable, searchable, sortable, and filterable.

- **Offline analysis:** Remote on-demand analysis of multiple fabrics available for customers.

- **Ease of deployment:** Seamless deployment using controller credentials with no additional sensors; deep linking with Cisco ACI fabric.

## Exam Preparation Tasks

As mentioned in the Introduction, you have a couple of choices for exam preparation: the exercises here, Chapter 21, "Final Preparation," and the exam simulation questions in the Pearson Test Prep software online.

## Review All Key Topics

Review the most important topics in the chapter, noted with the key topic icon in the outer margin of the page. Table 6-16 lists a reference to these key topics and the page numbers on which each is found.

**Table 6-16** Key Topics for Chapter 6

| Key Topic Element | Description | Page |
|---|---|---|
| Figure 6-2 | Nexus NX-OS Boot Sequence | 256 |
| Step list | Setup Utility section | 256 |
| Figure 6-4 | POAP Process Flow Diagram | 261 |
| Section | Nexus Nondisruptive In-Service Software Upgrade | 263 |
| Figure 6-5 | Nexus 9500 Parallel Upgrade Process | 264 |
| Section | Programmable Logical Devices Upgrade | 269 |
| Section | NX-OS Configuration Save and Backup | 272 |
| Section | Network Time Protocol | 275 |

| Key Topic Element | Description | Page |
|---|---|---|
| Figure 6-6 | NTP Stratum | 275 |
| Section | Network Infrastructure Monitoring | 284 |
| Section | NX-OS System Message Logging | 284 |
| Section | NX-OS Simple Network Management Protocol | 286 |
| Table 6-11 | SNMP Security Models and Levels | 288 |
| Section | Nexus NetFlow | 293 |
| Section | Switched Port Analyzer | 298 |
| Figure 6-12 | Management System with Streaming Telemetry | 306 |
| Figure 6-14 | Cisco Network Assurance Engine | 311 |

## Memory Tables

Print a copy of Appendix C, "Memory Tables" (found on the companion website), or at least the section for this chapter, and complete the tables and lists from memory. Appendix D, "Memory Tables Answer Key," also on the companion website, includes completed tables and lists to check your work.

## Define Key Terms

Define the following key terms from this chapter, and check your answers in the Glossary.

basic input/output system (BIOS), central processing unit (CPU), command-line interface (CLI), complex programmable logic device (CPLD), Coordinated Universal Time (UTC), Dynamic Host Configuration Protocol (DHCP), field-programmable gate array (FPGA), generic routing encapsulation (GRE), Google Protocol Buffers (GPB), Graceful Insertion and Removal (GIR), in-service software upgrade (ISSU), JavaScript Object Notation (JSON), Nonvolatile random-access memory (NVRAM), service-level agreement (SLA), Software Maintenance Updates (SMU), Tool command language (Tcl), Transport Layer Security/Secure Sockets Layer (TLS/SSL), Video Terminal 100 (VT100)

## References

Cisco Nexus 9000 Series NX-OS Software Upgrade and Downgrade Guide, Release 10.3(x): https://www.cisco.com/c/en/us/td/docs/dcn/nx-os/nexus9000/103x/upgrade/cisco-nexus-9000-nx-os-software-upgrade-downgrade-guide-103x.html

Cisco Nexus 9000 Series FPGA/EPLD Upgrade Release Notes, Release 10.2(5): https://www.cisco.com/c/en/us/td/docs/dcn/nx-os/nexus9000/102x/epld/nxos-n9k-epld-1025.html

Cisco Nexus 9000 Series NX-OS System Management Configuration Guide, Release 10.3(x): https://www.cisco.com/c/en/us/td/docs/dcn/nx-os/nexus9000/103x/configuration/system-management/cisco-nexus-9000-series-nx-os-system-management-configuration-guide-103x.html

Cisco Nexus 9000 NX-OS Fundamentals Configuration Guide, Release 10.3(x): https://www.cisco.com/c/en/us/td/docs/dcn/nx-os/nexus9000/103x/configuration/fundamentals/cisco-nexus-9000-nx-os-fundamentals-configuration-guide-103x.html

# CHAPTER 7

# Describe Cisco Nexus Dashboard

In this era of digital transformation and business resiliency, vast amounts of data are being generated every second, and networking infrastructure is becoming more complex and distributed. Network operations teams need the right tools to manage today's complex data center environments that include on-premises infrastructure and public cloud sites. Although many operational services and tools are available to manage data center operations, maneuvering through multiple applications has become a challenge in itself because IT teams must now correlate information from numerous tools across hybrid environments. Cisco Nexus Dashboard specifically addresses this pain point by providing a single pane of glass to manage a unified operations infrastructure based on the Cisco Nexus Dashboard platform.

**This chapter covers the following key topics:**

**Cisco Nexus Dashboard:** This section discusses various services/applications for the Cisco Nexus Dashboard platform including Cisco Nexus Dashboard Insights (NDI), Cisco Nexus Dashboard Orchestrator (NDO), Cisco Nexus Dashboard Fabric Controller (NDFC), and Cisco Nexus Dashboard Data Broker (NDDB), along with their features and benefits.

**Cisco Nexus Dashboard Platforms:** This section discusses various form factors for Cisco Nexus Dashboard deployment.

**Cisco Nexus Dashboard Cluster Nodes:** This section discusses various node types for Cisco Nexus Dashboard cluster deployment, such as master nodes, standby nodes, and worker nodes, including the Nexus Dashboard capacity planning tool.

**Cisco Nexus Dashboard External Networks:** This section discusses various external network types for the Cisco Nexus Dashboard platform. Later in the section, we discuss the round-trip time (RTT) requirements for various services deployed on the Cisco Nexus Dashboard platform.

**Cisco Nexus Dashboard GUI Overview:** This section discusses the graphical user interface (GUI) overview of the Cisco Nexus Dashboard platform, including the One View page, Admin Console page, Services page, and Sites page.

## "Do I Know This Already?" Quiz

The "Do I Know This Already?" quiz enables you to assess whether you should read this entire chapter thoroughly or jump to the "Exam Preparation Tasks" section. If you are in doubt about your answers to these questions or your own assessment of your knowledge of the topics, read the entire chapter. Table 7-1 lists the major headings in this chapter and their corresponding "Do I Know This Already?" quiz questions. You can find the answers in Appendix A, "Answers to the 'Do I Know This Already?' Quizzes."

**Table 7-1** "Do I Know This Already?" Section-to-Question Mapping

| Foundation Topics Section | Questions |
|---|---|
| Cisco Nexus Dashboard | 1–2 |
| Cisco Nexus Dashboard Platforms | 3–4 |
| Cisco Nexus Dashboard Cluster Nodes | 5 |
| Cisco Nexus Dashboard External Networks | 6 |
| Cisco Nexus Dashboard GUI Overview | 7–8 |

**CAUTION** The goal of self-assessment is to gauge your mastery of the topics in this chapter. If you do not know the answer to a question or are only partially sure of the answer, you should mark that question as wrong for purposes of the self-assessment. Giving yourself credit for an answer you correctly guess skews your self-assessment results and might provide you with a false sense of security.

1. Which Cisco Nexus Dashboard service offers streamlined data center network automation, control, and management for Cisco NX-OS–based VXLAN fabrics?

   a. Cisco Nexus Dashboard Insights

   b. Cisco Nexus Dashboard Orchestrator

   c. Cisco Nexus Dashboard Fabric Controller

   d. Cisco Nexus Dashboard Data Broker

2. Which of the following are NOT the Cisco Nexus Dashboard Fabric Controller personas?

   a. Fabric Discovery

   b. Fabric Controller

   c. SAN Controller

   d. Insights

3. In which of the following form factors can Cisco Nexus Dashboard be deployed? (Choose two answers.)

   a. .iso

   b. .app

   c. .arm

   d. .exe

4. Which of the following are the Cisco Nexus Dashboard virtual form factor resource profiles? (Choose two answers.)

   a. App node

   b. Data node

   c. Management node

   d. Control node

5. Which of the following nodes can be promoted to the role of a master node?

   **a.** Worker node

   **b.** Backup node

   **c.** Standby node

   **d.** Alternate node

6. Which Cisco Nexus Dashboard external network is used for service-to-service communication?

   **a.** Management Network

   **b.** Control Network

   **c.** Data Network

   **d.** Backup Network

7. Which of the following Cisco Nexus Dashboard menus are available from the Cisco Nexus Dashboard Home screen? (Choose two answers.)

   **a.** Admin console

   **b.** Administrative

   **c.** Infrastructure

   **d.** One View

8. Which submenus belong to the System Resources menu in Cisco Nexus Dashboard Admin Console? (Choose two answers.)

   **a.** Resource Utilization

   **b.** DaemonSets

   **c.** Users

   **d.** StatefulSets

## Foundation Topics

## Cisco Nexus Dashboard

Cisco Nexus Dashboard (ND) is a central management console for multiple data center sites and a common platform for hosting Cisco data center operation applications, such as Nexus Dashboard Insights and Nexus Dashboard Orchestrator. These applications are universally available for all the data center sites and provide real-time analytics, visibility, and assurance for network policies and operations. Nexus Dashboard provides a common platform and modern technology stack for these microservices-based applications, simplifying the life-cycle management of the different modern applications and reducing the operational over-head to run and maintain these applications. It also provides a central integration point for external third-party applications with the locally hosted applications.

Using the Cisco Nexus Dashboard, IT operations teams can navigate seamlessly all aspects of infrastructure life-cycle tasks from initial configuration and capacity planning to run-ning and troubleshooting the entire IT infrastructure by leveraging Cisco Nexus Dashboard Insights (formerly Nexus Insights) and Cisco Nexus Dashboard Orchestrator (formerly Cisco Multi-Site Orchestrator), Cisco Nexus Dashboard Data Broker (formerly Nexus Data Broker), and third-party applications for mission-critical multicloud data center environment.

Cisco Nexus Dashboard provides a common platform for the following services.

- **Insights:** Helps identify anomalies, provide root-cause analysis, plan capacity, manage change, and accelerate troubleshooting

- **Orchestrator:** Provides the visibility and connectivity to different fabric controllers and unifies them into one single orchestrator, ensuring that consistent intent-based policies are provisioned properly

- **Data Broker:** Enables NetOps to programmatically manage aggregating, filtering, and forwarding complete flows to custom analytics tools

- **Fabric Controller:** Offers streamlined data center network automation, control, and management for Cisco NX-OS based VXLAN fabrics

- **Fabric Discovery:** Monitors Cisco NX-OS fabrics

- **SAN Controller:** Offers streamlined data center network automation, control, and management for Cisco NX-OS–based SAN fabrics

Figure 7-1 illustrates the Cisco Nexus Dashboard.

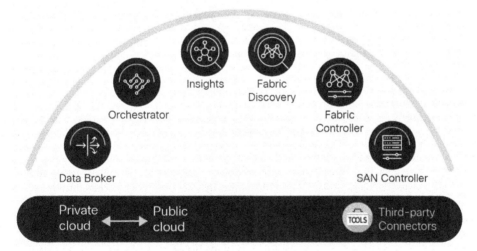

**Figure 7-1** *Cisco Nexus Dashboard*

Following are the benefits of the Cisco Nexus Dashboard:

- **Easy to use**

  - Provides a customizable role-based UI view to provide a focused view on network operator use cases

  - Provides single sign-on (SSO) for seamless user experience across operation services

  - Provides a single console for health monitoring and quick service turn-up

- **Easy to scale**

    - Ensures high availability, scale-out operations from a single dashboard

    - Scales use cases leveraging flexible deployment options

    - Provides operations that span across on-premises, multicloud, and edge networks

- **Easy to maintain**

    - Provides seamless integration and life-cycle management of operational services

    - Enables you to onboard and manage operational services across on-premises, cloud, or hybrid environments

    - Provides a single integration point for critical third-party applications and tools

## Cisco Nexus Dashboard Insights

Visibility, troubleshooting, root-cause analysis, and remediation of network issues are common challenges for day-to-day network operations. With the legacy networking operation tools, these tasks are manual, time consuming, and reactive. They require network operators to have years of experience, extensive domain expertise, and the ability to correlate different events in complex IT environments to prevent or fix issues while upholding the infrastructure uptime with minimum disruption. Cisco Nexus Dashboard Insights (formerly Nexus Insights) aims to simplify and automate these operation tasks.

Cisco Nexus Dashboard Insights (NDI) is an application that enables you to monitor, analyze, troubleshoot, and assure the networks in real time. It helps identify anomalies, provide root-cause analysis, plan capacity, manage change, and accelerate troubleshooting. By tracking historical context, collecting and processing hardware and software telemetry data, and correlating your designs with Cisco best practices, you can get excellent visibility and awareness of issues affecting your environment and take corrective actions.

NDI also includes network assurance capabilities that were formerly provided by the Cisco Network Assurance Engine (NAE) and enables you to continuously analyze and verify that the network state is consistent with intent. It ensures that network policies are compliant with business rules, validates network changes before deploying them, and determines network impact due to changes between any two points in time. You can perform natural language queries to gain in-depth connectivity knowledge of the network, of what policies enable which network elements and of the relationships between communication and virtual resources in real time.

### Cisco Nexus Dashboard Insights Features and Benefits

The key features of Cisco Nexus Dashboard Insights can be divided into three main groups:

- **Visibility and Monitoring:** These features help the operations team monitor the network infrastructure, anticipate risk, maintain compliance, and reduce downtime.

    - **Topology view:** From the topology view, you can explore, navigate, discover, and zoom into issues. You also can visualize logical constructs such as tenant, VRF, EPG, and more on top of the physical topology. In addition, you can perform rapid troubleshooting using filters to focus on problematic nodes.

- **Capacity planning:** This feature provides fabricwide visibility of resource utilization and historical trends, which helps in efficient capacity planning. You can detect components exceeding capacity thresholds ahead of time. Examples: TCAM, routes, ACL entries, ports, tenants, VRFs, EPGs, and many more.

- **Control plane statistics:** This feature provides detailed statistics and state information for PIM, IGMP, and IGMP-snooping protocols to monitor multicast control plane health.

- **Microburst detection:** This feature exposes and locates invisible microbursts and helps in finding out congestion hot spots and protects application performance.

- **Explorer queries:** This feature explores associations and connectivity across multiple sites and understands the state of network deployment using powerful natural-language querying.

- **Interface statistics:** This feature uses detailed data plane statistics to diagnose, locate, and remediate issues. You can monitor and use protocol anomalies and state information to remediate BGP, vPC, LACP, CDP, and LLDP problems.

- **Analytics and Correlation:** These features leverage artificial intelligence (AI)– and machine learning (ML)–based insights.

  - **Flow telemetry:** This feature uses Flow Table (FT)/Flow Table Events (FTE) to minimize troubleshooting time through automated root-cause analysis of data plane anomalies, such as packet drops, latency, workload movements, routing issues, ACL drops, and more. You can monitor flow rate usage to optimize FT performance.

  - **Assurance:** This feature validates low-level design configurations across your environment for both online and offline sites using assurance analysis.

  - **Endpoint analytics:** This feature locates virtual machines, bare-metal hosts, and other endpoints in the data center fabric. You can use historical data to track their movements.

  - **Integrations:** Cisco NDI provides a central integration point for API-driven third-party applications with the applications that are hosted on Nexus Dashboard.

  - **Delta analysis:** This feature provides a comprehensive view of health drift between any two points in time, minimizing the change window. It also provides a comprehensive view of policy/config drift between two points in time, minimizing troubleshooting time.

  - **Prechange analysis:** This feature predicts the impact of the intended configuration changes before deploying and leverage insight-driven change management.

  - **Anomalies:** This feature compares and contrasts time-synced data of multiple parameters to derive deeper understanding of issues and behaviors. You can learn the impacted endpoints, applications, and flows due to network anomalies. Cisco NDI also helps in anomaly assignment by tagging anomaly events to the right team member for faster resolution.

- **Advisories and Tools:** These features eliminate unplanned outages, plus improve uptime and SLA. These features require connection to Cisco Cloud.

  - **Conformance and life cycle:** This feature minimizes risk of running end-of-sale (EoS) or end-of-life (EoL) devices. You can view current status and project the future status of network software and hardware inventory against known EoS/EoL notices to ensure conformance.

  - **PSIRTs/bugs:** This feature notifies you so that you can take necessary action to stay secure and in compliance. You can get instant visibility into any applicable bugs and prevent unscheduled outages.

  - **Cisco TAC assist:** This feature automates the mundane, repetitive tasks of log collection, and attaches them to TAC service requests (SRs). You can delegate additional log collection to the TAC team and free yourself from dull work.

  - **Upgrade analysis:** This feature detects changes in configuration or operational state before and after switch upgrades and validates across 40+ checks.

  - **Field notices:** Cisco NDI can identify field notices that can potentially impact the network sites that it is monitoring and generate advisory alerts to the network operations team. The alerts consists of relevant impacts of the identified field notices as well as the affected devices in the network.

Figure 7-2 illustrates standard feature set of Cisco Nexus Dashboard Insights.

**Figure 7-2** *Nexus Dashboard Insights Features*

### Cisco Nexus Dashboard Insights GUI Overview

The key components of Cisco Nexus Dashboard Insights are shown in the left panel of the Cisco NDI graphical user interface (GUI) in Figure 7-3.

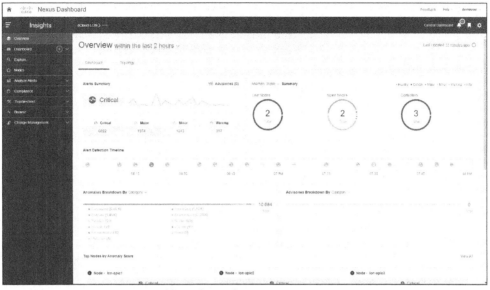

**Figure 7-3**  *Cisco Nexus Dashboard Insights Site Overview Page*

The Cisco NDI Site Overview page shown in Figure 7-3 provides a direct view into the site-level anomalies (issues) that need attention, all of which are calculated by Cisco Nexus Dashboard Insights. The anomalies are consolidated into the Overview screen and sorted by category and severity. The Insights service further groups the anomalies by top nodes, time-line view, site health score, and advisories. Lastly, a node inventory by roles and corresponding health score allows click access to the in-depth node-level visibility that gives all details on the nodes, including trends of anomalies observed.

Figure 7-4 shows the expanded form of the Cisco NDI main menu.

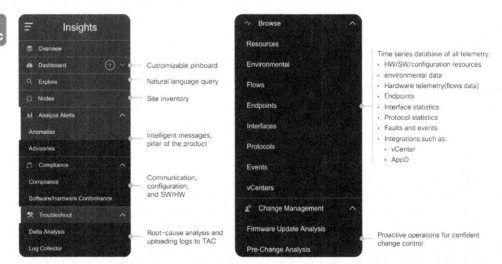

**Figure 7-4**  *Cisco Nexus Dashboard Insights Main Menu (Expanded)*

Cisco Nexus Dashboard Insights also allows users to create Custom Dashboards for any charts, as seen in the menu. In addition to viewing the rolled-up summary presentation of the anomalies and alerts, Nexus Dashboard Insights users can also interactively browse, search, and analyze the anomalies and advisory alerts generated by Cisco NDI service under the Analyze Alerts menu.

Most organizations have some types of compliance requirements for their networks. They can be industry regulatory compliance requirements, or the organizations' internal requirements for security or business functions. Additionally, the network teams often have their own established best practices, standard configuration, or standardized naming conventions that they would like to implement or enforce during the ongoing network operation. The compliance assurance functions in the Insights service give the network team one more place to directly describe and submit their intents for the network, then automatically and continuously verify and validate the intents in the network for them. Any deviation from the intents will be captured as compliance violation anomalies and reported to the network team immediately. With the automated, continuous security and configuration compliance analysis, Nexus Dashboard Insights enables true intent-based network operation.

Nexus Dashboard Insights can run network delta analysis. This capability is inherited from the Cisco NAE application. Users of the Insights service can select any two snapshots of the network site and ask Insights to analyze the differences between them, including configuration differences, and differences in anomalies and advisories that reveal the differences in how the network was operating at the two points in time. When you are troubleshooting a network incidence, the differences in the network configuration or operations can often help identify the cause of the issue. When you're performing network maintenance, such as configuration changes, software upgrades, or hardware replacement, it is helpful to check the differences in the network before and after the maintenance task. It can tell whether the network has converged or restored to how it should be after the task, or whether the task has resolved the issues that it is supposed to resolve, or if it has introduced any new issues. The Delta Analysis function increases network operation efficiency for these maintenance tasks and helps reduce the Mean Time to Resolution (MTRR) for troubleshooting.

Nexus Dashboard Insights can assist the network team to collect tech-support logs per node using Log Collector functionality. It turns the tedious task into a simple one-step automated job. These logs can be downloaded locally and optionally uploaded to Cisco Cloud to make them available for Cisco Support when opening a service request (SR).

Under the Browse functionality, all anomalies observed for any of the data sets mentioned in the Browse menu are rolled into the Dashboard view of the respective site. Resource utilization shows time-series–based trends of capacity utilization by correlating Software Telemetry data collected from nodes in each site. Persistent trends help identify burdened pieces of infrastructure and plan for resizing, restructuring, and repurposing. Environmental data provides anomaly-detection capabilities in hardware components such as CPU, memory, temperature, fan speed, power, and storage. Statistics are all about interfaces and routing protocols. Interface statistics provide a view into the trend of utilization, including errors such as CRC, FCS, and Stomped CRC. Protocol Statistics provide a view into what interface protocols are active, such as CDP, LLDP, LACP, BGP, PIM, IGMP, and IGMP snooping; protocol details like neighbors, incoming and outgoing interfaces (OIFs) for a (*,G), (S,G) entry; along with trends of errors like a lost connection or neighbor, OIF flaps, or invalid packet. The Flow Analytics dashboard attracts operator attention to key indicators of infrastructure data-plane health. Time-series data offers evidence of historical trends, specific patterns, and past issues and can help the operator build a case for audit, compliance, and capacity planning or infrastructure assessment. Endpoints shows time-series–based endpoint movement in the fabric, with endpoint details and endpoints with duplicate IPs. In virtualized data center environments, this keeps track of virtual machine movement, which is extremely useful to identify the virtual machine's current location and its historical movements in the fabric.

Integrating VMware vCenter server allows Nexus Dashboard Insights to collect data and metrics of the virtual machines and hosts monitored by VMware vCenter and then correlate the collected information with the data collected from the Cisco ACI or Cisco NDFC. The vCenter Dashboard presents a view of the of the Top Virtual Machines by Anomaly Score, along with various metrics. With application integrations such as Cisco AppDynamics and Cisco Nexus Dashboard Insights, users get a single pane of glass (SPOG) for application and network statistics and anomalies. Cisco Nexus Dashboard Insights consumes data streamed from the AppDynamics controller, and in addition to showing application, tier, node health, and metrics, Cisco Nexus Dashboard Insights derives the baseline of network statistics of these applications like TCP loss, round-trip time, latency, throughput, and performance impacting events (PIEs) and generates anomalies on threshold violations. For any AppDynamics flows, Cisco Nexus Dashboard Insights also provides an in-depth end-to-end path, latency, drops if any, and drop reasons to help users identify if app slowness or issues are resulting from network issues. The event analytics dashboard displays faults, events, and audit logs in a time-series fashion. Clicking any of these points in the history displays its historical state and detailed information. Further, all of these are correlated together to identify whether deletion of configuration led to a fault.

Firmware Update Analysis lists the intermittent upgrades to get to the destination software, upgrade impact, and release notes for each release linked directly in Cisco Nexus Dashboard Insights. Insights users can use the prechange verification capability to proactively validate the configuration changes against the latest snapshot of the network before implementing configuration changes in the network. You can simply submit your intended changes to the Insights service. The Insights service will analyze the impacts of the changes to the network, calling out any errors or potential issues. You, as a network engineer, get an opportunity to review and correct the errors and only implement the fully qualified configuration changes to the network. This prechange analysis function removes the guesswork from network configuration change management, minimizes the risks of change management, and therefore increases the availability of the entire network.

## Cisco Nexus Dashboard Orchestrator

Cisco Nexus Dashboard Orchestrator (NDO) provides consistent network and policy orchestration, scalability, and disaster recovery across multiple data centers through a single pane of glass while allowing the data center to go wherever the data is. NDO allows you to interconnect separate Cisco Application Centric Infrastructure (Cisco ACI) sites, Cisco Cloud ACI sites, and Cisco Nexus Dashboard Fabric Controller (NDFC) sites, each managed by its own controller (APIC cluster, NDFC cluster, or Cloud APIC instances in a public cloud). The on-premises sites (ACI or NDFC) can be extended to different public clouds for hybrid-cloud deployments while cloud-first installations can be extended to multicloud deployments without on-premises sites. In addition, NDO can be deployed as a service in Cisco Nexus Dashboard.

7

For Cisco ACI, NDO is the intersite policy manager. It provides single-pane management, enabling you to monitor the health-score state of all interconnected sites. It also allows you to define, in a centralized place, all intersite policies, which can then be pushed to different APIC domains for rendering them on the physical switches in those fabrics. This capability provides a high degree of control over when and where to deploy the policies, which in turn allows the tenant change domain separation that uniquely characterizes the Cisco Multi-Site architecture. With NDO, you can extend your policies to any site or multiple public clouds.

For Cisco NDFC, NDO enables network policy consistency and disaster recovery across multiple NDFC fabrics around the world through a single pane of glass and scale-out NDFC leaf switches to thousands of switches managed using one centralized policy.

Figure 7-5 shows the Cisco Nexus Dashboard overview.

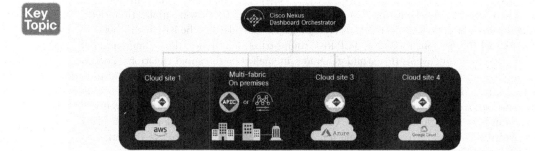

**Figure 7-5** *Cisco Nexus Dashboard Orchestrator Overview*

### Cisco Nexus Dashboard Orchestrator Features and Benefits

Following are the key features and benefits of Cisco Nexus Dashboard Orchestrator:

- Single pane of glass for administration and orchestration of multiple networking fabrics for both Cisco ACI and NDFC

- Automation of the configuration and management of intersite network interconnects across an IP backbone for both Cisco ACI and NDFC

- Consistent multitenant policy across multiple sites, which allows IP mobility, disaster recovery, and active/active use cases for data centers

- Capability to map tenants, applications, and associated networks to specific availability domains within the Cisco Multi-Site architecture for both Cisco ACI and NDFC

- Hybrid cloud and multicloud orchestration supporting on-premises Cisco ACI sites and public cloud sites (AWS and Azure)

- Capability to have multicloud ACI deployments without on-premises sites

- Scale-out sites and leaf switches based on resource growth

## Cisco Nexus Dashboard Fabric Controller

Cisco Nexus Dashboard Fabric Controller, or NDFC (formerly known as Data Center Network Manager, a.k.a. DCNM), is the comprehensive management solution for all NX-OS deployments spanning LAN Fabric, SAN, and IP Fabric for Media (IPFM) networks in data centers powered by Cisco. Cisco Nexus Dashboard Fabric Controller also supports other devices, such as IOS-XE switches, IOS-XR routers, and non-Cisco devices. Being a multifabric controller, Cisco Nexus Dashboard Fabric Controller manages multiple deployment models like VXLAN EVPN, Classic 3-Tier, FabricPath, and routed-based fabrics for LAN while providing ready-to-use control, management, monitoring, and automation capabilities for all these environments. In addition, Cisco NDFC, when enabled as a SAN Controller, automates Cisco MDS switches and Cisco Nexus family infrastructure in NX-OS mode with a focus on storage-specific features and analytics capabilities.

Cisco Nexus Dashboard Fabric Controller primarily focuses on control and management for three primary types of deployments:

- LAN networking including VXLAN, Multi-Site, Classic Ethernet, and External Fabrics supporting Cisco Nexus switches running standalone NX-OS, with additional support for IOS-XR, IOS-XE, and adjacent host, compute, virtual machine, and container management systems.

- SAN networking for Cisco MDS and Cisco Nexus switches running standalone NX-OS, including support for integration with storage arrays and additionally host, compute, virtual machine, and container orchestration systems.

- Media control for multicast video production networks running Cisco Nexus switches operated as standalone NX-OS, with additional integrations for third-party media control systems.

Cisco Nexus Dashboard Fabric Controller is available as an application running exclusively on top of the Cisco Nexus Dashboard Virtual or Physical Appliance. Virtual Nexus Dashboard deployment with OVA is also referred to as virtual Nexus Dashboard (vND) deployment, while the deployment of Nexus Dashboard on a physical appliance (service engine) is known as physical Nexus Dashboard (pND) deployment. You can find more on various deployment modes of Nexus Dashboard in later sections of this chapter.

Cisco Nexus Dashboard Fabric Controller has a single installation mode. Post-installation, it supports selection from multiple personas at runtime. After the Nexus Dashboard Fabric Controller is installed, you can choose from one of the following personas:

- **Fabric Discovery:** Discover, monitor, and visualize LAN deployments.

- **Fabric Controller:** LAN Controller for Classic Ethernet (vPC), routed, VXLAN, Multi-Site, and IP Fabric for Media Deployments.

- **SAN Controller:** SAN Controller for MDS and Nexus switches. Includes SAN Insights with streaming telemetry.

Figure 7-6 illustrates Cisco NDFC modes/personas.

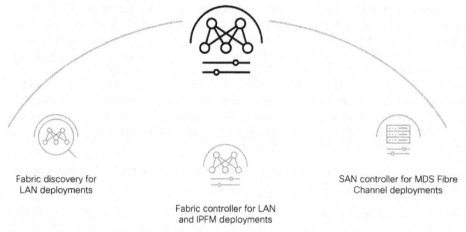

**Figure 7-6**  *Cisco NDFC modes/personas*

**NOTE**  For any given instance of Nexus Dashboard, only one version of NDFC service will be active. On the active NDFC service, you can configure only one persona at any given instance.

In Cisco NDFC, all features/services are modularized, broken into smaller microservices, and the required microservices are orchestrated based on the feature set or feature selections. Therefore, if any feature or microservice is down, only that microservice is restarted and recovered, resulting in minimal disruption.

## Cisco Nexus Dashboard Fabric Controller Features and Benefits

Following are the key features and benefits of Cisco Nexus Dashboard Fabric Controller.

- **Infrastructure and GUI:**
  - Provides modular, microservices-based architecture to enable scale-out models.
  - Provides React JS–based UI to simplify and enhance GUI interactions.
  - Supports active/active high availability for either LAN or SAN deployments.
  - Includes a runtime feature manager for LAN, SAN, and IPFM deployments.
  - Offers Nexus Dashboard Fabric Discovery mode for inventory, discovery, and monitoring only.
  - Provides user feedback tool integration to allow users to submit feedback/requests to be reviewed by product team.

- **Dashboards:**
  - Provides last 24 hours summary of events and top "talkers."
  - Offers custom summary view of LAN and SAN domains and topology groups.

- Provides host, switch, and fabric dashboards and provides views of configurations, control, events, and traffic and context-based searches from dashboards.

- Brings the NDFC computing dashboard into the VMware vCenter for dependency mapping and inventory, performance, configuration, and event views.

- **Customizable templates:**

  - Includes best-practice policy templates with Python support and built-in compliance checking for fabric builder.

  - Provides prebuilt templates for classic LAN mode provisioning.

  - Allows creation of new customizable templates using the template editor.

  - Allows import and conversion of configuration scripts to templates.

- **REST and JavaScript Object Notification (JSON) API:**

  - All northbound APIs are REST. NDFC's GUI uses these REST APIs for all GUI functions.

  - Includes self-documented "swagger"-style built-in documentation, with examples.

  - Enables integration with third-party or custom orchestration and automation tools like Ansible.

- **Configuration and change management for classic LAN Mode:**

  - Provides predeployment validation of configuration changes to help reduce human errors. (POAP also includes this feature.)

  - Provides a general configuration archive to track changes, allowing rollback to a last-known good state.

  - Provides the capability to back up configuration files from all switches for classic LAN-mode operations.

  - Provides Brownfield host port interface configuration sync-up feature, which supports resync of out-of-band host port configurations to NDFC.

- **Software image management:**

  - Includes support for Cisco in-service software upgrade (ISSU), Graceful Insertion and Removal (GIR), and Return Material Authorization (RMA) functions.

  - Includes installation/uninstallation of SMUs and RPMs for Cisco Nexus platforms.

  - Supports NX-OS image and EPLD installation and upgrades from the GUI.

Cisco NDFC provides the following features for LAN fabric with VXLAN EVPN.

- **Fabric control and overlay visibility and management:**

  - Provides fabric management for multiple types of LAN solutions, including VXLAN-EVPN, and traditional three-tier LAN deployments with workflows for provisioning LAN services such as VPCs.

7

- Includes intuitive overlay management with built-in best practices and maximum visibility for robust Cisco NX-OS configuration profiles.

- Autodetects unprovisioned switches for use in fabric builder with day-0 POAP for policy-based bootstrapping of fabric infrastructure.

- Offers compliance management to ensure that network is in sync with intended deployment and notify users when out of compliance, allowing users to deploy any corrections.

- Supports easy provisioning using interface groups; attaches overlay networks to groups in one go, allowing new interfaces added to the group to automatically inherit the configuration.

- Provides integration with Nexus Dashboard Orchestrator (NDO) to extend overlay networks or VRFs between VXLAN-EVPN fabrics managed by different NDFC instances.

- Supports overlay network and VRF provisioning using CLI.

- **Hybrid-cloud connectivity:**

  - Supports hybrid-cloud connectivity with AWS and Microsoft Azure public clouds.

  - Integrates with Cisco Nexus Dashboard Orchestrator (NDO) and Cisco Cloud Network Controller to provide L3 VRF stretch between private and public clouds.

- **Unified topology views and control:**

  - Presents topology views showing physical and overlay networks on the same page, helping IT administrators quickly identify the extent of virtual overlay networks on a programmable fabric.

  - In topology view, shows VXLAN details, VXLAN tunnel endpoint (VTEP) status, and VXLAN network identifier (VNI) status on a per-switch basis.

  - Presents smart topology views showing virtual port channels (vPCs) and virtual device contexts for Cisco Nexus networks. (Topology views include VXLAN search.)

- **Role-based access control (RBAC) for fabric objects:**

  - Allows role-based access control (RBAC) within the fabric to separate administrative tasks between functional domains.

  - Provides a granularized RBAC model, which supports the same user having different roles across different fabrics.

Cisco NDFC provides the following features for IP Fabric for Media (IPFM).

- **Flow Control**

  - Flow and host policy manager

- **Visualization and health**

  - Topology and endpoint visibility.

  - End-to-end flow visualization.

  - Network health monitoring.

  - RTP and EDI flow monitoring.

- **Provisioning and automation**

  - Fabric bootstrap: day-0 provisioning.

  - API gateway for broadcast controller.

  - Fabric builder for IPFM underlay network with nonblocking multicast.

Cisco NDFC provides the following features for storage area networking (SAN).

- **SAN Analytics integration with Cisco SAN Insights:**

  - Provides SAN Analytics visualization at scale, providing a single pane of glass into hundreds of thousands of FC flows.

  - Offers SAN Insights anomaly detection to find real-world issues and send alerts in real time.

  - Provides a fully customizable infrastructure to create and manage SAN Insights events.

  - Offers always-on and auto-learned approach for all FC flows.

- **Storage topology and visibility:**

  - Provides Switch, end device, VSAN, and zoning visualization on the topology maps.

  - Allows you to see trends and explore link bandwidth straight from the topology map.

  - Offers health color coding to quickly find and troubleshoot issues.

  - Provides device manager integration for all switches in the topology.

  - Provides storage and host visualization on the topology map.

- **SAN zoning:**

  - Offers a totally redesigned web-based zoning interface to drastically reduce the cycle time for common administration tasks. Also provides IVR zoning function on the same page.

  - Provides a web-based FC and device-alias configuration to ease transition to a web-based user interface for zoning and other management tasks.

7

- **Automated analysis:**

  - SAN host-path-redundancy feature to better organize and identify virtual and physical hosts with path-redundancy problems in the fabric.

  - Slow-drain analysis features to increase efficiency and reduce the time to discover the slow-drain devices.

- **Storage management:**

  - Provides visibility into all modern storage products to help provide information to storage administrators in the context of SAN management.

  - Offers port channel and VSAN management.

  - Offers FICON management.

Cisco NDFC provides the following features for visibility, monitoring, and troubleshooting.

- **Automated discovery:**

  - Provides automated network discovery for up-to-date physical and logical inventory information.

  - Tracks inventory and performance information in real time.

- **Topology overlays and views:**

  - Provides detailed visibility into real-time and historical performance statistics in the data center.

  - In topology views, shows link-layer and overlay status details alongside switch details to aid troubleshooting and visibility.

  - Provides general visibility into Layer-2 network connectivity mapped on the physical topology view.

  - Provides topology, configuration, and information for virtual machines, port groups, DVS/vSwitches, vNICs, and VMNICs correlated with the physical network topology.

  - Provides insight into port and bandwidth use, error count, traffic statistics, and so on.

- **Event management, reports, and alarms:**

  - Provides real-time network-health summary with detailed views of individual network components, enabling operations staff to respond quickly to events based on event severity.

  - Provides an alarm function for stateful alarm monitoring to show whether an error condition is active. Users can define an alarm policy for the device, interface, or syslog conditions and can email alarms to users.

- Provides easy-to-schedule reports using predefined templates, including inventory, health, and performance monitoring reports. These reports later can be exported for postprocessing or sent by email.

- Allows creation of custom port groups based on priority and severity level of the application and implementation of rule-based event forwarding to notify the system or user of traps and syslog messages generated for the custom port group.

## Cisco Nexus Dashboard Fabric Controller GUI Overview

The key components of Cisco Nexus Dashboard Fabric Controller are shown in the left panel of the Cisco NDFC graphical user interface in Figure 7-7.

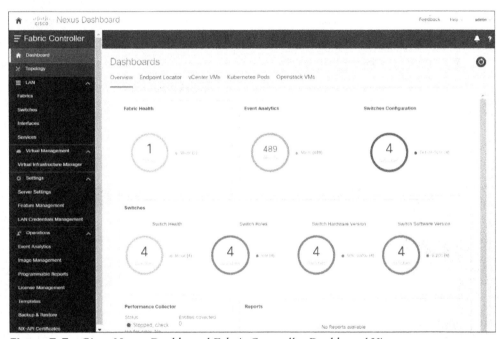

**Figure 7-7**   *Cisco Nexus Dashboard Fabric Controller Dashboard View*

The intent of the Dashboard is to enable network and storage administrators to focus on particular areas of concern around the health and performance of data center switching. This information is provided as 24-hour snapshots. The functional view of LAN switching consists of seven dynamic dashlets that display information in the context of the selected scope by default.

The following default dashlets appear in the Overview dashboard window:

- **Fabric Health:** Displays the fabric health summary of problems and number in the donut depicting total number of fabrics. Displays fabric health status with Critical and Healthy.

- **Events Analytics:** Displays events with Critical, Error, and Warning severity.

- **Switches Configuration:** Displays the switches' inventory summary information, such as the switch models and the corresponding count. It also displays the synchronization status of the switch configurations as compared to the intent defined in Cisco NDFC.

- **Switch Health:** Displays the switches' health summary Critical and Healthy with the corresponding count.

- **Switch Roles:** Displays the switches' roles summary and the corresponding count. Displays the number of access, spine, and leaf devices.

- **Switch Hardware Version:** Displays the switches' models and the corresponding count.

- **Switch Software Version:** Displays the switches' software version and the corresponding count.

- **Reports:** Displays switch reports.

The Topology window displays color-coded nodes and links that correspond to various network elements, including switches, links, fabric extenders, port channel configurations, virtual port channels, and more.

Figure 7-8 shows the Cisco NDFC Topology view.

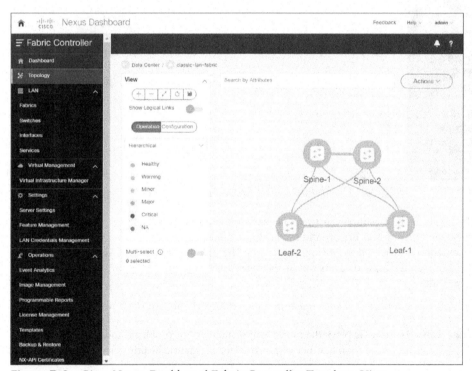

**Figure 7-8**  *Cisco Nexus Dashboard Fabric Controller Topology View*

Figure 7-9 shows the expanded form of the Cisco NDFC main menu for LAN deployments.

**Figure 7-9**    *Cisco Nexus Dashboard Fabric Controller Main Menu for LAN Deployments*

The Fabrics tab displays the fabric name, fabric technology based on the fabric template, and fabric type—Switch Fabric, LAN Monitor, or External—along with ASN for the fabric and fabric health. From the Fabrics tab, you can also create, edit, and delete fabric. In the Switches tab, you can verify the current switches' details, including name, IP address, serial number, associated fabric, and configuration status, including In-Sync or Out-of-sync and model number. From the Switches tab, you can add switches to the fabric and deploy configuration to the switches, plus assign various switch roles, such as spine, leaf, edge router, and border gateway. The Interfaces tab displays all the interfaces that are discovered for the switch, virtual port channels (vPCs), and intended interfaces missing on the device. You can create, deploy, view, edit and delete various interface configurations from this tab, including port channel, vPC, loopback, and subinterface. From the Services tab, you can add, edit, or delete various service nodes, such as Firewall, Load Balancer, and Virtual Networking Function (VNF).

From the Virtual Infrastructure Manager tab, you can add, edit, delete, and rediscover virtual infrastructure manager instances, such as vCenter, Kubernetes Cluster, and OpenStack Cluster. The Server Settings tab allows you to set the parameters of the NDFC server from the Cisco NDFC Web UI. Server settings are classified under different tabs, such as Alarms, Events, and SNMP. The Feature Management tab allows you to dynamically enable feature sets belonging to different personas such as Kubernetes Visualizer and Endpoint Locator. The LAN Credentials Management tab allows you to configure two sets of credentials:

- **Discovery Credentials:** Cisco Nexus Dashboard Fabric Controller uses these credentials during discovery and periodic polling of the devices. NDFC use discovery credentials with SSH and SNMPv3 to discover hardware or software inventory from the switches. Therefore, these are called discovery credentials. You can discover one inventory per switch. These are read-only and cannot make configuration changes on the switches.

- **Configuration Change Credentials:** Cisco Nexus Dashboard Fabric Controller uses these credentials when a user tries to use the features that change the device configuration.

The Event Analytics tab displays the alarms that are generated for various categories. This tab displays information such as ID (optional), Severity, Failure Source, Name, Category, Acknowledged, Creation Time, Last Updated (optional), Policy, and Message. You can specify the Refresh Interval in this tab. You can select one or more alarms and then acknowledge or unacknowledge their status using the Change Status drop-down list. From Image Management tab, you can automate the steps associated with upgrade planning, scheduling, downloading, and monitoring the devices. Image management is supported only for Cisco Nexus switches.

The Programmable Reports application enables the generation of reports using Python 2.7 scripts. Report jobs are run to generate reports, and each report job can generate multiple reports. You can schedule the report to run for a specific device or fabric. These reports are analyzed to obtain detailed information about the devices. The License Management tab displays the status of NDFC server license and licenses for each switch and also allows you to configure smart licensing. Cisco Smart Licensing is a flexible licensing model that provides you with an easier, faster, and more consistent way to purchase and manage software across the Cisco portfolio and across your organization. You can add, edit, delete, duplicate, import, and export templates that are configured across different Cisco Nexus, IOS-XE, IOS-XR, and Cisco MDS platforms using Templates tab. Templates support JavaScript. You can use the JavaScript function in a template to perform arithmetic operations and string manipulations in the template syntax. From the Backup and Restore tab, you can take a backup manually anytime, or you can configure a scheduler to back up all fabric configurations and intents. You can take a backup using either of the following formats:

- **Config only:** A config only backup is smaller. It contains the intent, dependent data, discovery information, credentials, and policies. A restore from this backup has functional fabrics, switch discovery, expected configurations, and other settings.

- **Full:** A full backup is large. It contains current data, historical data, alarms, host information, and everything in a config only backup. A restore from this backup has functional historical reports, metrics charts, and all base functionality.

When restoring a backup, you can choose to do a config only restore or a full restore.

Cisco NX-OS switches require an SSL certificate to function in NX-API HTTPS mode. You can generate the SSL certificates and get it signed by your CA. You can install the certificates manually using CLI commands on the switch console or use Cisco Nexus Dashboard Fabric Controller to install these on switches. The NX-API Certificates tab allows you to upload NX-API certificates to Nexus Dashboard Fabric Controller that can be used later to install on the switches that are managed by Nexus Dashboard Fabric Controller.

Figure 7-10 shows the expanded form of the Cisco NDFC main menu for SAN deployments.

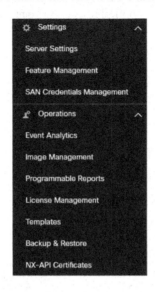

**Figure 7-10**   *Cisco Nexus Dashboard Fabric Controller Main Menu for SAN Deployments*

In the main menu of NDFC for SAN deployments, we see few new tabs under the SAN and Virtual Management drop-downs, such as Links, End Devices, Host Path Redundancy, Port Monitoring, Active Zones, Storage, and Zoning. The Links tab allows you to monitor the ISL traffic and errors and also view the performance of NPV links. The End Devices tab displays the list of host and storage devices and enclosures. The SAN Host Path Redundancy check enables you to view the nonredundant host storage paths. It helps you to identify the host enclosure errors along with the resolution to fix the errors. The Host Path Redundancy tab displays the hostpath errors along with a list of host enclosures, storage enclosures, and host-storage pairs that have been selected to be ignored during the redundancy check. The Port Monitoring tab allows you to save custom Port Monitoring policies in the Cisco SAN Controller database and to push the selected custom policy to one or more fabrics or Cisco MDS 9000 Series switches. The policy is designated as the active Port-Monitor policy in the switch. The Active Zones tab displays a list of regular zones and IVR zones configured on the SAN Controller. The Storage tab displays information about storage arrays. The Zoning tab under the Virtual Management drop-down enables you to set up access control between storage devices or user groups.

## Cisco Nexus Dashboard Data Broker

The Cisco Nexus Dashboard Data Broker (NDDB) is a simple, scalable, and cost-effective solution for data center, enterprise, and service provider customers who need to monitor high-volume and business-critical traffic. It replaces traditional purpose-built matrix switches with one or more Cisco Nexus 3000, 9300, or 9500 Series switches that you can interconnect to build a highly scalable TAP-Aggregation network that can help copy or mirror the production traffic using optical test access points (TAPs) and Cisco Switched Port Analyzer (SPAN).

Figure 7-11 shows the two key parts that form the Cisco Nexus Dashboard Data Broker solution. The first of these is the Cisco Nexus switches that provide aggregation, filtering, replication, and redirection capabilities. The second is the controller, which pushes the configuration to the switches to perform these functionalities.

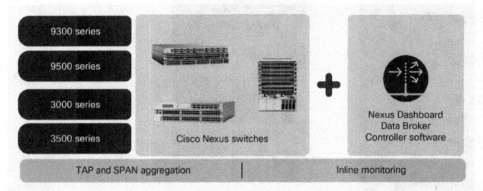

**Figure 7-11**   *Cisco Nexus Dashboard Data Broker Solution*

The Cisco Nexus switches form the Nexus Dashboard Data Broker (NDDB) switches, which connect to the production network to aggregate the copy traffic using TAP and SPAN methods. The aggregated traffic is filtered and redirected to tools as configured by the customer, as shown in Figure 7-12.

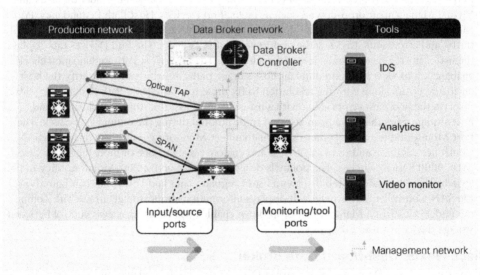

**Figure 7-12**   *Nexus Dashboard Data Broker Deployment Model*

The Data Broker Controller can be deployed in the following modes:

- **Centralized:** The controller is deployed on a VM/server/bare metal outside the TAP aggregation switches. In this mode, the controller can support a multiswitch TAP aggregation topology, as shown in Figure 7-12.

- **Embedded:** The controller is deployed on the TAP aggregation switch using a guest shell. In this mode, the controller can be used only as a single switch deployment.

- **Nexus Dashboard:** The controller is supported as an application on Cisco Nexus Dashboard.

- **Cisco ACI:** The controller is supported as an application on Cisco ACI APICs.

### Cisco Nexus Dashboard Data Broker Features and Benefits

Following are the key features and benefits of Cisco Nexus Dashboard Data Broker:

- Offers a simple, scalable, cost-effective solution for monitoring high-volume and business-critical traffic.

- Builds a TAP SPAN infrastructure with a wide range of port density and bandwidth ranging from 1 Gbps to 400 Gbps. Bandwidth supported includes 1, 10, 25, 40, 100, and 400 Gbps.

- Supports line-rate traffic filtering, replication, and forwarding functions.

- Supports inline traffic redirection to multiple security tools at the perimeter of the data center network.

- Deploys advanced functionalities such as time stamping, source port tagging, MPLS label stripping, VXLAN header stripping, packet slicing, and more.

- Generates sampled flow (sFlow) and NetFlow records.

- Copies and redirects traffic from remote or local sources to remote or local tools.

- Integrates with Cisco Application Centric Infrastructure (Cisco ACI) to configure access SPAN sessions using the Cisco Application Policy Infrastructure Controller (APIC) REST API.

- Runs as an application on APIC.

- Runs as an application on Nexus Dashboard.

- Integrates with Cisco DNA Center (DNAC) to configure SPAN on selected access switches in enterprise networks.

- Onboards a Cisco Nexus 3550 Series switch as a TAP device.

## Cisco Nexus Dashboard Platforms

Cisco Nexus Dashboard is offered as a cluster of specialized Cisco UCS servers (Nexus Dashboard platform) with the software framework (Nexus Dashboard) pre-installed on it. The Cisco Nexus Dashboard software stack can be decoupled from the hardware and deployed in a number of virtual form factors.

Cisco Nexus Dashboard can be deployed using a number of different form factors. Keep in mind, however, that you must use the same form factor for all nodes; mixing different form factors within the same cluster is not supported.

- **Cisco Nexus Dashboard physical appliance (.iso):** This form factor refers to the original physical appliance hardware that you can purchase with the Cisco Nexus Dashboard software stack pre-installed on it.

- **VMware ESXi (.ova):** This virtual form factor allows you to deploy a Nexus Dashboard cluster using VMware ESXi virtual machines with one of two resource profiles:

  - **Data node:** Node profile designed for data-intensive applications, such as Nexus Dashboard Insights.

  - **App node:** Node profile designed for non-data-intensive applications, such as Nexus Dashboard Orchestrator.

- **Linux KVM (.qcow2):** This virtual form factor allows you to deploy a Nexus Dashboard cluster using Linux KVM virtual machines.

- **Amazon Web Services (.ami):** This cloud form factor allows you to deploy a Nexus Dashboard cluster using AWS instances.

- **Microsoft Azure (.arm):** This cloud form factor allows you to deploy a Nexus Dashboard cluster using Azure instances.

- **In an existing Red Hat Enterprise Linux (RHEL) system:** You can run Nexus Dashboard node in an existing Red Hat Enterprise Linux server.

The physical appliance form factor is supported on the original Nexus Dashboard platform hardware only. Following is the list of specifications required for the physical appliance servers:

- UCS C220 M5 Chassis

- 2× 10-core 2.2G Intel Xeon Silver CPU

- 256 GB of RAM

- 4× 2.4TB HDDs

  400GB SSD

  1.2TB NVME drive

- UCS Virtual Interface Card 1455 (4×25G ports)

- 1050W power supply

A total of three servers with the preceding specifications is required to form a Nexus Dashboard cluster.

Table 7-2 lists the specifications for the virtual form factor Nexus Dashboard cluster deployment.

**Table 7-2**  Nexus Dashboard Virtual Form Factor Requirements

| Data Node Requirements | App Node Requirements |
|---|---|
| VMware ESXi 6.7 and above | VMware ESXi 6.7 and above |
| VMware vCenter 6.x and above, if deploying using vCenter | VMware vCenter 6.x and above, if deploying using vCenter |
| Each VM requires the following: | Each VM requires the following: |
| ■ 32 vCPUs with physical reservation<br>■ 128 GB of RAM with physical reservation<br>■ 3 TB SSD storage for the data volume and an additional 50 GB for the system volume<br><br>Data nodes must be deployed on storage with the following minimum performance requirements:<br><br>■ The SSD must be attached to the data store directly or in JBOD mode if using a RAID Host Bus Adapter (HBA).<br>■ The SSDs must be optimized for mixed use/application (not read-optimized).<br>■ 4K Random Read IOPS: 93000<br>■ 4K Random Write IOPS: 31000<br><br>It is recommended that each Nexus Dashboard node be deployed in a different ESXi server. | ■ 16 vCPUs with physical reservation<br>■ 64 GB of RAM with physical reservation<br>■ 500 GB HDD or SSD storage for the data volume and an additional 50 GB for the system volume<br><br>Some services require App nodes to be deployed on faster SSD storage while other services support HDD.<br><br>It is recommended that each Nexus Dashboard node be deployed in a different ESXi server. |

## Cisco Nexus Dashboard Cluster Nodes

Each Nexus Dashboard cluster typically consists of one or three master nodes. For three-node clusters, you can also provision a number of worker nodes to enable horizontal scaling and standby nodes for easy cluster recovery in case of a master node failure. Depending on the type and number of services you choose to run, you may be required to deploy additional worker nodes in your cluster after the initial deployment.

Following are the few guidelines for Nexus Dashboard cluster deployment:

■ Single-node clusters are supported for a limited number of services and cannot be extended to a three-node cluster after the initial deployment. If you deploy a single-node cluster and want to extend it to a three-node cluster or add worker nodes, you need to redeploy it as a base three-node cluster.

■ For three-node clusters, at least two master nodes are required for the cluster to remain operational. In case of two master node failure, the cluster enters an offline read-only mode and cannot be used until you recover it.

■ Only three-node clusters support additional worker nodes. After your initial cluster is up and running, you can configure and deploy additional nodes.

Table 7-3 lists the maximum verified scalability limits for the Nexus Dashboard nodes.

**Table 7-3**  Maximum Verified Scalability Limits for ND Nodes

| Category | Scale |
|---|---|
| Nodes in a physical cluster | Three master nodes |
| | Four worker nodes |
| | Two standby nodes |
| Nodes in a virtual cluster (ESXi) | Three master nodes |
| | Three worker nodes |
| | Two standby nodes |
| Nodes in a virtual cluster (KVM) | Three master nodes |
| Nodes in a cloud cluster (AWS or Azure) | Three master nodes |
| Nodes in a Red Hat Enterprise Linux (RHEL) | Three master nodes |

The Cisco Nexus Dashboard Capacity Planning tool, available on the web, provides cluster-izing guidelines based on the type and number of services you plan to run in your Nexus Dashboard as well as the target fabrics' sizes. Figure 7-13 shows the Cisco Nexus Dashboard Capacity Planning tool.

# Nexus Dashboard Capacity Planning

This page provides cluster sizing guidelines based on the type and number of services you plan to run in your Nexus Dashboard as well as the target fabrics' sizes. The provided information has been tested and validated by Cisco, Cisco partners, or both.

For feedback on this tool, send email to ciscodcnapps-docfeedback@cisco.com.

Nexus Dashboard Release: | 2.2.1/2.2.2 ˅ |

Cluster Form Factor:
- ◉ Physical
- ○ Virtual (vCenter/ESXi)
- ○ Virtual (KVM)
- ○ Cloud (AWS/Azure)
- ○ Linux (RHEL)

Nexus Dashboard Services:
- ☐ Insights
- ☐ Orchestrator
- ☐ Data Broker
- ☐ Fabric Controller

Total switches: ◉ 1-50  ○ 51-100  ○ 101-500

**Minimum cluster size:** 3 nodes.
High availability deployments require an additional 'standby' node.

**Figure 7-13**  *Nexus Dashboard Capacity Planning Tool*

Depending on the services (NDI/NDO/NDFC/NDDB) being deployed on top of a virtual Nexus Dashboard cluster, the number of required nodes and which node type must be deployed as master changes, as shown in Table 7-4. The following information is derived from the Cisco Nexus Dashboard Capacity Planning tool.

**Table 7-4**   Master Node Types

| Deployed Services | NDI | NDO | NDI and NDO | NDFC | NDDB |
|---|---|---|---|---|---|
| Total number of nodes needed | 6 | 3 | 6 | 3 | 3 |
| Type of master nodes | DATA | APP | DATA | APP | APP |
| Total number of DATA nodes needed | 3 | 0 | 3 | 0 | 0 |
| Total number of APP nodes needed | 3 | 3 | 3 | 3 | 3 |

**NOTE**   You can access the Nexus Dashboard Capacity Planning tool at https://www.cisco.com/c/dam/en/us/td/docs/dcn/tools/nd-sizing/index.html.

Nexus Dashboard supports distribution of cluster nodes across multiple sites. The following node distribution recommendations apply to both physical and virtual clusters:

- For Nexus Dashboard Insights, a centralized, single-site deployment is recommended. Although the NDI service does not gain redundancy benefits of distributed clusters, the single-site deployment model does stop the exposure of the cluster to interconnection failures when nodes are deployed in different sites.

- For Nexus Dashboard Orchestrator and Nexus Dashboard Fabric Controller, a distributed cluster is recommended. Because at least two Nexus Dashboard master nodes are required for the cluster to remain operational, when you are deploying a physical Nexus Dashboard cluster across two sites, it is recommended to deploy a standby node in the site with the single master node.

## Cisco Nexus Dashboard External Networks

Cisco Nexus Dashboard is deployed as a cluster, connecting each service node to two networks—the management network and the data network. When first configuring Nexus Dashboard, you need to provide two IP addresses for the two Nexus Dashboard interfaces— one connected to the data network and the other to the management network. Individual services installed in the Nexus Dashboard may utilize the two networks for additional purposes.

Table 7-5 lists the purpose of data and management network for Nexus Dashboard.

Connectivity between the Nexus Dashboard cluster nodes is required on both networks with the additional round-trip time (RTT) requirements shown in Table 7-6.

**Table 7-5**   Nexus Dashboard External Network Purpose

| Data Network | Management Network |
|---|---|
| ■ Nexus Dashboard node clustering.<br><br>■ Service-to-service communication.<br><br>■ Nexus Dashboard nodes to Cisco APIC, Cloud Network Controller, and NDFC/DCNM communication. For example, the network traffic for services such as Nexus Dashboard Insights. | ■ Accessing Nexus Dashboard GUI.<br><br>■ Accessing Nexus Dashboard CLI via SSH.<br><br>■ Accessing Cisco DC App Center (AppStore).<br><br>If you want to use the Nexus Dashboard App Store to install services, https://dcappcenter.cisco.com must be reachable via the Management Network.<br><br>■ DNS and NTP communication.<br><br>■ Nexus Dashboard firmware upload.<br><br>■ Intersight device connector.* |

*Device Connector provides a secure way for the connected devices to send information and receive control instructions from the Cisco Intersight portal, using a secure Internet connection.

**Table 7-6**   RTT Requirements

| Service | Connectivity | Maximum RTT |
|---|---|---|
| Nexus Dashboard cluster | Between nodes | 150 ms |
| Nexus Dashboard Orchestrator | Between nodes | 150 ms |
|  | To sites | For APIC sites: 500 ms<br>For NDFC sites: 150 ms |
| Nexus Dashboard Insights | Between nodes | 50 ms |
|  | To sites | 50 ms |
| Nexus Dashboard Fabric Controller | Between nodes | 50 ms |
|  | To sites | 50 ms |
| Nexus Dashboard Data Broker | Between nodes | 150 ms |
|  | To sites | 500 ms |

**NOTE**   You must always use the lowest RTT requirement when deploying the Nexus Dashboard cluster and services. For example, if you plan to cohost the Insights and Orchestrator services, site connectivity RTT must not exceed 50 ms.

## Cisco Nexus Dashboard GUI Overview

After you have deployed the Nexus Dashboard cluster, you can perform all remaining actions using its GUI. To access the Cisco Nexus Dashboard GUI, simply browse to any one of the nodes' management IP addresses:

```
https://<node-mgmt-ip>
```

**NOTE**   Depending on the permissions of the user logged in to the Nexus Dashboard GUI, the UI will display only the objects and settings the user is allowed to access.

## One View Page

The first page you see when you log in to your Nexus Dashboard cluster is the One View, as shown in Figure 7-14. This page provides information about the current Nexus Dashboard cluster's status, sites, services, and resources usage.

**Figure 7-14**  *Nexus Dashboard One View*

Here, you can have a single place for status overview of the entire cluster (or all clusters in case of multicluster connectivity) for Dashboard users. Note that the Nexus Snapshot information is available for Nexus Dashboard Insights service only. You can always access the One View page by clicking the Home icon in the top-left corner of the UI.

## Admin Console Page

You can navigate to your Nexus Dashboard cluster's Admin Console by clicking Admin Console in the One View page after you log in.

1. The global Home icon provides a convenient way of returning to the Nexus Dashboard's home screen (Figure 7-14). It allows you to navigate between different components:

   - **One View** page (Figure 7-14), which provides a single pane of glass view into all your connected clusters, sites, and services.

   - **Admin Console** (Figure 7-15), where you can configure and administer your Nexus Dashboard cluster.

   - **Services** for one-click access to every service available in your cluster. In multicluster deployments, Services include all services across all of your clusters.

   - **Sites** for one-click access to the controller UI of any site onboarded to your cluster. In multicluster deployments, Sites includes all sites across all of your clusters.

2. Current Cluster displays the name of the currently viewed cluster. In multicluster deployments, you can click the name of the cluster to quickly switch to another connected cluster.

3. The Intent icon allows you to access the most common tasks, such as adding sites or nodes, upgrading the cluster, and creating users.

Figure 7-15 shows the Nexus Dashboard Admin Console.

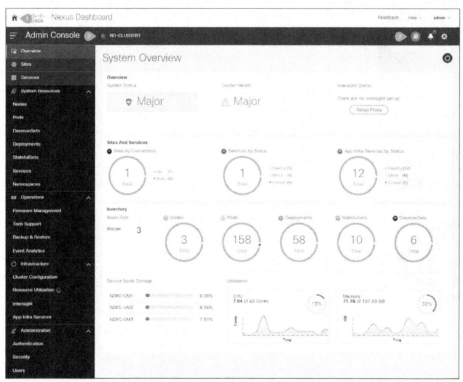

**Figure 7-15** *Nexus Dashboard Admin Console*

## Overview Page

The Overview page of the Admin Console shown in Figure 7-15 provides information about the current Nexus Dashboard cluster's status, sites, services, and resources usage:

■ The Overview tile displays System Status, Cluster Health, and Cisco Intersight Status. You can click the Cluster Health status to view specific details of any issues in your cluster.

■ The Sites and Services tile displays the Sites by Connectivity, as well as Services and App Infra Services by Status. Connectivity indicates whether the sites are up or down. Status is displayed in number of services that are healthy, have minor faults, or have critical faults.

■ The Inventory tile provides details of the nodes, pods, deployments, and other statistics about the currently selected cluster.

**NOTE**   You can click different areas in the System Overview tab to open the corresponding GUI screens where you can see additional details or make configuration changes.

### Sites Page

The Sites page in the left navigation pane allows you to onboard sites from a single location and then use those sites from any service deployed in your cluster. Figure 7-16 shows the Nexus Dashboard Sites page.

**Figure 7-16**   *Nexus Dashboard Sites Page*

Any site that is already onboarded is listed on this page, including the following:

- **Health Score:** Provides the current health status of the site as reported by the site's controller.

- **Name:** Indicates the name of the site as you provided it during onboarding.

- **Connectivity Status:** Indicates whether the site's connectivity is established (Up) or not (Down).

- **Firmware Version:** Lists the version of the controller software currently running in the site.

- **Services Used:** Provides a list of services currently using the specific site.

### Services Page

The Services page in the left navigation pane allows you to access and manage services in your Nexus Dashboard. Any service that is already installed and enabled is listed under the Installed Services tab, while the App Store tab provides an easy way to deploy additional services directly from the Cisco's Data Center App Center page, as shown in Figure 7-17.

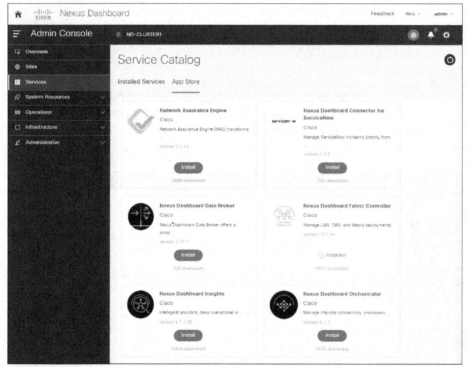

**Figure 7-17**   *Nexus Dashboard Services Page*

## System Resources Pages

The System Resources category in the left navigation pane displays the cluster resources, such as the nodes that make up your cluster and the Kubernetes API objects utilized by the cluster.

The System Resources category contains the following subcategories:

- **Nodes:** Provides information about all master, worker, and standby nodes in your cluster, along with their networking configuration and CPU/memory utilization, as shown in Figure 7-18.

- **Pods:** Provides information about pods, which are a fundamental unit of compute. A *pod* is a group of containers that are scheduled together and are generally static. When a service requires a change in how it is deployed, new pods are created with the new configuration, and the old pods are destroyed instead of changing the configuration of the existing pods in place.

   Deployments, DaemonSets, and StatefulSets provide service developers with ways to describe how and where to deploy sets of pods:

- **Deployments:** Deployments are the most general of these objects and simply define a set of pods with the ability to set constraints about how many copies of the pod are deployed and on what type of node.

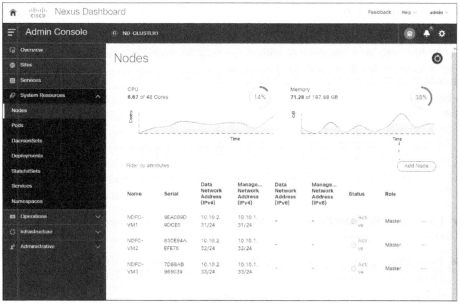

**Figure 7-18** *System Resources Nodes Page*

- **DaemonSets:** Define a pod that runs on every host in the Kubernetes cluster and is automatically created whenever a node is added to the cluster.

- **StatefulSets:** Define pods that need to be run on a predictable host with a specific storage volume. If these pods go down, they are re-created in the same place with the same persistent identifier so that they can use the same storage volume as their previous incarnation.

- **Services:** Provide information about services (or set of dynamically changing pods and containers) running in the cluster. Each service consists of multiple pods and containers, which may be created, destroyed, or changed during cluster scaling or recovery, but the service's names provide a static way of accessing the specific service irrespective of its underlying configuration.

- **Namespaces:** Provide information about Kubernetes namespaces used to organize groups of other API objects. Namespaces can be used to operate on all objects in the namespace at once or to restrict access to particular users or roles.

## Operations Pages

The Operations category in the left navigation pane displays the actions that can be performed on the Nexus Dashboard.

The Operations category contains the following subcategories:

- **Firmware Management:** Firmware Management is used to perform cluster (firmware) upgrades or downgrades.

- **Tech Support:** An administrator can perform technical support collections.

- **Backup and Restore:** Backup and Restore displays the backed-up and restored configuration.

- **Audit Logs:** Audit logs are user triggered configuration changes.

### Infrastructure Pages

The Infrastructure category in the left navigation pane allows you to manage the Nexus Dashboard cluster, Cisco Intersight connector, and Application Infra Services.

The Infrastructure category contains the following subcategories:

- **Cluster Configuration:** Provides cluster details (such as name, app subnet, and service subnet), allows you to configure clusterwide settings (such as DNS and NTP servers, persistent IP addresses, and routes), and displays any current issues in the cluster.

- **Resource Utilization:** Provides real-time information about the resource utilization of your Nexus Dashboard cluster.

- **Intersight:** Provides access to Cisco Intersight device connector configuration. The Cisco NI service depends on the Intersight Device Connector for the service to be configured and available on the service node.

- **App Infra Services:** Provides information about the infra services running on your Nexus Dashboard and allows you to restart individual microservices if needed.

### Administrative Pages

The Administrative category in the left navigation pane allows you to manage authentication and users.

The Administrative category contains the following subcategories:

- **Authentication:** Allows you to configure remote authentication domains.

- **Security:** Allows you to view and edit the security configurations, such as keys and certificates.

- **Users:** Allows you to create and update local Nexus Dashboard users or view the users configured on any remote authentication servers you added to the Nexus Dashboard.

## Exam Preparation Tasks

As mentioned in the Introduction, you have a couple of choices for exam preparation: the exercises here, Chapter 21, "Final Preparation," and the exam simulation questions in the Pearson Test Prep software online.

## Review All Key Topics

Review the most important topics in the chapter, noted with the key topic icon in the outer margin of the page. Table 7-7 lists a reference to these key topics and the page numbers on which each is found.

**Table 7-7**   Key Topics for Chapter 7

| Key Topic Element | Description | Page |
|---|---|---|
| Paragraph | Cisco Nexus Dashboard | 316 |
| Paragraph | Cisco Nexus Dashboard Insights | 318 |
| Figure 7-2 | Nexus Dashboard Insights Features | 320 |
| Figure 7-4 | Cisco Nexus Dashboard Insights Main Menu (Expanded) | 321 |
| Figure 7-5 | Cisco Nexus Dashboard Orchestrator Overview | 324 |
| List | Cisco Nexus Dashboard Fabric Controller | 325 |
| List | Cisco Nexus Dashboard Data Broker | 337 |
| List | Nexus Dashboard Platforms | 338 |
| List | Cisco Nexus Dashboard Cluster Nodes | 339 |
| Table 7-3 | Maximum Verified Scalability Limits for ND Nodes | 340 |
| Table 7-4 | Master Node Types | 341 |

## Memory Tables

Print a copy of Appendix B, "Memory Tables" (found on the companion website), or at least the section for this chapter, and complete the tables and lists from memory. Appendix C, "Memory Tables Answer Key," also on the companion website, includes completed tables and lists to check your work.

## Define Key Terms

Define the following key terms from this chapter, and check your answers in the Glossary.

Cisco Network Assurance Engine (NAE), Cisco Nexus Dashboard (ND), Cisco Nexus Dashboard Data Broker (NDDB), Cisco Nexus Dashboard Fabric Controller (NDFC), Cisco Nexus Dashboard Insights (NDI), Cisco Nexus Dashboard Orchestrator (NDO), graphical user interface (GUI), IP Fabric for Media (IPFM), Mean Time to Resolution (MTRR), round-trip time (RTT), single pane of glass (SPOG), storage area network (SAN)

## References

Cisco Nexus Dashboard At-a-Glance: https://www.cisco.com/c/en/us/products/collateral/data-center-analytics/nexus-dashboard-aag.html?ccid=cc001485&oid=aagdnc023707

Cisco Nexus Dashboard Data Sheet: https://www.cisco.com/c/en/us/products/collateral/data-center-analytics/nexus-dashboard/datasheet-c78-744371.html

Cisco Nexus Dashboard User Guide, Release 2.3.x: https://www.cisco.com/c/en/us/td/docs/dcn/nd/2x/user-guide-23/cisco-nexus-dashboard-user-guide-231.html

Nexus Dashboard Fabric Controller At-a-Glance: https://www.cisco.com/c/en/us/products/collateral/cloud-systems-management/prime-data-center-network-manager/at-a-glance-c45-741113.html?ccid=cc001485

Cisco Nexus Dashboard Fabric Controller 12 Data Sheet: https://www.cisco.com/c/en/us/products/collateral/cloud-systems-management/prime-data-center-network-manager/nb-06-ndfc-ds-cte-en.html

Cisco NDFC-Fabric Controller Configuration Guide, Release 12.1.2e: https://www.cisco.com/c/en/us/td/docs/dcn/ndfc/1212/configuration/fabric-controller/cisco-ndfc-fabric-controller-configuration-guide-1212.html

Cisco NDFC-SAN Controller Configuration Guide, Release 12.1.2e: https://www.cisco.com/c/en/us/td/docs/dcn/ndfc/1212/configuration/san-controller/cisco-ndfc-san-controller-configuration-guide-1212.html

Cisco Nexus Dashboard Insights White Paper, Release 6.0.1: https://www.cisco.com/c/en/us/td/docs/dcn/whitepapers/cisco-nexus-dashboard-insights-white-paper-601.html

Cisco Nexus Dashboard Insights for the Data Center Data Sheet: https://www.cisco.com/c/en/us/products/collateral/data-center-analytics/nexus-insights/datasheet-c78-742685.html

Cisco Nexus Dashboard Data Broker Data Sheet: https://www.cisco.com/c/en/us/products/collateral/cloud-systems-management/nexus-data-broker/data_sheet_c78-729452.html

Cost-Effective Traffic Monitoring with Cisco Nexus Dashboard Data Broker At-a-Glance: https://www.cisco.com/c/en/us/products/collateral/cloud-systems-management/nexus-data-broker/at-a-glance-c45-732727.html

Cisco Nexus Dashboard Orchestrator Overview: https://www.cisco.com/c/en/us/products/collateral/cloud-systems-management/multi-site-orchestrator/nb-06-mso-so-cte-en.html?ccid=cc001487&oid=sowdnc024734

Relevant Cisco Live Presentations: https://www.ciscolive.com

# CHAPTER 8

# Implement Fibre Channel

The main purpose of data centers is to provide the resources required to run applications and securely store data. As enterprises of every size move to digitize their businesses and adapt to new cloud-native workloads while preserving support for well-established applications, they need to rely on a storage network with no compromises. Most enterprise applications count on relational databases and block storage to host their data. In this context, Fibre Channel networking devices are the preferred choice for connecting computational resources to data repositories in the form of disk arrays and tape libraries. Even today, with a variety of file- and object-based storage solutions on the market and the block-based alternative offered by Small Computer System Interface over IP (iSCSI) technology, almost all financial institutions and most Fortune 500 companies rely on Fibre Channel, sometimes in combination with its derivative Fibre Channel over Ethernet (FCoE) protocol, as their trusted storage networking infrastructure, capable of functioning with almost no downtime.

## This chapter covers the following key topics:

**Cisco MDS 9000 Series Hardware:** This section discusses Cisco MDS 9000 Series hardware including Cisco MDS 9700 Series Multilayer Directors, 9300 Series Multilayer Fabric Switches, 9200 Series Multiservice Switches, and 9100 Series Multilayer Fabric Switches.

**Fibre Channel Basics:** This section discusses Fibre Channel topologies, port types, addressing, and switch fabric initialization. This section also discusses device registration, FLOGI, and FCNS databases.

**CFS:** This section discusses CFS features, CFS fabric lock, CFSoIP, and CFSoFC concepts, along with CFS Merge and CFS Regions concepts.

**VSAN:** This section discusses VSAN features, attributes, advantages, Dynamic Port VSAN Membership (DPVM), and VSAN Trunking concepts.

**SAN Port Channels:** This section discusses types of SAN port channels, port channel load balancing, and port channel modes.

**Zoning:** This section discusses zoning features, zone enforcement, full and active zone set, Autozone, zone merge, smart zoning, and enhanced zoning concepts.

**Device Alias:** This section discusses device alias features, modes, and distribution and compares zone aliases and device aliases.

**NPIV and NPV:** This section discusses the concepts of NPIV and NPV and includes a configuration example.

# "Do I Know This Already?" Quiz

The "Do I Know This Already?" quiz enables you to assess whether you should read this entire chapter thoroughly or jump to the "Exam Preparation Tasks" section. If you are in doubt about your answers to these questions or your own assessment of your knowledge of the topics, read the entire chapter. Table 8-1 lists the major headings in this chapter and their corresponding "Do I Know This Already?" quiz questions. You can find the answers in Appendix A, "Answers to the 'Do I Know This Already?' Quizzes."

**Table 8-1** "Do I Know This Already?" Section-to-Question Mapping

| Foundation Topics Section | Questions |
| --- | --- |
| Cisco MDS 9000 Series Hardware | 1 |
| Fibre Channel Basics | 2–4 |
| CFS | 5–6 |
| VSAN | 7–8 |
| SAN Port Channels | 9–10 |
| Zoning | 11–12 |
| Device Alias | 13–14 |
| NPV and NPIV | 15 |

**CAUTION** The goal of self-assessment is to gauge your mastery of the topics in this chapter. If you do not know the answer to a question or are only partially sure of the answer, you should mark that question as wrong for purposes of the self-assessment. Giving yourself credit for an answer you correctly guess skews your self-assessment results and might provide you with a false sense of security.

1. Which of the following MDS switches supports external supervisor modules?

   a. Cisco MDS 9706

   b. Cisco MDS 9396T

   c. Cisco MDS 9250i

   d. Cisco MDS 9148S

2. Which of the following is not a phase in the switched fabric initialization process?

   a. Fabric reconfiguration

   b. FCID allocation

   c. Domain ID distribution

   d. FCIP allocation

   e. Principal switch (PS) selection

3. How is the principal switch selected during the fabric initialization process?

   a. The lowest run-time priority is considered the highest priority.

   b. The highest run-time priority is considered the highest priority.

   c. The highest switch WWN is considered the highest priority.

   d. The highest port WWN is considered the lowest priority.

**4.** Which of the following are CORRECT regarding the fabric login (FLOGI) process? (Choose two answers.)

   **a.** FLOGI happens between the N port and an F port.

   **b.** FLOGI happens between two N ports.

   **c.** The N port sends the FLOGI request to the well-known directory service address 0xfffffc.

   **d.** The N port sends the FLOGI request to the well-known fabric login server address 0xfffffe.

**5.** Which of the following statements is NOT correct regarding CFS?

   **a.** CFS is a client/server protocol.

   **b.** CFS uses a proprietary SW_ILS (0x77434653) protocol for all CFS packets.

   **c.** Applications that use CFS are completely unaware of the lower layer transport.

   **d.** The N port virtualization feature on Cisco NX-OS uses the CFS infrastructure.

**6.** Which of the following are CFS modes of distribution? (Choose three answers.)

   **a.** Coordinated distributions

   **b.** Unrestricted coordinated distributions

   **c.** Uncoordinated distributions

   **d.** Unrestricted uncoordinated distributions

**7.** Which of the following statements is NOT correct regarding VSANs?

   **a.** Multiple VSANs cannot share the same physical topology.

   **b.** The same Fibre Channel identifiers (FCIDs) can be assigned to a host in another VSAN.

   **c.** Events causing traffic disruptions in one VSAN are contained within that VSAN and are not propagated to other VSANs.

   **d.** VSAN 1 cannot be deleted, but it can be suspended.

**8.** What is the maximum number of VSANs that can be configured on a switch?

   **a.** 128

   **b.** 256

   **c.** 512

   **d.** 1024

**9.** Which of the following ports will NOT form a SAN port channel?

   **a.** E ports and TE ports

   **b.** F ports and NP ports

   **c.** E ports and F ports

   **d.** TF ports and TNP ports

**10.** Which of the following is NOT CORRECT regarding Active mode of SAN port channels? (Choose two answers.)

   **a.** In Active mode, a port channel protocol negotiation is performed with the peer ports.

   **b.** In Active mode, when you add or modify a port channel member port configuration, you must explicitly disable (shut) and enable (no shut) the port channel member ports at either end.

    **c.** Active mode is the default mode in SAN port channels.

    **d.** You must explicitly configure this mode.

**11.** Which of the following statements is NOT CORRECT regarding zones?

    **a.** Devices can belong to only one zone at a time.

    **b.** Members in a zone can access each other; members in different zones cannot access each other.

    **c.** Zones can vary in size.

    **d.** If zoning is activated, any device that is not in an active zone (a zone that is part of an active zone set) is a member of the default zone.

**12.** Zone members can be defined using which of the following criteria? (Choose three answers.)

    **a.** Port World Wide Name (pWWN)

    **b.** IPv4 address

    **c.** FCIP address

    **d.** FCID

**13.** Which of the following statements is CORRECT regarding the device alias feature?

    **a.** The device alias information is dependent on the VSAN configuration.

    **b.** The device alias configuration and distribution are dependent on the zone server and the zone server database.

    **c.** The device alias application uses the Cisco Fabric Services (CFS) infrastructure to enable efficient database management and distribution.

    **d.** A device alias name is restricted to 68 alphanumeric characters.

**14.** What happens when you commit the changes made to the pending database of the device alias?

    **a.** The pending database content keeps a separate copy along with effective database content.

    **b.** The pending database is emptied of its contents.

    **c.** The fabric lock is implemented.

    **d.** The pending database is not distributed to the switches in the fabric, and the effective database on those switches is overwritten with the new changes.

**15.** Once the NPV edge switch registers itself with the NPV core switch (NPIV), the NPV edge switch converts all subsequent FLOGIs from end devices to which message type?

    **a.** NPV FLOGI

    **b.** FDISCs

    **c.** PLOGI

    **d.** PLRI

8

## Foundation Topics

# Cisco MDS 9000 Series Hardware

Cisco MDS 9000 multilayer SAN switches combine a robust, flexible hardware architecture with multiple layers of network and storage-management intelligence. You can use Cisco MDS 9000 Series multilayer switches to build highly available, scalable storage networks with advanced security and unified management.

The Cisco MDS 9000 family is composed of hardware products described in the following sections.

## Cisco MDS 9700 Series Multilayer Directors

Cisco MDS 9700 Series multilayer director class SAN switches support 16-Gbps, 32-Gbps, and 64-Gbps Fibre Channel switching modules. The high port density SAN director addresses storage requirements for large, virtualized data centers. These switches provide excellent availability, security, and scalability; simplified management; and the ability to flexibly integrate new technologies. Cisco MDS 9700 provides Ansible support for automated SAN provisioning and management. The MDS 9700 enables you to transparently deploy unified fabrics with Fibre Channel, IBM Fibre Connection (FICON), and Fibre Channel over Ethernet (FCoE) connectivity with a low total cost of ownership (TCO).

Table 8-2 summarizes the Cisco MDS 9700 Series multilayer director chassis form factors available at the time of this writing; see also Figure 8-1.

**Table 8-2** Cisco MDS 9700 Series Multilayer Directors Chassis

| | MDS 9718 | MDS 9710 | MDS 9706 |
|---|---|---|---|
| Maximum ports per chassis | $768 \times 2$-, 4-, 8-, 10-, 16-, and 32-Gbps FC | $384 \times 2$-, 4-, 8-, 10-, 16-, and 32-Gbps FC | $192 \times 2$-, 4-, 8-, 10-, 16-, and 32-Gbps FC |
| | $768 \times 10$-Gbps FCoE / $384 \times 40$-Gbps FCoE | $384 \times 10$-Gbps FCoE / $192 \times 40$-Gbps FCoE | $192 \times 10$-Gbps FCoE / $96 \times 40$-Gbps FCoE |
| Line card slots | 16 | 8 | 4 |
| Supervisor slots | 2 | 2 | 2 |
| Physical dimensions (RU) | 26 | 14 | 9 |

Designed to integrate multiprotocol switching and routing, intelligent SAN services, and storage applications onto highly scalable SAN switching platforms, the Cisco MDS 9700 Series supervisor modules enable intelligent, resilient, scalable, and secure high-performance multilayer SAN switching solutions.

Table 8-3 summarizes the Cisco MDS 9700 Series multilayer directors supervisor modules available at the time of this writing; see also Figure 8-2.

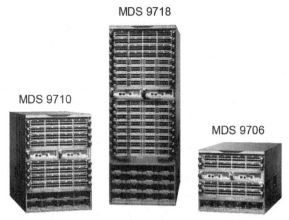

**Figure 8-1**    *Cisco MDS 9700 Series Multilayer Directors*

**Table 8-3**    Cisco MDS 9700 Series Multilayer Directors Supervisor Modules

|  | 9700 Series Supervisor-1 | 9700 Series Supervisor-1E | 9700 Series Supervisor-4 |
|---|---|---|---|
| Chassis | MDS 9706, MDS 9710 | MDS 9718 | MDS 9706, MDS 9710, MDS 9718 |
| Supervisors per chassis | Must be installed in pairs | Must be installed in pairs | Must be installed in pairs |
| Max Fibre Channel (FC) ports | Up to 384 FC ports per chassis | Up to 768 FC ports per chassis | Up to 768 FC ports per chassis |
| Fibre Channel port bandwidth | 2, 4, 8, 10, 16, and 32 Gbps | 2, 4, 8, 10, 16, and 32 Gbps | 2, 4, 8, 10, 16, and 32 Gbps |
| Fibre Channel over Ethernet (FCoE) | Yes | Yes | Yes |
| Fibre Channel over IP (FCIP) | Yes | Yes | Yes |
| Memory | 8-GB DDR3 | 32-GB DDR3 | 16-GB DDR4 |
| Number of cores | 4 | 8 | 8 |
| Clock speed | 2.1 GHz | 2.1 GHz | 2.0 GHz |

8

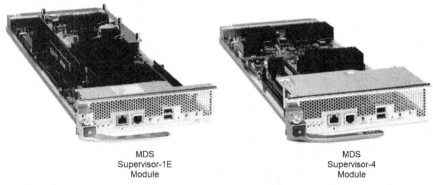

MDS
Supervisor-1E
Module

MDS
Supervisor-4
Module

**Figure 8-2**    *Cisco MDS 9700 Series Supervisor Modules*

With industry-leading port densities of linerate 16-Gbps Fibre Channel ports per director chassis, intelligent fabric services such as integrated VSANs, Inter-VSAN Routing (IVR), and PortChannels, the Cisco MDS 9700 48-port 16-Gbps Fibre Channel switching module enables deployment of large, scalable, and virtualized data centers. The Cisco MDS 9700 48-port 16-Gbps Fibre Channel switching module is designed for the most demanding storage networking environments. It delivers full-duplex aggregate performance of 768 Gbps, making it well suited for high-speed 16-Gbps storage subsystems, 16-Gbps inter-switch links (ISLs), and high-performance virtualized servers. The Cisco MDS 9700 48-port 16-Gbps Fibre Channel switching module also provides Cisco VMpath technology that enables advanced virtual machine-aware SAN provisioning and monitoring for virtualized data centers. With Cisco VMpath, you can monitor, manage, and control SAN resource allocation and performance on a per-virtual machine basis, and map paths all the way from the server to storage, enabling end-to-end tracking of mission-critical workloads.

The 32-Gbps 48-port Fibre Channel switching module provides 768 line-rate 32-Gbps Fibre Channel ports per director, thus meeting the high-performance needs for flash-memory and Non-Volatile Memory express (NVMe) over Fibre Channel workloads. It offers innovative services including virtual machine awareness, on-board Fibre Channel analytics engine, E-port and F-port diagnostics, integrated VSANs, Inter-VSAN Routing (IVR), and port channels. It delivers full-duplex aggregate performance of 1536 Gbps, making it well suited for high-speed 32-Gbps storage subsystems, 32-Gbps inter-switch links (ISLs), high-performance virtualized servers, and all-flash and NVMe arrays. This switching module ships with a built-in analytics engine. The engine can analyze real-time Fibre Channel exchanges and report on various metrics in detail, enabling comprehensive and timely monitoring of any potential performance problems among SAN edge devices.

The 64-Gbps 48-port Fibre Channel switching module meets the high-performance needs for Non-Volatile Memory Express (NVMe) over Fibre Channel and flash memory storage. It offers innovative services, including full end-to-end NVMe support, onboard advanced Fibre Channel analytics engine, virtual machine awareness, Dynamic Rate Limiting Ingestion (DIRL), E-port and F-port diagnostics, integrated VSANs, Advanced Inter-VSAN Routing (IVR), and port channels. It delivers full-duplex aggregate performance of 3072 Gbps, making it well suited for high-speed 64-Gbps storage subsystems, 64-Gbps inter-switch links (ISLs), high-performance virtualized servers, and NVMe and all-flash arrays.

Table 8-4 summarizes the Cisco MDS 9700 Series multilayer directors Fibre Channel switching modules available at the time of this writing.

**Table 8-4**   Cisco MDS 9700 Series Multilayer Directors Fibre Channel Switching Modules

|  | 48-Port 16-Gbps FC Module | 48-Port 32-Gbps FC Module | 48-Port 64-Gbps FC Module |
|---|---|---|---|
| Ports | 48 × 2-, 4-, 8-, 10-, 16-Gbps FC | 48 × 4-, 8-, 16-, 32-Gbps FC | 48 × 8-, 16-, 32-, 64-Gbps FC |
| Maximum ports per chassis | 768 × 2-, 4-, 8-, 10-, 16-Gbps FC | 768 × 4-, 8-, 16-, 32-Gbps FC | 768 × 8-, 16-, 32-, 64-Gbps FC |
| Oversubscription | Line rate | Line rate | Line rate |
| FC switching bandwidth | 768 Gbps | 1536 Gbps | 3072 Gbps |
| Intelligent fabric services | VSAN, IVR, up to 16 port channels | VSAN, IVR, up to 16 port channels | VSAN, IVR, up to 16 port channels |

Figure 8-3 shows Cisco MDS 9700 Fibre Channel switching modules.

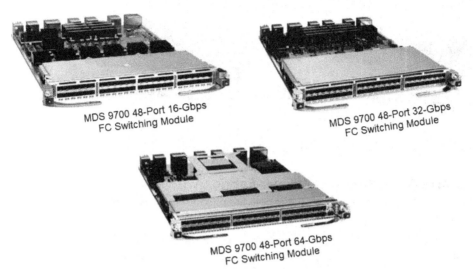

MDS 9700 48-Port 16-Gbps
FC Switching Module

MDS 9700 48-Port 32-Gbps
FC Switching Module

MDS 9700 48-Port 64-Gbps
FC Switching Module

**Figure 8-3**   *Cisco MDS 9700 Fibre Channel Switching Modules*

With the Cisco MDS 9700 48-port 10-Gbps Fibre Channel over Ethernet (FCoE) module, the Cisco MDS 9700 Series multilayer directors platform offers both 16-Gbps Fibre Channel and 10-Gbps FCoE capabilities, providing multiprotocol flexibility for SANs. You can extend the benefits of FCoE beyond the access layer to the data center core with a full line-rate FCoE module for the Cisco MDS 9700 Series.

The Cisco MDS 9700 40-Gbps 24-port Fibre Channel over Ethernet (FCoE) module provides Cisco Unified Fabric connectivity to the SAN core. It empowers midsize and large enterprises that are rapidly deploying cloud-scale applications with inter-switch link (ISL) consolidation by four to one over traditional 10-Gbps FCoE and three to one over 16-Gbps FC. Today's data center fabric is already using 40-Gbps connectivity in the core for more efficient convergence, higher performance, and lower total cost of ownership (TCO). With the entire Cisco Nexus family supporting 40-Gbps FCoE, this capability can be extended to the SAN core.

Table 8-5 summarizes the Cisco MDS 9700 Series multilayer directors Fibre Channel over Ethernet (FCoE) switching modules available at the time of this writing.

**Table 8-5**   Cisco MDS 9700 Series Multilayer Directors FCoE Switching Modules

|  | 48-Port 10-Gbps FCoE Module | 24-Port 40-Gbps FCoE Module |
|---|---|---|
| Ports | 48 × 10-Gbps FCoE | 24 × 40-Gbps FCoE |
| Maximum ports per chassis | 768 × 2-, 4-, 8-, 10-, 16-Gbps FC | 768 × 10-Gbps FCoE; 384 × 40-Gbps FCoE |
| Oversubscription | Line rate | Line rate |
| FCoE switching bandwidth | 480 Gbps | 960 Gbps |
| Intelligent fabric services | Up to 16 port channels | Up to 16 port channels |

Figure 8-4 shows Cisco MDS 9700 Fibre Channel over Ethernet (FCoE) switching modules.

MDS 9700 48-Port 10-Gbps FCoE Module

MDS 9700 24-Port 40-Gbps FCoE Module

**Figure 8-4** *Cisco MDS 9700 Fibre Channel Over Ethernet (FCoE) Switching Modules*

## Cisco MDS 9300 Series Multilayer Fabric Switches

Cisco MDS 9300 Series multilayer fabric switches provide enterprise-class features along with state-of-the-art analytics and telemetry capabilities.

The Cisco MDS 9396S 16G multilayer fabric switch combines high performance with exceptional flexibility and cost effectiveness. This powerful, compact, 2-rack-unit (2RU) switch scales from 48 to 96 line-rate 16-Gbps Fibre Channel ports.

The Cisco MDS 9396S is excellent for

- A standalone SAN in large departmental storage environments

- A middle-of-row or top-of-rack switch in medium-sized redundant fabrics

- An edge switch in enterprise data center core-edge topologies

The Cisco MDS 9396T 32-Gbps 96-port 2-rack unit Fibre Channel switch provides high-speed Fibre Channel connectivity in the SAN. This switch offers state-of-art analytics and telemetry capability built into its next-generation application-specific integrated circuit (ASIC) platform. The Non-Volatile Memory Express (NVMe)-ready switch allows seamless transition to Fibre Channel Non-Volatile Memory Express (FC-NVMe) workloads whenever available without any hardware upgrade in the SAN. This high-density, highly reliable and scalable, enterprise class switch is ideal for medium to large departmental SANs.

Table 8-6 summarizes the Cisco MDS 9300 Series multilayer fabric switches available at the time of this writing.

**Table 8-6** Cisco MDS 9300 Series Multilayer Fabric Switches

| | MDS 9396T 32-Gbps 96-Port Fibre Channel Switch | MDS 9396S 16-Gbps 96-Port Fibre Channel Switch |
|---|---|---|
| Ports (standard) | 48 × 4-, 8-, 16-, 32-Gbps | 48 × 2-, 4-, 8-, 16-Gbps FC |
| Ports (expansion) | License upgrade in 16-port increments up to 96 ports | License upgrade in 12-port increments up to 96 ports |
| Form factor | Fixed | Fixed |
| Advanced traffic management: VSAN, IVR, up to 16 links for port channels | Yes | Yes |

| | MDS 9396T 32-Gbps 96-Port Fibre Channel Switch | MDS 9396S 16-Gbps 96-Port Fibre Channel Switch |
|---|---|---|
| Fibre Channel over Ethernet (FCoE) | No | No |
| iSCSI | No | No |
| Rack Unit (RU) size: | 2 | 2 |

Figure 8-5 shows Cisco MDS 9300 Series multilayer fabric switches.

**Figure 8-5**   *Cisco MDS 9300 Series Multilayer Fabric Switches*

## Cisco MDS 9200 Series Multiservice Switches

Cisco MDS 9200 Series multiservice switches provide business continuance by delivering state-of-the-art multiprotocol and distributed multiservice convergence. They offer high-performance SAN extension and disaster-recovery solutions, intelligent fabric services, and cost-effective multiprotocol connectivity for both open systems and mainframe environments.

The Cisco MDS 9220i offers up to twelve 32-Gbps Fibre Channel ports, four 1/10-, two 25-, and one 40-Gigabit Ethernet IP storage services ports, in a fixed one-rack-unit (1RU) form factor. The Cisco MDS 9220i connects to existing native Fibre Channel networks, protecting current investments in storage networks. With a compact form factor and advanced capabilities, the Cisco MDS 9220i is an ideal solution for departmental and remote branch-office SANs as well as in large-scale SANs in conjunction with Cisco MDS 9700 Series Multilayer Directors.

The Cisco MDS 9250i offers up to forty 16-Gbps Fibre Channel ports, two 1/10-Gigabit Ethernet IP storage services ports, and eight 10-Gigabit Ethernet Fibre Channel over Ethernet (FCoE) ports in a fixed two-rack-unit (2RU) form factor. The Cisco MDS 9250i connects to existing native Fibre Channel networks, protecting current investments in storage networks. With a compact form factor and advanced capabilities normally available only on director-class switches, the Cisco MDS 9250i is an ideal solution for departmental and remote branch-office SANs as well as in large-scale SANs in conjunction with the Cisco MDS 9700 Series multilayer directors.

Table 8-7 summarizes the Cisco MDS 9200 Series multiservice switches available at the time of this writing.

8

**Table 8-7**    Cisco MDS 9200 Series Multiservice Switches

| | MDS 9220i Multiservice Multiprotocol Fabric Switch | MDS 9250i Multiservice Multiprotocol Fabric Switch |
|---|---|---|
| Ports (standard) | 4 × 4-, 8-, 16-, 32-Gbps FC, 2 × 1-Gbps IP | 20 × 2-, 4-, 8-, 16-Gbps FC, 8 × 10-Gbps FCoE, 2 × 1/10 GE |
| Ports (expansion) | 12 × 4-, 8-, 16-, 32-Gbps FC, 4 × 1/10-Gbps OR 2 × 25-Gbps OR 1 × 40-Gbps IP | License upgrade to 40 × 16-Gbps FC |
| Form factor | Fixed | Fixed |
| Advanced traffic management: VSAN, IVR, up to 16 links for port channels | Yes | Yes |
| Fibre Channel over Ethernet (FCoE) | No | Yes |
| iSCSI | No | Yes |
| Rack Unit (RU) size | 1 | 2 |

Figure 8-6 shows Cisco MDS 9200 Series multiservice switches.

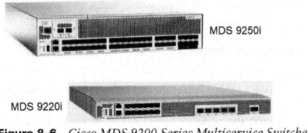

**Figure 8-6**    *Cisco MDS 9200 Series Multiservice Switches*

## Cisco MDS 9100 Series Multilayer Fabric Switches

Cisco MDS 9100 Series switches are affordable SAN solutions and are flexible, agile, highly available, highly secure, and easy to manage while providing visibility to every flow.

The Cisco MDS 9132T 32-Gbps 32-port Fibre Channel switch provides high-speed Fibre Channel connectivity from the server rack to the SAN core. It empowers small, midsize, and large enterprises that are rapidly deploying cloud-scale applications using extremely dense virtualized servers, providing the dual benefits of greater bandwidth and consolidation. Small-scale SAN architectures can be built from the foundation using this low-cost, low-power, nonblocking, line-rate, and low-latency, bidirectional airflow-capable, fixed stand-alone SAN switch connecting both storage and host ports. Medium-size to large-scale SAN architectures built with SAN core directors can expand 32-Gbps connectivity to the server rack using these switches either in switch mode or network port virtualization (NPV) mode.

The Cisco MDS 9124V 64-Gbps 24-port Fibre Channel switch provides high-speed Fibre Channel connectivity for all-flash arrays and high-performance hosts. This switch offers state-of-the-art analytics and telemetry capabilities built into its next-generation application-specific integrated circuit (ASIC) chipset. This switch allows seamless transition to Fibre Channel Non-Volatile Memory Express (NVMe/FC) workloads whenever available without any hardware upgrade in the SAN. It empowers small, midsize, and large enterprises that are rapidly deploying cloud-scale applications using extremely dense virtualized servers, providing the benefits of greater bandwidth, scale, and consolidation.

The Cisco MDS 9148S 16G multilayer fabric switch is the next generation of the highly reliable, flexible, and low-cost Cisco MDS 9100 Series switches. It combines high performance with exceptional flexibility and cost-effectiveness. This powerful, compact one-rack-unit (1RU) switch scales from 12 to 48 line-rate 16-Gbps Fibre Channel ports.

The Cisco MDS 9148S is excellent for

- A standalone SAN in small departmental storage environments

- A top-of-the-rack switch in medium-sized redundant fabrics

- An edge switch in enterprise data center core-edge topologies

Up to 48 autosensing Fibre Channel ports are capable of speeds of 2, 4, 8, and 16 Gbps, with 16 Gbps of dedicated bandwidth for each port. The base switch model comes with 12 ports enabled and can be upgraded as needed with the 12-port Cisco MDS 9148S On-Demand Port Activation license to support configurations of 24, 36, or 48 enabled ports. Only the Cisco MDS 9148S scales from 12 to 48 high-performance Fibre Channel ports in a single 1RU form factor.

The Cisco MDS 9148V 64-Gbps 48-port and Cisco MDS 9148T 32-Gbps 48-port Fibre Channel switch provides high-speed Fibre Channel connectivity for All-Flash arrays. This switch offers state-of-the-art analytics and telemetry capability built into its next-generation application-specific integrated circuit (ASIC) platform. This switch allows seamless transition to Fibre Channel Non-Volatile Memory Express (FC-NVMe) workloads whenever available without any hardware upgrade in the SAN.

The MDS 9148T Fibre Channel switch provides an option to deploy as few as twenty-four 32-Gbps Fibre Channel ports in the entry-level variant, which can grow in increments of 8 ports to up to 48 ports. This setup allows four possible configurations of 24, 32, 40, and 48 ports.

Table 8-8 summarizes the Cisco MDS 9100 Series multilayer fabric switches available at the time of this writing.

**Table 8-8** Cisco MDS 9100 Series Multilayer Fabric Switches

| | MDS 9132T 32-Gbps 32-Port Fibre Channel Switch | MDS 9124V 64-Gbps 24-Port Fibre Channel Switch | MDS 9148S 16-Gbps 48-Port Fibre Channel Switch | MDS 9148T 32-Gbps 48-Port Fibre Channel Switch | MDS 9148V 64-Gbps 48-Port Fibre Channel Switch |
|---|---|---|---|---|---|
| Ports (standard) | 8 × 4-, 8-, 16-, 32-Gbps FC | 8 × 8-, 16-, 32-, 64-Gbps FC | 12 × 2-, 4-, 8-, 16-Gbps FC | 24 ts] 4-, 8-, 16-, 32-Gbps FC | 24 × 8-,16-, 32-, 64-Gbps FC |
| Ports (expansion) | 16-port 32-Gbps expansion module to expand to 24 ports; 8-port license upgrade to 16 ports in base switch and up to 32 ports with expansion module | License upgrade in 8-port increments up to 24 ports | License upgrade in 12-port increments up to 48 ports | License upgrade in 8-port increments up to 48 ports | License upgrade in 8-port increments up to 48 ports |
| Form factor | Semi-modular | Fixed | Fixed | Fixed | Fixed |
| Advanced traffic management: VSAN, IVR, up to 16 links for port channels | Yes | Yes | Yes | Yes | Yes |
| Fibre Channel over Ethernet (FCoE) | No | No | No | No | No |
| iSCSI | No | No | No | No | No |
| Rack Unit (RU) size | 1 | 1 | 1 | 1 | 1 |

Figure 8-7 shows Cisco MDS 9100 Series multilayer fabric switches.

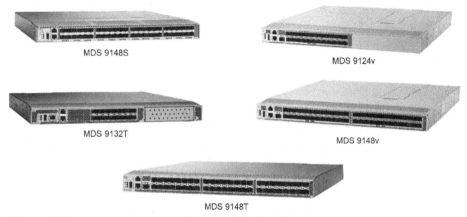

MDS 9148S

MDS 9124v

MDS 9132T

MDS 9148v

MDS 9148T

**Figure 8-7**   *Cisco MDS 9100 Series Multilayer Fabric Switches*

## Fibre Channel Basics

Fibre Channel (FC) is a high-speed data transfer protocol providing in-order, lossless delivery of raw block data, primarily used to connect computer data storage to servers. The lossless delivery of a raw data block is achieved based on a credit mechanism known as buffer-to-buffer credits, which we discuss later in this chapter. Fibre Channel typically runs on optical fiber cables within and between data centers but can also run on copper cabling. We will discuss copper cabling options in the next chapter when we dig deep into the FCoE proto-col. Fibre Channel networks form a switched fabric because they operate in unison as one big switch. Here we set the stage for the Fibre Channel switched fabric initialization process after discussing various Fibre Channel topologies and port types.

### Fibre Channel Topologies

It is common practice in SAN environments to build two separate, redundant physical fabrics (Fabric A and Fabric B) in case a single physical fabric fails. In the design of SANs, most environments fall into three types of topologies within a physical fabric: single-tier (collapsed-core), two-tier (core-edge design), and three-tier (edge-core-edge design):

■ **Collapsed-core topology:** Within the single-tier design, servers are connected to the core switches. Storage devices are also connected to one or more core switches, as shown in Figure 8-8. Core switches provide storage services. It has single management per fabric and is mostly deployed for small SAN environments.

The main advantage of this topology is the degree of scalability offered at a very effi-cient port usage. The collapsed-core design aims to offer very high port density while eliminating a separate physical layer of switches and their associated ISLs.

The only disadvantage of the collapsed-core topology is its scale limit relative to the core-edge topology. While the collapsed-core topology can scale quite large, the core-edge topology should be used for the largest of fabrics. However, to continually scale the collapsed-core design, you could convert the core to a core-edge design and add another layer of switches.

8

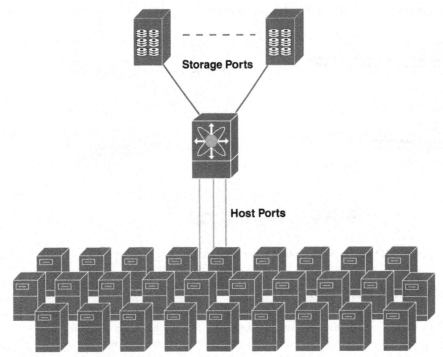

**Figure 8-8**  *Collapsed-Core Topology*

■ **Core-edge topology:** Within the two-tier design, servers connect to the edge switches, and storage devices connect to one or more core switches, as shown in Figure 8-9.
  This allows the core switch to provide storage services to one or more edge switches,
  thus servicing more servers in the fabric. The inter-switch links (ISLs) will have to be
  designed so that the overall fabric maintains both the fan-out ratio of servers to storage and the overall end-to-end oversubscription ratio. High availability is achieved
  using two physically separate, but identical, redundant SAN fabrics.

In the design of a core-edge topology, a major trade-off is made between three key
characteristics of the design. The first trade-off is the overall effective port density
that can be used to connect hosts or storage devices. For a given number of switches
in a core-edge design, the higher the effective port density, typically the higher ISL
oversubscription from the edge layer to the core layer. The second characteristic is
the oversubscription of the design. Oversubscription is a natural part of any network topology because the nature of a SAN is to "fan out" the connectivity and I/O
resources of storage devices. However, the higher the oversubscription of the design,
the more likely congestion may occur, thereby impacting a wide scope of applications
and their I/O patterns. The third characteristic that ties these other two together is
cost. The basic principle suggests the higher the oversubscription for a given effective
port density, the lower the overall cost of the solution.

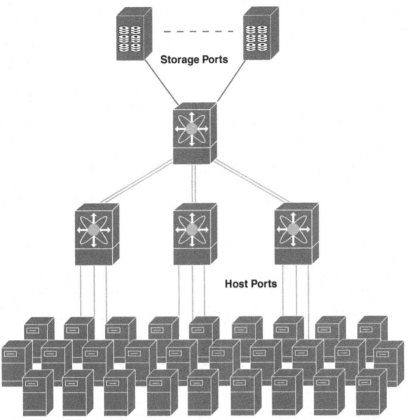

**Figure 8-9**  *Core-Edge Topology*

- **Edge-core-edge topology:** In environments where future growth of the network has the number of storage devices exceeding the number of ports available at the core switch, a three-tier design may be ideal. This type of topology still uses a set of edge switches for server connectivity but adds another set of edge switches for storage devices, as shown in Figure 8-10. Both sets of edge switches connect into a core switch via inter-switch links (ISLs). ISLs have to be designed in such a way that the overall fan-in ratio of servers to storage and overall end-to-end oversubscription are maintained. High availability is achieved using two physically separate, but identical, redundant SAN fabrics.

The resiliency of this topology is sufficiently high due to the redundant structure but without the excessive ISLs, as in the mesh topology. The performance of this topology is predictable, because paths between two communicating devices will not vary in length and hops; the direct path between two switches will always be chosen. Using ISL port channeling between the switches will provide for faster recovery time with no fabric-wide disruption. The port channels between the switches provide load sharing over a logical ISL link. This topology is simple to architect and implement and simple to maintain and troubleshoot.

8

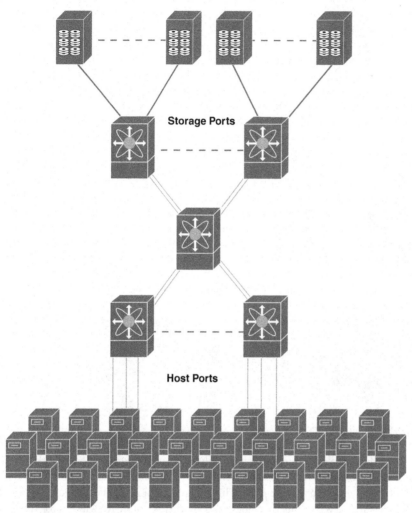

**Figure 8-10** *Edge-Core-Edge Topology*

## Fibre Channel Port Types

The main function of a switch is to relay frames from one data link to another. These frames are sent and received using Fibre Channel interfaces/ports.

Each Fibre Channel interface can be used as a downlink (connected to a server) or as an uplink (connected to the data center SAN). Each physical Fibre Channel interface in a switch may operate in one of several port modes, such as E port, F port, TE port, SD port, and ST port. SD and ST ports will be discussed in Chapter 11, "Describe Software Management and Infrastructure Monitoring." The use of NP, TF, and TNP modes will be more clear after we discuss the NPV and NPIV modes of fabric switches later in this chapter. Besides these modes, each interface may be configured in auto or Fx port modes. These two modes determine the port type during interface initialization. Interfaces are created in VSAN 1 by default. We discuss VSAN later in this chapter; for now let's just compare VSANs in the storage world with VLANs in the Ethernet world.

Each interface has an associated administrative configuration and an operational status. The administrative configuration does not change unless you modify it. Administrative mode has various attributes that you can configure. The operational status represents the current status of a specified attribute, such as the interface speed. This status cannot be changed and is read-only. Some values, for example, operational speed, may not be valid when the interface is down.

Figure 8-11 shows various Fibre Channel port types.

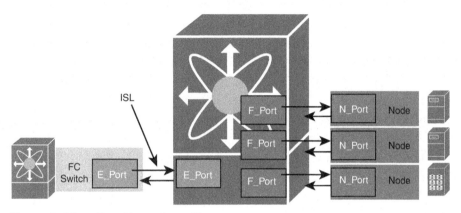

**Figure 8-11**   *Fibre Channel Port Types*

## E Port

In expansion port (E port) mode, an interface functions as a fabric expansion port. This port can be connected to another E port to create an inter-switch link between two switches. E ports carry frames between switches for configuration and fabric management. They serve as a conduit between switches for frames destined for remote N ports. An E port connected to another switch can also be configured to form a port channel.

## F Port

In fabric port (F port) mode, an interface functions as a fabric port. This port can be connected to a peripheral device (host or disk) operating as an N port. An F port can be attached to only one N port.

## NP Ports

An NP port is a port on a device that is in NPV mode and connected to the core switch via an F port. NP ports function like N ports, except that in addition to providing N port operations, they also function as proxies for multiple physical N ports.

## TE Port

In trunking E port (TE port) mode, an interface functions as a trunking expansion port. It can be connected to another TE port to create an extended ISL (EISL) between two switches. TE ports expand the functionality of E ports to support the following:

- VSAN trunking

- Transport quality of service (QoS) parameters

- Fibre Channel traceroute (fctrace) feature

In TE port mode, all the frames are transmitted in EISL frame format, which contains VSAN information. Interconnected switches use the VSAN ID to multiplex traffic from one or more VSANs across the same physical link.

### TF Port

In trunking F port (TF port) mode, an interface functions as a trunking expansion port. It can be connected to another trunked N port (TN port) or trunked NP port (TNP port) to create a link between a core switch and an NPV switch or a host bus adapter (HBA) in order to carry tagged frames. TF ports expand the functionality of F ports to support VSAN trunking.

In TF port mode, all the frames are transmitted in EISL frame format, which contains VSAN information. Interconnected switches use the VSAN ID to multiplex traffic from one or more VSANs across the same physical link.

### TNP Port

In trunking NP port (TNP port) mode, an interface functions as a trunking expansion port. It can be connected to a trunked F port (TF port) to create a link to a core NPIV switch from an NPV switch in order to carry tagged frames.

### Fx Port

Interfaces configured as Fx ports can operate in either F port mode or FL port mode. FL port mode is used in arbitrated loop topology, which we do not discuss in this book. The Fx port mode is determined during interface initialization depending on the attached N port. Fx port mode configuration disallows interfaces to operate in any other mode—for example, preventing an interface to connect to another switch.

### Auto Mode

Interfaces configured in auto mode can operate in F port, E port, TE port, or TF port mode. The port mode is determined during interface initialization. For example, if the interface is connected to a node (host or disk), it operates in F port mode depending on the N port mode. If the interface is attached to a third-party switch, it operates in E port mode. If the interface is attached to another FC switch—for example, Cisco MDS 9000 Series multilayer switches, it may become operational in TE port mode.

**NOTE**   Not all port modes are available in all types of Fibre Channel switches. Also, we skipped some port modes such as TL, NL, and FL port types because they are rarely used in today's FC SAN environment.

Port mode on Fibre Channel interfaces can be configured using the **switchport mode** *<port-type>* command, as shown in Example 8-1.

**Example 8-1**   *Fibre Channel Interface Configuration*

```
switch# configure terminal
switch(config)# interface fc1/1
switch(config-if)# switchport mode F
or
switch(config-if)# switchport mode auto
```

## Fibre Channel Addressing

In Fibre Channel fabric, there are two types of addresses: World Wide Names (WWNs) and Fibre Channel Identifiers (FCID). Every Fibre Channel port and node has a hard-coded address called the World Wide Name, which is assigned by the manufacturer. Each WWN is an 8- or 16-byte number, the length and format of which is determined by the most significant four bits, which are referred to as a Network Address Authority (NAA). The remainder of the value is derived from an IEEE organizational unique identifier (OUI) or from a company ID (CID) and vendor-supplied information. Each format defines a different way to arrange and/or interpret these components. When NAA = 1 or 2 or 5, the length of the WWN is 8 bytes. For NAA = 6, the length of the WWN is 16 bytes. In this book, we deal with only 8-byte WWNs.

There are two types of WWNs: port WWN (pWWN) and node WWN (nWWN), as depicted in Figure 8-12. The pWWN uniquely identifies a port in the FC fabric, whereas the nWWN uniquely identifies a node in the FC fabric. The node can be any switch, a disk drive, an HBA that contains more than one port, an array controller, and so on.

**Figure 8-12**   *Example of WWN, WWNN, and WWPN*

When a node connects to the fabric, it performs a fabric login during which it is assigned a 3-byte FC address, or FCID. This FCID is used for routing frames across the fabric using Fabric Shortest Path First (FSPF) protocol, which automatically calculates the best path between any two switches in a fabric. FSPF is based on link state protocol and dynamically computes routes throughout a fabric by establishing the shortest and quickest path between any two switches. FSPF selects an alternative path in the event of the failure of a given path. FSPF supports multiple paths and automatically computes an alternative path around a failed link.

FCID is composed of 24 bits (3 bytes), as shown in Figure 8-13. Each field has specific meaning in FCID.

- **Domain ID:** The domain ID is assigned to each FC switch in a fabric and is unique to that switch. Because the upper FCIDs are reserved for various FC fabric services, such as 0xFFFFFF for broadcast and 0xFFFFFC for name server, the domain ID field restricts the maximum number of FC switches that can be connected in a fabric or VSAN to 239. Routing decisions are made based on domain ID bits of FCID.

- **Area ID:** The area ID represents a set of devices connected to N ports on a switch. This field restricts the maximum number of ports on a single FC switch to 256.

- **Port ID:** The port ID identifies a specific FC object in the fabric. Cisco uses a combination of area ID and port ID to provide a unique 16-bit address for each device.

**Figure 8-13**   *Fibre Channel Identifier (FCID) Format*

Some of the reserved FCIDs are shown in Table 8-9.

**Table 8-9**   Reserved FCIDs

| Fibre Channel Services | Reserved Addresses |
|---|---|
| Management Server | 0xFFFFFA |
| Fabric Controller | 0xFFFFFD |
| F_Port Controller/Fabric Login Server | 0xFFFFFE |
| Broadcast Address/Server | 0xFFFFFF |
| N_Port Controller | 0xFFFFF0 |
| Multicast Server | 0xFFFFF5 |

**NOTE**   If you are coming from the Ethernet and IP world, you might compare WWNs with a MAC address and FCID with an IP address. But we recommend that you do not do that to avoid confusion in the future.

## Flow Control

Buffer-to-buffer credits (BB_credits) are a flow control mechanism to ensure that FC switches do not run out of buffers because switches must not drop frames. BB_credits are negotiated on a per-hop basis between ports when the link is brought up. When the transmitter sends a port login request, the receiver responds with an accept (ACC) frame that includes information on the size and number of frame buffers (BB_credits) the receiver has. The transmitter stores the BB_credits value and another value called buffer-to-buffer credits count (BB_credit_CNT) in a table. The BB_credits_CNT decreases with each packet placed on the wire from the transmitter side independent of the packet size. When a "receiver ready" acknowledgment signal is received from the receiver side, the BB_credits_CNT value is increased by one. The transmitting port keeps track of the BB_credits_CNT value to avoid overrunning the buffers on the receiving end. If the count becomes zero, no more packets are transmitted.

The BB_credit value can decrease the overall throughput of the link if insufficient BB_credits are available. The receive BB_credit value can be configured manually also for each FC interface. In most cases, you do not need to modify the default configuration. The receive BB_credit values depend on the switch/module type and the port mode. The range for assigning BB_credits is between 1 and 500 in all port modes. This value can be changed as required.

In Figure 8-14, the initiator has three transmit credits, and the receiver has three receive credits. When the initiator sends two frames on the wire, the transmit credits is decreased by two. When the initiator receives a "receiver ready" frame from the receiver, it increases its transmit credit by one and so on.

End-to-end credits are the maximum number of data frames a source port can send to a destination port without receiving an acknowledgment frame (ACK). This credit is granted during N port login and is replenished with the return of the ACK response frame. Buffer-to-buffer credits are negotiated on a per-hop basis between ports when the link is brought up, whereas end-to-end credits are negotiated between the source and destination port across the fabric.

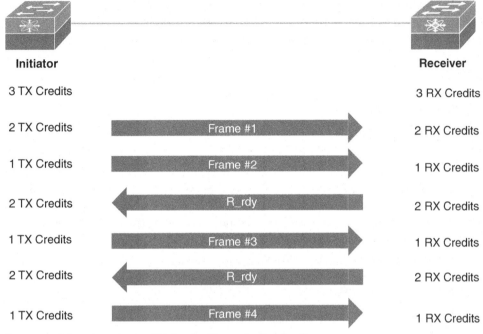

Initiator

3 TX Credits

2 TX Credits

1 TX Credits

2 TX Credits

1 TX Credits

2 TX Credits

1 TX Credits

**Figure 8-14**  *Flow Control Using Buffer-to-Buffer Credits*

## Switched Fabric Initialization

The fabric initialization process consists of four phases:

- **Principal switch selection:** This phase guarantees the selection of a unique principal switch (PS) across the fabric.

- **Domain ID distribution:** This phase guarantees each switch in the fabric obtains a unique domain ID.

- **FCID allocation:** This phase guarantees a unique FCID assignment to each device attached to the corresponding switch in the fabric.

- **Fabric reconfiguration:** This phase guarantees a resynchronization of all switches in the fabric to ensure they simultaneously restart a new principal switch selection phase.

Each switch in a fabric is assigned one or more unique domain IDs using a two-step process. First, one switch, called the principal switch, is selected from the switches of a fabric. Then the principal switch assigns domain IDs to the other switches of the fabric. FCID address assignment within a domain is performed by the switch to which that domain ID is granted. The domains are configured on a per-VSAN basis. If you do not configure a domain ID, the local switch uses a random ID.

> **NOTE** Changes to fcdomain parameters should not be performed on a daily basis. These changes should be made by an administrator or individual who is completely familiar with switch operations. Fibre Channel domain parameters can be configured using the **fcdomain** command.

### Principal Switch Selection

Each fabric has only one principal switch. The principal switch is responsible for distribution of domain IDs within the fabric.

Principal switch selection in a fabric is based on the following values:

- **Run-time priority:** The lowest run-time priority is considered the highest priority. By default, the configured priority is 128. The valid range to set the priority is between 1 and 254. The value 255 is accepted from other switches but cannot be locally configured.

- **Switch WWN:** The lowest switch WWN is given higher priority.

During the principal switch selection phase, the switch with the highest priority becomes the principal switch. If two switches have the same configured priority, the switch with the lower World Wide Name (WWN) becomes the principal switch.

As shown in Figure 8-15, when switch 1 is connected to switch 2, the principal switch election starts. Because both of the switches have the same configured priority, which is 128, the local WWN on both the switches is checked. Because switch 1 has the lowest WWN, it becomes the principal switch. When WWN is the principal switch election criterion, the runtime priority of the principal switch is automatically changed to 2.

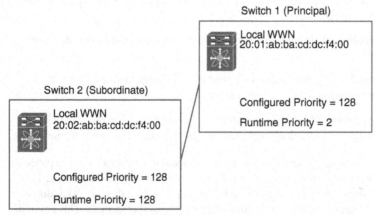

**Figure 8-15** *Principal Switch Selection*

The principal switch selection process is very complex. Figure 8-16 shows the messages exchanged during the principal switch selection process and domain ID distribution. For simplicity, let's consider only two switches in the fabric.

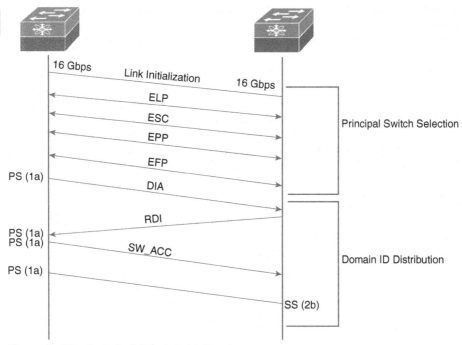

**Figure 8-16**  *Switched Fabric Initialization*

When the two switches are connected via a link, they enter into the link initialization phase where they negotiate the port speed at which the ports are capable of operating. When the link is initialized, the switches enter into the exchange link parameters (ELP) phase. Information about the interfaces such as buffer-to-buffer credits, timers, and class of service are exchanged between the two switches using controller addresses (0xFFFFFD). The switches enter the exchange switch capabilities (ESC) phase when the neighboring fabric controller agrees on the routing protocol and recognizes the vendor ID of the switch. If the switches are Cisco MDS 9000 Series devices, they use Cisco-specific feature negotiations such as virtual SAN trunks in the Cisco proprietary Exchange Peer Parameters (EPP) frame. In the Exchange Fabric Parameters (EFP) phase, the principal switch is selected.

### Domain ID Distribution

Domain IDs uniquely identify a switch in a VSAN. A switch may have different domain IDs in different VSANs. The domain ID is part of the overall FCID.

The configured domain ID can be preferred or static. When you assign a static domain ID type, you are requesting a particular domain ID. If the switch does not get the requested address, it will isolate itself from the fabric. When you specify a preferred domain ID, you are also requesting a particular domain ID; however, if the requested domain ID is unavailable, the switch will accept another domain ID. By default, the configured domain ID is 0 (zero) and the configured type is preferred. The 0 (zero) value can be configured only if the preferred option is used. If a domain ID is not configured, the local switch sends a random ID in its request. Static domain IDs are recommended.

When a subordinate switch requests a domain, the following process takes place:

- The local switch sends a configured domain ID request to the principal switch.

- The principal switch assigns the requested domain ID if available. Otherwise, it assigns another available domain ID.

The behavior for a subordinate switch changes based on three factors: the allowed domain ID lists, the configured domain ID, and the domain ID that the principal switch has assigned to the requesting switch. The valid range for an assigned domain ID list is from 1 to 239. You can specify a list of ranges to be in the allowed domain ID list and separate each range with a comma. The principal switch assigns domain IDs that are available in the locally configured allowed domain list.

When the received domain ID is not within the allowed list, the requested domain ID becomes the runtime domain ID, and all interfaces on that VSAN are isolated. When the assigned and requested domain IDs are the same, the preferred and static options are not relevant, and the assigned domain ID becomes the runtime domain ID.

When the assigned and requested domain IDs are different, the following cases apply:

- If the configured type is static, the assigned domain ID is discarded, all local interfaces are isolated, and the local switch assigns itself the configured domain ID, which becomes the runtime domain ID.

- If the configured type is preferred, the local switch accepts the domain ID assigned by the principal switch, and the assigned domain ID becomes the runtime domain ID.

**NOTE**   A static domain is specifically configured by the user and may be different from the runtime domain. If the domain IDs are different, the runtime domain ID changes to take on the static domain ID after the next restart, either disruptive or nondisruptive. If you perform a disruptive restart, reconfigure fabric (RCF) frames are sent to other switches in the fabric, and data traffic is disrupted on all the switches in the VSAN (including remotely segmented ISLs). If you perform a nondisruptive restart, build fabric (BF) frames are sent to other switches in the fabric, and data traffic is disrupted only on the switch.

If you change the configured domain ID, the change is accepted only if the new domain ID is included in all the allowed domain ID lists currently configured in the VSAN. Alternatively, you can also configure a zero-preferred domain ID.

Refer to Figure 8-16 for domain ID distribution phases. In the domain ID assigned (DIA) phase, the principal switch assigns itself a domain ID (1a) and floods the DIA frames with this information in the fabric. Each switch in the fabric that received the DIA frames from the principal switch requests a domain ID using a request domain identifier (RDI). The RDI request can contain a preferred (or static) domain ID depending on the configuration of the switch. In the next phase, the principal switch grants the requested domain ID or another from its domain list to the subordinate switch (SS). Lastly, the downstream switch accepts the domain ID (2b) if it is the same as the static ID or it belongs to its domain list. Finally, the fabric is formed. If the downstream switch doesn't accept the domain ID, it becomes an isolated switch.

In Figure 8-17, the principal switch, switch 1, has a runtime domain ID of 3. The subordinate switch, switch 2, is configured with a domain ID of 7 as preferred. Switch 2 requests configured domain ID 7 from the principal switch. Because the assignment of domain ID 7 is not restricted by the Unallowed domain IDs list, the principal switch assigns domain ID 7 to switch 2. If domain ID 7 were in the Unallowed domain ID list, the principal switch would assign another domain ID, in this example 51, to the subordinate switch.

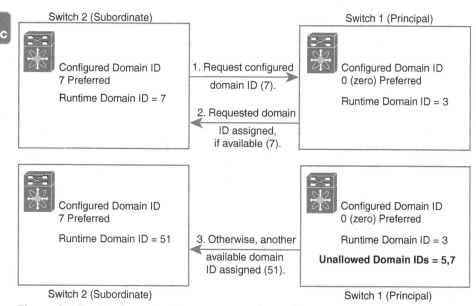

**Figure 8-17**   *Configuration Process Using the Preferred Option*

## FCID Allocation

In this phase, when an N port logs in to a SAN switch, it is assigned an FCID. By default, the persistent FCID feature is enabled. When persistent FCIDs are enabled, the current FCIDs in use in the fcdomain are saved across reboots. The fcdomain automatically populates the database with dynamic entries that the switch has learned about after a device (host or disk) is plugged into a port interface. A persistent FCID assigned to an F port can be moved across interfaces and can continue to maintain the same persistent FCID. If the persistent FCID feature is disabled, the FCIDs are stored in a volatile cache, and the contents of this volatile cache are not saved across reboots.

## Fabric Reconfiguration

In this phase, a resynchronization of all switches in the fabric happens to ensure they simultaneously restart a new principal switch selection phase. A new principal switch selection can be triggered in three ways: a switch reboot, a build fabric (BF) frame, or a reconfigure fabric (RCF) frame. A BF frame can be initiated manually, due to a link failure or when a configured fabric joins another configured fabric with nonoverlapping domain IDs. A BF frame requests a nondisruptive reconfiguration of the entire fabric where the connectivity is not lost. An RCF frame can be initiated manually or automatically if a switch is isolated. Most of the fabric switches have this automatic option disabled. An RCF frame requests a disruptive reconfiguration of the entire fabric, and the traffic is impacted in the fabric.

### Device Registration: FLOGI, PLOGI, PRLI

After the switched fabric is initialized, the end devices connected to the fabric register to the switched fabric. When a device is connected to the FC fabric, the following three types of login are possible to the switched fabric:

■ **Fabric login (FLOGI):** FLOGI happens between an N port and an F port. After an FC device (host) is attached to the FC fabric, it performs fabric login, as shown in Figure 8-18. The host (N port) sends the FLOGI request to the well-known fabric login server address 0xFFFFFE. The FLOGI frame contains its node name, N port name, and service parameters. When the fabric switch receives the FLOGI request, it responds with an accept (ACC) frame to the sender while setting appropriate bits on the ACC frame, indicating what service parameters are not supported. Once the fabric login is achieved, the switch assigns FCID to the node.

■ **Port login (PLOGI):** PLOGI happens between two N ports. The N port sends a PLOGI request to the well-known directory service address 0xFFFFFC. The PLOGI frame contains the port address, port name, node name, B2B_credit capability, and other service parameters. When both N ports inform about their capabilities to one another using PLOGI requests, they are able to establish logical sessions between the two nodes, as shown in Figure 8-18.

■ **Process login (PRLI):** PRLI happens between two processes originating from two different N ports. The processes that are involved can be system processes or a group of related processes.

### FLOGI and FCNS Databases

In the Ethernet world, an ARP table maintains a database for resolution between the MAC address (Layer 2) and IP address (Layer 3). Similarly, in the Fibre Channel world, every switch maintains an FLOGI and an FCNS database that maintains the resolution between WWNs (Layer 2) and FCIDs (Layer 3).

The FLOGI database logs every end device (server or storage) that has successfully performed a fabric login and obtained an FCID from the switch.

Fibre Channel switches share the FLOGI database information with each other using the Fibre Channel Name Service (FCNS). The name server functionality running on each switch maintains the FCNS database, which contains the attributes for all hosts and storage devices in each VSAN. Hence, each switch in the fabric learns where each WWN is and how to route traffic to specific WWNs. The name server permits an N port to register attributes during a PLOGI (to the name server) to obtain attributes of other hosts. These attributes are deregistered when the N port logs out either explicitly or implicitly.

In short, the FCNS database lists devices that are currently logged in to each VSAN, and the FLOGI database displays devices logged in to per switch. Example 8-2 shows sample output of the FLOGI and FCNS databases.

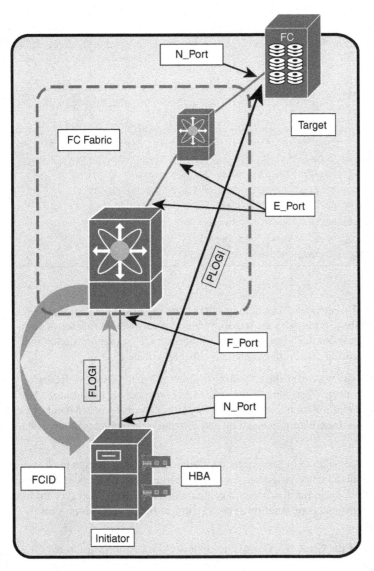

**Figure 8-18**   *FLOGI and PLOGI Processes*

**Example 8-2**   *Sample Output of* **show flogi database** *and* **show fcns database** *Commands*

```
switch# show flogi database
--------------------------------------------------------------------------------
INTERFACE   VSAN   FCID       PORT NAME                 NODE NAME
--------------------------------------------------------------------------------
sup-fc0     2      0xb30100   10:00:00:05:30:00:49:63   20:00:00:05:30:00:49:5e
fc9/13      1      0xb200e2   21:00:00:04:cf:27:25:2c   20:00:00:04:cf:27:25:2c
fc9/13      1      0xb200e1   21:00:00:04:cf:4c:18:61   20:00:00:04:cf:4c:18:61
fc9/13      1      0xb200d1   21:00:00:04:cf:4c:18:64   20:00:00:04:cf:4c:18:64
```

8

```
fc9/13        1      0xb200ce    21:00:00:04:cf:4c:16:fb    20:00:00:04:cf:4c:16:fb
fc9/13        1      0xb200cd    21:00:00:04:cf:4c:18:f7    20:00:00:04:cf:4c:18:f7
Total number of flogi = 6.


switch# show fcns database
------------------------------------------------------------------------------
FCID        TYPE  PWWN                    (VENDOR)       FC4-TYPE:FEATURE
------------------------------------------------------------------------------
0x010000    N     50:06:0b:00:00:10:a7:80                scsi-fcp fc-gs
0x010001    N     10:00:00:05:30:00:24:63 (Cisco)        ipfc
0x010002    N     50:06:04:82:c3:a0:98:52 (Company 1)    scsi-fcp 250
0x010100    N     21:00:00:e0:8b:02:99:36 (Company A)    scsi-fcp
0x020000    N     21:00:00:e0:8b:08:4b:20 (Company A)
0x020100    N     10:00:00:05:30:00:24:23 (Cisco)        ipfc
0x020200    N     21:01:00:e0:8b:22:99:36 (Company A)    scsi-fcp
```

# CFS

Cisco Fabric Services (CFS) provides a common infrastructure for automatic configuration synchronization in the fabric. It provides the transport function as well as a rich set of common services to the applications. CFS has the ability to discover CFS-capable switches in the fabric and discover application capabilities in all CFS-capable switches.

The Cisco MDS NX-OS software uses the CFS infrastructure to enable efficient database distribution and to foster device flexibility. It simplifies SAN provisioning by automatically distributing configuration information to all switches in a fabric. Several Cisco MDS NX-OS applications use the CFS infrastructure to maintain and distribute the contents of a particular application's database.

Many features in the Cisco MDS switches require configuration synchronization in all switches in the fabric. Maintaining configuration synchronization across a fabric is important to maintain fabric consistency. In the absence of a common infrastructure, such synchronization is achieved through manual configuration at each switch in the fabric. This process is tedious and error prone.

The following are some of the Cisco NX-OS features that use the CFS infrastructure:

- N port virtualization

- FlexAttach virtual pWWN

- NTP

- Dynamic port VSAN membership

- Distributed device alias services

- SAN device virtualization

- TACACS+ and RADIUS

- User and administrator roles

- Port security

- Call Home

- Syslog

- fctimer

- Saved startup configurations using the Fabric Startup Configuration Manager (FSCM)

- Allowed domain ID lists

- Registered state change notification (RSCN) timer

All CFS-based applications provide an option to enable or disable the distribution capabilities. The application configuration is not distributed by CFS unless distribution is explicitly enabled for that application.

The CFS functionality is independent of the lower-layer transport. CFS is a peer-to-peer protocol with no client/server relationship. CFS uses a proprietary SW_ILS (0x77434653) protocol for all CFS packets. CFS packets are sent to or from the switch domain controller addresses. CFS can also use IP to send information to other switches. Applications that use CFS are completely unaware of the lower layer transport.

## CFS Features

CFS has the following features:

- Peer-to-peer protocol with no client/server relationship at the CFS layer.

- Three scopes of distribution:

    - **Logical scope:** The distribution occurs within the scope of a VSAN.

    - **Physical scope:** The distribution spans the entire physical topology.

    - **Over a selected set of VSANs:** Some applications, such as Inter-VSAN Routing (IVR), require configuration distribution over some specific VSANs. These applications can specify to CFS the set of VSANs over which to restrict the distribution.

- Three modes of distribution:

    - **Coordinated distributions:** Only one distribution is allowed in the fabric at any given time. CFS uses locks to enforce this. A coordinated distribution is not allowed to start if locks are taken for the application anywhere in the fabric. Coordinated distribution can be CFS driven or application driven. In a CFS-driven distribution, the lock is executed by CFS in response to an application request without intervention from the application. In an application-driven distribution, the fabric lock is under the complete control of the application.

    - **Uncoordinated distributions:** Multiple parallel distributions are allowed in the fabric except when a coordinated distribution is in progress.

    - **Unrestricted uncoordinated distributions:** Unrestricted uncoordinated distributions allow multiple parallel distributions in the fabric in the presence of an existing

8

coordinated distribution. Unrestricted uncoordinated distributions are allowed to run in parallel with all other types of distributions.

- Support for a merge protocol that facilitates the merge of application configuration during a fabric merge event (when two independent fabrics merge).

### CFS Fabric Lock

When you configure (first-time configuration) a Cisco NX-OS feature (or application) that uses the CFS infrastructure, that feature starts a CFS session and locks the fabric. When a fabric is locked, the Cisco NX-OS software does not allow any configuration changes from a switch to this Cisco NX-OS feature, other than the switch holding the lock, and issues a message to inform the user about the locked status. The configuration changes are held in a pending database by that application.

If you start a CFS session that requires a fabric lock but forget to end the session, an administrator can clear the session. If you lock a fabric at any time, your username is remembered across restarts and switchovers. If another user (on the same machine) tries to perform configuration tasks, that user's attempts are rejected.

A commit operation saves the pending database for all application peers and releases the lock for all switches. In general, the commit function does not start a session; only a lock function starts a session. However, an empty commit is allowed if configuration changes were not previously made. In this case, a commit operation results in a session that acquires locks and distributes the current database.

When you commit configuration changes to a feature using the CFS infrastructure, you receive a notification about one of the following responses:

- **One or more external switches report a successful status:** The application applies the changes locally and releases the fabric lock.

- **None of the external switches report a successful state:** The application considers this state a failure and does not apply the changes to any switch in the fabric. The fabric lock is not released.

### CFSoIP and CFSoFC

A mixed fabric of different platforms such as the Cisco Nexus 7000 Series, Cisco Nexus 5000 Series, and Cisco MDS 9000 Series can interact with each other using CFS over IP (CFSoIP) and/or CFS over FC (CFSoFC).

You can configure CFS to distribute information over IP for networks containing switches that are not reachable over Fibre Channel. CFS distribution over IP supports the following features:

- Physical distribution over an entirely IP network.

- Physical distribution over a hybrid Fibre Channel and IP network with the distribution reaching all switches that are reachable over either Fibre Channel or IP.

- Distribution over IP version 4 (IPv4) or IP version 6 (IPv6).

- Keepalive mechanism to detect network topology changes using a configurable multicast address.

■ Compatibility with Cisco MDS NX-OS Release 4.x.

■ Distribution for logical scope applications is not supported because the VSAN implementation is limited to Fibre Channel.

The switch attempts to distribute information over Fibre Channel first and then over the IP network if the first attempt over Fibre Channel fails. CFS does not send duplicate messages if distribution over both IP and Fibre Channel is enabled.

Figure 8-19 shows a network with both Fibre Channel and IP connections. Node A forwards an event to node B over Fibre Channel. Node B forwards the event to nodes C and D using unicast IP. Node C forwards the event to node E using Fibre Channel.

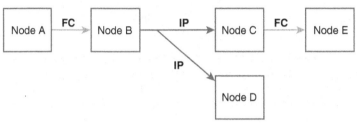

**Figure 8-19**   *Network Example 1 with Fibre Channel and IP Connections*

Figure 8-20 is the same as Figure 8-19 except that nodes D and E are connected using Fibre Channel. All processes are the same in this example because node B has node C and node D in the distribution list for IP. Node C does not forward to node D because node D is already in the distribution list from node B.

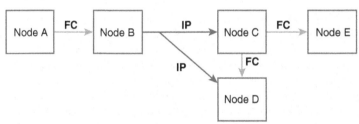

**Figure 8-20**   *Network Example 2 with Fibre Channel and IP Connections*

Figure 8-21 is the same as Figure 8-20 except that nodes D and E are connected using IP. Both nodes C and D forward the event to node E because node E is not in the distribution list from node B.

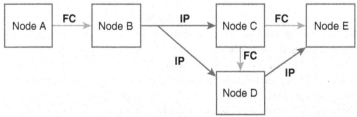

**Figure 8-21**   *Network Example 3 with Fibre Channel and IP Connections*

CFS over IP can also be used with static IP peers. In this case, dynamic discovery over IP multicast is disabled, and CFS distribution is done only on the peers configured statically. CFS uses the list of configured IP addresses to communicate with each peer and learn the peer switch WWN. After learning the peer switch WWN, CFS marks the switch as CFS-capable and triggers application-level merging and database distribution.

## CFS Merge

An application keeps the configuration synchronized in a fabric through CFS. Two such fabrics might merge as a result of an ISL coming up between them. These two fabrics could have two different sets of configuration information that need to be reconciled in the event of a merge. CFS provides notification each time an application peer comes online. If a fabric with M application peers merges with another fabric with N application peers, and if an application triggers a merge action on every such notification, a link-up event results in M*N merges in the fabric.

CFS supports a protocol that reduces the number of merges required to one by handling the complexity of the merge at the CFS layer. This protocol runs per application per scope. The protocol involves selecting one switch in a fabric as the merge manager for that fabric. The other switches do not play any role in the merge process.

During a merge, the merge manager in the two fabrics exchange their configuration databases with each other. The application on one of them merges the information, decides if the merge is successful, and informs all switches in the combined fabric of the status of the merge.

In case of a successful merge, the merged database is distributed to all switches in the combined fabric, and the entire new fabric remains in a consistent state.

## CFS Regions

A CFS region is a user-defined subset of switches for a given feature or application in its physical distribution scope. When a SAN is spanned across a vast geography, you may need to localize or restrict the distribution of certain profiles among a set of switches based on their physical proximity. CFS regions allow you to configure multiple islands of distribution within the fabric, for a given CFS feature or application. CFS regions are designed to restrict the distribution of a feature's configuration to a specific set or grouping of switches in a fabric.

**NOTE**   You can only configure a CFS region on physical switches in a SAN. You cannot configure a CFS region in a VSAN.

CFS regions are identified by numbers ranging from 0 through 200. Region 0 is reserved as the default region, and it contains every switch in the fabric. You can configure regions from 1 through 200. If the feature is moved—that is, assigned to a new region—its scope is restricted to that region; it ignores all other regions for distribution or merging purposes. The assignment of the region to a feature has precedence in distribution over its initial physical scope. You can configure a CFS region to distribute configurations for multiple features. However, on a given switch, you can configure only one CFS region at a time to distribute the configuration for a given feature. Once you assign a feature to a CFS region, its configuration cannot be distributed within another CFS region.

Let's discuss a scenario where CFS regions will be useful. Call Home is an application that triggers alerts to network administrators when a situation arises or something abnormal occurs. When the fabric covers many geographies and with multiple network administrators who are each responsible for a subset of switches in the fabric, the Call Home application sends alerts to all network administrators regardless of their location. For the Call Home application to send message alerts selectively to network administrators, the physical scope of the application has to be fine-tuned or narrowed down, which is achieved by implementing CFS regions.

Table 8-10 summarizes the NX-OS CLI commands that are related to CFS configuration and verification.

**Key Topic**

**Table 8-10**  Summary of NX-OS CLI Commands for CFS Configuration and Verification

| | |
|---|---|
| switch# **configure terminal** | Enters configuration mode. |
| switch(config)# **(no) cfs distribute** | Enables CFS distribution on the switch. |
| switch(config)# **(no) cfs ipv4 distribute** | Globally enables CFS over IPv4 for all applications on the switch. |
| switch(config)# **(no) cfs ipv6 distribute** | Globally enables CFS over IPv6 for all applications on the switch. |
| switch(config)# **(no) cfs ipv4 mcast-address 239.255.1.1** | Configures the IPv4 multicast address for CFS distribution over IPv4. The ranges of valid IPv4 addresses are 239.255.0.0 through 239.255.255.255 and 239.192/16 through 239.251/16. |
| switch(config)# **(no) cfs ipv6 mcast-address ff15::e244:4754** | Configures the IPv6 multicast address for CFS distribution over IPv6. The range of valid IPv6 addresses is ff15::/16 (ff15::0000:0000 through ff15::ffff:ffff) and ff18::/16 (ff18::0000:0000 through ff18::ffff:ffff). |
| switch(config)# **dpvm abort** | Clears the CFS locks for the Dynamic Port VSAN Membership (DPVM) application in the entire fabric. |
| switch(config)# **clear dpvm session** | Clears the CFS locks for the DPVM application. |
| switch(config)# **(no) cfs static-peers** | Enters CFS static peers configuration mode and disables dynamic discovery of peers using multicast forwarding. |
| switch(config-cfs-static)# **ip address 1.2.3.4** | Adds the IP address to the static peers list and marks the switch as CFS-capable. |
| switch(config)# **(no) cfs region 4** | Creates a region with the number 4. |
| switch(config-cfs-region)# **(no) callhome** | Adds the Call Home application to region 4. |
| switch# **show cfs status** | Displays the status of the CFS distribution on the switch. |
| switch# **show cfs application** | Displays the applications that are currently registered with CFS. |
| switch# **show cfs lock** | Displays all the locks that are currently acquired by any application. |
| switch# **show cfs region (brief)** | Displays detailed information about the CFS regions. |
| switch# **show cfs static peers** | Displays the IP address, WWN, and the status of the CFS static peer request. |

8

# VSAN

A VSAN is a virtual storage-area network (SAN). VSANs provide isolation among devices that are physically connected to the same fabric. With VSANs, you can create multiple logical SANs over a common physical infrastructure. Each VSAN is a logically and functionally separate SAN with its own set of Fibre Channel fabric services. This partitioning of fabric services greatly reduces network instability by containing fabric reconfigurations and error conditions within an individual VSAN. The strict traffic segregation provided by VSANs helps ensure that the control and data traffic of a specified VSAN are confined within the VSAN's own domain, increasing SAN security. VSANs help reduce costs by facilitating consolidation of isolated SAN islands into a common infrastructure without compromising availability.

Users can create administrator roles that are limited in scope to certain VSANs. For example, a network administrator role can be set up to allow configuration of all platform-specific capabilities, while other roles can be set up to allow configuration and management only within specific VSANs. This approach improves the manageability of large SANs and reduces disruptions due to human error by isolating the effect of a user action to a specific VSAN whose membership can be assigned based on switch ports or the World Wide Name (WWN) of attached devices.

## VSAN Features

With the introduction of VSANs, the network administrator can build a single topology containing switches, links, and one or more VSANs. Each VSAN in the topology has the same behavior and property as a SAN. A VSAN has the following additional features:

- Multiple VSANs can share the same physical topology.

- The same Fibre Channel identifiers (FCIDs) can be assigned to a host in another VSAN, thus increasing VSAN scalability.

- Every instance of a VSAN runs all required protocols such as FSPF, domain manager, and zoning (more on zoning later in this chapter).

- Fabric-related configurations in one VSAN do not affect the associated traffic in another VSAN.

- Events causing traffic disruptions in one VSAN are contained within that VSAN and are not propagated to other VSANs.

Figure 8-22 shows a physical Fibre Channel switching infrastructure with two defined VSANs: VSAN 2 (dashed) and VSAN 7 (solid). VSAN 2 includes hosts H1 and H2, application servers AS2 and AS3, and storage arrays SA1 and SA4. VSAN 7 connects H3, AS1, SA2, and SA3.

The four switches in this network are interconnected by trunk links that carry both VSAN 2 and VSAN 7 traffic. The inter-switch topology of both VSAN 2 and VSAN 7 are identical. This is not a requirement, and a network administrator can enable certain VSANs on certain links to create different VSAN topologies.

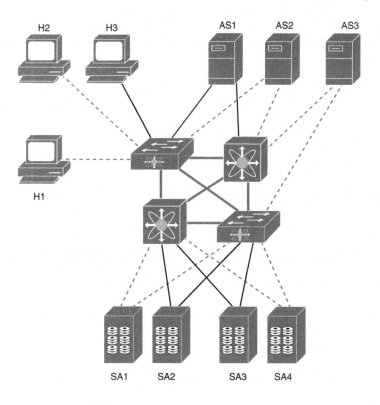

---- Link in VSAN 2

——— Link in VSAN 7

■■■ Trunk Link

**Figure 8-22**  *Example of Two VSANs*

Without VSANs, a network administrator would need separate switches and links for separate SANs. When VSANs are enabled, the same switches and links may be shared by multiple VSANs. VSANs allow SANs to be built on port granularity instead of switch granularity. Figure 8-22 illustrates that a VSAN is a group of hosts or storage devices that communicate with each other using a virtual topology defined on the physical SAN.

The primary use of VSANs is to separate traffic based on certain criteria such as customer traffic segregation or to meet the needs of a particular department or application.

## VSAN Attributes

VSANs have the following attributes:

- **VSAN ID:** The VSAN ID identifies the VSAN as the default VSAN (VSAN 1), user-defined VSANs (VSAN 2 to 4093), and the isolated VSAN (VSAN 4094).

- **State:** The administrative state of a VSAN can be configured to an active (default) or suspended state. When VSANs are created, they may exist in various conditions or states.

  - The active state of a VSAN indicates that the VSAN is configured and enabled. By enabling a VSAN, you activate the services for that VSAN. A VSAN is in the operational state if the VSAN is active and at least one port is up. This state indicates that traffic can pass through this VSAN.

■ The suspended state of a VSAN indicates that the VSAN is configured but not enabled. If a port is configured in this VSAN, it is disabled. Use this state to deactivate a VSAN without losing the VSAN's configuration. All ports in a suspended VSAN are disabled. By suspending a VSAN, you can preconfigure all the VSAN parameters for the whole fabric and activate the VSAN immediately.

■ **VSAN name:** This text string identifies the VSAN for management purposes. The name can be from 1 to 32 characters long, and it must be unique across all VSANs. By default, the VSAN name is a concatenation of VSAN and a four-digit string representing the VSAN ID. For example, the default name for VSAN 3 is VSAN0003. A VSAN name must be unique.

■ **Load-balancing attributes:** These attributes indicate the use of the source-destination ID (src-dst-id) or the originator exchange OX ID (src-dst-ox-id, the default) for load-balancing path selection.

**NOTE**   Up to 256 VSANs can be configured in a switch. Of these, one is a default VSAN (VSAN 1), and another is an isolated VSAN (VSAN 4094). User-specified VSAN IDs range from 2 to 4093. VSAN 1 cannot be deleted, but it can be suspended. When you configure a port in VSAN 4094 or move a port to VSAN 4094, that port is immediately isolated. Each VSAN can contain up to 239 switches and has an independent address space that allows identical Fibre Channel IDs (FCIDs) to be used simultaneously in different VSANs.

## VSAN Advantages

VSANs offer the following advantages:

■ **Traffic isolation:** Traffic is contained within VSAN boundaries, and devices reside only in one VSAN, thus ensuring absolute separation between user groups, if desired.

■ **Scalability:** VSANs are overlaid on top of a single physical fabric. The ability to create several logical VSAN layers increases the scalability of the SAN.

■ **Per-VSAN fabric services:** Replication of fabric services on a per-VSAN basis provides increased scalability and availability.

■ **Redundancy:** Several VSANs created on the same physical SAN ensure redundancy. If one VSAN fails, redundant protection (to another VSAN in the same physical SAN) is configured using a backup path between the host and the device.

■ **Ease of configuration:** Users can be added, moved, or changed between VSANs without changing the physical structure of a SAN. Moving a device from one VSAN to another only requires configuration at the port level, not at a physical level.

## Dynamic Port VSAN Membership (DPVM)

Port VSAN membership on the switch is assigned on a port-by-port basis. By default, each port belongs to the default VSAN. You can assign VSANs to ports either statically or dynamically. To assign dynamic VSAN membership to ports, you assign VSANs based on the device WWN. This method is referred to as Dynamic Port VSAN Membership (DPVM). DPVM offers flexibility and eliminates the need to reconfigure the port VSAN membership to maintain fabric topology when a host or storage device connection is moved between two Cisco fabric switches or two ports within a switch. DPVM retains the configured VSAN regardless of where a device is connected or moved.

DPVM configurations are based on port World Wide Name (pWWN) and node World Wide Name (nWWN) assignments. DPVM contains mapping information for each device pWWN/ nWWN assignment and the corresponding VSAN. The Cisco NX-OS software checks DPVM active configuration during a device FLOGI and obtains the required VSAN details.

The pWWN identifies the host or device, and the nWWN identifies a node consisting of multiple devices. You can assign any one of these identifiers or any combination of these identifiers to configure DPVM mapping. If you assign a combination, preference is given to the pWWN.

DPVM can be configured to automatically learn (autolearn) new devices within each VSAN. DPVM autolearn can be enabled or disabled at any time. Learned entries are created by populating device pWWNs and VSANs. DPVM should be activated before autolearn can be enabled. Autolearned entries can also be manually deleted. The autolearned entries become permanent when DPVM autolearn is disabled.

DPVM uses the Cisco Fabric Services infrastructure to allow efficient database management and distribution. DPVM uses the application-driven, coordinated distribution mode and the fabric-wide distribution scope.

## VSAN Trunking

VSAN trunking enables interconnected ports to transmit and receive frames in more than one VSAN. Trunking is supported on E ports and F ports. VSAN trunking is supported on native Fibre Channel interfaces and virtual Fibre Channel interfaces.

The trunking protocol is important for E port and TE port operations. It supports the following capabilities:

- Dynamic negotiation of operational trunk mode

- Selection of a common set of trunk-allowed VSANs

- Detection of a VSAN mismatch across an ISL

Trunking configurations are applicable only to E ports. If trunk mode is enabled in an E port and that port becomes operational as a trunking E port, it is referred to as a TE port, as shown in Figure 8-23. The trunk-allowed VSANs configured for TE ports are used by the trunking protocol to determine the allowed-active VSANs in which frames can be received or transmitted. If a trunking-enabled E port is connected to a third-party switch, the trunking protocol ensures seamless operation as an E port.

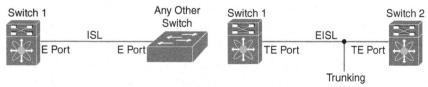

**Figure 8-23**  *VSAN Trunking Between Cisco-Cisco and Cisco-Third-Party Switches*

If you misconfigure VSAN configurations across E ports, issues can occur, such as the merging of traffic in two VSANs (causing both VSANs to mismatch), as shown in Figure 8-24. The VSAN trunking protocol validates the VSAN interfaces at both ends of an ISL to avoid merging VSANs. The trunking protocol cannot detect merging of VSANs when a third-party switch is placed in between two Cisco SAN switches, as shown in Figure 8-25.

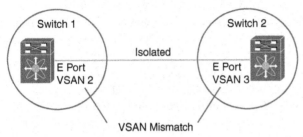

**Figure 8-24** *VSAN Mismatch Between Cisco Switches*

**Figure 8-25** *VSAN Mismatch Between Cisco Switches with Third-Party Switch in Between*

VSAN 2 and VSAN 3 are effectively merged with overlapping entries in the name server and the zone applications. Cisco MDS 9000 Fabric Manager helps detect such topologies.

By default, the VSAN trunking protocol is enabled. If the trunking protocol is disabled on a switch, no port on that switch can apply new trunk configurations. Existing trunk configurations are not affected: the TE port continues to function in trunk mode but only supports traffic in VSANs that it negotiated with previously (when the trunking protocol was enabled). Other switches that are directly connected to this switch are similarly affected on the connected interfaces. If you need to merge traffic from different port VSANs across a nontrunking ISL, disable the trunking protocol.

By default, trunk mode is enabled in all Fibre Channel interfaces. However, trunk mode configuration takes effect only in E port mode. You can configure trunk mode as on (enabled), off (disabled), or auto (automatic). The default trunk mode is on. The trunk mode configurations at the two ends of the link determine the trunking state of the link and the port modes at both ends, as shown in Table 8-11.

**Table 8-11** Trunk Mode Status Between Switches

| Switch 1 | Switch 2 | Trunking State | Port Mode |
|----------|----------|----------------|-----------|
| On | Auto or on | Trunking (EISL) | TE port |
| Off | Auto, on, or off | No trunking (ISL) | E port |
| Auto | Auto | No trunking (ISL) | E port |

**NOTE**  When connected to a third-party switch, the trunk mode configuration has no effect. The inter-switch link (ISL) is always in a trunking disabled state.

Each Fibre Channel interface has an associated trunk-allowed VSAN list. In TE port mode, frames are transmitted and received in one or more VSANs specified in this list. By default, the complete VSAN range (1 through 4093) is included in the trunk-allowed list. The common set of VSANs that are configured and active in the switch are included in the trunk-allowed VSAN list for an interface, and they are called *allowed-active VSANs*. The trunking protocol uses the list of allowed-active VSANs at the two ends of an ISL to determine the list of operational VSANs in which traffic is allowed. You can configure a selected set of VSANs (from the allowed-active list) to control access to the VSANs specified in a trunking ISL. The allowed VSANs are configured on a per-interface basis.

In Figure 8-26, switch 1 has VSANs 1 through 5; switch 2 has VSANs 1 through 3; and switch 3 has VSANs 1, 2, 4, and 5. However, only the common set of allowed-active VSANs at the ends of the ISL become operational. The ISL between switch 1 and switch 2 includes VSAN 1 and VSAN 3. The ISL between switch 2 and switch 3 includes VSAN 1 and VSAN 2. The ISL between switch 3 and switch 1 includes VSAN 1, 2, and 5. VSAN 2 can only be routed from switch 1 through switch 3 to switch 2.

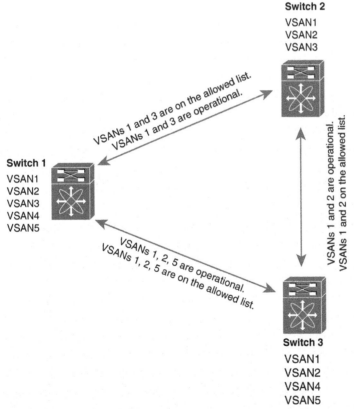

**Figure 8-26**  *Operational and Allowed VSAN Configuration*

Table 8-12 summarizes the NX-OS CLI commands that are related to VSAN configuration and verification.

**Table 8-12** Summary of NX-OS CLI Commands for VSAN Configuration and Verification

| Command | Purpose |
|---|---|
| switch# **config terminal** | Enters configuration mode. |
| switch(config)# **vsan database** | Configures the database for a VSAN. Application-specific VSAN parameters cannot be configured from this prompt. |
| switch(config-vsan-db)# **(no) vsan 2** | Creates a VSAN with the specified ID (2) if that VSAN does not exist already. |
| switch(config-vsan-db)# **vsan 2 name TechDoc** | Updates the VSAN with the assigned name (TechDoc) |
| switch(config-vsan-db)# **(no) vsan 2 suspend** | Suspends the selected VSAN. |
| switch(config-vsan-db)# **vsan 2 interface fc1/8** | Assigns the membership of the fc1/8 interface to the specified VSAN (VSAN 2) |
| switch(config-vsan-db)# **(no) vsan 2 loadbalancing src-dst-id** | Enables the load-balancing guarantee for the selected VSAN and directs the switch to use the source and destination ID for its path selection process. |
| switch(config-vsan-db)# **vsan 2 loadbalancing src-dst-ox-id** | Changes the path selection setting to use the source ID, the destination ID, and the OX ID (default) |
| switch(config-vsan-db)# **(no) vsan 2 suspend** | Suspends the selected VSAN. |
| switch(config-vsan-db)# **end** | Returns you to EXEC mode. |
| switch(config)# **(no) feature dpvm** | Enables DPVM on that switch. |
| switch(config)# **(no) dpvm database** | Creates the DPVM config database. |
| switch(config-dpvm-db)# **(no) pwwn 12:33:56:78:90:12:34:56 vsan 100** | Maps the specified device pWWN to VSAN 100. |
| switch(config-dpvm-db)# **(no) nwwn 14:21:30:12:63:39:72:81 vsan 101** | Maps the specified device nWWN to VSAN 101. |
| switch(config-dpvm-db)# **dpvm commit** | Is required to commit the configuration changes when DPVM distribute is enabled. |
| switch(config)# **(no) dpvm activate** | Activates the DPVM configuration. |
| switch(config)# **dpvm activate force** | Forcefully activates the DPVM configuration and overrides the conflicting entries. |
| switch(config)# **(no) dpvm auto-learn** | Enables autolearn on the switch. |
| switch(config)# **clear dpvm auto-learn** | Clears the list of autolearned entries. |
| switch(config)# **clear dpvm auto-learn pwwn** *pwwn* | Clears the list of autolearned pWWN entries in the distributed DPVM database. |
| switch(config)# **(no) dpvm distribute** | Enables (default) DPVM distribution to the neighboring switches. |

| Command | Purpose |
|---|---|
| switch(config)# **(no) trunk protocol enable** | Enables the trunking protocol (default). |
| switch(config)# **interface fc** *slot/port* | Selects the specified Fibre Channel interface. |
| switch(config)# **interface vfc** *vfc-id* | Selects the specified virtual Fibre Channel interface. |
| switch(config-if)# **switchport trunk mode on** | Enables (default) the trunk mode for the specified interface. |
| switch(config-if)# **switchport trunk mode off** | Disables the trunk mode for the specified interface. Trunk mode cannot be turned off for virtual Fibre Channel interfaces. |
| switch(config-if)# **switchport trunk mode auto** | Configures the trunk mode to **auto** mode, which provides automatic sensing for the interface. |
| switch(config-if)# **(no) switchport trunk allowed vsan** *vsan-id* - *vsan-id* | Changes the allowed list for the specified VSAN range. |
| switch(config-if)# **(no) switchport trunk allowed vsan add** *vsan-id* | Expands the specified VSAN to the new allowed list. |
| switch # **show vsan membership** | Displays static membership information for all VSANs. |
| switch # **show vsan 1 membership** | Displays membership information for the specified VSAN. |
| switch # **show vsan membership interface fc1/1** | Displays static membership information for a specified interface. |
| switch # **show vsan 4094 membership** | Displays all ports associated with the isolated VSAN. |
| switch# **show vsan 100** | Displays the configuration for a specific VSAN. |
| switch# **show vsan usage** | Displays the VSAN usage. |
| switch# **show vsan** | Displays all VSANs. |
| switch# **show fabric switch information vsan 100** | Displays information about all the switches in the fabric for VSAN 100. |
| switch# **show dpvm pending** | Holds all configuration changes until they are committed when DPVM distribute is enabled (it is enabled by default when the feature is enabled). The list of pending changes can be seen at any time using this command. |
| switch# **show dpvm database** | Displays DPVM static device configuration. |
| switch# **show dpvm database active** | Displays the enforced DPVM device configuration. |
| switch# **show dpvm status** | Displays the DPVM configuration status. |
| switch# **show dpvm ports vsan 10** | Displays the DPVM current dynamic ports for the specified VSAN. |
| switch# **show interface fc3/3** | Displays the trunk mode of the Fibre Channel interface fc3/3. |
| switch# **show trunk protocol** | Displays the trunk mode of a Fibre Channel interface. |
| switch# **show interface trunk vsan 1-1000** | Displays the VSAN information for all trunk interfaces on VSAN 1 to 1000. |

8

Example 8-3 shows how to configure and verify VSANs on the sample topology shown in Figure 8-27. The example shows the configuration only for MDS-9148S-1; the configuration for MDS9148S-2 is similar.

MDS-9148S-1

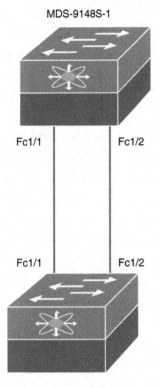

Fc1/1            Fc1/2

Fc1/1            Fc1/2

MDS-9148S-2

**Figure 8-27**   *Sample Topology for VSAN Creation and Verification*

**Example 8-3**   *VSAN Creation and Verification on MDS-9148S Switch*

```
| Initial configuration and entering the VSAN database
MDS-9148S-1# conf t
Enter configuration commands, one per line. End with CNTL/Z.
MDS-9148S-1(config)# vsan database

| Creating VSAN 11 with name VSAN11 and configuring interfaces for VSAN 11.
MDS-9148S-1(config-vsan-db)# vsan 11 name VSAN11
MDS-9148S-1(config-vsan-db)# vsan 11 interface fc1/1, fc1/2

| Configuring interfaces as E ports
MDS-9148S-1(config-vsan-db)# int fc 1/1, fc 1/2
MDS-9148S-1(config-if)# switchport mode E
MDS-9148S-1(config-if)# no shut
```

```
! Verifying status of the interfaces
MDS-9148S-1(config-if)# show interface fc 1/1, fc1/2 brief
```

| Interface | Vsan | Admin Mode | Admin Trunk Mode | Status | SFP | Oper Mode | Oper Speed (Gbps) | Port Channel | Logical Type |
|-----------|------|------------|------------------|--------|-----|-----------|-------------------|--------------|--------------|
| fc1/1 | 11 | E | on | trunking | swl | TE | 8 | -- | core |
| fc1/2 | 11 | E | on | trunking | swl | TE | 8 | -- | core |

```
! Verifying the VSAN membership
MDS-9148S-1(config)# show vsan membership

vsan 1 interfaces:
    fc1/4         fc1/5          fc1/6          fc1/7
    fc1/8         fc1/9          fc1/10         fc1/11
<....output omitted....>
    fc1/48

vsan 11 interfaces:
    fc1/1         fc1/2          fc1/3

vsan 4079(evfp_isolated_vsan) interfaces:

vsan 4094(isolated_vsan) interfaces:

! Verifying the VSAN usage
MDS-9148S-1(config)# show vsan usage
2 vsan configured
configured vsans:1,11
vsans available for configuration:2-10,12-4078,4080-4093

! Verifying all VSANs configured on the switch
MDS-9148S-1(config)# show vsan

vsan 1 information
        name:VSAN0001   state:active
        interoperability mode:default
        loadbalancing:src-id/dst-id/oxid
        operational state:down

vsan 11 information
        name:VSAN11   state:active
        interoperability mode:default
        loadbalancing:src-id/dst-id/oxid
        operational state:up
```

```
vsan 4079:evfp_isolated_vsan

vsan 4094:isolated_vsan

MDS-9148S-1(config)#
```

# SAN Port Channels

SAN port channels refer to the aggregation of multiple physical interfaces into one logical interface to provide higher aggregated bandwidth, load balancing, and link redundancy. Port channels can connect to interfaces across switching modules, so a failure of a switching module cannot bring down the port channel link.

In Figure 8-28, port channel A aggregates two links on two interfaces on the same switching module at each end of a connection. Port channel B also aggregates two links, but each link is connected to a different switching module. If the switching module goes down, traffic is not affected.

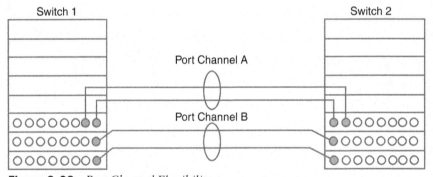

**Figure 8-28**   *Port Channel Flexibility*

## Types of SAN Port Channels

An E port channel provides a point-to-point connection over ISL (E ports) or EISL (TE ports), as shown in Figure 8-29. Multiple links can be combined into a port channel, and it increases the aggregate bandwidth on an ISL by distributing traffic among all functional links in the channel. It load balances across multiple links and maintains optimum bandwidth utilization. Load balancing is based on the source ID, destination ID, and exchange ID (OX ID). The E port channel provides high availability on an ISL. If one link fails, traffic previously carried on this link is switched to the remaining links. If a link goes down in a port channel, the upper protocol is not aware of it. To the upper protocol, the link is still there, although the bandwidth is diminished. The routing tables are not affected by link failure. Port channels may contain up to 16 physical links and may span multiple modules for added high availability. Trunking enables a link transmitting frames in the EISL format to carry (trunk) multiple VSAN traffic.

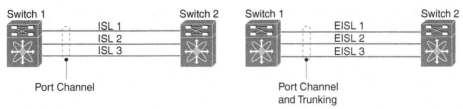

**Figure 8-29**  *Port Channel and Trunking*

An F port channel is also a logical interface that combines a set of F ports connected to the same Fibre Channel node and operates as one link between the F ports and the NP ports. F port channels are mainly used to connect NX-OS Core and NPV switches to provide optimal band-width utilization and transparent failover between the uplinks of a VSAN. An F port channel trunk combines the functionality and advantages of a TF port and an F port channel.

Port channels also can form between the following set of ports:

- E ports and TE ports

- F ports and NP ports

- TF ports and TNP ports

A port can be configured as a member of a static port channel only if the following configu-rations are the same in the port and the port channel:

- Speed

- Mode

- Rate mode

- Port VSAN

- Trunking mode

- Allowed VSAN list or VF-ID list

A compatibility check ensures that the same parameter settings are used in all physical ports in the channel. Otherwise, they cannot become part of a port channel. The compatibility check is performed before a port is added to the port channel.

The check ensures that the following parameters and settings match at both ends of a port channel:

- **Capability parameters** (type of interface, Gigabit Ethernet at both ends, or Fibre Channel at both ends).

- **Administrative compatibility parameters** (speed, mode, rate mode, port VSAN, allowed VSAN list, and port security). A port addition procedure fails if the capability and administrative parameters in the remote switch are incompatible with the capabil-ity and administrative parameters in the local switch.

- **Operational parameters** (remote switch WWN and trunking mode). If the operational parameters are incompatible, the compatibility check fails, and the interface is placed in a suspended (if On mode is configured) or isolated state (if Active mode is configured) based on the configured mode. We discuss port channel modes later in this chapter.

**NOTE**   Ports in Shared rate mode cannot form a port channel or a trunking port channel.

A port channel group can be automatically created when compatible links come up between two compatible switches if channel group autocreation is enabled in all ports at both ends using the **channel-group auto** command under the interface.

### Port Channel Load Balancing

Load-balancing functionality on SAN port channels can be provided using the following methods:

- **Flow based:** All frames between source and destination follow the same links for a given flow. That is, whichever link is selected for the first exchange of the flow is used for all subsequent exchanges.

- **Exchange based:** The first frame in an exchange is assigned to a link, and then subsequent frames in the exchange follow the same link. However, subsequent exchanges can use a different link. This method provides finer granularity for load balancing while preserving the order of frames for each exchange.

Figure 8-30 illustrates how flow-based load balancing works. When the first frame in a flow is received on an interface for forwarding, link 1 is selected. Each subsequent frame in that flow is sent over the same link. No frame in Source ID 1 (SID1) and Destination ID 1 (DID1) utilizes link 2. All the frames in SID2 and DID2 use link 2.

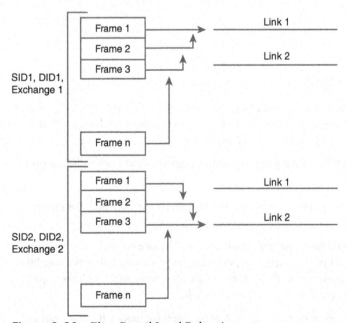

**Figure 8-30**   *Flow-Based Load Balancing*

Figure 8-31 illustrates how exchange-based load balancing works. When the first frame in an exchange is received for forwarding on an interface, link 1 is chosen by a hash algorithm. All remaining frames in that particular exchange are sent on the same link. For exchange 1, no frame uses link 2. For the next exchange, link 2 is chosen by the hash algorithm. Now all frames in exchange 2 use link 2.

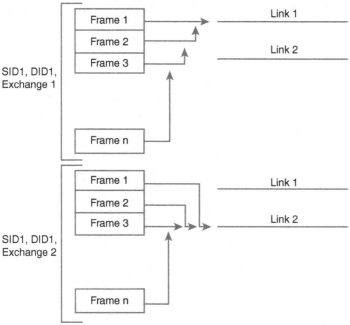

**Figure 8-31** *Exchange-Based Load Balancing*

## Port Channel Modes

You can configure each SAN port channel with a channel group mode parameter to determine the port channel protocol behavior for all member ports in this channel group. The possible values for a channel group mode are as follows:

- **On mode (default):** The member ports only operate as part of a SAN port channel or remain inactive. In this mode, the port channel protocol is not initiated. However, if a port channel protocol frame is received from a peer port, the software indicates its nonnegotiable status. Port channels configured in the On mode require you to explicitly enable and disable the port channel member ports at either end if you add or remove ports from the port channel configuration. You must physically verify that the local and remote ports are connected to each other.

- **Active mode:** The member ports initiate port channel protocol negotiation with the peer port(s) regardless of the channel group mode of the peer port. If the peer port, while configured in a channel group, does not support the port channel protocol or responds with a nonnegotiable status, it will default to the On mode behavior. The Active port channel mode allows automatic recovery without explicitly enabling and disabling the port channel member ports at either end.

**NOTE** An F port channel is supported only in Active mode.

Table 8-13 compares On and Active modes of the port channel.

**Table 8-13** Channel Group Configuration Differences

| On Mode | Active Mode |
|---|---|
| No protocol is exchanged. | A port channel protocol negotiation is performed with the peer ports. |
| Interfaces are moved to the suspended state if their operational values are incompatible with the SAN port channel. | Interfaces are moved to the isolated state if their operational values are incompatible with the SAN port channel. |
| When you add or modify a port channel member port configuration, you must explicitly disable (shut) and enable (no shut) the port channel member ports at either end. | When you add or modify a port channel interface, the SAN port channel automatically recovers. |
| Port initialization is not synchronized. | There is synchronized startup of all ports in a channel across peer switches. |
| No misconfigurations are detected because no protocol is exchanged. | Misconfigurations are consistently detected using a port channel protocol. |
| Misconfigured ports are transitioned to the suspended state. You must explicitly disable (shut) and enable (no shut) the member ports at either end. | Misconfigured ports are transitioned to the isolated state to correct the misconfiguration. Once you correct the misconfiguration, the protocol ensures automatic recovery. |
| This is the default mode. | You must explicitly configure this mode. |

Table 8-14 summarizes the NX-OS CLI commands that are related to port channel configuration and verification.

**Table 8-14** Summary of NX-OS CLI Commands for Port Channel Configuration and Verification

| Command | Purpose |
|---|---|
| switch# **config terminal** | Enters configuration mode. |
| switch(config)# **(no) interface port-channel 1** | Configures the specified port channel (1) using the default On mode in Cisco MDS NX-OS Release 8.3(1) and earlier releases. Configures the specified port channel (1) using the default Active mode from Cisco MDS NX-OS Release 8.4(1). |
| switch(config-if)# **switchport mode E/F** | Configures the administrative mode of the port. |
| switch(config-if)# **channel mode active/on** | Specifies the port mode for the link in a port channel. |

| Command | Purpose |
|---|---|
| switch(config)# **interface fc1/15** | Configures the specified port interface (fc1/15). |
| switch(config-if)# **switchport mode E/F** | Configures the administrative mode of the port. |
| switch(config-if)# **switchport speed 4000** | Configures the port speed of the interface to 4000 Mbps. |
| switch(config-if)# **switchport rate-mode dedicated** | Reserves dedicated bandwidth for the interface. |
| switch(config-if)# **switchport trunk mode on** | Enables (default) the trunk mode for the specified interface. |
| switch(config-if)# **(no) channel-group 1** | Adds physical Fibre Channel port 1/15 to channel group 1. If channel group 1 does not exist, it is created. The port is shut down. |
| switch(config-if)# **channel-group 1 force** | Forces the addition of the physical port for interface fc1/1 to channel group 1. The port is shut down. |
| switch(config- if)# **(no) channel-group auto** | Automatically creates the channel group for the selected interface(s). |
| switch# **show port-channel summary** | Displays a summary of port channels within the switch. |
| switch# **show port-channel database** | Cisco MDS NX-OS Release 8.3(1) and earlier: Displays the port channel configured in the On mode (default) and Active mode. Cisco MDS NX-OS Release 8.4(1) and later: Displays the port channel configured in the On mode and Active mode (default). |
| switch# **show port-channel consistency** | Displays the consistency status without details. |
| switch# **show port-channel consistency detail** | Displays the consistency status with details. |
| switch# **show port-channel usage** | Displays the port channel usage. |
| switch# **show port-channel compatibility-parameters** | Displays the port channel compatibility. |
| switch# **show interface fc** *slot/port* | Displays autocreated port channels. |
| switch# **show port-channel database interface port-channel** *number* | Displays the specified port channel interface. |

Let's continue from the previous example of VSAN creation. This example uses the same topology as shown in Figure 8-32. Now you will create a port channel between the two links fc1/1 and fc1/2. Example 8-4 shows configuration only for MDS-9148S-1; the configuration for MDS9148S-2 is similar.

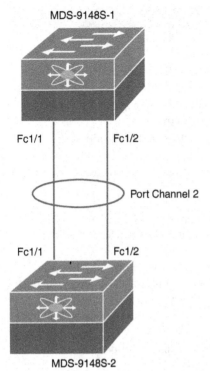

MDS-9148S-1

Fc1/1          Fc1/2

Port Channel 2

Fc1/1          Fc1/2

MDS-9148S-2

**Figure 8-32**  *Sample Topology for Port Channel Creation and Verification*

**Example 8-4**  *SAN Port Channel Creation and Verification on MDS-9148S Switch*

```
! Adding Physical Fibre Channel Ports to Port-Group 2 as E ports.
MDS-9148S-1(config)# int fc1/1, fc1/2
MDS-9148S-1(config-if)# switchport mode E
MDS-9148S-1(config-if)# channel-group 2
fc1/1 fc1/2 added to port-channel 2 and disabled
please do the same operation on the switch at the other end of the port-channel,
then do "no shutdown" at both ends to bring it up
MDS-9148S-1(config-if)# no shutdown

! Configuring Port Channel 2 as Trunk with allowed VSAN 11
MDS-9148S-1(config-if)# int port-channel 2
MDS-9148S-1(config-if)# switchport trunk allowed vsan 11
Warning: This command will remove all VSANs currently being trunked and trunk only
the specified VSANs.
Do you want to continue? (y/n) [n] y
MDS-9148S-1(config-if)# no shutdown

! Verifying Port Channel 2 summary and interface details
MDS-9148S_1(config-if)# show port-channel summary
```

```
-------------------------------------------------------------------------
Interface          Total Ports        Oper Ports        First Oper Port
-------------------------------------------------------------------------
port-channel 2          2                  2                 fc1/1

MDS-9148S-1(config-if)# show interface port-channel 2

port-channel2 is trunking
    Hardware is Fibre Channel
    Port WWN is 24:02:8c:60:4f:cf:7f:70
    Admin port mode is E, trunk mode is on
    snmp link state traps are enabled
    Port mode is TE
    Port vsan is 11
    Speed is 16 Gbps
    Logical type is core
    Trunk vsans (admin allowed and active) (11)
    Trunk vsans (up)                       (11)
    Trunk vsans (isolated)                 ()
    Trunk vsans (initializing)             ()
    5 minutes input rate 640 bits/sec,80 bytes/sec, 0 frames/sec
    5 minutes output rate 640 bits/sec,80 bytes/sec, 0 frames/sec
      1888 frames input,160664 bytes
        0 discards,0 errors
        0 invalid CRC/FCS,0 unknown class
        0 too long,0 too short
      1807 frames output,143428 bytes
        1 discards,0 errors
      26 input OLS,7  LRR,0 NOS,0 loop inits
      28 output OLS,47 LRR, 28 NOS, 4 loop inits
    Member[1] : fc1/1    [up] *
    Member[2] : fc1/2    [up]
    Interface last changed at Wed Jul 24 00:41:27 2019

! Verifying Port Channel Database. The asterisks (*) indicate which interface came
online first.
MDS-9148S-1# show port-channel database
port-channel2
    Administrative channel mode is on
    Operational channel mode is on
    Last membership update succeeded
    First operational port is fc1/1
    2 ports in total, 2 ports up
    Ports:   fc1/1    [up] *
             fc1/2    [up]
```

## Zoning

Zoning enables you to set up access control between storage devices or user groups. If you have administrator privileges in your fabric, you can create zones to increase network security and to prevent data loss or corruption. Zoning is enforced by examining the source-destination ID field.

### Zoning Features

Zoning has the following features:

- A *zone* consists of multiple zone members.

  - Members in a zone can access each other; members in different zones cannot access each other.

  - If zoning is not activated, all devices are members of the default zone.

  - If zoning is activated, any device that is not in an active zone (a zone that is part of an active zone set) is a member of the default zone.

  - Zones can vary in size.

  - Devices can belong to more than one zone.

- A *zone set* consists of one or more zones.

  - A zone set can be activated or deactivated as a single entity across all switches in the fabric.

  - Only one zone set can be activated at any time.

  - A zone can be a member of more than one zone set.

  - A zone switch can have a maximum of 1000 zone sets (Cisco MDS Series switches) or 500 zone sets (Cisco Nexus 5000 Series switches).

- *Zoning* can be administered from any switch in the fabric.

  - When you activate a zone (from any switch), all switches in the fabric receive the active zone set. Additionally, full zone sets are distributed to all switches in the fabric if this feature is enabled in the source switch.

  - If a new switch is added to an existing fabric, zone sets are acquired by the new switch.

- Zone changes can be configured nondisruptively. New zones and zone sets can be activated without interrupting traffic on unaffected ports or devices.

- *Zone membership* criteria are based mainly on WWNs or FCIDs. You can configure and use FC alias, also called the zone alias, while configuring zone membership of initiators and targets for specific zones. The following criteria can be used while defining zone members:

  - **Port World Wide Name (pWWN):** Specifies the pWWN of an N port attached to the switch as a member of the zone.

- **Fabric pWWN:** Specifies the WWN of the fabric port (the switch port's WWN). This membership is also referred to as port-based zoning.

- **FCID:** Specifies the FCID of an N port attached to the switch as a member of the zone.

- **Interface and switch WWN (sWWN):** Specifies the interface of a switch identified by the sWWN. This membership is also referred to as interface-based zoning.

- **Interface and domain ID:** Specifies the interface of a switch identified by the domain ID.

- **Domain ID and port number:** Specifies the domain ID of an MDS domain and additionally specifies a port belonging to a non-Cisco switch.

- **IPv4 address:** Specifies the IPv4 address (and optionally the subnet mask) of an attached device.

- **IPv6 address:** The IPv6 address of an attached device in 128 bits in colon-separated hexadecimal format.

- **Symbolic-nodename:** Specifies the member symbolic node name. The maximum length is 240 characters.

- Default zone membership includes all ports or WWNs that do not have a specific membership association. Access between default zone members is controlled by the default zone policy.

All members of a zone can communicate with each other. For a zone with $N$ members, $N*(N-1)$ access permissions need to be enabled. The best practice is to avoid configuring large numbers of targets or large numbers of initiators in a single zone. This type of configuration wastes switch resources by provisioning and managing many communicating pairs (initiator-to-initiator or target-to-target) that will never actually communicate with each other. For this reason, a single initiator with a single target is the most efficient approach to zoning.

The following specifics must be considered when creating zone members:

- Configuring only one initiator and one target for a zone provides the most efficient use of the switch resources.

- Configuring the same initiator to multiple targets is accepted.

- Configuring multiple initiators to multiple targets is not recommended.

- While configuring a zone member based on interface type, you should always select a fabric switch that potentially has the highest interface count in the fabric.

Figure 8-33 shows a zone set with two zones—zone 1 and zone 2—in a fabric. Zone 1 provides access from all three hosts (H1, H2, H3) to the data residing on storage systems S1 and S2. Zone 2 restricts the data on S3 to access only by H3. H3 resides in both zones.

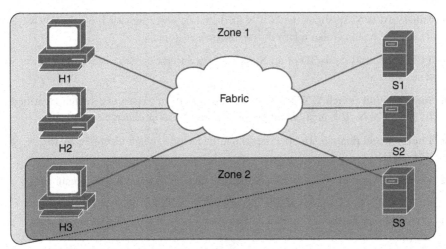

**Figure 8-33**   *Fabric with Two Zones*

Sometimes zones can be confused with VSANs. Two VSANs are equivalent to two uncon-
nected SANs; zone A on VSAN 1 is different and separate from zone A in VSAN 2. You can
also define multiple zones in a VSAN. Table 8-15 lists the differences between VSANs and
zones.

**Table 8-15**   VSAN and Zone Comparison

| VSAN Characteristic | Zone Characteristic |
| --- | --- |
| VSANs equal SANs with routing, naming, and zoning protocols. | Routing, naming, and zoning protocols are not available on a per-zone basis. |
| — | Zones are always contained within a VSAN. Zones never span two VSANs. |
| VSANs limit unicast, multicast, and broadcast traffic. | Zones limit unicast traffic. |
| Membership is typically defined using the VSAN ID to F ports. | Membership is typically defined by the pWWN. |
| An HBA or a storage device can belong only to a single VSAN—the VSAN associated with the F port. | An HBA or storage device can belong to multiple zones. |
| VSANs enforce membership at each E port, source port, and destination port. | Zones enforce membership only at the source and destination ports. |
| VSANs are defined for larger environments (storage service providers). | Zones are defined for a set of initiators and targets not visible outside the zone. |
| VSANs encompass the entire fabric. | Zones are configured at the fabric edge. |

## Zone Enforcement

Zoning can be enforced in two ways: soft and hard. Each end device (N port) discovers other
devices in the fabric by querying the name server. When a device logs in to the name server,
the name server returns the list of other devices that can be accessed by the querying device.
If an N port does not know about the FCIDs of other devices outside its zone, it cannot
access those devices.

In *soft zoning*, zoning restrictions are applied only during interaction between the name server and the end device. If an end device somehow knows the FCID of a device outside its zone, it can access that device.

In this mode, only control plane traffic is policed by the switch supervisor/CPU services. In particular, the Fibre Channel Name Server (FCNS) will limit the list of permitted devices in an FCNS reply to only those that are in the zone configuration. However, the end device data plane traffic is unpoliced. This means a rogue end device may connect to other devices it is not zoned with.

*Hard zoning* is enforced by the hardware on each frame sent by an N port. As frames enter the switch, source-destination IDs are compared with permitted combinations to allow the frame at wirespeed. Hard zoning is applied to all forms of zoning. Hard zoning enforces zoning restrictions on every frame and prevents unauthorized access.

In this mode, both control plane and data plane traffic are policed. Control plane traffic is policed by the switch supervisor/CPU, and data plane traffic is policed on each ingress port with hardware assistance. The policing rules are set by the zone set that is programmed into each linecard/port ASIC. The destination of each frame is checked by hardware and, if it is not permitted by zoning, it is dropped. In this mode, any device can communicate only with end devices it is authorized to.

Cisco SAN switches support both hard and soft zoning. By default, both types of zoning are enabled, with hard zoning used in priority over soft zoning. In the event that the system is unable to use hard zoning due to hardware resource exhaustion, it will be disabled and the system will fall back to use soft zoning.

## Full and Active Zone Set

Zones provide a method for specifying access control, while zone sets are a grouping of zones to enforce access control in the fabric. Zone sets are configured with the names of the member zones and the VSAN (if the zone set is in a configured VSAN). You can make a copy of a zone set and then edit it without altering the original zone set. You can copy an active zone set from the bootflash: directory, volatile: directory, or slot0, to one of the following areas:

- To the full zone set

- To a remote location (using FTP, SCP, SFTP, or TFTP)

The active zone set is not part of the full zone set. You cannot make changes to an existing zone set and activate it if the full zone set is lost or is not propagated.

Before configuring a zone set, consider these specifics:

- Each VSAN can have multiple zone sets, but only one zone set can be active at any given time.

- When you create a zone set, that zone set becomes a part of the full zone set.

- When you activate a zone set, a copy of the zone set from the full zone set is used to enforce zoning and is called the active zone set. An active zone set cannot be modified. A zone that is part of an active zone set is called an active zone.

8

- The administrator can modify the full zone set even if a zone set with the same name is active. However, the modification will be enforced only upon reactivation.

- When the activation is done, the active zone set is automatically stored in persistent configuration. This enables the switch to preserve the active zone set information across switch resets.

- All other switches in the fabric receive the active zone set so they can enforce zoning in their respective switches.

- Hard and soft zoning are implemented using the active zone set. Modifications take effect during zone set activation.

**NOTE**  If one zone set is active and you activate another zone set, the currently active zone set is automatically deactivated. You do not need to explicitly deactivate the currently active zone set before activating a new zone set.

Figure 8-34 shows a full zone set consisting of Z1 and Z2 zone sets. The Z1 zone set has zones A, B, and C as its zone members, and the Z2 zone set has zones C, D, and E as its zone members. Although two zone sets are configured on the switch, none of them are in an active state. When you activate zone set Z1, it becomes an active zone set in the fabric.

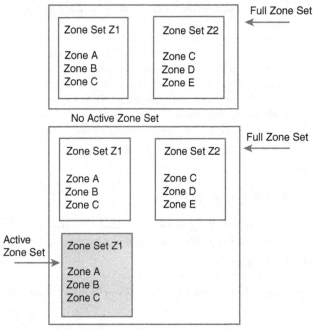

**Figure 8-34**  *Full and Active Zone Sets*

When zone D is added as a member of the currently active zone set Z1, as shown in Figure 8-35, it will not be part of the active zone set unless and until you activate zone set Z1 again.

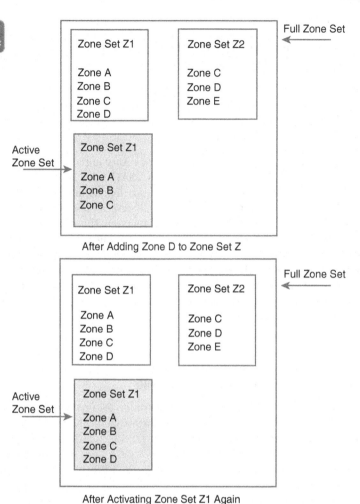

**Figure 8-35**  *Adding New Zone to Active Zone Sets*

You can distribute full zone sets using one of two methods: one-time distribution using the **zoneset distribute vsan** command at the EXEC mode level or full zone set distribution using the **zoneset distribute full vsan** command at the configuration mode level. The **zoneset distribute vsan** command only distributes the full zone set information; it does not save the information to the startup configuration. You must explicitly save the running configuration to the startup configuration.

One-time distribution distributes the full zone set information immediately. But it does not distribute the full zone set information along with the active zone set during the activation, deactivation, or merge process.

Full zone set distribution does not distribute the full zone set immediately. But it distributes the full zone set information along with the active zone set during activation, deactivation, and the merge processes.

## Autozone

The Autozone feature is a mechanism to automate zoning of devices. This feature can be used to reduce the administrative overhead of manually creating and updating the switch zone configuration each time a device is added to the SAN to a one-time command. An administrator has to configure the Autozone feature after the initial deployment and does not have to manually change or modify the zone configuration each time a new device is added to a fabric. The Autozone feature is intended for fabrics composed of a single fabric switch that has no more than 100 devices connected.

Initially, Autozone configures zoning that enables connectivity from every initiator to every target. The zones that are created are placed in a single zone set in VSAN 1 and activated. When in automatic mode, a Scheduler job is created to scan for newly logged-in devices every five minutes. New initiators are zoned with all the targets, and new targets are zoned with all the initiators. The new zones are then added to the active zone set. This process allows the switch to be administered with minimal effort by simply plugging in new devices and having automatic connectivity for the devices within minutes. The administrator can run Autozone manually if connectivity to the newly logged-in devices is required before the next scheduled scan. Autozone does not change the existing zones created either by Autozone or manually by an administrator. This prevents duplication of any existing zones by Autozone and allows an administrator to manually add specialized zones.

Autozone has two modes of operation:

- **Automatic mode:** The Autozone Scheduler job runs every five minutes, checking for changes in device logins, and updates the zone set accordingly.

- **Manual mode:** No Scheduler job is created. The administrator has to run the **autozone --update** command each time a new device is connected to a switch for the device to be added to the zoning configuration.

**NOTE**   Autozone works on single-switch fabrics. It works only for ports that are logged on to VSAN 1. If the administrator moves ports to other VSANs, Autozone does not move them back into VSAN 1 or zone them.

## Zone Merge

All Cisco SAN switches distribute active zone sets when new E port links come up or when a new zone set is activated in a VSAN. When two switches in a fabric are merged using a TE or E port, these TE and E ports may become isolated when the active zone set databases are different between the two switches or fabrics, as shown in Figure 8-36. When a TE port or an E port becomes isolated, you can recover that port from its isolated state using one of three options:

- Import the neighboring switch's active zone set database and replace the current active zone set.

- Export the current database to the neighboring switch.

- Manually resolve the conflict by editing the full zone set, activating the corrected zone set, and then bringing up the link.

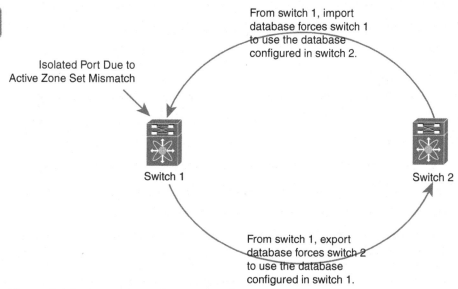

**Figure 8-36** *Importing and Exporting the Database*

On Cisco SAN switches, you cannot edit an active zone set. However, you can copy an active zone set to create a new zone set that you can edit. Also, you can back up the zone configuration to a workstation using TFTP. This zone backup file can then be used to restore the zone configuration on a switch. Restoring the zone configuration overwrites any existing zone configuration on a switch.

## Smart Zoning

Smart zoning implements hard zoning of large zones with fewer hardware resources than was previously required. The traditional zoning method allows each device in a zone to communicate with every other device in the zone, and the administrator is required to manage the individual zones. Smart zoning eliminates the need to create a single initiator to single target zones. By analyzing device-type information in the FCNS, the Cisco MDS NX-OS software can implement useful combinations at the hardware level, and the combinations that are not used are ignored. For example, initiator-target pairs are configured, but not initiator-initiator. The device is treated as unknown if during zone convert, the device is not logged in to the fabric, or when the zone is created, the initiator, target, or initiator and target are not specified.

The device-type information of each device in a smart zone is automatically populated from the Fibre Channel Name Server (FCNS) database as host, target, or both. This information allows more efficient utilization of switch hardware by identifying initiator-target pairs and configuring those only in hardware. In the event of a special situation, such as a disk controller that needs to communicate with another disk controller, the administrator can override smart zoning defaults to allow complete control.

After the zone set is converted to smart zoning, you need to activate the zone set. Smart zoning only supports PWWN, FCID, FCalias, and Device-alias zoning member configurations.

> **NOTE**    Smart zoning can be enabled at the VSAN level but can also be disabled at the zone level.

## Enhanced Zoning

There are two modes of zoning: basic (which is the default) and enhanced. You can enable enhanced zoning in a VSAN by using the **zone mode enhanced vsan** *vsan-id* command.

In enhanced zoning, modifications to the zone database are made within a session. A session is created at the time of the first successful configuration command. On creation of a session, a copy of the zone database is created. Any changes made within the session are performed on this copy of the zoning database. These changes in the copy zoning database are not applied to the effective zoning database until you commit the changes. When you apply the changes, the session is closed.

If the fabric is locked by another user, and for some reason the lock is not cleared, you can force the operation and close the session. You must have permission (role) to clear the lock in this switch and perform the operation on the switch from where the session was originally created. To release the session lock on the zoning database on the switches in a VSAN, use the **no zone commit vsan** command from the switch where the database was initially locked.

When two Fibre Channel (FC) switches that have already been configured with active zone sets and are not yet connected are brought together with an Extended ISL (EISL) link, the zone sets merge. In enhanced zoning, the merge method depends on the fabric-wide merge control setting:

■ **Restrict:** If the two databases are not identical, the ISLs between the switches are isolated.

■ **Allow:** The two databases are merged using the merge rules specified in Table 8-16.

**Table 8-16**    Database Zone Merge Status for **allow merge control** Setting

| Local Database | Adjacent Database | Merge Status | Results of the Merge |
|---|---|---|---|
| The databases contain zone sets with the same name but different zones, aliases, and attributes groups. | | Successful | The union of the local and adjacent databases. |
| The databases contain a zone, zone alias, or zone attribute group object with the same name but different members. | | Failed | ISLs are isolated. |
| Empty | Contains data | Successful | The adjacent database information populates the local database. |
| Contains data | Empty | Successful | The local database information populates the adjacent database. |

Table 8-17 lists the advantages of enhanced zoning.

**Table 8-17**  Advantages of Enhanced Zoning

| Basic Zoning | Enhanced Zoning | Enhanced Zoning Advantages |
|---|---|---|
| Administrators can make simultaneous configuration changes. Upon activation, one administrator can overwrite another administrator's changes. | Performs all configurations within a single configuration session. When you begin a session, the switch locks the entire fabric to implement the change. | One configuration session for the entire fabric to ensure consistency within the fabric. |
| If a zone is part of multiple zone sets, you create an instance of this zone in each zone set. | Zone set uses references to the zone as required once you define the zone. | Reduced payload size as the zone is referenced. The size is more significant with bigger databases. |
| The default zone policy is defined per switch. To ensure smooth fabric operation, all switches in the fabric must have the same default zone setting. | Enforces and exchanges the default zone setting throughout the fabric. | Fabric-wide policy enforcement to reduce troubleshooting time. |
| To retrieve the results of the activation per switch basis, the managing switch provides a combined status about the activation. It does not identify the failure switch. | Retrieves the activation results and the nature of the problem from each remote switch. | Enhanced error reporting to ease the troubleshooting process. |
| To distribute the zoning database, you must reactivate the same zone set. The reactivation may affect hardware changes for hard zoning on the local switch and on remote switches. | Implements changes to the zoning database and distributes it without reactivation. | Distribution of zone sets without activation to avoid hardware changes for hard zoning in the switches. |
| The Cisco-specific zone member types (symbolic node name, and other types) may be used by other non-Cisco switches. During a merge, the Cisco-specific types can be misunderstood by the non-Cisco switches. | Provides a vendor ID along with a vendor-specific type value to uniquely identify a member type. | Unique vendor type. |

Table 8-18 summarizes the NX-OS CLI commands that are related to zoning configuration and verification.

**Table 8-18** Summary of NX-OS CLI Commands for Zoning Configuration and Verification

| Command | Purpose |
|---|---|
| switch# **config terminal** | Enters configuration mode. |
| switch# **autozone --enable** | Enables Autozone to automatically create zones, add them to a zone set, and activate the zone set as needed every five minutes. |
| switch# **autozone --enableautosave** | Enables automatic saving of the Autozone configuration. |
| switch# **autozone --update** | Enables execution of Autozone in manual mode. |
| switch# **autozone --disable** | Prevents new devices from being zoned automatically and retaining the existing zone configuration. |
| switch# **autozone --delete** | Deletes all the zones and the zone set created by Autozone on VSAN 1. |
| switch(config)# **zone name Zone1 vsan 3** | Configures a zone called Zone1 for the VSAN called vsan 3. |
| switch(config-zone)# **member** *type value* | Configures a member for the specified zone (Zone1) based on the type (pWWN, fabric pWWN, FCID, fcalias, domain ID, IPv4 address, IPv6 address, or interface) and value specified. |
| switch(config)# **zoneset name Zoneset1 vsan 3** | Configures a zone set called Zoneset1. |
| switch(config-zoneset)# **member Zone1** | Adds Zone1 as a member of the specified zone set (Zoneset1). |
| switch(config)# **(no) zoneset activate name Zoneset1 vsan 3** | Activates the specified zone set. If full zone set distribution is configured for a VSAN, the zone set activation also distributes the full zoning database to the other switches in the fabric. If enhanced zoning is configured for a VSAN, the zone set activation is held until the **zone commit vsan** *vsan-id* command is enabled. The **show zone pending-diff vsan** *vsan-id* displays the pending changes. |
| switch(config)# **(no) zone default-zone permit vsan 1** | Permits traffic flow to default zone members. |
| switch(config)# **fcalias name AliasSample vsan 3** | Configures an alias name (AliasSample). |
| switch(config-fcalias)# **member** *type value* | Configures a member for the specified fcalias (AliasSample) based on the type (pWWN, fabric pWWN, FC ID, domain ID, IPv4 address, IPv6 address, or interface) and value specified. |
| switch(config)# **zoneset distribute full vsan 3** | Enables sending a full zone set along with an active zone set. |
| switch# **zoneset distribute vsan 3** | Enables a one-time distribution of the full zone set. |
| switch# **zoneset import interface fc1/3 vsan 2** | Imports the zone set from the adjacent switch connected through the fc1/3 interface for VSAN 2. |

| Command | Purpose |
|---|---|
| switch# **zoneset export vsan 5** | Exports the zone set to the adjacent switch connected through VSAN 5. |
| switch# **zone copy active-zoneset full-zoneset vsan 2** | Makes a copy of the active zone set in VSAN 2 to the full zone set. |
| switch(config)# **(no) zone smart-zoning enable vsan 1** | Enables smart zoning on a VSAN. |
| switch(config)# **(no) zone mode enhanced vsan 3** | Enables enhanced zoning in the specified VSAN. |
| switch(config)# **(no) zone commit vsan 3** | Applies the changes to the enhanced zone database and closes the session. The **no** form of the command releases the session lock on the zoning database. |
| switch(config)# **(no) zone merge-control restrict vsan 3** | Configures a restricted merge control setting for this VSAN. |
| switch# **autozone –show** | Displays the Autozone status, the existing zone and zone set configuration created by Autozone, and the zoning configuration that Autozone would create for unzoned devices that are currently logged in to a switch. |
| switch# **show zone** | Displays zone information for all VSANs. |
| switch(config)# **show zone status vsan 3** | Displays the status of the zone for the specified VSAN. |
| switch# **show zoneset active** | Displays the active zone set configuration. |
| switch# **show zoneset vsan 1** | Displays configured zone set information for the specified VSAN. |

Example 8-5 shows how to configure and verify zoning on the sample topology shown in Figure 8-37. This example shows configuration only for MDS-9148S-1; the configuration for MDS9148S-2 is similar.

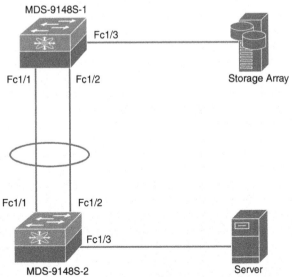

**Figure 8-37**  *Sample Topology for Zoning Creation and Verification*

**Example 8-5**   *Zoning Creation and Verification on MDS-9148S Switch*

```
! Checking current mode of Zoning.
MDS-9148S-1(config)# show zone status vsan 11
VSAN: 11 default-zone: deny distribute: active only Interop: default
    mode: basic merge-control: allow
    session:  none
    hard-zoning: enabled broadcast: unsupported
    smart-zoning: disabled
    rscn-format: fabric-address
    activation overwrite control: disabled
Default zone:
    qos: none broadcast: unsupported ronly: unsupported
Full Zoning Database :
    DB size: 124 bytes
    Zonesets:  0 Zones: 0 Aliases: 0
Active Zoning Database :
    Database Not Available
Current Total Zone DB Usage: 124 / 2097152 bytes (0 % used)
Pending (Session) DB size:
    Full DB Copy size: n/a
    Active DB Copy size: n/a
SFC size: 124 / 2097152 bytes (0 % used)
Status:

! Checking flogi database on MDS-9148S-1 for fabric login of Storage Array
MDS-9148S-1(config)# show flogi database
--------------------------------------------------------------------------------
INTERFACE    VSAN   FCID       PORT NAME            NODE NAME
--------------------------------------------------------------------------------
fc1/3        11     0x010000   50:0a:09:83:81:aa:aa:01   50:0a:09:80:81:aa:aa:01

Total number of flogi = 1.

! Checking fcns database on MDS-9148S-1 to verify fabric login of both Storage Array
and Server
MDS-9148S-1(config)# show fcns database

VSAN 11:
--------------------------------------------------------------------------------
FCID       TYPE   PWWN                    (VENDOR)   FC4-TYPE:FEATURE
--------------------------------------------------------------------------------
0x010000   N      50:0a:09:83:81:aa:aa:01  (NetApp)   scsi-fcp:target
0x470000   N      20:00:00:25:b5:10:70:10  (Cisco)    scsi-fcp:init fc-gs
```

```
Total number of entries = 2

! Configuring Zone with name ZONE_VSAN11 for vsan 11.
MDS-9148S-1(config)# zone name ZONE_VSAN11 vsan 1
! Checking the various methods by which zone member can be configured.
MDS-9148S-1(config-zone)# member ?
  device-alias        Add device-alias member to zone
  domain-id           Add member based on domain-id,port-number
  fcalias             Add fcalias to zone
  fcid                Add FCID member to zone
  fwwn                Add Fabric Port WWN member to zone
  interface           Add member based on interface
  ip-address          Add IP address member to zone
  pwwn                Add Port WWN member to zone
  symbolic-nodename   Add Symbolic Node Name member to zone


! Inserting FC target into Zone ZONE_VSAN11
MDS-9148S-1(config-zone)# member pwwn 50:0a:09:83:81:aa:aa:01
! Inserting FC initiator into Zone ZONE_VSAN11
MDS-9148S-1(config-zone)# member pwwn 20:00:00:25:b5:10:70:10
! Creating Zoneset with name ZONESET_VSAN11 for VSAN 11 with member ZONE_VSAN11
MDS-9148S-1(config-zone)# zoneset name ZONESET_VSAN11 vsan 11
MDS-9148S-1(config-zoneset)# member ZONE_VSAN11
! Verifying configured zone
MDS-9148S-1(config-zoneset)# show zone vsan 11
zone name ZONE_VSAN11 vsan 11

    pwwn 50:0a:09:83:81:aa:aa:01

    pwwn 20:00:00:25:b5:10:70:10
! Verifying active zone. Since we have not activated the zoneset, there is no active
zone in the fabric.
MDS-9148S-1(config-zoneset)# show zone active vsan 11
Zone not present


! Enabling full zoneset distribution on each activation of zoneset
MDS-9148S-1(config-zoneset)# zoneset distribute full vsan 11


! Activating Zoneset
MDS-9148S-1(config)# zoneset activate name ZONESET_VSAN11 vsan 11
Zoneset activation initiated. check zone status


! Verifying active zone after zoneset activation
MDS-9148S-1(config)# show zone active vsan 11
zone name ZONE_VSAN11 vsan 11
```

8

```
* fcid 0x010000 [pwwn 50:0a:09:83:81:aa:aa:01]

* fcid 0x470000 [pwwn 20:00:00:25:b5:10:70:10]


! Changing zone mode from basic to enhanced
MDS-9148S-1(config)# zone mode enhanced vsan 11
WARNING: This command would distribute the zoning database of this switch throughout
the fabric. Do you want to continue? (y/n) [n] y
Set zoning mode command initiated. Check zone status


! Verifying zone mode.
MDS-9148S-1(config)# show zone status vsan 11
VSAN: 11 default-zone: deny distribute: full Interop: default
    mode: enhanced merge-control: allow
    session: none
    hard-zoning: enabled broadcast: unsupported
    smart-zoning: disabled
    rscn-format: fabric-address
    activation overwrite control: disabled
Default zone:
    qos: none broadcast: unsupported ronly: unsupported
Full Zoning Database :
    DB size: 280 bytes
    Zonesets: 1 Zones: 1 Aliases: 0 Attribute-groups: 1
Active Zoning Database :
    DB Size: 88 bytes
    Name: ZONESET_VSAN11 Zonesets: 1 Zones: 1
Current Total Zone DB Usage: 368 / 2097152 bytes (0 % used)
Pending (Session) DB size:
    Full DB Copy size: 0 bytes
    Active DB Copy size: 0 bytes
SFC size: 0 / 2097152 bytes (0 % used)
Status: Set zoning mode complete at 04:21:45 UTC Jul 23 2019
MDS-9148S-1(config)#
```

## Device Alias

Cisco SAN switches support Distributed Device Alias Services (device aliases) on a per-VSAN basis and on a fabric-wide basis. Device alias distribution allows you to move host bus adapters (HBAs) between VSANs without manually reentering alias names.

While the port WWN (pWWN) of a device has to be specified to configure different features (zoning, QoS, and port security) in a SAN switch, you must assign the correct device name each time you configure these features. An incorrect device name may cause unexpected results. You can avoid this if you define a user-friendly name for a pWWN and use this name in all of the configuration commands, as required. These user-friendly names are called *device aliases*.

## Device Alias Features

Device aliases have the following features:

- The device alias information is independent of the VSAN configuration.

- The device alias configuration and distribution are independent of the zone server and the zone server database.

- You can import legacy zone alias configurations without losing data.

- The device alias application uses the Cisco Fabric Services (CFS) infrastructure to enable efficient database management and distribution. Device aliases use the coordinated distribution mode and the fabric-wide distribution scope.

- Device aliases support basic and enhanced modes.

- Device aliases used to configure zones, IVR zones, or port security features are displayed automatically with their respective pWWNs in the **show** command output.

Device aliases can be assigned only to pWWNs. There must be a one-to-one relationship between the pWWN and the device alias that maps to it.

A device alias name is restricted to 64 alphanumeric characters and may include one or more of the following characters:

- *a* to *z* and *A* to *Z* (Device alias names must begin with an alphabetic character—*a* to *z* or *A* to *Z*.)

- 1 to 9

- - (hyphen) and _ (underscore)

- $ (dollar sign) and ^ (up caret)

## Device Alias Modes

A device alias supports the following two modes:

- **Basic mode:** When operating in basic mode, which is the default, the device alias is immediately expanded to a pWWN. This operation continues until the mode is changed to enhanced. In basic mode, when device aliases are changed to point to a new HBA, for example, that change is not reflected in the zone server. Users must remove the previous HBA's pWWN, add the new HBA's pWWN, and then reactivate the zone set.

- **Enhanced mode:** When operating in enhanced mode, applications accept a device alias name in its native format. Instead of expanding the device alias to a pWWN, the device alias name is stored in the configuration and distributed in its native device alias format. So, applications such as zone server, PSM, or DPVM can automatically keep track of the device alias membership changes and enforce them accordingly. The primary benefit of operating in enhanced mode is that you have a single point of change.

Whenever you change device alias modes, the change is distributed to other switches in the network only if device alias distribution is enabled, or on. Otherwise, the mode change takes place only on the local switch.

If two fabrics running in different device alias modes are joined together, the device alias merge fails. There is no automatic conversion to one mode or the other during the merge process. In this situation, you must select one mode over the other. Before changing from enhanced to basic mode, you must first explicitly remove all native device alias-based configurations from both local and remote switches or replace all device alias-based configuration members with the corresponding pWWN. If you remove a device alias from the device alias database, all applications automatically stop enforcing the corresponding device alias.

Renaming the device alias not only changes the device alias name in the device alias database but also replaces the corresponding device alias configuration in all of the applications. When a new device alias is added to the device alias database, and the application configuration is present on that device alias, it automatically takes effect.

### Device Alias Distribution

By default, device alias distribution is enabled. The device alias feature uses CFS to distribute the modifications to all switches in a fabric.

If device alias distribution is disabled, database changes are not distributed to the switches in the fabric. The same changes would have to be performed manually on all switches in the fabric to keep the device alias database up-to-date. Database changes immediately take effect, so there would also not be any pending database and commit or abort operations. If you have not committed the changes and you disable distribution, a commit task will fail. But if you modify the device alias configuration, you will need to commit or discard the changes because the fabric remains locked during this period. Device alias database changes are validated with the applications. If any of the applications cannot accept the device alias database changes, those changes will be rejected; this applies to device alias database changes resulting from either a commit or merge operation.

The device alias feature uses two databases to accept and implement device alias configurations.

- **Effective database:** This is the database currently used by the fabric.

- **Pending database:** Your subsequent device alias configuration changes are stored in the pending database.

When you perform any device alias configuration task (regardless of which device alias task), the fabric is automatically locked for the device alias feature. After you lock the fabric, no other user can make any configuration changes to this feature. A copy of the effective database is obtained and used as the pending database. Subsequent modifications are made to the pending database. The pending database remains in use until you commit the modifications to the pending database or discard (abort) the changes to the pending database.

If you commit the changes made to the pending database, the following events occur:

- The pending database content overwrites the effective database content.

- The pending database is distributed to the switches in the fabric, and the effective database on those switches is overwritten with the new changes.

- The pending database is emptied of its contents.

- The fabric lock is released for this feature.

If you discard the changes made to the pending database, the following events occur:

- The effective database contents remain unaffected.

- The pending database is emptied of its contents.

- The fabric lock is released for this feature.

You can use locking operations (clear, commit, abort) only when device alias distribution is enabled. If you have performed a device alias task and have forgotten to release the lock by either committing or discarding the changes, an administrator can release the lock from any switch in the fabric. If the administrator performs this task, your changes to the pending database are discarded and the fabric lock is released. The changes are available only in the volatile directory and may be discarded if the switch is restarted.

If a switch with an existing device alias database is being added to an existing fabric, conflicts might arise if the same device alias name is used but with different pWWNs in the two fabrics, or if the same pWWN is used but with different device alias names. To resolve the merge status, use the **show device-alias merge status** and **show cfs merge status name device-alias** commands to verify the status of the merge. Use the **show device-alias merge conflicts** command to display the device alias and pWWNs that are causing a merge failure.

## Zone Aliases (FC Aliases) Versus Device Aliases

Legacy zone aliases, also called FC aliases, which are used in zoning configuration, are different from device aliases. Table 8-19 compares the configuration differences between zone-based alias configuration and device alias configuration.

**Table 8-19**  Comparison Between Zone Aliases and Device Aliases

| Zone-Based Aliases | Device Aliases |
|---|---|
| Aliases are limited to the specified VSAN. | You can define device aliases without specifying the VSAN number. You can also use the same definition in one or more VSANs without any restrictions. |
| Zone aliases are part of the zoning configuration. The alias mapping cannot be used to configure other features. | Device aliases can be used with any feature that uses the pWWN. |
| You can use any zone member type to specify the end devices. | Only pWWNs are supported along with new device aliases such as IP addresses. |
| Configuration is contained within the Zone Server database and is not available to other features. | Device aliases are not restricted to zoning. Device alias configuration is available to the FCNS, zone, fcping, traceroute, and IVR applications. |
| FC aliases are not displayed with the associated WWNs in the show command output like **show zoneset active, show flogi database**, and **show fcns database**. | Device aliases are displayed with the associated WWNs in the show command outputs like **show zoneset active, show flogi database**, and **show fcns database**. |

8

| Zone-Based Aliases | Device Aliases |
|---|---|
| FC aliases are not distributed as part of active zone set and are distributed only as part of the full zone database as per the FC standards. | Device aliases are distributed through CFS. |

You can import legacy zone alias configurations to use the device alias feature without losing data, if each zone alias has only one member with type pWWN, and the name and definition of the zone alias are not the same as any existing device alias name.

Table 8-20 summarizes the NX-OS CLI commands that are related to device alias configuration and verification.

**Table 8-20**    Summary of NX-OS CLI Commands for Device Alias Configuration and Verification

| Command | Purpose |
|---|---|
| switch# **config terminal** | Enters configuration mode. |
| switch(config)# **device-alias database** | Enters the pending database configuration submode. |
| switch(config-device-alias-db)# **device-alias name Device1 pwwn 21:01:00:e0:8b:2e:80:93** | Specifies a device name (Device1) for the device that is identified by its pWWN. Starts writing to the pending database and simultaneously locks the fabric because this is the first-issued device alias configuration command. |
| switch(config-device-alias-db)# **no device-alias name Device1** | Removes the device name (Device1) for the device that is identified by its pWWN. |
| switch(config-device-alias-db)# **device-alias rename Device1 Device2** | Renames an existing device alias (Device1) with a new name (Device2). |
| switch(config)# **(no) device-alias distribute** | Enables the distribution (default). |
| switch(config)# **device-alias commit** | Commits the changes made to the currently active session. |
| switch(config)# **device-alias abort** | Discards the currently active session. |
| switch(config)# **clear device-alias session** | Clears the device alias fabric lock session. |
| switch(config)# **clear device-alias database** | Clears all database content. |
| switch(config)# **device-alias import fcalias vsan 3** | Imports the fcalias information for the specified VSAN. |
| switch# **show device-alias name Device1** | Displays the device alias configuration for Device1. |
| switch# **show device-alias status** | Displays configuration information for the device-alias service, including whether fabric distribution is enabled, the number of device aliases in the database, lock information, and the database mode (Basic or Enhanced). |
| switch# **show device-alias session status** | Returns the status of the last CFS command, such as **clear**, **commit**, or **terminate**. The results of the last-used CFS command and reason fields help identify the reason for the failure. |

| Command | Purpose |
|---------|---------|
| switch# **show cfs merge status name device-alias** | Displays information about the status of the CFS merge for the device alias database. |
| switch# **show device-alias database** | Displays the entire device alias database. |
| switch# **show device-alias database pending** | Displays all configured device aliases from the pending database. |
| switch# **show device-alias internal validation info** | Displays information about the status of the validation process (part of a commit or merge). |
| switch# **show device-alias merge conflicts** | Displays the device alias names or pWWNs causing a merge failure. |
| switch# **show device-alias merge status** | Displays the result of the device alias merge operation and the reason for the result. |

Example 8-6 shows how to configure and verify the device alias on the sample topology shown in Figure 8-38.

MDS-9148S                                    Storage Array

**Figure 8-38**  *Sample Topology for Device Alias Configuration and Verification*

**Example 8-6**  *Device Alias Creation and Verification on MDS-9148S Switch*

```
! Setting the Device Alias mode to enhanced and committing the changes.
MDS-9148S(config)# device-alias mode enhanced
MDS-9148S(config)# device-alias commit
WARNING: Device-alias DB is empty in this switch. Initiating a commit from this
switch will clear [wipe out] Device-alias DB across all the switches in the fabric,
losing Device-alias full DB config permanently. Do you want to continue? (y/n) [n] y


! Verifying the flogi database to configure Device Alias for Storage pWWN.
MDS-9148S(config)# show flogi database
--------------------------------------------------------------------------------
INTERFACE     VSAN    FCID      PORT NAME                NODE NAME
--------------------------------------------------------------------------------
fc1/3         11      0x010000  50:0a:09:82:80:aa:aa:01 50:0a:09:80:80:aa:aa:01

Total number of flogi = 1.


! Configuring device alias for Storage pwwn as STORAGE
MDS-9148S(config)# device-alias database
MDS-9148S(config-device-alias-db)# device-alias name STORAGE pwwn
50:0a:09:82:80:aa:aa:01
```

8

```
! Since we have not committed the changes, the device alias will show up only as
pending configuration and not in device-alias active database
MDS-9148S(config-device-alias-db)# show device-alias database
There are no entries in the database
MDS-9148S(config-device-alias-db)# show device-alias pending
device-alias name STORAGE pwwn 50:0a:09:82:80:aa:aa:01


Total number of entries = 1


! Once we commit the changes, STORAGE device alias is populated in both device-alias
database and flogi database.
MDS-9148S(config-device-alias-db)# device-alias commit
MDS-9148S(config)# show device-alias database
device-alias name STORAGE pwwn 50:0a:09:82:80:aa:aa:01


Total number of entries = 1
MDS-9148S(config)# show flogi database
--------------------------------------------------------------------------------

INTERFACE    VSAN    FCID    PORT NAME               NODE NAME
--------------------------------------------------------------------------------

fc1/3        11      0x010000  50:0a:09:82:80:aa:aa:01 50:0a:09:80:80:aa:aa:01
                                        [STORAGE]


Total number of flogi = 1.


! Verifying Device Alias mode.


MDS-9148S(config)# show device-alias status
Fabric Distribution : Enabled
Database:- Device Aliases 1 Mode: Enhanced
        Checksum: 0xcf406e8ea08acd95f3de38e8541a311
MDS-9148S(config)#
```

## NPIV and NPV

In fabric mode, the NX-OS switches provide the standard Fibre Channel switching capability and features. In this mode, each switch that joins a SAN is assigned a domain ID. Each SAN (or VSAN) supports a maximum of 239 domain IDs, so the SAN has a limit of 239 switches. In a SAN topology with a large number of edge switches, the SAN may need to grow beyond this limit. N port virtualization (NPV) alleviates the domain ID limit by sharing the domain ID of the core switch among multiple edge switches.

The NPV core switch, with the N port identifier virtualization (NPIV) feature enabled, provides a means to assign multiple FCIDs to a single N port. This feature allows multiple applications on the N port to use different identifiers and allows access control, zoning, and port security to be implemented at the application level.

An NPV edge switch relays all traffic from server-side ports to the core switch. The core switch provides F port functionality (such as login and port security) and all the Fibre Channel switching capabilities. The edge switch shares the domain ID of the core switch. The edge switch appears as a Fibre Channel host to the core switch and as a regular Fibre Channel switch to its connected devices.

Figure 8-39 shows an interface-level view of an NPV configuration.

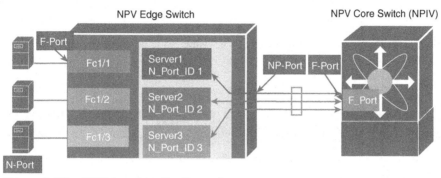

**Figure 8-39** *NPV Interface Configuration*

In NPV mode, a subset of fabric mode CLI commands and functionality is supported. For example, commands related to fabric login and name server registration are not required on the edge switch because these functions are provided in the core switch. To display the fabric login and name server registration databases, you must enter the **show flogi database** and **show fcns database** commands on the core switch.

All interfaces from the edge switch to the core switch are configured as proxy N ports (NP ports). An NP uplink is a connection from an NP port on the edge switch to an F port on the core switch. When an NP uplink is established, the edge switch sends a fabric login message (FLOGI) to the core switch, and then (if the FLOGI is successful) it registers itself with the name server on the core switch. Subsequent FLOGIs from end devices connected to this NP uplink are converted to fabric discovery messages (FDISCs). In Cisco Nexus devices, NP uplink interfaces must be native Fibre Channel interfaces.

When an NP port becomes operational, the switch first logs itself in to the core switch by sending an FLOGI request (using the port WWN of the NP port). After completing the FLOGI request, the switch registers itself with the fabric name server on the core switch (using the symbolic port name of the NP port and the IP address of the edge switch).

Server interfaces are F ports on the edge switch that connect to the servers. A server interface may support multiple end devices by enabling the N port identifier virtualization (NPIV) feature on the core switch. NPIV provides a means to assign multiple FCIDs to a single N port, which allows the server to assign unique FCIDs to different applications. To use the NPIV feature, you have to enable the NPIV feature. Server interfaces are automatically distributed among the NP uplinks to the core switch. All of the end devices connected to a server interface are mapped to the same NP uplink. In Cisco Nexus devices, server interfaces can be physical or virtual Fibre Channel interfaces.

**NOTE**  Zoning is not enforced at the edge switch (rather, it is enforced on the core switch). Multiple devices attached to an edge switch log in through the same F port on the core, so they cannot be separated into different zones.

When you enable NPV on an edge switch using the **npv enable** command, the system configuration is erased and the switch reboots. After you enable NPV, you should configure the NP uplink interfaces and the server interfaces using the **switchport mode NP** and **switchport mode F** commands, respectively. You cannot configure NPV mode on a per-interface basis. NPV mode applies to the entire switch.

On NPV switches, by default, trunk mode is disabled. You can configure trunk mode as on (enabled), off (disabled), or auto (automatic). The trunk mode configuration at the two ends of an ISL, between two switches, determine the trunking state of the link and the port modes at both ends as listed in Table 8-21.

**Table 8-21**    Trunk Mode Status Between NPV and NPIV Switches

| Port Type | NPV Core Switch (NPIV) | NPV Edge Switch | Trunking State | Link Mode |
|---|---|---|---|---|
| F and NP ports | On | Auto or On | Trunking | TF-TNP link |
| | Auto | On | Trunking | TF-TNP link |
| | Off | Auto, on, or off | No Trunking | F-NP link |

Table 8-22 summarizes the NX-OS CLI commands that are related to NPV and NPIV configuration and verification.

**Table 8-22**    Summary of NX-OS CLI Commands for NPV and NPIV Configuration and Verification

| Command | Purpose |
|---|---|
| switch# **config terminal** | Enters configuration mode. |
| switch(config)# **(no) feature npiv** | Enables NPIV for all VSANs on the switch. |
| switch(config)# **vsan database** | Configures the port VSANs for the F port on the NPIV core switch. |
| switch(config)# **interface fc 2/1** | Configures the NPIV core switch port as an F port. |
| switch(config-if)# **switchport mode F** | Configures the interface as an F port. |
| switch(config)# **(no) feature npv** | Enables NPV mode on an NPV device. The module or switch is rebooted, and when it comes back up, it is in NPV mode. |
| switch(config)# **vsan database** | Configures the port VSANs for the NP port on the NPV device. |
| switch(config)# **interface fc 1/1** | On the NPV device, selects the interfaces that will be connected to the aggregator switch and configures them as NP ports. |
| switch(config-if)# **switchport mode NP** | Configures the interface as an NP port. |

| Command | Purpose |
|---|---|
| switch# **show fcns database** | Displays all the NPV devices in all the VSANs that the aggregator switch belongs to. |
| switch# **show fcns database detail** | Displays additional details such as IP addresses, switch names, and interface names about the NPV devices. |
| switch# **show npv flogi-table** | Displays a list of the NPV devices that are logged in, along with VSANs, source information, pWWNs, and FCIDs. |
| switch# **show npv status** | Displays the status of the different servers and external interfaces. |

Example 8-7 shows how to configure and verify NPV and NPIV on the sample topology shown in Figure 8-40.

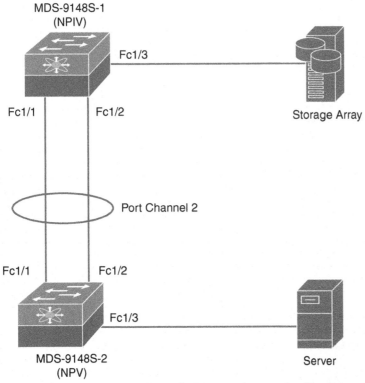

**Figure 8-40**  *Sample Topology for NPV and NPIV Configuration and Verification*

**Example 8-7**  *NPV and NPIV Creation and Verification on MDS-9148S Switches*

```
MDS-9148S-2: (NPV)
=================
! Enabling Feature NPV.
MDS-9148S-2(config)# feature npv
Verify that boot variables are set and the changes are saved. Changing to npv mode
erases the current configuration and reboots the switch in npv mode. Do you want to
continue? (y/n):y


! Configuring fc 1/1 and fc 1/2 interfaces as part of Port Channel 2.
MDS-9148S-2(config)# int fc 1/1, fc 1/2
MDS-9148S-2(config-if)# channel-group 2 force
fc1/1 fc1/2 added to port-channel 2 and disabled
please do the same operation on the switch at the other end of the port-channel,
then do "no shutdown" at both ends to bring it up
MDS-9148S-2(config-if)# no shut


! Configuring channel mode of Port Channel 2 as active mode and interface as NP port
which indirectly configures fc 1/1 and fc 1/2 as NP port.
MDS-9148S-2(config-if)# int port-channel 2
MDS-9148S-2(config-if)# switchport mode np
MDS-9148S-2(config-if)# channel mode active
MDS-9148S-2(config-if)# no shut


! Checking status of Port Channel 2 for port mode and active interfaces
MDS-9148S-2# show interface port-channel 2
port-channel 2 is up
    Hardware is Fibre Channel
    Port WWN is 24:02:8c:60:4f:2d:de:c0
    Admin port mode is NP, trunk mode is off
    snmp link state traps are enabled
    Port mode is NP
    Port vsan is 11
    Speed is 16 Gbps
    1 minute input rate 0 bits/sec, 0 bytes/sec, 0 frames/sec
    1 minute output rate 0 bits/sec, 0 bytes/sec, 0 frames/sec
      111 frames input, 10496 bytes
        0 discards, 0 errors
        0 CRC,  0 unknown class
        0 too long, 0 too short
      90 frames output, 8732 bytes
        0 discards, 0 errors
      0 input OLS, 0 LRR, 0 NOS, 0 loop inits
      6 output OLS, 4 LRR, 0 NOS, 0 loop inits
```

```
      last clearing of "show interface" counters never
      Member[1] : fc1/1
      Member[2] : fc1/2
      Interface last changed at Mon Jul 22 05:35:04 2019


! Checking npv status for External interface and Server Interfaces status
MDS-9148S-2# show npv status


npiv is disabled

disruptive load balancing is disabled

External Interfaces:
====================
  Interface: port-channel 2, State: Up
        VSAN:    11, State: Up, FCID: 0x010100


  Number of External Interfaces: 1

Server Interfaces:
==================
<span epub:type="pagebreak" id="page_414"/>
Interface: fc1/3, VSAN:    11, State: Up


  Number of Server Interfaces: 1

! Checking npv flogi-table to confirm the flogi for directly connected Server


MDS-9148S-2# show npv flogi-table
--------------------------------------------------------------------------------------
SERVER                                                                        EXTERNAL
INTERFACE  VSAN   FCID    PORT NAME            NODE NAME            INTERFACE
--------------------------------------------------------------------------------------
fc1/3      11     0x010101  20:00:00:25:b5:10:70:10  21:00:00:25:b5:10:70:10      po2

Total number of flogi = 1.


MDS-9148S-1: (NPIV)
==================

! Enabling feature npiv.
MDS-9148S-1(config)# feature npiv
```

```
! Configuring interfaces fc 1/1 and fc 1/2 as part of port channel 2
MDS-9148S-1(config)# int fc 1/1, fc 1/2
MDS-9148S-1(config-if)# channel-group 2 force
MDS-9148S-1(config-if)# no shutdown


! Configuring port channel 2 interface as F port with channel mode active
MDS-9148S-1(config-if)# int port-channel 2
MDS-9148S-1(config-if)# switchport mode F
MDS-9148S-1(config-if)# channel mode active
MDS-9148S-1(config-if)# no shut


! Verifying status of port channel 2 for port mode and active interfaces
MDS-9148S-1(config)# show interface port-channel 2
port-channel2 is up
    Hardware is Fibre Channel
    Port WWN is 24:02:00:de:fb:25:b8:80
    Admin port mode is F, trunk mode is on
    snmp link state traps are enabled
    Port mode is F
    Port vsan is 11
    Speed is 16 Gbps
    Logical type is core
    5 minutes input rate 160 bits/sec,20 bytes/sec, 0 frames/sec
    5 minutes output rate 192 bits/sec,24 bytes/sec, 0 frames/sec
      1022 frames input,90236 bytes
        0 discards,0 errors
        0 invalid CRC/FCS,0 unknown class
        0 too long,0 too short
      1117 frames output,96364 bytes
        0 discards,0 errors
      42 input OLS,17  LRR,0 NOS,0 loop inits
      50 output OLS,44 LRR, 30 NOS, 0 loop inits
    Member[1] : fc1/1     [up] *
    Member[2] : fc1/2     [up]
  Interface last changed at Tue Jul 23 06:49:24 2019


! Verifying npiv status
MDS-9148S-1# show npiv status
NPIV is enabled


! Verifying flogi and fcns table to see if MDS-9148S-2 has logged in to NPIV router.
The second entry in both the following tables belong to MDS-9148S-2 switch.
```

```
MDS-9148S-1(config)# show flogi database
-----------------------------------------------------------------------------
INTERFACE        VSAN    FCID        PORT NAME              NODE NAME
-----------------------------------------------------------------------------
fc1/3            11      0x010000    50:0a:09:83:81:aa:aa:01   50:0a:09:80:81:aa:aa:01
port-channel2    11      0x010100    24:02:8c:60:4f:2d:de:c0   20:0b:8c:60:4f:2d:de:c1
port-channel2    11      0x010101    20:00:00:25:b5:10:70:10   21:00:00:25:b5:10:70:10

Total number of flogi = 3.


MDS-9148S-1(config)# show fcns database

VSAN 11:
-----------------------------------------------------------------------------
FCID          TYPE    PWWN                       (VENDOR)    FC4-TYPE:FEATURE
-----------------------------------------------------------------------------
0x010000      N       50:0a:09:83:81:aa:aa:01    (NetApp)    scsi-fcp:target
0x010100      N       24:02:8c:60:4f:2d:de:c0    (Cisco)     npv
0x010101      N       20:00:00:25:b5:10:70:10    (Cisco)     scsi-fcp:init fc-gs

Total number of entries = 3
```

## Exam Preparation Tasks

As mentioned in the Introduction, you have a couple of choices for exam preparation: the exercises here, Chapter 21, "Final Preparation," and the exam simulation questions in the Pearson Test Prep software online.

## Review All Key Topics

Review the most important topics in the chapter, noted with the key topic icon in the outer margin of the page. Table 8-23 lists a reference to these key topics and the page numbers on which each is found.

**Table 8-23**   Key Topics for Chapter 8

| Key Topic Element | Description | Page |
|---|---|---|
| Section | Fibre Channel Port Types | 368 |
| Table 8-9 | Reserved FCIDs | 372 |
| Figure 8-14 | Flow Control Using Buffer-to-Buffer Credits | 373 |
| List | Fabric initialization process | 373 |
| List | Principal switch selection | 374 |
| Figure 8-16 | Switched Fabric Initialization | 375 |
| Figure 8-17 | Configuration Process Using the Preferred Option | 377 |
| List | Device registration | 378 |
| Paragraph | FLOGI database and FCNS database | 378 |

| Key Topic Element | Description | Page |
|---|---|---|
| List | CFS features | 381 |
| Table 8-10 | Summary of NX-OS CLI Commands for CFS Configuration and Verification | 385 |
| List | VSAN features | 386 |
| List | VSAN attributes | 387 |
| Table 8-11 | Trunk Mode Status Between Switches | 390 |
| Table 8-12 | Summary of NX-OS CLI Commands for VSAN Configuration and Verification | 392 |
| List | Valid port channel combinations | 397 |
| List | Port channel load balancing | 398 |
| Table 8-13 | Channel Group Configuration Differences | 400 |
| Table 8-14 | Summary of NX-OS CLI Commands for Port Channel Configuration and Verification | 400 |
| List | Zoning features | 404 |
| Paragraph | Soft zoning and hard zoning | 407 |
| Figure 8-34 | Full and Active Zone Sets | 408 |
| Figure 8-35 | Adding New Zone to Active Zone Sets | 409 |
| Figure 8-36 | Importing and Exporting the Database | 411 |
| Table 8-18 | Summary of NX-OS CLI Commands for Zoning Configuration and Verification | 414 |
| List | Device alias effective and pending database | 420 |
| Table 8-20 | Summary of NX-OS CLI Commands for Device Alias Configuration and Verification | 422 |
| Paragraph | NPV and NPIV | 424 |
| Table 8-22 | Summary of NX-OS CLI Commands for NPV and NPIV Configuration and Verification | 426 |

## Memory Tables

Print a copy of Appendix C, "Memory Tables" (found on the companion website), or at least the section for this chapter, and complete the tables and lists from memory. Appendix D, "Memory Tables Answer Key," also on the companion website, includes completed tables and lists to check your work.

## Define Key Terms

Define the following key terms from this chapter, and check your answers in the Glossary.

Cisco Fabric Services (CFS), Dynamic Port VSAN Membership (DPVM), Exchange Peer Parameter (EPP), F port channel trunk, fabric login (FLOGI), fan-in ratio, fan-out ratio, host bus adapter (HBA), inter-switch links (ISLs), N port identifier virtualization (NPIV), N port virtualization (NPV), port login (PLOGI), port World Wide Name (pWWN), process login (PRLI), switch World Wide Name (sWWN), virtual storage-area network (VSAN), World Wide Node Name (WWNN), World Wide Port Name (WWPN), zoning

## References

Relevant Cisco Live Presentations: https://www.ciscolive.com/

Cisco MDS 9000 Series Interfaces Configuration Guide, Release 8.x: https://www.cisco.com/c/en/us/td/docs/switches/datacenter/mds9000/sw/8_x/config/interfaces/cisco_mds9000_interfaces_config_guide_8x.html

Gustavo A. A. Santana, *Data Center Virtualization Fundamentals* (Indianapolis: Cisco Press, 2014).

Cisco MDS 9000 Series Fabric Configuration Guide, Release 8.x: https://www.cisco.com/c/en/us/td/docs/switches/datacenter/mds9000/sw/8_x/config/fabric/cisco_mds9000_fabric_config_guide_8x.html

Cisco MDS 9000 Series System Management Configuration Guide, Release 8.x: https://www.cisco.com/c/en/us/td/docs/switches/datacenter/mds9000/sw/8_x/config/system-management/cisco_mds9000_system_management_config_guide_8x.html

Fibre Channel Fabric Address Manager MIB: https://tools.ietf.org/html/draft-desanti-fc-domain-manager-02

Relevant Cisco Community Pages: https://community.cisco.com

Cisco Nexus 5600 Series NX-OS SAN Switching Configuration Guide, Release 7.x: https://www.cisco.com/c/en/us/td/docs/switches/datacenter/nexus5600/sw/san_switching/7x/b_5600_SAN_Switching_Config_7x.html

Cisco Nexus 9000 Series NX-OS SAN Switching Configuration Guide, Release 10.3(x): https://www.cisco.com/c/en/us/td/docs/dcn/nx-os/nexus9000/103x/configuration/san-switching/cisco-nexus-9000-series-nx-os-san-switching-configuration-guide-release-103x.html

8

# CHAPTER 9

# Implement FCoE Unified Fabric

Simply defined, I/O consolidation is the ability to carry different types of traffic with different traffic characteristics and handling requirements over the same physical media. The most difficult challenge of I/O consolidation is to satisfy the requirements of different traffic classes within a single network. Because Fibre Channel is the dominant storage protocol in the data center, any viable I/O consolidation solution for storage must allow for transparent integration of the Fibre Channel model. Fibre Channel over Ethernet (FCoE) meets this requirement in part by encapsulating each Fibre Channel frame inside an Ethernet frame. The goal of FCoE is to provide I/O consolidation over Ethernet, allowing Fibre Channel and Ethernet networks to share a single, integrated infrastructure, thereby reducing network complexities in the data center. FCoE consolidates both storage-area networks (SANs) and Ethernet traffic onto one converged network adapter (CNA), eliminating the need for using separate host bus adapters (HBAs) and network interface cards (NICs).

## This chapter covers the following key topics:

**FCoE Overview:** This section discusses Ethernet enhancements including PFC, ETS, and DCBX, along with FCoE frame format, virtual Fibre Channel (VFC), FCoE elements, and port types. Later in the section, we discuss FCoE addressing and forwarding, FCoE Initialization Protocol (FIP), and the benefits of FCoE.

**FCoE Topology Options:** This section discusses various FCoE topology options, including single-hop and multi-hop topologies.

**FCoE Implementations:** This section discusses FCoE configuration on Cisco Nexus 7000 Series, 5000 Series, 9000 Series, FCoE over FEX, and FCoE NPV configuration and verification.

## "Do I Know This Already?" Quiz

The "Do I Know This Already?" quiz enables you to assess whether you should read this entire chapter thoroughly or jump to the "Exam Preparation Tasks" section. If you are in doubt about your answers to these questions or your own assessment of your knowledge of the topics, read the entire chapter. Table 9-1 lists the major headings in this chapter and their corresponding "Do I Know This Already?" quiz questions. You can find the answers in Appendix A, "Answers to the 'Do I Know This Already?' Quizzes."

**Table 9-1** "Do I Know This Already?" Section-to-Question Mapping

| Foundation Topics Section | Questions |
|---|---|
| FCoE Overview | 1–4 |
| FCoE Topology Options | 5 |
| FCoE Implementations | 6–7 |

1. Which of the following statements is TRUE regarding Enhanced Transmission Selection (ETS)?

   a. ETS automatically discovers and negotiates DCB capabilities between the NIC and switch.

   b. ETS manages end-to-end congestion.

   c. ETS enables multiple traffic types to share the same link.

   d. ETS manages bandwidth between different types of traffic on the same link.

2. What is the Ethertype of FCoE and FIP frames?

   a. FCoE = 0x8906; FIP = 0x8914

   b. FCoE = 0x8906; FIP = 0x8916

   c. FCoE = 0x8914; FIP = 0x8906

   d. FCoE = 0x8916; FIP = 0x8906

3. Which action is performed in the FCF discovery phase in the FIP process?

   a. CNA broadcasts a solicitation to find FCF to log in to. Broadcasts go out on the FCoE VLAN.

   b. CNA begins normal FC data commands using Ethertype 0x8906.

   c. CNA performs fabric login using FLOGI or FLOGI with NPV FDISC.

   d. An end device (CNA) broadcasts a request for FCoE VLAN. The request occurs on the native VLAN.

4. Which of the following statements is CORRECT regarding the virtual Fibre Channel interface? (Choose three answers.)

   a. Each virtual Fibre Channel interface must be bound to an FCoE-enabled Ethernet interface.

   b. Each virtual Fibre Channel interface can be associated with multiple VSANs.

   c. Any VSAN with associated virtual Fibre Channel interfaces must be mapped to a dedicated FCoE-enabled VLAN.

   d. The Fibre Channel portion of FCoE is configured with the help of a virtual Fibre Channel (vFC) interface.

5. Which of the following is not a FCoE single-hop topology?

   a. FCoE direct-attached topology

   b. FCoE remote-attached topology

   c. FCoE FEX topology

   d. FCoE remote-attached FEX topology

**6.** Which of the following commands disables LAN traffic on an FCoE link?

   **a.** `switch(config)# interface Ethernet 2/1`
   `switch(config-if)# shutdown lan`

   **b.** `switch(config)# interface Ethernet 2/1`
   `switch(config-if)# lan shutdown`

   **c.** `switch(config)# interface Ethernet 2/1`
   `switch(config-if)# shutdown switchport`

   **d.** `switch(config)# interface Ethernet 2/1`
   `switch(config-if)# switchport shutdown`

**7.** Which of the following statements are CORRECT regarding FCoE NPV? (Choose three answers.)

   **a.** FCoE NPV implements FIP snooping as an extension to the NPV function while retaining the traffic-engineering, vsan-management, administration, and trouble-shooting aspects of NPV.

   **b.** Connectivity from an FCoE NPV bridge to the FCF is supported only over point-to-multipoint links.

   **c.** From a control plane perspective, FCoE NPV performs proxy functions toward the FCF and the hosts in order to load-balance logins from the hosts evenly across the available FCF uplink ports.

   **d.** An FCoE NPV bridge is VSAN-aware and capable of assigning VSANs to the hosts.

## Foundation Topics

## FCoE Overview

A typical data center has two separate networks: one for Ethernet and one for Fibre Channel storage. These networks are physically and logically separated from each other, as shown on the left in Figure 9-1. Here, a SAN leverages dual fabric with multipathing failover initiated by the client, and a LAN leverages single fully meshed fabric with higher levels of component redundancy. Both networks have a redundant pair of switches at each layer, which results in increased CAPEX and OPEX as well as reduced business functionality.

The consolidation of I/O traffic in the data center brings the Fibre Channel and Ethernet networks into a single integrated infrastructure, as shown on the right in Figure 9-1. This results in decreased CAPEX and OPEX. An access switch in the consolidated topology is Fibre Channel over Ethernet Forwarder (FCF). Dual fabrics are still deployed for redundancy.

Servers used to have three types of NICs: Ethernet NICs for LAN traffic, management traffic, backup traffic, and so on; host channel adapter (HCA) for Inter-Process Communication (IPC) traffic; and HBAs for Fibre Channel/storage traffic, as shown in Figure 9-2. With the development of FCoE, converged network adapters (CNAs) were introduced; they can handle all the previous three types of traffic over single high-speed 10G links, resulting in a lesser number of interfaces for servers.

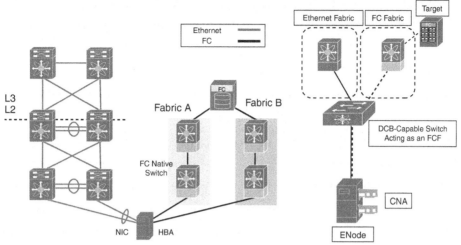

**Figure 9-1**  *Traditional LAN and SAN Infrastructure (Left); Converged LAN and SAN Infrastructure (Right)*

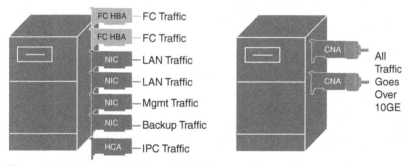

**Figure 9-2**  *Converged Network Adapter*

Fibre Channel over Ethernet (FCoE) allows Fibre Channel traffic to be encapsulated over a physical Ethernet link. FCoE frames use a unique Ethertype so that FCoE traffic and standard Ethernet traffic can be carried on the same link.

Classic Ethernet is a best-effort protocol; in the event of congestion, Ethernet will discard packets, relying on higher-level protocols to provide retransmission and other reliability mechanisms. Fibre Channel traffic requires a lossless transport layer; because it is a data storage protocol, it is unacceptable to lose a single data packet. Native Fibre Channel implements a lossless service at the transport layer using a buffer-to-buffer credit system.

For FCoE traffic, the Ethernet link must provide a lossless service. Ethernet links on Cisco Nexus devices provide two mechanisms to ensure lossless transport for FCoE traffic: link-level flow control (LLFC) and priority-based flow control (PFC). For FCoE, PFC is recommended.

IEEE 802.3x link-level flow control allows a congested receiver to signal the far end to pause the data transmission for a short period of time. The pause functionality is applied to all the traffic on the link.

9

The priority flow control feature applies pause functionality to specific classes of traffic on the Ethernet link. For example, PFC can provide lossless service for the FCoE traffic and best-effort service for the standard Ethernet traffic. PFC can provide different levels of service to specific classes of Ethernet traffic. We discuss these enhancements to Ethernet protocol in detail in the next section.

## Ethernet Enhancements

The T11 organization's FC-BB-5 standard defines FCoE and also defines running FC over other media types. The IEEE 802.1 organization facilitates FCoE by defining enhancements to Ethernet. These enhancements fall under the DCB umbrella, specifically, three enabling standards for Ethernet to support FCoE:

1. Priority-based flow control (PFC)
2. Enhanced Transmission Selection (ETS)
3. Data Center Bridging Exchange (DCBX)

Figure 9-3 identifies the T11 and IEEE standards.

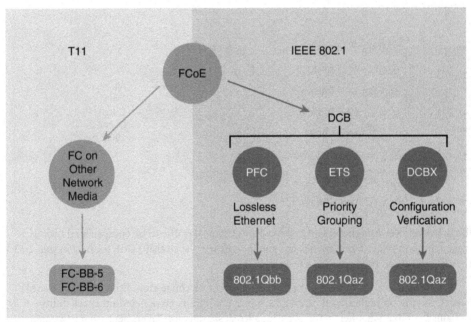

**Figure 9-3**   *T11 and IEEE 802.1 FCoE Standards*

### Priority-Based Flow Control (PFC)

PFC is defined in IEEE 802.1Qbb. Link sharing is critical to I/O consolidation. For link sharing to succeed, large bursts from one traffic type must not affect other traffic types, large queues of traffic from one traffic type must not starve other traffic types' resources, and optimization for one traffic type must not create large latency for small messages of other traffic types. The Ethernet pause mechanism can be used to control the effects of one traffic type over another.

PFC creates eight separate virtual links, each belonging to a CoS priority value, on the physical link and allows any of these links to be paused and restarted independently. This approach can enable the network to create a no-drop class of service for an individual virtual link that can coexist with other traffic types on the same interface. In native FC, the network is designed not to drop traffic (lossless). PFC can enable Ethernet to support FC by providing a lossless fabric. Figure 9-4 shows the eight virtual data lanes on a single wire that make up PFC. One virtual lane of data (for example, FC) can be paused while the remaining lanes continue to transmit.

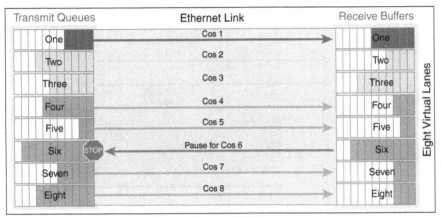

**Figure 9-4** *Priority-Based Flow Control (PFC)*

The Ethernet frames that are sent by the switch to the adapter may include the IEEE 802.1Q tag. This tag includes a field for the class of service (CoS) value used by the priority-based flow control (PFC). The IEEE 802.1Q tag also includes a virtual LAN (VLAN) field.

### Enhanced Transmission Selection (ETS)

ETS is defined in IEEE 802.1Qaz. PFC can create eight distinct virtual link types on a physical link, and it can be advantageous to have different traffic classes defined within each virtual link. Traffic within the same PFC IEEE 802.1p class can be grouped together yet treated differently within each group. ETS provides prioritized processing based on bandwidth allocation, low latency, or best effort, resulting in per-group traffic class allocation.

Extending the virtual link concept, the network interface card (NIC) provides virtual interface queues: one for each traffic class. Each virtual interface queue is accountable for managing its allotted bandwidth for its traffic group but has flexibility within the group to dynamically manage the traffic. For example, virtual link 3 for the IP class of traffic may have a high-priority designation and a best effort within that same class, with the virtual link 3 class sharing a percentage of the overall link with other traffic classes. ETS allows differentiation among traffic of the same priority class, thus creating a priority group. The capability to apply differentiated treatment to different traffic within the same priority class is enabled by implementing ETS.

Figure 9-5 shows three classes of traffic sharing the same 10-Gbps ETS-enabled connection with the following predefined percentages:

- Server Cluster Traffic: 30 percent

- Storage Traffic: 30 percent

- LAN Traffic: 40 percent

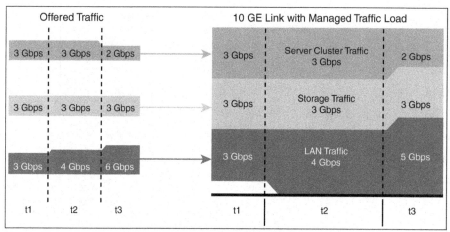

**Figure 9-5**  *Enhanced Transmission Selection (ETS)*

In Figure 9-5

- During interval T1, Server Cluster Traffic, Storage Traffic, and LAN Traffic each use 3-Gbps bandwidth, hence not saturating the 10-Gbps link.

- During interval T2, when the offered traffic reaches the 10-Gbps limit of the connection, ETS is activated to distribute the traffic with the predefined percentages (30, 30, and 40 for Server Cluster Traffic, Storage Traffic, and LAN Traffic, respectively).

- During interval T3, Server Cluster Traffic only requires 2 Gbps of traffic, thus enabling another class of traffic (LAN Traffic) to share the unused bandwidth.

## Data Center Bridging Exchange (DCBX)

DCBX is defined in IEEE 802.1Qaz. DCBX is a discovery and capability exchange protocol that IEEE DCBs use to discover peers and exchange configuration information between DCB-compliant bridges (see Figure 9-6). The following parameters can be exchanged with DCBX:

- Priority groups in ETS

- PFC

- Congestion notification

- Applications

- Logical link-down

- Network interface virtualization

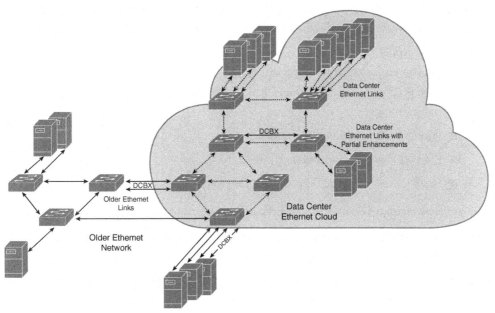

**Figure 9-6**   *Data Center Bridging Exchange*

DCBX allows network devices to advertise their identities and capabilities over the network. It enables end devices to pick up proper configuration from the network and for switches to verify proper configuration.

The DCBX protocol is an extension of the Link Layer Discovery Protocol (LLDP). DCBX endpoints exchange request and acknowledgment messages. For flexibility, parameters are coded in a type-length-value (TLV) format. DCBX runs on the physical Ethernet link between the Cisco Nexus device and the CNA. By default, DCBX is enabled on Ethernet interfaces. When an Ethernet interface is brought up, the switch automatically starts to communicate with the CNA. During the normal operation of FCoE between the switch and the CNA, DCBX provides link-error detection. DCBX is also used to negotiate capabilities between the switch and the CNA and to send configuration values to the CNA.

The CNAs that are connected to a Cisco Nexus device are programmed to accept the configuration values sent by the switch, allowing the switch to distribute configuration values to all attached CNAs. This reduces the possibility of configuration errors and simplifies CNA administration.

Data Center Bridging Exchange Protocol (DCBXP) is enabled by default when you enable LLDP. When LLDP is enabled, DCBXP can be enabled or disabled using the **[no] lldp tlv-select dcbxp** command. DCBXP is disabled on ports where LLDP transmit or receive is disabled.

You can enable LLDP on each FCoE switch by issuing the **feature lldp** command. On the Cisco Nexus 7000, LLDP is enabled when the FCoE feature set is installed (in the storage VDC). You cannot disable LLDP while the FCoE feature is installed.

9

The switch and CNA exchange capability information and configuration values. Cisco Nexus devices support the following capabilities:

- FCoE: If the CNA supports FCoE capability, the switch sends the IEEE 802.1p CoS value to be used with FCoE packets.

- PFC: If the adapter supports PFC, the switch sends the IEEE 802.1p CoS values to be enabled with PFC.

- Priority group type, length, and values (TLV).

- Ethernet logical link up and down signal.

- FCoE logical link up and down signal for pre-FIP CNAs.

The following rules determine whether the negotiation results in a capability being enabled:

- If a capability and its configuration values match between the switch and the CNA, the feature is enabled.

- If a capability matches, but the configuration values do not match, the following occurs:

  - If the CNA is configured to accept the switch configuration value, the capability is enabled using the switch value.

  - If the CNA is not configured to accept the switch configuration value, the capability remains disabled.

  - If the CNA does not support a DCBX capability, that capability remains disabled.

  - If the CNA does not implement DCBX, all capabilities remain disabled.

## FCoE Frame Format

FCoE is implemented by encapsulating an FC frame in an Ethernet packet with the dedicated Ethertypes 0x8906(FCoE) and 0x8914(FIP). An FC frame, encapsulated inside the FCoE header, consists of 24 bytes of headers and up to 2112 bytes of data. The encapsulated FC frame has all the standard headers, which allow it to be passed to the storage network without further modification.

Figure 9-7 details the FC encapsulation into Ethernet frames.

In the FCoE header with Ethertype 0x8906, the first 48 bits consists of the destination MAC address, and the next 48 bits consist of the source MAC address. The 32-bit IEEE 802.1Q tag defines the VLAN. FCoE has its own Ethertype as designated by the next 16 bits followed by the 4-bit version field. The next 100 bits are reserved; they pad the FCoE frame to the IEEE 802.3 minimum packet length of 64 bytes and are followed by the 8-bit start-of-frame. The actual Fibre Channel frame is followed by the start-of-frame. The 8-bit end-of-frame delimiter is followed by 24 reserved bits. Lastly, the frame ends with 32 bits dedicated to the FCS function that provides error detection functionality for the Ethernet frame.

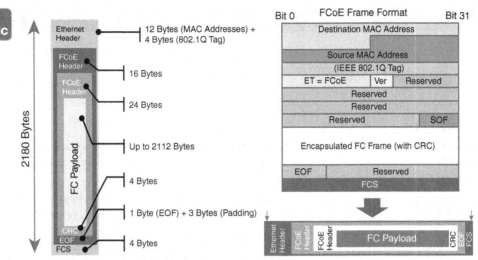

**Figure 9-7**   *FCoE Frame Format*

FIP is encapsulated in an Ethernet packet with a dedicated Ethertype: 0x8914. The packet has a 4-bit version field, as shown in Figure 9-8. Along with the source and destination MAC addresses, the FIP packet also contains an FIP operation code and an FIP operation subcode. Table 9-2 describes the FIP operation codes and subcodes.

**Figure 9-8**   *FIP Frame Format*

**Table 9-2**   FIP Operation Codes and Subcodes

| FIP Operation Code | FIP Subcode | FIP Operation |
|---|---|---|
| 0x0001 | 0x01 | Discovery Solicitation |
| | 0x02 | Discovery Advertisement |
| 0x0002 | 0x01 | Virtual Link Instantiation Request |
| | 0x02 | Virtual Link Instantiation Reply |

| FIP Operation Code | FIP Subcode | FIP Operation |
|---|---|---|
| 0x0003 | 0x01 | FIP Keepalive |
| | 0x02 | FIP Clear Virtual Links |
| 0x0004 | 0x01 | FIP VLAN Request |
| | 0x02 | FIP VLAN Notification |

## Virtual Fibre Channel (VFC)

In a native FC storage-area network (SAN), physical FC switches and end devices (such as hosts with host bus adapters [HBAs]) are connected with fiber cable. The FC protocol runs natively on the SAN, and both the switches and end devices communicate through it.

With FCoE, that FC SAN is overlaid onto a physical Ethernet network, creating a VFC SAN running over Ethernet. In the previous section, we discussed the enhancements to Ethernet needed to facilitate this. In addition to these enhancements, a new process is needed on Cisco Nexus switches to support FC. This process is known as FCoE Manager or fcoe_mgr. The fcoe_mgr process controls all the FCoE components and configuration. The fcoe_mgr process is started by installing the FCoE feature set. Virtual SANs (VSANs) are then associated with designated FCoE VLANs and bind virtual Fibre Channel (vFC) interfaces to physical Ethernet interfaces. FCoE configuration is discussed later in this chapter.

With FCoE, HBAs are replaced with CNAs. CNAs enable converged I/O by supporting both FC and classical Ethernet data traffic on the same Ethernet wire. CNAs, along with proper drivers on the host end device, support FCoE.

Figure 9-9 is an illustration of a VSAN over Ethernet.

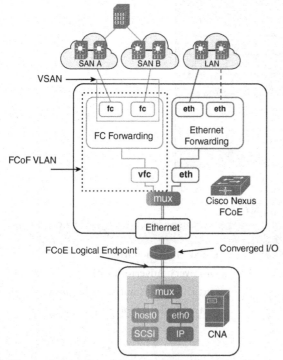

**Figure 9-9**  *Virtual FC over Ethernet*

The Fibre Channel portion of FCoE is configured with the help of a virtual Fibre Channel (vFC) interface. In FCoE, there are only physical Ethernet interfaces. You don't have any physical Fibre Channel interfaces, so you actually need to create a logical instance of those Fibre Channel interfaces. To do that, you create a virtual Fibre Channel interface and bind it to both a VSAN that it's associated with and a physical Ethernet interface on a switch, so that when that interface comes up, the vFC comes up. Logical Fibre Channel features can be configured on virtual Fibre Channel interfaces.

Following are some guidelines that you must follow when creating a virtual Fibre Channel interface:

- Each virtual Fibre Channel interface must be bound to an FCoE-enabled Ethernet interface. FCoE is supported on 10-Gigabit Ethernet interfaces.

- Each virtual Fibre Channel interface is associated with only one VSAN.

- Any VSAN with associated virtual Fibre Channel interfaces must be mapped to a dedicated FCoE-enabled VLAN.

- FCoE is not supported on private VLANs.

The Ethernet interface to which you bind the virtual Fibre Channel interface must be a trunk port. The FCoE VLAN that corresponds to the virtual Fibre Channel's VSAN must be in the allowed VLAN list and must not be configured as the native VLAN of the trunk port. Also, the Ethernet interface must be configured as portfast using the **spanning-tree port type edge trunk** command.

Example 9-1 shows how to configure the VLAN on a physical Ethernet address, create virtual Fibre Channel interface 6, bind vFC 6 to the physical Ethernet interface, enable associated VLAN 600, and map VLAN 600 to VSAN 6.

**Example 9-1**  *Virtual Fibre Channel Interface Configuration*

```
switch# configure terminal
switch(config)# interface ethernet 1/2
switch(config-if)# switchport mode trunk
switch(config-if)# switchport trunk allowed vlan 1,600
switch(config)# interface vfc 6
switch(config-if)# bind interface ethernet 1/2
switch(config-if)# exit
switch(config)# vlan 600
switch(config-vlan)# fcoe vsan 6
switch(config-vlan)# exit
switch(config)# vsan database
switch(config-vsan)# vsan 6 interface vfc 6
```

## FCoE Elements and Port Types

The FCoE standard defines two types of endpoints: FCoE Ethernet Nodes (ENodes) and Fibre Channel Forwarders (FCFs). Figure 9-10 shows a simplified version of an ENode. An ENode (also called a CNA adapter) is a Fibre Channel HBA implemented within an Ethernet

NIC. The data-forwarding component that handles FC frame encapsulation/decapsulation is called an FCoE Link EndPoint (LEP). An FCoE LEP is a virtual FC interface mapped onto the physical Ethernet interface. An FCoE controller is the functional entity that performs the FIP and instantiates VN_Port/FCoE_LEP pairs. We discuss the FCoE Initialization Protocol (FIP) in the next section.

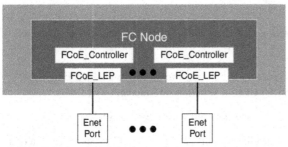

**Figure 9-10**    *Simplified ENode*

**NOTE**    Only second-generation CNAs support the FCoE control plane protocol called FIP. FIP support is required to build certain types of topologies in FCoE; for example, use of FEXs in the FCoE topology requires FIP support.

Figure 9-11 shows a simplified version of the FCoE switch. FCF is the forwarding entity inside an FCoE switch. An FCF switch is one that actually contains both a Fibre Channel switch and an Ethernet switch—for example, the Cisco Nexus 5000 Series switch. A Cisco MDS switch with FCoE module installed can act as an FCF switch also. The FCF processes the Fibre Channel logins and consumes one domain ID. FCF performs the encapsulation and decapsulation of the FCoE frames and forwards the FCoE traffic based on Fibre Channel information that the frames contain.

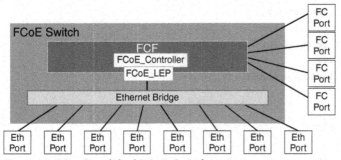

**Figure 9-11**    *Simplified FCoE Switch*

ENodes present virtual FC interfaces in the form of VN_Ports, which can establish FCoE virtual links with FCFs' VF_Ports, as shown in Figure 9-12. FCFs present virtual FC interfaces in the form of VF_Ports or VE_Ports; a VF_Port establishes FCoE virtual links with a CNA's VN_Port or FCoE NPV's VNP_Port, and VE_Ports enable FCFs to establish FCoE virtual links with other FCFs. These interface types have their equivalents in native Fibre Channel's N_Ports, F_Ports, and E_Ports. A virtual fabric (VF) port in an FCoE network acts as a fabric port that connects to a peripheral device (host or disk) operating as a VN_port. A VF_port can be attached to only one VN_port. A virtual expansion (VE) port acts as an expansion port in an FCoE network and can connect to multiple FCoE switches together in the network.

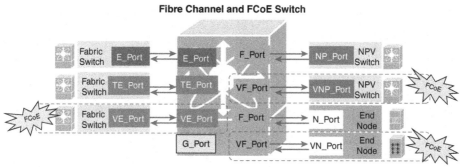

**Figure 9-12**  *FC and FCoE Switch Port Types*

Ethernet devices communicate using a MAC address, whereas Fibre Channel devices communicate using FCIDs. Because FCoE switches support both Ethernet and Fibre Channel, it needs to able to translate between them. Because Ethernet uses a 48-bit MAC address and Fibre Channel uses a 24-bit FCID, a direct translation between them is not possible.

## FCoE Addressing and Forwarding

FCoE uses a Fabric Provided MAC Address (FPMA) for SAN traffic. The ENode still gets a 24-bit FCID. FPMA is built by concatenating a 24-bit FCoE MAC address prefix (FC-MAP), ranging from 0x0E-FC-00 to 0x0E-FC-FF, to the 24-bit FCID, as shown in Figure 9-13. Being able to build a unique MAC address for the ENode directly from its FCID saves the switch from having to maintain a table that associates FCID and MAC addresses.

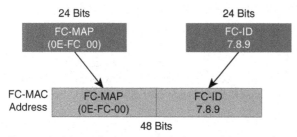

**Figure 9-13**  *Fabric-Provided MAC Address (FPMA)*

The FC-MAP range was introduced so that different values can be assigned to different SANs. For example, SAN A would be associated with 0x0EFC00 and SAN B with 0x0EFC01. This additional configuration ensures the uniqueness of the produced FPMA in the whole network. FC-MAPs are different for different SANs, FCIDs are uniquely assigned within a SAN, and the resulting FC-MAP and FCID are unique across the different SANs in the entire network.

Figure 9-14 shows a Fibre Channel frame traversing native Fibre Channel SAN and FCoE SAN. For simplicity, only the header information is displayed in the figure. The FCoE forwarding in Figure 9-14 can be summarized in the following steps:

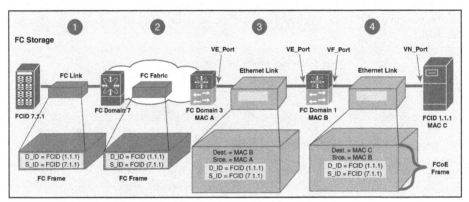

**Figure 9-14**   *FCoE Forwarding*

1.  The Fibre Channel N_port on the storage array sends out the FC frame to the VN port on the CNA adapter with Source FCID (S_ID) as 7.1.1 and Destination FCID (D_ID) as 1.1.1. The frame is switched by the first Fibre Channel Switch.

2.  Because the destination ID (D_ID) is not in FC domain 7 of the receiving switch, the switch forwards the frame to the port associated with the shortest path to the destination, using the FSPF algorithm. The Fibre Channel switch with domain ID 7 sends the frame to the FCoE switch with domain ID 3.

3.  The FCoE switch with domain 3 receives the frame. Because the destination ID (D_ID) is not in the FC domain 3 of the receiving switch, the switch forwards the frame to the port associated with the shortest path to the destination, using the FSPF algorithm. In this case, the frame will be transmitted to the FCoE-enabled Ethernet fabric. The FC frame is encapsulated inside an Ethernet frame with source MAC address (MAC A) of VE_port of switch with FC domain 3 and destination MAC address (MAC B) of VE_port of switch with FC domain 1.

4.  When the frame arrives at the FCoE switch with the FC domain 1, the frame is decapsulated, and the switch determines that the FC frame destination is within its domain. The FC frame is reencapsulated with a source MAC address of MAC B and a destination MAC address of MAC C. The frame is then transmitted out to the appropriate port where MAC C and FCID 1.1.1 are connected.

5.  When the HBA adapter with MAC C receives the frame, it decapsulates the frame and accepts the FC frame with FCID 1.1.1

## FCoE Initialization Protocol (FIP)

FCoE Initialization Protocol (FIP) is the FCoE control protocol responsible for establishing and maintaining Fibre Channel virtual links between pairs of FCoE devices (ENodes or FCFs). During the virtual link establishment phase, FIP first discovers FCoE VLANs and remote virtual FC interfaces; then it performs virtual link initialization functions (fabric login [FLOGI] and fabric discovery [FDISC], or exchange link parameters [ELP]) similar to their native Fibre Channel equivalents. After the virtual link is established, Fibre Channel payloads can be exchanged on the virtual link, and FIP remains in the background to perform virtual link maintenance functions; it continuously verifies reachability between the two virtual FC interfaces on the Ethernet network, and it offers primitives to delete the virtual link in response to administrative actions to that effect.

FIP aims to establish virtual FC links between VN_Ports and VF_Ports (ENode to FCF), as well as between pairs of VE_Ports (FCF to FCF), because these are the only legal combinations supported by native Fibre Channel fabrics. This section focuses on FIP in the context of virtual FC links between VN_Ports and VF_Ports.

Cisco NX-OS supports the T11-compliant FIP on Cisco Nexus devices. FIP is used to perform device discovery, initialization, and link maintenance. FIP performs the following protocol steps:

- **FIP VLAN discovery:** FIP discovers the FCoE VLAN that will be used by all other FIP protocols and the FCoE encapsulation for Fibre Channel payloads on the established virtual link. FIP VLAN discovery occurs in the native VLAN used by the initiator or target to exchange Ethernet traffic. The FIP VLAN discovery protocol is the only FIP protocol running on the native VLAN; all other FIP protocols run on the discovered FCoE VLANs.

- **FIP discovery:** When an FCoE device is connected to the fabric, it sends out a Discovery Solicitation message. A Fibre Channel Forwarder (FCF) or a switch responds to the message with a Solicited Advertisement that provides an FCF MAC address to use for subsequent logins.

- **FCoE virtual link instantiation:** FIP defines the encapsulation of FLOGI, fabric discovery (FDISC), logout (LOGO), and exchange link parameter (ELP) frames, along with the corresponding reply frames. The FCoE devices use these messages to perform a fabric login.

- **FCoE virtual link maintenance:** FIP periodically sends maintenance messages between the switch and the CNA to ensure the connection is still valid. This is referred to as the FCoE Keepalive (FKA).

Figure 9-15 shows a typical FIP protocol exchange resulting in the establishment of a virtual link between an ENode's VN_Port and an FCF's VF_Port.

The CNA initiates an FIP VLAN request, broadcasting to destination MAC 01:10:18:01:00:02. This well-known MAC address is referred to as the ALL-FCF-MACs address, meaning FCoE-enabled switches will recognize and respond to it. Keep in mind that FIP uses Ethertype 0x8914. In this step, the CNA requests the FCoE VLAN. The VLAN request from the host should be received on the native VLAN. The native VLAN cannot be an FCoE VLAN.

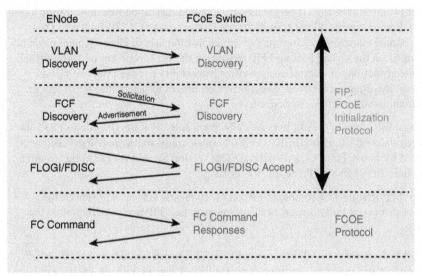

**Figure 9-15**  *FCoE Initialization Protocol (FIP)*

The CNA next performs an FIP discovery by looking for an FCF switch to log in to. The CNA broadcasts again to the All-FCF-MACs address. This request, however, is transmitted on the FCoE VLAN that was learned from the previous request. In this discovery, the CNA provides information about itself, such as the maximum FCoE frame size it supports, its World Wide Name (WWN), and that it supports the Fabric Provided MAC Address (FPMA).

The switch advertises its capabilities. The advertisement contains the virtual fabric ID (VSAN), the switch FC MAP ID, and the FC Keepalive (FKA) period. The total frame size in the advertisement equals the maximum FCoE frame size the CNA sent in its discovery. The switch pads the Advertisement frame to ensure it matches what the CNA expects, and this will confirm the network path indeed supports full FC frame sizes (encapsulated in Ethernet).

Now that the CNA has a valid FCF that will support fabric logins, it initiates the FLOGI. In the screen image shown in Figure 9-15, the Ethertype is still 0x8914 (FIP). The rest of the frame contains standard FC FLOGI information.

The switch accepts the CNA's FLOGI. This is the last step for the FIP VFC instantiation process and Ethertype 0x8914. All communication after this FLOGI Accept will be Ethertype 0x8906, which is the FCoE's data plane.

Table 9-3 summarizes the FIP process.

**Table 9-3**   FIP Virtual Instantiation Summary

| FIP Step | Action | Response |
|---|---|---|
| VLAN discovery | An end device (CNA) broadcasts a request for FCoE VLAN. The request occurs on the native VLAN. | A switch responds with the FCoE VLAN. |
| FCF discovery | A CNA broadcasts a solicitation to find the FCF to log in to. Broadcasts go out on the FCoE VLAN. | A switch responds with an advertisement. |

| FIP Step | Action | Response |
|----------|--------|----------|
| FLOGI/FDISC | A CNA performs fabric login using FLOGI or FLOGI with NPV FDISC for NPV setup. | A switch accepts the FLOGI/FDISC. |
| FC commands | A CNA begins normal FC data commands using Ethertype 0x8906. | A switch forwards encapsulated FCoE frames. |

### Benefits of FCoE

I/O consolidation in the fabric using FCoE provides several benefits. The benefits are as follows:

- Reduction in the number of adapters and network infrastructure devices

- Reduction in the number of cables:

    - Allows economical blend of inexpensive copper and longer-link optical technologies

    - Reduces cable installation expenses

    - Significantly reduces the number of long cables

    - Can increase server density if server deployment is impeded by cable bulk or airflow concerns

    - Reduces the possibility of air dams in the data center

    - Reduces cable maintenance and provisioning concerns in the data center

- Reduction in the amount of power used

- Reduction in space used due to switch equipment rack occupancy

- Reduction in server height due to fewer add-in card slot requirements if servers are I/O bound

- Redeployment of power and space savings to provisioning of additional servers, extending the life of the data center

- Interoperation with existing SANs; management of SANs remains constant

- No Stateful Gateway requirement; simply maps FC traffic onto lossless Ethernet

## FCoE Topology Options

FCoE supported topologies can be broadly classified into two groups:

- FCoE single-hop topology

- FCoE multi-hop topology

### FCoE Single-Hop Topology

Three single-hop solutions are possible when FCoE is deployed using Cisco Nexus switches:

- **FCoE direct-attached topology:** The host is directly connected to the first-hop converged access switch.

- **FCoE FEX topology:** A FEX is deployed between the server and the first hop converged access switch.

- **FCoE remote-attached topology:** A server is connected to a non-FCF switch that acts as an FCoE passthrough.

### FCoE Direct-Attached Topology

In the topology shown in Figure 9-16, a CNA is directly attached to the FCF, and FCoE extends from the CNA to the FCF and then is broken out to Native FC and Ethernet. Trunking is not required on the host driver because all FCoE frames are tagged by the CNA. A VLAN can be dedicated for every virtual fabric in the SAN. FIP discovers the FCoE VLAN and signals it to the hosts. Because FIP uses native VLAN, you should not use it for FCoE VLANs. FCoE VLANs are mostly pruned on pure Ethernet links. If you are using MST, generally three instances are defined: one for Ethernet VLAN and one for each SAN fabric VLAN.

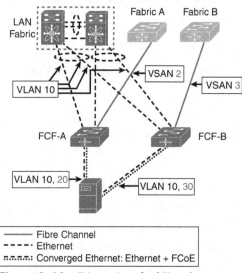

**Figure 9-16**   *Direct-Attached Topology*

Figure 9-16 shows a host connected to two FCFs (A and B). Three logical topologies in the figure are independent of each other: the first one for native Ethernet LAN using VLAN 10, the second one for Fabric A using VSAN 2, and the third and final one for Fabric B using VSAN 3. VSAN 2 is carried over VLAN 20, and VSAN 3 is carried over VLAN 30. The converged Ethernet between the host and the FCFs provides transport for both native Ethernet and Fibre Channel traffic.

The host can be connected to FCFs using vPC for improved resiliency, as shown in Figure 9-17. However, this might disrupt SAN traffic because SAN A traffic might leak to SAN B using a vPC peer-link and vice versa. Therefore, FCoE VLANs and FIP Ethertype are not allowed to cross the vPC peer-link although the Ethernet VLAN can cross the vPC peer-link.

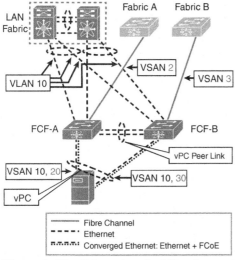

**Figure 9-17**    *Direct-Attached Topology with vPC*

## FCoE FEX Topology

FCoE FEX topology is another variant of single-hop topology. In this topology, you extend the FCoE edge by using FEXs. A host can be connected to FEXs using either individual links or vPC. For vPC connectivity, native Ethernet traffic uses both the uplinks, but Fibre Channel traffic uses a single link and does not participate in vPC. FEXs, in turn, are connected to the northbound FCFs using either static pinning of individual links or using a single-homed port channel, as shown in Figure 9-18.

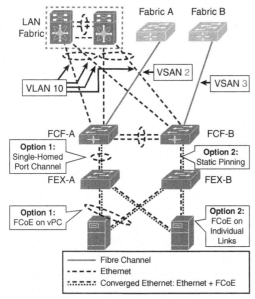

**Figure 9-18**    *FCoE FEX Topology*

**NOTE** Not all FEXs support the preceding FCoE setup. Refer to the capability of different FEXs by using the appropriate data sheet for the FEX model. Also, only second-generation CNAs support FEX FCoE design because FIP is a requirement for this design.

### FCoE Remote-Attached Topology

FCoE remote-attached topology is another variant of single-hop topology. In this topology, the host is connected to FCFs via FCoE passthrough switches, as shown in Figure 9-19. The virtual link between the VN port and VF port is established through the Ethernet path that crosses one or more passthrough switches.

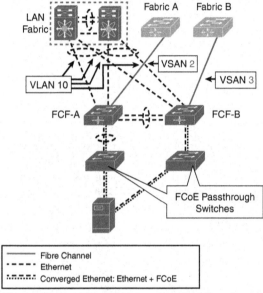

**Figure 9-19**  *FCoE Remote-Attached Topology*

Passthrough switches make forwarding decisions using Ethernet semantics and are not capable of forwarding Fibre Channel frames. Passthrough switches pose a security risk because someone can intercept the traffic through such a switch. To overcome the security concerns, you can either configure FIP snooping or a manual access control list. FIP snooping locks down the forwarding path from a CNA to FCFs using automatic configuration of ACLs. You can also configure access control lists manually to stop an attacker from spoofing MAC addresses, although this results in more administrative overhead.

## FCoE Multi-Hop Topology

Multi-hop FCoE makes use of VE ports to expand the FCoE fabric. VE ports are similar to E ports in the Fibre Channel world. Two VE ports are connected using either a single link or port channel in a point-to-point fashion, as shown in Figure 9-20. For each of the FCF-connected Ethernet interfaces, a vFC interface is created and binds to the Ethernet interface.

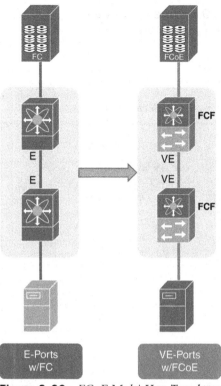

**Figure 9-20**  *FCoE Multi-Hop Topology*

In FCoE multi-hop topology, the usual traffic is from north-south from the initiator to the target, but east-west traffic could be an issue in this design. Because the FCoE infrastructure is increased from the edge access layer switch to multi-hops, the advantage of this topology is the decreased number of cables between servers and switches.

## FCoE Implementations

Cisco Nexus devices support FCoE implementation including the Cisco Nexus 5000, 7000, 7700, 6000, and 9000 Series switches. Cisco MDS 9000 Series multilayer switches also support FCoE implementation.

In the Cisco Nexus 7000/7700 Series switches, each F Series module that runs FCoE requires an FCoE license. Also, FCoE does not require an additional VDC and is enabled in the storage VDC by default. On Cisco Nexus 5000 Series switches, FCoE capability is included in the Storage Protocol Services License, which needs to be activated by entering the **feature fcoe** command. FCoE is enabled on Cisco MDS Series switches by default, although Cisco MDS series switches are mostly used for Fibre Channel connectivity. The Cisco NX-OS software supports FCoE with 10-Gigabit and 40-Gigabit Ethernet interfaces.

Because the implementation of FCoE is a little bit different in different NX-OS devices, we look at Cisco Nexus 7000 Series, Cisco Nexus 5000 Series, and Cisco Nexus 9000 Series implementations separately.

## FCoE Configuration on Cisco Nexus 7000 Series Switches

Let's first look into the configuration steps required to configure FCoE on Cisco Nexus 7000 Series switches.

Example 9-2 shows configuration tasks that need to be performed while you are configuring FCoE on Cisco Nexus 7000 Series switches.

**Example 9-2**   *Sample FCoE Configuration on Nexus 7000 Series Switches*

```
Step 1: Preparing the Switch for Configuring FCoE


! Firstly, you will need to install FCoE feature set and associate an FCoE license
with an FCoE module to configure FCoE. You need one license for each module configured
for FCoE. Then enable no drop queue for FCoE class.


switch# configure terminal
switch(config)# install feature-set fcoe
switch(config)# feature lldp
switch(config)# license fcoe module 2
switch(config)# system qos
switch(config-sys-qos)# service-policy type network-qos default-nq-7e-policy



Step 2: Creating and configuring Storage VDC

! Create a dedicated storage VDC and enable storage features in a storage VDC. You
do not need to allow the feature-set or enable it in the storage VDC because this
process is handled automatically for a storage VDC. Also you will need to allocate
interfaces to the storage VDC as a dedicated FCoE port. You must allocate all inter-
faces in the port group. You must configure these interfaces in switchport trunk
mode as Spanning Tree Protocol (STP) edge ports. Also ensure that you have allocated
the FCoE VLAN range.


switch(config)# vdc fcoe type storage
switch(config-vdc)# allocate interface ethernet 2/1
switch(config-vdc)# allocate fcoe-vlan-range 10-30


switch(config)# interface ethernet 2/1
switch(config-if)# switchport mode trunk
switch(config-if)# spanning-tree port type edge trunk


! Enable LLDP feature and unshut the FCoE ports on storage VDC.


switch# switchto vdc fcoe type storage
switch-fcoe# configure terminal
switch-fcoe(config)# feature lldp
switch-fcoe(config)# interface ethernet 2/1
switch-fcoe(config-if)# no shutdown


Step 3: Configuring FCoE VLANs and Virtual Fibre Channel Interfaces
```

! A unique, dedicated VLAN must be configured at every converged access switch to carry traffic for each virtual fabric (VSAN) in the SAN (for example, VLAN 200 for VSAN 200, VLAN 300 for VSAN 300, and so on). If you enable MST, you must use a separate Multiple Spanning Tree (MST) instance for FCoE VLANs. In the following example we allow VLAN 200 which will later be mapped to FCoE VSAN 200

```
switch-fcoe(config)# interface ethernet 2/1
switch-fcoe(config-if)# switchport trunk allowed vlan 1,200

switch-fcoe(config)# vsan database
switch-fcoe(config-vsan-db)# vsan 200

switch-fcoe(config)# vlan 200
switch-fcoe(config-vlan)# fcoe vsan 200
```

! To use FCoE, you must first create Virtual Fibre Channel (vFC) interfaces. Then, you must bind the VFC interfaces to physical interfaces before FCoE can be used.

```
switch-fcoe(config)# interface vfc 2
switch-fcoe(config-if)# switchport mode e
switch-fcoe(config-if)# bind interface ethernet 2/1
```

! Configure the association between the VSAN and virtual Fibre Channel interface or virtual Fibre Channel port channel.

```
switch-fcoe(config)# vsan database
switch-fcoe(config-vsan-db)# vsan 200 interface vfc 2
switch-fcoe(config-vsan-db)# exit
```

### Miscellaneous FCoE Configuration

DCBX allows the switch to send a LAN Logical Link Status (LLS) message to a directly connected CNA. To disable LAN traffic on an FCoE link, enter the **shutdown lan** command to send an LLS-Down message to the CNA. This command causes all VLANs on the interface that are not enabled for FCoE to be brought down. If a VLAN on the interface is enabled for FCoE, it continues to carry SAN traffic without any interruption.

```
switch(config)# interface Ethernet 2/1
switch(config-if)# shutdown lan
```

The FCoE switch advertises its priority. The priority is used by the CNAs in the fabric to determine the best switch to connect to. You can configure the global fabric priority using the following command. The default value is 128. The range is from 0 (higher) to 255 (lower).

```
switch-fcoe(config)# fcoe fcf-priority 42
```

9

You can configure the interval for Fibre Channel fabric advertisement on the switch using the following command:

```
switch-fcoe(config)# fcoe fka-adv-period 8
```

The VFID check verifies that the VSAN configuration is correct on both ends of a VE link. You can turn off the VFID check for VE ports to allow VE loopback configuration between two VE ports on the same switch.

```
switch-fcoe(config)# fcoe veloopback
```

## FCoE Configuration on Cisco Nexus 5000 Series Switches

Because there is no concept of storage VDC on Cisco Nexus 5000 Series switches, the configuration is a little bit different when it comes to FCoE configuration on these switches.

Example 9-3 shows configuration tasks that need to be performed while you are configuring FCoE on Cisco Nexus 5000 Series switches.

**Example 9-3**  *Sample FCoE Configuration on Nexus 5000 Series Switches*

```
Step 1: Configure QoS


! Before enabling FCoE on a Cisco Nexus device, you must attach the pre-defined FCoE
policy maps to the type qos, type network-qos, and type queuing policy maps.


switch(config)# system qos
switch(config-sys-qos)# service-policy type {network-qos | qos |queuing } [input |
output ] fcoe-default policy-name


! The previous command specifies the default FCoE policy map to use as the service
policy for the system. There are four pre-defined policy-maps for FCoE.


switch(config-sys-qos)# service-policy type queuing input fcoe-default-in-policy
switch(config-sys-qos)# service-policy type queuing output fcoe-default-out-policy
switch(config-sys-qos)# service-policy type qos input fcoe-default-in-policy
switch(config-sys-qos)# service-policy type network-qos fcoe-default-nq-policy


! You can configure the default Ethernet system class to support the jumbo MTU using
the following commands


switch(config)# policy-map type network-qos jumbo
switch(config-pmap-nq)# class type network-qos class-fcoe
switch(config-pmap-c-nq)# pause no-drop
switch(config-pmap-c-nq)# mtu 2158
switch(config-pmap-c-nq)# class type network-qos class-default
switch(config-pmap-c-nq)# mtu 9216
switch(config-pmap-c-nq)# exit
switch(config-pmap-nq)# exit
```

```
switch(config)# system qos
switch(config-sys-qos)# service-policy type network-qos jumbo


Step 2: Enable the FCoE and LLDP feature

switch# configure terminal
switch(config)# feature fcoe
switch(config)# feature lldp


Step 3: Enable the associated VLAN and map the VLAN to a VSAN.

switch(config)# vlan 200
switch(config-vlan)# fcoe vsan 2
switch(config-vlan)# exit


Step 4: Configure the VLAN on a physical Ethernet interface.

switch# configure terminal
switch(config)# interface ethernet 1/4
switch(config-if)# spanning-tree port type edge trunk
switch(config-if)# switchport mode trunk
switch(config-if)# switchport trunk allowed vlan 1,200
switch(config-if)# exit


Step 5: Create a virtual Fibre Channel interface and bind it to a physical Ethernet
interface.

switch(config)# interface vfc 4
switch(config-if)# bind interface ethernet 1/4
switch(config-if)# exit


Step 6: Associate the virtual Fibre Channel interface to the VSAN.

switch(config)# vsan database
switch(config-vsan)# vsan 2 interface vfc 4
switch(config-vsan)# exit
```

Other miscellaneous configurations, such as disabling LAN traffic on an FCoE link, config-uring fabric-priority, and setting the advertisement interval, are the same as discussed for the Cisco Nexus 7000 Series configuration.

## FCoE Configuration on Cisco Nexus 9000 Series Switches

Example 9-4 shows configuration tasks that need to be performed while you are configuring FCoE on Cisco Nexus 9000 Series switches.

**Example 9-4** *Sample FCoE Configuration on Nexus 9000 Series Switches*

```
Step 1: Configure TCAM carving.


! Perform TCAM carving to assign TCAM space to ingress Port-based ACL (ing-ifacl) and
ingress redirect (ing-redirect) regions. These TCAM resources are required for the
FCoE to work on Nexus 9000 Series switches. Here we will pull these TCAM resources
from ingress Router ACL (ing-racl) by reducing the ing-racl TCAM space from 2304 to
1536 and assign the freed-up (512) TCAM space to ing-ifacl and ing-redirect, 256
each. Once the TCAM configuration is done, you need to save the configuration and
reload the switch.


switch# configure terminal
switch(config)# hardware access-list tcam region ing-racl 1536
switch(config)# hardware access-list tcam region ing-ifacl 256
switch(config)# hardware access-list tcam region ing-redirect 256

switch(config)# show hardware access-list tcam region | in racl|ifacl|redirect
                       Ingress PACL [ing-ifacl] size =   256
                       Ingress RACL [ing-racl] size = 1536
                        Egress RACL [egr-racl] size = 1792
                    Ingress Redirect [ing-redirect] size =   256
        Ingress Flow Redirect [ing-flow-redirect] size =     0
    Ingress PACL IPv4 Lite [ing-ifacl-ipv4-lite] size =     0
    Ingress PACL IPv6 Lite [ing-ifacl-ipv6-lite] size =     0
switch(config)#

switch(config)# copy running-config startup-config
switch(config)# reload


Step 2: Enable the FCoE and LLDP feature.


! Install and enable the FCoE feature on the switch. There are four types of FCoE
default QoS policies in Nexus 9000 Series switches: network QoS, output queuing,
input queuing, and QoS. The FCoE default policies are enabled when you enable the
FCoE feature using the feature-set fcoe command. The default QoS ingress policy,
default-fcoe-in-policy, is implicitly attached to all FC and SAN-port-channel
interfaces to enable FC to FCoE traffic.


switch# configure terminal
switch(config)# install feature-set fcoe
switch(config)# feature-set fcoe



! Enable LLDP feature.


switch(config)# feature lldp
```

**Step 3:** Enable the associated VLAN and map the VLAN to a VSAN.

```
switch(config)# vlan 200
switch(config-vlan)# fcoe vsan 2
switch(config-vlan)# exit
```

**Step 4:** Configure the VLAN on a physical Ethernet interface.

```
switch# configure terminal
switch(config)# interface ethernet 1/4
switch(config-if)# spanning-tree port type edge trunk
switch(config-if)# switchport mode trunk
switch(config-if)# switchport trunk allowed vlan 1,200
switch(config-if)# exit
```

**Step 5:** Create a virtual Fibre Channel interface and bind it to a physical Ethernet interface.

```
switch(config)# interface vfc 4
switch(config-if)# bind interface ethernet 1/4
switch(config-if)# exit
```

**Step 6:** Associate the virtual Fibre Channel interface to the VSAN.

```
switch(config)# vsan database
switch(config-vsan)# vsan 2 interface vfc 4
switch(config-vsan)# exit
```

Other miscellaneous configurations, such as disabling LAN traffic on an FCoE link, configuring fabric-priority, and setting the advertisement interval, are the same as discussed for the Cisco Nexus 7000 Series configuration.

**NOTE** The Cisco MDS 9700 Series, MDS 9500 Series, and MDS 9250i switches automatically enables the FCoE feature when an FCoE-capable module is present in the chassis. The Cisco MDS 9250i switches already have fixed FCoE ports. These FCoE ports can be enabled only if a minimum of two power supply units (PSUs) are online. For FCoE configuration on Cisco MDS 9000 Series switches, refer to "Cisco MDS 9000 Series FCoE Configuration Guide, Release 9.x."

9

## FCoE over FEX

If you are using FEX in between an FCF and a host, then the additional configuration steps are as shown in Example 9-5.

Example 9-5 shows configuration tasks that need to be performed while you are configuring FCoE over FEX on Cisco Nexus 5000 Series switches.

**Example 9-5** *Sample FCoE over FEX Configuration on Nexus 5000 Series Switches*

```
Step 1: Enable FCoE, FEX, and LLDP features, and FEX for FCoE.

switch(config)# feature fcoe
switch(config)# feature fex
switch(config)# feature lldp
switch(config)# fex 200
switch(config-fex)# fcoe

Step 2: Configure switch physical interface in fex-fabric mode and associate the
fex.

switch(config)# interface Ethernet 2/1
switch(config-if)# switchport mode fex-fabric
switch(config-if)# fex associate 200

Step 3: Configure the VLAN on the Physical Interface

switch(config)# interface Ethernet 200/1/1
switch(config-if)# switchport mode trunk
switch(config-if)# switchport trunk native vlan 24
switch(config-if)# switchport trunk allowed vlan 24, 200
switch(config-if)# spanning-tree port type edge trunk

Step 4: Associate FCoE VSAN to FCoE VLAN.

switch(config)# vlan 200
switch(config-vlan)# fcoe vsan 200

Step 5: Create a virtual Fibre Channel interface and bind it to a physical Ethernet
interface.

switch(config)# interface vfc200
switch(config-if)# bind interface Ethernet 200/1/1
switch(config-if)# no shutdown

Step 6: Associate the virtual Fibre Channel interface to the VSAN.

switch(config)# vsan database
switch(config-vsan)# vsan 200 interface vfc 200
```

The FCoE over FEX configuration on Nexus 9000 Series switches is similar to the configuration shown in Example 9-5. However, the only difference is that in Nexus 9000 Series switches, you need to enable the FEX and FCoE features using different commands. To install and enable the FEX feature on the Nexus 9000 Series switch, you use the commands **install feature-set fex** and **feature-set fex**, respectively. To install and enable the FCoE feature on the Nexus 9000 Series switch, you use the commands **install feature-set fcoe** and **feature-set fcoe**, respectively.

## FCoE NPV

FCoE NPV is supported on the Cisco Nexus devices. It functions similarly to traditional FCoE. The FCoE NPV feature is an enhanced form of FIP snooping that provides a secure method to connect FCoE-capable hosts to an FCoE-capable FCoE forwarder (FCF) switch.

The FCoE NPV feature provides the following benefits:

■ FCoE NPV does not have the management and troubleshooting issues that are inherent to managing hosts remotely at the FCF.

■ FCoE NPV implements FIP snooping as an extension to the NPV function while retaining the traffic-engineering, vsan-management, administration, and troubleshooting aspects of NPV.

■ FCoE NPV and NPV together allow communication through FC and FCoE ports at the same time. This provides a smooth transition when moving from FC to FCoE topologies.

From a control plane perspective, FCoE NPV performs proxy functions toward the FCF and the hosts in order to load-balance logins from the hosts evenly across the available FCF uplink ports. An FCoE NPV bridge is VSAN-aware and capable of assigning VSANs to the hosts.

VSANs from the hosts must be created, and for each VSAN, a dedicated VLAN must also be created and mapped. The mapped VLAN is used to carry FIP and FCoE traffic for the corresponding VSAN. The VLAN-VSAN mapping must be configured consistently in the entire fabric.

For each host directly connected over Ethernet interfaces on the FCoE NPV bridge, a virtual Fibre Channel (vFC) interface must be created and bound to the Ethernet interface. By default, the vFC interface is configured in the F mode (VF port).

Connectivity from an FCoE NPV bridge to the FCF is only supported over point-to-point links. These links can be individual Ethernet interfaces or members of an Ethernet port channel interface. For each FCF-connected Ethernet interface, a vFC interface must be created and bound to the Ethernet interface. These vFC interfaces must be configured as VNP ports. On the VNP port, an FCoE NPV bridge emulates an FCoE-capable host with multiple ENodes, each with a unique ENode MAC address. By default, the VNP port is enabled in trunk mode.

Example 9-6 shows configuration tasks that need to be performed while you are configuring FCoE NPV on Cisco Nexus 5000 Series switches on the sample topology shown in Figure 9-21.

9

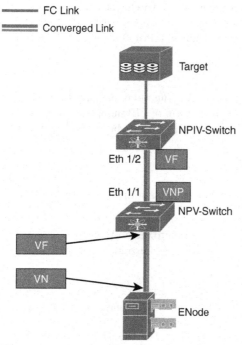

**Figure 9-21** *Sample Topology for FCoE NPV*

**Example 9-6** *Sample FCoE NPV Configuration on Nexus 5000 Series Switches*

```
Step 1: Enable FCoE NPV

! You can enable FCoE NPV using the feature fcoe-npv command.

npv-switch# configure terminal
npv-switch(config)# feature fcoe-npv



Step 2: Enable FCoE QoS

npv-switch(config)# system qos
npv-switch(config-sys-qos)# service-policy type qos input fcoe-default-in-policy
npv-switch(config-sys-qos)# service-policy type queuing input fcoe-default-in-policy
npv-switch(config-sys-qos)# service-policy type queuing output fcoe-default-out-policy
npv-switch(config-sys-qos)# service-policy type network-qos fcoe-default-nq-policy

Step 3: Configuring VLAN to VSAN mapping

npv-switch(config)# vsan database
npv-switch(config-vsan-db)# vsan 50
```

```
npv-switch(config-vsan-db)# vlan 50
npv-switch(config-vlan)# fcoe vsan 50


Step 4: VNP Port configuration

npv-switch(config)# int e1/1
npv-switch(config-if)# switchport mode trunk
npv-switch(config-if)# switchport trunk allowed vlan 50
npv-switch(config-if)# no shut

! Create a vFC port and bind it to an Ethernet port. Set the port mode to NP and
bring up the port.

npv-switch# config t
npv-switch(config)# interface vfc 20
npv-switch(config-if)# switchport mode NP
npv-switch(config-if)# bind interface ethernet 1/1
npv-switch(config-if)# switchport trunk allowed vsan 50
npv-switch(config-if)# no shutdown

Step 5: VF Port configuration

! A similar configuration must be applied to the NPIV side of the link. The primary
difference is that the vFC is configured for the VF mode and NPIV is enabled.

npiv-switch(config)# feature npiv
npiv-switch(config)# interface Ethernet1/2
npiv-switch(config-if)# switchport
npiv-switch(config-if)# switchport mode trunk
npiv-switch(config-if)# switchport trunk allowed vlan 50
npiv-switch(config-if)# no shutdown

! Create a vFC port and bind it to an Ethernet port. Set the port mode to F and
bring up the port.

npiv-switch(config-if)# interface vfc20
npiv-switch(config-if)# switchport mode F
npiv-switch(config-if)# bind interface Ethernet1/2
npiv-switch(config-if)# switchport trunk allowed vsan 50
npiv-switch(config-if)# no shutdown
```

The FCoE NPV configuration on Nexus 9000 Series switches is similar to the configuration shown in Example 9-6; however, the only difference is that in Nexus 9000 Series switches, the FCoE NPV feature is installed and enabled on the npv-switch using the commands **install feature-set fcoe-npv** and **feature-set fcoe-npv**, respectively.

## FCoE Verification

The verification commands are the same for Cisco Nexus switches and Cisco MDS switches. We discuss some of the verification commands in this section. You can find a list of useful FCoE verification commands in Table 9-4.

Example 9-7 shows some verification commands along with output. Note that the output in Example 9-7 does not reflect any of the previous configuration examples and is provided only to acquaint you with various verification commands.

**Example 9-7** *FCoE Verification Commands*

```
! To verify that the FCoE capability is enabled, use the show fcoe command.

switch# show fcoe
Global FCF details
        FCF-MAC is 00:0d:ec:6d:95:00
        FC-MAP is 0e:fc:00
        FCF Priority is 128
        FKA Advertisement period for FCF is 8 seconds
! To display the FCoE database, use the show fcoe database command

switch# show fcoe database
------------------------------------------------------------------------
INTERFACE      FCID        PORT NAME             MAC ADDRESS
------------------------------------------------------------------------
vfc3           0x490100    21:00:00:1b:32:0a:e7:b8   00:c0:dd:0e:5f:76

! To display the FCoE settings for an interface, use the show interface <interface
number> fcoe command.

switch# show interface ethernet 1/37 fcoe
Ethernet1/37 is FCoE UP
    vfc3 is Up
        FCID is 0x490100
        PWWN is 21:00:00:1b:32:0a:e7:b8
        MAC addr is 00:c0:dd:0e:5f:76

! To display a virtual Fibre Channel interface bound to an Ethernet interface, use
the show interface vfc <vfc-id> command.

switch# show interface vfc 3
vfc3 is up
    Bound interface is Ethernet1/37
    Hardware is Virtual Fibre Channel
    Port WWN is 20:02:00:0d:ec:6d:95:3f
    Admin port mode is F, trunk mode is on
```

```
    snmp link state traps are enabled
    Port mode is F, FCID is 0x490100
    Port vsan is 931
    1 minute input rate 0 bits/sec, 0 bytes/sec, 0 frames/sec
    1 minute output rate 0 bits/sec, 0 bytes/sec, 0 frames/sec
      0 frames input, 0 bytes
        0 discards, 0 errors
      0 frames output, 0 bytes
        0 discards, 0 errors
    Interface last changed at Thu May 21 04:44:42 2019
```

! To display the mapping between the VLANs and VSANs on the switch, use the show vlan fcoe command.

```
switch# show vlan fcoe
VLAN      VSAN     Status
--------  -------- --------
15        15       Operational
20        20       Operational
25        25       Operational
30        30       Non-operational
```

! To verify VSAN membership of Virtual Interface, use the show vsan <vsan-id> membership command.

```
switch# show vsan 11 membership
vsan 11 interfaces:
    fc1/47          fc1/48         vfc1011
```

! To verify the information about the NPV FLOGI session, use the show npv flogi-table command.

```
switch# show npv flogi-table
--------------------------------------------------------------------------------
SERVER                                                               EXTERNAL
INTERFACE VSAN   FCID    PORT NAME          NODE NAME              INTERFACE
--------------------------------------------------------------------------------
vfc1       20    0x670000   21:01:00:1b:32:2a:e5:b8 20:01:00:1b:32:2a:e5:b8     fc2/6
Total number of flogi = 1.
```

```
! To verify the status of the NPV configuration including information about VNP
ports, use the show npv status command.

switch# show npv status


npiv is enabled

disruptive load balancing is disabled

External Interfaces:
====================
  Interface:  fc2/5, State: Trunking
        VSAN:    1, State: Up
        VSAN:  200, State: Up
        VSAN:  400, State: Up
        VSAN:   20, State: Up
        VSAN:  100, State: Up
        VSAN:  300, State: Up
        VSAN:  500, State: Up, FCID: 0xa10000
  Interface:  fc2/6, State: Trunking
        VSAN:    1, State: Up
        VSAN:  200, State: Up
        VSAN:  400, State: Up
        VSAN:   20, State: Up
        VSAN:  100, State: Up
        VSAN:  300, State: Up
        VSAN:  500, State: Up, FCID: 0xa10001
  Interface: vfc90,  State: Down
  Interface: vfc100, State: Down
  Interface: vfc110, State: Down
  Interface: vfc111, State: Down
  Interface: vfc120, State: Down
  Interface: vfc130, State: Trunking
        VSAN:    1, State: Waiting For VSAN Up
        VSAN:  200, State: Up
        VSAN:  400, State: Up
        VSAN:  100, State: Up
        VSAN:  300, State: Up
        VSAN:  500, State: Up, FCID: 0xa10002

  Number of External Interfaces: 8

Server Interfaces:
==================
```

```
Interface:    vfc1, VSAN:   20, State: Up
Interface:    vfc2, VSAN: 4094, State: Down
Interface:    vfc3, VSAN: 4094, State: Down
Interface: vfc5000, VSAN: 4094, State: Down
Interface: vfc6000, VSAN: 4094, State: Down
Interface: vfc7000, VSAN: 4094, State: Down
Interface: vfc8090, VSAN: 4094, State: Down
Interface: vfc8191, VSAN: 4094, State: Down

Number of Server Interfaces: 8
```

Table 9-4 summarizes the NX-OS CLI commands that are related to FCoE configuration and verification.

**Table 9-4**   Summary of NX-OS CLI Commands for FCoE Configuration and Verification

| Command | Purpose |
|---|---|
| switch# **config terminal** | Enters configuration mode. |
| switch(config)# **install feature-set fcoe** | Installs the FCoE feature set in the default VDC on Nexus 7000 Series switches. |
| switch(config)# **(no) feature fcoe** | Enables the FCoE capability on Nexus 5000 Series switches. |
| switch(config)# **feature lldp** | Enables the Link Layer Discovery Protocol (LLDP) feature in the default VDC. This feature is required for FCoE operation. |
| switch(config)# **feature lacp** | Enables the Link Aggregation Control Protocol (LACP) feature in the default VDC. This feature is considered a best practice for FCoE operation. |
| switch(config)# **license fcoe module 2** | Associates an FCoE license with a module on Nexus 7000 Series switches. |
| switch(config)# **system qos** | Enters quality of service (QoS) configuration mode. |
| switch(config-sys-qos)# **service-policy type network-qos default-nq-7e-policy** | Enables the QoS policy that supports FCoE traffic. The *policy-name* default is default-nq-8e-policy. |
| switch(config)# **vdc** *fcoe* **type storage** | Enters VDC configuration mode. The *vdc_id* can be any case-sensitive, alphanumeric string up to 32 characters. |
| switch(config-vdc)# **allocate interface ethernet** *2/1-2* | Allocates interfaces to the storage VDC as a dedicated FCoE port. You must allocate all interfaces in the port group. You must configure these interfaces in Switchport trunk mode as Spanning Tree Protocol (STP) edge ports. |
| switch(config-vdc)# **allocate fcoe-vlan-range** *10-30* | Allows the VLAN to be used in the storage VDC, and allocates the VLANs that can be used for FCoE and mapped to a VSAN. |

9

| Command | Purpose |
|---|---|
| switch(config-vdc)# **switchto vdc** *fcoe* | Switches to the storage VDC. |
| fcoe(config)# **(no) fcoe fcf-priority** *42* | Configures the global fabric priority. The default value is 128. The range is from 0 (higher) to 255 (lower). |
| fcoe(config)# **(no) fcoe fka-adv-period** *8* | Configures the advertisement interval for the fabric. The default value is 8 seconds. The range is from 4 to 60 seconds. |
| fcoe(config)# **fcoe veloopback** | Enables the VFID check for all VE ports. |
| switch(config)# **interface** *e 2/1* | Specifies an interface to configure, and enters interface configuration mode. |
| switch(config-if)# **switchport mode trunk** | Puts the Ethernet interface into trunk mode. |
| switch(config-if)# **spanning-tree port type edge trunk** | Sets the interface to STP-type edge port to support STP Lite for loop prevention. |
| switch(config-if)# **no shutdown** | Administratively enables the Ethernet shared interface. |
| switch(config-if)# **(no) shutdown lan** | Shuts down Ethernet traffic on the interface. If the interface is part of an FCoE VLAN, the shutdown has no impact on the FCoE traffic. |
| switch(config)# **vsan database** | Enters VSAN database configuration mode. |
| switch(config-vsan-db)# **vsan** *200* | Defines the VSAN. The VSAN number range is from 1 to 4094. |
| switch(config-vsan-db)# **(no) vsan** *2* **interface vfc** *4* | Configures the association between the VSAN and virtual Fibre Channel interface or virtual Fibre Channel port channel. The *vsan-id* must map to a VLAN on the physical Ethernet interface or port channel that is bound to the virtual Fibre Channel interface or virtual Fibre Channel port channel. |
| switch(config)# **vlan** *200* | Enters VLAN configuration mode. The VLAN number range is from 1 to 4096. |
| switch(config-vlan)# **fcoe vsan** *200* | Enables FCoE for the specified VLAN and configures the mapping from this VLAN to the specified VSAN. If you do not specify a VSAN number, a mapping is created from this VLAN to the VSAN with the same number. |
| switch(config)# **interface vfc** *4* | Creates a virtual Fibre Channel interface (if it does not already exist) and enters interface configuration mode. The *vfc-id* range is from 1 to 8192. |
| switch(config-if)# **switchport** *mode e* | Configures the switchport mode for a virtual Fibre Channel interface. The *mode* is E or F. The default is F mode. |
| switch(config-if)# **(no) bind interface ethernet** *1/4* | Binds the virtual Fibre Channel interface to the specified interface. |

| Command | Purpose |
|---|---|
| switch(config)# **fex** *101* | Enters configuration mode for the specified FEX. The range for *fex-chassis_ID* is from 100 to 199. |
| switch(config-fex)# **fcoe** | Enables Fibre Channel over Ethernet traffic on the FEX. |
| switch(config)# **interface Ethernet** *2/1* | Specifies an interface to configure, and enters interface configuration mode. |
| switch(config-if)# **(no) switchport mode fex-fabric** | Sets the interface to support an external Fabric Extender. |
| switch(config-if)# **fex associate** *200* | Associates the FEX-number to the Fabric Extender unit attached to the interface. The range of the FEX-number is from 100 to 199. |
| switch# **show feature** | Displays information about the enabled features. |
| switch# **show feature-set** | Displays information about the feature sets. |
| switch# **show license usage FCOE-N7K-F132XP** | Displays the F1 line card usage used by a storage VDC on Nexus 7000 Series switches. |
| switch# **show vdc fcoe-vlan-range** | Displays information about the VLAN range allocated for FCoE. |
| switch# **show vdc shared membership** | Switches to the storage VDC. |
| switch# **show vlan fcoe** | Displays information about the FCoE configuration for a VLAN. |
| switch# **show interface vfc** *4* | Displays the detailed configuration of the specified Fibre Channel interface. |
| switch# **show interface vfc-port-channel 2** | Displays information about the virtual Fibre Channel interfaces bound to port channel interfaces. |
| switch# **show vsan** | Displays information about the VSAN. |
| switch# **show vsan** *11* **membership** | Displays the specified VSAN membership. |
| switch# **show interface ethernet** *1/37* **fcoe** | Displays the FCoE settings for an interface. |
| switch# **show fcoe database** | Displays information about the FCoE database. |
| switch# **show npv status** | Displays the status of the NPV configuration including information about VNP ports. |
| switch# **show npv flogi-table** | Displays information about N port virtualization (NPV) fabric login (FLOGI) session |

Example 9-8 begins the configuration and verification of FCoE on the sample topology shown in Figure 9-22. This example shows configuration for N5K because after configuring the link between the parent switch (N5K) and FEX as FEX fabric, you basically consider interfaces on FEX as they are on the parent switch.

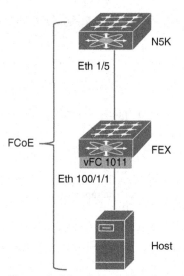

**Figure 9-22** *Sample Topology for FCoE Configuration and Verification*

**Example 9-8** *FCoE Configuration and Verification*

```
! Verifying if FCoE and lldp feature is enabled on N5K
N5K# show feature | in e
fcoe          1          enabled
fcoe-npv      1          disabled
lldp          1          enabled


! Verifying if appropriate FCoE-aware QoS is enabled
N5K# show policy-map type network-qos

  Type network-qos policy-maps
  ================================

  policy-map type network-qos default-nq-policy
    class type network-qos class-default

      mtu 1500
  policy-map type network-qos fcoe-default-nq-policy
    class type network-qos class-fcoe

      pause no-drop
      mtu 2158
    class type network-qos class-default

      mtu 1500
  policy-map type network-qos fcoe-default-nq-policy-jumbo
    class type network-qos class-fcoe
```

```
      pause no-drop
        mtu 2158
     class type network-qos class-default

       mtu 9216

! Verifying the status of VSAN 11

N5K# show vsan 11
vsan 11 information
         name:VSAN0011  state:active
         interoperability mode:default
         loadbalancing:src-id/dst-id/oxid
         operational state:up

! Enabling FCoE for FEX

N5K# configure terminal
Enter configuration commands, one per line. End with CNTL/Z.
N5K(config)# fex 100
N5K(config-fex)# fcoe

! Assigning VSAN 11 to FCoE VLAN 1011
N5K(config-fex)# vlan 1011
N5K(config-vlan)# fcoe vsan 11

! Configuring Physical Interface on N5K connected to FEX
N5K(config-vlan)# interface Ethernet1/5
N5K(config-if)# switchport mode fex-fabric
N5K(config-if)# fex associate 100

 Configuring FEX interface populated on N5K
N5K(config-if)# interface Ethernet100/1/1
N5K(config-if)# switchport mode trunk
N5K(config-if)# switchport trunk native vlan 27
N5K(config-if)# switchport trunk allowed vlan 27, 1011

! Configuring Virtual Interface and binding Physical Interface to it
N5K(config-if)# interface vfc1011
N5K(config-if)# bind interface ethernet 100/1/1
N5K(config-if)# switchport mode F
N5K(config-if)# switchport trunk allowed vsan 11
Warning: This command will remove all VSANs currently being trunked and trunk only
the specified VSANs.
Do you want to continue? (y/n) [n] y
N5K(config-if)# no shutdown
```

9

```
! Binding Virtual Interface to VSAN 11
N5K(config-if)# vsan database
N5K(config-vsan-db)# vsan 11 interface vfc1011
N5K(config-vsan-db)# end

! Verifying status of FCoE VLAN
N5K(config-if)# show vlan fcoe

Original VLAN ID       Translated VSAN ID      Association State
-----------------      ------------------      ------------------
    1011                      11                   Operational


! Verifying VSAN membership of Virtual Interface

N5K# show vsan 11 membership
vsan 11 interfaces:
    fc1/47            fc1/48            san-port-channel 7  vfc1011

! Verifying FEX interface FCoE status connected to the host.

N5K# show interface ethernet 100/1/1 fcoe
   vfc1011 is Up
Ethernet100/1/1 is FCoE UP
        FCID is 0x470000
        PWWN is 20:00:00:25:b5:10:70:10
        MAC addr is d4:c9:3c:fe:d2:be
! Verifying the status of vFC interface

N5K# show interface vfc 1011
vfc1011 is trunking
    Bound interface is Ethernet100/1/1
    Hardware is Ethernet
    Port WWN is 23:f2:8c:60:4f:2d:de:ff
    Admin port mode is F, trunk mode is on
    snmp link state traps are enabled
    Port mode is TF
    Port vsan is 11
    Trunk vsans (admin allowed and active) (11)
    Trunk vsans (up)                        (11)
    Trunk vsans (isolated)                  ()
    Trunk vsans (initializing)              ()
    1 minute input rate 256 bits/sec, 32 bytes/sec, 0 frames/sec
    1 minute output rate 272 bits/sec, 34 bytes/sec, 0 frames/sec
      17 frames input, 1904 bytes
```

```
        0 discards, 0 errors
  18 frames output, 2020 bytes
        0 discards, 0 errors
  last clearing of &#8220;show interface&#8221; counters Sun Aug  4 22:23:42 2019

  Interface last changed at Sun Aug  4 22:23:42 2019

! Verifying fabric login status of the host using vFC interface

N5K# show flogi database
--------------------------------------------------------------------------------
INTERFACE    VSAN    FCID      PORT NAME               NODE NAME
--------------------------------------------------------------------------------
vfc1011      11      0x470000  20:00:00:25:b5:10:70:10  21:00:00:25:b5:10:70:10

Total number of flogi = 1.
```

## Exam Preparation Tasks

As mentioned in the Introduction, you have a couple of choices for exam preparation: the exercises here, Chapter 21, "Final Preparation," and the exam simulation questions in the Pearson Test Prep software online.

## Review All Key Topics

Review the most important topics in the chapter, noted with the key topic icon in the outer margin of the page. Table 9-5 lists a reference to these key topics and the page numbers on which each is found.

 **Key Topic**

**Table 9-5**   Key Topics for Chapter 9

| Key Topic Element | Description | Page |
|---|---|---|
| Paragraph | Priority-Based Flow Control (PFC) | 439 |
| Paragraph | Enhanced Transmission Selection (ETS) | 439 |
| Paragraph | Data Center Bridging Exchange (DCBX) | 440 |
| Figure 9-7 | FCoE Frame Format | 443 |
| Figure 9-8 | FIP Frame Format | 443 |
| List | Virtual Fibre Channel | 445 |
| Figure 9-12 | FC and FCoE Switch Port Types | 447 |
| Paragraph | FCoE Addressing and Forwarding | 447 |
| List | FCoE Initialization Protocol (FIP) | 449 |
| Figure 9-15 | FCoE Initialization Protocol (FIP) | 450 |
| Table 9-3 | FIP Virtual Instantiation Summary | 450 |
| List | Benefits of FCoE | 451 |

9

| Key Topic Element | Description | Page |
|---|---|---|
| Example 9-2 | Sample FCoE Configuration on Nexus 7000 Series Switches | 456 |
| Example 9-3 | Sample FCoE Configuration on Nexus 5000 Series Switches | 458 |
| Example 9-4 | Sample FCoE Configuration on Nexus 9000 Series Switches | 460 |
| Example 9-5 | Sample FCoE over FEX Configuration on Nexus 5000 Series Switches | 462 |
| Example 9-6 | Sample FCoE NPV Configuration on Nexus 5000 Series Switches | 464 |
| Table 9-4 | Summary of NX-OS CLI Commands for FCoE Configuration and Verification | 469 |

## Memory Tables

Print a copy of Appendix C, "Memory Tables" (found on the companion website), or at least the section for this chapter, and complete the tables and lists from memory. Appendix D, "Memory Tables Answer Key," also on the companion website, includes completed tables and lists to check your work.

## Define Key Terms

Define the following key terms from this chapter, and check your answers in the Glossary.

converged network adapter (CNA), data center bridging (DCB), Data Center Bridging Exchange (DCBX), Enhanced Transmission Selection (ETS), Fabric Shortest Path First (FSPF), Fibre Channel over Ethernet (FCoE), Fibre Channel over Ethernet N-Port ID Virtualization (FCoE-NPIV), Fibre Channel over Ethernet N-Port Virtualization (FCoE-NPV), host bus adapter (HBA), IEEE 802.1Qaz, IEEE 802.1Qbb, Inter-Process Communication (IPC), multi-hop FCoE, priority-based flow control (PFC), type-length-value (TLV)

## References

Cisco MDS 9000 Series FCoE Configuration Guide, Release 9.x: https:// www.cisco.com/c/en/us/td/docs/dcn/mds9000/sw/9x/configuration/fcoe/cisco-mds-9000-nx-os-fcoe-configuration-guide-9x.html

Cisco Nexus 5600 Series NX-OS Fibre Channel over Ethernet Configuration Guide, Release 7.x: https://www.cisco.com/c/en/us/td/docs/switches/datacenter/nexus5600/sw/ fcoe/7x/b_5600_FCoE_Config_7x.html

Fibre Channel over Ethernet (FCoE) Configuration and Troubleshooting Guide: https:// www.cisco.com/c/dam/en/us/products/collateral/storage-networking/mds-9700-series-multilayer-directors/guide-c07-733622.pdf

Evaluating Multi-hop FCoE: https://www.cisco.com/c/en/us/td/docs/solutions/Enterprise/ Data_Center/VMDC/tech_eval/mFCoEwp.html

Relevant Cisco Live Presentations: https://www.ciscolive.com

Cisco Nexus 5000 Series NX-OS FCoE Operations Guide, Release 5.1(3)N1(1): https://www.cisco.com/c/en/us/td/docs/switches/datacenter/nexus5000/sw/operations/fcoe/513_n1_1/ops_fcoe.html

Cisco Nexus 7000 Series FCoE Configuration Guide 8.x: https://www.cisco.com/c/en/us/td/docs/switches/datacenter/nexus7000/sw/fcoe/config/cisco_nexus7000_fcoe_config_guide_8x.html

Unified Fabric White Paper—Fibre Channel over Ethernet (FCoE): https://www.cisco.com/c/en/us/td/docs/solutions/Enterprise/Data_Center/UF_FCoE_final.html

Gustavo A. A. Santana, *Data Center Virtualization Fundamentals*. (Indianapolis: Cisco Press, 2014)

Cisco Nexus 5600 Series NX-OS SAN Switching Configuration Guide, Release 7.x: https://www.cisco.com/c/en/us/td/docs/switches/datacenter/nexus5600/sw/san_switching/7x/b_5600_SAN_Switching_Config_7x.html

Cisco Nexus 9000 Series NX-OS SAN Switching Configuration Guide, Release 10.3(x): https://www.cisco.com/c/en/us/td/docs/dcn/nx-os/nexus9000/103x/configuration/san-switching/cisco-nexus-9000-series-nx-os-san-switching-configuration-guide-release-103x.html

9

# CHAPTER 10

# Describe NFS and NAS Concepts

As small companies move from paper-based processes to digital applications, they become more vulnerable to the huge costs and disruptions that can result from losing vital business information. Small businesses are also challenged to comply with growing regulatory requirements governing the storage of customer information. They need strong data security, advanced encryption capabilities, and tools to control the way users access sensitive data. The common data storage solutions used in many small businesses—backup disks and flash drives, primitive tape backup systems, and simple hard drives directly attached to employee PCs—cannot provide the advanced security and control features that today's small businesses require. Such ad hoc storage solutions can also diminish productivity by impeding employees' ability to easily transfer and share files. Network File System (NFS) and network-attached storage (NAS) provide robust security and advanced data backup capabilities at a price that small companies can afford.

## This chapter covers the following key topics:

**Describe NFS Concepts:** This section provides an overview of different NFS versions including NFS version 2, 3, and 4.

**Describe NAS Concepts:** This section covers NAS concepts along with NAS benefits and Cisco NSS3000 Series Network Storage System.

## "Do I Know This Already?" Quiz

The "Do I Know This Already?" quiz enables you to assess whether you should read this entire chapter thoroughly or jump to the "Exam Preparation Tasks" section. If you are in doubt about your answers to these questions or your own assessment of your knowledge of the topics, read the entire chapter. Table 10-1 lists the major headings in this chapter and their corresponding "Do I Know This Already?" quiz questions. You can find the answers in Appendix A, "Answers to the 'Do I Know This Already?' Quizzes."

**Table 10-1**  "Do I Know This Already?" Section-to-Question Mapping

| Foundation Topics Section | Questions |
|---|---|
| Describe NFS Concepts | 1–2 |
| Describe NAS Concepts | 3–4 |

**CAUTION**  The goal of self-assessment is to gauge your mastery of the topics in this chapter. If you do not know the answer to a question or are only partially sure of the answer, you should mark that question as wrong for purposes of the self-assessment. Giving yourself credit for an answer you correctly guess skews your self-assessment results and might provide you with a false sense of security.

1. Which of the following features was introduced in NFSv4.2?

   a. Support for larger files and file systems such as 64-bit file sizes and offsets

   b. pNFS extension

   c. NFS multipathing

   d. Server-side clone and copy

2. Which of the following versions of NFS supports only TCP as its transport protocol?

   a. NFS version 1

   b. NFS version 2

   c. NFS version 3

   d. NFS version 4

3. Which of the following file- and data-sharing protocols are supported by NAS? (Choose two answers.)

   a. NFS

   b. FCoE

   c. FC

   d. CIFS

4. Which of the following is NOT an advantage of the NAS storage system?

   a. It has the ability to use existing IP connectivity Ethernet infrastructure.

   b. With 10- and 40-Gbps Ethernet connectivity, NAS supports faster data backup and restoration.

   c. NAS is a block-level data storage server that can provide connectivity over Fibre Channel infrastructure.

   d. NAS provides disk-level resiliency by using RAID mirroring.

## Foundation Topics

## Describe NFS Concepts

Network File System (NFS) is a distributed file system protocol originally developed by Sun Microsystems in 1984. NFS allows remote hosts to mount file systems over a network and interact with those file systems as though they are mounted locally. NFS uses a client/server model, in which a server makes directories on its storage accessible to one or more clients; and clients mount the directories to access the files in them. NFS uses remote procedure calls (RPCs) to route requests between clients and server, and TCP/IP as a transport protocol. NFS is hierarchical in nature, where directories (a special type of file) can contain further directories and files.

NFS (unlike Server Message Block, or SMB, which is a proprietary protocol) is an industry standard, defined by the IETF, and has several versions defined in different Requests for Comments (RFCs). Sun Microsystems used version 1 only for in-house experimental purposes. When the NFS protocol was released for general use, it was called NFS version 2. NFS version 2 supports both UDP and TCP. NFS version 2 with UDP as its transport protocol provides a stateless network connection between the server and the client. In the stateless condition, a server need not maintain any protocol state information about any of its clients in order to function correctly. Stateless servers have a distinct advantage over stateful servers in the event of a failure. With stateless servers, a client only needs to retry a request until the server responds; it does not even need to know that the server has crashed or that the network temporarily went down. The client of a stateful server, on the other hand, needs to either detect a server failure and rebuild the server's state when it comes back up, or cause client operations to fail. NFS version 3 supports both UDP and TCP. NFS version 3 introduces support for larger files and file systems such as 64-bit file sizes and offsets, support for asynchronous writes on the server to improve write performance, and additional file attributes in many replies to avoid the need to refetch them. NFS version 3 provides backward compatibility with the existing installed base of NFS version 2 protocol implementations.

NFS version 4 uses the TCP protocol to communicate with the server. NFS version 4 offers advanced file caching for performance improvements and strong authentication, and it introduces a stateful protocol where client usage information of an object is maintained by the server. NFS version 4.1 provides protocol support to take advantage of clustered server deployments, including the ability to provide scalable parallel access to files distributed among multiple servers (pNFS extension). Version 4.1 also includes a session trunking mechanism (also known as NFS Multipathing) and is available in some enterprise solutions such as VMware ESXi. When the trunking is available, you can use multiple IP addresses to access a single NFS volume. NFS version 4.2 introduces new features including server-side clone and copy, application I/O advise, sparse files, space reservation, application data block (ADB), labeled NFS with sec_label that accommodates any MAC security system, and two new operations for pNFS (LAYOUTERROR and LAYOUTSTATS). A traditional file copy of a remotely accessed file, whether from one server to another or between locations in the same server, results in the data being put on the network twice—from the source to the client and then from the client to the destination. NFS version 4.2 allows unnecessary traffic to be eliminated, and a file can be copied between servers without copying it to the client first, as shown in Figure 10-1. Applications and clients want to advise the server to expected I/O behavior. Using IO_ADVISE to communicate future I/O behavior—such as whether a file will be accessed sequentially or randomly and whether a file will be accessed in the near future—allows servers to optimize future I/O requests for a file by, for example, prefetching or evicting data. Sparse files are those that have unallocated or uninitialized data blocks as holes in the file. Such holes are typically transferred as zeros when read from the file. Sparse files are very efficient because they do not store the zeros on disk; instead, they hold enough data describing how many zeros need to be generated while reading the file. To read more about the other features on NFS version 4.2, refer to RFC 7862 (https://tools.ietf.org/html/rfc7862).

The advantage of NFSv4 over its predecessors is that only one IP port, 2049, is used to run the service, which simplifies using the protocol across firewalls. NFS is supported in a heterogenous environment: Windows, Linux, and even VMware clients support NFS shares (exports) of directories and files.

Server-Side Copy (SSC)

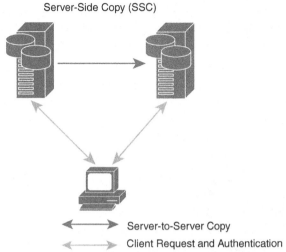

Server-to-Server Copy

Client Request and Authentication

**Figure 10-1** *NFS v4.2 Server-to-Server Copy*

## Describe NAS Concepts

Network-attached storage (NAS) is a centralized file-level (as opposed to block-level) external data storage server connected to a network providing data access to a heterogeneous group of clients such as Microsoft Windows, Apple, Macintosh, UNIX, and Linux platforms. NAS typically uses the existing network infrastructure based on IP and Ethernet. The management of the file system resides with the NAS storage system. With NAS, you can access data that might be stored across different platforms as if it were on your own computer. NAS can be used for public, private, and hybrid cloud storage for big data, virtual desktop infrastructure (VDI), high-performance computing (HPC), and so on. NAS systems contain one or more hard drives, often arranged into logical redundant storage containers or Redundant Array of Independent Disks (RAID).

NAS storage appliances provide terabytes of additional storage capacity while providing automated, redundant data backups. Today's NAS storage systems require minimal maintenance, reduce data storage costs, and provide fast file access from a centralized, secure data repository.

Figure 10-2 shows typical NAS server connectivity to a network infrastructure.

NAS supports two file- and data-sharing protocols—Common Internet File System (CIFS) and Network File System (NFS). CIFS is a version of the Server Message Block (SMB) protocol and was developed by Microsoft for Windows-based clients. SMB allows UNIX-based clients to access CIFS shares. CIFS and SMB are often used interchangeably because CIFS is a form of SMB. CIFS uses a client/server model where servers "share" and clients "use" or "map" the share. NFS was developed by Sun Microsystems for UNIX-based clients. Windows-based clients can also access NFS exports. NFS also uses a client/server model where servers "export" and clients "mount" the export. NFS is not compatible with CIFS/SMB; therefore, NFS clients cannot communicate directly with the SMB servers. However, UNIX and Linux clients can access CIFS shares by using SAMBA, which provides name resolution, file serving, and so on.

10

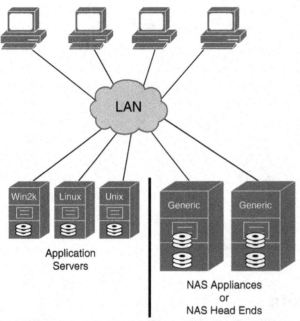

**Figure 10-2**  *Typical NAS Server Connectivity*

The top features to look for in an NAS storage appliance include

- **Redundant data backup:** Ideally, one should be able to set up the NAS storage appliance as a RAID system. For example, in a RAID1 configuration, the same data is simultaneously stored on two hard drives. If one drive crashes, the data is still accessible from the second.

- **Fast data backup/restoration:** For maximum performance, the NAS storage appliance should support the Gigabit Ethernet interface.

- **Lockability:** For extra data security, most NAS storage appliances have a lockable front panel to prevent theft or tampering.

- **Small size and quiet operation:** Some network storage appliances are small enough to fit on a shelf. Ideally, you should look for a quiet appliance that will not disturb nearby workers.

- **Support for Microsoft Distributed File System (MDFS):** This feature allows you to map multiple storage devices, so users see them as one drive. Users do not have to remember which drive their data is stored on.

- **Automatic file encryption/decryption:** This feature protects data if a hard drive within the NAS system is stolen. For robust security, look for an NAS solution offering 256-bit AES file encryption.

- **Ability to constantly back up from multiple computers:** This feature can be centralized in a network storage appliance. It simplifies backup management while helping ensure that valuable information is not lost.

## NAS Benefits

Following are the benefits of the NAS storage system:

- **Centralized management:** It is easier to manage a centralized storage server than multiple direct-attached storage devices connected to individual servers or computers.

- **IP connectivity:** One of the major advantages of NAS is that it can use the existing IP connectivity infrastructure, which reduces the cost of migration from access to shared storage.

- **Centralized backup:** It is easier to take backups from one centralized server rather than from multiple individual servers. NAS can automatically do continuous backups from multiple computers.

- **Disk utilization:** In traditional direct-attached storage, the average utilization of the disk is around 30 to 40 percent, but in centralized NAS storage, the average utilization is closer to 80 percent.

- **Thin provisioning:** NAS provides the ability to allocate storage as and when needed by servers rather than assigning dedicated storage to start with.

- **Deduplication and compression:** NAS offers improved disk utilization by removing duplicate blocks and using compression.

- **Resiliency:** Disk failures are taken care of by RAID mirroring.

- **Snapshots:** Because the NAS system controls the file system, it enables the use of advanced storage options such as snapshots.

- **Faster data backup/restoration:** With 10- and 40-Gbps Ethernet connectivity, NAS supports faster data backup and restoration.

- **Automatic file encryption/decryption:** This feature protects data if a hard drive within the NAS system is stolen.

## Cisco UCS S-Series Storage Servers

Cisco offers Cisco UCS S3260 Storage Server, which can be used as NAS or SAN storage. The Cisco UCS S3260 Storage Server is a modular, high-density, high-availability, dual-node storage-optimized server well suited for service providers, enterprises, and industry-specific environments. It provides dense, cost-effective storage to address ever-growing data needs. It is optimized for large datasets used in environments such as big data, cloud, object storage, video surveillance, and content delivery.

The Cisco UCS S3260 server helps you achieve the highest levels of data availability and performance. With dual-node capability that is based on the 2nd Gen Intel Xeon Scalable processors, the server features up to 1080 TB of local storage in a compact 4-rack-unit (4RU) form factor. The drives can be configured with enterprise-class RAID redundancy or with a pass-through Host Bus Adapter (HBA) controller. Network connectivity is provided up to 100G using Cisco VIC or third-party adapters, with expanded unified I/O capabilities for data migration between NAS and SAN environments.

Figure 10-3 and Figure 10-4 show the front view and rear view of Cisco UCS S3260 Storage Server, respectively.

**10**

**Figure 10-3**   *Front View of Cisco UCS S3260 Storage Server*

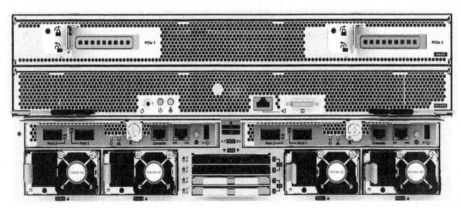

**Figure 10-4**   *Rear View of Cisco UCS S3260 Storage Server*

The following are the product highlights:

- Dual two-socket server nodes based on second Gen Intel Xeon scalable processors with up to 48 cores per server node.

- Up to 1.5 TB of DDR4 memory per M5 server node, and up to 1 TB of Intel Optane DC persistent memory.

- Support for high-performance Nonvolatile Memory Express (NVMe) and flash memory.

- Massive 1080-TB data storage capacity that easily scales to petabytes with Cisco UCS Manager software.

- Policy-based storage management framework for zero-touch capacity on demand.

- Dual-port 40-Gbps system I/O controllers with a Cisco UCS Virtual Interface Card 1300 platform embedded chip or PCIe-based system I/O controller for Quad Port 10/25G Cisco VIC 1455 or Dual Port 40/100G Cisco VIC 1495 or third-party PCIe adapters.

- Unified I/O for Ethernet or fibre channel to existing NAS or SAN storage environments.

- Support for Cisco bidirectional transceivers, with 40-Gbps connectivity over existing 10-Gbps cabling infrastructure.

Cisco UCS management provides enhanced storage management functions for the Cisco UCS S3260 and all Cisco UCS servers. Storage profiles give you the flexibility in defining the number of storage disks and the roles and uses of those disks and other storage parameters. You can select and configure the disks to be used for storage by a virtual drive.

A logical collection of physical disks is called a disk group, and a disk group configuration policy defines the way a disk group is created and configured. A disk group can be partitioned into virtual drives. Each virtual drive appears as an individual physical device to the operating system. The policy specifies the RAID level to be used for the disk group and either manual or automatic selection of disks for the disk group and roles for the disks. This feature allows optimization of the storage resources without additional overhead and licensing costs.

## Exam Preparation Tasks

As mentioned in the Introduction, you have a couple of choices for exam preparation: the exercises here, Chapter 21, "Final Preparation," and the exam simulation questions in the Pearson Test Prep software online.

## Review All Key Topics

Review the most important topics in the chapter, noted with the key topic icon in the outer margin of the page. Table 10-2 lists a reference to these key topics and the page numbers on which each is found.

**Table 10-2**   Key Topics for Chapter 10

| Key Topic Element | Description | Page |
|---|---|---|
| Paragraph | Describe NFS concepts | 480 |
| Paragraph | Describe NAS concepts | 481 |
| List | NAS features | 482 |
| List | NAS benefits | 483 |

## Define Key Terms

Define the following key terms from this chapter, and check your answers in the Glossary.

Common Internet File System (CIFS), network-attached storage (NAS), Network File System (NFS), Redundant Array of Independent Disks (RAID), Server Message Block (SMB)

10

## References

SNIA NFSv4 Overview: http://www.snia.org/sites/default/files/SNIA_An_Overview_of_NFSv4-3_0.pdf

SNIA NFS Introduction: https://www.snia.org/sites/default/files/ESF/What_is_NFS_Final2.pdf

SNIA What's New in NFSv4.2: https://www.snia.org/sites/default/files/NFS_4.2_Final.pdf

Cisco NAS Storage: https://www.cisco.com/c/en/us/solutions/small-business/resource-center/tools-tips/nas-storage.html

Cisco UCS S3260 Storage Server Data Sheet: https://www.cisco.com/c/en/us/products/collateral/servers-unified-computing/ucs-s-series-storage-servers/datasheet-c78-738059.html

Relevant Cisco Live Presentation: https://www.ciscolive.com/

IETF NFSv2 RFC: https://tools.ietf.org/html/rfc1094

IETF NFSv3 RFC: https://tools.ietf.org/html/rfc1813

IETF NFSv4 RFC: https://tools.ietf.org/html/rfc7530

# CHAPTER 11

# Describe Software Management and Infrastructure Monitoring

The Cisco MDS 9000 Series of multilayer directors and fabric switches provides best-in-class high availability, scalability, security, and management, allowing you to deploy high-performance storage-area networks (SANs). Layering a rich set of intelligent features onto a high-performance switch fabric, the Cisco MDS 9000 Series addresses the stringent requirements of large data center storage environments: high availability, security, scalability, ease of management, and seamless integration of new technologies.

## This chapter discusses the following key topics:

**Cisco MDS NX-OS Setup Utility:** This section discusses the Cisco MDS NX-OS Setup Utility and shows how it allows you to build an initial configuration file using the System Configuration dialog.

**Cisco MDS NX-OS Software Upgrade and Downgrade:** This section discusses the Cisco MDS NX-OS software disruptive and nondisruptive upgrade and downgrade procedures along with the electrical programmable logical device (EPLD) upgrade procedure.

**Infrastructure Monitoring:** This section discusses various system management features used to monitor and manage a switch using Cisco MDS NX-OS software including system messages, Call Home, Embedded Event Manager, RMON, SPAN, and RSPAN features.

## "Do I Know This Already?" Quiz

The "Do I Know This Already?" quiz enables you to assess whether you should read this entire chapter thoroughly or jump to the "Exam Preparation Tasks" section. If you are in doubt about your answers to these questions or your own assessment of your knowledge of the topics, read the entire chapter. Table 11-1 lists the major headings in this chapter and their corresponding "Do I Know This Already?" quiz questions. You can find the answers in Appendix A, "Answers to the 'Do I Know This Already?' Quizzes."

**Table 11-1**  "Do I Know This Already?" Section-to-Question Mapping

| Foundation Topics Section | Questions |
|---|---|
| Cisco MDS NX-OS Setup Utility | 1 |
| Cisco MDS NX-OS Software Upgrade and Downgrade | 2–4 |
| Infrastructure Monitoring | 5–6 |

1. Which of the following statements is INCORRECT regarding the Cisco MDS NX-OS Setup Utility?

    a. The Cisco MDS NX-OS Setup Utility is an interactive command-line interface (CLI) mode that guides you through a basic (also called a startup) configuration of the system.

    b. You can press Ctrl+C at any prompt to skip the remaining configuration options and proceed with what you have configured up to that point, except for the administrator password.

    c. You use the setup utility mainly for configuring the system initially, when no configuration is present. However, you can use the setup utility at any time for basic device configuration.

    d. You can configure only out-of-band and not in-band management using the Cisco MDS NX-OS Setup Utility.

2. Which of the following are types of software images that the Cisco MDS 9000 Series of switches use? (Choose two answers.)

    a. Kickstart image

    b. System image

    c. Flash image

    d. Supervisor image

3. You are upgrading Cisco MDS switches in your infrastructure. Before upgrading, you want to make sure that all features currently configured in your infrastructure are compatible with the destination upgrade release. Which of the following commands will you use to confirm the same?

    a. **show compatibility matrix system bootflash:** *system image filename*

    b. **show incompatibility-all system bootflash:** *system image filename*

    c. **show compatibility-all system bootflash:** *system image filename*

    d. **show incompatibility matrix system bootflash:** *system image filename*

4. You can upgrade any switch in the Cisco MDS 9000 Family by using which of the following methods? (Choose two answers.)

    a. Automatically upgrading by using the **install all** command

    b. Copying the image into bootflash and using the **reload** command

    c. Manually upgrading by changing the boot statements to point to the destination upgrade image and using the **reload** command

    d. Using the **upgrade system** command

5. Which of the following statements is INCORRECT regarding system messages on Cisco MDS switches?

   a. They provide logging information for monitoring and troubleshooting.

   b. System messages configuration allows the user to select the types of captured logging information.

   c. System messages configuration allows the user to select the destination server to forward the captured logging information.

   d. All log messages are saved across system reboots.

6. Which of the following statements are CORRECT regarding the SPAN destination (SD) port? (Choose two answers.)

   a. It allows data traffic only in the egress (Tx) direction.

   b. Multiple sessions can't share the same destination ports.

   c. If the SD port is shut down, all shared sessions stop generating SPAN traffic.

   d. The SD port always has a port VSAN 1 configured automatically.

## Foundation Topics

## Cisco MDS NX-OS Setup Utility

The Cisco MDS NX-OS Setup Utility is an interactive command-line interface (CLI) mode that guides you through a basic (also called a startup) configuration of the system. The setup utility allows you to configure only enough connectivity for system management. The setup utility allows you to build an initial configuration file using the System Configuration dialog. The setup starts automatically when a device has no configuration file in NVRAM. The dialog guides you through initial configuration. After the file is created, you can use the CLI to perform additional configuration.

You can press Ctrl+C at any prompt to skip the remaining configuration options and proceed with what you have configured up to that point, except for the administrator password. If you want to skip answers to any questions, press Enter. If a default answer is not available (for example, the device host name), the device uses what was previously configured and skips to the next question. Figure 11-1 shows how to enter and exit the setup script.

You use the setup utility mainly for configuring the system initially, when no configuration is present. However, you can use the setup utility at any time for basic device configuration. The setup utility keeps the configured values when you skip steps in the script. For example, if you have already configured the mgmt0 interface, the setup utility does not change that configuration if you skip that step. However, if there is a default value for the step, the setup utility changes to the configuration using that default, not the configured value. Be sure to carefully check the configuration changes before you save the configuration.

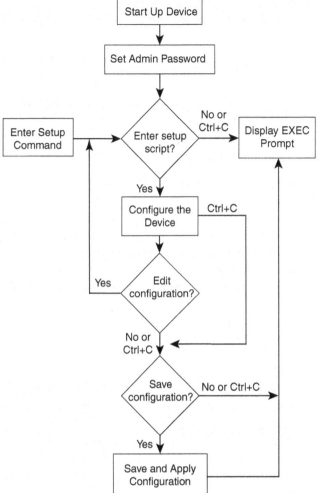

**Figure 11-1**  *Setup Script Flow*

Before starting the setup utility, make sure you perform the following steps:

**Step 1.**  Connect the console port on the supervisor module to the network. If you have dual supervisor modules, connect the console ports on both supervisor modules to the network.

**Step 2.**  Connect the Ethernet management (mgmt) port on the supervisor module to the network. If you have dual supervisor modules, connect the Ethernet management ports on both supervisor modules to the network.

The first time you access a switch in the Cisco MDS 9000 Family, it runs a setup program that prompts you for the IP address and other configuration information necessary for the switch to communicate over the supervisor module Ethernet interface (mgmt).

11

This information is required to configure and manage the switch. The IP address can only be configured from the CLI. You can configure out-of-band management on the mgmt0 interface.

The in-band management logical interface is VSAN 1. This management interface uses the Fibre Channel infrastructure to transport IP traffic. An interface for VSAN 1 is created on every switch in the fabric. Each switch should have its VSAN 1 interface configured with either an IPv4 address or an IPv6 address in the same subnetwork. A default route that points to the switch providing access to the IP network should be configured on every switch in the Fibre Channel fabric.

Following are the steps to configure out-of-band management on the mgmt0 interface:

**Step 1.**   Power on the switch. Switches in the Cisco MDS 9000 Family boot automatically.

**Step 2.**   Enter **yes** (yes is the default) to enable the secure password standard.

```
Do you want to enforce secure password standard (yes/no): yes
```

You can also enable the secure password standard using the **password strength-check** command. A secure password should contain characters from at least three of the classes: lowercase letters, uppercase letters, digits, and special characters.

**Step 3.**   Enter the new password for the administrator.

```
Enter the password for admin: admin-password


Confirm the password for admin: admin-password
```

If a password is trivial (short, easy-to-decipher), your password configuration is rejected. Be sure to configure a strong password. Passwords are case sensitive.

**Step 4.**   Enter **yes** to enter the setup mode.

```
This setup utility will guide you through the basic configuration of
the system. Setup configures only enough connectivity for management
of the system.


*Note: setup is mainly used for configuring the system initially,
when no configuration is present. So setup always assumes system
defaults and not the current system configuration values.


Press Enter at anytime to skip a dialog. Use ctrl-c at anytime
to skip the remaining dialogs.


Would you like to enter the basic configuration dialog (yes/no): yes
```

The setup utility guides you through the basic configuration process. Press Ctrl+C at any prompt to end the configuration process.

**Step 5.**   Enter **yes** (no is the default) if you wish to create additional accounts.

```
Create another login account (yes/no) [no]: yes
```

While configuring your initial setup, you can create an additional user account (in the network-admin role) besides the administrator's account.

```
Enter the user login ID: user_name
Enter the password for user_name: user-password
Confirm the password for user_name: user-password
Enter the user role [network-operator]: network-admin
```

**Step 6.**    Configure the read-only or read-write SNMP community string.

    **a.**    Enter **yes** (no is the default) to configure the read-only SNMP community string.

```
Configure read-only SNMP community string (yes/no) [n]: yes
```

    **b.**    Enter the SNMP community string.

```
SNMP community string: snmp_community
```

**Step 7.**    Enter a name for the switch. The switch name is limited to 32 alphanumeric characters. The default is switch.

```
Enter the switch name: switch_name
```

**Step 8.**    Enter **yes** (yes is the default) at the configuration prompt to configure out-of-band management.

```
Continue with Out-of-band (mgmt0) management configuration? [yes/no]: yes
```

    **a.**    Enter the mgmt0 IPv4 address.

```
Mgmt0 IPv4 address: ip_address
```

    **b.**    Enter the mgmt0 IPv4 subnet mask.

```
Mgmt0 IPv4 netmask: subnet_mask
```

**Step 9.**    Enter **yes** (yes is the default) to configure the default gateway.

```
Configure the default-gateway: (yes/no) [y]: yes
```

    **a.**    Enter the default gateway IP address.

```
IP address of the default gateway: default_gateway
```

**Step 10.**    Enter **yes** (no is the default) to configure advanced IP options such as in-band management, static routes, default network, DNS, and domain name.

```
Configure Advanced IP options (yes/no)? [n]: yes
```

    **a.**    Enter **no** (no is the default) at the in-band management configuration prompt.

```
Continue with in-band (VSAN1) management configuration? (yes/no)
[no]: no
```

    **b.**    Enter **yes** (yes is the default) to enable IPv4 routing capabilities.

```
Enable ip routing capabilities? (yes/no) [y]: yes
```

    **c.**    Enter **yes** (yes is the default) to configure a static route.

```
Configure static route: (yes/no) [y]: yes
```

    Enter the destination prefix.

```
Destination prefix: dest_prefix
```

    Enter the destination prefix mask.

```
Destination prefix mask: dest_mask
```

11

Enter the next hop IP address.

```
Next hop ip address: next_hop_address
```

**d.**   Enter **yes** (yes is the default) to configure the default network.

```
Configure the default-network: (yes/no) [y]: yes
```

Enter the default network IPv4 address. The default network IPv4 address is the destination prefix provided in step 10c.

```
Default network IP address [dest_prefix]: dest_prefix
```

**e.**   Enter **yes** (yes is the default) to configure the DNS IPv4 address.

```
Configure the DNS IP address? (yes/no) [y]: yes
```

Enter the DNS IP address.

```
DNS IP address: name_server
```

**f.**   Enter **yes** (no is the default) to configure the default domain name configuration.

```
Configure the default domain name? (yes/no) [n]: yes
```

Enter the default domain name.

```
Default domain name: domain_name
```

**Step 11.**   Enter **yes** (yes is the default) to enable the SSH service.

```
Enabled SSH service? (yes/no) [n]: yes
```

Enter the SSH key type.

```
Type the SSH key you would like to generate (dsa/rsa)? rsa
```

Enter the number of key bits within the specified range.

```
Enter the number of key bits? (768-2048) [1024]: 2048
```

**Step 12.**   Enter **yes** (no is the default) to configure the Telnet service.

```
Enable the telnet service? (yes/no) [n]: yes
```

**Step 13.**   Enter **yes** (yes is the default) to configure congestion or no_credit drop for FC interfaces.

```
Configure congestion or no_credit drop for fc interfaces? (yes/no)
[q/quit] to quit [y]:yes
```

**Step 14.**   Enter **con** or **no** (con is the default) to configure congestion or no_credit drop.

```
Enter the type of drop to configure congestion/no_credit drop? (con/no)
[c]:con
```

**Step 15.**   Enter a value from 100 to 1000 (d is the default) to calculate the number of milliseconds for congestion or no_credit drop.

```
Enter number of milliseconds for congestion/no_credit drop[100 - 1000]
or [d/default] for default:100
```

**Step 16.**   Enter a mode for congestion or no_credit drop.

```
Enter mode for congestion/no_credit drop[E/F]:
```

**Step 17.**   Enter **yes** (no is the default) to configure the NTP server.

```
Configure NTP server? (yes/no) [n]: yes
```

Enter the NTP server IPv4 address.

NTP server IP address: *ntp_server_IP_address*

**Step 18.** Enter **shut** (shut is the default) to configure the default switch port interface to the shut (disabled) state.

```
Configure default switchport interface state (shut/noshut) [shut]: shut
```

The management Ethernet interface is not shut down at this point. Only the Fibre Channel, iSCSI, FCIP, and Gigabit Ethernet interfaces are shut down.

**Step 19.** Enter **on** (off is the default) to configure the switch port trunk mode.

```
Configure default switchport trunk mode (on/off/auto) [off]: on
```

**Step 20.** Enter **yes** (yes is the default) to configure the switchport mode F.

```
Configure default switchport mode F (yes/no) [n]: yes
```

**Step 21.** Enter **on** (off is the default) to configure the Port Channel auto-create state.

```
Configure default port-channel auto-create state (on/off) [off]: on
```

**Step 22.** Enter **permit** (deny is the default) to deny a default zone policy configuration.

```
Configure default zone policy (permit/deny) [deny]: permit
```

This configuration permits traffic flow to all members of the default zone.

**Step 23.** Enter **yes** (no is the default) to disable a full zone set distribution. This overrides the switch-wide default for the full zone set distribution feature.

```
Enable full zoneset distribution (yes/no) [n]: yes
```

You see the new configuration. Review and edit the configuration that you have just entered.

**Step 24.** Enter **enhanced** (basic is the default) to configure default-zone mode as enhanced. This overrides the switch-wide default zone mode as enhanced.

```
Configure default zone mode (basic/enhanced) [basic]: enhanced
```

**Step 25.** Enter **no** (no is default) if you are satisfied with the configuration.

```
The following configuration will be applied:
  username admin password admin_pass role network-admin
  username user_name password user_pass role network-admin
  snmp-server community snmp_community ro
  switchname switch
  interface mgmt0
   ip address ip_address subnet_mask
   no shutdown
  ip routing
  ip route dest_prefix dest_mask dest_address
  ip default-network dest_prefix
  ip default-gateway default_gateway
  ip name-server name_server
  ip domain-name domain_name
  telnet server disable
  ssh key rsa 2048 force
  ssh server enable
  ntp server ipaddr ntp_server
```

11

```
                    system default switchport shutdown
                    system default switchport trunk mode on
                    system default switchport mode F
                    system default port-channel auto-create
                    zone default-zone permit vsan 1-4093
                    zoneset distribute full vsan 1-4093
                    system default zone mode enhanced
                  Would you like to edit the configuration? (yes/no)  [n]: no
```

**Step 26.**   Enter **yes** (yes is default) to use and save this configuration.

```
                  Use this configuration and save it? (yes/no) [y]: yes
```

If you do not save the configuration at this point, none of your changes are updated the next time the switch is rebooted. Type **yes** to save the new configuration. This ensures that the kickstart and system images are also automatically configured.

**Step 27.**   Log in to the switch using the new username and password and verify that the switch is running the software version that you installed using the previous procedure issuing the **show version** command.

Example 11-1 displays the **show version** output.

**Example 11-1**   *Verifying NX-OS Version on an MDS 9100 Switch*

```
switch# show version
Cisco Nexus Operating System (NX-OS) Software
TAC support: http://www.cisco.com/tac
Documents: http://www.cisco.com/en/US/products/ps9372/tsd_products_support_series_
  home.html
Copyright (c) 2002-2018, Cisco Systems, Inc. All rights reserved.
The copyrights to certain works contained herein are owned by
other third parties and are used and distributed under license.
Some parts of this software are covered under the GNU Public
License. A copy of the license is available at
http://www.gnu.org/licenses/gpl.html.


Software
  BIOS:      version 2.1.17
  loader:    version N/A
  kickstart: version 8.3(1)
  system:    version 8.3(1)
  BIOS compile time:       01/08/14
  kickstart image file is: bootflash:///m9100-s5ek9-kickstart-mz.8.3.1.bin
  kickstart compile time:  7/30/2018 12:00:00 [07/12/2018 04:40:49]
  system image file is:    bootflash:///m9100-s5ek9-mz.8.3.1.bin
  system compile time:     7/30/2018 12:00:00 [07/12/2018 08:32:46]


Hardware
  cisco MDS 9148S 16G 48 FC (1 Slot) Chassis ("2/4/8/16 Gbps FC/Supervisor")
```

```
   Motorola, e500v2 with 4088556 kB of memory.
   Processor Board ID JAE1948007Z


 Device name: MDS-2
   bootflash:    4001760 kB


Kernel uptime is 5 day(s), 21 hour(s), 28 minute(s), 7 second(s)


Last reset at 312523 usecs after Thu Aug 22 04:58:00 2019
   Reason: Reset Requested by CLI command reload
   System version: 8.3(1)
   Service:


plugin
   Core Plugin
switch#
```

You can configure both in-band and out-of-band configuration together by entering **yes** in steps 10a, 10c, and 10d in the previous procedure, as shown in the following excerpt.

The following is the initial setup procedure for configuring the in-band management logical interface on VSAN 1:

**Step 10.**  Enter **yes** (no is the default) to configure advanced IP options such as in-band management, static routes, default network, DNS, and domain name.

```
Configure Advanced IP options (yes/no)? [n]: yes
```

  **a.**  Enter **yes** (no is the default) at the in-band management configuration prompt.

```
Continue with in-band (VSAN1) management configuration? (yes/no)
[no]: yes
```

  Enter the VSAN 1 IPv4 address.

```
VSAN1 IPv4 address: ip_address
```

  Enter the IPv4 subnet mask.

```
VSAN1 IPv4 net mask: subnet_mask
```

  **b.**  Enter **no** (yes is the default) to enable IPv4 routing capabilities.

```
Enable ip routing capabilities? (yes/no) [y]: no
```

  **c.**  Enter **no** (yes is the default) to configure a static route.

```
Configure static route: (yes/no) [y]: no
```

  **d.**  Enter **no** (yes is the default) to configure the default network

```
Configure the default-network: (yes/no) [y]: no
```

  **e.**  Enter **no** (yes is the default) to configure the DNS IPv4 address.

```
Configure the DNS IP address? (yes/no) [y]: no
```

  **f.**  Enter **no** (no is the default) to skip the default domain name configuration.

```
Configure the default domain name? (yes/no) [n]: no
```

11

**NOTE**  If you are executing the setup script after issuing a **write erase** command, you must explicitly change the default zoning mode to enhanced for VSAN 1 after finishing the script by using the following commands:

```
switch# configure terminal
switch(config)# zone mode enhanced vsan 1
```

# Cisco MDS NX-OS Software Upgrade and Downgrade

A Cisco MDS switch is shipped with the Cisco MDS NX-OS operating system for the Cisco MDS 9000 Series multilayer directors and fabric switches. The Cisco MDS NX-OS software consists of two images: the kickstart image and the system image.

The software image install procedure depends on the following factors:

- **Software images:** The kickstart and system image files reside in directories or folders that can be accessed from the Cisco MDS 9000 Series multilayer switch prompt.

- **Image version:** Each image file has a version.

- **Flash disks on the switch:** The bootflash: resides on the supervisor module, and the CompactFlash disk is inserted into the slot0: device.

- **Supervisor modules:** Either single or dual supervisor modules are present. To realize the benefits of a nondisruptive upgrade on the Cisco MDS 9700 Series multilayer directors, you should install dual supervisor modules per the Cisco recommendation.

To determine the version of the Cisco MDS NX-OS software that is currently running on a Cisco MDS 9000 switch using the CLI, log in to the switch and run the **show version** command in privileged EXEC mode.

Use the **show incompatibility-all system bootflash:** *system image filename* command to determine which features are incompatible with the destination upgrade release, as follows:

```
switch(config)# show incompatibility-all system bootflash:m9700-sf4ek9-mz.8.4.1.bin


Checking incompatible configuration(s):

No incompatible configurations


Checking dynamic incompatibilities:

No incompatible configurations
```

No payload encryption (NPE) images are also available with the Cisco MDS NX-OS software. The NPE images are intended for countries that have import restrictions on products that encrypt payload data. To differentiate an NPE image from a standard software image, the letters NPE are included in the image. Nondisruptive software upgrades or downgrades between NPE images and non-NPE images are not supported.

You can upgrade any switch in the Cisco MDS 9000 Family using one of the following methods:

- **Automated, one-step upgrade using the install all command:** This upgrade is nondisruptive. The **install all** command upgrades all modules in any Cisco MDS 9000 Family switch. Cisco recommends having dual supervisors installed on the MDS switch while performing a nondisruptive upgrade. Although a nondisruptive update doesn't require a switch reload, it disrupts the control plane for about 80 seconds.

- **Quick, one-step upgrade using the reload command:** This upgrade is disruptive and requires a switch reload. Before running the **reload** command, copy the correct kickstart and system images to the correct location in bootflash and change the boot commands in your configuration.

**NOTE** An upgrade or downgrade of control plane software that results in the data plane going down for any period of time is called a *disruptive* (or *hitful*) *upgrade* or *downgrade*, respectively. This includes a stateless restart. An upgrade or downgrade of control plane software that does not take down the data plane for any period of time is called a *nondisruptive* (or *hitless*) *upgrade* or *downgrade*, respectively. This includes a stateful restart.

When the Cisco MDS Series switch is first switched on or during reboot, the switch follows the boot sequence shown in Figure 11-2.

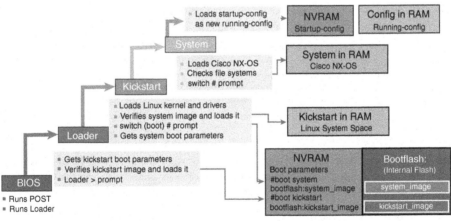

**Figure 11-2** *Boot Sequence*

The BIOS on the supervisor module first runs power-on self-test (POST) diagnostics and then runs the loader bootstrap function. The boot parameters are held in NVRAM and point to the location and name of both the kickstart and system images. The loader obtains the location of the kickstart file, usually on bootflash, and verifies the kickstart image before loading it.

The kickstart loads the Linux kernel and device drivers and then needs to load the system image. Again, the boot parameters in NVRAM should point to the location and name of the system image, usually on bootflash. The kickstart then verifies the system image and loads it.

11

Finally, the system image loads the Cisco NX-OS software, checks the file systems, and proceeds to load the startup configuration, containing the switch configuration, from NVRAM.

If the boot parameters are missing or have an incorrect name or location, the boot process fails at the last stage. If this happens, the administrator must recover from the error and reload the switch. The **install all** command is a script that greatly simplifies the boot procedure and checks for errors and the upgrade impact before proceeding.

We discuss the disruptive and nondisruptive upgrade and downgrade procedures in detail in the following sections.

## Nondisruptive Upgrade on a Cisco MDS Fabric Switch

Let's first look at the process for a nondisruptive upgrade on a Cisco MDS fabric switch.

Before performing an upgrade, use the **show install all impact** command to view the effect of updating the system from the running image to another specified image.

**Step 1.** Verify that the system image files for the upgrade are present on the active supervisor module bootflash:

```
switch# dir bootflash:

25863680 Sep 23 12:02:16 2017 m9250-s5ek9-kickstart-mz.8.2.1.bin
25864704 Sep 05 12:21:26 2018 m9250-s5ek9-kickstart-mz.8.2.1.bin
25869312 Apr 01 12:29:34 2018 m9250-s5ek9-kickstart-mz.8.2.2.bin
25869312 Apr 12 01:55:22 2018 m9250-s5ek9-kickstart-mz.8.2.2.bin
25947136 Nov 09 13:41:43 2018 m9250-s5ek9-kickstart-mz.8.3.1.bin
25970176 Jan 17 14:10:47 2019 m9250-s5ek9-kickstart-mz.8.3.2.bin
26126848 May 07 11:51:20 2019 m9250-s5ek9-kickstart-mz.8.4.1.bin


Usage for bootflash://sup-local

2838728704 bytes used
520916992 bytes free
3359645696 bytes total
```

**Step 2.** If the software image file is not present, download it from an FTP or TFTP server to bootflash. You can obtain the software image file from the Cisco.com Software Download Center at http://www.cisco.com/cisco/software/navigator.html.

```
switch# copy tftp://tftpserver.cisco.com/MDS/m9250-s5ek9-kickstart-
mz.8.4.1.bin bootflash:m9250-s5ek9-kickstart-mz.8.4.1.bin
switch# copy tftp://tftpserver.cisco.com/MDS/m9250-s5ek9-mz.8.4.1.bin
bootflash:m9250-s5ek9-mz.8.4.1.bin
```

**Step 3.** Ensure that the required space is available on the switch:

```
switch# dir bootflash:
25863680 Sep 23 12:02:16 2017 m9250-s5ek9-kickstart-mz.8.2.1.bin
25864704 Sep 05 12:21:26 2018 m9250-s5ek9-kickstart-mz.8.2.1.bin
25869312 Apr 01 12:29:34 2018 m9250-s5ek9-kickstart-mz.8.2.2.bin
25869312 Apr 12 01:55:22 2018 m9250-s5ek9-kickstart-mz.8.2.2.bin
25947136 Nov 09 13:41:43 2018 m9250-s5ek9-kickstart-mz.8.3.1.bin
```

```
25970176 Jan 17 14:10:47 2019 m9250-s5ek9-kickstart-mz.8.3.2.bin
26126848 May 07 11:51:20 2019 m9250-s5ek9-kickstart-mz.8.4.1.bin


Usage for bootflash://sup-local
120695976 bytes used
63863640 bytes free
184559616 bytes total
```

**Step 4.**   If you need more space on the switch, delete the files that are not required:

```
switch# delete bootflash: m9250-s5ek9-kickstart-mz.8.2.1.bin
switch# delete bootflash: m9250-s5ek9-kickstart-mz.8.2.1.bin
```

**Step 5.**   Save the configuration using the **copy running-config startup-config** command:

```
switch# copy running-config startup-config
```

You can also back up your existing configuration to a file, using the **copy running-config bootflash:backup_config.txt** command. You can add a date reference to the .txt filename to identify the file later.

**Step 6.**   Perform the upgrade by running the **install all** command:

```
switch# install all kickstart m9250-s5ek9-kickstart-mz.8.4.1.bin system
m9250-s5ek9-mz.8.4.1.bin
Installer will perform compatibility check first. Please wait.
y
Verifying image bootflash:/m9250-s5ek9-kickstart-mz.8.4.1.bin for boot
variable "kickstart".
[# ] 0%
[####################] 100% -- SUCCESS
Verifying image bootflash:/m9250-s5ek9-mz.8.4.1.bin for boot variable
"system".
[####################] 100% -- SUCCESS
Performing module support checks.
[####################] 100% -- SUCCESS
Verifying image type.
[####################] 100% -- SUCCESS
Extracting "system" version from image bootflash:/
m9250-s5ek9-mz.8.4.1.bin
[####################] 100% -- SUCCESS
Extracting "kickstart" version from image bootflash:/
m9250-s5ek9-kickstart-mz.8.4.1.bin
[####################] 100% -- SUCCESS
Extracting "bios" version from image bootflash:/m9250-s5ek9-mz.8.4.1.bin
[####################] 100% -- SUCCESS
Performing Compact Flash and TCAM sanity test.
[####################] 100% -- SUCCESS
Notifying services about system upgrade.
[####################] 100% -- SUCCESS
Compatibility check is done:
```

11

```
Module bootable Impact Install-type   Reason
------ -------- ------ --------------  ------
1                yes    non-disruptive reset


Other miscellaneous information for installation:
Module info
------ ----------------------------------
1       FC ports 1-40 and FCoE ports 1-8 are hitless, IPS 1-2 are hitful,
        and Intelligent Applications running are hitful


Images will be upgraded according to following table:
Module Image     Running-Version          New-Version  Upg-Required
------ --------  --------------------      ------------ -----------
1      system    8.1(1)                    8.4(1)       yes
1      kickstart 8.1(1)                    8.4(1)       yes
1      bios      v2.1.17(01/08/14):v2.1.17(01/08/14)   v2.1.17(01/08/14)
                                                        no


Do you want to continue with the installation (y/n)? [n] y
Install is in progress, please wait.
Performing runtime checks.
[####################] 100% -- SUCCESS
Notifying services about the upgrade.
[####################] 100% -- SUCCESS
Setting boot variables.
[####################] 100% -- SUCCESS
Performing configuration copy.
[####################] 100% -- SUCCESS
Module 1: Refreshing compact flash and Upgrading bios/loader/bootrom/
power-seq.
Warning: please do not remove or power off the module at this time.
[####################] 100% -- SUCCESS
Upgrade can no longer be aborted, any failure will result in a
disruptive upgrade.
Freeing memory in the file system.
[####################] 100% -- SUCCESS
Loading images into memory.
[####################] 100% -- SUCCESS
Saving linecard runtime state.
[####################] 100% -- SUCCESS
Saving supervisor runtime state.
[####################] 100% -- SUCCESS
Saving mts state.
[####################] 100% -- SUCCESS
Reloading the kernel to proceed with the upgrade.
<output omitted>
Loading system software
```

```
Uncompressing system image: bootflash:///m9250-s5ek9-mz.8.4.1.bin
ccccccccccccccccccccccccccccccccccccccccccccccccccccccccccccccccc
Load plugins that defined in image conf: /isan/plugin_img/img.conf
<output omitted>Continuing with installation process, please wait.
The login will be disabled until the installation is completed.
Status for linecard upgrade.
[####################] 100% -- SUCCESS
Performing supervisor state verification.
[####################] 100% -- SUCCESS
Supervisor non-disruptive upgrade successful.
Install has been successful.
```

**Step 7.**    Log in to the switch:

```
MDS Switch
x.x.x.x login: admin
Cisco Nexus Operating System (NX-OS) Software
TAC support: http://www.cisco.com/tac
Copyright (c) 2002-2014, Cisco Systems, Inc. All rights reserved.
The copyrights to certain works contained in this software are
owned by other third parties and used and distributed under
license. Certain components of this software are licensed under
the GNU General Public License (GPL) version 2.0 or the GNU
Lesser General Public License (LGPL) Version 2.1. A copy of each
such license is available at
http://www.opensource.org/licenses/gpl-2.0.php and
http://www.opensource.org/licenses/lgpl-2.1.php
```

**Step 8.**    Run the **show version** command to verify the upgraded image version:

```
switch# show version
Cisco Nexus Operating System (NX-OS) Software
TAC support: http://www.cisco.com/tac
Documents: http://www.cisco.com/en/US/products/ps9372/ tsd_products_
support_series_home.html
Copyright (c) 2002-2019, Cisco Systems, Inc. All rights reserved.
The copyrights to certain works contained herein are owned by
other third parties and are used and distributed under license.
Some parts of this software are covered under the GNU Public
License. A copy of the license is available at
http://www.gnu.org/licenses/gpl.html.
Software
BIOS: version 2.1.17
loader: version N/A
kickstart: version 8.4(1) [build 8.4(1)]
system: version 8.4(1) [build 8.4(1)]
BIOS compile time: 01/08/14
kickstart image file is: bootflash:///m9250-s5ek9-kickstart-mz.8.4.1.bin
kickstart compile time: 6/1/2019 23:00:00 [05/07/2019 04:18:10]
```

11

```
486system image file is: bootflash:///m9250-s5ek9-mz.8.4.1.bin
system compile time: 6/1/2019 23:00:00 [05/07/2019 07:09:57]
Hardware
cisco MDS 9250i 40 FC 2 IPS 8 FCoE (2 RU) Chassis
("40FC+8FCoE+2IPS Supervisor")
Motorola, e500v2 with 4088636 kB of memory.
Processor Board ID JAF1804AAFG
Device name: MDS9250i
bootflash: 4001760 kB
Kernel uptime is 0 day(s), 0 hour(s), 7 minute(s), 42 second(s)
Last reset at 288238 usecs after Thu May 9 11:40:56 2019
Reason: Reset due to upgrade
System version: 8.1(1)
Service:
plugin
Core Plugin
```

**Step 9.** Verify the status of the modules on the switch, using the **show module** command:

```
switch# show module

Mod Ports Module-Type                   Model           Status
--- ----- --------------------------- --------------- ---------
1   50    40FC+8FCoE+2IPS Supervisor   DS-C9250I-K9-SUP active *
Mod Sw      Hw    World-Wide-Name(s) (WWN)
--- ------  ----  -------------------------------------------------
1   8.4(1)  1.0   20:01:00:2a:6a:1b:64:d0 to 20:28:00:2a:6a:1b:64:d0
Mod MAC-Address(es)                      Serial-Num
--- ------------------------------------  ------------
1   b8-38-61-4a-25-c0 to b8-38-61-4a-25-cf JAF1804AAFG
```

**Step 10.** To display the status of a nondisruptive upgrade on a fabric switch, use the **show install all status** command. The command output displays the status only after the switch has rebooted with the new image. All the actions preceding the reboot are not captured in this output because when you enter the **install all** command using a Telnet session, the session is disconnected when the switch reboots. When you reconnect to the switch through a Telnet session, the upgrade may already be complete, in which case, the output displays the status of the upgrade.

```
switch# show install all status

This is the log of last installation.

Continuing with installation process, please wait.
The login will be disabled until the installation is completed.

Status for linecard upgrade.
```

```
-- SUCCESS

Performing supervisor state verification.
-- SUCCESS

Install has been successful
```

## Disruptive Upgrade on a Cisco MDS Fabric Switch

Now let's look at the process for a disruptive upgrade on a Cisco MDS fabric switch.

**Step 1.** Verify that the system image files for the upgrade are present on the active supervisor module bootflash:

```
switch# dir bootflash:

25863680 Sep 23 12:02:16 2017 m9250-s5ek9-kickstart-mz.8.2.1.bin
25864704 Sep 05 12:21:26 2018 m9250-s5ek9-kickstart-mz.8.2.1.bin
25869312 Apr 01 12:29:34 2018 m9250-s5ek9-kickstart-mz.8.2.2.bin
25869312 Apr 12 01:55:22 2018 m9250-s5ek9-kickstart-mz.8.2.2.bin
25947136 Nov 09 13:41:43 2018 m9250-s5ek9-kickstart-mz.8.3.1.bin
25970176 Jan 17 14:10:47 2019 m9250-s5ek9-kickstart-mz.8.3.2.bin
26126848 May 07 11:51:20 2019 m9250-s5ek9-kickstart-mz.8.4.1.bin

Usage for bootflash://sup-local

2838728704 bytes used
520916992 bytes free
3359645696 bytes total
```

**Step 2.** If the software image file is not present, download it from an FTP or TFTP server to bootflash. You can obtain the software image file from the Cisco.com Software Download Center at http://www.cisco.com/cisco/software/navigator.html.

```
switch# copy tftp://tftpserver.cisco.com/MDS/m9250-s5ek9- kickstart-
mz.8.4.1.bin bootflash:m9250-s5ek9-kickstart- mz.8.4.1.bin
switch# copy tftp://tftpserver.cisco.com/MDS/m9250-s5ek9-mz.8.4.1.bin
bootflash:m9250-s5ek9-mz.8.4.1.bin
```

**Step 3.** Ensure that the required space is available on the switch:

```
switch# dir bootflash:
25863680 Sep 23 12:02:16 2017 m9250-s5ek9-kickstart-mz.8.2.1.bin
25864704 Sep 05 12:21:26 2018 m9250-s5ek9-kickstart-mz.8.2.1.bin
25869312 Apr 01 12:29:34 2018 m9250-s5ek9-kickstart-mz.8.2.2.bin
25869312 Apr 12 01:55:22 2018 m9250-s5ek9-kickstart-mz.8.2.2.bin
25947136 Nov 09 13:41:43 2018 m9250-s5ek9-kickstart-mz.8.3.1.bin
25970176 Jan 17 14:10:47 2019 m9250-s5ek9-kickstart-mz.8.3.2.bin
26126848 May 07 11:51:20 2019 m9250-s5ek9-kickstart-mz.8.4.1.bin

Usage for bootflash://sup-local
120695976 bytes used
63863640 bytes free
184559616 bytes total
```

11

**Step 4.**  If you need more space on the switch, delete the files that are not required:

```
switch# delete bootflash: m9250-s5ek9-kickstart-mz.8.2.1.bin
switch# delete bootflash: m9250-s5ek9-kickstart-mz.8.2.1.bin
```

**Step 5.**  Change the boot statements on the switch to reflect the new system software.

```
switch# configure terminal
switch(config)# no boot kickstart bootflash:/
m9250-s5ek9- kickstart-mz.8.2.1.bin
switch(config)# no boot system bootflash:/m9250-s5ek9-mz. 8.2.1.bin
switch(config)# boot kickstart bootflash:/
m9250-s5ek9- kickstart-mz.8.4.1.bin
switch(config)# boot system bootflash:/m9250-s5ek9-mz.8.4.1.bin
switch(config)# exit
```

**Step 6.**  Save the configuration using the **copy running-config startup-config** command:

```
switch# copy running-config startup-config
```

You can also back up your existing configuration to a file by using the **copy running-config bootflash:backup_config.txt** command. You can add a date reference to the .txt filename to identify the file later.

**Step 7.**  Reload the switch using the **reload** command:

```
switch# reload
!!!WARNING! there is unsaved configuration!!!
This command will reboot the system. (y/n)? [n] y
```

**Step 8.**  Log in to the switch:

```
MDS Switch
x.x.x.x login: admin
Cisco Nexus Operating System (NX-OS) Software
TAC support: http://www.cisco.com/tac
Copyright (c) 2002-2014, Cisco Systems, Inc. All rights reserved.
The copyrights to certain works contained in this software are
owned by other third parties and used and distributed under
license. Certain components of this software are licensed under
the GNU General Public License (GPL) version 2.0 or the GNU
Lesser General Public License (LGPL) Version 2.1. A copy of each
such license is available at
http://www.opensource.org/licenses/gpl-2.0.php and
http://www.opensource.org/licenses/lgpl-2.1.php
```

**Step 9.**  Run the **show version** command to verify the new image on the switch:

```
switch# show version
Cisco Nexus Operating System (NX-OS) Software
TAC support: http://www.cisco.com/tac
Documents: http://www.cisco.com/en/US/products/ps9372/ tsd_products_
support_series_home.html
Copyright (c) 2002-2019, Cisco Systems, Inc. All rights reserved.
```

```
The copyrights to certain works contained herein are owned by
other third parties and are used and distributed under license.
Some parts of this software are covered under the GNU Public
License. A copy of the license is available at
http://www.gnu.org/licenses/gpl.html.
Software
BIOS: version 2.1.17
loader: version N/A
kickstart: version 8.4(1) [build 8.4(1)]
system: version 8.4(1) [build 8.4(1)]
BIOS compile time: 01/08/14
kickstart image file is: bootflash:///m9250-s5ek9-kickstart-mz.8.4.1.bin
kickstart compile time: 6/1/2019 23:00:00 [05/07/2019 04:18:10]
system image file is: bootflash:///m9250-s5ek9-mz.8.4.1.bin
system compile time: 6/1/2019 23:00:00 [05/07/2019 07:09:57]
Hardware
cisco MDS 9250i 40 FC 2 IPS 8 FCoE (2 RU) Chassis
("40FC+8FCoE+2IPS Supervisor")
Motorola, e500v2 with 4088636 kB of memory.
Processor Board ID JAF1804AAFG
Device name: MDS9250i
bootflash: 4001760 kB
Kernel uptime is 0 day(s), 0 hour(s), 7 minute(s), 42 second(s)
Last reset at 288238 usecs after Thu May 9 11:40:56 2019
Reason: Reset due to upgrade
System version: 8.1(1)
Service:
plugin
Core Plugin
```

**Step 10.** Verify the status of the modules on the switch, using the **show module** command:

```
switch# show module


Mod Ports Module-Type               Model            Status
--- ----- ------------------------- ---------------- ----------
1   50    40FC+8FCoE+2IPS Supervisor DS-C9250I-K9-SUP active *
Mod Sw     Hw   World-Wide-Name(s) (WWN)
--- ------ ---- ----------------------------------------------------
1   8.4(1) 1.0  20:01:00:2a:6a:1b:64:d0 to 20:28:00:2a:6a:1b:64:d0
Mod MAC-Address(es)                      Serial-Num
--- ------------------------------------ ----------
1   b8-38-61-4a-25-c0 to b8-38-61-4a-25-cf JAF1804AAFG
```

11

## Nondisruptive Downgrade on a Cisco MDS Fabric Switch

Next, let's look at the process for a nondisruptive downgrade on a Cisco MDS fabric switch.

**Step 1.** Verify that the system image files for the downgrade are present in the active supervisor module bootflash:

```
switch# dir bootflash:

26126848 May 07 11:51:20 2019 m9250-s5ek9-kickstart-mz.8.4.1.bin
20090368 Apr 06 05:25:31 2001 m9250-s5ek9-kickstart-mz.7.3.1.DY.1.bin
20044800 Mar 30 15:42:05 2014 m9250-s5ek9-kickstart-mz.6.2.7.bin
107197681 Apr 06 05:26:53 2001 m9250-s5ek9-mz.6.2.5.bin.S68
107587249 Mar 30 15:42:52 2014 m9250-s5ek9-mz.6.2.7.bin
```

**Step 2.** If the software image file is not present, download it from an FTP or TFTP server to the active supervisor module bootflash. You can obtain the software image file from the Cisco.com Software Download Center: http://www.cisco.com/cisco/software/navigator.html.

```
switch# copy tftp://tftpserver.cisco.com/MDS/m9250-s5ek9- kickstart-
mz.7.3.1.DY.1.bin bootflash:m9250-s5ek9-kickstart-mz.7.3.1.DY.1.bin
switch# copy tftp://tftpserver.cisco.com/MDS/m9250-s5ek9- kickstart-
mz.7.3.1.DY.1.bin bootflash:m9250-s5ek9-kickstart-mz.7.3.1.DY.1.bin
```

**Step 3.** Ensure that the required space is available in the active supervisor:

```
switch# dir bootflash:

26126848 May 07 11:51:20 2019 m9250-s5ek9-kickstart-mz.8.4.1.bin
12288 Aug 26 19:06:14 2011 lost+found/
18939904 Jul 01 10:54:49 2011 m9250-s5ek9-kickstart-mz.6.2.5.bin
101756072 Jul 01 10:33:52 2011 m9250-s5ek9-mz.6.2.5.bin

Usage for bootflash://sup-local
120695976 bytes used
63863640 bytes free
184559616 bytes total
```

**Step 4.** If you need more space in the active supervisor module bootflash, delete the files that are not required, to make space available:

```
switch# delete bootflash: m9250-s5ek9-kickstart-mz.6.2.5.bin
switch# delete bootflash: m9250-s5ek9-kickstart-mz.6.2.5.bin
```

**Step 5.** Run the **show incompatibility system** *image-filename* command to determine whether you must disable the features not supported by a release earlier than the release that is installed.

```
switch# show incompatibility system
bootflash:m9250-s5ek9-kickstart-mz.7.3.1.DY.1.bin
no incompatible configuration
```

**Step 6.** Save the configuration using the **copy running-config startup-config** command:

```
switch# copy running-config startup-config
```

**Step 7.**    Run the **install all** command to downgrade the software:

```
switch(config)# install all kickstart m9250-s5ek9-kickstart-
mz.7.3.1.DY.1.bin system m9250-s5ek9-mz.7.3.1.DY.1.bin
Installer will perform compatibility check first. Please wait.


Verifying image bootflash:/m9250-s5ek9-kickstart-mz.7.3.1.DY.1.bin for
boot variable "kickstart".
[####################] 100% -- SUCCESS


Verifying image bootflash:/m9250-s5ek9-mz.7.3.1.DY.1.bin for boot
variable "system".
[####################] 100% -- SUCCESS


Performing module support checks.
[####################] 100% -- SUCCESS


Verifying image type.
[####################] 100% -- SUCCESS


Extracting "system" version from image bootflash:/
m9250-s5ek9-mz.7.3.1.DY.1.bin.
[####################] 100% -- SUCCESS


Extracting "kickstart" version from image bootflash:/
m9250-s5ek9-kickstart-mz.7.3.1.DY.1.bin.
[####################] 100% -- SUCCESS


Extracting "bios" version from image bootflash:/
m9250-s5ek9-mz.7.3.1.DY.1.bin.
[####################] 100% -- SUCCESS


Performing Compact Flash and TCAM sanity test.
[####################] 100% -- SUCCESS


Notifying services about system upgrade.
[####################] 100% -- SUCCESS




Compatibility check is done:

Module bootable Impact Install-type   Reason
------ -------- ------ -------------  ------
1               yes    non-disruptive reset
```

```
Other miscellaneous information for installation:

Module info
------ ----------------------------------
1       FC ports 1-40 and FCoE ports 1-8 are hitless, IPS 1-2 are
        hitful, and Intelligent Applications running are hitful

Images will be upgraded according to following table:
Module Image       Running-Version    New-Version    Upg-Required
------ ---------   ------------------  ------------   --------------
1      system      8.1(1b)             7.3(1)DY(1)             yes
1      kickstart   8.1(1b)             7.3(1)DY(1)             yes
1      bios v2.1.17(01/08/14):v2.1.17(01/08/14) v2.1.17(01/08/14) no

Do you want to continue with the installation (y/n)?  [n] y

Install is in progress, please wait.

Performing runtime checks.
[####################] 100% -- SUCCESS

Notifying services about the upgrade.
[####################] 100% -- SUCCESS

Setting boot variables.
[####################] 100% -- SUCCESS

Performing configuration copy.
[####################] 100% -- SUCCESS

Module 1: Refreshing compact flash and Upgrading bios/loader/bootrom/
power-seq.
Warning: please do not remove or power off the module at this time.
[####################] 100% -- SUCCESS

Converting startup config.
[####################] 100% -- SUCCESS

Upgrade can no longer be aborted, any failure will result in a
disruptive upgrade.

Freeing memory in the file system.
[####################] 100% -- SUCCESS

Loading images into memory.
[####################] 100% -- SUCCESS
```

```
Saving linecard runtime state.
[####################] 100% -- SUCCESS

Saving supervisor runtime state.
[####################] 100% -- SUCCESS

Saving mts state.
[####################] 100% -- SUCCESS

Reloading the kernel to proceed with the upgrade.
All telnet and ssh connections will now be temporarily terminated.
<output omitted>

Status for linecard upgrade.
[####################] 100% -- SUCCESS

Performing supervisor state verification.
[####################] 100% -- SUCCESS

Install has been successful.
```

**Step 8.**   Run the **show version** command to verify the successful downgrade:

```
switch# show version

Cisco Nexus Operating System (NX-OS) Software
TAC support: http://www.cisco.com/tac
Documents: http://www.cisco.com/en/US/products/ps9372/ tsd_products_
support_series_home.html
Copyright (c) 2002-2016, Cisco Systems, Inc. All rights reserved.
The copyrights to certain works contained herein are owned by
other third parties and are used and distributed under license.
Some parts of this software are covered under the GNU Public
License. A copy of the license is available at
http://www.gnu.org/licenses/gpl.html.

Software
BIOS: version 2.1.17
loader: version N/A
kickstart: version 7.3(1)DY(1)
system: version 7.3(1)DY(1)
BIOS compile time: 01/08/14
kickstart image file is: bootflash:///m9250-s5ek9-kickstart-
mz.7.3.1.DY.1.bin.S21
kickstart compile time: 1/11/2016 16:00:00 [02/11/2016 10:35:42]
system image file is: bootflash:///m9250-s5ek9-mz.7.3.1.DY.1.
bin.S21
```

11

```
system compile time: 1/11/2016 16:00:00 [02/11/2016 13:08:53]


Hardware
cisco MDS 9250i 40 FC 2 IPS 8 FCoE (2 RU) Chassis
("40FC+8FCoE+2IPS Supervisor")
Motorola, e500v2, core 0 with 4155752 kB of memory.
Processor Board ID JAF1626BCQH

Device name: alishan-dr
bootflash: 4013856 kB

Kernel uptime is 0 day(s), 17 hour(s), 18 minute(s), 58 second(s)

Last reset at 443194 usecs after Wed Aug 31 10:58:41 2016

Reason: Reset due to upgrade
System version: 7.3(1)DY(1)
Service:

plugin
Core Plugin
switch#
```

**Step 9.**    Verify the status of the modules in the switch, using the **show module** command:

```
switch# show module

Mod Ports Module-Type                    Model               Status
--- ----- -------------------------- ------------------- ---------
1    50    40FC+8FCoE+2IPS Supervisor DS-C9250i-22PK9-SUP active *


Mod Sw         Hw World-Wide-Name(s) (WWN)
--- ---------- --- -------------------------------------------------
1   7.3(1)DY(1) 0.9 20:01:54:7f:ee:1b:14:a0 to 20:28:54:7f:ee:1b:14:a0


Mod MAC-Address(es)                      Serial-Num
--- ------------------------------------ ----------
1    f0-f7-55-29-50-60 to f0-f7-55-29-50-6f   JAF1626BCQH

* this terminal session

switch#
```

## Disruptive Downgrade on a Cisco MDS Fabric Switch

Finally, let's look at the process for a disruptive downgrade on a Cisco MDS fabric switch.

**Step 1.** Verify that the system image files for the downgrade are present in the active supervisor module bootflash:

```
switch# dir bootflash:

26126848 May 07 11:51:20 2019 m9250-s5ek9-kickstart-mz.8.4.1.bin
20090368 Apr 06 05:25:31 2001 m9250-s5ek9-kickstart-mz.7.3.1.DY.1.bin
20044800 Mar 30 15:42:05 2014 m9250-s5ek9-kickstart-mz.6.2.7.bin
107197681 Apr 06 05:26:53 2001 m9250-s5ek9-mz.6.2.5.bin.S68
107587249 Mar 30 15:42:52 2014 m9250-s5ek9-mz.6.2.7.bin
```

**Step 2.** If the software image file is not present, download it from an FTP or TFTP server to the active supervisor module bootflash. You can obtain the software image file from the Cisco.com Software Download Center: http://www.cisco.com/cisco/software/navigator.html.

```
switch# copy tftp://tftpserver.cisco.com/MDS/m9250-s5ek9- kickstart-
mz.7.3.1.DY.1.bin bootflash:m9250-s5ek9-kickstart-mz.7.3.1.DY.1.bin
switch# copy tftp://tftpserver.cisco.com/MDS/m9250-s5ek9-kickstart-
mz.7.3.1.DY.1.bin bootflash:m9250-s5ek9-kickstart-mz.7.3.1.DY.1.bin
```

**Step 3.** Ensure that the required space is available in the active supervisor:

```
switch# dir bootflash:

26126848 May 07 11:51:20 2019 m9250-s5ek9-kickstart-mz.8.4.1.bin
12288 Aug 26 19:06:14 2011 lost+found/
18939904 Jul 01 10:54:49 2011 m9250-s5ek9-kickstart-mz.6.2.5.bin
101756072 Jul 01 10:33:52 2011 m9250-s5ek9-mz.6.2.5.bin

Usage for bootflash://sup-local
120695976 bytes used
63863640 bytes free
184559616 bytes total
```

**Step 4.** If you need more space in the active supervisor module bootflash, delete the files that are not required to make space available:

```
switch# delete bootflash: m9250-s5ek9-kickstart-mz.6.2.5.bin
switch# delete bootflash: m9250-s5ek9-kickstart-mz.6.2.5.bin
```

**Step 5.** Run the **show incompatibility system** *image-filename* command to determine whether you must disable the features not supported by a release earlier than the release that is installed:

```
switch# show incompatibility system
bootflash:m9250-s5ek9-kickstart-mz.7.3.1.DY.1.bin
no incompatible configuration
```

**Step 6.** Change the boot statements on the switch to reflect the new system software:

```
switch# configure terminal
```

11

```
switch(config)# no boot kickstart bootflash:/
m9250-s5ek9- kickstart-mz.8.2.1.bin
switch(config)# no boot system bootflash:/m9250-s5ek9-mz.8.2.1.bin
switch(config)# boot kickstart bootflash:/
m9250-s5ek9- kickstart-mz.7.3.1.DY.1.bin
switch(config)# boot system bootflash:/
m9250-s5ek9-kickstart- mz.7.3.1.DY.1.bin
switch(config)# exit
```

**Step 7.** Save the configuration using the **copy running-config startup-config** command:

```
switch# copy running-config startup-config
```

You can also back up your existing configuration to a file, using the **copy running-config bootflash:backup_config.txt** command. You can add a date reference to the .txt filename to identify the file later.

**Step 8.** Reload the switch using the **reload** command:

```
switch# reload
!!!WARNING! there is unsaved configuration!!!
This command will reboot the system. (y/n)? [n] y
```

**Step 9.** Run the **show version** command to verify the successful downgrade:

```
switch# show version

Cisco Nexus Operating System (NX-OS) Software
TAC support: http://www.cisco.com/tac
Documents: http://www.cisco.com/en/US/products/ps9372/ tsd_products_
support_series_home.html
Copyright (c) 2002-2016, Cisco Systems, Inc. All rights reserved.
The copyrights to certain works contained herein are owned by
other third parties and are used and distributed under license.
Some parts of this software are covered under the GNU Public
License. A copy of the license is available at
http://www.gnu.org/licenses/gpl.html.


Software
BIOS: version 2.1.17
loader: version N/A
kickstart: version 7.3(1)DY(1)
system: version 7.3(1)DY(1)
BIOS compile time: 01/08/14
kickstart image file is: bootflash:///m9250-s5ek9-kickstart-
mz.7.3.1.DY.1.bin.S21
kickstart compile time: 1/11/2016 16:00:00 [02/11/2016 10:35:42]
system image file is: bootflash:///m9250-s5ek9-mz.7.3.1.DY.
1.bin.S21
system compile time: 1/11/2016 16:00:00 [02/11/2016 13:08:53]
```

```
Hardware
cisco MDS 9250i 40 FC 2 IPS 8 FCoE (2 RU) Chassis
("40FC+8FCoE+2IPS Supervisor")
Motorola, e500v2, core 0 with 4155752 kB of memory.
Processor Board ID JAF1626BCQH

Device name: alishan-dr
bootflash: 4013856 kB

Kernel uptime is 0 day(s), 17 hour(s), 18 minute(s), 58 second(s)

Last reset at 443194 usecs after Wed Aug 31 10:58:41 2016

Reason: Reset due to upgrade
System version: 7.3(1)DY(1)
Service:

plugin
Core Plugin
switch#
```

**Step 10.**   Verify the status of the modules in the switch, using the **show module** command:

```
switch# show module

Mod Ports Module-Type                  Model              Status
--- ----- -------------------------    ------------------ -------
1   50    40FC+8FCoE+2IPS Supervisor   DS-C9250i-22PK9-SUP active *

Mod Sw          Hw    World-Wide-Name(s) (WWN)
--- ----------- ----  --------------------------------------------
1   7.3(1)DY(1) 0.9   20:01:54:7f:ee:1b:14:a0 to 20:28:54:7f:ee:1b:14:a0

Mod MAC-Address(es)                      Serial-Num
--- ------------------------------------ ----------
1   f0-f7-55-29-50-60 to f0-f7-55-29-50-6f JAF1626BCQH

* this terminal session

switch#
```

## EPLD Upgrade on Cisco MDS 9000 Series Switches

Switches and directors in the Cisco MDS 9000 Series contain several electrical program-mable logical devices (EPLDs) that provide hardware functionalities in all of the modules. Cisco periodically provides EPLD image upgrades to include enhanced hardware functional-ity or to resolve known issues.

11

EPLD images are released as part of a Cisco MDS NX-OS release. Therefore, the EPLD images have a version number that matches the Cisco MDS NX-OS release they are part of.

An EPLD image is a package containing updates for each type of EPLD. Because EPLD changes are infrequent, an EPLD image may contain new updates for only some EPLDs. The remaining EPLD updates will be the same version as the previous EPLD image. You do not need to update your EPLD images unless otherwise advised by the Technical Assistance Center (TAC).

You can use the **show version module** *slot* **epld** command to view all current EPLD versions on a specified module, as shown in Example 11-2.

**Example 11-2**  *Displaying Current EPLD Versions for a Module*

```
switch# show version module 1 epld


EPLD Device Version

-------------------------------------

Power Manager 1.003
IO SPI 1.003
IO SPI 2 1.002
```

You can use the **show version fan** *slot* **epld** command to view all current EPLD versions on a specific fan module. Example 11-3 shows the currently installed EPLD versions on a fan module.

**Example 11-3**  *Displaying Current EPLD Versions for a Fan Module*

```
switch# show version fan 1 epld


EPLD Device Version

-------------------------------------

Fan Controller (1) 0.006
Fan Controller (2) 0.006
```

To view all current EPLD versions on a fabric module, you can use the **show version xbar** *slot* **epld** command. Example 11-4 shows the currently installed EPLD versions on a fabric module.

**Example 11-4**  *Displaying Current EPLD Versions for a Fabric Module*

```
switch# show version xbar 2 epld


EPLD Device Version

-------------------------------------

Power Manager 1.002
```

You can use the **show version epld** *uri* command to view all the updates contained in an EPLD package. Example 11-5 shows the available EPLD versions.

**Example 11-5**   *Displaying EPLD Versions in an EPLD Image for a Cisco MDS 9700 Series Switch*

```
switch# show version epld bootflash:m9000-pkg2.8.2.1.epld

Retrieving EPLD versions... Please wait.

EPLD image file 8.2.1 built on Wed Sep 27 04:43:59 2017

Module Type Model EPLD Device Version
-------------------------------------------------------------------------
Supervisor Module-3 DS-X97-SF1-K9 Power Manager SPI 20.000

Supervisor Module-3 DS-X97-SF1E-K9 Power Manager SPI 20.000

Fabric Module 1 DS-X9718-FAB1 Power Manager 1.002

Fabric Module 1 DS-X9710-FAB1 Power Manager 1.003

Fabric Module 1 DS-X9706-FAB1 Power Manager 1.002

Fabric Module 2 DS-X9710-FAB-2 Power Manager 0.001

16 Gbps Advanced FC Module DS-X9448-768K9 Power Manager 8.000
16 Gbps Advanced FC Module DS-X9448-768K9 IO 15.000
10 Gbps FCoE Module DS-X9848-480K9 Power Manager 0.006
10 Gbps FCoE Module DS-X9848-480K9 IO 0.005

40 Gbps FCoE Module DS-X9824-960K9 Power Manager SPI 1.005
40 Gbps FCoE Module DS-X9824-960K9 IO SPI 2 0.028
40 Gbps FCoE Module DS-X9824-960K9 IO SPI 0.031

Fan DS-C9718-FAN Fan Controller (1) 0.006
Fan DS-C9718-FAN Fan Controller (2) 0.006
Fan DS-C9710-FAN Fan Controller (1) 0.006
Fan DS-C9710-FAN Fan Controller (2) 0.006

Fan DS-C9706-FAN Fan Controller (1) 0.006
Fan DS-C9706-FAN Fan Controller (2) 0.006

2/4/8/16G Fabric Switch DS-C9396S-K9 IO SPI 2 1.002
2/4/8/16G Fabric Switch DS-C9396S-K9 IO SPI 1.003
```

**11**

```
32 Gbps Advanced FC Module DS-X9648-1536K9 Power Manager SPI 0.002
32 Gbps Advanced FC Module DS-X9648-1536K9 SFP SPI 0.005
32 Gbps Advanced FC Module DS-X9648-1536K9 IO SPI 0.038


4/8/16/32G 1 RU Fabric Switch DS-C9132T IO SPI 2 0.022
4/8/16/32G 1 RU Fabric Switch DS-C9132T MI IO SPI 0.017
4/8/16/32G 1 RU Fabric Switch DS-C9132T LEM IO SPI 0.0
```

EPLDs can be installed, upgraded, or downgraded using CLI commands. Installing a module EPLD update includes the updating of both supervisors and switching modules. At the end of this process, the target module is reloaded. For switching modules, this disrupts traffic on all ports of the module for the duration of the reload. You can use the **install all epld** *uri* **parallel module** slot command to update EPLD images for a module in the Cisco MDS 9700 Series switches, as shown in Example 11-6.

**Example 11-6** *Updating Module EPLDs on a Cisco MDS 9700 Series Switch*

```
switch# install all epld bootflash:m9000-pkg2.8.2.1.epld parallel module 6

WARNING!!!: Executing the "install all epld" command
may result in multiple modules going offline and
affect redundant links.


It is strongly recommended to use one of the following
when EPLD upgrade is attempted on a system carrying
production traffic.
1) "install module <mod#> epld"
2) "install all epld <uri> parallel module <mod#>"
where <mod#> is on a single module


For EPLD upgrade best practices, please refer to the link-

http://www.cisco.com/en/US/docs/switches/datacenter/
sw/best_practices/cli_mgmt_guide/epld_upgrade.html
 Do you want to continue (y/n) ? [n] y
Copy complete, now saving to disk (please wait)...


EPLD image signature verification passed
 Compatibility check:
Module Type Upgradable Impact      Reason
------ ---- ---------- ----------- -----------------
6      SUP  Yes        disruptive  Module Upgradable


Retrieving EPLD versions... Please wait.
```

```
Images will be upgraded according to following table:
Module Type EPLD                 Running-Version New-Version Upg-Required
------ ---- ----------------- ---------------- ----------- -------------
6      SUP  Power Manager SPI  18.000           19.000      Yes


The above modules require upgrade.
Do you want to continue (y/n) ? [n] y


Starting Module 6 EPLD Upgrade
Module 6 : Power Manager SPI [Upgrade Started ]
Module 6 : Power Manager SPI [Erasing ] : 100.00%
Module 6 : Power Manager SPI [Programming ] : 100.00% (6020818 of 6020818 total
bytes)


Module 6 Upgrade Done.


Waiting for Module 6 to come online.


Module 6 EPLD upgrade is successful.


EPLD Upgrade Completed.
Module Type Upgrade-Result
------ ---- --------------
6      SUP  Succes
```

You can use the **install module** *slot* **epld** *uri* command to update EPLD images for a module in the Cisco MDS switches except the Cisco MDS 9700 Series switches, as shown in Example 11-7. If the module number specified in the **install module** *slot* **epld** *uri* command is not present, the update is aborted. If the module is present but not online, the module state is reported and the switch software prompts you to continue. If you continue, the module is brought online, and all the EPLDs on the module are updated, regardless of whether or not they require it.

**Example 11-7**  *Updating Module EPLDs on a Cisco MDS 9396S Switch*

```
switch# install module 1 epld bootflash:m9000-pkg2-8.2.1.epld
Retrieving EPLD versions... Please wait.


Images will be upgraded according to following table:
Module Type EPLD       Running-Version New-Version Upg-Required
------ ---- -------- --------------- ----------- -------------
1      SUP  IO SPI    0.034           1.003       Yes
1      SUP  IO SPI 2  0.005           1.002       Yes
```

11

```
Data traffic on the switch will be affected!!
The switch will reload after the upgrade process.
Do you want to continue (y/n) ? [n] y


Module 1 : IO SPI [Programming ] : 100.00% ( 12970 of 12970 total bytes)

Module 1 : IO SPI 2 [Programming ] : 100.00% ( 3137 of 3137 total bytes)


Waiting for Module to come online.


Module 1 EPLD upgrade is successful.



Reconfiguring Active Supervisor EPLDs.
The Supervisor will reset.
Module 1 : IO SPI 2 [Programming ] : 0.70% ( 22 of 3137 total bytes)
Module 1 EPLD upgrade is successful.
```

You can use the **install all epld** *uri* **parallel fan-module** *slot* command to upgrade EPLD images for the fan modules. The EPLD update for the fan module is nondisruptive, and a power cycle is not required after the update.

The Cisco MDS 9700 Series and Cisco MDS 9513 director-class switch have dedicated fabric modules. These modules contain EPLDs, which can be upgraded. All other Cisco MDS switches do not have these modules, so this process is not applicable for them.

For the Cisco MDS 9700 Series of switches, use the **install all epld** *uri* **parallel xbar-module** *slot* command to update EPLD images on the fabric modules. This process reloads the updated module. To ensure that the data traffic performance is not affected while the module is reloading, check the fabric bandwidth utilization by using the **show hardware fabric-utilization detail** command. If there is adequate reserve fabric bandwidth available before the update starts, the update will be nondisruptive.

On the Cisco MDS 9513 Multilayer Director switch, there is no command to directly update the fabric module EPLD. The fabric module EPLD is updated as part of the corresponding supervisor module EPLD update; that is, fabric module 1 is updated as part of the slot 7 supervisor module update, and fabric module 2 is updated as part of the slot 8 supervisor module update.

To update the EPLDs on supervisor modules of the director class switches in a nondisruptive manner, use the following steps:

**Step 1.**   Update the EPLD on the standby supervisor module. From the active supervisor module, enter the **install module** *slot* **epld** *uri* CLI command, specifying the current standby supervisor module number. After the EPLD update is complete, the standby supervisor module will reboot.

**Step 2.**   When the standby supervisor module is online, physically remove the standby supervisor module and reinstall it. The standby supervisor module will come up with the new EPLD version.

**Step 3.**   After the standby supervisor module reaches the ha-standby state, perform a switchover and wait until the new standby supervisor module reaches the ha-standby state.

**Step 4.**   From the active supervisor module, repeat steps 1 through 3.

> **NOTE**   An EPLD update of the supervisor module of fabric switches (Cisco MDS 9100, Cisco MDS 9200, and Cisco MDS 9300 Series switches) is disruptive because there is no redundant supervisor to take over while the update is in progress. All traffic through the system is stopped for the duration of the update, and the switch is rebooted after the upgrade has completed. The update may take up to 30 minutes to complete.

# Infrastructure Monitoring

System management features are used to monitor and manage a switch using Cisco MDS NX-OS software. These features are described next.

## System Messages

System messages are monitored remotely by accessing the switch through Telnet, SSH, or the console port, or by viewing the logs on a system message logging server. The system message logging software saves the messages in a log file or directs the messages to other devices. This feature has the following capabilities:

- Provides logging information for monitoring and troubleshooting

- Allows the user to select the types of captured logging information

- Allows the user to select the destination server to forward the captured logging information

By default, the switch logs normal but significant system messages to a log file and sends these messages to the system console. You can specify which system messages should be saved based on the type of facility and the severity level. Messages are time-stamped to enhance real-time debugging and management.

You can access the logged system messages using the CLI or by saving them to a correctly configured system message logging server. The switch software saves system messages in a file that can save up to 1200 entries.

Log messages are not saved across system reboots. However, a maximum of 100 log messages with a severity level of critical and below (levels 0, 1, and 2) is saved in NVRAM.

## Call Home

Call Home provides email-based notification of critical system events. A versatile range of message formats is available for optimal compatibility with pager services, standard email, or XML-based automated parsing applications. Common uses of this feature may include direct paging to a network support engineer, email notification to a Network Operations Center, and utilization of Cisco Smart Call Home services for direct case generation with the Technical Assistance Center.

11

The Call Home functionality is available directly through the Cisco MDS 9000 Series switches and the Cisco Nexus 5000 Series switches. It provides multiple Call Home messages, each with separate potential destinations. You can define your own destination profiles in addition to predefined profiles; you also can configure up to 50 email addresses for each destination profile. Flexible message delivery and format options make it easy to integrate specific support requirements.

The Call Home feature offers the following advantages:

- A fixed set of predefined alerts for trigger events on the switch.

- Automatic execution and attachment of relevant command output.

- Multiple message format options:

  - **Short Text:** Suitable for pagers or printed reports.

  - **Plain Text:** Full formatted message information suitable for human reading.

  - **XML:** Matching readable format using Extensible Markup Language (XML) and document type definitions (DTDs) named Messaging Markup Language (MML). The XML format enables communication with the Cisco Systems Technical Assistance Center.

- Multiple concurrent message destinations. You can configure up to 50 email destination addresses for each destination profile.

- Multiple message categories including system, environment, switching module hardware, supervisor module, hardware, inventory, syslog, RMON, and test.

- Secure messages transport directly from your device or through an HTTP proxy server or a downloadable transport gateway (TG). You can use a TG aggregation point to support multiple devices or in cases where security requires that your devices not be connected directly to the Internet.

Smart Call Home is a component of Cisco SMARTnet Service that offers proactive diagnostics, real-time alerts, and personalized web-based reports on selected Cisco devices. Smart Call Home provides fast resolution of system problems by analyzing Call Home messages sent from your devices and providing a direct notification path to Cisco customer support.

## Embedded Event Manager

The Embedded Event Manager (EEM) monitors events that occur on your device and takes action to recover or troubleshoot these events, based on your configuration. EEM consists of three major components:

- **Event statements:** Events to monitor from Cisco NX-OS component that may require some action, workaround, or notification.

- **Action statements:** An action that the EEM can take, such as sending an email or disabling an interface, to recover from an event.

- **Policies:** An event paired with one or more actions to troubleshoot or recover from the event.

To learn more about EEM configuration, refer to Chapter 16, "Automation and Scripting Tools."

## RMON

Remote Network Monitoring (RMON) is an Internet Engineering Task Force (IETF) standard monitoring specification that allows various network agents and console systems to exchange network monitoring data. RMON is disabled by default, and no events or alarms are configured in the switch. You can configure your RMON alarms and events by using the CLI or an SNMP-compatible network management station to monitor Cisco MDS 9000 Family switches.

All switches in the Cisco MDS 9000 Family support the following RMON functions (defined in RFC 2819):

- **Alarm:** Each alarm monitors a specific management information base (MIB) object for a specified interval. When the MIB object value exceeds a specified value (rising threshold), the alarm condition is set, and only one event is triggered regardless of how long the condition exists. When the MIB object value falls below a certain value (falling threshold), the alarm condition is cleared. This allows the alarm to trigger again when the rising threshold is crossed again.

- **Event:** Determines the action to take when an event is triggered by an alarm. The action can be to generate a log entry, an SNMP trap, or both.

## SPAN

The Switched Port Analyzer (SPAN) feature is supported by switches in the Cisco MDS 9000 Family. It monitors network traffic through a Fibre Channel interface. Traffic through any Fibre Channel interface can be replicated to a special port called the SPAN destination port (SD port). Any Fibre Channel port in a switch can be configured as an SD port. When an interface is in SD port mode, it cannot be used for normal data traffic. You can attach a Fibre Channel analyzer to the SD port to monitor SPAN traffic, as shown in Figure 11-3.

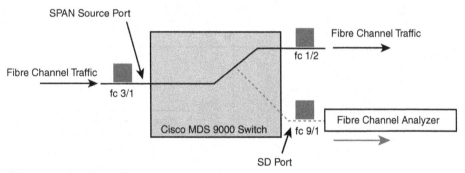

**Figure 11-3** *SPAN Transmission*

SD ports do not receive frames; they only transmit a copy of the SPAN source traffic. The SPAN feature is nonintrusive and does not affect switching of network traffic for any SPAN source ports.

SPAN sources refer to the interfaces from which traffic can be monitored. You can also specify VSAN as a SPAN source, in which case, all supported interfaces in the specified VSAN are included as SPAN sources. When a VSAN as a source is specified, all physical ports and port channels in that VSAN are included as SPAN sources. A TE port is included only when the port VSAN of the TE port matches the source VSAN. A TE port is excluded even if the configured allowed VSAN list may have the source VSAN, but the port VSAN is different. You cannot configure source interfaces (physical interfaces, port channels, or sup-fc interfaces) and source VSANs in the same SPAN session.

You can choose the SPAN traffic in the ingress direction, the egress direction, or both directions for any source interface:

■ **Ingress source (Rx):** Traffic entering the switch fabric through this source interface is *spanned*, or copied, to the SD port, as shown in Figure 11-4.

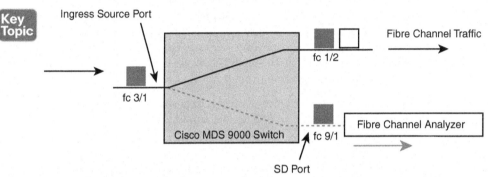

**Figure 11-4**   *SPAN Traffic from the Ingress Direction*

■ **Egress source (Tx):** Traffic exiting the switch fabric through this source interface is spanned, or copied, to the SD port, as shown in Figure 11-5.

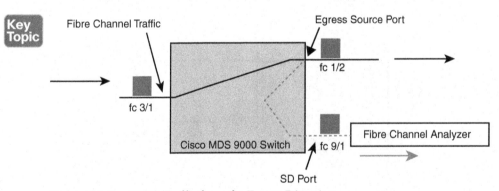

**Figure 11-5**   *SPAN Traffic from the Egress Direction*

The SPAN feature is available for the following interface types:

■ **Physical ports:** These port types include F, FL, TE, E, and TL ports.

■ **Interface sup-fc0 (traffic to and from the supervisor):**

   ■ The Fibre Channel traffic from the supervisor module to the switch fabric through the sup-fc0 interface is called ingress traffic. It is spanned when sup-fc0 is chosen as an ingress source port.

■ The Fibre Channel traffic from the switch fabric to the supervisor module through the sup-fc0 interface is called egress traffic. It is spanned when sup-fc0 is chosen as an egress source port.

■ **Port channels:**

■ All ports in the port channel are included and spanned as sources.

■ You cannot specify individual ports in a port channel as SPAN sources. Previously configured SPAN-specific interface information is discarded.

■ **IPS module-specific Fibre Channel interfaces:**

■ iSCSI interfaces

■ FCIP interfaces

Each SPAN session represents an association of one destination with a set of source(s) along with various other parameters that you specify to monitor the network traffic. One destination can be used by one or more SPAN sessions. You can configure up to 16 SPAN sessions in a switch. Each session can have several source ports and one destination port. To activate any SPAN session, at least one source and the SD port must be up and functioning. Otherwise, traffic is not directed to the SD port. You can temporarily deactivate (suspend) any SPAN session. The traffic monitoring is stopped during this time.

**NOTE**   A source can be shared by two sessions; however, each session must be in a different direction—one ingress and one egress.

You can perform VSAN-based filtering to selectively monitor network traffic on specified VSANs. You can apply this VSAN filter to all sources in a session. Only VSANs present in the filter are spanned. These filters are bidirectional.

An SD port has the following characteristics:

■ It ignores BB_credits.

■ It allows data traffic only in the egress (Tx) direction.

■ It does not require a device or an analyzer to be physically connected.

■ It supports only 1 Gbps or 2 Gbps speeds. The auto-speed option is not allowed. In Cisco MDS 9700 Series switches, the SD port supports 2 Gbps, 4 Gbps, 8 Gbps, and 16 Gbps speeds only.

■ Multiple sessions can share the same destination ports.

■ If the SD port is shut down, all shared sessions stop generating SPAN traffic.

■ The outgoing frames can be encapsulated in Extended Inter-Switch Link (EISL) format.

■ The SD port does not have a port VSAN.

■ SD ports cannot be configured using Storage Services Modules (SSMs).

11

■ The port mode cannot be changed if it is being used for a SPAN session. If you need to change an SD port mode to another port mode, first remove the SD port from all sessions and then change the port mode using the **switchport mode** command.

### SPAN Configuration Example

Example 11-8 shows a sample configuration of a SPAN session.

**Key Topic**

**Example 11-8**  *SPAN Configuration*

**Step 1.**    Configure an SD port for SPAN monitoring:

```
switch# configure terminal
switch(config)# interface fc9/2
switch(config-if)# switchport mode SD
switch(config-if)# switchport speed 1000
switch(config-if)# no shutdown
switch(config-if)# exit
```

**Step 2.**    Configure a SPAN session:

```
switch(config)# span session 1
switch(config-span)# destination interface fc9/2
switch(config-span)# source interface fc7/2
switch(config-span)# source filter vsan 1-2
switch(config-span)# no shutdown
```

**NOTE**   Source interfaces can be VSAN, port channel, iSCSI interface, FCIP interface, interface ranges, and so on.

```
# To temporarily suspend or reactivate a SPAN session, you can use (no) suspend command.
switch(config-span)# (no) suspend
```

**Step 3.**    Verify SPAN configuration:

```
switch# show span session 1
Session 1 (active)
   Destination is fc9/2
   Session filter vsans are 1-2
   Ingress (rx) sources are
     fc7/2,
   Egress (tx) sources are
     fc7/2,
```

### Remote SPAN

The Remote SPAN (RSPAN) feature enables you to remotely monitor traffic for one or more SPAN sources distributed in one or more source switches in a Fibre Channel fabric. The SPAN destination (SD) port is used for remote monitoring in a destination switch. A destination switch is usually different from the source switch(es) but is attached to the same Fibre

Channel fabric. You can replicate and monitor traffic in any remote Cisco MDS 9000 Family switch or director, just as you would monitor traffic in a Cisco MDS source switch.

The RSPAN feature is nonintrusive and does not affect network traffic switching for those SPAN source ports. Traffic captured on the remote switch is tunneled across a Fibre Channel fabric that has trunking enabled on all switches in the path from the source switch to the destination switch. The Fibre Channel tunnel is structured using trunked ISL (TE) ports. In addition to TE ports, the RSPAN feature uses two other interface types, as shown in Figure 11-6.

- **SD ports:** A passive port. The FC analyzer can obtain remote SPAN traffic from these passive ports.

- **ST ports:** SPAN tunnel (ST) ports are entry point ports in the source switch for the RSPAN Fibre Channel tunnel. ST ports are special RSPAN ports and cannot be used for normal Fibre Channel traffic.

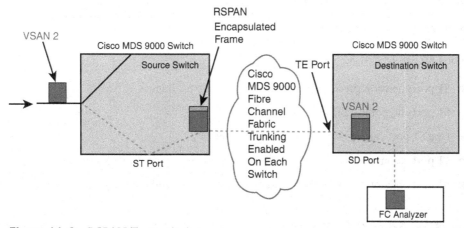

**Figure 11-6**   *RSPAN Transmission*

RSPAN has the following advantages:

- Enables nondisruptive traffic monitoring at a remote location

- Provides a cost-effective solution by using one SD port to monitor remote traffic on multiple switches

- Works with any Fibre Channel analyzer

- Is compatible with the Cisco MDS 9000 Port Analyzer adapters

- Does not affect traffic in the source switch but shares the ISL bandwidth with other ports in the fabric

An FC tunnel is a logical data path between a source switch and a destination switch. The FC tunnel originates from the source switch and terminates at the remotely located destination switch. RSPAN uses a special Fibre Channel tunnel (FC tunnel) that originates at the

11

ST port in the source switch and terminates at the SD port in the destination switch. You must bind the FC tunnel to an ST port in the source switch and map the same FC tunnel to an SD port in the destination switch. After the mapping and binding are configured, the FC tunnel is referred to as an RSPAN tunnel, as shown in Figure 11-7.

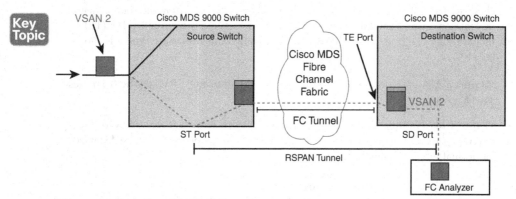

**Figure 11-7**  *FC and RSPAN Tunnel*

ST ports have the following characteristics:

- ST ports perform the RSPAN encapsulation of the FC frame.

- ST ports do not use BB_credits.

- One ST port can be bound to only one FC tunnel.

- ST ports cannot be used for any purpose other than to carry RSPAN traffic.

- ST ports cannot be configured using Storage Services Modules (SSMs).

## Exam Preparation Tasks

As mentioned in the Introduction, you have a couple of choices for exam preparation: the exercises here, Chapter 21, "Final Preparation," and the exam simulation questions in the Pearson Test Prep software online.

## Review All Key Topics

Review the most important topics in the chapter, noted with the key topic icon in the outer margin of the page. Table 11-2 lists a reference to these key topics and the page numbers on which each is found.

**Table 11-2**  Key Topics for Chapter 11

| Key Topic Element | Description | Page |
|---|---|---|
| Figure 11-1 | Setup Script Flow | 491 |
| List | Nondisruptive Upgrade on a Cisco MDS Fabric Switch | 500 |
| List | Disruptive Upgrade on a Cisco MDS Switch | 505 |

| Key Topic Element | Description | Page |
|---|---|---|
| List | Nondisruptive Downgrade on a Cisco MDS Fabric Switch | 508 |
| List | Disruptive Downgrade on a Cisco MDS Fabric Switch | 513 |
| Example 11-6 | Updating Module EPLDs on a Cisco MDS 9700 Series Switch | 518 |
| Example 11-7 | Updating Module EPLDs on a Cisco MDS 9396S Switch | 519 |
| Figure 11-4 | SPAN Traffic from the Ingress Direction | 524 |
| Figure 11-5 | SPAN Traffic from the Egress Direction | 524 |
| Example 11-8 | SPAN Configuration | 526 |
| Figure 11-7 | FC and RSPAN Tunnel | 528 |

## Define Key Terms

Define the following key terms from this chapter, and check your answers in the Glossary.

Call Home, electrical programmable logical devices (EPLD), in-band, out-of-band, Remote Network Monitoring (RMON), Remote SPAN (RSPAN), Switched Port Analyzer (SPAN)

## References

Cisco MDS 9000 NX-OS Software Upgrade and Downgrade Guide, Release 8.x: https://www.cisco.com/c/en/us/td/docs/switches/datacenter/mds9000/sw/8_x/upgrade/upgrade.html

Cisco MDS 9000 Family Release Notes for Cisco MDS 9000 EPLD Images, Release 8.x: https://www.cisco.com/c/en/us/td/docs/switches/datacenter/mds9000/sw/8_x/release_notes/epld/epld_rn_8x.html

Cisco MDS 9000 Series System Management Configuration Guide, Release 8.x: https://www.cisco.com/c/en/us/td/docs/switches/datacenter/mds9000/sw/8_x/config/system-management/cisco_mds9000_system_management_config_guide_8x.html

Cisco MDS 9000 Series Fundamentals Configuration Guide, Release 8.x: https://www.cisco.com/c/en/us/td/docs/switches/datacenter/mds9000/sw/8_x/config/fundamentals/cisco_mds9000_fundamentals_config_guide_8x.html

11

# CHAPTER 12

# Cisco Unified Computing Systems Overview

The Cisco Unified Computing System (UCS) is the industry's first converged data center platform. The Cisco UCS delivers smart, programmable infrastructure that simplifies and speeds enterprise-class applications and service deployment in bare-metal, virtualized, and cloud-computing environments.

The Cisco UCS is an integrated computing infrastructure with intent-based management to automate and accelerate deployment of all applications, including virtualization and cloud computing, scale-out and bare-metal workloads, and in-memory analytics, in addition to edge computing that supports remote and branch locations and massive amounts of data from the Internet of Things (IoT).

### This chapter covers the following key topics:

**Cisco UCS Architecture:** This section provides an overview of UCS B-Series, C-Series, and Fabric Interconnect (FI) architecture and connectivity.

**Cisco UCS Initial Setup and Management:** This section covers UCS B-Series and C-Series initial setup and configuration.

**Cisco UCS Network Management:** This section discusses UCS LAN management, including VLANs, pools, polices, quality of service (QoS), and templates.

**Cisco UCS Storage:** This section discusses UCS SAN management, including SAN connectivity (iSCSI, Fibre Channel, FCoE), VSANs, WWN pools, and zoning.

## "Do I Know This Already?" Quiz

The "Do I Know This Already?" quiz enables you to assess whether you should read this entire chapter thoroughly or jump to the "Exam Preparation Tasks" section. If you are in doubt about your answers to these questions or your own assessment of your knowledge of the topics, read the entire chapter. Table 12-1 lists the major headings in this chapter and their corresponding "Do I Know This Already?" quiz questions. You can find the answers in Appendix A, "Answers to the 'Do I Know This Already?' Quizzes."

**Table 12-1** "Do I Know This Already?" Section-to-Question Mapping

| Foundation Topics Section | Questions |
|---|---|
| Cisco UCS Architecture | 1–2 |
| Cisco UCS Initial Setup and Management | 3–5 |
| Cisco UCS Network Management | 6–7 |
| Cisco UCS Storage | 8–9 |

1. What are the Cisco UCS Mini main infrastructure components? (Choose two answers.)

   a. Fabric Interconnect

   b. Blade Server

   c. Power Supply

   d. I/O module

2. What type of connections does UCS blade chassis FEX fabric support? (Choose two answers.)

   a. Basic mode

   b. Discrete mode

   c. Port mode

   d. Port channel mode

3. When a host firmware package policy is created, what must it be associated with to upgrade the BIOS?

   a. Blade or blade pool

   b. Boot policy

   c. Service profile

   d. Service template

4. Which commands allow you to view the state of high availability between the two clustered fabric interconnects? (Choose two answers.)

   a. **show cluster HA status**

   b. **show cluster state extended**

   c. **show cluster extended-state**

   d. **show cluster state**

5. What is the correct path to verify the overall status of Chassis 1 | Server 3?

   a. Servers tab > Chassis > Server 3 General tab

   b. Status tab > Chassis > Chassis 1 > Servers > Server 3

   c. Equipment tab > Chassis > Chassis 1 > Servers > Server 3 FSM tab

   d. Equipment tab > Chassis > Chassis 1 > Servers > Server 3 Status tab

   e. Admin tab > Chassis > Chassis 1 > Servers > Server 3 General tab

   f. Equipment tab > Chassis > Chassis 1 > Servers > Server 3 General tab

6. If the virtual local area network (VLAN) is deleted from the fabric interconnect using the Cisco UCS Manager, what happens?

   a. The port belonging to the VLAN is assigned to the default VLAN.

   b. The port belonging to the VLAN is pinned to a native VLAN.

   c. You cannot delete the VLAN because an interface member belongs to that VLAN.

   d. The port changes to a shutdown state.

7. Which of the following characteristics are true in the Cisco UCS unicast traffic path in end-host switching mode? (Choose two answers.)

   a. Each server link is pinned as one-to-many uplink ports.

   b. Server-to-server Layer 2 traffic is pinned to an uplink port.

   c. Server-to-network traffic goes out on its pinned uplink port.

   d. Server-to-server Layer 2 traffic is locally switched.

   e. Server-to-network traffic is locally switched.

8. Which TCP/IP-based protocol for storage communication is supported by the Cisco UCS?

   a. iFCP

   b. FCIP

   c. iSCSI

   d. FCoE

9. What type of UCS network storage provides maximum reliability, expandability, and performance?

   a. Network-attached storage (NAS)

   b. Direct-attached storage (DAS)

   c. RAID storage

   d. Storage-area network (SAN)

## Foundation Topics

## Cisco UCS Architecture

The Cisco Unified Computing System (UCS) has a unique architecture that integrates compute, data network access, and storage network access into a common set of components under a single management portal (single-pane-of-glass portal). The Cisco UCS combines access layer networking and servers. This high-performance, next-generation server system provides a data center with a high degree of workload agility and scalability. The hardware and software components support Cisco's unified fabric, which runs multiple types of data center traffic over a single converged network adapter. Figure 12-1 shows UCS management and network connectivity.

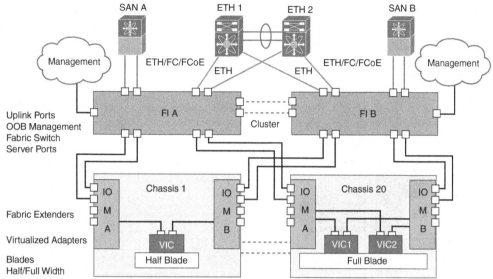

**Figure 12-1** *Cisco Unified Computing System Architecture*

The simplified architecture of the Cisco UCS reduces the number of required devices and centralizes switching resources. By eliminating switching inside a chassis, Cisco significantly reduced the network access layer fragmentation. The Cisco UCS implements a Cisco unified fabric within racks and groups of racks, supporting Ethernet and Fibre Channel protocols. This simplification reduces the number of switches, cables, adapters, and management points by up to two-thirds. All devices in a Cisco UCS domain remain under a single management domain, which remains highly available through the use of redundant components. The Cisco UCS architecture provides the following features (see Figure 12-2):

- **High availability:** The management and data plane of the Cisco UCS is designed for high availability and redundant access layer fabric interconnects. In addition, the Cisco UCS supports existing high-availability and disaster recovery solutions for the data center, such as data replication and application-level clustering technologies.

- **Scalability:** A single Cisco UCS domain supports multiple chassis and their servers, all of which are administered through one Cisco UCS Manager.

- **Flexibility:** A Cisco UCS domain allows you to quickly align computing resources in the data center with rapidly changing business requirements. This built-in flexibility is determined by whether you choose to fully implement the stateless computing feature. Pools of servers and other system resources can be applied as necessary to respond to workload fluctuations, support new applications, scale existing software and business services, and accommodate both scheduled and unscheduled downtime. Server identity can be abstracted into a mobile service profile that can be moved from server to server with minimal downtime and no need for additional network configuration.

With this level of flexibility, you can quickly and easily scale server capacity without having to change the server identity or reconfigure the server, LAN, or SAN. During a maintenance window, you can quickly do the following:

- Deploy new servers to meet unexpected workload demand and rebalance resources and traffic.

- Shut down an application, such as a database management system, on one server and then boot it up again on another server with increased I/O capacity and memory resources.

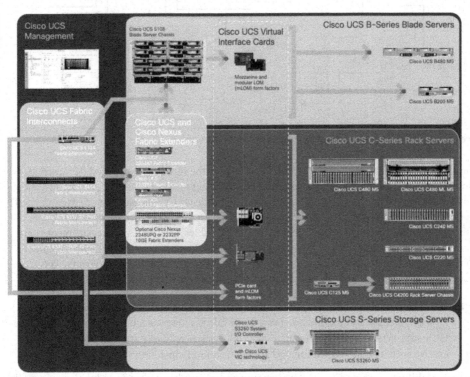

**Figure 12-2**   *Cisco UCS Components and Connectivity*

## Cisco UCS Components and Connectivity

The main components of the Cisco UCS are as follows:

- **Cisco Intersight:** Cisco Intersight allows for the cloud-based management of Cisco UCS systems, which provides better scalability and visibility over multiple geographically distributed data centers. It is cloud-based Software as a Service (SaaS); it has a broad scope that extends to complete infrastructure and application lifecycle management. It has limitless scale so you can manage all of your infrastructure from a single control point with role- and policy-based automation.

- **Cisco UCS Manager:** The Cisco UCS Manager is the centralized management interface for the Cisco UCS.

- **Cisco UCS Fabric Interconnects:** The Cisco UCS Fabric Interconnect is the core component of Cisco UCS deployments, providing both network connectivity and management capabilities for the Cisco UCS system. The Cisco UCS Fabric Interconnects run the Cisco UCS Manager control software and consist of the following components:

  - Cisco UCS 6500/6400/6300 Series Fabric Interconnects, and Cisco UCS Mini

  - Transceivers for network and storage connectivity

  - Expansion modules for the various Fabric Interconnects

  - Cisco UCS Manager software

- **Cisco UCS I/O modules and Cisco UCS Fabric Extender:** I/O modules (or IOMs) are also known as Cisco Fabric Extenders (FEXs) or simply FEX modules. These modules serve as line cards to the FIs in the same way that Nexus series switches can have remote line cards. I/O modules also provide interface connections to blade servers. They multiplex data from blade servers and provide this data to FIs and do the same in the reverse direction. In production environments, I/O modules are always used in pairs to provide redundancy and failover.

- **Cisco UCS blade server chassis:** The Cisco UCS 5100 Series Blade Server Chassis is a crucial building block of the Cisco UCS, delivering a scalable and flexible architecture for current and future data center needs, while helping reduce total cost of ownership.

- **Cisco UCS blade servers:** Cisco UCS blade servers, also known as the B-Series servers, are at the heart of the Cisco UCS solution. They come in various system resource configurations in terms of CPU, memory, and hard disk capacity. All blade servers are based on Intel Xeon processors. There is no AMD option available.

- **Cisco UCS rack servers:** The Cisco UCS C-Series servers are rack-mount standalone servers that can be installed and controlled individually. This means that these servers can behave as any traditional rack server, bringing all the benefits of the independent management hardware of the Cisco Integrated Management Controller (CIMC), or they can be integrated in a Cisco UCS under the management of Cisco UCS Manager and can support flexible designs for the needs of the customers. Cisco provides FEXs for the rack-mount servers. FEXs can be used to connect and manage rack-mount servers from FIs. Rack-mount servers can also be directly attached to the fabric interconnect. Small and medium businesses (SMBs) can choose from different blade configurations as per business needs.

- **Cisco UCS S-Series:** Storage servers are modular servers that support up to 60 large-form-factor internal drives to support storage-intensive workloads including big data, content streaming, online backup, and storage-as-a-service applications. The servers support one or two computing nodes with up to two CPUs each, and with up to 160 Gbps of unified fabric connectivity per node. These features simplify the process of deploying just the right amount of resources to most efficiently support your applications.

- **Cisco UCS Mini solutions:** These solutions can be created by using Cisco UCS 6324 Fabric Interconnects in the blade server chassis instead of rack-mount FEXs. This creates a standalone Cisco UCS instance that can connect to blade servers, rack servers, and external storage systems.

## Cisco UCS 5108 Blade Server Chassis

The Cisco UCS 5108 Blade Server Chassis is six rack units (6RU) high, can mount in an industry-standard 19-inch rack, and uses standard front-to-back cooling (see Figure 12-3). A chassis can accommodate up to eight half-width or four full-width Cisco UCS B-Series blade servers form factors within the same chassis. By incorporating unified fabric and fabric-extender technology, the Cisco Unified Computing System enables the chassis to

- Have fewer physical components

- Require no independent management

- Be more energy efficient than a traditional blade server chassis

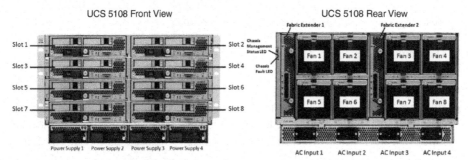

**Figure 12-3**  *UCS 5108 Blade Server Chassis*

The Cisco UCS 5108 Blade Server Chassis is supported with all generations of fabric interconnects.

## UCS Blade Servers

Cisco UCS B-Series blade servers are based on Intel Xeon processors (see Figure 12-4). They work with virtualized and nonvirtualized applications to increase performance, energy efficiency, flexibility, and administrator productivity.

Cisco UCS B200 M5 Blade Server

- 2nd Gen Intel® Xeon® Scalable processors or Intel Xeon Scalable processors
- 2 sockets
- Up to 9 TB of memory
- Up to 2 GPUs
- Intel® Optane™ DC persistent memory

Cisco UCS B480 M5 Blade Server

- 2nd Gen Intel® Xeon® Scalable processors or Intel Xeon Scalable processors
- 4 sockets
- Up to 18 TB of memory
- Up to 4 GPUs
- Intel® Optane™ DC persistent memory

**Figure 12-4**  *UCS B200 M5 and B480 M5 Blade Servers*

With the Cisco UCS blade server, you can quickly deploy stateless physical and virtual workloads with the programmability that the Cisco UCS Manager and Cisco Single Connect technology enables.

Cisco UCS B480 M5 is a full-width server that uses second-generation Intel Xeon Scalable processors or Intel Xeon Scalable processors with up to 12 TB of memory, or up to 18 TB of Intel Optane DC persistent memory; up to four SAS, SATA, and NVMe drives; M.2 storage; up to four GPUs; and 160-Gigabit Ethernet connectivity. It offers exceptional levels of performance, flexibility, and I/O throughput to run the most demanding applications.

Cisco UCS B200 M5 is a half-width server that uses second-generation Intel Xeon Scalable processors or Intel Xeon Scalable processors with up to 3 TB of memory or 6 TB of Intel Optane DC persistent memory; up to two SAS, SATA, and NVMe drives; plus M.2 storage; up to two GPUs; and up to 80-Gigabit Ethernet. The Cisco UCS B200 M5 blade server offers exceptional levels of performance, flexibility, and I/O throughput to run applications.

A new addition to the Cisco B-Series servers is the sixth generation of blade servers, which comes in the form of the B200 M6 blade server. Building on the legacy of the B200 servers, it provides extended support for up to 12 TB of memory, up to 40 cores per socket, four M.2 drives with RAID support, and two Cisco VIC 1400. The sixth generation B200 servers have two CPU sockets and support for the third generation of Intel-scalable CPUs.

> **NOTE**   The central processing unit (CPU) is designed to control all computer parts, improve performance, and support parallel processing. The current CPU is a multicore processor. A graphic processing unit (GPU) is used in computer graphic cards and image processing. The GPU can be used as a coprocessor to accelerate CPUs. In today's IT world, distributed applications (such as artificial intelligence, or AI) or deep learning applications require high-speed and parallel processing. GPUs are the best solution for distributed applications because GPUs contain high-core density (256 cores or more) compared to CPUs that contain 8 or 16 or a maximum of 32 cores. CPUs can offload some of the compute-intensive and time-consuming portions of the code to the GPU.

## Cisco UCS Rack Servers

UCS C-Series rack servers deliver unified computing in an industry-standard form factor to increase agility (see Figure 12-5). Each server addresses varying workload challenges through a balance of processing, memory, I/O, and internal storage resources.

## Cisco UCS Storage Servers

The Cisco UCS S3260 storage server is a modular dual-node x86 server designed for investment protection (see Figure 12-6). Its architectural flexibility provides high performance or high capacity for your data-intensive workloads. Using a storage server combined with the Cisco UCS Manager, you can easily deploy storage capacity from terabytes to petabytes within minutes.

C220 M5/M6/M7

- Up to 4th Gen Intel Xeon Scalable CPUs
- 2 sockets, up to 52 cores per socket
- Up to 8/9/12 TB memory
- Support for Cisco UCS VIC 15000 Series adapters as well as third-party options
- Up to 10 SAS/SATA or NVMe disk drives
- Up to 3 GPUs supported

C5000 M5/M6/M7

- Up to 4th Gen Intel Xeon Scalable CPUs
- 2 sockets, up to 60 cores per socket
- Up to 8/9/12 TB memory
- Support for Cisco UCS VIC 15000 Series adapters as well as third-party options
- Up to 28 SAS/SATA or NVMe disk drives
- Up to 5 GPUs supported

C480 M5

- 2nd Gen Intel Xeon Scalable CPUs
- 4 sockets, up to 28 cores per socket
- Up to 18 TB memory
- Support for Cisco UCS VIC 15000 Series adapters as well as third-party options
- Up to 32 SFF disk drives
- Up to 6 GPUs supported

C125 M5

- AMD® EPYC™ 7001 and 7002 series processors
- 2 sockets, 64 cores per socket
- Up to 2 TB memory
- Support for Cisco UCS VIC 1400 Series adapters

C225 M6

- AMD® EPYC™ 7003 and 7002 series processors
- 2 sockets, 64 cores per socket
- Up to 8 TB memory
- Up to 10 NVMe drives
- Up to 4 PCIe Generation 4 slots

C5005 M6

- AMD® EPYC™ 7003 and 7002 series processors
- 2 sockets, 64 cores per socket
- Up to 8 TB memory
- Up to 28 small form-factor (SFF) drives
- Up to 8 PCIe Generation 4 slots

**Figure 12-5** *UCS C-Series Rack Servers*

## Cisco UCS S3260 Storage Server

FRONT

BACK

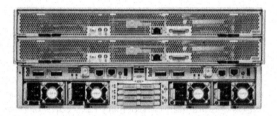

- Dual 2-socket server nodes based on 2nd Gen Intel Xeon Scalable processors with up to 48 cores per server node
- Up to 1.5 TB of DDR4 memory per M5 server node and up to 1 TB of Intel Optane™ DC Persistent Memory
- Support for high-performance Nonvolatile Memory Express (NVMe) and flash memory
- Massive 1,080-TB data storage capacity that easily scales to petabytes with Cisco UCS Manager software
- Policy-based storage management framework for zero-touch capacity on demand
- Dual-port 40-Gbps system I/O controllers with a Cisco UCS Virtual Interface Card 1300 platform embedded chip or PCIe-based system I/O controller for Quad Port 10/25G Cisco VIC 1455 or Dual Port 40/100G Cisco VIC 1495 or 3rd party PCIe adapters
- Unified I/O for Ethernet or Fibre Channel to existing NAS or SAN storage environments
- Support for Cisco bidirectional transceivers, with 40-Gbps connectivity over existing 10-Gbps cabling infrastructure

**Figure 12-6** *Cisco UCS Storage Server*

12

The Cisco UCS S3260 server is designed as a storage server to support storage and processing of huge amounts of data in the data canter. It provides dual-node capability, based on the second-generation Intel Xeon Scalable processor; it features up to 1080 TB of local storage in a compact four-rack-unit (4RU) form factor. The drives can be configured with enterprise-class Redundant Array of Independent Disks (RAID) redundancy or with a pass-through host bus adapter (HBA) controller. Network connectivity is provided with dual-port up to 40-Gbps nodes in each server, with expanded unified I/O capabilities for data migration between network-attached storage (NAS) and SAN environments. This storage-optimized server comfortably fits in a standard 32-inch-depth rack, such as the Cisco R 42610 rack.

 ## Cisco UCS Mini

The Cisco UCS Mini solution extends the Cisco UCS architecture into environments that requires smaller domains, including branch and remote offices, point-of-sale locations, and smaller IT environments.

The Cisco UCS Mini has three main infrastructure components:

- Cisco UCS 6324 Fabric Interconnect

- Cisco UCS blade server chassis

- Cisco UCS blade or rack-mount servers

In the Cisco UCS Mini solution, the Cisco UCS 6324 Fabric Interconnect is collapsed into the I/O module form factor and is inserted into the IOM slot of the blade server chassis. The Cisco UCS 6324 Fabric Interconnect has 24 10G ports available on it. Sixteen of these ports are server facing, providing two 10G dedicated ports to each of the eight half-width blade slots. The remaining eight ports are divided into groups of four 1/10G Enhanced Small Form-Factor Pluggable (SFP+) ports and one 40G Quad Small Form-Factor Pluggable (QSFP) port, which is called the *scalability port*. Figure 12-7 shows UCS Mini connectivity.

**NOTE**   Currently, the Cisco UCS Manager supports only one extended chassis for the Cisco UCS Mini.

## Cisco UCS Fabric Infrastructure

Cisco UCS Fabric Interconnects are top-of-rack devices and provide unified access to the Cisco UCS domain. The Cisco UCS Fabric Interconnect hardware is now in its fourth generation. The following fabric interconnects are available in the Cisco UCS Fabric Interconnects product family:

- Cisco UCS 6500 Series Fabric Interconnects (Model: 6536)

- Cisco UCS 6400 Series Fabric Interconnects (Models: 6454, 64108)

- Cisco UCS 6300 Series Fabric Interconnects (Models: 6332, 6332-16UP and 6324)

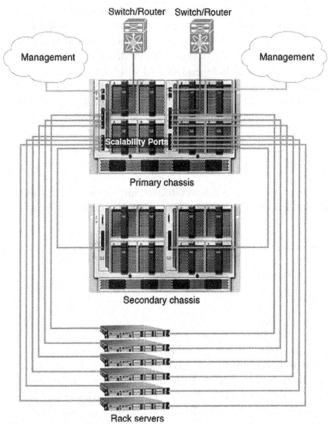

**Figure 12-7**    *The Cisco UCS Mini Infrastructure*

## Cisco UCS 6536 Fabric Interconnect

The Cisco UCS 6536 Fabric Interconnect builds the communication and management connectivity for the UCS X9508 X-Series and UCS 5108 B-Series server chassis, in this way integrating the Cisco UCS X-Series compute nodes, UCS B-Series blade servers, and UCS C-Series rack servers. All servers attached to a Cisco UCS 6536 Fabric Interconnect become part of a single, highly available management domain. (See Figure 12-8.)

**Figure 12-8**    *Cisco UCS 6536 Fabric Interconnect*

From a networking perspective, the Cisco UCS 6536 uses a cut-through architecture, low-latency, line-rate 10/25/40/100-Gigabit Ethernet ports. The switching capacity is 7.42 Tbps per FI, or 14.84 Tbps per unified fabric domain. It supports 1600-Gbps bandwidth per X9508 chassis with X9108-IFM-100G, in addition to enabling end-to-end 100G Ethernet and 200G aggregate bandwidth per X210c compute node. With the X9108-IFM-25G and the IOM 2408, the supported connectivity is up to 400 Gbps per chassis.

12

The characteristics of the Cisco 6536 Fabric Interconnect are

- 1 RU

- 36 × 10/25/40/100-Gbps FCoE fixed ports

- Max 4× unified ports (33–36)

- Max 2× ports supporting 1-Gbps (ports 9 and 10)

- Max 36 ports supporting 40/100-Gbps

- Max 16× 8/16/32-Gbps FC ports

- 7.42 Tbps throughput

- 2× AC power supplies 1100W

- 6× fan modules

- Up to 20× blade chassis

- Front-to-back cooling (fan-side intake, port-side exhaust)

- Supported chassis: UCSX-9508 and UCSB-5108

## Cisco UCS 6454 Fabric Interconnect

The Cisco UCS 6454 Fabric Interconnect provides both network connectivity and management capabilities to the Cisco UCS system. The fabric interconnect provides Ethernet and Fibre Channel to the servers in the system. The servers connect to the fabric interconnect and then to the LAN or SAN.

Each Cisco UCS 6454 Fabric Interconnect runs the Cisco UCS Manager to fully manage all Cisco UCS elements. The fabric interconnect supports 10/25-Gigabit Ethernet ports in the fabric with 40/100-Gigabit Ethernet uplink ports. High availability can be achieved when a Cisco UCS 6454 Fabric Interconnect is connected to another Cisco UCS 6454 Fabric Interconnect through the L1 or L2 port on each device. UCS 6454 FI is a 1RU top-of-rack switch that mounts in a standard 19-inch rack, such as the Cisco R Series rack. It has 44 10/25-Gigabit Ethernet SFP28 ports (16 unified ports), 4 1/10/25-Gigabit Ethernet ports and 6 40/100-Gigabit Ethernet QSFP28 ports. Each 40/100-Gigabit Ethernet port can break out into 4 10/25-Gigabit Ethernet uplink ports. The 16 unified ports support 10/25-Gigabit Ethernet or 8/16/32-Gbps Fibre Channel speeds.

> **NOTE**   The Cisco UCS 6454 Fabric Interconnect supported 8 unified ports (ports 1–8) with Cisco UCS Manager 4.0(1) and 4.0(2), but with release 4.0(4) and later it supports 16 unified ports (ports 1–16).

The Cisco UCS 6454 Fabric Interconnect supports a maximum of eight FCoE port channels or four SAN ports, or a maximum of eight SAN port channels and FCoE port channels (four each). It also has one network management port, one console port for setting the initial configuration, and one USB port for saving or loading configurations. The FI also includes

L1/L2 ports for connecting two fabric interconnects for high availability. The fabric interconnect contains a CPU board that consists of the following:

- Intel Xeon D-1528 v4 Processor, 1.6 GHz

- 64 GB of RAM

- 8 MB of NVRAM (4  NVRAM chips)

- 128-GB SSD (bootflash)

The ports on the Cisco UCS 6454 Fabric Interconnect can be configured to carry either Ethernet or Fibre Channel traffic. You can configure only the first 16 ports to carry Fibre Channel traffic. The ports cannot be used by a Cisco UCS domain until you configure them.

**NOTE**   When you configure a port on a fabric interconnect, the administrative state is automatically set to enabled. If the port is connected to another device, this may cause traffic disruption. The port can be disabled and enabled after it has been configured.

Ports on the Cisco UCS 6454 Fabric Interconnect are numbered and grouped according to their function. The ports are numbered top to bottom and left to right. Figure 12-9 shows the port numbering, which is as follows:

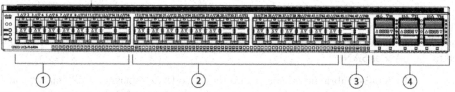

**Figure 12-9**   *Cisco UCS 6454 Fabric Interconnect*

1. **Ports 1–16:** Unified ports can operate as 10/25-Gigabit Ethernet or 8/16/32-Gbps Fibre Channel. FC ports are converted in groups of four.

2. **Ports 17–44:** Each port can operate as either a 10-Gbps or 25-Gbps SFP28 port.

**NOTE**   When you use Cisco UCS Manager releases earlier than 4.0(4), ports 9–44 are 10/25-Gbps Ethernet or FCoE.

3. **Ports 45–48:** Each port can operate as a 1-Gigabit Ethernet, 10-Gigabit Ethernet, or 25-Gigabit Ethernet or FCoE port.

4. **Uplink Ports 49–54:** Each port can operate as either a 40-Gbps or 100-Gbps Ethernet or FCoE port. When you use a breakout cable, each of these ports can operate as 4 × 10-Gigabit Ethernet or 4 × 25-Gigabit Ethernet or FCoE ports. Ports 49–54 can be used only to connect to Ethernet or FCoE uplink ports, and not to UCS server ports.

Cisco UCS 6454 Fabric Interconnects support splitting a single 40/100-Gigabit Ethernet QSFP port into four 10/25-Gigabit Ethernet ports using a supported breakout cable. These ports can be used only as uplink ports connecting to a 10/25G switch. On the UCS 6454

Fabric Interconnect, by default, there are six ports in the 40/100G mode. These are ports 49 to 54. These 40/100G ports are numbered in a 2-tuple naming convention. For example, the second 40G port is numbered as 1/50. The process of changing the configuration from 40G to 10G, or from 100G to 25G is called *breakout*, and the process of changing the configuration from 4 × 10G to 40G or from 4 × 25G to 100G is called *unconfigure*.

When you break out a 40G port into 10G ports or a 100G port into 25G ports, the resulting ports are numbered using a 3-tuple naming convention. For example, the breakout ports of the second 40-Gigabit Ethernet port are numbered as 1/50/1, 1/50/2, 1/50/3, and 1/50/4. Figure 12-9 shows the rear view of the Cisco UCS 6454 Fabric Interconnect and includes the ports that support breakout port functionality (Group 4).

## Cisco UCS 6300 Series Fabric Interconnects

The Cisco UCS 6300 Series Fabric Interconnect joins next-generation UCS products, including the following hardware:

- Cisco UCS 6332 Fabric Interconnect, an Ethernet or Fibre Channel over Ethernet (FCoE) chassis with 32 40-Gigabit Ethernet QSFP+ ports

- Cisco UCS 6332-16UP Fabric Interconnect, an Ethernet, FCoE, and Fibre Channel chassis with 16 1- or 10-Gigabit Ethernet SFP+ ports or 16 4-, 8-, or 16-Gbps Fibre Channel ports, 24 40-Gigabit Ethernet QSFP+ ports

- Cisco 2304 IOM or Cisco 2304V2, I/O modules with eight 40-Gigabit backplane ports and four 40-Gigabit Ethernet uplink ports

- Multiple VICs

UCS 6332 Fabric Interconnect is a 1RU, top-of-rack switch with 32 40-Gigabit Ethernet QSFP+ ports, one 100/1000 network management port, one RS-232 console port for setting the initial configuration, and two USB ports for saving or loading configurations (see Figure 12-10). The switch also includes an L1 port and an L2 port for connecting two fabric interconnects to provide high availability. The switch mounts in a standard 19-inch rack, such as the Cisco R-Series rack. Cooling fans pull air front-to-rear. That is, air intake is on the fan side, and air exhaust is on the port side.

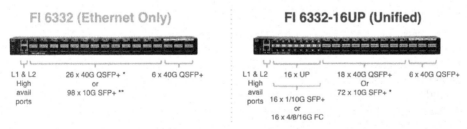

**Figure 12-10**   *Cisco UCS Fabric Interconnect 6332*

Ports on the Cisco UCS 6300 Series Fabric Interconnects can be configured to carry either Ethernet or Fibre Channel traffic. These ports are not reserved. They cannot be used by a Cisco UCS domain until you configure them. When you configure a port on a fabric interconnect, the administrative state is automatically set to enabled. If the port is connected to another device, this may cause traffic disruption. You can disable the port after it has been configured.

The Cisco UCS Fabric Interconnect 6300 Series supports splitting a single QSFP port into four 10-Gigabit Ethernet ports using a supported breakout cable. By default, there are 32 ports in the 40-Gigabit mode. These 40-Gigabit Ethernet ports are numbered in a 2-tuple naming convention. For example, the second 40-Gigabit Ethernet port is numbered as 1/2. The process of changing the configuration from 40-Gigabit Ethernet to 10-Gigabit Ethernet is called *breakout*, and the process of changing the configuration from 4 10-Gigabit Ethernet to 40-Gigabit Ethernet is called *unconfigure*. When you break out a 40-Gigabit Ethernet port into 10-Gigabit Ethernet ports, the resulting ports are numbered using a 3-tuple naming convention. For example, the breakout ports of the second 40-Gigabit Ethernet port are numbered as 1/2/1, 1/2/2, 1/2/3, and 1/2/4. Table 12-2 summarizes the constraints for breakout functionality for Cisco UCS 6300 Series Fabric Interconnects.

**Table 12-2**   Cisco UCS 6300 Port Breakout Summary

| Cisco UCS 6300 Series Fabric Interconnect Series | Breakout Configurable Ports | Ports Without Breakout Functionality Support |
| --- | --- | --- |
| Cisco UCS 6332 | 1–12, 15–26 | 13–14, 27–32<br>**Note:** Autonegotiate behavior is not supported on ports 27–32. |
| Cisco UCS 6332-16UP | 17–34 | 1–16, 35–40<br>**Note:** Autonegotiate behavior is not supported on ports 35–40. |

**NOTE**   Up to four breakout ports are allowed if QoS jumbo frames are used.

## Fabric Interconnect and Fabric Extender Connectivity

Fabric Extenders (FEs) are extensions of the fabric interconnects (FIs) and act as remote line cards to form a distributed modular fabric system. The fabric extension is accomplished through the FEX fabric link, which is the connection between the fabric interconnect and the FEX. A minimum of one connection between the FI and FEX is required to provide server connectivity. Depending on the FEX model, subsequent connections can be up to eight links, which provides added bandwidth to the servers.

The latest generation of the Cisco UCS Fabric Extenders is the Cisco UCS 2408 FEX. It is used in the Cisco UCS 5108 chassis and allows for connectivity to the Cisco 6454, 64108, and 6536 Fabric Interconnects. The external connectivity is provided by 8× 25-Gbps FcoE SFP28 ports. This allows for up to 200 Gbps of bandwidth between the Cisco UCS 2408 FEX and the Cisco UCS 6400 and 6500 Series Fabric Interconnects. As in a Cisco UCS 5108 blade chassis, there are always two FEXs—one for connectivity to each of the Fabric Interconnects. The combined bandwidth available to the chassis will be 400 Gbps.

The internal connectivity is supported by 32× 10-Gbps ports, which through the mid-plane provide 4× 10-Gbps bandwidth per server slot, per Cisco UCS 2408 FEX. Again, looking at the redundant connectivity of the Cisco UCS 5108, this secures a total of 80 Gbps of redundant bandwidth for each blade server in the chassis. The internal to external communication is delivered by the 1.04 Tbps of hardware forwarding capability of the FEX.

The Cisco UCS 2304 IOM (Fabric Extender) is an I/O module with 8× 40-Gigabit backplane ports and 4× 40-Gigabit uplink ports (see Figure 12-11). It can be hot-plugged into the rear of a Cisco UCS 5108 blade server chassis. A maximum of two UCS 2304 IOMs can be installed in a chassis. The Cisco UCS 2304 IOM provides chassis management control and blade management control, including control of the chassis, fan trays, power supply units, and blades. It also multiplexes and forwards all traffic from the blade servers in the chassis to the 10-Gigabit Ethernet uplink network ports that connect to the fabric interconnect. The IOM can also connect to a peer IOM to form a cluster interconnect.

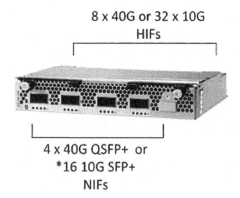

*with QSFP+ to SFP+ Breakout cable

**Figure 12-11**  *Cisco UCS 2300 IOM*

Figure 12-12 shows how the FEX modules in the blade chassis connect to the FIs. The 5108 chassis accommodates the following FEXs:

■ Cisco UCS 2408

■ Cisco UCS 2304

**NOTE**   The Cisco UCS 2304 Fabric Extender is not compatible with the Cisco UCS 6200 Fabric Interconnect series.

■ Cisco UCS 2208XP

■ Cisco UCS 2204XP

In a blade chassis, the FEX fabric link (the link between the FEX and the FI) supports two different types of connections:

■ Discrete mode

■ Port channel mode

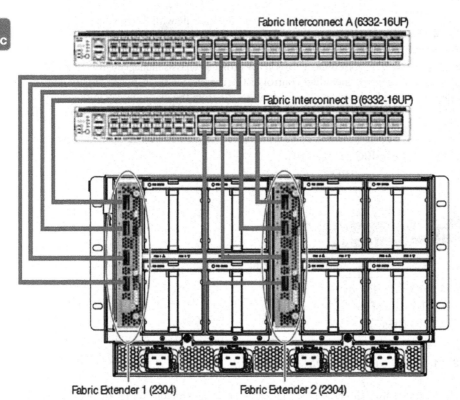

**Figure 12-12**  *Connecting Blade Chassis Fabric Extenders to Fabric Interconnect*

In discrete mode, a half-width server slot is pinned to a given FEX fabric link. The supported numbers of links are 1, 2, 4, and 8, as shown in Table 12-3. Figure 12-13 shows an example of four FEX fabric link connections. Figure 12-14 shows an example of discrete mode FEX fabric link per slot, and Figures 12-15 and 12-16 show an example of different options for the FEX fabric link connections.

**Table 12-3**  Blade Chassis Slot to Link Mapping

| FEX Type | Number of FEX Links | Half-Width Server Slot to Link |
|---|---|---|
| Cisco UCS 2304, Cisco UCS 2208XP, and Cisco UCS 2204XP | 1 | Server slots 1–8 merged to link 1 |
| | 2 | Server slots 1, 3, 5, 7 merged to link 1 |
| | | Server slots 2, 4, 6, 8 merged to link 2 |
| | 4 | Server slots 1, 5 merged to link 1 |
| | | Server slots 2, 6 merged to link 2 |
| | | Server slots 3, 7 merged to link 3 |
| | | Server slots 4, 8 merged to link 4 |
| Cisco UCS 2208XP only | 8 | 1:1 mapping. Each half-width server slot is pinned to a single FEX fabric link. |

Blade Chassis

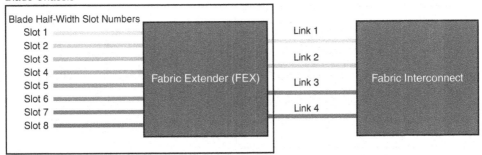

**Figure 12-13**  *Discrete Mode FEX Fabric Link Slot*

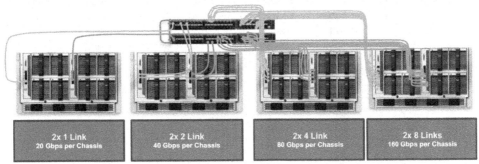

**Figure 12-14**  *UCS 10-Gigabit Ethernet FEX to FI Connectivity*

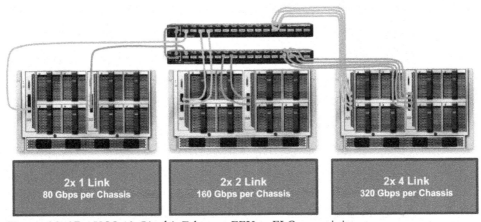

**Figure 12-15**  *UCS 40-Gigabit Ethernet FEX to FI Connectivity*

In port channel mode, the FEX fabric links are bundled into a single logical link (see Figure 12-16) to provide higher bandwidth to the servers. Depending on the FEX, up to eight links can be port channeled.

Blade Chassis

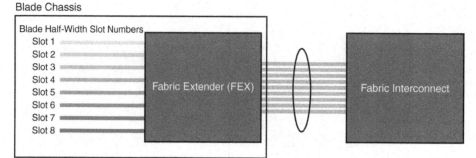

**Figure 12-16** *FEX Fabric Links in Port Channel Mode*

The Adapter-FEX uses a mechanism to divide a single physical link into multiple virtual links or channels, as shown in Figure 12-17. Each channel is identified by a unique channel number, and its scope is limited to the physical link.

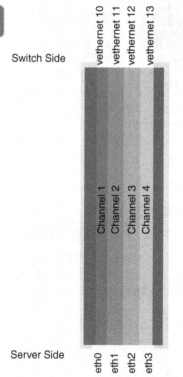

**Figure 12-17** *UCS FEX Virtual Links*

The physical link connects a port on a server network adapter with an Ethernet port on the device, which allows the channel to connect a virtual network interface card (vNIC) on the server with a virtual Ethernet interface on the device.

Packets on each channel are tagged with a virtual network tag (VNTag) with a specific source virtual interface identifier (VIF). The VIF allows the receiver to identify which channel the source transmit is using to the packet.

A rack-mount server has a different connectivity method. The Cisco C-Series supports two types of connections:

- Single-wire management

- Dual-wire management

Cisco UCS Manager single-wire management supports an additional option to integrate the C-Series rack-mount server with the Cisco UCS Manager using the Network Controller Sideband Interface (NC-SI). This option enables the Cisco UCS Manager to manage the C-Series rack-mount servers using a single wire for both management traffic and data traffic. When you use the single-wire management mode, one host-facing port on the FEX is sufficient to manage one rack-mount server instead of the two ports you would use in the Shared-LOM (LAN On Motherboard) mode. This connection method allows you to connect more rack-mount servers with the Cisco UCS Manager for integrated server management. You should make sure you have the correct server firmware for integration with the Cisco UCS Manager. If not, upgrade your server firmware before integrating the server with the Cisco UCS Manager. Figure 12-18 shows how the C-Series rack-mount chassis connects to the FEXs and FIs for single-wire management, with numbered elements as follows:

1. Cisco UCS 6332-16UP FI (Fabric A)
2. Cisco Nexus 2232PP, 2232TM-E, or 2348UPQ (Fabric A)
3. Cisco UCS 6332-16UP FI (Fabric B)
4. Cisco Nexus 2232PP, 2232TM-E, or 2348UPQ (Fabric B)
5. Cisco UCS C-Series server
6. Cisco UCS VIC1225 in PCIe slot 1

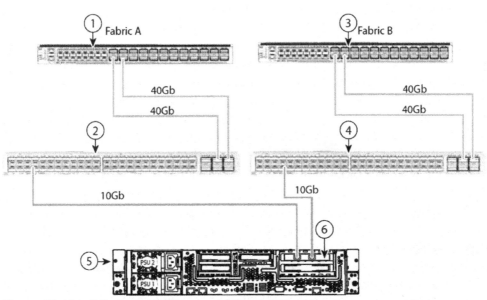

**Figure 12-18** *C-Series Rack Chassis with Single-Wire Management*

The Cisco UCS dual-wire manager supports the existing rack server integration and management option through shared LOM, using two separate cables for data traffic and management traffic, as shown in Figure 12-19. The prerequisites for integration with the Cisco UCS Manager are built into the C-Series servers. You should make sure you have the correct server firmware for integration with the Cisco UCS Manager. If not, you need to upgrade your server firmware before integrating the server with the Cisco UCS Manager. Figure 12-19 shows how the C-Series rack-mount chassis connect to the FEXs and FIs for dual-wire management, with numbered elements as follows:

1.    Cisco UCS 6332-16UP FI (Fabric A)

2.    GLC-TE transceiver in FEX port (Fabric A)

3.    Cisco Nexus 2232PP, 2232TM-E, or 2348UPQ (Fabric A)

4.    Cisco UCS 6332-16UP FI (Fabric B)

5.    GLC-TE transceiver in FEX port (Fabric B)

6.    Cisco Nexus 2232PP, 2232TM-E, or 2348UPQ (Fabric B)

7.    Cisco UCS C-Series server

8.    1-Gb Ethernet LOM ports

9.    10-Gb Adapter card in PCIe slot 1

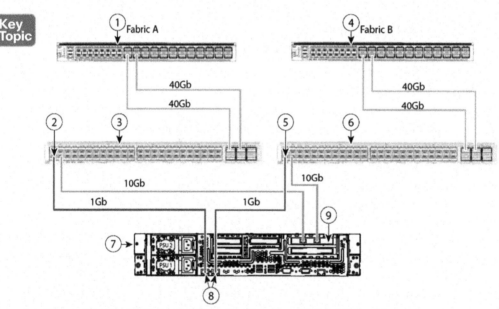

**Figure 12-19**    *C-Series Rack-Mount Chassis with Dual-Wire Management*

## Cisco UCS Virtualization Infrastructure

The Cisco UCS is a single integrated system with switches, cables, adapters, and servers all tied together and managed by unified management software. Thus, you are able to virtualize every component of the system at every level. The switch port, cables, adapter, and servers can all be virtualized.

Because of the virtualization capabilities at every component of the system, you have the unique ability to provide rapid provisioning of any service on any server on any blade through a system that is wired once. Figure 12-20 illustrates these virtualization capabilities.

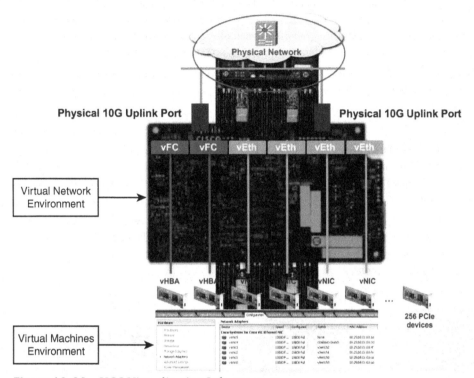

**Figure 12-20**   *UCS Virtualization Infrastructure*

The Cisco UCS Virtual Interface Card 1400/14000 Series (Figure 12-20) extends the network fabric directly to both servers and virtual machines so that a single connectivity mechanism can be used to connect both physical and virtual servers with the same level of visibility and control. Cisco VICs provide complete programmability of the Cisco UCS I/O infrastructure, with the number and type of I/O interfaces configurable on demand with a zero-touch model.

Cisco VICs support Cisco Single Connect technology, which provides an easy, intelligent, and efficient way to connect and manage computing in the data center. Cisco Single Connect unifies LAN, SAN, and systems management into one simplified link for rack servers, blade servers, and virtual machines. This technology reduces the number of network adapters, cables, and switches needed and radically simplifies the network, reducing complexity. Cisco VICs can support 256 PCI Express (PCIe) virtual devices, either virtual network interface cards (vNICs) or virtual host bus adapters (vHBAs), with a high rate of I/O operations per second (IOPS), support for lossless Ethernet, and 10/25/40/100-Gbps connection to servers. The PCIe Generation 3 × 16 interface helps ensure optimal bandwidth to the host for network-intensive applications, with a redundant path to the fabric interconnect. Cisco VICs support NIC teaming with fabric failover for increased reliability and availability. In addition, it provides a policy-based, stateless, agile server infrastructure for your data center.

The VIC 1400/14000 Series is designed exclusively for the M5 generation of UCS B-Series blade servers, C-Series rack servers, and S-Series storage servers. The adapters are capable of supporting 10/25/40/100-Gigabit Ethernet and Fibre Channel over Ethernet. It incorporates Cisco's next-generation converged network adapter (CNA) technology and offers a comprehensive feature set. In addition, the VIC supports Cisco's Data Center Virtual Machine Fabric Extender (VM-FEX) technology. This technology extends the Cisco UCS Fabric Interconnect ports to virtual machines, simplifying server virtualization deployment.

The Cisco UCS VIC 1400/14000 Series provides the following features and benefits (see Figure 12-21):

- **Stateless and agile platform:** The personality of the card is determined dynamically at boot time using the service profile associated with the server. The number, type (NIC or HBA), identity (MAC address and World Wide Name [WWN]), failover policy, bandwidth, and quality of service (QoS) policies of the PCIe interfaces are all determined using the service profile. The capability to define, create, and use interfaces on demand provides a stateless and agile server infrastructure.

- **Network interface virtualization:** Each PCIe interface created on the VIC is associated with an interface on the Cisco UCS Fabric Interconnect, providing complete network separation for each virtual cable between a PCIe device on the VIC and the interface on the fabric interconnect.

Cisco UCS VIC 1440

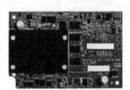
Cisco UCS VIC 1480

Cisco UCS VIC 1455

Cisco UCS VIC 1457

Cisco UCS VIC 1495

Cisco UCS VIC 1497

**Figure 12-21**  *Cisco UCS 1400 Virtual Interface Cards (VICs)*

UCS M5 B-Series VIC:

- **Cisco VIC 1440**

  - Single-port 40-Gigabit Ethernet or 4 × 10-Gbps Ethernet/FCoE capable modular LAN On Motherboard (mLOM).

  - Cisco UCS VIC 1440 capabilities are enabled for two ports of 40-Gbps Ethernet.

- UCS VIC 1440 enables a policy-based, stateless, agile server infrastructure that can present to the host PCIe standards-compliant interfaces that can be dynamically configured as either NICs or HBAs.

- **Cisco VIC 1480**

  - Single-port 40-Gigabit Ethernet s or 4 × 10-Gigabit Ethernet/FCoE capable mezzanine card (mezz).

  - UCS VIC 1480 enables a policy-based, stateless, agile server infrastructure that can present PCIe standards-compliant interfaces to the host that can be dynamically configured as either NICs or HBAs.

UCS M5 C-Series VIC:

- **Cisco VIC 1455**

  - Quad-port Small Form-Factor Pluggable (SFP28) half-height PCIe card.

  - Supports 10/25-Gigabit Ethernet or FCoE. The card can present PCIe standards-compliant interfaces to the host, and these can be dynamically configured as either NICs or HBAs.

- **Cisco VIC 1457**

  - Quad-port Small Form-Factor Pluggable (SFP28) mLOM card.

  - Supports 10/25-Gigabit Ethernet or FCoE. The card can present PCIe standards-compliant interfaces to the host, and these can be dynamically configured as either NICs or HBAs.

- **Cisco VIC 1467**

  - Quad-port Small Form-Factor Pluggable (SFP28) mLOM card for Cisco UCS C-Series M6 rack servers.

  - Supports 10/25-Gigabit Ethernet or FCoE. The card can present PCIe standards-compliant interfaces to the host, and these can be dynamically configured as either NICs or HBAs.

- **Cisco VIC 1477**

  - Quad-port Small Form-Factor Pluggable (SFP28) mLOM card for Cisco UCS C-Series M6 rack servers.

  - Supports 40/100-Gigabit Ethernet or FCoE. The card can present PCIe standards-compliant interfaces to the host, and these can be dynamically configured as either NICs or HBAs.

- **Cisco VIC 1495**

  - Dual-port Quad Small Form-Factor (QSFP28) PCIe.

  - Supports 40/100-Gigabit Ethernet or FCoE. The card can present PCIe standards-compliant interfaces to the host, and these can be dynamically configured as NICs or HBAs.

- Cisco VIC 1497

    - Dual-port Quad Small Form-Factor (QSFP28) mLOM card.

    - The card supports 40/100-Gigabit Ethernet or FCoE. The card can present PCIe standards-compliant interfaces to the host, and these can be dynamically configured as NICs or HBAs.

- Cisco VIC 14425

    - Modular LAN On Motherboard (mLOM) designed for Cisco UCS X210c M6 compute node.

    - 4× 25-Gbps Ethernet/FcoE interfaces. A total bandwidth of 100 Gbps for the server with 50-Gbps connectivity to each fabric.

- Cisco VIC 14825

    - Mezzanine card (mezz) designed for Cisco UCS X210c M6 compute node.

    - 4× 25-Gbps Ethernet/FcoE interfaces. A total bandwidth of 100 Gbps for the server with 50-Gbps connectivity to each fabric.

The latest generation of the Cisco VICs is the family of the Cisco VIC 15000 adapters, which offer models for the B-Series, C-Series, and the X-system compute nodes. The available models are

- Cisco VIC 15231

    - Modular LAN On Motherboard (mLOM) designed for the Cisco UCS X210 Compute Node

    - 2× 100-Gbps Ethernet/FCoE interfaces

- Cisco VIC 15420

    - Modular LAN On Motherboard (mLOM) designed for Cisco UCS X210c M6/M7 Compute Node

    - 4× 25-Gbps Ethernet/FCoE interfaces

- Cisco VIC 15422

    - Mezzanine card (mezz) designed for Cisco UCS X210c M6/M7 Compute Node

    - 4× 25-Gbps Ethernet/FCoE interfaces

- Cisco VIC 15428

    - Quad-port Small Form-Factor Pluggable (SFP+/SFP28/SFP56) mLOM card designed for Cisco UCS C-Series M6/M7 rack servers

    - 4× 10/25/50-Gbps Ethernet/FCoE interfaces

- Cisco VIC 15238

    - Dual-port Small Form-Factor Pluggable (SFP+/SFP28/SFP56) mLOM card designed for Cisco UCS C-Series M6/M7 rack servers

    - 2× 40/100/200-Gbps Ethernet/FCoE interfaces

■ Cisco VIC **15411**

    ■ Dual-port Modular LAN On Motherboard (mLOM) designed for Cisco UCS B-Series M6 blade servers

    ■ 2× 40-Gbps Ethernet/FCoE interfaces

## Cisco UCS-X System

The Cisco UCS X-Series Modular system, shown Figure 12-22, is the latest generation of the Cisco UCS. It is a modular system managed from the Cisco Intersight cloud. Here are the major new features:

■ The system operates in Intersight Managed Mode (IMM) because it is managed from the Cisco Intersight.

■ The new Cisco UCS X9508 chassis has a midplane-free design. The I/O connectivity for the X9508 chassis is accomplished via frontloading, with vertically oriented compute nodes intersecting with horizontally oriented I/O connectivity modules in the rear of the chassis.

■ Cisco UCS 9108 Intelligent Fabric modules provide connectivity to the upstream Cisco UCS 6400/6500 Fabric Interconnects.

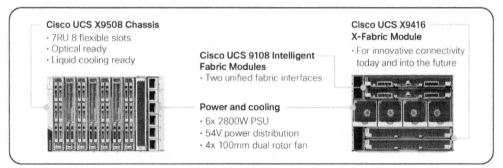

**Figure 12-22**  *Cisco UCS X-System with Cisco Intersight*

The new Cisco UCS X9508 chassis provides a new and adaptable substitute for the first generation of the UCS chassis. It is designed to be expandable in the future. As proof of this, the X-Fabric slots are intended for future use. It has optimized cooling flows to support reliable operation for longer times. The major features are as follows:

■ A seven-rack-unit (7RU) chassis has eight front-facing flexible slots. They can house a combination of compute nodes and a pool of future I/O resources, which may include GPU accelerators, disk storage, and nonvolatile memory.

■ The 2× Cisco UCS 9108 Intelligent Fabric Modules (IFMs) at the top of the chassis connect the chassis to upstream Cisco UCS 6400/6500 Series Fabric Interconnects. Each IFM has the following features:

    ■ It includes up to 200 Gbps of unified fabric connectivity per compute node.

- The Cisco UCS 9108 25G IFM supports 8× 25-Gbps SFP28 uplink ports, while the 100G option supports 8× 100-Gbps QSFP uplink ports. The unified fabric carries management traffic to the Cisco Intersight cloud operations platform, Fibre Channel over Ethernet (FCoE) traffic, and production Ethernet traffic to the fabric interconnects.

- At the bottom are slots, ready to house future I/O modules that can flexibly connect the compute modules with I/O devices. This connectivity is called Cisco UCS X-Fabric technology because X is a variable that can evolve with new technology developments.

- The 6× 2800W power supply units (PSUs) provide 54V power to the chassis with N, N+1, and N+N redundancy. A higher voltage allows efficient power delivery with less copper and reduced power loss.

- Efficient, 4× 100mm, dual counter-rotating fans deliver industry-leading airflow and power efficiency. Optimized thermal algorithms enable different cooling modes to best support the network environment. Cooling is modular so that future enhancements can potentially handle open- or closed-loop liquid cooling to support even higher-power processors.

The X-Fabric Technology supports 32 lanes of PCIe Gen 4 connectivity to each compute node. Using the Cisco UCS X9416 X-Fabric Modules, each blade can access PCIe devices, including up to four GPUs in a Cisco UCS X440p PCIe node. Combined with two onboard cards, the compute nodes can accelerate workloads with up to six GPUs per node.

The available compute nodes for the Cisco UCS X-System are

- **Cisco UCS X210× M6 Compute Node**

  - **CPU:** Up to 2× third-generation Intel Xeon Scalable Processors with up to 40 cores per processor and 1.5 MB Level 3 cache per core.

  - **Memory:** Up to 32× 256 GB DDR4-3200 DIMMs for up to 8 TB of main memory. Configuring up to 16× 512-GB Intel Optane persistent memory DIMMs can yield up to 12 TB of memory.

- **Cisco UCS X210× M7 Compute Node**

  - **CPU:** Up to 2× fourth-generation Intel Xeon Scalable Processors with up to 60 cores per processor and up to 2.625 MB Level 3 cache per core and up to 112.5 MB per CPU.

  - **Memory:** Up to 32× 256 GB DDR5-4800 DIMMs for up to 8 TB of main memory.

- **Cisco UCS X410× M7 Compute Node**

  - **CPU:** 4× fourth-generation Intel Xeon Scalable Processors with up to 60 cores per processor and up to 2.625 MB Level 3 cache per core and up to 112.5 MB per CPU.

  - **Memory:** Up to 64× 256 GB DDR5-4800 DIMMs for up to 16 TB of main memory.

# Cisco UCS Initial Setup and Management

The Cisco UCS Manager enables you to manage general and complex server deployments. For example, you can manage a general deployment with a pair of fabric interconnects, which is the redundant server access layer that you get with the first chassis that can scale up to 20 chassis and up to 160 physical servers. This can be a combination of blades and rack-mount servers to support the workload in your environment. As you add more servers, you can continue to perform server provisioning, device discovery, inventory, configuration, diagnostics, monitoring, fault detection, and auditing.

Beginning with release 4.0(2a), the Cisco UCS Manager extends support for all existing features on the following Cisco UCS hardware unless specifically noted:

- Cisco UCS C480 M5 ML Server

- Cisco UCS VIC 1495

- Cisco UCS VIC 1497

- Cisco UCS 6454 Fabric Interconnect

- Cisco UCS VIC 1455

- Cisco UCS VIC 1457

- Cisco UCS C125 M5 Server

By default, the Cisco UCS 6454 Fabric Interconnect, the Cisco UCS 6332 FIs, the Cisco UCS Mini 6324 FIs, and the UCS 6200 Series FIs include centralized management. You can manage the Cisco UCS blade servers and rack-mount servers that are in the same domain from one console. You can also manage the Cisco UCS Mini from the Cisco UCS Manager.

To ensure optimum server performance, you can configure the amount of power that you allocate to servers. You can also set the server boot policy, the location from which the server boots, and the order in which the boot devices are invoked. You can create service profiles for the Cisco UCS B-Series blade servers and the Cisco UCS Mini to assign to servers. Service profiles enable you to assign BIOS settings, security settings, the number of vNICs and vHBAs, and anything else that you want to apply to a server. Initial configuration of fabric interconnects is performed using the console connection. It is essential to maintain symmetric Cisco UCS Manager versions between the fabric interconnects in a domain.

Follow these steps to perform the initial configuration for the Cisco UCS Manager:

**Step 1.** Power on the fabric interconnect. You see the power-on self-test messages as the fabric interconnect boots.

**Step 2.** If the system obtains a lease IPv4 or IPv6 address, go to step 6; otherwise, continue to the next step.

**Step 3.** Connect to the console port.

**Step 4.** At the installation method prompt, enter **GUI**.

**Step 5.**    If the system cannot access a DHCP server, you are prompted to enter the following information:

■ IPv4 or IPv6 address for the management port on the fabric interconnect

■ IPv4 subnet mask or IPv6 prefix for the management port on the fabric interconnect

■ IPv4 or IPv6 address for the default gateway assigned to the fabric interconnect

**NOTE**  In a cluster configuration, both fabric interconnects must be assigned the same management interface address type during setup.

**Step 6.**    Copy the web link from the prompt into a web browser and go to the Cisco UCS Manager GUI launch page.

**Step 7.**    On the Cisco UCS Manager GUI launch page, select **Express Setup**.

**Step 8.**    On the Express Setup page, select **Initial Setup** and click **Submit**.

**Step 9.**    In the Cluster and Fabric Setup area, do the following:

■ Click the **Enable Clustering** option.

■ For the Fabric Setup option, select **Fabric A**.

■ In the Cluster IP Address field, enter the IPv4 or IPv6 address that the Cisco UCS Manager will use.

**Step 10.**  In the System Setup area, complete the following fields:

| Name | Description |
|------|-------------|
| System Name | The name assigned to the Cisco UCS domain. In a standalone configuration, the system adds "-A" to the system name. In a cluster configuration, the system adds "-A" to the fabric interconnect assigned to Fabric A, and "-B" to the fabric interconnect assigned to Fabric B. |
| Admin Password | The password used for the Admin account on the fabric interconnect. Choose a strong password that meets the guidelines for Cisco UCS Manager passwords. This password cannot be blank |
| Confirm Admin Password | The password used for the Admin account on the fabric interconnect. |
| Mgmt IP Address | The static IPv4 or IPv6 address for the management port on the fabric interconnect. |
| Mgmt IP Netmask or Mgmt IP Prefix | The IPv4 subnet mask or IPv6 prefix for the management port on the fabric interconnect. |
| Default Gateway | The IPv4 or IPv6 address for the default gateway assigned to the management port on the fabric interconnect |
| DNS Server IP | The IPv4 or IPv6 address for the DNS Server assigned to the fabric |
| Domain Name | The name of the domain in which the fabric interconnect resides |

**Step 11.**  Click **Submit**. A page then displays the results of your setup operation.

Another option is to use the command-line interface (CLI) to configure the primary fabric interconnect as follows:

**Step 1.**  Connect to the console port.

**Step 2.**  Power on the fabric interconnect. You see the power-on self-test messages as the fabric interconnect boots.

**Step 3.**  When the unconfigured system boots, it prompts you for the setup method to be used. Enter **console** to continue the initial setup using the console CLI.

**Step 4.**  Enter **setup** to continue as an initial system setup.

**Step 5.**  Enter **y** to confirm that you want to continue the initial setup.

**Step 6.**  Enter the password for the admin account.

**Step 7.**  To confirm, reenter the password for the admin account.

**Step 8.**  Enter **yes** to continue the initial setup for a cluster configuration.

**Step 9.**  Enter the fabric interconnect fabric (either A or B).

**Step 10.**  Enter the system name.

**Step 11.**  Enter the IPv4 or IPv6 address for the management port of the fabric interconnect. If you enter an IPv4 address, you are prompted to enter an IPv4 subnet mask. If you enter an IPv6 address, you are prompted to enter an IPv6 network prefix.

**Step 12.**  Enter the respective IPv4 subnet mask or IPv6 network prefix; then press Enter. You are prompted for an IPv4 or IPv6 address for the default gateway, depending on the address type you entered for the management port of the fabric interconnect.

**Step 13.**  Enter either of the following:

- IPv4 address of the default gateway

- IPv6 address of the default gateway

**Step 14.**  Enter **yes** if you want to specify the IP address for the DNS server or **no** if you do not.

**Step 15.**  (Optional) Enter the IPv4 or IPv6 address for the DNS server. The address type must be the same as the address type of the management port of the fabric interconnect.

**Step 16.**  Enter **yes** if you want to specify the default domain name or **no** if you do not.

**Step 17.**  (Optional) Enter the default domain name.

**Step 18.**  Review the setup summary and enter **yes** to save and apply the settings, or enter **no** to go through the Setup wizard again to change some of the settings. If you choose to go through the Setup wizard again, it provides the values you previously entered, and the values appear in brackets. To accept previously entered values, press Enter.

Example 12-1 sets up the first fabric interconnect for a cluster configuration using the console to set IPv4 management addresses.

**Example 12-1**   *UCS FI IPv4 Initialization*

```
Enter the installation method (console/gui)? console
Enter the setup mode (restore from backup or initial setup) [restore/setup]? setup
You have chosen to setup a new switch. Continue? (y/n): y
Enter the password for "admin": adminpassword
Confirm the password for "admin": adminpassword
Do you want to create a new cluster on this switch (select 'no' for standalone setup
or if you want this switch to be added to an existing cluster)? (yes/no) [n]: yes
Enter the switch fabric (A/B): A
Enter the system name: dccor
Mgmt0 IPv4 address: 192.168.10.11
Mgmt0 IPv4 netmask: 255.255.255.0
IPv4 address of the default gateway: 192.168.0.1
Virtual IPv4 address: 192.168.0.10
Configure the DNS Server IPv4 address? (yes/no) [n]: yes
DNS IPv4 address: 198.18.133.200
Configure the default domain name? (yes/no) [n]: yes
Default domain name: domainname.com
Join centralized management environment (UCS Central)? (yes/no) [n]: no
Following configurations will be applied:
  Switch Fabric=A
  System Name=dccor
  Management IP Address=192.168.0.11
  Management IP Netmask=255.255.255.0
  Default Gateway=192.168.0.1
  Cluster Enabled=yes
  Virtual Ip Address=192.168.0.10
  DNS Server=198.18.133.200
  Domain Name=domainname.com
Apply and save the configuration (select 'no' if you want to re-enter)? (yes/no): yes
```

Example 12-2 sets up the first fabric interconnect for a cluster configuration using the
console to set IPv6 management addresses:

**Example 12-2**   *UCS FI IPv6 Initialization*

```
Enter the installation method (console/gui)? console
Enter the setup mode (restore from backup or initial setup) [restore/setup]? setup
You have chosen to setup a new switch. Continue? (y/n): y
Enter the password for "admin": adminpassword
Confirm the password for "admin": adminpassword
Do you want to create a new cluster on this switch (select 'no' for standalone setup
or if you want this switch to be added to an existing cluster)? (yes/no) [n]: yes
Enter the switch fabric (A/B): A
Enter the system name: dccor
Mgmt0 address: 2020::207
```

```
Mgmt0 IPv6 prefix: 64
IPv6 address of the default gateway: 2020::1
Configure the DNS Server IPv6 address? (yes/no) [n]: yes
DNS IP address: 2020::201
Configure the default domain name? (yes/no) [n]: yes
Default domain name: domainname.com
Join centralized management environment (UCS Central)? (yes/no) [n]: no
Following configurations will be applied:
Switch Fabric=A
System Name=dccor
Enforced Strong Password=no
Physical Switch Mgmt0 IPv6 Address=2020::207
Physical Switch Mgmt0 IPv6 Prefix=64
Default Gateway=2020::1
Ipv6 value=1
DNS Server=2020::201
Domain Name=domainname.com
Apply and save the configuration (select 'no' if you want to re-enter)? (yes/no): yes
```

To configure the subordinate fabric interconnect using the GUI, follow these steps:

**Step 1.** Power up the fabric interconnect. You see the power-on self-test message as the fabric interconnect boots.

**Step 2.** If the system obtains a lease, go to step 6; otherwise, continue to the next step.

**Step 3.** Connect to the console port.

**Step 4.** At the installation method prompt, enter **GUI**.

**Step 5.** If the system cannot access a DHCP server, you are prompted to enter the following information:

■ IPv4 or IPv6 address for the management port on the fabric interconnect

■ IPv4 subnet mask or IPv6 prefix for the management port on the fabric interconnect

■ IPv4 or IPv6 address for the default gateway assigned to the fabric interconnect

**NOTE** In a cluster configuration, both fabric interconnects must be assigned the same management interface address type during setup.

**Step 6.** Copy the web link from the prompt into a web browser and go to the Cisco UCS Manager GUI launch page.

**Step 7.** On the Cisco UCS Manager GUI launch page, select **Express Setup**.

**Step 8.** On the Express Setup page, select **Initial Setup** and click **Submit**. The fabric interconnect should detect the configuration information for the first fabric interconnect.

**Step 9.**    In the Cluster and Fabric Setup Area, do the following:

■ Select the **Enable Clustering** option.

■ For the Fabric Setup option, make sure **Fabric B** is selected.

**Step 10.**    In the System Setup Area, enter the password for the Admin account into the Admin Password of Master field. The Manager Initial Setup Area is displayed.

**Step 11.**    In the Manager Initial Setup Area, the field that is displayed depends on whether you configured the first fabric interconnect with an IPv4 or IPv6 management address. Complete the field that is appropriate for your configuration, as follows:

■ **Peer FI is IPv4 Cluster enabled. Please Provide Local fabric interconnect Mgmt0 IPv4 Address:** Enter an IPv4 address for the Mgmt0 interface on the local fabric interconnect.

■ **Peer FI is IPv6 Cluster Enabled. Please Provide Local fabric interconnect Mgmt0 IPv6 Address:** Enter an IPv6 address for the Mgmt0 interface on the local fabric interconnect.

**Step 12.**    Click **Submit**. A page displays the results of your setup operation.

To configure the subordinate fabric interconnect using the CLI, follow these steps:

**Step 1.**    Connect to the console port.

**Step 2.**    Power up the fabric interconnect. You see the power-on self-test messages as the fabric interconnect boots.

**Step 3.**    When the unconfigured system boots, it prompts you for the setup method to be used. Enter **console** to continue the initial setup using the console CLI.

**NOTE**    The fabric interconnect should detect the peer fabric interconnect in the cluster. If it does not, check the physical connections between the L1 and L2 ports, and verify that the peer fabric interconnect has been enabled for a cluster configuration.

**Step 4.**    Enter **y** to add the subordinate fabric interconnect to the cluster.

**Step 5.**    Enter the admin password of the peer fabric interconnect.

**Step 6.**    Enter the IP address for the management port on the subordinate fabric interconnect.

**Step 7.**    Review the setup summary and enter **yes** to save and apply the settings, or enter **no** to go through the Setup wizard again to change some of the settings. If you choose to go through the Setup wizard again, it provides the values you previously entered, and the values appear in brackets. To accept previously entered values, press Enter.

Example 12-3 sets up the second fabric interconnect for a cluster configuration using the console and the IPv4 address of the peer.

**Example 12-3**  *UCS Second FI IPv4 Initialization*

```
Enter the installation method (console/gui)? console

Installer has detected the presence of a peer Fabric interconnect. This Fabric
interconnect will be added to the cluster. Continue (y/n) ? y

Enter the admin password of the peer Fabric Interconnect: adminpassword

Peer Fabric interconnect Mgmt0 IPv4 Address: 192.168.10.11

Apply and save the configuration (select 'no' if you want to re-enter)? (yes/no): yes
```

Example 12-4 sets up the second fabric interconnect for a cluster configuration using the console and the IPv6 address of the peer.

**Example 12-4**  *UCS Second FI IPv6 Initialization*

```
Enter the installation method (console/gui)? console

Installer has detected the presence of a peer Fabric interconnect. This Fabric
interconnect will be added to the cluster. Continue (y/n) ? y

Enter the admin password of the peer Fabric Interconnect: adminpassword

Peer Fabric interconnect Mgmt0 IPv6 Address: 2020::207

Apply and save the configuration (select 'no' if you want to re-enter)? (yes/no): yes
```

You can verify that both fabric interconnect configurations are complete by logging in to the fabric interconnect via the SSH or GUI and verifying the cluster status through the CLI as the commands in Table 12-4 or through the GUI, as shown in Figure 12-23.

**Table 12-4**  Cluster Verification CLI

| Command | Purpose | Sample Output |
|---|---|---|
| show cluster state | Displays the operational state and leadership role for both fabric interconnects in a high-availability cluster. | The following example shows that both fabric interconnects are in the Up state, HA is in the Ready state, Fabric Interconnect A has the primary role, and Fabric Interconnect B has the subordinate role:<br><br>```<br>UCS-A# show cluster state<br>Cluster Id:<br>0x4432f72a371511de-0xb97c000de1b1ada4<br>A: UP, PRIMARY<br>B: UP,<br>SUBORDINATE HA READY<br>``` |

| Command | Purpose | Sample Output |
|---------|---------|---------------|
| **show cluster extended-state** | Displays extended details about the cluster state and typically used when troubleshooting issues. | The following example shows how to view the extended state of a cluster:<br><br>```<br>UCSC# show cluster<br>extended-state<br>0x2e95deacbd0f11e2-0x8ff35147e84f3de2 Start<br>time: Thu May 16 06:54:22 2018 Last election<br>time: Thu May 16 16:29:28 2019<br>System Management<br>Viewing the Cluster State<br>A: UP, PRIMARY<br>B: UP, SUBORDINATE<br>A: memb state UP, lead state<br>PRIMARY, mgmt services state: UP<br>B: memb state UP, lead state<br>SUBORDINATE,<br>mgmt services state: UP<br>heartbeat state PRIMARY_OK<br>HA READY<br>Detailed state of the device<br>selected for HA quorum data:<br>Device 1007, serial:<br>a66b4c20-8692-11df-bd63-1b72ecd12d4,<br>state: active<br>Device 1010, serial:<br>00e3e6d0-8693-11df-9e10-0f4428ee3289,<br>state: active<br>Device 1012, serial:<br>1d8922c8-8693-11df-9133-89334345c,<br>state: active<br>``` |

**Figure 12-23** *Cisco UCS Manager Cluster Verification*

## Fabric Interconnect Connectivity and Configurations

A fully redundant Cisco Unified Computing System consists of two independent fabric planes: Fabric A and Fabric B. Each plane consists of a central fabric interconnect connected to an I/O module (Fabric Extender) in each blade chassis. The two fabric interconnects are completely independent from the perspective of the data plane; the Cisco UCS can function with a single fabric interconnect if the other fabric is offline or not provisioned (see Figure 12-24).

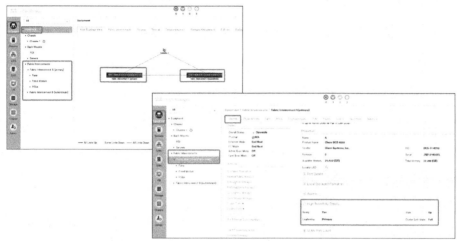

**Figure 12-24**   *UCS Fabric Interconnect (FI) Status*

The following steps show how to determine the primary fabric interconnect:

**Step 1.**   In the Navigation pane, click **Equipment.**

**Step 2.**   Expand **Equipment > Fabric Interconnects.**

**Step 3.**   Click the fabric interconnect for which you want to identify the role.

**Step 4.**   In the Work pane, click the **General** tab.

**Step 5.**   In the General tab, click the down arrows on the High Availability Details bar to expand that area.

**Step 6.**   View the Leadership field to determine whether the fabric interconnect is primary or subordinate.

> **NOTE**   If the admin password is lost, you can determine the primary and secondary roles of the fabric interconnects in a cluster by opening the Cisco UCS Manager GUI from the IP addresses of both fabric interconnects. The subordinate fabric interconnect fails with the following message: "UCSM GUI is not available on secondary node."

The fabric interconnect is the core component of the Cisco UCS. Cisco UCS Fabric Interconnects provide uplink access to LAN, SAN, and out-of-band management segments, as shown in Figure 12-25. Cisco UCS infrastructure management is handled through the embedded management software, the Cisco UCS Manager, for both hardware and software management. The Cisco UCS Fabric Interconnects are top-of-rack devices and provide unified access to the Cisco UCS domain.

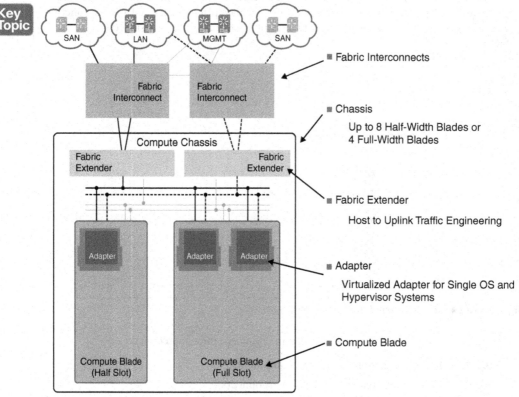

**Figure 12-25** *Cisco UCS Components Logical Connectivity*

All network endpoints, such as host bus adapters (HBAs) and management entities such as Cisco Integrated Management Controllers (CIMCs), are dual-connected to both fabric planes and thus can work in an active-active configuration.

Virtual port channels (vPCs) are not supported on the fabric interconnects, although the upstream LAN switches to which they connect can be vPC or Virtual Switching System (VSS) peers.

Cisco UCS Fabric Interconnects provide network connectivity and management for the connected servers. They run the Cisco UCS Manager control software and consist of expansion modules for the Cisco UCS Manager software.

### Uplink Connectivity

Fabric interconnect ports configured as uplink ports are used to connect to upstream network switches. You can connect these uplink ports to upstream switch ports as individual links or as links configured as port channels. Port channel configurations provide bandwidth aggregation as well as link redundancy.

You can achieve northbound connectivity from the fabric interconnect through a standard uplink, a port channel, or a virtual port channel configuration. The port channel name and ID configured on the fabric interconnect should match the name and ID configuration on the upstream Ethernet switch.

It is also possible to configure a port channel as a vPC, where port channel uplink ports from a fabric interconnect are connected to different upstream switches. After all uplink ports are configured, you can create a port channel for these ports.

### Downlink Connectivity

Each fabric interconnect is connected to I/O modules in the Cisco UCS chassis, which provides connectivity to each blade server. Internal connectivity from blade servers to IOMs is transparently provided by the Cisco UCS Manager using the 10BASE-KR Ethernet standard for backplane implementations, and no additional configuration is required. You must configure the connectivity between the fabric interconnect server ports and IOMs. Each IOM, when connected with the fabric interconnect server port, behaves as a line card to fabric interconnect; hence, IOMs should never be cross-connected to the fabric interconnect. Each IOM is connected directly to a single fabric interconnect.

The Fabric Extender (also referred to as the IOM, or FEX) logically extends the fabric interconnects to the blade server. The best analogy is to think of it as a remote line card that's embedded in the blade server chassis, allowing connectivity to the external world. IOM settings are pushed via the Cisco UCS Manager and are not managed directly. The primary functions of this module are to facilitate blade server I/O connectivity (internal and external), multiplex all I/O traffic up to the fabric interconnects, and help monitor and manage the Cisco UCS infrastructure. You should configure fabric interconnect ports that should be connected to downlink IOM cards as server ports. You need to make sure there is physical connectivity between the fabric interconnect and IOMs. You must also configure the IOM ports and the global chassis discovery policy.

## Fabric Interconnect Port Modes

The port mode determines whether a unified port on the fabric interconnect is configured to carry Ethernet or Fibre Channel traffic. You configure the port mode in the Cisco UCS Manager. However, the fabric interconnect does not automatically discover the port mode.

Changing the port mode deletes the existing port configuration and replaces it with a new logical port. Any objects associated with that port configuration, such as VLANs and VSANs, are also removed. There is no restriction on the number of times you can change the port mode for a unified port.

When you set the port mode to Ethernet, you can configure the following Ethernet port types:

- Server ports

- Ethernet uplink ports

- Ethernet port channel members

- FCoE ports

- Appliance ports

- Appliance port channel members

■ SPAN destination ports

■ SPAN source ports

> **NOTE**   For SPAN source ports, you configure one of the port types and then configure the port as a SPAN source.

For Fibre Channel, you can configure the following port types:

■ Fibre Channel uplink ports

■ Fibre Channel port channel members

■ Fibre Channel storage ports

■ FCoE Uplink ports

■ SPAN source ports

A port must be explicitly defined as a specific type, and this type defines the port behavior. For example, discovery of components such as Fabric Extenders or blades is performed only on server ports. Similarly, uplink ports are automatically configured as IEEE 802.1Q trunks for all VLANs defined on the fabric interconnect.

The following steps show how to verify fabric interconnect neighbors:

**Step 1.**   In the Navigation pane, click **Equipment**.

**Step 2.**   In the Equipment tab, expand **Equipment > Fabric Interconnects**.

**Step 3.**   Click the fabric interconnect for which you want to view the LAN or SAN or LLDP neighbors.

**Step 4.**   In the Work pane, click the **Neighbors** tab.

**Step 5.**   Click the **LAN** or **SAN** or **LLDP** subtab. This subtab lists all the LAN or SAN or LLDP neighbors of the specified Fabric Interconnect. (See Figure 12-26.)

**Figure 12-26**   *UCS Fabric Interconnect (FI) Neighbors Detail*

**NOTE**   In either Ethernet switching mode, a fabric interconnect does not require an upstream switch for Layer 2 traffic between two servers connected to it on the same fabric.

An external switch is required for switching Layer 2 traffic between servers if vNICs belonging to the same VLAN are mapped to different fabric interconnects (see Figure 12-27).

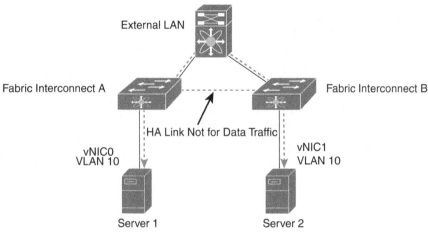

**Figure 12-27**   *UCS FI to External LAN Connection*

## Fabric Failover for Ethernet: High-Availability vNIC

To understand the switching mode behavior, you need to understand the fabric-based failover feature for Ethernet in the Cisco UCS. Each adapter in the Cisco UCS is a dual-port adapter that connects to both fabrics (A and B). The two fabrics in the Cisco UCS provide failover protection in the event of planned or unplanned component downtime in one of the fabrics. Typically, host software—such as NIC teaming for Ethernet and PowerPath or multipath I/O (MPIO) for Fibre Channel—provides failover across the two fabrics (see Figure 12-28).

A vNIC in the Cisco UCS is a host-presented PCI device that is centrally managed by the Cisco UCS Manager. The fabric-based failover feature, which you enable by selecting the high-availability vNIC option in the service profile definition, allows network interface virtualization (NIV)-capable adapters (Cisco virtual interface card, or VIC) and the fabric interconnects to provide active-standby failover for Ethernet vNICs without any NIC-teaming software on the host.

For unicast traffic failover, the fabric interconnect in the new path sends gratuitous Address Resolution Protocols (gARPs). This process refreshes the forwarding tables on the upstream switches.

For multicast traffic, the new active fabric interconnect sends an Internet Group Management Protocol (IGMP) Global Leave message to the upstream multicast router. The upstream multicast router responds by sending an IGMP query that is flooded to all vNICs. The host OS responds to these IGMP queries by rejoining all relevant multicast groups. This process forces the hosts to refresh the multicast state in the network in a timely manner.

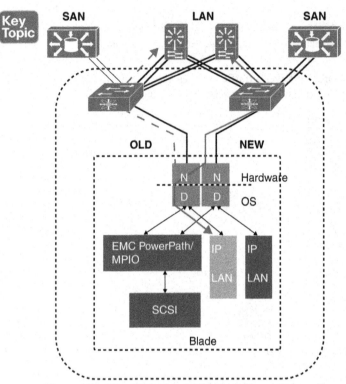

**Figure 12-28** *UCS Fabric Traffic Failover Example*

Cisco UCS fabric failover is an important feature because it reduces the complexity of defining NIC teaming software for failover on the host. It does this transparently in the fabric based on the network property that is defined in the service profile.

## Ethernet Switching Mode

The Ethernet switching mode determines how the fabric interconnect behaves as a switching device between the servers and the network. The fabric interconnect operates in either of the following Ethernet switching modes:

- End-host mode
- Switching mode

In end-host mode, the Cisco UCS presents an end host to an external Ethernet network. The external LAN sees the Cisco UCS Fabric Interconnect as an end host with multiple adapters (see Figure 12-29).

End-host mode allows the fabric interconnect to act as an end host to the network, representing all servers (hosts) connected to it through vNICs. This behavior is achieved by pinning (either dynamically pinning or hard pinning) vNICs to uplink ports, which provides redundancy to the network, and makes the uplink ports appear as server ports to the rest of the fabric.

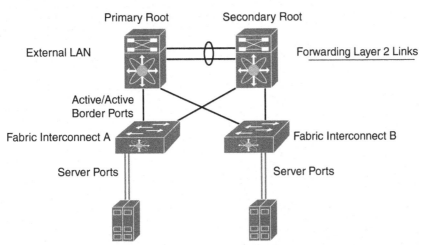

**Figure 12-29**  *UCS FI End-Host Mode Ethernet*

In end-host mode, the fabric interconnect does not run the Spanning Tree Protocol (STP), but it avoids loops by denying uplink ports from forwarding traffic to each other and by denying egress server traffic on more than one uplink port at a time. End-host mode is the default Ethernet switching mode and should be used if either of the following is used upstream:

■ Layer 2 switching for Layer 2 aggregation

■ vPC or VSS aggregation layer

**NOTE**   When you enable end-host mode, if a vNIC is hard pinned to an uplink port and this uplink port goes down, the system cannot repin the vNIC, and the vNIC remains down.

Server links (vNICs on the blades) are associated with a single uplink port, which may also be a port channel. This association process is called *pinning*, and the selected external interface is called a *pinned uplink port*. The pinning process can be statically configured when the vNIC is defined or dynamically configured by the system. In end-host mode, pinning is required for traffic flow to a server.

Static pinning is performed by defining a pin group and associating the pin group with a vNIC. Static pinning should be used in scenarios in which a deterministic path is required. When the target (as shown on Figure 12-30) on Fabric Interconnect A goes down, the corresponding failover mechanism of the vNIC goes into effect, and traffic is redirected to the target port on Fabric Interconnect B.

If the pinning is not static, the vNIC is pinned to an operational uplink port on the same fabric interconnect, and the vNIC failover mechanisms are not invoked until all uplink ports on that fabric interconnect fail. In the absence of Spanning Tree Protocol, the fabric interconnect uses various mechanisms for loop prevention while preserving an active-active topology.

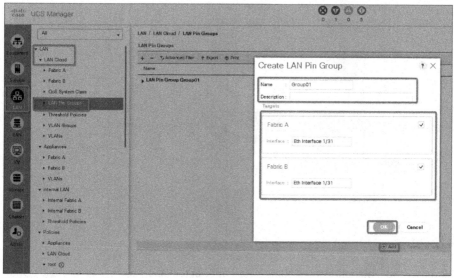

**Figure 12-30**  *UCS LAN Pinning Group Configuration*

In the Cisco UCS, two types of Ethernet traffic paths will have different characteristics—
Unicast and Multicast/Broadcast:

- Unicast traffic paths in the Cisco UCS are shown in Figure 12-31. Characteristics of
  unicast traffic in the Cisco UCS include the following:

  - Each server link is pinned to exactly one uplink port (or port channel).

  - Server-to-server Layer 2 traffic is locally switched.

  - Server-to-network traffic goes out on its pinned uplink port.

  - Network-to-server unicast traffic is forwarded to the server only if it arrives on a
    pinned uplink port. This feature is called the Reverse Path Forwarding (RPF) check.

  - Server traffic received on any uplink port, except its pinned uplink port, is dropped
    (called the *deja-vu check*).

  - The server MAC address must be learned before traffic can be forwarded to it.

- Multicast/broadcast traffic paths in the Cisco UCS are shown in Figure 12-32.
  Characteristics of multicast/broadcast traffic in the Cisco UCS include the following:

  - Broadcast traffic is pinned on exactly one uplink port in the Cisco UCS Manager,
    and the incoming broadcast traffic is pinned on a per-VLAN basis, depending on
    uplink port VLAN membership.

  - IGMP multicast groups are pinned based on IGMP snooping. Each group is pinned
    to exactly one uplink port.

  - Server-to-server multicast traffic is locally switched.

  - RPF and deja-vu checks also apply to multicast traffic.

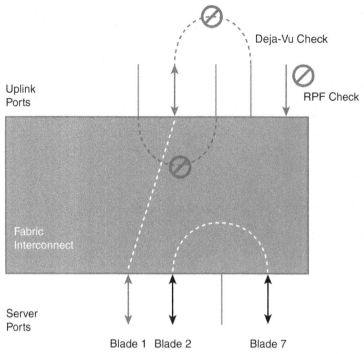

**Figure 12-31**   *UCS Unicast Traffic Path*

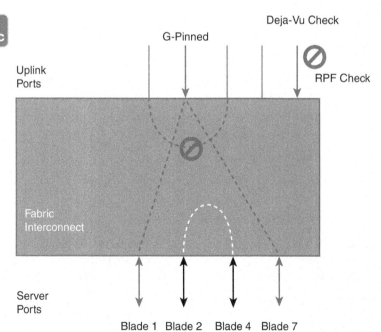

**Figure 12-32**   *Multicast and Broadcast Traffic Summary*

In switching mode the fabric interconnect runs STP to avoid loops; broadcast and multicast packets are handled in the traditional way. You should use the switching mode only if the fabric interconnect is directly connected to a router or if either of the following is used upstream:

■ Layer 3 aggregation

■ VLAN in a box

In Ethernet switching mode (see Figure 12-33), the Cisco UCS Fabric Interconnects act like traditional Ethernet switches with support for Spanning Tree Protocol on the uplink ports.

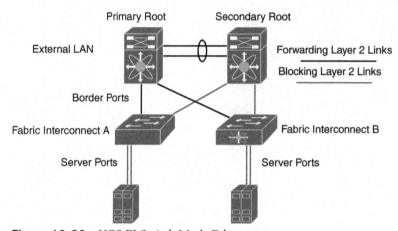

**Figure 12-33**   *UCS FI Switch Mode Ethernet*

The following are Ethernet switching mode features:

■ Spanning Tree Protocol is run on the uplink ports per VLAN as defined by Cisco Per-VLAN Spanning Tree Plus (PVST+).

■ Configuration of Spanning Tree Protocol parameters (such as bridge priority and hello timers) is not supported.

■ VLAN Trunk Protocol (VTP) is not supported.

■ MAC address learning and aging occur on both the server and uplink ports as in a typical Layer 2 switch.

■ Upstream links are blocked according to Spanning Tree Protocol rules.

■ In most cases, end-host mode is preferable because it offers scalability and simplicity for server administrators when connecting to an upstream network. However, there are other factors to consider when selecting the appropriate switching mode, including the following:

■ Scalability

■ Efficient use of bandwidth

- Fabric failover

- Active-active link utilization

- Disjoint Layer 2 domain or a loop-free topology

- Optimal network behavior for the existing network topology

- Application-specific requirements

**NOTE**   For both Ethernet switching modes, even when vNICs are hard-pinned to uplink ports, all server-to-server unicast traffic in the server array is sent only through the fabric interconnect and is never sent through uplink ports. Server-to-server multicast and broadcast traffic is sent through all uplink ports in the same VLAN.

**NOTE**   Cisco UCS Manager Release 4.0(2) and later releases support Ethernet and Fibre Channel switching modes on Cisco UCS 6454 Fabric Interconnects.

To configure Ethernet switching mode (see Figure 12-34), follow these steps:

**Step 1.**    In the Navigation pane, click **Equipment**.

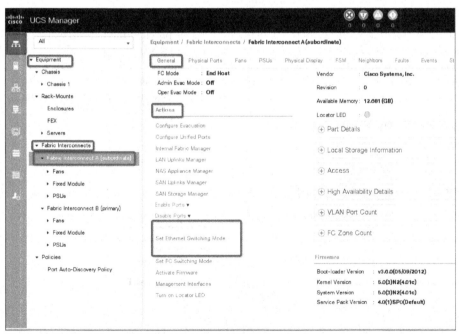

**Figure 12-34**   *Cisco UCS Switch Fabric Mode Configuration*

**Step 2.**    Expand **Equipment > Fabric Interconnects > Fabric_Interconnect_Name**.

**Step 3.**    In the Work pane, click the **General** tab.

**Step 4.**    In the Actions area of the General tab, click one of the following links:

■ **Set Ethernet Switching Mode**

■ **Set Ethernet End-Host Mode**

**NOTE**   The link for the current mode is dimmed.

**Step 5.**    In the dialog box, click **Yes**. The Cisco UCS Manager restarts the fabric interconnect, logs you out, and disconnects the Cisco UCS Manager GUI.

**NOTE**   When you change the Ethernet switching mode, the Cisco UCS Manager logs you out and restarts the fabric interconnect. For a cluster configuration, the Cisco UCS Manager restarts both fabric interconnects. The subordinate fabric interconnect reboots first as a result of the change in switching mode. The primary fabric interconnect reboots only after you acknowledge it in Pending Activities. The primary fabric interconnect can take several minutes to complete the change in Ethernet switching mode and become system ready. The existing configuration is retained. While the fabric interconnects are rebooting, all blade servers lose LAN and SAN connectivity, causing a complete outage of all services on the blades. This might cause the operating system to fail.

In some commonly deployed LAN topologies, switch mode provides the best network behavior. A typical example is a switch directly connected to a pair of Hot Standby Router Protocol (HSRP) routers that are the Spanning Tree Protocol roots on different VLANs. Switch mode provides the optimal path because of the use of Spanning Tree Protocol. For example, a vNIC belonging to an odd-numbered VLAN can be dynamically pinned to link X on Fabric Interconnect A (see Figure 12-35). As a result of this process, traffic traverses an extra hop to the HSRP master.

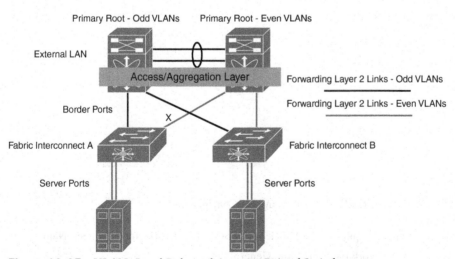

**Figure 12-35**   *VLANs Load-Balanced Across a Pair of Switches*

When a switch is directly connected to a pair of HSRP routers, the recommended Ethernet switching mode is switch mode because it provides the optimal path. End-host mode can be used if static pinning is employed.

## UCS Device Discovery

The chassis connectivity policy determines whether a specific chassis is included in a fabric port channel after chassis discovery. This policy is helpful for users who want to configure one or more chassis differently from what is specified in the global chassis discovery policy. The chassis connectivity policy also allows for different connectivity modes per fabric interconnect, further expanding the level of control offered with regards to chassis connectivity.

By default, the chassis connectivity policy is set to global. This means that connectivity control is configured when the chassis is newly discovered, using the settings configured in the chassis discovery policy. Once the chassis is discovered, the chassis connectivity policy controls whether the connectivity control is set to none or port channel.

## Chassis/FEX Discovery

The chassis discovery policy determines how the system reacts when you add a new chassis. The Cisco UCS Manager uses the settings in the chassis discovery policy to determine the minimum threshold for the number of links between the chassis and the fabric interconnect and whether to group links from the IOM to the fabric interconnect in a fabric port channel. In a Cisco UCS Mini setup, chassis discovery policy is supported only on the extended chassis.

The Cisco UCS Manager cannot discover any chassis that is wired for fewer links than are configured in the chassis/FEX discovery policy. For example, if the chassis/FEX discovery policy is configured for four links, the Cisco UCS Manager cannot discover any chassis that is wired for one link or two links. Reacknowledgement of the chassis resolves this issue.

## Rack Server Discovery Policy

The rack server discovery policy determines how the system reacts when you add a new rack-mount server. The Cisco UCS Manager uses the settings in the rack server discovery policy to determine whether any data on the hard disks is scrubbed and whether server discovery occurs immediately or needs to wait for explicit user acknowledgment.

The Cisco UCS Manager cannot discover any rack-mount server that has not been correctly cabled and connected to the fabric interconnects. The steps to configure rack server discovery are as follows:

**Step 1.**   In the Navigation pane, click **Equipment**.

**Step 2.**   Click the **Equipment** node. In the Work pane, click the **Policies** tab.

**Step 3.**   Click the **Global Policies** subtab.

**Step 4.**   In the Rack Server Discovery Policy area, specify the action that you want to occur when a new rack server is added and specify the scrub policy. Then click **Save Changes**.

## Initial Server Setup for Standalone UCS C-Series

Use the following procedure to perform initial setup on a UCS C-Series server:

**Step 1.**  Power up the server. Wait for approximately two minutes to let the server boot in standby power during the first bootup. You can verify power status by looking at the Power Status LED:

- **Off:** There is no AC power present in the server.

- **Amber:** The server is in standby power mode. Power is supplied only to the CIMC and some motherboard functions.

- **Green:** The server is in main power mode. Power is supplied to all server components.

**NOTE**  Verify server power requirements because some servers (UCS C-240, for example) require 220V instead of 110V.

**NOTE**  During bootup, the server beeps once for each USB device that is attached to the server. Even if no external USB devices are attached, there is a short beep for each virtual USB device, such as a virtual floppy drive, CD/DVD drive, keyboard, or mouse. A beep is also emitted if a USB device is hot-plugged or hot-unplugged during the BIOS power-on self-test (POST) or while you are accessing the BIOS Setup utility or the EFI shell.

**Step 2.**  Connect a USB keyboard and VGA monitor by using the supplied Kernel-based Virtual Machine (KVM) cable connected to the KVM connector on the front panel. You can use the VGA and USB ports on the rear panel. However, you cannot use the front-panel VGA and the rear-panel VGA at the same time. If you are connected to one VGA connector and you then connect a video device to the other connector, the first VGA connector is disabled.

**Step 3.**  Open the Cisco IMC Configuration Utility as follows:

- Press the Power button to boot the server. Watch for the prompt to press F8.

- During bootup, press F8 when prompted to open the Cisco IMC Configuration Utility, as shown in Figure 12-36.

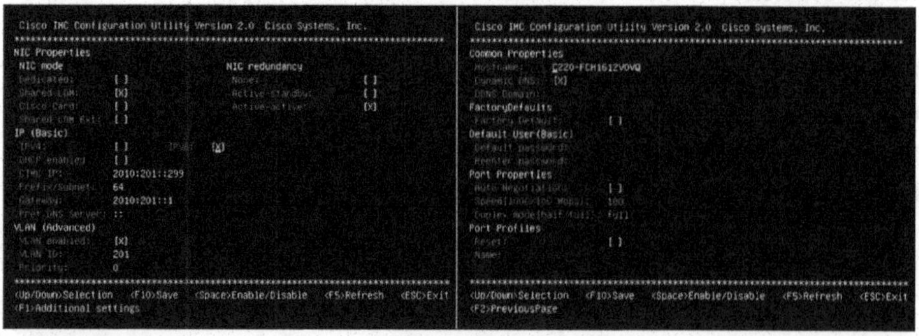

**Figure 12-36**  *Standalone UCS CIMC Configuration Utility*

**NOTE**   The first time that you enter the Cisco IMC Configuration Utility, you are prompted to change the default password. The default password is *password*.

The following are the requirements for a strong password:

- The password can have a minimum of 8 characters and a maximum of 14 characters.

- The password must not contain the user's name.

- The password must contain characters from three of the following four categories:
  - English uppercase letters (A through Z)
  - English lowercase letters (a through z)
  - Base 10 digits (0 through 9)
  - Nonalphabetic characters (!, @, #, $, %, ^, &, *, -, _, =, ")

**Step 4.**   Set NIC mode and NIC redundancy as follows:

- Set the NIC mode to your choice for which ports to use to access the CIMC for server management:

  - **Shared LOM EXT (default):** This is shared LOM extended mode. This is the factory-default setting, along with Active-active NIC redundancy and DHCP-enabled. With this mode, the shared LOM and Cisco card interfaces are both enabled.

  - In this mode, DHCP replies are returned to both the shared LOM ports and the Cisco card ports. If the system determines that the Cisco card connection is not getting its IP address from a Cisco UCS Manager system because the server is in standalone mode, further DHCP requests from the Cisco card are disabled. Use the Cisco card NIC mode if you want to connect to the CIMC through a Cisco card in standalone mode.

  - **Dedicated:** The dedicated management port is used to access the CIMC. You must select a NIC redundancy and IP setting.

  - **Shared LOM:** The 1-Gigabit Ethernet ports are used to access the CIMC. You must select a NIC redundancy and IP setting.

  - **Cisco Card:** The ports on an installed Cisco UCS virtual interface card are used to access the CIMC. You must select a NIC redundancy and IP setting.

- Use this utility to change the NIC redundancy to your preference. This server has three possible NIC redundancy settings:

  - **None:** The Ethernet ports operate independently and do not fail over if there is a problem.

  - **Active-standby:** If an active Ethernet port fails, traffic fails over to a standby port.

  - **Active-active:** All Ethernet ports are utilized simultaneously.

**Step 5.** Choose whether to enable DHCP for dynamic network settings or to enter static network settings. The static IPv4 and IPv6 settings include the following:

■ The Cisco IMC IP address.

■ The prefix/subnet. For IPv6, valid values are 1–127.

■ The gateway. For IPv6, if you do not know the gateway, you can set it as none by typing :: (two colons).

■ The preferred DNS server address. For IPv6, you can set this as none by typing :: (two colons).

**Step 6.** (Optional) Use this utility to make VLAN settings.

**Step 7.** (Optional) Set a host name for the server.

**Step 8.** (Optional) Enable dynamic DNS and set a dynamic DNS (DDNS) domain.

**Step 9.** (Optional) If you select the Factory Default check box, the server is set back to the factory defaults.

**Step 10.** (Optional) Set a default user password.

**Step 11.** (Optional) Enable autonegotiation of port settings or set the port speed and duplex mode manually. Autonegotiation is applicable only when you use the Dedicated NIC mode. Autonegotiation sets the port speed and duplex mode automatically based on the switch port to which the server is connected. If you disable autonegotiation, you must set the port speed and duplex mode manually.

**Step 12.** (Optional) Reset port profiles and the port name.

**Step 13.** Press F5 to refresh the settings you made. You might have to wait about 45 seconds until the new settings appear and the "Network settings configured" message is displayed before you reboot the server in the next step.

**Step 14.** Press F10 to save your settings and reboot the server. If you chose to enable DHCP, the dynamically assigned IP and MAC addresses are displayed on the console screen during bootup.

**Step 15.** Connect to the CIMC for server management. Connect Ethernet cables from your LAN to the server, using the ports that you selected by your NIC mode setting in step 4. The Active-active and Active-passive NIC redundancy settings require you to connect to two ports.

**Step 16.** Use a browser and the IP address of the CIMC to connect to the CIMC Setup Utility. The IP address is based on the settings that you made in step 4 (either a static address or the address assigned by your DHCP server). The default username for the server is *admin*. The default password is *password*.

The following steps explain how to install the operating system on the Cisco UCS C-Series Standalone server:

**Step 1.** Launch CIMC from a web browser (use the static IP you configured during initial setup or DHCP IP if you enabled DHCP) as shown in Figure 12-37. Accept all the certification alerts that you get.

**Figure 12-37**   *C-Series Standalone CIMC GUI*

**Step 2.**   To prepare the storage, navigate to **Storage**, as shown in Figure 12-38.

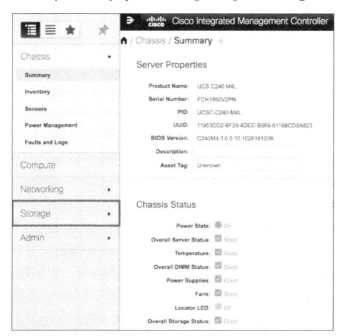

**Figure 12-38**   *C-Series Standalone Storage Configuration*

**Step 3.**   Navigate to **Storage > Controller Info**. Then from Controller Info, select **Create Virtual Drive from Unused Physical Drives**, as shown in Figure 12-39.

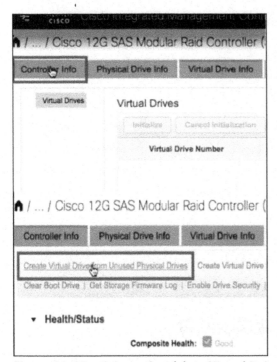

**Figure 12-39**  *C-Series Standalone Virtual Drive Configuration*

**Step 4.**    Select RAID Level 5 from the drop-down option (to enable RAID5). Then
select **Physical Drives**. (Note that you need to select at least three HDDs for
Raid 5.) Next, from the Virtual Drive Properties tab, set the RAID5 drive name
and properties (access policy, read policy, strip size, size, and so on) and then
click **Create Virtual Drive** to create the drive. From the Virtual Drive Info
tab, verify the RAID5 drive health from the Virtual Drive info, as shown in
Figure 12-40.

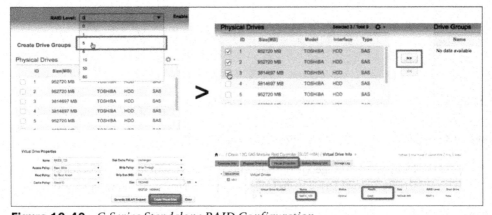

**Figure 12-40**  *C-Series Standalone RAID Configuration*

**Step 5.** To install any operating system (ESXi, for example), you need to map the operating system ISO image to a DVD. From the Fabric Interconnect Setup CIMC, select **Launch KVM**. (Ensure JRE 1.7 or higher is installed on the PC if you use a Java-based KVM.) In this case, you use an HTML-based KVM, as shown in the Figure 12-41.

**Figure 12-41**  *C-Series Standalone KVM*

**Step 6.** Mount the Virtual ISO with the KVM Console, as shown in Figure 12-42.

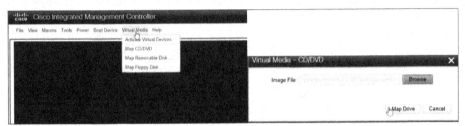

**Figure 12-42**  *C-Series Standalone CD/DVD Mapping*

**Step 7.** Reboot the Cisco UCS server from the KVM. Press F6 on startup, choose the **Virtual CD/DVD** option, and then press Enter (see Figure 12-43).

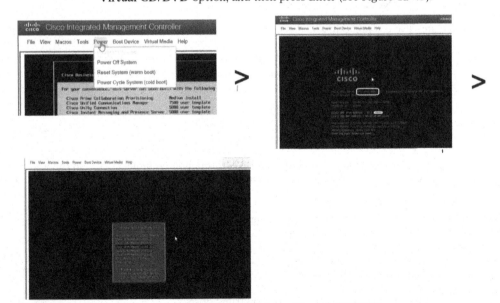

**Figure 12-43**  *C-Series Standalone Boot OS from Virtual CD/DVD*

# Cisco UCS Network Management

The Cisco UCS Fabric Interconnect behaves as a switching device between the servers and the network, and the Cisco UCS Manager is embedded in the fabric interconnect, providing server hardware state abstraction. This section covers switching and server network profile configurations.

## UCS Virtual LAN

A virtual LAN (VLAN) is a switched network that is logically segmented by function, project team, or application, without regard to the physical locations of the users. VLANs have the same attributes as physical LANs, but you can group end stations even if they are not physically located on the same LAN segment.

Any switch port can belong to a VLAN. Unicast, broadcast, and multicast packets are forwarded and flooded only to end stations in the VLAN. Each VLAN is considered a logical network, and packets destined for stations that do not belong to the VLAN must be forwarded through a router or bridge.

VLANs are typically associated with IP subnetworks. For example, all of the end stations in a particular IP subnet belong to the same VLAN. To communicate between VLANs, you must route the traffic. By default, a newly created VLAN is operational. Additionally, you can configure VLANs to be in the active state, which is passing traffic, or in the suspended state, in which the VLANs are not passing packets. By default, the VLANs are in the active state and pass traffic.

You can use the Cisco UCS Manager to manage VLANs by doing the following:

- Configure named VLANs

- Assign VLANs to an access or trunk port

- Create, delete, and modify VLANs

VLANs are numbered from 1 to 4094. All configured ports belong to the default VLAN when you first bring up a switch. The default VLAN (VLAN 1) uses only default values. You cannot create, delete, or suspend activity in the default VLAN.

The native VLAN and the default VLAN are not the same. *Native* refers to VLAN traffic without an 802.1Q header and can be assigned or not. The native VLAN is the only VLAN that is not tagged in a trunk, and the frames are transmitted unchanged.

You can tag everything and not use a native VLAN throughout your network, and the VLAN or devices are reachable because switches use VLAN 1 as the native by default.

The UCS Manager - LAN Uplink Manager configuration page enables you to configure VLANs and to change the native VLAN setting. Changing the native VLAN setting requires a port flap for the change to take effect; otherwise, the port flap is continuous. When you change the native VLAN, there is a loss of connectivity for approximately 20–40 seconds.

Native VLAN guidelines are as follows:

- You can configure native VLANs only on trunk ports.

- You can change the native VLAN on a UCS vNIC; however, the port flaps and can lead to traffic interruptions.

- Cisco recommends using the native VLAN 1 setting to prevent traffic interruptions if using the Cisco Nexus 1000v switches. The native VLAN must be the same for the Nexus 1000v port profiles and your UCS vNIC definition.

- If the native VLAN 1 setting is configured, and traffic routes to an incorrect interface, there is an outage, or the switch interface flaps continuously, your disjoint Layer 2 network configuration might have incorrect settings.

- Using the native VLAN 1 for management access to all of your devices can potentially cause problems if someone connects another switch on the same VLAN as your management devices.

You configure a VLAN by assigning a number to it. You can delete VLANs or move them from the active operational state to the suspended operational state. If you attempt to create a VLAN with an existing VLAN ID, the switch goes into the VLAN sub-mode but does not create the same VLAN again. Newly created VLANs remain unused until you assign ports to the specific VLAN. All of the ports are assigned to VLAN 1 by default. Depending on the range of the VLAN, you can configure the following parameters for VLANs (except for the default VLAN):

- VLAN name

- Shut down or not shut down

When you delete a specified VLAN, the ports associated with that VLAN are shut down and no traffic flows. However, the system retains all of the VLAN-to-port mappings for that VLAN. When you re-enable or re-create the specified VLAN, the system automatically reinstates all of the original ports to that VLAN.

If a VLAN group is used on a vNIC and also on a port channel assigned to an uplink, you cannot delete and add VLANs in the same transaction. The act of deleting and adding VLANs in the same transaction causes an ENM pinning failure on the vNIC. vNIC configurations are done first, so the VLAN is deleted from the vNIC and a new VLAN is added, but this VLAN is not yet configured on the uplink. Hence, the transaction causes a pinning failure.

Access ports only send untagged frames and belong to and carry the traffic of only one VLAN. Traffic is received and sent in native formats with no VLAN tagging. Anything arriving on an access port is assumed to belong to the VLAN assigned to the port.

You can configure a port in access mode and specify the VLAN to carry the traffic for that interface. If you do not configure the VLAN for a port in access mode or an access port, the interface carries the traffic for the default VLAN, which is VLAN 1.

You can change the access port membership in a VLAN by configuring it. You must create the VLAN before you can assign it as an access VLAN for an access port. If you change the access VLAN on an access port to a VLAN that is not yet created, the Cisco UCS Manager shuts down that access port.

If an access port receives a packet with an 802.1Q tag in the header other than the access VLAN value, that port drops the packet without learning its MAC source address. If you assign an access VLAN that is also a primary VLAN for a private VLAN, all access ports with that access VLAN receive all the broadcast traffic for the primary VLAN in the private VLAN mode.

Trunk ports allow multiple VLANs to transport between switches over that trunk link. A trunk port can carry untagged packets simultaneously with the 802.1Q tagged packets. When you assign a default port VLAN ID to the trunk port, all untagged traffic travels on the default port VLAN ID for the trunk port, and all untagged traffic is assumed to belong to this VLAN. This VLAN is referred to as the native VLAN ID for a trunk port. The native VLAN ID is the VLAN that carries untagged traffic on trunk ports.

The trunk port sends an egressing packet with a VLAN that is equal to the default port VLAN ID as untagged; all the other egressing packets are tagged by the trunk port. If you do not configure a native VLAN ID, the trunk port uses the default VLAN.

**NOTE**   Changing the native VLAN on a trunk port or an access VLAN of an access port flaps the switch interface.

### Named VLANs

The name that you assign to a VLAN ID adds a layer of abstraction that allows you to globally update all servers associated with service profiles that use the named VLAN. You do not need to reconfigure the servers individually to maintain communication with the external LAN.

You can create more than one named VLAN with the same VLAN ID. For example, if servers that host business services for Human Resources and Finance need to access the same external LAN, you can create VLANs named HR and Finance with the same VLAN ID. Then, if the network is reconfigured and Finance is assigned to a different LAN, you only have to change the VLAN ID for the named VLAN for Finance. The VLAN name is case sensitive.

In a cluster configuration, you can configure a named VLAN to be accessible only to one fabric interconnect or to both fabric interconnects.

**NOTE**   You cannot create VLANs with IDs from 3915 to 4042. These ranges of VLAN IDs are reserved. The VLAN IDs you specify must also be supported on the switch that you are using. For example, on Cisco Nexus 5000 Series switches, the VLAN ID range from 3968 to 4029 is reserved. Before you specify the VLAN IDs in the Cisco UCS Manager, make sure that the same VLAN IDs are available on your switch.

**NOTE**   VLAN 4048 is user configurable. However, the Cisco UCS Manager uses VLAN 4048 for the following default values. If you want to assign 4048 to a VLAN, you need to change the FCoE default VLAN. The FCoE VLAN for the default VSAN uses VLAN 4048 by default. The FCoE storage port native VLAN uses VLAN 4049.

The following types of ports are counted in the VLAN port calculation:

- Border uplink Ethernet ports
- Border uplink Ether-channel member ports

- FCoE ports in a SAN cloud

- Ethernet ports in a NAS cloud

- Static and dynamic vNICs created through service profiles

- VM vNICs created as part of a port profile in a hypervisor in hypervisor domain

Based on the number of VLANs configured for these ports, the Cisco UCS Manager tracks the cumulative count of VLAN port instances and enforces the VLAN port limit during validation. The Cisco UCS Manager reserves some predefined VLAN port resources for control traffic. These include management VLANs configured under HIF and NIF ports.

The Cisco UCS Manager validates VLAN port availability during the following operations:

- Configuring and unconfiguring border ports and border port channels

- Adding or removing VLANs from a cloud

- Configuring or unconfiguring SAN or NAS ports

- Associating or disassociating service profiles that contain configuration changes

- Configuring or unconfiguring VLANs under vNICs or vHBAs

- Receiving creation or deletion notifications from a VMWare vNIC and from an ESX hypervisor

- Fabric interconnect reboot

- Cisco UCS Manager upgrade or downgrade

The Cisco UCS Manager strictly enforces the VLAN port limit on service profile operations. If the Cisco UCS Manager detects that the VLAN port limit is exceeded, the service profile configuration fails during deployment.

Exceeding the VLAN port count in a border domain is less disruptive. When the VLAN port count is exceeded in a border domain, the Cisco UCS Manager changes the allocation status to Exceeded. To change the status back to Available, complete one of the following actions:

- Unconfigure one or more border ports

- Remove VLANs from the LAN cloud

- Unconfigure one or more vNICs or vHBAs

Use the following steps to configure named VLANs:

**Step 1.** In the Navigation pane, click **LAN**.

**Step 2.** On the LAN tab, click the **LAN** node. Then in the Work pane, click the **VLANs** tab. On the icon bar to the right of the table, click **+** (the plus sign). If the **+** icon is disabled, click an entry in the table to enable it.

**Step 3.** In the Create VLANs dialog box, as shown in Figure 12-44, fill in the following information:

| Name | Description |
|---|---|
| VLAN Nam/Profile Field | For a single VLAN, this is the VLAN name. For a range of VLANs, this is the prefix that the system uses for each VLAN name. The VLAN name is case sensitive. |
| | This name can be between 1 and 32 alphanumeric characters. You cannot use spaces or any special characters other than - (hyphen), _ (underscore), : (colon), and . (period), and you cannot change this name after the object is saved. |
| Multicast Policy drop-down list | The multicast policy associated with this VLAN. |
| Configuration options | You can choose one of the following: |
| | ■ **Common/Global:** The VLANs apply to both fabrics and use the same configuration parameters in both cases. |
| | ■ **Fabric A:** The VLANs only apply to fabric A. |
| | ■ **Fabric B:** The VLAN only apply to fabric B. |
| | ■ **Both Fabrics Configured Differently:** The VLANs apply to both fabrics, but you can specify different VLAN IDs for each fabric. |
| | For upstream disjoint L2 networks, Cisco recommends that you choose Common/Global to create VLANs that apply to both fabrics. |
| VLAN IDs field | To create one VLAN, enter a single numeric ID. To create multiple VLANs, enter individual IDs or ranges of IDs separated by commas. A VLAN ID can |
| | ■ Be between 1 and 3967 |
| | ■ Be between 4048 and 4093 |
| | ■ Overlap with other VLAN IDs already defined on the system |
| | For example, to create six VLANs with the IDs 4, 22, 40, 41, 42, and 43, enter 4, 22, 40-43. |
| | **NOTE:** VLANs with IDs from 4030 to 4047 and from 4094 to 4095 are reserved. You cannot create VLANs with IDs from this range. Until Cisco UCS Manager Release 4.0(1d), VLAN ID 4093 was in the list of reserved VLANs. VLAN 4093 has been removed from the list of reserved VLANs and is available for configuration. |
| | The VLAN IDs you specify must also be supported on the switch that you are using. For example, on Cisco Nexus 5000 Series switches, the VLAN ID range from 3968 to 4029 is reserved. Before you specify the VLAN IDs in Cisco UCS Manager, make sure that the same VLAN IDs are available on your switch. |
| | VLANs in the LAN cloud and FCoE VLANs in the SAN cloud must have different IDs. Using the same ID for a VLAN and an FCoE VLAN in a VSAN results in a critical fault and traffic disruption for all vNICs and uplink ports using that VLAN. Ethernet traffic is dropped on any VLAN that has an ID that overlaps with an FCoE VLAN ID. |

| Name | Description |
|------|-------------|
| Sharing Type field | Whether this VLAN is subdivided into private or secondary VLANs. This can be one of the following:<br><br>■ **None:** This VLAN does not have any secondary or private VLANs.<br><br>■ **Primary:** This VLAN can have one or more secondary VLANs, as shown in the Secondary VLANs area.<br><br>■ **Isolated:** This is a private VLAN. The primary VLAN with which it is associated is shown in the Primary VLAN drop-down list. |

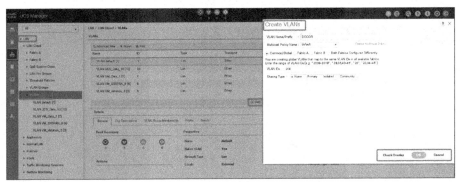

**Figure 12-44** *Name VLAN Configuration*

**Step 4.** If you clicked the Check Overlap button, do the following:

■ Click the **Overlapping VLANs** tab and review the fields to verify that the VLAN ID does not overlap with any IDs assigned to existing VLANs.

■ Click the **Overlapping VSANs** tab and review the fields to verify that the VLAN ID does not overlap with any FCoE VLAN IDs assigned to existing VSANs.

■ Click **OK.**

■ If the Cisco UCS Manager identified any overlapping VLAN IDs or FCoE VLAN IDs, change the VLAN ID to one that does not overlap with an existing VLAN.

**Step 5.** Click **OK.**

The Cisco UCS Manager adds the VLAN to one of the following VLANs nodes:

■ The LAN Cloud > VLANs node for a VLAN accessible to both fabric interconnects.

■ The Fabric_Interconnect_Name > VLANs node for a VLAN accessible to only one fabric interconnect.

Use the following steps to delete named VLANs:

**Step 1.** In the Navigation pane, click **LAN**. Then on the LAN tab, click the **LAN** node. In the Work pane, click the **VLANs** tab.

**Step 2.** Click one of the following subtabs, based on the VLAN that you want to delete (see Figure 12-45).

| Subtab | Description |
|--------|-------------|
| All | Displays all VLANs in the Cisco UCS domain. |
| Dual Mode | Displays the VLANs that are accessible to both fabric interconnects. |
| Fabric A | Displays the VLANs that are accessible to only Fabric Interconnect A. |
| Fabric B | Displays the VLANs that are accessible to only Fabric Interconnect B. |

**Figure 12-45** *Deleting a Named VLAN*

**Step 3.** In the table, click the VLAN that you want to delete. You can use the Shift key or Ctrl key to select multiple entries.

**Step 4.** Right-click the highlighted VLAN or VLANs and click Delete. If a confirmation dialog box is displayed, click **Yes**.

**NOTE** If the Cisco UCS Manager includes a named VLAN with the same VLAN ID as the one you delete, the VLAN is not removed from the fabric interconnect configuration until all named VLANs with that ID are deleted.

**NOTE** If you are deleting a private primary VLAN, ensure that you reassign the secondary VLANs to another working primary VLAN.

**NOTE**   Before you delete a VLAN from a fabric interconnect, ensure that the VLAN was removed from all vNICs and vNIC templates. If you delete a VLAN that is assigned to a vNIC or vNIC template, the vNIC might allow that VLAN to flap.

## UCS Identity Pools

The Cisco UCS Manager can classify servers into resource pools based on criteria including physical attributes (such as processor, memory, and disk capacity) and location (for example, blade chassis slot). Server pools can help automate configuration by identifying servers that can be configured to assume a particular role (such as web server or database server) and automatically configuring them when they are added to a pool.

Resource pools are collections of logical resources that can be accessed when configuring a server. These resources include universally unique IDs (UUIDs), MAC addresses, and WWNs.

The Cisco UCS platform utilizes a dynamic identity instead of hardware burned-in identities. A unique identity is assigned from identity and resource pools. Computers and peripherals extract these identities from service profiles. A service profile has all the server identities including UUIDs, MACs, WWNNs, firmware versions, BIOS settings, policies, and other server settings. A service profile is associated with the physical server that assigns all the settings in a service profile to the physical server.

In case of server failure, the failed server needs to be removed, and the replacement server needs to be associated with the existing service profile of the failed server. In this service profile association process, the new server automatically picks up all the identities of the failed server, and the operating system or applications that depend on these identities do not observe any change in the hardware. In case of peripheral failure, the replacement peripheral automatically acquires the identities of the failed components. This significantly improves the system recovery time in case of a failure. Server profiles include many identity pools:

- UUID suffix pools
- MAC pools
- IP pools
- Server pools

### Universally Unique Identifier Suffix Pools

A universally unique identifier suffix pool is a collection of System Management BIOS (SMBIOS) UUIDs that are available to be assigned to servers. The first number of digits that constitute the prefix of the UUID is fixed. The remaining digits, the UUID suffix, are variable. A UUID suffix pool ensures that these variable values are unique for each server associated with a service profile which uses that particular pool to avoid conflicts.

If you use UUID suffix pools in service profiles, you do not have to manually configure the UUID of the server associated with the service profile.

An example of creating UUID pools is as follows:

**Step 1.**   In the Navigation pane, click **Servers.**

**Step 2.**   Expand **Servers > Pools.**

**Step 3.** Expand the node for the organization where you want to create the pool. If the system does not include multitenancy, expand the root node.

**Step 4.** Right-click **UUID Suffix Pools** and select **Create UUID Suffix Pool**.

**Step 5.** In the Define Name and Description page of the Create UUID Suffix Pool wizard, complete the following fields (see Figure 12-46):

| Name | Description |
|------|-------------|
| Name field | The name of the UUID pool. This name can be between 1 and 32 alphanumeric characters. You cannot use spaces or any special characters other than - (hyphen), _ (underscore), : (colon), and . (period), and you cannot change this name after the object is saved. |
| Description field | The user-defined description of the pool. Enter up to 256 characters. You can use any characters or spaces except ` (accent mark), \ (backslash), ^ (caret), " (double quote), = (equal sign), > (greater than), < (less than), or ' (single quote). |
| Prefix field | This can be one of the following:<br><br>■ **Derived:** The system creates the suffix.<br>■ **Other:** You specify the desired suffix. If you select this option, the Cisco UCS Manager GUI displays a text field where you can enter the desired suffix, in the format *XXXXXXXX-XXXX-XXXX*. |
| Assignment Order field | This can be one of the following:<br><br>■ **Default:** The Cisco UCS Manager selects a random identity from the pool.<br>■ **Sequential:** The Cisco UCS Manager selects the lowest available identity from the poll. |

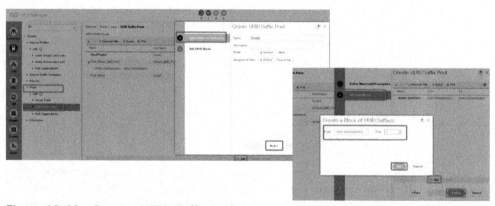

**Figure 12-46** *Creating UUID Suffix Pool*

**Step 6.** Click **Next**.

**Step 7.** In the Add UUID Blocks page of the Create UUID Suffix Pool wizard, click **Add**.

**Step 8.**    In the Create a Block of UUID Suffixes dialog box, complete the following fields:

| Name | Description |
|---|---|
| From field | The first UUID in the block. |
| Size field | The number of UUIDs in the block. |

**Step 9.**    Click **OK**.

**Step 10.**    Click **Finish** to complete the wizard.

You need to assign the UUID suffix pool to a service profile and/or template.

## MAC Pools

A MAC pool is a collection of network identities, or MAC addresses, that are unique in their Layer 2 environment and are available to be assigned to vNICs on a server. If you use MAC pools in service profiles, you do not have to manually configure the MAC addresses to be used by the server associated with the service profile.

In a system that implements multitenancy, you can use the organizational hierarchy to ensure that MAC pools can only be used by specific applications or business services. The Cisco UCS Manager uses the name resolution policy to assign MAC addresses from the pool. To assign a MAC address to a server, you must include the MAC pool in a vNIC policy. The vNIC policy is then included in the service profile assigned to that server. You can specify your own MAC addresses or use a group of MAC addresses provided by Cisco.

An example of creating a Management IP pool is as follows:

**Step 1.**    In the Navigation pane, click the **LAN** tab. In the LAN tab, expand **LAN > Pools** and then expand the node for the organization where you want to create the pool. If the system does not include multitenancy, expand the root node.

**Step 2.**    Right-click **MAC Pools** and select **Create MAC Pool**.

**Step 3.**    In the first page of the Create MAC Pool wizard, do the following:

■ Enter a unique name and description for the MAC Pool.

■ Click **Next**.

**Step 4.**    In the second page of the Create MAC Pool wizard, do the following:

■ Click **Add**.

■ In the Create a Block of MAC Addresses page, enter the first MAC address in the pool and the number of MAC addresses to include in the pool.

■ Click **OK**.

■ Click **Finish**.

## IP Pools

IP pools are collections of IP addresses that do not have a default purpose. You can create IPv4 or IPv6 address pools in the Cisco UCS Manager to do the following:

■ Replace the default management IP pool ext-mgmt for servers that have an associated service profile. The Cisco UCS Manager reserves each block of IP addresses in the

IP pool for external access that terminates in the Cisco Integrated Management Controller (CIMC) on a server. If there is no associated service profile, you must use the ext-mgmt IP pool for the CIMC to get an IP address.

■ Replace the management in-band or out-of-band IP addresses for the CIMC.

**NOTE**  You cannot create iSCSI boot IPv6 pools in the Cisco UCS Manager.

You can create IPv4 address pools in the Cisco UCS Manager to do the following:

■ Replace the default iSCSI boot IP pool iscsi-initiator-pool. The Cisco UCS Manager reserves each block of IP addresses in the IP pool that you specify.

■ Replace both the management IP address and iSCSI boot IP addresses.

**NOTE**  The IP pool must not contain any IP addresses that were assigned as static IP addresses for a server or service profile.

An example of creating a management IP pool is as follows:

**Step 1.**  In the Navigation pane, click the **LAN** tab. In the LAN tab, expand **LAN > Pools > Organization_Name**.

**Step 2.**  Right-click **IP Pools** and select **Create IP Pool**.

**Step 3.**  In the Define Name and Description page of the Create IP Pool wizard, complete the following fields:

| Name | Description |
|---|---|
| Name field | The name of the IP address pool. This name can be between 1 and 32 alphanumeric characters. You cannot use spaces or any special characters other than - (hyphen), _ (underscore), : (colon), and . (period), and you cannot change this name after the object is saved. |
| Description field | The user-defined description of the IP address pool. Enter up to 256 characters. You can use any characters or spaces except ` (accent mark), \ (backslash), ^ (caret), " (double quote), = (equal sign), > (greater than), < (less than), or ' (single quote). |
| Assignment Order field | This can be one of the following:<br><br>■ **Default:** The Cisco UCS Manager selects a random identity from the pool.<br><br>■ **Sequential:** The Cisco UCS Manager selects the lowest available identity from the pool. |

**Step 4.**  Click **Next**.

**Step 5.**  In the Add IPv4 Blocks page of the Create IP Pool wizard, click **Add**.

**Step 6.**    In the Create a Block of IPv4 Addresses dialog box, complete the following fields (see Figure 12-47):

| Name | Description |
| --- | --- |
| From field | The first IPv4 address in the block. |
| Size field | The number of IP addresses in the pool. |
| Subnet Mask field | The subnet mask associated with the IPv4 addresses in the block. |
| Default Gateway field | The default gateway associated with the IPv4 addresses in the block. |
| Primary DNS field | The primary DNS server that this block of IPv4 addresses should access. |
| Secondary DNS field | The secondary DNS server that this block of IPv4 addresses should access. |
| From field | The first IPv4 address in the block. |

**Figure 12-47**    *Creating an IP Pool*

**Step 7.**    Click **Next**.

**Step 8.**    In the Add IPv6 Blocks page of the Create IP Pool wizard, click **Add**.

**Step 9.**    In the Create a Block of IPv6 Addresses dialog box, complete the following fields:

| Name | Description |
| --- | --- |
| From field | The first IPv6 address in the block. |
| Size field | The number of IP addresses in the pool. |
| Prefix | The network address prefix associated with the IPv6 addresses in the block. |
| Default Gateway field | The default gateway associated with the IPv6 addresses in the block. |
| Primary DNS field | The primary DNS server that this block of IPv6 addresses should access. |
| Secondary DNS field | The secondary DNS server that this block of IPv6 addresses should access. |

**Step 10.**    Click **OK**, and then click **Finish** to complete the wizard.

## Server Pools

A server pool contains a set of servers. These servers typically share the same characteristics. Those characteristics can be their location in the chassis or an attribute such as server type, amount of memory, local storage, type of CPU, or local drive configuration. You can manually assign a server to a server pool, or you can use server pool policies and server pool policy qualifications to automate the assignment.

If your system implements multitenancy through organizations, you can designate one or more server pools to be used by a specific organization. For example, a pool that includes all servers with two CPUs could be assigned to the Marketing organization, while all servers with 64-GB memory could be assigned to the Finance organization. A server pool can include servers from any chassis in the system, and a given server can belong to multiple server pools.

An example of creating a server pool using Cisco UCS Manager is as follows:

**Step 1.**    In the Navigation pane, click **Servers**.

**Step 2.**    Expand **Servers > Pools**.

**Step 3.**    Expand the node for the organization where you want to create the pool. If the system does not include multitenancy, expand the **root** node.

**Step 4.**    Right-click the **Server Pools** node and select **Create Server Pool**.

**Step 5.**    On the Set Name and Description page of the Create Server Pool wizard, complete the following fields:

| Name | Description |
|---|---|
| Name field | The name of the server pool. |
| Description field | A user-defined description of the server pool. |

**Step 6.**    Click **Next**.

**Step 7.**    On the Add Servers page of the Create Server Pool wizard:

- Select one or more servers from the **Available Servers** table.

- Click the >> button to add the servers to the server pool.

- When you have added all desired servers to the pool, click **Finish**.

## Service Profiles

Every server that is provisioned in the Cisco Unified Computing System is specified by a service profile. A service profile is a software definition of a server and its LAN and SAN network connectivity; in other words, a service profile defines a single server and its storage and networking characteristics. Service profiles are stored in the Cisco UCS Fabric Interconnects. When a service profile is deployed to a server, the Cisco UCS Manager automatically configures the server, adapters, Fabric Extenders, and fabric interconnects to match the configuration specified in the service profile. This automation of device configuration reduces the number of manual steps required to configure servers, network interface cards, host bus adapters, and LAN and SAN switches.

A service profile typically includes four types of information:

- **Server definition:** It defines the resources (for example, a specific server or a blade inserted to a specific chassis) that are required to apply to the profile.

- **Identity information:** Identity information includes the UUID, MAC address for each virtual NIC (vNIC), and WWN specifications for each HBA.

- **Firmware revision specifications:** These are used when a certain tested firmware revision is required to be installed or for some other reason a specific firmware is used.

- **Connectivity definition:** It is used to configure network adapters, Fabric Extenders, and parent interconnects; however, this information is abstract because it does not include the details of how each network component is configured.

A service profile is created by the Cisco UCS server administrator. This service profile leverages configuration policies that were created by the server, network, and storage administrators. Server administrators can also create a service profile template that can be used later to create service profiles in an easier way. A service template can be derived from a service profile, with server and I/O interface identity information abstracted. Instead of specifying exact UUID, MAC address, and WWN values, a service template specifies where to get these values. For example, a service profile template might specify the standard network connectivity for a web server and the pool from which its interface's MAC addresses can be obtained. Service profile templates can be used to provision many servers with the same simplicity as creating a single one.

There are two types of service profiles in a UCS system:

- **Service profiles that inherit server identity:** These service profiles are similar in concept to a rack-mounted server. These service profiles use the burned-in values (such as MAC addresses, WWN addresses, BIOS version and settings) of the hardware. Due to the nature of using these burned-in values, these profiles are not easily portable and can't be used for moving from one server to the other. In other words, these profiles exhibit the nature of 1:1 mapping and thus require changes to be made to them when moving from one server to another.

- **Service profiles that override server identity:** These service policies exhibit the nature of stateless computing in the Cisco UCS system. These service profiles take the resources (such as MAC addresses, WWN addresses, BIOS version) from a resource pool already created in the Cisco UCS Manager. The settings or values from these resource pools override the burned-in values of the hardware. Hence, these profiles are very flexible and can be moved from one server to the other easily, and this movement is transparent to the network. In other words, these profiles provide a one-to-many mapping and require no change to be made to them when moving from one server to another.

To create a service profile, navigate to the Servers tab, right-click Service Profiles, and choose Create Service Profile, as shown in Figure 12-48.

**Figure 12-48**    *Creating a Service Profile*

The vNIC creation for servers is part of the server profile or server profile template creation. After a service profile (Expert) is started for the blade servers, creating the vNIC is the second step in the configuration wizard.

Using a vNIC template is the recommended method for configuring the NIC settings once, for each template, and then quickly creating new vNICs with the desired configuration. The vNIC configuration settings can be optimized for various operating systems, storage devices, and hypervisors. A vNIC template can be configured as either of the following:

- **Initiating template:** This vNIC template provides one-time configuration for the vNICs created using this template. Any subsequent changes to the template are not propagated to abstracted vNICs.

- **Updating template:** This vNIC template provides initial configuration for the vNICs created using this template. Any subsequent changes to the template are also propagated to abstracted vNICs. It is a good practice to create a vNIC template for production environments.

vNIC MAC addresses can be assigned manually or by configuring a MAC address pool. It is possible to either use the burned-in MAC addresses or abstract MAC addresses from an identity pool with system-defined prefixes. Stateless computing is the salient feature of the Cisco UCS platform. Therefore, it is a good practice to abstract vNIC MAC addresses for server profiles and consequently use server vNIC MAC addresses from MAC address identity pools instead of using burned-in NIC MAC addresses. The benefit of abstracting the MAC identity is that in case of physical server failure, the server profile can be easily associated with the replacement server. The new server acquires all the identities associated with the old server, including the vNIC MAC addresses. From the operating system perspective, there is no change at all.

A good exercise is to create vNIC templates with different configurations and create individual vNICs from vNIC templates as required. Also, you can define MAC address pools and assign MAC addresses to individual vNICs using those MAC address pools.

A vNIC is typically abstracted from the physical mezzanine card. The Cisco mezzanine NIC card, also known as a Palo card or virtual interface card (VIC), provides dynamic server interfaces. Cisco VIC cards provide up to 256 dynamic interfaces. vNICs can be created within server profiles or by using a vNIC template. Using a vNIC template is the recommended method for configuring the NIC settings, doing so once for each template and then quickly creating additional vNICs with the desired configurations. The vNIC configuration settings can be optimized for various operating systems, storage devices, and hypervisors.

## UCS Server Policies

The Cisco UCS Manager uses server policies to assign settings and to define behavior of several server components. These policies include BIOS policies, boot policies, host firmware policies, maintenance policies, local disk policies, power control polices, scrub policies, vNIC/vHBA placement policies, and so on, as shown in Figure 12-49.

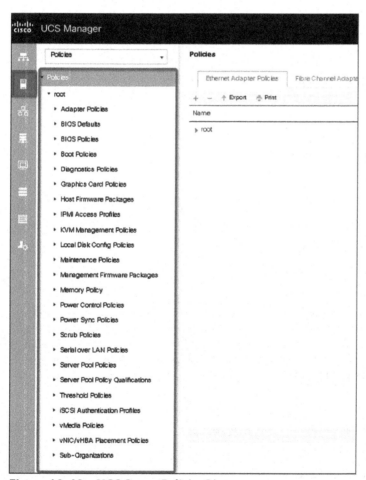

**Figure 12-49**  *UCS Server Policies List*

- **BIOS policy:** The Cisco UCS provides two methods for making global modifications to the BIOS settings on servers in a Cisco UCS domain.

    - You can create one or more BIOS policies that include a specific grouping of BIOS settings that match the needs of a server or set of servers.

■ You can use the default BIOS settings for a specific server platform.

Both the BIOS policy and the default BIOS settings for a server platform enable you to fine-tune the BIOS settings for a server managed by the Cisco UCS Manager.

Depending on the needs of the data center, you can configure BIOS policies for some service profiles and use the BIOS defaults in other service profiles in the same Cisco UCS domain, or you can use only one of them. You can also use the Cisco UCS Manager to view the actual BIOS settings on a server and determine whether they are meeting current needs. BIOS policies include

■ Main BIOS Settings

■ Processor BIOS Settings

■ Intel Directed I/O BIOS Settings

■ RAS Memory BIOS Settings

■ Serial Port BIOS Settings

■ USB BIOS Settings

■ PCI Configuration BIOS Settings

■ QPI BIOS Settings

■ LOM and PCIe Slots BIOS Settings

■ Graphics Configuration BIOS Settings

■ Boot Options BIOS Settings

■ Server Management BIOS Settings

> **NOTE** The Cisco UCS Manager pushes BIOS configuration changes through a BIOS policy or default BIOS settings to the CIMC buffer. These changes remain in the buffer and do not take effect until the server is rebooted. We recommend that you verify the support for BIOS settings in the server that you want to configure. Some settings, such as Mirroring mode for RAS Memory, are not supported by all Cisco UCS servers.

■ **Boot policy:** The Cisco UCS Manager boot policy overrides the boot order in the BIOS setup menu and determines the following:

■ Selection of the boot device

■ Location from which the server boots

■ Order in which boot devices are invoked

For example, you can choose to have associated servers boot from a local device, such as a local disk or CD-ROM (VMedia), or you can select a SAN boot or a LAN (PXE) boot. You must include this policy in a service profile, and that service profile must be associated with a server for it to take effect. If you do not include a boot policy in a service profile, the Cisco UCS Manager applies the default boot policy.

**NOTE**    Changes to a boot policy might be propagated to all servers created with an updating service profile template that includes that boot policy. Reassociation of the service profile with the server to rewrite the boot order information in the BIOS is automatically triggered.

- **Host firmware policies:** Use host firmware policy to associate qualified or well-known versions of the BIOS, adapter ROM, or local disk controller with logical service profiles, as described earlier. A best practice is to create one policy, based on the latest packages that correspond with the Cisco UCS Manager infrastructure and server software release, and to reference that host firmware package for all service profiles and templates created. This best practice helps ensure version consistency of a server's lowest-level firmware, regardless of physical server failures that may cause reassociation of service profiles on other blades.

- **Maintenance policy:** Use the maintenance policy to specify how the Cisco UCS Manager should proceed for configuration changes that will have a service impact or require a server reboot. Values for the maintenance policy can be "immediate," "user-ack," or "timer automatic." The best practice is to not use the "default" policy and instead to create and use maintenance policies for either "user-ack" or "timer automatic," and to always have these as elements of the service profile or service profile template definition.

- **Power control policy:** The Cisco UCS uses the priority set in the power control policy along with the blade type and configuration to calculate the initial power allocation for each blade within a chassis. During normal operation, the active blades within a chassis can borrow power from idle blades within the same chassis. If all blades are active and reach the power cap, service profiles with higher priority power control policies take precedence over service profiles with lower priority power control policies.

  Priority is ranked on a scale of 1 to 10, where 1 indicates the highest priority and 10 indicates lowest priority. The default priority is 5.

  For mission-critical applications, a special priority called no-cap is also available. Setting the priority to no-cap prevents the Cisco UCS from leveraging unused power from a particular server. With this setting, the server is allocated the maximum amount of power possible for that type of server.

- **Local disk policies:** A local disk policy specifies how to configure any local disks on the blade. A best practice is to specify no local storage for SAN boot environments, thereby precluding any problems at service profile association time, when local disks may present themselves to the host OS during installation. You can also remove or unseat local disks from blades completely, especially blades used for OS installation.

- **Scrub policies:** A scrub policy determines what happens to local disks and the BIOS upon service profile disassociation. The default policy is no scrubbing. A best practice is to set the policy to scrub the local disk, especially for service providers, multitenant customers, and environments in which network installation to a local disk is used.

- **vNIC/vHBA placement policies:** vNIC/vHBA placement policies are used to determine what types of vNICs or vHBAs can be assigned to the physical adapters on a server. Each vNIC/vHBA placement policy contains four virtual network interface connections (vCons) that are virtual representations of the physical adapters. When a vNIC/vHBA placement policy is assigned to a service profile, and the service profile is associated with a server, the vCons in the vNIC/vHBA placement policy are assigned to the physical adapters.

  If you do not include a vNIC/vHBA placement policy in the service profile or you use the default configuration for a server with two adapters, the Cisco UCS Manager defaults to the All configuration and equally distributes the vNICs and vHBAs between the adapters.

  You can use this policy to assign vNICs or vHBAs to either of the two vCons. The Cisco UCS Manager uses the vCon assignment to determine how to assign the vNICs and vHBAs to the physical adapter during service profile association.

  - **All:** All configured vNICs and vHBAs can be assigned to the vCon, whether they are explicitly assigned to it, unassigned, or dynamic.

  - **Assigned Only:** vNICs and vHBAs must be explicitly assigned to the vCon. You can assign them explicitly through the service profile or the properties of the vNIC or vHBA.

  - **Exclude Dynamic:** Dynamic vNICs and vHBAs cannot be assigned to the vCon. The vCon can be used for all static vNICs and vHBAs, whether they are unassigned or explicitly assigned to it.

  - **Exclude Unassigned:** Unassigned vNICs and vHBAs cannot be assigned to the vCon. The vCon can be used for dynamic vNICs and vHBAs and for static vNICs and vHBAs that are explicitly assigned to it.

## UCS Service Profile Templates

With a service profile template, you can quickly create several service profiles with the same basic parameters, such as the number of vNICs and vHBAs, and with identity information drawn from the same pools.

For example, if you need several service profiles with similar values to configure servers to host database software, you can create a service profile template, either manually or from an existing service profile. You then use the template to create the service profiles. The Cisco UCS supports the following types of service profile templates:

- **Initial template:** Service profiles created from an initial template inherit all the properties of the template. However, after you create the profile, it is no longer connected to the template. If you need to make changes to one or more profiles created from this template, you must change each profile individually.

- **Updating template:** Service profiles created from an updating template inherit all the properties of the template and remain connected to the template. Any changes to the template automatically update the service profiles created from the template.

The following steps show how to create a service profile template:

**Step 1.**    In the Navigation pane, click the **Servers**.

**Step 2.**    Expand **Servers > Service Profiles Templates**.

**Step 3.**    Expand the node for the organization where you want to create the service profile template. If the system does not include multitenancy, expand the root node.

**Step 4.**    Right-click the organization and select **Create Service Profile Template**, as shown in Figure 12-50.

**Figure 12-50**    *Creating a Service Profile Template*

**Step 5.**    In the Create Service Profile Template wizard, complete the following:

- Page 1: Identifying the Service Profile Template, as in Figure 12-51.

- Page 2: Configuring the Storage Options, as in Figure 12-52.

- Page 3: Configuring the Networking Options, as in Figure 12-53.

- Page 4: Setting the vNIC/vHBA Placement, as in Figure 12-54.

- Page 8: Setting the Server Boot Order, as in Figure 12-55.

- Page 9: Adding the Maintenance Policy, as in Figure 12-56.

- Page 10: Specifying the Server Assignment, as in Figure 12-57.

- Page 11: Adding Operational Policies, as in Figure 12-58.

**Figure 12-51**  *Service Profile Template Wizard Page 1*

**Figure 12-52**  *Service Profile Template Wizard Page 2*

**Figure 12-53**  *Service Profile Template Wizard Page 3*

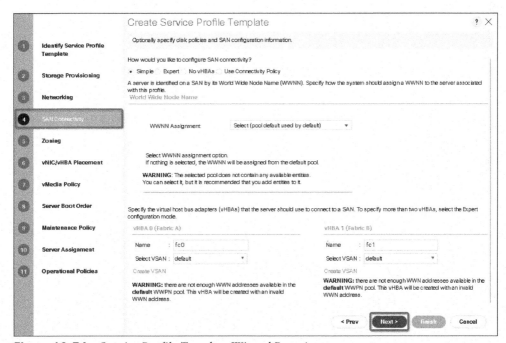

**Figure 12-54**  *Service Profile Template Wizard Page 4*

**Figure 12-55** *Service Profile Template Wizard Page 8*

**Figure 12-56** *Service Profile Template Wizard Page 9*

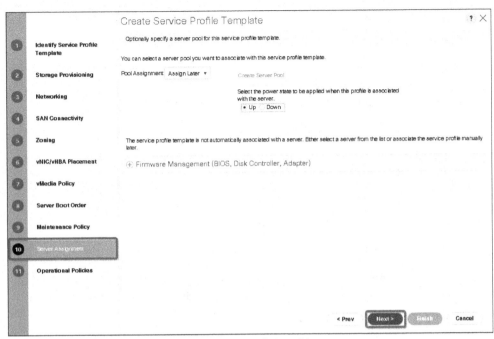

**Figure 12-57**   *Service Profile Template Wizard Page 10*

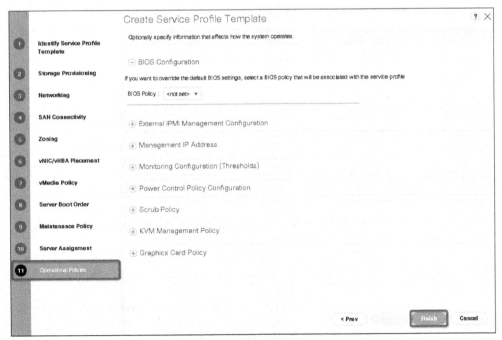

**Figure 12-58**   *Service Profile Template Wizard Page 11*

## Quality of Service

The Cisco UCS provides the following methods to implement quality of service:

- System classes that specify the global configuration for certain types of traffic across the entire system

- QoS policies that assign system classes for individual vNICs

- Flow control policies that determine how uplink Ethernet ports handle pause frames

Global QoS changes made to the QoS system class may result in brief data-plane interruptions for all traffic. Some examples of such changes are

- Changing the MTU size for an enabled class

- Changing packet drop for an enabled class

- Changing the class of service (CoS) value for an enabled class

### QoS System Classes

The Cisco UCS uses Data Center Ethernet (DCE) to handle all traffic inside a Cisco UCS domain. This industry standard enhancement to Ethernet divides the bandwidth of the Ethernet pipe into eight virtual lanes. Two virtual lanes are reserved for internal system and management traffic, and you can configure QoS for the other six virtual lanes.

System classes determine how the DCE bandwidth in these six virtual lanes is allocated across the entire Cisco UCS domain. Each system class reserves a specific segment of the bandwidth for a specific type of traffic, which provides a level of traffic management, even in an oversubscribed system. For example, you can configure the Fibre Channel Priority system class to determine the percentage of DCE bandwidth allocated to FCoE traffic. Table 12-5 describes the system classes that you can configure.

**Table 12-5**  UCS System QoS Class

| System Class | Description |
|---|---|
| Platinum<br>Gold<br>Silver<br>Bronze | A configurable set of system classes that you can include in the QoS policy for a service profile. Each system class manages one lane of traffic. |
| | All properties of these system classes are available for you to assign custom settings and policies. |
| | For Cisco UCS Mini, packet drop can only be disabled on the platinum and gold classes. Only one platinum and one gold class can be configured as a no-drop class at a time. |
| Best Effort | A system class that sets the quality of service for the lane reserved for basic Ethernet traffic. |
| | Some properties of this system class are preset and cannot be modified. For example, this class has a drop policy that allows it to drop data packets if required. You cannot disable this system class. |

| System Class | Description |
|---|---|
| Fibre Channel | A system class that sets the quality of service for the lane reserved for Fibre Channel over Ethernet traffic. |
| | Some properties of this system class are preset and cannot be modified. For example, this class has a no-drop policy that ensures it never drops data packets. You cannot disable this system class. |
| | **NOTE:** FCoE traffic has a reserved QoS system class that should not be used by any other type of traffic. If any other type of traffic has a CoS value that is used by FCoE, the value is remarked to 0. |

## QoS System Classes Configurations

The type of adapter in a server might limit the maximum MTU supported. For example, network MTU above the maximums might cause the packet to drop for some adapters.

**NOTE**   Under the network QoS policy, the MTU is used only for buffer carving when no-drop classes are configured. No additional MTU adjustments are required under the network QoS policy to support jumbo MTU.

You need to use the same CoS values on UCS and Nexus 5000 for all the no-drop policies. To ensure that end-to-end priority-based flow control (PFC) works correctly, have the same QoS policy configured on all intermediate switches.

An example of configuring and enabling LAN QoS is as follows:

**Step 1.**   In the Navigation pane, click **LAN**. Expand **LAN > LAN Cloud**.

**Step 2.**   Select the **QoS System Class** node. The packet drop should be unchecked to configure MTU. MTU is not configurable for drop-type QoS system classes and is always set to 9216. MTU is only configurable for no-drop-type QoS system classes.

**Step 3.**   In the Work pane, click the **General** tab. Update the properties for the system class that you want to configure to meet the traffic management needs of the system.

**Step 4.**   (Optional) To enable the system class, check the **Enabled** check box for the QoS system that you want to enable. Then click **Save Changes** (see Figure 12-59).

**NOTE**   Some properties might not be configurable for all system classes. The maximum value for MTU is 9216.

**NOTE**   The Best Effort or Fibre Channel system classes are enabled by default. You cannot disable these two system classes. All QoS policies that are associated with a disabled system class default to Best Effort or, if the disabled system class is configured with a CoS of 0, to the CoS 0 system class.

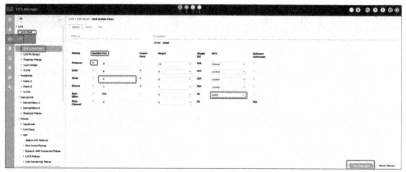

**Figure 12-59**  *UCS LAN QoS System Class Configuration*

## Configuring Quality of Service Policies

A QoS policy assigns a system class to the outgoing traffic for a vNIC or vHBA. This system class determines the quality of service for that traffic. For certain adapters, you can also specify additional controls on the outgoing traffic, such as burst and rate.

You must include a QoS policy in a vNIC policy or vHBA policy and then include that policy in a service profile to configure the vNIC or vHBA.

The following steps show how to create a QoS policy:

**Step 1.**    In the Navigation pane, click **LAN**. Next, expand **LAN > Policies**. Then expand the node for the organization where you want to create the pool. If the system does not include multitenancy, expand the root node.

**Step 2.**    Right-click **QoS Policy** and select **Create QoS Policy**. In the Create QoS Policy dialog box, complete the required fields, as shown in Figure 12-60. Then click **OK**. Include the QoS policy in a vNIC or vHBA template.

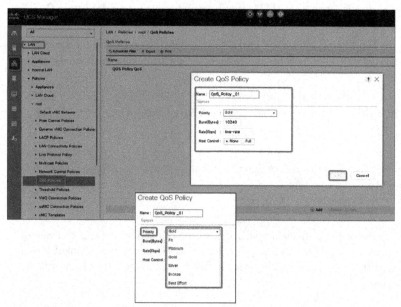

**Figure 12-60**  *UCS LAN QoS Policy Configuration*

12

# Cisco UCS Storage

The Cisco UCS support storage types are as follows:

- **Direct-attached storage (DAS):** This is the storage available inside a server and is directly connected to the system through the motherboard within a parallel SCSI implementation. DAS is commonly described as captive storage. Devices in a captive storage topology do not have direct access to the storage network and do not support efficient sharing of storage. To access data with DAS, you must go through a front-end network. DAS devices provide little or no mobility to other servers and little scalability.

  DAS devices limit file sharing and can be complex to implement and manage. For example, to support data backups, DAS devices require resources on the host and spare disk systems that other systems cannot use. The cost and performance of this storage depend on the disks and RAID controller cards inside the servers. DAS is less expensive and is simple to configure; however, it lacks the scalability, performance, and advanced features provided by high-end storage.

- **Network-attached storage (NAS):** This storage is usually an appliance providing file system access. This storage could be as simple as a Network File System (NFS) or Common Internet File System (CIFS) share available to the servers. Typical NAS devices are cost-effective devices that do not provide very high performance but have very high capacity with some redundancy for reliability. NAS is usually moderately expensive and simple to configure; plus it provides some advanced features. However, it also lacks scalability, performance, and advanced features provided by SAN.

- **Storage-area network (SAN):** A SAN is a specialized high-speed network that attaches servers and storage devices. A SAN allows an any-to-any connection across the network by using interconnect elements, such as switches and directors. It eliminates the traditional dedicated connection between a server and storage, and the concept that the server effectively owns and manages the storage devices. It also eliminates any restriction to the amount of data that a server can access, currently limited by the number of storage devices that are attached to the individual server. Instead, a SAN introduces the flexibility of networking to enable one server or many heterogeneous servers to share a common storage utility. A network might include many storage devices, including disk, tape, and optical storage. Additionally, the storage utility might be located far from the servers that it uses. This type of storage provides maximum reliability, expandability, and performance. The cost of a SAN is also very high compared to other storage options. A SAN is the most resilient, highly scalable, and high-performance storage; however, it is also the most expensive and complex to manage.

## UCS SAN Connectivity

The Cisco Unified Computing System model supports different methods to connect to centralized storage. The first storage connectivity method uses a pure Ethernet IP network to connect the servers to both their user community and the shared storage array. Communication between the servers and storage over IP can be accomplished by using a Small Computer System Interface over IP (iSCSI), which is a block-oriented protocol encapsulated over IP, or traditional network-attached storage (NAS) protocols such as Common Internet

File System (CIFS) or Network File System (NFS). LAN-based storage access follows the path through the Cisco Nexus 9000 Series Switching Fabric shown in Figure 12-61. A more traditional but advanced second method is using a Fibre Channel SAN using the Data Center Core Cisco Nexus 9000 switches or the Cisco MDS Series for larger SAN environments. Fibre Channel over Ethernet (FCoE) builds on the lossless Ethernet infrastructure to provide a converged network infrastructure.

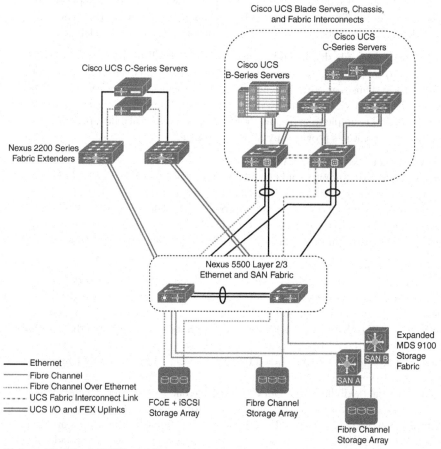

**Figure 12-61**  *LAN-Based Storage*

For resilient access, SANs are normally built with two distinct fabric switches that are not cross connected. Currently, Fibre Channel offers the widest support for various disk-array platforms and also support for boot-from-SAN. Cisco UCS Fabric Interconnects maintain separate Fibre Channel fabrics, so each fabric is attached to one of the Data Center Core switches running either SAN A or SAN B, as shown in Figure 12-62. When Fibre Channel is used for storage access from Cisco UCS B-Series blade servers, the system provides virtual host bus adapters to the service profiles to be presented to the host operating system. A Cisco UCS Fabric Interconnect can connect to the Data Center Core switches with FCoE uplinks.

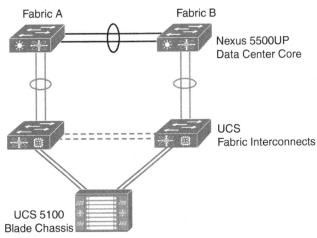

**Figure 12-62** *Fibre Channel–Based Storage*

On the Cisco UCS Fabric Interconnect, the Fibre Channel ports that connect to the Data Center Core SAN operate in N-port virtualization mode. All Fibre Channel switching happens upstream at the Data Center Core switches running N-port identifier virtualization (NPIV). NPIV allows multiple Fibre Channel port IDs to share a common physical port although there are multiple Fibre Channel ports on the fabric interconnects. You can connect the Cisco UCS C-Series rack-mount servers to the Fibre Channel SAN by using dedicated host bus adapters that attach directly to the SAN switches. Alternatively, you can use a converged network adapter, which allows Ethernet data FCoE storage traffic to share the same physical set of cabling. This Unified Wire approach allows these servers to connect directly to the Cisco Nexus 5500UP Series switches or a Cisco Nexus Fabric Extender for data traffic, as well as SAN A and SAN B highly available storage access, as shown in Figure 12-63. The Cisco Nexus 5500UP switch fabric is responsible for splitting FCoE traffic off to the Fibre Channel attached storage array. Many storage arrays now include FCoE connectivity as an option and can be directly connected to the Data Center Core.

Many available shared storage systems offer multiprotocol access to the system, including iSCSI, Fibre Channel, FCoE, CIFS, and NFS. Multiple methods can be combined on the same storage system to meet the access requirements of a variety of server implementations. This flexibility also helps facilitate migration from legacy third-party server implementations onto the Cisco UCS. The Cisco UCS main storage protocols are as follows:

- **iSCSI:** An industry standard protocol for attaching various I/O peripherals such as printers, scanners, tape drives, and storage devices. The most common SCSI devices are disks and tape libraries.

  SCSI is the core protocol to connect raw hard disk storage with the servers. To control remote storage with the SCSI protocol, different technologies are used as wrappers to encapsulate commands, such as FC and iSCSI. The Fibre Channel protocol provides the infrastructure to encapsulate SCSI traffic and provides connectivity between computers and storage. FC operates at speeds of 2, 4, 8, and 16 Gbps.

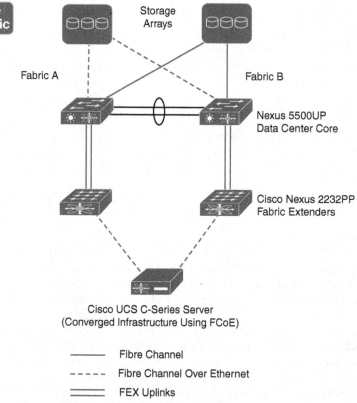

Figure 12-63  *Storage High Availability*

- **Fibre Channel (FC):** Fibre Channel identifies infrastructure components with World Wide Names (WWNs). WWNs are 64-bit addresses that uniquely identify the FC devices. Like MAC addresses, FC has bits assigned to vendors to identify their devices. Each end device (like an HBA port) is given a World Wide Port Name (WWPN), and each connectivity device (like a fabric switch) is given a World Wide Node Name (WWNN). A Fibre Chanel HBA used for connecting to a SAN is known as an *initiator*, and a Fibre Channel SAN providing disks as LUNs is known as a *target*. The Fibre Channel protocol is different from Ethernet or TCP/IP protocols. Fibre Channel consists of the following:

  - Hard disk arrays that provide raw storage capacity.

  - Storage processors to manage hard disks and provide storage LUNs and masking for the servers.

  - Fibre Channel switches (also known as *fabric*) that provide connectivity between storage processors and server HBAs.

  - Fibre Channel Host Bus Adapters that are installed in the computer and provide connectivity to the SAN.

- **Fibre Channel over Ethernet (FCoE):** FCoE transport replaces the Fibre Channel cabling with 10-Gigabit Ethernet cables and provides lossless delivery over unified I/O. Ethernet is widely used in networking. With some advancements such as Data Center Ethernet (DCE) and priority-based flow control (PFC) in Ethernet to make it more reliable for the data center, Fibre Channel is now also implemented on top of Ethernet. This implementation is known as FCoE.

## UCS SAN Configuration

The Cisco UCS Manager has a SAN tab that enables you to create, modify, and delete configuration elements related to SANs (FC, iSCSI) or direct-attached FC/FCoE or NAS appliances and communications, as shown in Figure 12-64. The major configurations under SAN are the following:

- **SAN Cloud:** This node allows you to

    - Configure SAN uplinks, including storage ports and port channels and SAN pin groups.

    - View the FC identity assignment.

    - Configure WWN pools, including WWPN, WWxN, and WWxN, and iSCSI Qualified Name (IQN) pools.

    - View the FSM details for a particular endpoint to determine if a task succeeded or failed and use the FSM to troubleshoot any failures.

    - Monitor storage events and faults for health management.

**Figure 12-64**   *The Cisco UCS Manager's SAN Tab*

- **Storage Cloud:** This node allows you to

    - Configure storage FC links and storage FCoE interfaces (using the SAN Storage Manager).

- Configure VSAN settings.

- Monitor SAN cloud events for health management.

- **Policies:** This node allows you to

- Configure threshold policies, classes, and properties and monitor events.

- Configure threshold organization and suborganization storage policies, including default VHBA, behavior, FC adapter, LACP, SAN connectivity, SAN connector, and VHBA templates.

- **Pools:** This node allows you to configure pools defined in the system, including IQN, IQN suffix, WWNN, WWPN, and WWxN.

- **Traffic Monitoring Sessions:** This node allows you to configure port traffic monitoring sessions defined in the system.

## Virtual Storage-Area Networks

A virtual storage-area network, or VSAN, is a logical partition in a storage-area network. The VSAN isolates traffic to that external SAN, including broadcast traffic. The Cisco UCS supports a maximum of 32 VSANs. The Cisco UCS uses named VSANs, which are similar to named VLANs. The name that you assign to a VSAN ID adds a layer of abstraction that allows you to globally update all servers associated with service profiles that use the named VSAN. You do not need to reconfigure the servers individually to maintain communication with the external SAN. You can create more than one named VSAN with the same VSAN ID. Then you can use the VSAN name used in the profile. The traffic on one named VSAN knows that the traffic on another named VSAN exists but cannot read or access that traffic.

### Named VSANs Configurations

In a cluster configuration, a named VSAN can be configured to be accessible only to the Fibre Channel uplink ports on one fabric interconnect or to the Fibre Channel uplink ports on both fabric interconnects. You must configure each named VSAN with an FCoE VLAN 599ID. This property determines which VLAN is used for transporting the VSAN and its Fibre Channel packets.

The following steps show how to create a named VSAN:

**Step 1.**    In the Navigation pane, click **SAN**. Then expand **SAN > SAN Cloud**.

**Step 2.**    In the Work pane, click the **VSANs** tab. On the icon bar to the right of the table, click + (the plus sign). If the + icon is disabled, click an entry in the table to enable it.

**Step 3.**    In the Create VSAN dialog box, complete the required fields, as shown in Figure 12-65. Then click **OK**.

> **NOTE**    FCoE VLANs in the SAN cloud and VLANs in the LAN cloud must have different IDs. Using the same ID for FCoE VLANs in a VSAN and a VLAN results in a critical fault and traffic disruption for all vNICs and uplink ports using that FCoE VLAN. Ethernet traffic is dropped on any VLAN with an ID that overlaps with an FCoE VLAN ID.

**Figure 12-65**  *Creating Storage VSANs*

The Cisco UCS Manager GUI adds the VSAN to one of the following VSANs nodes:

■ The SAN Cloud > VSANs node for a storage VSAN accessible to both fabric interconnects, as shown in Figure 12-66

■ The SAN Cloud > Fabric_Name > VSANs node for a VSAN accessible to only one fabric interconnect

**Figure 12-66**  *Named VSANs List*

The following steps show how to create a storage VSAN:

**Step 1.**    In the Navigation pane, click **SAN**. On the SAN tab, expand **SAN > Storage Cloud**.

**Step 2.**    In the Work pane, click the **VSANs** tab. On the icon bar to the right of the table, click **+**. If the + icon is disabled, click an entry in the table to enable it.

**Step 3.**    In the Create VSAN dialog box, complete the required fields, as shown in Figure 12-67. Then click **OK**.

**Figure 12-67**  *Creating Storage VSANs*

The Cisco UCS Manager GUI adds the VSAN to one of the following VSANs nodes:

- The Storage Cloud > VSANs node for a storage VSAN accessible to both fabric interconnects, as shown in Figure 12-68

- The Storage Cloud > Fabric_Name > VSANs node for a VSAN accessible to only one fabric interconnect

**Figure 12-68**  *Storage VSANs List*

## Zones and Zone Sets

A *zone* is a collection of ports that can communicate between them over the SAN. Zoning allows you to partition the Fibre Channel fabric into one or more zones. Each zone defines the set of Fibre Channel initiators and Fibre Channel targets that can communicate with each other in a VSAN. Zoning also enables you to set up access control between hosts and storage devices or user groups. A zone has the following characteristics:

- Members in a zone can access each other; members in different zones cannot access each other.

- Zones can vary in size.

- Devices can belong to more than one zone.

- A physical fabric can have a maximum of 8000 zones.

A *zone set* consists of one or more zones. Zone sets provide you with flexibility to activate or deactivate all zone members in a single activity. Any changes to a zone set are not applied until the zone set is activated. A zone can be a member of more than one zone set, but only one zone set can be activated at any time. You can use zone sets to enforce access control within the Fibre Channel fabric.

The Cisco UCS Manager supports switch-based Fibre Channel zoning and Cisco UCS Manager-based Fibre Channel zoning. You cannot configure a combination of zoning types in the same Cisco UCS domain. However, you can configure a Cisco UCS domain with one of the following types of zoning:

- **Cisco UCS Manager-based Fibre Channel zoning:** This configuration combines direct-attached storage with local zoning. Fibre Channel or FCoE storage is directly connected to the fabric interconnects, and zoning is performed in the Cisco UCS

Manager using Cisco UCS local zoning. Any existing Fibre Channel or FCoE uplink connections need to be disabled. The Cisco UCS does not currently support active Fibre Channel or FCoE uplink connections coexisting with the utilization of the UCS Local Zoning feature.

■ **Switch-based Fibre Channel zoning:** This configuration combines direct-attached storage with uplink zoning. The Fibre Channel or FCoE storage is directly connected to the fabric interconnects, and zoning is performed externally to the Cisco UCS domain through an MDS or Nexus 5000 switch. This configuration does not support local zoning in the Cisco UCS domain.

**NOTE**   Zoning is configured on a per-VSAN basis. You cannot enable zoning at the fabric level.

The following steps show how to create a new Fibre Channel zone profile:

**Step 1.**   In the Navigation pane, click **SAN**.

**Step 2.**   On the SAN tab, click **Storage Cloud**.

**Step 3.**   Right-click **FC Zone Profiles** and choose **Create FC Zone Profile**, as shown in Figure 12-69.

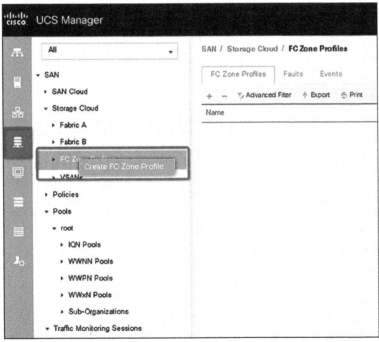

**Figure 12-69**   *Creating an FC Zone Profile*

**Step 4.** In the Create FC Zone Profile dialog box, complete the following fields (see Figure 12-70):

| Field | Description |
|---|---|
| Name field | A name for the profile. This name can be between 1 and 32 alphanumeric characters. You cannot use spaces or any special characters other than – (hyphen), _(underscore), : (colon), and . (period), and you cannot change this name after the object is saved. |
| Description field | This field is optional. Enter a brief description of the zone profile. |
| FC Zoning radio button | Select the desired state of the zone profile. |
| FC User Zones | Click the + icon on the right of the table to create FC user zone. The Create FC User Zone window is displayed. Continue to the next step for details to create FC user zone. |

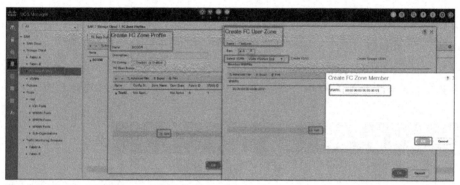

**Figure 12-70** *Adding an FC Zone Member*

**Step 5.** Complete the following fields in the Create FC User Zone dialog box:

| Field | Description |
|---|---|
| Name field | A name for the FC user zone. This name can be between 1 and 32 alphanumeric characters. You cannot use spaces or any special characters other than - (hyphen), _(underscore), : (colon), and . (period), and you cannot change this name after the object is saved. |
| Path radio button | The VSAN path configuration. Click the radio button to determine how the VSAN should be configured. The following options are available:<br><br>■ **Path A:** The VSAN path to the VSAN ID that exists only in Fabric A.<br><br>■ **Path B:** The VSAN path to the VSAN ID that exists only in Fabric B. |
| Select VSAN drop-down list | The unique identifier assigned to the VSANs that exists already in the network.<br><br>The ID can be between 1 and 4078, or between 4080 and 4093. The number 4079 is a reserved VSAN ID. You cannot configure Fibre Channel zoning in end-host mode. |
| Create VSAN link | Click the + icon to create a new VSAN in a new window. This allows you to create a VSAN for Fibre Channel zoning. After creating the VSAN, you can return and continue creating a channel zone profile. |

| Field | Description |
|---|---|
| Create Storage VSAN link | Click the + icon to create a new storage VSAN in a new window. This allows you to create a VSAN for Fibre Channel zoning. After creating the VSAN, you can return and continue creating a channel zone profile. |
| Member WWPNs | Click the + icon on the right of the table to create World Wide Port Name (WWPN). The Create FC Zone Member window is displayed. Enter the WWPN for this zone. |

**Step 6.**   Click **OK** to close the Create FC Zone Member window. Then click **OK** again to close the Create FC User Zone window. Then click **OK** to close the Create FC Zone Profile window. The new Fibre Channel zone profile is created and listed under FC Zone Profiles, as shown in Figure 12-71.

**Figure 12-71**   *Zone Profile List*

## World Wide Name Pool

A World Wide Name pool is a collection of WWNs for use by the Fibre Channel vHBAs in a Cisco UCS domain. If you use WWN pools in service profiles, you do not have to manually configure the WWNs that will be used by the server associated with the service profile. In a system that implements multitenancy, you can use a WWN pool to control the WWNs used by each organization.

■ A WWNN pool is a WWN pool that contains only World Wide Node Names. If you include a pool of WWNNs in a service profile, the associated server is assigned a WWNN from that pool.

■ A WWPN pool is one that contains only World Wide Port Names. If you include a pool of WWPNs in a service profile, the port on each vHBA of the associated server is assigned a WWPN from that pool.

- A WWxN pool is a WWN pool that contains both World Wide Node Names and World Wide Port Names. You can specify how many ports per node are created with WWxN pools. The pool size must be a multiple of ports-per-node + 1. For example, if you specify 7 ports per node, the pool size must be a multiple of 8. If you specify 63 ports per node, the pool size must be a multiple of 64.

You can use a WWxN pool whenever you select a WWNN or WWPN pool. The WWxN pool must be created before it can be assigned.

You create separate pools for the following:

- World Wide Node Names assigned to the vHBA

- World Wide Port Names assigned to the vHBA

- Both World Wide Node Names and World Wide Port Names

The following steps show how to create a WWxN pool:

**Step 1.**    In the Navigation pane, click **SAN**. Then in the SAN tab, expand **SAN > Pools**.

**Step 2.**    Expand the node for the organization where you want to create the pool. If the system does not include multitenancy, expand the root node, right-click **WWxN Pools**, and select **Create WWxN Pool**.

**Step 3.**    In the Define Name and Description page of the Create WWxN Pool wizard, complete the following fields (see Figure 12-72):

| Name | Description |
|---|---|
| Name field | The name of the World Wide Port Name pool. This name can be between 1 and 32 alphanumeric characters. You cannot use spaces or any special characters other than - (hyphen), _ (underscore), : (colon), and . (period), and you cannot change this name after the object is saved. |
| Description field | A description of the pool. Enter up to 256 characters. You can use any characters or spaces except ` (accent mark), \ (backslash), ^ (caret), " (double quote), = (equal sign), > (greater than), < (less than), or ' (single quote). |
| Max Ports per Node field | The maximum number of ports that can be assigned to each node name in this pool. You cannot change this value once the object has been saved. |
| Assignment Order field | This can be one of the following: <br> ■ **Default:** The Cisco UCS Manager selects a random identity from the pool. <br> ■ **Sequential:** The Cisco UCS Manager selects the lowest available identity from the pool. |

**Step 4.**    Click **Next**.

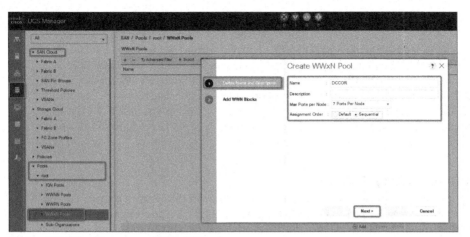

**Figure 12-72**   *Creating a WWxN Pool*

**Step 5.**    In the Add WWN Blocks page of the Create WWxN Pool wizard, click **Add**. In the Create WWN Block dialog box, complete the following fields (see Figure 12-73):

| Name | Description |
|------|-------------|
| From field | The first WWN in the block. |
| Size field | The number of WWNs in the block. |
| | For WWxN pools, the pool size must be a multiple of *ports-per-node* + 1. For example, if there are 7 ports per node, the pool size must be a multiple of 8. If there are 63 ports per node, the pool size must be a multiple of 64. |

**Step 6.**    Click **OK** and then click **Finish**.

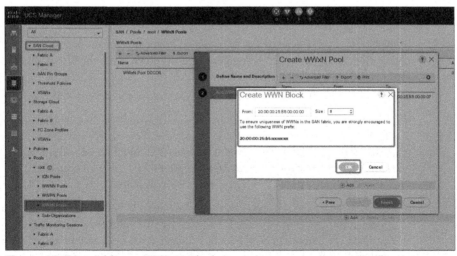

**Figure 12-73**   *Adding a WWxN Block*

**NOTE**  A WWN pool can include only WWNNs or WWPNs in the ranges from 20:00:00:00:00:00:00:00 to 20:FF:00:FF:FF:FF:FF:FF or from 50:00:00:00:00:00:00:00 to 5F:FF:00:FF:FF:FF:FF:FF. All other WWN ranges are reserved. When Fibre Channel traffic is sent through the Cisco UCS infrastructure, the source WWPN is converted to a MAC address. You cannot use WWPN pool that can translate to a source multicast MAC address. To ensure the uniqueness of the Cisco UCS WWNNs and WWPNs in the SAN fabric, Cisco recommends using the following WWN prefix for all blocks in a pool: 20:00:00:25:B5:XX:XX:XX.

## SAN Connectivity Policies

SAN connectivity policies determine the connections and the network communication resources between the server and the SAN. These policies use pools to assign WWNs and WWPNs to servers and to identify the vHBAs that the servers use to communicate with the network. You can configure SAN connectivity for a service profile through any of the following methods:

- Local vHBAs that are created in the service profile

- Local SAN connectivity policy

- Local vHBAs connectivity policy

The Cisco UCS maintains mutual exclusivity between connectivity policies and local vHBA configuration in the service profile. You cannot have a combination of connectivity policies and locally created vHBAs. When you include a SAN connectivity policy, all existing vHBA configuration in that service profile is erased.

The following steps show how to create a SAN connectivity policy:

**Step 1.**  In the Navigation pane, click **SAN**. Then expand **SAN > Policies**. Expand the node for the organization where you want to create the policy. If the system does not include multitenancy, expand the root node. Right-click **SAN Connectivity Policies** and choose **Create SAN Connectivity Policy**.

**Step 2.**  In the Create SAN Connectivity Policy dialog box, enter a name and optional description. From the WWNN Assignment drop-down list in the World Wide Node Name area, do one of the following:

- Choose **Select** (pool default used by default) to use the default WWN pool.

- Choose one of the options listed under Manual Using OUI and then enter the WWN in the World Wide Node Name field. You can specify a WWNN in the range from 20:00:00:00:00:00:00:00 to 20:FF:FF:FF:FF:FF:FF:FF or from 50:00:00:00:00:00:00:00 to 5F:FF:FF:FF:FF:FF:FF:FF. You can click the link to verify that the WWNN you specified is available.

- Choose a WWN pool name from the list to have a WWN assigned from the specified pool. Each pool name is followed by two numbers in parentheses that show the number of WWNs still available in the pool and the total number of WWNs in the pool.

**Step 3.**   In the vHBAs table, click **Add.** In the Create vHBAs dialog box, enter the name and an optional description. Then choose the Fabric ID, Select VSAN, Pin Group, Persistent Binding, and Max Data Field Size. You can also create a VSAN or SAN pin group from this area.

**Step 4.**   In the Operational Parameters area, choose the **Stats Threshold Policy.** In the Adapter Performance Profile area, choose the **Adapter Policy** and **QoS Policy.** You can also create a Fibre Channel adapter policy or QoS policy from this area.

**Step 5.**   After you have created all the vHBAs you need for the policy, click **OK.**

# Exam Preparation Tasks

As mentioned in the Introduction, you have a couple of choices for exam preparation: the exercises here, Chapter 21, "Final Preparation," and the exam simulation questions in the Pearson Test Prep software online.

## Review All Key Topics

Review the most important topics in the chapter, noted with the key topic icon in the outer margin of the page. Table 12-6 lists a reference to these key topics and the page numbers on which each is found.

**Table 12-6**   Key Topics for Chapter 12

| Key Topic Element | Description | Page |
|---|---|---|
| Figure 12-1 | Cisco Unified Computing System Architecture | 533 |
| Figure 12-2 | Cisco UCS Components and Connectivity | 534 |
| Section | Cisco UCS Components and Connectivity | 534 |
| Section | Cisco UCS Mini | 539 |
| Section | Fabric Interconnect and Fabric Extender Connectivity | 544 |
| Figure 12-12 | Connecting Blade Chassis Fabric Extenders to Fabric Interconnect | 546 |
| Table 12-3 | Blade Chassis Slot to Link Mapping | 546 |
| Figure 12-17 | UCS FEX Virtual Links | 548 |
| Figure 12-18 | C-Series Rack Chassis with Single-Wire Management | 549 |
| Figure 12-19 | C-Series Rack-Mount Chassis with Dual-Wire Management | 550 |
| Section | Cisco UCS Virtualization Infrastructure | 550 |
| Table 12-4 | Cluster Verification CLI | 563 |
| Figure 12-25 | Cisco UCS Components Logical Connectivity | 566 |
| Section | Fabric Interconnect Port Modes | 567 |
| List | Port Types | 567 |

| Key Topic Element | Description | Page |
|---|---|---|
| Figure 12-28 | UCS Fabric Traffic Failover Example | 570 |
| Figure 12-31 | UCS Unicast Traffic Path | 573 |
| Figure 12-32 | Multicast and Broadcast Traffic Summary | 573 |
| Section | Named VLANs | 586 |
| Section | UCS Identity Pools | 591 |
| Section | UCS Server Policies | 599 |
| Paragraph | Maintenance Policy | 601 |
| Paragraph | Power Control Policy | 601 |
| Section | QoS System Classes | 608 |
| Section | UCS SAN Connectivity | 611 |
| Figure 12-63 | Storage High Availability | 614 |

## Define Key Terms

Define the following key terms from this chapter, and check your answers in the Glossary.

Fibre Channel (FC), Fibre Channel over Ethernet (FCoE), host bus adapter (HBA), Internet of Things (IoT), just a bunch of disks (JBOD), Kernel-based Virtual Machine (KVM), Quad Small Form-Factor Pluggable (QSFP), Small Computer System over IP (iSCSI), Small Form-Factor Pluggable Plus (SFP+), virtual interface card (VIC), virtual storage-area network (VSAN), World Wide Node Name (WWNN), World Wide Port Name (WWPN), zoning

## References

Cisco Servers—Unified Computing System (UCS): https://www.cisco.com/site/us/en/products/computing/servers-unified-computing-systems/resources.html

Cisco Live UCS Fundamentals BRKCOM 1001: https://www.ciscolive.com/c/dam/r/ciscolive/apjc/docs/2016/pdf/BRKCOM-1001.pdf

Cisco Live UCS Networking Deep Dive BRKCOM-2003: https://www.alcatron.net/Cisco%20Live%202015%20Melbourne/Cisco%20Live%20Content/Data%20Centre/BRKCOM-2003%20UCS%20Networking%20Deep%20Dive.pdf

# CHAPTER 13

# Cisco Unified Computing Infrastructure Monitoring

Today, data center architectures are transitioning to highly virtualized, highly dynamic, internal cloud forms. Monitoring activity from the computing perspective is an essential source of operational intelligence. Monitoring tools must provide sufficient capacity and flexibility to handle rapidly growing traffic volumes and a dynamic computing resource. Cisco UCS Monitoring enables the data center administrator to monitor the physical computing environment in conjunction with the virtual environment and helps reduce the corresponding management complexities, thus increasing IT agility.

## This chapter covers the following key topics:

**Cisco UCS System Monitoring:** This section discusses various UCS monitoring features, including SNMP, Call Home, NetFlow, and traffic monitoring (known as Switched Port Analyzer, or SPAN).

**Cisco Intersight:** This section covers the Cisco Intersight Software-as-a-Service management platform, which provides global management of the Cisco Unified Computing System (UCS) and Cisco HyperFlex hyperconverged infrastructure anywhere.

## "Do I Know This Already?" Quiz

The "Do I Know This Already?" quiz enables you to assess whether you should read this entire chapter thoroughly or jump to the "Exam Preparation Tasks" section. If you are in doubt about your answers to these questions or your own assessment of your knowledge of the topics, read the entire chapter. Table 13-1 lists the major headings in this chapter and their corresponding "Do I Know This Already?" quiz questions. You can find the answers in Appendix A, "Answers to the 'Do I Know This Already?' Quizzes."

**Table 13-1** "Do I Know This Already?" Section-to-Question Mapping

| Foundation Topics Section | Questions |
|---|---|
| Cisco UCS System Monitoring | 1–3 |
| Cisco Intersight | 4–5 |

**CAUTION**   The goal of self-assessment is to gauge your mastery of the topics in this chapter. If you do not know the answer to a question or are only partially sure of the answer, you should mark that question as wrong for purposes of the self-assessment. Giving yourself credit for an answer you correctly guess skews your self-assessment results and might provide you with a false sense of security.

1. What types of UCS interfaces support destination traffic monitoring? (Choose two answers.)

   a. Ethernet

   b. vNIC

   c. Fibre Channel

   d. FCoE Port

2. If you suspect some changes have been made to the UCS configuration and want to check who initiated them, what log do you check?

   a. Syslog

   b. System event logs

   c. SNMP

   d. Audit logs

3. The UCS system event log resides on the Cisco Integrated Management Controller (CIMC) in NVRAM. What will happen if the logs reach their maximum file limits?

   a. The system event log (SEL) will be rotated, and the old log will be archived automatically.

   b. The system event log file has circular logging, which means that new data will delete the old data.

   c. No further events can be recorded when the logs are full, unless files are backed up and cleared manually or via policy.

   d. Files will be deleted, and the system event log will be lost.

4. Which Cisco Intersight license required for on-premises server (an Intersight virtual appliance)? (Choose two answers.)

   a. Standard

   b. Essentials

   c. Advantage

   d. Base

5. What is the Intersight upgrade process?

   a. Manually download the upgrade files from Cisco.com, upload them to the Intersight server via SCP or SFTP, and run the command-line interface (CLI) command to update the server.

   b. Upgrades to Cisco Intersight are delivered automatically without requiring the resources of traditional management tool upgrades and disruption to your operations.

   c. Manually download the upgrade files from Cisco.com, and then use the browser to upload the files and upgrade the server.

   d. Only the Cisco Technical Assistance Center (TAC) can upgrade the Intersight server.

## Foundation Topics

# Cisco UCS System Monitoring

The Cisco Unified Computing System (UCS) Manager can detect all system faults. Normally, system faults are categorized as critical, major, minor, and warnings. Cisco recommends that you monitor all critical and major severity faults. As in Cisco NX-OS, the Cisco UCS supports different monitoring protocols, such as standard syslog, SNMP, NetFlow, Call Home, and SPAN traffic monitoring. In addition, the Cisco UCS provides monitoring for the computing environment, such as XML application programming interface (API), audit logs, statistics collection, database health monitoring, and computing hardware monitoring.

The Cisco UCS Manager core is made up of three elements: the data management engine, application gateway, and user-accessible northbound interface. The northbound interface is composed of SNMP, syslog, XML API, and UCSM CLI.

You can monitor the Cisco UCS Manager servers through XML API, SNMP, and syslog. Both SNMP and syslog are interfaces used only for monitoring because they are read-only, so no configuration changes are allowed from these interfaces. Alternatively, the XML API is a monitoring interface that is read-write, which allows you to monitor the Cisco UCS Manager and change the configuration if needed. Figure 13-1 shows the core and monitoring interfaces.

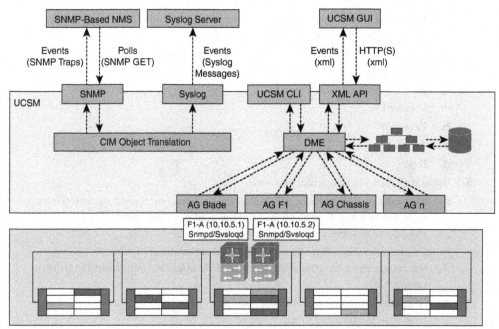

**Figure 13-1** *Cisco UCS Manager Core and Monitoring Interfaces*

## Data Management Engine

The data management engine (DME) is the center of the Cisco UCS Manager system, which maintains the following components:

- The Cisco UCS XML database, which houses the inventory database of all physical elements (blade and rack mount servers, chassis, modules, and fabric interconnects)

- The logical configuration data for profiles, policies, pools, vNIC, and vHBA templates

- The various networking-related configuration details like VLANs, VSANs, port channels, network uplinks, and server downlinks

The DME monitors

- The current health and state of all components of all physical and logical elements in a Cisco UCS domain

- The transition information of all finite state machine (FSM) tasks occurring

The Cisco UCS XML database stores only the current inventory, health, and managed end-points config information, resulting in a near real-time XML data file. By default, the DME does not store a historical log of faults that have occurred on a Cisco UCS domain. As fault conditions are raised on the endpoints, the DME creates faults in the Cisco UCS XML database. As those faults are mitigated, the DME clears and removes the faults from the Cisco UCS XML database.

## Application Gateway

Application gateways (AGs) are software agents that communicate directly with the end-points to relay the health and state of the endpoints to the DME. AG-managed endpoints include servers, chassis, modules, fabric extenders, fabric interconnects, and NX-OS. The AGs actively monitor the server through the IPMI and SELs using the Cisco Integrated Management Controller (CIMC). They provide the DME with the health, state, configuration, and potential fault conditions of a device. The AGs manage configuration changes from the current state to the desired state during FSM transitions when changes are made to the Cisco UCS XML database.

The module AG and chassis AG communicate with the chassis management controller (CMC) to get information about the health, state, configuration, and fault conditions observed by the CMC. The fabric interconnect NX-OS AG communicates directly with NX-OS to get information about the health, state, configuration, statistics, and fault conditions observed by NX-OS on the fabric interconnects. All AGs provide inventory details about the endpoints to the DME during the various discovery processes. The AGs perform the state changes necessary to configure endpoints during FSM-triggered transitions, monitor the health and state of the endpoints, and notify the DME of any faults.

## Northbound Interfaces

The northbound interfaces include SNMP, syslog, CLI, and XML API. The XML API present in the Apache web server layer sends login, logout, query, and configuration requests using HTTP or HTTPS. SNMP and syslog are both consumers of data from the DME.

SNMP INFORMs and TRAPs are translated directly from the fault information stored in the Cisco UCS XML database. SNMP GET requests are sent through the same object translation engine in reverse, where the DME receives a request from the object translation engine. The data is translated from the XML database to an SNMP response.

Syslog messages use the same object translation engine as SNMP, where the source of the data (faults, events, audit logs) is translated from XML into a Cisco UCS Manager–formatted syslog message.

## Cisco UCS Monitoring Events and Logs

The Cisco UCS Manager generates system log, or *syslog*, messages to record the following incidents that take place in the Cisco UCS Manager system:

- Routine system operations

- Failures and errors

- Critical and emergency conditions

There are three kinds of syslog entries: Fault, Event, and Audit. Each syslog message identifies the Cisco UCS Manager process that generated the message and provides a brief description of the operation or error that occurred. The syslog is useful both in routine troubleshooting, incident handling, and management.

The Cisco UCS Manager collects and logs syslog messages internally. Also, you can send them to external syslog servers running a syslog daemon. Logging to a central syslog server helps in aggregation of logs and alerts. Some syslog messages include DIMM problems, equipment failures, thermal problems, voltage problems, power problems, high availability (HA) cluster problems, and link failures.

Syslog messages contain event codes and fault codes. To monitor syslog messages, you can define syslog message filters. These filters can parse the syslog messages based on the criteria you choose. You can use the following criteria to define a filter:

- **By event or fault codes:** Define a filter with a parsing rule to include only the specific codes that you intend to monitor. Messages that do not match these criteria are discarded.

- **By severity level:** Define a filter with a parsing rule to monitor syslog messages with specific severity levels. You can set syslog severity levels individually for OS functions, to facilitate logging and display of messages ranging from brief summaries to detailed information for debugging.

Cisco devices can send their log messages to a UNIX-style syslog service. A syslog service simply accepts messages and then stores them in files or prints them according to a simple configuration file. This form of logging is the best available for Cisco devices because it can provide protected long-term storage of logs. Figure 13-2 shows UCS syslog configurations.

**Figure 13-2**  *UCS Syslog Configurations*

UCS generates system event logs (SELs) as well. An SEL is used to troubleshoot system health. It records most server-related events, such as instances of over- or under-voltage, temperature events, fan events, and BIOS events. The types of events supported by SEL include BIOS events, memory unit events, processor events, and motherboard events.

The SELs are stored in the CIMC NVRAM, through an SEL log policy. It is best practice to periodically download and clear the SELs. The SEL file is approximately 40 KB in size, and no further events can be recorded after it is full. It must be cleared before additional events can be recorded.

You can use the SEL policy to back up the SEL to a remote server and optionally to clear the SEL after a backup operation occurs. Backup operations can be triggered based on specific actions, or they can be set to occur at regular intervals. You can also manually back up or clear the SEL. Figure 13-3 shows UCS SEL configurations for specific chassis because SELs will be saved in CIMC NVRAM.

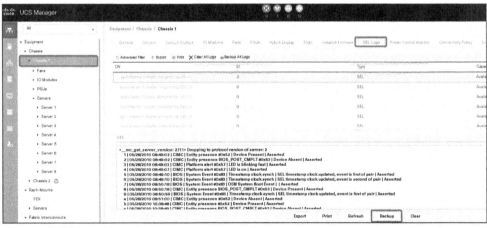

**Figure 13-3**  *UCS System Event Logs*

The backup file is automatically generated. The filename format is *sel-SystemName-ChassisID-ServerID-ServerSerialNumber-Timestamp*—for example, sel-UCS-A-ch01-serv01-QCI12522939-20091121160736.

Because the UCS is a computer device, it will record any user activity. Audit logs record system events that occurred, where they occurred, and which users initiated them, as shown in Figure 13-4.

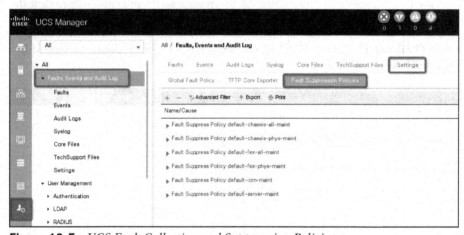

**Figure 13-4**  *UCS Audit Logs*

## Cisco UCS Monitoring Policies

Cisco UCS has two monitoring policies. The first monitoring policy is fault collection and suppression; this global fault policy controls the life cycle of a fault in a Cisco UCS domain, including when faults are cleared, the flapping interval (the length of time between the fault being raised and the condition being cleared), and the retention interval (the length of time a fault is retained in the system), as shown in Figure 13-5.

**Figure 13-5**  *UCS Fault Collection and Suppression Policies*

A fault in Cisco UCS has the following life cycle:

1.  A condition occurs in the system, and the Cisco UCS Manager raises a fault. This is the active state.

2.  When the fault is alleviated, it enters a flapping or soaking interval that is designed to prevent flapping. *Flapping* occurs when a fault is raised and cleared several times in rapid succession. During the flapping interval, the fault retains its severity for the length of time specified in the global fault policy.

3. If the condition reoccurs during the flapping interval, the fault returns to the active state. If the condition does not reoccur during the flapping interval, the fault is cleared.

4. The cleared fault enters the retention interval. This interval ensures that the fault reaches the attention of an administrator even if the condition that caused the fault has been alleviated and the fault has not been deleted prematurely. The retention interval retains the cleared fault for the length of time specified in the global fault policy.

5. If the condition reoccurs during the retention interval, the fault returns to the active state. If the condition does not reoccur, the fault is deleted.

The second monitoring policy is the statistics collection policy, which defines how frequently statistics are collected (collection interval) and how frequently they are reported (reporting interval). Reporting intervals are longer than collection intervals so that multiple statistical data points can be collected during the reporting interval. This provides the Cisco UCS Manager with sufficient data to calculate and report minimum, maximum, and average values.

For NIC statistics, the Cisco UCS Manager displays the average, minimum, and maximum of the change since the last collection of statistics. If the values are 0, there has been no change since the last collection.

As shown in Figure 13-6, statistics can be collected and reported for the following five functional areas of the Cisco UCS system:

- **Adapter:** Statistics related to the adapters

- **Chassis:** Statistics related to the chassis

- **Host:** A placeholder for future support

- **Port:** Statistics related to the ports, including server ports, uplink Ethernet ports, and uplink Fibre Channel ports

- **Server:** Statistics related to servers

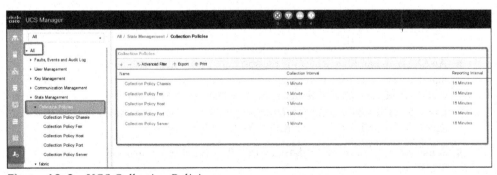

**Figure 13-6**  *UCS Collection Policies*

> **NOTE**   The Cisco UCS Manager has one default statistics collection policy for each of the five functional areas. You cannot create additional statistics collection policies, and you cannot delete the existing default policies. You can only modify the default policies.

The values that are displayed for the delta counter in the Cisco UCS Manager are calculated as the difference between the last two samples in a collection interval. In addition, the Cisco UCS Manager displays the average, minimum, and maximum delta values of the samples in the collection interval.

### Cisco UCS Simple Network Management Protocol

The Simple Network Management Protocol (SNMP) is an application layer protocol that provides a message format for communication between SNMP managers and agents. SNMP provides a standardized framework and a common language for monitoring and managing devices in a network. Figure 13-7 shows a UCS Manager SNMP configuration example.

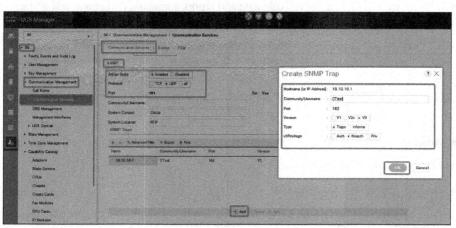

**Figure 13-7**   *UCS SNMP Configuration Example*

Cisco UCS SNMP framework consists of three parts:

- **An SNMP manager:** The system used to control and monitor the activities of network devices using SNMP.

- **An SNMP agent:** SNMP agent is the software component within Cisco UCS that maintains the data for Cisco UCS and reports this data as needed to the SNMP manager. Cisco UCS includes the agent and a collection of MIBs (management information base). To enable the SNMP agent and create the relationship between the manager and agent, enable and configure SNMP in the Cisco UCS Manager.

- **A management information base (MIB):** The collection of managed objects on the SNMP agent.

### Cisco UCS Call Home and Smart Call Home

Call Home provides an email-based notification for critical system policies. A range of message formats is available for compatibility with pager services or XML-based automated parsing applications. You can use this feature to page a network support engineer, email a network operations center, or use Cisco Smart Call Home services to generate a case with the Technical Assistance Center (TAC).

The Call Home feature can deliver alert messages containing information about diagnostics and environmental faults, and events also can deliver alerts to multiple recipients. Each profile includes configurable message formats and content categories. A predefined destination profile is provided for sending alerts to the Cisco TAC, but you also can define your own destination profiles.

When you configure Call Home to send messages (see Figure 13-8), the Cisco UCS Manager executes the appropriate CLI **show** command and attaches the command output to the message.

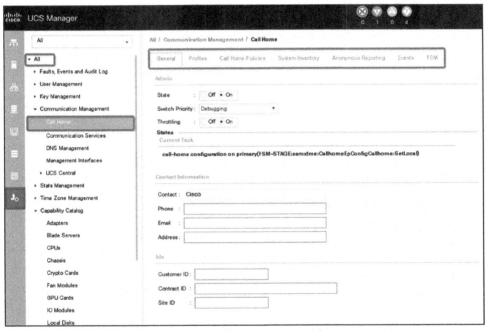

**Figure 13-8**  *Cisco UCS Call Home Configuration Example*

Cisco UCS delivers Call Home messages in the following formats:

■ Short text format, which provides a one- or two-line description of the fault that is suitable for pagers or printed reports.

■ Full text format, which provides fully formatted messages with detailed information that is suitable for human reading.

■ XML machine-readable format, which uses Extensible Markup Language (XML) and Adaptive Messaging Language (AML) XML Schema Definition (XSD). The AML XSD is published on the Cisco.com website. The XML format enables communication with the Cisco Systems Technical Assistance Center.

### Cisco UCS Manager Database Health and Hardware Monitoring

The Cisco UCS Manager uses the SQLite database stored on the fabric interconnects to persist configuration and inventory. Data corruption on both the Flash and NVRAM storage devices can cause failures and loss of configuration data. The Cisco UCS Manager provides several proactive health check and recovery mechanisms to improve the integrity of the Cisco UCS Manager database. These mechanisms enable active monitoring of the database health:

- **Periodic health check:** A periodic check of database integrity ensures that any corruption is caught and recovered proactively.

- **Periodic backup:** A periodic internal full state backup of the system ensures a smoother route to recovery in the case of any unrecoverable errors.

Example 13-1 shows the command-line interface to change the time interval for the health check to run every two days and commits the transaction.

**Example 13-1**  *UCS CLI Configuration to Change the Health Check Interval*

```
UCS-A# scope system
UCS-A /system # set mgmt-db-check-policy health-check-interval 2
UCS-A /system* # commit-buffer
UCS-A /system #
```

The Cisco UCS consists of different hardware components; the Cisco UCS Manager provides hardware monitoring for the following components (see Figure 13-9):

- Monitoring a fabric interconnect

- Monitoring a blade server

- Monitoring a rack-mount server

- Monitoring an IO module

- Managing the interface's monitoring policy

- Monitoring local storage

- Managing transportable flash module and supercapacitor

- Monitoring the trusted platform module (TPM)

### Cisco UCS NetFlow Monitoring

NetFlow is a standard network protocol for collecting IP traffic data. NetFlow enables you to define a flow in terms of unidirectional IP packets that share certain characteristics. All packets that match the flow definition are collected and exported to one or more external NetFlow Collectors, where they can be further aggregated, analyzed, and used for application-specific processing.

**Figure 13-9**  *UCS Hardware Health Report*

The Cisco UCS Manager uses NetFlow-capable adapters (Cisco UCS VIC 1240, Cisco UCS VIC 1280, Cisco UCS VIC 1225, Cisco UCS VIC 1300 Series, and Cisco UCS VIC 1440 Series) to communicate with the routers and switches that collect and export flow information.

**NOTE**   NetFlow monitoring is not supported on Cisco UCS 6454 Fabric Interconnects. Also, for Release 3.0(2), NetFlow monitoring is supported for end-host mode only.

NetFlow components include

- **Network flows:** A flow is a set of unidirectional IP packets that have common properties such as the source or destination of the traffic, routing information, and protocol used. Flows are collected when they match the definitions in the flow record definition.

- **Flow record definitions:** A flow record definition contains information about the properties used to define the flow, which can include both characteristic properties and measured properties. Characteristic properties, also called flow keys, are the properties that define the flow. The Cisco UCS Manager supports IPv4, IPv6, and Layer 2 keys. Measured characteristics, also called flow values or nonkeys, are measurable values such as the number of bytes contained in all packets of the flow or the total number of packets.

  A flow record definition is a specific combination of flow keys and flow values. The two types of flow record definitions are

  - **System-defined:** Default flow record definitions supplied by the Cisco UCS Manager

  - **User-defined:** Flow record definitions that you can create yourself

- **Flow exporters, flow exporter profiles, and flow collectors:** Flow exporters transfer the flows to the flow connector based on the information in a flow exporter profile. The flow exporter profile contains the networking properties used to export NetFlow packets. The networking properties include a VLAN, the source IP address, and the subnet mask for each fabric interconnect.

**NOTE**   In the Cisco UCS Manager GUI, the networking properties are defined in an exporter interface that is included in the profile. In the Cisco UCS Manager CLI, the properties are defined in the profile.

Flow collectors receive the flows from the flow exporter. Each flow collector contains an IP address, port, external gateway IP, and VLAN that defines where the flows are sent.

■ **Flow monitors and flow monitor sessions:** A flow monitor consists of a flow definition, one or two flow exporters, and a timeout policy (see Figure 13-10). You can use a flow monitor to specify which flow information you want to gather and where you want to collect it from. Each flow monitor operates in either the egress or ingress direction.

A flow monitor session contains up to four flow monitors—two flow monitors in the ingress direction and two flow monitors in the egress direction. A flow monitor session can also be associated with a vNIC.

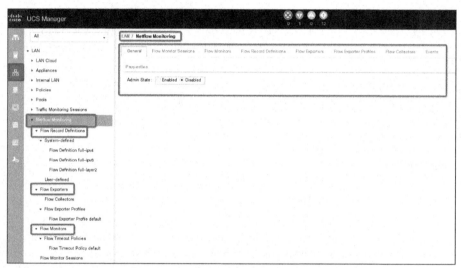

**Figure 13-10**  *UCS NetFlow Configuration Example*

## Traffic Monitoring

Today the infrastructure in data centers is distributed. With layers of virtual and physical devices and systems, the data center infrastructure has become more complex to troubleshoot. The accelerating adoption of IP-based services like cloud computing, virtual desktop infrastructure, and unified communications has further compounded this complexity, massively increasing the scope of the network. As a result, network or application problems could have a major impact on business operations.

Network administrators will need better visibility into network traffic across the data center infrastructure. Traffic visibility will improve troubleshooting and help you find the root cause of network problems. Because network performance has become more critical, if network performance drops even slightly, IP-based services will start to fail. Consequently, poor network performance has the potential to cause outages across the data center, with unpredictable and unpleasant results.

Network administrators can use traffic monitoring to detect, diagnose, and resolve network performance issues. The Cisco UCS Manager offers traffic monitoring that copies traffic from one or more source ports and sends the copied traffic to a dedicated destination port for analysis by a network analyzer. This feature is also known as Switched Port Analyzer (SPAN).

There are two types of monitoring sessions:

- Ethernet

- Fibre Channel

The type of destination port determines what kind of monitoring session you need. For an Ethernet traffic monitoring session, the destination port must be an unconfigured physical port. For a Fibre Channel traffic monitoring session, the destination port must be a Fibre Channel uplink port, except when you are using Cisco UCS 6454 Fabric Interconnects and 6300 Series Fabric Interconnects.

**NOTE**  For Cisco UCS 6332, 6332-16UP, and 6454 Fabric Interconnects, you cannot choose Fibre Channel destination ports. The destination port must be an unconfigured physical Ethernet port.

### Traffic Monitoring Across Ethernet

An Ethernet traffic monitoring session can monitor any of the source and destination ports listed in Table 13-2.

**Table 13-2**    UCS Ethernet Traffic Monitoring Ports

| Source Ports | Destination Ports |
|---|---|
| Uplink Ethernet port | Unconfigured Ethernet port |
| Ethernet port channel | |
| VLAN | |
| Service profile vNIC | |
| Service profile vHBA | |
| FCoE port | |
| Port channels | |
| Unified uplink port | |
| VSAN | |

**NOTE**  All traffic sources must be located within the same switch as the destination port. A port configured as a destination port cannot also be configured as a source port. A member port of a port channel cannot be configured individually as a source. If the port channel is configured as a source, all member ports are source ports.

A server port can be a source only if it is a nonvirtualized rack server adapter-facing port.

- **Traffic monitoring for Cisco UCS 6400 and 6500 Fabric Interconnects**

    - Cisco UCS 6400 and 6500 do not support a Fibre Channel port as a destination port. Therefore, an Ethernet port is the only option for configuring any traffic monitoring session on this fabric interconnect.

- Cisco UCS 6400 and 6500 support monitoring traffic in the transmit direction for more than two sources per fabric interconnect.

- You can monitor or use SPAN on port channel sources for traffic in the transmit and receive directions.

- You can configure a port as a destination port for only one monitor session.

- You can monitor the port channel as a source in the transmit direction.

- You cannot monitor vEth as a source in the transmit direction.

- **Traffic monitoring for Cisco UCS 6300 Interconnects**

  - Cisco UCS 6300 Fabric Interconnect supports port-based mirroring.

  - Cisco UCS 6300 Fabric Interconnect supports VLAN SPAN only in the receive direction.

  - Ethernet SPAN is a port based on the Cisco UCS 6300 Fabric Interconnect.

- **Traffic monitoring for Cisco UCS 6200 Interconnects**

  - Cisco UCS 6200 and 6324 support monitoring traffic in the transmit direction for up to two sources per fabric interconnect.

  - Cisco UCS 6200 SPAN traffic is rate-limited by the SPAN destination port speed. This can be either 1 or 10 Gbps.

**NOTE** (For 6200 and 6324 Fabric Interconnects) You can monitor or use SPAN on port channels only for ingress traffic.

### Traffic Monitoring Across Fibre Channel

You can monitor Fibre Channel traffic using either a Fibre Channel traffic analyzer or an Ethernet traffic analyzer. When Fibre Channel traffic is monitored with an Ethernet traffic monitoring session, at an Ethernet destination port, the destination traffic is FCoE. The Cisco UCS 6300 Fabric Interconnect supports FC SPAN only on the ingress side. A Fibre Channel port on a Cisco UCS 6248 Fabric Interconnect cannot be configured as a source port.

A Fibre Channel traffic monitoring session can monitor any source and destination ports listed in Table 13-3.

**Table 13-3**  UCS Fibre Channel Traffic Monitoring Ports

| Source Ports | Destination Ports |
| --- | --- |
| FC port | Fibre Channel uplink port |
| FC port channel | Unconfigured Ethernet port (Cisco UCS 6536, 64108, 6454, 6332, and 6332-16UP Fabric Interconnects) |
| Uplink Fibre Channel port | |
| SAN port channel | |
| VSAN | |
| Service profile vHBA | |
| Fibre Channel storage port | |

When configuring or activating traffic monitoring, consider the following points:

- **Traffic monitoring sessions:** A traffic monitoring session is disabled by default when created. To begin monitoring traffic, first activate the session. A traffic monitoring session must be unique on any fabric interconnect within the Cisco UCS pod. Create each monitoring session with a unique name and unique VLAN source. To monitor traffic from a server, add all vNICs from the service profile corresponding to the server.

**13**

- **Maximum number of supported active traffic monitoring sessions per fabric interconnect:** You can create and store up to 16 traffic monitoring sessions, but only four can be active at the same time. For each Cisco UCS 6454 and 6300 Fabric Interconnect, you can monitor only up to four traffic directions. The receive and transmit directions each count as one monitoring session, while the bidirectional monitoring session is counted as two. For example:

  - Four active sessions: If each session is configured to monitor traffic in only one direction

  - Two active sessions: If each session is configured to monitor traffic bidirectionally

  - Three active sessions: If one session is unidirectional and the second session is bidirectional

**NOTE**  Traffic monitoring can impose a significant load on your system resources. To minimize the load, select sources that carry as little unwanted traffic as possible and disable traffic monitoring when it is not needed.

- **vNIC:** Because a traffic monitoring destination is a single physical port, a traffic monitoring session can monitor only a single fabric. To monitor uninterrupted vNIC traffic across a fabric failover, create two sessions, one per fabric, and connect two analyzers. Add the vNIC as the traffic source using the exact same name for both sessions. If you change the port profile of a virtual machine, any associated vNICs being used as source ports are removed from monitoring, and you must reconfigure the monitoring session. If a traffic monitoring session was configured on a dynamic vNIC under a release earlier than the Cisco UCS Manager Release 2.0, you must reconfigure the traffic monitoring session after upgrading. Cisco UCS 6200 supports traffic monitoring from a vNIC in the transmit direction. However, Cisco UCS 6454 does not support traffic monitoring from a vNIC in the transmit direction.

- **vHBA:** A vHBA can be a source for either an Ethernet or Fibre Channel monitoring session, but it cannot be a source for both simultaneously. When a vHBA is set as the SPAN source, the SPAN destination receives only VN-tagged frames. It does not receive direct FC frames. Cisco UCS 6200 supports traffic monitoring from a vHBA in the transmit direction. However, Cisco UCS 6454 does not support traffic monitoring traffic from a vHBA in the transmit direction.

The following steps show how to create an Ethernet traffic monitoring session:

**Step 1.**    In the Navigation pane, click **LAN**, then from the LAN tab, expand LAN > Traffic Monitoring Sessions > *Fabric_Interconnect_Name*.

**Step 2.** Click **Add** to open the Create Traffic Monitoring Session dialog. Then complete the fields in Table 13-4.

**Table 13-4**    Ethernet Traffic Monitoring Session Fields

| Name | Description |
|---|---|
| Name field | Enter the name of the traffic monitoring session. |
| | This name can be between 1 and 16 alphanumeric characters. You cannot use spaces or any special characters other than the - (hyphen), _ (underscore), : (colon), or . (period), and you cannot change this name after the object is saved. |
| Admin State field | Choose whether traffic will be monitored for the physical port selected in the Destination field. This can be one of the following: |
| | **Enabled:** Cisco UCS begins monitoring the port activity as soon as some source components are added to the session. |
| | **Disabled:** Cisco UCS does not monitor the port activity. |
| Destination drop-down list | Choose the physical port to be monitored. |
| | Click the link in this field to view the port properties. |
| Admin Speed field | Select the data transfer rate of the port channel to be monitored. |
| | The available data rates depend on the fabric interconnect installed in the Cisco UCS domain. For Ethernet traffic monitoring sessions in 6332 and 6332-16UP FIs, you cannot use the 1-Gbps speed configuration for the configured Ethernet destination port. |

**Step 3.** Click **OK** (see Figure 13-11).

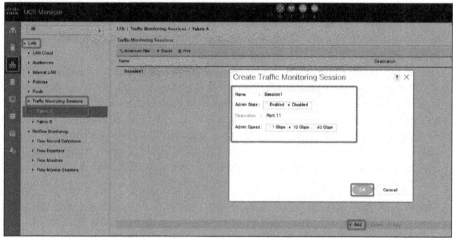

**Figure 13-11**    *Creating a UCS Ethernet Traffic Monitoring Session*

The following steps show how to create a Fibre Channel traffic monitoring session:

**Step 1.** In the Navigation pane, click **SAN**. Then expand SAN > Traffic Monitoring Sessions > *Fabric_Interconnect_Name*.

**Step 2.** Right-click *Fabric_Interconnect_Name* and choose **Create Traffic Monitoring Session**.

**Step 3.**   In the Create Traffic Monitoring Session dialog box, complete the fields shown in Table 13-5.

**Table 13-5**   SAN Traffic Monitoring Session Fields

| Name | Description |
|---|---|
| Name field | Enter a name for the traffic monitoring session.<br><br>This name can be between 1 and 16 alphanumeric characters. You cannot use spaces or any special characters other than the - (hyphen), _ (underscore), : (colon), or . (period), and you cannot change this name after the object is saved. |
| Admin State field | Choose whether traffic will be monitored for the physical port selected in the Destination field. This can be one of the following:<br><br>**Enabled:** Cisco UCS begins monitoring the port activity as soon as some source components are added to the session.<br><br>**Disabled:** Cisco UCS does not monitor the port activity. |
| Destination drop-down list | Select the physical port where you want to monitor all the communication from the sources. |
| Admin Speed drop-down list | Select the data transfer rate of the port channel to be monitored. The available data rates depend on the fabric interconnect installed in the Cisco UCS domain. This can be one of the following:<br><br>1 Gbps<br><br>2 Gbps<br><br>4 Gbps<br><br>8 Gbps<br><br>16 Gbps<br><br>32 Gbps |

**Step 4.**   Click **OK** (see Figure 13-12).

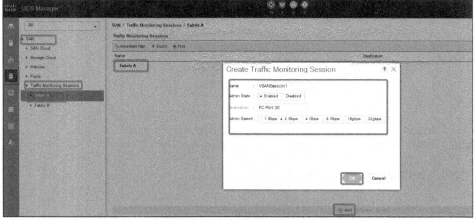

**Figure 13-12**   *Creating UCS SAN Traffic Monitoring Session*

The following steps show how to add traffic sources to a monitoring session. You can choose multiple sources from more than one source type to be monitored by a traffic monitoring session. The available sources depend on the components configured in the Cisco UCS domain.

> **NOTE**   This procedure describes how to add sources for Ethernet traffic monitoring sessions. To add sources for a Fibre Channel monitoring session, select the SAN tab instead of the LAN tab in step 2.

**Step 1.**   Make sure that a traffic monitoring session is created.

**Step 2.**   In the Navigation pane, click **LAN**. Then expand LAN > Traffic Monitoring Sessions > *Fabric_Interconnect_Name*.

**Step 3.**   Expand *Fabric_Interconnect_Name* and click the monitor session that you want to configure. Then in the Work pane, click the **General** tab.

**Step 4.**   In the Sources area, expand the section for the type of traffic source that you want to add.

**Step 5.**   To see the components that are available for monitoring, click the + button to open the Add Monitoring Session Source dialog box.

**Step 6.**   Select a source component and click **OK**. You can repeat the preceding three steps as needed to add multiple sources from multiple source types. Then click **Save** to save the changes (see Figure 13-13).

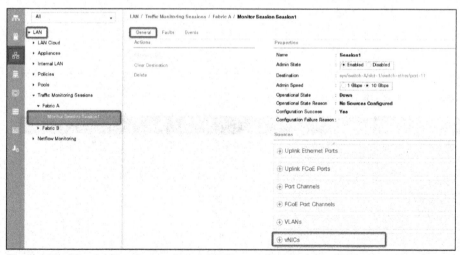

**Figure 13-13**   *Adding Source Port (vNIC) to an Existing Traffic Monitoring Session*

The following steps show how to activate and deactivate a traffic monitoring session.

> **NOTE**   This procedure describes how to activate an Ethernet traffic monitoring session. To activate a Fibre Channel monitoring session, select the SAN tab instead of the LAN tab in step 1.

**Step 1.** In the Navigation pane, click **LAN**. Then expand LAN > Traffic Monitoring Sessions > *Fabric_Interconnect_Name*.

**Step 2.** Expand *Fabric_Interconnect_Name* and click the monitor session that you want to activate or deactivate.

**Step 3.** In the Work pane, click the **General** tab. Then in the Properties area, click the **Enabled** or **Disabled** radio button for Admin State.

**Step 4.** Click **Save Changes** (see Figure 13-14).

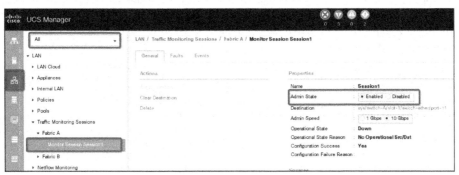

**Figure 13-14** *Activating a Traffic Monitoring Session*

## Cisco Intersight

Cisco Intersight provides intelligent cloud-based infrastructure management, configuration, and orchestration with embedded analytics for the Cisco Unified Computing System (UCS) and Cisco HyperFlex platforms.

Intersight provides management as a service and is designed to be easy to implement and scale. Cisco UCS and Cisco HyperFlex systems are fully programmable infrastructures with a unified API, as illustrated in Figure 13-15. Cisco Intersight is API driven, so the platform and the connected systems are DevOps-enabled to facilitate continuous delivery. Users from operations and development teams can access the platform through portals that are designed for various personas.

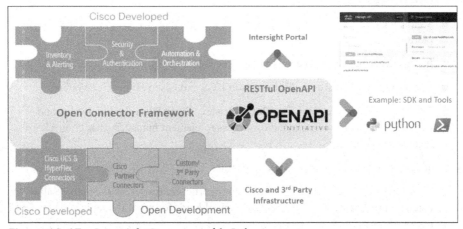

**Figure 13-15** *Intersight Programmable Infrastructure*

This platform enables IT organizations to analyze, simplify, and automate their environments in ways that were not possible with prior generations of tools. This capability empowers organizations to deliver applications faster, so they can support new business initiatives.

Cisco UCS and Cisco HyperFlex platforms use model-based management to provision servers and the associated storage and fabric automatically, regardless of form factor. Cisco Intersight works in conjunction with the Cisco UCS Manager and Cisco Integrated Management Controller. By simply associating a model-based configuration with a resource through server profiles, IT staff can consistently align policy, server personality, and workloads. These policies can be created once and used by IT staff with minimal effort to deploy servers. The result is improved productivity and compliance and lower risk of failures due to inconsistent configuration.

Cisco Intersight is integrated with data center and hybrid-cloud platforms and services to securely deploy and manage infrastructure resources across data center and edge environments. In addition, Cisco provides future integrations to third-party operations tools to allow customers to use their existing solutions more effectively.

Cisco Intersight offers flexible deployment either as Software as a Service (SaaS) on Intersight.com or running on your premises with the Cisco Intersight virtual appliance. The virtual appliance provides users with the benefits of Cisco Intersight while allowing more flexibility for those with additional data locality and security requirements.

## Intersight Management as a Service

Cisco Intersight builds on the Cisco UCS and Cisco HyperFlex platforms to provide an intuitive infrastructure with cloud-powered intelligence. Instead of managing from your own on-site system management console, you can use Cisco's cloud-based management platform at Intersight.com or through the Cisco Intersight virtual appliance. This capability allows you to focus on managing your systems rather than your management tools. It also allows you to take advantage of new features as they become available from Cisco. In addition, Cisco Intersight allows you to manage systems both in your data center and at remote edge and branch office locations.

Following are Cisco Intersight features and benefits:

- Unified management

  - Simplify Cisco UCS and Cisco HyperFlex management with a single management platform.

  - Increase scale across data centers and remote locations without additional complexity.

  - Use a single dashboard to monitor Cisco UCS and Cisco HyperFlex systems.

  - The Cisco UCS Manager, Cisco IMC software, Cisco HyperFlex Connect, and Cisco UCS Director tunneling allow access to element managers that do not have local network access.

- Configuration, provisioning, and server profiles

  - Treat Cisco UCS servers and storage as infrastructure resources that can be allocated and reallocated among application workloads for more dynamic and efficient use of server capacity.

**13**

- Create multiple server profiles with just a few clicks or through the available API, automating the provisioning process.

- Clone profiles to quickly provision Cisco UCS C-Series servers in standalone mode.

- Create, deploy, and manage your Cisco HyperFlex configurations.

- Ensure consistency and eliminate configuration drift, maintaining standardization across many systems.

- Inventory information and status

  - Display and report inventory information for Cisco UCS and Cisco HyperFlex systems.

  - Use global search to rapidly identify systems based on names, identifiers, and other information.

  - Use tagging to associate custom attributes with systems.

  - Monitor Cisco UCS and Cisco HyperFlex server alerts and health status across data centers and remote locations.

  - View your Cisco HyperFlex configurations.

  - Track and manage firmware versions across all connected Cisco UCS and Cisco HyperFlex systems.

  - Track and manage software versions and automated patch updates for all claimed Cisco UCS Director software installations.

- Enhanced support experience

  - Get automated alerts about failure notifications.

  - Automate the generation and forwarding of technical support files to the Cisco Technical Assistance Center to accelerate the troubleshooting process.

- Open API

  - A RESTful API supports the OpenAPI Specification (OAS) to provide full programmability and deep integrations systems.

  - The Python and PowerShell SDKs enable integrations with Ansible, Chef, Puppet, and other DevOps and IT Operations Management (ITOM) tools.

- Seamless integration and upgrades

  - Upgrades are available for Cisco UCS, Cisco HyperFlex systems, and Cisco UCS Director software running supported firmware and software versions.

  - Upgrades to Cisco Intersight are delivered automatically without requiring the resources of traditional management tool upgrades and disruption to your operations.

## Intersight as a Telemetry Data Collection

To support the complex environments created by modern applications and the dramatically increasing number of endpoints, enterprises require analytics integrated tightly with their operations management tools. To enable these analytics capabilities, Cisco UCS servers, Cisco HyperFlex systems, and Cisco UCS Director software are configured to automatically connect and transmit to Cisco Intersight certain telemetry information (including server serial numbers and IP addresses, the types of software installed on an endpoint, and feature use data; see Figure 13-16). This telemetry information will be used to power the Cisco Intersight recommendation engine. The Cisco Intersight recommendation engine will use the telemetry information to proactively review customer metadata to identify potential issues in customers' environments to prevent problems and improve system uptime in the future.

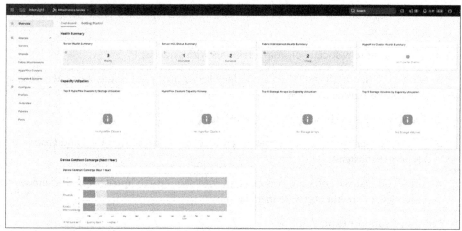

**Figure 13-16** *Intersight Dashboard*

### Cisco Intersight Supported Software

Cisco Intersight supports Cisco UCS and Cisco HyperFlex platforms with the software versions listed in Table 13-6.

**Table 13-6** Supported Software

| Platform | Versions Supported |
|---|---|
| Cisco UCS Fabric Interconnects and connected HyperFlex and UCS B, C, S Series Servers | For 6200 and 6300 Series Fabric Interconnects: Cisco UCS Manager 3.2 and later<br><br>For 6400 Series Fabric Interconnects: Cisco UCS Manager 4.0 and later<br><br>For 6500 Series Fabric Interconnects: Cisco UCS Manager 4.2(2a) and later |
| Cisco UCS C-Series Standalone and HyperFlex HX-Series Edge Servers | For M7 Servers: Cisco IMC Software 4.3(1) and later; recommended version 4.3(1.230124)<br><br>For M6 Servers: Cisco IMC Software 4.2 and later<br><br>For M5 Servers: Cisco IMC Software 3.1 and later<br><br>For M4 Servers: Cisco IMC Software 3.0(4) and later |

| Platform | Versions Supported |
|---|---|
| Cisco UCS S3260 Standalone Servers | Cisco IMC Software 4.0(4e) and later |
| Cisco HyperFlex Clusters | Requires HyperFlex Data Platform 4.0(2e) and later for Cisco HyperFlex Connect launch |
| Cisco UCS Director | Cisco UCS Director 6.6.0.0 and later |
| Dell PowerEdge Servers | iDRAC v5.10.00.0 and later |
| HPE ProLiant Servers | iLO 5 version 2.55 and later |
| NetApp AFF-Series, FAS-Series, All SAN Arrays | ONTAP version 9.7p1 and later |
| NetApp Active IQ Unified Manager for NetApp ONTAP | Latest version of AIQUM is required (currently 9.12 GA) |
| Pure Storage FlashArray | Purity version FA 4.8 to FA 6.0.2 (REST API 1.x only)<br><br>Purity version FA 6.0.3 or later (REST API 1.x and REST API 2.x) |
| VMware vCenter | 6.5, 6.7, and 7.0 |
| Hitachi Ops Center API Configuration Manager | 10.1.0-00 and later |
| Cisco Nexus Switch | Supported devices:<br>Cisco Nexus 9200 Series<br>Cisco Nexus 9300 Series<br>Cisco Nexus 9400 Series<br>Cisco Nexus 9500 Series<br>Cisco Nexus 9800 Series<br><br>Certified devices:<br>N9K-C9332PQ<br>N9K-C9336C-FX2<br>N9K-C9372PX<br>N9K-C9396TX<br>N9K-C93108TC-EX<br>N9K-C93120TX<br>N9K-C93128TX<br>N9K-93180YC-EX<br>N9K-C93180YC-FX<br>N9K-C93600CD-GX<br>N9K-C93360YC-FX2<br>N9K-C9316D-GX<br>N9K-C9516<br>N9K-C9504<br>Requires NX-OS Release 9.3(9) or later. |

13

| Platform | Versions Supported |
|---|---|
| Cisco MDS Switch | Supported devices: |
| | Cisco MDS 9100 Series |
| | Cisco MDS 9200 Series |
| | Cisco MDS 9300 Series |
| | Cisco MDS 9700 Series |
| | |
| | Certified devices: |
| | DS-C9132T-MEK9 |
| | DS-C9132T-MIK9 |
| | DS-C9148S-K9 |
| | DS-C9148T-K9 |
| | DS-C9396S-K9 |
| | DS-C9396T-K9 |
| | Requires NX-OS Release 8.4(2a) or later. |

## Cisco Intersight Licensing

Cisco Intersight uses a subscription-based license for the following services:

- **Infrastructure Service and Cloud Orchestrator:** The services to manage Cisco endpoints such as the Cisco UCS server and Cisco HyperFlex system.

- **Cisco Nexus Cloud:** The service to manage your cloud-native and hybrid-cloud data center environments.

- **Workload Optimizer:** The service to optimize workloads across the hybrid infrastructure containers.

The Infrastructure Service and Cloud Orchestrator service use a subscription-based license with multiple tiers.

The Cisco Intersight Infrastructure Services, used to manage and monitor Cisco UCS servers, Cisco HyperFlex systems, and Cisco UCS Director software, licensing model, offer the following two tiers:

- **Cisco Intersight Infrastructure Services Essentials:** The Essentials license tier offers server management with global health monitoring, inventory, proactive support through Cisco TAC integration, multifactor authentication, along with SDK and API access.

- **Cisco Intersight Infrastructure Services Advantage:** The Advantage license tier offers advanced server management with extended visibility, ecosystem integration, and automation of Cisco and third-party hardware and software, along with multidomain solutions.

Table 13-7 shows the differences between the Cisco Infrastructure Services license tiers for Cisco Intersight.

**Table 13-7**    Cisco Intersight Infrastructure Services License Tiers

| Category | Feature | Essentials | Advantage |
|---|---|---|---|
| Lifecycle Operations | Global Monitoring and Inventory | Yes | Yes |
| | Custom Dashboards | Yes | Yes |
| | Policy-based Configuration with Server Profiles | Yes | Yes |
| | Firmware Management | Yes | Yes |
| | HCL for Compliance | Yes | Yes |
| | Third-party Server Ops | Yes | Yes |
| | UCS-Manager and UCS-Central Entitlements | Yes | Yes |
| Proactive Support | Proactive RMA | Yes | Yes |
| | Connected TAC | Yes | Yes |
| | Advisories | Yes | Yes |
| | Sustainability (Power Policy Management for Servers, BIOS and OS, Dynamic Power Rebalancing) | Yes | Yes |
| In-Platform Automation | Tunneled vKVM | | Yes |
| | Operating System Install Automation | | Yes |
| | Storage/Virtualization/Network Automation | | Yes |
| | Workflow Designer | | Yes |
| Ecosystem Integrations | Ecosystem Visibility and Operations, Network (Nexus, MDS), Storage (NetApp, Pure Storage, Hitachi, Cohesity), Hybrid Cloud (VMware, Red Hat), Automation (Ansible, Terraform) | | Yes |
| | ITOM Integrations (ServiceNow) | | Yes |

The following steps show the procedure for adding UCS to Cisco Intersight:

**Step 1.**    Log in to Cisco Intersight using the Chrome browser (see Figure 13-17).

**Step 2.**    To add Cisco UCS to Intersight, you need the UCS Manager device ID and device claim code. To get these, you need to log in to the UCS Manager then expand Admin > Device Connecter > Connection (see Figure 13-18).

**Figure 13-17**  *Logging In to Cisco Intersight*

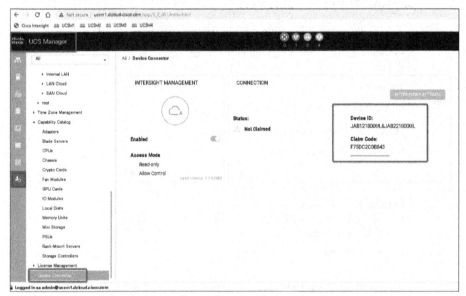

**Figure 13-18**  *UCS Manager Device ID and Device Claim Code*

**NOTE**   The Device claim code is a token, and its value changes about every 60 seconds. You need to make sure you have the latest code.

**Step 3.**    To add a new UCS device in Cisco Intersight, go to **System >Admin > Targets**, click **Claim a New Target** (see Figure 13-19). You also need to get the UCS device ID and device claim code (from step 2). Then click **Direct Claim**.

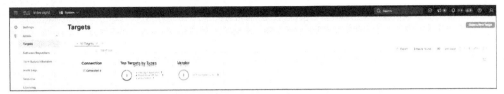

**Figure 13-19**  *Cisco Intersight Claim Target*

**Step 4.**  Select what target you are going to add (see Figure 13-20).

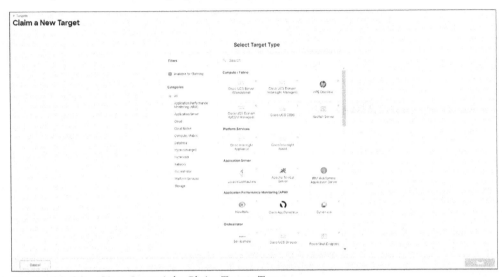

**Figure 13-20**  *Cisco Intersight Claim Target Type*

**Step 5.**  Add the Device ID and Claim code for the Cisco UCS Manager (see Figure 13-21).

**Figure 13-21**  *Adding the Cisco UCS Manager as a Target in Cisco Intersight*

**Step 6.**  Verify the Cisco UCS's inventory and alerts from **Infrastructure Service > Servers** and select the newly added Cisco UCS Manager (see Figure 13-22). Make sure all servers are listed and can be managed from the Intersight dashboard.

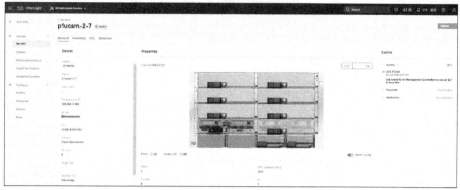

**Figure 13-22**  *Cisco UCS Manager in Cisco Intersight*

## Exam Preparation Tasks

As mentioned in the Introduction, you have a couple of choices for exam preparation: the exercises here, Chapter 21, "Final Preparation," and the exam simulation questions in the Pearson Test Prep Software Online.

## Review All Key Topics

Review the most important topics in the chapter, noted with the key topic icon in the outer margin of the page. Table 13-8 lists a reference to these key topics and the page numbers on which each is found.

**Table 13-8**  Key Topics for Chapter 13

| Key Topic Element | Description | Page |
|---|---|---|
| Section | Cisco UCS Monitoring Events and Logs | 632 |
| Figure 13-2 | UCS Syslog Configurations | 633 |
| Figure 13-4 | UCS Audit Logs | 634 |
| Figure 13-7 | UCS SNMP Configuration Example | 636 |
| Section | Cisco UCS Manager Database Health and Hardware Monitoring | 638 |
| Section | Cisco UCS NetFlow Monitoring | 638 |
| Figure 13-9 | UCS Hardware Health Report | 639 |
| Section | Traffic Monitoring | 640 |
| Section | Traffic Monitoring Across Ethernet | 641 |
| Table 13-2 | UCS Ethernet Traffic Monitoring Ports | 641 |
| Table 13-3 | UCS Fibre Channel Traffic Monitoring Ports | 642 |
| Section | Intersight Management as a Service | 648 |
| Section | Intersight as a Telemetry Data Collection | 650 |
| Section | Cisco Intersight Licensing | 652 |
| Table 13-7 | Cisco Intersight Infrastructure Services License Tiers | 653 |
| List | Adding Cisco UCS Manager to Intersight | 653 |

## Define Key Terms

Define the following key terms from this chapter and check your answers in the Glossary.

application programming interface (API), Cisco Integrated Management Controller (CIMC), Cisco Nexus, Cisco NX-OS, DevOps, dual in-line memory module (DIMM), Extensible Markup Language (XML), nonvolatile random-access memory (NVRAM), Software as a Service (SaaS), software development kit (SDK), system event log (SEL), trusted platform module (TPM), UCS Manager (UCSM), virtual interface card (VIC), virtual storage-area network (VSAN)

## References

Cisco UCS Manager: https://www.cisco.com/c/en/us/support/servers-unified-computing/ucs-manager/series.html

Cisco Intersight Help Center: https://intersight.com/help/saas/home

# CHAPTER 14

# Cisco Unified Compute Software and Configuration Management

Cisco Unified compute software and configuration management will help an operation to easily back up system configurations and firmware upgrades. Any computer hardware can fail or be lost due to natural disasters. If that happens, the operation will lose all configurations and will require an extensive and time-consuming process to recover computers. A backup can help you restore or replace them in a short time.

This chapter discusses configuration backup/restore and firmware upgrade aspects of the Cisco UCS family relevant to the certification exam. It is assumed that you are familiar with the Cisco UCS product family.

### This chapter covers the following key topics:

**Cisco UCS Configuration Management:** This section covers UCS configuration backup and restore methods and policies and provides examples.

**UCS Firmware and Software Updates:** This section covers UCS firmware and software updates using the Cisco Unified Computing System (UCS) Manager and Cisco Integrated Management Controller (CIMC) and provides examples.

## "Do I Know This Already?" Quiz

The "Do I Know This Already?" quiz enables you to assess whether you should read this entire chapter thoroughly or jump to the "Exam Preparation Tasks" section. If you are in doubt about your answers to these questions or your own assessment of your knowledge of the topics, read the entire chapter. Table 14-1 lists the major headings in this chapter and their corresponding "Do I Know This Already?" quiz questions. You can find the answers in Appendix A, "Answers to the 'Do I Know This Already?' Quizzes."

**Table 14-1** "Do I Know This Already?" Section-to-Question Mapping

| Foundation Topics Section | Questions |
|---|---|
| Cisco UCS Configuration Management | 1–3 |
| UCS Firmware and Software Updates | 4–5 |

1. What are the types of Cisco UCS backup policies? (Choose two answers.)
   a. All Configuration
   b. Incremental backup
   c. Full State
   d. Differential backup

2. A UCS administrator deleted two service profiles by mistake. Now you need to restore them from your daily backup. What type of backup will have service profiles?
   a. All Configuration
   b. Full State
   c. Logical Configuration
   d. System Configuration

3. What are the two import types supported by the Cisco UCS Manager? (Choose two answers.)
   a. Merge
   b. Incremental
   c. Differentiator
   d. Replace

4. You cannot use Auto Install to upgrade the infrastructure components to one version of Cisco UCS and upgrade the chassis and server components to a different version.
   a. True
   b. False

5. You cannot cancel a server firmware upgrade process after you complete the configuration in the Install Server Firmware wizard because the Cisco UCS Manager applies the changes immediately.
   a. True
   b. False

## Foundation Topics

# Cisco UCS Configuration Management

Cisco UCS configuration management allows you to perform a backup through the Cisco UCS Manager. You can take a snapshot of all or part of the system configuration and export that file to a location on your network. You cannot use the Cisco UCS Manager to back up data on the servers; however, you can perform a backup while the system is up and running. The backup operation saves information only from the management plane. It does not have any impact on the server or network traffic.

As with any backup operation, before you start the backup, you need to consider the following factors:

- **Backup locations:** The backup location is the destination or folder on the network where you want the Cisco UCS Manager to export the backup file. You can maintain only one backup operation for each location where you plan to save a backup file.

- **Potential to overwrite backup files:** If you rerun a backup operation without changing the filename, the Cisco UCS Manager overwrites the existing file on the server. To avoid overwriting existing backup files, you need to change the filename in the backup operation or copy the existing file to another location.

- **Backup type:** You can run and export more than one type of backup to the same location. The UCS Manager supports the following types:

    - **Full State:** A binary file that includes a snapshot of the entire system. You can use the file generated from this backup to restore the system during disaster recovery. This file can restore or rebuild the configuration on the original fabric interconnect or re-create the configuration on a different fabric interconnect. You cannot use this file for an import.

**NOTE** You can only use a full state backup file to restore a system that is running the same version as the system from which the backup file was exported.

    - **All Configuration:** An XML file that includes all system and logical configuration settings. You can use the file generated from this backup to import these configuration settings to the original fabric interconnect or to a different fabric interconnect. You cannot use this file for a system restore. This file does not include passwords for locally authenticated users.

    - **System Configuration:** An XML file that includes all system configuration settings such as usernames, roles, and locales. You can use the file generated from this backup to import these configuration settings to the original fabric interconnect or to a different fabric interconnect. You cannot use this file for a system restore.

■ **Logical Configuration:** An XML file that includes all logical configuration settings such as service profiles, VLANs, VSANs, pools, and policies. You can use the file generated from this backup to import these configuration settings to the original fabric interconnect or to a different fabric interconnect. You cannot use this file for a system restore.

You should change the backup type before you rerun the backup operation. It is a good practice to change the filename for easier identification and to avoid overwriting the existing backup file.

> **NOTE**  Incremental backups are not supported.

■ **Backup schedules:** You can create a backup operation in advance and leave the admin state disabled until you are ready to run the backup. The Cisco UCS Manager does not run the backup operation, save, or export the configuration file until you set the admin state of the backup operation to Enabled.

■ **Encryption of full state backups:** Full state backups are encrypted so that passwords and other sensitive information are not exported as clear text.

### Creating and Running a Backup Operation

The following steps show how to create a new backup operation:

**Step 1.** In the Navigation pane, click **Admin > All**. In the Work pane, click the **General** tab. In the Actions area, click **Backup Configuration**.

**Step 2.** In the Backup Configuration dialog box, click **Create Backup Operation**.

**Step 3.** In the Create Backup Operation dialog box, complete the fields shown in Table 14-2. Then click **OK** (see Figure 14-1).

**Table 14-2**  Backup Operation Creation Fields

| Name | Description |
|---|---|
| Admin State field | This can be one of the following:<br><br>**Enabled:** The Cisco UCS Manager runs the backup operation as soon as you click OK.<br><br>**Disabled:** The Cisco UCS Manager does not run the backup operation when you click OK. If you select this option, all fields in the dialog box remain visible. However, you must manually run the backup from the Backup Configuration dialog box. |
| Type field | The information saved in the backup configuration file. This can be one of the following:<br><br>Full State<br><br>All Configuration<br><br>System Configuration<br><br>Logical Configuration |

| Name | Description |
|---|---|
| Preserve Identities check box | This check box remains selected for an All Configuration or System Configuration type of backup operation and provides the following functionality: |
| | **All Configuration:** The backup file preserves all identities derived from pools, including vHBAs, WWPNs, WWNN, vNICs, MACs, and UUIDs. Also, the identities for chassis, FEX, rack servers, and user labels for chassis, FEX, rack servers, I/O modules, and blade servers are preserved. |
| | **NOTE:** If this check box is not selected, the identities will be reassigned and user labels will be lost after a restore. |
| | **System Configuration:** The backup file preserves identities for chassis, FEX, rack servers and user labels for chassis, FEX, rack servers, I/O modules, and blade servers. |
| | **NOTE:** If this check box is not selected, the identities will be reassigned and user labels will be lost after a restore. |
| | **Logical Configuration:** If this check box is selected for the Logical Configuration type of backup operation, the backup file preserves all identities derived from pools, including vHBAs, WWPNs, WWNN, vNICs, MACs, and UUIDs. |
| | **NOTE:** If this check box is not selected, the identities will be reassigned and user labels will be lost after a restore. |
| Location of the Backup File field | Where the backup file should be saved. This can be one of the following: |
| | **Remote File System:** The backup XML file is saved to a remote server. The Cisco UCS Manager GUI displays the following fields that allow you to specify the protocol, host, filename, username, and password for the remote system. |
| | **Local File System:** The backup XML file is saved locally. |
| | The HTML-based Cisco UCS Manager GUI displays the Filename field. Enter a name for the backup file in *<filename>*.xml format. The file is downloaded and saved to a location depending on your browser settings. |
| Protocol field | The protocol to use when communicating with the remote server. This can be one of the following: |
| | FTP |
| | TFTP |
| | SCP |
| | SFTP |
| | USB A: The USB drive inserted into fabric interconnect A. This option is available only for certain system configurations. |
| | USB B: The USB drive inserted into fabric interconnect B. This option is available only for certain system configurations. |
| Hostname field | The host name, IPv4, or IPv6 address of the location where the backup file is stored. This can be a server, storage array, local drive, or any read/write media that the fabric interconnect can access through the network. |

| Name | Description |
|------|-------------|
| | **NOTE:** If you use a host name rather than an IPv4 or IPv6 address, you must configure a DNS server. If the Cisco UCS domain is not registered with Cisco UCS Central or DNS management is set to Local, configure a DNS server in the Cisco UCS Manager. If the Cisco UCS domain is registered with Cisco UCS Central and DNS management is set to Global, configure a DNS server in Cisco UCS Central. |
| Remote File field | The full path to the backup configuration file. This field can contain the filename as well as the path. If you omit the filename, the backup procedure assigns a name to the file. |
| User field | The username the system should use to log in to the remote server. This field does not apply if the protocol is TFTP or USB. |
| Password field | The password for the remote server username. This field does not apply if the protocol is TFTP or USB. |
| | The Cisco UCS Manager does not store this password. Therefore, you do not need to enter this password unless you intend to enable and run the backup operation immediately. |

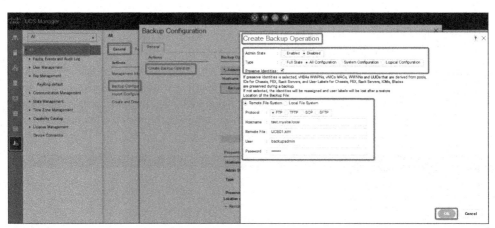

**Figure 14-1**   *Backup Creation Snapshot*

**Step 4.**   If the Cisco UCS Manager displays a confirmation dialog box, click **OK**. If you set the Admin State field to Enabled, the Cisco UCS Manager takes a snapshot of the configuration type that you selected and exports the file to the network location. The backup operation is displayed in the Backup Operations table in the Backup Configuration dialog box.

**Step 5.**   (Optional) To view the progress of the backup operation, do the following:

If the operation is not displayed in the Properties area, click the operation in the Backup Operations table. In the Properties area, click the down arrows on the FSM Details bar. The FSM Details area expands and displays the operation status (see Figure 14-2).

**Figure 14-2**   *UCS Current Backup Operation*

**Step 6.**   Click **OK** to close the Backup Configuration dialog box.

The backup operation will not start if the admin state is set to Disable during the creation. To run the backup operations, follow these steps:

**Step 1.**   In the Navigation pane, click **Admin > All**. In the Work pane, click the **General** tab. In the Actions area, click **Backup Configuration**. In the Backup Operations table of the Backup Configuration dialog box, click the backup operation that you want to run. The details of the selected backup operation are displayed in the Properties area, as shown in Figure 14-3.

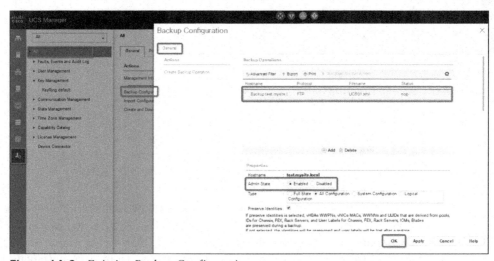

**Figure 14-3**   *Existing Backup Configurations*

**Step 2.**   In the Properties area, complete the fields shown in Table 14-3.

**Table 14-3**   Backup Running Fields

| Name | Description |
|---|---|
| Admin State field | This can be one of the following:<br>**Enabled:** The Cisco UCS Manager runs the backup operation as soon as you click OK. |
| Protocol field | You need to enter the password for the username in the Password field for the following protocols:<br>FTP<br>SCP<br>SFTP |
| (Optional) | Change the content of the other available fields that configured during backup creation<br>**NOTE:** If you change other fields—such as resetting a scheduled backup from weekly to daily—you must re-enter your username and password. Otherwise, an FI backup will fail. |

**Step 3.**   Click **Apply.** The Cisco UCS Manager takes a snapshot of the configuration type that you selected and exports the file to the network location. The backup operation is displayed in the Backup Operations table in the Backup Configuration dialog box.

**Step 4.**   (Optional) To view the progress of the backup operation, click the down arrows on the FSM Details bar. The FSM Details area expands and displays the operation status (see Figure 14-4). Click **OK** to close the Backup Configuration dialog box.

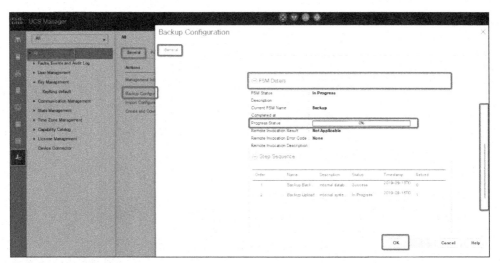

**Figure 14-4**   *Backup Status*

The backup operation continues to run until it is completed. To view the progress, reopen the Backup Configuration dialog box, as shown in Figure 14-4.

## Backup Policies

You can automate the backup by using backup polices. Policies will schedule the backup job to run regularly at a certain time without administrative involvement.

There are two types of backup polices:

■ All Configuration

■ Full State

## Backup Policy Configuration

To configure a backup policy, follow these steps:

**Step 1.**   In the Navigation pane, click **Admin > All**. In the Work pane, click the **Backup and Export Policy** tab.

**Step 2.**   For a Full State Backup, complete the fields under Full State Backup Policy. For an All Configuration, complete only the fields under All Configuration Backup Policy, as shown in Figure 14-5 and Table 14-4.

**Figure 14-5**   *Backup Policy Configuration*

**Table 14-4**   Policy Backup and Export Fields

| Name | Description |
|---|---|
| Hostname field | The host name, IPv4, or IPv6 address of the location where the policy backup file is stored. This can be a server, storage array, local drive, or any read/write media that the fabric interconnect can access through the network. |
| | **NOTE:** If you use a host name rather than an IPv4 or IPv6 address, you must configure a DNS server. If the Cisco UCS domain is not registered with Cisco UCS Central or DNS management is set to Local, configure a DNS server in the Cisco UCS Manager. If the Cisco UCS domain is registered with Cisco UCS Central and DNS management is set to Global, configure a DNS server in Cisco UCS Central. |
| Protocol field | The protocol to use when communicating with the remote server. This can be one of the following: |
| | FTP |
| | TFTP |
| | SCP |
| | SFTP |
| | USB A: The USB drive inserted into fabric interconnect A. This option is available only for certain system configurations. |
| | USB B: The USB drive inserted into fabric interconnect B. This option is available only for certain system configurations. |
| User field | The username the system should use to log in to the remote server. This field does not apply if the protocol is TFTP or USB. |
| Password field | The password for the remote server username. This field does not apply if the protocol is TFTP or USB. |
| Remote File field | The full path to the policy backup file. This field can contain the filename as well as the path. If you omit the filename, the backup procedure assigns a name to the file. |
| Admin State field | This can be one of the following: |
| | **Enable:** The Cisco UCS Manager backs up all policy information using the schedule specified in the Schedule field. |
| | **Disable:** The Cisco UCS Manager does not back up policy information. |
| Schedule field | The frequency with which the Cisco UCS Manager backs up policy information. |
| Max Files field | The maximum number of backup files that the Cisco UCS Manager maintains. This value cannot be changed. |
| Description field | The description of the backup policy. The default description is Database Backup Policy. |
| | You can enter up to 256 characters using any characters or spaces except ` (accent mark), \ (backslash), ^ (caret), " (double quote), = (equal sign), > (greater than), < (less than), or ' (single quote). |

14

**Step 3.** (Optional) In the Backup/Export Config Reminder area, complete the fields as shown in Figure 14-6 and Table 14-5.

**Table 14-5** Backup Policy Reminder Options

| Name | Description |
|------|-------------|
| Admin State column | This can be one of the following:<br>**Enable:** The Cisco UCS Manager raises a fault if a backup is not taken during the specified time period.<br>**Disable:** The Cisco UCS Manager does not raise a fault if a backup is not taken during the specified time period. |
| Remind Me After (days) column | The number of days before you are reminded to make a backup. Enter an integer between 1 and 365. The default value is 30 days. |

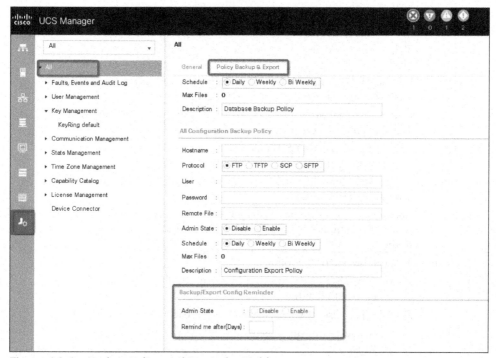

**Figure 14-6** *Backup Policy and Reminder Fields*

**Step 4.** Click **Save Changes** to save the configuration.

## Import Backups

The Cisco UCS Manager supports two methods to import backup data. You can use one of the following methods to import and update a system configuration through Cisco UCS:

■ **Merge:** The information in the imported configuration file is compared with the existing configuration information. If there are conflicts, the import operation overwrites the information on the Cisco UCS domain with the information in the import configuration file.

■ **Replace:** The current configuration information is replaced with the information in the imported configuration file one object at a time.

### Enable the Import Operation

You cannot import a full state backup file. You can import any of the following configuration files:

■ All Configuration

■ System Configuration

■ Logical Configuration

The import backup operation procedure is as follows:

**Step 1.** In the Navigation pane, click **Admin > All**. In the Work pane, click the **General** tab. In the Actions area, click **Import Configuration**.

**Step 2.** In the Import Operations table of the Import Configuration dialog box, click the operation that you want to run. The details of the selected import operation are displayed in the Properties area.

**Step 3.** In the Properties area, complete the fields as shown in Table 14-6.

**Table 14-6** Backup Modification Fields

| Name | Description |
|------|-------------|
| Admin State field | This can be one of the following: **Enabled:** The Cisco UCS Manager runs the backup operation as soon as you click OK. |
| Protocol field | You need to enter the password for the username in the Password field for the following protocols: FTP SCP SFTP |
| (Optional) | Change the content of the other available fields |

**Step 4.** Click **Apply**. The Cisco UCS Manager imports the configuration file from the network location. Depending on which action you selected, the information in the file is either merged with the existing configuration or replaces the existing configuration. The import operation is displayed in the Import Operations table of the Import Configuration dialog box (see Figure 14-7).

**Step 5.** (Optional) To view the progress of the import operation, click the down arrows on the FSM Details bar. The FSM Details area expands and displays the operation status.

**Step 6.** Click **OK** to close the Import Configuration dialog box.

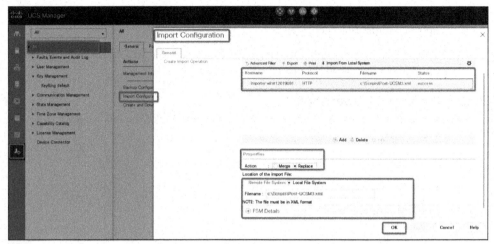

**Figure 14-7**  *UCS Backup Import Configurations*

The import operation continues to run until it is completed. To view the progress, reopen the Import Configuration dialog box.

### System Restore

You can use the restore function for disaster recovery. You can restore a system configuration from any full state backup file that was exported from Cisco UCS. The file does not need to have been exported from Cisco UCS on the system that you are restoring. When you are restoring using a backup file that was exported from a different system, we recommend that you use a system with the same or similar system configuration and hardware, including fabric interconnects, servers, adapters, and I/O module or FEX connectivity. Mismatched hardware and system configurations can lead to the restored system not fully functioning. If there is a mismatch between the I/O module links or servers on the two systems, acknowledge the chassis and servers after the restore operation.

In Cisco UCS Manager Release 4.0(1) and later releases, if a full state backup is collected on a UCS 6200 Series Fabric Interconnect with the following unsupported features, then full state restore cannot be used to restore this file on a Cisco UCS 6454 Fabric Interconnect:

■ Chassis Discovery Policy and Chassis Connectivity Policy are in non port-channel mode.

■ Switching mode is either Ethernet or FC.

■ Virtual Machine Management is enabled - VMware, Linux KVM, or Microsoft Hypervisor.

**NOTE**  You can only use a full state backup file to restore a system that is running the same version as the system from which the backup file was exported.

## Restoring the Configuration for a Fabric Interconnect

It is recommended that you use a full state backup file to restore a system that is running the same version as the system from which the backup file was exported. You can also use a full state backup to restore a system if they have the same release train. For example, you can use a full state backup taken from a system running Release 4.0(2a) to restore a system running Release 4.0(4d).

To avoid issues with VSAN or VLAN configuration, you should restore a backup on the fabric interconnect that was the primary fabric interconnect at the time of backup.

You will need to collect the following information before you start to restore the system configuration:

- Fabric interconnect management port IPv4 address and subnet mask, or IPv6 address and prefix

- Default gateway IPv4 or IPv6 address

- Backup server IPv4 or IPv6 address and authentication credentials

- Fully qualified name of a full state backup file

**NOTE**   You must have access to a full state configuration file to perform a system restore. You cannot perform a system restore with any other type of configuration or backup file.

The system restoration procedure is as follows:

**Step 1.**   Connect to the console port. If the fabric interconnect is off, power on the fabric interconnect. You will see the power-on self-test message as the fabric interconnect boots.

**Step 2.**   At the installation method prompt, enter **GUI**. If the system cannot access a DHCP server, you may be prompted to enter the information as shown in Table 14-7.

**Table 14-7**   Fabric Interconnect Management Fields

| Name | Description |
| --- | --- |
| IP address | The IPv4 or IPv6 address for the management port on the fabric interconnect. |
| Subnet Mask or Prefix | Subnet mask or prefix for the management port on the fabric interconnect. |
| Default Gateway | The IPv4 or IPv6 address for the default gateway assigned to the fabric interconnect. |

**Step 3.**   Copy the web link from the prompt into a web browser and go to the Cisco UCS Manager GUI launch page. On the launch page, select **Express Setup** and then **Restore From Backup**. Click **Submit**.

**Step 4.**    In the Protocol area of the Cisco UCS Manager Initial Setup page, select the protocol you want to use to upload the full state backup file:

- SCP

- TFTP

- FTP

- SFTP

**Step 5.**    In the Server Information area, complete the fields shown in Table 14-8.

**Table 14-8**    Server Information Fields

| Name | Description |
|------|-------------|
| Server IP | The IP address of the computer where the full state backup file is located. This can be a server, storage array, local drive, or any read/write media that the fabric interconnect can access through the network. |
| Backup File Path | Backup File Path, the file path where the full state backup file is located, including the folder names and filename. |
|  | **NOTE:** You can only use a full state backup file to restore a system that is running the same version as the system from which the backup file was exported. |
| User ID | The username the system should use to log in to the remote server. This field does not apply if the protocol is TFTP or USB. |
| Password | The password for the remote server username. This field does not apply if the protocol is TFTP. |

**Step 6.**    Click **Submit**.

You can return to the console to watch the progress of the system restore.

The fabric interconnect logs in to the backup server, retrieves a copy of the specified full state backup file, and restores the system configuration.

For a cluster configuration, you do not need to restore the secondary fabric interconnect. As soon as the secondary fabric interconnect reboots, the Cisco UCS Manager synchronizes the configuration with the primary fabric interconnect.

# UCS Firmware and Software Updates

The firmware is the program that controls the operation and functionality of various UCS components. It is the combination of software and hardware that has program code and data stored in it in order for the device to function. Upgrading the firmware improves the performance of the UCS, which could provide enhanced security, new features, and bug fixes.

Cisco UCS contains many different hardware components. Each component will have firmware. UCS firmware can be categorized as one of four types:

- **Infrastructure software bundle:** This bundle is also called the *A bundle*. It contains the firmware images that the fabric interconnects, I/O modules, and the Cisco UCS Manager require to function.

■ **B-Series server software bundle:** Also called the *B bundle*, this bundle contains the firmware images that the B-Series blade servers require to function, such as adapter, BIOS, CIMC, and board controller firmware. The "Release Bundle Contents for Cisco UCS Manager, Release 4.0" provides details about the contents of the B-Series server software bundle.

> **NOTE**   Starting with Cisco UCS Manager Release 3.1(2), the firmware for endpoints that are common to both the B-Series and C-Series server software bundles, such as local disk, is available in both the B-Series and C-Series server software bundles.

■ **C-Series server software bundle:** Also called the *C bundle*, this bundle contains the firmware images that the C-Series rack-mount servers require to function, such as adapter, BIOS, CIMC, and board controller firmware. The C bundle also contains the firmware images for Cisco UCS S3260 storage servers. The "Release Bundle Contents for Cisco UCS Manager, Release 4.0" provides details about the contents of the C-Series server software bundle.

■ **Capability catalog software bundle:** Also called the *T bundle*, this bundle specifies implementation-specific tunable parameters, hardware specifics, and feature limits. The capability catalog is an asset of tunable parameters, strings, and rules. Cisco UCS uses the catalog to update the display and configurability of components such as newly qualified DIMMs and disk drives for servers. The catalog is divided by hardware components, such as the chassis, CPU, local disk, and I/O module. You can use the catalog to view the list of providers available for that component. There is one provider per hardware component. Each provider is identified by the vendor, model (PID), and revision. For each provider, you can also view details of the equipment manufacturer and the form factor.

The capability catalog includes the following contents:

■ Implementation-specific tunable parameters

   ■ Power and thermal constraints

   ■ Slot ranges and numbering

   ■ Adapter capacities

■ Hardware-specific rules

   ■ Firmware compatibility for components such as the BIOS, CIMC, RAID controller, and adapters

   ■ Diagnostics

   ■ Hardware-specific reboot

- User display strings

  - Part numbers, such as the CPN, PID/VID

  - Component descriptions

  - Physical layout/dimensions

  - OEM information

If you want to achieve maximum UCS efficiency with the new UCS manager updates, Cisco recommends that you upgrade UCS hardware firmware. One of the many benefits of UCS is the ease with which firmware upgrades/downgrades can be applied. The Cisco UCS Manager simplifies this process by utilizing an auto-install procedure that takes a lot of the manual firmware application out of the equation.

Beginning with Cisco UCS Manager Release 4.0(1), Cisco released unified Cisco UCS Manager software and firmware upgrades for each of the following platforms with every release of the Cisco UCS Manager:

- Cisco UCS 6454 Fabric Interconnect with Cisco UCS B-Series and C-Series servers

- Cisco UCS 6300 Series Fabric Interconnect with Cisco UCS B-Series and C-Series servers

- Cisco UCS 6200 Series Fabric Interconnect with Cisco UCS B-Series and C-Series servers

- Cisco UCS 6324 Fabric Interconnect with Cisco UCS B-Series and C-Series servers, which is also known as UCS Mini

The upgrade order for the endpoints in a Cisco UCS domain depends on the upgrade path. Cisco maintains a set of best practices for managing firmware images and updates.

Here are some best practices to consider when you manage images:

- Before you perform firmware updates, use the UCS Manager image management interfaces to download relevant images to the fabric interconnect.

- The Cisco UCS Manager maintains an inventory of available firmware images.

- Images are stored in the /bootflash partition in the fabric interconnect.

- The /bootflash partition is dedicated solely to firmware images managed by the UCS Manager.

- Each fabric interconnect ships preloaded with one firmware package.

- Faults are raised when the /bootflash partition exceeds 70 percent and 90 percent capacity.

- Each image represents an individual firmware package specific to one hardware component—for example, I/O module image, BMC image, and UCS Manager image.

- Multiple images are bundled together to form an image package.

- An image package is meant only for ease of distribution and download.

- Unlike an individual image, image packages do not have versions.

- Cisco publishes both individual images and image packages.

Here are some best practices to consider when you download images:

- The Cisco UCS Manager allows you to download both individual images and image packages.

- You can use these SCP, FTP, SFTP, and TFTP to transfer images to the Cisco UCS.

- Image download can be initiated from the UCS command-line interface (CLI) and graphical user interface (GUI):

  - To download the image from the CLI, use the **download image** command in scope firmware mode.

  - In the GUI, click **Installed Firmware** under Equipment.

- A download task is created that can be used to monitor the download progress; use the **show download-task** command.

- When you download a package, the package is unpacked, and individual images are extracted from it.

- The same image can be downloaded multiple times.

- A failed (or successful) download task can be restarted.

  - In the CLI, use the **restart** command in scope download-task mode or execute the same download command again to start the download process.

  - In the GUI, click the **Restart** link under Download Task to resume the download process.

- Download tasks can be deleted at any time. When you delete a download task, downloaded images are not deleted.

Here are some best practices to consider when you delete images:

- You can use the UCS Manager GUI or the CLI to remove unused images.

- Image deletion is asynchronous. When the administrator removes an image, the object is marked as Deleted. The delete process is performed in the background.

- In the case of an HA cluster, images are automatically deleted on both fabric interconnects.

- Packages are read-only, and they cannot be deleted.

- You can delete multiple images in either the UCS Manager GUI or CLI:

  - Select multiple images in the GUI.

  - Execute the **delete image** command in the CLI.

  - You can delete by type or version. For example, the **delete image version 1.1(0.47)** command deletes all images versioned as 1.1(0.47).

Here are some best practices to consider for packages and images:

- The UCS Manager maintains an inventory of all available images.

- The image catalog contains a list of images and packages.

- A package is a read-only object that is created when it is downloaded.

- A package does not occupy disk space. It represents a list or collection of images that were unpacked as part of the package download.

- A package cannot be deleted. Packages are automatically purged when all the images that are part of the package are removed.

- When an individual image is downloaded, the package name is the same as the image name.

- You can use the **show image** and **show package** commands to view the contents of a catalog.

- The **show image** command is available at each endpoint scope. Corresponding filters are applied. For example, the **show image** command under I/O module scope displays all available I/O module images.

- The **show system firmware expand** command displays firmware versions that run on all endpoints.

- The **show** *<endpoint>* **firmware** command displays all firmware details for that endpoint. For example, the **show server firmware** command displays firmware details for all servers in the system.

Be sure to take special considerations into account when you download images in a UCS high-availability cluster configuration with multiple fabric interconnects. Here are some best practices to consider when you download images to an HA cluster:

- In a fabric interconnect cluster, images on both fabric interconnects are automatically synced.

- When you download images or packages during cluster setup, images are automatically downloaded to both clustered fabric interconnects.

- When two previously separated fabric interconnects join to form a cluster, all images are synced from the primary fabric interconnect to the secondary.

- If images are deleted from the primary fabric interconnect when the subordinate is down, the images will be removed from the subordinate when it comes back up.

For firmware updates, you can use either of these methods:

- **Direct update:** Direct updates at the endpoints.

- **Firmware policy:** Updates to server components through service profiles that include a host firmware package policy and a management firmware package policy.

The Cisco UCS Manager separates the direct update process into stages to ensure that you can push the firmware to a component while the system runs without affecting uptime on the server or other components. Because you do not need to reboot the server until after you activate the firmware update, you can perform that task overnight or during other maintenance windows.

These stages occur when you manually update firmware:

- **Update:** During this stage, the system pushes the selected firmware version to the component. The update process overwrites the firmware in the backup slot on the component.

- **Activate:** During this stage, the system sets the backup slot as active and reboots the endpoint. When the endpoint is rebooted, the backup slot becomes the active slot, and the active slot becomes the backup slot. The firmware in the new active slot becomes the startup version and the running version.

If the component cannot boot from the startup firmware, it defaults to the backup version and raises an alarm.

Here are some best practices to consider for firmware updates:

- Many of the components in UCS can store more than one firmware image.

- The image with which the endpoint is booted is called the running version.

- The other nonactive image is called the backup version.

- The image with which the endpoint would boot next time is called the startup version.

- The UCS Manager provides update operations to push a new version of the firmware to replace the backup image.

- The UCS Manager provides activate operations to change the running version to a new version.

- For some endpoints, you can use the set-startup option during activation to set the component boot image without resetting the device. The next reset will result in the component booting to the selected software image.

- For the fabric interconnect firmware and the Cisco UCS Manager, no update is needed because the image is already present locally.

- The LSI firmware, option ROM, host-facing adapter firmware, and BIOS cannot be updated directly like other components. These components can be updated only through firmware policies associated with the service profile.

- The Cisco UCS Manager provides interfaces to update and activate. There is no ordering for endpoint resets during the activation.

- While updates can be issued simultaneously, Cisco recommends that software and firmware activations be issued in a logical, methodical order.

- Firmware that is activated must pass compatibility checks; otherwise, the activation fails.

> **NOTE**   For capability catalog upgrades, updates and activations occur simultaneously. You only need to update or activate those upgrades. You do not need to perform both steps.

Various platforms that are supported by the Cisco UCS Manager have different components that require firmware upgrades:

- Fabric interconnects:
  - Cisco UCS 6454
  - Cisco UCS 6332
  - Cisco UCS 6332-16 UP
  - Cisco UCS 6248 UP
  - Cisco UCS 6296 UP
  - Cisco UCS 6324
- Chassis components:
  - Cisco UCS S3260 chassis:
    - Chassis Management Controller (CMC)
    - Chassis Adapter
    - SAS Expander
    - Board Controller
  - Blade server chassis:
    - I/O modules
    - Power supply unit

> **NOTE**   I/O modules are not supported on the primary Cisco UCS Mini chassis. However, they are supported on the secondary Cisco UCS Mini chassis.

- Server components:
  - Blade and rack server:
    - Adapter
    - Cisco Integrated Management Controller (CIMC)

- BIOS

- Storage controller

- Board controller

■ Cisco UCS S3260 storage server node:

- Cisco Integrated Management Controller (CIMC)

- BIOS

- Board controller

- Storage controller

**NOTE**   The Storage controller is not a supported server component in the Cisco UCS Mini.

## Firmware Version Terminology

The firmware version terminology used depends on the type of endpoint. Each CIMC, I/O module, BIOS, CIMC, and Cisco adapter has two slots for firmware in flash. Each slot holds a version of firmware. One slot is active, and the other is the backup slot. A component boots from whichever slot is designated as active.

The following firmware version terminology is used in the Cisco UCS Manager:

- **Running version:** The running version is the firmware that is active and in use by the endpoint.

- **Startup version:** The startup version is the firmware that will be used when the endpoint next boots up. The Cisco UCS Manager uses the activate operation to change the startup version.

- **Backup version:** The backup version is the firmware in the other slot and not in use by the endpoint. This version can be firmware that you have updated to the endpoint but have not yet activated, or it can be an older firmware version that was replaced by a recently activated version. The Cisco UCS Manager uses the update operation to replace the image in the backup slot. If the endpoint cannot boot from the startup version, it boots from the backup version.

- **Firmware versions in the fabric interconnect and the Cisco UCS Manager:** You can only activate the fabric interconnect firmware and the Cisco UCS Manager on the fabric interconnect. The fabric interconnect and the Cisco UCS Manager firmware do not have backup versions because all the images are stored on the fabric interconnect. As a result, the number of bootable fabric interconnect images is not limited to two, like the server CIMC and adapters. Instead, the number of bootable fabric interconnect images is limited by the available space in the memory of the fabric interconnect and the number of images stored there.

  The fabric interconnect and the Cisco UCS Manager firmware have running and startup versions of the kernel and system firmware. The kernel and system firmware must run the same versions of firmware.

## Firmware Upgrades Through Auto Install

Auto Install enables you to automatically upgrade a Cisco UCS domain to the firmware versions contained in a single package, in the following stages:

■ **Install Infrastructure Firmware:** Uses the Cisco UCS Infrastructure Software Bundle to upgrade the infrastructure components, such as the fabric interconnects, the I/O modules, and the Cisco UCS Manager. Figure 14-8 illustrates the recommended process flow to automatically install infrastructure firmware.

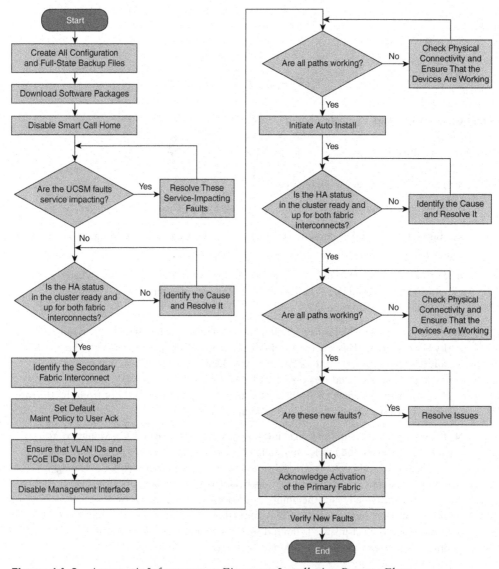

**Figure 14-8** *Automatic Infrastructure Firmware Installation Process Flow*

- **Install Server Firmware:** Uses the Cisco UCS B-Series Blade Server Software Bundle to upgrade all blade servers in the Cisco UCS domain and/or the Cisco UCS C-Series Rack-Mount UCS-Managed Server Software Bundle to upgrade all rack servers.

These two stages are independent and can be run or scheduled to run at different times.

You can use Auto Install to upgrade the infrastructure components to one version of Cisco UCS and server components to a different version.

- **Direct Upgrade After Auto Install:** During Auto Install, the startup version of the default infrastructure pack is configured. To successfully complete a direct upgrade or activation of the Cisco UCS Manager, fabric interconnects, and I/O modules after Auto Install, ensure that the startup version is cleared before starting a direct upgrade or activation. If the startup version of the default infrastructure pack is configured, you cannot directly upgrade or activate the Cisco UCS Manager, fabric interconnects, and I/O modules. Clearing the startup version of the Default Infrastructure Pack provides detailed steps for clearing the startup version.

- **Install Infrastructure Firmware:** Install Infrastructure Firmware upgrades all infrastructure components in a Cisco UCS domain, including the Cisco UCS Manager, and all fabric interconnects and I/O modules. All components are upgraded to the firmware version included in the selected Cisco UCS Infrastructure software bundle. Install Infrastructure Firmware does not support a partial upgrade to only some infrastructure components in a Cisco UCS domain.

  You can schedule an infrastructure upgrade for a specific time to accommodate a maintenance window. However, if an infrastructure upgrade is already in progress, you cannot schedule another infrastructure upgrade. You must wait until the current upgrade is complete before scheduling the next one.

**NOTE**   You can cancel an infrastructure firmware upgrade if it is scheduled to occur at a future time. However, you cannot cancel an infrastructure firmware upgrade after the upgrade has begun.

- **Install Server Firmware:** Install Server Firmware uses host firmware packages to upgrade all servers and their components in a Cisco UCS domain. All servers whose service profiles include the selected host firmware packages are upgraded to the firmware versions in the selected software bundles, as follows:

  - Cisco UCS B-Series Blade Server Software Bundle for all blade servers in the chassis
  - Cisco UCS C-Series Rack-Mount UCS-Managed Server Software Bundle for all rack-mount servers that are integrated into the Cisco UCS domain

**NOTE**   You cannot cancel a server firmware upgrade process after you complete the configuration in the Install Server Firmware wizard. The Cisco UCS Manager applies the changes immediately. However, the timing of the actual reboot of servers occurs depends on the maintenance policy in the service profile associated with the server.

If you want to upgrade all components in a Cisco UCS domain to the same package version, you must run the stages of Auto Install in the following order:

1. Install Infrastructure Firmware
2. Install Server Firmware

This order enables you to schedule the server firmware upgrades during a different maintenance window than the infrastructure firmware upgrade.

Before you start the upgrade, first you need to obtain your UCS software bundles from Cisco. The following steps explain how to get Cisco software bundles:

**Step 1.**   You need to determine which of the following software bundles you need to be able to update the Cisco UCS domain:

■ **Cisco UCS Infrastructure Software Bundle for Cisco UCS 6536 fabric interconnect, 6454 fabric interconnect, 6300 Series fabric interconnects, 6200 Series fabric interconnects, and 6324 fabric interconnects:** Required for all Cisco UCS domains.

■ **Cisco UCS B-Series Blade Server Software Bundle:** Required for all Cisco UCS domains that include blade servers.

■ **Cisco UCS C-Series Rack-Mount UCS-Managed Server Software Bundle:** Required only for Cisco UCS domains that include integrated rack-mount servers. This bundle contains firmware to enable the Cisco UCS Manager to manage those servers and is not applicable to standalone C-Series rack-mount servers.

**Step 2.**   Navigate to Cisco.com. Click **Download Software**. Search for **UCS Infrastructure**.

**Step 3.**   In the right pane, click the link for UCS Infrastructure and UCS Manager Software (see Figure 14-9).

**Step 4.**   On the first page from which you download a software bundle, click the **Release Notes** link to download the latest version of the Release Notes.

**Step 5.**   Read the Release Notes before upgrading your Cisco UCS domain.

**Step 6.**   After downloading the software from the Cisco website, you must upload firmware images to the fabric interconnect from either a local file system (local computer) or a remote system.

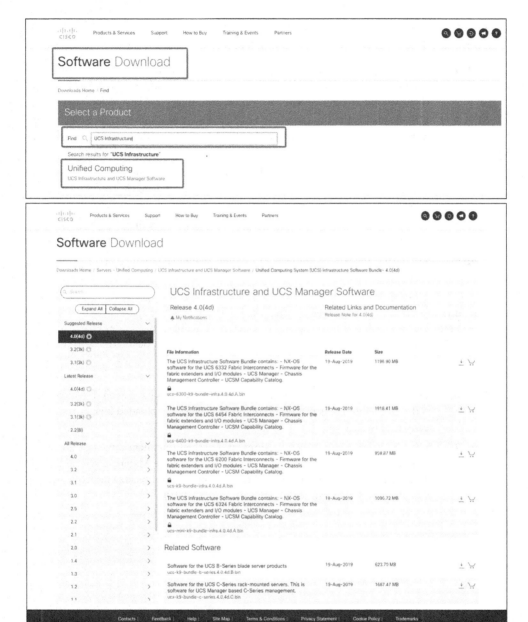

**Figure 14-9** *Cisco Software Download Page*

**NOTE**   In a cluster setup, the image file for the firmware bundle is downloaded to both fabric interconnects, regardless of which fabric interconnect is used to initiate the download. The Cisco UCS Manager maintains all firmware packages and images in both fabric interconnects in sync. If one fabric interconnect is down, the download finishes successfully. The images are synced to the other fabric interconnect when it comes back online.

### Direct Upgrade After Auto Install Procedure

To perform a direct upgrade after the Auto Install procedure, follow these steps:

**Step 1.** In the Navigation pane, click **Equipment**. On the Equipment tab, click the **Equipment** node. Then in the work pane, click the **Firmware Management** tab. Then click the **Installed Firmware** subtab, and then click **Download Firmware**.

**Step 2.** In the Download Firmware dialog box, click the **Local File System** radio button in the Location of the Image File field for a local file or **Remote File System** for a remote device.

**Step 3.** In the Filename field, type the full path and name of the image file. For a local file, if you do not know the exact path to the folder where the firmware image file is located, click **Browse** and navigate to the file.

**Step 4.** Click **OK**. The Cisco UCS Manager GUI begins downloading the firmware bundle to the fabric interconnect.

**Step 5.** (Optional) Monitor the status of the firmware bundle download on the Download Tasks tab.

> **NOTE**   If the Cisco UCS Manager reports that the bootflash is out of space, delete obsolete bundles on the Packages tab to free up space. To view the available space in bootflash, navigate to the fabric interconnect on the Equipment tab and expand the Local Storage Information area on the General tab.

**Step 6.** Repeat this task until all the required firmware bundles have been downloaded to the fabric interconnect. Next, you need to prepare uploaded images to be ready for installation.

**Step 7.** In the Navigation pane, click **Equipment**. On the Equipment tab, click the **Equipment** node. In the work pane, click the **Firmware Management** tab. Then click the **Firmware Auto Install** subtab, and in the Actions area under General, click **Prepare for Firmware Install** (see Figure 14-10).

**Figure 14-10**   *Preparation for Firmware Installation*

**Step 8.**   On the Select Package Versions page of the Prepare for Firmware Install wizard, do the following:

- To update the infrastructure components in the Cisco UCS domain, choose the software bundle to which you want to upgrade from the New Version drop-down list in the A-Series Infrastructure Firmware area.

- To update the blade servers in the Cisco UCS domain, choose the software bundle to which you want to upgrade from the New Version drop-down list in the B-Series Blade Server Firmware area.

- To update the rack-mount servers and S3260 chassis in the Cisco UCS domain, choose the software bundle to which you want to upgrade from the New Version drop-down list in the C-Series Chassis/Rack-Mount Server Firmware area.

- If the Cisco UCS domain includes both blade servers and rack servers, we recommend that you choose a new firmware version for the B-Series blade servers and C-Series rack-mount servers in the Select Package Versions page and upgrade all servers in the domain.

Then click **Next** (see Figure 14-11).

> **NOTE**   If you update the default host firmware package, you might cause the upgrade of firmware on unassociated servers and on servers with associated service profiles that do not include a host firmware package. This firmware upgrade may cause the reboot of those servers according to the maintenance policy defined in the service profile.

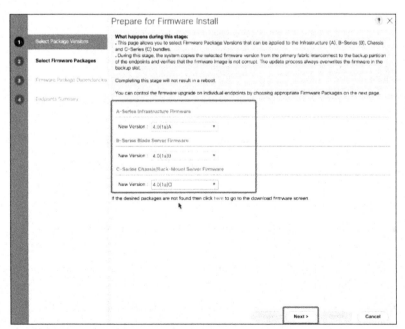

**Figure 14-11**   *Firmware Package Selection*

**Step 9.** On the Select Firmware Packages page of the Prepare for Firmware Install wizard, do the following:

- Expand the node for each organization that contains a firmware package you want to update with the selected software.

- Click the check box next to the name of each firmware package that you want to update.

- This step modifies all the selected infra, host, and chassis firmware packages with the new version of firmware.

Click **Next** (see Figure 14-12).

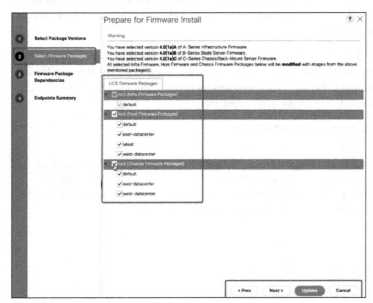

**Figure 14-12** *Firmware Selection*

**Step 10.** On the Firmware Package Dependencies page of the Prepare for Firmware Install wizard, do the following:

- Expand the node for each host firmware package listed in the table.

- Review the list of service or chassis profiles that include the host or chassis firmware package.

- If desired, click a link in one of the following columns:

  - **Host/Chassis Pack DN column:** Opens the navigator for the host or chassis firmware package.

  - **Service/Chassis Profile DN column:** Opens the navigator for the service or chassis profile.

- To start the firmware update immediately, click **Update** (see Figure 14-13).

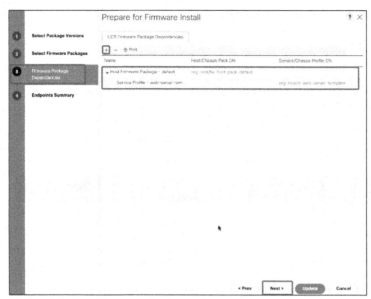

**Figure 14-13**   *Firmware Packages Dependencies*

**Step 11.**   On the Endpoints Summary page of the Prepare for Firmware Install wizard, do the following:

■ Click the appropriate check boxes to filter the results in the UCS Firmware Pack Endpoints table.

■ If you are satisfied that you have selected the appropriate firmware packages and want to start the server upgrade, click **Update** (see Figure 14-14). That will start the firmware upgrade.

**Figure 14-14**   *Firmware Preparation Summary*

## Install Infrastructure Firmware Procedure

To proceed with a firmware upgrade only, follow these steps:

**Step 1.**   If your Cisco UCS domain does not use an NTP server to set the time, make sure that the clocks on the primary and secondary fabric interconnects are in sync. You can do this by configuring an NTP server in the Cisco UCS Manager or by syncing the time manually.

**Step 2.**   In the Navigation pane, click **Equipment**. On the Equipment tab, click the **Equipment** node. In the work pane, click the **Firmware Management** tab (see Figure 14-15).

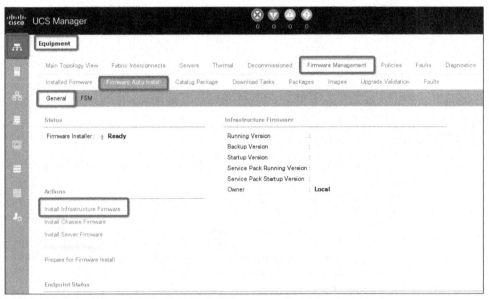

**Figure 14-15**   *Infrastructure Installation*

**Step 3.**   In the subtab, click the **Firmware Auto Install** tab. In the Actions area, click **Install Infrastructure Firmware**.

**Step 4.**   In the Prerequisites page of the Install Infrastructure Firmware dialog box, ensure that you address the warnings before proceeding.

Warnings are given in the following categories:

- Whether there are any current critical or major faults

- Whether a configuration backup has been taken recently

- Whether the management interface monitoring policy is enabled

- Whether there is pending fabric interconnect reboot activity

- Whether NTP is configured

You can click the hyperlinks for each warning to address them directly. Click the check box for each warning that you have addressed, or click the **Ignore All** check box to continue without addressing the warnings (see Figure 14-16).

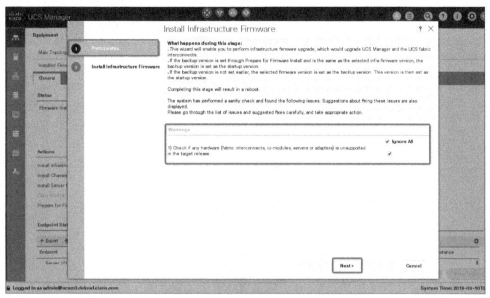

**Figure 14-16**   *Infrastructure Firmware Prerequisites*

**Step 5.**   In the Properties area of the Install Infrastructure Firmware dialog box, complete the fields shown in Table 14-9.

**Table 14-9**   Infrastructure Firmware Fields

| Name | Description |
|---|---|
| Name field | The name of the infrastructure pack created and maintained by Cisco UCS. You cannot change the default name in this field or create a custom infrastructure pack. |
| Description field | A user-defined description of the infrastructure pack. This field is completed by default. However, you can enter your own description if you prefer.<br><br>You can enter up to 256 characters using any characters or spaces except ` (accent mark), \ (backslash), ^ (caret), " (double quote), = (equal sign), > (greater than), < (less than), or ' (single quote). |
| Version drop-down list | A list of the software bundles that are available for you to upgrade the firmware on the infrastructure components. |
| Force check box | If this box is checked, Cisco UCS attempts the installation even if a previous attempt to install the selected version failed or was interrupted. |

**Step 6.**   In the Infrastructure Schedule area of the Install Infrastructure Firmware dialog box, complete the fields shown in Table 14-10. Then click **Finish** (see Figure 14-17).

**Table 14-10** Infrastructure Firmware Schedule Fields

| Option | Description |
|--------|-------------|
| Start Time field | The date and time that the occurrence will run. Click the down arrow at the end of the field to select the date from a calendar. |
| Upgrade Now check box | If this box is checked, the Cisco UCS Manager ignores the Start Time field and upgrades the infrastructure firmware as soon as you click OK. |

**Figure 14-17** *Infrastructure Firmware Configurations*

The Firmware Installer field on the Firmware Auto Install tab displays the status of the infrastructure firmware upgrade (see Figure 14-18).

**NOTE** If there is not enough space under bootflash, a warning will be displayed, and the upgrade process will stop.

**Figure 14-18** *Infrastructure Firmware Update Status*

You need to acknowledge the reboot of the primary fabric interconnect. If you do not acknowledge that reboot, the Cisco UCS Manager cannot complete the infrastructure upgrade, and the upgrade will remain pending indefinitely.

**NOTE** To upgrade with minimal disruption, you must confirm the following:

■ Ensure that all the I/O modules that are attached to the fabric interconnect are up before you acknowledge the reboot of the fabric interconnect. If all I/O modules are not up, all the servers connected to the fabric interconnect will immediately be rediscovered and cause a major disruption.

■ Ensure that both of the fabric interconnects and the service profiles are configured for failover.

■ Verify that the data path has been successfully restored from the secondary fabric interconnect before you acknowledge the reboot of the primary fabric interconnect.

After you upgrade the infrastructure firmware, Install Infrastructure Firmware automatically reboots the secondary fabric interconnect in a cluster configuration. However, you must acknowledge the reboot of the primary fabric interconnect. If you do not acknowledge the reboot, Install Infrastructure Firmware will wait indefinitely for that acknowledgment rather than complete the upgrade.

**Step 7.** On the toolbar, click **Pending Activities**. In the Pending Activities dialog box, click the **User Acknowledged Activities** tab. In the table, locate the row for the pending reboot of the primary fabric interconnect.

**Step 8.** In the Reboot Now column for that row, click the **Acknowledge All** check box, and then click **OK**.

The Cisco UCS Manager immediately reboots the primary fabric interconnect. You cannot stop this reboot after you click OK.

## Upgrading the Server Firmware with Auto Install

You cannot cancel a server firmware upgrade process after you complete the configuration in the Install Server Firmware wizard. The Cisco UCS Manager applies the changes immediately. However, the timing of the actual reboot of servers depends on the maintenance policy in the service profile associated with the server.

Steps to upgrading server firmware are similar to the steps for upgrading infrastructure firmware with some minor changes. The steps are as follows:

**Step 1.** In the Navigation pane, click **Equipment**. On the Equipment tab, click the **Equipment** node. In the work pane, click the **Firmware Management** tab. In the subtab, click the **Firmware Auto Install** tab. In the Actions area, click **Install Server Firmware**.

**Step 2.** On the Prerequisites page of the Install Server Firmware wizard, carefully review the prerequisites and guidelines listed on this page and then do one of the following:

■ If you have completed all of the prerequisites, click **Next**.

■ If you have not completed all of the prerequisites, click **Cancel** and complete the prerequisites before you upgrade the server firmware.

**Step 3.**    On the Select Package Versions page of the Install Server Firmware wizard, do the following:

- If the Cisco UCS domain contains blade servers, choose the software bundle to which you want to upgrade these servers from the New Version drop-down list in the B-Series Blade Server Software area.

- If the Cisco UCS domain contains rack-mount servers, choose the software bundle to which you want to upgrade these servers from the New Version drop-down list in the C-Series Rack-Mount Server Software area.

- If the Cisco UCS domain includes both blade servers and rack servers, we recommend that you choose a new firmware version for the B-Series blade servers and C-Series rack-mount servers in the Select Package Versions page and upgrade all servers in the domain.

Then click **Next**.

**NOTE**    If you update the default host firmware package, you might cause the upgrade of firmware on unassociated servers and on servers with associated service profiles that do not include a host firmware package. This firmware upgrade may cause the reboot of those servers according to the maintenance policy defined in the service profile.

**Step 4.**    On the Select Host Firmware Packages page of the Install Server Firmware wizard, do the following:

- Expand the node for each organization that contains a host firmware package you want to update with the selected software.

- Select the check box next to the name of each host firmware package that you want to update.

This step updates the selected host firmware package with the new version of firmware. You must choose the host firmware packages included in the service profiles associated with all servers in the Cisco UCS domain to update all servers. Then click **Next**.

**Step 5.**    On the Host Firmware Package Dependencies page of the Install Server Firmware wizard, do the following:

- Expand the node for each host firmware package listed in the table.

- Review the list of service profiles that include the host firmware package.

- If desired, click a link in one of the following columns:

  - **Host Pack DN column:** Opens the navigator for the host firmware package.

  - **Service Profile DN column:** Opens the navigator for the service profile.

- Do one of the following:

  - If you want to change one or more of the selected host firmware packages, click **Prev**.

■ If you are satisfied that you have selected the appropriate host firmware packages and want to review the impact of the server firmware upgrade on the endpoints, click **Next**.

■ If you want to start the server upgrade immediately, click **Install**.

**Step 6.** On the Impacted Endpoints Summary page of the Install Server Firmware wizard, do the following:

■ Click the appropriate check boxes to filter the results in the Impacted Endpoints table. You can filter the results by the type of endpoint and by whether the impact of the upgrade is disruptive.

■ Review the list of impacted endpoints.

■ If desired, click the link in the Maintenance Policy column to open the navigator for that policy.

■ Do one of the following:

■ If you want to change one or more of the selected host firmware packages, click **Prev**.

■ If you are satisfied that you have selected the appropriate host firmware packages and want to start the server upgrade, click **Install**.

**Step 7.** (Optional) To check on the progress of the server firmware upgrade, check the FSM tab for each server that you are upgrading. The Firmware Installer field on the Firmware Auto Install tab shows only the status of an infrastructure firmware upgrade.

## Standalone Cisco UCS C-Series Server Firmware Upgrade Using the Host Upgrade Utility (HUU)

The Cisco Host Upgrade Utility (hereafter referred to as HUU) is a tool that you can use to upgrade the firmware on a Cisco UCSC-Series server. HUU includes an option that enables you to download a container for a selected platform on a Windows operating system. You can download the container from the HUU ISO disk image by burning the ISO on a physical media. When you insert the physical media into the server, auto-run launches an Index.html page in your browser. This Index.html page provides access to the location from where you can download the container. You also can download the container from the ISO using the standard ISO extraction utilities.

After upgrading the Cisco Integrated Management Controller (CIMC) firmware, you must check the compatibility matrix to verify whether the drivers are compliant with the upgraded version of CIMC. If the driver versions are noncompliant, you must upgrade the driver versions to match the CIMC version.

UCS hardware and software interoperability websites at https://ucshcltool.cloudapps.cisco.com/public/ and https://www.cisco.com/c/en/us/products/servers-unified-computing/interoperability.html#%7Etab-storage enable you to search easily to find driver compatibility (see Figure 14-19).

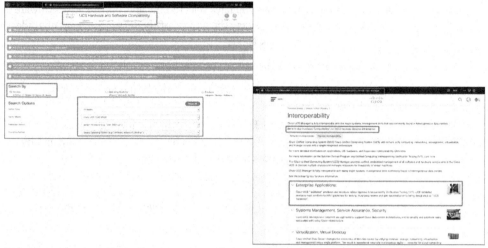

**Figure 14-19**  *UCS Hardware Compatibility Web Page*

## Downloading and Preparing the ISO for an Upgrade

To prepare your ISO for an upgrade, you first need to download the right firmware. Make sure you download HUU ISO image because you will need to map the ISO as a CD and boot from the CD to start HUU utility. Follow these steps:

**Step 1.**   Download the firmware from the Cisco website. Open software.cisco.com/download/home.

**Step 2.**   Enter **UCS** and select the appropriate version for UCS here. In this UCS, C220 M3 Rack Server Software is selected, as shown in Figure 14-20.

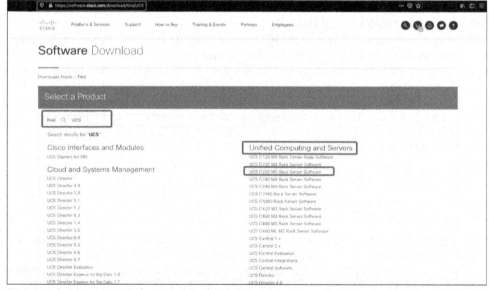

**Figure 14-20**  *Cisco Software Download Page*

**Step 3.**    Click **Unified Computing System (UCS) Server Firmware** (see Figure 14-21).

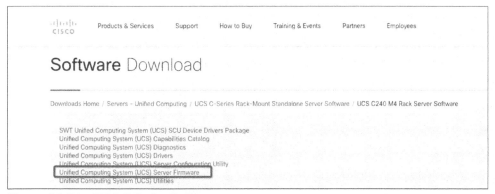

**Figure 14-21**    *UCS C-Series Software*

**Step 4.**    Select the release that you want and then download it (see Figure 14-22). Make sure it is an HUU ISO.

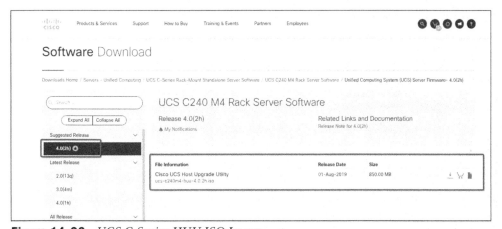

**Figure 14-22**    *UCS C-Series HUU ISO Image*

**Step 5.**    Navigate to the CIMC URL, enter the credentials, and then click **Login**.

**Step 6.**    When you are logged in, check the CIMC version prior to the upgrade (see Figure 14-23).

**Step 7.**    Click **Launch KVM Console**. When a dialog box appears, click **OK** (see Figure 14-24).

**Step 8.**    Map the ISO as a CD/DVD (see Figure 14-25).

**Step 9.**    To begin the installation, as shown in Figure 14-26, you have to power off the server first. Then power on the server as shown in the figure.

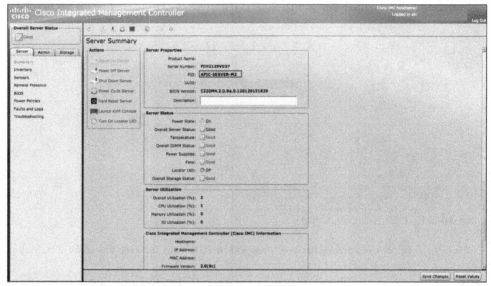

**Figure 14-23**  *CIMC Firmware Verification*

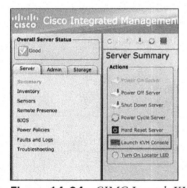

**Figure 14-24**  *CIMC Launch KVM Console*

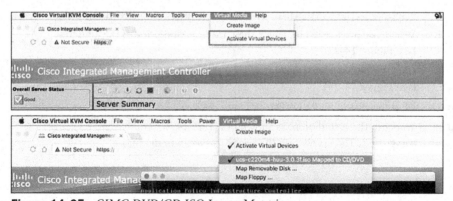

**Figure 14-25**  *CIMC DVD/CD ISO Image Mapping*

**Figure 14-26**   *CIMC Power Cycle Option*

**Step 10.**   After the bootup process, which usually takes 30–40 seconds, access the bootup mode by pressing F6 to open the boot selection menu.

**Step 11.**   After the server enters the boot selection menu, click **Cisco vKVM-Mapped vDVD1.22** (see Figure 14-27). This then loads the new file.

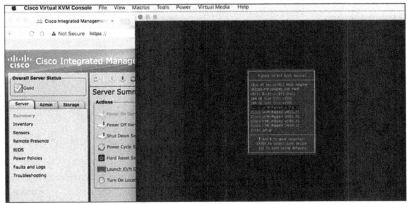

**Figure 14-27**   *Change Boot Sequence to Boot from vDVD/CD*

**Step 12.**   After a few minutes of boot time, you see the screen shown in Figure 14-28.

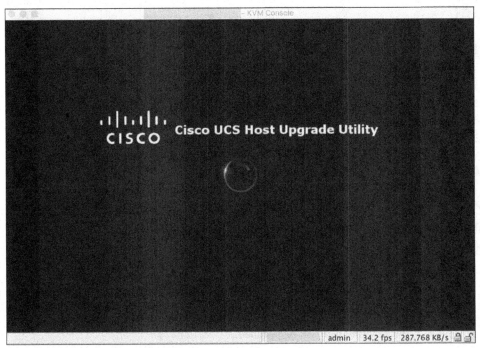

**Figure 14-28**   *Cisco HUU Bootup*

**Step 13.**   After the server boots successfully, click **I agree**, as shown in Figure 14-29, to agree to terms of use.

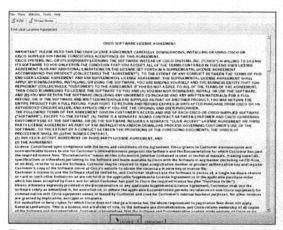

**Figure 14-29**   *End-User License Agreement*

**Step 14.**   On the following screen, click **Update All** (see Figure 14-30). Now click **Yes** twice, and then click **No**.

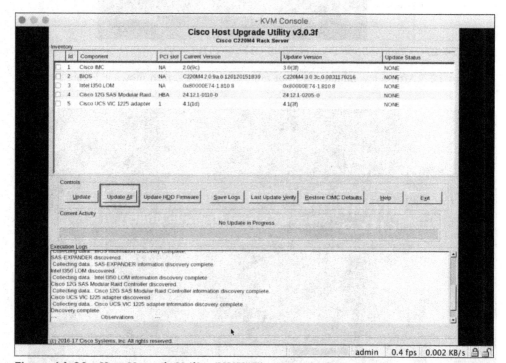

**Figure 14-30**   *Host Upgrade Utility (HUU) Firmware Options*

**Step 15.**   The upgrade process will begin and can take 20–30 minutes to complete. When it is finished, log out from the session, and then when you try to log in again, the new firmware will be installed.

**Step 16.** Verify the new firmware version. There is currently no verification procedure available for this configuration. Just log in and check the version (see Figure 14-31).

**Figure 14-31** *CIMC Firmware Verification After Upgrade*

**Step 17.** If for some reason the upgrade process is stuck or fails, collect CIMC logs from **Admin > Utilities > General Technical Support Data for Local Download > Generate Technical Support Data > Generate > Download to local PC** (see Figure 14-32).

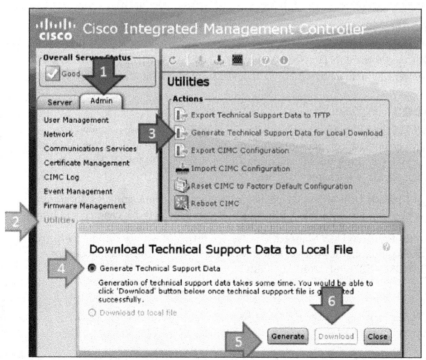

**Figure 14-32** *Technical Support Data*

## Exam Preparation Tasks

As mentioned in the Introduction, you have a couple of choices for exam preparation: the exercises here, Chapter 21, "Final Preparation," and the exam simulation questions in the Pearson Test Prep software online.

## Review All Key Topics

Review the most important topics in the chapter, noted with the key topic icon in the outer margin of the page. Table 14-11 lists a reference to these key topics and the page numbers on which each is found.

**Table 14-11**    Key Topics for Chapter 14

| Key Topic Element | Description | Page |
|---|---|---|
| List | Creating and Running a Backup Operation | 661 |
| Section | Backup Policies | 666 |
| Section | Enable the Import Operation | 669 |
| Section | Firmware Version Terminology | 679 |
| Section | Firmware Upgrades Through Auto Install | 680 |
| Section | Standalone Cisco UCS C-Series Server Firmware Upgrade Using the Host Upgrade Utility (HUU) | 693 |

## Define Key Terms

Define the following key terms from this chapter, and check your answers in the Glossary.

basic input/output system (BIOS), Extensible Markup Language (XML), File Transfer Protocol (FTP), finite-state machine (FSM), firmware, input/output module (I/O module), Network Time Protocol (NTP), Secure Copy Protocol (SCP), Trivial File Transfer Protocol (TFTP), universally unique identifier (UUID), virtual network interface card (vNIC)

## References

Cisco UCS Manager Firmware Management Guide, Release 4.0: https://www.cisco.com/c/en/us/td/docs/unified_computing/ucs/ucs-manager/GUI-User-Guides/Firmware-Mgmt/4-0/b_UCSM_GUI_Firmware_Management_Guide_4-0/b_UCSM_GUI_Firmware_Management_Guide_4-0_chapter_010.html

Cisco Host Upgrade Utility User Guide: https://www.cisco.com/c/en/us/td/docs/unified_computing/ucs/c/sw/lomug/2-0-x/3_0/b_huu_3_0_1/b_huu_2_0_13_chapter_011.html

Release Notes for Cisco UCS Manager, Release 4.2: https://www.cisco.com/c/en/us/td/docs/unified_computing/ucs/release/notes/cisco-ucs-manager-rn-4-2.html#concept_DC9C47F7CB5D4EB7B96F216B1ABCE3BC

# CHAPTER 15

# Cisco HyperFlex Overview

Cisco HyperFlex is a platform designed to offer a flexible infrastructure that can power mission-critical applications with multicloud services to extend and distribute customer applications to any cloud. Cisco HyperFlex was designed to address the next boundary of placing computing anywhere customers and data reside.

While enterprise applications have been migrating to centralized data centers and to the cloud, Cisco HyperFlex systems deliver hyperconvergence with power and simplicity for any application, on any cloud, anywhere. Cisco HyperFlex systems deliver the agility, scalability, and pay-as-you-grow economics of the cloud with the benefits of multisite, distributed computing on a global scale.

With Cisco HyperFlex systems, you have flexible pools of computing, network, and storage resources that are easy to deploy and maintain. The system offers one-click integration with VMware vSphere, allowing your IT staff to extend their virtualization skills to storage and management; the purpose is to get better visibility into and control over computing, network, and storage resources from a single console, improving productivity and infrastructure operation.

### This chapter covers the following key topics:

**Cisco HyperFlex Solution and Benefits:** This section provides a high-level overview of Cisco flexible hyperconverged infrastructure (HyperFlex) solutions, along with Hyper-Flex benefits, automation, management, and resource scaling.

**HyperFlex as Edge, Hybrid, and All-Flash Nodes:** This section discusses different HyperFlex deployments, including the HyperFlex as Edge platform, HyperFlex as multicloud platform, and HyperFlex as NVMe, and includes HyperFlex platform management examples.

## "Do I Know This Already?" Quiz

The "Do I Know This Already?" quiz enables you to assess whether you should read this entire chapter thoroughly or jump to the "Exam Preparation Tasks" section. If you are in doubt about your answers to these questions or your own assessment of your knowledge of the topics, read the entire chapter. Table 15-1 lists the major headings in this chapter and their corresponding "Do I Know This Already?" quiz questions. You can find the answers in Appendix A, "Answers to the 'Do I Know This Already?' Quizzes."

**Table 15-1**  "Do I Know This Already?" Section-to-Question Mapping

| Foundation Topics Section | Questions |
|---|---|
| Cisco HyperFlex Solution and Benefits | 1–2 |
| HyperFlex as Edge, Hybrid, and All-Flash Nodes | 3–6 |

**CAUTION**  The goal of self-assessment is to gauge your mastery of the topics in this chapter. If you do not know the answer to a question or are only partially sure of the answer, you should mark that question as wrong for purposes of the self-assessment. Giving yourself credit for an answer you correctly guess skews your self-assessment results and might provide you with a false sense of security

1. HyperFlex offers one-click integration with which of the following?

   a. VMware vSphere

   b. Microsoft Hyper-V

   c. Linux KVM

   d. All of the above

2. A HyperFlex solution will provide you with which of the following?

   a. Unified management

   b. Resource optimizations

   c. Lower traffic latency

   d. All of the above

3. Through which of the following can you automate HyperFlex processes by yourself with interfaces to the Cisco UCS Manager? (Choose two answers.)

   a. Cisco UCS Manager CLI

   b. Microsoft PowerShell

   c. Python

   d. XML

4. Cisco HyperFlex offers deep learning capabilities at the edge, utilizing up to eight CPUs.

   a. True

   b. False

5. The Cisco Unified Computing System provides a single point of connectivity that integrates the Cisco HyperFlex HX-Series All-Flash or hybrid nodes and a variety of Cisco UCS servers into a single unified cluster. Cisco offers you the flexibility to choose a combination of which of the following? (Choose three answers.)

   a. CPU

   b. Flash memory

   c. Server chassis

   d. Power supply

   e. Disk storage resources

   **6.** Cisco provides an architectural performance edge with NVMe drives connected indirectly to the CPU rather than through a latency-inducing PCIe switch.

   **a.** True

   **b.** False

## Foundation Topics

# Cisco HyperFlex Solution and Benefits

A traditional data center infrastructure is developed on compute, storage, and virtualization control planes, and these three silos are monitored and managed by different admin groups, as shown in Figure 15-1.

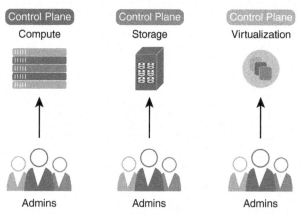

**Figure 15-1** *Traditional Data Center Control Plane*

You need an infrastructure that can follow your data and increase the speed of business, regardless of where it takes place: from your core data center (enterprise applications, big data, and deep learning) to private and public clouds (virtualized and containerized applications) and edge locations (remote offices, branch offices, retail and industrial sites). Cisco HyperFlex systems deliver hyperconvergence, as shown in Figure 15-2, with power and simplicity for any application on any cloud.

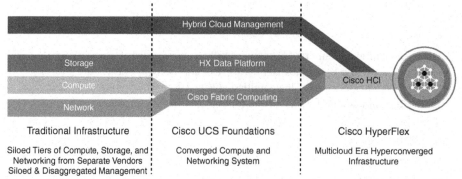

**Figure 15-2** *Cisco HyperFlex Hyperconverged Infrastructure (HCI)*

Cisco HyperFlex was designed with an end-to-end software-defined infrastructure. The platform eliminates the compromises found in other hyperconverged products. It combines software-defined computing using Cisco UCS servers, software-defined storage using the Cisco HyperFlex HX Data Platform, and software-defined networking (SDN) using Cisco Unified Fabric.

The Cisco UCS fabric interconnects provide a single point of connectivity integrating Cisco HyperFlex HX-Series All-Flash, all-NVMe, or hybrid nodes and other Cisco UCS servers into a single unified cluster. You can choose the combination of CPU, flash memory, graphics acceleration, and disk storage resources you need to deliver an optimal infrastructure for your applications. Incremental scalability allows you to start small and scale up and out as your needs grow. The Cisco HyperFlex HX Data Platform combines the cluster's solid-state drives (SSDs), hard disk drives (HDDs), and NVMe drives into a single distributed, multitier, object-based data store, as shown in Figure 15-3.

**15**

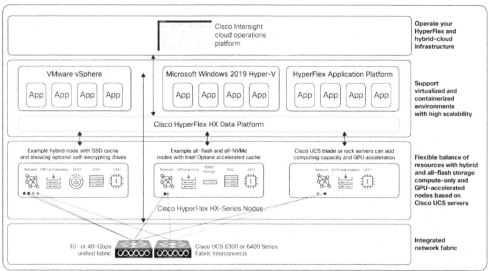

**Figure 15-3**   *Cisco HyperFlex System Interconnection, Virtualization, and Management*

The Cisco HyperFlex solution was engineered on Cisco UCS technology. The HyperFlex systems include rack and blade servers built with Intel Xeon processors, built-in networking, integrated management, and a high-performance and highly available data platform, with pre-installed software, as shown in Figure 15-4. You can mix and match blade and rack servers to tune the cluster with the right mix of processing and storage capacity for their workloads. Cisco networking interconnects the system from a single point, eliminating the do-it-yourself projects of previous-generation systems. The replication factor determines how many copies of information will be kept in the Cisco HyperFlex cluster. Replication factor 2 (RF2) will have two copies available, distributed across two nodes. Replication factor 3 (RF3) means that there will be three copies available on the cluster.

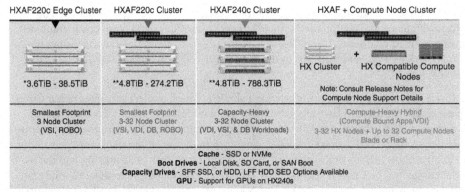

| HXAF220c Edge Cluster | HXAF220c Cluster | HXAF240c Cluster | HXAF + Compute Node Cluster |
|---|---|---|---|
| *3.6TiB - 38.5TiB | **4.8TiB - 274.2TiB | **4.8TiB - 788.3TiB | HX Cluster   HX Compatible Compute Nodes<br>Note: Consult Release Notes for Compute Node Support Details |
| Smallest Footprint 3 Node Cluster (VSI, ROBO) | Smallest Footprint 3-32 Node Cluster (VSI, VDI, DB, ROBO) | Capacity-Heavy 3-32 Node Cluster (VDI, VSI, & DB Workloads) | Compute-Heavy Hybrid (Compute Bound Apps/VDI)<br>3-32 HX Nodes + Up to 32 Compute Nodes Blade or Rack |

**Cache** - SSD or NVMe
**Boot Drives** - Local Disk, SD Card, or SAN Boot
**Capacity Drives** - SFF SSD, or HDD, LFF HDD SED Options Available
**GPU** - Support for GPUs on HX240s

*Edge Does Not Support RF3. Usable Capacity w/RF2 Before Compression and Deduplication.
**Usable Capacity w/RF3 Before Compression and Deduplication.

**Figure 15-4** *HyperFlex Configuration Options*

The Cisco HyperFlex HX Data Platform makes your data instantly accessible and highly available, with always-on deduplication and compression that reduce your storage needs. In addition, the preinstalled VMware ESXi hypervisor accelerates both provisioning and scaling. With Cisco HyperFlex systems, you have flexible pools of computing, network, and storage resources that are easy to deploy and maintain. You can bring the pay-as-you-grow economics of the cloud to your data center to support diverse application needs and help you propel business innovation, as shown in Figure 15-5. The system offers one-click integration with VMware vSphere, allowing your IT staff to extend their virtualization skills to storage and management; the purpose is to get better visibility into and control over your computing, network, and storage resources from a single console, improving productivity and infrastructure operation.

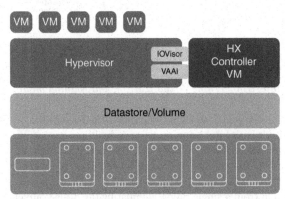

**Figure 15-5** *HyperFlex Infrastructure*

In the VMware vSphere environment, the controller occupies a virtual machine with a dedicated number of processor cores and amount of memory, allowing it to deliver consistent performance and not affect the performance of the other virtual machines on the cluster. The controller can access all storage without hypervisor intervention through the VMware

VM_DIRECT_PATH feature. It uses the node's memory and SSD drives as part of a distributed caching layer, and it uses the node's HDDs for distributed capacity storage. The controller integrates the data platform into VMware software through the use of two preinstalled VMware ESXi vSphere Installation Bundles (VIBs):

- **IO Visor:** This VIB provides a Network File System (NFS) mount point so that the ESXi hypervisor can access the virtual disk drives that are attached to individual virtual machines. From the hypervisor's perspective, it is simply attached to an NFS.

- **VMware vStorage API for Array Integration (VAAI):** This storage offload API allows vSphere to request advanced file system operations such as snapshots and cloning. The controller causes these operations to occur through manipulation of metadata rather than actual data copying, providing rapid response and thus rapid deployment of new application environments.

The Hypervisor datastore provides the storage capacity and datastore capacity. This is the combined consumable physical storage available to the storage cluster through datastores and managed by the HX Data Platform. Datastores are logical containers that the HX Data Platform uses to manage storage use and storage resources. Datastores are where the host places virtual disk files and other VM files. Datastores hide the specifics of physical storage devices and provide a uniform model for storing VM files.

With systems designed to be upgraded as new technologies become available, you have an infrastructure that is easy to deploy, scale, and manage, while providing investment protection.

## HyperFlex Benefits

Cisco HyperFlex systems include a purpose-built, high-performance, low-latency hyperconverged platform that adapts to support any application, in any cloud, anywhere (see Figure 15-6). HyperFlex integrates hardware and software nodes, and it enables you to innovate across the entire stack.

HyperFlex is a unique hardware data compression accelerator with full bare-metal deployment, and software installation is managed from the cloud. It provides more GPU acceleration in virtual desktop environments or artificial intelligence (AI) and machine learning (ML) inferencing applications. HyperFlex delivers

- Intelligent end-to-end automation, including networking

- Unified management

- Resource scaling

- Bigger virtual machine density and lower jitter and latency

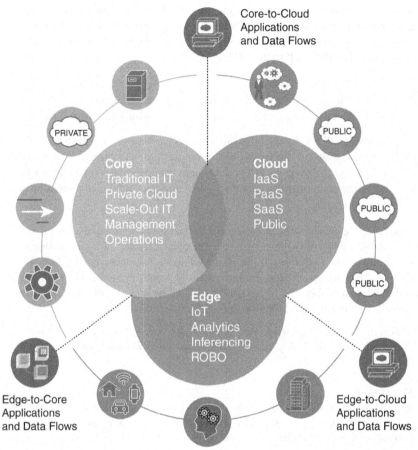

**Figure 15-6**  *HyperFlex Supports Any Application, in Any Cloud, Anywhere*

### Intelligent End-to-End Automation

Cisco HyperFlex systems provide comprehensive end-to-end automation across computing, storage, and networking resources. Using a simple and intuitive wizard, the entire deployment process takes minutes to complete. The process uses Cisco UCS Manager service profile templates optimized for hyperconverged environments to help ensure rapid deployment and expansion.

Cisco fabric interconnects create a redundant dual-network fabric that connects to Cisco UCS virtual interface cards (VICs) in server nodes. These cards establish a programmable I/O infrastructure. You can configure the number and type of I/O interfaces on demand with a zero-touch model that increases staff efficiency and accelerates operations. You can preconfigure Cisco UCS service profiles to automatically create the appropriate devices to support your cluster with no guesswork required, as shown in Figure 15-7.

Intelligent
Automation

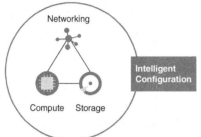

HX Optimized Service Profiles
For Rapid Cluster Deployment and Expansion

Intuitive User Interface
Simple Wizard Installer for the Entire Process

**Figure 15-7**  *End-to-End HyperFlex Automation*

The Cisco programmable I/O infrastructure dramatically reduces the number of network adapters, cables, and switches you need. Cisco VICs support up to 256 PCI Express (PCIe) devices with a high rate of I/O operations per second (IOPS), lossless Ethernet, and 20-Gbps connectivity to each server. Network interface card (NIC) teaming with automated fabric failover increases reliability and availability. That will simplify deployment by preconfiguring the network with automated workflows. The network fabric gives you the following:

- Traffic segmentation and security through dedicated virtual links connecting each server to the fabric interconnect. HyperFlex automatically creates the multiple interfaces used by VMware networking in accordance with VMware best practices.

- Storage and management traffic shared on the network fabric. This approach enables optimal performance.

- Quality of service (QoS) policies enabled for well-defined and predictable service. Policies include no-drop and jumbo frame policies for optimal performance.

- Multicast policy for Cisco HyperFlex system clusters. This feature is a part of the Cisco automated configuration process that other vendors do not even consider.

- No need to configure IPv6 or IPv4 multicasting or Internet Group Management Protocol (IGMP) snooping on your upstream switches as a network prerequisite. HyperFlex will keep all the required networking configuration information in the fabric interconnect and automatically configure it all for you.

### Unified Management for All Workloads

If your data center supports virtualized environments, you already use VMware vCenter to manage your virtual infrastructure. With Cisco HyperFlex systems, you can continue to do so without creating another management silo. With a single vCenter plug-in, you can manage your physical and virtual hyperconverged infrastructure through a single, intuitive interface. If you have already started to manage your data center infrastructure with workflow-based Cisco UCS Director, you can use it to manage and automate your hyperconverged environment as well. The reason for this flexibility is that each management approach uses a unified API provided by the Cisco UCS Manager. This integrated, model-based management software is built into all your Cisco server and storage infrastructure (see Figure 15-8).

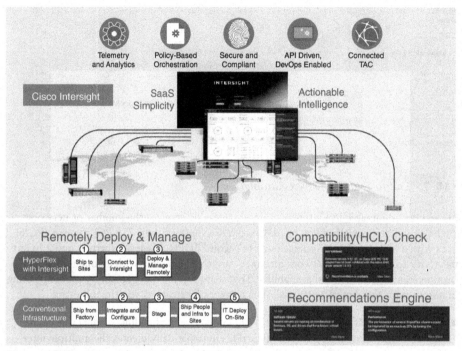

**Figure 15-8**  *HyperFlex Centralized Management*

If you want to manage your entire data center infrastructure with a single workflow-based automation tool, you can use the Cisco UCS Director. This single tool can manage your full application lifecycle, whether applications are deployed in your hyperconverged environment; on your blade or rack servers; or on your networking, storage, or third-party systems.

Cisco management automates tasks to reduce the chance of errors that can cause downtime. The Cisco UCS Director provides easy-to-use automation, extends to heterogeneous environments, maintains its awareness of your environments, and organizes your environments into a holistic unified view so that you can see and control everything.

Cisco UCS management encompasses all your Cisco UCS infrastructure, whether it is converged, hyperconverged, or bare metal. You can even automate processes yourself with interfaces to Cisco UCS Manager through Microsoft PowerShell and Python. In addition, you can integrate the Cisco CloudCenter solution with your Cisco HyperFlex system to facilitate hybrid cloud mobility across clouds, further increasing your infrastructure agility.

### Independent Resource Scaling

Cisco HyperFlex systems include a purpose-built, high-performance distributed file system that expands the boundaries of the hyperconverged infrastructure. You can scale your environment simply by adding nodes to the configuration. You can also choose to independently scale computing or storage capacity to meet the specific needs of your applications. Cisco predefined networking resources expand to incorporate the new nodes (see Figure 15-9). All this is accomplished without the need for you to change or adjust your software or networking configuration or interrupt your cluster operations. The new node is efficiently and automatically added to your environment with no downtime.

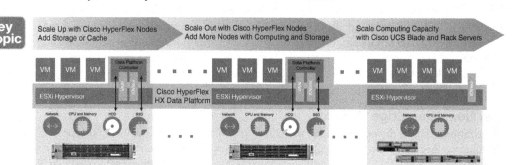

**Figure 15-9**  *HyperFlex Resource Optimization*

With Cisco HyperFlex systems, you can scale your storage by adding a Cisco UCS rack server–based storage node to the cluster. You can scale your computing performance by adding Cisco UCS blade server–based computing nodes. Clusters can scale up to 576 CPUs and 12 TB of RAM, 1024 virtual machines per host, and 64 nodes per cluster. You can scale with a graphics-processing-intensive computing node by adding Cisco UCS C240 or C220 rack servers to the cluster.

### Superior Virtual Machine Density with Lower and Consistent Latency

The Cisco HyperFlex HX Data Platform is a file system that is specifically built for hyperconverged systems. It uses dynamic data distribution, in which data is striped and distributed across the cluster, using all available resources for optimal I/O performance. As a result, Cisco HyperFlex systems achieve significantly greater performance, allowing you to run up to three times more virtual machines, dramatically lowering your overall total cost of ownership (TCO), and providing more flexibility for your environment, as shown in Figure 15-10.

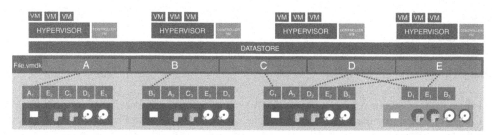

- Stripe Blocks of a File Across Servers
- Replicate One or Two Additional Copies to Other Servers
- Handle Entire Server or Disk Failures
- Restore Back to Original Number of Copies
- Rebalance VMs and Data Post Replacement
- Rolling Software Upgrades

**Figure 15-10**  *HyperFlex Dynamic Data Distribution*

Cisco HyperFlex Systems deliver more than low latency; they deliver more consistent latency between virtual machines. This is important when hosting enterprise applications that must meet specific service-level agreements. If your latency for traffic between virtual machines varies, so will your application performance and your user experience.

# HyperFlex as an Edge, Hybrid, and All-Flash Nodes

HyperFlex edge, All-Flash, and all-NVMe configurations provide an integrated network fabric and powerful data optimization features that bring the full potential of hyperconvergence to a wide range of workloads and use cases. These faster-to-deploy, simpler-to-manage, and easier-to-scale systems provide a unified pool of infrastructure resources to power any application anywhere.

## HyperFlex as an Edge Device

Digitization expands the network edge to millions of IoT devices; the number and types of things connecting and communicating through the Internet increase every day. Business growth and success favor those who fully embrace IT innovation and create improved digital experiences for customers. Applications are increasingly housed in the data center and in cloud platforms, and the Internet edge is moving to the branch and user devices.

There are certainly benefits to consolidating apps and services like this and delivering them over a WAN or the Internet, as shown in Figure 15-11. Such centralization gives you consistent security policy enforcement.

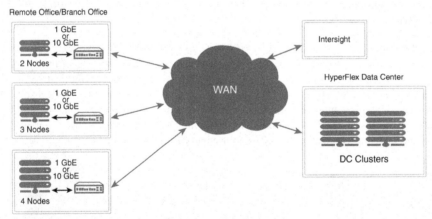

**Figure 15-11**  *HyperFlex Edge*

For small and medium-sized businesses (SMBs) and remote offices, branch offices (ROBO), Cisco offers a solution to these challenges. The solution is hybrid, All-Flash, all-NVMe, and edge HyperFlex configurations. This solution offers an integrated network fabric and powerful data optimization features that bring the full potential of hyperconvergence to a wide range of workloads and use cases.

A hyperconverged solution that is tailor-made for small businesses and ROBOs is one that takes into consideration existing networking and virtualization licenses.

When you are running a clustered file system such as the Cisco HyperFlex HX Data Platform, data consistency across nodes is of paramount importance. Cisco HyperFlex systems are built on a quorum mechanism that can help guarantee consistency whenever that quorum is available.

A quorum in Cisco HyperFlex systems traditionally is based on a node majority in which each node in the system casts a single vote, with a simple majority required for the cluster to remain operational. This mechanism works well for three-node and larger clusters that can tolerate one or more node losses and still be able to obtain a majority consensus and continue operations. However, fault tolerance and file system consistency become more challenging when only two nodes are deployed at a customer's ROBO location. In this scenario, if one of the two nodes fails, a quorum can no longer be established using a node majority algorithm alone.

In the unlikely event that the communication pathway between the two nodes is disrupted, a "split brain" condition may occur if both nodes continue to process data without obtaining a quorum. The opposite outcome, the loss of availability, is also possible. You must avoid both scenarios to help prevent the introduction of data inconsistency while also maintaining high availability. For these reasons, hyperconverged two-node architectures require an additional component, sometimes referred to as a *witness* or an *arbiter*, that can vote if a failure occurs within the cluster. This traditional and burdensome deployment architecture requires the additional witness to be provisioned on existing infrastructure and connected to the remote cluster over the customer's network. Typically, these external witnesses are packaged as either virtual machines or standalone software that is installable within a guest operating system.

Cisco HyperFlex Anywhere has the following capabilities:

■ It offers flexibility and scalability at the edge. Two-, three-, and four-node edge configurations support a wider set of use cases, as shown in Figure 15-12. Template-based lights-out deployment, configuration, management, and monitoring speed anywhere deployment at scale, anywhere.

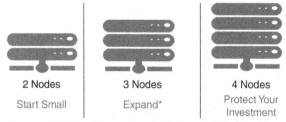

**2 Nodes**
Start Small

**3 Nodes**
Expand*

**4 Nodes**
Protect Your
Investment

**Figure 15-12**  *HyperFlex Multinode Edge*

■ Cisco Intersight provides an invisible cloud witness. The automatic, cloud-based witness for two-node clusters eliminates the complexity of configuring and maintaining a witness node for each edge site (see Figure 15-13).

15

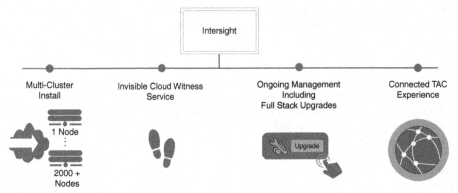

**Figure 15-13** *HyperFlex with Invisible Cloud Witness Service*

- It provides inferencing at the edge. You can perform deep learning on GPU-only nodes in the data center and drive inferencing with up to two NVIDIA Tesla T4 and P6 GPUs in edge nodes and up to six NVIDIA Tesla GPUs in Cisco HyperFlex HX240c nodes.

## HyperFlex Hyperconverged Multicloud Platform (Hybrid or All-Flash)

The Cisco HyperFlex platform offers hybrid or All-Flash configurations, a solution that integrates the network fabric, and powerful data optimization features to bring the full potential of hyperconvergence from enterprise applications to edge computing. This Cisco solution is faster to deploy, simpler to manage, and easier to scale than the current generation of systems. It provides a unified pool of infrastructure resources to power applications as your business needs dictate (see Figure 15-14).

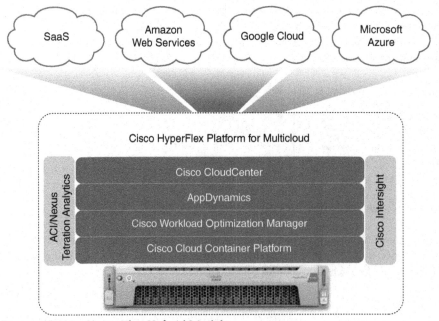

**Figure 15-14** *HyperFlex Hybrid Model*

With hybrid or All-Flash-memory storage configurations and a choice of management tools, Cisco HyperFlex Systems deliver a preintegrated cluster with a unified pool of resources that you can quickly deploy, adapt, scale, and manage to efficiently power your applications (see Figure 15-15).

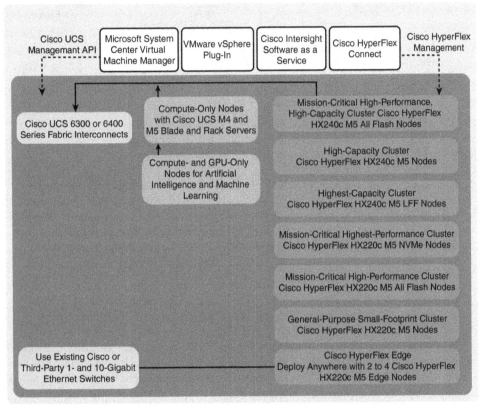

**Figure 15-15**  *HyperFlex Hardware and Management Flexibility*

Cisco UCS provides a single point of connectivity that integrates Cisco HyperFlex HX Series All-Flash or hybrid nodes and a variety of Cisco UCS servers into a single unified cluster. Cisco offers the flexibility to choose the combination of CPU, flash memory, graphics acceleration, and disk storage resources you need to deliver an optimal infrastructure for your applications. Incremental scalability allows you to start small and scale up as your needs grow. You gain the cost savings and performance advantages of Cisco UCS with the flexibility to choose among the solutions offered by the broad Cisco UCS management partner ecosystem.

## HyperFlex All NVMe

All-NVMe nodes deliver the highest performance for mission-critical data center workloads. Cisco provides an architectural performance edge with NVMe drives connected directly to the CPU rather than through a latency-inducing PCIe switch (see Figure 15-16).

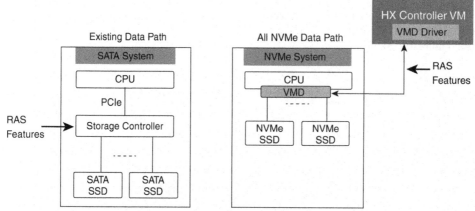

**Figure 15-16** *SATA RAS Compared to All-NVMe Storage Connectivity*

Intel Optane SSDs also connect to the PCIe bus to accelerate caching for even greater performance than NVMe drives alone. NVMe drives yield impressive performance gains over SATA and SAS SSDs, which has driven their adoption in the server market. In the simplest terms, the reason is that it involves much more than a drive qualification. SATA- and SAS-based SSDs require dramatically different server designs than NVMe drives, so bringing an all-NVMe node to market required platform-level hardware and software optimization.

Cisco owns the entire HyperFlex solution stack from the node hardware, the Hyperconverged Infrastructure (HCI) software, to the networking. Taking this fully engineered approach to HCI is what enabled Cisco to address key areas such as the reliability, availability, and serviceability (RAS) challenges that the NVMe architecture introduces. It's also why Cisco was able to leverage its tight partnership with Intel to not just use Intel SSDs but incorporate other Intel innovations like the Intel Volume Management Device (VMD). Cisco used the Intel VMD as a key ingredient to overcome RAS challenges such as surprise drive removal errors and firmware management, and to enable features like LED status lights on the drives and even hot-pluggable NVMe drives.

## Cisco HyperFlex Data Platform

The Cisco HX Data Platform has many integrated components. They include Cisco fabric interconnects (FIs), Cisco UCS Manager, Cisco HX specific servers, and Cisco compute-only servers; VMware vSphere, ESXi servers, and vCenter; and the Cisco HX Data Platform installer, controller VMs, HX Connect, vSphere HX Data Platform plug-in, and stcli commands.

The Cisco HX Data Platform is installed on a virtualized platform such as VMware vSphere. During installation, after specifying the Cisco HyperFlex HX cluster name, the HX Data Platform creates a hyperconverged storage cluster on each of the nodes. As your storage needs increase and you add nodes in the HX cluster, the HX Data Platform balances the storage across the additional resources. You can add compute-only nodes to increase compute-only resources to the storage cluster, as shown in Figure 15-17.

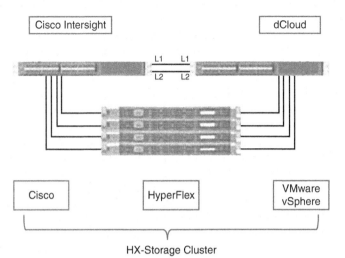

**Figure 15-17**   *HyperFlex Lab Cluster Infrastructure*

## HX Storage Cluster Physical Components

Cisco HyperFlex storage clusters contain the following objects. These objects are monitored by the HX Data Platform for the storage cluster. They can be added and removed from the HX storage cluster.

■ **Converged nodes:** Converged nodes are the physical hardware on which the VM runs. They provide computing and storage resources such as disk space, memory, processing, power, and network I/O. When a converged node is added to the storage cluster, a storage controller VM is installed. The HX Data Platform services are handled through the storage controller VM. Converged nodes add storage resources to your storage cluster through their associated drives.

■ **Compute nodes:** Compute nodes add compute resources but not storage capacity to the storage cluster. They are used as a means to add compute resources, including CPU and memory. They do not need to have any caching (SSD) or storage (HDD) drives. Compute nodes are optional in an HX storage cluster.

■ **Drives:** There are two types of drives that are required for any node in the storage cluster: SSDs and HDDs. HDDs typically provide the physical storage units associated with converged nodes. SSDs typically support management. Adding or removing disks on your converged nodes is not performed through the HX Data Platform.

■ **Datastores:** These datastores provide storage capacity and datastore capacity. This is the combined consumable physical storage available to the storage cluster through datastores and managed by the HX Data Platform. Datastores are logical containers that are used by the HX Data Platform to manage your storage use and storage resources. Datastores are where the host places virtual disk files and other VM files. Datastores hide the specifics of physical storage devices and provide a uniform model for storing VM files.

## HX Data Platform High Availability

The HX Data Platform high availability feature ensures that the storage cluster maintains at least two copies of all your data during normal operation with three or more fully functional nodes.

If nodes or disks in the storage cluster fail, the cluster's ability to function is affected. If more than one node fails or one node and disk(s) on a different node fail, it is called a simultaneous failure.

The number of nodes in the storage cluster and the Data Replication Factor and Access Policy settings determine the state of the storage cluster that results from node failures.

HX Data Platform storage cluster status information is available through HX Connect, the HX Data Platform plug-in, and the storage controller VM stcli commands. Storage cluster status is described through resiliency and operational status values. Storage cluster status is described through the following reported status elements:

- **Operational status:** Describes the ability of the storage cluster to perform the storage management and storage cluster management functions of the cluster. Describes how well the storage cluster can perform operations.

- **Resiliency status:** Describes the ability of the storage clusters to tolerate node failures within the storage cluster. Describes how well the storage cluster can handle disruptions.

The following settings take effect when the storage cluster transitions into particular operational and resiliency status states:

- **Data replication factor:** Sets the number of redundant data replicas.

- **Cluster access policy:** Sets the level of data protection and data loss.

- **Operational status values:** Cluster operational status indicates the operational status of the storage cluster and the ability for the applications to perform I/O. The operational status options are

  - **Online:** The cluster is ready for I/O.

  - **Offline:** The cluster is not ready for I/O.

  - **Out of space:** Either the entire cluster is out of space, or one or more disks are out of space. In both cases, the cluster cannot accept write transactions but can continue to display static cluster information.

  - **Readonly:** The cluster cannot accept write transactions but can continue to display static cluster information.

  - **Unknown:** This is a transitional state while the cluster is coming online.

- **Resiliency status values:** Resiliency status is the data resiliency health status and ability of the storage cluster to tolerate failures. Resiliency status options are

  - **Healthy:** The cluster is healthy with respect to data and availability.

- **Warning:** Either the data or the cluster availability is being adversely affected.

- **Unknown:** This is a transitional state while the cluster is coming online.

## HX Data Platform Cluster Tolerated Failures

If nodes or disks in the HX storage cluster fail, the cluster's ability to function is affected. If more than one node fails or one node and disk(s) on a different node fail, it is called a simultaneous failure. How the number of node failures affect the storage cluster depends on the following:

- **Number of nodes in the cluster:** The response by the storage cluster is different for clusters with three to four nodes and five or greater nodes.

- **Data replication factor:** This number is set during HX Data Platform installation and cannot be changed. The options are two or three redundant replicas of your data across the storage cluster.

**NOTE**  A data replication factor of 3 is recommended.

- **Access policy:** This can be changed from the default setting after the storage cluster is created. The options are strict, for protecting against data loss, or lenient, to support longer storage cluster availability.

## HX Data Platform Ready Clones

HX Data Platform Ready Clones is a storage technology that enables you to rapidly create and customize multiple cloned VMs from a host VM. It enables you to create multiple copies of VMs that can then be used as standalone VMs.

A Ready Clone, similar to a standard clone, is a copy of an existing VM. The existing VM is called the host VM. When the cloning operation is complete, the Ready Clone is a separate guest VM.

Changes made to a Ready Clone do not affect the host VM. A Ready Clone's MAC address and UUID are different from that of the host VM.

Installing a guest operating system and applications can be time consuming. With Ready Clone, you can make many copies of a VM from a single installation and configuration process. Clones are useful when you deploy many identical VMs to a group.

## HX Data Platform Native Snapshots

HX Data Platform Native Snapshots is a backup feature that saves versions (states) of working VMs. VMs can be reverted back to native snapshots.

Use the HX Data Platform plug-in to take native snapshots of your VMs. HX Data Platform Native Snapshot options include creating a native snapshot, reverting to any native snapshot, and deleting a native snapshot. Timing options include Hourly, Daily, and Weekly, all in 15-minute increments.

A native snapshot is a reproduction of a VM that includes the state of the data on all VM disks and the VM power state (on, off, or suspended) at the time the native snapshot is taken. Take a native snapshot to save the current state of the VM so that you can revert to the saved state.

## HX Cluster Interfaces

Each HyperFlex interface provides access to information about and a means to perform actions upon the HX storage cluster. The HX storage cluster interfaces include

- **HX Connect:** Enables you to use monitoring, performance charts, and tasks for upgrade, encryption, replication, datastores, nodes, disks, and VM-ready clones.

- **HX Data Platform Plug-in:** Enables you to use monitoring, performance charts, and tasks for datastores, hosts (nodes), and disks.

- **Storage Controller VM command line:** Enables you to run the HX Data Platform stcli commands.

- **HyperFlex Systems RESTful APIs:** Enables authentication, replication, encryption, monitoring, and management of HyperFlex Systems through an on-demand stateless protocol.

Additional interfaces include

- **Cisco HX Data Platform Installer:** Enables you to install the HX Data Platform, deploy and expand the HX storage cluster, deploy stretched clusters, and deploy Hyper-V clusters.

- **Cisco UCS Manager:** Provides tasks for networking, storage and storage access, and managing resources in the HX storage cluster.

- **VMware vSphere Web Client and vSphere Client:** Enables you to manage all the VMware ESXi servers in the vCenter cluster.

- **VMware ESXi:** Enables you to manage the individual ESXi host, providing a host command line.

## HX Self-Encrypting Drives

Self-encrypting drives (SEDs) have special hardware that encrypts incoming data and decrypts outgoing data in real-time. The data on the disk is always stored in encrypted form. A media encryption key controls this encryption and decryption. This key is never stored in the processor or memory.

A security key, also known as key-encryption key or an authentication passphrase, is used to encrypt the media encryption key. To enable SED, you must provide a security key. No key is required to fetch the data, if the disk is not locked.

The Cisco HyperFlex system enables you to configure security keys locally or remotely. When you configure the key locally, you must remember the key. In case you forget the key, it cannot be retrieved, and the data is lost if the drive power cycles. You can configure the key remotely by using a key management server (also known as KMIP server). This method addresses the issues related to safe-keeping and retrieval of the keys in the local management.

The encryption/decryption for SEDs is done through the hardware. Thus, it does not affect the overall system performance. SEDs reduce the disk retirement and redeployment costs through instantaneous cryptographic erasure. Cryptographic erasure is done by changing the media encryption key. When the media encryption key of a disk is changed, the data on the disk cannot be decrypted and is immediately rendered unusable.

### Configuring a Local Encryption Key

To configure a local encryption key, follow these steps:

**Step 1.** On the Cisco HyperFlex Connect navigation pane, choose **Encryption**.

**Step 2.** On the Encryption page, click **Configure Encryption**.

**Step 3.** Enter the Cisco UCS Manager credentials shown in Table 15-2.

**Table 15-2** Local Encryption Cisco UCS Manager Credentials Information

| UI Element | Essential Information |
|---|---|
| **UCS Manager host name** field | Cisco UCS Manager cluster host name. <br> Enter an IP address or FQDN. <br> *<eng.storvisor.com>* |
| **User name** field | *<admin>* username |
| **Password** field | *<admin>* password |

Click **Next**.

**Step 4.** To secure the HyperFlex cluster using an encryption key generated and stored locally, select **Local Key**. Then click **Next**.

**Step 5.** Enter the encryption key (passphrase) for this cluster.

**NOTE** Enter exactly 32 alphanumeric characters.

**Step 6.** Click **Enable Encryption**.

### Managing HX Disks in the Cluster

Disks, whether SSDs or HDDs, might fail. If this occurs, you need to remove the failed disk and replace it. Follow the server hardware instructions for removing and replacing the disks in the host. The HX Data Platform identifies the SSD or HDD and incorporates it into the storage cluster. To increase the datastore capacity of a storage cluster, add the same size and type SSDs or HDDs to each converged node in the storage cluster. For hybrid servers, add HDDs. For All-Flash servers, add SSDs.

**NOTE**   When performing a hot-plug pull and replace on multiple drives from different vendors or of different types, pause for a few moments (30 seconds) between each action. Pull, pause for about 30 seconds, replace a drive, and pause for 30 seconds. Then pull, pause for 30 seconds, and replace the next drive. Sometimes, when a disk is removed, it continues to be listed in the cluster summary information. To refresh this, restart the HX cluster.

Disk requirements vary between converged nodes and compute-only nodes. To increase the available CPU and memory capacity, you can expand the existing cluster with compute-only nodes as needed. These compute-only nodes provide no increase to storage performance or storage capacity.

Alternatively, adding converged nodes increases storage performance and storage capacity alongside CPU and memory resources. Servers with only solid-state disks are All-Flash servers. Servers with both SSDs and HDDs are hybrid servers. The following applies to all the disks in a HyperFlex cluster:

- All the disks in the storage cluster must have the same amount of storage capacity. All the nodes in the storage cluster must have the same number of disks.

- All SSDs must support TRIM and have TRIM enabled.

- All HDDs can be either SATA or SAS type. All SAS disks in the storage cluster must be in a pass-through mode.

- Disk partitions must be removed from SSDs and HDDs. Disks with partitions are ignored and not added to your HX storage cluster.

- Optionally, you can remove or back up existing data on disks. All existing data on a provided disk is overwritten.

**NOTE**   New factory servers are shipped with the appropriate disk partition settings. Do not remove disk partitions from new factory servers.

- Only the disks ordered directly from Cisco are supported.

- On servers with self-encrypting drives (SEDs), both the cache and persistent storage (capacity) drives must be SED capable. These servers support Data at Rest Encryption (DARE).

In addition to the disks listed in Table 15-3, all M4 converged nodes have 2x 64-GB SD FlexFlash cards in a mirrored configuration with ESX installed. All M5 and M6 converged nodes have M.2 SATA SSD with ESXi installed.

**Table 15-3**  HX Servers Disk Types

| Platform | Component | Qty | Hybrid | All Flash | Hybrid SED | All Flash SED |
|---|---|---|---|---|---|---|
| MX240 M5 Servers | System SSD for logs | 1 | 240 GB SSD | 240 GB SSD | 240 GB SSD | 240 GB SSD |
| | Cache SSD | 1 (back) | 1.6 TB SSD | 1.6 TB NVMe 400 GB SSD | 1.6 TB SSD | 800 GB SSD |
| | Persistent | 6-23 | 1.2 TB HDD 1.8 TB HDD | 960 GB SSD 3.8 TB SSD | 1.2 TB HDD | 800 GB SSD 960 GB SSD 3.8 TB SSD |
| MX240 M4 Servers | System SSD for logs | 1 | 120 GB SSD 240 GB SSD | 120 GB SSD 240 GB SSD | 120 GB SSD 240 GB SSD | 120 GB SSD 240 GB SSD |
| | Cache SSD | 1 | 1.6 TB SSD | 1.6 TB NVMe 400 GB SSD | 1.6 TB SSD | 1.6 TB NVMe 800 GB SSD |
| | Persistent | 6-23 | 1.2 TB HDD 1.8 TB HDD | 960 GB SSD 3.8 TB SSD | 1.2 TB HDD | 800 GB SSD 960 GB SSD 3.8 TB SSD |
| MX220 M5 Servers | System SSD for logs | 1 | 240 GB SSD | 240 GB SSD | 240 GB SSD | 240 GB SSD |
| | Cache SSD | 1 | 480 GB SSD 800 GB SSD | 1.6 TB NVMe 400 GB SSD | 800 GB SSD | 800 GB SSD |
| | Persistent | 6-8 | 1.2 TB HDD 1.8 TB HDD | 960 GB SSD 3.8 TB SSD | 1.2 TB HDD | 800 GB SSD 960 GB SSD 3.8 TB SSD |
| MX220 M4 Servers | System SSD for logs | 1 | 120 GB SSD 240 GB SSD | 120 GB SSD 240 GB SSD | 120 GB SSD 240 GB SSD | 120 GB SSD 240 GB SSD |
| | Cache SSD | 1 | 480 GB SSD | 400 GB SSD | 800 GB SSD | 800 GB SSD |
| | Persistent | 6 | 1.2 TB HDD 1.8 TB HDD | 960 GB SSD 3.8 TB SSD | 1.2 TB HDD | 800 GB SSD 960 GB SSD 3.8 TB SSD |
| HX220 M5 Servers for Edge Clusters | System SSD for logs | 1 | 240 GB SSD | 240 GB SSD | 240 GB SSD | 240 GB SSD |
| | Cache SSD | 1 | 480 GB SSD 800 GB SSD | 1.6 TB NVMe 400 GB SSD | 800 GB SSD | 800 GB SSD |
| | Persistent | 3-8 | 1.2 TB HDD | 960 GB SSD 3.8 TB SSD | 1.2 TB HDD | 800 GB SSD 960 GB SSD 3.8 TB SSD |

15

**NOTE**   Do not mix storage disk types or storage sizes on a server or across the storage cluster. Mixing storage disk types is not supported.

- When replacing cache or persistent disks, always use the same type and size as the original disk.
- Do not mix any of the persistent drives. Use all HDD or SSD and the same size drives in a server.
- Do not mix hybrid and All-Flash cache drive types. Use the hybrid cache device on hybrid servers and All-Flash cache devices on All-Flash servers.
- Do not mix encrypted and nonencrypted drive types. Use SED hybrid or SED All-Flash drives. On SED servers, both the cache and persistent drives must be the SED type.
- All nodes must use the same size and quantity of SSDs. Do not mix SSD types.

### Managing HX Datastores

Datastores are logical containers used by the HX Data Platform to manage your storage usage and storage resources. Datastores are where the host places virtual disk files and other VM files. Datastores hide the specifics of physical storage devices and provide a uniform model for storing VM files.

You can add, refresh the list, edit name and size, delete, mount, and unmount datastores from either the HX Connect UI or the HX Data Platform Plug-in UI. You can only rename an unpaired datastore that is unmounted. Do not rename a datastore using the vCenter administrator interface.

**NOTE**   Use as few datastores as possible to avoid startup delay and to keep clone savings high. Configuring more than 10 datastores could result in excessive startup delay.

To add a datastore, follow these steps:

**Step 1.**   Choose an interface. From the vSphere Web Client Navigator, select **vCenter Inventory Lists > Cisco HyperFlex Systems > Cisco HX Data Platform > cluster > Manage > Datastores**. Then from HX Connect, select **Datastores**.

**Step 2.**   Select the **create datastore**.

**Step 3.**   Enter a name for the datastore. vSphere Web Client enforces a 42-character limit for the datastore name. Assign each datastore a unique name.

**Step 4.**   Specify the datastore size. Choose **GB** or **TB** from the drop-down list.

**Step 5.**   Specify the data blocksize. From HX Connect, choose **8K** or **4K**. The default is 8K. In the HX Data Platform Plug-in, the default is assumed. For VDI workloads, the default is 4K.

**Step 6.**   Click **OK** to accept your changes or **Cancel** to cancel all changes.

**Step 7.**   Verify the datastore. Click the **Refresh** icon if needed to display your new datastore. From the HX Data Platform plug-in, click the **Manage > Datastores > Hosts** tab to see the mount status of the new datastore.

If you check the datastore through the vSphere Client application, **Host > Configuration> Datastores,** the Drive Type is listed as Unknown. Listing NFS datastores as Unknown is expected vSphere behavior.

Next, prepare to mount a datastore:

■ No VM, template, snapshot, or CD/DVD image resides on the datastore. This is the most common error while unmounting.

■ Storage I/O control is disabled for the datastore.

■ The datastore is not used for vSphere HA heartbeat.

■ The datastore is not used to host RDM metadata files. RDM is not supported.

■ The datastore is not used as a scratch location.

**NOTE** You cannot select an NFS datastore as a destination for the persistent scratch location on ESXi. If you select the HX datastore for the persistent scratch location, it will be removed after the ESXi host reloads.

For all M5 servers, M.2 boot SSD is automatically selected for use as scratch. This is configured out of the box on any new install.

For HX240M4 (non-SED), Intel SSD is used for persistent logs/scratch (the same applies on 220M5/240M5, but on a different local SSD).

For HX220M4 and HX240M4 (SED), there is no location to store the scratch partition. So, the only option is to use syslog for persistent logging over the network.

To mount a datastore, follow these steps:

**Step 1.** Choose an interface. From the vSphere Web Client Navigator, select **vCenter Inventory Lists > Cisco HyperFlex Systems > Cisco HX Data Platform > cluster > Manage > Datastores.** Then from HX Connect, select **Datastores.**

**Step 2.** Select a **datastore.**

**Step 3.** Click **Mount.**

**Step 4.** Confirm to mount the datastore; then click **OK.**

## Expand Cisco HX System Clusters

A compute-only node can be added to a HyperFlex cluster, after cluster creation. It is added to provide extra compute resources. The Cisco UCS server does not need to have any caching or persistent drives because they do not contribute any storage capacity to the cluster.

Before you start adding a compute-only node, make sure that the following prerequisites are met:

■ Ensure that the storage cluster state is healthy.

■ Ensure that the new node meets the compute-only system requirements listed in Installation Prerequisites, including network and disk requirements.

- Install the ESXi hypervisor after service profile association.

- Ensure that the new node uses the same configuration as the other nodes in the storage cluster. This includes VLAN IDs and switch types (whether vSwitches), VLAN tagging with External Switch VLAN Tagging (EST), VLAN tagging with Virtual Switch Tagging (VST), or Virtual Distributed Switch.

**NOTE** If the storage cluster is in an out-of-space condition, when you add a new node, the system automatically rebalances the storage cluster. This is in addition to the rebalancing that is performed every 24 hours.

- Enable Enhanced vMotion (EVC) if the new node to be added has a different CPU family than what is already used in the HX cluster.

- Ensure that the software version on the node matches the Cisco HX Data Platform version, the ESXi version, and the vCenter version. To identify the software version, go to the Storage Cluster Summary tab in vCenter and check the HX Data Platform version in the top section. Upgrade if necessary.

- Ensure that the new node has at least one valid DNS and NTP server configured.

- If you are using SSO or Auto Support, ensure that the node is configured for SSO and SMTP services.

- ESXi installation is supported on SD cards for M4 converged nodes and M.2 SATA SSD for M5 converged nodes. For compute-only nodes, ESXi installation is supported for SD Cards, SAN boot, or front SSD/HDD. Installing ESXi on USB Flash is not supported for compute-only nodes.

### Enabling HX Logical Availability Zones

Logical availability zones (LAZ) provide multiple logical grouping of nodes and distribute the data across these groups in such a way that no single group has more than one copy of the data. This enables enhanced protection from node failures, allowing for more nodes to fail while the overall cluster remains online. After you have successfully configured your HyperFlex cluster, refer to the commands in Table 15-4 to enable or disable logical availability zones.

**NOTE** Wait for at least 10 seconds between successive invocations of LAZ disable and LAZ enable operations in that order.

In case of a fresh cluster installation, for best results, it is recommended that LAZ is enabled during cluster creation.

**Table 15-4**   LAZ Enable and Disable **stcli** Commands

| Command | Description |
|---|---|
| stcli cluster get-zone | Checks whether zones are enabled. |
| stcli cluster set-zone --zone 0 | Disables zones. |
| stcli cluster set-zone --zone 1<br><br>stcli rebalance start | (Recommended) Enables and creates zones (default number of zones).<br><br>**NOTE:** A cluster created without zoning enabled will become zone compliant only after enabling zoning and successful completion of rebalance.<br><br>You must execute the **rebalance start** command after you enable and create zones.<br><br>Triggering rebalance activity may involve large-scale data movements across several nodes in the cluster, which may decrease the IO performance in the cluster. |
| stcli cluster set-zone --zone 1<br>--numzones *<integer-value>*<br><br>stcli rebalance start | Enables zones and creates a specific number of zones.<br><br>**NOTE:** You must execute the **rebalance start** command after you enable and create zones. |

There are several requirements and guidelines for configuring logical availability zones in a cluster. If you choose to ignore these requirements, you can expand the cluster with the following procedure:

**Step 1.**   Disable LAZ:

```
stcli cluster --set-zone 0
```

You must wait for a few minutes—roughly around five minutes—for LAZ to be disabled.

**Step 2.**   Add nodes to the cluster.

**Step 3.**   After the nodes are added to the cluster, enable LAZ:

```
stcli cluster set-zone --zone 1
```

If the number of zones is not set explicitly, by default, four zones are created.

**Step 4.**   Initiate rebalancing in the cluster:

```
stcli rebalance start
```

**NOTE**   Rebalancing nodes may decrease the performance of the cluster by about 30 to 40 percent. The time taken to rebalance the nodes in the cluster depends on the cluster size and the data within the cluster. You can use the **stcli rebalance status** command to review the progress of the rebalancing activity.

**Step 5.**   Review the cluster configuration and determine if the cluster is zone compliant:

```
stcli cluster --get-zone
```

15

## Exam Preparation Tasks

As mentioned in the Introduction, you have a couple of choices for exam preparation: the exercises here, Chapter 21, "Final Preparation," and the exam simulation questions in the Pearson Test Prep software online.

## Review All Key Topics

Review the most important topics in the chapter, noted with the key topic icon in the outer margin of the page. Table 15-5 lists a reference to these key topics and the page numbers on which each is found.

**Table 15-5**  Key Topics for Chapter 15

| Key Topic Element | Description | Page |
|---|---|---|
| Figure 15-3 | Cisco HyperFlex System Interconnection, Virtualization, and Management | 705 |
| Section | Intelligent End-to-End Automation | 708 |
| Figure 15-7 | End-to-End HyperFlex Automation | 709 |
| Section | Unified Management for All Workloads | 709 |
| Section | Independent Resource Scaling | 710 |
| Figure 15-9 | HyperFlex Resource Optimization | 711 |
| Section | HyperFlex as an Edge Device | 712 |
| Figure 15-15 | HyperFlex Hardware and Management Flexibility | 715 |

## Define Key Terms

Define the following key terms from this chapter, and check your answers in the Glossary.

branch office (ROBO); Cisco Unified Computing System (UCS); graphical processing unit (GPU); input/output operations per second (IOPS); Logical Availability Zones (LAZ); Peripheral Component Interconnect Express (PCIe); reliability, availability, and service-ability (RAS); remote office; replication factor (RF); solid-state drive (SSD); tebibyte (TiB); Virtual Desktop Infrastructure (VDI); virtual interface cards (VICs); Virtual Server Infra-structure (VSI); Volume Management Device (VMD)

## References

Cisco HyperFlex HX-Series: https://www.cisco.com/c/en/us/products/hyperconverged-infrastructure/hyperflex-hx-series/index.html

Cisco Live HyperFlex presentations: https://www.ciscolive.com/

Cisco HyperFlex Systems Solution Overview: https://www.cisco.com/c/en/us/products/collateral/hyperconverged-infrastructure/hyperflex-hx-series/solution-overview-c22-744674.html

# CHAPTER 16

# Automation and Scripting Tools

Network automation can make your life easier. There are many reasons why IT organizations of all shapes and sizes are adopting network automation. Following are some of them:

■ **Reduced operational costs:** Automation can give a return on investment for every dollar spent. Automation has the potential to reduce IT department staffing costs while potentially redirecting IT staff efforts to more proactive, business value–generating projects.

■ **Deterministic outcomes:** Automation of the network decreases manual, error-prone processes on network configuration and deployment.

■ **Resilient networks:** Automation can detect and fix network errors on the fly without manual intervention. This results in more resilient networks.

■ **Faster deployment:** Network automation can deploy and upgrade network devices in the network faster without requiring any manual intervention or configuration.

## This chapter discusses the following key topics:

**EEM Overview:** This section discusses EEM policies, event statements, and action statements, along with EEM configuration and verification.

**Scheduler:** This section discusses the Scheduler concepts, along with Scheduler configuration and verification.

**Bash Shell for Cisco NX-OS:** This section discusses Bourne Again SHell (Bash) for Cisco NX-OS along with managing feature and patch RPMs.

**Guest Shell for Cisco NX-OS:** This section discusses how to access the Guest Shell for Cisco NX-OS, the resources used, and the capabilities of the Guest Shell. Later in this section, we discuss how to manage the Guest Shell.

**XML:** This section discusses XML syntax in detail and includes an example.

**JSON:** This section briefly discusses JSON syntax and includes an example.

**Rest API:** This section discusses the concepts of Rest API, including Rest API authentication and Rest API response data. Later in this section, we discuss NX-API in detail, including request and response elements for NX-API. At the end of this section, we describe the NX-API Developer Sandbox.

## "Do I Know This Already?" Quiz

The "Do I Know This Already?" quiz enables you to assess whether you should read this entire chapter thoroughly or jump to the "Exam Preparation Tasks" section. If you are in doubt about your answers to these questions or your own assessment of your knowledge of the topics, read the entire chapter. Table 16-1 lists the major headings in this chapter and their corresponding "Do I Know This Already?" quiz questions. You can find the answers in Appendix A, "Answers to the 'Do I Know This Already?' Quizzes."

**Table 16-1** "Do I Know This Already?" Section-to-Question Mapping

| Foundation Topics Section | Questions |
|---|---|
| EEM Overview | 1–2 |
| Scheduler | 3–4 |
| Bash Shell for Cisco NX-OS | 5 |
| Guest Shell for Cisco NX-OS | 6 |
| XML | 7 |
| JSON | 8 |
| Rest API | 9–10 |

**CAUTION** The goal of self-assessment is to gauge your mastery of the topics in this chapter. If you do not know the answer to a question or are only partially sure of the answer, you should mark that question as wrong for purposes of the self-assessment. Giving yourself credit for an answer you correctly guess skews your self-assessment results and might provide you with a false sense of security.

1. What are the major components of the Embedded Event Manager (EEM)? (Choose two answers.)

   a. Event statements

   b. Job statements

   c. Action statements

   d. Schedule statements

2. Which of the following actions are NOT supported on EEM configuration? (Choose three answers.)

   a. Generate a syslog message.

   b. Reload the device.

   c. Generate a Python script.

   d. Update a counter.

3. Which of the following statements are NOT correct for the Scheduler? (Choose two answers.)

   a. You must have network-admin user privileges to configure a scheduled job.

   b. You must enable any conditional features before you can configure those features in a job.

   c. If you create a schedule and assign jobs and do not configure the time, the job still starts as the Scheduler applies a default timetable.

   d. Scheduler features are enabled by default.

**4.** Which types of timetables for job scheduling are possible in the Scheduler? (Choose three answers.)

   **a.** Monthly

   **b.** Yearly

   **c.** Delta

   **d.** One-time mode

**5.** Which command enables the Bash shell on Nexus 9000 Series switches?

   **a.** run bash

   **b.** feature bash-shell

   **c.** run bash sudo su

   **d.** username foo shelltype bash

**6.** Which of the following capabilities is NOT provided to network-admin from within the Guest Shell?

   **a.** Access to Nexus switch bootflash

   **b.** Access to Cisco Nexus switch CLI

   **c.** The ability to install and run 32-bit and 64-bit Windows applications

   **d.** The ability to install and run 32-bit and 64-bit Linux applications

**7.** Which of the following statements are CORRECT regarding XML? (Choose two answers.)

   **a.** Each XML element must have a start-tag and end-tag.

   **b.** Each XML document can have multiple root elements.

   **c.** XML is not case sensitive.

   **d.** An empty-element tag (or standalone tag) must be properly closed.

**8.** Which of the following statements is correct with respect to JavaScript Object Notation (JSON)?

   **a.** JSON is more verbose than XML.

   **b.** JSON is used to describe structured data, which doesn't include arrays, whereas XML includes arrays.

   **c.** JSON is an unordered set of name/value pairs, so it tends to be self-explanatory.

   **d.** A proper JSON object begins with a left bracket [ and ends with a right bracket ].

**9.** Which of the following are allowed HTTP methods for RESTful API requests? (Choose three answers.)

   **a.** GET

   **b.** POST

   **c.** DOWN

   **d.** PUT

**10.** Which of the following elements does NOT belong to NX-API Response?

   **a.** chunk

   **b.** output

   **c.** outputs

   **d.** msg

## Foundation Topics

## EEM Overview

This section describes how to configure the Embedded Event Manager (EEM) to detect and handle critical events on Cisco NX-OS devices.

The EEM monitors events that occur on the device and takes action to recover or troubleshoot these events based on the configuration.

The EEM consists of three major components:

- **Event statements:** Events to monitor from another Cisco NX-OS component that may require some action, workaround, or notification.

- **Action statements:** Actions that the EEM can take, such as sending an email or disabling an interface, to recover from an event.

- **Policies:** Events paired with one or more actions to troubleshoot or recover from the event.

### Policies

An EEM policy consists of an event statement and one or more action statements. The event statement defines the event to look for as well as the filtering characteristics for the event. The action statement defines the action EEM takes when the event occurs.

Figure 16-1 shows the two basic statements in an EEM policy.

| **Event Statement** | | **Action Statement** |
|---|---|---|
| Tells your system: Look for this specific event to happen.<br><br>For example, when a card is removed. |  | Tells your system: If that event happens, do these things.<br><br>For example, when a card is removed, log the details. |

**Figure 16-1**  *EEM Policy Statements*

EEM policies can be configured using the command-line interface (CLI) or a VSH script.

The EEM gives a device-wide view of policy management. EEM policies are configured on the supervisor, and the EEM pushes the policy to the correct module based on the event type. The EEM takes any actions for a triggered event either locally on the module or on the supervisor (the default option). The EEM maintains event logs on the supervisor.

Cisco NX-OS has a number of preconfigured system policies. These system policies define many common events and actions for the device. System policy names begin with two underscore characters (__). You can create user policies to suit your network. If you create a user policy, any actions in your policy occur after EEM triggers any system policy actions related to the same event as your policy. You can also override some system policies. The overrides that you configure take the place of the system policy. You can override the event or the actions.

16

Use the **show event manager system-policy** command to view the preconfigured system policies and determine which policies that you can override.

Table 16-2 provides some examples of system policies.

**Table 16-2**   System Policies

| Event | Description |
|---|---|
| __ethpm_link_flap | More than 30 link flaps in a 420-second interval. Action: Error. Disable the port. |
| __lcm_module_failure | Power cycle two times and then power down. |
| __pfm_fanbad_all_systemfan | Syslog when fan goes bad. |

## Event Statements

An event is any device activity for which some action, such as a workaround or a notification, should be taken. In many cases, these events are related to faults in the device such as when an interface or a fan malfunctions.

The EEM defines event filters so only critical events or multiple occurrences of an event within a specified time period trigger an associated action. Event statements specify the event that triggers a policy to run. You can configure multiple event triggers. The EEM schedules and runs policies on the basis of event statements. The EEM examines the event and action commands and runs them as defined. If you want to allow the triggered event to process any default actions, you must configure the EEM policy to allow the event default action statement.

Table 16-3 describes some of the EEM events you can use on the device.

**Table 16-3**   EEM Events

| EEM Event | Description |
|---|---|
| cli | A CLI command is entered that matches a pattern with a wildcard. |
| interface | The interface counter exceeds a threshold. |
| module | A specified module enters the selected status. |
| module-failure | A module failure is generated. |
| syslog | The event monitors syslog messages and invokes the policy based on the search string in the policy. |
| track | A tracked object changes state. |

## Action Statements

Action statements describe the action triggered by a policy. Each policy can have multiple action statements. If no action is associated with a policy, EEM still observes events but takes no actions.

EEM supports the following actions in action statements:

- Execute any CLI commands.

- Update a counter.

- Log an exception.

- Force the shutdown of any module.

- Reload the device.

- Shut down specified modules because the power is over budget.

- Generate a syslog message.

- Generate a Call Home event.

- Generate an SNMP notification.

- Use the default action for the system policy.

If you want to allow the triggered event to process any default actions, you must configure the EEM policy to allow the default action. For example, if you match a CLI command in a match statement, you must add the event-default action statement to the EEM policy; otherwise, EEM will not allow the CLI command to execute.

Verify that your action statements within your user policy or overriding policy do not negate each other or adversely affect the associated system policy.

**NOTE**   The username: admin (with network-admin or vdc-admin user privileges) is required to configure EEM on a nondefault VDC.

## Configuring EEM

EEM configuration is a three-step process:

**Step 1.**   Register the applet with the EEM and enter applet configuration mode.

`event manager applet` *applet-name*

**Step 2.**   Configure the event statement for the policy. Repeat this step for multiple event statements.

`event` *event-statement*

**Step 3.**   Configure an action statement for the policy. Repeat this step for multiple action statements.

`action` *number[.number2] action-statement*

You can define environment variables for EEM that are available for all policies. Environment variables are useful for configuring common values that you can use in multiple policies. For example, you can create an environment variable for the IP address of an external email server:

`event manager environment` *variable-name variable-value*

The *variable-name* can be any case-sensitive alphanumeric string up to 29 characters. The *variable-value* can be any quoted alphanumeric string up to 39 characters.

You can also override a system policy using the following command:

`event manager applet` *applet-name* `override` *system-policy*

The *applet-name* can be any case-sensitive alphanumeric string up to 29 characters. The *system-policy* must be one of the existing system policies.

Example 16-1 shows how to monitor a module powerdown.

**Example 16-1** *EEM Script for Monitoring Module Powerdown*

```
switch# configure terminal
Enter configuration commands, one per line. End with CNTL/Z.
switch(config)# event manager applet monitorPoweroff
switch(config-applet)# description "Monitors module power down."
switch(config-applet)# event cli match "conf t ; poweroff *"
switch(config-applet)# action 1.0 cli show module
```

### Verifying the EEM Configuration

You can use the following commands to verify the EEM configuration:

**show running-config eem:** Displays information about the running configuration for EEM.

**show event manager system-policy [all]:** Displays information about the predefined system policies.

**show event manager policy active detailed:** Displays the EEM policies that are executing.

# Scheduler

In regular day-to-day network operations, you need to perform multiple routine maintenance activities on a regular basis—for example, backing up data or saving a configuration. You can achieve these goals by using the Scheduler. The Scheduler uses jobs that consist of a single command or multiple commands that define routine activities. Jobs can be scheduled one time or at periodic intervals.

The Scheduler defines a job and its timetable as follows:

- **Job:** A routine task defined as a command list and completed according to a specified schedule.

- **Schedule:** The timetable for completing a job. You can assign multiple jobs to a schedule. A schedule is defined as either periodic or one-time only.

  - **Periodic mode:** A recurring interval that continues until you delete the job. You can configure the following types of intervals:

    - **Daily:** A job is completed once a day.

    - **Weekly:** A job is completed once a week.

    - **Monthly:** A job is completed once a month.

    - **Delta:** A job begins at the specified start time and then at specified intervals (days:hours:minutes).

  - **One-time mode:** A job is completed only once at a specified time.

Before starting a job, the Scheduler authenticates the user who created the job. Because user credentials from a remote authentication are not retained long enough to support a scheduled job, you need to locally configure the authentication passwords for users who create jobs. These passwords are part of the Scheduler configuration and are not considered a locally configured user. Before starting the job, the Scheduler validates the local password against the password from the remote authentication server.

The Scheduler maintains a log file containing the job output. If the size of the job output is greater than the size of the log file, the output is truncated.

**NOTE**   The Scheduler requires no license.

The Scheduler has the following prerequisites:

- You must enable any conditional features before you can configure those features in a job.

- You must have a valid license installed for any licensed features that you want to configure in the job.

- You must have network-admin user privileges to configure a scheduled job.

## Configuring Scheduler

The Scheduler has the following configuration guidelines and limitations:

- The Scheduler can fail if it encounters one of the following while performing a job:

  - If the license has expired for a feature at the time the job for that feature is scheduled

  - If a feature is disabled at the time when a job for that feature is scheduled

  - If you have removed a module from a slot and a job for that slot is scheduled

- Verify that you have configured the time. The Scheduler does not apply a default timetable. If you create a schedule and assign jobs and do not configure the time, the job is not started.

- While defining a job, verify that no interactive or disruptive commands (for example, **copy bootflash:** *file* **ftp:** *URI*, **write erase**, and other similar commands) are specified because the job is started and conducted noninteractively.

You can enable the Scheduler feature so that you can configure and schedule jobs, or you can disable the Scheduler feature after it has been enabled:

```
switch(config)# [no] feature scheduler
```

You can configure the log file size for capturing jobs, schedules, and job output:

```
switch(config)# scheduler logfile size value
```

In this command, *value* defines the scheduler log file size in kilobytes. The range is from 16 to 1024. The default is 16.

> **NOTE**   If the size of the job output is greater than the size of the log file, the output is truncated.

You can configure the scheduler to use remote authentication for users who want to configure and schedule jobs. The following command configures a cleartext password for the user who is currently logged in:

```
switch(config)# scheduler aaa-authentication password [0 | 7] password
```

The following command configures a cleartext password for a remote user:

```
switch(config)# scheduler aaa-authentication username name
password [0 | 7] password
```

> **NOTE**   Remote users must authenticate with their cleartext password before creating and configuring jobs.

You can define a job including the job name and the command sequence. The following two commands create a job and define the sequence of commands for the specified job:

```
switch(config)# scheduler job name string
```

```
switch(config-job)# command1 ;[command2;command3 ;...]
```

You can define a timetable in the Scheduler to be used with one or more jobs. If you do not specify the time for the **time** commands, the Scheduler assumes the current time. You can start a job daily at a designated time specified as HH:MM. You can also start a job on a specified day of the week specified as follows:

- An integer such as 1 = Sunday, 2 = Monday, and so on.

- An abbreviation such as Sun = Sunday.

You can also start a job on a specified day each month (dm). If you specify either 29, 30, or 31, the job is started on the last day of each month.

```
switch(config)# scheduler schedule name string
```

```
switch(config-schedule)# job name string
```

```
switch(config-schedule)# time daily time
```

or

```
switch(config-schedule)# time weekly [[dm:]HH:]MM
```

or

```
switch(config-schedule)# time monthly [[dm:]HH:]MM
```

You can clear the Scheduler log file using the **clear scheduler logfile** command.

Example 16-2 shows how to create a Scheduler job that saves the running configuration to a file in bootflash and then copies the file from bootflash to a TFTP server (the filename is created using the current timestamp and switch name).

**Example 16-2**   *Scheduler Job to Back Up Configuration*

```
switch# configure terminal
switch(config)# scheduler job name backup-cfg
switch(config-job)# cli var name timestamp $(TIMESTAMP) ;copy running-config
bootflash:/$(SWITCHNAME)-cfg.$(timestamp) ;copy bootflash:/$(SWITCHNAME)-cfg.$
(timestamp) tftp://1.2.3.4/ vrf management
switch(config-job)# end
switch(config)#
```

Example 16-3 shows how to schedule a Scheduler job called backup-cfg to run daily at 1 a.m.

**Example 16-3**   *Scheduler Job to Back Up Configuration at Specified Time*

```
switch# configure terminal
switch(config)# scheduler schedule name daily
switch(config-schedule)# job name backup-cfg
switch(config-schedule)# time daily 1:00
switch(config-schedule)# end
switch#
```

### Verifying Scheduler Configuration

You can verify the Scheduler configuration using the commands shown in Table 16-4.

**Table 16-4**   Scheduler Verification Commands

| Command | Purpose |
|---|---|
| show scheduler config | Displays the Scheduler configuration. |
| show scheduler job [name *string*] | Displays the jobs configured. |
| show scheduler logfile | Displays the contents of the Scheduler log file. |
| show scheduler schedule [name *string*] | Displays the schedules configured. |

Example 16-4 shows how to display the job schedule and the results of Scheduler jobs that have been executed by the Scheduler.

**Example 16-4**   *Displaying Job Schedule and the Result of Scheduler Jobs*

```
switch# show scheduler schedule
Schedule Name : daily
---------------------------
User Name : admin
Schedule Type : Run every day at 1 Hrs 00 Mins
Last Execution Time : Fri Jan 2 1:00:00 2019
Last Completion Time: Fri Jan 2 1:00:01 2019
Execution count : 2
```

```
--------------------------------------------------
Job Name Last Execution Status
--------------------------------------------------
back-cfg Success (0)
switch#


switch# show scheduler logfile
Job Name : back-cfg Job Status: Failed (1)
Schedule Name : daily User Name : admin
Completion time: Fri Jan 1 1:00:01 2019
----------------------------- Job Output -----------------------------
'cli var name timestamp 2019-01-01-01.00.00'
'copy running-config bootflash:/$(HOSTNAME)-cfg.$(timestamp)'
'copy bootflash:/switch-cfg.2019-01-01-01.00.00 tftp://1.2.3.4/ vrf management '
copy: cannot access file '/bootflash/switch-cfg.2019-01-01-01.00.00'
==============================================================================
Job Name : back-cfg Job Status: Success (0)
Schedule Name : daily User Name : admin
Completion time: Fri Jan 2 1:00:01 2019
----------------------------- Job Output -----------------------------
'cli var name timestamp 2019-01-02-01.00.00'
'copy running-config bootflash:/switch-cfg.2019-01-02-01.00.00'
'copy bootflash:/switch-cfg.2019--01-02-01.00.00 tftp://1.2.3.4/ vrf management '
Connection to Server Established.
[ ] 0.50KBTrying to connect to tftp server......
[###### ] 24.50KB
TFTP put operation was successful
==============================================================================
switch#
```

# Bash Shell for Cisco NX-OS

In addition to the NX-OS CLI, Cisco Nexus 9000, 3000, 3500, 3600, 7000, and 7700 Series switches support access to the Bourne Again SHell (Bash). Bash interprets commands that you enter or commands that are read from a shell script. Using Bash enables access to the underlying Linux system on the device and to manage the system.

In Cisco NX-OS, Bash is accessible from user accounts that are associated with the Cisco NX-OS dev-ops role or the Cisco NX-OS network-admin role.

Example 16-5 shows the authority of the dev-ops role and the network-admin role.

**Example 16-5**  *Displaying Authority of the dev-ops and network-admin Roles*

```
switch# show role name dev-ops


Role: dev-ops
  Description: Predefined system role for devops access. This role
  cannot be modified.
  Vlan policy: permit (default)
  Interface policy: permit (default)
  Vrf policy: permit (default)
  ----------------------------------------------------------------
  Rule    Perm    Type      Scope          Entity
  ----------------------------------------------------------------
  4       permit  command                  conf t ; username *
  3       permit  command                  bcm module *
  2       permit  command                  run bash *
  1       permit  command                  python *

switch# show role name network-admin


Role: network-admin
  Description: Predefined network admin role has access to all commands
  on the switch
  ----------------------------------------------------------------
  Rule    Perm    Type      Scope          Entity
  ----------------------------------------------------------------
  1       permit  read-write
switch#
```

You can enable Bash by running the **feature bash-shell** command. The **run bash** command loads Bash and begins at the home directory for the user.

Example 16-6 shows how to enable the Bash shell feature and how to run Bash.

**Example 16-6**  *Enabling bash-shell and Running Bash*

```
switch# configure terminal
switch(config)# feature bash-shell
switch# run bash
bash-4.2$ whoami
admin
bash-4.2$ pwd
/bootflash/home/admin
bash-4.2$
```

You can also execute Bash commands by using the **run bash** command. For instance, you can run **whoami** using the **run bash** *command*:

```
run bash whoami
```

You can also run Bash by configuring the user **shelltype**:

```
username foo shelltype bash
```

This command puts you directly into the Bash shell upon login. This does not require **feature bash-shell** to be enabled. You can also run NX-OS CLI commands from the Bash shell using the **vsh -c** command.

## Managing Feature RPMs

Features on the Nexus 9000, 3000, and 3500 Series are distributed as packages. You can use the Bash shell to manage those packages. Before installing the RPM package, you need to verify the system readiness for the same by using the following command:

```
switch# show logging logfile | grep -i "System ready"

2018 Mar 27 17:24:22 switch %ASCII-CFG-2-CONF_CONTROL: System ready
```

If you see "System ready" output, you are all set.

Table 16-5 provides some of the commands that you can use to manage RPM packages using Bash.

**Table 16-5**  Commands to Manage RPM Packages Using Bash

| Command or Action | Purpose |
|---|---|
| **run bash sudo su** | Loads Bash. |
| **yum list available** | Displays a list of the available RPMs. YUM (Yellowdog Updater Modified) is a package management tool for RPM (RedHat Package Manager) based on Linux systems. |
| **sudo yum installed \| grep** *platform* | Displays a list of the NX-OS feature RPMs installed on the switch. |
| **sudo yum -y install** *rpm* | Installs an available RPM. |
| **sudo yum -y upgrade** *rpm* | Upgrades an installed RPM. |
| **sudo yum -y downgrade** *rpm* | Downgrades the RPM if any of the YUM repositories have a lower version of the RPM. |
| **sudo yum -y erase** *rpm* | Erases the RPM. |

## Managing Patch RPMs

Table 16-6 shows some of the commands that you can use to manage Patch RPMs using Bash.

**Table 16-6**  Commands to Manage Patch RPMs Using Bash

| Command or Action | Purpose |
|---|---|
| **yum list --patch-only** | Displays a list of the patch RPMs present on the switch. |
| **sudo yum install --add** *URL_of_patch* | Adds the patch to the repository, where *URL_of_patch* is a well-defined format, such as bootflash:/*patch*, not in standard Linux format, such as /bootflash/*patch*. |

| Command or Action | Purpose |
|---|---|
| **yum list --patch-only available** | Displays a list of the patches that are added to the repository but are in an inactive state. |
| **sudo yum install** *patch_RPM* **--nocommit** | Activates the patch RPM, where *patch_RPM* is a patch that is located in the repository. Do not provide a location for the patch in this step. Adding the **--nocommit** flag to the command means that the patch RPM is activated in this step, but not committed. |
| **sudo yum install** *patch_RPM* **--commit** | Commits the patch RPM. The patch RPM must be committed to keep it active after reloads. |
| **sudo yum erase** *patch_RPM* **--nocommit** | Deactivates the patch RPM. |
| **sudo yum install --remove** *patch_RPM* | Removes an inactive patch RPM. |

## Guest Shell for Cisco NX-OS

In addition to the NX-OS CLI and Bash access on the underlying Linux environment, the Cisco Nexus 9000 Series devices support access to a decoupled execution space running within a Linux Container (LXC) called the Guest Shell. When running in the Guest Shell, you have network-admin privileges.

From within the Guest Shell, the network-admin has the following capabilities:

- Access to the network over Linux network interfaces

- Access to Cisco Nexus switch bootflash

- Access to Cisco Nexus switch volatile tmpfs

- Access to Cisco Nexus switch CLI

- Access to Cisco NX-API REST

- The ability to install and run Python scripts

- The ability to install and run 32-bit and 64-bit Linux applications

Decoupling the execution space from the native host system allows customization of the Linux environment to suit the needs of the applications without impacting the host system or applications running in other Linux Containers.

### Accessing the Guest Shell

You can use the **run guestshell** CLI command to access the Guest Shell on the Cisco Nexus device; the **run guestshell** command parallels the **run bash** command that is used to access the host shell. This command allows you to access the Guest Shell and get a Bash prompt or run a command within the context of the Guest Shell. The command uses password-less SSH to an available port on the localhost in the default network namespace.

The Cisco NX-OS automatically installs and enables the Guest Shell by default on systems with sufficient resources. Subsequent upgrades to the Cisco Nexus series switch software will not automatically upgrade the Guest Shell. The Guest Shell is based on a CentOS 7 root file system.

**NOTE** Systems with 4 GB of RAM will not enable the Guest Shell by default. The Guest Shell is automatically enabled on systems with more than 4 GB of RAM.

The Guest Shell starts an OpenSSH server upon bootup. The server listens on a randomly generated port on the localhost IP address interface 127.0.0.1 only. This provides the password-less connectivity into the Guest Shell from the NX-OS virtual-shell when the **guestshell** keyword is entered. If this server is killed or its configuration (residing in /etc/ssh/sshd_config-cisco) is altered, access to the Guest Shell from the NX-OS CLI might not work.

Starting in 2.2(0.2), the Guest Shell will dynamically create user accounts with the same username with which the user logged in to the switch. However, all other information is NOT shared between the switch and the Guest Shell user accounts.

In addition, the Guest Shell accounts are not automatically removed, so they must be removed by the network administrator when no longer needed.

### Resources Used for the Guest Shell

By default, the resources for the Guest Shell have a small impact on resources available for normal switch operations. If the network-admin requires additional resources for the Guest Shell, the **guestshell resize**{cpu | memory | rootfs} command changes these limits.

Table 16-7 shows the Guest Shell resource limits.

**Table 16-7** Guest Shell Resource Limits

| Resource | Default | Minimum/Maximum |
|----------|---------|-----------------|
| CPU | 1% | 1/20% |
| Memory | 256 MB | 256/3840 MB |
| Storage | 200 MB | 200/2000 MB |

The CPU limit is the percentage of the system compute capacity that tasks running within the Guest Shell are given when there is contention with other compute loads in the system. When there is no contention for CPU resources, the tasks within the Guest Shell are not limited.

**NOTE** A Guest Shell reboot is required after changing the resource allocations. This can be accomplished with the **guestshell reboot** command.

Misbehaving or malicious application code can cause DoS as the result of overconsumption of connection bandwidth, disk space, memory, and other resources. The host provides resource-management features that ensure fair allocation of resources between the Guest Shell and services on the host.

### Capabilities in the Guest Shell

The Guest Shell is populated with CentOS 7 Linux, which provides the ability to YUM install software packages built for this distribution. The Guest Shell is prepopulated with many of the common tools that would naturally be expected on a networking device, including **net-tools**, **iproute**, **tcpdump**, and OpenSSH. Python 2.7.5 is included by default, as is the PIP for installing additional Python packages.

The Guest Shell has access to the Linux network interfaces used to represent the management and data ports of the switch. Typical Linux methods and utilities like **ifconfig** and **ethtool** can be used to collect counters, as shown in Example 16-7. When an interface is placed into a Virtual Routing and Forwarding (VRF) in the NX-OS CLI, the Linux network interface is placed into a network namespace for that VRF. You can see the name spaces at /var/run/netns and can use the **ip netns** utility to run in the context of different namespaces. A couple of utilities, **chvrf** and **vrfinfo**, are provided as a convenience for running in a different namespace and getting information about which namespace or VRF a process is running in.

**Example 16-7**   *Displaying Counters for Ethernet 1/47 Interface Inside Guest Shell*

```
switch# guestshell
[guestshell@guestshell ~]$ ifconfig Eth1-47
Eth1-47: flags=4163<UP,BROADCAST,RUNNING,MULTICAST> mtu 1500
inet 13.0.0.47 netmask 255.255.255.0 broadcast 13.0.0.255
ether 54:7f:ee:8e:27:bc txqueuelen 100 (Ethernet)
RX packets 311442 bytes 21703008 (20.6 MiB)
RX errors 0 dropped 185 overruns 0 frame 0
TX packets 12967 bytes 3023575 (2.8 MiB)
TX errors 0 dropped 0 overruns 0 carrier 0 collisions 0
```

The Guest Shell provides an application to allow the user to issue NX-OS commands from the Guest Shell environment to the host network element. The **dohost** application accepts any valid NX-OS configuration or exec commands and issues them to the host network element.

When you are invoking the **dohost** command, each NX-OS command may be in single or double quotes:

**dohost** *"<NXOS CLI>"*

Example 16-8 shows how to use the **dohost** command.

**Example 16-8**   *Using the **dohost** Command*

```
[guestshell@guestshell ~]$ dohost "sh lldp time | in Hold" "show cdp global"
Holdtime in seconds: 120
Global CDP information:
CDP enabled globally
Refresh time is 21 seconds
Hold time is 180 seconds
CDPv2 advertisements is enabled
DeviceID TLV in System-Name(Default) Format
[guestshell@guestshell ~]$
```

Python can be used interactively, or Python scripts can be run in the Guest Shell, as shown in Example 16-9.

**Example 16-9**   *Running Python Inside the Guest Shell*

```
guestshell:~$ python
Python 2.7.5 (default, Jun 24 2019, 00:41:19)
[GCC 4.8.3 20140911 (Red Hat 4.8.3-9)] on linux2
Type "help", "copyright", "credits" or "license" for more information.
>>>
guestshell:~$
```

The Pip Python Package Manager is included in the Guest Shell to allow the network-admin to install new Python packages, as shown in Example 16-10.

**Example 16-10**   *Using Pip Python Package Manager to Install a Python Package*

```
[guestshell@guestshell ~]$ sudo su
[root@guestshell guestshell]# pip install Markdown
Collecting Markdown
Downloading Markdown-2.6.2-py2.py3-none-any.whl (157kB)
100% |################################| 159kB 1.8MB/s
Installing collected packages: Markdown
Successfully installed Markdown-2.6.2
[root@guestshell guestshell]# pip list | grep Markdown
Markdown (2.6.2)
[root@guestshell guestshell]#
```

To preserve the integrity of the files within the Guest Shell, the file systems of the Guest Shell are not accessible from the NX-OS CLI. For the host, bootflash: and volatile: are mounted as /bootflash and /volatile within the Guest Shell. A network-admin can access files on this media using the NX-OS exec commands from the host or using Linux commands from within the Guest Shell.

## Managing the Guest Shell

Table 16-8 lists commands to manage the Guest Shell.

**Table 16-8**   Commands to Manage the Guest Shell

| Commands | Description |
|---|---|
| **guestshell enable** | Installs and activates the Guest Shell. |
| **guestshell disable** | Shuts down and disables the Guest Shell. |
| **guestshell upgrade** | Deactivates and upgrades the Guest Shell. |
| **guestshell reboot** | Deactivates the Guest Shell and then reactivates it. |
| **guestshell destroy** | Deactivates and uninstalls the Guest Shell. |
| **guestshell run** *command* | Executes a Linux/UNIX command within the context of the Guest Shell environment. After execution of the command, you are returned to the switch prompt. |
| **guestshell resize [cpu \| memory \| rootfs ]** | Changes the allotted resources available for the Guest Shell. The changes take effect the next time the Guest Shell is enabled or rebooted. |

The **guestshell disable** command shuts down and disables the Guest Shell, as shown in Example 16-11.

**Example 16-11**   *Using the* **guestshell disable** *Command*

```
switch# guestshell disable
You will not be able to access your guest shell if it is disabled. Are you sure you
want to disable the guest shell? (y/n) [n] y
2019 Jul 30 19:47:23 switch %$ VDC-1 %$ %VMAN-2-ACTIVATION_STATE: Deactivating
virtual service 'guestshell+'
2019 Jul 30 18:47:29 switch %$ VDC-1 %$ %VMAN-2-ACTIVATION_STATE: Successfully
deactivated virtual service 'guestshell+'
```

The **guestshell destroy** command uninstalls the Guest Shell and its artifacts, as shown in Example 16-12.

**Example 16-12**   *Using the* **guestshell destroy** *Command*

```
switch# guestshell destroy
You are about to destroy the guest shell and all of its contents. Be sure to save
your work. Are you sure you want to continue? (y/n) [n] y
2019 Jul 30 18:49:10 switch %$ VDC-1 %$ %VMAN-2-INSTALL_STATE: Destroying virtual
service
 'guestshell+'
2019 Jul 30 18:49:10 switch %$ VDC-1 %$ %VMAN-2-INSTALL_STATE: Successfully destroyed
virtual service 'guestshell +'
```

The **guestshell enable** command installs the Guest Shell from a Guest Shell software package, as shown in Example 16-13. By default, the package embedded in the system image is used for the installation. The command is also used to reactivate the Guest Shell if it has been disabled.

**Example 16-13**   *Using the* **guestshell enable** *Command*

```
switch# guestshell enable
2019 Jul 30 18:50:27 switch %$ VDC-1 %$ %VMAN-2-INSTALL_STATE: Installing virtual
service 'guestshell+'
2019 Jul 30 18;50;42 switch %$ VDC-1 %$ %VMAN-2-INSTALL_STATE: Install success
virtual service 'guestshell+'; Activating
2019 Jul 30 18:50:42 switch %$ VDC-1 %$ %VMAN-2-ACTIVATION_STATE: Activating virtual
service 'guestshell+'
2019 Jul 30 18:51:16 switch %$ VDC-1 %$ %VMAN-2-ACTIVATION_STATE: Successfully
activated
virtual service 'guestshell+'
```

The output of the **show guestshell detail** command displays details about the guestshell package (such as version, signing resources, and devices), as shown in Example 16-14.

16

**Example 16-14**   *Using the* guestshell detail *Command*

```
switch# show guestshell detail
Virtual service guestshell+ detail
  State                : Activated
  Package information
    Name               : guestshell.ova
    Path               : /isan/bin/guestshell.ova
    Application
      Name             : GuestShell
      Installed version : 2.2(0.2)
      Description      : Cisco Systems Guest Shell
    Signing
      Key type         : Cisco key
      Method           : SHA-1
    Licensing
      Name             : None
      Version          : None
  Resource reservation
    Disk               : 250 MB
    Memory             : 256 MB
    CPU                : 1% system CPU


  Attached devices
    Type           Name        Alias
    ---------------------------------------------
    Disk           _rootfs
    Disk           /cisco/core
    Serial/shell
    Serial/aux
    Serial/Syslog              serial2
    Serial/Trace               serial3
```

# XML

Extensible Markup Language (XML) is a markup language that defines a set of rules for
encoding documents in a format that is both human-readable and machine-readable. XML
follows a specific format and helps give structure to data. Because XML is platform-neutral,
computer-language-neutral, and text-based, it is useful for data exchange between computers
and for data storage.

Example 16-15 displays a fragment from an XML document that shows how you might
structure some simple data about a network device.

**Example 16-15**  *XML Structure of a Network Device*

```
<device>
        <interface>mgmt0</interface>
        <state>up</state>
        <eth_ip_addr>192.168.10.175</eth_ip_addr>
        <eth_ip_mask>24</eth_ip_mask>
<device>
```

The XML fragment has a root element called device. The device element has four child elements:

- interface

- state

- eth_ip_addr

- eth_ip_mask

You can think of each element as a data field. XML provides structure to those data fields. XML doesn't do anything with the data. To manipulate that data, a piece of software has to send, receive, store, or display it. One example of such software is Google Postman.

## Example

Example 16-16 displays an XML document that has a root node element called ciscopress. Notice that the ciscopress element contains one child element: book.

**Example 16-16**  *XML Structure Example*

```
<?xml version ="1.0" encoding="UTF-8"?>
  <ciscopress>
    <book isbn="1587052024">
      <title>Routing TCP/IP</title>
      <author>Jeff Doyle</author>
      <category></category>
      <year>2005</year>
      <edition>2</edition>
      <price>72</price>
    </book>
  </ciscopress>
```

Figure 16-2 shows a visual representation of the sample XML document as a tree.

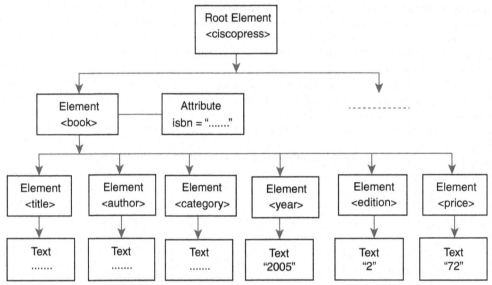

**Figure 16-2** *Visual Representation of XML Document as a Tree*

Note the following points:

- The book element contains multiple child elements.

- The book element contains metadata in the form of an attribute called isbn. An element can contain multiple attributes.

- The <category> element in the sample XML document contains no character data. It's an "empty element." This is valid if the underlying schema allows it.

One aspect of the XML language that sets it apart from a markup language like HTML is that it has no predefined tags. The elements in Figure 16-2, such as <ciscopress> and <price>, are not defined in the XML standard. These elements and the document structure are created by the author of the XML document. That's different from the way HTML works with predefined tags such as <p>, <h1>, and <table>.

An XML document that contains data is also sometimes referred to as an XML payload.

## XML Syntax

The basic unit of an XML document is called an element. Each XML element must conform to the following rules to be considered "well formed":

- Each XML element must have a start-tag and an end-tag. The tags are enclosed in angle brackets—for example, <device>...</device>. Unlike HTML, the closing tag is mandatory.

- An empty-element tag (or standalone tag) must be properly closed—for example, <interface></interface>.

- An XML element includes its start-tag, enclosing character data and/or child elements, and the end-tag.

- The element's name can contain letters, numbers, and other Unicode characters, but NOT white spaces.

- The element's name must start with a letter, an underscore "_", or a colon ":", but cannot start with certain reserved words such as xml.

- Each XML document must have one (and only one) root element. XML elements must be properly nested. For example, <device><interface>... </device></interface is incorrectly nested. The correct nesting is <device><interface>...</interface></device>.

- XML is case sensitive. For example, <Interface> and <interface> are considered two different elements.

- The start-tag may contain attributes in the form of attribute_name="attribute_value". Attributes are used to provide extra information about the element. Unlike HTML, the attribute_value of an XML attribute must be properly quoted (either in double quotes or single quotes).

- Certain characters, such as <, >, which are used in XML syntax, must be replaced with entity references in the form of &entity_name;. XML has five predefined entity references:

  - &lt; (<)

  - &gt; (>)

  - &amp; (&)

  - &quot; (")

  - &apos; (').

- XML comments can be used in the form <!-- comment texts -->, which is the same as HTML.

- Unlike HTML, white spaces in the text are preserved.

- A new-line character is represented by a Line Feed (LF) character (0AH).

## JSON

JavaScript Object Notation (JSON) is a lightweight text-based open standard designed for human-readable data interchange.

JSON objects contain data in a consistent format that can be passed and programmatically consumed more easily than the data in report formats. A JSON object is an unordered set of name/value pairs, so it tends to be self-explanatory, like XML, but it is less bulky.

Parameters for JSON objects are passed in the following format:
ParameterName:parameterValue. A proper JSON object begins with a left brace { and ends with a right brace }. Each name in a pair is followed by a colon (:) and then the corresponding value. The name/value pairs are separated by commas.

16

Example 16-17 displays a fragment from a JSON document that shows how you might structure some simple data about a network device.

**Example 16-17**   *JSON Structure of a Network Device*

```
{
    "device": {
      "interface": "mgmt0",
      "state": "up",
      "eth_ip_addr": "192.168.10.175",
      "eth_ip_mask": 24,
                  }
}
```

Both JSON and XML are human-readable formats. They are both independent of any specific programming language. However, there are a few differences:

- **Verbose:** XML is more verbose than JSON and usually uses more characters to express the same data than JSON.

- **Arrays:** XML is used to describe structured data, which doesn't include arrays, whereas JSON includes arrays.

- **Parsing:** Although most programming languages contain libraries that can parse both JSON and XML data, evaluating specific data elements can be more difficult in XML (although more powerful) compared to JSON.

## Rest API

An application programming interface (API) is a way for two pieces of software to talk to each other. An API allows for the development of rich applications with a wide variety of functionality. Let's go through an example.

Suppose you are the creator of an online marketplace named Jack's Shop, where people can come to buy stuff and get it delivered to their home/office. How do you track which user purchased what? You need to maintain a database with user accounts and user order history. But you don't want to maintain a user credentials database in-house. You would like your users to log in using their Google or Facebook accounts. How do you achieve this? A simple answer to this question would be using the Facebook API or Google API to authenticate users.

REST is centered around the HTTP request and response model. Consuming an API is just as simple as making an HTTP request. For example, if you make a request to an API Service, the result of the request will be returned in the response. The data returned in the response is usually JSON or XML.

To construct a request, you need to know the following information for the API that you are calling. You can find this information in the API reference documentation.

- **Method**

  - GET: Retrieve data

- POST: Create something new

- PUT: Update data

- DELETE: Delete data

- URL

  - The URL for the endpoint you want to call

  - Example: http://apic/api/aaaLogin.xml

- URL Parameters

  - The parameters that you can pass as part of the URL

- Authentication

  - Authentication type (Basic HTTP, token-based, and OAuth are common)

  - Authentication credentials

- Additional HTTP Headers

  - Additional HTTP headers required by the specific API

  - Example: Content-Type: application/json

- Request Body

  - JSON or XML containing the HTTP Message Body data bytes that are needed to complete the request

- Response Body

  - JSON or XML containing the HTTP Message Body data bytes transmitted in an HTTP transaction message response

Figure 16-3 shows the REST API request and response process.

**Figure 16-3**  *REST API Request and Response*

## Authentication

There are different types of authentication for REST APIs. Authentication is used to control access and access rights to the REST APIs. For example, some users might have read-only access, which means that they can use only the parts of the API that read data. Other users might have both read and write access. This means they can use the API to perform operations that not only read data but also add, edit, and delete data. These access rights are typically based on user-assigned roles such as Administrator that would have full rights to change data, whereas a plain User role might have read-only access rights.

The following list shows the types of authentication controls:

- **None:** The Web API resource is public; anybody can place a call. Generally, the case for GET methods, rarely for POST, PUT, DELETE.

- **Basic HTTP:** The username and password are passed to the server in an encoded string.

    - Authorization: Basic ENCODEDSTRING.

- **Token:** A secret key generally retrieved from the Web API developer portal.

    - The keyword may change from one Web API to another: Bearer, token.

    - Passed with each API call.

- **OAuth:** A sequence flow is initiated to retrieve an access token from an identity provider. The token is then passed with each API call.

    - Open standard. User rights are associated with the token (OAuth scope).

    - The token expires. It can be revoked. It can also be reissued via a refresh token.

## Response

The returned data is defined in the Response portion, which includes the HTTP status codes along with the data format and attributes.

- HTTP status codes

    - HTTP status codes are used to return success, error, or other statuses. (See http://www.w3.org/Protocols/HTTP/HTRESP.html.)

    - Some common examples are

        - 200 OK

        - 202 Accepted/Processing

        - 401 Not Authorized

- Content

    - Often returned in different formats based on the request. Common formats are JSON, XML, and Text.

Figure 16-4 shows a REST API request and response all in the same window using Postman.

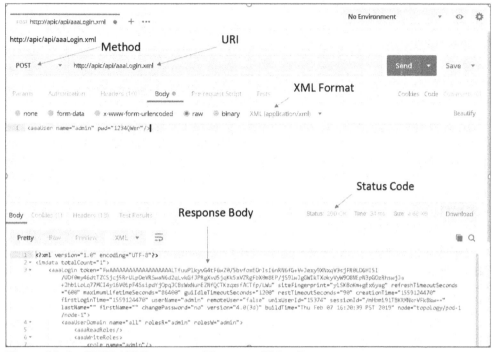

**Figure 16-4**  *REST API Request and Response Using Postman*

## NX-API

CLI commands are mostly run on the Nexus devices. NX-API enables you to access these CLIs by making them available outside the switch by using HTTP/HTTPS. You can use this extension to the existing Cisco Nexus CLI system on the Cisco Nexus 9000, 3000, 3500, 3600, and 7000 Series devices. NX-API supports show commands, configurations, and Linux Bash. NX-API uses HTTP/HTTPS as its transport. CLIs are encoded into the HTTP/HTTPS POST body.

The NX-API back end uses the Nginx HTTP server. The Nginx process, and all of its children processes, are under Linux cgroup protection where the CPU and memory usage are capped. If the Nginx memory usage exceeds the cgroup limitations, the Nginx process is restarted and restored.

NX-API is integrated into the authentication system on the device. Users must have appropriate accounts to access the device through NX-API. NX-API uses HTTP basic authentication. All requests must contain the username and password in the HTTP header. You should consider using HTTPS to secure your user's login credentials.

NX-API provides a session-based cookie, nxapi_auth, when users first successfully authenticate. With the session cookie, the username and password are included in all subsequent NX-API requests that are sent to the device. The username and password are used with the session cookie to bypass performing the full authentication process again. If the session cookie is not included with subsequent requests, another session cookie is required and is provided by the authentication process. Avoiding unnecessary use of the authentication process helps reduce the workload on the device.

**NOTE**   A nxapi_auth cookie expires in 600 seconds (10 minutes). This value is a fixed and cannot be adjusted.

The commands, command type, and output type for the Cisco Nexus 9000 Series devices are entered using NX-API by encoding the CLIs into the body of an HTTP/HTTPS POST. The response to the request is returned in XML or JSON output format.

NX-API CLI is enabled by default for local access. The remote HTTP access is disabled by default. First, you need to enable the NX-API feature before you can send any API requests to the NX-OS software.

To enable the NX-API nxapi feature, enter these commands:

```
switch# conf t

switch(config)# feature nxapi
```

Example 16-18 shows a request and its response in XML format.

**Example 16-18**   *Request and Response in XML Format*

```
Request:
<?xml version="1.0"?>
<ins_api>
  <version>1.2</version>
  <type>cli_show</type>
  <chunk>0</chunk>
  <sid>sid</sid>
  <input>show clock</input>
  <output_format>xml</output_format>
</ins_api>


Response:
<?xml version="1.0"?>
<ins_api>
  <type>cli_show</type>
  <version>1.2</version>
  <sid>eoc</sid>
  <outputs>
    <output>
      <body>
        <simple_time>01:30:58.810 UTC Thu May 30 2019</simple_time>
      </body>
      <input>show clock</input>
      <msg>Success</msg>
      <code>200</code>
    </output>
  </outputs>
</ins_api>
```

Example 16-19 shows a request and its response in JSON format.

**Example 16-19**   *Request and Response in JSON Format*

```
Request:
{
  "ins_api": {
    "version": "1.2",
    "type": "cli_show",
    "chunk": "0",
    "sid": "1",
    "input": "show clock",
    "output_format": "json"
  }
}
Response:
{
  "ins_api": {
    "type": "cli_show",
    "version": "1.2",
    "sid": "eoc",
    "outputs": {
      "output": {
        "input": "show clock",
        "msg": "Success",
        "code": "200",
        "body": {
          "simple_time": "01:29:16.684 UTC Thu May 30 2019"
        }
      }
    }
  }
}
```

## NX-API Request and Response Elements

NX-API request elements are sent to the device in XML format or JSON format. The HTTP header of the request must identify the content type of the request.

You can use the NX-API request elements shown in Table 16-9 to specify a CLI command for XML or JSON format.

**Table 16-9**   NX-API Request Elements

| NX-API Request Element | Description |
|---|---|
| version | This element specifies the NX-API version. |
| type | This request specifies the type of command to be executed—for example, cli_show, cli_conf, bash. |

| NX-API Request Element | Description |
|---|---|
| chunk | Some **show** commands can return a large amount of output. For the NX-API client to start processing the output before the entire command completes, NX-API supports output chunking for **show** commands. In this case, 1 enables chunk output, whereas 0 denotes not to chunk the output. |
| rollback | This element is valid only for configuration CLIs, not for show commands. It specifies the configuration rollback options—for example, Stop-on-error, Continue-on-error, Rollback-on-error. |
| sid | The session ID element is valid only when the response message is chunked. To retrieve the next chunk of the message, you must specify an *sid* to match the *sid* of the previous response message. |
| input | Input can be one command or multiple commands. However, you should not mix commands that belong to different message types. For example, **show** commands are cli_show message type and are not supported in cli_conf mode. |
| output_format | The available output message formats are xml and json. |

The NX-API elements that respond to a CLI command are listed in Table 16-10.

**Table 16-10**   NX-API Response Element

| NX-API Response Element | Description |
|---|---|
| version | NX-API version. |
| type | Type of command to be executed. |
| sid | Session ID of the response. This element is valid only when the response message is chunked. |
| outputs | Tag that encloses all command outputs.<br>When multiple commands are in cli_show or cli_show_ascii, each command output is enclosed by a single output tag.<br>When the message type is cli_conf or bash, there is a single output tag for all the commands because cli_conf and bash commands require context. |
| output | Tag that encloses the output of a single command output.<br>For cli_conf and bash message types, this element contains the outputs of all the commands. |
| input | Tag that encloses a single command that was specified in the request. |
| body | Body of the command response. |
| code | Error code returned from the command execution. |
| msg | Error message associated with the returned error code. |

Table 16-11 provides some of the possible NX-API errors, error codes, and messages of an NX-API response.

**Table 16-11**   NX-API Response and Error Codes

| NX-API Response | Code | Message |
|---|---|---|
| SUCCESS | 200 | Success. |
| CLI_CLIENT_ERR | 400 | CLI execution error. |
| CLI_CMD_ERR | 400 | Input CLI command error. |
| IN_MSG_ERR | 400 | Request message is invalid. |
| NO_INPUT_CMD_ERR | 400 | No input command. |
| PERM_DENY_ERR | 401 | Permission denied. |
| XML_TO_JSON_CONVERT_ERR | 500 | XML to JSON conversion error. |
| JSON_NOT_SUPPORTED_ERR | 501 | JSON not supported due to large amount of output. |
| MSG_TYPE_UNSUPPORTED_ERR | 501 | Message type not supported. |
| STRUCT_NOT_SUPPORTED_ERR | 501 | Structured output unsupported. |

### NX-API Developer Sandbox

The Cisco NX-API Developer Sandbox is a web form hosted on the switch. It translates NX-OS CLI commands into equivalent XML or JSON payloads and converts NX-API REST payloads into their CLI equivalents. The web form is a single screen with three panes—Command (top pane), Request (bottom-left pane), and Response (bottom-right pane)—as shown in Figure 16-5.

**Figure 16-5**   *NX-API Sandbox GUI*

The Request pane also has a series of tabs. Each tab represents a different language: Python, Java, and JavaScript. Each tab enables you to view the request in the respective language. For example, after converting CLI commands into an XML or JSON payload, click the Python tab to view the request in Python, which you can use to create scripts.

Controls in the Command pane enable you to choose a supported command type, such as cli_show, cli_show_ascii, cli_conf, and a message format, such as XML or JSON. The available options vary depending on the chosen method.

When you type or paste one or more CLI commands into the Command pane, the web form converts the commands into a REST API payload, checking for configuration errors, and displays the resulting payload in the Request pane. If you then choose to post the payload directly from the sandbox to the switch (by choosing the POST option), the Response pane displays the API response.

## Exam Preparation Tasks

As mentioned in the Introduction, you have a couple of choices for exam preparation: the exercises here, Chapter 21, "Final Preparation," and the exam simulation questions in the Pearson Test Prep software online.

## Review All Key Topics

Review the most important topics in the chapter, noted with the key topic icon in the outer margin of the page. Table 16-12 lists a reference to these key topics and the page numbers on which each is found.

**Table 16-12** Key Topics for Chapter 16

| Key Topic Element | Description | Page |
|---|---|---|
| Paragraph | EEM Overview | 731 |
| Figure 16-1 | EEM Policy Statements | 731 |
| Table 16-2 | System Policies | 732 |
| Table 16-3 | EEM Events | 732 |
| List | Action Statements | 732 |
| List | Configuring EEM | 733 |
| Paragraph | Verifying EEM Configuration | 734 |
| List | Scheduler | 734 |
| Example 16-2 | Scheduler Job to Back Up Configuration | 737 |
| Example 16-3 | Scheduler Job to Back up Configuration at Specified Time | 737 |
| Table 16-4 | Scheduler Verification Commands | 737 |
| Example 16-6 | Enabling bash-shell and Running Bash | 739 |
| Table 16-5 | Commands to Manage RPM Packages Using Bash | 740 |
| Table 16-6 | Commands to Manage Patch RPMs Using Bash | 740 |
| Paragraph | Accessing the Guest Shell | 741 |
| Paragraph | Capabilities in the Guest Shell | 743 |
| Table 16-8 | Commands to Manage the Guest Shell | 744 |
| Example 16-15 | XML Structure of a Network Device | 747 |
| List | XML Syntax | 748 |
| Paragraph | JSON | 749 |

| Key Topic Element | Description | Page |
|---|---|---|
| Example 16-17 | JSON Structure of a Network Device | 750 |
| List | XML and JSON Differences | 750 |
| Paragraph | REST API | 750 |
| List | REST API Request Components | 750 |
| List | REST API Authentication Types | 752 |
| List | REST API Response Components | 752 |
| Table 16-9 | NX-API Request Elements | 755 |
| Table 16-10 | NX-API Response Elements | 756 |
| Table 16-11 | NX-API Response and Error Codes | 757 |

## Memory Tables

Print a copy of Appendix C, "Memory Tables" (found on the companion website), or at least the section for this chapter, and complete the tables and lists from memory. Appendix D, "Memory Tables Answer Key," also on the companion website, includes completed tables and lists to check your work.

## Define Key Terms

Define the following key terms from this chapter, and check your answers in the Glossary.

action statements, application programming interface (API), Bourne Again SHell (Bash Shell), Embedded Event Manager (EEM), event statements, Extensible Markup Language (XML), Guest Shell, JavaScript Object Notation (JSON), job, NX-API, NX-API Developer Sandbox, policies, Representational State Transfer (REST), RPM Package Manager (RPM), Scheduler, Yellowdog Updater Modified (YUM)

## References

Cisco Nexus 7000 Series NX-OS System Management Configuration Guide 8.x: https://www.cisco.com/c/en/us/td/docs/switches/datacenter/nexus7000/sw/system-management/config/cisco_nexus7000_system-management_config_guide_8x.html

Cisco Nexus 9000 Series NX-OS System Management Configuration Guide, Release 9.2(x): https://www.cisco.com/c/en/us/td/docs/switches/datacenter/nexus9000/sw/92x/system-management/b-cisco-nexus-9000-series-nx-os-system-management-configuration-guide-92x/b-cisco-nexus-9000-series-nx-os-system-management-configuration-guide-92x_chapter_01001.html

Cisco Nexus 9000 Series NX-OS Programmability Guide, Release 9.2(x): https://www.cisco.com/c/en/us/td/docs/switches/datacenter/nexus9000/sw/92x/programmability/guide/b-cisco-nexus-9000-series-nx-os-programmability-guide-92x.html

Cisco DevNet: https://developer.cisco.com/

16

# CHAPTER 17

# Evaluate Automation and Orchestration Technologies

Most of the early automation tools were developed for server automation. As use cases of automation increased, many companies developed products that supported automation from day one. Cisco is no different; it developed several products such as the Cisco UCS Server, Cisco Nexus switches, and Cisco ACI, which now support automation tools such as Ansible and HashiCorp Terraform. Automation tools help maintain consistent configuration throughout a network with no or minimal human intervention. Some automation tools are agentless, such as Ansible, which utilizes device-specific APIs or SSH to push configuration to network devices, and do not require installation of an agent. However, some automation tools work with the help of an agent, meaning they are installed on the network devices, which are responsible for converting configuration details to a device-specific configuration.

## This chapter discusses the following key topics:

**Ansible:** This section discusses Ansible concepts, components, and Ansible command-line interface (CLI) tools. Later in this section, we look at a Cisco NX-OS Ansible example.

**Python:** This section discusses the Python packages supported on-box for Cisco Nexus devices, CLI command APIs, Python in interactive and noninteractive mode, UCS Manager Python SDK, and the Convert to UCS Python API.

**PowerOn Auto Provisioning (POAP):** This section discusses limitations and network requirements for POAP, POAP configuration scripts, POAP processes, and how to configure a switch using POAP.

**Terraform:** This section discusses the HashiCorp Terraform IaC tool and its support on Cisco ACI.

**PowerShell:** This section explains the UCS PowerShell modules, also referred to as UCS PowerTool Suite.

## "Do I Know This Already?" Quiz

The "Do I Know This Already?" quiz enables you to assess whether you should read this entire chapter thoroughly or jump to the "Exam Preparation Tasks" section. If you are in doubt about your answers to these questions or your own assessment of your knowledge of the topics, read the entire chapter. Table 17-1 lists the major headings in this chapter and their corresponding "Do I Know This Already?" quiz questions. You can find the answers in Appendix A, "Answers to the 'Do I Know This Already?' Quizzes."

**Table 17-1** "Do I Know This Already?" Section-to-Question Mapping

| Foundation Topics Section | Questions |
|---|---|
| Ansible | 1–2 |
| Python | 3–4 |
| PowerOn Auto Provisioning (POAP) | 5–6 |
| Terraform | 7–8 |
| PowerShell | 9 |

**CAUTION** The goal of self-assessment is to gauge your mastery of the topics in this chapter. If you do not know the answer to a question or are only partially sure of the answer, you should mark that question as wrong for purposes of the self-assessment. Giving yourself credit for an answer you correctly guess skews your self-assessment results and might provide you with a false sense of security.

1. Which structured format are Ansible playbooks written in?

   a. JSON

   b. XML

   c. YAML

   d. TOML

2. Which statements are CORRECT for the Ansible automation tool? (Choose two answers.)

   a. Engineers create Ansible playbooks in JSON that describe a workflow or the configuration of the infrastructure.

   b. Ansible scripts run on Cisco devices using Ansible Agent installed on the remote hosts.

   c. When the control station runs the Ansible playbooks, they typically copy modules written in Python to remote hosts.

   d. Ansible runs the modules on the remote hosts to perform the work described in playbooks.

3. What is the name of the Python package for Cisco?

   a. cisco

   b. cisco_secret

   c. cisco_socket

   d. cisco.acl

4. When it is used for executing CLI commands, which API prints the command output directly to stdout and returns nothing to Python?

   a. cli()

   b. clid()

   c. clip()

   d. clistdout()

5. Which of the following statements about POAP are INCORRECT? (Choose two answers.)

   a. For the POAP feature to function, the switch software image must support POAP.

   b. Checking for a USB device containing the configuration script file in POAP mode is supported on the Cisco Nexus 9000 Series switches.

   c. The POAP process requires a minimum DHCP lease period of 1800 seconds (30 minutes).

   d. POAP does not support provisioning of the switch after it has been configured and is operational.

6. Which of the following is NOT a phase of the POAP process?

   a. DHCP discovery phase

   b. Configuration loading phase

   c. Script execution phase

   d. Post-installation reload phase

7. Which Terraform command is used to define what steps need to be taken and the dependencies between the resources for the successful application of a Terraform plan?

   a. **terraform destroy**

   b. **terraform init**

   c. **terraform apply**

   d. **terraform plan**

8. What is used for Terraform to be able to communicate correctly with the managed resources' APIs?

   a. Variables file

   b. API key token

   c. Provider plug-in

   d. Applications

9. Where do you get the Cisco PowerShell modules?

   a. Cisco Software download site

   b. Microsoft download Site

   c. PowerShell Gallery

   d. Subscription to MS Office 365

## Foundation Topics

## Ansible

Created by Michael DeHaan and acquired by Red Hat in 2015, Ansible is an open-source, agentless tool for software provisioning, configuration management, and application deployment. Users have the flexibility to turn their laptops into an Ansible control station to automate basic tasks, or they can deploy a dedicated host to use Ansible as an orchestration tool to roll out application updates while ensuring minimal downtime. Ansible provides a simple domain-specific language (DSL) to enable these different use cases. Ansible is popular among infrastructure engineers and developers because it requires minimal time and effort to get up and running. Before describing the specifics of Ansible, the following sections provide a high-level overview of how Ansible works.

A basic workflow for Ansible using playbooks looks something like that shown in Figure 17-1:

1. Engineers create Ansible playbooks in YAML that describe a workflow or the configuration of infrastructure.

2. Ansible playbooks are deployed to an Ansible control station.

3. When the control station runs the Ansible playbooks, they typically copy modules written in Python to remote hosts.

4. Finally, Ansible runs the modules on the remote hosts to perform the work described in playbooks.

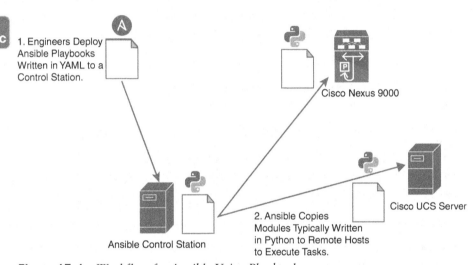

1. Engineers Deploy Ansible Playbooks Written in YAML to a Control Station.

Cisco Nexus 9000

Cisco UCS Server

2. Ansible Copies Modules Typically Written in Python to Remote Hosts to Execute Tasks.

Ansible Control Station

**Figure 17-1**  *Workflow for Ansible Using Playbooks*

## Ansible Components

Ansible requires a control machine to run the Ansible tool. By default, Ansible uses a push model to push changes to remote hosts from the Ansible control machine. The control machine can be any Linux/UNIX host with a Python interpreter that supports SSH or the required transport to devices managed by Ansible. Some of the important components of the Ansible control machine are as follows:

- **Modules** are typically written in Python. They are typically copied to remote hosts and run by the Ansible tool. Ansible modules are referenced as tasks in Ansible playbooks or using CLI arguments in the Ansible ad hoc CLI tool.

- **Inventory files** contain the hosts operated by Ansible. They contain group and host definitions that can be referenced by Ansible playbooks or using CLI arguments from the Ansible ad hoc CLI tool. A host can belong to multiple groups.

- **Playbooks** are written in YAML and contain Ansible domain-specific language. To enable reuse, playbooks can be modularized much like software. Variables containing data for playbooks can be separated into YAML files residing on the Ansible control machine.

- **Configuration files** control how the tool runs. For example, the configuration file can change the default directories of the modules.

## Important Ansible Concepts

Following are the important Ansible components:

- **Authentication:** Ansible uses SSH primarily for transport. Given that, you must have a way to handle authentication. By default, Ansible assumes engineers use public key infrastructure (SSH keys) instead of usernames and passwords for authentication. This enables engineers to access hosts without typing out passwords every time playbooks are run. If needed, this default behavior can be overridden.

- **Ansible play:** An Ansible play is a component of the Ansible DSL created within Ansible playbooks. A play is a mapping of hosts to tasks in a playbook. Hosts are typically identified by groups that are defined in inventory files. Tasks are lists of the Ansible modules that are run against groups of hosts.

- **Variables:** Ansible playbooks use double curly braces {{ }} to enclose variables. This enables the Ansible tool to perform variable substitution. Let's look at an example: different data centers use different ports for a services such as web applications. Every data center has different configuration parameters for AD/DNS servers, NTP servers, and so on. When automating tasks using Ansible, you provide these unique combinations to playbooks using variables. There are two ways to provide variables to the Ansible tool:

  - **CLI prompt:** The Ansible DSL contains an option, vars_prompt:, that enables the operator to provide variable data using a CLI. This is primarily useful when running simple playbooks manually to automate tasks.

  - **Variable files:** Variables can also be defined in YAML files and referenced in playbooks. There are different types of variable files. Some variables have global scope using the vars_files: Ansible DSL. Other variables, called group variables, can be applied to specific groups defined in the inventory file. Others, called host variables, are applied to specific hosts in the inventory.

- **Jinja templates:** Ansible can use jinja2 template functionality to autogenerate configuration for network devices. While doing so, templates replace the variables defined with appropriate values.

- **Roles:** One common approach is to organize playbooks using roles, which enable reuse. To enable reuse, roles provide a structure for variables, playbooks, templates, and other required files.

## Ansible CLI Tools

Ansible provides CLI tools that enable automation. The most useful CLI tools that Ansible provides include the following:

- The *ansible* CLI tool runs modules against targeted hosts. This is commonly referred to as the ad hoc CLI. Engineers can run tasks against targeted hosts without creating playbooks containing Ansible DSL.

- The *ansible-playbook* CLI tool runs playbooks against targeted hosts. Playbooks contain Ansible domain-specific language in YAML.

- The *ansible-vault* CLI tool enables engineers to encrypt sensitive data. If a playbook requires access to data that engineers do not want to expose in plain text, the *ansible-vault* tool can be used to create an encrypted YAML file containing the sensitive data. When data needs to be accessed, a password is provided.

- The *ansible-pull* tool enables clients to "pull" modules from a centralized server. (Normally, Ansible pushes modules out from a control station to the managed hosts.)

- The *ansible-docs* CLI tool enables engineers to parse the docstrings of Ansible modules to see sample syntax and the parameters that modules require.

- The *ansible-galaxy* tool can create or download roles from the Ansible community. Ansible Galaxy is a public repository of Ansible playbooks grouped into roles from the community. Roles provide a method to package Ansible playbooks for reuse.

## Cisco NX-OS and Ansible Example

All the Cisco NX-OS modules are included in Ansible Core as of Ansible 2.2, so no additional effort is required to begin automating your Nexus devices. Because Ansible has an agentless architecture, when the NXAPI feature is enabled, and a username and password are configured, the devices can be managed through Ansible. The username provided in the playbook must have the requisite role privilege to allow device configuration changes.

Example 17-1 shows an Ansible playbook that is written using the YAML format, ensuring that VLANs 2, 15, and 20 are created with proper names.

**Example 17-1**   *Ansible Playbook Example*

```
---

- name: vlan provisioning
  hosts: n9kv-1
  connection: local
  gather_facts: no

vars:
  nxos_provider:
  username: "{{ un }}"
  password: "{{ pwd }}"
  transport: nxap
```

```
  host: "{{ inventory_hostname }}"

tasks:

- name: CREATE VLANS AND ASSIGN A NAME, USING VLAN_ID
nxos_vlan:
 vlan_id: "{{ item.vlan_id }}"
 name: "{{ item.name }} "
 provider: "{{ nxos_provider }}"
with_items:
 - vlan_id: 2
   name: native
 - vlan_id: 15
   name: web
 - vlan_id: 20
   name: ap
```

The playbook has these fields:

- The **name:** field defines the playbook name.

- The **hosts: n9kv-1** field specifies the set of hosts that will be configured by the playbook.

- The **connection: local** field denotes that the task will be handled by Ansible, just like a local action.

- The **gather_facts: no** field denotes that no information from the device will be collected.

- The **tasks:** field specifies the task that will be run on the Nexus device.

- The **vars:** field defines the username and password and transport method to achieve the tasks at hand. In this example, the configuration will be done using NXAPI as the transport method.

Ansible is *idempotent*, in that it will only make a change on the devices if a change is necessary. If the configuration is already present, no changes will be made.

**NOTE** For Cisco UCS Servers, the UCS Manager Software Development Kit (UCSMSDK) is required to be present on the host against which the playbook is executed. Ansible 2.5 and later versions support Cisco UCS modules. The Ansible module uses the UCS API to execute automation tasks on Cisco UCS Servers.

# Python

Python is a programming language that has high-level data structures and a simple approach to object-oriented programming. Python's syntax and dynamic typing, together with its interpreted nature, make it an ideal language for scripting and rapid application development in many areas on most platforms.

The Python interpreter and the standard library are freely available in source or binary form for all major platforms from the Python website at www.python.org. The Python website also distributes and links to many free third-party Python modules, programs and tools, and additional documentation.

The Cisco Nexus Series devices support Python in both interactive and noninteractive (script) modes. This means that the Python interpreter is now embedded in the Cisco NX-OS, and you can execute Python commands and scripts directly on the switch. This is also referred to as the on-box Python. Python is also supported in the Guest Shell environment.

The initial version of Python that was supported was 2.7, but because it is end-of-life and end-of-support, currently the supported version is v3. The command that you need to use is **python3**.

The Python scripting capability provides programmatic access to the device's CLI to perform various tasks and PowerOn Auto Provisioning (POAP) or Embedded Event Manager (EEM) actions. Python can also be accessed from the Bash shell.

The Python scripting capability on Cisco Nexus switches enables you to perform the following tasks:

- Run a script to verify configuration on switch bootup

- Back up a configuration

- Perform proactive congestion management by monitoring and responding to buffer utilization characteristics

- Perform integration with the PowerOn Auto Provisioning or EEM modules

- Perform a job at a specific time interval (such as Port Auto Description)

- Programmatically access the switch command-line interface to perform various tasks

## Python Package for Cisco

Cisco NX-OS provides a Python package named cisco package that enables access to many core network device modules, such as interfaces, VLANs, VRFs, ACLs, and routes. After you have imported the cisco package, you can display its help by entering **help (cisco)** at the Python prompt. To display help on a specific module in the Cisco Python package, enter **help (cisco.**_module_name_**)**, where _module_name_ is the name of the module. For example, to display help on the Cisco ACL module, enter **help (cisco.acl)**.

Example 17-2 shows how to display information about the Python package for Cisco.

**Example 17-2**  *Python Package for Cisco*

```
>>> import cisco
>>> help(cisco)
Help on package cisco:

NAME
    cisco
```

```
FILE
      /isan/python/scripts/cisco/__init__.py

PACKAGE CONTENTS
    acl
    bgp
    cisco_secret
    cisco_socket
    feature
    interface
    key
    line_parser
    md5sum
    nxcli
    ospf
    routemap
    routes
    section_parser
    ssh
    system
    tacacs
    vrf

CLASSES
    __builtin__.object
    cisco.cisco_secret.CiscoSecret
    cisco.interface.Interface
    cisco.key.Ke
```

The methods and functions in the Python package named cisco are implemented in Python source files included with the software development kit (SDK) package. Many of these files have documentation embedded within the source code. In the Python source files, documentation is contained in documentation strings, bracketed by three backticks, or ```. Some source files and methods are for internal use and do not have embedded documentation.

Table 17-2 shows the functionality that the cisco package provides.

**Table 17-2**   Cisco Package Functions

| Function | Description |
|---|---|
| acl | Adds the ability to create, delete, and modify access control lists |
| bgp | Functions around configuring BGP |
| cisco_secret | Adjusts Cisco passwords |
| feature | Gets information about supported and enabled features on NX-OS |
| interface | Functions around manipulating interfaces |
| nxcli | Contains useful CLI interaction utilities |

| Function | Description |
|----------|-------------|
| ospf | Functions around configuring OSPF |
| ssh | Generates SSH key information |
| tacacs | Runs and parses TACACS+ status information |
| vrf | Creates and deletes virtual routing and forwarding (VRF) tables |

From the cisco package, you can import individual modules as needed using

```
from cisco.module_name import *
```

where *module_name* is the name of the individual module. In the example, the ACL module is imported.

```
>>> import cisco
>>> from cisco.acl import *
```

Other useful modules include the cli package and the json package. The cli package is used to allow Python scripts running on the NX-OS device to interact with the CLI to get and set configuration on the device. This library has one function within it named cli. The input parameters to the function are the CLI commands the user wants to run, and the output is a string representing the parser output from the CLI command.

```
>>> from cli import *
>>> import json
```

After starting Python and importing the required packages and modules, you can run Python scripts directly, or you can enter blocks of Python code and run the code.

## Using the CLI Command APIs

The Python programming language uses three APIs that can execute CLI commands. The APIs are available from the Python CLI module.

You must enable the APIs with the **from cli import** * command. The arguments for these APIs are strings of CLI commands. To execute a CLI command through the Python interpreter, you enter the CLI command as an argument string of one of the following APIs:

- **cli()** returns the raw output of CLI commands, including control or special characters. The interactive Python interpreter prints control or special characters "escaped." A carriage return is printed as '\n' and gives results that can be difficult to read. The **clip()** API gives results that are more readable.

   ```
   Example: string = cli ("cli-command")
   ```

- **clid()** returns JSON output for the CLI command, if XML support exists for the command; otherwise, an exception is thrown. This API can be useful when searching the output of **show** commands.

   ```
   Example: json_string = clid ("cli-command")
   ```

- **clip()** prints the output of the CLI command directly to stdout and returns nothing to Python.

   ```
   Example: clip ("cli-command")
   ```

When two or more commands are run individually, the state is not persistent from one command to subsequent commands.

In the following example, the second command fails because the state from the first command does not persist for the second command:

```
>>> cli("conf t")
>>> cli("interface eth4/1")
```

When two or more commands are run together, the state is persistent from one command to subsequent commands.

In the following example, the second command is successful because the state persists for the second and third commands:

```
>>> cli("conf t ; interface eth4/1 ; shut")
```

**NOTE**   Commands are separated with " ; " as shown in the example. The semicolon ( ; ) must be surrounded with single blank characters.

## Python in Interactive Mode

To enter the Python shell, enter the **python** command from the NX-OS command line with no parameters. You can enter lines of Python code to execute a block of code. A colon (:) at the end of a line tells the Python interpreter that the subsequent lines will form a code block. After the colon, you must indent the subsequent lines in the block, following Python indentation rules. After you have typed the block, press Return or Enter twice to execute the code.

**NOTE**   The Python interpreter is designated with the >>> or ... prompt.

Example 17-3 shows how to invoke Python from the CLI and run Python commands interactively.

**Example 17-3**   *Interactive Python Example*

```
switch# python
Python 2.7.5 (default, Feb 8 2019, 23:59:43)
[GCC 4.6.3] on linux2
Type "help", "copyright", "credits" or "license" for more information.
>>> from cli import *
>>> import json
>>> cli('configure terminal ; interface loopback 5 ; no shut')
''
>>> intflist=json.loads(clid('show interface brief'))
>>> i=0
>>> while i < len(intflist['TABLE_interface']['ROW_interface']):
...   intf=intflist['TABLE_interface']['ROW_interface'][i]
...   i=i+1
...   if intf['state'] == 'up':
```

```
... print intf['interface']
...
mgmt0
Ethernet2/7
Ethernet4/7
loopback0
loopback5
>>>
```

The preceding example brings the loopback 5 interface UP and shows how to query the interfaces running on the switch.

To exit the Python shell, type **exit()**:

```
>>>exit()

switch#
```

## Python in Noninteractive Mode

You can run a Python script in noninteractive mode by providing the Python script name as an argument to the Python CLI command. Python scripts must be placed under the boot-flash or volatile scheme. A maximum of 32 command-line arguments for the Python script are allowed with the Python CLI command.

To execute a Python script, enter the **python** command, followed by the filename of the script, followed by any arguments for the script, as shown in this example:

```
switch# python bootflash:scripts/deltaCounters.py Ethernet1/1 1 5
```

The Cisco Nexus switches also support the **source** CLI command for running Python scripts. The bootflash:scripts directory is the default script directory for the source CLI command.

```
switch# source deltaCounters Ethernet1/1 1 5
```

You can display the script source using the **show file** CLI command, as in Example 17-4.

**Example 17-4**   show file *Command*

```
switch# show file bootflash:scripts/deltaCounters.py

#!/isan/bin/python

from cli import *
import sys, time

ifName = sys.argv[1]
delay = float(sys.argv[2])
count = int(sys.argv[3])
cmd = 'show interface ' + ifName + ' counters'

out = json.loads(clid(cmd))
rxuc = int(out['TABLE_rx_counters']['ROW_rx_counters'][0]['eth_inucast'])
rxmc = int(out['TABLE_rx_counters']['ROW_rx_counters'][1]['eth_inmcast'])
rxbc = int(out['TABLE_rx_counters']['ROW_rx_counters'][1]['eth_inbcast'])
```

```
txuc = int(out['TABLE_tx_counters']['ROW_tx_counters'][0]['eth_outucast'])
txmc = int(out['TABLE_tx_counters']['ROW_tx_counters'][1]['eth_outmcast'])
txbc = int(out['TABLE_tx_counters']['ROW_tx_counters'][1]['eth_outbcast'])
print 'row rx_ucast rx_mcast rx_bcast tx_ucast tx_mcast tx_bcast'
print '======================================================='
print ' %8d %8d %8d %8d %8d %8d' % (rxuc, rxmc, rxbc, txuc, txmc, txbc)
print '======================================================='


i = 0
while (i < count):
    time.sleep(delay)
    out = json.loads(clid(cmd))
    rxucNew = int(out['TABLE_rx_counters']['ROW_rx_counters'][0]['eth_inucast'])
    rxmcNew = int(out['TABLE_rx_counters']['ROW_rx_counters'][1]['eth_inmcast'])
    rxbcNew = int(out['TABLE_rx_counters']['ROW_rx_counters'][1]['eth_inbcast'])
    txucNew = int(out['TABLE_tx_counters']['ROW_tx_counters'][0]['eth_outucast'])
    txmcNew = int(out['TABLE_tx_counters']['ROW_tx_counters'][1]['eth_outmcast'])
    txbcNew = int(out['TABLE_tx_counters']['ROW_tx_counters'][1]['eth_outbcast'])
    i += 1
    print '%-3d %8d %8d %8d %8d %8d %8d' % \
    (i, rxucNew - rxuc, rxmcNew - rxmc, rxbcNew - rxbc, txucNew - txuc, txmcNew -
txmc, txbcNew - txbc)
```

The preceding output for the deltaCounters.py script shows the increment in receive and transmit counters for a specified interface over a period.

The usage is

```
deltaCounters.py interface seconds count
```

For example, **deltaCounters.py Ethernet1/1 1 5** displays the counters for the Ethernet1/1 interface every 1 second for 5 periods.

Example 17-5 shows the counter values when the deltaCounters.py script is run.

**Example 17-5**  *Counter Values When deltaCounters.py Script Is Run*

```
switch# python bootflash:scripts/deltaCounters.py Ethernet1/1 1 5
row rx_ucast rx_mcast rx_bcast tx_ucast tx_mcast tx_bcast
=========================================================
         0      791        1        0   212739        0
=========================================================
1        0        0        0        0       26        0
2        0        0        0        0       27        0
3        0        1        0        0       54        0
4        0        1        0        0       55        0
5        0        1        0        0       81        0
switch#
```

The source command is helpful when executing compound commands from the CLI. Example 17-6 shows a source command following a pipe operator (|), allowing a Python script to receive input from another CLI command.

**Example 17-6**   *Example of Compound Source Command*

```
switch# show running-config | source sys/cgrep policy-map

policy-map type network-qos nw-pfc
policy-map type network-qos no-drop-2
policy-map type network-qos wred-policy
policy-map type network-qos pause-policy
policy-map type qos foo
policy-map type qos classify
policy-map type qos cos-based
policy-map type qos no-drop-2
policy-map type qos pfc-tor-port
```

In the preceding example, *policy-map* is an argument to the Python script named cgrep.

## UCS Manager Python SDK

The Cisco UCS Python SDK is a Python module that helps automate all aspects of Cisco UCS management, including server, network, storage, and hypervisor management.

The bulk of the Cisco UCS Python SDK works on the UCS Manager's Management Information Tree (MIT), performing create, modify, or delete actions on the managed objects (MO) in the tree.

Install Python 3 and above and pip before installing ucsmsdk. After Python and pip are installed, install the latest version of the SDK from pypi using the following command:

```
pip install ucsmsdk
```

You can also install the latest developer version from GitHub using the following commands:

```
git clone https://github.com/CiscoUcs/ucsmsdk/

cd ucsmsdk

sudo make install
```

For login and logout from the UCS Manager, you need to import the UCSHandle class. The following example shows how to create a connection handle before you can log in and log out from the server.

```
from ucsmsdk.ucshandle import UCSHandle


# Create a connection handle
handle = UcsHandle("192.168.1.1", "admin", "password")
```

```
# Login to the server
handle.login()
```

```
# Logout from the server
handle.logout()
```

The SDK provides APIs to enable CRUD operations:

■ Create an object: add_mo

■ Retrieve an object: query_dn, query_classid, query_dns, query_classids

■ Update an object: set_mo

■ Delete an object: delete_mo

The preceding APIs can be bunched together in a transaction (All or None). The commit_mo operation commits the changes made using the preceding APIs. All these methods are invoked on a UCSHandle instance.

The following example creates a new service profile (LsServer) object under the parent org-root. You create managed objects by using the add_mo API:

```
from ucsmsdk.mometa.ls.LsServer import LsServer
sp = LsServer(parent_mo_or_dn="org-root", name="sp_demo")
handle.add_mo(sp)
```

The following example shows how to query an existing Mo using a distinguished name (DN) and update it:

```
# Query for an existing Mo
sp = handle.query_dn("org-root/ls-sp_demo")
```

```
# Update description of the service profile
sp.descr = "demo_descr"
```

```
# Add it to the on-going transaction
handle.set_mo(sp)
```

The following example shows the use of remove_mo in removing an object:

```
# Query for an existing Mo
sp = handle.query_dn("org-root/ls-sp_demo")
```

```
# Remove the object
handle.remove_mo(sp)
```

**NOTE**   API operations are batched together by default until a **commit()** is invoked.

In the following code, the objects are created only when a **commit()** is invoked. If there is a failure in one of the steps, no changes are committed to the server.

```
from ucsmsdk.mometa.ls.LsServer import LsServer

sp1 = LsServer(parent_mo_or_dn="org-root", name="sp_demo1")

handle.add_mo(sp1)


sp2 = LsServer(parent_mo_or_dn="org-root", name="sp_demo2")

handle.add_mo(sp2)


# commit the changes to server

handle.commit()
```

### Convert to UCS Python

Wouldn't it be cool if you didn't have to know much about the SDK to be able to automate operations based off it?

Welcome the convert_to_ucs_python API!

The steps involved to generate a Python script equivalent to the steps performed on the UCSM GUI are as follows:

**Step 1.**   Launch the Java-based UCSM user interface (UI).

**Step 2.**   Launch the Python shell and invoke convert_to_ucs_python on the same machine.

**Step 3.**   Perform the desired operation on the UI.

**Step 4.**   The convert_to_ucs_python API monitors the operation and generates an equivalent Python script for it.

The UCSM GUI logs all the activities that are performed through it, and the Python shell monitors that log to generate the equivalent Python script. Because the logging is local to the machine where the UI is running, convert_to_ucs_python also must run on the same machine.

## PowerOn Auto Provisioning (POAP)

PowerOn Auto Provisioning (POAP) automates the process of upgrading software images and installing configuration files on devices that are being deployed in the network for the first time.

When a device with the POAP feature boots and does not find the startup configuration, the device enters POAP mode, locates a DHCP server, and bootstraps itself with its interface IP address, gateway, and DNS server IP addresses. The device also obtains the IP address of a TFTP server and downloads a configuration script that enables the switch to download and install the appropriate software image and configuration file.

**NOTE**   The DHCP information is used only during the POAP process.

## Limitations of POAP

The switch software image must support POAP for this feature to function.

POAP does not support provisioning of the switch after it has been configured and is operational. Only autoprovisioning of a switch with no startup configuration is supported.

## Network Requirements for POAP

POAP requires the following network infrastructure, as shown in Figure 17-2:

- A DHCP server to bootstrap the interface IP address, gateway address, and Domain Name System (DNS) server

- A TFTP server that contains the configuration script used to automate the software image installation and configuration process

- One or more servers that contain the desired software images and configuration files

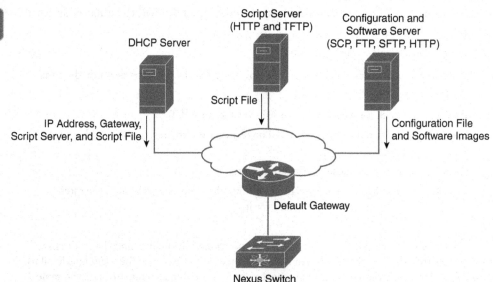

**Figure 17-2**   *POAP Network Infrastructure*

**NOTE**   Checking for a USB device containing the configuration script file in POAP mode is not supported on Cisco Nexus 9000 Series switches.

## POAP Configuration Script

Cisco has sample configuration scripts that were developed using the Python programming language and Tool command language (Tcl). You can customize one of these scripts to meet the requirements of your network environment.

The reference script supplied by Cisco supports the following functionality:

- Retrieves the switch-specific identifier—for example, the serial number.

- Downloads the software image (system and kickstart images) if the files do not already exist on the switch. The software image is installed on the switch and is used at the next reboot.

- Schedules the downloaded configuration to be applied at the next switch reboot.

- Stores the configuration as the startup configuration.

For Cisco Nexus 9000 Series switches, the POAP script can be found at https://github.com/datacenter/nexus9000/blob/master/nx-os/poap/poap.py.

To modify the script using Python, see the *Cisco NX-OS Python API Reference Guide* for your platform.

## POAP Process

The POAP process has the following phases:

1. Power up
2. USB discovery
3. DHCP discovery
4. Script execution
5. Post-installation reload

Within these phases, other process and decision points occur. Figure 17-3 shows a flow diagram of the POAP process.

### Power-Up Phase

When you power up the device for the first time, it loads the software image that is installed at manufacturing and tries to find a configuration file from which to boot. When a configuration file is not found, the POAP mode starts.

During startup, a prompt appears asking if you want to abort POAP and continue with a normal setup. You can choose to exit or continue with POAP.

If you exit POAP mode, you enter the normal interactive setup script. If you continue in POAP mode, all the front-panel interfaces are set up in the default configuration.

**NOTE** No user intervention is required for POAP to continue. The prompt that asks if you want to abort POAP remains available until the POAP process is complete.

### USB Discovery Phase

When POAP starts, the process searches the root directory of all accessible USB devices for the POAP configuration script file, configuration files, and system and kickstart images. If the configuration script file is found on a USB device, POAP begins running the configuration script. If the configuration script file is not found on the USB device, POAP executes DHCP discovery.

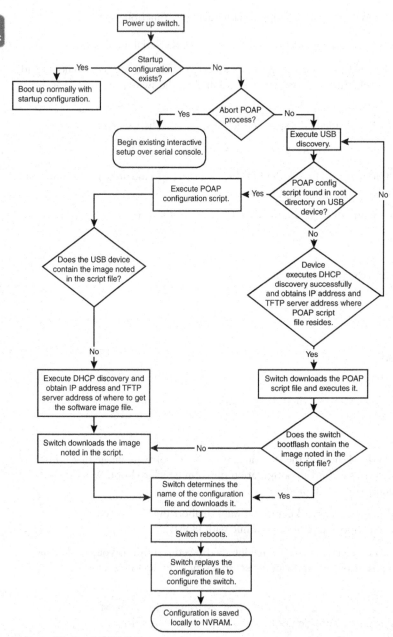

**Figure 17-3** *POAP Process*

If the software image and switch configuration files specified in the configuration script are present, POAP uses those files to install the software and configure the switch. If the software image and switch configuration files are not on the USB device, POAP starts the DHCP phase from the beginning.

### DHCP Discovery Phase

The switch sends out DHCP discover messages on the front-panel interfaces or the MGMT interface that solicits DHCP offers from the DHCP server or servers (see Figure 17-4). The DHCP client on the Cisco Nexus switch uses the switch serial number in the client-identifier option to identify itself to the DHCP server. The DHCP server can use this identifier to send information, such as the IP address and script filename, back to the DHCP client.

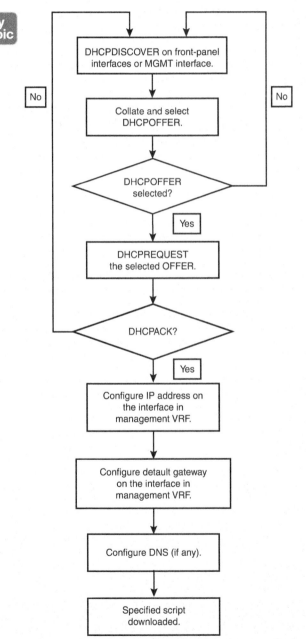

**Figure 17-4**  *DHCP Discovery Process*

POAP requires a minimum DHCP lease period of 3600 seconds (1 hour). POAP checks the DHCP lease period. If the DHCP lease period is set to less than 3600 seconds (1 hour), POAP does not complete the DHCP negotiation.

The DHCP discover message also solicits the following options from the DHCP server:

- **TFTP server name or TFTP server address:** The DHCP server relays the TFTP server name or TFTP server address to the DHCP client. The DHCP client uses this information to contact the TFTP server to obtain the script file.

- **Bootfile name:** The DHCP server relays the bootfile name to the DHCP client. The bootfile name includes the complete path to the bootfile on the TFTP server. The DHCP client uses this information to download the script file.

When multiple DHCP offers that meet the requirement are received, the one arriving first is honored, and the POAP process moves to the next stage. The device completes the DHCP negotiation (request and acknowledgment) with the selected DHCP server, and the DHCP server assigns an IP address to the switch. If a failure occurs in any of the subsequent steps in the POAP process, the IP address is released back to the DHCP server.

Figure 17-4 shows a flow diagram of the DHCP Discovery process.

### Script Execution Phase

After the device bootstraps itself using the information in the DHCP acknowledgment, the script file is downloaded from the TFTP server.

The switch runs the configuration script, which downloads and installs the software image and downloads a switch-specific configuration file.

However, the configuration file is not applied to the switch at this point because the software image that currently runs on the switch might not support all of the commands in the configuration file. After the switch reboots, it begins running the new software image, if an image was installed. At that point, the configuration is applied to the switch.

**NOTE** If the switch loses connectivity, the script stops, and the switch reloads its original software images and bootup variables.

### Post-Installation Reload Phase

The switch restarts and applies (replays) the configuration on the upgraded software image. Afterward, the switch copies the running configuration to the startup configuration.

## Configuring a Switch Using POAP

Before configuring a switch using POAP, make sure that the network environment is set up to use POAP. The procedure to configure a switch using POAP is as follows:

**Step 1.** Install the switch in the network.

**Step 2.** Power on the switch.

If no configuration file is found, the switch boots in POAP mode and displays a prompt asking if you want to abort POAP and continue with a normal setup. No entry is required to continue to boot in POAP mode.

**Step 3.**   (Optional) If you want to exit POAP mode and enter the normal interactive setup script, enter **y** (yes).

**Step 4.**   The switch boots, and the POAP process begins.

**Step 5.**   Verify the device configuration using the commands shown in Table 17-3.

**Table 17-3**   POAP Verification Commands

| Command | Purpose |
|---|---|
| show running-config | Displays the running configuration. |
| show startup-config | Displays the startup configuration. |
| show time-stamp running-config last-changed | Displays the timestamp when the running configuration was last changed. |

# HashiCorp Terraform

Terraform is an Infrastructure as Code (IaC) open-source tool created by HashiCorp. Terraform is used to automate and orchestrate the provisioning, configuration, and management of resources and infrastructures across data centers and hybrid cloud environments. It can manage low-level components like compute, storage, and networking resources, as well as high-level components from the application stack and SaaS features.

Terraform is compatible with various operating systems, including Windows, macOS, and many Linux distributions and can make API calls on your behalf to one or more providers, such as Cisco, Amazon Web Services (AWS), Azure, Google Cloud, Digital Ocean, and others.

To learn more about Terraform, visit https://www.terraform.io.

If you want to use it, you need to download and install the binary package from HashiCorp. You can do this by downloading it from their repository, or you can use some of the popular package managers.

For the manual installation, the procedure is as follows:

1. Download the appropriate package for your operating system as a zip archive.

2. Unzip the package to get the single binary named Terraform, with the accompanying files.

3. Make sure that the Terraform binary is included in your PATH.

Alternate methods are to use package managers, and the decision which one to use depends mostly on the operating system that you use. An example is the Chocolatey package manager for Windows. It's an open-source package management, and after you have it installed, you can start the Terraform installation with the following command:

```
$choco install terraform
```

To verify the installation of Terraform, from the command line, just use the command

```
$terraform -help
```

If the installation was successful, it will list the available Terraform sub-commands.

More information and installation options are available at https://developer.hashicorp.com/terraform/tutorials/aws-get-started/install-cli.

17

## Terraform Concept

Terraform communicates with the managed resources using application programming interfaces (APIs). To know how exactly to communicate with the different resources, Terraform uses providers, which are open-source plug-ins that expose the implementation for specific services and infrastructures. They abstract the API layer of real resources, allowing Terraform to create, manage, and update the needed resources. Each provider has its documentation describing the resource types and their arguments. Providers must be declared in the configurations for Terraform to install and use them. They can be categorized as Official, Partner, or Community providers. The publicly available providers can be found in the Terraform Registry. There are providers for different vendors and service providers, such as Cisco Systems, Amazon AWS, Microsoft Azure, Google Cloud Platform, and many others.

The workflow can be summarized in three separate stages:

- **Write:** During this initial stage, the resources and the needed configuration are defined.

- **Plan:** Based on the write stage definitions, Terraform will create an execution plan, which will contain the steps and needed configuration that will be applied to the managed resources.

- **Apply:** After the plan has been approved, Terraform will perform the needed steps accordingly, and it will apply the needed configurations and changes, as it respects the dependencies among the different resources.

For each of these stages, different commands and components are used. After the apply stage is done, you can perform additional steps, such removing unneeded resources and getting the current state of the infrastructure.

## Terraform Components

Terraform uses a declarative approach to describe the desired state of the devices in configuration files. Then the configuration files are organized into an execution plan. The plan contains all the needed information regarding the devices and how to reach the desired state. Before a Terraform plan can be executed, it needs to be confirmed. The configuration files are created using a proprietary syntax called HashiCorp Configuration Language (HCL), and there is also JSON support.

The Terraform configuration files use the .tf extension, and some are special:

- **terraform-provider.tf:** This file describes the providers that will be used. Multiple providers can be listed.

- **terraform.tfvars:** This file defines the variables. It can have different extensions, such as .tfvars, .tfvar.json, .auto.tfvars, and .auto.tfvars.json.

- **terraform.tfstate:** This file maintains the state of the managed infrastructure and objects, because it stores the bindings between the objects and the resource instances declared in the configuration.

- **Terraform-main.tf:** This is the main configuration file. It defines the resources and the configuration that needs to be created.

The Terraform configuration file works with resources as the fundamental construct. The resources are organized in blocks. A resource block describes an infrastructure object, along with the needed characteristics and the intent.

The target infrastructure is defined as providers, which contain the target IP address, URL, credentials, and so on.

Cisco is an official provider for HashiCorp, and the Terraform software can be used for automation and integration of the Cisco Data Center, Cloud, Security, and Enterprise products.

The Cisco ACI Terraform provider contains the needed information to define how Terraform will interact with the Cisco APIC. The provider needs to be configured with the correct credentials to be able to authenticate successfully against the Cisco APIC. In Example 17-7, you can see how to include the Cisco ACI provider.

**Example 17-7**   *Cisco ACI Terraform Provider Definition*

```
terraform {
  required_providers {
    aci = {
      source = "CiscoDevNet/aci"
      version = "2.8.0"
    }
  }
}


provider "aci" {
  # Configuration options
}
```

As mentioned previously, the configuration file defines the blocks of resources and what their configuration needs to be. Example 17-8 shows how you can start the basic configuration of a Cisco ACI to define the creation of the tenant, bridge domain, and subnet.

**Example 17-8**   *Cisco ACI Resources in a Terraform Configuration File*

```
provider "aci" {
  # cisco-aci user name
  username = "${var.username}"
  # cisco-aci password
  password = "${var.password}"
  # cisco-aci url
  url      = "${var.apic_url}"
  insecure = true
}


resource "aci_tenant" "terraform_tenant" {
  name          = "tenant_for_terraform"
```

```
    description = "This tenant is created by the Terraform ACI provider"
}


resource "aci_bridge_domain" "bd_for_subnet" {
  tenant_dn   = "${aci_tenant.terraform_tenant.id}"
  name        = "bd_for_subnet"
  description = "This bridge domain is created by the Terraform ACI provider"
}


resource "aci_subnet" "demosubnet" {
  bridge_domain_dn                 = "${aci_bridge_domain.bd_for_subnet.id}"
  ip                               = "10.10.1.1/24"
  scope                            = "private"
  description                      = "This subject is created by Terraform"
}
```

When this plan is run against the Cisco APIC, Terraform does a cross-check. This means that it first checks whether these resources already exist on the system. If there are such resources, no changes are made. But if Terraform finds a difference between the configuration file and the state on the target infrastructure, the Cisco ACI in this example, it forces the needed changes, or the creation or removal of resources, as required by the definitions in the configuration file.

### Terraform Commands

After a Terraform configuration file is created, or cloned, the first thing that needs to happen is to initialize the directory. This is done with the command **terraform init**. During the initialization, Terraform looks for information regarding the providers that need to be used with this configuration file and attempts to load the providers' plug-ins. The output of the command is shown in Figure 17-5.

```
Initializing the backend...

Initializing provider plugins...
- Finding ciscodevnet/aci versions matching "2.8.0"...
- Installing ciscodevnet/aci v2.8.0...
- Installed ciscodevnet/aci v2.8.0 (signed by a HashiCorp partner, key ID 433649E2C56309DE)

Partner and community providers are signed by their developers.
If you'd like to know more about provider signing, you can read about it here:
https://www.terraform.io/docs/cli/plugins/signing.html

Terraform has created a lock file .terraform.lock.hcl to record the provider
selections it made above. Include this file in your version control repository
so that Terraform can guarantee to make the same selections by default when
you run "terraform init" in the future.

Terraform has been successfully initialized!

You may now begin working with Terraform. Try running "terraform plan" to see
any changes that are required for your infrastructure. All Terraform commands
should now work.

If you ever set or change modules or backend configuration for Terraform,
rerun this command to reinitialize your working directory. If you forget, other
commands will detect it and remind you to do so if necessary.
```

**Figure 17-5**  *Output of the* terraform init *Command*

The creation of the configuration files and the initialization of the working directory conclude the write stage.

The plan stage is started with the command **terraform plan**. It generates an execution plan, which determines the needed steps to perform the required configuration. In Figure 17-6, you can see the output of the **terraform plan** command.

```
Terraform will perform the following actions:

  # aci_bridge_domain.my_terraform_bd will be created
  + resource "aci_bridge_domain" "my_terraform_bd" {
      + annotation                 = "orchestrator:terraform"
      + arp_flood                  = (known after apply)
      + bridge_domain_type         = (known after apply)
      + description                = "This bridge domain is created by the Terraform ACI provider"
      + ep_clear                   = (known after apply)
      + ep_move_detect_mode        = (known after apply)
      + host_based_routing         = (known after apply)
      + id                         = (known after apply)
      + intersite_bum_traffic_allow = (known after apply)
      + intersite_l2_stretch       = (known after apply)
      + ip_learning                = (known after apply)
      + ipv6_mcast_allow           = (known after apply)
      + limit_ip_learn_to_subnets  = (known after apply)
      + ll_addr                    = (known after apply)
      + mac                        = (known after apply)
      + mcast_allow                = (known after apply)
      + multi_dst_pkt_act          = (known after apply)
      + name                       = "bd_for_subnet"
      + name_alias                 = (known after apply)
      + optimize_wan_bandwidth     = (known after apply)
      + relation_fv_rs_bd_to_ep_ret = (known after apply)
      + relation_fv_rs_bd_to_nd_p  = (known after apply)
      + relation_fv_rs_ctx         = (known after apply)
      + relation_fv_rs_igmpsn      = (known after apply)
      + relation_fv_rs_mldsn       = (known after apply)
      + tenant_dn                  = (known after apply)
      + unicast_route              = (known after apply)
      + unk_mac_ucast_act          = (known after apply)
      + unk_mcast_act              = (known after apply)
      + v6unk_mcast_act            = (known after apply)
      + vmac                       = (known after apply)
    }

  # aci_tenant.my_terraform_tenant will be created
  + resource "aci_tenant" "my_terraform_tenant" {
      + annotation                 = "orchestrator:terraform"
      + description                = (known after apply)
      + id                         = (known after apply)
      + name                       = "tenant_for_terraform"
      + name_alias                 = (known after apply)
      + relation_fv_rs_tenant_mon_pol = (known after apply)
    }

Plan: 2 to add, 0 to change, 0 to destroy.
```

**Figure 17-6**  *Output from the* **terraform plan** *Command*

After the plan is verified and approved, for the apply stage, you use the command **terraform apply**. It carries the needed actions defined in the execution plan to achieve the desired state using the managed resources. Figure 17-7 shows the output of applying a **terraform plan** on Cisco ACI.

In addition to these major commands, there is the **terraform destroy** command. It is used to remove resources managed by Terraform. Figure 17-8 shows the output of this command run against a Cisco APIC; it destroys two resources.

```
Terraform will perform the following actions:

  # aci_bridge_domain.my_terraform_bd will be created
  + resource "aci_bridge_domain" "my_terraform_bd" {
      + annotation                 = "orchestrator:terraform"
      + arp_flood                  = (known after apply)
      + bridge_domain_type         = (known after apply)
      + description                = "This bridge domain is created by the Terraform ACI provider"
      + ep_clear                   = (known after apply)
      + ep_move_detect_mode        = (known after apply)
      + host_based_routing         = (known after apply)
      + id                         = (known after apply)
      + intersite_bum_traffic_allow = (known after apply)
      + intersite_l2_stretch       = (known after apply)
      + ip_learning                = (known after apply)
      + ipv6_mcast_allow           = (known after apply)
      + limit_ip_learn_to_subnets  = (known after apply)
      + ll_addr                    = (known after apply)
      + mac                        = (known after apply)
      + mcast_allow                = (known after apply)
      + multi_dst_pkt_act          = (known after apply)
      + name                       = "bd_for_subnet"
      + name_alias                 = (known after apply)
      + optimize_wan_bandwidth     = (known after apply)
      + relation_fv_rs_bd_to_ep_ret = (known after apply)
      + relation_fv_rs_bd_to_nd_p  = (known after apply)
      + relation_fv_rs_ctx         = (known after apply)
      + relation_fv_rs_igmpsn      = (known after apply)
      + relation_fv_rs_mldsn       = (known after apply)
      + tenant_dn                  = (known after apply)
      + unicast_route              = (known after apply)
      + unk_mac_ucast_act          = (known after apply)
      + unk_mcast_act              = (known after apply)
      + v6unk_mcast_act            = (known after apply)
      + vmac                       = (known after apply)
    }

  # aci_tenant.my_terraform_tenant will be created
  + resource "aci_tenant" "my_terraform_tenant" {
      + annotation                 = "orchestrator:terraform"
      + description                = (known after apply)
      + id                         = (known after apply)
      + name                       = "tenant_for_terraform"
      + name_alias                 = (known after apply)
      + relation_fv_rs_tenant_mon_pol = (known after apply)
    }

Plan: 2 to add, 0 to change, 0 to destroy.

Do you want to perform these actions?
  Terraform will perform the actions described above.
  Only 'yes' will be accepted to approve.

  Enter a value:
```

**Figure 17-7**  *Output from the* **terraform apply** *Command*

```
aci_tenant.my_terraform_tenant: Refreshing state... [id=uni/tn-tenant_for_terraform]
aci_bridge_domain.my_terraform_bd: Refreshing state... [id=uni/tn-tenant_for_terraform/BD-bd_for_subnet]

Terraform used the selected providers to generate the following execution plan. Resource actions are indicated with the following symbols:
  - destroy

Terraform will perform the following actions:

  # aci_bridge_domain.my_terraform_bd will be destroyed
  - resource "aci_bridge_domain" "my_terraform_bd" {
      - annotation                 = "orchestrator:terraform" -> null
      - arp_flood                  = "no" -> null
      - bridge_domain_type         = "regular" -> null
      - description                = "This bridge domain is created by the Terraform ACI provider" -> null
      - ep_clear                   = "no" -> null
      - ep_move_detect_mode        = "disable" -> null
      - host_based_routing         = "no" -> null
      - id                         = "uni/tn-tenant_for_terraform/BD-bd_for_subnet" -> null
      - intersite_bum_traffic_allow = "no" -> null
      - intersite_l2_stretch       = "no" -> null
      - ip_learning                = "yes" -> null
      - ipv6_mcast_allow           = "no" -> null
      - limit_ip_learn_to_subnets  = "yes" -> null
      - ll_addr                    = "::" -> null
      - mac                        = "00:22:BD:F8:19:FF" -> null
      - mcast_allow                = "no" -> null
      - multi_dst_pkt_act          = "bd-flood" -> null
      - name                       = "bd_for_subnet" -> null
      - optimize_wan_bandwidth     = "no" -> null
      - tenant_dn                  = "uni/tn-tenant_for_terraform" -> null
      - unicast_route              = "yes" -> null
      - unk_mac_ucast_act          = "proxy" -> null
      - unk_mcast_act              = "flood" -> null
      - v6unk_mcast_act            = "flood" -> null
      - vmac                       = "not-applicable" -> null
    }

  # aci_tenant.my_terraform_tenant will be destroyed
  - resource "aci_tenant" "my_terraform_tenant" {
      - annotation = "orchestrator:terraform" -> null
      - id         = "uni/tn-tenant_for_terraform" -> null
      - name       = "tenant_for_terraform" -> null
    }

Plan: 0 to add, 0 to change, 2 to destroy.

Do you really want to destroy all resources?
  Terraform will destroy all your managed infrastructure, as shown above.
  There is no undo. Only 'yes' will be accepted to confirm.

  Enter a value:                                                    Go to Line/Column
```

**Figure 17-8**  *Output from the* **terraform destroy** *Command.*

In conclusion, HashiCorp Terraform is a powerful IaC tool, which is supported across multiple Cisco products. As the support dynamically changes, the best approach is to check the latest Cisco providers available and the supported capabilities.

# PowerShell

Microsoft PowerShell is a complex automation tool that can be used across platforms. It can be used in different ways, such as a command-line shell, where it provides convenient features such as command-line history or support for command and parameter aliases and command pipelining. It can be used as a scripting language, as a component of a CI-CD pipeline, where it can be used for the automation of management systems by supporting common data formats like CSV, JSON, and XML. PowerShell is also a powerful automation platform. It supports modules for different providers and vendors, and at the same time the PowerShell Desired State Configuration (DSC) framework makes it extremely convenient and easy to provision infrastructures, such as an IaC tool.

Cisco has developed PowerShell modules, which allow the Cisco UCS Manager, the Cisco Integrated Management Controller (CIMC), and Cisco Intersight to be managed and provisioned and configured with the help of PowerShell.

The Cisco PowerShell modules from the different supported systems are available at the PowerShell Gallery at https://www.powershellgallery.com/profiles/Cisco.

**NOTE** The local version of PowerShell must be at least 5.1!

The Cisco UCS PowerTool suite is a set of PowerShell modules that communicate via the UCS XML API. The Cisco UCS is an integrated compute solution, in which the management is built as XML objects structured in a hierarchical object model using an XML schema. More than 98 percent of that schema is built in the UCS PowerTool library. This allows the PowerShell to communicate, manage, and provision the Cisco compute solutions. With the release of Cisco Intersight, as a cloud-based SaaS management platform for the Cisco compute solutions, there is also a PowerShell module that supports the Intersight APIs.

The modules in the UCS PowerTool library consist of Microsoft PowerShell cmdlets, which enable the communication, the retrieval, and the change of UCS managed objects. The PowerShell cmdlets are created to work in the following categories:

- Sessions

- Methods

- Queries and filters

- Configurations and transactions

To start working with the UCS PowerShell modules, you need to check your version of the PowerShell, as shown in Example 17-9).

17

**Example 17-9**   *Checking the PowerShell Version*

```
PS /> $PSVersionTable

Name                          Value
----                          -----
PSVersion                     7.1.4
PSEdition                     Core
GitCommitId                   7.1.4
OS                            Linux 4.15.0-29-generic #31-Ubuntu SMP Tue Jul 17
15:39:52 UTC 2018
Platform                      Unix
PSCompatibleVersions          {1.0, 2.0, 3.0, 4.0…}
PSRemotingProtocolVersion     2.3
SerializationVersion          1.1.0.1
WSManStackVersion             3.0
```

To install the UCS PowerTool library, you need to install the Cisco.UCS.Core and
Cisco.UCSManager packages. The installation is demonstrated in Example 17-10.

**Example 17-10**   *Installing the Cisco UCS PowerShell Library*

```
PS /> Install-Module 'Cisco.ucs.core' -RequiredVersion 2.5.3.0

Untrusted repository
You are installing the modules from an untrusted repository. If you trust this
repository, change its InstallationPolicy value by running the Set-PSRepository cmd-
let. Are you sure you want to install the modules from
'PSGallery'?
[Y] Yes  [A] Yes to All  [N] No  [L] No to All  [S] Suspend  [?] Help (default is "N"): A


<... output omitted ...>


Do you accept the license terms for module 'Cisco.UCS.Core'.
[Y] Yes  [A] Yes to All  [N] No  [L] No to All  [S] Suspend  [?] Help (default is "N"): A
PS />
PS /> Get-Package -Name Cisco.UCS.Core

Name              Version     Source                         ProviderName
----              -------     ------                         ------------
Cisco.UCS.Core    2.5.3.0     https://www.powershellgallery... PowerShellGet
PS /> Install-Module 'Cisco.UCSManager' -RequiredVersion 3.0.1.2

Untrusted repository
You are installing the modules from an untrusted repository. If you trust this
repository, change its
InstallationPolicy value by running the Set-PSRepository cmdlet. Are you sure you
want to install the modules from
```

```
'UcsRepository'?
[Y] Yes  [A] Yes to All  [N] No  [L] No to All  [S] Suspend  [?] Help (default is "N"): A


<... output omitted ...>


Do you accept the license terms for module 'Cisco.UCS.Common'.
[Y] Yes  [A] Yes to All  [N] No  [L] No to All  [S] Suspend  [?] Help (default is "N"): A
PS /> Get-Package -Name Cisco.UCSManager


Name                Version         Source                          ProviderName
----                -------         ------                          ------------
Cisco.UCSManager    3.0.1.2         https://www.powershellgallery... PowerShellGet
```

After the successful installation of the UCS modules, the next step is to add the modules to the path and import them. After that, you can start using the UCS cmdlets. The examples show the installation of the Cisco UCS modules, but the procedure to install the modules for the Cisco IMC is similar.

After the UCS PowerShell library modules are installed in PowerShell, you can start managing Cisco UCS infrastructures. The first step is to connect to the UCS, as demonstrated in Example 17-11. This example demonstrates how to find the needed command, to connect, and to verify the status of the connection.

**Example 17-11**  *Checking the PowerShell Version*

```
PS /> Get-Help Connect-Ucs

NAME
    Connect-Ucs

SYNOPSIS
    Connects to a UCS



SYNTAX
    Connect-Ucs [-Name] <string[]> [-Credential] <PSCredential> [-Port <ushort>]
[-NoSsl] [-NotDefault] [-Proxy <WebProxy>] [<CommonParameters>]


    Connect-Ucs -LiteralPath <string> -Key <SecureString> [-NotDefault]
[-Proxy <WebProxy>] [<CommonParameters>]


    Connect-Ucs -Path <string> -Key <SecureString> [-NotDefault] [-Proxy <WebProxy>]
[<CommonParameters>]
```

17

```
DESCRIPTION
    Connects to a UCS. The cmdlet starts a new session using the specified parameters.
One can have more than one connections to a server. PowerTool Supports working with
multiple default servers. This can be enabled by
    setting SupportMultipleDefaultUcs using Set-UcsPowerToolConfiguration.
<... output omitted ...>
PS /> Connect-Ucs -name 10.10.1.131


cmdlet Connect-Ucs at command pipeline position 1
Supply values for the following parameters:
Credential
User: admin
Password for user admin: ********



NumPendingConfigs              : 0
Ucs                            : UCSPE-10-10-1-131
Cookie                         : 1628081939/11413e70-ca6a-4557-bb86-e7525d4c1a34
Domains                        : org-root
LastUpdateTime                 : 8/25/2021 1:01:27 PM
Name                           : 10.10.1.131
NoSsl                          : False
NumWatchers                    : 0
Port                           : 443
Priv                           : {admin, read-only}
PromptOnCompleteTransaction    : False
Proxy                          :
RefreshPeriod                  : 600
SessionId                      :
TransactionInProgress          : False
Uri                            : https://10.10.1.131
UserName                       : admin
Version                        : 4.1(2c)
VirtualIpv4Address             : 10.10.1.131
WatchThreadStatus              : None


PS /> Get-UcsPSSession
NumPendingConfigs              : 0
Ucs                            : UCSPE-10-10-1-131
Cookie                         : 1628081939/11413e70-ca6a-4557-bb86-e7525d4c1a34
Domains                        : org-root
LastUpdateTime                 : 8/25/2021 1:01:27 PM
Name                           : 10.10.1.131
NoSsl                          : False
```

```
NumWatchers                   : 0
Port                          : 443
Priv                          : {admin, read-only}
PromptOnCompleteTransaction   : False
Proxy                         :
RefreshPeriod                 : 600
SessionId                     :
TransactionInProgress         : False
Uri                           : https://10.10.1.131
UserName                      : admin
Version                       : 4.1(2c)
VirtualIpv4Address            : 10.10.1.131
WatchThreadStatus             : None
```

And finally, when the work is done and the connection is no longer needed, you can use the command **Disconnect-Ucs.**

After the modules of the UCS PowerTool library are installed, you can query the available commands. In Example 17-12, you can see the commands related to working with VLANs are listed.

**Example 17-12** *List UCS PowerShell Cmdlets*

```
PS /> Get-Command -Verb Get | Select-String Vlan

Get-UcsAdaptorVlan
Get-UcsFabricBHVlan
Get-UcsFabricOrgVlanPolicy
Get-UcsFabricPooledVlan
Get-UcsFabricReservedVlan
Get-UcsFabricVlanEp
Get-UcsFabricVlanGroupReq
Get-UcsFabricVlanReq
Get-UcsSwVlan
Get-UcsSwVlanPortNs
Get-UcsSwVlanPortNsOverride
Get-UcsVlan
Get-UcsVlanMemberPort
Get-UcsVlanMemberPortChannel
Get-UcsVmVlan
Get-UcsVnicLifVlan
Get-UcsVnicVlan
```

By using the command **Get-UcsVlan**, you can retrieve information for the existing VLANs on the UCS, as shown in Example 17-13.

17

**Example 17-13**  *Listing UCS PowerShell Cmdlets*

```
PS /> Get-UcsVlan



PS /> Get-UcsVlan


AssocPrimaryVlanState     : ok
AssocPrimaryVlanSwitchId  : NONE
Cloud                     : ethestclan
CompressionType           : included
ConfigIssues              :
ConfigOverlap             : ok
DefaultNet                : no
EpDn                      :
Global                    : 0
Id                        : 1
IfRole                    : nas-storage
IfType                    : virtual
Local                     : 0
Locale                    : external
McastPolicyName           :
Name                      : default
OperMcastPolicyName       : org-root/mc-policy-default
OperState                 : ok
OverlapStateForA          : active
OverlapStateForB          : not-active
PeerDn                    :
PolicyOwner               : local
PubNwDn                   :
PubNwId                   : 1
PubNwName                 :
Sacl                      :
Sharing                   : none
SwitchId                  : dual
Transport                 : ether
Type                      : lan
Ucs                       : UCSPE-10-10-1-131
Dn                        : fabric/eth-estc/net-default
Rn                        : net-default
Status                    :
XtraProperty              : {}
```

```
AssocPrimaryVlanState     : ok
AssocPrimaryVlanSwitchId  : NONE
Cloud                     : ethestclan
CompressionType           : included
ConfigIssues              :
ConfigOverlap             : ok
DefaultNet                : no
EpDn                      :
Global                    : 0
Id                        : 163
IfRole                    : nas-storage
IfType                    : virtual
Local                     : 0
Locale                    : external
McastPolicyName           :
Name                      : test_vlan163
OperMcastPolicyName       : org-root/mc-policy-default
OperState                 : ok
OverlapStateForA          : active
OverlapStateForB          : not-active
```

From the output in this example, you can see that there is a VLAN named test_vlan163 that exists and is operational on Fabric Interconnect A.

The UCS PowerTool library can be used with the standalone Cisco UCS C-series servers by installing the Cisco.IMC PowerShell modules. You still need to have the Cisco.ucs.core module. The way that the communication happens and how the information is retrieved and manipulated is the same.

Using PowerShell for the purposes of automating Cisco UCS infrastructure can be convenient, and it depends on your skills, preferences, and the CI/CD solution used.

## Exam Preparation Tasks

As mentioned in the Introduction, you have a couple of choices for exam preparation: the exercises here, Chapter 21, "Final Preparation," and the exam simulation questions in the Pearson Test Prep software online.

## Review All Key Topics

Review the most important topics in the chapter, noted with the key topic icon in the outer margin of the page. Table 17-4 lists a reference to these key topics and the page numbers on which each is found.

**Table 17-4**　Key Topics for Chapter 17

| Key Topic Element | Description | Page |
|---|---|---|
| Figure 17-1 | Workflow for Ansible Using Playbooks | 765 |
| List | Important Components of Ansible Control Machine | 765 |
| List | CLI Command APIs | 771 |
| Paragraph | Python in Interactive Mode | 772 |
| Paragraph | Python in Noninteractive Mode | 773 |
| Figure 17-2 | POAP Network Infrastructure | 778 |
| Figure 17-3 | POAP Process | 780 |
| Figure 17-4 | DHCP Discovery Process | 781 |
| Section | Terraform Commands | 786 |
| Section | PowerShell | 789 |

## Memory Tables

Print a copy of Appendix C, "Memory Tables" (found on the companion website), or at least the section for this chapter, and complete the tables and lists from memory. Appendix D, "Memory Tables Answer Key," also on the companion website, includes completed tables and lists to check your work.

## Define Key Terms

Define the following key terms from this chapter, and check your answers in the Glossary.

Advanced Message Queuing Protocol (AMQP), application programming interface (API), Cisco Integrated Management Controller (CIMC), Cisco MDS, Cisco NX-OS, Cisco UCS Manager SDK (UCSMSDK), Credential Security Support Provider Protocol (CredSSP), Distributed Virtual Switch (DVS), Domain Name System (DNS), domain-specific language (DSL), Dynamic Host Configuration Protocol (DHCP), Elastic Sky X integrated (ESXi), Ethernet VPN (EVPN), Extensible Markup Language (XML), Git/GitHub, Graceful Insertion and Removal (GIR), graphical user interface (GUI), Hypertext Transfer Protocol (HTTP), hypervisor, in-service software upgrade (ISSU), Integrated Lights-Out (iLO), Intelligent Platform Management Interface (IPMI), Inter-Switch Link (ISL), JavaScript Object Notation (JSON), managed object (MO), Management Information Base (MIB), Management Information Tree (MIT), multitenancy, network interface card (NIC), Network Time Protocol (NTP), NX-API, Open Agent Container (OAC), orchestration, PowerOn Auto Provisioning (POAP), PowerShell agent (PSA), PowerShell session (PSSession), Preboot Execution Environment (PXE), Prime Network Service Controller (PNSC), RecoverPoint, RPM Package Manager (RPM), Rubygems, Simple Network Management Protocol (SNMP), software development kit (SDK), Software Maintenance Upgrade (SMU), UCS Manager (UCSM), Unified Computing System (UCS), Virtual Extensible LAN (VXLAN), virtual interface card (VIC), virtual LAN (VLAN), virtual machine network interface card (VMNIC), virtual network interface card (vNIC), virtual port channel (vPC), Virtual Routing and Forwarding (VRF), VNX, VPLEX, VXLAN network identifier (VNID), VXLAN tunnel endpoint (VTEP), Web Services-Management (WSMAN), WHIPTAIL, Windows Remote Management (WinRM), Windows Remote Shell (WinRS), workflow, Workflow Designer, YAML Ain't Markup Language (YAML)

# References

Ansible Documentation: https://docs.ansible.com/ansible/latest/index.html

Cisco Devnet: https://developer.cisco.com

Data Center GitHub: https://github.com/datacenter

Cisco GitHub: https://github.com/cisco

Cisco UCS GitHub: https://github.com/CiscoUcs

Cisco Nexus 9000 Series NX-OS Programmability Guide, Release 9.2(x): https://www.cisco.com/c/en/us/td/docs/switches/datacenter/nexus9000/sw/92x/programmability/guide/b-cisco-nexus-9000-series-nx-os-programmability-guide-92x.html

Cisco Nexus 9000 Series NX-OS Fundamentals Configuration Guide, Release 9.2(x): https://www.cisco.com/c/en/us/td/docs/switches/datacenter/nexus9000/sw/92x/fundamentals/configuration/guide/b-cisco-nexus-9000-nx-os-fundamentals-configuration-guide-92x.html

Relevant Cisco Live Sessions: http://www.ciscolive.com

Cisco Developer: https://developer.cisco.com/

17

# Network Security

Securing network access and data center devices has never been a simple task. However, it's always challenging and hard to define user access privileges and apply appropriate network policies, network controls, and so on. The new network security module is Zero Trust (ZT); it is a guiding concept that implies the network is always assumed to be hostile and both external and internal threats exist at all times. Zero Trust mandates a "never trust, always verify, enforce least privilege" approach, granting least privilege access based on a dynamic evaluation of the trustworthiness of users and their devices and of any transaction risk before they are allowed to connect to network resources.

## This chapter covers the following key topics:

**Authentication, Authorization, and Accounting (AAA):** This section discusses the Cisco NX-OS authentication, authorization, and accounting concepts. Later in this section, we discuss server groups, server monitoring, remote and local AAA services, and AAA network configurations.

**Role-Based Access Control (RBAC):** This section discusses user roles, rules, and policies related to user roles and includes RBAC commands in a sample configuration.

**Nexus First-Hop Security:** This section discusses Nexus first-hop security, including DAI, DHCP snooping, and port security; it also includes configuration examples and verifications.

**Nexus Control Plane Policing (CoPP):** This section discusses Nexus Control Plane Policing (CoPP) usage, recommendations, and configuration; it also includes a customized CoPP example.

**Cisco ACI Contracts:** This section discusses Application Centric Infrastructure (ACI) contracts and microsegmentation and includes graphical user interface (GUI) and command-line interface (CLI) configuration examples.

**Keychain Authentication:** This section discusses keychain management that allows administrators to create and maintain keychains, which are sequences of keys (sometimes called shared secrets). Keychains are used to secure communications with other devices by using key-based authentication.

## "Do I Know This Already?" Quiz

The "Do I Know This Already?" quiz enables you to assess whether you should read this entire chapter thoroughly or jump to the "Exam Preparation Tasks" section. If you are in doubt about your answers to these questions or your own assessment of your knowledge of the topics, read the entire chapter. Table 18-1 lists the major headings in this chapter and their corresponding "Do I Know This Already?" quiz questions. You can find the answers in Appendix A, "Answers to the 'Do I Know This Already?' Quizzes."

**Table 18-1** "Do I Know This Already?" Section-to-Question Mapping

| Foundation Topics Section | Questions |
|---|---|
| Authentication, Authorization, and Accounting | 1–3 |
| Role-Based Access Control | 4 |
| Nexus First-Hop Security | 5–7 |
| Nexus Control Plane Policing | 8 |
| Cisco ACI Contracts | 9–10 |
| Keychain Authentication | 11 |

**CAUTION** The goal of self-assessment is to gauge your mastery of the topics in this chapter. If you do not know the answer to a question or are only partially sure of the answer, you should mark that question as wrong for purposes of the self-assessment. Giving yourself credit for an answer you correctly guess skews your self-assessment results and might provide you with a false sense of security.

1. What are the most common AAA protocols? (Choose two answers.)

    a. TCP/IP

    b. RADIUS

    c. TACACS+

    d. LDAP

2. What command would you enter to set up authentication on your router to query the TACACS+ servers and, if unable to communicate to the servers, authenticate from the local password?

    a. aaa authentication login default group radius enable

    b. aaa authentication login default group tacacs+ local

    c. aaa authentication login default group tacacs+ enable

    d. aaa authentication login default group tacacs+ none

3. What ports are used by RADIUS protocols? (Choose two answers.)

    a. UDP 49

    b. UDP 1645/1646

    c. TCP 1645/1646

    d. UDP 1812/1813

4. By default, the user accounts without an administrator role can access the
    _____. (Choose two answers.)

    a. show command

    b. config terminal command

    c. Interface <interface name>

    d. Router OSPF

5. When you enable DHCP snooping, what does an untrusted port filter out?

   a. DHCP replies from a legitimate DHCP server

   b. DHCP replies from a rogue server

   c. DHCP requests from a legitimate client

   d. DHCP requests from rogue clients

6. Dynamic ARP inspections help mitigate an attack based on which one of the following parameters with an ARP reply packet?

   a. Source IP address

   b. MAC address

   c. Destination IP address

   d. Sequence number

7. By default, how many MAC addresses are permitted to be learned on a switch port with port security enabled?

   a. Eight

   b. Four

   c. Two

   d. One

8. What does Control Plane Policing (CoPP) protect?

   a. The CPU against DDoS

   b. Memory against memory leaks

   c. The NX-OS against unauthorized access

   d. All of the above

9. Microsegmentation improves network performance.

   a. True

   b. False

10. If no contract is applied between intra-endpoints, no traffic flow is allowed between the provider and the consumer.

   a. True

   b. False

11. What is the key start time in the keychain?

   a. The absolute time that the lifetime ends

   b. The absolute time that the lifetime begins

   c. The number of seconds after the start time

   d. Infinite lifetime (no end time)

## Foundation Topics

# Authentication, Authorization, and Accounting

Authentication, Authorization, and Accounting (AAA) is a protocol used to secure access to a Cisco Nexus device. The AAA model answers three questions:

1. Who is on the network (authentication)?

2. What are they allowed to do on the network (authorization)?

3. What have they been doing on the network (accounting)?

- **Authentication:** Identifies users, including the login and password dialog, challenge and response, messaging support, and encryption. Authentication is the process of verifying the identity of the person or device accessing the Cisco NX-OS device, which is based on the user ID and password combination provided by the entity trying to access the Cisco NX-OS device. Cisco NX-OS devices allow you to perform local authentication (using the local lookup database) or remote authentication (using one or more RADIUS or TACACS+ servers).

- **Authorization:** Provides access control. Authorization is the process of assembling a set of attributes that describe what the user is authorized to perform. Authorization in the Cisco NX-OS software is provided by attributes that are downloaded from AAA servers. Remote security servers, such as RADIUS and TACACS+, authorize users for specific rights by associating attribute-value (AV) pairs, which define those rights with the appropriate user.

- **Accounting:** Provides the method for collecting information, logging the information locally, and sending the information to the AAA server for billing, auditing, and reporting. The accounting feature tracks and maintains a log of every management session used to access the Cisco NX-OS device. You can use this information to generate reports for troubleshooting and auditing purposes. You can store accounting logs locally or send them to remote AAA servers.

AAA allows for a granular approach to securing the devices by setting policies for either a group or individual and by allowing the administrator to use different method lists for different access types. For example, the engineer could create a method list for authentication that states the TACACS+ server at 10.10.10.1 should be used for console access and should fall back to the local database. A different method list can be used for the VTY lines stating that a RADIUS server should be used and fall back to the local database. If the default method list is used, it applies to all device access methods. AAA can be used with both RADIUS and TACACS+ servers to provide secure services. There are some noteworthy differences between the two protocols:

1. TACACS+ uses TCP port 49 for communication, whereas RADIUS uses UDP port 1645/1646 or 1812/1813.

2. TACACS+ encrypts the entire contents of the packet. RADIUS encrypts only the password.

3. TACACS+ is more flexible in the protocols that it can support.

4. TACACS+ is Cisco proprietary. RADIUS is defined in RFC 2138 and is an open standard.

Nexus devices support local and remote AAA. Remote AAA services are provided through RADIUS and TACACS+ protocols. Remote services have the following advantages over local AAA services:

- It is easier to manage user password lists for each Cisco NX-OS device in the fabric.

- AAA servers are already deployed widely across enterprises and can be easily used for AAA services.

- You can centrally manage the accounting log for all Cisco NX-OS devices in the fabric.

- It is easier to manage user attributes for each Cisco NX-OS device in the fabric than using the local databases on the Cisco NX-OS devices.

You can specify remote AAA servers for authentication, authorization, and accounting using server groups. A server group is a set of remote AAA servers that implement the same AAA protocol. The purpose of a server group is to provide for failover servers in case a remote AAA server fails to respond. If the first remote server in the group fails to respond, the next remote server in the group is tried until one of the servers sends a response. If all the AAA servers in the server group fail to respond, that server group option is considered a failure. If required, you can specify multiple server groups. If the Cisco NX-OS device encounters errors from the servers in the first group, it tries the servers in the next server group.

Configuring AAA on the command line is fairly simple, but the commands can be quite lengthy depending on the optional parameters used within the command set itself.

## AAA Service Configuration Options

AAA configuration in Cisco NX-OS devices is service based, which means that you can have separate AAA configurations for the following services:

- User Telnet or Secure Shell (SSH) login authentication

- Console login authentication

- Cisco TrustSec authentication

- 802.1X authentication

- Extensible Authentication Protocol over User Datagram Protocol (EAPoUDP) authentication for Network Admission Control (NAC)

- User management session accounting

- 802.1X accounting

Table 18-2 shows some of the most-used AAA service configuration commands. For a full list of commands, refer to the Nexus Security Configuration Guide links in the "Reference" section at the end of the chapter.

**Table 18-2**   AAA Service Global Configuration Commands

| AAA Service Configuration Option | Related Command |
|---|---|
| Telnet or SSH login | **aaa authentication login default** |
| Fallback to local authentication for the default login. | **aaa authentication login default fallback error local** |

| AAA Service Configuration Option | Related Command |
|---|---|
| Console login | **aaa authentication login console** |
| Cisco TrustSec authentication | **aaa authentication cts default** |
| 802.1X authentication | **aaa authentication dot1x default** |
| EAPoUDP authentication | **aaa authentication eou default** |
| User session accounting | **aaa accounting default** |
| 802.1X accounting | **aaa accounting dot1x default** |

You can specify the following authentication methods for the AAA services:

- **All RADIUS servers:** Uses the global pool of RADIUS servers for authentication

- **Specific Server Groups:** Specifies a single remote group or specific remote groups

- **Local:** Uses the local username or password database for authentication

- **None:** Specifies that no AAA authentication be used

**NOTE**  If you specify the All RADIUS servers method rather than a specified server group method, the Cisco NX-OS device chooses the RADIUS server from the global pool of configured RADIUS servers, in the order of configuration. Servers from this global pool are the servers that can be selectively configured in a RADIUS server group on the Cisco NX-OS device.

## Authentication and Authorization User Login Process

The authentication and authorization process is as follows:

1. When a user logs in to the required Cisco NX-OS device, that user can use the Telnet, SSH, or console login option.

**NOTE**  It is recommended that you disable the Telnet service and only allow SSH for remote access. Telnet is insecure because it sends passwords and commands in clear text.

2. If you configured the AAA server groups using the server group authentication method, the Cisco NX-OS device sends an authentication request to the first AAA server in the group as follows:

   - If the AAA server fails to respond, the next AAA server is tried and so on until the remote server responds to the authentication request.

   - If all AAA servers in the server group fail to respond, the servers in the next server group are tried.

   - If all configured methods fail, the local database is used for authentication.

3. If the Cisco NX-OS device successfully authenticates users through a remote AAA server, the following possibilities apply:

   - If the AAA server protocol is RADIUS, user roles specified in the cisco-av-pair attribute are downloaded with an authentication response.

18

- If the AAA server protocol is TACACS+, another request is sent to the same server to get the user roles specified as custom attributes for the shell.

4. If the username and password are successfully authenticated locally, the Cisco NX-OS device logs in the user and assigns the roles configured in the local database.

For the Nexus 7000 Series with virtual device context (VDC), all AAA configurations and operations are local to the VDC, except the default console methods and the AAA accounting log. The configuration and operation of the AAA authentication methods for the console login apply only to the default VDC. The AAA accounting log is only in the default VDC. You can display the contents from any VDC, but you must clear it in the default VDC.

## AAA NX-OS Configurations

The Cisco NX-OS feature does not require a license. Any feature not included in a license package is bundled with the Cisco NX-OS system images. It is recommended that you configure AAA with a remote server. Remote AAA servers have the following prerequisites:

- Ensure that the Cisco NX-OS device is configured as a client of the AAA servers.

- Ensure that the secret key is configured on the Cisco NX-OS device and the remote AAA servers.

- Ensure that the remote server responds to AAA requests from the Cisco NX-OS device.

**NOTE**  If you have a user account configured on a local Cisco NX-OS device that has the same name as a remote user account on an AAA server, the Cisco NX-OS software applies the user roles for the local user account to the remote user, not the user roles configured on the AAA server.

Table 18-3 lists the default settings for AAA parameters. You can alter these parameters as necessary.

**Table 18-3**   Default Settings for AAA Parameters

| Parameters | Default |
|---|---|
| Console authentication method | Local |
| Default authentication method | Local |
| Login authentication failure messages | Disabled |
| MSCHAP authentication | Disabled |
| Default accounting method | Local |
| Accounting log display length | 250 KB |

Tables 18-4 through 18-6 show some of the most-used AAA configuration commands. For a full list of commands, refer to the Nexus Security Configuration Guide links in the "References" section at the end of this chapter.

**Table 18-4**   Global AAA Commands

| Command | Purpose |
|---|---|
| **aaa authentication login console** {**group** *group-list* [**none** ] \| **local** \| **none** } | Configures login authentication methods for the console.<br><br>The *group-list* argument consists of a space-delimited list of group names. The group names are the following:<br><br>**Radius** uses the global pool of RADIUS servers for authentication. |
|  | The **local** method uses the local database for authentication, and the **none** method specifies that no AAA authentication be used.<br><br>The default console login method is **local**, which is used when no methods are configured or when all the configured methods fail to respond. |
| **aaa authentication login default** { **fallback error local** \|**group** *group-list* [**none** ] \| **local** \| **none** } | Configures the default authentication methods.<br><br>The **fallback error local** method enables fallback to local authentication for the default login if remote authentication is configured and all AAA servers are unreachable. Fallback to local authentication is enabled by default.<br><br>**NOTE:** Disabling fallback to local authentication can lock your Cisco NX-OS device, forcing you to perform a password recovery to gain access. To prevent being locked out of the device, we recommend that you disable fallback to local authentication for only the default login or the console login, not both.<br><br>The *group-list* argument consists of a space-delimited list of group names. The group names are the following:<br><br>**Radius** uses the global pool of RADIUS servers for authentication.<br><br>The **local** method uses the local database for authentication, and the **none** method specifies that no AAA authentication be used.<br><br>The default login method is **local**, which is used when no methods are configured or when all the configured methods fail to respond.<br><br>You can configure one of the following:<br><br>■ AAA authentication groups<br>■ AAA authentication groups with no authentication<br>■ Local authentication<br>■ No authentication<br><br>**NOTE:** The **local** keyword is not supported (and is not required) when configuring AAA authentication groups because local authentication is the default if remote servers are unreachable. For example, if you configure **aaa authentication login default group g1**, local authentication is tried if you are unable to authenticate using AAA group g1. In contrast, if you configure **aaa authentication login default group g1 none**, no authentication is performed if you are unable to authenticate using AAA group g1. |

18

| Command | Purpose |
|---|---|
| **aaa user default-role** | Enables the default user role for AAA authentication. The default is enabled. You can disable the default user role feature by using the **no** form of this command. |
| **aaa authentication login error-enable** | Enables login authentication failure messages. The default is disabled. |
| **no aaa authentication login ascii-authentication** | Disables ASCII authentication. |
| **aaa authentication login {mschap \| mschapv2 } enable** | Enables MSCHAP or MSCHAP V2 authentication. The default is disabled. **NOTE:** You cannot enable both MSCHAP and MSCHAP V2 on your Cisco NX-OS device. |
| **aaa accounting default {group** *group-list* \| **local }** | Configures the default accounting method. The *group-list* argument consists of a space-delimited list of group names. The group names are the following: **radius:** Uses the global pool of RADIUS servers for accounting. **named-group:** Uses a named subset of TACACS+ or RADIUS servers for accounting. The **local** method uses the local database for accounting. The default method is **local**, which is used when no server groups are configured or when all the configured server groups fail to respond. |

**Table 18-5**   AAA Passphrase and Locking User Accounts Commands

| Command | Purpose |
|---|---|
| **userpassphrase { min-length <8 ? 127> \| max-length <80 ? 127> }** | Allows the admin to configure either minimum or maximum passphrase length. |
| **userpassphrase { min-length & max-length }** | Allows the admin to configure both minimum and maximum passphrase length. |
| **userpassphrase { default-lifetime \| default-warntime \| default-gracetime }** | Allows the admin to update the default configurations. |
| **username** *<username>* **passphrase { lifetime \| warntime \| gracetime }** | Allows the admin to configure passphrase lifetimes for any user. |
| **username** *<username>* **lock-user-account** | Allows the admin to lock any user account. |
| **username** *<username>* **expire-userpassphrase** | Allows the admin to set any user passphrase to expire immediately. |
| **password prompt username** | Enables the login knob. If this command is enabled and the user enters the **username** command without the **password** option, the password is prompted. The password accepts hidden characters. Use the **no** form of this command to disable the login knob. |

**Table 18-6**   AAA Verification and Monitoring Commands

| Command | Purpose |
|---------|---------|
| **show accounting log [size | last-index | start-seqnum number | start-time year month day hh: mm: ss]** | Displays the accounting log contents. <br><br> By default, the command output contains up to 250,000 bytes of the accounting log. You can use the size argument to limit command output. The range is from 0 to 250,000 bytes. You can also specify a starting sequence number or a starting time for the log output. The range of the starting index is from 1 to 1,000,000. Use the **last-index** keyword to display the value of the last index number in the accounting log file. |
| **show aaa accounting** | Displays AAA accounting configuration. |
| **show aaa authentication [login {ascii-authentication | error-enable | mschap | mschapv2 }]** | Displays AAA authentication login configuration information. |
| **show aaa groups** | Displays the AAA server group configuration. |
| **show running-config aaa [all ]** | Displays the AAA configuration in the running configuration. |
| **show startup-config aaa** | Displays the AAA configuration in the startup configuration. |
| **show userpassphrase all** | Lists all the parameter values under **userpassphrase**. |
| **show username** *<username>* **passphrase timevalues** | Allows any user to view the passphrase lifetimes configured and the admin to view for any user. |
| **show locked-users** | Allows the admin to view and unlock all the locked users. |

Example 18-1 shows how to configure the AAA login and console using a remote RADIUS server with a fallback option set to local.

**Example 18-1**   *NX-OS AAA Configuration*

```
Switch(config)# radius-server host 10.10.10.134 key cisco123
switch(config)# aaa group server radius radius-1
switch(config-radius)# server 10.10.10.134

switch(config)# aaa authentication login default group radius-1
switch(config)# aaa authentication login console group radius-1
switch(config)# aaa authentication login default fallback error local
switch(config)# aaa accounting default group radius-1
```

# Role-Based Access Control

One of the most challenging problems in managing a large data center is the complexity of security administration. Role-based access control (RBAC) allows you to determine the commands and resources available to each user. In RBAC, users are associated with roles and rules. User roles determine a user's privileges, and a rule defines what operations the role allows the user to perform.

18

You can create and manage user accounts and assign roles that limit access to operations on the Cisco NX-OS device. RBAC allows you to define the rules for an assigned role that restricts the authorization that the user has to access management operations.

You can configure up to a maximum of 256 user accounts. By default, the user account does not expire unless you explicitly configure it to expire. The **expire** option determines the date when the user account is disabled. For Nexus 7000 Series with virtual device context (VDC), users can have user accounts on multiple VDCs. These users can move between VDCs after an initial connection to a VDC. The Cisco NX-OS software provides two default user accounts: admin and admin backup.

**NOTE**    The following words are reserved and cannot be used to configure users: bin, daemon, adm, lp, sync, shutdown, halt, mail, news, uucp, operator, games, gopher, ftp, nobody, nscd, mailnull, root, rpc, rpcuser, xfs, gdm, mtsuser, ftpuser, man, and sys.

**NOTE**    The Cisco NX-OS software does not support all numeric usernames, whether created with TACACS+ or RADIUS, or created locally. Local users with all-numeric names cannot be created. If an all-numeric username exists on the AAA server and is entered during login, the user is not logged in.

**NOTE**    Usernames must begin with an alphanumeric character and can contain only these special characters: ( + = . _ \ -). The # and ! symbols are not supported. If the username contains characters that are not allowed, the specified user is unable to log in.

A good security practice is to enable password-strength checking to force users to use strong passwords. A strong password has the following characteristics:

- Is at least eight characters long

- Does not contain many consecutive characters (such as abcd)

- Does not contain many repeating characters (such as aaabbb)

- Does not contain dictionary words

- Does not contain proper names

- Contains both uppercase and lowercase characters

- Contains numbers

The following are examples of strong passwords:

- M!C15c0!@345

- 2020Ccn980ok

- D@taC3ntr3Ex@m

If a password is trivial (such as a short, easy-to-decipher password), the Cisco NX-OS software rejects the password configuration if password-strength checking is enabled. Be sure to configure a strong password as shown in the preceding examples. Passwords are case sensitive.

**NOTE**  Clear-text passwords cannot contain dollar signs ($) or spaces anywhere in the password. Also, they cannot include these special characters at the beginning of the password: quotation marks (" or '), vertical bars (|), or right-angle brackets (>).

**NOTE**  All printable ASCII characters are supported in the password string if they are enclosed in quotation marks.

## NX-OS User Roles and Rules

User roles contain rules that define the operations allowed for the user who is assigned the role. Each user role can contain multiple rules, and each user can have multiple roles. For example, if role1 allows access only to configuration operations, and role2 allows access only to debug operations, users who belong to both role1 and role2 can access configuration and debug operations. You can also limit access to specific Virtual Routing and Forwarding (VRF) instances, VLANs, and interfaces.

The Cisco NX-OS software provides the following user roles:

- **network-admin:** Complete read-and-write access to the entire Cisco NX-OS device (for Nexus 7000, only available in the default VDC)

- **network-operator:** Complete read access to the entire Cisco NX-OS device (for Nexus 7000, only available in the default VDC)

- **vdc-admin:** Read-and-write access limited to a VDC

- **vdc-operator:** Read access limited to a VDC

**18**

**NOTE**  Only Cisco Nexus 7000 Series switches support multiple VDCs; however, the vdc-operator role is available on all Nexus switches and has the same privileges and limitations as the network-operator role.

**NOTE**  All Cisco Nexus Series switches except Nexus 7000 support a single VDC; consequently the vdc-admin has the same privileges and limitations as the network-admin.

By default, the user accounts without an administrator role can access only the **show, exit, end,** and **configure terminal** commands. You can add rules to allow users to configure features.

**NOTE**   If you belong to multiple roles, you can execute a combination of all the commands permitted by these roles. Access to a command takes priority over being denied access to a command. For example, suppose a user has role1, which is denied access to the configuration commands. However, the user also has role2, which has access to the configuration commands. In this case, the user has access to the configuration commands.

**NOTE**   Only the network-admin user can perform a checkpoint or rollback in the RBAC roles. Though other users have these commands as a permit rule in their role, user access is denied when you try to execute these commands.

The rule is the basic element of a role. A rule defines what operations the role allows the user to perform. You can apply rules for the following parameters:

- **Command:** A command or group of commands defined in a regular expression
- **Feature:** A command or group of commands defined in a regular expression
- **Feature group:** Default or user-defined group of features
- **OID:** An SNMP object identifier (OID)

The command, feature, and feature group parameters create a hierarchical relationship. The most basic control parameter is the command. The next control parameter is the feature, which represents all commands associated with the feature. The last control parameter is the feature group. The feature group combines related features and allows you to easily manage the rules. The Cisco NX-OS software also supports the predefined feature group L3 that you can use.

You can configure up to 256 rules for each role. The user-specified rule number determines the order in which the rules are applied. Rules are applied in descending order. For example, if a role has three rules, rule 3 is applied before rule 2, which is applied before rule 1.

For Nexus 7000 with virtual device context, the users with the network-admin and network-operator roles can operate in all VDCs when logged in from the default VDC and use the 805**switchto vdc** command to access other VDCs. All other user roles are local to the VDC. Roles are not shared between VDCs. Each VDC maintains an independent user role database.

The following guidelines and limitations apply to the **switchto vdc** command:

- Only users with the network-admin or network-operator role can use the switchto vdc command. No other users are permitted to use it.
- No user can grant permission to another role to use the **switchto vdc** command.
- After a network-admin uses the **switchto vdc** command, this user becomes a vdc-admin for the new VDC. Similarly, after a network-operator uses the **switchto vdc** command, this user becomes a vdc-operator for the new VDC. Any other roles associated with the user are not valid after the **switchto vdc** command is entered.
- After a network-admin or network-operator uses the **switchto vdc** command, this user cannot use this command to switch to another VDC. The only option is to use the **switchback** command to return to the original VDC.

## NX-OS RBAC Configurations

The RBAC feature does not require a license. Any feature not included in a license package is bundled with the Cisco NX-OS system images. RBAC configuration recommendations and limitations include the following:

- You can create up to 64 user-defined roles in a VDC in addition to the four default user roles in the default VDC and the two default user roles in the nondefault VDCs.

- You can add up to 256 rules to a user role.

- You can add up to 64 user-defined feature groups to a VDC in addition to the default feature group, L3.

- You can configure up to 256 users in a VDC.

- You can assign a maximum of 64 user roles to a user account.

- If you have a user account configured on the local Cisco NX-OS device that has the same name as a remote user account on an AAA server, the Cisco NX-OS software applies the user roles for the local user account to the remote user, not the user roles configured on the AAA server.

- You cannot delete the default admin and SNMP user accounts.

- You cannot remove the default user roles from the default admin user accounts.

- The network-operator and vdc-operator roles cannot run the **show running-config** and **show startup-config** commands.

- RBAC is not supported for traffic between F1 Series module ports and M1 Series module ports in the same VLAN.

- When you use the **rule rule-id permit command** *command-string* command, the *command-string* argument should be complete or it should contain an asterisk (*) after the command name—for example, **show** * or **show running-config** *.

- If you are adding more than one command in the *command-string* argument, the commands should be separated by a command separator (;), and whitespace should be added.

- When you are specifying interfaces, it is recommended that you specify the entire media type keyword such as **Ethernet** or **loopback**. However, if you are using the short form of the media type keyword, it should be followed by an asterisk (*)—for example, **"rule 22 permit command show run int Ethernet4/1"**, **"rule 22 permit command show run int loopback1"**, or **"rule 22 permit command show run int eth*"**. Rules that do not follow this guideline are not accepted—for example, **"rule 22 permit command show run int Eth1/4"** and **"rule 22 permit command show run int loop1"**.

Table 18-7 shows NX-OS user account default parameters. You can alter these parameters as necessary.

18

**Table 18-7**   Default User Accounts and RBAC Parameters

| Parameters | Default |
|---|---|
| User account password | Undefined. |
| User account expiry date | None. |
| User account role in the default VDC (Nexus 7000 only) | Network-operator if the creating user has the network-admin role, or vdc-operator if the creating user has the vdc-admin role. |
| User account role in the non-VDCs | Vdc-operator if the creating user has the vdc-admin role. |
| Default user roles in the default VDC (Nexus 7000 only) | Network-operator. |
| Default user roles in the nondefault VDCs | Vdc-operator. |
| Interface policy | All interfaces are accessible. |
| VLAN policy | All VLANs are accessible. |
| VRF policy | All VRFs are accessible. |
| Feature group | L3. |

Tables 18-8 and 18-9 show some of the most-used user account and RBAC configuration commands. For a full list of commands, refer to the Nexus Security Configuration Guide links in the "References" section at the end of this chapter.

**Table 18-8**   User Account and RBAC Global Commands

| Command | Purpose |
|---|---|
| **password strength-check** | Enables password-strength checking. |
| | The default is enabled. |
| | You can disable password-strength checking by using the **no** form of this command. |
| **username** *user-id*<br>[**password** [0 \| 5 ] *password*]<br>[**expire** *date*] [**role** *role-name*] | Configures a user account. |
| | The **user-id** argument is a case-sensitive, alphanumeric character string with a maximum length of 28 characters. Valid characters are uppercase letters *A* through *Z*, lowercase letters *a* through *z*, numbers 0 through 9, hyphen (-), period (.), underscore (_), plus sign (+), and equal sign (=). |
| | The default password is undefined. The 0 option indicates that the password is clear text, and the 5 option indicates that the password is encrypted. The default is 0 (clear text). |
| | **NOTE:** If you do not specify a password, the user might not be able to log in to the Cisco NX-OS device. |
| | **NOTE:** If you create a user account with the encrypted password option, the corresponding SNMP user is not created. |

| Command | Purpose |
|---------|---------|
| | The **expire date** option format is YYYY-MM-DD. The default is no expiry date. |
| | User accounts can have a maximum of 64 user roles. |
| **role name** *role-name* | Specifies a user role and enters role configuration mode. |
| | The role-name argument is a case-sensitive, alphanumeric character string with a maximum length of 16 characters. |
| **rule** *number* {**deny** \| **permit** } **command** *command-string* | Configures a command rule. |
| | The *command-string* argument can contain spaces and regular expressions. For example, **interface ethernet** includes all Ethernet interfaces. |
| | Repeat this command for as many rules as needed. |
| **rule** *number* {**deny** \| **permit** } {**read** \| **read-write** } **feature** *feature-name* | Configures a read-only or read-and-write rule for a feature. |
| | Use the **show role feature** command to display a list of features. |
| | Repeat this command for as many rules as needed. |
| **rule** *number* {**deny** \| **permit** } {**read** \| **read-write** } **feature-group** *group-name* | Configures a read-only or read-and-write rule for a feature group. |
| | Use the **show role feature-group** command to display a list of feature groups. |
| | Repeat this command for as many rules as needed. |
| **rule** *number* {**deny** \| **permit** } {**read** \| **read-write** } **oid** *snmp_oid_name* | Configures a read-only or read-and-write rule for an SNMP object identifier. |
| | You can enter up to 32 elements for the OID. This command can be used to allow SNMP-based performance monitoring tools to poll devices but restrict their access to system-intensive branches such as the IP routing table, ARP cache, MAC address tables, specific MIBs, and so on. |
| | **NOTE:** The deepest OID can be at the scalar level or at the table root level. |
| | Repeat this command for as many rules as needed. |
| **description** *text* | (Optional) Configures the role description. You can include spaces in the description. |
| **interface policy deny** | Enters role interface policy configuration mode. |
| **permit interface** *interface-list* | Specifies a list of interfaces that the role can access. |
| | Repeat this command for as many interfaces as needed. |
| **vlan policy deny** | Enters role VLAN policy configuration mode. |
| **permit vlan** *vlan-list* | Specifies a range of VLANs that the role can access. |
| | Repeat this command for as many VLANs as needed. |

18

**Table 18-9**   User Account and RBAC Verification Commands

| Command | Purpose |
|---|---|
| show role | Displays the user role configuration. |
| show role feature | Displays the feature list. |
| show role feature-group | Displays the feature group configuration. |
| show startup-config security | Displays the user account configuration in the startup configuration. |
| show running-config security [all ] | Displays the user account configuration in the running configuration. The **all** keyword displays the default values for the user accounts. |
| show user-account | Displays user account information. |

Example 18-2 shows how to configure a user role named User-Role-1.

**Example 18-2**   *Creating a User Role Named User-Role-1*

```
Switch(config)# role name User-Role-1
Switch(config-role)# rule 3 permit read-write feature l2nac
Switch(config-role)# rule 2 permit read-write feature dot1x
Switch(config-role)# rule 1 deny command clear *
```

Example 18-3 shows how to create a user role that can configure an interface to enable and show the Hot Standby Router Protocol (HSRP) and Gateway Load Balancing Protocol (GLBP). Rule 1 allows you to configure HSRP on an interface, rule 2 allows you to configure the **config hsrp** commands and enable the exec-level **show** and **debug** commands for HSRP, and rule 3 allows you to enable the exec-level **show** and **debug glbp** commands.

**Example 18-3**   *Creating a User Role Named MyTest*

```
Switch(config)# role name MyTest
Switch(config-role)# rule 1 permit command config t; interface *; hsrp *
Switch(config-role)# rule 2 permit read-write feature hsrp
Switch(config-role)# rule 3 permit read feature glbp
```

Example 18-4 shows how to configure a user role that can configure only a specific interface (Interface E1/4).

**Example 18-4**   *Creating a User Role Named Int_Eth1_4_only*

```
Switch(config)# role name Int_Eth1_4_only
Switch(config-role)# rule 1 permit command configure terminal; interface *
Switch(config-role)# interface policy deny
Switch(config-role-interface)# permit interface Ethernet1/4
```

Example 18-5 shows how to configure a user role feature group to enable or disable specific features.

**Example 18-5**  *Creating a User Group Named Security-features*

```
Switch(config)# role feature-group name Security-features
Switch(config-featuregrp)# feature radius
Switch(config-featuregrp)# feature tacacs
Switch(config-featuregrp)# feature vpc
Switch(config-featuregrp)# feature aaa
Switch(config-featuregrp)# feature bgp
Switch(config-featuregrp)# feature acl
Switch(config-featuregrp)# feature access-list
```

Example 18-6 shows how to configure a user account.

**Example 18-6**  *Creating a User Account*

```
Switch(config)# username user1 password C1sc0@2020 role User-role-1
```

Example 18-7 shows how to add an OID rule to restrict access to part of the OID subtree.

**Key Topic**

**Example 18-7**  *Creating a User Role Named User1*

```
Switch(config)# role name User1
Switch(config-role)# rule 1 permit read feature snmp
```
```
Switch(config-role)# rule 2 deny read oid 1.3.6.1.2.1.1.9
Switch(config-role)# role name User1


Role: User1
Description: new role
  Vlan policy: permit (default)
  Interface policy: permit (default)
  Vrf policy: permit (default)
  ------------------------------------------------------------------
  Rule    Perm    Type    Scope          Entity
  ------------------------------------------------------------------
  2       deny    read    oid            1.3.6.1.2.1.1.9
  1       permit  read    feature        snmp
```

18

# Nexus First-Hop Security

Information theft can result from router impersonation (man-in-the-middle attacks), address theft, address spoofing, and remote address resolution cache exhaustion (denial-of-service attacks). These security breaches can come from malicious or misconfigured users and can severely disrupt Layer 2 domains and networks in general.

Nexus First-Hop Security (FHS) features enable better IPv4 and IPv6 link security and management over the Layer 2 links. In a service provider environment, these features closely control address assignment and derived operations, such as Duplicate Address Detection (DAD) and Address Resolution (AR).

The following supported FHS features secure the protocols and help build a secure endpoint database on the fabric leaf switches that are used to mitigate security threats such as man-in-the-middle (MITM) attacks and IP thefts:

- **ARP inspection:** Allows a network administrator to intercept, log, and discard ARP packets with invalid MAC address-to-IP address bindings.

- **ND inspection:** Learns and secures bindings for stateless autoconfiguration addresses in Layer 2 neighbor tables.

- **DHCP inspection:** Validates DHCP messages received from untrusted sources and filters out invalid messages.

- **RA Guard:** Allows the network administrator to block or reject unwanted or rogue router advertisement (RA) guard messages.

- **IPv4 and IPv6 Source Guard:** Blocks any data traffic from an unknown source.

- **Trust Control:** A trusted source is a device that is under your administrative control. These devices include the switches, routers, and servers in the fabric. Any device beyond the firewall or outside the network is an untrusted source. Generally, host ports are treated as untrusted sources.

FHS features provide the following security measures:

- **Role enforcement:** Prevents untrusted hosts from sending messages that are out of the scope of their role.

- **Binding enforcement:** Prevents address theft.

- **DoS attack mitigations:** Prevents malicious endpoints from growing the endpoint database to the point where the database could stop providing operation services.

- **Proxy:** Acts as proxy to increase the efficiency of address resolution.

## Nexus Dynamic ARP Inspection

Dynamic ARP inspection (DAI) ensures that only valid ARP requests and responses are relayed. The Address Resolution Protocol (ARP) provides IP communication within a Layer 2 broadcast domain by mapping an IP address to a MAC address. For example, host B wants to send information to host A but does not have the MAC address of host A in its ARP cache. In ARP terms, host B is the sender and host A is the target.

To get the MAC address of host A, host B generates a broadcast message for all hosts within the broadcast domain to obtain the MAC address associated with the IP address of host A. All hosts within the broadcast domain receive the ARP request, and host A responds with its MAC address.

An ARP spoofing attack can affect hosts, switches, and routers connected to your Layer 2 network by sending false information to the ARP caches of the devices connected to the subnet. Sending false information to an ARP cache is known as ARP cache poisoning. Spoof attacks can also intercept traffic intended for other hosts on the subnet.

As in Figure 18-1, hosts A, B, and C are connected to the device on interfaces A, B, and C, which are on the same subnet. Their IP and MAC addresses are shown in parentheses; for example, host A uses IP address IA and MAC address MA. When host A needs to send IP data to host B, it broadcasts an ARP request for the MAC address associated with IP address IB. When the device and host B receive the ARP request, they populate their ARP caches with an ARP binding for a host with the IP address IA and a MAC address MA; for example, IP address IA is bound to MAC address MA. When host B responds, the device and host A populate their ARP caches with a binding for a host with the IP address IB and the MAC address MB.

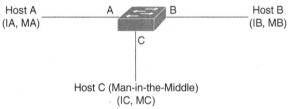

**Figure 18-1** *Man-in-the-Middle Attack*

Host C can poison the ARP caches of the device, host A, and host B by broadcasting two forged ARP responses with bindings: one for a host with an IP address of IA and a MAC address of MC and another for a host with the IP address of IB and a MAC address of MC. Host B and the device then use the MAC address MC as the destination MAC address for traffic intended for IA, which means that host C intercepts that traffic. Likewise, host A and the device use the MAC address MC as the destination MAC address for traffic intended for IB.

Because host C knows the true MAC addresses associated with IA and IB, it can forward the intercepted traffic to those hosts by using the correct MAC address as the destination. This topology, in which host C has inserted itself into the traffic stream from host A to host B, is an example of a man-in-the-middle attack.

To prevent traffic interception, Cisco Nexus performs DAI activities:

- Intercepts all ARP requests and responses on untrusted ports.

- Verifies that each of these intercepted packets has a valid IP-to-MAC address binding before updating the local ARP cache or before forwarding the packet to the appropriate destination.

- Drops invalid ARP packets.

DAI can determine the validity of an ARP packet based on valid IP-to-MAC address bindings stored in a Dynamic Host Configuration Protocol (DHCP) snooping binding database. This database is built by DHCP snooping if DHCP snooping is enabled on the VLANs and on the device. It can also contain static entries that you create. If the ARP packet is received on a trusted interface, the device forwards the packet without any checks. On untrusted interfaces, the device forwards the packet only if it is valid.

DAI can validate ARP packets against user-configured ARP access control lists (ACLs) for hosts with statically configured IP addresses. The device logs dropped packets.

18

You can configure DAI to drop ARP packets when the IP addresses in the packets are invalid or when the MAC addresses in the body of the ARP packets do not match the addresses specified in the Ethernet header.

DAI associates a trust state with each interface on the device. Packets that arrive on trusted interfaces bypass all DAI validation checks, and packets that arrive on untrusted interfaces go through the DAI validation process.

In a typical network configuration, the guidelines for configuring the trust state of interfaces are as follows:

■ **Untrusted:** Interfaces that are connected to hosts

■ **Trusted:** Interfaces that are connected to devices

With this configuration, all ARP packets that enter the network from a device bypass the security check. No other validation is needed at any other place in the VLAN or in the network.

> **NOTE**   Use the trust state configuration carefully. Configuring interfaces as untrusted when they should be trusted can result in a loss of connectivity.

As an example, let's assume device A and device B are running DAI on the VLAN that includes host 1 and host 2, as shown in Figure 18-2. If host 1 and host 2 acquire their IP addresses from the DHCP server connected to device A, only device A binds the IP-to-MAC address of host 1. If the interface between device A and device B is untrusted, the ARP packets from host 1 are dropped by device B, and connectivity between host 1 and host 2 is lost.

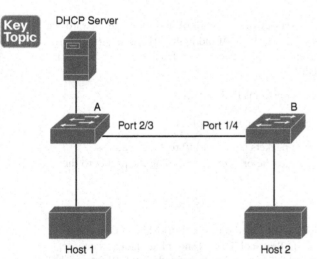

**Figure 18-2**   *ARP Packet Validation on a VLAN Enabled for DAI*

If you configure interfaces as trusted when they should be untrusted, you may open a security hole in a network. If device A is not running DAI, host 1 can easily poison the ARP cache of device B (and host 2, if you configured the link between the devices as trusted). This condition can occur even though device B is running DAI.

DAI ensures that hosts (on untrusted interfaces) connected to a device that runs DAI do not poison the ARP caches of other hosts in the network; however, DAI does not prevent hosts in other portions of the network from poisoning the caches of the hosts that are connected to a device that runs DAI.

If some devices in a VLAN run DAI and other devices do not, the guidelines for configuring the trust state of interfaces on a device that runs DAI become the following:

- **Untrusted:** Interfaces that are connected to hosts or to devices that are not running DAI

- **Trusted:** Interfaces that are connected to devices that are running DAI

To validate the bindings of packets from devices that do not run DAI, configure ARP ACLs on the device that runs DAI. When you cannot determine the bindings, isolate at Layer 3 the devices that run DAI from devices that do not run DAI.

## NX-OS DAI Configurations

The DAI feature does not require a license. Any feature not included in a license package is bundled with the Cisco NX-OS system images. DAI configuration recommendations and limitations are as follows:

> **NOTE**   You must enable the DHCP feature before you can configure DAI.

- DAI is an ingress security feature; it does not perform any egress checking.

- DAI is not effective for hosts connected to devices that do not support DAI or that do not have this feature enabled. Because man-in-the-middle attacks are limited to a single Layer 2 broadcast domain, you should separate the domain with DAI from domains without DAI. This separation secures the ARP caches of hosts in the domain with DAI.

- DAI depends on the entries in the DHCP snooping binding database to verify IP-to-MAC address bindings in incoming ARP requests and ARP responses. If you want DAI to use static IP-MAC address bindings to determine if ARP packets are valid, you need to enable DHCP snooping. If you want DAI to use dynamic IP-MAC address bindings to determine if ARP packets are valid, you must configure DHCP snooping on the same VLANs on which you configure DAI.

- When you use the **feature dhcp** command to enable the DHCP feature, there is a delay of approximately 30 seconds before the I/O modules receive the DHCP or DAI configuration. This delay occurs regardless of the method that you use to change from a configuration with the DHCP feature disabled to a configuration with the DHCP feature enabled. For example, if you use the Rollback feature to revert to a configuration that enables the DHCP feature, the I/O modules receive the DHCP and DAI configuration approximately 30 seconds after you complete the rollback.

- When DHCP snooping is disabled or used in a non-DHCP environment, you should use ARP ACLs to permit or to deny packets and disable DAI.

- DAI is supported on access ports, trunk ports, port-channel ports, and private VLAN (PVLAN) ports.

18

■ The DAI trust configuration of a port channel determines the trust state of all physical ports that you assign to the port channel. For example, if you have configured a physical port as a trusted interface and then you add that physical port to a port channel that is an untrusted interface, the physical port becomes untrusted.

■ When you remove a physical port from a port channel, the physical port does not retain the DAI trust state configuration of the port channel.

■ When you change the trust state on the port channel, the device configures a new trust state on all the physical ports that comprise the channel.

■ If you want DAI to use static IP-MAC address bindings to determine whether ARP packets are valid, ensure that DHCP snooping is enabled and that you have configured the static IP-MAC address bindings.

■ If you want DAI to use dynamic IP-MAC address bindings to determine whether ARP packets are valid, ensure that DHCP snooping is enabled.

Table 18-10 lists the default settings for DAI parameters. You can alter these parameters as necessary.

**Table 18-10** Default DAI Parameters

| Parameters | Default |
|---|---|
| DAI | Disabled on all VLANs. |
| Interface trust state | All interfaces are untrusted. |
| ARP ACLs for non-DHCP environments | No ARP ACLs are defined. |
| Validation checks | No checks are performed. |
| Log buffer | When DAI is enabled, all denied or dropped ARP packets are logged. The number of entries in the log is 32. The number of system messages is limited to 5 per second. The logging-rate interval is 1 second. |
| Per-VLAN logging | All denied or dropped ARP packets are logged. |

Tables 18-11 through 18-13 show some of the most-used DAI configuration commands. For a full list of commands, refer to the Nexus Security Configuration Guide links in the "References" section at the end of this chapter.

**Table 18-11** DAI Global Commands

| Command | Purpose |
|---|---|
| **ip arp inspection vlan** *list* | Enables DAI for the specified list of VLANs. The **no** option disables DAI for the specified VLANs. |
| **ip arp inspection filter** *acl-name* **vlan** *list* | Applies the ARP ACL to the list of VLANs, or if you use the no option, removes the ARP ACL from the list of VLANs. |

| Command | Purpose |
|---------|---------|
| **ip arp inspection validate {[src-mac ] [dst-mac ] [ip ]}** | Enables additional DAI validation, or if you use the **no** option, disables additional DAI validation. |
| **ip arp inspection log-buffer entries** *number* | Configures the DAI logging buffer size. The **no** option reverts to the default buffer size, which is 32 messages. The buffer size can be between 1 and 1024 messages. |

**Table 18-12**   DAI Interface-Level Commands

| Command | Purpose |
|---------|---------|
| **ip arp inspection trust** | Configures the interface as a trusted ARP interface. The **no** option configures the interface as an untrusted ARP interface. |

**Table 18-13**   DAI Verification Commands

| Command | Purpose |
|---------|---------|
| **show ip arp inspection** | Displays the status of DAI. |
| **show ip arp inspection interface ethernet** | Displays the trust state. |
| **show ip arp inspection vlan** | Displays the DAI configuration for a specific VLAN. |
| **show arp access-lists** | Displays ARP ACLs. |
| **show ip arp inspection log** | Displays the DAI log configuration. |
| **show ip arp inspection statistics** | Displays DAI statistics. |
| **clear ip arp inspection statistics vlan** *<id>* | Clears DAI statistics. |

18

Figure 18-3 shows a network topology example. Host 1 is connected to switch A, and host 2 is connected to switch B. Both Nexus switches are running DAI on VLAN 1, where the hosts are located. A DHCP server is connected to switch A. Both hosts acquire their IP addresses from the same DHCP server. Switch A has the bindings for host 1 and host 2, and switch B has the binding for host 2. Switch A's Ethernet interface E2/3 is connected to switch B's Ethernet interface E1/4.

**Key Topic**

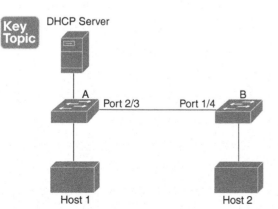

**Figure 18-3**   *Nexus DAI Network Topology*

DAI depends on the entries in the DHCP snooping binding database to verify IP-to-MAC address bindings in incoming ARP requests and ARP responses. You must make sure to enable DHCP snooping to permit ARP packets that have dynamically assigned IP addresses. This configuration does not work if the DHCP server is moved from switch A to a different location.

To ensure that this configuration does not compromise security, configure interface E2/3 on switch A and interface E1/4 on switch B as trusted.

To enable DAI and configure interface E2/3 on switch A as trusted, follow these steps:

**Step 1.** While logged in to switch A, verify the connection between switch A and switch B using the **cdp neighbors** command, as shown in Example 18-8.

**Example 18-8** *Switch A CDP Neighbors*

```
switchA# show cdp neighbors
Capability Codes: R - Router, T - Trans-Bridge, B - Source-Route-Bridge
                  S - Switch, H - Host, I - IGMP, r - Repeater,
                  V - VoIP-Phone, D - Remotely-Managed-Device,
                  s - Supports-STP-Dispute
Device ID            Local Intrfce   Hldtme  Capability  Platform     Port ID
switchB              Ethernet2/3     177     R S I       WS-C2960-24TC Ethernet1/4
switchA#
```

**Step 2.** Enable DAI on VLAN 1 and verify the configuration, as shown in Example 18-9.

**Example 18-9** *Switch A Enabling IP ARP Inspection on VLAN 1*

```
switchA# config t
switchA(config)# ip arp inspection vlan 1
switchA(config)# show ip arp inspection vlan 1
Source Mac Validation : Disabled
Destination Mac Validation : Disabled
IP Address Validation : Disabled
Vlan : 1
-----------
Configuration : Enabled
Operation State : Active
switchA(config)#
```

**Step 3.** Configure Ethernet interface 2/3 as trusted, as shown in Example 18-10.

**Example 18-10** *Switch A Enabling IP ARP Trust on Interface E2/3*

```
switchA(config)# interface ethernet 2/3
switchA(config-if)# ip arp inspection trust
switchA(config-if)# exit
switchA(config)# exit
switchA# show ip arp inspection interface ethernet 2/3
 Interface        Trust State    Rate (pps)    Burst Interval
 ------------     -----------    ----------    --------------
 Ethernet2/3      Trusted        15            5
```

**Step 4.**    Verify DHCP bindings, as shown in Example 18-11.

**Example 18-11**  *Switch A DHCP Binding*

```
switchA# show ip dhcp snooping binding
MacAddress          IpAddress        LeaseSec  Type          VLAN  Interface
-----------------   ---------------  --------  ------------  ----  ------------
00:60:0b:00:12:89   10.0.0.1         0         dhcp-snooping  1    Ethernet2/3
switchA#
```

**Step 5.**    Check the statistics before and after DAI, as shown in Example 18-12.

**Example 18-12**  *Switch A ARP Inspection Statistics*

```
switchA# show ip arp inspection statistics vlan 1
Vlan : 1
-----------
ARP Req Forwarded  = 0
ARP Res Forwarded  = 0
ARP Req Dropped    = 0
ARP Res Dropped    = 0
DHCP Drops         = 0
DHCP Permits       = 0
SMAC Fails-ARP Req = 0
SMAC Fails-ARP Res = 0
DMAC Fails-ARP Res = 0
IP Fails-ARP Req   = 0
IP Fails-ARP Res   = 0
switchA#
!! If host 1 sends out two ARP requests with an IP address of 10.0.0.1 and a MAC
address of 0002.0002.0002, both requests are permitted,

switchA# show ip arp inspection statistics vlan 1
Vlan : 1
-----------
ARP Req Forwarded  = 2
ARP Res Forwarded  = 0
ARP Req Dropped    = 0
ARP Res Dropped    = 0
DHCP Drops         = 0
DHCP Permits       = 2
SMAC Fails-ARP Req = 0
SMAC Fails-ARP Res = 0
DMAC Fails-ARP Res = 0
IP Fails-ARP Req   = 0
IP Fails-ARP Res   = 0
```

18

If host 1 tries to send an ARP request with an IP address of 10.0.0.3, the packet is dropped and an error message is logged, as shown in Example 18-13.

**Example 18-13**  *Switch A DIA DHCP Logs*

```
00:12:08: %SW_DAI-4-DHCP_SNOOPING_DENY: 2 Invalid ARPs (Req) on Ethernet2/3, vlan
1.([0002.0002.0002/10.0.0.3/0000.0000.0000/0.0.0.0/02:42:35 UTC Fri Aug 16 2019])
```

ARP request drop statistics can be displayed, as shown in Example 18-14.

**Example 18-14**  *Switch A ARP Inspection Drop Statistics*

```
switchA# show ip arp inspection statistics vlan 1
switchA#
Vlan : 1
-----------
ARP Req Forwarded  = 2
ARP Res Forwarded  = 0
ARP Req Dropped    = 2
ARP Res Dropped    = 0
DHCP Drops         = 2
DHCP Permits       = 2
SMAC Fails-ARP Req = 0
SMAC Fails-ARP Res = 0
DMAC Fails-ARP Res = 0
IP Fails-ARP Req   = 0
IP Fails-ARP Res   = 0
switchA#
```

To enable DAI and configure Ethernet interface 1/4 on switch B as trusted, follow these steps:

**Step 1.**    While logged in to switch B, verify the connection between switch A and switch B, as shown in Example 18-15.

**Example 18-15**  *Switch B CDP Neighbors*

```
switchB# show cdp neighbors
Capability Codes: R - Router, T - Trans-Bridge, B - Source-Route-Bridge
                  S - Switch, H - Host, I - IGMP, r - Repeater,
                  V - VoIP-Phone, D - Remotely-Managed-Device,
                  s - Supports-STP-Dispute
Device ID           Local Intrfce   Hldtme  Capability  Platform       Port ID
switchA             Ethernet1/4     120     R S I       WS-C2960-24TC  Ethernet2/3
switchB#
```

**Step 2.**    Enable DAI on VLAN 1, and verify the configuration, as shown in Example 18-16.

**Example 18-16**  *Switch B Enabling IP ARP Inspection on VLAN 1*

```
switchB# config t
switchB(config)# ip arp inspection vlan 1
switchB(config)# show ip arp inspection vlan 1
Source Mac Validation      : Disabled
Destination Mac Validation : Disabled
IP Address Validation      : Disabled
Vlan : 1
-----------
Configuration   : Enabled
Operation State : Active
switchB(config)#
```

**Step 3.**   Configure Ethernet interface 1/4 as trusted, as shown in Example 18-17.

**Example 18-17**  *Switch B Enabling IP ARP Trust on Interface E1/4*

```
switchB(config)# interface ethernet 1/4
switchB(config-if)# ip arp inspection trust
switchB(config-if)# exit
switchB(config)# exit
switchB# show ip arp inspection interface ethernet 1/4
 Interface        Trust State    Rate (pps)    Burst Interval
 -------------    -----------    ----------    --------------
 Ethernet1/4      Trusted           15              5
switchB#
```

**Step 4.**   Verify the list of DHCP snooping bindings, as shown in Example 18-18.

**Example 18-18**  *Switch B DHCP Binding*

```
switchB# show ip dhcp snooping binding
MacAddress          IpAddress        LeaseSec  Type          VLAN  Interface
-----------------   ---------------  --------  ------------  ----  -------------
00:01:00:01:00:01   10.0.0.2         4995      dhcp-snooping  1    Ethernet1/4
switchB#
```

**Step 5.**   Check the statistics before and after DAI processes, as shown in Example 18-19.

**Example 18-19**  *Switch B ARP Inspection Statistics*

```
switchB# show ip arp inspection statistics vlan 1
Vlan : 1
-----------
ARP Req Forwarded  = 0
ARP Res Forwarded  = 0
ARP Req Dropped    = 0
ARP Res Dropped    = 0
```

18

```
DHCP Drops          = 0
DHCP Permits        = 0
SMAC Fails-ARP Req = 0
SMAC Fails-ARP Res = 0
DMAC Fails-ARP Res = 0
IP Fails-ARP Req   = 0
IP Fails-ARP Res   = 0
switchB#
!! If Host 2 sends out an ARP request with the IP address 10.0.0.2 and the MAC
address 0001.0001.0001, the packet is forwarded and the statistics are updated.

switchB# show ip arp inspection statistics vlan 1
Vlan : 1
-----------
ARP Req Forwarded  = 1
ARP Res Forwarded  = 0
ARP Req Dropped    = 0
ARP Res Dropped    = 0
DHCP Drops         = 0
DHCP Permits       = 1
SMAC Fails-ARP Req = 0
SMAC Fails-ARP Res = 0
DMAC Fails-ARP Res = 0
IP Fails-ARP Req   = 0
IP Fails-ARP Res   = 0
switchB#
```

If host 2 attempts to send an ARP request with the IP address 10.0.0.1, DAI drops the request and logs the system message, as shown in Example 18-20.

**Example 18-20**   *Switch B DIA DHCP Logs*

```
00:18:08: %SW_DAI-4-DHCP_SNOOPING_DENY: 1 Invalid ARPs (Req) on Ethernet1/4, vlan 1.
([0001.0001.0001/10.0.0.1/0000.0000.0000/0.0.0.0/01:53:21 UTC Fri Aug 16 2019])
```

ARP request drop statistics can be displayed, as shown in Example 18-21.

**Example 18-21**   *Switch B ARP Inspection Drop Statistics*

```
switchB# show ip arp inspection statistics vlan 1
Vlan : 1
-----------
ARP Req Forwarded  = 1
ARP Res Forwarded  = 0
ARP Req Dropped    = 1
```

```
ARP Res Dropped    = 0
DHCP Drops         = 1
DHCP Permits       = 1
SMAC Fails-ARP Req = 0
SMAC Fails-ARP Res = 0
DMAC Fails-ARP Res = 0
IP Fails-ARP Req   = 0
IP Fails-ARP Res   = 0
switchB#
```

## NX-OS DHCP Snooping

DHCP snooping acts like a firewall between untrusted hosts and trusted DHCP servers. DHCP snooping performs the following activities:

- Validates DHCP messages received from untrusted sources and filters out invalid messages.

- Builds and maintains the DHCP snooping binding database, which contains information about untrusted hosts with leased IP addresses.

- Uses the DHCP snooping binding database to validate subsequent requests from untrusted hosts.

DHCP snooping can be enabled globally and on a per-VLAN basis. By default, the feature is disabled globally and on all VLANs. You can enable the feature on a single VLAN or a range of VLANs.

### DHCP Snooping Trusted and Untrusted Sources

The DHCP snooping feature determines whether traffic sources are trusted or untrusted. An untrusted source may initiate traffic attacks or other hostile actions. To prevent such attacks, DHCP snooping filters messages from untrusted sources.

In an enterprise network, a trusted source is a device that is under your administrative control. These devices include the switches, routers, and servers in the network. Any device beyond the firewall or outside the network is an untrusted source. Generally, host ports are treated as untrusted sources.

In a service provider environment, any device that is not in the service provider network is an untrusted source (such as a customer switch); host ports are untrusted sources.

In the Cisco NX-OS device, you can indicate that a source is trusted by configuring the trust state of its connecting interface. The default trust state of all interfaces is untrusted. You must configure DHCP server interfaces as trusted. You can also configure other interfaces as trusted if they connect to devices (such as switches or routers) inside your network. You usually do not configure host port interfaces as trusted. Figure 18-4 shows trusted and untrusted ports.

18

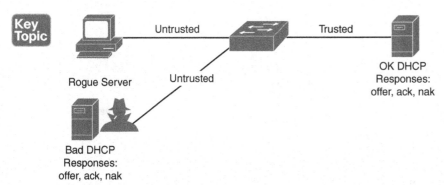

**Figure 18-4**  *DHCP Snooping Trusted and Untrusted Ports*

**NOTE**   For DHCP snooping to function properly, all DHCP servers must be connected to the device through trusted interfaces.

DHCP snooping updates the database when the device receives specific DHCP messages. For example, the feature adds an entry to the database when the device receives a DHCPACK message from the server. The feature removes the entry in the database when the IP address lease expires, or the device receives a DHCPRELEASE message from the host.

Each entry in the DHCP snooping binding database includes the MAC address of the host, the leased IP address, the lease time, the binding type, and the VLAN number and interface information associated with the host. Dynamic ARP inspection and IP Source Guard also use information stored in the DHCP snooping binding database.

You can remove entries from the binding database by using the **clear ip dhcp snooping binding** command.

### DHCP Snooping Packet Validation

The device validates DHCP packets received on the untrusted interfaces of VLANs that have DHCP snooping enabled. The device forwards the DHCP packet unless any of the following conditions occur (in which case, the packet is dropped):

- The device receives a DHCP response packet (such as a DHCPACK, DHCPNAK, or DHCPOFFER packet) on an untrusted interface.

- The device receives a packet on an untrusted interface, and the source MAC address and the DHCP client hardware address do not match. This check is performed only if the DHCP snooping MAC address verification option is turned on.

- The device receives a DHCPRELEASE or DHCPDECLINE message from an untrusted host with an entry in the DHCP snooping binding table, and the interface information in the binding table does not match the interface on which the message was received.

In addition, you can enable strict validation of DHCP packets, which checks the options field of DHCP packets, including the "magic cookie" value in the first four bytes of the options field. By default, strict validation is disabled. When you enable it, by using the **ip dhcp packet strict-validation** command, if DHCP snooping processes a packet that has an invalid options field, it drops the packet.

## DHCP Snooping Option 82 Data Insertion

DHCP can centrally manage the IP address assignments for a large number of subscribers. When you enable Option 82, the device identifies a subscriber device that connects to the network (in addition to its MAC address). Multiple hosts on the subscriber LAN can connect to the same port on the access device and are uniquely identified.

When you enable Option 82 on the Cisco NX-OS device, the following sequence of events occurs:

1. The host (DHCP client) generates a DHCP request and broadcasts it on the network.

2. When the Cisco NX-OS device receives the DHCP request, it adds the Option 82 information in the packet. The Option 82 information contains the device MAC address (the remote ID suboption) and the port identifier, vlan-mod-port, from which the packet is received (the circuit ID suboption). For hosts behind the port channel, the circuit ID is filled with the if_index of the port channel.

3. The device forwards the DHCP request that includes the Option 82 field to the DHCP server.

4. The DHCP server receives the packet. If the server is Option 82 capable, it can use the remote ID, the circuit ID, or both to assign IP addresses and implement policies, such as restricting the number of IP addresses that can be assigned to a single remote ID or circuit ID. The DHCP server echoes the Option 82 field in the DHCP reply.

5. The DHCP server sends the reply to the Cisco NX-OS device. The Cisco NX-OS device verifies that it originally inserted the Option 82 data by inspecting the remote ID and possibly the circuit ID fields. The Cisco NX-OS device removes the Option 82 field and forwards the packet to the interface that connects to the DHCP client that sent the DHCP request.

## NX-OS DHCP Snooping Configuration

The DHCP snooping feature does not require a license. Any feature not included in a license package is bundled with the Cisco NX-OS system images. DHCP snooping configuration recommendations and limitations are as follows:

■ If you are using both the Unicast Reverse Path Forwarding (uRPF) strict mode in your client vPC VLANs and the First Hop Redundancy Protocol (FHRP) with the DHCP relay feature, the DHCP requests are sourced from the physical egress IP address interface (not the FHRP VIP) by default. Consequently, if your DHCP server is not on a directly connected subnet and you have multiple ECMP routes back to your vPC pair, some packets might land on the neighbor switch instead of the originating switch and be dropped by RPF. This behavior is expected. To avoid this scenario, perform one of the following workarounds:

  ■ Use the uRPF loose mode, not uRPF strict.

  ■ Configure static routes for the interface address on the affected FHRP interfaces and redistribute the static routes into IGP.

■ Using the **ip dhcp relay source-interface** *interface-name* command, you can configure a different interface as the source interface.

- After System Switchover, DHCP Global stats show incorrect values as they get erased because they are not stored in persistent storage service (PSS). The PSS component works with system services to recover states in the event of a service restart. Updating stats in PSS during packet path will affect scale.

- If you use DHCP relay where DHCP clients and servers are in different VRF instances, use only one DHCP server within a VRF.

- Before globally enabling DHCP snooping on the device, make sure that the devices acting as the DHCP server and the DHCP relay agent are configured and enabled.

- DHCP snooping does not work with DHCP relay configured on the same Nexus device.

- If a VLAN ACL (VACL) is configured on a VLAN that you are configuring with DHCP snooping, ensure that the VACL permits DHCP traffic between DHCP servers and DHCP hosts. When both DHCP snooping and DHCP relay are enabled on a VLAN and the SVI of that VLAN, DHCP relay takes precedence.

- If an ingress router ACL is configured on a Layer 3 interface that you are configuring with a DHCP server address, ensure that the router ACL permits DHCP traffic between DHCP servers and DHCP hosts.

- ACL statistics are not supported if the DHCP snooping feature is enabled.

- Before using POAP, make sure that DHCP snooping feature is enabled and firewall rules are set to block unintended or malicious DHCP servers.

- When you configure DHCPv6 server addresses on an interface, a destination interface cannot be used with global IPv6 addresses.

Table 18-14 shows the default settings for DHCP snooping parameters. You can alter these parameters as necessary.

**Table 18-14**   DHCP Snooping Default Parameters

| Parameters | Default |
|---|---|
| DHCP feature | Disabled |
| DHCP snooping | Disabled |
| DHCP snooping on VLANs | Disabled |
| DHCP snooping MAC address verification | Enabled |
| DHCP snooping Option 82 support | Disabled |

Tables 18-15 through 18-17 show some of the most-used DHCP snooping configuration commands. For a full list of commands, refer to the Nexus Security Configuration Guide links in the "References" section at the end of this chapter.

**Table 18-15**   DHCP Snooping Global Commands

| Commands | Purpose |
|---|---|
| feature dhcp | Enables the DHCP feature. The **no** option disables the DHCP feature and erases all DHCP configuration. |

| Commands | Purpose |
|---|---|
| **ip dhcp snooping** | Enables DHCP snooping globally. The **no** option disables DHCP snooping. |
| **ip dhcp snooping vlan** *vlan-list* | Enables DHCP snooping on the VLANs specified by *vlan-list*. The **no** option disables DHCP snooping on the VLANs specified. |
| **ip dhcp snooping verify mac-address** | Enables DHCP snooping MAC address verification. The **no** option disables MAC address verification. |
| **ip dhcp snooping information option** | Enables the insertion and removal of Option 82 information for DHCP packets. The **no** option disables the insertion and removal of Option 82 information. |

**Table 18-16**   DHCP Snooping Interface-Level Command

| Commands | Purpose |
|---|---|
| **ip dhcp snooping trust** | Configures the interface as a trusted interface for DHCP snooping. The **no** option configures the port as an untrusted interface. |

**Table 18-17**   DHCP Snooping Verification and Clearing Commands

| Commands | Purpose |
|---|---|
| **show running-config dhcp [all ]** | Displays the DHCP configuration in the running configuration. |
| **show ip dhcp snooping** | Displays general information about DHCP snooping. |
| **show startup-config dhcp [all ]** | Displays the DHCP configuration in the startup configuration. |
| **show ip dhcp snooping binding** | Displays the DHCP snooping binding database. |
| **clear ip dhcp snooping binding** | Clears all entries from the DHCP snooping binding database. |
| **clear ip dhcp snooping binding interface ethernet** *slot/port* [*.subinterface-number*] | Clears entries associated with a specific Ethernet interface from the DHCP snooping binding database. |
| **clear ip dhcp snooping binding vlan** *vlan-id* **mac** *mac-address* **ip** *ip-address* **interface** {**ethernet** slot/port[*.subinterface-number* \| **port-channel** *channel-number* [*.subchannel-number*] } | Clears a single, specific entry from the DHCP snooping binding database. |

Example 18-22 shows how to enable the NX-OS IP DHCP snooping feature on VLAN 125 and configure interface E1/32 as a trusted interface.

**Example 18-22**   *NX-OS DHCP Snooping Configuration*

```
Switch(config)# feature dhcp
Switch(config)# ip dhcp snooping
Switch(config)# ip dhcp snooping vlan 125
Switch(config)# interface ethernet 1/32
Switch(config-if)# ip dhcp snooping trust
```

18

## Port Security

Port security prevents rogue network extensions via hub or wireless access points (APs) from connecting to your switch. Because it limits the number of MAC addresses to a port, port security can also be used as a mechanism to prevent users from adding extensions to the IT-created network.

For example, if a user plugs a computer or a device into a user-facing port or data port with port security defined for a single MAC address, the computer or device itself would occupy that MAC address and not allow any devices behind it to access the network, as shown in Figure 18-5. Generally, a configuration appropriate to stop MAC flooding is also appropriate to inhibit rogue access.

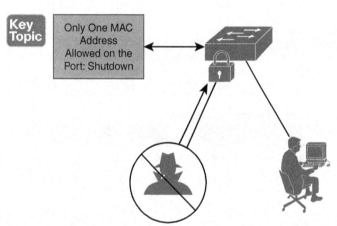

**Figure 18-5**   *Port Security Limits MAC Address to Prevent Rogue Access*

Port security also allows you to configure Layer 2 physical interfaces and Layer 2 port channel interfaces to allow inbound traffic from only a restricted set of MAC addresses. The MAC addresses in the restricted set are called *secure* MAC addresses. In addition, the device does not allow traffic from these MAC addresses on another interface within the same VLAN. The number of MAC addresses that the device can secure is configurable per interface.

The process of securing a MAC address is called *learning*. A MAC address can be a secure MAC address on one interface only. For each interface on which you enable port security, the device can learn a limited number of MAC addresses by using the static, dynamic, or sticky methods. The way that the device stores secure MAC addresses varies depending on how the device learned the secure MAC address.

- **Static method:** The static learning method allows you to manually add or remove secure MAC addresses to the running configuration of an interface. If you copy the running configuration to the startup configuration, static secure MAC addresses are unaffected if the device restarts. A static secure MAC address entry remains in the configuration of an interface until one of the following events occurs:

  - You explicitly remove the address from the configuration.

  - You configure the interface to act as a Layer 3 interface.

**NOTE**   Adding secure addresses by using the static method is not affected by whether dynamic or sticky address learning is enabled.

- **Dynamic method:** By default, when you enable port security on an interface, you enable the dynamic learning method. With this method, the device secures MAC addresses as ingress traffic passes through the interface. If the address is not yet secured and the device has not reached any applicable maximum, it secures the address and allows the traffic. The device stores dynamic secure MAC addresses in memory. A dynamic secure MAC address entry remains in the configuration of an interface until one of the following events occurs:

  - The device restarts.

  - The interface restarts.

  - The address reaches the age limit that you configured for the interface.

  - You explicitly remove the address.

  - You configure the interface to act as a Layer 3 interface.

- **Sticky method:** If you enable the sticky method, the device secures MAC addresses in the same manner as dynamic address learning, but the device stores addresses learned by this method in nonvolatile RAM (NVRAM). As a result, addresses learned by the sticky method persist through a device restart. Sticky secure MAC addresses do not appear in the running configuration of an interface. Dynamic and sticky address learning are mutually exclusive. When you enable sticky learning on an interface, the device stops dynamic learning and performs sticky learning instead. If you disable sticky learning, the device resumes dynamic learning.

  A sticky secure MAC address entry remains in the configuration of an interface until one of the following events occurs:

  - You explicitly remove the address.

  - You configure the interface to act as a Layer 3 interface.

## Nexus Port Secure MAC Address Maximum and Dynamic Address Aging

By default, an interface can have only one secure MAC address. You can configure the maximum number of MAC addresses permitted per interface or per VLAN on an interface. Maximums apply to secure MAC addresses learned by any method: dynamic, sticky, or static. The following three limits can determine how many secure MAC addresses are permitted on an interface:

- **System maximum:** The device has a nonconfigurable limit of 8192 secure MAC addresses. If learning a new address would violate the device maximum, the device does not permit the new address to be learned, even if the interface or VLAN maximum has not been reached.

18

- **Interface maximum:** You can configure a maximum number of 1025 secure MAC addresses for each interface protected by port security. The default interface maximum is one address. The sum of all interface maximums on a switch cannot exceed the system maximum.

- **VLAN maximum:** You can configure the maximum number of secure MAC addresses per VLAN for each interface protected by port security. The sum of all VLAN maximums under an interface cannot exceed the configured interface maximum. VLAN maximums are useful only for trunk ports. There are no default VLAN maximums.

The device ages MAC addresses learned by the dynamic method and drops them after the age limit is reached. You can configure the age limit on each interface. The range is from 0 to 1440 minutes, where 0 disables aging.

The method that the device uses to determine that the MAC address age is also configurable. The two methods of determining address age are as follows:

- **Inactivity:** The length of time after the device last received a packet from the address on the applicable interface.

- **Absolute:** The length of time after the device learned the address. This is the default aging method; however, the default aging time is 0 minutes, which disables aging.

**NOTE**   When the absolute aging time is configured, MAC aging occurs even when the traffic from the source MAC is flowing. However, during MAC aging and relearning, there could be a transient traffic drop.

## Port Security Violations and Actions

Port security triggers security violations when one of the following events occurs:

- **MAC count violation:** Ingress traffic arrives at an interface from a nonsecure MAC address and learning the address would exceed the applicable maximum number of secure MAC addresses.

- **Shutdown:** Port security shuts down the interface that received the packet triggering the violation. The interface is error disabled. This action is the default. After you reenable the interface, it retains its port security configuration, including its secure MAC addresses.

- **Restrict:** Port security drops ingress traffic from any nonsecure MAC addresses.

- **MAC move violation:** Ingress traffic from a secure MAC address arrives at a different interface in the same VLAN as the interface on which the address is secured.

**NOTE**   If an interface is errDisabled, you can bring it up only by flapping the interface.

## Nexus Port Types and Port Security

You can configure port security only on Layer 2 interfaces. Details about port security and different types of interfaces or ports are as follows:

- **Access ports:** You can configure port security on interfaces that you have configured as Layer 2 access ports. On an access port, port security applies only to the access VLAN. VLAN maximums are not useful for access ports.

- **Trunk ports:** You can configure port security on interfaces that you have configured as Layer 2 trunk ports. The device allows VLAN maximums only for VLANs associated with the trunk port.

- **SPAN ports:** You can configure port security on Switched Port Analyzer (SPAN) source ports but not on SPAN destination ports.

- **Ethernet port channels:** You can configure port security on Layer 2 Ethernet port channels in either access mode or trunk mode.

- **Fabric Extender (FEX) ports:** Port security is supported on GEM (Generic Expansion Module) and FEX ports.

- **Private VLAN enabled ports:** Port security is supported on ports that are enabled as private VLAN ports.

**NOTE**   You cannot configure port security on VXLAN interfaces.

## NX-OS Port Security Configuration

The port security feature does not require a license. Any feature not included in a license package is bundled with the Cisco NX-OS system images. Port security configuration recommendations and limitations are as follows:

- Port security is supported on PVLAN ports.

- Port security does not support SPAN destination ports.

- Port security does not depend on other features.

- If any member link in a port channel is in the preprovisioned state—that is, the module is offline—the port security feature cannot be disabled on the port channel.

- Port security is not supported on vPC ports.

- Port security operates with 802.1X on Layer 2 Ethernet interfaces.

Table 18-18 lists the default settings for NX-OS port security parameters. You can alter these parameters as necessary.

18

**Table 18-18**   NX-OS Port Security Default Parameters

| Parameters | Default |
|---|---|
| Port security enablement globally | Disabled |
| Port security enablement per interface | Disabled |
| MAC address learning method | Dynamic |
| Interface maximum number of secure MAC addresses | 1 |
| Security violation action | Shutdown |
| Aging type | Absolute |
| Aging time | 0 |

Tables 18-19 through 18-21 show some of the most-used NX-OS port security configuration commands. For a full list of commands, refer to the Nexus Security Configuration Guide links in the "References" section at the end of this chapter.

**Table 18-19**   NX-OS Port Security Global Commands

| Command | Purpose |
|---|---|
| **feature port-security** | Enables port security globally. The **no** option disables port security globally. |
| **clear port-security dynamic** {**interface** *ethernet slot/port* \| **address** *address*} [**vlan** *vlan-ID*] | Removes dynamically learned, secure MAC addresses, as specified. If you use the **interface** keyword, you remove all dynamically learned addresses on the interface that you specify. If you use the **address** keyword, you remove the single, dynamically learned address that you specify. Use the **vlan** keyword if you want to further limit the command to removing an address or addresses on a particular VLAN. |

**Table 18-20**   NX-OS Port Security Interface-Level Commands

| Command | Purpose |
|---|---|
| **switchport** | Configures the interface as a Layer 2 interface. |
| **switchport port-security** | Enables port security on the interface. The no option disables port security on the interface. |
| **switchport port-security mac-address sticky** | Enables sticky MAC address learning on the interface. The no option disables sticky MAC address learning. |
| **switchport port-security mac-address** *address* [**vlan** *vlan-ID*] | Configures a static MAC address for port security on the current interface. Use the **vlan** keyword if you want to specify the VLAN on which traffic from the address is allowed. |
| **clear port-security dynamic address** *address* | Removes the dynamic secure MAC address that you specify. |
| **switchport port-security maximum** *number* [**vlan** *vlan-ID*] | Configures the maximum number of MAC addresses that can be learned or statically configured for the current interface. The highest valid number is 1025. The **no** option resets the maximum number of MAC addresses to the default, which is 1. If you want to specify the VLAN that the maximum applies to, use the **vlan** keyword. |

| Command | Purpose |
|---|---|
| switchport port-security aging type {absolute \| inactivity } | Configures the type of aging that the device applies to dynamically learned MAC addresses. The **no** option resets the aging type to the default, which is absolute aging.<br><br>**NOTE:** F1 series modules do not support the inactivity aging type. |
| switchport port-security aging time *minutes* | Configures the number of minutes that a dynamically learned MAC address must age before the device drops the address. The maximum valid number of minutes is 1440. The **no** option resets the aging time to the default, which is 0 minutes (no aging). |
| switchport port-security violation {protect \| restrict \| shutdown} | Configures the security violation action for port security on the current interface. The **no** option resets the violation action to the default, which is to shut down the interface. |

**Table 18-21**   NX-OS Port Security Verification Commands

| Command | Purpose |
|---|---|
| show running-config port-security | Displays the port security configuration. |
| show port-security | Displays the port security status of the device. |
| show port-security interface | Displays the port security status of a specific interface. |
| show port-security address | Displays secure MAC addresses. |

Example 18-23 enables port security on interface E3/2 to limit the number of total MAC addresses learned to six. It allows a maximum of three MAC addresses for VLAN10 and a maximum of two MAC addresses for VLAN 20. A violation drops all packets from an insecure host.

**Example 18-23**   *NX-OS Port Security Configuration*

```
Switch(config)# feature port-security
Switch(config-if)# interface Ethernet 3/2
Switch(config-if)# switchport
Switch(config-if)# switchport port-security
Switch(config-if)# switchport port-security maximum 6
Switch(config-if)# switchport port-security maximum 3 vlan 10
Switch(config-if)# switchport port-security maximum 2 vlan 20
Switch(config-if)# switchport port-security violation restrict
```

## Nexus Control Plane Policing

Nexus Series switches are deployed as data center and campus switches. A Nexus control plane CPU is the brain of the network and handles the maximum load of the network, which includes frequent bursts of control traffic, such as OSPF, OTV, ARP, LISP, BGP, and so on.

Control Plane Policing (CoPP) protects the control plane and separates it from the data plane, which ensures network stability, reachability, and packet delivery.

CoPP allows a policy map to be applied to the control plane. This policy map looks like a normal QoS policy and is applied to all traffic entering the switch from a nonmanagement port. A common attack vector for network devices is the denial-of-service (DoS) attack, where excessive traffic is directed at the device interfaces.

Cisco NX-OS devices provide CoPP to prevent DoS attacks from impacting performance. Such attacks, which can be perpetrated either inadvertently or maliciously, typically involve high rates of traffic destined to the supervisor module or CPU itself.

The supervisor module divides the traffic that it manages into three functional components or planes:

- **Data plane:** Handles all the data traffic. The basic functionality of a Cisco NX-OS device is to forward packets from one interface to another. The packets that are not meant for the switch itself are called the *transit packets*. These packets are handled by the data plane.

- **Control plane:** Handles all routing protocol control traffic. These protocols, such as the Border Gateway Protocol (BGP) and Open Shortest Path First (OSPF), send control packets between devices. These packets are destined to router addresses and are called *control plane packets*.

- **Management plane:** Runs the components meant for Cisco NX-OS device management purposes, such as the command-line interface (CLI) and Simple Network Management Protocol (SNMP).

The supervisor module has both the management plane and control plane and is critical to the operation of the network. Any disruption or attacks to the supervisor module result in serious network outages. For example, excessive traffic to the supervisor module could overload and slow down the performance of the entire Cisco NX-OS device. Traffic hitting the CPU on the supervisor module can come in through three paths, as shown in Figure 18-6. Only traffic sent through an *Inband* interface is subject to CoPP or hardware rate limit (HWRL) because it is the only traffic that reaches the supervisor via forwarding engines.

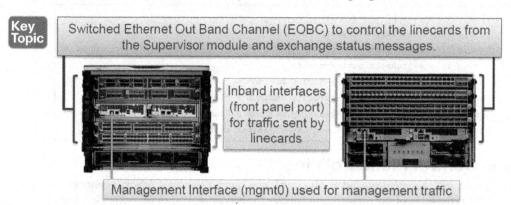

**Figure 18-6** *Cisco Nexus Supervisor*

DoS attacks on the supervisor module could generate IP traffic streams to the control plane at a very high rate, forcing the control plane to spend a large amount of time handling these packets and preventing the control plane from processing genuine traffic. Examples of DoS attacks include

- Internet Control Message Protocol (ICMP) echo requests

- IP fragments

- TCP SYN flooding

These attacks can impact the device performance and have the following negative effects:

- Reduced service quality (such as poor voice, video, or critical applications traffic)

- High route processor or switch processor CPU utilization

- Route flaps due to loss of routing protocol updates or keepalives

- Unstable Layer 2 topology

- Slow or unresponsive interactive sessions with the CLI

- Processor resource exhaustion, such as the memory and buffers

- Indiscriminate drops of incoming packets

**NOTE**   It is important to ensure that you protect the supervisor module from accidental or malicious attacks by configuring control plane protection.

To protect the control plane, the Cisco NX-OS device segregates different packets destined for the control plane into different classes. After these classes are identified, the Cisco NX-OS device polices the packets, which ensures that the supervisor module is not overwhelmed.

## Control Plane Packet

Control plane packets are the packets that are handled by the CPU. Control plane packets and some data packets punt to the CPU (or traffic destined to the CPU). These packets are as follows:

- **Receive packets:** Packets that have the destination address of a router. The destination address can be a Layer 2 address (such as a router MAC address) or a Layer 3 address (such as the IP address of a router interface). These packets include router updates and keepalive messages. Multicast packets can also be in this category where packets are sent to multicast addresses that are used by a router.

- **Exception packets:** Packets that need special handling by the supervisor module. For example, if a destination address is not present in the Forwarding Information Base (FIB) and results in a miss, the supervisor module sends an ICMP unreachable packet back to the sender. Another example is a packet with IP options set.

- **Redirected packets:** Packets that are redirected to the supervisor module. Features such as Dynamic Host Configuration Protocol (DHCP) snooping or dynamic Address Resolution Protocol (ARP) inspection redirect some packets to the supervisor module.

- **Glean packets:** If a Layer 2 MAC address for a destination IP address is not present in the FIB, the supervisor module receives the packet and sends an ARP request to the host.

All of these different packets could be maliciously used to attack the control plane and overwhelm the Cisco NX-OS device. CoPP classifies these packets to different classes and provides a mechanism to individually control the rate at which the supervisor module receives these packets.

## Classification for CoPP

For effective protection, the Cisco NX-OS device classifies the packets that reach the supervisor modules to allow you to apply different rate-controlling policies based on the type of the packet. For example, you might want to be less strict with a protocol packet such as Hello messages but stricter with a packet that is sent to the supervisor module because the IP option is set.

### Rate-Controlling Mechanisms

After the packets are classified, the Cisco NX-OS device has different mechanisms to control the rate at which packets arrive at the supervisor module. Two mechanisms control the rate of traffic to the supervisor module. One is called *policing*, and the other is called *rate limiting*.

Using hardware policers, you can define separate actions for traffic that conforms to, exceeds, or violates certain conditions. The actions can transmit the packet, mark down the packet, or drop the packet.

You can configure the following parameters for policing:

- **Committed information rate (CIR):** Desired bandwidth specified as a bit rate or a percentage of the link rate

- **Peak information rate (PIR):** Desired bandwidth specified as a bit rate or a percentage of the link rate

- **Committed burst (BC):** Size of a traffic burst that can exceed the CIR within a given unit of time and not impact scheduling

- **Extended burst (BE):** Size that a traffic burst can reach before all traffic exceeds the PIR

In addition, you can set separate actions such as transmit or drop for conform, exceed, and violate traffic.

When you bring up your Cisco NX-OS device for the first time, the Cisco NX-OS software installs the default copp-system-p-policy-strict policy to protect the supervisor module from DoS attacks. You can set the level of protection by choosing one of the following CoPP policy options from the initial setup utility:

- **Strict:** This policy is 1 rate and 2 color and has a BC value of 250 ms (except for the important class, which has a value of 1000 ms).

- **Moderate:** This policy is 1 rate and 2 color and has a BC value of 310 ms (except for the important class, which has a value of 1250 ms). These values are 25 percent greater than the strict policy.

- **Lenient:** This policy is 1 rate and 2 color and has a BC value of 375 ms (except for the important class, which has a value of 1500 ms). These values are 50 percent greater than the strict policy.

- **Dense:** This policy is 1 rate and 2 color. The classes critical, normal, redirect, exception, undesirable, L2-default, and default have a BC value of 250 ms. The classes important, management, normal-dhcp, normal-dhcp-relay-response, and monitoring have a BC value of 1000 ms. The class l2-unpoliced has a BC value of 5 MB.

**NOTE** It is recommend that you use dense as a default policy when the chassis is fully loaded with F2 Series modules or loaded with more F2 Series modules than any other I/O modules.

- **Skip:** No control plane policy is applied.

If you do not select an option or choose not to execute the setup utility, the Cisco NX-OS software applies strict policing. We recommend that you start with the strict policy and later modify the CoPP policies as required.

The copp-system-p-policy policy has optimized values suitable for basic device operations. You must add specific class and ACL rules that meet your DoS protection requirements. The default CoPP policy does not change when you upgrade the Cisco NX-OS software.

**NOTE** Selecting the Skip option and not subsequently configuring CoPP protection can leave your Cisco NX-OS device vulnerable to DoS attacks.

Figure 18-7 shows a Nexus 7000 CoPP strict profile example.

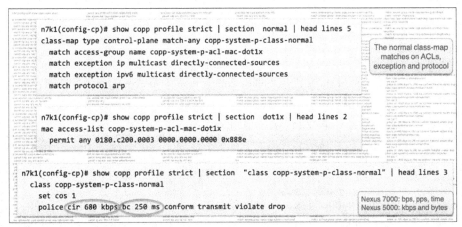

**Figure 18-7** *Nexus 7000 CoPP Strict Profile*

### Modular QoS Command-Line Interface

CoPP uses the Modular Quality of Service Command-Line Interface (MQC). MQC is a CLI structure that allows you to define a traffic class, create a traffic policy (policy map), and attach the traffic policy to an interface. The traffic policy contains the CoPP feature that will be applied to the traffic class. Steps to configure CoPP are as follows:

**Step 1.** Define a traffic class using the **class-map** command. A traffic class is used to classify traffic. Example 18-24 shows how to create a new class-map called copp-sample-class.

**Example 18-24** *NX-OS CoPP Class Map Configuration*

```
Switch(config)# class-map type control-plane copp-sample-class
```

**Step 2.** Create a traffic policy using the **policy-map** command. A traffic policy (policy map) contains a traffic class and one or more CoPP features that will be applied to the traffic class. The CoPP features in the traffic policy determine how to treat the classified traffic.

**Step 3.** Attach the traffic policy (policy map) to the control plane using the **control-plane** and **service-policy** commands. Example 18-25 shows how to attach the policy map to the control plane.

**Example 18-25** *NX-OS CoPP Service Policy Configuration*

```
Switch(config)# control-plane
Switch(config-cp)# service-policy input copp-system-policy
```

**NOTE** The copp-system-policy is always configured and applied. You do not need to use this command explicitly.

**NOTE** A Cisco NX-OS device supports only hardware-based CoPP that does not support the management interface (mgmt0). The out-of-band mgmt0 interface connects directly to the CPU and does not pass through the in-band traffic hardware where CoPP is implemented. On the mgmt0 interface, ACLs can be configured to give or deny access to a particular type of traffic.

Tables 18-22 through 18-24 show NX-OS class comparison for preconfigured control plane policies.

**Table 18-22** Nexus 9000 CoPP Class Comparison

| class copp-system-p-class | | strict | | moderate | | lenient | | dense | |
|---|---|---|---|---|---|---|---|---|---|
| | | cir (pps) | bc (pkt) | cir (pps) | bc (pkt) | cir (pps) | bc (pkt) | cir (pps) | bc (pkt) |
| critical | cos 7 | 19000 | 128 | 19000 | 192 | 19000 | 256 | 2500 | 128 |
| important | cos 6 | 3000 | 128 | 3000 | 192 | 3000 | 256 | 1200 | 128 |
| multicast-router | cos 6 | 3000 | 128 | 3000 | 192 | 3000 | 256 | 1200 | 128 |

| class copp-system-p-class | | strict | | moderate | | lenient | | dense | |
|---|---|---|---|---|---|---|---|---|---|
| | | cir (pps) | bc (pkt) | cir (pps) | bc (pkt) | cir (pps) | bc (pkt) | cir (pps) | bc (pkt) |
| management | cos 2 | 3000 | 32 | 3000 | 48 | 3000 | 64 | 1200 | 128 |
| l3mc-data | cos 1 | 3000 | 32 | 3000 | 32 | 3000 | 32 | 1200 | 32 |
| l3uc-data | cos 1 | 250 | 32 | 250 | 32 | 250 | 32 | 250 | 32 |
| normal | cos 1 | 1500 | 32 | 1500 | 48 | 1500 | 64 | 750 | 32 |
| normal-dhcp | cos 1 | 300 | 32 | 300 | 48 | 300 | 64 | 150 | 128 |
| normal-dhcp-relay-response | cos 1 | 400 | 64 | 400 | 96 | 400 | 128 | 200 | 128 |
| normal-igmp | cos 3 | 6000 | 64 | 6000 | 64 | 6000 | 64 | 2500 | 128 |
| redirect | cos 1 | 1500 | 32 | 1500 | 48 | 1500 | 64 | 1500 | 32 |
| exception | cos 1 | 50 | 32 | 50 | 48 | 50 | 64 | 50 | 32 |
| exception-diag | cos 1 | 50 | 32 | 50 | 48 | 50 | 64 | 50 | 32 |
| monitoring | cos 1 | 75 | 128 | 75 | 192 | 75 | 256 | 50 | 128 |
| l2-unpoliced | cos 7 | 20000 | 8192 | 20000 | 8192 | 20000 | 8192 | 20000 | 8192 |
| undesirable | cos 0 | 15 | 32 | 15 | 48 | 15 | 64 | 15 | 32 |
| l2-default | cos 0 | 50 | 32 | 50 | 48 | 50 | 64 | 25 | 32 |
| class class-default | cos 0 | 50 | 32 | 50 | 48 | 50 | 64 | 25 | 32 |

**Table 18-23**  Nexus 7000 CoPP Class Comparison

| class copp-system-p-class | | strict | | moderate | | lenient | | dense | |
|---|---|---|---|---|---|---|---|---|---|
| | | cir (kbps) | bc (ms) | cir (kbps) | bc (ms) | cir (kbps) | bc (ms) | cir (kbps) | bc (ms) |
| critical | cos 7 | 36000 | 250 | 36000 | 310 | 36000 | 375 | 4500 | 250 |
| important | cos 6 | 1400 | 1500 | 1400 | 1500 | 1400 | 1500 | 1400 | 1500 |
| multicast-router | cos 6 | 2600 | 1000 | 2600 | 1000 | 2600 | 1000 | 370 | 1000 |
| management | cos 2 | 10000 | 250 | 10000 | 310 | 10000 | 375 | 2500 | 1000 |
| multicast-host | cos 1 | 1000 | 1000 | 1000 | 1000 | 1000 | 1000 | 190 | 1000 |
| redirect | cos 1 | 280 | 250 | 280 | 310 | 280 | 375 | 200 | 250 |
| normal | cos 1 | 680 | 250 | 680 | 310 | 680 | 375 | 300 | 250 |
| ndp | cos 6 | 680 | 250 | 680 | 310 | 680 | 375 | 300 | 250 |
| dhcp | cos 1 | 1500 | 250 | 1500 | 310 | 1500 | 375 | 660 | 1000 |
| dhcp-relay-response | cos 1 | 1800 | 500 | 1800 | 620 | 1800 | 750 | 800 | 1000 |
| exception | cos 1 | 360 | 250 | 360 | 310 | 360 | 375 | 200 | 250 |
| monitoring | cos 1 | 130 | 1000 | 130 | 1250 | 130 | 1500 | 130 | 1000 |
| undesirable | cos 0 | 32 | 250 | 32 | 310 | 32 | 375 | 32 | 250 |

| class copp-system-p-class | | strict | | moderate | | lenient | | dense | |
|---|---|---|---|---|---|---|---|---|---|
| | | cir (kbps) | bc ms) | cir (kbps) | bc (ms) | cir (kbps) | bc (ms) | cir (kbps) | bc (ms) |
| fcoe | cos 6 | 1060 | 1000 | 1060 | 1250 | 1060 | 1500 | 600 | 1000 |
| l2-default | | 100 | 250 | 100 | 310 | 100 | 375 | 250 | |
| default | cos 0 | 100 | 250 | 100 | 250 | 100 | 250 | 50 | 250 |
| | | cir (gbps) | bc (mbytes) | cir (gbps) | bc (mbytes) | cir (gbps) | bc (mbytes) | cir (gbps) | bc (mbytes) |
| l2-unpoliced | | 8 | 5 | 8 | 5 | 8 | 5 | 8 | |

**Table 18-24** Nexus 5000 CoPP Class Comparison

| copp-system-policy | default | | scaled-l2 | | scaled-l3 | | customized | |
|---|---|---|---|---|---|---|---|---|
| | cir (kbps) | bc (bytes) | cir (kbps) | bc (bytes) | cir (kbps) | bc (bytes) | cir (kbps) | bc (bytes) |
| igmp | 1024 | 65,535 | 4096 | 264,000 | 4096 | 264,000 | 1024 | 65,535 |
| pim-hello | 1024 | 4,800,000 | 1024 | 4,800,000 | 1024 | 4,800,000 | 1024 | 4,800,000 |
| bridging | 20000 | 4,800,000 | 20000 | 4,800,000 | 20000 | 4,800,000 | 20000 | 4,800,000 |
| arp | 1024 | 3,600,000 | 1024 | 3,600,000 | 4000 | 3,600,000 | 1024 | 3,600,000 |
| dhcp | 1024 | 4,800,000 | 1024 | 4,800,000 | 1024 | 4,800,000 | 1024 | 4,800,000 |
| wccp | 1060 | 4,800,000 | 1060 | 4,800,000 | 1060 | 4,800,000 | 1060 | 4,800,000 |
| mgmt | 12000 | 4,800,000 | 12000 | 4,800,000 | 12000 | 4,800,000 | 12000 | 4,800,000 |
| ecp | 6400 | 3,200,000 | 6400 | 3,200,000 | 6400 | 3,200,000 | 6400 | 3,200,000 |
| lacp | 1024 | 4,800,000 | 1024 | 4,800,000 | 1024 | 4,800,000 | 1024 | 4,800,000 |
| lldp | 2048 | 4,800,000 | 2048 | 4,800,000 | 2048 | 4,800,000 | 2048 | 4,800,000 |
| udld | 2048 | 4,800,000 | 2048 | 4,800,000 | 2048 | 4,800,000 | 2048 | 4,800,000 |
| isis | 1024 | 4,800,000 | 2048 | 4,800,000 | 2048 | 4,800,000 | 1024 | 4,800,000 |
| msdp | 9600 | 4,800,000 | 9600 | 4,800,000 | 9600 | 4,800,000 | 9600 | 4,800,000 |
| cdp | 1024 | 4,800,000 | 1024 | 4,800,000 | 1024 | 4,800,000 | 1024 | 4,800,000 |
| fip | 1024 | 4,800,000 | 1024 | 4,800,000 | 1024 | 4,800,000 | 1024 | 4,800,000 |
| bgp | 9600 | 4,800,000 | 9600 | 4,800,000 | 9600 | 4,800,000 | 9600 | 4,800,000 |
| eigrp | 9600 | 4,800,000 | 9600 | 4,800,000 | 9600 | 4,800,000 | 9600 | 4,800,000 |

## NX-OS CoPP Configuration

The Control Plane Policing feature does not require a license. Any feature not included in a license package is bundled with the Cisco NX-OS system images. CoPP configuration recommendations and limitations are as follows:

- CoPP classification does not work for the Layer 2 control traffic in native VLAN in the following scenarios:

  - When the **native vlan** (ID other than 1) command is configured on the interface and the native VLAN ID is missing in the configuration.

  - If the **vlan dot1q tag native exclude control** command is configured.

■ Customizing CoPP is an ongoing process. CoPP must be configured according to the protocols and features used in your specific environment as well as the supervisor features that are required by the server environment. As these protocols and features change, CoPP must be modified.

■ We recommend that you continuously monitor CoPP. If drops occur, determine if CoPP dropped traffic unintentionally or in response to a malfunction or attack. In either event, analyze the situation and evaluate the need to modify the CoPP policies.

■ All the traffic that you do not specify in the other class maps is put into the last class, the default class. Monitor the drops in this class and investigate if these drops are based on traffic that you do not want or the result of a feature that was not configured and you need to add.

■ All broadcast traffic is sent through CoPP logic to determine which packets (for example, ARP and DHCP) need to be redirected through an ACL to the router processor. Broadcast traffic that does not need to be redirected is matched against the CoPP logic, and both conforming and violated packets are counted in the hardware but not sent to the CPU. Broadcast traffic that needs to be sent to the CPU and broadcast traffic that does not need to be sent to the CPU must be separated into different classes.

■ After you have configured CoPP, delete anything that is not being used, such as old class maps and unused routing protocols.

■ You must ensure that the CoPP policy does not filter critical traffic such as routing protocols or interactive access to the device. Filtering this traffic could prevent remote access to the Cisco NX-OS device and require a console connection.

■ The Cisco NX-OS software does not support egress CoPP or silent mode. CoPP is supported only on ingress (you cannot use the **service-policy output copp** command to the control plane interface).

■ You can use the access control entry (ACE) hit counters in the hardware only for ACL logic. Use the software ACE hit counters and the **show access-lists** and **show policy-map type control-plane** commands to evaluate CPU traffic.

■ The Cisco NX-OS device hardware performs CoPP on a per-forwarding-engine basis. CoPP does not support distributed policing. Therefore, you should choose rates so that the aggregate traffic does not overwhelm the supervisor module.

■ If multiple flows map to the same class, individual flow statistics are not available.

Table 18-25 lists the default settings for NX-OS CoPP parameters. You can alter these parameters as necessary.

18

**Table 18-25**   NX-OS CoPP Default Parameters

| Parameters | Default |
|---|---|
| Default policy | Strict. |
| Default policy | Nine policy entries.<br><br>**NOTE:** The maximum number of supported policies with associated class maps is 128. |
| Scale factor value | 1.00. |

Tables 18-26 through 18-29 show some of the most-used CoPP class and policy configuration commands. For a full list of commands, refer to the Nexus Security Configuration Guide links in the "References" section at the end of this chapter.

**Table 18-26**   NX-OS CoPP Control Plane Class Map Commands

| Command | Purpose |
|---|---|
| switch(config)# **class-map type control-plane [match-all \| match-any ]** *class-map-name* | Specifies a control plane class map and enters class map configuration mode. The default class matching is **match-any**. The name can be a maximum of 64 characters long and is case sensitive.<br><br>**NOTE:** You cannot use **class-default**, **match-all**, or **match-any** as class map names. |
| switch(config-cmap)# **match access-group name** *access-list-name* | (Optional) Specifies matching for an IP ACL.<br><br>**NOTE:** The **permit** and **deny** ACL keywords are ignored in the CoPP matching. |
| switch(config-cmap)# **match exception {ip \| ipv6 } icmp redirect** | (Optional) Specifies matching for IPv4 or IPv6 ICMP redirect exception packets. |
| switch(config-cmap)# **match exception {ip \| ipv6 } icmp unreachable** | (Optional) Specifies matching for IPv4 or IPv6 ICMP unreachable exception packets. |
| switch(config-cmap)# **match exception {ip \| ipv6 } option** | (Optional) Specifies matching for IPv4 or IPv6 option exception packets. |
| switch(config-cmap)# **match exception {ip \| ipv6 } unicast rpf-failure** | (Optional) Specifies matching for IPv4 or IPv6 Unicast Reverse Path Forwarding (Unicast RPF) exception packets. For any CoPP class map, you can rate-limit the IPv4 or IPv6 URPF exception packets as per the class map's rate-limit configuration. |
| switch(config-cmap)# **match protocol arp** | Specifies matching for IP Address Resolution Protocol (ARP) and Reverse Address Resolution Protocol (RARP) packets. |
| switch(config-cmap)# **match redirect arp-inspect** | (Optional) Specifies matching for ARP inspection redirected packets. |
| switch(config-cmap)# **match redirect dhcp-snoop** | (Optional) Specifies matching for DHCP snooping redirected packets. |
| switch(config-cmap)# **exit** | Exits class map configuration mode. |

**Table 18-27**   NX-OS CoPP Control Plane Policy Map Commands

| Command | Purpose |
|---|---|
| switch# **policy-map type control-plane** *policy-map-name* | Specifies a control plane policy map and enters policy map configuration mode. The policy map name can have a maximum of 64 characters and is case sensitive. |
| switch(config-pmap)# **class** {*class-map-name* [**insert-before** *class-map-name2*] \| **class-default** } | Specifies a control plane class map name or the class default and enters control plane class configuration mode. <br><br> The **class-default** class map is always at the end of the class map list for a policy map. |
| switch(config-pmap-c)# **police** [**cir** ] {*cir-rate* [**bps** \| **gbps** \| **kbps** \| **mbps** \| **pps** ]} | Specifies the committed information rate (CIR). The rate range is from 0 to 80,000,000,000. The default CIR unit is bps. |
| switch(config-pmap-c)# **police** [**cir** ] {*cir-rate* [**bps** \| **gbps** \| **kbps** \| **mbps** \| **pps** ]} [**bc** ] *burst-size* [**bytes** \| **kbytes** \| **mbytes** \| **ms** \| **packets** \| **us** ] | Specifies the CIR with the committed burst (BC). The CIR range is from 0 to 80,000,000,000, and the BC range is from 0 to 512,000,000. The default CIR unit is bps, and the default BC size unit is bytes. |
| switch(config-pmap-c)# **police** [**cir** ] {*cir-rate* [**bps** \| **gbps** \| **kbps** \| **mbps** \| **pps** ]} **conform** {**drop** \| **set-cos-transmit** *cos-value* \| **set-dscp-transmit** *dscp-value* \| **set-prec-transmit** *prec-value* \| **transmit** } [**exceed** {**drop** \| **set dscp dscp table cir-markdown-map** \| **transmit** ]] [**violate** {**drop** \| **set dscp dscp table pir-markdown-map** \| **transmit** ]] | Specifies the CIR with the conform action. The CIR range is from 0 to 80,000,000,000. The default rate unit is bps. The range for the *cos-value* and *prec-value* arguments is from 0 to 7. The range for the *dscp-value* argument is from 0 to 63. <br><br> The options are as follows: <br><br> **drop:** Drops the packet. <br><br> **set-cos-transmit:** Sets the class of service (CoS) value. <br><br> **set-dscp-transmit:** Sets the differentiated services code point (DSCP) value. <br><br> **set-prec-transmit:** Sets the precedence value. <br><br> **transmit:** Transmits the packet. <br><br> **set dscp dscp table cir-markdown-map:** Sets the exceed action to the CIR markdown map. <br><br> **set dscp dscp table pir-markdown-map:** Sets the violate action to the PIR markdown map. <br><br> **NOTE:** You can specify the BC and conform action for the same CIR. |
| switch(config-pmap-c)# **police** [**cir** ] {*cir-rate* [**bps** \| **gbps** \| **kbps** \| **mbps** \| **pps** ]} **pir** *pir-rate* [**bps** \| **gbps** \| **kbps** \| **mbps** ] [[**be** ] *burst-size* [**bytes** \| **kbytes** \| **mbytes** \| **ms** \| **packets** \| **us** ]] | Specifies the CIR with the peak information rate (PIR). The CIR range is from 0 to 80,000,000,000, and the PIR range is from 1 to 80,000,000,000. You can optionally set an extended burst (BE) size. The BE range is from 1 to 512,000,000. The default CIR unit is bps, the default PIR unit is bps, and the default BE size unit is bytes. <br><br> **NOTE:** You can specify the BC, conform action, and PIR for the same CIR. |

18

| Command | Purpose |
|---|---|
| switch(config-pmap-c)# **set cos [inner ]** *cos-value* | (Optional) Specifies the 802.1Q class of service (CoS) value. Use the inner keyword in a Q-in-Q environment. The range is from 0 to 7. The default value is 0. |
| switch(config-pmap-c)# **set dscp [tunnel ] {***dscp-value* **\| af11 \| af12 \| af13 \| af21 \| af22 \| af23 \| af31 \| af32 \| af33 \| af41 \| af42 \| af43 \| cs1 \| cs2 \| cs3 \| cs4 \| cs5 \| cs6 \| cs7 \| ef \| default }** | (Optional) Specifies the differentiated services code point value in IPv4 and IPv6 packets. Use the **tunnel** keyword to set tunnel encapsulation. The range is from 0 to 63. The default value is 0. |
| switch(config-pmap-c)# **set precedence [tunnel ] {***prec-value* **\| critical \| flash \| flash-override \| immediate \| internet \| network \| priority \| routine }** | (Optional) Specifies the precedence value in IPv4 and IPv6 packets. Use the **tunnel** keyword to set tunnel encapsulation. The range is from 0 to 7. The default value is 0. |
| switch(config-pmap-c)# **exit** | Exits policy map class configuration mode. |
| switch(config-pmap)# **exit** | Exits policy map configuration mode. |

**Table 18-28**   NX-OS CoPP Control Plane Service Map Commands

| Command | Purpose |
|---|---|
| switch# **policy-map type control-plane** *policy-map-name* | Specifies a control plane policy map and enters policy map configuration mode. The policy map name can have a maximum of 64 characters and is case sensitive. |
| switch(config-cp)# **service-policy input** *policy-map-name* | Specifies a policy map for the input traffic. Repeat this step if you have more than one policy map. You cannot disable CoPP. If you enter the no form of this command, packets are rate limited at 50 packets per seconds. |
| switch(config-pmap)# **class {***class-map-name* **[insert-before** *class-map-name2***] \| class-default }** | Specifies a control plane class map name or the class default and enters control plane class configuration mode. The **class-default** class map is always at the end of the class map list for a policy map. |
| switch(config-pmap-c)# **police [cir ] {***cir-rate* **[bps \| gbps \| kbps \| mbps \| pps ]}** | Specifies the committed information rate (CIR). The rate range is from 0 to 80,000,000,000. The default CIR unit is bps. |
| switch(config-pmap-c)# **police [cir ] {***cir-rate* **[bps \| gbps \| kbps \| mbps \| pps ]} [bc ]** *burst-size* **[bytes \| kbytes \| mbytes \| ms \| packets \| us ]** | Specifies the CIR with the committed burst (BC). The CIR range is from 0 to 80,000,000,000, and the BC range is from 0 to 512,000,000. The default CIR unit is bps, and the default BC size unit is bytes. |
| switch(config-pmap-c)# **police [cir ] {***cir-rate* **[bps \| gbps \| kbps \| mbps \| pps ]} conform {drop \| set-cos-transmit** *cos-value* **\| set-dscp-transmit** *dscp-value* **\| set-prec-transmit** *prec-value* **\| transmit } [exceed {drop \| set dscp dscp table cir-markdown-map \| transmit }] [violate {drop \| set dscp dscp table pir-markdown-map \| transmit }]** | Specifies the CIR with the conform action. The CIR range is from 0 to 80,000,000,000. The default rate unit is bps. The range for the *cos-value* and *prec-value* arguments is from 0 to 7. The range for the *dscp-value* argument is from 0 to 63. The options are as follows: **drop:** Drops the packet. **set-cos-transmit:** Sets the class of service (CoS) value. **set-dscp-transmit:** Sets the differentiated services code point value. |

| Command | Purpose |
|---|---|
| | **set-prec-transmit:** Sets the precedence value. |
| | **transmit:** Transmits the packet. |
| | **set dscp dscp table cir-markdown-map:** Sets the exceed action to the CIR markdown map. |
| | **set dscp dscp table pir-markdown-map:** Sets the violate action to the PIR markdown map. |
| | **NOTE:** You can specify the BC and conform action for the same CIR. |
| switch(config-pmap-c)# **police [cir ]** {*cir-rate* **[bps | gbps | kbps | mbps | pps ]} pir** *pir-rate* **[bps | gbps | kbps | mbps ] [[be ]** *burst-size* **[bytes | kbytes | mbytes | ms | packets | us ]]** | Specifies the CIR with the peak information rate (PIR). The CIR range is from 0 to 80,000,000,000, and the PIR range is from 1 to 80,000,000,000. You can optionally set an extended burst (BE) size. The BE range is from 1 to 512,000,000. The default CIR unit is bps, the default PIR unit is bps, and the default BE size unit is bytes. **NOTE:** You can specify the BC, conform action, and PIR for the same CIR, |
| switch(config-pmap-c)# **set cos [inner ]** *cos-value* | (Optional) Specifies the 802.1Q class of service (CoS) value. Use the inner keyword in a Q-in-Q environment. The range is from 0 to 7. The default value is 0. |
| switch(config-pmap-c)# **set dscp [tunnel ]** {*dscp-value* **| af11 | af12 | af13 | af21 | af22 | af23 | af31 | af32 | af33 | af41 | af42 | af43 | cs1 | cs2 | cs3 | cs4 | cs5 | cs6 | cs7 | ef | default }** | (Optional) Specifies the differentiated services code point value in IPv4 and IPv6 packets. Use the **tunnel** keyword to set tunnel encapsulation. The range is from 0 to 63. The default value is 0. |
| switch(config-pmap-c)# **set precedence [tunnel ]** {*prec-value* **| critical | flash | flash-override | immediate | internet | network | priority | routine }** | (Optional) Specifies the precedence value in IPv4 and IPv6 packets. Use the **tunnel** keyword to set tunnel encapsulation. The range is from 0 to 7. The default value is 0. |
| switch(config-pmap-c)# **exit** | Exits policy map class configuration mode. |
| switch(config-pmap)# **exit** | Exits policy map configuration mode. |

**Table 18-29**  NX-OS CoPP Global Command and Verification

| Command | Purpose |
|---|---|
| **copp profile [strict | moderate | lenient | dense ]** | Applies the CoPP best practice policy. |
| **copp copy profile {strict | moderate | lenient| dense } {prefix | suffix }** *string* | Copies the default profile to a new profile to make modifications. |
| **show copp status** | Displays the CoPP status, including the last configuration operation and its status. This command also enables you to verify that the CoPP best practice policy is attached to the control plane. |
| **show policy-map type control-plane [expand ] [name** *policy-map-name*] | Displays the control plane policy map with associated class maps and CIR and BC values. |

| Command | Purpose |
|---|---|
| **show policy-map interface control-plane** [class *class-map* \| **module** *slot*] | Displays the policy values with associated class maps and drops per policy or class map. It also displays the scale factor values when a CoPP policy is applied. When the scale factor value is the default (1.00), it is not displayed. <br><br> **NOTE:** The scale factor changes the CIR, BC, PIR, and BE values internally on each module, but the display shows the configured CIR, BC, PIR, and BE values only. The actual applied value on a module is the scale factor multiplied by the configured value. |
| **show class-map type control-plane** [*class-map-name*] | Displays the control plane class map configuration, including the ACLs that are bound to this class map. |
| **show ip access-lists** [*acl-name*] | Displays the access lists, including the ACLs. If the **statistics per-entry** command is used, it also displays hit counts for specific entries. |
| **show policy-map interface control-plane** {[**module** *module-number* [**inst-all** ]] [**class** {*class-map* \| **violated** }] \| [**class** {*class-map* \| **violated** }] [**module** *module-number* [**inst-all** ]]} | Displays packet-level statistics for all classes that are part of the applied CoPP policy. <br><br> Statistics are specified in terms of OutPackets (packets admitted to the control plane) and DropPackets (packets dropped because of rate limiting). <br><br> **NOTE:** With Supervisor 3 or F2e Series modules, the output of this command uses Layer 3 packet lengths when displaying the byte count. With M1, M2, or F2 Series modules, the command output uses Layer 2 packet lengths for the byte count. <br><br> From Cisco NX-OS Release 8.1(1), you can display the per-instance statistics for all classes that are part of the applied CoPP policy for a module by using the **inst-all** keyword. |

To create a new CoPP, it is recommended that you copy an existing CoPP (strict, moderate, lenient, or dense) and modify it as shown in the following steps. (These steps apply on Nexus 9000 or Nexus 7000 Series switches only.)

**Step 1.** Copy one of the predefined policies, as shown in Example 18-26.

**Key Topic**

**Example 18-26** *Copy a Predefined NX-OS Nexus 7000 CoPP*

```
Switch-A# copp copy profile dense prefix dccore

Switch-A# show run | begin policy
policy-map type control-plane dccore-copp-policy-dense
  class dccore-copp-class-critical
    set cos 7
    police cir 4500 kbps bc 250 ms conform transmit violate drop
  class dccore-copp-class-important
```

**Step 2.** Modify any class map or policy map, as shown in Example 18-27.

**Example 18-27** *Modify a CoPP by Adding a New Class*

```
Switch-A(config)# policy-map type control-plane dccore-copp-policy-dense
Switch-A(config-pmap)# class dccore-copp-class-critical
Switch-A(config-pmap-c)# police cir 9000 kbps bc 450 ms conform transmit violate drop

Switch -A# show run | begin policy
policy-map type control-plane dccore-copp-policy-dense
  class dccore-copp-class-critical
    set cos 7
    police cir 9000 kbps bc 450 ms conform transmit violate drop
  class dccore-copp-class-important
    set cos 6
    police cir 1400 kbps bc 1500 ms conform transmit violate drop
```

## Cisco ACI Contracts

Network and application security best practices are required to control traffic flows and permit specific traffic between two applications or devices. ACI contracts provide a way for the Cisco Application Centric Infrastructure (ACI) administrator to control traffic flow within the ACI fabric between endpoint groups (EPGs). These contracts are built using a provider-consumer model where one endpoint group provides the services it wants to offer, and another endpoint group consumes them. Contracts are assigned a scope of Global, Tenant, VRF, or Application Profile, which limit the accessibility of the contract (see Figure 18-8).

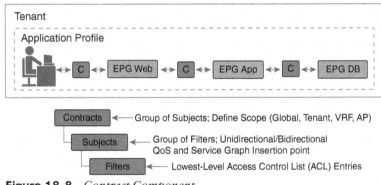

**Figure 18-8** *Contract Component*

Contracts contain the following items:

- **Subjects:** A group of filters for a specific application or service.

- **Filters:** A technique to classify traffic based on Layer 2 to Layer 4 attributes (such as Ethernet type, protocol type, TCP flags, and ports).

- **Actions:** Tasks to be taken on the filtered traffic. The following actions are supported:

  - Permit the traffic (regular contracts, only).

  - Mark the traffic (DSCP/CoS) (regular contracts, only).

- Redirect the traffic (regular contracts, only, through a service graph).

- Copy the traffic (regular contracts, only, through a service graph or SPAN).

- Block the traffic (taboo contracts, only).

- Log the traffic (taboo contracts, only).

- **Labels:** (Optional) A method to group objects such as subjects and endpoint groups for the purpose of increasing granularity in policy enforcement.

In the ACI security model, contracts contain the policies that govern the communication between EPGs. The contract specifies what can be communicated, and the EPGs specify the source and destination of the communications. Contracts link EPGs, as shown here:

```
EPG 1 -------------- CONTRACT -------------- EPG 2
```

Endpoints in EPG 1 can communicate with endpoints in EPG 2 and vice versa if the contract allows it. This policy construct is very flexible. Many contracts can exist between EPG 1 and EPG 2, more than two EPGs can use a contract, and contracts can be reused across multiple sets of EPGs, and more.

There is also directionality in the relationship between EPGs and contracts. EPGs can either provide or consume a contract. An EPG that provides a contract is typically a set of endpoints that provide a service to a set of client devices. The protocols used by that service are defined in the contract. An EPG that consumes a contract is typically a set of endpoints that are clients of that service. When the client endpoint (consumer) tries to connect to a server endpoint (provider), the contract checks to see if that connection is allowed. Unless otherwise specified, that contract would not allow a server to initiate a connection to a client. However, another contract between the EPGs could easily allow a connection in that direction.

This providing/consuming relationship is typically shown graphically with arrows between the EPGs and the contract. Note the direction of the arrows shown here:

```
EPG 1 <------consumes------- CONTRACT <------provides------- EPG 2
```

The contract is constructed in a hierarchical manner. It consists of one or more subjects, each subject contains one or more filters, and each filter can define one or more protocols, as shown in Figure 18-9.

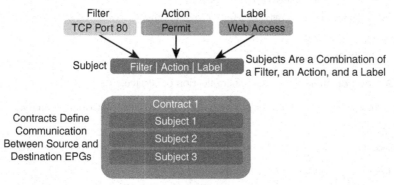

Contracts Are Groups of Subjects That Define Communication Between EPGs

**Figure 18-9**  *ACI Subjects and Contracts*

While different endpoint groups can only communicate with other endpoint groups based on the contract rules defined, no contract is required for intra-endpoint group communication. Intra-endpoint group communication from endpoint to endpoint in the same endpoint group is allowed by default.

If a filter allows traffic from any consumer port to a provider port (such as 8080), and if reverse port filtering is enabled and the contract is applied in both directions (say for TCP traffic), either the consumer or the provider can initiate communication. The provider could open a TCP socket to the consumer using port 8080, whether the provider or consumer sent traffic first.

## Cisco ACI Contract Configuration Parameters

When configuring contracts, you can define the following options:

- **Application-profile:** This contract can be applied to any endpoint groups in the same application profile.

- **Contract scope:** The scope of a service contract between two or more participating peer entities or endpoint groups. The contract is not applied to any consumer endpoint group outside the scope of the provider endpoint group. The states are

  - **Private network:** This contract can be applied to any endpoint groups within the same VRF. (This is the default.)

  - **Tenant:** This contract can be applied to any endpoint groups within the same tenant.

  - **Global:** This contract can be applied to any endpoint groups throughout the fabric.

- **QoS class:** You can set the priority level of the service contract. The priority level can be

  - Unspecified (this is the default).

  - Level1: Class 1 differentiated services code point (DSCP) value.

  - Level2: Class 2 DSCP value.

  - Level3: Class 3 DSCP value.

- **Tags (labels):** (Optional) The search keyword or term that is assigned to the application profile. A tag allows you to group multiple objects by a descriptive name. You can assign the same tag name to multiple objects, and you can assign one or more tag names to an object. When contracts are assigned to an endpoint group as either a consumer or provider, by default all subjects within a contract apply to the endpoint group. With tags, only endpoint groups in application profiles with matching criteria implement the subject of the contract.

- **Match:** The subject match criteria across consumer endpoint groups. Labels can be applied to a variety of provider and consumer-managed objects, including endpoint groups, contracts, bridge domains, DHCP relay policies, and DNS policies. When you

18

are checking for a match of provider labels and consumer labels, the match setting is determined by the provider endpoint group. The different options are

- **AtleastOne:** At least one label matches on provider and consumer endpoint groups. Blank labels are considered a match. (This is the default.)

- **AtmostOne:** The setting matches only when all labels on the endpoint groups are exactly the same. Blank labels are considered a match.

- **None:** None of the subject labels match.

- **All:** The setting matches only when both endpoint groups have all labels, excluding blank labels.

## Create, Modify, or Remove Regular Contracts

You can create or modify or remove tenant contracts to control traffic flow between endpoint groups. Only users with the administrator privilege can create, modify, or remove a contract.

To create a contract using the ACI GUI, follow these steps:

**Step 1.** On the menu bar, choose **Tenants > ALL TENANTS**. In the Work pane, choose **Tenant_Name**.

**Step 2.** In the Navigation pane, choose **Tenant_Name > Contracts**.

**Step 3.** In the Work pane, choose **Actions > Create Contract**.

**Step 4.** In the Create Contract dialog box, perform the following actions:

- Enter a Contract Name.

- Choose a Contract Scope (optional).

- Choose a QoS Class (optional).

- Click + (the plus sign) next to the Subject to add a Contract Subject.

- In the Create Contract Subject dialog box, perform the following actions:

 - Enter a Contract Subject Name.

 - Click + in the Filter Chain field.

**Step 5.** Click **Update**, click **OK**, and then click **Submit**.

To create a contract using the Cisco NX-OS, follow these steps:

**Step 1.** Get into the configuration mode using the Cisco NX-OS CLI. Then enter the following:

```
apic1# configure
apic1(config)#
```

**Step 2.** To create the contracts and assign an access group (filters) for HTTPS traffic between EPGs, enter the following:

```
apic1(config)# tenant <tenant name>
apic1(config-tenant)# contract <contract name>
apic1(config-tenant-contract)# subject <subject name>
```

```
apic1(config-tenant-contract-subj)# access-group <access group name> both
apic1(config-tenant-contract-subj)# exit
apic1(config-tenant-contract)# exit
```

To modify an existing contract using the ACI GUI, follow these steps:

**Step 1.**    On the menu bar, choose **Tenants > ALL TENANTS.** Then in the Work pane, choose **Tenant_Name.**

**Step 2.**    In the Navigation pane, choose **Tenant_Name > Contracts > Contract_Name.**

**Step 3.**    In the Work pane, choose the **Policy** tab. Then do the following:

■ Choose a Contract Scope (optional).

■ Choose a QoS Class (optional).

■ Click + next to the Subject field to add a Contract Subject.

■ In the Create Contract Subject dialog box, perform the following actions:

■ Enter a Contract Subject Name.

■ Click + next to Filter Chain.

**Step 4.**    Click **Update**, click **OK**, and then click **Submit.**

To remove a contract using the ACI GUI, follow these steps:

**Step 1.**    On the menu bar, choose **Tenants > ALL TENANTS.** In the Work pane, choose **Tenant_Name.**

**Step 2.**    In the Navigation pane, choose **Tenant_Name > Contracts > Contract_Name.**

**Step 3.**    In the Work pane, choose **Actions > Delete.**

To verify a contract using the ACI API or shell command, you can use these commands:

```
REST API: /api/node/class/vzBrCP.xml
```

```
Shell Command : admin@apic1:~> moquery -c vzBrCP
```

To apply a contract to an EPG using the ACI GUI, follow these steps:

**Step 1.**    On the menu bar, choose **Tenants > ALL TENANTS.** In the Work pane, choose **Tenant_Name.**

**Step 2.**    In the Navigation pane, choose **Tenant_Name > Application Profiles > Application_Profile_Name > Application EPGs > EPG_Name > Contracts.**

**Step 3.**    In the Work pane, choose **Actions > Add Provided Contract** or **Actions > Add Consumed Contract.**

**NOTE**    Choose the action depending on how the contract is to be deployed.

In the Add Contract dialog box, perform the following actions:

- Enter a Contract_Name.

- Choose a QOS policy (optional).

- Choose a Label (optional).

**Step 4.** Click **Submit**.

## Apply or Remove VRF Contracts

To apply contracts to all endpoint groups within a VRF, you can apply the contract directly to the VRF. This concept is also referred as a *vzAny* endpoint group. It simplified contract management by allowing the contract configuration for all endpoint groups within a VRF, also optimizing hardware resource consumption.

For example, if a Cisco ACI administrator has 100 endpoint groups that are all part of the same VRF, he can apply the contracts to this one vzAny group under the VRF rather than to each endpoint group.

Traditionally, VRF-wide contracts allow established traffic, allowing endpoint group contracts to define traffic in only one direction—from consumer to provider—without the need to have reverse port forwarding enabled for TCP traffic. Because all endpoint groups within the VRF allow established traffic, reverse port forwarding is unnecessary in the contract applied to the endpoint group directly.

A quick trick to see if contracts, or the lack thereof, are blocking traffic within the VRF in an ACI fabric is to unenforce the VRF. This technique allows communication between all endpoint groups within the VRF without the need for contracts. This is equivalent to applying the common tenant contract vzAny to the VRF endpoint group.

**NOTE** If a very large number of contracts exists within the VRF, reimplementing the contracts in the leaf switches can take up to an hour or more when the VRF is moved back to enforced.

To apply a contract to a VRF (vzAny) using the GUI, follow these steps:

**Step 1.** On the menu bar, choose **Tenants > ALL TENANTS**. In the Work pane, choose **Tenant_Name**.

**Step 2.** In the Navigation pane, choose **Tenant_Name > Networking > Private Networks > Private_Network_Name > EPG Collection for Context**.

**Step 3.** In the Work pane, click + next to either Add Provided Contract or Add Consumed Contract.

**NOTE** Make a selection depending on how the contract is to be deployed.

Then do the following:

- Enter a Contract_Name.

- Choose a QOS Type.

- Choose Match Criteria.

**Step 4.** Click **Update**.

To verify a contract using the ACI API or shell command, you can use these commands:

```
REST API: /api/node/class/vzBrCP.xml

Shell Command : admin@apic1:~> moquery -c vzBrCP
```

## Inter-Tenant Contracts

Some services, such as DNS for name resolution and Active Directory for user management, are common or shared across tenants. Because these services are shared, you need to allow their traffic across the whole fabric. Communication between EPGs that belong to different tenants is allowed only when they share the same contract. To use the same contract, you need to export the source tenant to the appropriate destination tenant. That contract appears under the Imported Contract section in the Security Policies of the destination tenant.

A consumed contract interface is used to associate an EPG from the destination tenant with the imported contract.

> **NOTE** A consumed contract interface represents one or more subjects defined under the contract. By associating to an interface, an endpoint group starts consuming all the subjects represented by the interface.

In the following example, EPG-1 in tenant Cisco-1 requires communication with EPG-2 in tenant Cisco-2. This is accomplished by utilizing contact interfaces. As illustrated in Figure 18-10, the tenant Cisco-1 user exports the intended contract interfaces and selects a provider to provide the contrast to EPG-2. The user then confirms the imported contract in tenant Cisco-2 and selects the contract as consumed. To advertise the routes from the source VRF to the intended VRF, the user must create the subnet within the EPG.

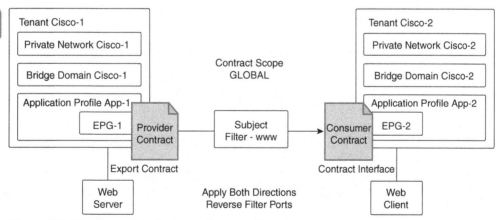

**Figure 18-10** *Exporting Contracts Between Tenants*

To export the contract from Cisco-1/EPG-1 to Cisco-2/EPG-2, follow these steps:

**Step 1.** From tenant Cisco-1/EPG-1, do the following:

- Create an export contract under Security Policies.

- Create the host subnet (default Gateway IP) under EPG1 - subnet scope shared.

- Add the contract under EPG1 - contract type provider.

- Create the host subnet under the bridge domain - subnet scope private/ public.

**Step 2.** From tenant Cisco-2/EPG-2, do the following:

- Confirm the exported contract is listed under Imported Contracts.

- Create the host subnet (default Gateway IP) under EPG2 - subnet scope shared.

- Add the interface contract under EPG2 - contract type consumed.

- Create the host subnet (default Gateway IP) under the bridge domain - subnet scope private/public.

## Inter-Private Network Contracts Communication

In the following example, EPG-1 in VRF Cisco-1 requires communication with EPG-2 in VRF Cisco-2. This is accomplished by utilizing the subnet field within the EPG, as shown in Figure 18-11. When you create the subnet under the EPG and select shared, the route is leaked to the VRF noted within the Tenant scoped contract.

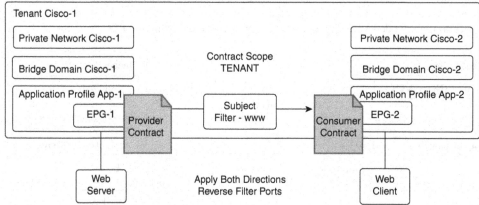

**Figure 18-11** *Exporting Contracts Between Private Networks*

To create a subnet and share it, use the following steps:

**Step 1.** Create the contract under Security Policies - contract scope Tenant.

**Step 2.** (Tenant Cisco-1/EPG-1) Create the host subnet (default Gateway IP) under EPG1 - subnet scope shared.

**Step 3.**    Add the contract under EPG1 - contract type provider.

**Step 4.**    (Tenant Cisco-1/EPG-2) Create the host subnet (default Gateway IP) under EPG2 - subnet scope shared.

**Step 5.**    Add the contract under EPG2 - contract type provider.

## Single Contract Bidirectional Reverse Filter

A single contract bidirectional reverse filter is useful when implementing a contract with the option to apply the contract subject in both directions and with the option to apply the reverse filter. This is the most common filter because it allows a single subject/filter to be implemented with a single provider/consumer relationship.

In this example, EPG-1 provides a contract with a subject of www, and EPG-2 consumes the contract, as shown in Figure 18-12. This allows the web client in EPG-2 to access the web server in EPG-1. That is, EPG-1 provides a service to EPG-2. The web server in EPG-1 does not have access to port 80 of the web client in EPG-2. This results in a single contract with one subject and one filter (www) with a single provider and a single consumer.

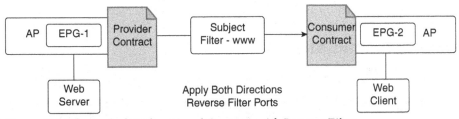

**Figure 18-12**    *Default Bidirectional Contract with Reverse Filter*

## Single Contract Unidirectional with Multiple Filters

This example involves implementing a contract without the option to apply the contract subject in both directions. When selecting this option, the user no longer has the option to select the reverse filter option.

In this example, EPG-1 provides a contract with a subject of icmp, and EPG-2 consumes the contract, as shown in Figure 18-13. This allows the host in EPG-1 to access the host in EPG-2 via icmp. When utilizing a single subject without the use of "Apply Both Directions," the user must then configure two filters, one in each direction. This results in a single contract with one subject, two filters (icmp), and a single provider and a single consumer.

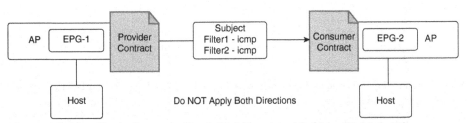

**Figure 18-13**    *Single Contract, Single Unidirectional Subject, Multiple Filters*

### Multiple Contracts Unidirectional Single Filter

For high granularity, contracts can be implemented unidirectionally, as shown a Figure 18-14. In this example, EPG-1 provides a contract with an icmp subject, and EPG-2 consumes the contract. This allows Client 2 in EPG-2 to access the host in EPG-1 via icmp. That is, EPG-1 provides a service to EPG-2. The result is two contracts with one subject and one filter. Each contract has a single provider and a single consumer referencing the same contract. The difference here is that the contract is explicitly applied in *both* directions.

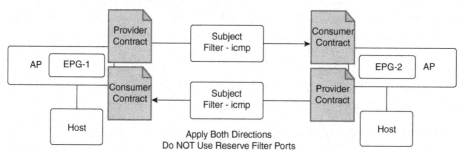

**Figure 18-14**  *Multiple Contracts, Unidirectional Subjects, Single Filters*

# ACI Microsegmentation

Microsegmentation is a security requirement to reduce attack surfaces by minimizing the possibilities for lateral movement in the event of a security breach. With traditional networking technologies, this is very hard to accomplish. Network flow and categorized devices depend on functionality or criticality and segment them into zones, but ACI enables a new approach, by allowing degrees of flexibility and automation not possible with traditional network management and operations, making microsegmentation a distinct possibility.

Cisco ACI microsegmentation (uSeg) enables you to automatically assign endpoints to logical security zones called endpoint groups. These EPGs are based on various network-based or virtual machine–based attributes.

Microsegmentation with Cisco ACI supports virtual endpoints attached to the following:

- Cisco ACI Virtual Edge

- Cisco Application Virtual Switch (AVS)

- Microsoft vSwitch

- VMware vSphere Distributed Switch (VDS)

Microsegmentation with network-based attributes also supports bare-metal environments.

> **NOTE**  You can configure microsegmentation with Cisco ACI for physical and virtual endpoints, and you can share the same EPGs for both physical and virtual endpoints.

Microsegmentation using the Cisco ACI involves the Cisco APIC, vCenter, or Microsoft System Center Virtual Machine Manager (SCVMM), and leaf switches. The workflow for microsegmentation using the Cisco ACI Virtual Edge, Cisco AVS, VMware VDS, or Microsoft vSwitch is shown here.

The APIC workflow is as follows:

1. The user configures a VMM domain for the Cisco ACI Virtual Edge, Cisco AVS, VMware VDS, or Microsoft vSwitch in the Cisco APIC.

2. The Cisco APIC connects to vCenter or SCVMM and does the following:

   ■ Creates an instance of the Cisco ACI Virtual Edge, Cisco AVS, VMware VDS, or Microsoft vSwitch.

   ■ Pulls VM and hypervisor inventory information from the associated VMware vCenter or Microsoft SCVMM.

3. The user creates an application EPG and associates it with a vCenter/SCVMM domain. In each vCenter/SCVMM domain, a new encapsulation is allocated for this application EPG. The application EPG does not have any attributes. The vCenter/SCVMM administrator assigns virtual endpoints to this application EPG—not to any microsegment EPGs. It is the application EPG that appears in vCenter/SCVMM as a port group.

4. The user creates a uSeg EPG and associates it with the VMM domain. The uSeg EPG does not appear in vCenter/SCVMM as a port group; it has a special function:

   ■ The uSeg EPG has VM-based attributes to match filter criteria. If a match occurs between the uSeg EPG VM attributes and VMs, the Cisco APIC dynamically assigns the VMs to the uSeg EPG.

   ■ The endpoints are transferred from the application EPG to the uSeg EPG. If the uSeg EPG is deleted, the endpoints are assigned back to the application EPG.

   ■ The uSeg EPG must be assigned to a VMM domain in order for it to take effect. When you associate the uSeg EPG to a VMM domain, its criteria are applied for that VMM domain only. If you have VMware VDS, you also must assign the uSeg EPG to the same bridge domain as the application EPG.

In the case of VMware VDS, its criteria are applied for that VMM domain and bridge domain.

The leaf switch and the Cisco ACI Virtual Edge, Cisco AVS, or Microsoft vSwitch workflow is as follows:

1. The physical leaf switch pulls the attribute policies from the Cisco APIC.

2. The Cisco ACI Virtual Edge, Cisco AVS, or Microsoft vSwitch sends a VM attach message to the physical leaf switch using the OpFlex protocol when a VM attaches to the Cisco ACI Virtual Edge, Cisco AVS, or Microsoft vSwitch.

3. The physical leaf switch matches the VM against the configured attribute policies for the tenant.

4. If the VM matches the configured VM attributes, the physical leaf switch pushes the uSeg EPG—along with the corresponding encapsulation—to the Cisco ACI Virtual Edge, Cisco AVS, or Microsoft vSwitch.

18

Note that this action does not change the original port-group assignment for the VM in vCenter/SCVMM.

Packet forwarding for the Cisco ACI Virtual Edge, Cisco AVS, or Microsoft vSwitch workflow is as follows:

1. When the VM sends the data packets, the Cisco ACI Virtual Edge, Cisco AVS, or Microsoft vSwitch tags the packets using encapsulation corresponding to the uSeg EPG, not the application EPG.

2. The physical leaf hardware sees an attribute-based encapsulated VM packet and matches it with the configured policy.

The VM is dynamically assigned to a uSeg EPG, and the packet is forwarded based on the policy defined for that particular uSeg EPG.

## Example: ACI Microsegmentation with VMs from a Single Application EPG

You can use microsegmentation with Cisco ACI to create new uSeg EPGs to contain VMs from a single application EPG. By default, VMs within an application EPG can communicate with each other; however, you might want to prevent communication between groups of VMs if VRF is in enforced mode and there is no contract between uSeg EPGs.

For this example, let's assume that you need to deploy a virtual desktop infrastructure (VDI) for the Human Resources, Finance, and Operations departments. The VDI virtual desktop VMs are part of a single application EPG called EPG_VDI with identical access requirements to the rest of the application EPGs.

Service contracts are built in such a way that the EPG-VDI has access to Internet resources and internal resources. But at the same time, the company must ensure that each of the VM groups—Human Resources, Finance, and Operations—cannot access the others even though they belong to the same application EPG, EPG_VDI.

To meet this requirement, you can create filters in the Cisco APIC that would check the names of the VMs in the application EPG, EPG_VDI. If you create a filter with the value "HR_VM," the Cisco APIC creates a uSeg EPG—a microsegment—for all Human Resource VMs. The Cisco APIC looks for matching values in all the EPGs in a tenant even though you want to group the matching VMs within one EPG. So, when you create VMs, it is recommended that you choose names unique within the tenant.

Similarly, you can create filters with the keyword "FIN_VMs" for Finance virtual desktops and "OPS_VMs" for Operations virtual desktops. These uSeg EPGs are represented as new EPGs within the Cisco APIC policy model. You can then apply contracts and filters to control access between the VM groups even though they belong to the same application EPG.

As shown in Figure 18-15, all the virtual desktop VMs from the Human Resources, Finance, and Operations groups have been moved from the application EPG, EPG_VDI, to new uSeg EPGs: EPG_OPS_MS, EPG_FIN_MS, and EPG_HR_MS. Each uSeg EPG has the attribute type VM Name with a value to match key parts of the VM's name. EPG_OPS_MS has the value OPS_VM, so all VMs in the tenant containing OPS_VM in their names become part of EPG_OPS_MS. The other uSeg EPGs have corresponding values, resulting in the movement of VMs in the tenant with matching names to the uSeg EPGs.

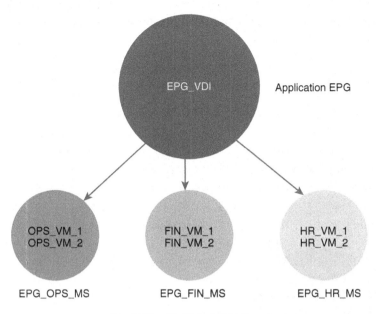

**Figure 18-15** *Microsegmentation with Cisco ACI with VMs from a Single Application EPG*

You can configure microsegmentation with the Cisco ACI to put VMs that belong to different application EPGs into a new uSeg EPG. You might want to do this to apply policy to VMs that share a certain characteristic although they belong to different application EPGs.

## Example: ACI Microsegmentation with VMs in Different Application EPGs

For this next example, let's assume that you need to deploy a three-tier web application. The application is built on VMs that run different operating systems and different versions of the same operating system. For example, the VMs might run Linux, Windows 2012 R2, and Windows 2016. The application is distributed, so the company has divided the VMs into three different EPGs: EPG_Web, EPG_App, and EPG_DB.

Because of a recent vulnerability in the Windows 2012 R2 operating system, your company's security team decided to quarantine VMs running Windows 2012 R2 in case those VMs are compromised. The security team also decided to upgrade all Windows 2012 R2 VMs to Windows 2016. It also wants to microsegment all production VMs across all EPGs and restrict external connectivity to those VMs.

To meet this requirement, you can configure a uSeg EPG in the Cisco APIC. The attribute would be Operating System, and the value of the attribute would be Windows 2012 R2.

You can now quarantine the VMs running Windows 2012 R2 and upgrade them to Windows 2016. When the upgrade is complete, the VMs will no longer be part of the uSeg EPG you created for VMs running Windows 2012 R2. This change is reflected dynamically to the Cisco APIC, and those virtual machines revert to their original EPGs.

As shown in Figure 18-16, the new uSeg EPG EPG_Windows_2012 has the attribute type Operating System and the value Windows 2012 R2. The VMs App_VM_2, DB_VM_1, DB_VM_2, and Web_VM_2 run Windows 2012 R2 as their operating system—and so have been moved to the new uSeg EPG EPG_Windows_2012. However, the VMs App_VM_1, DB_VM_3, and Web_VM_1 run Linux or Windows 2016, so they remain in their application EPGs.

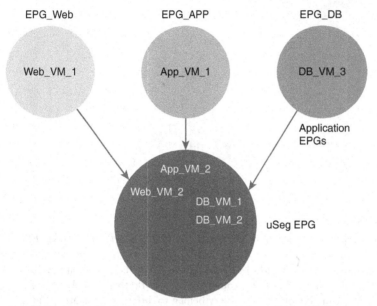

EPG Windows with Attribute Type Operating System and Value Windows

**Figure 18-16** *Microsegmentation with Cisco ACI in Different Application EPGs*

## ACI Microsegmentation Configurations

You can use the Cisco ACI to configure microsegmentation with the Cisco APIC to put VMs that belong to different application EPGs or the same EPG into a new uSeg EPG. The task is essentially the same for the Cisco ACI Virtual Edge, Cisco AVS, VMware VDS, and Microsoft vSwitch; the slight differences are noted in the procedure.

To configure new microsegmentation using the ACI GUI, use the following steps:

**Step 1.**    Log in to the Cisco ACI.

**Step 2.**    Choose **Tenants** and then choose the tenant where you want to create a microsegment.

**Step 3.**    In the Navigation pane for the tenant, expand the Tenant folder, the Application Profiles folder, and the Profile folder.

**Step 4.**    Complete one of the following actions:

If you are using VMware VDS, complete the following substeps; if you are using the Cisco ACI Virtual Edge, Cisco AVS, or Microsoft vSwitch, skip the following substeps and continue with step 5.

■ Expand the **Application EPGs** folder and the folder for the application EPG.

■ Right-click the **Domains (VMs and Bare-Metals)** folder.

- In the Add VMM Domain Association dialog box, select the **Allow Micro-Segmentation** check box.

- If you are using VMware VDS, you also need to configure all the required parameters.

- Click **Submit**.

**Step 5.** In the Navigation pane for the tenant, right-click the **uSeg EPGs** folder, and then choose **Create Useg EPG**.

**Step 6.** In the Create USeg EPG Step 1 > Identity dialog, complete the following steps to begin creating a uSeg EPG for a group of VMs:

- In the Name field, enter a name. We recommend that you choose a name indicating that the new uSeg EPG is a microsegment.

- In the intra-EPG isolation field, select **Enforced** or **Unenforced**. If you select Enforced, the Cisco ACI prevents all communication between the endpoint devices within this uSeg EPG.

- In the Bridge Domain area, choose a bridge domain from the drop-down list.

**NOTE**   For VMware VDS, you must choose the same bridge domain that is used for the application EPG. Otherwise, the VDS uSeg will not match VM attributes and will not place the VM into a uSeg EPG.

- (Optional) In the EPG Match Precedence field, choose an integer to set the precedence for the uSeg EPG among other VM-based attribute uSeg EPGs, overriding default rules. The larger the integer, the higher the precedence.

- Click **Next**.

**18**

**Step 7.** In the Create uSeg EPG Step 2 > Domains dialog, complete the following steps to associate the uSeg EPG with a VMM domain:

- Click the + (plus) icon at the right of the dialog box.

- From the Domain Profile drop-down list, choose a profile.

- If you have a Cisco ACI Virtual Edge, Cisco AVS, or a VMware VDS, choose a VMware domain; if you have a Microsoft vSwitch, choose a Microsoft domain.

**NOTE**   You must choose the same domain that is used by the application EPG.

- From the Deploy Immediacy drop-down list, accept the default **On Demand** if you have the Cisco ACI Virtual Edge, Cisco AVS, or Microsoft vSwitch; choose **Immediate** if you have VMware VDS.

- From the Resolution Immediacy drop-down list, accept the default **Immediate**.

- In the Encap Mode drop-down list, accept the default **Auto**.

- In the Port Encap (or Secondary VLAN for Micro-Seg) field, accept the default value.

- If you have Cisco ACI Virtual Edge, from the Switching Mode drop-down list, choose a mode.

- Choose **AVE** to switch the uSeg EPG through Cisco ACI Virtual Edge; choose **Native** to switch the uSeg EPG through the VMware VDS.

- Click **Update**, and then click **Finish.**

**Step 8.**    In the Navigation page for the tenant, open the folder for the uSeg EPG that you just created.

**Step 9.**    Click the uSeg **Attributes** folder.

The uSeg Attributes work pane appears, where you configure attributes to filter for VMs that you want to put into the uSeg EPG.

**Step 10.**    (Optional) If you will filter using VM-based attributes, in the uSeg Attributes work pane, from the match drop-down list, choose **Match Any** or **Match All.** The Match feature enables you to use multiple attributes to filter VMs for the uSeg EPG. The default is Match Any. The Match All feature is supported for VM-based attributes only.

**Step 11.**    Click the "+" or the "+(" icon to add a filtering statement. The "+" icon allows you to create a simple statement, one that creates a filter for a single attribute. You can add multiple simple statements to filter for multiple attributes. The "+(" icon allows you to create a block, or nested, statement, which allows you to set attributes in a hierarchy, which filters for the highest-level attribute first and then filters for lower-level attributes.

**Step 12.**    Complete one of the following series of steps to configure the filter.

You can configure an *IP-based* attribute:

- From the Select a Type drop-down list, choose **IP.**

- From the Use EPG Subnet? drop-down list, choose **Yes** or **No.**

   If you choose Yes, you will use a previously defined subnet as the IP attribute filter.

   If you choose No, enter the VM IP address or a subnet with the appropriate subnet mask in the field to the right of the Use EPG Subnet drop-down list.

- (Optional) Create a second IP Address filter by repeating the preceding substeps. You might want to do this to include discontinuous IP addresses in the microsegment.

- Click **Submit.**

Or a *MAC-based* attribute:

- From the Select a Type drop-down list, choose **MAC.**

- In the right field, enter the MAC address of the VM.

- Click **Submit.**

Or a *VM-based* custom attribute:

■ From the Select a Type drop-down list, choose **VM - Custom Attribute**.

■ Click the search icon next to the field to the right of the Select a Type drop-down list.

■ In the Select Custom Attribute dialog box, choose a controller from the Controller drop-down list.

■ From the VM drop-down list, choose a VM.

■ From the Attribute Name drop-down list, choose the name, and then click **SELECT**.

■ From the Operator drop-down list, choose an operator, and then enter a value in the field to the right of the drop-down list.

■ Click **Submit**.

Or a *VM-based* tag attribute (Cisco ACI Virtual Edge, Cisco AVS, and VMware VDS only):

■ From the Select a Type drop-down list, choose **VM - Tag**.

■ Click the magnifying glass icon next to the Category field, and in the Select VM Category dialog box, choose the category from the Category Name drop-down list, and then click **SELECT**. The category that you enter must be identical to the one assigned earlier for the tag in VMware vCenter.

■ From the Operator drop-down list, choose the appropriate operator.

■ Click the magnifying glass icon next to the field on the right, and in the Select VM Tag dialog box, select a tag from the Tag Name drop-down list and then click **SELECT**.

■ Click **Submit**.

Or *any another VM-based* attribute:

■ From the Select a Type drop-down list, choose a VM attribute.

■ From the Operator drop-down list, choose the appropriate operator.

■ Complete one of the following steps:

   ■ If you chose the Datacenter VM-based attribute, enter the name of the data center in the field to the right of the Operator drop-down list.

   ■ If you chose any other VM-based attribute, click the search icon next to the field to the right of the operator drop-down list, choose appropriate values for the attribute in the Select dialog box, and then click **SELECT**.

■ Click **Submit**.

**Step 13.**  Click the "+" or the "+(" icon to add additional attributes for the uSeg EPG.

**Step 14.**  Repeat step 2 through step 13 to create additional uSeg EPGs.

# Keychain Authentication

Public key infrastructure (PKI) services provide a scalable and trusted method of authentication. UCS Manager supports PKI only for the web sessions (https) to establish secure communication between the client's browser and UCS Manager for management purposes. To learn more about UCS Manager Communication Services, refer to the "Cisco UCS Manager Administration Management Guide."

The 350-601 DCCOR blueprint includes Keychain Authentication under Compute Security, whereas it should be part of Network Security. We are placing this section here to reflect the blueprint flow of topics. This section discusses keychain management on NX-OS and not UCS.

NX-OS keychain management allows you to create and maintain keychains, which are sequences of keys (sometimes called shared secrets). You can use keychains with features that secure communications with other devices by using key-based authentication. The device allows you to configure multiple keychains.

Some routing protocols that support key-based authentication can use a keychain to implement a hitless key rollover for authentication.

To maintain stable communications, each device that uses a protocol that is secured by key-based authentication must be able to store and use more than one key for a feature at the same time. Based on the send and accept lifetimes of a key, keychain management provides a secure mechanism to handle key rollover. The device uses the lifetimes of keys to determine which keys in a keychain are active. Each key in a keychain has two lifetimes, as follows:

- **Accept lifetime:** The time interval within which the device accepts the key during key exchange with another device.

- **Send lifetime:** The time interval within which the device sends the key during key exchange with another device.

You define the send and accept lifetimes of a key by using the following parameters:

- **Start-time:** The absolute time that the lifetime begins.

- **End-time:** The end time can be defined in one of the following ways:

  - The absolute time that the lifetime ends

  - The number of seconds after the start time that the lifetime ends

  - Infinite lifetime (no end-time)

During a key send lifetime, the device sends routing update packets with the key. The device does not accept communication from other devices when the key sent is not within the accept lifetime of the key on the device.

It is recommended that you configure key lifetimes that overlap within every keychain. This practice avoids failure of neighbor authentication due to the absence of active keys.

## NX-OS Keychain Configurations

Keychain configuration does not require a license. Any feature not included in a license package is bundled with the Cisco NX-OS system images.

**NOTE**   Changing the system clock impacts when keys are active.

Tables 18-30 and 18-31 describe the keychain commands.

**Table 18-30**   Keychain Commands

| Command | Purpose |
|---|---|
| **key chain** *name* | Creates the keychain and enters keychain configuration mode. |
| **key** *key-ID* | Enters key configuration mode for the key that you specified. The *key-ID* argument must be a whole number between 0 and 65,535. |
| **key-string** [*encryption-type*] *text-string* | Configures the text string for the key. The *text-string* argument is alphanumeric, case sensitive, and supports special characters. |
| | The *encryption-type* argument can be one of the following values: |
| | **0:** The *text-string* argument that you enter is unencrypted text. This is the default. |
| | **7:** The *text-string* argument that you enter is encrypted. The encryption method is a Cisco proprietary method. This option is useful when you are entering a text string based on the encrypted output of a **show key chain** command that you ran on another NX-OS device. |
| **accept-lifetime** [**local**] *start-time* **duration** *duration-value* \| **infinite** \| *end-time*] | Configures an accept lifetime for the key. By default, the device treats the *start-time* and *end-time* arguments as UTC. If you specify the **local** keyword, the device treats these times as local times. |
| | The *start-time* argument is the time of day and date that the key becomes active. |
| | Specify the end of the lifetime with one of the following options: |
| | **duration** *duration-value*: The length of the lifetime in seconds. The maximum length is 2,147,483,646 seconds (approximately 68 years). |
| | **infinite:** The accept lifetime of the key never expires. |
| | *end-time*: The *end-time* argument is the time of day and date that the key becomes inactive. |
| **send-lifetime** [**local**] *start-time* **duration** *duration-value* \| **infinite** \| *end-time*] | Configures a send lifetime for the key. By default, the device treats the *start-time* and *end-time* arguments as UTC. If you specify the local keyword, the device treats these times as local times. |
| | The *start-time* argument is the time of day and date that the key becomes active. |
| | You can specify the end of the send lifetime with one of the following options: |
| | **duration** *duration-value*: The length of the lifetime in seconds. The maximum length is 2,147,483,646 seconds (approximately 68 years). |
| | **infinite:** The send lifetime of the key never expires. |
| | *end-time*: The *end-time* argument is the time of day and date that the key becomes inactive. |

18

**Table 18-31**    AAA Passphrase and Locking User Accounts Commands

| Command | Purpose |
|---|---|
| show key chain | Displays the keychains configured on the device. |
| show key chain *name* | (Optional) Shows the keychain configuration, including the key configuration. |
| show key chain *name* [mode decrypt] | (Optional) Shows the keychain configuration, including the key text configuration. The mode decrypt option, which can be used by a device administrator only, displays the keys in cleartext. |

Example 18-28 shows how to configure key chains with four keys. First, key 0 has a lifetime of one day (August 19, 2019) with one-day activation. Second, key 1 has a three-month lifetime but will be active for only two months. Key 2 has a lifetime of seven months and will be active for six months, and key 3 has a lifetime of seven months and will be active for seven months as well.

**Example 18-28**    *NX-OS Keychain Configuration*

```
SWITCH-A(config)# key chain dccor
SWITCH-A(config-keychain)# key 0
SWITCH-A(config-keychain-key)# key-string CIsC@123
SWITCH-A(config-keychain-key)# accept-lifetime 00:00:00 aug 19 2019 23:59:59 aug 19
2019
SWITCH-A(config-keychain-key)# send-lifetime 00:00:00 aug 19 2019 23:59:59 aug 19
2019
SWITCH-A(config-keychain-key)# exit
SWITCH-A(config-keychain)# key 1
SWITCH-A(config-keychain-key)# key-string My&3t2918
SWITCH-A(config-keychain-key)# accept-lifetime 00:00:00 aug 19 2019 23:59:59 oct 19
2019
SWITCH-A(config-keychain-key)# send-lifetime 00:00:00 sep 19 2019 23:59:59 oct 19
2019
SWITCH-A(config-keychain-key)# exit
SWITCH-A(config-keychain)# key 2
SWITCH-A(config-keychain-key)# key-string DC4C0r
SWITCH-A(config-keychain-key)# accept-lifetime 00:00:00 aug 12 2019 23:59:59 feb 12
2020
SWITCH-A(config-keychain-key)# send-lifetime 00:00:00 aug 12 2019 23:59:59 jan 12
2020
SWITCH-A(config-keychain)# key 3
SWITCH-A(config-keychain-key)# key-string N3tr0kP@Ss
SWITCH-A(config-keychain-key)# accept-lifetime 00:00:00 aug 12 2019 23:59:59 feb 12
2020
SWITCH-A(config-keychain-key)# send-lifetime 00:00:00 aug 12 2019 23:59:59 feb 12
2020
```

## Key Selection

To select a key, the router looks through its entire list of keys and sends the key-string of the lowest key number that is currently valid. Assuming today is September 15, 2019, both key 2 and key 3 would be the only valid keys of the four keys shown in Figure 18-17. Because key 2 is the lowest numbered key, this is the key that will be used to attempt authentication with the neighboring router.

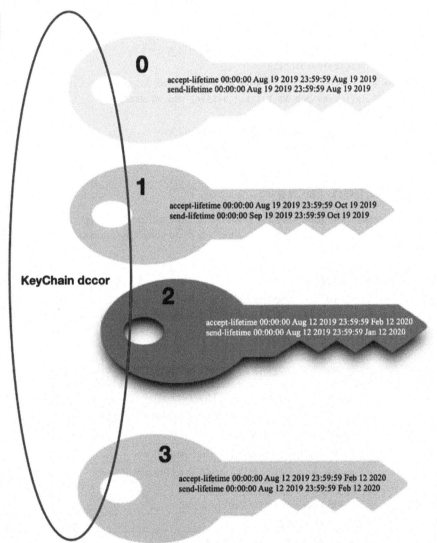

**Figure 18-17**  *Authentication Key Selection*

Based on the same information, if this router were to receive a key string as part of the authentication process, it would try to validate that key against the same key number in its own key chain. If the received key matched the same key number (key 2), the authentication would be validated, as in Example 18-29.

**Example 18-29** *Keychain Authentication Selection Result*

```
SWITCH A(config-keychain-key)# show key chain
Key-Chain dccor
  Key 0 -- text 7 "072c605f6d29485744"
    accept lifetime UTC (00:00:00 Aug 19 2019)-(23:59:59 Aug 19 2019)
    send lifetime UTC (00:00:00 Aug 19 2019)-(23:59:59 Aug 19 2019)
  Key 1 -- text 7 "0f498fdadde485741"
    accept lifetime UTC (00:00:00 Aug 19 2019)-(23:59:59 Oct 19 2019)
    send lifetime UTC (00:00:00 Sep 19 2019)-(23:59:59 Oct 19 2019)
  Key 2 -- text 7 "071a20495f0d000c031d"
    accept lifetime UTC (00:00:00 Sep 12 2019)-(23:59:59 Feb 12 2020) [active]
    send lifetime UTC (00:00:00 Oct 12 2019)-(23:59:59 Jan 12 2020)
Key 3 -- text 7 "212c605ead29235733"
    accept lifetime UTC (00:00:00 Aug 12 2019)-(23:59:59 Feb 12 2019)
    send lifetime UTC (00:00:00 Aug 12 2019)-(23:59:59 Feb 12 2019)
```

# Exam Preparation Tasks

As mentioned in the Introduction, you have a couple of choices for exam preparation: the exercises here, Chapter 21, "Final Preparation," and the exam simulation questions in the Pearson Test Prep software online.

## Review All Key Topics

Review the most important topics in the chapter, noted with the key topic icon in the outer margin of the page. Table 18-32 lists a reference to these key topics and the page numbers on which each is found.

**Table 18-32**   Key Topics for Chapter 18

| Key Topic Element | Description | Page |
|---|---|---|
| Example 18-7 | Creating a User Role Named User1 | 815 |
| Figure 18-2 | ARP Packet Validation on a VLAN Enabled for DAI | 818 |
| Figure 18-3 | Nexus DAI Network Topology | 821 |
| Figure 18-4 | DHCP Snooping Trusted and Untrusted Ports | 828 |
| Figure 18-5 | Port Security Limits MAC Address to Prevent Rogue Access | 832 |
| Example 18-23 | NX-OS Port Security Configuration | 837 |
| Figure 18-6 | Cisco Nexus Supervisor | 838 |
| Paragraph | Modular QoS Command-Line Interface | 842 |
| Example 18-26 | Copy a Predefined NX-OS Nexus 7000 CoPP | 850 |
| Example 18-27 | Modify a CoPP by Adding a New Class | 851 |
| Section | Cisco ACI Contract Configuration Parameters | 853 |
| Figure 18-10 | Exporting Contracts Between Tenants | 857 |

| Key Topic Element | Description | Page |
|---|---|---|
| Figure 18-11 | Exporting Contracts Between Private Networks | 858 |
| Section | Example: ACI Microsegmentation with VMs from a Single Application EPG | 862 |
| Section | Example: ACI Microsegmentation with VMs in Different Application EPGs | 863 |
| Section | Keychain Authentication | 868 |
| Paragraph | Key Selection | 871 |
| Figure 18-17 | Authentication Key Selection | 871 |

## Define Key Terms

Define the following key terms from this chapter, and check your answers in the Glossary.

authentication, authorization, and accounting (AAA); committed information rate (CIR); differentiated services code point (DSCP); Duplicate Address Detection (DAD); Extensible Authentication Protocol over User Datagram Protocol (EAPoUDP); Lightweight Directory Access Protocol (LDAP); Microsoft Challenge-Handshake Authentication Protocol (MSC-HAP); Network Admission Control (NAC); peak information rate (PIR); Remote Authentication Dial-In User Service (RADIUS); role-based access control (RBAC); Secure Shell (SSH); software-defined networking (SDN); Terminal Access Controller Access Control System (TACACS+); virtual machine (VM); Zero Trust (ZT)

## References

Cisco Nexus 9000 Series NX-OS Security Configuration Guide, Release 9.2(x): https://www.cisco.com/c/en/us/support/switches/nexus-9000-series-switches/ products-installation-and-configuration-guides-list.html

The Comprehensive Guide to Securing NX-OS Devices: https://www.ciscolive.com/c/dam/r/ciscolive/emea/docs/2016/pdf/BRKDCT-3102.pdf

Cisco Application Centric Infrastructure Best Practices Guide: https://www.cisco.com/c/en/us/td/docs/switches/datacenter/aci/apic/sw/1-x/ACI_Best_Practices/b_ACI_Best_Practices/b_ACI_Best_Practices_chapter_010.html

Cisco ACI Virtualization Guide, Release 3.1(1) and 3.1(2): https://www.cisco.com/c/en/us/td/docs/switches/datacenter/aci/apic/sw/3-x/virtualization/b_ACI_Virtualization_Guide_3_1_1/b_ACI_Virtualization_Guide_3_1_1_chapter_0100.html

Cisco UCS Manager Administration Management Guide 4.0: https://www.cisco.com/c/en/us/td/docs/unified_computing/ucs/ucs-manager/GUI-User-Guides/Admin-Management/4-0/b_Cisco_UCS_Admin_Mgmt_Guide_4-0.html

18

# CHAPTER 19

# Compute Security

Most computing platforms are designed to meet performance and function requirements with little or no attention to security. Compute hardening is an important security requirement for any data center platform. As a result, Cisco released a UCS hardening guide to help users secure Cisco Unified Computing System (Cisco UCS) platform devices to improve network security.

## This chapter covers the following key topics:

**Securing UCS Management Using Authentication, Authorization, and Accounting (AAA):** This section discusses the concepts of Cisco UCS authentication, authorization, and accounting. Later in this section, we discuss user attributes; two-factor authentications; LDAP, RADIUS, and TACACS+ providers; and group configurations.

## "Do I Know This Already?" Quiz

The "Do I Know This Already?" quiz enables you to assess whether you should read this entire chapter thoroughly or jump to the "Exam Preparation Tasks" section. If you are in doubt about your answers to these questions or your own assessment of your knowledge of the topics, read the entire chapter. Table 19-1 lists the major headings in this chapter and their corresponding "Do I Know This Already?" quiz questions. You can find the answers in Appendix A, "Answers to the 'Do I Know This Already?' Quizzes."

**Table 19-1** "Do I Know This Already?" Section-to-Question Mapping

| Foundation Topics Section | Questions |
|---|---|
| Securing UCS Management Using Authentication, Authorization, and Accounting (AAA) | 1–3 |

**CAUTION** The goal of self-assessment is to gauge your mastery of the topics in this chapter. If you do not know the answer to a question or are only partially sure of the answer, you should mark that question as wrong for purposes of the self-assessment. Giving yourself credit for an answer you correctly guess skews your self-assessment results and might provide you with a false sense of security.

1. What are the UCS authentication protocols that support dual-factor authentications? (Choose two answers.)

   a. LDAP

   b. RADIUS

   c. TACACS+

   d. Local

2. Which UCS authentication protocol does not require user attributes?

   a. LDAP with group mapping

   b. RADIUS

   c. TACACS+

   d. Keychain authentication

3. What port is used by LDAP SSL protocols?

   a. UDP 49

   b. UDP 1645/1646

   c. TCP 636

   d. TCP 389

## Foundation Topics

# Securing UCS Management Using Authentication, Authorization, and Accounting

The authentication, authorization, and accounting (AAA) framework is vital to securing network devices. The AAA framework provides authentication of management sessions, limits users to specific administrator-defined commands, and logs all commands entered by all users.

RADIUS and TACACS+ are both supported on the UCS compute system. TACACS+ encrypts the entire TCP payload, which includes both the username and password. RADIUS only encrypts the password. Therefore, TACACS+ is more secure. Additionally, you can use LDAP for user authentication. To encrypt the LDAP authentication exchange, enable the SSL option.

1. **Authentication:** Authentication is the process of establishing whether a client is who or what it claims to be in a particular context. A client can be an end user, a machine, or an application. Authentication mechanisms differ depending on the components that are communicating.

Cisco UCS provides two methods of user authentication:

■ Local accounts on the Cisco UCS Manager

■ Remote authentication using LDAP, RADIUS, or TACACS+

2. **Authorization:** Role management helps to manage authorization, which enables you to specify the resources that users are allowed to access. Role management lets you treat groups of users as a unit by assigning users to roles such as manager, sales, or member.

After you have established roles, you can create access rules. By using roles, you can establish these types of rules independent from individual users. Users can belong to more than one role.

Cisco UCS user roles include the following:

■ **AAA administrator:** Read/write access to users, roles, and AAA configuration. Read access to the rest of the system.

■ **Facility Manager:** Read-and-write access to power management operations through the power management privilege. Read access to the remaining system.

■ **Server Compute:** Read and write access to most aspects of service profiles. However, the user cannot create, modify or delete vNICs or vHBAs.

■ **Administrator:** Complete read/write access to the entire system. The default admin account is assigned this role by default and cannot be changed.

■ **Network administrator:** Read/write access to the fabric interconnect infrastructure and network security operations. Read access to the rest of the system.

■ **Operations:** Read/write access to system logs, including the syslog servers, and faults. Read access to the rest of the system.

■ **Read-only:** Read-only access to the system configuration with no privileges to modify the system state.

■ **Server equipment administrator:** Read/write access to physical server-related operations. Read access to the rest of the system.

■ **Server profile administrator:** Read/write access to logical server-related operations. Read access to the rest of the system.

■ **Server security administrator:** Read/write access to server security-related operations. Read access to the rest of the system.

■ **Storage administrator:** Read/write access to storage operations. Read access to the rest of the system.

## User RADIUS and TACACS+ Attributes

For RADIUS and TACACS+ configurations, you must configure a user attribute in each remote authentication provider through which users log in to the Cisco UCS Manager. This user attribute holds the roles and locales assigned to each user.

**NOTE** This step is not required for LDAP configurations that use LDAP group mapping to assign roles and locales.

When a user logs in, the Cisco UCS Manager does the following:

1. Queries the remote authentication service.

2. Validates the user.

3. If the user is validated, checks for the roles and locales assigned to that user.

Table 19-2 compares the user attribute requirements for the remote authentication providers supported by Cisco UCS.

**Table 19-2**  Comparison of User Attributes by Remote Authentication Provider

| Authentication Provider | Custom Attribute | Schema Extension | Attribute ID Requirements |
|---|---|---|---|
| LDAP | Not required if group mapping is used.<br><br>Optional if group mapping is not used. | Optional. You can choose to do one of the following:<br><br>■ Do not extend the LDAP schema and configure an existing, unused attribute that meets the requirements.<br><br>■ Extend the LDAP schema and create a custom attribute with a unique name, such as CiscoAVPair. | The Cisco LDAP implementation requires a Unicode type attribute.<br><br>If you choose to create the CiscoAVPair custom attribute, use the following attribute ID: 1.3.6.1.4.1.9.287247.1. |
| RADIUS | Optional. | (Optional) You can choose to do one of the following:<br><br>■ Do not extend the RADIUS schema and use an existing unused attribute that meets the requirements.<br><br>■ Extend the RADIUS schema and create a custom attribute with a unique name, such as cisco-avpair. | The vendor ID for the Cisco RADIUS implementation is 009, and the vendor ID for the attribute is 001.<br><br>The following syntax example shows how to specify multiple user roles and locales if you choose to create the cisco-avpair attribute:<br><br>shell:roles="admin,aaa"<br>shell:locales="L1,abc"<br><br>Use a comma (,) as the delimiter to separate multiple values. |

19

| Authentication Provider | Custom Attribute | Schema Extension | Attribute ID Requirements |
|---|---|---|---|
| TACACS+ | Required. | Required. You must extend the schema and create a custom attribute with the name cisco-av-pair. | The cisco-av-pair name is the string that provides the attribute ID for the TACACS+ provider. The following syntax example shows how to specify multiple user roles and locales when you create the cisco-av-pair attribute: cisco-av-pair=shell:roles="admin aaa" shell:locales* "L1 abc" Using an asterisk (*) in the cisco-av-pair attribute syntax flags the locale as optional, preventing authentication failures for other Cisco devices that use the same authorization profile. Use a space as the delimiter to separate multiple values. |

Example 19-1 shows an OID sample for a custom Cisco AVPair attribute.

**Example 19-1**  *Cisco AVPair Attribute Sample*

```
CN=CiscoAVPair,CN=Schema,
CN=Configuration,CN=X
objectClass: top
objectClass: attributeSchema
cn: CiscoAVPair
distinguishedName: CN=CiscoAVPair,CN=Schema,CN=Configuration,CN=X
instanceType: 0x4
uSNCreated: 26318654
attributeID: 1.3.6.1.4.1.9.287247.1
attributeSyntax: 2.5.5.12
isSingleValued: TRUE
showInAdvancedViewOnly: TRUE
adminDisplayName: CiscoAVPair
adminDescription: UCS User Authorization Field
oMSyntax: 64
LDAPDisplayName: CiscoAVPair
name: CiscoAVPair
objectCategory: CN=Attribute-Schema,CN=Schema,CN=Configuration,CN=X
```

## Two-Factor Authentication

The Cisco UCS Manager supports two-factor authentication for remote user logins, which adds a level of security to account logins. Two-factor authentication login requires a username, a token, and a password combination in the password field. You can provide a PIN, certificate, or token.

Two-factor authentication uses authentication applications that maintain token servers to generate one-time tokens for users during the login process and to store passwords in the AAA server. Requests are sent to the token server to retrieve a vendor-specific attribute. The Cisco UCS Manager expects the token server to integrate with the AAA server; therefore, it forwards the request to the AAA server. The password and token are validated at the same time by the AAA server. Users must enter the token and password sequence in the same order as it is configured in the AAA server.

Two-factor authentication is supported by associating RADIUS or TACACS+ provider groups with designated authentication domains and enabling two-factor authentication for those domains. Two-factor authentication does not support IPM and is not supported when the authentication realm is set to LDAP, local, or none.

## UCS Web Session Refresh and Session Timeout Period

The Web Session Refresh Period is the maximum amount of time allowed between refresh requests for a Cisco UCS Manager GUI web session. The Web Session Timeout is the maximum amount of time that can elapse after the last refresh request before a Cisco UCS Manager GUI web session becomes inactive.

You can increase the Web Session Refresh Period to a value greater than 60 seconds up to 172,800 seconds to avoid frequent session timeouts that require regenerating and re-entering a token and password multiple times. The default value is 7200 seconds when two-factor authentication is enabled and 600 seconds when two-factor authentication is not enabled.

You can specify a value between 300 and 172,800 for the Web Session Timeout Period. The default is 8000 seconds when two-factor authentication is enabled and 7200 seconds when two-factor authentication is not enabled.

## UCS LDAP Providers and Groups

UCS LDAP supports nested LDAP. You can add an LDAP group as a member of another group and nest groups to consolidate member accounts and to reduce the replication of traffic. Cisco UCS Manager release 2.1(2) and higher enable you to search LDAP groups that are nested within another group defined in an LDAP group map.

> **NOTE**   Nested LDAP search support is supported only for Microsoft Active Directory servers. The supported versions are Microsoft Windows 2003 SP3, Microsoft Windows 2008 R2, and Microsoft Windows 2012.

By default, *user rights are inherited* when you nest an LDAP group within another group. For example, if you make Group 1 a member of Group 2, the users in Group 1 have the same permissions as the members of Group 2. You can then search users that are members of Group 1 by choosing only Group 2 in the LDAP group map, instead of having to search Group 1 and Group 2 separately. You do not always need to create subgroups in a group map in the Cisco UCS Manager.

19

The LDAP group rule determines whether Cisco UCS should use LDAP groups when assigning user roles and locales to a remote user. The following scenario shows step by step how to create, modify, and delete a default LDAP provider.

The following scenario describes default LDAP provider configurations.

> **NOTE**   The properties that you configure in this example are default settings for all provider connections of this type defined in the Cisco UCS Manager. If an individual provider includes a setting for any of these properties, Cisco UCS uses that setting and ignores the default setting.

Before you start, if you are using Active Directory as your LDAP server, create a user account in the Active Directory server to bind it with Cisco UCS. Give this account a nonexpiring password.

- In the LDAP server, perform one of the following configurations:
    - Configure LDAP groups. LDAP groups contain user role and locale information.
    - Configure users with the attribute that holds the user role and locale information for the Cisco UCS Manager. You can choose whether to extend the LDAP schema for this attribute. If you do not want to extend the schema, use an existing LDAP attribute to hold the Cisco UCS user roles and locales. If you prefer to extend the schema, create a custom attribute, such as the CiscoAVPair attribute. Cisco LDAP implementation requires a Unicode type attribute. If you choose to create the CiscoAVPair custom attribute, use the following attribute ID: 1.3.6.1.4.1.9.287247.1.
    - For a cluster configuration, add the management port IPv4 or IPv6 addresses for both fabric interconnects. This configuration ensures that remote users can continue to log in if the first fabric interconnect fails and the system fails over to the second fabric interconnect. All login requests are sourced from these IP addresses, not the virtual IPv4 or IPv6 address used by the Cisco UCS Manager.
- If you want to use secure communications, create a trusted point containing the certificate of the root certificate authority (CA) of the LDAP server in the Cisco UCS Manager.
- If you need to change the LDAP providers or add or delete them, change the authentication realm for the domain to local, make the changes to the providers, and then change the domain authentication realm back to LDAP.

> **NOTE**   LDAP remote usernames that include special characters cannot log in to systems that are running NX-OS versions 2.2(3a) and later. The user cannot log in because of the NX-OS limitations where special characters (!, %, ^) are not supported in the username.

The following steps show how to create the LDAP provider:

**Step 1.**   In the Navigation pane, click **Admin**.

**Step 2.**   Expand **All > User Management > LDAP**, as in Figure 19-1.

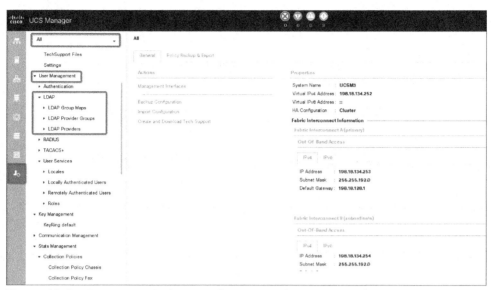

**Figure 19-1**   *Creating an LDAP Provider Main Page*

**Step 3.**   In the Work pane, click the **General** tab.

**Step 4.**   In the Actions area, click **Create LDAP Provider**.

**Step 5.**   On the Create LDAP Provider page of the wizard, complete all fields with appropriate LDAP service information. Complete the fields shown in Table 19-3 with information about the LDAP service you want to use, as in Figure 19-2, and then click **Next**.

**Table 19-3**   LDAP Provider Fields

| Name | Description |
|---|---|
| Hostname/FDQN (or IP Address) field | The hostname, or IPv4 or IPv6 address, on which the LDAP provider resides. If SSL is enabled, this field must exactly match a Common Name (CN) in the security certificate of the LDAP database. |
| | **NOTE:** If you use a host name rather than an IPv4 or IPv6 address, you must configure a DNS server. If the Cisco UCS domain is not registered with Cisco UCS Central or DNS management is set to local, configure a DNS server in the Cisco UCS Manager. If the Cisco UCS domain is registered with Cisco UCS Central and DNS management is set to global, configure a DNS server in Cisco UCS Central. |
| Order field | The order that the Cisco UCS uses this provider to authenticate users. |
| | Enter an integer between 1 and 16, or enter lowest-available or 0 (zero) if you want Cisco UCS to assign the next available order based on the other providers defined in this Cisco UCS domain. |
| Bind DN field | The distinguished name (DN) for an LDAP database account that has read and search permissions for all objects under the base DN. |
| | The maximum supported string length is 255 ASCII characters. |

19

| Name | Description |
|------|-------------|
| Base DN field | The specific distinguished name in the LDAP hierarchy where the server begins a search when a remote user logs in and the system attempts to obtain the user's DN based on the username. You can set the length of the base DN to a maximum of 255 characters minus the length of CN=username, where username identifies the remote user attempting to access the Cisco UCS Manager using LDAP authentication. |
| | This value is required unless a default base DN has been set on the LDAP General tab. |
| Port field | The port through which Cisco UCS communicates with the LDAP database. The standard port number is 389. |
| Enable SSL check box | If this box is checked, encryption is required for communications with the LDAP database. If it is unchecked, authentication information will be sent as clear text. |
| | LDAP uses STARTTLS. This allows encrypted communication using port 389. |
| | If it is checked, do not change the port to 636; leave it as 389. Cisco UCS negotiates a TLS session on port 636 for SSL, but initial connection starts unencrypted on 389. |
| Filter field | The LDAP search is restricted to those usernames that match the defined filter. |
| | This value is required unless a default filter has been set on the LDAP General tab. |
| Attribute field | An LDAP attribute that stores the values for the user roles and locales. This property is always a name-value pair. The system queries the user record for the value that matches this attribute name. |
| | If you do not want to extend your LDAP schema, you can configure an existing, unused LDAP attribute with the Cisco UCS roles and locales. Alternatively, you can create an attribute named CiscoAVPair in the remote authentication service with the following attribute ID: 1.3.6.1.4.1.9.287247.1. |
| | This value is required unless a default attribute has been set on the LDAP General tab. |
| Password field | The password for the LDAP database account specified in the Bind DN field. You can enter any standard ASCII characters except for space, [ss] (section sign), ? (question mark), or = (equal sign). |
| Confirm Password field | The LDAP database password repeated for confirmation purposes. |

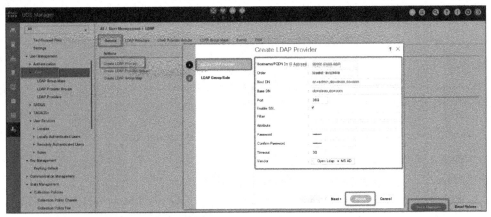

**Figure 19-2**  *LDAP Provider Fields*

**Step 6.**    On the LDAP Group Rule page of the wizard, complete all fields with the appropriate LDAP group rule information as shown in Figure 19-3.

**NOTE**   Role and locale assignment is cumulative. If a user is included in multiple groups, or has a role or locale specified in the LDAP attribute, Cisco UCS assigns that user all the roles and locales mapped to any of those groups or attributes.

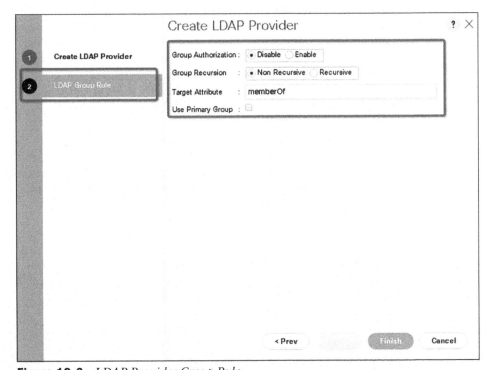

**Figure 19-3**  *LDAP Provider Group Rule*

**Step 7.**    Click **Finish**, and then **Save Changes**.

> **NOTE**   If your implementations involve a single LDAP database, select LDAP as the authentication service, but if your implementations involve multiple LDAP databases, you need to configure an LDAP provider group.

The following steps show how to modify an existing LDAP group rule:

**Step 1.**    In the Navigation pane, click **Admin**.

**Step 2.**    Expand **All > User Management > LDAP**.

**Step 3.**    Expand **LDAP Providers** and choose the LDAP provider for which you want to change the group rule.

**Step 4.**    In the Work pane, click the **General** tab.

**Step 5.**    In the LDAP Group Rules area, complete the fields shown in Table 19-4.

**Table 19-4**    LDAP Provider Fields

| Name | Description |
|---|---|
| Group Authorization field | Whether Cisco UCS also searches LDAP groups when authenticating and assigning user roles and locales to remote users. This can be one of the following: |
| | **Disable:** Cisco UCS does not access any LDAP groups. |
| | **Enable:** Cisco UCS searches all LDAP groups mapped in this Cisco UCS domain. If the remote user is found, Cisco UCS assigns the user roles and locales defined for that LDAP group in the associated LDAP group map. |
| | **NOTE:** Role and locale assignment is cumulative. If a user is included in multiple groups, or has a role or locale specified in the LDAP attribute, Cisco UCS assigns that user all the roles and locales mapped to any of those groups or attributes. |
| Group Recursion field | Whether Cisco UCS searches both the mapped groups and their parent groups. This can be one of the following: |
| | **Non-Recursive:** Cisco UCS searches only the groups mapped in this Cisco UCS domain. If none of the groups containing the user explicitly set the user's authorization properties, Cisco UCS uses the default settings. |
| | **Recursive:** Cisco UCS searches each mapped group and all its parent groups for the user's authorization properties. These properties are cumulative, so for each group Cisco UCS finds with explicit authorization property settings, it applies those settings to the current user. Otherwise, it uses the default settings. |
| Target Attribute field | The attribute Cisco UCS uses to determine group membership in the LDAP database. The supported string length is 63 characters. |
| Use Primary Group field | The attribute Cisco UCS uses to determine whether the primary group can be configured as an LDAP group map for membership validation. With this option, the Cisco UCS Manager can download and verify the primary group membership of the user. |

**Step 6.**    Click **Save Changes** (see Figure 19-4).

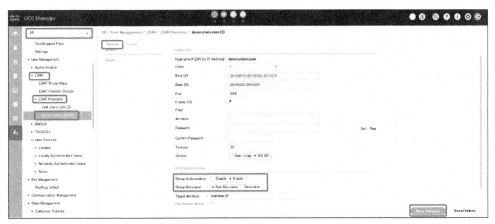

**Figure 19-4**    *LDAP Group Rules*

The following steps show how to delete an existing LDAP group:

**Step 1.**    In the Navigation pane, click **Admin**.

**Step 2.**    Expand **All > User Management > LDAP**.

**Step 3.**    Expand **LDAP Providers**.

**Step 4.**    Right-click the LDAP provider that you want to delete and choose **Delete**.

**Step 5.**    If a confirmation dialog box displays, click **Yes** (see Figure 19-5).

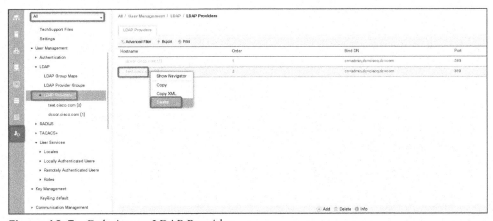

**Figure 19-5**    *Deleting an LDAP Provider*

## LDAP Group Mapping

LDAP group mapping eliminates the requirement to define role or locale information in the LDAP user object. The UCS Manager can use group membership information to assign a role or locale to an LDAP user during login for organizations using LDAP groups to restrict access to LDAP databases.

When a user logs in to the Cisco UCS Manager, the LDAP group map pulls information about the user's role and locale. If the role and locale criteria match the information in the policy, access is granted. The Cisco UCS Manager supports a maximum of 28, 128, or 160 LDAP group maps depending on the release version.

> **NOTE** Cisco UCS Manager Release 3.1(1) supports a maximum of 128 LDAP group maps, and Release 3.1(2) and later support a maximum of 160 LDAP group maps.

The role and locale definitions that you configure locally in the Cisco UCS Manager do not update automatically based on changes to an LDAP directory. When deleting or renaming LDAP groups in an LDAP directory, you must also update the Cisco UCS Manager with the change.

You can configure an LDAP group map to include any of the following combinations of roles and locales:

- Roles only
- Locales only
- Both roles and locales

For example, consider an LDAP group representing a group of server administrators at a specific location. The LDAP group map might include user roles such as server profile and server equipment. To restrict access to server administrators at a specific location, you can set the locale to a particular site name. The following scenario shows how to create and delete the LDAP group map.

> **NOTE** The Cisco UCS Manager includes out-of-the-box user roles but does not include any locales. Mapping an LDAP provider group to a locale requires that you create a custom locale.

This example shows step by step how to create and delete LDAP group maps. Before adding an LDAP group map, you need to configure the LDAP server. The LDAP server configuration requirements are as follows:

- Create an LDAP group in the LDAP server.
- Configure the distinguished name for the LDAP group in the LDAP server.
- Create locales in the Cisco UCS Manager (optional).
- Create custom roles in the Cisco UCS Manager (optional).

After configuring the LDAP server, follow these steps to create an LDAP group mapping:

**Step 1.** In the Navigation pane, click **Admin.**

**Step 2.** Expand **All > User Management > LDAP.**

**Step 3.**   Right-click **LDAP Group Maps** and choose **Create LDAP Group Map**.

**Step 4.**   In the Create LDAP Group Map dialog box, specify all LDAP group map information as appropriate (see Figure 19-6).

**NOTE**   The name that you specify in the LDAP Group DN field must match the name in the LDAP database.

**NOTE**   If you use a special character in the LDAP Group DN field, you must prefix the special character with an escape character \ (single backslash).

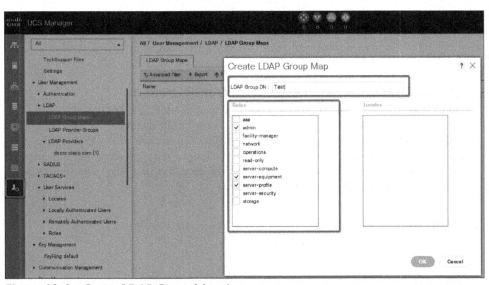

**Figure 19-6**   *Create LDAP Group Mapping*

The following steps show how to delete an existing LDAP group map:

**Step 1.**   In the Navigation pane, click **Admin**.

**Step 2.**   Expand **All > User Management > LDAP**.

**Step 3.**   Expand LDAP Group Maps.

**Step 4.**   Right-click the LDAP group map that you want to delete and choose **Delete**.

**Step 5.**   If a confirmation dialog box displays, click **Yes** (see Figure 19-7).

**Figure 19-7**  *Deleting LDAP Group Mapping*

## RADIUS and TACACS+ Authentication Configurations

To add a RADIUS or TACACS+ provider, first you need to configure RADIUS/TACACS+ properties, and after that to add RADIUS/TACACS+ server information. You can configure default settings; default properties apply to all provider connections of this type defined in the Cisco UCS Manager. If an individual provider includes a setting for any of these properties, Cisco UCS uses provider setting and ignores the default setting. The following scenario shows step by step how to create a UCS provider.

> **NOTE**  RADIUS authentication uses the Password Authentication Protocol (PAP).

> **NOTE**  The Cisco UCS Manager supports a maximum of 16 RADIUS providers.

This example shows you step by step how to create RADIUS/TACACS+ remote authentication. Before adding a RADIUS provider, you need to perform the following RADIUS server configurations:

■ Configure users with the attribute that holds the user role and locale information for the Cisco UCS Manager. You can choose whether to extend the RADIUS schema for this attribute. If you do not want to extend the schema, use an existing RADIUS attribute to hold the Cisco UCS user roles and locales. If you prefer to extend the schema, create a custom attribute, such as the cisco-avpair attribute.

The vendor ID for the Cisco RADIUS implementation is 009, and the vendor ID for the attribute is 001.

The following syntax example shows how to specify multiple user roles and locales if you choose to create the cisco-avpair attribute: shell:roles="admin,aaa" shell:locales="L1,abc". Use a comma (,) as the delimiter to separate multiple values.

■ For a cluster configuration, add the management port IPv4 or IPv6 addresses for both fabric interconnects. This configuration ensures that remote users can continue to log in if the first fabric interconnect fails and the system fails over to the second fabric interconnect. All login requests are sourced from these IP addresses, not the virtual IP address used by the Cisco UCS Manager.

Similar for TACACS+, before adding the provider, you need to perform the following TACACS+ server configurations:

■ Create the cisco-av-pair attribute. You cannot use an existing TACACS+ attribute.

■ The cisco-av-pair name is the string that provides the attribute ID for the TACACS+ provider.

■ The following syntax example shows how to specify multiple user roles and locales when you create the cisco-av-pair attribute: cisco-av-pair=shell:roles="admin aaa" shell:locales*"L1 abc". Using an asterisk (*) in the cisco-av-pair attribute syntax flags the locale as optional, preventing authentication failures for other Cisco devices that use the same authorization profile. Use a space as the delimiter to separate multiple values.

■ For a cluster configuration, add the management port IPv4 or IPv6 addresses for both fabric interconnects. This configuration ensures that remote users can continue to log in if the first fabric interconnect fails and the system fails over to the second fabric interconnect. All login requests are sourced from these IP addresses, not the virtual IP address used by the Cisco UCS Manager.

After configuring the remote authentication server (RADIUS or TACACS+), you can configure authentication server properties. The following steps show how to configure the RADIUS server default properties:

**Step 1.**　In the Navigation pane, click **Admin**.

**Step 2.**　Expand **User Management > RADIUS**.

**Step 3.**　In the Properties area, complete all fields.

**Step 4.**　Click **Save Changes**.

The following steps show how to configure TACACS+ server default properties:

**Step 1.**　In the Navigation pane, click **Admin**.

**Step 2.**　Expand **User Management > TACACS+**.

**Step 3.**　In the Properties area, complete the **Timeout** field.

**Step 4.**　Click **Save Changes**.

After configuring remote authentication server properties, the next step is to configure the authentication server provider. The following steps show how to configure the UCS RADIUS server provider:

**Step 1.**　In the Navigation pane, click **Admin**.

**Step 2.**　Expand **All > User Management > RADIUS**.

**Step 3.** In the Create RADIUS Provider dialog box, specify all appropriate RADIUS service information.

**NOTE** If you use a host name rather than an IPv4 or IPv6 address, you must ensure that a DNS server is configured for the host name.

**Step 4.** Click **OK** and then **Save Changes** (see Figure 19-8).

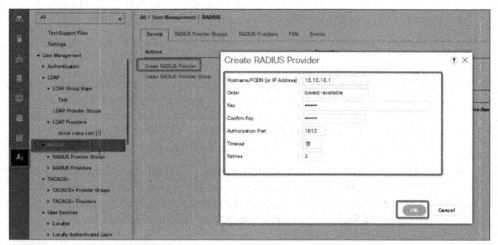

**Figure 19-8** *Creating a RADIUS Provider*

**NOTE** If your implementations involve a single RADIUS database, select RADIUS as the primary authentication service, but if your implementations involve multiple RADIUS databases, configure a RADIUS provider group.

The following steps show how to configure the UCS TACACS+ server provider:

**Step 1.** In the Navigation pane, click **Admin**.

**Step 2.** Expand **All > User Management > TACACS+**.

**Step 3.** In the Actions area of the General tab, click **Create TACACS+ Provider**.

**Step 4.** In the Create TACACS+ Provider dialog box, do the following:

■ Complete all fields with TACACS+ service information, as appropriate.

**NOTE** If you use a host name rather than an IPv4 or IPv6 address, you must ensure a DNS server is configured for the host name.

■ Click **OK**.

**Step 5.** Click **Save Changes**.

**NOTE**  If your implementations involve a single TACACS+ database, select TACACS+ as the primary authentication service, but if your implementations involve multiple TACACS+ databases, configure a TACACS+ provider group.

The final step to activate a remote authentication server is to assign an authentication method to management.

The following steps show how to add remote access authentication to management:

**Step 1.**  In the Navigation pane, click **Admin**.

**Step 2.**  Expand **All > User Management > Authentication**.

**Step 3.**  Click **Native Authentication**.

**Step 4.**  In the Work pane, click the **General** tab.

**Step 5.**  To set the console, you can select the **Console Authentication** area, as in Figure 19-9. To set a default authentication, select **Default Authentication**, as in Figure 19-10. Then complete the fields described in Table 19-5.

**Table 19-5**  Authentication Method Fields

| Name | Description |
|---|---|
| Realm field | The method by which a user logging in to the console is authenticated. This can be one of the following: |
| | **Local:** The user account must be defined locally in this Cisco UCS domain. |
| | **RADIUS:** The user must be defined on the RADIUS server specified for this Cisco UCS domain. |
| | **TACACS+:** The user must be defined on the TACACS+ server specified for this Cisco UCS domain. |
| | **LDAP:** The user must be defined on the LDAP server specified for this Cisco UCS domain. |
| | **None:** If the user account is local to this Cisco UCS domain, no password is required when the user logs in to the console. |
| Provider Group drop-down list | The provider group to be used to authenticate a user logging in to the console. |
| | **NOTE:** The Provider Group drop-down list is displayed when you select LDAP, RADIUS, or TACACS+ as the method by which a user is authenticated. |
| Two-Factor Authentication | Two-factor authentication is available only when the Realm is set to RADIUS or TACACS+. When this check box is selected, the Console requires users whose accounts are authenticated by RADIUS or TACACS+ servers to enter a token plus a password to log in. |

**19**

**Step 6.**  Click **Save Changes**.

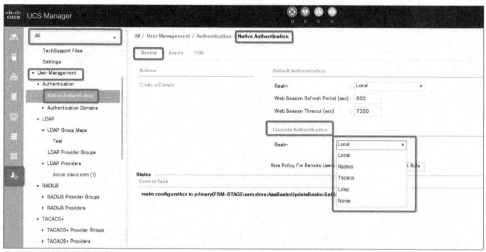

**Figure 19-9** *Setting UCS Management Console Authentication*

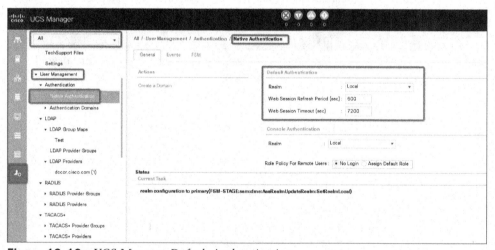

**Figure 19-10** *UCS Manager Default Authentication*

## UCS Remote Users Role Policy

By default, if user roles are not configured in the Cisco UCS Manager, read-only access is granted to all users logging in to the Cisco UCS Manager from a remote server using the LDAP, RADIUS, or TACACS+ protocols. For security reasons, it might be desirable to restrict access to those users matching an established user role in the Cisco UCS Manager.

You can configure the role policy for remote users in the following ways:

- **assign-default-role:** Does not restrict user access to the Cisco UCS Manager based on user roles. Read-only access is granted to all users unless other user roles have been defined in Cisco UCS Manager. This is the default behavior.

- **no-login:** Restricts user access to the Cisco UCS Manager based on user roles. If user roles have not been assigned for the remote authentication system, access is denied.

The following steps show how to configure the remote user role policy:

**Step 1.** In the Navigation pane, click **Admin**.

**Step 2.** Expand **All > User Management > Authentication**.

**Step 3.** Click **Native Authentication**.

**Step 4.** In the Work pane, click the **General** tab and complete the parameters shown in Table 19-6.

**Table 19-6** Remote Users Role Policy Fields

| Name | Description |
|---|---|
| Realm drop-down list | The default method by which a user is authenticated during remote login. This can be one of the following:<br>**Local:** The user account must be defined locally in this Cisco UCS domain.<br>**RADIUS:** The user account must be defined on the RADIUS server specified for this Cisco UCS domain.<br>**TACACS+:** The user account must be defined on the TACACS+ server specified for this Cisco UCS domain.<br>**LDAP:** The user account must be defined on the LDAP server specified for this Cisco UCS domain.<br>**None:** If the user account is local to this Cisco UCS domain, no password is required when the user logs in remotely. |
| Provider Group drop-down list | The default provider group to be used to authenticate the user during remote login.<br>**NOTE:** The Provider Group drop-down is displayed when you select LDAP, RADIUS, or TACACS+ as the method by which a user is authenticated. |
| Web Session Refresh Period (sec) | When a web client connects to Cisco UCS Manager, the client must send refresh requests to the Cisco UCS Manager to keep the web session active. This option specifies the maximum amount of time allowed between refresh requests for a user in this domain.<br>If this time limit is exceeded, the Cisco UCS Manager considers the web session inactive, but it does not terminate the session.<br>Specify an integer between 60 and 172,800. The default is 600 seconds when Two-Factor Authentication is not enabled and 7200 seconds when it is enabled. |
| Web Session Timeout (sec) | The maximum amount of time that can elapse after the last refresh request before the Cisco UCS Manager considers a web session as inactive. If this time limit is exceeded, the Cisco UCS Manager automatically terminates the web session.<br>Specify an integer between 300 and 172,800. The default is 7200 seconds when Two-Factor Authentication is not enabled and 8000 seconds when it is enabled. |

19

| Name | Description |
|------|-------------|
| Two Factor Authentication check box | Two-Factor Authentication is available only when the Realm is set to RADIUS or TACACS+. When you select this check box, the Cisco UCS Manager and the KVM Launch Manager require users whose accounts are authenticated by RADIUS or TACACS+ servers to enter a token plus a password to log in. When 60 seconds remain for the Web Session Refresh Period to expire, users must generate a new token and enter the token plus their password to continue the session. |
| | **NOTE:** After you enable two-factor authentication and save the configuration, the default Web Session Refresh Period (sec) changes to 7200, and the default Web Session Timeout (sec) changes to 8000. |

**Step 5.** In the Role Policy for Remote Users field, click one of the following radio buttons to determine what happens when a user attempts to log in and the remote authentication provider does not supply a user role with the authentication information:

- **No Login:** The user is not allowed to log in to the system, even if the username and password are correct.

- **Assign Default Role:** The user is allowed to log in with a read-only user role.

**Step 6.** Click **Save Changes.**

## Multiple Authentication Services Configuration

You can configure Cisco UCS to use multiple authentication services by configuring the following features:

- Provider groups

- Authentication domains

A provider group is a set of providers that the Cisco UCS accesses during the authentication process. All of the providers within a provider group are accessed in the order that the Cisco UCS provider uses to authenticate users. If all of the configured servers are unavailable or unreachable, the Cisco UCS Manager automatically falls back to the local authentication method using the local username and password.

The Cisco UCS Manager allows you to create a maximum of 16 provider groups, with a maximum of 8 providers allowed per group.

## Exam Preparation Tasks

As mentioned in the Introduction, you have a couple of choices for exam preparation: the exercises here, Chapter 21, "Final Preparation," and the exam simulation questions in the Pearson Test Prep software online.

## Review All Key Topics

Review the most important topics in the chapter, noted with the key topic icon in the outer margin of the page. Table 19-9 lists a reference to these key topics and the page numbers on which each is found.

**Table 19-9**    Key Topics for Chapter 19

| Key Topic Element | Description | Page |
|---|---|---|
| Section | User RADIUS and TACACS+ Attributes | 876 |
| Table 19-2 | Comparison of User Attributes by Remote Authentication Provider | 877 |
| Section | Two-Factor Authentication | 879 |
| Paragraph | LDAP provider configurations | 880 |
| Figure 19-2 | LDAP Provider Fields | 883 |
| Figure 19-6 | Create LDAP Group Mapping | 887 |

## Define Key Terms

Define the following key terms from this chapter, and check your answers in the Glossary.

American Standard Code for Information Interchange (ASCII); authentication, authorization, and accounting (AAA); Cisco attribute-value pair (Cisco AVPair); Cisco Nexus; Cisco NX-OS; Domain Name System (DNS); Lightweight Directory Access Protocol (LDAP); Password Authentication Protocol (PAP); Remote Authentication Dial-In User Service (RADIUS); role-based access control (RBAC); Terminal Access Controller Access Control System (TACACS+); virtual device context (VDC)

## References

Cisco Nexus 9000 Series NX-OS Security Configuration Guide, Release 9.2(x): https://www.cisco.com/c/en/us/support/switches/nexus-9000-series-switches/products-installation-and-configuration-guides-list.html

Cisco Nexus 7000 Series NX-OS Security Configuration Guide: https://www.cisco.com/c/en/us/td/docs/switches/datacenter/nexus7000/sw/security/config/cisco_nexus7000_security_config_guide_8x.html

Cisco UCS Manager Administration Management Guide 4.0: https://www.cisco.com/c/en/us/td/docs/unified_computing/ucs/ucs-manager/GUI-User-Guides/Admin-Management/4-0/b_Cisco_UCS_Admin_Mgmt_Guide_4-0.html

19

# CHAPTER 20

# Storage Security

Like IP infrastructure, the storage infrastructure must be protected from security vulnerabilities such as denial of service (DoS) and other malware attacks. In addition, elevation of privileges can also occur if a guest's account is not managed properly. These security risks can result in data being stolen and corrupted and applications not functioning properly. Because of its broad capabilities, unique security considerations must be addressed when deploying the storage infrastructure in your network. The Cisco MDS 9000 NX-OS software supports advanced security features that provide security within a storage-area network (SAN). These features protect your network against deliberate or unintentional disruptions from internal or external threats.

## This chapter discusses the following key topics:

**Authentication, Authorization, and Accounting (AAA):** This section discusses the concepts of authentication, authorization, and accounting. Later in this section, we discuss server groups, server monitoring, remote and local AAA services, server distribution using CFS, and implications of merging RADIUS and TACACS+ configurations.

**User Accounts and RBAC:** This section discusses user roles, rules, and policies related to user roles, along with RBAC sample configuration.

**Port Security:** This section discusses port security configuration and verification.

**Fabric Binding:** This section discusses fabric binding configuration and verification. Later in this section, we compare port security with fabric binding features.

## "Do I Know This Already?" Quiz

The "Do I Know This Already?" quiz enables you to assess whether you should read this entire chapter thoroughly or jump to the "Exam Preparation Tasks" section. If you are in doubt about your answers to these questions or your own assessment of your knowledge of the topics, read the entire chapter. Table 20-1 lists the major headings in this chapter and their corresponding "Do I Know This Already?" quiz questions. You can find the answers in Appendix A, "Answers to the 'Do I Know This Already?' Quizzes."

**Table 20-1** "Do I Know This Already?" Section-to-Question Mapping

| Foundation Topics Section | Questions |
|---|---|
| Authentication, Authorization, and Accounting (AAA) | 1–2 |
| User Accounts and RBAC | 3 |
| Port Security | 4–5 |
| Fabric Binding | 6–7 |

1. Which of the following statements are INCORRECT regarding TACACS+? (Choose two answers.)

    a. TACACS+ uses the TCP transport protocol to send data between the AAA client and server, making reliable transfers with a connection-oriented protocol.

    b. TACACS+ provides independent, modular AAA facilities. Authorization can be done without authentication.

    c. TACACS+ encrypts passwords only.

    d. TACACS+ is an open protocol supported by multiple vendors.

2. The LDAP client/server protocol uses which TCP port number for transport requirements?

    a. 2003

    b. 1812

    c. 389

    d. 49

3. Which of the following statements are CORRECT regarding user roles on Cisco MDS 9000 Series Switches? (Choose two answers.)

    a. User roles contain rules that define the operations allowed for the user who is assigned the role.

    b. Each user role can contain multiple rules, but each user cannot have multiple roles.

    c. Up to 16 rules can be configured for each role.

    d. User roles cannot be used to create VSAN administrators.

4. Which of the following statements are TRUE regarding the port security feature? (Choose two answers.)

    a. Port security binds the fabric at the switch level.

    b. Port security requires activation on a per-VSAN basis.

    c. Port security cannot be distributed by CFS.

    d. Port security uses pWWNs/nWWNs or fWWNs/sWWNs.

5. Port security can be configured using which of the following methods? (Choose three answers.)

    a. Manual Database Configuration

    b. Auto-Learning without CFS Distribution

    c. Fabric Binding

    d. Auto-Learning with CFS Distribution

6. Which statements are TRUE regarding the fabric binding feature? (Choose two answers.)

   a. The fabric binding feature helps prevent unauthorized switches from joining the fabric or disrupting current fabric operations.

   b. Fabric binding is configured on a per-VSAN basis.

   c. Fabric binding can be distributed by CFS and hence configured automatically on each switch in the fabric.

   d. Fabric binding uses pWWNs/nWWNs.

7. Which databases are managed by the fabric binding feature? (Choose two answers.)

   a. Configuration database

   b. Inactive database

   c. Active database

   d. Startup database

## Foundation Topics

# Authentication, Authorization, and Accounting

The authentication, authorization, and accounting (AAA) feature verifies the identity of, grants access to, and tracks the actions of users managing a switch. All Cisco MDS 9000 Series Switches use Remote Authentication Dial-In User Service (RADIUS), Terminal Access Controller Access Control System Plus (TACACS+), or Lightweight Directory Access Protocol (LDAP) protocols to provide solutions using remote AAA servers. The AAA Services can also be provided locally by the switch. This security feature provides a centralized user account management capability for AAA servers.

AAA uses security protocols to administer its security functions. If your router or access server is acting as a network access server, the communication between your network access server and the RADIUS, TACACS+, or LDAP security server is through AAA.

Based on the user ID and password combination provided, switches perform local authentication or authorization using the local database or remote authentication or authorization using an AAA server. A preshared secret key provides security for communication between the switch and AAA servers. This secret key can be configured for all AAA servers or for only a specific AAA server. This security feature provides a central management capability for AAA servers.

In this chapter, we concentrate on AAA functionality on Cisco MDS switches. Cisco MDS switches can be accessed using various methods, including the command-line interface (CLI) or Simple Network Management Protocol (SNMP). You can access the CLI using the console (serial connection), Telnet, or Secure Shell (SSH). You can secure the access to any switch in the Cisco MDS 9000 Series Switches using the AAA switch functionalities. AAA switch functionality on any switch in the Cisco MDS 9000 Series Switches can be configured using the CLI, Data Center Network Manager (DCNM), or an SNMP application.

## Authentication

Authentication is the process of verifying the identity of the person or device accessing the switch. This identity verification is based on the user ID and password combination provided by the entity trying to access the switch. Cisco MDS 9000 Series Switches allow you to perform local authentication (using the local lookup database) or remote authentication (using one or more RADIUS or TACACS+ servers).

## Authorization

Authorization provides access control. It is the process of assembling a set of attributes that describe what the user is authorized to perform. Based on the user ID and password combination, the user is authenticated and authorized to access the network as per the assigned role. We discuss user roles later in this chapter. You can configure parameters that can prevent unauthorized access by a user, provided the switches use the TACACS+ protocol.

AAA authorization is the process of assembling a set of attributes that describe what the user is authorized to perform. Authorization in the Cisco NX-OS software is provided by attributes that are downloaded from AAA servers. Remote security servers, such as RADIUS, TACACS+, and LDAP, authorize users for specific rights by associating attribute-value (AV) pairs, which define those rights with the appropriate user.

The following authorization roles exist in all Cisco MDS switches:

- **Network operator (network-operator):** Has permission to view the configuration only. The operator cannot make any configuration changes.

- **Network administrator (network-admin):** Has permission to execute all commands and make configuration changes. The administrator can also create and customize up to 64 additional roles.

- **Default-role:** Has permission to use the GUI (DCNM and Device Manager). This access is automatically granted to all users for accessing the GUI.

- **server-admin:** Predefined system role for server administrators.

These roles cannot be changed or deleted. You can create additional roles and configure the following options:

- Configure role-based authorization by assigning user roles locally or using remote AAA servers.

- Configure user profiles on a remote AAA server to contain role information. This role information is automatically downloaded and used when the user is authenticated through the remote AAA server.

**NOTE**   If a user belongs to only one of the newly created roles and that role is subsequently deleted, the user immediately defaults to the network-operator role.

20

## Accounting

The accounting feature tracks and maintains a log of every management configuration used to access the switch. This information can be used to generate reports for troubleshooting and auditing purposes. Accounting logs can be stored locally or sent to remote AAA servers. The default maximum size of the accounting log is 250,000 bytes and cannot be changed.

Configuration operations are automatically recorded in the accounting log if they are performed in configuration mode. Additionally, important system events (for example, configuration save and system switchover) are also recorded in the accounting log.

## Server Groups

You can specify remote AAA servers for authentication, authorization, and accounting using server groups. A server group is a set of remote AAA servers implementing the same AAA protocol. The purpose of a server group is to provide for failover servers in case a remote AAA server fails to respond. If the first remote server in the group fails to respond, the next remote server in the group is tried until one of the servers sends a response. If all the AAA servers in the server group fail to respond, that server group option is considered a failure. If required, you can specify multiple server groups.

## AAA Service Configuration Options

AAA configuration in Cisco MDS 9000 Series Switches is service based. You can have separate AAA configurations for the following services:

- Telnet or SSH login (DCNM and Device Manager login)
- Console login
- iSCSI authentication
- FC-SP authentication
- Accounting

In general, server group, local, and none are the three options that can be specified for any service in an AAA configuration. Each option is tried in the order specified. If all the options fail, local is tried.

> **NOTE**  Even if local is not specified as one of the options, it is tried by default if all AAA servers configured for authentication are unreachable. The user has the flexibility to disable this fallback.

## AAA Server Monitoring

An unresponsive AAA server introduces a delay in the processing of AAA requests. An MDS switch can periodically monitor an AAA server to check whether it is responding (or alive) to save time in processing AAA requests. The switch marks unresponsive AAA servers as dead and does not send AAA requests to any dead AAA servers. The switch periodically monitors dead AAA servers and brings them to the alive state when they respond. This monitoring process verifies that an AAA server is in a working state before real AAA requests are sent its way. Whenever an AAA server changes to the dead or alive state, an SNMP trap is generated, and the MDS switch warns the administrator that a failure is taking place before it can impact performance.

Figure 20-1 depicts AAA server states.

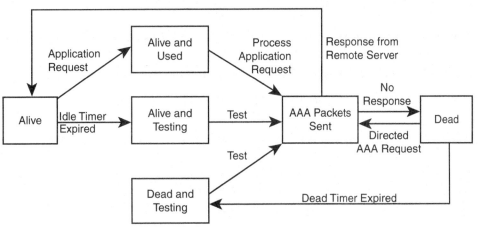

**Figure 20-1**   *AAA Server States*

The monitoring interval for alive servers and dead servers is different and can be configured by the user. AAA server monitoring is performed by sending a test authentication request to the AAA server.

The AAA server monitoring parameters can be configured globally for all servers or individually for a specific server. The global configurations will apply to all servers that do not have individual monitoring parameters defined. For any server, the individual test parameter defined for that particular server will always get precedence over the global settings.

## Remote AAA Services

Remote AAA services provided through RADIUS and TACACS+ protocols have the following advantages over local AAA services:

- User password lists for each switch in the fabric can be managed more easily.

- AAA servers are already deployed widely across enterprises and can be easily adopted.

- The accounting log for all switches in the fabric can be centrally managed.

- User role mapping for each switch in the fabric can be managed more easily.

If you prefer using remote AAA servers, follow these guidelines:

- Ensure that a minimum of one AAA server should be IP reachable.

- Be sure to configure a desired local AAA policy because this policy is used if all AAA servers are not reachable.

- Make sure AAA servers are easily reachable if an overlay Ethernet LAN is attached to the switch.

- Ensure SANs connected to the switch have at least one gateway switch connected to the Ethernet LAN reaching the AAA servers.

20

## RADIUS

RADIUS is a distributed client and server system implemented through AAA that secures networks against unauthorized access. In the Cisco implementation, RADIUS clients run on Cisco switches and send authentication requests to a central RADIUS server that contains all user authentication and network service access information.

You can add up to 64 RADIUS servers. RADIUS keys are always stored in encrypted form in persistent storage. The running configuration also displays encrypted keys.

Example 20-1 shows the steps required to configure RADIUS on MDS Switch.

**Example 20-1** *RADIUS Configuration on MDS Switch*

```
! Entering configuration mode

switch# configure terminal

! Configuring the host IP and the preshared key for the selected RADIUS server. In
this example, the host is 10.71.58.91 and the key is RadKey.

switch(config)# radius-server host 10.71.58.91 key RadKey

! Configuring the destination UDP port number to which the RADIUS authentication
messages should be sent. In this example, the host is 10.71.58.91 and the authenti-
cation port is 2003. The default authentication port is 1812, and the valid range is
0 to 65366.

switch(config)# radius-server host 10.71.58.91 auth-port 2003

! Configuring the destination UDP port number to which RADIUS accounting messages
should be sent. The default accounting port is 1813, and the valid range is 0 to
65366.

switch(config)# radius-server host 10.71.58.91 acct-port 2004

! Configuring the AAA server to be used for accounting purposes. If neither the
authentication nor the accounting options are specified, the server is used for both
accounting and authentication purposes.

switch(config)# radius-server host 10.71.58.91 accounting

! Configuring the global timeout period in seconds for the switch to wait for a
response from all RADIUS+ servers before the switch declares a timeout failure. The
time ranges from 1 to 1440 seconds.

switch(config)# radius-server timeout 30
```

```
! Configuring the number of times (3) the switch tries to connect to a RADIUS
server(s) before reverting to local authentication. By default, a switch retries
transmission to a RADIUS server only once before reverting to local authentication.
You can increase this number up to a maximum of five retries per server.

switch(config)# radius-server retransmit 3

! Configuring the dead timer interval value in minutes. The valid range is 1 to
1440 minutes. The dead timer specifies the interval that the MDS switch waits, after
declaring that a RADIUS server is dead, before sending out a test packet to deter-
mine if the server is now alive.

switch(config)# radius-server deadtime 5
switch(config)# end

! Verifying RADIUS server details

switch# show radius-server
retransmission count:3
timeout value:30
deadtime value:5
total number of servers:1

following RADIUS servers are configured:
        10.71.58.91:
                available for authentication on port:2003
                available for accounting on port:2004
                RADIUS shared secret:********

! Verifying the radius-server statistics

switch# show radius-server statistics 10.71.58.91
Server is not monitored

Authentication Statistics
        failed transactions: 0
        sucessfull transactions: 0
        requests sent: 0
        requests timed out: 0
        responses with no matching requests: 0
        responses not processed: 0
        responses containing errors: 0

Accounting Statistics
        failed transactions: 0
        sucessfull transactions: 0
```

20

```
    requests sent: 0
    requests timed out: 0
    responses with no matching requests: 0
    responses not processed: 0
    responses containing errors: 0


! Creating a server group named DCCORE and configuring the radius server at IPv4
address 10.71.58.91 to be tried first within the server group DCCORE.

switch(config)# aaa group server radius DCCORE
switch(config-radius)# server 10.71.58.91
switch(config-radius)# end


! Verifying radius-server groups

switch# show radius-server groups
total number of groups:2

following RADIUS server groups are configured:
        group radius:
                server: all configured radius servers
                deadtime is 5
        group DCCORE:
                server: 10.71.58.91 on auth-port 2003, acct-port 2004
                deadtime is 5
```

## TACACS+

TACACS+ is a security application implemented through AAA that provides a centralized validation of users who are attempting to gain access to a router or network access server. TACACS+ services are maintained in a database on a TACACS+ daemon that typically runs on a UNIX or Windows NT workstation. TACACS+ provides for separate and modular authentication, authorization, and accounting facilities.

TACACS+ is a client/server protocol that uses TCP (TCP port 49) for transport requirements. All switches in the Cisco MDS 9000 Series Switches provide centralized authentication using the TACACS+ protocol. TACACS+ has the following advantages over RADIUS authentication:

- Provides independent, modular AAA facilities. Authorization can be done without authentication.

- Uses the TCP transport protocol to send data between the AAA client and server, making reliable transfers with a connection-oriented protocol.

- Encrypts the entire protocol payload between the switch and the AAA server to ensure higher data confidentiality. The RADIUS protocol only encrypts passwords.

You need to configure the TACACS+ preshared key to authenticate the switch to the TACACS+ server. The length of the key is restricted to 64 characters and can include any printable ASCII characters (white spaces are not allowed). You can configure a global key to be used for all TACACS+ server configurations on the switch. You can override this global key assignment by explicitly using the **key** option when configuring an individual TACACS+ server.

By default, the TACACS+ feature is disabled in all switches in the Cisco MDS 9000 Series Switches. You must explicitly enable the TACACS+ feature to access the configuration and verification commands for fabric authentication. When you disable this feature, all related configurations are automatically discarded.

Example 20-2 shows the steps required to configure TACACS+ on an MDS Switch.

**Example 20-2**   *TACACS+ Configuration on MDS Switch*

```
! Entering configuration mode.

switch# configure terminal

! Enabling TACACS+ in the switch.

switch(config)# feature tacacs+

! Configuring the TACACS+ server identified by the specified IPv4 address.

switch(config)# tacacs-server host 171.71.58.91
warning: no key is configured for the host

! Configuring the TCP port for all TACACS+ requests.

switch(config)# tacacs-server host 171.71.58.91 port 2
warning: no key is configured for the host

! Configuring the TACACS+ server identified by the specified IPv4 address and
assigning the secret key.

switch(config)# tacacs-server host 171.71.58.91 key TacKey

! Configuring the timeout period for the switch to wait for a response from the
specified server before it declares a timeout failure.

switch(config)# tacacs-server host 171.71.58.91 timeout 25

! Assigning the global secret key (in encrypted format) to access the TACACS+ server.
This example specifies 7 to indicate the encrypted format being used. If this global
key and the individual server keys are not configured, clear text
messages are sent to the TACACS+ server(s).
```

20

```
switch(config)# tacacs-server key 7 3sdaA3daKUngd
```

! Configuring the global timeout period in seconds for the switch to wait for a
response from all TACACS+ servers before the switch declares a timeout failure. The
time ranges from 1 to 1440 seconds.

```
switch(config)# tacacs-server timeout 30
```

! Configuring the dead-time interval value in minutes. The valid range is 1 to 1440
minutes. The dead timer specifies the interval that the MDS switch waits, after
declaring a TACACS+ server is dead, before sending out a test packet to determine if
the server is now alive.

```
switch(config)# tacacs-server deadtime 5
switch(config)# end
```

! Verifying TACACS+ server Configuration

```
switch# show tacacs-server
Global TACACS+ shared secret:********
timeout value:30
deadtime value:5
total number of servers:1

following TACACS+ servers are configured:
        171.71.58.91:
                available on port:2
                TACACS+ shared secret:********
                timeout:25
```

! Verifying tacacs-server statistics

```
switch# show tacacs-server statistics 171.71.58.91
Server is not monitored

Authentication Statistics
        failed transactions: 0
        successful transactions: 0
        requests sent: 0
        requests timed out: 0
        responses with no matching requests: 0
        responses not processed: 0
        responses containing errors: 0

Authorization Statistics
        failed transactions: 0
        successful transactions: 0
```

```
        requests sent: 0
        requests timed out: 0
        responses with no matching requests: 0
        responses not processed: 0
        responses containing errors: 0

Accounting Statistics
        failed transactions: 0
        successful transactions: 0
        requests sent: 0
        requests timed out: 0
        responses with no matching requests: 0
        responses not processed: 0
        responses containing errors: 0


! Creating a server group named DCCORE and configuring TACACS+ server at IPv4
address 171.71.58.91 to be tried first within the server group called the DCCORE.

switch(config)# aaa group server tacacs+ DCCORE
switch(config-tacacs+)# server 171.71.58.91
switch(config-tacacs+)# end


! Verifying tacacs-server groups

switch# show tacacs-server groups

following TACACS+ server groups are configured:
total number of groups:1
        group DCCORE:
                server 171.71.58.91 on port 2
                deadtime is 5
```

## LDAP

The LDAP provides centralized validation of users who attempt to gain access to a Cisco MDS 9000 switch. LDAP services are maintained in a database on an LDAP daemon that typically runs on a UNIX or Windows NT workstation. You must have access to and must configure an LDAP server before the configured LDAP features on your Cisco switch are available.

LDAP provides for separate authentication and authorization facilities. LDAP allows for a single access control server (the LDAP daemon) in order to provide each service authentication and authorization independently. Each service can be tied into its own database in order to take advantage of other services available on that server or on the network, depending on the capabilities of the daemon.

The LDAP client/server protocol uses TCP (TCP port 389) for transport requirements. Cisco MDS devices provide centralized authentication with use of the LDAP protocol.

Clients establish a TCP connection and authentication session with an LDAP server through a simple bind (username and password). As part of the authorization process, the LDAP server searches its database to retrieve the user profile and other information.

You can configure the bind operation to first bind and then search, where authentication is performed first and authorization next, or to first search and then bind. The default method is to first search and then bind.

The advantage of searching first and binding later is that the distinguished name (DN) received in the search result can be used as the user DN during binding rather than forming a DN by prepending the username (cn attribute) with the baseDN. This method is especially helpful when the user DN is different from the username plus the baseDN. For the user bind, the bindDN is constructed as baseDN + append-with-baseDN, where append-with-baseDN has a default value of cn=$userid.

LDAP has the following guidelines and limitations:

- You can configure a maximum of 64 LDAP servers on the Cisco NX-OS device.

- Cisco NX-OS supports only LDAP version 3.

- Cisco NX-OS supports only these LDAP servers:

  - OpenLDAP

  - Microsoft Active Directory

- LDAP over Secure Sockets Layer (SSL) supports only SSL version 3 and Transport Layer Security (TLS) version 1.

- If you have a user account configured on the local Cisco NX-OS device that has the same name as a remote user account on an AAA server, the Cisco NX-OS software applies the user roles for the local user account to the remote user, not the user roles configured on the AAA server.

To access a remote LDAP server, first create a profile for it on the Cisco NX-OS device. Parameters specific to a server can be added to its profile. These include the use of SSL transport, the target port number on the server, the request timeout period, the root distinguished name (the bind user) and password, and search referrals.

Connectivity to LDAP servers over TLS (via SSL) is RFC4513 compliant. This requires that the identity presented by the server during secure transport negotiation must exactly match both the server profile name and the certificate on the switch. Matching may be by IP address or host name in the certificate "Subject Alternative Name." This is the preferred method. If there is no match, the common name (CN) in the certificate "Subject" is checked. Server certificates are installed separately on the Cisco NX-OS devices.

NOTE   By default, when you configure an LDAP server IP address or host name on a Cisco NX-OS device, the LDAP server is added to the default LDAP server group. You can also add the LDAP server to another LDAP server group. Starting from Cisco MDS NX-OS Release 8.2(1), when TCP port 636 is configured, the connection establishment securely starts with an SSL or TLS negotiation. For other ports, this is done explicitly using the **enable-ssl** keyword.

You can specify one or more remote AAA servers to authenticate users using server groups. All members of a group must be configured to use LDAP. The servers are tried in the same order in which you configure them. You can configure these server groups at any time, but they take effect only when you apply them to an AAA service.

Cisco MDS 9000 Series switches support group-based user roles. You can create a group on the LDAP servers and also create a group with the exact same name on the Cisco MDS switch and then add users to the group. The user role attribute is inherited by the user from the group that is configured. This can be accomplished using the Microsoft LDAP Server's built-in memberOf attribute. If you want to use the memberOf attribute, ensure that you create a role name on the switch. The role name must be the same as the group name on the LDAP server. A user can be part of multiple groups, but only one group should be part of the switch role.

Example 20-3 shows the steps required to configure LDAP on an MDS switch.

**Example 20-3**   *LDAP Configuration on MDS Switch*

> Key Topic

```
! Entering configuration mode.

switch# configure terminal

! Enabling LDAP. By default, the LDAP feature is disabled on the Cisco NX-OS device.
You must explicitly enable the LDAP feature to access the configuration and
verification commands for authentication.

switch(config)# feature ldap

! Configuring the IPv4 or IPv6 address or hostname for an LDAP server. The
enable-ssl keyword ensures the integrity and confidentiality of the transferred
data by causing the LDAP client to establish a Secure Sockets Layer (SSL) session
prior to sending the bind or search request.

switch(config)# ldap-server host 10.10.1.1 enable-ssl

! Configuring the rootDN for the LDAP server database and the bind password for the
root. The rootDN is used to bind to the LDAP server to verify its state. You can
also configure the TCP port to use for LDAP messages to the server. The range is
from 1 to 65535, and the default TCP port is the global value or 389 if a global
value is not configured.
```

20

```
switch(config)# ldap-server host 10.10.1.1 rootDN cn=manager,dc=dccore,dc=com
password S5M3Tm timeout 30
```

! Configuring the global TCP port to use for LDAP messages to the server. The
default TCP port is 389. The range is from 1 to 65535.

```
switch(config)# ldap-server port 5
```

! Configuring a global timeout interval that determines how long the Cisco NX-OS
device waits for responses from all LDAP servers before declaring a timeout failure.

```
switch(config)# ldap-server timeout 7
```

! Configuring the global dead-time interval. The dead-time interval specifies the
time that the Cisco NX-OS device waits, after declaring that an LDAP server is
dead, before sending out a test packet to determine if the server is now alive. The
default value is 0 minutes. The range is from 1 to 60 minutes.

```
switch(config)# ldap-server deadtime 6
```

! Creating an LDAP server group and configuring the LDAP server as a member of the
LDAP server group.

```
switch(config)# aaa group server ldap DCCOREServer1
switch(config-ldap)# server 10.10.1.1
switch(config-ldap)# exit
```

! Configuring the default AAA authorization method for the LDAP servers. DCCOREServer1
is a server group. The ssh-certificate keyword configures LDAP or local authorization
with certificate authentication, and the ssh-publickey keyword configures LDAP or
local authorization with the SSH public key.

```
switch(config)# aaa authorization ssh-certificate default group DCCOREServer1
switch(config)# exit
```

! Verifying the AAA authorization configuration

```
switch# show aaa authorization
        pki-ssh-cert: group DCCOREServer1
        pki-ssh-pubkey: local
AAA command authorization:
```

! Verifying LDAP server

```
switch# show ldap-server
timeout     : 7
```

```
port          : 5
deadtime      : 6
total number of servers : 1


following LDAP servers are configured:
    10.10.1.1:
                idle time:0
                test user:test
                test password:********
                test DN:dc=test,dc=com
        timeout: 30    port: 389    rootDN: cn=manager,dc=dccore,dc=com
        enable-ssl: true
```

! Verifying the LDAP server group configuration

```
switch# show ldap-server groups
total number of groups: 1


following LDAP server groups are configured:
    group DCCOREServer1:
        Mode: UnSecure
        Authentication: Search and Bind
        Bind and Search : append with basedn (cn=$userid)
        Authentication: Do bind instead of compare
        Bind and Search : compare passwd attribute userPassword
        Authentication Mech: Default(PLAIN)
        server: 10.10.1.1 port: 389 timeout: 30
        Search map:
```

## Local AAA Services

When remote AAA servers time out, a local login is attempted, depending on the fallback configuration. For this local login to be successful, a local account for the user with the same password should exist. The system stores the password information in encrypted form. The user is authenticated if the username and password exist in the local authentication configuration. The **username** command configures local users and their roles.

You can enable/disable fallback to a local database in case the remote authentication is set and all AAA servers are unreachable (authentication error). The fallback is set to local by default in case of an authentication error. You can disable this fallback for both console and ssh/telnet login. Disabling this fallback will tighten the security of authentication. You can enable/disable the fallback using the **(no) aaa authentication login default fallback error local** command. Replace **default** with **console** in this command to disable fallback to the console.

20

> **NOTE**   If fallback is disabled for both default and console, remote authentication is enabled, and servers are unreachable, the switch will be locked.

## AAA Authentication and Authorization Process

The following steps explain the authentication and authorization process:

1. When you try to log in to the Cisco MDS 9000 Series Switches using the Telnet, SSH, DCNM or Device Manager, or console login options, the authentication process starts.

2. After you have configured server groups using the server group authentication method, an authentication request is sent to the first AAA server in the group.

   ■ If the AAA server fails to respond, the next AAA server is contacted and so on until the remote server responds to the authentication request.

   ■ If all AAA servers in the server group fail to respond, the servers in the next server group are contacted.

   ■ If all configured methods fail, by default, the local database is used for authentication.

3. When you are successfully authenticated through a remote AAA server, the following possible actions are taken:

   ■ If the AAA server protocol is RADIUS, user roles specified in the **cisco-av-pair** attribute are downloaded with an authentication response.

   ■ If the AAA server protocol is TACACS+, another request is sent to the same server to get the user roles specified as custom attributes for the shell.

   ■ If user roles are not successfully retrieved from the remote AAA server, the user is assigned the network-operator role if the **aaa user default-role** command is enabled. You are denied access if this command is disabled.

4. When your username and password are successfully authenticated locally, you are allowed to log in, and you are assigned the roles configured in the local database.

Figure 20-2 shows a flow chart of the authorization and authentication process for RADIUS remote AAA service.

You can enable or disable fallback to a local database in case the remote authentication is set and all AAA servers are unreachable (authentication error). The fallback is set to local by default in case of an authentication error. You can disable this fallback for both console and ssh/telnet login. Disabling this fallback will tighten the security of authentication.

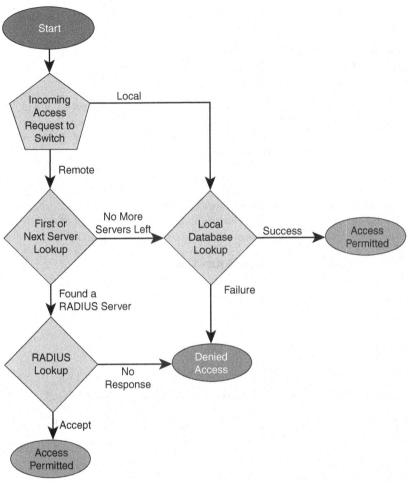

**Figure 20-2**  *Switch Authentication and Authorization Flow for RADIUS Remote AAA Service*

## AAA Server Distribution

Configuration for RADIUS and TACACS+ AAA on a Cisco MDS switch can be distributed using the Cisco Fabric Services (CFS). The distribution is disabled by default.

After the distribution is enabled, the first server or global configuration starts an implicit session. All server configuration commands entered thereafter are stored in a temporary database and applied to all switches in the fabric (including the originating one) when you explicitly commit the database. The various server and global parameters are distributed, except the server and global keys. These keys are unique secrets to a switch and should not be shared with other switches.

Only switches where distribution is enabled can participate in the distribution activity. A distribution session starts the moment you begin a RADIUS/TACACS+ server or global configuration.

**20**

Radius configuration distribution can be configured using the **radius distribute** command, and TACACS+ server distribution can be configured using the **tacacs+ distribute** command.

After the implicit distribution session has started, you can check the session status using the **show tacacs+ distribution status** and **show radius distribution status** commands for TACACS+ and RADIUS server distribution, respectively.

After you issue the first configuration command related to AAA servers, all server and global configurations that are created (including the configuration that caused the distribution session start) are stored in a temporary buffer, not in the running configuration. To commit the configuration changes, you can use the **radius commit** or **tacacs+ commit** command.

Discarding the distribution of a session in progress causes the configuration in the temporary buffer to be dropped, and the distribution is not applied. To discard the RADIUS session in-progress distribution, use the **radius abort** or **tacacs+ abort** command. To clear the ongoing CFS distribution session (if any) and to unlock the fabric for the RADIUS or TACACS+ feature, use the **clear radius session** or **clear tacacs+ session** command.

### Merging RADIUS and TACACS+ Configurations

The RADIUS and TACACS+ server and global configuration are merged when two fabrics merge. The merged configuration is applied to CFS distribution-enabled switches.

When merging the fabric, be aware of the following conditions:

- The server groups are not merged.

- The server and global keys are not changed during the merge.

- The merged configuration contains all servers found on all CFS-enabled switches.

- The timeout and retransmit parameters of the merged configuration are the largest values found per server and global configuration.

**NOTE** If a conflict occurs between two switches in the server ports that are configured, the merge fails.

Use the **show radius distribution status** or **show tacacs+ distribution status** command to view the status of the RADIUS or TACACS+ fabric merge.

## User Accounts and RBAC

Cisco MDS 9000 Series switches use role-based access control (RBAC) to define the amount of access that each user has when the user logs in to the switch.

With RBAC, you define one or more user roles and then specify which management operations each user role is allowed to perform. When you create a user account for the switch, you associate that account with a user role, which then determines what the individual user is allowed to do on the switch.

## User Roles

User roles contain rules that define the operations allowed for the user who is assigned the role. Each user role can contain multiple rules, and each user can have multiple roles. For example, if role1 allows access only to configuration operations, and role2 allows access only to debug operations, users who belong to both role1 and role2 can access configuration and debug operations. You can also limit access to specific VSANs, VLANs, and interfaces.

If you belong to multiple roles, you can execute a combination of all the commands permitted by these roles. Access to a command takes priority over being denied access to a command. For example, suppose a user has RoleA, which denied access to the configuration commands. However, the user also has RoleB, which has access to the configuration commands. In this case, the user has access to the configuration commands.

The Cisco MDS 9000 Series Switches provides the following default user roles:

- **network-admin (superuser):** Complete read and write access to the entire switch.

- **network-operator:** Complete read access to the switch. However, the network-operator role cannot run the **show running-config** and **show startup-config** commands.

- **server-admin:** Predefined system role for server administrators.

Roles can be used to create VSAN administrators. Depending on the configured rules, these VSAN administrators can configure storage features (for example, zone, fcdomain, or VSAN properties) for their VSANs without affecting other VSANs. Also, if the role permits operations in multiple VSANs, the VSAN administrators can change VSAN membership of F or FL ports among these VSANs.

A custom role user with network-admin privileges is restricted to modify the account of other users. However, only the admin can modify all user accounts.

You can modify the user privileges by performing the following tasks:

1. Modify the role using console authentication.

   If you set up the console authentication as local, log on using the local-admin user and modify the user.

2. Modify the role using remote authentication.

   Turn off the remote authentication. Log on using the local-admin privileges and modify the user. Turn on remote authentication.

3. Modify the role using LDAP/AAA.

   Create a group in LDAP/AAA and rename the group network-admin. Add the required users to this group. The users of this group will now have complete network-admin privileges.

## Rules

The rule is the basic element of a role. A rule defines what operations the role allows the user to perform.

**20**

Up to 16 rules can be configured for each role. The user-specified rule number determines the order in which the rules are applied. Rules are applied in ascending order. For example, rule 1 is applied before rule 2, which is applied before rule 3, and so on. A user not belonging to the network-admin role cannot perform commands related to roles.

**NOTE**  A deny-all statement is assumed as rule 0 so that no action is possible for a user role unless explicitly permitted.

Each rule consists of a rule number, a rule type (permit or deny), a command type (for example, **config**, **clear**, **show**, **exec**, **debug**), and an optional feature name (for example, FSPF, zone, VSAN, fcping, or interface).

Regardless of the **read-write** rule configured for a user role, some commands can be executed only through the predefined network-admin role. For example, if user A is permitted to perform all **show** commands, user A cannot view the output of the **show role** command if user A does not belong to the network-admin role.

In cases where a default role is applicable to all users, and a configured role is applicable for specific users, consider the following scenarios:

- **Same rule type (permit or deny):** If the default role and the configured role for a specific user have the same rule type, the specific user will have access to all the rules of both the default role and the configured role.

  If the default role, say A, has the following rules:

  rule 5 permit show feature environment

  rule 4 permit show feature hardware

  rule 3 permit config feature ssh

  rule 2 permit config feature ntp

  rule 1 permit config feature tacacs+

  and a specific user is assigned to the following role, say B, with one rule:

  rule 1 permit config feature dpvm

  the specific user will have access to the rules of both A and B.

- **Different rule type:** If the default role and the configured role for a specific user have different rule types for a particular rule, the default role will override the conflicting rule statement of the configured role.

  If the default role, say A, has the following rules:

  rule 5 permit show feature environment

  rule 4 permit show feature hardware

  rule 3 permit config feature ssh

rule 2 permit config feature ntp

rule 1 permit config feature tacacs+

and a specific user is assigned to the following role, say B, with two rules:

rule 6 permit config feature dpvm

rule 2 deny config feature ntp

rule 2 of A and B are in conflict. In this case, A overrides the conflicting rule of B, and the user is assigned the remaining rules of A and B, including the overridden rule:

rule 6 permit config feature dpvm

rule 5 permit show feature environment

rule 4 permit show feature hardware

rule 3 permit config feature ssh

rule 2 permit config feature ntp → Overridden rule

rule 1 permit config feature tacacs+

## User Role Policies

You can define user role policies to limit the switch resources that the user can access, or to limit access to interfaces, VLANs, and VSANs.

User role policies are constrained by the rules defined for the role. For example, if you define an interface policy to permit access to specific interfaces, the user does not have access to the interfaces unless you configure a command rule for the role to permit the **interface** command.

If a command rule permits access to specific resources (interfaces, VLANs, or VSANs), the user is permitted to access these resources, even if the user is not listed in the user role policies associated with that user.

Configuring the VSAN policy on Cisco MDS 9000 Series Switches requires the ENTERPRISE_PKG license.

You can configure a role so that it allows tasks to be performed only for a selected set of VSANs. By default, the VSAN policy for any role is permit, which allows tasks to be performed for all VSANs. To selectively allow VSANs for a role, set the VSAN policy to deny and then set the configuration to permit or the appropriate VSANs.

Users configured in roles where the VSAN policy is set to deny cannot modify the configuration for E ports. They can only modify the configuration for F or FL ports (depending on whether the configured rules allow such configuration to be made). This is to prevent such users from modifying configurations that may impact the core topology of the fabric.

20

### RBAC Sample Configuration

Example 20-4 shows the steps required to configure RBAC on an MDS switch.

**Example 20-4**   *RBAC Configuration on MDS Switch*

```
! Entering configuration mode.

switch# config terminal

! Creating a role and entering role submode to configure description for the role.

switch(config)# role name sangroup
switch(config-role)# description Selective SAN group

! Configuring rules for the sangroup role. Allowing users belonging to the sangroup
role to perform all configuration commands except fspf config commands.

switch(config-role)# rule 1 permit config
switch(config-role)# rule 2 deny config feature fspf
switch(config-role)# rule 3 permit debug feature zone
switch(config-role)# rule 4 permit exec feature fcping

! Deleting rule 3

switch(config-role)# no rule 3

! Configuring VSAN policy for sangroup role to deny and permitting selective VSANs
from VSAN 15 through 20.

switch(config-role)# vsan policy deny
switch(config-role-vsan)# permit vsan 15-20
switch(config-role-vsan)# end

! Verifying sangroup role

switch# show role name sangroup
Role: sangroup
  Description: Selective SAN group
  Vsan policy: deny
  Permitted vsans: 15-20
  -------------------------------------------------
  Rule    Type      Command-type      Feature
  -------------------------------------------------
  1       permit    config            *
  2       deny      config            fspf
  4       permit    exec              fcping
```

# Port Security

All switches in the Cisco MDS 9000 Series Switches provide port security features that reject intrusion attempts and report these intrusions to the administrator. Typically, any Fibre Channel device in a SAN can attach to any SAN switch port and access SAN services based on zone membership. Port security features prevent unauthorized access to a switch port in the following ways:

- Login requests from unauthorized Fibre Channel devices (Nx ports) and switches (xE ports) are rejected.

- All intrusion attempts are reported to the SAN administrator through system messages.

- Configuration distribution uses the CFS infrastructure and is limited to those switches that are CFS capable. Distribution is disabled by default.

- Configuring the port security policy requires the ENTERPRISE_PKG license.

To enforce port security, configure the devices and switch port interfaces through which each device or switch is connected, and activate the configuration.

- Use the port World Wide Name (pWWN) or the node World Wide Name (nWWN) to specify the Nx port connection for each device.

- Use the switch World Wide Name (sWWN) to specify the xE port connection for each switch.

Each Nx and xE port can be configured to restrict a single port or a range of ports. Port security policies are enforced on every activation and when the port tries to come up. The port security feature uses two databases to accept and implement configuration changes:

- **Configuration database:** All configuration changes are stored in the configuration database.

- **Active database:** This database is currently enforced by the fabric. The port security feature requires all devices connecting to a switch to be part of the port security active database. The software uses this active database to enforce authorization.

You can instruct the switch to automatically learn (auto-learn) the port security configurations over a specified period. This feature allows any switch in the Cisco MDS 9000 Series Switches to automatically learn about devices and switches that connect to it. Use this feature when you activate the port security feature for the first time because it saves tedious manual configuration for each port. You must configure auto-learning on a per-VSAN basis. If enabled, devices and switches that are allowed to connect to the switch are automatically learned, even if you have not configured any port access.

When auto-learning is enabled, learning happens for the devices or interfaces that were already logged in to the switch and the new devices or interfaces that need to be logged in in the future. Learned entries on a port are cleaned up after you shut down that port if auto-learning is still enabled.

Learning does not override the existing configured port security policies. So, for example, if an interface is configured to allow a specific pWWN, auto-learning will not add a new

20

entry to allow any other pWWN on that interface. All other pWWNs will be blocked even in auto-learning mode.

No entries are learned for a port in the shutdown state. When you activate the port security feature, auto-learning is also automatically enabled. You cannot reactivate port security until auto-learning is disabled or deactivated and activated again.

By default, the port security feature is not activated in any switch in the Cisco MDS 9000 Series Switches. When you activate the port security feature, the following apply:

- Auto-learning is also automatically enabled, which means

  - From this point, auto-learning happens for the devices or interfaces that were already logged in to the switch and also for the new devices that will log in in the future.

  - You cannot activate the database until you disable auto-learning.

- All the devices that are already logged in are learned and are added to the active database.

- All entries in the configured database are copied to the active database.

After the database is activated, subsequent device login is subject to the activated port-bound WWN pairs, excluding the auto-learned entries. You must disable auto-learning before the auto-learned entries become activated.

When you activate the port security feature, auto-learning is also automatically enabled. You can choose to activate the port security feature and disable auto-learning.

If a port is shut down because of a denied login attempt, and you subsequently configure the database to allow that login, the port does not come up automatically. You must explicitly issue a **no shutdown** CLI command to bring that port back online.

The port security feature can also use the Cisco Fabric Services infrastructure to enable efficient database management, providing a single point of configuration for the entire fabric in the VSAN, and enforce the port security policies throughout the fabric.

All the configurations performed in CFS distributed mode are stored in a pending (temporary) database. If you modify the configuration, you need to commit or discard the pending database changes to the configurations. The fabric remains locked during this period. Changes to the pending database are not reflected in the configurations until you commit the changes.

The first action that modifies the existing configuration creates the pending database and locks the feature in the VSAN. After you lock the fabric, the following situations apply:

- No other user can make any configuration changes to this feature.

- A copy of the configuration database becomes the pending database.

If you commit the changes made to the configurations, the configurations in the pending database are distributed to other switches. On a successful commit, the configuration change is applied throughout the fabric, and the lock is released.

Learned entries are temporary and do not have any role in determining whether a login is authorized. As such, learned entries do not participate in distribution. When you disable learning and commit the changes in the pending database, the learned entries become static entries in the active database and are distributed to all switches in the fabric. After the commit, the active database on all switches is identical.

If you discard (abort) the changes made to the pending database, the configuration remains unaffected, and the lock is released.

**NOTE**  Port activation or deactivation and auto-learning enable or disable do not take effect until after a CFS commit if CFS distribution is enabled.

## Port Security Configuration

Port security can be configured using the following three methods:

- Method 1: Manual Database Configuration

- Method 2: Auto-Learning without CFS Distribution

- Method 3: Auto-Learning with CFS Distribution

### Method 1: Manual Database Configuration

Example 20-5 shows the steps required to configure port security by manually configuring the port security database.

**Example 20-5**  *Manual Port Security Configuration on MDS Switch*

```
Step 1 Enable port security.

switch# configure terminal
switch(config)# feature port-security

Step 2 Manually configure all port security entries into the configure database
on each VSAN. You can add the port security entries by various ways. Some of the
samples are shown below.

switch(config)# port-security database vsan 2

! Configuring the specified sWWN to only log in through port channel 10.
switch(config-port-security)# swwn 20:01:33:11:00:2a:4a:66 interface port-channel 10

! Configuring any WWN to log in through the specified interfaces.
switch(config-port-security)# any-wwn interface fc1/1 - fc1/6

! Configuring the specified pWWN to only log in through the specified fWWN.
switch(config-port-security)# pwwn 20:11:00:33:11:00:2a:4a fwwn
20:81:00:44:22:00:4a:9e
```

20

```
! Configuring the specified nWWN to log in through the specified fWWN.
switch(config-port-security)# nwwn 26:33:22:00:55:05:3d:4c fwwn
20:81:00:44:22:00:4a:9e


! Configuring the specified pWWN to log in through any port in the fabric.
switch(config-port-security)# pwwn 20:11:33:11:00:2a:4a:66


! Configuring the specified pWWN to log in through the specified interface in the
specified switch
switch(config-port-security)# pwwn 20:11:33:11:00:2a:4a:66 swwn
20:00:00:0c:85:90:3e:80 interface fc2/1


! Configuring any WWN to log in through the specified interface in any switch.
switch(config-port-security)# any-wwn interface fc2/1


Step 3 Activate port security on each VSAN. This turns on auto-learning by default.


switch(config)# port-security activate vsan 2


Step 4 Disable auto-learn on each VSAN.


switch(config)# no port-security auto-learn vsan 2


Note: You can combine step 3 and 4 using the command port-security activate vsan 1
no-auto-learn


Step 5 Copy the running configuration to the startup configuration This saves the
port security configure database to the startup configuration.


switch(config)# copy running-config startup-config


Step 6 Repeat Step 1 through Step 5 for all switches in the fabric.
```

### Method 2: Auto-Learning Without CFS Distribution

Example 20-6 shows the steps required to configure port security using auto-learning without CFS distribution.

**Example 20-6**  *Auto-Learning Port Security Configuration Without CFS Distribution*

```
Step 1 Enable port security.


switch# configure terminal
switch(config)# feature port-security


Step 2 Activate port security on each VSAN. This turns on auto-learning by default.


switch(config)# port-security activate vsan 2
```

```
Step 3 Wait until all switches and all hosts are automatically learned.

Step 4 Disable auto-learn on each VSAN.

switch(config)# no port-security auto-learn vsan 2

Step 5 Copy the active database to the configure database on each VSAN.

switch# port-security database copy vsan 2

Step 6 Copy the running configuration to the startup configuration. This saves the
port security configure database to the startup configuration.

switch# copy running-config startup-config

Step 7 Repeat Step 1 through Step 6 for all switches in the fabric.
```

### Method 3: Auto-Learning with CFS Distribution

Example 20-7 shows the steps required to configure port security with auto-learning and CFS distribution.

**Example 20-7**  *Auto-Learning Port Security Configuration with CFS Distribution*

```
Step 1 Enable port security.

switch# configure terminal
switch(config)# feature port-security

Step 2 Enable CFS distribution.

switch(config)# port-security distribute

Step 3 Activate port security on each VSAN. This turns on auto-learning by default.

switch(config)# port-security activate vsan 2

Step 4 Issue a CFS commit to copy this configuration to all switches in the fabric.
At this point, all switches are activated, and auto-learning.

switch(config)# port-security commit vsan 2

Step 5 Wait until all switches and all hosts are automatically learned.
```

20

Step 6 Disable auto-learn on each VSAN.

```
switch(config)# no port-security auto-learn vsan 2
```

Step 7 Issue a CFS commit to copy this configuration to all switches in the fabric.
At this point, the auto-learned entries from every switch are combined into a static
active database that is distributed to all switches.

```
switch(config)# port-security commit vsan 2
```

Step 8 Copy the active database to the configure database on each VSAN.

```
switch# port-security database copy vsan 2
```

Step 9 Issue a CFS commit to copy this configuration to all switches in the fabric.
This ensures that the configure database is the same on all switches in the fabric.

```
switch(config)# port-security commit vsan 2
```

Step 10 Copy the running configuration to the startup configuration, using the fabric option. This saves the port security configure database to the startup configuration on all switches in the fabric.

```
switch# copy running-config startup-config fabric
```

## Verification of Port Security

Port security can be verified using the commands shown next.

The **show port-security database** commands display the configured port security information as shown in Example 20-8.

**Example 20-8**  *Verification of Port Security Database*

```
switch# show port-security database

---------------------------------------------------------------------------------------
VSAN   Logging-in Entity                 Logging-in Point            (Interface)
---------------------------------------------------------------------------------------
1      21:00:00:e0:8b:07:d9:1d(pwwn)     20:0d:00:05:30:00:95:de     (fc1/7)
1      50:06:04:82:bc:02:c3:84(pwwn)     20:0c:00:05:30:00:95:de     (fc1/6)
2      20:00:00:05:30:00:95:df(swwn)     20:0c:00:05:30:00:95:de     (port-channel 5)
3      20:00:00:05:30:00:95:de(swwn)     20:01:00:05:30:00:95:de     (fc1/1)
[Total 4 entries]
```

The **show port-security database active** command displays the activated database as shown in Example 20-9.

**Example 20-9** *Verification of Port Security Active Database*

```
switch# show port-security database active


------------------------------------------------------------------------------
VSAN  Logging-in Entity            Logging-in Point            (Interface)     Learnt
------------------------------------------------------------------------------
1      21:00:00:e0:8b:06:d9:1d(pwwn)  20:0d:00:05:30:00:95:de  (fc1/7)          Yes
1      50:06:04:82:bc:02:c3:84(pwwn)  20:0c:00:05:30:00:95:de  (fc1/6)          Yes
2      20:00:00:05:30:00:95:df(swwn)  20:0c:00:05:30:00:95:de  (port-channel 5) Yes
3      20:00:00:05:30:00:95:de(swwn)  20:01:00:05:30:00:95:de  (fc1/1)
[Total 4 entries]
```

The **show port-security status** command displays the port security status as shown in Example 20-10.

**Example 20-10** *Verification of Port Security Status*

```
switch# show port-security status

Fabric Distribution Enabled
VSAN 1 :No Active database, learning is disabled, Session Lock Taken
VSAN 2 :No Active database, learning is disabled, Session Lock Taken
...
```

The **show port-security violations** command displays the violations in the port security database as shown in Example 20-11.

**Example 20-11** *Verification of Port Security Violations*

```
switch# show port-security violations


------------------------------------------------------------------------------
VSAN Interface    Logging-in Entity            Last-Time            [Repeat count]
------------------------------------------------------------------------------
--
1    fc1/7        21:00:00:e0:8b:07:d9:1d(pwwn)  Jul  9 08:32:20 2019       [20]
                  20:00:00:e0:8b:07:d9:1d(nwwn)
1    fc1/6        50:06:04:82:bc:02:c3:84(pwwn   Jul  9 08:32:20 2019       [1]
                  50:06:04:82:bc:02:c3:84(nwwn)
2    port-channel 5 20:00:00:05:30:00:95:de(sww  Jul  9 08:32:40 2019       [1]
[Total 2 entries]
```

20

# Fabric Binding

The fabric binding feature helps prevent unauthorized switches from joining the fabric or disrupting current fabric operations. It ensures ISLs are enabled only between specified switches in the fabric binding configuration. Fabric binding is configured on a per-VSAN basis. It uses the Exchange Fabric Membership Data (EFMD) protocol to ensure that the list of authorized switches is identical in all switches in the fabric.

Fabric binding binds the fabric at the switch level. It authorizes only the configured sWWN stored in the fabric binding database to participate in the fabric. Fabric binding cannot be distributed by CFS and must be configured manually on each switch in the fabric.

The switch login uses both port security binding and fabric binding for a given VSAN. While port security complements fabric binding, they are independent features and can be enabled or disabled separately.

On Cisco MDS 9000 Series Switches, fabric binding requires either the MAINFRAME_PKG license or the ENTERPRISE_PKG license.

The fabric binding feature must be enabled in each switch in the fabric that participates in the fabric binding. By default, this feature is disabled in all switches in the Cisco MDS 9000 Series Switches. A user-specified fabric binding list contains a list of switch WWNs (sWWNs) within a fabric. If an sWWN attempts to join the fabric and that sWWN is not on the list, the ISL between the switch and the fabric is automatically isolated in that VSAN, and the switch is denied entry into the fabric.

To enforce fabric binding, configure the sWWN to specify the xE port connection for each switch. Enforcement of fabric binding policies is done on every activation and when the port tries to come up. In a Fibre Channel VSAN, the fabric binding feature requires all sWWNs connected to a switch to be part of the fabric binding active database; the domain ID is optional.

The fabric binding feature maintains a configuration database (config-database) and an active database. The config-database is a read-write database that collects the configurations you perform. These configurations are enforced only upon activation. This activation overwrites the active database with the contents of the config-database. The active database is read-only and is the database that checks each switch that attempts to log in. You cannot activate the fabric binding database on the switch if entries existing in the configured database conflict with the current state of the fabric. For example, one of the already logged-in switches may be denied login by the config-database. You can choose to forcefully override these situations. When you save the fabric binding configuration, the config database is saved to the running configuration.

## Fabric Binding Configuration

Example 20-12 shows the steps required to configure fabric binding on an MDS switch.

**Example 20-12**   *Fabric Binding Configuration on MDS Switch*

```
Step 1 Enable the fabric-binding feature.

switch# configure terminal
switch(config)# feature fabric-binding

Step 2 Configure a list of sWWNs for devices that are allowed to access the fabric.
You can also add the sWWN of another switch for a specific domain ID to the
configured database list.

switch(config)# fabric-binding database vsan 2
switch(config-fabric-binding)# swwn 21:00:05:30:23:22:22:22
switch(config-fabric-binding)# swwn 20:00:00:05:30:00:4a:1e domain 101

Step 3 Activate the fabric binding database. To forcefully activate the fabric
binding database, use the force option.

switch(config)# fabric-binding activate vsan 2 [force]

Step 4 Copy the fabric binding active database to the fabric binding config database.

switch# fabric-binding database copy vsan 2

Step 5 Save the fabric binding configuration.

switch# copy running-config startup-config

Step 6 Verify the fabric binding configuration.

! Verifying the fabric-binding database

switch# show fabric-binding database
-------------------------------------------------
Vsan   Logging-in Switch WWN     Domain-id
-------------------------------------------------
2      20:00:00:de:fb:25:b8:80   0xb1(177) [Local]
2      21:00:05:30:23:22:22:22         Any
2      20:00:00:05:30:00:4a:1e   0x65(101)
[Total 3 entries]

! Verifying the fabric-binding active database
switch# show fabric-binding database active
-------------------------------------------------
Vsan   Logging-in Switch WWN     Domain-id
-------------------------------------------------
```

20

```
2       20:00:00:de:fb:25:b8:80   0xb1(177)  [Local]
2       21:00:05:30:23:22:22:22       Any
2       20:00:00:05:30:00:4a:1e   0x65(101)
[Total 3 entries]
```

! Verifying the fabric-binding statistics
```
switch# show fabric-binding statistics


Statistics For VSAN: 2
------------------------------------
Number of sWWN permit: 0
Number of sWWN deny  : 0
Total Logins permitted  : 0
Total Logins denied     : 0
```

! Verifying the fabric-binding status
```
switch# show fabric-binding status


VSAN 2 :Activated database
```

! Verifying the fabric-binding violations. In VSAN 2, the switch was found in the
list, but has a domain ID mismatch.

```
switch# show fabric-binding violations


--------------------------------------------------------------------------------
VSAN Switch WWN[domain]          Last-Time          [Repeat count]    Reason
--------------------------------------------------------------------------------
2    20:00:00:05:30:00:4a:1e  [0xeb] Nov 25 05:46:14 2003    [2]      Domain mismatch
```

## Port Security Versus Fabric Binding

Port security and fabric binding are two independent features that can be configured to complement each other. Table 20-2 compares the two features.

**Table 20-2**   Fabric Binding and Port Security Comparison

| Fabric Binding | Port Security |
|---|---|
| Binds the fabric at the switch level. | Binds devices at the interface level. |
| Authorizes only the configured sWWN stored in the fabric binding database to participate in the fabric. | Allows a preconfigured set of Fibre Channel devices to logically connect to SAN ports. The switch port, identified by a WWN or interface number, connects to a Fibre Channel device (a host or another switch), also identified by a WWN. By binding these two devices, you lock these two ports into a group (or list). |
| Requires activation on a per-VSAN basis. | Requires activation on a per-VSAN basis. |

| Fabric Binding | Port Security |
|---|---|
| Allows specific user-defined switches that are allowed to connect to the fabric, regardless of the physical port to which the peer switch is connected. | Allows specific user-defined physical ports to which another device can connect. |
| Does not learn about switches that are logging in. | Learns about switches or devices that are logging in if learning mode is enabled. |
| Cannot be distributed by CFS and must be configured manually on each switch in the fabric. | Can be distributed by CFS. |
| Uses a set of sWWNs. | Uses pWWNs/nWWNs or fWWNs/sWWNs. |

# Exam Preparation Tasks

As mentioned in the Introduction, you have a couple of choices for exam preparation: the exercises here, Chapter 21, "Final Preparation," and the exam simulation questions in the Pearson Test Prep software online.

## Review All Key Topics

Review the most important topics in the chapter, noted with the key topic icon in the outer margin of the page. Table 20-3 lists a reference to these key topics and the page numbers on which each is found.

**Table 20-3**   Key Topics for Chapter 20

| Key Topic Element | Description | Page |
|---|---|---|
| Section | Authentication | 899 |
| Section | Authorization | 899 |
| Section | Accounting | 900 |
| Figure 20-1 | AAA Server States | 901 |
| Section | RADIUS | 902 |
| Example 20-1 | RADIUS Configuration on MDS Switch | 902 |
| Paragraph | TACACS+ | 904 |
| Example 20-2 | TACACS+ Configuration on MDS Switch | 905 |
| Example 20-3 | LDAP Configuration on MDS Switch | 909 |
| List | AAA Authentication and Authorization Process | 912 |
| Section | User Roles | 915 |
| Paragraph | Rules | 915 |
| Example 20-4 | RBAC Configuration on MDS Switch | 918 |
| Section | Port Security | 919 |

20

| Key Topic Element | Description | Page |
|---|---|---|
| List | Port Security Configuration | 921 |
| Section | Fabric Binding | 926 |
| Example 20-12 | Fabric Binding Configuration on MDS Switch | 927 |
| Table 20-2 | Fabric Binding and Port Security Comparison | 928 |

## Memory Tables and Lists

Print a copy of Appendix C, "Memory Tables" (found on the companion website), or at least the section for this chapter, and complete the tables and lists from memory. Appendix D, "Memory Tables Answer Key," also on the companion website, includes completed tables and lists to check your work.

## Define Key Terms

Define the following key terms from this chapter, and check your answers in the Glossary.

AAA Server, Secure Shell (SSH); authentication, authorization, and accounting (AAA); base DN; bind DN; cisco-av-pair; Cisco Fabric Services (CFS); distinguished name (DN); DPVM Exchange Fabric Membership Data (EFMD); fabric port WWN (fWWN); fcping; Fibre Channel Security Protocol (FC-SP); FSPF; Internet Small Computer Interface (iSCSI); Lightweight Directory Access Protocol (LDAP); memberOf attribute; Microsoft Active Directory; node World Wide Name (nWWN); OpenLDAP; port World Wide Name (pWWN); Remote Authentication Dial-In User Service (RADIUS); Secure Sockets Layer (SSL); switch World Wide Name (sWWN); Terminal Access Controller Access Control System Plus (TACACS+); Transport Layer Security (TLS)

## References

Cisco MDS 9000 Series Security Configuration Guide, Release 8.x: https://www.cisco.com/c/en/us/td/docs/switches/datacenter/mds9000/sw/8_x/config/security/cisco_mds9000_security_config_guide_8x.html

Cisco Nexus 5600 Series NX-OS System Management Configuration Guide, Release 7.x: https://www.cisco.com/c/en/us/td/docs/switches/datacenter/nexus5600/sw/system_management/7x/b_5600_System_Mgmt_Config_7x.html

Configure MDS LDAP TechNotes: https://www.cisco.com/c/en/us/support/docs/voice/mds/118979-config-mds-00.html

# Final Preparation

The first 20 chapters of this book cover the technologies, protocols, design concepts, and considerations required to be prepared to pass the 350-601 CCNP and CCIE Data Center Core DCCOR exam. While these chapters supply the detailed information, most people need more preparation than simply reading the first 20 chapters of this book. This chapter details a set of tools and a study plan to help you complete your preparation for the exams.

This short chapter has three main sections. The first section lists the exam preparation tools useful at this point in the study process. The second section lists the different types of questions you can encounter in the exam. The third and final section lists a suggested study plan now that you have completed all the earlier chapters in this book.

## Getting Ready

Here are some important tips to keep in mind to ensure you are ready for this rewarding exam!

- **Build and use a study tracker:** Consider taking the exam objectives shown in the chapters and build yourself a study tracker. This will help ensure you have not missed anything and that you are confident for your exam! As a matter of fact, this book offers a sample Study Planner as a website supplement.

- **Think about your time budget for questions in the exam:** If you do the math, you will realize that on average you have about one minute per question. Although this does not sound like enough time, realize that many of the questions are very straightforward, and you may take 15 to 30 seconds on those. This way, you build time for other questions as you take your exam.

- **Watch the clock:** Check in on the time remaining periodically as you are taking the exam. You might even find that you can slow down pretty dramatically as you have built up a nice block of extra time.

- **Get some ear plugs:** The testing center might provide ear plugs, but get some just in case and bring them along. There might be other test takers in the center with you, and you do not want to be distracted by their screams. I personally have no issue blocking out the sounds around me, so I never worry about this, but I know it is an issue for some.

- **Plan your travel time:** Give yourself extra time to find the center and get checked in. Be sure to arrive early. As you test more at that center, you can certainly start cutting it closer time-wise.

- **Get rest:** Most students report success with getting plenty of rest the night before the exam. All-night cram sessions are not typically successful.

- **Bring in valuables but get ready to lock them up:** The testing center will take your phone, your smart watch, your wallet, and other such items. It will provide a secure place for them.

- **Take notes:** You will be given note-taking implements, so do not be afraid to use them. For example, I always end up jotting down any questions I struggled with. I then memorize these at the end of the test by reading my notes over and over again. I then always make sure I have a pen and paper in the car. I write down the issues in there just after the exam. When I get home with a pass or fail, I research those items!

## Tools for Final Preparation

This section lists some information about the available tools and how to access the tools.

### Pearson Test Prep Practice Test Software and Questions on the Website

Register this book to get access to the Pearson IT Certification Test Prep practice test software (software that displays and grades a set of exam-realistic, multiple-choice questions). Using the Pearson Test Prep Engine, you can either study by going through the questions in Study mode or take a simulated (timed) CCNP and CCIE Data Center Core exam.

The Pearson Test Prep practice test software comes with two full practice exams. These practice tests are available to you either online or as an offline Windows application. To access the practice exams that were developed with this book, please follow the instructions below.

## How to Access the Pearson Test Prep (PTP) App

You have two options for installing and using the Pearson Test Prep application: a web app and a desktop app. To use the Pearson Test Prep application, start by finding the registration code that comes with the book. You can find the code in these ways:

- **Print book or bookseller eBook versions:** You can get your access code by registering the print ISBN (9780138228088) on ciscopress.com/register. Make sure to use the print book ISBN regardless of whether you purchased an eBook or the print book. Once you register the book, your access code will be populated on your account page under the Registered Products tab. Instructions for how to redeem the code are available on the book's companion website by clicking the Access Bonus Content link.

- **Premium Edition:** If you purchase the Premium Edition eBook and Practice Test directly from the Cisco Press website, the code will be populated on your account page after purchase. Just log in at www.ciscopress.com, click Account to see details of your account, and click the digital purchases tab.

**NOTE** After you register your book, your code can always be found in your account under the Registered Products tab.

Once you have the access code, to find instructions about both the PTP web app and the desktop app, follow these steps:

**Step 1.**   Open this book's companion website, as shown earlier in this Introduction under the heading "How to Access the Companion Website."

**Step 2.**   Click the Practice Exams button.

**Step 3.**   Follow the instructions listed there both for installing the desktop app and for using the web app.

Note that if you want to use the web app only at this point, just navigate to www.pearson-testprep.com, establish a free login if you do not already have one, and register this book's practice tests using the registration code you just found. The process should take only a couple of minutes.

## Customizing Your Exams

Once you are in the exam settings screen, you can choose to take exams in one of three modes:

- Study mode

- Practice Exam mode

- Flash Card mode

Study mode allows you to fully customize your exams and review answers as you are taking the exam. This is typically the mode you would use first to assess your knowledge and identify information gaps. Practice Exam mode locks certain customization options because it is presenting a realistic exam experience. Use this mode when you are preparing to test your exam readiness. Flash Card mode strips out the answers and presents you with only the question stem. This mode is great for late-stage preparation when you really want to challenge yourself to provide answers without the benefit of seeing multiple-choice options. This mode will not provide the detailed score reports that the other two modes will, so you should not use it if you are trying to identify knowledge gaps.

In addition to these three modes, you will be able to select the source of your questions. You can choose to take exams that cover all of the chapters, or you can narrow your selection to just a single chapter or the chapters that make up specific parts in the book. All chapters are selected by default. If you want to narrow your focus to individual chapters, simply deselect all the chapters and then select only those on which you want to focus in the Objectives area.

You can also select the exam banks on which to focus. Each exam bank comes complete with a full exam of questions that cover topics in every chapter. The two exams printed in the book are available to you as well as two additional exams of unique questions. You can have the test engine serve up exams from all four banks or just from one individual bank by selecting the desired banks in the exam bank area.

You can make several other customizations to your exam from the exam settings screen, such as the time of the exam, the number of questions served up, whether to randomize questions and answers, whether to show the number of correct answers for multiple-answer questions, or whether to serve up only specific types of questions. You can also create custom test banks by selecting only questions that you have marked or questions on which you have added notes.

## Updating Your Exams

If you are using the online version of the Pearson Test Prep software, you should always have access to the latest version of the software as well as the exam data. If you are using the Windows desktop version, every time you launch the software, it will check to see if there are any updates to your exam data and automatically download any changes that were made since the last time you used the software. This requires that you are connected to the Internet at the time you launch the software.

Sometimes, due to many factors, the exam data may not fully download when you activate your exam. If you find that figures or exhibits are missing, you may need to manually update your exams.

To update a particular exam you have already activated and downloaded, simply select the **Tools** tab and select the **Update Products** button. Again, this is only an issue with the desktop Windows application.

If you want to check for updates to the Pearson Test Prep exam engine software, Windows desktop version, simply select the **Tools** tab and select the **Update Application** button. This will ensure you are running the latest version of the software engine.

### Premium Edition

In addition to the free practice exam provided on the website, you can purchase additional exams with expanded functionality directly from Pearson IT Certification. The Premium Edition of this title contains an additional two full practice exams and an e-book (in both PDF and ePub format). In addition, the Premium Edition title also has remediation for each question to the specific part of the e-book that relates to that question.

Because you have purchased the print version of this title, you can purchase the Premium Edition at a deep discount. There is a coupon code in the book sleeve that contains a one-time-use code and instructions for where you can purchase the Premium Edition.

To view the premium edition product page, go to www.informit.com/title/9780138228217.

## Chapter-Ending Review Tools

Chapters 1 through 20 include several features in the "Exam Preparation Tasks" section at the end of the chapter. You might have already worked through them in each chapter. It can also be helpful to use these tools again as you make your final preparations for the exam.

# Learn the Question Types Using the Cisco Certification Exam Tutorial

In the weeks leading up to your exam, you should think more about the different types of exam questions and have a plan for how to approach those questions. One of the best ways to learn about the exam questions is to use the Cisco Exam Tutorial.

To find the Cisco Certification Exam Tutorial, go to http://www.cisco.com/ and search for "exam tutorial." You can simply google "Cisco Certification Exam Tutorial Videos" also. The tutorial sits inside a web page with a video presentation of the exam user interface. The tutorial walks you through the different types of exam questions. The sample questions in this section are from the Cisco Certification Exam Tutorial, and they have nothing to do with the actual 350-601 CCNP and CCIE Data Center DCCOR exam content. You can expect to find the following types of questions on the exam:

- **Multiple-choice, single-answer:** The question has several possible answers but only one correct answer. In the real exam, if you click Next on the multi-choice, single-answer question without clicking an answer, the testing software tells you that you have too few answers. Figure 21-1 shows an example.

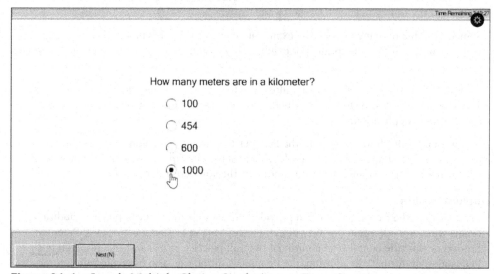

**Figure 21-1**    *Sample Multiple-Choice, Single-Answer Exam Question*

- **Multiple-choice, multiple-answer:** The question has several possible answers, with a given number of correct ones. In the real exam, if you select too few answers and click Next, you can see how the user interface responds. Figure 21-2 shows an example.

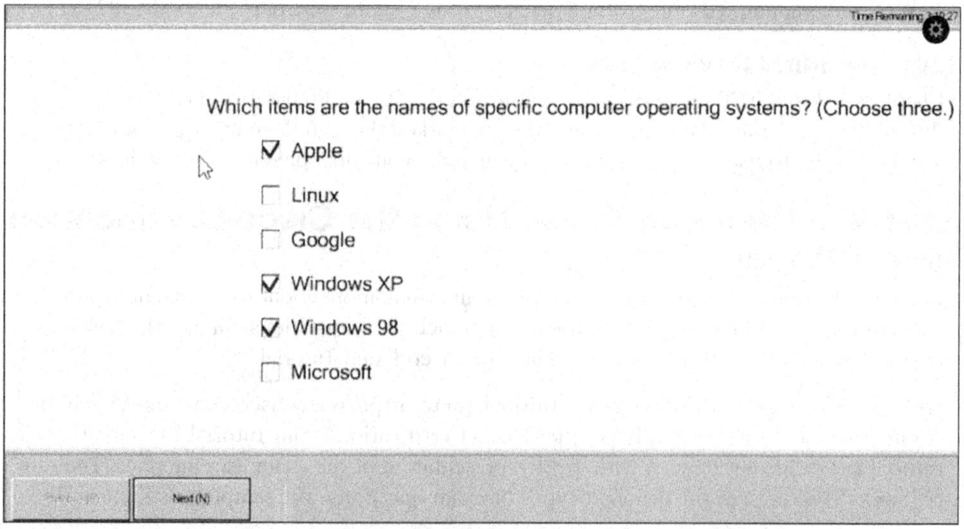

**Figure 21-2**    *Sample Multiple-Choice, Multiple-Answer Exam Question*

■ **Drag-and-drop:** In the drag-and-drop questions, you can drag the answers to the obvious answer locations but then drag them back to the original location. (You might do this on the real exam, if you change your mind when answering the question.) Figure 21-3 shows an example.

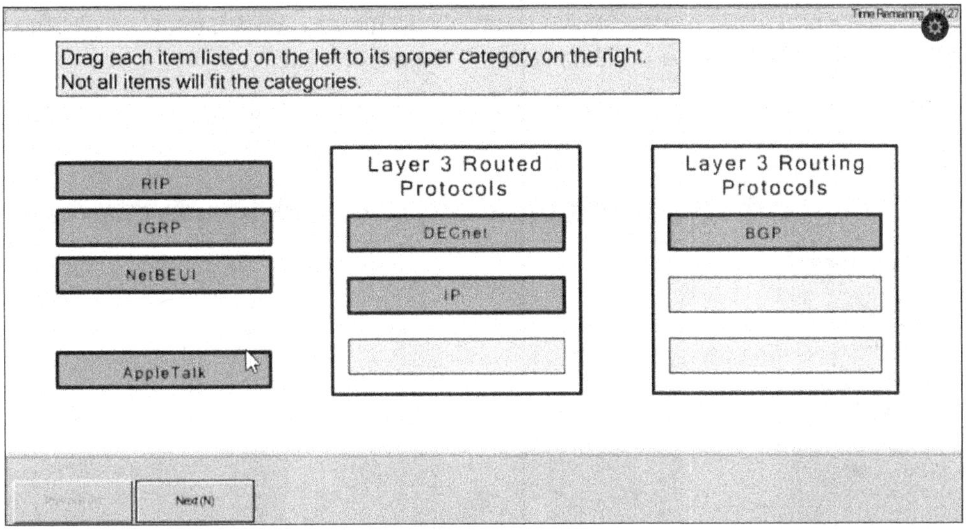

**Figure 21-3**  *Sample Drag-and-Drop Exam Question*

■ **Fill-in-the-blank:** In this type of question, you will find one or more blank answers that you must fill in. Figure 21-4 shows an example.

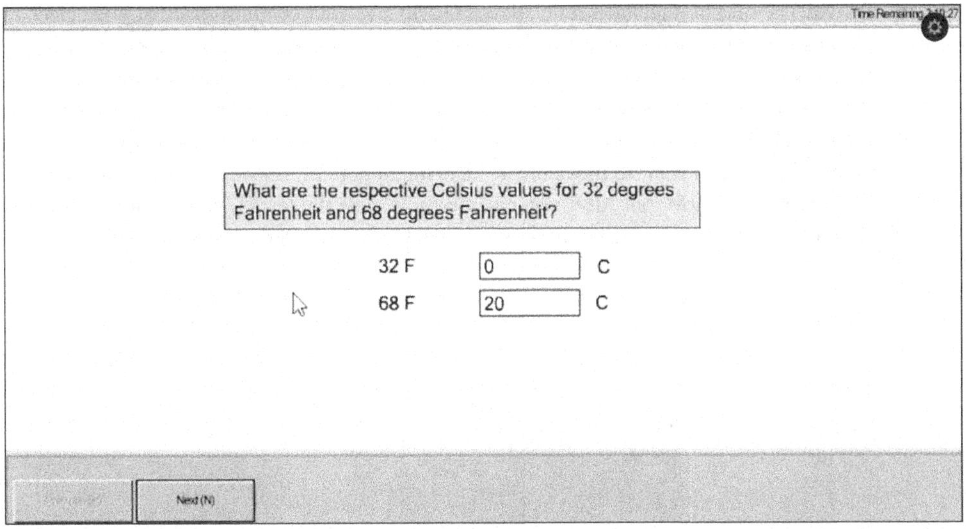

**Figure 21-4**  *Sample Fill-in-the-Blank Exam Question*

- **Simulation:** The question includes a description and a network diagram. You can click a network device and interact with it through a simulated command-line interface (CLI). On the simulation question, first make sure that you can get to the CLI on one of the routers. To do so, you have to click the PC icon for a PC connected to the router console; the console cable appears as a dashed line, and network cables are solid lines. (Note that the exam tutorial uses the IOS CLI, not NX-OS, but it is similar enough for you to get the idea.) Figure 21-5 shows an example.

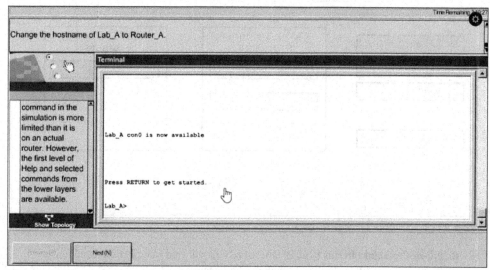

**Figure 21-5** *Sample Router Simulation Question*

- **Testlet:** The question includes a detailed scenario and a set of questions that you select and answer. On the testlet question, answer one multiple-choice question, move to the second and answer it, and then move back to the first question, confirming that inside a testlet, you can move around between questions. In the real exam, on the testlet question, if you click the Next button, you will see the pop-up window that Cisco uses as a prompt to ask whether you want to move on. Testlets might actually allow you to give too few answers and still move on. After you click to move past the testlet, you cannot go back to change your answer for any of these questions. Figure 21-6 shows an example.

This is a "Testlet" - it contains 4 questions that relate to the scenario below.

**Scenario**

An employee who uses a laptop as a workstation at the office is having trouble establishing a connection to the company network. The employee calls the technical support help desk. After a series of questions, the technical support person has the employee ping the gateway address 192.168.0.1. The support person then has the employee ping the loopback address 127.0.0.1. What the

**Question #1**

Of the choices below, what is the only certain conclusion that can be drawn from the ping to the laptop loopback address?

○ The laptop has a network card installed.

○ The laptop has a wireless NIC.

○ The laptop will have no trouble making a connection to the rest of the network.

○ The TCP/IP stack is installed on the laptop.

○ The TCP/IP stack is not installed on the laptop.

1
2
3
4

Next (N)

**Figure 21-6**  *Sample Testlet Question*

■ **Simlet:** The question includes a scenario and a set of questions that you must answer based on interaction with a simulated network device. Make sure that you look at the scroll area. On the Sim question, make sure that you can toggle between the topology window and the terminal emulator window by clicking Show Topology and Hide Topology. Figure 21-7 shows an example.

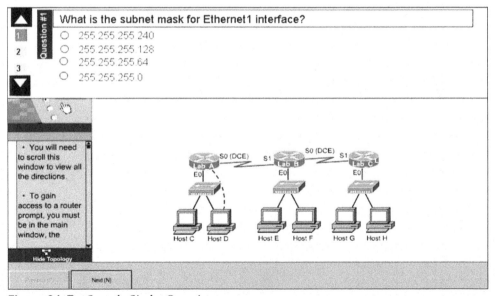

**Question #1**

What is the subnet mask for Ethernet1 interface?

○  255.255.255.240
○  255.255.255.128
○  255.255.255.64
○  255.255.255.0

1
2
3

• You will need to scroll this window to view all the directions.

• To gain access to a router prompt, you must be in the main window, the

Hide Topology

Next (N)

S0 (DCE)  S1   S0 (DCE)  S1
Lab A      Lab B       Lab C
E0         E0          E0

Host C   Host D   Host E   Host F   Host G   Host H

21

**Figure 21-7**  *Sample Simlet Question*

## Suggested Plan for Final Review/Study

This section lists a suggested study plan from the point at which you finish reading through Chapter 20, until you take the 350-601 CCNP and CCIE Data Center Core DCCOR exam. Certainly, you can ignore this plan, use it as is, or just take suggestions from it.

The plan uses two steps:

**Step 1.** **Review key topics and DIKTA? questions:** You can use the table that lists the key topics in each chapter or just flip the pages looking for key topics. Also, reviewing the DIKTA? questions from the beginning of the chapter can be helpful for review.

**Step 2.** **Use the Pearson Cert Practice Test Engine to practice:** The Pearson Cert Practice Test Engine can be used to study using a bank of unique exam-realistic questions available only with this book.

## Summary

The tools and suggestions listed in this chapter have been designed with one goal in mind: to help you develop the skills required to pass the 350-601 CCNP and CCIE Data Center Core DCCOR exam. This book has been developed from the beginning to not only tell you the facts but also to help you learn how to apply the facts. No matter how much experience you have leading up to when you take the exams, it is our hope that the broad range of preparation tools, and even the structure of the book, helps you pass the exam with ease. We hope you do well on the exam.

# CCNP and CCIE Data Center Core DCCOR 350-601 Official Cert Guide Exam Updates

## The Purpose of This Chapter

For all the other chapters, the content should remain unchanged throughout this edition of the book. Instead, this chapter will change over time, with an updated online PDF posted so you can see the latest version of the chapter even after you purchase this book.

Why do we need a chapter that updates over time? For two reasons:

- To add more technical content to the book before it is time to replace the current book edition with the next edition. This chapter will include additional technology content and possibly additional PDFs containing more content.

- To communicate detail about the next version of the exam, to tell you about our publishing plans for that edition, and to help you understand what that means to you.

After the initial publication of this book, Cisco Press will provide supplemental updates as digital downloads for minor exam updates. If an exam has major changes or accumulates enough minor changes, we will then announce a new edition. We will do our best to provide any updates to you free of charge before we release a new edition. However, if the updates are significant enough in between editions, we may release the updates as a low-priced standalone eBook.

If we do produce a free updated version of this chapter, you can access it on the book's companion website. Simply go to the companion website page and go to the "Exam Updates Chapter" section of the page.

If you have not yet accessed the companion website, follow this process below:

**Step 1.** Browse to www.ciscopress.com/register.

**Step 2.** Enter the print book ISBN (even if you are using an eBook): **9780138228088**.

**Step 3.** After registering the book, go to your account page and select the **Registered Products** tab.

**Step 4.** Click the **Access Bonus Content** link to access the companion website. Select the **Exam Updates Chapter** link or scroll down to that section to check for updates.

## About Possible Exam Updates

Cisco introduced CCNA and CCNP in 1998. For the first 25 years of those certification tracks, Cisco updated the exams on average every 3–4 years. However, Cisco did not pre-announce the exam changes, so they felt very sudden. Usually, a new exam would be announced, with new exam topics, giving you 3–6 months before your only option was to take the new exam. As a result, you could be studying with no idea about Cisco's plans, and the next day, you had a 3–6 month timeline to either pass the old exam or pivot to prepare for the new exam.

Thankfully, Cisco changed its exam release approach in 2023. Called the Cisco Certification Roadmap (https://cisco.com/go/certroadmap), the new plan includes these features:

- Cisco considers changes to all exam tracks (CCNA, CCNP Enterprise, CCNP Security, and so on) annually.

- Cisco uses a predefined annual schedule for each track, so even before any announcements, you know the timing of possible changes to the exam you are studying for.

- The schedule moves in a quarterly sequence:

    - Privately review the exam to consider what to change.

    - Publicly announce whether an exam is changing, and if so, announce details like exam topics and release date.

    - Release the new exam.

- Exam changes might not occur each year. If changes occur, Cisco characterizes them as minor (less than 20% change) or major (more than 20% change).

The specific dates for a given certification track can be confusing because Cisco organizes the work by fiscal year quarters. Figure 22-1 spells out the quarters with an example 2024 fiscal year. Their fiscal year begins in August, so, for example, the first quarter (Q1) of fiscal year (FY) 2024 begins in August 2023.

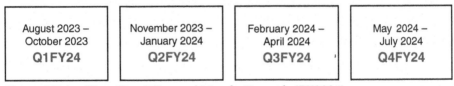

| August 2023 – October 2023 **Q1FY24** | November 2023 – January 2024 **Q2FY24** | February 2024 – April 2024 **Q3FY24** | May 2024 – July 2024 **Q4FY24** |

**Figure 22-1**  *Cisco Fiscal Year and Months Example (FY2024)*

Focus more on the sequence of the quarters to understand the plan. Over time, Cisco may make no changes in some years and minor changes in others.

## Impact on You and Your Study Plan

The new Cisco policy helps you plan, but it also means that the exam might change before you pass the current exam. That impacts you, affecting how we deliver this book to you. This chapter gives us a way to communicate in detail about those changes as they occur. But you should watch other spaces as well.

For those other information sources to watch, bookmark and check these sites for news. In particular:

- **Cisco:** Check the Certification Roadmap page: cisco.com/go/certroadmap. Make sure to sign up for automatic notifications from Cisco on that page.

- **Publisher:** Check their page about new certification products, offers, discounts, and free downloads related to the more frequent exam updates: ciscopress.com/newcert.

- **Cisco Learning Network:** Subscribe to the CCNA Community at http://cs.co/9780138228088, where we expect ongoing discussions about exam changes over time. If you have questions, search for "roadmap" in the CCNA community, and if you do not find an answer, ask a new question!

As changes arise, we will update this chapter with more detail about exam and book content. At that point, we will publish an updated version of this chapter, listing our content plans. That detail will likely include the following:

- Content removed, so if you plan to take the new exam version, you can ignore those when studying.

- New content planned per new exam topics, so you know what's coming.

The remainder of the chapter shows the new content that may change over time.

## News About the Next Exam Release

The next exam release for 350-601 DCCOR exam is scheduled for Q1FY24 (August 2023–October 2023).

At the most recent version of this chapter, the 350-601 DCCOR: Implementing and Operating Cisco Data Center Core Technologies exam blueprint/exam topics version was Version 1.1.

## Updated Technical Content

The current version 1.0 of this chapter has no additional technical content.

# Answers to the "Do I Know This Already?" Quizzes

## Chapter 1

1. B. The area ID, authentication, hello/dead intervals, stub flag, and maximum transmission unit (MTU) size must match to form OSPF adjacencies.

2. B, C. The router with the highest OSPF priority will be elected as the DR. If there is a tie, the router with the higher ID will be elected as the DR.

3. B, C. When multiple OSPF routers are connected to a multi-access medium such as Ethernet or nonbroadcast multiple access (NBMA), a designated router (DR), and a backup designated router (BDR) are elected. DRs reduce network traffic because only they maintain the complete OSPF database and then send updates to the other routers on the shared network segment.

4. B, D. The OSPF IPv6 interface to a link can have more than one IPv6 address. In fact, a single link can belong to multiple subnets, and two interfaces attached to the same link but belonging to different IPv6 subnets can still communicate. OSPFv3 changes the OSPFv2 language of "subnet" to "link" and allows the exchange of packets between two neighbors on the same link but belonging to different IPv6 subnets.

5. A. IPv6 routing uses link-local addresses to form routing adjacencies.

6. C. BGP path selection 1. Weight, 2. Local_Pref, 3. Local path, 4. AS_Path, 5. Origin type, 6. multi-exit discriminator (MED), 7. eBGP/iBGP, 8. Metric.

7. D. The **show ip bgp summary** command displays summarized information about the status of all BGP connections.

8. A. External BGP (eBGP) is used to establish sessions and exchange route information between two or more autonomous systems. Internal BGP (iBGP) is used by routers that belong to the same autonomous system (AS).

9. C. A detect multiplier is the number of missing BFD hello messages from another BFD device before this local device detects a fault in the forwarding path.

10. B. MLDv1 is similar to IGMPv2, and MLDv2 is similar to IGMPv3.

11. A, C. In multicast routing, the decision to forward traffic is based on the source address, not on the destination address as in unicast routing.

12. A, D, E. The HSRP default hello time is 3 seconds, and the default hold time is 10 seconds. Virtual IP must be on same subnet as the interface IP address. HSRP version 1 supports group numbers from 0 to 255.

13. A. In HSRP version 1, group numbers are restricted to the range from 0 to 255. HSRP version 2 expands the group number range from 0 to 4095.

**14.** A. The **standby preempt** command enables the Hot Standby Router Protocol (HSRP) router with the highest priority to immediately become the active router.

**15.** B. VRRP object tracking provides a way to ensure the best VRRP router is the virtual router master for the group by altering VRRP priorities to the status of tracked objects, such as the interface or IP route states.

# Chapter 2

**1.** C. The smallest numeric bridge ID wins the election.

**2.** E. Enabling the PortFast feature causes a switch or a trunk port to enter the STP forwarding state immediately or upon a linkup event, thus bypassing the listening and learning states.

**3.** B, D. The IEEE 802.1w standard, called Rapid STP or RSTP, provides faster STP.

**4.** B. When Rapid PVST+ detects a topology change, the protocol does the following: it starts the topology change (TC) while a timer with a value equal to twice the hello time for all the non-edge root and designated ports, if necessary, then flushes the MAC addresses associated with all these ports.

**5.** A, C, D. The Link Aggregation Control Protocol (LACP) is part of the IEEE specification 802.3ad, so it can be used on non-Cisco devices.

With the mode active, the switch sends LACP packets, initiates negotiations with remote ports, and can form a port channel if it receives a response.

The LACP uses the port priority with the port number to form the port identifier. The port priority determines which ports should be put in standby mode when there is a hardware limitation that prevents all compatible ports from aggregating. A higher port priority number indicates a lower priority.

**6.** A. The port channel interface represents the whole bundle, and all the configurations on this interface are applied to all physical ports that are assigned to this logical interface.

**7.** A, C. Fabric Extender (FEX) supports the port channel and virtual port channel for uplink aggregation.

**8.** B. vPC peers use the Cisco Fabric Services protocol to synchronize forwarding-plane information and implement necessary configuration checks.

**9.** B. There are two types of consistency check failures: the ones that will bring down the entire port channel (these are type 1s) and the ones that only cause an error or keep a single VLAN or group of VLANs from becoming active on the port channel (type 2). MTU is type 1 consistency check failure, whereas QoS, SVI, and ACL all are type 2.

**10.** B, D. From vPC general guidelines, a vPC must be configured on a pair of Cisco Nexus switches of the same type. For example, you can deploy a vPC on a pair of Cisco Nexus 5000 Series switches or Cisco Nexus 7000 Platform switches but not on a combination of them. A vPC keepalive should not run across a vPC peer link. A vPC domain, by definition, consists of a pair of switches that are identified by a shared vPC domain ID. You can use vPC as a Layer 2 link to establish a routing adjacency between two external routers.

# Chapter 3

1.   C. The underlay network—the bottom of that layer—provides a foundation for all other network services. The underlay transmits VXLAN and other overlay packets, so administrators must understand a different way to address connectivity issues.

2.   D. Virtual Extensible LAN extends the VLAN address space and adds a 24-bit segment ID, increasing available IDs to 16 million. Millions of isolated Layer 2 VXLAN networks can coexist on a common Layer 3 infrastructure because the VXLAN segment ID in each frame segregates individual logical networks.

3.   B. For VXLAN gateway redundancy, both vPC VTEP switches need to have the identical secondary IP address configured under the loopback interface.

# Chapter 4

1.   B, C. In a two-tier CLOS architecture, every lower-tier switch (leaf layer) is connected to each of the top-tier switches (spine layer) in a full-mesh topology. Every leaf switch connects to every spine switch in the fabric. The ACI fabric provides consistent low-latency forwarding across high-bandwidth links (40 Gbps and 100 Gbps). APIC connects to leaf devices only.

2.   C, D. The Cisco APIC uses the concept of endpoints and policies. The endpoints are virtual machines (VMs) or physical servers.

3.   C. The APIC discovers the IP address and node information of other Cisco APIC controllers in the cluster using the Link Layer Discovery Protocol (LLDP)-based discovery process.

4.   D. All traffic in the ACI fabric is normalized as VXLAN packets. At ingress, the ACI encapsulates external VLAN, VXLAN, and NVGRE packets in a VXLAN packet.

5.   B. The APIC manages the fabric. It is recommended to have a minimum of three APIC controllers in a cluster (N+2 redundancy).

6.   A. The Virtual Machine Manager (VMM) domain profile groups VM controllers with similar networking policy requirements. For example, VM controllers can share VLAN pools and application endpoint groups (EPGs). The APIC communicates with the controller to publish network configurations such as port groups that are then applied to the virtual workloads.

7.   A, C. Contract filters are used to classify traffic based on Layer 2 to Layer 4 attributes (such as Ethernet type, protocol type, TCP flags, and ports).

# Chapter 5

1.   A. The National Institute of Standards and Technology (NIST) defines cloud computing as a model for enabling ubiquitous, convenient, on-demand network access to a shared pool of configurable computing resources (e.g., networks, servers, storage, applications and services) that can be rapidly provisioned and released with minimal management effort or service provider interaction.

2.   D. NIST identifies cloud computing with five essential characteristics: on-demand self-service, broad network access, resource pooling, rapid elasticity, and measured service.

3. A, B, D. The most popular cloud computing service models are Infrastructure as a Service (IaaS), Platform as a Service (PaaS), and Software as a Service (SaaS).

4. B. PaaS delivers the Networking, Storage, Servers, Virtualization, Operating System, Middleware, and Runtime layers as a service to cloud consumers.

5. A, B, C. The four most popular cloud deployment models are the private cloud, public cloud, hybrid cloud, and community cloud.

6. D. In the private cloud, the infrastructure is provisioned for a single organization; therefore, it provides better data security and regulatory compliance compared to the public, hybrid, and community clouds where the infrastructure is shared between multiple cloud consumers.

## Chapter 6

1. B, D. When a boot is successful, you can use the setup utility to build an initial configuration file using the System Configuration dialog. The setup starts automatically when a device has no configuration file in NVRAM. The dialog guides you through the initial configuration.

2. B, C. For POAP, Cisco offers sample configuration scripts that were developed using the Python programming language and Tool command language (Tcl).

3. B. Because Cisco NX-OS cannot connect to a radio or atomic clock and act as a stratum 1 server, Cisco recommends that you use the public NTP servers available on the Internet.

4. A, C. Cisco NX-OS can automatically generate system checkpoints to help you avoid a loss of configuration information. System checkpoints are generated by the following events:

   ■ When an enabled feature is disabled with the **no feature** command

   ■ When an instance of a Layer 3 protocol is removed, such as with the **no router bgp** command or the **no ip pim sparse-mode** command

   ■ When a feature's license expires

5. B. The default NTP port is UDP 161.

6. A, B. Cisco NX-OS streaming telemetry allows you to push data off the device to a defined endpoint as JavaScript Object Notation (JSON) or using Google Protocol Buffers (GPB) at a much higher frequency and more efficiently.

7. A, D. With the Cisco Network Assurance Engine, you can predict the impact of changes, verify networkwide behavior, and assure network security policy and compliance.

## Chapter 7

1. C. Cisco NDFC offers streamlined data center network automation, control, and management for Cisco NX-OS–based VXLAN fabrics. Cisco NDI helps identify anomalies, provide root-cause analysis, plan capacity, manage change, and accelerate

troubleshooting. Cisco NDO provides the visibility and connectivity to different fabric controllers and unifies them into one single orchestrator, ensuring that consistent intent-based policies are provisioned properly. NDDB enables NetOps to programmatically manage aggregating, filtering, and forwarding complete flows to custom analytics tools.

2.  D. After the Nexus Dashboard Fabric Controller is installed, you can choose from one of the following personas: Fabric Discovery, Fabric Controller, and SAN Controller. Cisco Nexus Dashboard Insights is a separate service like Cisco Nexus Dashboard Fabric Controller and is not part of Cisco NDFC personas.

3.  A, C. Cisco Nexus Dashboard can be deployed using a number of different form factors: Cisco Nexus Dashboard physical appliance (.iso), VMware ESXi (.ova), Linux KVM (.qcow2), Amazon Web Services (.ami), Microsoft Azure (.arm), and in an existing Red Hat Enterprise Linux (RHEL) system.

4.  A, B. Virtual form factor allows you to deploy a Nexus Dashboard cluster using VMware ESXi virtual machines with one of two resource profiles:

    ■ **Data node:** A node profile designed for data-intensive applications, such as Nexus Dashboard Insights.

    ■ **App node:** A node profile designed for non-data-intensive applications, such as Nexus Dashboard Orchestrator.

5.  C. Each Nexus Dashboard cluster typically consists of one or three master nodes. For three-node clusters, you can also provision a number of worker nodes to enable horizontal scaling and standby nodes for easy cluster recovery in case of a master node failure.

6.  C. Cisco Nexus Dashboard is deployed as a cluster, connecting each service node to two networks—the management network and the data network. Service-to-service communication utilizes Data Network, whereas installation of services utilizes Management Network.

7.  A, D. Cisco Nexus Dashboard Home screen allows you to navigate between different components. One View page provides a single pane of glass (SPOG) view into all your connected cluster, sites, and services. Admin Console page enables you to configure and administer your Nexus Dashboard cluster. Services page provides one-click access to every service available in your cluster. Sites page provides one-click access to the controller UI of any site onboarded to your cluster.

8.  B, D. The System Resources category contains the following subcategories: Node, Pods, Deployments, StatefulSets, DaemonSets, Services, and Namespaces. DaemonSets define a pod that runs on every host in the Kubernetes cluster and is automatically created whenever a node is added to the cluster. StatefulSets define pods that need to be run on a predictable host with a specific storage volume. If StatefulSets pods go down, they are re-created in the same place with the same persistent identifier so that they can use the same storage volume as their previous incarnation.

# Chapter 8

1. A. Cisco MDS 9706 chassis supports external Supervisor-1 and Supervisor-4 modules. Cisco MDS 9396T, 9250i, and 9148S are fixed switches and don't support external supervisor modules.

2. D. The fabric initialization process consists of four phases: principal switch selection, domain ID distribution, FCID allocation, and fabric reconfiguration.

3. A. The lowest run-time priority is considered the highest priority during the principal switch selection process. By default, the configured priority is 128. The valid range to set the priority is between 1 and 254.

4. A, D. FLOGI happens between the N port and an F port. After an FC device (host) is attached to the FC fabric, it performs fabric login. The host (N port) sends the FLOGI request to the well-known fabric login server address 0xfffffe. The FLOGI frame contains its node name, N port name, and service parameters.

5. A. CFS is a peer-to-peer protocol with no client/server relationship.

6. A, C, D. CFS uses three modes of distribution: coordinated distributions, uncoordinated distributions, and unrestricted uncoordinated distributions. Coordinated distributions allow only one distribution in the fabric at any given time. Uncoordinated distributions allow multiple parallel distributions in the fabric except when a coordinated distribution is in progress. Unrestricted uncoordinated distributions allow multiple parallel distributions in the fabric in the presence of an existing coordinated distribution.

7. A. Multiple VSANs can share the same physical topology.

8. B. Theoretically, up to 256 VSANs can be configured in a switch. Of these, one is a default VSAN (VSAN 1), and another is an isolated VSAN (VSAN 4094). User-specified VSAN IDs range from 2 to 4093.

9. C. Port channel can be formed between E ports and TE ports, F ports and NP ports, and TF ports and TNP ports. E ports and F ports will not form a port channel because the E port is used to connect to another switch and the F port is used to connect a peripheral device (host or disk).

10. B, C. In Active mode, when you add or modify a port channel interface, the SAN port channel automatically recovers. Also, the ON mode is the default mode in SAN port channels, not the Active mode.

11. A. Devices can belong to more than one zone.

12. A, B, D. Zone membership can be defined using the port World Wide Name (pWWN), Fabric pWWN, FCID, interface and switch WWN (sWWN), interface and domain ID, domain ID and port number, IPv4 address, IPv6 address, and symbolic-nodename.

13. C. The device alias information is independent of the VSAN configuration. The device alias configuration and distribution are independent of the zone server and the zone server database. A device alias name is restricted to 64 alphanumeric characters.

**14.** B. When you commit the changes made to the pending database of the device alias, the pending database content overwrites the effective database content. The pending database is distributed to the switches in the fabric, and the effective database on those switches is overwritten with the new changes. Also, the fabric lock is released.

**15.** B. When an NP uplink is established, the edge switch sends a fabric login message (FLOGI) to the core switch, and then (if the FLOGI is successful) it registers itself with the name server on the core switch. Subsequent FLOGIs from end devices connected to this NP uplink are converted to fabric discovery messages (FDISCs).

# Chapter 9

**1.** D. IEEE 802.1Q defines eight priorities but not a simple, effective, and consistent scheduling mechanism between them. IEEE 802.11 Qaz ETS (Enhanced Transmission Selection) allows assignment of bandwidth to each priority group.

**2.** A. FCoE is implemented by encapsulating an FC frame in an Ethernet packet with the dedicated Ethertypes 0x8906(FCoE) and 0x8914(FIP).

**3.** A. In the VLAN discovery phase, an end device (CNA) broadcasts a request for FCoE VLAN. The request occurs on the native VLAN. In the FCF discovery phase, the CNA broadcasts a solicitation to find FCF to log in to. Broadcasts go out on the FCoE VLAN. In the FLOGI/DISC phase, CNA performs a fabric login using FLOGI or FLOGI with NPV FDISC. In the FC commands phase, the CNA begins normal FC data commands using Ethertype 0x8906.

**4.** A, C, D. Each virtual Fibre Channel interface is associated with only one VSAN.

**5.** D. Three single-hop solutions are possible when FCoE is deployed using Cisco Nexus switches: FCoE direct-attached topology, FCoE FEX topology, and FCoE remote-attached topology.

**6.** A. DCBX allows the switch to send a LAN Logical Link Status (LLS) message to a directly connected CNA. To disable LAN traffic on an FCoE link, you can use the **shutdown lan** command to send an LLS-Down message to the CNA. This command causes all VLANs on the interface that are not enabled for FCoE to be brought down. If a VLAN on the interface is enabled for FCoE, it continues to carry SAN traffic without any interruption.

**7.** A, C, D. Connectivity from an FCoE NPV bridge to the FCF is supported only over point-to-point links.

# Chapter 10

**1.** D. NFS version 3 introduced support for larger files and file systems such as 64-bit file sizes and offsets. NFSv4.1 introduced pNFS extension and NFS multipathing (or session trunking mechanism). NFSv4.2 introduced the server-side clone and copy feature, which allows a file to be copied between servers without copying it to the client first.

**2.** D. NFS versions 2 and 3 support both TCP and UDP. NFS version 4 supports only TCP as its transport protocol.

3. **A, D.** NAS supports two file- and data-sharing protocols: Common Internet File System (CIFS) and Network File System (NFS).

4. **C.** Network-attached storage (NAS) is a centralized file-level (as opposed to block-level) external data storage server connected to a network providing data access to a heterogeneous group of clients.

## Chapter 11

1. **D.** You can configure both in-band and out-of-band configuration using the Cisco MDS NX-OS Setup Utility.

2. **A, B.** The Cisco MDS NX-OS software consists of two images: the kickstart image and the system image.

3. **B.** The **show incompatibility-all system bootflash:** *system image filename* command determines which features are incompatible with the destination upgrade release.

4. **A, C.** You can upgrade any switch in the Cisco MDS 9000 Family by using the auto-mated, one-step upgrade using the **install all** command or by doing a manual upgrade by changing the boot statements to point to the destination upgrade image and using the **reload** command. An automated upgrade using the **install all** command is nondis-ruptive and doesn't require a switch reload, but it disrupts the control plane for about 80 seconds.

5. **D.** Log messages are not saved across system reboots. However, a maximum of 100 log messages with a severity level of critical and below (levels 0, 1, and 2) is saved in NVRAM.

6. **A, C.** Each SPAN session represents an association of one destination with a set of sources along with various other parameters that you specify to monitor the network traffic. One destination can be used by one or more SPAN sessions. The SD port does not have a port VSAN.

## Chapter 12

1. **A, B.** The Cisco UCS Mini solution extends the Cisco UCS architecture into envi-ronments that require smaller domains, including branch and remote offices, point-of-sale locations, and smaller IT environments. The Cisco UCS Mini has three main infrastructure components:

   ■ Cisco UCS 6324 Fabric Interconnect

   ■ Cisco UCS blade server chassis

   ■ Cisco UCS blade or rack-mount servers

2. **B, D.** In a blade chassis, the FEX fabric link (the link between the FEX and the FI) supports two different types of connections:

   ■ Discrete mode

   ■ Port channel mode

3. C. A service profile typically includes four types of information:

   ■ **Server definition:** It defines the resources (for example, a specific server or a blade inserted to a specific chassis) that are required to apply to the profile.

   ■ **Identity information:** Identity information includes the universally unique identifier (UUID), Media Access Control (MAC) address for each virtual network interface card (vNIC), and World Wide Name (WWN) specifications for each host bus adapter (HBA).

   ■ **Firmware revision specifications:** These specifications are used when a certain tested firmware revision is required to be installed or for some other reason a specific firmware is used.

   ■ **Connectivity definition:** This definition is used to configure network adapters, Fabric Extenders, and parent interconnects; however, this information is abstract because it does not include the details of how each network component is configured.

4. C, D. The command-line interface cluster verification commands are **show cluster extended-state** and **show cluster state**.

5. F. You can verify the server status by clicking the Equipment tab, Chassis, and then the Server General tab.

6. D. When you delete a specified VLAN, the ports associated with that VLAN are shut down, and no traffic flows from it.

7. C, D. Unicast traffic in Cisco UCS has the following characteristics:

   ■ Each server link is pinned to exactly one uplink port (or port channel).

   ■ Server-to-server Layer 2 traffic is locally switched.

   ■ Server-to-network traffic goes out on its pinned uplink port.

8. C. The Cisco Unified Computing System model supports multiple ways to connect with centralized storage. The first storage connectivity method uses a pure Ethernet IP network to connect the servers to both their user community and the shared storage array. Communication between the servers and storage over IP can be accomplished by using a Small Computer System Interface over IP (iSCSI).

9. D. A storage-area network (SAN) introduces the flexibility of networking to enable one server or many heterogeneous servers to share a common storage utility. A network might include many storage devices, including disk, tape, and optical storage. Additionally, the storage utility might be located far from the servers that it uses. This type of storage provides maximum reliability, expandability, and performance. The SAN is the most resilient, highly scalable, and high-performance storage.

# Chapter 13

1. A, C. The type of destination port determines what kind of monitoring session you need. For an Ethernet traffic monitoring session, the destination port must be an unconfigured physical port. For a Fibre Channel traffic monitoring session, the

destination port must be a Fibre Channel uplink port, except when you are using Cisco UCS 6454 Fabric Interconnects and 6300 Series Fabric Interconnects.

2. **D.** Audit logs record system events that occurred, where they occurred, and which users initiated them.

3. **C.** The SELs are stored in the CIMC NVRAM through an SEL log policy. It is best practice to periodically download and clear the SELs. The SEL file is approximately 40 KB in size, and no further events can be recorded when it is full. It must be cleared before additional events can be recorded.

4. **B, C.** Only Essential and Advanced support the Intersight virtual appliance.

5. **B.** Upgrades to Intersight are delivered automatically and do not require any resources.

## Chapter 14

1. **A, C.** The two types of backup policies are All Configuration and Full State.

2. **C.** In a logical configuration, an XML file includes all logical configuration settings such as service profiles, VLANs, VSANs, pools, and policies. You can use the file generated from this backup to import these configuration settings to the original fabric interconnect or to a different fabric interconnect. You cannot use this file for a system restore.

3. **A, D.** The Cisco UCS Manager uses one of the following methods to import and update a system configuration:

   ■ **Merge:** The information in the imported configuration file is compared with the existing configuration information. If there are conflicts, the import operation overwrites the information on the Cisco UCS domain with the information in the import configuration file.

   ■ **Replace:** The current configuration information is replaced with the information in the imported configuration file one object at a time.

4. **B.** You can use Auto Install to upgrade the infrastructure components to one version of Cisco UCS and upgrade the chassis and server components to a different version.

5. **A.** You cannot cancel a server firmware upgrade process after you complete the configuration in the Install Server Firmware wizard. The Cisco UCS Manager applies the changes immediately. However, the timing of the actual reboot of servers depends on the maintenance policy in the service profile associated with the server.

## Chapter 15

1. **A.** The HyperFlex system offers one-click integration with VMware vSphere, allowing your IT staff to extend their virtualization skills to storage and management; the purpose is to get better visibility into and control over your computing, network, and storage resources from a single console.

2. **D.** HyperFlex delivers

   ■ Intelligent end-to-end automation, including networking

   ■ Unified management

- Resource scaling

- Bigger virtual machine density and lower jitter and latency

3. B, C. You can automate processes yourself with interfaces to the Cisco UCS Manager through Microsoft PowerShell and Python.

4. B. You can perform deep learning on GPU-only nodes in the data center and drive inferencing with up to two NVIDIA Tesla T4 and P6 GPUs in edge nodes and up to six NVIDIA Tesla GPUs in Cisco HyperFlex HX240c nodes.

5. A, B, E. Cisco UCS provides a single point of connectivity that integrates Cisco HyperFlex HX-Series All-Flash or hybrid nodes and a variety of Cisco UCS servers into a single unified cluster. Cisco offers you the flexibility to choose a combination of CPU, flash memory, graphics acceleration, and disk storage resources.

6. B. Cisco provides an architectural performance edge with NVMe drives connected directly to the CPU rather than through a latency-inducing PCIe switch.

# Chapter 16

1. A, C. In the EEM, event statements monitor events on Cisco NX-OS components that may require some action, workaround, or notification. Action statements take action, such as sending an email or disabling an interface, to recover from an event.

2. A, B, D. EEM supports the following actions in action statements: generate a syslog message, reload the device, and update a counter. EEM can't generate a Python script by itself.

3. C, D. The Scheduler does not apply a default timetable. If you create a schedule and assign jobs and do not configure the time, the job is not started. Scheduler features need to be enabled first before a Scheduler can be configured.

4. A, C, D. You can configure only Daily, Weekly, Monthly, Delta (the job begins at a specified start time and then at specified intervals), and one-time mode intervals for job scheduling in the Scheduler.

5. B. You enable the Bash shell by running the command **feature bash-shell**. The **run bash** command loads Bash and begins at the home directory for the user.

6. C. The Guest Shell runs within a Linux Container (LXC), a decoupled execution space on the underlying Linux environment. It doesn't support Windows applications.

7. A, D. Each XML document must have one and only one root element. Also, XML is case sensitive. For example, <Device> and <device> are considered two different elements.

8. C. XML is more verbose than JSON and usually uses more characters to express the same data than JSON. JSON includes arrays, whereas XML doesn't include arrays. A proper JSON object begins with a left brace { and ends with a right brace }.

9. A, B, D. GET, POST, PUT, and DELETE are the allowed HTTP methods for REST API requests.

10. A. NX-API response elements consist of version, type, sid, outputs, output, input, body, code and msg; chunk belongs to the NX-API request element.

# Chapter 17

1. C. Ansible playbooks are written in YAML structured format.

2. C, D. Ansible playbooks are written in YAML structured format and contain Ansible domain-specific language (DSL). Ansible is agentless; therefore, Ansible playbooks are deployed to an Ansible control station and not an Ansible agent.

3. A. The python package for Cisco is named *cisco*. The cisco package contains various modules, including cisco_secret, cisco_socket, and acl.

4. C. **clip()** prints the output of the CLI command directly to stdout and returns nothing to Python. **cli()** returns the raw output of CLI commands, including control or special characters. **clid()** returns JSON output for the CLI command, if XML support exists for the command; otherwise, an exception is thrown. **clistdout()** is not an API.

5. B, C. Checking for a USB device containing the configuration script file in POAP mode is NOT supported on the Cisco Nexus 9000 series switches. POAP requires a minimum DHCP lease period of 3600 seconds (1 hour). POAP checks the DHCP lease period. If the DHCP lease period is set to less than 3600 seconds (1 hour), POAP does not complete the DHCP negotiation.

6. B. The POAP process has the following phases: (1) Power-up phase, (2) USB discovery phase, (3) DHCP discovery phase, (4) Script execution phase, and (5) Post-installation phase.

7. D. The **terraform plan** command specifies the steps and the dependencies that will occur during the execution of a Terraform plan.

8. C. Terraform uses providers, which are open-source plug-ins that expose the implementation for specific services and infrastructures. They abstract the API layer of real resources, allowing Terraform to create, manage, and update the needed resources.

9. C. You go to the PowerShell Gallery to get the Cisco PowerShell modules for all the supported systems.

# Chapter 18

1. B, C. Nexus devices support local and remote AAA. Remote AAA services are provided through the RADIUS and TACACS+ protocols. TCP/IP is not an AAA protocol, and LDAP is not commonly used for network authentication.

2. B. The **aaa authentication login default group tacacs+ local** command uses AAA as a default login and tries the TACACS+ group because it is first in the list; then it tries the local account.

3. B, D. RADIUS uses the UDP 1645/1646 and 1812/1813 ports.

4. A, B. By default, the user accounts without an administrator role can access only the **show**, **exit**, **end**, and **configure terminal** commands. You can add rules to allow users to configure features.

5. B. The device validates DHCP packets received on the untrusted interfaces of VLANs that have DHCP snooping enabled. The device forwards the DHCP packet unless any of the following conditions occur (in which case, the packet is dropped):

   ■ The device receives a DHCP response packet (such as a DHCPACK, DHCPNAK, or DHCPOFFER packet) on an untrusted interface.

   ■ The device receives a packet on an untrusted interface, and the source MAC address and the DHCP client hardware address do not match. This check is performed only if the DHCP snooping MAC address verification option is turned on.

   ■ The device receives a DHCPRELEASE or DHCPDECLINE message from an untrusted host with an entry in the DHCP snooping binding table, and the interface information in the binding table does not match the interface on which the message was received.

6. B. ARP inspections allow a network administrator to intercept, log, and discard ARP packets with invalid MAC address-to-IP address bindings.

7. D. When port security is enabled, the default maximum number of permitted MAC address is one.

8. A. The Cisco NX-OS device provides CoPP to prevent denial-of-service (DoS) attacks from impacting performance. Such attacks, which can be perpetrated either inadvertently or maliciously, typically involve high rates of traffic destined to the supervisor module or CPU itself.

9. A. When the network is microsegmented, there are fewer end devices per subnetwork, thus minimizing traffic flow and optimizing the network.

10. B. While different endpoint groups (EPGs) can only communicate with other endpoint groups based on the contract rules defined, no contract is required for intra-endpoint group communication. Intra-endpoint group communication from endpoint to endpoint in the same endpoint group is allowed by default.

11. B. Start time: The absolute time that the lifetime begins.

    End time: The end time can be defined in one of the following ways:

    ■ The absolute time that the lifetime ends

    ■ The number of seconds after the start time that the lifetime ends

    ■ Infinite lifetime (no end time)

# Chapter 19

1. B, C. Two-factor authentication is supported by associating RADIUS or TACACS+ provider groups with designated authentication domains and enabling two-factor authentication for those domains. Two-factor authentication does not support IPM and is not supported when the authentication realm is set to LDAP, local, or none.

2. A. For RADIUS and TACACS+ configurations, you must configure a user attribute in each remote authentication provider through which users log in to the Cisco UCS

Manager. This user attribute holds the roles and locales assigned to each user. This step is not required for LDAP configurations that use LDAP group mapping to assign roles and locales.

**3.** C. LDAP uses STARTTLS. This allows encrypted communication using port 389. Cisco UCS negotiates a TLS session on port 636 for SSL, but initial connection starts unencrypted on 389.

# Chapter 20

**1.** C, D. TACACS+ is a Cisco proprietary protocol. TACACS+ encrypts the entire protocol payload between the switch and the AAA server to ensure higher data confidentiality. RADIUS encrypts passwords only.

**2.** C. The LDAP client/server protocol uses TCP (TCP port 389) for transport requirements.

**3.** A, C. Each user role can contain multiple rules, and each user can have multiple roles. Roles can be used to create VSAN administrators. Depending on the configured rules, these VSAN administrators can configure MDS features (for example, zone, fcdomain, or VSAN properties) for their VSANs without affecting other VSANs. Also, if the role permits operations in multiple VSANs, the VSAN administrators can change VSAN membership of F or FL ports among these VSANs.

**4.** B, D. Port security binds devices at the interface level. Port security can be distributed by CFS.

**5.** A, B, D. Fabric binding binds the fabric at the switch level, whereas port security binds devices at the interface level.

**6.** A, B. Fabric binding cannot be distributed by CFS and must be configured manually on each switch in the fabric. Fabric binding uses a set of sWWNs.

**7.** A, C. The fabric binding feature maintains a configuration database (config-database) and an active database. The config-database is a read-write database that collects the configurations you perform. These configurations are enforced only upon activation. This activation overwrites the active database with the contents of the config-database. The active database is read-only and is the database that checks each switch that attempts to log in.

# GLOSSARY

**802.1Qaz**　The IEEE standard for data center bridging (DCB) enhancements to Ethernet local-area networks for Enhanced Transmission Selection (ETS). It provides a common management framework for assignment of bandwidth to frame priorities.

**802.1Qbb**　The IEEE standard for data center bridging (DCB) enhancements to Ethernet local-area networks for priority-based flow control (PFC). It provides a link-level flow control mechanism that can be controlled independently for each frame priority. The purpose of this mechanism is to ensure zero traffic loss under congestion in DCB networks.

# A

**AAA server**　The server/host responsible for running RADIUS or TACACS services.

**action statements**　Statements that describe the action triggered by a policy. Each policy can have multiple action statements.

**Adaptive Security Virtual Appliances (ASAv)**　A Cisco virtual security solution for traditional multitier and fabric environments. In multitenant environments, ASAv provides tenant edge security services.

**Address Resolution Protocol (ARP)**　An Internet protocol used to map an IP address to a MAC address. Defined in RFC 826.

**Advanced Message Queuing Protocol (AMQP)**　An open standard application layer protocol for message-oriented middleware. AMQP mandates the behavior of the messaging provider and client to the extent that implementations from different vendors are interoperable, in the same way as SMTP, HTTP, FTP, and so on have created interoperable systems.

**any-source multicast (ASM)**　A method that allows multiple senders to be on the same group/channel, as opposed to a source-specific multicast where a single particular source is specified.

**application programming interface (API)**　A way to specify a software component in terms of its operations, its inputs and outputs, and its underlying types. Cisco UCS, Cisco Nexus switches in NX-OS, and ACI mode expose APIs to the external world for programmatic control.

**application virtual switch (AVS)**　A hypervisor-resident virtual network switch that is specifically designed for the application centric infrastructure (ACI) architecture. Based on the Cisco Nexus 1000V virtual switch, AVS provides feature support for the ACI application policy model, full switching capabilities, and more advanced telemetry features.

**American Standard Code for Information Interchange (ASCII)**　An 8-bit code for character representation (7 bits plus parity).

**authentication, authorization, and accounting (AAA)**　A feature that verifies the identity of, grants access to, and tracks the actions of users managing a switch. Authentication confirms the identity of the user or device. Authorization determines what the user or device is allowed to do. Accounting records information about access attempts, including inappropriate requests.

**autonomous system (AS)**    A collection of networks under a common administration sharing a common routing strategy. Autonomous systems are subdivided by areas. An autonomous system must be assigned a unique 16-bit number by the IANA. Sometimes abbreviated AS.

# B

**base DN**    The point from where a server will search for users.

**basic input/output system (BIOS)**    In a computer system, it performs the power-on self-test procedure, searches, and loads to the master boot record in the system booting process.

**Bidirectional Forwarding Detection (BFD)**    A detection protocol designed to provide fast forwarding path failure detection times for all media types, encapsulations, topologies, and routing protocols. In addition to fast forwarding path failure detection, BFD provides a consistent failure detection method for network administrators.

**bind DN**    A distinguished name that is composed of the user and the location of the user in the LDAP directory tree.

**Bourne Again SHell (Bash Shell)**    A Unix shell and command language written by Brian Fox for the GNU Project as a free software replacement for the Bourne shell. Bash enables access to the underlying Linux system on the Cisco Nexus device, which is used to manage the system.

**bridge protocol data units (BPDUs)**    A frame that contains information about the Spanning Tree Protocol (STP). Switches send BPDUs using a unique MAC address from its origin port and a multicast address as destination MAC (01:80:C2:00:00:00). For STP algorithms to function, the switches need to share information about themselves and their connections, which are BPDUs. BPDUs are sent out as multicast frames to which only other Layer 2 switches or bridges are listening.

**Broadcast, Unknown unicast, and Multicast (BUM)**    A type of traffic transmitted using one of three methods to a destination of which the sender does not know the network address. This is achieved by sending the network traffic to multiple destinations on an Ethernet domain.

# C

**Call Home**    Call Home provides an email-based notification of critical system events. A versatile range of message formats is available for optimal compatibility with pager services, standard email, or XML-based automated parsing applications.

**central processing unit (CPU)**    The CPU executes instructions in the operating system. Among these functions are system initialization, routing functions, and network interface control. The CPU is a microprocessor. Large routers can have multiple CPUs.

**Cisco attribute-value pair (cisco-av-pair)**    The Internet Engineering Task Force (IETF) draft standard specifies a method for communicating vendor-specific information between the network access server and the RADIUS server by using the vendor-specific attribute (attribute 26). Attribute 26 encapsulates vendor-specific attributes (VSA), thereby allowing vendors to support their own extended attributes otherwise not suitable for general use.

**Cisco Discovery Protocol (CDP)**   A media- and protocol-independent device-discovery protocol that runs on most Cisco-manufactured equipment, including routers, access servers, and switches. Using CDP, a device can advertise its existence to other devices and receive information about other devices on the same LAN or on the remote side of a WAN.

**Cisco Fabric Services (CFS)**   A common infrastructure for automatic configuration synchronization in the network. It provides the transport function and a set of common services to the features. CFS has the ability to discover CFS-capable switches in the network and discover feature capabilities in all CFS-capable switches.

**Cisco Integrated Management Controller (CIMC)**   A controller present in both Cisco UCS blade chassis and blade/rack servers, allowing integrated management control of the Cisco UCS infrastructure without needing separate hardware modules.

**Cisco MDS**   A family of Cisco storage-area network switches supporting Fibre Channel, Fibre Channel over Ethernet, and Fibre Channel over IP-based storage environments.

**Cisco Network Assurance Engine (NAE)**   A comprehensive intent-assurance solution that mathematically verifies the entire data center network for correctness.

**Cisco Nexus**   A family of Cisco network physical and virtual switches primarily targeted at the data center environments.

**Cisco Nexus Dashboard (ND)**   A unified automation platform that provides unprecedented simplicity by integrating operational services to manage customers' on-premises, cloud, and hybrid data center networks through a single pane of glass.

**Cisco Nexus Dashboard Data Broker (NDDB)**   A software-defined, programmable solution to aggregate copies of network traffic using Switched Port Analyzer (SPAN) or network test access point (TAP) for monitoring and visibility.

**Cisco Nexus Dashboard Fabric Controller (NDFC)**   A comprehensive management and automation solution for all Cisco Nexus and Cisco Multilayer Distributed Switching (MDS) platforms powered by Cisco NX-OS. NDFC provides management, automation, control, monitoring, and integration for deployments spanning LAN, SAN, and IP Fabric for Media (IPFM) fabrics.

**Cisco Nexus Dashboard Insights (NDI)**   An application that monitors, analyzes, troubleshoots, and assures a network in real time. It helps identify anomalies, provide root-cause analysis, plan capacity, manage change, and accelerate troubleshooting.

**Cisco Nexus Dashboard Orchestrator (NDO)**   An application that provides the visibility and connectivity to different fabric controllers and unifies them into one single orchestrator, ensuring that consistent intent-based policies are provisioned properly.

**Cisco NX-OS**   A device operating system running on the Cisco Nexus data center family of switches.

**Cisco Unified Computing System (Cisco UCS)**   An (x86) architecture data center server platform, introduced in 2009, that is composed of computing hardware, virtualization support, switching fabric, and management software.

**command-line interface (CLI)**    An interface that enables the user to interact with the operating system by entering commands and optional arguments.

**committed information rate (CIR)**    The rate at which data is expected to be transmitted, on average, under normal conditions.

**Common Internet File System (CIFS)**    CIFS is a particular implementation of the Server Message Block protocol, created by Microsoft. *See also* Server Message Block.

**community cloud**    A cloud computing environment that provides shared infrastructure resources to specific groups that share common interests or have common concerns. A community cloud can be deployed either on-premises or off-premises, and it can be owned and operated by either a third-party managing service provider, the participating organizations themselves, or a combination of both.

**complex programmable logic device (CPLD)**    Similar to FPGA, this is an integrated circuit designed to be configured by an integrator or an end user after manufacturing.

**converged network adapter (CNA)**    A computer input/output device that combines the functionality of a host bus adapter (HBA) with a network interface controller (NIC). In other words, it "converges" access to a storage-area network and a general-purpose computer network.

**Coordinated Universal Time (UTC)**    The time zone at zero degrees longitude, previously called Greenwich Mean Time (GMT) and Zulu time. UTC replaced GMT in 1967 as the world time standard. UTC is based on an atomic time scale rather than an astronomical time scale.

**Council of Oracles Protocol (COOP)**    A protocol used to communicate the mapping information (location and identity) to the spine proxy. An iLeaf will forward endpoint address information to spine Oracle using ZeroMQ (Zero Message Queue). COOP running on the spine nodes will ensure all spine nodes maintain a consistent copy of end point address and location information and maintain the DHT repository of endpoint identity to location mapping database.

**Credential Security Support Provider Protocol (CredSSP)**    A security support provider that is implemented by using the Security Support Provider Interface (SSPI). CredSSP lets an application delegate the user's credentials from the client to the target server for remote authentication.

**cyclic redundancy check (CRC)**    An error-detecting code commonly used in digital networks and storage devices to detect accidental changes to raw data.

# D

**data center bridging (DCB)**    A set of IEEE standards enhancing Ethernet networks to be able to accommodate convergence of network and storage traffic.

**Data Center Bridging Exchange (DCBX)**    A discovery and capability exchange protocol to discover peers and exchange configuration information between DCB-compliant bridges. DCBX leverages functionality provided by IEEE 802.1AB (LLDP).

**Data Center Network Manager (DCNM)**  A network platform designed to help efficiently implement, visualize, and manage Cisco Unified Fabric. It includes a comprehensive feature set, along with a customizable dashboard that provides enhanced visibility and automated fabric provisioning of dynamic data centers.

**DevOps**  A set of software development practices that combine software development (Dev) and information-technology operations (Ops) to shorten the systems-development life cycle while delivering features, fixes, and updates frequently in close alignment with business objectives.

**Dynamic Host Configuration Protocol (DHCP)**  A protocol used by hosts to dynamically discover and lease an IP address and learn the correct subnet mask, default gateway, and DNS server IP addresses.

**differentiated services code point (DSCP)**  The six most significant bits of the 1-byte IP type of service (ToS) field. The per-hop behavior represented by a particular DSCP value is configurable. DSCP values range between 0 and 63.

**distinguished name (DN)**  A name that includes an object's entire path to the root of the LDAP namespace.

**Distributed Virtual Switch (DVS)**  A virtual switch that is used to configure, monitor, and administer virtual machine access switching.

**Domain Name System (DNS)**  An application layer protocol used throughout the Internet for translating hostnames into their associated IP addresses.

**domain-specific language (DSL)**  A computer language specialized to a particular application domain. This is in contrast to a general-purpose language (GPL), which is broadly applicable across domains.

**dual in-line memory module (DIMM)**  Small circuit boards carrying memory integrated circuits, with signal and power pins on both sides of the board, in contrast to single-in-line memory modules (SIMMs).

**Duplicate Address Detection (DAD)**  A proxy feature responds to the DAD queries on behalf of a node that owns the queried address. It is useful in environments where nodes cannot communicate directly on the link.

**Dynamic Host Configuration Protocol (DHCP)**  A client/server protocol that automatically provides a host with its IP address and other related configuration information, such as the subnet mask, default gateway IP address, and DNS server IP address.

**dynamic load balancing (DLB)**  A form of traffic-based load balancing in which cable modems are balanced among upstream and downstream channels after they come online, while they are passing traffic. Dynamic load balancing must be enabled by using the enforce option of the cable load-balance group threshold command.

**Dynamic Port VSAN Membership (DPVM)**  A method that dynamically assigns VSAN membership to ports by assigning VSANs based on the device WWN.

# E

**Elastic Sky X integrated (ESXi)**    A bare-metal hypervisor from VMware that installs directly onto a physical server. With direct access to and control of underlying resources, a VMware ESXi effectively partitions hardware to consolidate applications and cut costs.

**electrical programmable logical devices (EPLD)**    Hardware components such as ASICs on I/O modules that can be upgraded without having to replace the hardware. EPLD upgrades are typically not required, but in some cases, such as new chassis installs or chassis redeployments, it is recommended that you upgrade to the latest EPLD version to ensure that all upgradable hardware components have the latest feature enhancements and caveat fixes.

**Embedded Event Manager (EEM)**    Tool that detects and handles critical events on Cisco NX-OS devices. It monitors events that occur on the device and takes action to recover or troubleshoot these events, based on the configuration.

**Enhanced Transmission Selection (ETS)**    *See* 802.1Qaz.

**equal-cost multipath (ECMP)**    Multiple routing paths of equal cost that may be used for packet forwarding.

**Ethernet VPN (EVPN)**    A standards-based technology that provides virtual multipoint bridged connectivity between different Layer 2 domains over an IP or IP/MPLS backbone network.

**event statements**    Statements that specify the event that triggers an EEM policy to run. You can configure multiple event triggers.

**Exchange Peer Parameters (EPP)**    Fibre Channel port channel protocol that uses EPP SW_ILS frames. SW_ILS frames are special Fibre Channel frames exchanged between storage switches on ISL links. There are many kinds of SW_ILS frames, and EPP is one of them.

**Extensible Authentication Protocol over User Datagram Protocol (EAPoUDP)**    A protocol used by Network Admission Control (NAC) to query the Cisco Trust Agent on the PC. It enables a PC to access the network after it has passed the validation.

**Extensible Markup Language (XML)**    A markup language that defines a set of rules for encoding documents in a format that is both human-readable and machine-readable. It is defined in the XML 1.0 specification produced by the W3C, and several other related specifications, all free open standards.

# F

**F port channel trunk**    A type of trunk between F ports that allows interconnected ports to transmit and receive tagged frames in more than one VSAN over the same physical link.

**fabric login (FLOGI)**    A host's N port establishes a 24-bit address for the device logging in and establishes buffer-to-buffer credits and the class of service supported.

**fabric port WWN (fWWN)**    Each port on a fabric has an fWWN that is sometimes also called a Fabric Port WWN (FPWNNN).

**Fabric Shortest Path First (FSPF)**   The standard path selection protocol used by Fibre Channel fabrics. FSPF automatically calculates the best path between any two switches in a fabric.

**fan-in ratio**   The ratio of how many storage ports can be served from a single host channel.

**fan-out ratio**   The relationship in quantity between a single port on a storage device and the number of servers that are attached to it.

**fcping**   A feature that verifies reachability of a node by checking its end-to-end connectivity. You can invoke the fcping feature by providing the FC ID, the destination port WWN, or the device alias information.

**Fibre Channel (FC)**   A high-speed network technology (commonly running at 2-, 4-, 8-, and 16-gigabit per second rates) primarily used to connect computer data storage. Fibre Channel is standardized in the T11 Technical Committee of the International Committee for Information Technology Standards (INCITS), an American National Standards Institute (ANSI)-accredited standards committee.

**Fibre Channel over Ethernet (FCoE)**   A computer network technology that encapsulates Fibre Channel frames over Ethernet networks. This allows Fibre Channel to use 10-Gigabit Ethernet networks (or higher speeds) while preserving the Fibre Channel protocol characteristics. The specification is part of the International Committee for Information Technology Standards T11 FC-BB-5 standard published in 2009. FCoE maps Fibre Channel directly over Ethernet while being independent of the Ethernet forwarding scheme.

**Fibre Channel over Ethernet N-port ID Virtualization (FCoE-NPIV)**   Fibre Channel mechanism to assign multiple Fibre Channel IDs on the same physical interface. FCoE-NPIV can work with FCoE-NPV to enable scaled-out SAN access layer.

**Fibre Channel over Ethernet N-port Virtualization (FCoE-NPV)**   Secure method to connect FCoE-capable hosts to an FCoE-capable FCoE forwarder (FCF) device. Switches operating in FCoE-NPV mode proxy all Fibre Channel processing and functions to the upstream switch operating in FCoE-NPIV mode.

**Fibre Channel Security Protocol (FC-SP)**   A protocol that provides switch-switch and host-switch authentication capabilities to overcome security challenges for enterprise-wide fabrics. Diffie-Hellman Challenge Handshake Authentication Protocol (DHCHAP) is an FC-SP protocol that provides authentication between Cisco MDS 9000 Family switches and other devices.

**field-programmable gate array (FPGA)**   An integrated circuit designed to be configured by a customer or a designer after manufacturing; hence, "field-programmable."

**File Transfer Protocol (FTP)**   Application protocol, part of the TCP/IP protocol stack, used for transferring files between network nodes. FTP is defined in RFC 959.

**finite-state machine (FSM)**   Cisco UCS Finite State Machines that monitor the state transition of Cisco UCS objects.

**firmware**   A program written to the read-only memory (ROM) of a computing device.

**First Hop Redundancy Protocol (FHRP)**   A networking protocol that offers default gateway redundancy by allowing two or more routers to provide backup for the IP address of the default gateway.

# G

**Gateway Load Balancing Protocol (GLBP)**   A Cisco proprietary protocol feature that provides automatic router backup for IP hosts configured with a single default gateway on an IEEE 802.3 LAN.

**generic routing encapsulation (GRE)**   A tunneling protocol developed by Cisco that can encapsulate a wide variety of network layer protocols inside a virtual point-to-point link to Cisco routers at remote points over an IP internetwork. By connecting multiprotocol subnetworks in a single-protocol backbone environment, IP tunneling using GRE allows network expansion across a single-protocol backbone environment.

**Git/GitHub**   A web-based Git repository hosting service. It offers all the distributed revision control and source code management (SCM) functionality of Git and adds its own features. Unlike Git, which is strictly a command-line tool, GitHub provides a web-based graphical interface and desktop as well as mobile integration.

**Google Protocol Buffers (GPB)**   Provides an alternative encoding mechanism, streaming the data in GPB format over UDP or TCP. It can be configured by CLI and XML and uses the same policy files as those of JSON. Additionally, a GPB encoder requires metadata in the form of compiled .proto files to translate the data into GPB format.

**Graceful Insertion and Removal (GIR)**   A function that provides an easy method for isolating a switch for maintenance windows and then bringing it back into service with little service disruption.

**graphical processing unit (GPU)**   An embedded system used in personal computers, workstations, and game consoles. GPUs are very efficient in computer graphics and image processing. GPUs structure designed on parallel possessing, which makes them more efficient than CPUs for artificial intelligence (AI) or big data applications that process large amounts of data.

**graphical user interface (GUI)**   A type of computing interface that allows users to interact with electronic devices through graphical icons and visual indicators such as secondary notation, as opposed to text-based interfaces, typed command labels, or text navigation. GUIs were introduced in reaction to the perceived steep learning curve of command-line interfaces (CLIs), which require commands to be typed on the keyboard.

**Guest Shell**   A decoupled execution space running within a Linux Container (LXC) on Cisco Nexus devices. The Guest Shell gives network-admin level privileges.

# H

**host bus adapter (HBA)**   Also called host controller or host adapter, this connects a host system to other network or storage devices.

**Hot Standby Router Protocol (HSRP)**   A Cisco proprietary redundancy protocol for establishing a fault-tolerant default gateway, described in detail in RFC 2281.

**hybrid cloud**   A cloud computing environment that offers a hybrid approach between the private and public cloud. The premise of the hybrid cloud is to extend the existing private cloud environment into the public cloud as needed, on demand, and with consistent network and security policies.

**Hypertext Transfer Protocol (HTTP)**  The protocol used by web browsers and web servers to transfer files, such as text and graphics files.

**hypervisor**  Software that allows multiple operating systems, known as guest operating systems, to share a single physical server. Guest operating systems run inside virtual machines and have fair scheduled access to underlying server physical resources.

# I

**IaaS**  Infrastructure as a Service. A form of cloud computing that provides virtualized computing resources over the Internet. IaaS is one of three main categories of cloud computing services, alongside Software as a Service (SaaS) and Platform as a Service (PaaS).

**ICMP Router Discovery Protocol (IRDP)**  Also known as Internet Router Discovery Protocol. A protocol that enables hosts to locate routers. When operating as a client, router discovery packets are generated. When operating as a host, router discovery packets are received. IRDP is only useful in the presence of host computers that are running it. Note that routers do not receive IRDP packets; therefore, unlike CDP, IRDP is not useful in a router-only environment.

**in-band**  A storage virtualization method that places the virtualization engine directly in the data path so that both block data and the control information that governs its virtual appearance transit the same link.

**in-service software upgrade (ISSU)**  The industry's first comprehensive, transparent software upgrade capability for the IP/Multiprotocol Label Switching edge router.

**input/output module (I/O module)**  A computer term for a module that controls the communication between the computer and the outside world. Inputs are the data received by the system, and outputs are the data sent from it.

**input/output operations per second (IOPS)**  A performance measurement used to benchmark computer storage devices like storage-area networks (SAN), hard disk drives (HDD), and solid state drives (SSD).

**Integrated Lights-Out (iLO)**  A proprietary embedded server management technology by HP Inc. that provides out-of-band management facilities.

**Intelligent Platform Management Interface (IPMI)**  A set of computer interface specifications for an autonomous computer subsystem that provides management and monitoring capabilities independently of the host system's CPU, firmware (BIOS or UEFI), and operating system.

**interior gateway protocol (IGP)**  Internet protocol used to exchange routing information within an autonomous system.

**Internet Assigned Numbers Authority (IANA)**  An organization that owns the rights to assign many operating numbers and facts about how the global Internet works, including public IPv4 and IPv6 addresses.

**Internet Control Message Protocol (ICMP)**    A TCP/IP network layer protocol that reports errors and provides other information relevant to IP packet processing.

**Internet Group Management Protocol (IGMP)**    Used by IP routers and their immediately connected hosts to communicate multicast group membership states.

**Internet protocol (IP)**    The network layer protocol in the TCP/IP stack, providing routing and logical addressing standards and services.

**Internet Small Computer System Interface (iSCSI)**    An Internet Protocol–based storage networking standard for linking data storage facilities. By carrying SCSI commands over IP networks, iSCSI is used to facilitate data transfers over intranets and manage storage over long distances. iSCSI can be used to transmit data over local-area networks (LANs), wide-area networks (WANs), or the Internet and can enable location-independent data storage and retrieval. The protocol allows clients (called initiators) to send SCSI commands (CDBs) to SCSI storage devices (targets) on remote servers. It is a storage-area network (SAN) protocol, allowing organizations to consolidate storage into data center storage arrays while providing hosts (such as database and web servers) with the illusion of locally attached disks. iSCSI can be run over long distances using existing network infrastructure. iSCSI was pioneered by IBM and Cisco in 1998 and submitted as a draft standard in March 2000.

**Internet of Things (IoT)**    The network of physical devices, vehicles, buildings, and other items—embedded with electronics, software, sensors, and network connectivity—that enables these objects to collect and exchange data.

**Inter-Process Communication (IPC)**    A platform-independent mechanism through which route processors, line cards, or redundant components communicate with each other. IPC is a point-to-point communication protocol.

**inter-switch link (ISL)**    A Cisco-proprietary protocol that maintains VLAN information as traffic flows between switches and routers.

**intra-fabric messaging (IFM)**    A process used for communication between different devices on the ACI fabric. The software layer that tries to deliver messages between the various DME addresses for each agent is called an *identity*. An identity has the following format: system-type:system-id:service:slot.

**IP Fabric for Media (IPFM)**    An IP-based infrastructure for transporting audio and video signals including 4k and 8k ultra HD videos.

# J–K–L

**JavaScript Object Notation (JSON)**    A lightweight data-interchange format that is based on a subset of JavaScript programming language. It can be considered an alternative to XML.

**job**    A routine task defined as a command list and completed according to a specified schedule.

**just a bunch of disks (JBOD)**    A group of external disks that can be used individually without interdependency.

**Kernel-based Virtual Machine (KVM)**    A virtualization package for Linux on an x86 hardware platform. KVM uses x86 hardware virtualization extensions (for example, Intel

VT-x) to implement a hypervisor that hosts VMs as user space processes. Cisco UCS servers support the KVM-based Red Hat Enterprise Virtualization (RHEV) as the hypervisor in a server virtualization system.

**Lightweight Directory Access Protocol (LDAP)**   The protocol used for gathering/managing information from an LDAP-accessible directory/database. An example of its use is having an AAA server use an LDAP request to Active Directory to verify the credentials of a user.

**Link Aggregation Control Protocol (LACP)**   The IEEE standard for Ethernet. LACP (802.3ad) for the gigabit interfaces feature bundles individual Gigabit Ethernet links into a single logical link that provides the aggregate bandwidth of up to four physical links.

**Link Layer Discovery Protocol (LLDP)**   A vendor-independent link layer protocol used by network devices to advertise their identity and capabilities to neighbors on a LAN segment. LLDP is specified in IEEE 802.1AB.

**link-state advertisements (LSAs)**   The link-state advertisement created by the OSPF designated router (DR) or pseudonode that represents a group of routers on the same interface. The network LSA advertises summary information to represent the group of routers on the network.

**local-area network (LAN)**   A computer network that interconnects computers within a limited area, such as a home, school, computer laboratory, or office building, using network media. The defining characteristics of LANs, in contrast to wide-area networks (WANs), include their smaller geographic area and noninclusion of leased telecommunication lines.

**logical availability zones (LAZ)**   A logical data center that groups two or more HyperFlex nodes into a logically defined zone. A minimum of three zones is created, and the data in the cluster is distributed in such a way that no blocks are written to the nodes within a single zone more than once. Due to this enhanced distribution pattern of data across zones, wherein each zone has multiple servers, clusters with LAZ enabled can typically withstand more failures than clusters that operate without this feature enabled. The number of failures that can be tolerated varies depending on the number of zones in the cluster and the number of servers in each of the zones. Generally, multiple node failures across one or two zones will be tolerated better and with less risk than multiple nodes failing across three or more zones.

# M

**managed object (MO)**   An object that is identified by a name and contains a set of typed values or properties. It specifies whether the target of the operation is a managed object or an object class. Everything in the Cisco Nexus switches is represented as a class or a managed object.

**Multicast Routing Information Base (MRIB)**   A topology table that is also known as the multicast route table (mroute), which derives from the unicast routing table and PIM.

**Management Information Base (MIB)**   A database used for managing the entities in a communications network. Most often associated with the Simple Network Management Protocol (SNMP), the term is also used more generically in contexts such as in the OSI/ISO network management model.

**Management Information Tree (MIT)**   A tree with parent-child relationships in which Cisco Nexus switches' managed object instances can contain other instances.

**maximum transmission unit (MTU)**   In computer networking, the MTU of a communications protocol of a layer is the size (in bytes) of the largest protocol data unit that the layer can pass onward.

**Mean Time to Resolution (MTRR)**   The average time it takes to fully resolve a failure.

**Media Access Control (MAC) address**   A standardized data link layer address that is required for every device that connects to a LAN. Ethernet MAC addresses are 6 bytes long and are controlled by the IEEE. Also known as a hardware address, a MAC layer address, and a physical address.

**memberOf attribute**   An attribute that specifies the DN of the groups to which the object belongs.

**message digest 5 (MD5)**   A one-way hashing algorithm that produces a 128-bit hash. Both MD5 and SHA-1 are variations on MD4 and are designed to strengthen the security of the MD4 hashing algorithm. SHA-1 is more secure than MD4 and MD5. Cisco uses hashes for authentication within the IPsec framework. Also used for message authentication in SNMPv2. MD5 verifies the integrity of the communication, authenticates the origin, and checks for timeliness. MD5 has a smaller digest and is considered to be slightly faster than SHA-1.

**Microsegmentation (uSeg)**   A process that enables users to create microsegments across multiple VMs and physical domains in a consistent policy-driven framework. It allows operational flexibility and choice for customers.

**Microsoft Active Directory(AD)**   Microsoft implementation of LDAP directory services for use in Windows-based environments. Active Directory provides administrators with the means for assigning networkwide policies, deploying programs to many computer systems concurrently, and applying critical updates to an entire organization. Active Directory stores information and settings related to an organization in a centralized and accessible database.

**Microsoft Challenge-Handshake Authentication Protocol (MSCHAP)**   An authentication method used by the Microsoft Windows operating system. Cisco routers that support this authentication method enable Microsoft Windows operating system users to establish remote PPP sessions without configuring an authentication method on the client. MSCHAP V2 authentication introduced an additional feature not available with MSCHAP V1 or standard CHAP authentication: the Change Password feature. This feature enables the client to change the account password if the RADIUS server reports that the password has expired.

**Multicast Listener Discovery (MLD)**   In IPv6, multicast group management is accomplished with a set of ICMPv6 messages that comprise the Multicast Listener Discovery (MLD) protocol. MLDv1 is similar to IGMPv2 and MLDv2 is similar to IGMPv3. Like IGMP, MLDv2 is backward compatible with MLDv1.

**Multicast Source Discovery Protocol (MSDP)**   A mechanism to connect multiple PIM sparse-mode (SM) domains. MSDP enables multicast sources for a group to be known to all rendezvous points in different domains. Each PIM-SM domain uses its own rendezvous points and does not need to depend on them in other domains. A rendezvous point runs MSDP over TCP to discover multicast sources in other domains. MSDP is also used to announce sources sending to a group. These announcements must originate at the domain's rendezvous point. MSDP depends heavily on MP-BGP for interdomain operation.

**Multichassis EtherChannel trunk (MCT)**  A type of link aggregation group (LAG) where port channel members terminate on separate chassis. The purpose is to provide a redundancy in the event one of the chassis fails.

**multi-hop FCoE**  A set of technologies and designs to extend convergence of network and storage traffic beyond the data center access layer.

**Multiprotocol BGP (MBGP)**  Also known as BGP+, MP-BGP represents multicast extensions to the BGP Unicast interdomain protocol. It adds capabilities to BGP to enable multicast routing policy throughout the Internet and to connect multicast topologies within and between BGP autonomous systems. That is, MP-BGP is an enhanced BGP that carries IP multicast routes. MP-BGP carries two sets of routes, one set for unicast routing and one set for multicast routing. The routes associated with multicast routing are used by Protocol Independent Multicast (PIM) to build multicast data distribution trees.

**multitenancy**  A mode of operation whereby IT resources are securely shared among multiple users. It utilizes virtualization technologies to create logical segments of a physical resource to create isolation between the users.

# N

**N port identifier virtualization (NPIV)**  A technique that enables the sharing of a single Fibre Channel N port between multiple N ports. It is used in storage networking techniques that utilize Fibre Channel–based ports to send and receive data between virtual machines (VMs) and virtual storage-area networks (SANs). NPIV is a component of the Fibre Channel Link Services (FC-LS) specification.

**N port virtualization (NPV)**  A technology that allows SAN switches to essentially become N port proxies. In a traditional SAN fabric, each switch gets assigned a domain ID. The domain ID is an 8-bit field in the FCID. There are officially 255 domain IDs. In reality, some of these IDs are reserved and can't be assigned to switches, leaving 239 switches. In large environments, that hard limit can become a serious issue as you try to scale the fabric. The solution to this problem is NPV.

**Neighbor Discovery (ND)**  A protocol that defines several mechanisms that are built into IPv6, such as prefix advertisement, duplicate address detection, ARP replacement, and router redirection. NDP uses ICMPv6 message types 133 through 137.

**Neighbor Unreachability Detection (NUD)**  An IPv6 mechanism used for tracking neighbor reachability.

**Network Admission Control (NAC)**  A solution that enables you to authenticate wired, wireless, and VPN users and devices to the network; evaluate and remediate a device for policy compliance before permitting access to the network; differentiate access based on roles; and then audit and report on who is on the network.

**network-attached storage (NAS)**  File-oriented storage networking implementation, deployed in the form of customized storage appliances that are connected to the IP network.

Due to the file abstraction layer, NAS offers both storage and data sharing services across multiple platforms and protocols.

**Network File System (NFS)**   A distributed file system protocol originally developed by Sun Microsystems in 1984, which allows a user on a client computer to access files over a computer network much like local storage is accessed. The NFS is an open standard defined in a Request for Comments (RFC), allowing anyone to implement the protocol.

**network interface card (NIC)**   A computer card, sometimes an expansion card, and sometimes integrated into the motherboard of the computer that provides the electronics and other functions to connect to a computer network. Today, most NICs are specifically Ethernet NICs, and most have an RJ-45 port, the most common type of Ethernet port.

**Network Load Balancing Services (NLBS)**   A service that enables you to balance traffic across two or more WAN links without using complex routing protocols like BGP.

**Network Time Protocol (NTP)**   A protocol used to synchronize time-of-day clocks so that multiple devices use the same time of day, which allows log messages to be more easily matched based on their timestamps.

**Network Virtualization using Generic Routing Encapsulation (NVGRE)**   A network virtualization technology similar to VXLAN; it allows creating Layer 2 overlay networks on top of Layer 3 underlying networks by encapsulating original frames in GRE tunnels.

**NIST**   The National Institute of Standards and Technology (NIST) is a physical sciences laboratory, and a nonregulatory agency of the United States Department of Commerce. NIST's activities are organized into laboratory programs that include nanoscale science and technology, engineering, information technology, neutron research, material measurement, and physical measurement.

**node World Wide Name (nWWN)**   *See* World Wide Node Name (WWNN).

**nonvolatile random-access memory (NVRAM)**   A type of random-access memory (RAM) that retains its contents when a unit is powered off.

**NX-API**   An API that enables users to access the Nexus-OS CLI by making them available outside the switch by using HTTP/HTTPS.

**NX-API Developer Sandbox**   A web form hosted on the Nexus-OS switch. It translates NX-OS CLI commands into equivalent XML or JSON payloads and converts NX-API REST payloads into their CLI equivalents.

# O

**Open Agent Container (OAC)**   A 32-bit CentOS-based container created specifically for running Puppet agent software on Cisco Nexus devices.

**OpenLDAP**   A free, open-source implementation of the Lightweight Directory Access Protocol (LDAP).

**orchestration**   Coordination of multiple lower-level automation tasks to deliver an IT resource or set of IT resources "as a service."

**out-of-band**  A storage virtualization method that provides separate paths for data and control, presenting an image of virtual storage to the host by one link and allowing the host to directly retrieve data blocks from physical storage on another.

# P

**PaaS**  Platform as a Service. A category of cloud computing services that provides a platform allowing customers to develop, run, and manage applications without the complexity of building and maintaining the infrastructure typically associated with developing and launching an app.

**Password Authentication Protocol (PAP)**  Authentication protocol that allows PPP peers to authenticate one another. The remote router attempting to connect to the local router is required to send an authentication request. Unlike CHAP, PAP passes the password and host name or username in the clear (unencrypted). PAP does not itself prevent unauthorized access but merely identifies the remote end. The router or access server then determines whether that user is allowed access.

**Path MTU Discovery (PMTUD)**  A standardized technique in computer networking for determining the maximum transmission unit (MTU) size on the network path between two Internet Protocol (IP) hosts, usually with the goal of avoiding IP fragmentation. PMTUD was originally intended for routers in Internet Protocol Version 4 (IPv4).

**peak information rate (PIR)**  The maximum rate at which data can be transmitted. It is related to committed information rate (CIR), which is a committed rate speed that is guaranteed/capped.

**Peripheral Component Interconnect Express (PCIe)**  A high-speed serial computer bus standard that offers a high-speed interconnect between the server motherboard and other peripherals such as Ethernet and storage device.

**policies**  EEM policies consisting of an event statement and one or more action statements. The event statement defines the event to look for as well as the filtering characteristics for the event. The action statement defines the action EEM takes when the event occurs.

**port login (PLOGI)**  A host's N port requests login to another N port, before any data exchange between ports. This is done with port login at the address 0xFFFFFC.

**port VLAN ID (PVID)**  A default VLAN ID that is assigned to an access port to designate the virtual LAN segment to which this port is connected. The PVID places the port into the set of ports that are connected under the designated VLAN ID. Also, if a trunk port has not been configured with any VLAN memberships, the virtual switch's PVID becomes the default VLAN ID for the port's connection.

**port World Wide Name (pWWN)**  *See* World Wide Port Name (WWPN).

**PowerOn Auto Provisioning (POAP)**  A feature that automates the process of upgrading software images and installing configuration files on Cisco MDS and Nexus switches that are being deployed in the network.

**PowerShell agent (PSA)**  A virtual appliance used with the UCS Director to manage applications that expose Windows PowerShell–based northbound API calls. The PSA acts as an interfacing layer between the Cisco UCS Director and applications such as XenDesktop Controller and Microsoft SCVMM that are managed through Windows PowerShell.

**PowerShell session (PSSession)**   A connection created using the PSSession cmdlet. PowerShell establishes a persistent connection to the remote computer where you can run multiple commands that share data, such as a function or the value of a variable.

**Preboot Execution Environment (PXE)**   An industry standard protocol used for booting a machine via the network. In the data center, this protocol is often used to automate installation of an operating system on new servers.

**Prime Network Service Controller (PNSC)**   Management platform software for virtual network appliances. PNSC can be used to execute configuration changes quickly and consistently on virtual services elements like firewalls, load balancers, routers, and switches.

**priority-based flow control (PFC)**   *See* 802.1Qbb.

**private cloud**   A cloud computing environment provisioned for internal organizational use, which may include various internal divisions, business units, internal consumers, and so on.

**process login (PRLI)**   Processes establish communication between two different N ports.

**Protocol Independent Multicast (PIM)**   A multicast routing architecture that enables the addition of IP multicast routing on existing IP networks. PIM is unicast routing protocol independent and can be operated in two modes: dense and sparse.

**public cloud**   A cloud computing environment usually owned and operated by a service provider and offered as a service to customers.

# Q–R

**Quad Small Form-Factor Pluggable (QSFP)**   A high-density and low-power 40-Gigabit Ethernet connectivity option for data center, high-performance computing networks, enterprise core and distribution layers, and service provider applications.

**Quality of Service (QoS)**   The overall performance of a telephony or computer network, particularly the performance seen by the users of the network.

**Rapid per VLAN Spanning Tree (Rapid PVST+)**   A protocol that is based on the Rapid STP (RSTP) IEEE 802.1W standard. RSTP (IEEE 802.1w) natively includes most of the Cisco proprietary enhancements to the 802.1D Spanning Tree, such as BackboneFast and UplinkFast. Rapid-PVST+ uses RSTP to provide faster convergence. When any RSTP port receives legacy 802.1D BPDU, it falls back to legacy STP, and the inherent fast convergence benefits of 802.1W are lost when it interacts with legacy bridges. Cisco recommends that Rapid PVST+ be configured for best convergence.

**RecoverPoint**   A continuous data protection product offered by Dell EMC that supports asynchronous and synchronous data replication of block-based storage.

**Redundant Array of Independent Disks (RAID)**   RAID is a data storage virtualization technology that combines multiple physical disk drive components into one or more logical units for the purposes of data redundancy, performance improvement, or both.

**reliability, availability, and serviceability (RAS)**   A hardware design definition that means a reliable, highly available, and serviceable hardware design.

**Remote Authentication Dial-In User Service (RADIUS)**   A networking protocol that provides centralized authentication, authorization, and accounting (AAA) management for users who connect to and use a network service.

**Remote Network Monitoring (RMON)**   A standard monitoring specification that defines a set of statistics and functions that can be exchanged between RMON-compliant console systems and network probes. RMON provides comprehensive network-fault diagnosis, planning, and performance-tuning information.

**remote office, branch office (ROBO)**   Remote offices or satellite smaller business offices that usually get connected to the main enterprise via a wide area network (WAN).

**Remote SPAN (RSPAN)**   A feature that enables you to remotely monitor traffic for one or more SPAN sources distributed in one or more source switches in a fabric. The SPAN destination (SD) port is used for remote monitoring in a destination switch. A destination switch is usually different from the source switch but is attached to the same switched/Fibre Channel fabric.

**replication factor (RF)**   A number that indicates the total number of data copies made in the cluster to protect the data.

**Representational State Transfer (REST)**   An architectural style consisting of a coordinated set of architectural constraints applied to components, connectors, and data elements, within a distributed hypermedia system. REST ignores the details of component implementation and protocol syntax to focus on the roles of components, the constraints on their interaction with other components, and their interpretation of significant data elements.

**Reverse Path Forwarding (RPF)**   A technique used in routers to ensure loop-free multicast packet forwarding in multicast routing and to help prevent IP address spoofing in unicast routing.

**role-based access control (RBAC)**   An approach to restricting system access to authorized users for the purpose of computer systems security. It can implement mandatory access control (MAC) or discretionary access control (DAC).

**round-trip time (RTT)**   The time it takes for the source to receive a response of the request packet.

**Router Advertisement (RA)**   An ICMPv6 type 134 message sent periodically on the local link by an IPv6 router or upon request of a router solicitation message. The router advertisement message in IPv6 contains the IPv6 prefixes, valid and preferred lifetimes of prefixes, default router information, and some flags and options for nodes.

**RPM Package Manager (RPM)**   (Originally Red Hat Package Manager; now a recursive acronym.) A free and open-source package management system. The name RPM refers to the .rpm file format and the package manager program itself.

**Rubygems**   A package manager for the Ruby programming language that provides a standard format for distributing Ruby programs and libraries (in a self-contained format called a *gem*), a tool designed to easily manage the installation of gems, and a server for distributing them.

# S

**SaaS**  Software as a Service. A software licensing and delivery model in which software is licensed on a subscription basis and is centrally hosted. It is sometimes referred to as "on-demand software." SaaS is typically accessed by users using a thin client via a web browser.

**Scheduler**  Tool that uses jobs, which consist of a single command or multiple commands that define routine activities. Jobs can be scheduled one time or at periodic intervals.

**Secure Copy Protocol (SCP)**  Relying on SSH for security, SCP support allows the secure and authenticated copying of anything that exists in the Cisco IOS XE File Systems. SCP is derived from rcp.

**Secure Shell (SSH)**  A TCP/IP application layer protocol that supports terminal emulation between a client and a server, using dynamic key exchange and encryption to keep the communications private.

**Secure Sockets Layer (SSL)**  The original security method for HTTPS. Although succeeded by TLS, this term is still widely used and assumed. It is a secure alternative to HTTP.

**Server Message Block (SMB)**  SMB is a network communication protocol for providing shared access to files, printers, and serial ports between nodes on a network. Most usage of SMB involves computers running Microsoft Windows.

**service-level agreement (SLA)**  An agreement between an IT service provider and a customer. The SLA describes the IT service, documents service-level targets, and specifies the responsibilities of the IT service provider and the customer. A single SLA may cover multiple IT services or multiple customers.

**shortest path first (SPF)**  A routing algorithm that iterates on length of path to determine a shortest-path spanning tree. Commonly used in link-state routing algorithms. Sometimes called Dijkstra's algorithm.

**shortest path tree (SPT)**  The simplest form of a multicast distribution tree is a source tree with its root at the source and branches forming a spanning tree through the network to the receivers. Because this tree uses the shortest path through the network, it is also referred to as a shortest path tree (SPT).

**Simple Network Management Protocol (SNMP)**  An Internet-standard protocol for managing devices on IP networks. Devices that typically support SNMP include routers, switches, servers, workstations, printers, modem racks, and more.

**single pane of glass (SPOG)**  A single management dashboard that presents data from multiple sources in a unified display to manage a complex network infrastructure.

**Small Form-Factor Pluggable (SFP+)**  An enhanced version of the SFP that supports data rates up to 10 Gbps. The SFP+ specification was first published on May 9, 2006, and version 4.1 was published on July 6, 2009.

**software-defined networking (SDN)**  A collective name for network modernization technologies that intend to introduce characteristics such as automation and programmability into data center, campus, backbone, and wide-area networks.

**software development kit (SDK)**  A set of software development tools that allows the creation of applications for a certain software package, software framework, hardware platform, computer system, video game console, operating system, or similar development platform.

**software maintenance update (SMU)**  A software package that can be installed on a system to provide a patch fix or security resolution to a released image.

**Software Maintenance Upgrade (SMU)**  A package file that contains fixes for a specific defect. SMUs are created to respond to immediate issues and do not include new features.

**solid-state drive (SSD)**  A data storage device using integrated circuit memory that saves data permanently. SSD technology uses interfaces compatible with hard disk input/output (I/O) blocks.

**source-specific multicast (SSM)**  A datagram delivery model that best supports one-to-many applications, also known as broadcast applications. SSM is the core networking technology for the Cisco implementation of the IP Multicast Lite suite of solutions targeted for audio and video broadcast application environments.

**Spanning Tree Protocol (STP)**  A protocol that uses the Spanning Tree algorithm, allowing a switch to dynamically work around loops in a network topology by creating a spanning tree. Switches exchange bridge protocol data unit (BPDU) messages with other switches to detect loops and then remove the loops by blocking selected switch interfaces.

**storage area network (SAN)**  A dedicated high-speed network that makes storage devices accessible to servers by attaching storage directly to an operating system.

**switch World Wide Name (sWWN)**  A name assigned to a switch in a Fibre Channel fabric.

**Switched Port Analyzer (SPAN)**  A feature that monitors network traffic through a switch interface. Traffic through any switch port can be replicated to a special port called the SPAN destination port (SD port).

**switched virtual interface (SVI)**  A virtual interface (and port) that transmits only an untagged-VLAN packet for a managed switch.

**System Center Virtual Machine Manager (SCVMM)**  Forms part of Microsoft's System Center line of virtual machine management and reporting tools, alongside previously established tools such as System Center Operations Manager and System Center Configuration Manager. SCVMM is designed for management of large numbers of virtual servers based on Microsoft Virtual Server and Hyper-V.

**system event log (SEL)**  Log that records events taking place in the execution of a system in order to provide an audit trail that can be used to understand the activity of the system and to diagnose problems. It is essential to understand the activities of complex systems, particularly in the case of applications with little user interaction (such as server applications).

# T

**tebibyte (TiB)**  A unit used to measure memory or storage capacity. One tebibyte equals $2^{40}$ or 1,099,511,627,776 bytes.

**Terminal Access Controller Access Control System Plus (TACACS+)**  One of the protocols that can be used to communicate between an AAA server and its client.

**time-to-live (TTL)**   A field in an IP header that indicates how long a packet is considered valid.

**tool command language (Tcl)**   A scripting language that increases the flexibility of CLI commands. You can use Tcl to extract certain values in the output of a **show** command, perform switch configurations, run Cisco NX-OS commands in a loop, or define Embedded Event Manager (EEM) policies in a script.

**topology change (TC)**   RSTP topology change flag.

**Transmission Control Protocol (TCP)**   A connection-oriented transport layer TCP/IP protocol that provides reliable data transmission.

**Transport Layer Security (TLS)**   Based on SSL but more widely adopted as an IETF standard in RFC 5246.

**Transport Layer Security/Secure Sockets Layer (TLS/SSL)**   A protocol that resides between the application layer and TCP/IP to provide transparent encryption of data traffic.

**Trivial File Transfer Protocol (TFTP)**   A simplified version of FTP that allows files to be transferred from one computer to another over a network.

**trusted platform module (TPM)**   A specialized chip on an endpoint device that stores RSA encryption keys specific to the host system for hardware authentication.

**type-length-value (TLV)**   A dynamic format for storing data in any order. Used by the Cisco Generic ID PROM for storing asset information.

# U

**UCS Manager (UCSM)**   A platform emulator, where the full logical configuration of a server can be created from the user interface or the API methods and later applied to the physical hardware.

**UCS Manager SDK (UCSMSDK)**   A Python module that helps automate all aspects of Cisco UCS management, including server, network, storage, and hypervisor management.

**Unified Computing System (UCS)**   An (x86) architecture data center server platform, introduced in 2009, that is composed of computing hardware, virtualization support, switching fabric, and management software.

**universally unique identifier (UUID)**   Defined in the RFC 4122. UUIDs are applied for identification purposes.

**User Datagram Protocol (UDP)**   A connectionless transport layer protocol in the TCP/IP protocol stack. UDP is a simple protocol that exchanges datagrams without acknowledgments or guaranteed delivery.

# V

**Video Terminal 100 (VT100)**   A network application in which a computer runs software that makes it appear to a remote host as a directly attached terminal.

**Virtual Desktop Infrastructure (VDI)**  An architecture that allows users to use their desktops, laptops, and iPads as dumb terminals, while the actual application and data run securely on servers in the data center.

**virtual device context (VDC)**  Partitions a single physical device into multiple logical devices that provide fault isolation, management isolation, address allocation isolation, service differentiation domains, and adaptive resource management. A VDC instance can be managed within a physical device independently. Each VDC appears as a unique device to the connected users. A VDC runs as a separate logical entity within the physical device, maintains its own unique set of running software processes, has its own configuration, and can be managed by a separate administrator.

**Virtual Extensible LAN (VXLAN)**  Uses the MAC in User Datagram Protocol (MAC-in-UDP) encapsulation technique, which allows extending Layer 2 and Layer 3 connectivity services over an IP routed network. The VXLAN header carries a 24-bit identifier, known as a VXLAN VNID, which enables you to build more than 16 million logical segments.

**virtual interface card (VIC)**  A converged adapter that extends the network fabric directly to both servers and virtual machines so that a single connectivity mechanism can be used to connect both physical and virtual servers with the same level of visibility and control. This adapter provides acceleration for the various new operational modes introduced by server virtualization.

**virtual Internet routing lab (VIRL)**  Cisco virtual machines running the same network operating systems as used in the Cisco physical routers and switches.

**virtual LAN (VLAN)**  A group of devices, connected to one or more switches, with the devices grouped into a single broadcast domain through switch configuration. VLANs allow switch administrators to separate the devices connected to the switches into separate VLANs without requiring separate physical switches, gaining design advantages of separating the traffic without the expense of buying additional hardware.

**virtual machine (VM)**  Allocation of computing resources with other users. It isolates the operating system or application to avoid changing the end-user experience.

**Virtual Machine Manager (VMM)**  A piece of computer software, firmware, or hardware that creates and runs virtual machines.

**virtual machine network interface card (VMNIC)**  In VMware, a physical NIC that is assigned to a hypervisor as an uplink or trunked interface.

**virtual network interface card (vNIC)**  The virtual representation of a typical network interface card, used to connect to an Ethernet network.

**virtual port channel (vPC)**  Allows links that are physically connected to two different Cisco Nexus 5000, 7000, 9000, and UCS Series devices to appear as a single port channel to a third device. The third device can be a Cisco Nexus 2000 Series Fabric Extender, a switch, a server, or any other networking device. vPC can provide Layer 2 multipathing, which allows creating redundancy by increasing bandwidth, enabling multiple parallel paths between nodes, and load-balancing traffic where alternative paths exist.

**virtual private network (VPN)**  A private virtual network that extends across a public network such as the Internet.

**Virtual Router Redundancy Protocol (VRRP)**   The protocol controlling the IP address(es) associated with a virtual router, the router called the master. The election process provides dynamic failover in the forwarding responsibility if the master becomes unavailable. This allows any of the virtual router IP addresses on the LAN to be used as the default first-hop router by end-hosts.

**virtual routing and forwarding (VRF)**   A VPN routing and forwarding instance. A VRF consists of an IP routing table, a derived forwarding table, a set of interfaces that use the forwarding table, and a set of rules and routing protocols that determine what goes into the forwarding table.

**Virtual Server Infrastructure (VSI)**   The same machine can be used to run multiple server instances, each with independent operating system configurations.

**virtual storage-area network (VSAN)**   A collection of ports from a set of connected Fibre Channel switches that form a virtual fabric. Ports within a single switch can be partitioned into multiple VSANs, despite sharing hardware resources. Conversely, multiple switches can join a number of ports to form a single VSAN.

**VNX**   A series of storage arrays developed by EMC Corporation that unifies EMC's file-based and block-based offerings into a single product that can be managed with a single GUI.

**Volume Management Device (VMD)**   A new technology to enhance RAS capabilities for PCIe storage, VMD supported multi-SSD vendors, and multi virtualization operating systems like Windows/HyperV, Linux, and ESXi.

**VPLEX**   A virtual computer data storage product introduced by EMC Corporation. VPLEX implements a distributed "virtualization" layer within and across geographically disparate Fibre Channel storage-area networks and data centers.

**VXLAN network identifier (VNID)**   The 24-bit value used in the VXLAN packet header to identify virtual segments.

**VXLAN tunnel endpoint (VTEP)**   VXLAN tunnel endpoints are physical or virtual switch ports that terminate VXLAN tunnels and perform VXLAN encapsulation and deencapsulation. Each VTEP function has two interfaces: one is a switch interface on the local LAN segment to support local endpoint communication through bridging, and the other is an IP interface to the transport IP network.

# W

**Web Services-Management (WSMAN)**   A DMTF open standard defining a SOAP-based protocol for the management of servers, devices, applications, and various web services. WSMAN provides a common way for systems to access and exchange management information across the IT infrastructure.

**WHIPTAIL**   A company that built data storage systems out of solid-state drive components. It was later acquired by Cisco.

**wide-area network (WAN)**   A part of a larger network that implements mostly OSI Layer 1 and 2 technology, connects sites that typically sit far apart, and uses a business model in which a consumer (individual or business) must lease the WAN from a service provider (often a telco).

**Windows Remote Management (WinRM)** A feature of the Windows operating system that allows administrators to remotely run management scripts. WinRM is the "server" component of this remote management application.

**Windows Remote Shell (WinRS)** A feature of the Windows operating system that allows administrators to remotely run management scripts. WinRS is the client for WinRM, which runs on the remote computer attempting to remotely manage the WinRM server.

**workflow** The sequence of tasks that are required to fulfill a user request. The UCS Director workflow is built using a series of automation tasks linked together to perform a complex IT operation. It also determines the order in which the tasks are executed, and if required, it can link output of one task into the input of another.

**Workflow Designer** A tool provided by the UCS Director to build workflows. It provides a drag-and-drop user interface to design workflows. Workflows can be built by dragging tasks from the task library, placing them in required sequence, and defining their input and outputs. When the workflow design is complete, you can save it, test it, and publish it to a catalog for user consumption.

**World Wide Node Name (WWNN)** A name assigned to a node (an endpoint, a device) in a Fibre Channel fabric. It is valid for the same WWNN to be seen on many different ports (different addresses) on the network, identifying the ports as multiple network interfaces of a single network node.

**World Wide Port Name (WWPN)** A name assigned to a port in a Fibre Channel fabric. Used on storage-area networks, it performs a function equivalent to the MAC address in the Ethernet protocol because it is supposed to be a unique identifier in the network.

# X–Y–Z

**YAML Ain't Markup Language (YAML)** A human-readable data-serialization language. It is commonly used for configuration files but could be used in many applications where data is being stored (for example, debugging output) or transmitted (for example, document headers).

**Yellowdog Updater, Modified (YUM)** A free and open-source command-line package-management utility for computers or network devices running the Linux operating system using the RPM Package Manager. Though YUM has a command-line interface, several other tools provide graphical user interfaces to YUM functionality.

**Zero Trust (ZT)** A comprehensive approach to securing all access across the networks, applications, and environment. This approach helps secure access from users, end-user devices, APIs, IoT, microservices, containers, and more. It protects workforce, workloads, and workplace.

**zoning** In storage networking, the partitioning of a Fibre Channel fabric into smaller subsets to restrict interference, add security, and simplify management. While a SAN makes available several devices and/or ports to a single device, each system connected to the SAN should be allowed access only to a controlled subset of these devices/ports. Zoning applies only to the switched fabric topology (FC-SW); it does not exist in simpler Fibre Channel topologies.

# Index

## A

AAA model, 801
  accounting, 801, 900
  authentication, 801, 803–804, 899
  authorization, 801, 803–804, 899
  computer security, 875–876
  configuring AAA service options,
    802–803
  default parameter settings, 804
  global commands, 804–806
  local AAA services, 911–912
  locking user accounts, 806
  NX-OS configurations, 804–807
  passphrase commands, 806
  RADIUS, 801–802
  remote AAA services, 802, 901
  servers
    distribution, 913–914
    groups, 900
    monitoring, 900–901
  storage security, 898
    accounting, 900
    authentication, 899, 912–913
    authorization, 899, 912–913
    local AAA services, 911–912
    remote AAA services, 901
    server distribution, 913–914
    server groups, 900
    server monitoring, 900–901
    service configuration, 900

TACACS+801–802
  verification commands, 807
ABR, OSPF verification, 18–22
access
  Cisco ACI
    in-band management access, 214
    out-of-band management access,
      214–215
  fabric access policies, Cisco ACI,
    190–195
  Guest Shell, 743–744
  PTP, 933–934
  RBAC, 807–809
    Cisco NX-OS configurations,
      811–815
    user accounts, 914–919
accounting
  AAA model, 801
  storage security, 900
action statements, 733, 734–735
active zone sets, 407–409
addressing
  FC, 371–372
  FCoE, 447–448
adjacency, OSPF, 7
Admin Console page, ND GUI,
  343–344
Administrative pages, ND GUI, 348
AEP, Cisco ACI, 207–208
AG (Application Gateways), 631
All-Flash configuration, Cisco
  HyperFlex, 714–715

All-NVMe, Cisco HyperFlex, 715–716

Ansible

authentication, 766

Cisco NX-OS example, 767–768

CLI

*prompt, 766*

*tools, 767*

components, 765–766

configuration files, 766

important concepts, 766

inventory files, 765

Jinja templates, 766

modules, 765

playbooks, 765–766

*Cisco NX-OS example, 767–768*

*workflows using playbooks,
764–765*

plays, 766

roles, 766

variable files, 766

variables, 766

workflows using playbooks, 764–765

Anywhere, Cisco HyperFlex, 713

API (Application Programming
Interface)

CLI command API, Python, 771–772

NX-API

*Cisco NX-API Developer
Sandbox, 759–760*

*error codes, 758–759*

*Requests/Responses elements,
757–759*

*Requests/Responses in JSON, 757*

*Requests/Responses in XML,
756–757*

REST API, 752–753

*authentication, 753–754*

*Responses, 754–755*

APIC (Application Policy Infrastructure
Controllers), 176–179, 184–187

application profiles, Cisco ACI,
206–207

areas, OSPF, 10–12

ARP synchronization, vPC, 131

AS 65100, BGP configurations, 33

ASM (Any-Source Multicast), 51

attacks, man-in-the-middle, 817

authentication

AAA model, 801, 803–804, 875–876,
912–913

Ansible, 766

Cisco UCS Manager, multiple
authentication services
configuration, 892–894

keychain authentication, 868

*Cisco NX-OS configurations,
868–870*

*commands, 869–870*

*key selection, 871–872*

OSPF, 13

RADIUS, 888–892

REST API, 753–754

storage security, 899

TACACS+888–892

two-factor authentication, Cisco UCS
Manager, 879

VRRP, 77

authorization

AAA model, 801, 803–804, 876,
896–912

dev-ops role authority, displaying,
740–741

network-admin roles, displaying,
740–741

storage security, 899

Auto Install, firmware upgrades,
680–687

**automation**

Ansible

*authentication, 766*

*Cisco NX-OS example, 767–768*

*CLI prompt, 766*

*CLI tools, 767*

*components, 765–766*

*configuration files, 766*

*important concepts, 766*

*inventory files, 765*

*Jinja templates, 766*

*modules, 765*

*playbooks, 765–766, 767–768*

*plays, 766*

*roles, 766*

*variable files, 766*

*variables, 766*

*workflows using playbooks, 764–765*

benefits, 730

Cisco HyperFlex, 708–709

EEM

*action statements, 733, 734–735*

*configuring, 735–736*

*event statements, 733, 734*

*monitoring module powerdowns, 736*

*overview, 733*

*policies, 733–734*

*verifying configurations, 736*

POAP, 777–778

*configuration scripts, 778–779*

*DHCP discovery phase, 781–782*

*limitations, 778*

*network requirements, 778*

*post-installation reload phase, 782*

*power-up phase, 779*

*processes (overview), 779–780*

*script execution phase, 782*

*switch configurations, 782–783*

*USB discovery phase, 779–780*

*verification commands, 783*

PowerShell, 789

*installing, 789–795*

*listing UCS PowerShell cmdlets, 793–795*

*UCS PowerShell Library installations, 790–791*

*versions of, 789–790, 791–793*

Python, 768–769

*Cisco NX-OS, Python packages, 769–771*

*CLI command API, 771–772*

*interactive mode, 772–773*

*noninteractive mode, 773–775*

*UCS Manager Python SDK, 775–777*

Scheduler

*backups, 739*

*configuring, 737–740*

*displaying jobs/schedules, 739–740*

*job definitions, 736*

*overview, 736–737*

*prerequisites, 737*

*timetable definitions, 736*

*verifying configurations, 739–740*

Terraform, 783

*commands, 786–789*

*components, 784–786*

*concept, 784*

*workflows, 784*

**Autozone, 410**

**availability, LAZ and Cisco HyperFlex data platforms, 726–727**

# B

**backups**

Cisco UCS configuration management, 661–670

configuring, 663–665

creating, 661–663

import backups, 668–670

NX-OS, 272

policies, 666–668

Scheduler configurations, 739

status, 665–666

**bandwidth, port channels, 118**

**Bash Shell, 740**

displaying

*dev-ops role authority, 740–741*

*network-admin role authority, 740–741*

enabling, 741–742

feature RPM, 742

patch RPM, 742–743

running, 741–742

**BB_credits, 372**

**BDR, OSPF, 12–13**

**BFD (Bidirectional Forwarding Detection), 37**

configuring, 38–42

default parameter settings, 38–39

failure detection, 38

global commands, 39–40

interface commands, 40

neighbor relationships, 37–38

network topologies, 40–41

routing commands, 40

verification commands, 40

verifying configurations, 40–42

**BGP (Border Gateway Protocol), 24–25**

AS 65100 configurations, 33

clear commands, 32–33

configuring, 30–37

default parameter settings, 30

feature-based licenses, 30

global commands, 31

interface configurations, 34

multiprotocol BGP, 29–30

network topologies, 33

path selection, 26–29

peering, 25–26

routing commands, 31–32

verification commands, 32–33

verifying configurations, 34–37

**Bidir (Bidirectional shared trees), 51–52**

**blade chassis FEX, FI connections, 545–546**

**blade servers, Cisco UCS, 536–537**

**blocking duplicate frames, vPC, 129–131**

**boot sequences, NX-OS, 255–256**

**BPDU Filtering, 95, 96**

**BPDU Guard, 95, 96**

**Bridge Assurance, 95–96**

**bridge domains, Cisco ACI, 200–202**

**budgeting time, exam preparation, 932**

# C

**Call Home**

Cisco UCS Manager system monitoring, 636–637

infrastructure monitoring, 521–522

**centralized management, Cisco HyperFlex, 709–710**

**CFS (Cisco Fabric Services), 380–381**

CFSoFC, 382–384

CFSoIP, 382–384

fabric lock, 382

features, 381–382

merges, 384

regions, 384–385

**channel code matrix, port channels, 119**

**chapter-ending review tools, 935**

**checkpoints, NX-OS, 272–274**

**Cisco ACI (Application Centric Infrastructure)**

access

*in-band management access, 214*

*out-of-band management access, 214–215*

AEP, 207–208

APIC, 176–179, 184–187

application profiles, 206–207

architectural building blocks, 176

benefits, 174–175

bridge domains, 200–202

components, 175–176

configuring

*APIC, 184–187*

*initial setup, 182–187*

*LAB configurations, 221–223*

contracts, 208–209

*creating, 230–233*

*filters, 213, 230–233*

*taboo contracts, 209–210*

*vzAny rule, 210–212*

design best practices, 221

endpoint groups, 201–203

fabric

*access policies, 190–195*

*building, 224–227*

*building blocks, 195–196*

*discovery, 182, 187–189*

*loop detection, 220*

*overview, 179*

*traffic load balancing, 219–220*

*traffic storms, 219*

*upgrading, 189–190*

filters, creating, 230–233

initial setup, 182–187

LAB configurations, 221–223

leaf switches, 179–182

management tenants, 213

microsegmentations, 207

multitier topologies, 179–180

overview, 174–176

policy identification/enforcement, 218

policy models, 197–198

SCVMM integration, 204–205

spine switches, 179–182

tenants, 198–200

*creating, 227–230*

*intersubnet tenant traffic, 217–218*

*management tenants, 213*

three-tier applications, 233–235

vCenter integration, 235–238

Virtual Edge, 206

VMM domains, 203–204

VMware overlays, 206

VMware vCenter integration, 205

VRF, 200

VXLAN, 215–216

vzAny rule, 210–212

**Cisco ACI Contracts, 852–853**

applying, 855–856

components, 851–852

configuring, 853–854

creating, 854–855

exporting between networks, 858–859

inter-private network contracts communication, 858–859

Inter-Tenant Contracts, 857–858

microsegmentation, 860–867

modifying, 855

multiple contracts unidirectional single filters, 860

removing, 855

single contract bidirectional reverse filters, 859

single contract unidirectional with multiple filters, 859

verifying, 855

VRF Contracts, 856–857

**Cisco AVPair attribute, 878**

**Cisco Certification Exam Tutorial, types of questions, 935–939**

**Cisco, fiscal year and months example, 943**

**Cisco HyperFlex, 702, 704**

All-Flash configuration, 714–715

All-NVMe, 715–716

Anywhere, 713

automation, 708–709

benefits, 707–712

centralized management, 709–710

configuring, 705–706

data platforms, 716

   *cluster interfaces, 720*

   *cluster tolerated failures, 719*

   *datastores, 724–725*

   *disk management, 721–724*

   *HA, 718–719*

   *LAB clusters, 716–717*

   *LAZ, 726–727*

   *local encryption keys, 721*

   *Native Snapshots, 719–720*

   *Ready Clones, 719*

   *SED, 720–721*

   *server disk types, 722–723*

   *storage clusters, 717*

   *system clusters, 725–727*

Dynamic Data Distribution, 711–712

edges, 712–714

flexibility, 715

hardware, 715

HCI, 704

hybrid models, 714–715

hyperconvergence, 704

independent resource scaling, 710–711

infrastructures, 705, 706–707

interconnections, 705

invisible cloud witness services, 713–714

IO Visor, 707

latency, 711–712

multinode edges, 713

resource optimization, 710–711

SATA RAS, 715–716

unified management, 709–710

VAAI, 707

VM density, 711–712

**Cisco Intersight, 648**

benefits, 648–649

dashboards, 650

features, 648–649

infrastructure, 647

invisible cloud witness services, 713–714

licensing, 652–656

management as a service, 648–649

supported software, 650–652

telemetry data collection, 650

**Cisco MDS 9100 series multilayer fabric switches, 362–365**

**Cisco MDS 9200 series multiservice switches, 361–362**

**Cisco MDS 9300 series multilayer fabric switches, 360–361**

**Cisco MDS 9700 series multilayer directors, 356–360**

**Cisco MDS NX-OS Setup Utility,
490–498**

**Cisco NX-API Developer Sandbox,
759–760**

**Cisco NX-OS**

Ansible, 767–768

Bash Shell, 740

*displaying dev-ops role
authority, 740–741*

*displaying network-admin role
authority, 740–741*

*enabling, 741–742*

*feature RPM, 742*

*patch RPM, 742–743*

*running, 741–742*

CoPP configurations, 844–851

DAI configurations, 819–827

DHCP snooping, 827–831

Guest Shell, 743

*access, 743–744*

*capabilities, 744–746*

*displaying Ethernet 1/47
interface counters, 745*

*dohost command, 745*

*guestshell destroy command, 747*

*guestshell disable command, 747*

*guestshell enable command, 747*

*installing Python packages, 746*

*managing, 746–748*

*resource limits, 744*

*running Python in Guest Shell,
745–746*

*show guestshell detail command,
747–748*

keychain authentication, 868–870

port security, 832–837

Python packages, 769–771

RBAC configurations, 811–815

rules, 809–810

user roles, 809–810

**Cisco UCS (Unified Computing
System), 530**

5108 Blade Server Chassis, 536

architecture, 532–534

blade servers, 536–537

chassis discovery, 577

Cisco UCS Mini, 539–540

Cisco X-Series system, 555–556

components, 534–535

configuration management, 660–661

*backups, 661–670*

*system restore, 670–672*

configuring, 557–564

*FI, GUI configurations, 561–562*

*initial setup, 578–583*

connectivity, 534–535

fabric failover for Ethernet, 569–570

fabric infrastructure, 539

*Cisco UCS 6300 Series fabric
interconnect, 543–544*

*Cisco UCS 6454 fabric
interconnect, 541–543*

*Cisco UCS 6536 fabric
interconnect, 540–541*

FEX, 544–550, 577

FI, 544–550

*cluster verifications, 563–564*

*configuring, 565–567*

*connectivity, 565–567*

*Ethernet switching mode,
570–577*

*fabric failover for Ethernet,
569–570*

*GUI configurations, 561–562*

*IPv4 initialization, 559–560, 563*

*IPv6 initialization, 560–561, 563*

port modes, 567–569

vNIC, 569–570

firmware

  infrastructure installations, 688–691

  server upgrades, 691–699

  updates, 672–679

  upgrades through Auto Install, 680–687

  version terminology, 679

flexibility, 533–534

high availability, 533

identity pools, 591–596

initial setup, 557–564, 578–583

IP pools, 593–595

MAC pools, 593

managing, 557–564

network management, VLAN, 584–591

QoS, 608–610

rack servers, 537–538, 577

SAN, connectivity, 611–616, 624–625

scalability, 533

servers

  pools, 596

  profiles, 599–602

service profiles, 596–599, 602–607

software updates, 672–679

storage, 611

storage servers, 537–539

UUID pools, 591–593

virtualization, 550–555

vNIC, 569–570

VSAN, 616–621

WWN pools, 621–624

**Cisco UCS Manager**

  AAA model, 875–876

  Cisco AVPair attribute example, 878

LDAP, 877

  groups, 879–888

  nested LDAP, 879

  providers, 879–888

  user accounts, 880

multiple authentication services configuration, 894

RADIUS, 876, 877, 888–892

remote user role policies, 892–894

Session Timeout Period, 879

system monitoring, 630

  AG, 631

  Call Home, 636–637

  database health, 638

  DME, 631

  events, 632–634

  hardware, 638

  logs, 632–634

  NetFlow, 638–640

  northbound interfaces, 631–632

  policies, 634–640

  Smart Call Home, 636–637

  SNMP, 636

  traffic monitoring, 640–647

TACACS+877–878, 888–894

two-factor authentication, 879

Web Session Refresh Period, 879

**Cisco UCS S-Series storage servers, 483–484**

**clear commands, BGP, 32–33**

**clear-text passwords, 809**

**CLI (Command-Line Interface)**

  Ansible

    prompt, 766

    tools, 767

  modular QoS CLI, 842–844

  Python command API, 771–772

clocks
  PTP, 281–282, 283–284
  watching, exam preparation, 932
cloud computing
  benefits, 243
  characteristics, 243–244
  community clouds, 250
  defined, 242–244
  hybrid clouds, 249–250
  IaaS, 246–248
  PaaS, 246
  private clouds, 248
  public clouds, 248–249
  SaaS, 245
clusters
  Cisco HyperFlex data platforms
    cluster interfaces, 720
    LAB clusters, 716–717
    storage clusters, 717
    system clusters, 725–727
    tolerated failures, 719
  Cisco UCS FI verification, 563–564
  ND cluster nodes, 339–341
  storage clusters
    Cisco HyperFlex data
      platforms, 717
    compute nodes, 717
    converged nodes, 717
    datastores, 717
    drives, 717
  system clusters, Cisco HyperFlex data
    platforms, 725–727
  tolerated failures, Cisco HyperFlex
    data platforms, 719
CNA (Converged Network Adapters),
  436–437
collapsed-core topologies, FC, 365
commands

AAA model
  global commands, 804–806
  locking user accounts, 806
  passphrase commands, 806
  verification commands, 807
BFD
  global commands, 39–40
  interface commands, 40
  routing commands, 40
  verification commands, 40
BGP
  clear commands, 32–33
  global commands, 31
  routing commands, 31–32
  verification commands, 32–33
FCoE, verification commands, 466
FHS, port security, 836–837
HSRP
  global commands, 80
  interface commands, 80
  verification commands, 82
keychain authentication, 869–870
multicast routing
  global commands, 58–59
  interface commands, 59–61
NTP
  global commands, 276–278
  verification commands, 278
OSPF
  global commands, 14
  interface commands, 15
  process clear commands, 15–16
  routing commands, 14–15
port channels
  global commands, 134–135
  interface commands, 135
  verification commands, 137

PTP

    *global commands, 282*

    *interface commands, 283*

SAN port channels, verification commands, 400–401

SNMP

    *global commands, 288–289*

    *specific notation commands, 291*

    *verification commands, 291–292*

STP

    *global commands, 105*

    *interface commands, 106–107*

    *verification commands, 108*

Terraform, 786–789

verification commands, PTP, 283

vPC

    *domain commands, 136*

    *global commands, 134–135*

    *interface commands, 135*

    *verification commands, 137*

VRRP

    *global commands, 79–86*

    *interface commands, 80*

    *verification commands, 82*

VSAN, 392–393

VXLAN

    *global commands, 159–161*

    *interface commands, 161–162*

    *NVE config commands, 162*

    *verification commands, 162*

community clouds, **250**

compute nodes, storage clusters, **717**

computer security

    AAA model, 875–876

    Cisco AVPair attribute example, 878

    LDAP, 877

        *groups, 879–888*

        *nested LDAP, 879*

        *providers, 879–888*

        *user accounts, 880*

    multiple authentication services configuration, 892–894

    RADIUS, 876, 877, 888–892

    remote user role policies, 892–894

    TACACS+877–878, 888–894

    two-factor authentication, 879

configuration consistency, vPC, **128–129**

configuration files, Ansible, **766**

configuration scripts, POAP, **778–779**

configuring

    AAA model

        *NX-OS configurations, 804–807*

        *service options, 802–803*

    AAA services, storage security, 900

    ACI Contracts, 853–854

    All-Flash configuration, Cisco HyperFlex, 714–715

    backups, 663–665

    BFD, 38–42

    BGP, 30–37

    Cisco ACI

        *APIC, 184–187*

        *initial setup, 182–187*

        *LAB configurations, 221–223*

    Cisco HyperFlex, 705–706, 714–715

    Cisco NX-OS

        *DAI configurations, 819–827*

        *keychain authentication, 868–870*

        *port security, 832–837*

        *RBAC configurations, 811–815*

    Cisco UCS, 557–564, 660–661

        *backups, 661–670*

        *FI configurations, 561–562, 565–567*

*initial setup, 578–583*

*system restore, 670–672*

device alias, 422–423

EEM, 735–736

FCoE, 469–474

*Nexus 5000 switches, 458–459*

*Nexus 7000 switches, 456–458*

*Nexus 9000 switches, 459–461*

HSRP, 79–86

local encryption keys, 721

multicast routing, 56–69

named VLAN, 589–590

NTP, 279–280

NX-OS, 271

*basic management, 256–259*

*saves/backups, 272*

OSPF, 13–24

PIM, 164–167

port channels, 132–146

port security, 921–924

PTP, 283

RBAC, user accounts, 918–919

SAN port channels, 400–403

Scheduler, 737–740

SNMP, 292

STP, 102–117

switches, POAP configurations, 782–783

vPC, 132–146

VRRP, 79–86

VSAN, 391–394

VXLAN, 159–169

zoning, 414–417

consistency checks, vPC, 129

contracts, Cisco ACI, 208–209

creating, 230–233

filters, 213

taboo contracts, 209–210

vzAny rule, 210–212

control plane topologies, VXLAN, 159–161

converged nodes, storage clusters, 717

converting to UCS Manager Python SDK, 777

CoPP (Control Plane Policing), 837–839

Cisco NX-OS configurations, 844–851

classification, 840–844

control plane packets, 839–840

creating, 850–851

modifying, 851

modular QoS CLI, 842–844

Nexus 5000, 844

Nexus 7000 comparisons, 843–844

Nexus 9000 comparisons, 842–843

rate control, 840–841

core-edge topologies, FC, 366

CRUD operations, UCS Manager Python SDK, 776

customizing exams, 934–935

## D

DAI (Dynamic ARP Inspection), 816, 817–819

Cisco NX-OS configurations, 819–827

DHCP snooping, 827–831

man-in-the-middle attacks, 817

data platforms, Cisco HyperFlex, 716

clusters

*interfaces, 720*

*LAB clusters, 716–717*

*storage clusters, 717*

*system clusters, 725–727*

*tolerated failures, 719*

datastores, 724–725

disk management, 721–724

HA, 718–719

LAZ, 726–727

local encryption keys, 721

Native Snapshots, 719–720

Ready Clones, 719

SED, 720–721

server disk types, 722–723

database health, Cisco UCS Manager system monitoring, 638

datastores

Cisco HyperFlex data platforms, 724–725

storage clusters, 717

DCBX (Data Center Bridging Exchange), 440–442

deleting

LDAP providers, 885

named VLAN, 590–591

device alias, 418

configuring, 422–423

distributions, 420–421

features, 419

modes, 419–420

verifying configurations, 422–423

zone alias comparisons, 421–422

device registration, switched fabric initialization and FC, 378–380

dev-ops roles, displaying authority, 740–741

DHCP (Dynamic Host Configuration Protocol)

discovery phase, POAP, 781–782

snooping, 827–831

direct-attached topologies, FCoE, 452–453

disk management, Cisco HyperFlex data platforms, 721–724

displaying

dev-ops role authority, 740–741

Ethernet 1/47 interface counters with Guest Shell, 745

jobs/schedules in Scheduler, 739–740

disruptive downgrades, MDS switches, 513–515

disruptive upgrades, MDS switches, 505–507

DITKA? questions, 940

DME (Data Management Engine), 631

dohost command, 745

domains

ID, principal switch selection and FC, 375–377

vPC, 124, 136

downgrading MDS switches

disruptive downgrades, 513–515

nondisruptive downgrades, 508–512

software, 498–500

downlink connectivity, Cisco UCS FI, 567

DPVM (Dynamic Port VSAN Membership), 388–389

DR, OSPF, 12–13

drag-and-drop questions, 937

drives

SED, Cisco HyperFlex data platforms, 720–721

storage clusters, 717

dual-control plane, vPC, 126

duplicate frame prevention, vPC, 129–131

Dynamic Data Distribution, Cisco HyperFlex, 711–712

# E

ear plugs, exam preparation, 932

edge ports, STP, 94

edge-core-edge topologies, FC, 367–368

edges, Cisco HyperFlex, 712–714

EEM (Embedded Event Manager), 522

action statements, 733, 734–735

configuring, 735–736

event statements, 733, 734

monitoring module powerdowns, 736

overview, 733

policies, 733–734

verifying configurations, 736

enabling Bash Shell, 741–742

encapsulation, VXLAN, 151–152

encryption

local encryption keys, configuring, 721

SED, Cisco HyperFlex data platforms, 720–721

endpoint groups, Cisco ACI, 201–203

end-to-end automation, Cisco HyperFlex, 708–709

enhanced zoning, 412–413

ENodes, FCoE, 445–447

EPLD (Electrical Programmable Logical Devices)

MDS 9000 series switches, upgrades, 515–521

upgrading, 269–271

error codes, NX-API, 758–759

Ethernet

1/47 interface counters, displaying with Guest Shell, 745

Ethernet switching mode, Cisco UCS FI, 570–577

fabric failover for Ethernet, high availability vNIC, 569–570

FCoE, 434

addressing, 447–448

benefits, 451

CNA, 436–437

configuring, 469–474

DCBX, 440–442

direct-attached topologies, 452–453

ENodes, 445–447

ETS, 439–440

FCF, 445–447

FEX topologies, 453–454, 461–463

FIP, 448–451

forwarding, 447–448

FPMA, 447

frame format, 442–444

IEEE 802.1 standard, 438

implementing, 455

multi-hop topologies, 454–455

Nexus 5000 switch configurations, 458–459

Nexus 7000 switch configurations, 456–458

Nexus 9000 switch configurations, 459–461

NPV, 463–465

overview, 436–438

PFC, 438–439

ports, 445–447

remote-attached topologies, 454

single-hop topologies, 451–454

T11 standard, 438

verification commands, 466

verifying, 466–474

VFC, 444–445

traffic monitoring, 641–642

ETS (Enhanced Transmission Selection), 439–440

events

monitoring, Cisco UCS Manager, 632–634

statements, 733, 734

EVPN control plane, VXLAN, 156–157

exams

Cisco fiscal year and months example, 943

customizing, 934–935

news on releases, 944

preparing for, 932

*budgeting time, 932*

*chapter-ending review tools, 935*

*Cisco Certification Exam Tutorial questions, 935–939*

*clock watching, 932*

*customizing exams, 934–935*

*DITKA? questions, 940*

*drag-and-drop questions, 937*

*ear plugs, 932*

*fill-in-the-blank questions, 937*

*final reviews, 940*

*getting rest, 932*

*multiple-choice, multiple-answer questions, 936*

*multiple-choice, single answer questions, 936*

*PTP, 933–935*

*simlet questions, 939*

*simulation questions, 938*

*study plans, 940*

*study trackers, 932*

*taking notes, 933*

*testlet questions, 938–939*

*travel time, 932*

study plans, 943–944

updates, 942–943, 944

exporting contracts between networks, 858–859

extensions, STP, 94–95

# F

fabric

binding, 926–929

CFS, 380–381

*CFSoFC, 382–384*

*CFSoIP, 382–384*

*fabric lock, 382*

*features, 381–382*

*merges, 384*

*regions, 384–385*

Cisco ACI

*access policies, 190–195*

*building, 224–227*

*building blocks, 195–196*

*fabric discovery, 182, 187–189*

*loop detection, 220*

*overview, 179*

*traffic load balancing, 219–220*

*traffic storms, 219*

*upgrading, 189–190*

Cisco MDS 9100 series multilayer fabric switches, 362–365

Cisco MDS 9300 series multilayer fabric switches, 360–361

Cisco UCS, 539

*Cisco UCS 6300 Series fabric interconnect, 543–544*

*Cisco UCS 6454 fabric interconnect, 541–543*

*Cisco UCS 6536 fabric interconnect, 540–541*

fabric failover for Ethernet, high availability vNIC, 569–570

FLOGI, 378–380

FPMA, 447

MDS switches

*Cisco MDS NX-OS Setup Utility, 490–498*

disruptive downgrades, 513–515

disruptive upgrades, 505–507

nondisruptive downgrades, 508–512

nondisruptive upgrades, 500–505

upgrading/downgrading software, 498–500

NDFC, 325–326

features/benefits, 326–331

GUI, 331–335

switched fabric initialization, FC

device registration, 378–380

domain ID, 375–377

fabric reconfiguration, 377

FCID, 377

FCNS databases, 378–380

FLOGI, 378–380

overview, 373–374

PLOGI, 378

principal switch selection, 374–377

PRLI, 378

failure detection, BFD, 38

fault-tolerant links, vPC, 124

FC (Fibre Channel)

addressing, 371–372

basics, 365

BB_credits, 372

CFS, 380–381

CFSoFC, 382–384

CFSoIP, 382–384

fabric lock, 382

features, 381–382

merges, 384

regions, 384–385

Cisco MDS 9100 series multilayer fabric switches, 362–365

Cisco MDS 9200 series multiservice switches, 361–362

Cisco MDS 9300 series multilayer fabric switches, 360–361

Cisco MDS 9700 series multilayer directors, 356–360

collapsed-core topologies, 365

core-edge topologies, 366

device alias, 418

configuring, 422–423

distributions, 420–421

features, 419

modes, 419–420

verifying configurations, 422–423

zone alias comparisons, 421–422

edge-core-edge topologies, 367–368

FCID, 371–372, 377

flow control, 372

NPIV, 424–431

NPV, 424–431

ports, 368–370

SAN port channels, 396

configuring, 400–403

load balancing, 398–399

modes, 399–400

trunking, 396–397

types of, 396–398

verification commands, 400–401

verifying configurations, 400–403

switched fabric initialization

device registration, 378–380

domain ID, 375–377

fabric reconfiguration, 377

FCID, 377

FCNS databases, 378–380

FLOGI, 378–380

overview, 373–374

PLOGI, 378

principal switch selection, 374–377

PRLI, 378

topologies, 365–368

traffic monitoring, 642–647

VSAN, 386

    *advantages of, 388*

    *attributes, 387–388*

    *commands, 392–393*

    *configuring, 391–394*

    *DPVM, 388–389*

    *features, 386–387*

    *ID, 387*

    *names, 388*

    *states, 387–388*

    *switches, 388*

    *trunking, 389–394*

    *verifying configurations, 391–394*

    *zoning comparisons, 406*

zone alias, device alias comparisons, 421–422

zoning, 404

    *active zone sets, 407–409*

    *Autozone, 410*

    *configuring, 414–417*

    *enforcement, 406–407*

    *enhanced zoning, 412–413*

    *features, 404–406*

    *full zone sets, 407–409*

    *hard zoning, 407*

    *merges, 410–411*

    *smart zoning, 411–412*

    *verifying configurations, 414–417*

    *VSAN comparisons, 406*

FCF (Fibre Channel Forwarders), 445–447

FCID (Fibre Channel Identification), 371–372, 377

FCNS databases, 378–380

FCoE (Fibre Channel over Ethernet), 434

    addressing, 447–448

    benefits, 451

    CNA, 436–437

    configuring, 469–474

        *Nexus 5000 switches, 458–459*

        *Nexus 7000 switches, 456–458*

        *Nexus 9000 switches, 459–461*

    DCBX, 440–442

    direct-attached topologies, 452–453

    ENodes, 445–447

    ETS, 439–440

    FCF, 445–447

    FEX topologies, 453–454, 461–463

    FIP, 448–451

    forwarding, 447–448

    FPMA, 447

    frame format, 442–444

    IEEE 802.1 standard, 438

    implementing, 455

    multi-hop topologies, 454–455

    NPV, 463–465

    overview, 436–438

    PFC, 438–439

    ports, 445–447

    remote-attached topologies, 454

    single-hop topologies, 451–454

    T11 standard, 438

    verification commands, 466

    verifying, 466–474

    VFC, 444–445

feature RPM, managing with Bash Shell, 742

feature-based licenses

    BGP, 30

    multicast routing, 57–58

    OSPF, 14

    VXLAN, 159

**FEX (Fabric Extenders)**

blade chassis FEX, FI connections, 545–546

Cisco UCS, 544–550, 577

port channel mode, 547–548

topologies, FCoE, 453–454, 461–463

virtual links, 548

**FHS (First-Hop Security)**

DAI, 816, 817–819

*Cisco NX-OS configurations, 819–827*

*DHCP snooping, 827–831*

*man-in-the-middle attacks, 817*

features, 815–816

port security, 832–837

**FI (Fabric Interconnects)**

blade chassis FEX connections, 545–546

Cisco UCS, 544–550

*cluster verifications, 563–564*

*connectivity, 565–567*

*Ethernet switching mode, 570–577*

*fabric failover for Ethernet, 569–570*

*FI configurations, 565–567*

*GUI configurations, 561–562*

*IPv4 initialization, 559–560, 563*

*IPv6 initialization, 560–561, 563*

*port modes, 567–569*

*vNIC, 569–570*

system restore, 671–672

files, NFS, 479–480

fill-in-the-blank questions, 937

filters, Cisco ACI contracts, 213, 230–233

final reviews, exam preparation, 940

FIP (FCoE Initialization Protocol), 448–451

**firmware**

infrastructure installations, 688–691

server upgrades, 691–699

updates, Cisco UCS, 672–679

upgrades

*server upgrades, 691–699*

*through Auto Install, 680–687*

version terminology, 679

**fiscal year and months example, Cisco, 943**

**flexibility**

Cisco HyperFlex, 715

Cisco UCS, 533–534

**FLOGI (Fabric Login), 378–380**

**Flood and Learn Multicast-based control plane, VXLAN, 154–156**

**flow control, FC, 372**

**FPMA (Fabric-Provided MAC Addresses), 447**

**full zone sets, 407–409**

# G

**gateways**

AG, 631

VXLAN, 157

**global commands**

AAA model, 804–806

BFD, 39–40

BGP, 31

FHS, port security, 836–837

HSRP, 80

multicast routing, 58–59

NTP, 276–278

OSPF, 14

port channels, 134–135

PTP, 282

SNMP, 288–289

STP, 105

vPC, 134–135

VRRP, 79–86

VXLAN, 159–161

**Guest Shell, 743**

access, 743–744

capabilities, 744–746

displaying Ethernet 1/47 interface counters, 745

dohost command, 745

guestshell destroy command, 747

guestshell disable command, 747

guestshell enable command, 747

managing, 746–748

Python

*installing packages, 746*

*running in Guest Shell, 745–746*

resource limits, 744

show guestshell detail command, 747–748

**GUI (Graphical User Interfaces)**

Cisco UCS FI configurations, 561–562

ND

*Admin Console page, 343–344*

*Administrative pages, 348*

*Infrastructure pages, 348*

*One View page, 343*

*Operations pages, 347–348*

*overview, 342–348*

*Overview page, 344*

*Services page, 345–346*

*Sites page, 345*

*System Resources pages, 346–347*

NDFC, 331–335

NDI, 320–323

## H

**HA, Cisco HyperFlex data platforms, 718–719**

hard zoning, 407

hardware

Cisco HyperFlex, 715

Cisco UCS Manager system monitoring, 638

**HashiCorp Terraform, 783**

commands, 786–789

components, 784–786

concept, 784

workflows, 784

**HCI (HyperConverged Infrastructure), 704**

hello packets, 7

**high availability**

Cisco UCS, 533

vNIC, 569–570

VXLAN, 157–159

**HSRP (Hot Standby Router Protocol), 69–72**

configuring, 79–86

global commands, 79–86

interface commands, 80

load sharing, 72

network topologies, 70–71, 82–83

verification commands, 82

verifying configurations, 79–86

vPC gateways, 131

**HX Data Platform, 716**

Clusters

*interfaces, 720*

*tolerated failures, 719*

datastores, 724–725

disk management, 721–724

HA, 718–719

LAB clusters, 716–717

LAZ, 726–727

local encryption keys, 721

Native Snapshots, 719–720

Ready Clones, 719

SED, 720–721

server disk types, 722–723

storage clusters, 717

system clusters, 725–727

hybrid clouds, 249–250


# I

IaaS (Infrastructure as a Service), 246–248

identity pools, Cisco UCS, 91–596

IEEE 802.1 FCoE standard, 438

IGMP (Internet Group Management Protocol), 43–46

default parameter settings, 56

interface commands, 59–61

switch IGMP snooping, 46

images, NX-OS, 254

import backups, 668–670

in-band management access, Cisco ACI, 214

independent resource scaling, Cisco HyperFlex, 710–711

infrastructure monitoring, 284, 521

Call Home, 521–522

EEM, 522

RMON, 523

SPAN, 523–528

system messages, 521

Infrastructure pages, ND GUI, 348

installing

PowerShell, 789–795

Python packages, 746

UCS PowerShell Library, 790–791

VIB

IO Visor, 707

VAAI, 707

interactive mode, Python, 772–773

interface commands

BFD, 40

HSRP, 80–82

multicast routing, 59–61

OSPF, 15

port channels, 135

PTP, 283

STP, 106–107

vPC, 135

VRRP, 80

VXLAN, 161–162

interface configurations

BGP, 34

OSPF, 17–18

inter-private network contracts communication, 858–859

intersubnet tenant traffic, Cisco ACI, 217–218

Inter-Tenant Contracts, 857–858

inventory files, Ansible, 765

invisible cloud witness services, Cisco HyperFlex, 713–714

IO Visor, 707

IP pools, Cisco UCS, 593–595

IPv4, Cisco UCS FI initialization, 559–560, 563

IPv6 (Internet Protocol version 6)

Cisco UCS FI initialization, 560–561, 563

First Hop Redundancy, VRRP, 77–79

ISSU, NX-OS, 263–265

# J

Jinja templates, Ansible, 766
Job, Scheduler
  definitions, 736
  displaying, 739–740
JSON (JavaScript Object Notation),
  751–752, 757

# K

keychain authentication, 868
  Cisco NX-OS configurations, 868–870
  commands, 869–870
  key selection, 871–872

# L

LAB clusters, Cisco HyperFlex data
  platforms, 716–717
latency, Cisco HyperFlex, 711–712
LAZ, Cisco HyperFlex data platforms,
  726–727
LDAP (Lightweight Directory Access
  Protocol)
  Cisco UCS Manager, 877
  groups, 879–888
  MDS switches, 909–911
  nested LDAP, 879
  providers, 879–888
  storage security, 907–911
  user accounts, 880
leaf switches, Cisco ACI, 179–182
licensing, Cisco Intersight, 652–656
lifecycle management, NX-OS
  software, 263
link modes, port channels, 119
listing UCS PowerShell cmdlets, 793–795

load balancing
  Cisco ACI fabric traffic, 219–220
  port channels, 120–122
  SAN port channels, 398–399
  VSAN, 388
load sharing
  HSRP, 72
  VRRP, 75–76
local AAA services, 911–912
local encryption keys, configuring, 721
locking
  up valuables, exam preparation,
    932–933
  user accounts, AAA model
    commands, 806
logins
  FLOGI, 378–380
  PLOGI, 378
  PRLI, 378
logs
  Cisco UCS Manager system
    monitoring, 632–634
  system message logging, NX-OS,
    284–285
loop detection, Cisco ACI fabric, 220
Loop Guard, 95, 96–97
LSA (Link-State Advertisements), 7–10

# M

MAC (Media Access Control)
  addresses, FPMA, 447
  pools, Cisco UCS, 593
management access, Cisco ACI,
  214–215
management tenants, 213
managing
  Cisco HyperFlex

*centralized management,*
*709–710*

*disk management, 721–724*

*flexibility, 715*

*unified management, 709–710*

Cisco UCS, 557–564, 660–661

*backups, 661–670*

*networks, VLAN, 584–591*

*system restore, 670–672*

feature RPM with Bash Shell, 742

Guest Shell, 746–748

networks, SNMP, 286

Nexus consoles, 254–255

out-of-band management

*access, Cisco ACI, 214–215*

*Cisco MDS NX-OS Setup Utility,*
*492–496*

patch RPM with Bash Shell, 742–743

software

*Cisco MDS NX-OS Setup Utility,*
*490–498*

*lifecycles, NX-OS, 263*

*MDS switch upgrades/*
*downgrades, 498–500*

time management, networks, 274–275

*NTP, 275–280*

*PTP, 280–284*

**man-in-the-middle attacks, 817**

**MDS switches**

9000 series switches, EPLD upgrades,
515–521

**9100 series multilayer fabric switches,**
**362–365**

**9200 series multiservice switches,**
**361–362**

**9300 series multilayer fabric switches,**
**360–361**

9700 series multilayer directors,
356–360

Cisco MDS NX-OS Setup Utility,
490–498

disruptive downgrades, 513–515

disruptive upgrades, 505–507

LDAP, 909–911

nondisruptive downgrades, 508–512

nondisruptive upgrades, 500–505

NX-OS Setup Utility, 490–498

RADIUS, 902–904

RBAC, 918–919

TACACS+905–907

upgrading/downgrading software,
498–500

verifying NX-OS version, 496–497

**MDT (Multicast Distribution Trees),**
**47–49**

**member ports, vPC, 124**

**merges**

CFS, 384

zoning, 410–411

**MIB, SNMP, 289–291**

**microsegmentation, Cisco ACI, 207,**
**860–867**

**MLD (Multicast Listener Directory),**
**46–47**

**modular QoS CLI, CoPP, 842–844**

**modules**

Ansible, 765

monitoring powerdowns, 736

**monitoring**

events, Cisco UCS Manager, 632–634

infrastructure monitoring, 284, 521

*Call Home, 521–522*

*EEM, 522*

*RMON, 523*

*SPAN, 523–528*

*system messages, 521*

logs, Cisco UCS Manager, 632–634

module powerdowns, 736

NetFlow, Cisco UCS Manager system monitoring, 638–640

network infrastructures, 284

RMON, 523

servers, AAA, 900–901

system monitoring, Cisco UCS Manager, 630

    *AG, 631*

    *Call Home, 636–637*

    *database health, 638*

    *DME, 631, 638–640*

    *events, 632–634*

    *hardware, 638*

    *logs, 632–634*

    *northbound interfaces, 631–632*

    *policies, 634–640*

    *Smart Call Home, 636–637*

    *SNMP, 636*

    *traffic monitoring, 640–647*

traffic monitoring, 640–641

    *Ethernet, 641–642*

    *FC, 642–647*

**MPBGP EVPN control plane, VXLAN, 156–157**

**multicast forwarding, 55–56**

**multicast routing, 42–43**

  configuring, 56–69

  default parameter settings, 56–57

  feature-based licenses, 57–58

  global commands, 58–59

  IGMP, 43–46

    *default parameter settings, 56*

    *interface commands, 59–61*

  interface commands, 59–61

  MDT, 47–49

  MLD, 46–47

  network topologies, 61–62

PIM, 49–51

  *ASM, 51*

  *Bidir, 51–52*

  *configuring, 164–167*

  *default parameter settings, 56–57*

  *designated routers/forwarders, 54–55*

  *distribution modes, 58*

  *RP, 53–54*

  *SSM, 52–53*

  *verifying, 164–167*

RPF, 55–56

switch IGMP snooping, 46

TRM, 159

verifying configurations, 61–69

**multi-hop topologies, FCoE, 454–455**

**multinode edges, Cisco HyperFlex, 713**

**multiple contracts unidirectional single filters, 860**

**multiple-choice, multiple-answer questions, 936**

**multiple-choice, single answer questions, 936**

**multiprotocol BGP, 29–30**

**multitier topologies, Cisco ACI, 179–180**

# N

**named VLAN, 586–589**

  configuring, 589–590

  deleting, 590–591

**named VSAN, 616–618**

**NAS (Network-Attached Storage), 481–482**

  benefits, 483

  Cisco UCS S-Series storage servers, 483–484

**Native Snapshots, Cisco HyperFlex data platforms, 719–720**

ND (Nexus Dashboard), 316–317
benefits, 317–318
cluster nodes, 339–341
external networks, 341–342
GUI
   *Admin Console page, 343–344*
   *Administrative pages, 348*
   *Infrastructure pages, 348*
   *One View page, 343*
   *Operations pages, 347–348*
   *overview, 342–348*
   *Overview page, 344*
   *Services page, 345–346*
   *Sites page, 345*
   *System Resources pages, 346–347*
NDDB, 335–337
NDFC, 325–326
   *features/benefits, 326–331*
   *GUI, 331–335*
NDI, 318–323
NDO, 323–324
platforms, 337–339
virtual form factors, 339
NDDB (Nexus Dashboard Data Broker), 335–337
NDFC (Nexus Dashboard Fabric Controller), 325–326
features/benefits, 326–331
GUI, 331–335
NDI (Nexus Dashboard Insights), 318–323
NDO (Nexus Dashboard Orchestrator), 323–324
neighbor relationships, BFD, 37–38
nested LDAP, Cisco UCS Manager, 879
NetFlow, 293–298, 638–640
network-admin roles, displaying authority, 740–741

Network Assurance Engine, 310–312
networks
ACI Contracts, exporting between networks, 858–859
Cisco UCS, VLAN, 584–591
CNA, 436–437
infrastructure monitoring, 284, 521
   *Call Home, 521–522*
   *EEM, 522*
   *RMON, 523*
   *SPAN, 523–528*
   *system messages, 521*
inter-private network contracts communication, 858–859
monitoring infrastructures, 284
ND external networks, 341–342
POAP, requirements, 778
ports, STP, 94
RMON, 523
SNMP, 286
   *configuring, 292*
   *global commands, 288–289*
   *MIB, 289–291*
   *security, 287–288*
   *specific notation commands, 291*
   *traps, 286–287*
   *verification commands, 291–292*
time management, 274–275
   *NTP, 275–280*
   *PTP, 280–284*
topologies
   *BFD, 40–41*
   *BGP, 33*
   *HSRP, 82–83*
   *multicast routing, 61–62*
   *OSPF, 16*
   *port channels, 137–138*

*STP, 108*

*VRRP, 74, 82–83*

VSAN, *386*

*advantages of, 388*

*attributes, 387–388*

*commands, 392–393*

*configuring, 391–394*

*DPVM, 388–389*

*features, 386–387*

*ID, 387*

*names, 388*

*states, 387–388*

*switches, 388*

*trunking, 389–394*

*verifying configurations, 391–394*

*zoning comparisons, 406*

**networks, security**

AAA model, *801*

*accounting, 801*

*authentication, 801, 803–804*

*authorization, 801, 803–804*

*configuring AAA service options, 802–803*

*default parameter settings, 804*

*global commands, 804–806*

*locking user accounts, 806*

*passphrase commands, 806*

*RADIUS, 801–802*

*remote AAA services, 802*

*TACACS+801–802*

*verification commands, 807*

ACI Contracts, *852–853*

*applying, 855–856*

*components, 851–852*

*configuring, 853–854*

*creating, 854–855*

*exporting between networks, 858–859*

*inter-private network contracts communication, 858–859*

*Inter-Tenant Contracts, 857–858*

*microsegmentation, 860–867*

*modifying, 855*

*multiple contracts unidirectional single filters, 860*

*removing, 855*

*single contract bidirectional reverse filters, 859*

*single contract unidirectional with multiple filters, 859*

*verifying, 855*

*VRF Contracts, 856–857*

CoPP, *837–839*

*Cisco NX-OS configurations, 844–851*

*classification, 840–844*

*control plane packets, 839–840*

*creating, 850–851*

*modifying, 851*

*modular QoS CLI, 842–844*

*Nexus 5000, 844*

*Nexus 7000 comparisons, 843–844*

*Nexus 9000 comparisons, 842–843*

*rate control, 840–841*

FHS

*DAI, 816–827*

*features, 815–816*

keychain authentication, *868*

*Cisco NX-OS configurations, 868–870*

*commands, 869–870*

*key selection, 871–872*

NX-OS configurations, *804–807*

RBAC, *807–809, 811–815*

**news on exam releases, 944**

**Nexus**

console management, 254–255

ND, 316–317

   *benefits, 317–318*

   *cluster nodes, 339–341*

   *external networks, 341–342*

   *GUI, 342–348*

   *NDDB, 335–337*

   *NDFC, 325–335*

   *NDI, 318–323*

   *NDO, 323–324*

   *platforms, 337–339*

   *virtual form factors, 339*

NDDB, 335–337

NDFC, 325–326

   *features/benefits, 326–331*

   *GUI, 331–335*

NDI, 318–323

NDO, 323–324

NX-OS

   *boot sequences, 255–256*

   *checkpoints, 272–274*

   *configuring, 271–274*

   *configuring basic management,
   256–259*

   *images, 254*

   *ISSU, 263–265*

   *NetFlow, 293–298*

   *NTP, 275–280*

   *PLD upgrades, 269–271*

   *PTP, 280–284*

   *rollbacks, 272–274*

   *saves/backups, 272*

   *Smart Call Home, 292–293*

   *SNMP, 286–292*

   *software lifecycle management, 263*

   *SPAN, 298–306*

   *streaming telemetry, 306–309*

   *system message logging, 284–285*

   *time management, 274–284*

   *upgrade/downgrade procedures,
   265–269*

routing support, 5–6

switches, POAP configurations,
259–263

**Nexus 5000 switches**

CoPP comparisons, 844

FCoE configurations, 458–459

**Nexus 7000 switches**

CoPP comparisons, 843–844

FCoE configurations, 456–458

**Nexus 9000 switches**

CoPP comparisons, 842–843

FCoE configurations, 459–461

leaf switches, 179–182

spine switches, Cisco ACI, 179–182

**Nexus 9300 series, 181–182**

**Nexus 9500 series, 181, 264**

**Nexus CoPP (Control Plane Policing),
837–839**

Cisco NX-OS configurations, 844–851

classification, 840–844

control plane packets, 839–840

creating, 850–851

modifying, 851

modular QoS CLI, 842–844

Nexus 5000, 844

Nexus 7000 comparisons, 843–844

Nexus 9000 comparisons, 842–843

rate control, 840–841

**Nexus DAI (Dynamic ARP Inspection),
816, 817–819**

Cisco NX-OS configurations, 819–827

DHCP snooping, 827–831

man-in-the-middle attacks, 817

**Nexus FHS (First-Hop Security)**

DAI, 816, 817–819

*Cisco NX-OS configurations, 819–827*

*DHCP snooping, 827–831*

*man-in-the-middle attacks, 817*

features, 815–816

port security, 832–837

**NFS (Network File Systems), 479–480**

**NIC (Network Interface Cards), vNIC and high availability, 569–570**

**nondisruptive downgrades, MDS switches, 508–512**

**nondisruptive upgrades, MDS switches, 500–505**

**noninteractive mode, Python, 773–775**

**non-vPC ports, 124**

**normal ports, STP, 94**

**northbound interfaces, 631–632**

**note taking, exam preparation, 933**

**NPIV (N Port Identifier Virtualization), 424–431**

**NPV (N Port Virtualization), 424–431**

**NTP (Network Time Protocol), 275**

configuring, 279–280

default parameter settings, 275–276

global commands, 276–278

verification commands, 278

**numeric usernames, 808**

**NVE config commands, VXLAN, 162**

**NX-API**

Cisco NX-API Developer Sandbox, 759–760

error codes, 758–759

Requests/Responses

*elements, 757–759*

*in JSON, 757*

*in XML, 756–757*

**NX-OS**

AAA model configurations, 804–807

boot sequences, 255–256

checkpoints, 272–274

configuring, 271

*basic management, 256–259*

*saves/backups, 272*

images, 254

NetFlow, 293–298

PLD, upgrading, 269–271

rollbacks, 272–274

Smart Call Home, 292–293

SNMP, 286

*configuring, 292*

*global commands, 288–289*

*MIB, 289–291*

*security, 287–288*

*specific notation commands, 291*

*traps, 286–287*

*verification commands, 291–292*

software

*ISSU, 263–265*

*lifecycle management, 263*

*upgrade/downgrade procedures, 265–269*

SPAN, 298–306

streaming telemetry, 306–309

system message logging, 284–285

time management, 274–275

*NTP, 275–280*

*PTP, 280–284*

## O

One View page, ND GUI, 343

Operations pages, ND GUI, 347–348

optimizing Cisco HyperFlex resources, 710–711

orchestration

Ansible

*authentication, 766*

*Cisco NX-OS example, 767–768*

*CLI prompt, 766*

*CLI tools, 767*

*components, 765–766*

*configuration files, 766*

*important concepts, 766*

*inventory files, 765*

*Jinja templates, 766*

*modules, 765*

*playbooks, 765–766, 767–768*

*plays, 766*

*roles, 766*

*variable files, 766*

*variables, 766*

*workflows using playbooks, 764–765*

POAP, 777–778

*configuration scripts, 778–779*

*DHCP discovery phase, 781–782*

*limitations, 778*

*network requirements, 778*

*post-installation reload phase, 782*

*power-up phase, 779*

*processes (overview), 779–780*

*script execution phase, 782*

*switch configurations, 782–783*

*USB discovery phase, 779–780*

*verification commands, 783*

PowerShell, 789

*installing, 789–795*

*listing UCS PowerShell cmdlets, 793–795*

*UCS PowerShell Library installations, 790–791*

*versions of, 789–790, 791–793*

Python, 768–769

*Cisco NX-OS, Python packages, 769–771*

*CLI command API, 771–772*

*interactive mode, 772–773*

*noninteractive mode, 773–775*

*UCS Manager Python SDK, 775–777*

Terraform, 783

*commands, 786–789*

*components, 784–786*

*concept, 784*

*workflows, 784*

**orphaned ports, vPC, 124**

**OSPF (Open Shortest Path First), 6–7**

ABR verification, 18–22

adjacency, 7

areas, 10–12

authentication, 13

BDR, 12–13

configuring, 13–24

DR, 12–13

feature-based licenses, 14

global commands, 14

hello packets, 7

interface commands, 15

interface configurations, 17–18

LSA, 7–10

network topology, 16

OSPFv2 and OSPF3 comparisons, 7

process clear commands, 15–16

router configuration, 22–24

routing commands, 14–15

verifying configurations, 15–16

virtual links, 12

**out-of-band management**

access, Cisco ACI, 214–215

Cisco MDS NX-OS Setup Utility, 492–496

overlay protocols, VXLAN

configuring, 159–169

control plane topologies, 159–161

encapsulation, 151–152

EVPN control plane, 156–157

feature-based licenses, 159

Flood and Learn Multicast-based control plane, 154–156

gateways, 157

global commands, 159–161

high availability, 157–159

interface commands, 161–162

MPBGP EVPN control plane, 156–157

NVE config commands, 162

overview, 151–152

packet formats, 151–152

TRM, 159

verification commands, 162

verifying configurations, 164–169

VNI, 153–154

VTEP, 152–153

Overview page, ND GUI, 344

# P

PaaS (Platform as a Service), 246

packet formats, VXLAN, 151–152

passphrase commands, AAA model, 806

passwords

clear-text passwords, 809

strong passwords, 808–809

patch RPM, managing with Bash Shell, 742–743

peer gateways, vPC, 131–132

peer links, vPC, 124

peer switches, vPC, 124

peering, BGP, 25–26

peer-keepalives, vPC, 124

PFC (Priority-based Flow Control), 438–439

PIM (Protocol Independent Multicast), 49–51

ASM, 51

Bidir, 51–52

configuring, 164–167

default parameter settings, 56–57

designated routers/forwarders, 54–55

distribution modes, 58

RP, 53–54

SSM, 52–53

verifying, 164–167

Pip Python Package Manager, installing Python packages with Guest Shell, 746

playbooks, Ansible, 765–766

Cisco NX-OS example, 767–768

workflows using playbooks, 764–765

plays, Ansible, 766

PLD (Programmable Logical Devices), 269–271

PLOGI (Port Login), 378

POAP (PowerOn Auto Provisioning), 777–778

configuration scripts, 778–779

DHCP discovery phase, 781–782

limitations, 778

network requirements, 778

Nexus switches, 259–263

post-installation reload phase, 782

power-up phase, 779

processes (overview), 779–780

script execution phase, 782

switch configurations, 782–783

USB discovery phase, 779–780

verification commands, 783

**policies**

backups, 666–668

Cisco ACI

*policy identification/ enforcement, 218*

*policy models, 197–198*

Cisco UCS Manager system monitoring, 634–640

EEM, 733–734

**port channels, 117–118, 119–120**

bandwidth, 118

benefits, 118

channel code matrix, 119

configuring, 132–146

default parameter settings, 132–133

FEX, 547–548

global commands, 134–135

interface commands, 135

link modes, 119

load balancing, 120–122

network topologies, 137–138

redundancy, 118

SAN port channels, 396

*configuring, 400–403*

*load balancing, 398–399*

*modes, 399–400*

*trunking, 396–397*

*types of, 396–398*

*verification commands, 400–401*

*verifying configurations, 400–403*

STP, 118

verification commands, 137

**ports**

Cisco UCS FI port modes, 567–569

DPVM, 388–389

FC ports, 368–370

FCoE, 445–447

member ports, vPC, 124

NPIV, 424–431

NPV, 424–431

PLOGI, 378

security, 832–837, 919–921

*configuring, 921–924*

*fabric binding comparison, 928–929*

*verifying, 924–926*

SPAN, 298–306, 523–526

*configuring, 526*

*remote SPAN, 526–528*

STP ports

*edge ports, 94*

*network ports, 94*

*normal ports, 94*

vPC

*non-vPC ports, 124*

*orphaned ports, 124*

**post-installation reload phase, POAP, 782**

**PowerShell, 789**

installing, 789–795

listing UCS PowerShell cmdlets, 793–795

UCS PowerShell Library installations, 790–791

versions of, 789–790, 791–793

**power-up phase, POAP, 779**

**preparing for exams, 932**

chapter-ending review tools, 935

customizing exams, 934–935

DITKA? questions, 940

drag-and-drop questions, 937

ear plugs, 932

fill-in-the-blank questions, 937

final reviews, 940

getting rest, 932

multiple-choice, multiple-answer questions, 936

multiple-choice, single answer questions, 936

PTP

   *access, 933–934*

   *Cisco Certification Exam Tutorial questions, 935–939*

   *customizing exams, 934–935*

   *Premium Edition, 935*

   *updating exams, 935*

simlet questions, 939

simulation questions, 938

study plans, 940

study trackers, 932

taking notes, 933

testlet questions, 938–939

time

   *budgeting, 932*

   *clock watching, 932*

   *travel time, 932*

**primary roles, vPC, 127–128**

**private clouds, 248**

**PRLI (Process Login), 378**

**process clear commands, OSPF, 15–16**

**PTP (Pearson Test Prep)**

access, 933–934

customizing exams, 934–935

Premium Edition, 935

updating exams, 935

**PTP (Precision Time Protocol), 280**

clocks, 281–282, 283–284

configuring, 283

default parameter settings, 282

global commands, 282

interface commands, 283

verification commands, 283

**public clouds, 248–249**

**Python, 768–769**

Cisco NX-OS, Python packages, 769–771

CLI command API, 771–772

Guest Shell, running Python in, 745–746

installing packages with Guest Shell, 746

interactive mode, 772–773

noninteractive mode, 773–775

Pip Python Package Manager, installing Python packages with Guest Shell, 746

UCS Manager Python SDK, 775–777

   *converting to, 777*

   *CRUD operations, 776*

# Q

**QoS (Quality of Service)**

Cisco UCS, 608–610

modular QoS CLI, CoPP, 842–844

**questions**

Cisco Certification Exam Tutorial, 935–939

DITKA? questions, 940

drag-and-drop questions, 937

fill-in-the-blank questions, 937

multiple-choice, multiple-answer questions, 936

multiple-choice, single answer questions, 936

simlet questions, 939

simulation questions, 938

testlet questions, 938–939

# R

rack servers, Cisco UCS, 537–538, 577

RADIUS, 801–802

  authentication, 888–892

  Cisco UCS Manager, 876, 877, 888–892

  MDS switches, 902–904

  storage security, 902–904

  TACACS+ mergers, 914

Rapid PVST+98–105

rate control, CoPP, 840–841

RBAC (Role-Based Access Control), 807–809

  Cisco NX-OS configurations, 811–815

  MDS switches, 918–919

  user accounts, 914

    *roles, 915, 917*

    *rules, 915–917*

    *sample configuration, 918–919*

Ready Clones, Cisco HyperFlex data platforms, 719

redundancy, port channels, 118

regions, CFS, 384–385

registering devices, switched fabric initialization and FC, 378–380

remote AAA services, 802, 901

remote-attached topologies, FCoE, 454

remote SPAN, 526–528

remote users, Cisco UCS Manager role policies, 892–894

removing ACI Contracts, 855

Requests, NX-API

  elements, 757–759

  in JSON, 757

  in XML, 756–757

reserved FDIC, 372

resources

  limits, Guest Shell, 744

optimization, Cisco HyperFlex, 710–711

scaling, Cisco HyperFlex, 710–711

Responses

  NX-API

    *elements, 757–759*

    *in JSON, 757*

    *in XML, 756–757*

  REST API, 754–755

rest, exam preparation, 932

REST API, 752–753

  authentication, 753–754

  Responses, 754–755

RMON (Remote Network Monitoring), 523

roles

  Ansible, 766

  Cisco NX-OS, user roles, 809–810

  RBAC, 807–809, 915, 917

rollbacks, NX-OS, 272–274

Root Guard, 95, 97

routing

  BFD, 37

    *configuring, 38–42*

    *default parameter settings, 38–39*

    *failure detection, 38*

    *global commands, 39–40*

    *interface commands, 40*

    *neighbor relationships, 37–38*

    *network topologies, 40–41*

    *routing commands, 40*

    *verification commands, 40*

    *verifying configurations, 40–42*

  BGP, 24–25

    *AS 65100 configurations, 33*

    *clear commands, 32–33*

    *configuring, 30–37*

    *default parameter settings, 30*

*feature-based licenses, 30*
*global commands, 31*
*interface configurations, 34*
*multiprotocol BGP, 29–30*
*network topologies, 33*
*path selection, 26–29*
*peering, 25–26*
*routing commands, 31–32*
*verification commands, 32–33*
*verifying configurations, 34–37*
HSRP, 69–72
   *configuring, 79–86*
   *global commands, 79–86*
   *interface commands, 80*
   *load sharing, 72*
   *network topologies, 70–71, 82–83*
   *verification commands, 82*
   *verifying configurations, 79–86*
multicast routing, 42–43
   *configuring, 56–69*
   *default parameter settings, 56–57*
   *feature-based licenses, 57–58*
   *global commands, 58–59*
   *IGMP, 43–46, 56, 59–61*
   *interface commands, 59–61*
   *MDT, 47–49*
   *MLD, 46–47*
   *network topologies, 61–62*
   *PIM, 49–55, 56–61, 164–167*
   *RPF, 55–56*
   *switch IGMP snooping, 46*
   *TRM, 159*
   *verifying, 62–69*
   *verifying configurations, 61–69*
Nexus support, 5–6
OSPF, 6–7
   *ABR verification, 18–22*

*adjacency, 7*
*areas, 10–12*
*authentication, 13*
*BDR, 12–13*
*configuring, 13–24*
*DR, 12–13*
*feature-based licenses, 14*
*global commands, 14*
*hello packets, 7*
*interface commands, 15*
*interface configurations, 17–18*
*LSA, 7–10*
*network topology, 16*
*OSPFv2 and OSPF3
   comparisons, 7*
*process clear commands, 15–16*
*router configuration, 22–24*
*routing commands, 14–15*
*verifying configurations, 15–16*
*virtual links, 12*
VRRP, 73, 74
   *authentication, 77*
   *benefits, 75*
   *configuring, 79–86*
   *global commands, 79–86*
   *groups, 75*
   *interface commands, 80*
   *IPv6 First Hop Redundancy,
      77–79*
   *load sharing, 75–76*
   *network topologies, 74, 82–83*
   *operation, 73–75*
   *router priority/preemption,
      76–77*
   *tracking, 77*
   *verification commands, 82*
   *verifying configurations,
      79–86*

RP, PIM, 53–54

RPF (Reverse Path Forwarding), 55–56

RPM, managing with Bash Shell

feature RPM, 742

patch RPM, 742–743

rules

Cisco NX-OS, 809–810

RBAC, user accounts, 915–917

running

Bash Shell, 741–742

Python in Guest Shell, 745–746

# S

SaaS (Software as a Service), 245

SAN (Storage Area Networks)

Cisco UCS, connectivity, 611–616, 624–625

port channels, 396

configuring, 400–403

load balancing, 398–399

modes, 399–400

trunking, 396–397

types of, 396–398

verification commands, 400–401

verifying configurations, 400–403

SATA RAS, Cisco HyperFlex, 715–716

saves/backups, NX-OS, 272

scalability, Cisco UCS, 533

Scheduler

backups, 739

configuring, 737–740

displaying jobs/schedules, 739–740

job definitions, 736

overview, 736–737

prerequisites, 737

timetable definitions, 736

verifying configurations, 739–740

scripting

Bash Shell, enabling, 741–742

EEM, monitoring module powerdowns, 736

execution phase, POAP, 782

Guest Shell

*displaying Ethernet 1/47 interface counters, 745*

*dohost command, 745*

*guestshell destroy command, 747*

*guestshell disable command, 747*

*guestshell enable command, 747*

*installing Python packages, 746*

*show guestshell detail command, 747–748*

JSON, 751–752, 757

NX-API

*Cisco NX-API Developer Sandbox, 759–760*

*error codes, 758–759*

*Requests/Responses elements, 757–759*

*Requests/Responses in JSON, 757*

*Requests/Responses in XML, 756–757*

POAP, 777–778

*configuration scripts, 778–779*

*DHCP discovery phase, 781–782*

*limitations, 778*

*network requirements, 778*

*post-installation reload phase, 782*

*power-up phase, 779*

*processes (overview), 779–780*

*script execution phase, 782*

*switch configurations, 782–783*

*USB discovery phase, 779–780*

*verification commands, 783*

Python, 768–769
  Cisco NX-OS, Python packages, 769–771
  CLI command API, 771–772
  interactive mode, 772–773
  noninteractive mode, 773–775
  UCS Manager Python SDK, 775–777
REST API, 752–753
  authentication, 753–754
  Responses, 754–755
Scheduler
  backups, 739
  displaying jobs/schedules, 739–740
setup scripts, Cisco MDS NX-OS Setup Utility, 490–491
XML, 748–749
  Requests/Responses and REST API, 756–757
  structure example, 749–750
  syntax, 750–751
SCVMM, Cisco ACI integration, 204–205
secondary roles, vPC, 127–128
security
  Cisco UCS Manager
    AAA model, 875–876
    Cisco AVPair attribute example, 878
    LDAP, 877
    LDAP providers/groups, 879–888
    multiple authentication services configuration, 892–894
    RADIUS, 876, 877, 888–892
    remote user role policies, 892–894
    Session Timeout Period, 879

    TACACS+877–878, 888–894
    two-factor authentication, 879
    Web Session Refresh Period, 879
  clear-text passwords, 809
  computer security
    AAA model, 875–876
    Cisco AVPair attribute example, 878
    LDAP, 877
    LDAP providers/groups, 879–888
    multiple authentication services configuration, 892–894
    RADIUS, 876, 877, 888–892
    remote user role policies, 892–894
    TACACS+877–878, 888–894
    two-factor authentication, 879
  encryption
    local encryption keys, 721
    SED, 720–721
  FHS
    DAI, 816–827
    features, 815–816
  locking up valuables, exam preparation, 932–933
  network security
    AAA model, 801–807
    ACI Contracts, 851–867
    CoPP, 837–851
    FHS, 815–837
    Keychain Authentication, 868–872
    RBAC, 807–815
  passwords
    clear-text passwords, 809
    strong passwords, 808–809
  ports, 832–837
  ports, security, 919–921

configuring, 921–924

fabric binding comparison, 928–929

verifying, 924–926

SED, Cisco HyperFlex data platforms, 720–721

SNMP, 287–288

storage security

AAA model, 898–901

fabric binding, 926–929

LDAP, 907–911

port security, 919–926

RADIUS, 902–904, 914

RBAC, 914–919

TACACS+ 904–907, 914

strong passwords, 808–809

**SED, Cisco HyperFlex data platforms, 720–721**

**servers**

Cisco HyperFlex disk types, 722–723

Cisco UCS

5108 Blade Server Chassis, 536

blade servers, 536–537

Cisco UCS Mini, 539–540

pools, 596

profiles, 599–602

rack servers, 537–538, 577

storage servers, 537–539

firmware upgrades, 691–699

monitoring, AAA, 900–901

**services**

CFS, 380–381

CFSoFC, 382–384

CFSoIP, 382–384

fabric lock, 382

features, 381–382

merges, 384

regions, 384–385

Cisco Intersight management as a service, 648–649

IaaS, 246–248

PaaS, 246

profiles, Cisco UCS, 596–599, 602–607

SaaS, 245

**Services page, ND GUI, 345–346**

**Session Timeout Period, Cisco UCS Manager, 879**

**setup scripts, Cisco MDS NX-OS Setup Utility, 490–491**

**shells**

Bash Shell, 740

displaying dev-ops role authority, 740–741

displaying network-admin role authority, 740–741

enabling, 741–742

feature RPM, 742

patch RPM, 742–743

running, 741–742

Guest Shell, 743

access, 743–744

capabilities, 744–746

displaying Ethernet 1/47 interface counters, 745

dohost command, 745

guestshell destroy command, 747

guestshell disable command, 747

guestshell enable command, 747

installing Python packages, 746

managing, 746–748

resource limits, 744

running Python in Guest Shell, 745–746

show guestshell detail command, 747–748

**show guestshell detail command, 747–748**

simlet questions, 939

simulation questions, 938

single contract bidirectional reverse filters, 859

single contract unidirectional with multiple filters, 859

single-hop topologies, FCoE, 451–454

Sites page, ND GUI, 345

Smart Call Home, 292–293, 636–637

smart zoning, 411–412

snapshots, Cisco HyperFlex data platforms, 719–720

SNMP (Simple Network Management Protocol), 286

    Cisco UCS Manager system monitoring, 636

    configuring, 292

    global commands, 288–289

    MIB, 289–291

    security, 287–288

    specific notation commands, 291

    traps, 286–287

    verification commands, 291–292

software

    Cisco Intersight supported software, 650–652

    EPLD, upgrading, 269–271

    managing

        *Cisco MDS NX-OS Setup Utility, 490–498*

        *MDS switch upgrades/ downgrades, 496–497*

    MDS switches, upgrading/ downgrading software, 498–500

    NX-OS

        *ISSU, 263–265*

        *lifecycle management, 263*

        *upgrade/downgrade procedures, 265–269*

PLD, upgrading, 269–271

updates, Cisco UCS, 672–679

SPAN (Switched Port Analyzers), 298–306, 523–526

    configuring, 526

    remote SPAN, 526–528

special characters in usernames, 808

specific notation commands, SNMP, 291

spine switches, Cisco ACI, 179–182

SSM (Source-Specific Multicast), 52–53

storage

    Cisco UCS, 611

        *S-Series storage servers, 483–484*

        *storage servers, 537–539*

    datastores, Cisco HyperFlex data platforms, 724–725

    NAS, 481–482

        *benefits, 483*

        *Cisco UCS S-Series storage servers, 483–484*

    VSAN, 386

        *advantages of, 388*

        *attributes, 387–388*

        *commands, 392–393*

        *configuring, 391–394*

        *DPVM, 388–389*

        *features, 386–387*

        *ID, 387*

        *names, 388*

        *states, 387–388*

        *switches, 388*

        *trunking, 389–394*

        *verifying configurations, 391–394*

        *zoning comparisons, 406*

**storage clusters**

Cisco HyperFlex data platforms, 717

compute nodes, 717

converged nodes, 717

datastores, 717

drives, 717

**storage security**

AAA model, 898

  *accounting, 900*

  *authentication, 899, 912–913*

  *authorization, 899, 912–913*

  *local AAA services, 911–912*

  *remote AAA services, 901*

  *server distribution, 913–914*

  *server groups, 900*

  *server monitoring, 900–901*

  *service configuration, 900*

fabric binding, 926–929

LDAP, 907–911

port security, 919–921

  *configuring, 921–924*

  *fabric binding comparison, 928–929*

  *verifying, 924–926*

RADIUS, 902–904, 914

RBAC, 914–919

TACACS+904–907, 914

**STP (Spanning Tree Protocol), 93**

BPDU Filtering, 95, 96

BPDU Guard, 95, 96

Bridge Assurance, 95–96

configuring, 102–117

edge ports, 94

extension default settings, 102

extensions (overview), 94–95

global commands, 105

interface commands, 106–107

Loop Guard, 95, 96–97

network ports, 94

network topologies, 108

normal ports, 94

port channels, 118

Rapid PVST+98–105

Root Guard, 95, 97

topologies, 93–94, 108

UDLD, 97–98, 102–105

verification commands, 108

verifying configurations, 109–117

**streaming telemetry, NX-OS, 306–309**

**strong passwords, 808–809**

**structure example, XML, 749–750**

**study plans, exams, 940, 943–944**

**study trackers, 932**

**switched fabric initialization, FC**

device registration, 378–380

domain ID, 375–377

fabric reconfiguration, 377

FCID, 377

FCNS databases, 378–380

FLOGI, 378–380

overview, 373–374

PLOGI, 378

principal switch selection, 374–377

PRLI, 378

**switches**

Cisco MDS

FCoE configurations

  *Nexus 5000 switches, 458–459*

  *Nexus 7000 switches, 456–458*

  *Nexus 9000 switches, 459–461*

IGMP snooping, 46

leaf switches, Cisco ACI, 179–182

MDS switches

  *9000 series switches, EPLD upgrades, 515–521*

9100 series multilayer fabric
    switches, 362–365
9200 series multiservice
    switches, 361–362
9300 series multilayer fabric
    switches, 360–361
disruptive downgrades, 513–515
disruptive upgrades, 505–507
nondisruptive downgrades,
    508–512
nondisruptive upgrades, 500–505
NX-OS Setup Utility, 490–498
upgrading/downgrading
    software, 498–500
verifying NX-OS version,
    496–497
peer switches, vPC, 124
POAP configurations, 259–263,
    782–783
port security, 919–921
    configuring, 921–924
    fabric binding comparison,
        928–929
    verifying, 924–926
spine switches, Cisco ACI, 179–182
VSAN, 388
switching protocols
port channels, 117–118, 119–120
    bandwidth, 118
    benefits, 118
    channel code matrix, 119
    configuring, 132–146
    default parameter settings,
        132–133
    global commands, 134–135
    interface commands, 135
    link modes, 119
    load balancing, 120–122
    network topologies, 137–138

redundancy, 118
STP, 118
verification commands, 137
vPC, 134–135
STP, 93
    BPDU Filtering, 95, 96
    BPDU Guard, 95, 96
    Bridge Assurance, 95–96
    configuring, 102–117
    edge ports, 94
    extension default settings, 102
    extensions (overview), 94–95
    global commands, 105
    interface commands, 106–107
    Loop Guard, 95, 96–97
    network ports, 94
    network topologies, 108
    normal ports, 94
    port channels, 118
    Rapid PVST+98–102
    Root Guard, 95, 97
    topologies, 93–94, 108
    UDLD, 97–98, 102–105
    verification commands, 108
    verifying configurations,
        109–117
vPC, 122
    ARP synchronization, 131
    components, 124–125
    configuration consistency,
        128–129
    configuring, 132–146
    consistency checks, 129
    domain commands, 136
    domains, 124
    dual-control plane, 126
    duplicate frame prevention,
        129–131

*fault-tolerant links, 124*

*HSRP gateways, 131*

*implementing, 133–134*

*interface commands, 135*

*member ports, 124*

*non-vPC ports, 124*

*orphaned ports, 124*

*peer gateways, 131–132*

*peer links, 124*

*peer switches, 124*

*peer-keepalives, 124*

*primary roles, 127–128*

*secondary roles, 127–128*

*topologies, 122–123*

*traffic flows, 125–126*

*verification commands, 137*

syntax, XML, 750–751

system clusters, Cisco HyperFlex data platforms, 725–727

system messages

  infrastructure monitoring, 521

  logging, NX-OS, 284–285

system monitoring, Cisco UCS Manager, 630

  AG, 631

  Call Home, 636–637

  database health, 638

  DME, 631

  events, 632–634

  hardware, 638

  logs, 632–634

  NetFlow, 638–640

  northbound interfaces, 631–632

  policies, 634–640

  Smart Call Home, 636–637

  SNMP, 636

  traffic monitoring, 640–647

System Resources pages, ND GUI, 346–347

system restore, Cisco UCS configuration management, 670–672

# T

T11 FCoE standard, 438

taboo contracts, 209–210

TACACS+ 801–802

  authentication, 888–892

  Cisco UCS Manager, 876, 888–892

  MDS switches, 905–907

  RADIUS mergers, 914

  remote user role policies, 892–894

  storage security, 904–907, 914

telemetry data collection, Cisco Intersight, 650

tenants

  ACI Contracts, 857–858

  Cisco ACI, 198–200

    *creating, 227–230*

    *intersubnet tenant traffic, 217–218*

    *management tenants, 213*

  intersubnet tenant traffic, 217–218

  management tenants, 213

Terraform, 783

  commands, 786–789

  components, 784–786

  concept, 784

  workflows, 784

testlet questions, 938–939

three-tier Cisco ACI applications, 233–235

time

  exam preparation

    *budgeting time, 932*

*clock watching, 932*

*travel time, 932*

management, networks, 274–275

    *NTP, 275–280*

    *PTP, 280–284*

timetable definitions, **Scheduler, 736**

topologies

  FC, 365–368

  FCoE

    *direct-attached topologies, 452–453*

    *FEX topologies, 453–454, 461–463*

    *multi-hop topologies, 454–455*

    *remote-attached topologies, 454*

    *single-hop topologies, 451–454*

  multitier topologies, Cisco ACI, 179–180

  network topologies

    *BFD, 40–41*

    *BGP, 33*

    *HSRP, 70–71, 82–83*

    *multicast routing, 61–62*

    *OSPF, 16*

    *port channels, 137–138*

    *STP, 108*

    *VRRP, 74, 82–83*

  STP, 93–94, 108

  vPC, 122–123

  VXLAN control plane, 163

tracking, **VRRP, 77**

traffic flows, **vPC, 125–126**

traffic load balancing, **Cisco ACI fabric, 219–220**

traffic monitoring

  Cisco UCS Manager system monitoring, 640–641

  Ethernet, 641–642

  FC, 642–647

traffic storms, Cisco ACI fabric, 219

traps, SNMP, 286–287

travel time, exam preparation, 932

**TRM (Tenant Routed Multicast), 159**

trunking

  SAN port channels, 396–397

  VSAN, 389–394

two-factor authentication, **Cisco UCS Manager, 879**

# U

**UCS Manager Python SDK, 775–777**

  converting to, 777

  CRUD operations, 776

**UCS PowerShell cmdlets, listing, 793–795**

**UCS PowerShell Library, installing, 790–791**

**UDLD (Unidirectional Link Detection), 97–98, 102–105**

unified management, **Cisco HyperFlex, 709–710**

updates

  exams, 935, 942–943, 944

  firmware, Cisco UCS, 672–679

  software, Cisco UCS, 672–679

upgrading

  EPLD, 269–271

  fabric, Cisco ACI, 189–190

  firmware, through Auto Install, 680–687

  MDS 9000 series switches, EPLD upgrades, 515–521

  MDS switches

    *disruptive upgrades, 505–507*

    *nondisruptive upgrades, 500–505*

    *software, 498–500*

  Nexus 9500 series, 264

NX-OS, 265–269

PLD, upgrading, 269–271

**uplink connectivity, Cisco UCS FI, 567**

**USB discovery phase, POAP, 779–780**

**user accounts**

LDAP, 880

locking commands, AAA model, 806

numeric usernames, 808

RBAC, 914

*roles, 915, 917*

*rules, 915–917*

*sample configuration, 918–919*

special characters in usernames, 808

**usernames**

numeric usernames, 808

special characters in usernames, 808

**UUID pools, Cisco UCS, 591–593**

# V

**VAAI (vStorage API for Array Installation), 707**

**valuables (exam preparation), locking up, 932–933**

**variables, Ansible, 766**

**vCenter, Cisco ACI integration, 235–238**

**verification commands**

FCoE, 466

HSRP, 82

NTP, 278

port channels, 137

PTP, 283

SAN port channels, 400–401

SNMP, 291–292

STP, 108

vPC, 137

VRRP, 82

VXLAN, 162

**verifying**

AAA verification commands, 807

ACI Contracts, 855

BFD, 40–42

BGP configurations, 34–37

Cisco UCS FI, cluster verifications, 563–564

device alias configurations, 422–423

EEM configurations, 736

FCoE, 466–474

HSRP, 79–86

multicast routing, 62–69

multicast routing configurations, 61–69

NX-OS version, MDS switches, 496–497

OSPF configurations, 15–16

PIM, 164–167

POAP verification commands, 783

port security, 924–926

SAN port channel configurations, 400–403

Scheduler configurations, 739–740

STP configurations, 109–117

VRRP configurations, 79–86

VSAN configurations, 391–394

VXLAN configurations, 164–169

zoning configurations, 414–417

**VFC (Virtual Fibre Channel), 444–445**

**VIB (vSphere Installation Bundles)**

IO Visor, 707

VAAI, 707

**VIC (Virtual Interface Cards), 552–555**

**Virtual Edge, Cisco ACI, 206**

**virtual links**

FEX, 548

OSPF, 12

virtualization
    Cisco UCS, 550–555
    NPIV, 424–431
    NPV, 424–431
VLAN (Virtual LAN)
    Cisco UCS network management,
        584–591
    named VLAN, 586–589
        configuring, 589–590
        deleting, 590–591
VM, Cisco HyperFlex, VM density,
    711–712
VMM, Cisco ACI VMM domains,
    203–204
VMware overlays, Cisco ACI
    integration, 206
VMware vCenter, Cisco ACI
    integration, 205
VNI (Virtual Network Identifiers),
    153–154
vNIC, high availability, 569–570
vPC (Virtual Port Channels), 122
    ARP synchronization, 131
    components, 124–125
    configuration consistency, 128–129
    configuring, 132–146
    consistency checks, 129
    domain commands, 136
    domains, 124
    dual-control plane, 126
    duplicate frame prevention, 129–131
    fault-tolerant links, 124
    global commands, 134–135
    HSRP gateways, 131
    implementing, 133–134
    interface commands, 135
    non-vPC ports, 124
    orphaned ports, 124

    peer gateways, 131–132
    peer links, 124
    peer switches, 124
    peer-keepalives, 124
    primary roles, 127–128
    secondary roles, 127–128
    topologies, 122–123
    traffic flows, 125–126
    verification commands, 137
    vPC ports, member ports, 124
VRF (Virtual Routing and Forwarding)
    Cisco ACI, 200
    Contracts, 856–857
VRRP (Virtual Router Redundancy
    Protocol), 73, 74
    authentication, 77
    benefits, 75
    configuring, 79–86
    global commands, 79–86
    groups, 75
    interface commands, 80
    IPv6 First Hop Redundancy, 77–79
    load sharing, 75–76
    network topologies, 74, 82–83
    operation, 73–75
    router priority/preemption, 76–77
    tracking, 77
    verification commands, 82
    verifying configurations, 79–86
VSAN (Virtual Storage-Area
    Networks), 386
    advantages of, 388
    attributes, 387–388
    Cisco UCS, 616–621
    commands, 392–393
    configuring, 391–394
    DPVM, 388–389

features, 386–387

ID, 387

named VSAN, 616–618

names, 388

states, 387–388

switches, 388

trunking, 389–394

verifying configurations, 391–394

zone sets, 618–621

zones, 618–621

zoning comparisons, 406

**VTEP (VXLAN Tunnel Endpoints), 152–153**

**VXLAN (Virtual Extensible LAN)**

Cisco ACI, 215–216

configuring, 159–169

control plane topologies, 159–161

encapsulation, 151–152

EVPN control plane, 156–157

feature-based licenses, 159

Flood and Learn Multicast-based control plane, 154–156

gateways, 157

global commands, 159–161

high availability, 157–159

interface commands, 161–162

MPBGP EVPN control plane, 156–157

NVE config commands, 162

overview, 151–152

packet formats, 151–152

TRM, 159

verification commands, 162

verifying configurations, 164–169

VNI, 153–154

VTEP, 152–153

**vzAny rule, 210–212**

# W

Web Session Refresh Period, Cisco UCS Manager, 879

workflows

Ansible, 764–765

Terraform, 784

**WWN pools, Cisco UCS, 621–624**

# X

**XML (Extensible Markup Language), 748–749**

Requests/Responses and REST API, 756–757

structure example, 749–750

syntax, 750–751

# Y - Z

**zone alias, device alias comparisons, 421–422**

**zone sets, VSAN, 618–621**

**zones, VSAN, 618–621**

**zoning, 404**

active zone sets, 407–409

Autozone, 410

configuring, 414–417

enforcement, 406–407

enhanced zoning, 412–413

features, 404–406

full zone sets, 407–409

hard zoning, 407

merges, 410–411

smart zoning, 411–412

verifying configurations, 414–417

VSAN comparisons, 406

Register your product at **ciscopress.com/register**
to unlock additional benefits:

- Save 35%* on your next purchase with an exclusive discount code

- Find companion files, errata, and product updates if available

- Sign up to receive special offers on new editions and related titles

Get more when you shop at **ciscopress.com**:

- Everyday discounts on books, eBooks, video courses, and more

- Free U.S. shipping on all orders

- Multi-format eBooks to read on your preferred device

- Print and eBook Best Value Packs

**Cisco Press**